CRIME STATE RANKINGS
2006

Crime in the 50 United States

Editors:
Kathleen O'Leary Morgan and Scott Morgan

Morgan Quitno Press
© Copyright 2006, All Rights Reserved

512 East 9th Street, P.O. Box 1656
Lawrence, KS 66044-8656
USA

800-457-0742 or 785-841-3534
www.statestats.com

Thirteenth Edition

ISBN:
0-7401-1701-7
ISSN:
1077-4408

Crime State Rankings 2006 sells for $59.95 ($6 shipping) and is only available in paper binding. For those who prefer ranking information tailored to a particular state, we also offer *Crime State Perspectives*, state-specific reports for each of the 50 states.   These individual guides provide information on a state's data and rank for each of the categories featured in the national *Crime State Rankings* volume.   Perspectives sell for $19 or $9.50 if ordered with *Crime State Rankings*. If you are interested in city and metropolitan crime data, we offer *City Crime Rankings* ($49.95 paper).   Those interested in health statistics should check out our annual *Health Care State Rankings* ($59.95 paper).   For a general view of the states, please ask about our annual *State Rankings* reference book ($59.95 paper) or our annual *State Trends* ($59.95 paper).   Also available is *Education State Rankings*. This view of preK-12 education at the state level is $49.95. All of our books are available on CD-ROM in PDF format (same price as printed book) or with both PDF format and data sets in various database formats ($99.95).   Shipping and handling is $6 per order. For information, please visit our website at www.statestats.com.

Thirteenth Edition
Printed in the United States of America
March 2006

PREFACE

Community safety is a top concern of most Americans. While the incidence of crime has decreased throughout the United States in recent years, it still is an important factor to both businesses and individuals in choosing where to live or work.

Having access to straightforward, easy-to-understand crime information is essential in making these decisions. This 13th edition of *Crime State Rankings* provides researchers and concerned citizens with a huge collection of comparative crime and law enforcement statistics. State-by-state tables are featured, reporting crime numbers, rates and trends; consumer fraud and identity theft data; prison and corrections statistics; law enforcement personnel and finance data; juvenile crime numbers; and information on drugs and alcohol, arrests and crime clearances. In all, 511 tables provide answers to hundreds of the most commonly asked crime-related questions.

Important Notes About *Crime State Rankings 2006*

Crime State Rankings translates thousands of crime statistics available through federal and state governments into easy-to-understand, meaningful state comparisons. With each new edition, we reexamine every table to determine whether the information is of interest and relevant to our readers. Most tables in this 2006 edition have been updated, while others were removed and new data were added. The end product is an easy-to-use reference book featuring more than 500 tables of state crime comparisons.

While we have made a number of changes and updates to *Crime State Rankings,* many of the organizational features that have made this book so popular with both reviewers and researchers have not changed. Data are presented in both alphabetical and rank order so that readers may quickly find information for a particular state and then just as quickly learn which states rank above and below that state. Source information and other important footnotes are clearly shown at the bottom of each page and national totals, rates and percentages are prominently displayed at the top of each table. Every other line is shaded in gray for easier reading. In addition, numerous information-finding tools are provided: a thorough table of contents, table listings at the beginning of each chapter, a detailed index and a chapter thumb index. Also included is a roster of sources showing addresses, phone numbers and websites.

For the ease of our readers, the statistics in *Crime State Rankings 2006* require no additional calculations to convert numbers from thousands, millions, etc. All states are ranked on a high to low basis. Ties among states are shown alphabetically for a given ranking. Numbers reported in parentheses "( )" are negative numbers. For tables with national totals (as opposed to rates, per capita's, etc.) we include a separate column showing what percent of the national total each individual state's total represents. This column is headed by "% of USA." This percentage figure is particularly interesting when compared with a state's share of the nation's population for a particular year. The appendix contains population tables to aid in these comparisons.

For those interested in focusing on crime information for just one state, we once again offer our *Crime State Perspective* series of publications. These 21-page, comb-bound reports feature data and ranking information for an individual state pulled from *Crime State Rankings 2006.* (For example, *New York Crime in Perspective* contains crime information about the state of New York only.) When purchased individually, *Crime State Perspectives* sell for $19. When purchased with a copy of *Crime State Rankings 2006,* these handy quick reference guides are just $9.50.

Other Books from Morgan Quitno Press

Crime State Rankings is one of six annual reference books published by Morgan Quitno Press.

For up-to-date crime information for cities, our *City Crime Rankings* reference book compares cities of 75,000 population or more and all metropolitan areas (some as small as 65,000 population) in 40 categories of crime. Crime numbers, rates and trends are presented for all major crime categories reported by the FBI. Also featured in *City Crime Rankings* are the results of Morgan Quitno's "Safest City Award," an annual study that compares crime in 369 U.S. cities. (most recent version is the 12th edition featuring 2004 crime statistics; 49.95 + $6 S/H; paper.)

Our original and most popular reference book, now in its 17th edition, is *State Rankings 2006*. This annual volume compares states in a wide array of subject areas, such as agriculture, transportation, taxes, health, crime, education and housing. If K-12 education is your interest, *Education State Rankings 2005-2006* provides up-to-date information on teachers' salaries, class sizes, graduation rates, test scores and more. For state health information, *Health Care State Rankings 2006* includes data on health care facilities, providers, insurance and finance, incidence of disease, mortality, physical fitness, natality and reproductive health. *State Trends* provides a quick and easy way to track important quality of life changes in the 50 United States. One, five, 10 and 20-year trends are measured in health, taxes, crime, education and more.

The data in all of our reference books are available on CD-ROM. These electronic editions provide a searchable PDF version of each book as well as the raw data in .dbf, Excel and ASCII formats. Additional information about all of our publications is available online at www.statestats.com or by calling 1-800-457-0742.

Finally, a huge "thank you" goes out to our readers. We appreciate your comments and feedback that help keep our books relevant and usable. Please send your thoughts and ideas via email (information@morganquitno. com) or by phone at 1-800-457-0742. We look forward to hearing from you.　　　　　　　- THE EDITORS

WHICH STATE IS THE MOST DANGEROUS?

Nevada held firmly to the designation as the nation's Most Dangerous State for the third consecutive year and the sixth time out of the 14 years we have given this award. The only change in the "top" five states was the return of New Mexico to the contenders after a three year absence. Otherwise our 14th annual Most Dangerous State designation found Louisiana still in second place, followed by New Mexico, Arizona, and Maryland.

On the safer end of the ranking scale, North Dakota held off a challenge from Maine and remained our Safest State for the ninth time in ten years. Rounding out the safest five states were Vermont, New Hampshire and Wyoming.

The Methodology

The Safest and Most Dangerous States rankings are determined using a four-step process. First, rates for six crime categories — murder, rape, robbery, aggravated assault, burglary and motor vehicle theft — are plugged into a formula that measures how a state compares to the national average for a given crime category.

Second, the product of this equation is then multiplied by a weight assigned to each crime category. For this year's award, we again gave each crime category equal weight. This way, state comparisons are based purely on crime rates and how the rates stack up to the national average for a given crime category.

Third, the weighted numbers are added together to achieve the state's score ("SUM"). In the fourth and final step, these composite scores are ranked from highest to lowest to determine which states are the most dangerous and safest. Thus the farther below the national average a state's crime rate is, the lower (and safer) it ranks. The farther above the national average, the higher (and more dangerous) a state ranks in the final list.

2006 MOST DANGEROUS STATE

RANK	STATE	SUM	05	RANK	STATE	SUM	05
1	Nevada	50.68	1	26	Hawaii	(14.13)	25
2	Louisiana	40.43	2	27	Oregon	(14.60)	28
3	New Mexico	38.28	9	28	Indiana	(17.48)	27
4	Arizona	34.85	3	29	Pennsylvania	(18.37)	30
5	Maryland	34.41	4	30	Massachusetts	(19.73)	29
6	South Carolina	30.98	5	31	New York	(24.29)	31
7	Florida	25.06	6	32	New Jersey	(24.94)	32
8	Tennessee	24.22	7	33	Kentucky	(27.54)	37
9	Alaska	23.22	8	34	Nebraska	(30.12)	35
10	California	18.48	10	35	Minnesota	(30.67)	36
11	Texas	15.46	11	36	Utah	(32.28)	34
12	Michigan	13.60	12	37	Virginia	(33.81)	38
13	Georgia	10.30	13	38	Rhode Island	(34.23)	33
14	Oklahoma	7.81	14	39	Connecticut	(35.96)	39
15	Arkansas	6.99	22	40	Idaho	(39.27)	41
16	Washington	6.14	20	41	West Virginia	(40.74)	44
17	North Carolina	5.16	18	42	Montana	(42.90)	40
18	Alabama	2.19	19	43	Iowa	(43.71)	43
19	Illinois	2.16	16	44	Wisconsin	(47.36)	42
20	Missouri	(0.34)	21	45	South Dakota	(48.57)	46
21	Mississippi	(3.43)	17	46	Wyoming	(50.71)	45
22	Colorado	(3.63)	24	47	New Hampshire	(52.90)	47
23	Ohio	(5.08)	23	48	Vermont	(57.69)	49
24	Delaware	(7.90)	15	49	Maine	(62.58)	48
25	Kansas	(13.40)	26	50	North Dakota	(66.81)	50

FACTORS CONSIDERED (all given equal weight):
(all rates per 100,000 population)

1. Murder Rate (Table 323)
2. Rape Rate (Table 342)
3. Robbery Rate (Table 348)
4. Aggravated Assault Rate (Table 363)
5. Burglary Rate (Table 383)
6. Motor Vehicle Theft Rate (Table 393)

Morgan Quitno Press' primary objective is to present facts in a nonbiased, objective manner. While a central theme of our books is our clear presentation of data with the analysis and interpretation left to our readers, we stray from this policy once a year and issue our awards. The Safest and Most Dangerous States have been named annually since 1994. We have awarded the Most Livable State title since 1991, based on data from our *State Rankings* series. In 1993, we began the Healthiest State Award based on our *Health Care State Rankings* series. In 1994, we initiated the annual Safest and Most Dangerous City Award based on data in the annual *City Crime Rankings* volume. In 2002, we announced the Smartest State Award using data from, *Education State Rankings*. In 2004, we began the Most Improved State based on our newest annual, *State Trends*.

The story for Nevada and North Dakota remain much the same as last year. Nevada continues to be the nation's fastest growing state. With that rapid growth, comes a continuing struggle with crime. The good news is that its violent crime rate stayed the same as the year before. However, most of the country saw a declining violent crime rate.

North Dakota still may lack large numbers of people but it also has very little crime. As usual, it boasts the lowest violent crime rate in the nation by a significant margin. The Peace Garden State is still is at peace.

— THE EDITORS

TABLE OF CONTENTS

I. Arrests

II. Corrections

TABLE OF CONTENTS (continued)

TABLE OF CONTENTS (continued)

TABLE OF CONTENTS (continued)

V. Juveniles

TABLE OF CONTENTS (continued)

TABLE OF CONTENTS (continued)

TABLE OF CONTENTS (continued)

Urban/Rural Crime

TABLE OF CONTENTS (continued)

2000 Crimes

TABLE OF CONTENTS (continued)

VIII. Appendix

IX. Sources

X. Index

I. ARRESTS

Important Note Regarding Arrest Numbers

The state arrest numbers reported by the FBI and shown in tables 1 to 36 are only from those law enforcement agencies that submitted complete arrests reports for 12 months in 2004. The arrest rates were calculated by the editors using population totals provided by the FBI for those jurisdictions reporting. Reports from law enforcement agencies in Illinois, Kentucky and South Carolina represented 25% or less of their state populations and rates were not calculated. Reports from Georgia represented just over 35% its state population and reports from Arkansas, Mississippi, New York, South Dakota and West Virginia represented just over half of their state population. Rates for these states should be interpreted with caution. No arrest data were available for Montana or the District of Columbia.

Reported Arrests in 2004

National Total = 11,076,112 Reported Arrests*

ALPHA ORDER

RANK	STATE	ARRESTS	% of USA
20	Alabama	208,312	1.9%
42	Alaska	36,864	0.3%
10	Arizona	315,007	2.8%
31	Arkansas	98,086	0.9%
1	California	1,414,732	12.8%
17	Colorado	229,977	2.1%
27	Connecticut	116,805	1.1%
44	Delaware	31,048	0.3%
3	Florida	1,028,856	9.3%
21	Georgia	205,472	1.9%
39	Hawaii	49,456	0.4%
36	Idaho	72,204	0.7%
22	Illinois	200,447	1.8%
19	Indiana	215,441	1.9%
29	Iowa	110,513	1.0%
35	Kansas	80,262	0.7%
37	Kentucky	69,483	0.6%
16	Louisiana	232,704	2.1%
38	Maine	55,345	0.5%
11	Maryland	309,630	2.8%
30	Massachusetts	101,430	0.9%
8	Michigan	331,479	3.0%
26	Minnesota	132,255	1.2%
28	Mississippi	113,350	1.0%
12	Missouri	273,415	2.5%
NA	Montana**	NA	NA
32	Nebraska	93,098	0.8%
25	Nevada	148,909	1.3%
40	New Hampshire	43,769	0.4%
7	New Jersey	379,625	3.4%
33	New Mexico	92,672	0.8%
9	New York	315,889	2.9%
5	North Carolina	393,819	3.6%
47	North Dakota	26,010	0.2%
13	Ohio	271,838	2.5%
23	Oklahoma	158,957	1.4%
24	Oregon	155,202	1.4%
4	Pennsylvania	441,127	4.0%
41	Rhode Island	43,576	0.4%
46	South Carolina	26,540	0.2%
48	South Dakota	24,475	0.2%
14	Tennessee	269,127	2.4%
2	Texas	1,116,524	10.1%
34	Utah	90,811	0.8%
49	Vermont	12,074	0.1%
15	Virginia	267,765	2.4%
18	Washington	216,541	2.0%
45	West Virginia	30,257	0.3%
6	Wisconsin	383,306	3.5%
43	Wyoming	35,849	0.3%

RANK ORDER

RANK	STATE	ARRESTS	% of USA
1	California	1,414,732	12.8%
2	Texas	1,116,524	10.1%
3	Florida	1,028,856	9.3%
4	Pennsylvania	441,127	4.0%
5	North Carolina	393,819	3.6%
6	Wisconsin	383,306	3.5%
7	New Jersey	379,625	3.4%
8	Michigan	331,479	3.0%
9	New York	315,889	2.9%
10	Arizona	315,007	2.8%
11	Maryland	309,630	2.8%
12	Missouri	273,415	2.5%
13	Ohio	271,838	2.5%
14	Tennessee	269,127	2.4%
15	Virginia	267,765	2.4%
16	Louisiana	232,704	2.1%
17	Colorado	229,977	2.1%
18	Washington	216,541	2.0%
19	Indiana	215,441	1.9%
20	Alabama	208,312	1.9%
21	Georgia	205,472	1.9%
22	Illinois	200,447	1.8%
23	Oklahoma	158,957	1.4%
24	Oregon	155,202	1.4%
25	Nevada	148,909	1.3%
26	Minnesota	132,255	1.2%
27	Connecticut	116,805	1.1%
28	Mississippi	113,350	1.0%
29	Iowa	110,513	1.0%
30	Massachusetts	101,430	0.9%
31	Arkansas	98,086	0.9%
32	Nebraska	93,098	0.8%
33	New Mexico	92,672	0.8%
34	Utah	90,811	0.8%
35	Kansas	80,262	0.7%
36	Idaho	72,204	0.7%
37	Kentucky	69,483	0.6%
38	Maine	55,345	0.5%
39	Hawaii	49,456	0.4%
40	New Hampshire	43,769	0.4%
41	Rhode Island	43,576	0.4%
42	Alaska	36,864	0.3%
43	Wyoming	35,849	0.3%
44	Delaware	31,048	0.3%
45	West Virginia	30,257	0.3%
46	South Carolina	26,540	0.2%
47	North Dakota	26,010	0.2%
48	South Dakota	24,475	0.2%
49	Vermont	12,074	0.1%
NA	Montana**	NA	NA
	District of Columbia**	NA	NA

Source: Federal Bureau of Investigation
"Crime in the United States 2004" (Uniform Crime Reports, October 17, 2005)
By law enforcement agencies submitting complete reports to the F.B.I. for 12 months in 2004. The F.B.I. estimates
14,004,327 reported and unreported arrests occurred in 2004. See important note at beginning of this chapter.
**Not available.*

Reported Arrest Rate in 2004

National Rate = 4,865.4 Reported Arrests per 100,000 Population*

ALPHA ORDER

RANK ORDER

RANK	STATE	RATE		RANK	STATE	RATE
21	Alabama	5,207.6		1	Wisconsin	8,441.4
14	Alaska	5,784.0		2	Mississippi	7,609.7
18	Arizona	5,631.4		3	Louisiana	7,400.8
5	Arkansas	6,673.2		4	Wyoming	7,276.1
32	California	4,215.4		5	Arkansas	6,673.2
12	Colorado	5,834.1		6	Nevada	6,607.1
39	Connecticut	4,003.3		7	Georgia	6,530.2
36	Delaware	4,126.9		8	North Carolina	6,502.0
11	Florida	5,916.3		9	New Mexico	6,421.8
7	Georgia	6,530.2		10	Utah	5,926.5
29	Hawaii	4,480.7		11	Florida	5,916.3
17	Idaho	5,711.6		12	Colorado	5,834.1
NA	Illinois**	NA		13	South Dakota	5,819.2
24	Indiana	4,707.2		14	Alaska	5,784.0
31	Iowa	4,397.8		15	Missouri	5,757.2
34	Kansas	4,139.5		16	Nebraska	5,737.9
NA	Kentucky**	NA		17	Idaho	5,711.6
3	Louisiana	7,400.8		18	Arizona	5,631.4
33	Maine	4,204.7		19	Maryland	5,574.6
19	Maryland	5,574.6		20	Tennessee	5,559.7
46	Massachusetts	2,208.3		21	Alabama	5,207.6
41	Michigan	3,525.1		22	North Dakota	5,086.4
40	Minnesota	3,722.2		23	Texas	5,013.0
2	Mississippi	7,609.7		24	Indiana	4,707.2
15	Missouri	5,757.2		25	Oklahoma	4,665.8
NA	Montana**	NA		26	Washington	4,572.7
16	Nebraska	5,737.9		27	Oregon	4,534.4
6	Nevada	6,607.1		28	New Jersey	4,496.5
30	New Hampshire	4,414.1		29	Hawaii	4,480.7
28	New Jersey	4,496.5		30	New Hampshire	4,414.1
9	New Mexico	6,421.8		31	Iowa	4,397.8
43	New York	3,221.0		32	California	4,215.4
8	North Carolina	6,502.0		33	Maine	4,204.7
22	North Dakota	5,086.4		34	Kansas	4,139.5
42	Ohio	3,477.8		35	Virginia	4,132.0
25	Oklahoma	4,665.8		36	Delaware	4,126.9
27	Oregon	4,534.4		37	Pennsylvania	4,119.7
37	Pennsylvania	4,119.7		38	Rhode Island	4,032.5
38	Rhode Island	4,032.5		39	Connecticut	4,003.3
NA	South Carolina**	NA		40	Minnesota	3,722.2
13	South Dakota	5,819.2		41	Michigan	3,525.1
20	Tennessee	5,559.7		42	Ohio	3,477.8
23	Texas	5,013.0		43	New York	3,221.0
10	Utah	5,926.5		44	West Virginia	2,873.0
45	Vermont	2,322.3		45	Vermont	2,322.3
35	Virginia	4,132.0		46	Massachusetts	2,208.3
26	Washington	4,572.7		NA	Illinois**	NA
44	West Virginia	2,873.0		NA	Kentucky**	NA
1	Wisconsin	8,441.4		NA	Montana**	NA
4	Wyoming	7,276.1		NA	South Carolina**	NA
					District of Columbia**	NA

Source: Morgan Quitno Press using data from Federal Bureau of Investigation
"Crime in the United States 2004" (Uniform Crime Reports, October 17, 2005)
*By law enforcement agencies submitting complete reports to the F.B.I. for 12 months in 2004. These rates based on population estimates for areas under the jurisdiction of those agencies reporting. Arrest rate based on the F.B.I. estimate of total arrests is 4,769.0 reported and unreported arrests per 100,000 population. See important note at beginning of this chapter. **Not available.

2

Reported Arrests for Crime Index Offenses in 2004

National Total = 1,796,731 Reported Arrests*

ALPHA ORDER

RANK	STATE	ARRESTS	% of USA
23	Alabama	26,633	1.5%
42	Alaska	5,458	0.3%
7	Arizona	50,911	2.8%
32	Arkansas	12,921	0.7%
1	California	287,003	16.0%
18	Colorado	35,877	2.0%
27	Connecticut	20,317	1.1%
39	Delaware	6,689	0.4%
2	Florida	177,436	9.9%
21	Georgia	33,836	1.9%
40	Hawaii	6,375	0.4%
38	Idaho	7,821	0.4%
17	Illinois	36,140	2.0%
20	Indiana	34,651	1.9%
29	Iowa	16,084	0.9%
36	Kansas	10,687	0.6%
35	Kentucky	10,701	0.6%
16	Louisiana	38,280	2.1%
37	Maine	8,230	0.5%
8	Maryland	50,461	2.8%
28	Massachusetts	18,676	1.0%
12	Michigan	46,590	2.6%
26	Minnesota	20,866	1.2%
31	Mississippi	13,425	0.7%
11	Missouri	46,851	2.6%
NA	Montana**	NA	NA
33	Nebraska	11,765	0.7%
24	Nevada	24,450	1.4%
45	New Hampshire	3,153	0.2%
10	New Jersey	47,696	2.7%
34	New Mexico	10,808	0.6%
6	New York	62,052	3.5%
5	North Carolina	64,169	3.6%
47	North Dakota	2,313	0.1%
14	Ohio	43,228	2.4%
25	Oklahoma	23,096	1.3%
19	Oregon	35,420	2.0%
4	Pennsylvania	77,145	4.3%
41	Rhode Island	5,746	0.3%
43	South Carolina	5,077	0.3%
48	South Dakota	2,072	0.1%
13	Tennessee	44,422	2.5%
3	Texas	165,375	9.2%
30	Utah	15,445	0.9%
49	Vermont	1,360	0.1%
22	Virginia	31,848	1.8%
15	Washington	41,207	2.3%
44	West Virginia	4,549	0.3%
9	Wisconsin	48,101	2.7%
46	Wyoming	3,142	0.2%

RANK ORDER

RANK	STATE	ARRESTS	% of USA
1	California	287,003	16.0%
2	Florida	177,436	9.9%
3	Texas	165,375	9.2%
4	Pennsylvania	77,145	4.3%
5	North Carolina	64,169	3.6%
6	New York	62,052	3.5%
7	Arizona	50,911	2.8%
8	Maryland	50,461	2.8%
9	Wisconsin	48,101	2.7%
10	New Jersey	47,696	2.7%
11	Missouri	46,851	2.6%
12	Michigan	46,590	2.6%
13	Tennessee	44,422	2.5%
14	Ohio	43,228	2.4%
15	Washington	41,207	2.3%
16	Louisiana	38,280	2.1%
17	Illinois	36,140	2.0%
18	Colorado	35,877	2.0%
19	Oregon	35,420	2.0%
20	Indiana	34,651	1.9%
21	Georgia	33,836	1.9%
22	Virginia	31,848	1.8%
23	Alabama	26,633	1.5%
24	Nevada	24,450	1.4%
25	Oklahoma	23,096	1.3%
26	Minnesota	20,866	1.2%
27	Connecticut	20,317	1.1%
28	Massachusetts	18,676	1.0%
29	Iowa	16,084	0.9%
30	Utah	15,445	0.9%
31	Mississippi	13,425	0.7%
32	Arkansas	12,921	0.7%
33	Nebraska	11,765	0.7%
34	New Mexico	10,808	0.6%
35	Kentucky	10,701	0.6%
36	Kansas	10,687	0.6%
37	Maine	8,230	0.5%
38	Idaho	7,821	0.4%
39	Delaware	6,689	0.4%
40	Hawaii	6,375	0.4%
41	Rhode Island	5,746	0.3%
42	Alaska	5,458	0.3%
43	South Carolina	5,077	0.3%
44	West Virginia	4,549	0.3%
45	New Hampshire	3,153	0.2%
46	Wyoming	3,142	0.2%
47	North Dakota	2,313	0.1%
48	South Dakota	2,072	0.1%
49	Vermont	1,360	0.1%
NA	Montana**	NA	NA
	District of Columbia**	NA	NA

Source: Morgan Quitno Press using data from Federal Bureau of Investigation
"Crime in the United States 2004" (Uniform Crime Reports, October 17, 2005)
*By law enforcement agencies submitting complete reports to the F.B.I. for 12 months in 2004. The F.B.I. estimates 2,240,083 reported and unreported arrests for crime index offenses occurred in 2004. Crime index offenses consist of murder, forcible rape, robbery, aggravated assault, burglary, larceny-theft, motor vehicle theft and arson. See important note at beginning of this chapter. **Not available.

3

Reported Arrest Rate for Crime Index Offenses in 2004

National Rate = 789.2 Reported Arrests per 100,000 Population*

ALPHA ORDER

RANK	STATE	RATE
27	Alabama	665.8
18	Alaska	856.4
11	Arizona	910.1
16	Arkansas	879.1
19	California	855.2
11	Colorado	910.1
25	Connecticut	696.3
15	Delaware	889.1
7	Florida	1,020.3
3	Georgia	1,075.4
34	Hawaii	577.6
32	Idaho	618.7
NA	Illinois**	NA
20	Indiana	757.1
28	Iowa	640.1
37	Kansas	551.2
NA	Kentucky**	NA
1	Louisiana	1,217.4
31	Maine	625.3
13	Maryland	908.5
44	Massachusetts	406.6
39	Michigan	495.5
33	Minnesota	587.3
14	Mississippi	901.3
9	Missouri	986.5
NA	Montana**	NA
23	Nebraska	725.1
2	Nevada	1,084.9
45	New Hampshire	318.0
35	New Jersey	564.9
21	New Mexico	749.0
30	New York	632.7
4	North Carolina	1,059.4
42	North Dakota	452.3
36	Ohio	553.0
26	Oklahoma	677.9
6	Oregon	1,034.8
24	Pennsylvania	720.5
38	Rhode Island	531.7
NA	South Carolina**	NA
40	South Dakota	492.6
10	Tennessee	917.7
22	Texas	742.5
8	Utah	1,008.0
46	Vermont	261.6
41	Virginia	491.5
17	Washington	870.2
43	West Virginia	431.9
5	Wisconsin	1,059.3
29	Wyoming	637.7

RANK ORDER

RANK	STATE	RATE
1	Louisiana	1,217.4
2	Nevada	1,084.9
3	Georgia	1,075.4
4	North Carolina	1,059.4
5	Wisconsin	1,059.3
6	Oregon	1,034.8
7	Florida	1,020.3
8	Utah	1,008.0
9	Missouri	986.5
10	Tennessee	917.7
11	Arizona	910.1
11	Colorado	910.1
13	Maryland	908.5
14	Mississippi	901.3
15	Delaware	889.1
16	Arkansas	879.1
17	Washington	870.2
18	Alaska	856.4
19	California	855.2
20	Indiana	757.1
21	New Mexico	749.0
22	Texas	742.5
23	Nebraska	725.1
24	Pennsylvania	720.5
25	Connecticut	696.3
26	Oklahoma	677.9
27	Alabama	665.8
28	Iowa	640.1
29	Wyoming	637.7
30	New York	632.7
31	Maine	625.3
32	Idaho	618.7
33	Minnesota	587.3
34	Hawaii	577.6
35	New Jersey	564.9
36	Ohio	553.0
37	Kansas	551.2
38	Rhode Island	531.7
39	Michigan	495.5
40	South Dakota	492.6
41	Virginia	491.5
42	North Dakota	452.3
43	West Virginia	431.9
44	Massachusetts	406.6
45	New Hampshire	318.0
46	Vermont	261.6
NA	Illinois**	NA
NA	Kentucky**	NA
NA	Montana**	NA
NA	South Carolina**	NA
	District of Columbia**	NA

Source: Morgan Quitno Press using data from Federal Bureau of Investigation
    "Crime in the United States 2004" (Uniform Crime Reports, October 17, 2005)
*By law enforcement agencies submitting complete reports to the F.B.I. for 12 months in 2004. These rates based
on population estimates for areas under the jurisdiction of those agencies reporting. Arrest rate based on the F.B.I.
estimate of reported and unreported arrests for crime index offenses is 762.8 arrests per 100,000 population. See
important note at beginning of this chapter. **Not available.

4

Reported Arrests for Violent Crime in 2004

National Total = 475,501 Reported Arrests*

ALPHA ORDER

RANK	STATE	ARRESTS	% of USA
23	Alabama	6,068	1.3%
38	Alaska	1,485	0.3%
16	Arizona	9,017	1.9%
31	Arkansas	2,976	0.6%
1	California	117,860	24.8%
22	Colorado	6,143	1.3%
26	Connecticut	4,964	1.0%
34	Delaware	1,894	0.4%
2	Florida	50,838	10.7%
15	Georgia	9,393	2.0%
42	Hawaii	1,176	0.2%
40	Idaho	1,297	0.3%
14	Illinois	9,525	2.0%
12	Indiana	10,848	2.3%
28	Iowa	3,735	0.8%
33	Kansas	2,055	0.4%
35	Kentucky	1,791	0.4%
13	Louisiana	9,603	2.0%
44	Maine	864	0.2%
11	Maryland	12,139	2.6%
20	Massachusetts	7,009	1.5%
8	Michigan	14,206	3.0%
30	Minnesota	3,001	0.6%
32	Mississippi	2,249	0.5%
9	Missouri	12,469	2.6%
NA	Montana**	NA	NA
37	Nebraska	1,563	0.3%
25	Nevada	5,293	1.1%
46	New Hampshire	514	0.1%
6	New Jersey	14,853	3.1%
29	New Mexico	3,396	0.7%
7	New York	14,363	3.0%
5	North Carolina	16,422	3.5%
49	North Dakota	192	0.0%
18	Ohio	7,514	1.6%
24	Oklahoma	5,627	1.2%
27	Oregon	4,810	1.0%
4	Pennsylvania	23,576	5.0%
41	Rhode Island	1,257	0.3%
36	South Carolina	1,594	0.3%
47	South Dakota	318	0.1%
10	Tennessee	12,398	2.6%
3	Texas	33,453	7.0%
39	Utah	1,440	0.3%
48	Vermont	291	0.1%
21	Virginia	6,265	1.3%
19	Washington	7,121	1.5%
43	West Virginia	1,009	0.2%
17	Wisconsin	8,990	1.9%
45	Wyoming	549	0.1%

RANK ORDER

RANK	STATE	ARRESTS	% of USA
1	California	117,860	24.8%
2	Florida	50,838	10.7%
3	Texas	33,453	7.0%
4	Pennsylvania	23,576	5.0%
5	North Carolina	16,422	3.5%
6	New Jersey	14,853	3.1%
7	New York	14,363	3.0%
8	Michigan	14,206	3.0%
9	Missouri	12,469	2.6%
10	Tennessee	12,398	2.6%
11	Maryland	12,139	2.6%
12	Indiana	10,848	2.3%
13	Louisiana	9,603	2.0%
14	Illinois	9,525	2.0%
15	Georgia	9,393	2.0%
16	Arizona	9,017	1.9%
17	Wisconsin	8,990	1.9%
18	Ohio	7,514	1.6%
19	Washington	7,121	1.5%
20	Massachusetts	7,009	1.5%
21	Virginia	6,265	1.3%
22	Colorado	6,143	1.3%
23	Alabama	6,068	1.3%
24	Oklahoma	5,627	1.2%
25	Nevada	5,293	1.1%
26	Connecticut	4,964	1.0%
27	Oregon	4,810	1.0%
28	Iowa	3,735	0.8%
29	New Mexico	3,396	0.7%
30	Minnesota	3,001	0.6%
31	Arkansas	2,976	0.6%
32	Mississippi	2,249	0.5%
33	Kansas	2,055	0.4%
34	Delaware	1,894	0.4%
35	Kentucky	1,791	0.4%
36	South Carolina	1,594	0.3%
37	Nebraska	1,563	0.3%
38	Alaska	1,485	0.3%
39	Utah	1,440	0.3%
40	Idaho	1,297	0.3%
41	Rhode Island	1,257	0.3%
42	Hawaii	1,176	0.2%
43	West Virginia	1,009	0.2%
44	Maine	864	0.2%
45	Wyoming	549	0.1%
46	New Hampshire	514	0.1%
47	South Dakota	318	0.1%
48	Vermont	291	0.1%
49	North Dakota	192	0.0%
NA	Montana**	NA	NA
	District of Columbia**	NA	NA

Source: Federal Bureau of Investigation
   "Crime in the United States 2004" (Uniform Crime Reports, October 17, 2005)
*By law enforcement agencies submitting complete reports to the F.B.I. for 12 months in 2004. The F.B.I. estimates
590,258 reported and unreported arrests for violent crimes occurred in 2004. Violent crimes are offenses of murder,
forcible rape, robbery and aggravated assault. See important note at beginning of this chapter.
**Not available.

Reported Arrest Rate for Violent Crime in 2004

National Rate = 208.9 Reported Arrests per 100,000 Population*

ALPHA ORDER

RANK	STATE	RATE
23	Alabama	151.7
12	Alaska	233.0
20	Arizona	161.2
15	Arkansas	202.5
1	California	351.2
21	Colorado	155.8
18	Connecticut	170.1
8	Delaware	251.8
4	Florida	292.3
3	Georgia	298.5
33	Hawaii	106.5
35	Idaho	102.6
NA	Illinois**	NA
9	Indiana	237.0
28	Iowa	148.6
34	Kansas	106.0
NA	Kentucky**	NA
2	Louisiana	305.4
43	Maine	65.6
14	Maryland	218.6
22	Massachusetts	152.6
24	Michigan	151.1
41	Minnesota	84.5
25	Mississippi	151.0
6	Missouri	262.6
NA	Montana**	NA
37	Nebraska	96.3
11	Nevada	234.9
45	New Hampshire	51.8
17	New Jersey	175.9
10	New Mexico	235.3
29	New York	146.5
5	North Carolina	271.1
46	North Dakota	37.5
38	Ohio	96.1
19	Oklahoma	165.2
30	Oregon	140.5
13	Pennsylvania	220.2
31	Rhode Island	116.3
NA	South Carolina**	NA
42	South Dakota	75.6
7	Tennessee	256.1
27	Texas	150.2
40	Utah	94.0
44	Vermont	56.0
36	Virginia	96.7
26	Washington	150.4
39	West Virginia	95.8
16	Wisconsin	198.0
32	Wyoming	111.4

RANK ORDER

RANK	STATE	RATE
1	California	351.2
2	Louisiana	305.4
3	Georgia	298.5
4	Florida	292.3
5	North Carolina	271.1
6	Missouri	262.6
7	Tennessee	256.1
8	Delaware	251.8
9	Indiana	237.0
10	New Mexico	235.3
11	Nevada	234.9
12	Alaska	233.0
13	Pennsylvania	220.2
14	Maryland	218.6
15	Arkansas	202.5
16	Wisconsin	198.0
17	New Jersey	175.9
18	Connecticut	170.1
19	Oklahoma	165.2
20	Arizona	161.2
21	Colorado	155.8
22	Massachusetts	152.6
23	Alabama	151.7
24	Michigan	151.1
25	Mississippi	151.0
26	Washington	150.4
27	Texas	150.2
28	Iowa	148.6
29	New York	146.5
30	Oregon	140.5
31	Rhode Island	116.3
32	Wyoming	111.4
33	Hawaii	106.5
34	Kansas	106.0
35	Idaho	102.6
36	Virginia	96.7
37	Nebraska	96.3
38	Ohio	96.1
39	West Virginia	95.8
40	Utah	94.0
41	Minnesota	84.5
42	South Dakota	75.6
43	Maine	65.6
44	Vermont	56.0
45	New Hampshire	51.8
46	North Dakota	37.5
NA	Illinois**	NA
NA	Kentucky**	NA
NA	Montana**	NA
NA	South Carolina**	NA
	District of Columbia**	NA

Source: Morgan Quitno Press using data from Federal Bureau of Investigation
   "Crime in the United States 2004" (Uniform Crime Reports, October 17, 2005)
*By law enforcement agencies submitting complete reports to the F.B.I. for 12 months in 2004. These rates based on population estimates for areas under the jurisdiction of those agencies reporting. Arrest rate based on the F.B.I. estimate of reported and unreported arrests for violent crimes is 201.0 arrests per 100,000 population. See important note at beginning of this chapter. **Not available.

Reported Arrests for Murder in 2004

National Total = 10,691 Reported Arrests*

RANK	STATE	ARRESTS	% of USA
13	Alabama	280	2.6%
39	Alaska	31	0.3%
17	Arizona	252	2.4%
38	Arkansas	33	0.3%
1	California	1,894	17.7%
23	Colorado	145	1.4%
28	Connecticut	88	0.8%
44	Delaware	10	0.1%
3	Florida	693	6.5%
18	Georgia	248	2.3%
32	Hawaii	40	0.4%
41	Idaho	24	0.2%
7	Illinois	433	4.1%
19	Indiana	232	2.2%
32	Iowa	40	0.4%
37	Kansas	35	0.3%
29	Kentucky	55	0.5%
10	Louisiana	303	2.8%
45	Maine	8	0.1%
11	Maryland	295	2.8%
30	Massachusetts	54	0.5%
8	Michigan	364	3.4%
35	Minnesota	38	0.4%
22	Mississippi	156	1.5%
9	Missouri	321	3.0%
NA	Montana**	NA	NA
36	Nebraska	36	0.3%
24	Nevada	143	1.3%
48	New Hampshire	6	0.1%
15	New Jersey	270	2.5%
27	New Mexico	92	0.9%
16	New York	263	2.5%
5	North Carolina	536	5.0%
46	North Dakota	7	0.1%
20	Ohio	212	2.0%
21	Oklahoma	173	1.6%
25	Oregon	125	1.2%
5	Pennsylvania	536	5.0%
42	Rhode Island	19	0.2%
34	South Carolina	39	0.4%
48	South Dakota	6	0.1%
12	Tennessee	290	2.7%
2	Texas	834	7.8%
31	Utah	45	0.4%
46	Vermont	7	0.1%
13	Virginia	280	2.6%
26	Washington	123	1.2%
40	West Virginia	25	0.2%
4	Wisconsin	538	5.0%
43	Wyoming	14	0.1%

RANK	STATE	ARRESTS	% of USA
1	California	1,894	17.7%
2	Texas	834	7.8%
3	Florida	693	6.5%
4	Wisconsin	538	5.0%
5	North Carolina	536	5.0%
5	Pennsylvania	536	5.0%
7	Illinois	433	4.1%
8	Michigan	364	3.4%
9	Missouri	321	3.0%
10	Louisiana	303	2.8%
11	Maryland	295	2.8%
12	Tennessee	290	2.7%
13	Alabama	280	2.6%
13	Virginia	280	2.6%
15	New Jersey	270	2.5%
16	New York	263	2.5%
17	Arizona	252	2.4%
18	Georgia	248	2.3%
19	Indiana	232	2.2%
20	Ohio	212	2.0%
21	Oklahoma	173	1.6%
22	Mississippi	156	1.5%
23	Colorado	145	1.4%
24	Nevada	143	1.3%
25	Oregon	125	1.2%
26	Washington	123	1.2%
27	New Mexico	92	0.9%
28	Connecticut	88	0.8%
29	Kentucky	55	0.5%
30	Massachusetts	54	0.5%
31	Utah	45	0.4%
32	Hawaii	40	0.4%
32	Iowa	40	0.4%
34	South Carolina	39	0.4%
35	Minnesota	38	0.4%
36	Nebraska	36	0.3%
37	Kansas	35	0.3%
38	Arkansas	33	0.3%
39	Alaska	31	0.3%
40	West Virginia	25	0.2%
41	Idaho	24	0.2%
42	Rhode Island	19	0.2%
43	Wyoming	14	0.1%
44	Delaware	10	0.1%
45	Maine	8	0.1%
46	North Dakota	7	0.1%
46	Vermont	7	0.1%
48	New Hampshire	6	0.1%
48	South Dakota	6	0.1%
NA	Montana**	NA	NA
	District of Columbia**	NA	NA

Source: Federal Bureau of Investigation
    "Crime in the United States 2004" (Uniform Crime Reports, October 17, 2005)
*By law enforcement agencies submitting complete reports to the F.B.I. for 12 months in 2004. The F.B.I. estimates 14,004 reported and unreported arrests for murder occurred in 2004. Murder includes nonnegligent manslaughter. See important note at beginning of this chapter.
**Not available.

Reported Arrest Rate for Murder in 2004

National Rate = 4.7 Reported Arrests per 100,000 Population*

ALPHA ORDER				RANK ORDER		
RANK	STATE	RATE		RANK	STATE	RATE
6	Alabama	7.0		1	Wisconsin	11.8
16	Alaska	4.9		2	Mississippi	10.5
17	Arizona	4.5		3	Louisiana	9.6
33	Arkansas	2.2		4	North Carolina	8.8
11	California	5.6		5	Georgia	7.9
21	Colorado	3.7		6	Alabama	7.0
26	Connecticut	3.0		7	Missouri	6.8
41	Delaware	1.3		8	New Mexico	6.4
19	Florida	4.0		9	Nevada	6.3
5	Georgia	7.9		10	Tennessee	6.0
24	Hawaii	3.6		11	California	5.6
35	Idaho	1.9		12	Maryland	5.3
NA	Illinois**	NA		13	Indiana	5.1
13	Indiana	5.1		13	Oklahoma	5.1
38	Iowa	1.6		15	Pennsylvania	5.0
36	Kansas	1.8		16	Alaska	4.9
NA	Kentucky**	NA		17	Arizona	4.5
3	Louisiana	9.6		18	Virginia	4.3
45	Maine	0.6		19	Florida	4.0
12	Maryland	5.3		20	Michigan	3.9
43	Massachusetts	1.2		21	Colorado	3.7
20	Michigan	3.9		21	Oregon	3.7
44	Minnesota	1.1		21	Texas	3.7
2	Mississippi	10.5		24	Hawaii	3.6
7	Missouri	6.8		25	New Jersey	3.2
NA	Montana**	NA		26	Connecticut	3.0
33	Nebraska	2.2		27	Utah	2.9
9	Nevada	6.3		28	Wyoming	2.8
45	New Hampshire	0.6		29	New York	2.7
25	New Jersey	3.2		29	Ohio	2.7
8	New Mexico	6.4		31	Washington	2.6
29	New York	2.7		32	West Virginia	2.4
4	North Carolina	8.8		33	Arkansas	2.2
39	North Dakota	1.4		33	Nebraska	2.2
29	Ohio	2.7		35	Idaho	1.9
13	Oklahoma	5.1		36	Kansas	1.8
21	Oregon	3.7		36	Rhode Island	1.8
15	Pennsylvania	5.0		38	Iowa	1.6
36	Rhode Island	1.8		39	North Dakota	1.4
NA	South Carolina**	NA		39	South Dakota	1.4
39	South Dakota	1.4		41	Delaware	1.3
10	Tennessee	6.0		41	Vermont	1.3
21	Texas	3.7		43	Massachusetts	1.2
27	Utah	2.9		44	Minnesota	1.1
41	Vermont	1.3		45	Maine	0.6
18	Virginia	4.3		45	New Hampshire	0.6
31	Washington	2.6		NA	Illinois**	NA
32	West Virginia	2.4		NA	Kentucky**	NA
1	Wisconsin	11.8		NA	Montana**	NA
28	Wyoming	2.8		NA	South Carolina**	NA
					District of Columbia**	NA

Source: Morgan Quitno Press using data from Federal Bureau of Investigation
"Crime in the United States 2004" (Uniform Crime Reports, October 17, 2005)
*By law enforcement agencies submitting complete reports to the F.B.I. for 12 months in 2004. These rates based on population estimates for areas under the jurisdiction of those agencies reporting. Arrest rate based on the F.B.I. estimate of reported and unreported arrests for murder is 4.8 arrests per 100,000 population. See important note at beginning of this chapter. **Not available.

8

Reported Arrests for Rape in 2004

National Total = 20,850 Reported Arrests*

RANK	STATE	ARRESTS	% of USA
16	Alabama	457	2.2%
41	Alaska	82	0.4%
25	Arizona	222	1.1%
36	Arkansas	112	0.5%
3	California	2,099	10.1%
18	Colorado	434	2.1%
24	Connecticut	239	1.1%
39	Delaware	101	0.5%
2	Florida	2,157	10.3%
23	Georgia	286	1.4%
43	Hawaii	73	0.4%
37	Idaho	106	0.5%
11	Illinois	561	2.7%
26	Indiana	219	1.1%
35	Iowa	123	0.6%
31	Kansas	149	0.7%
32	Kentucky	143	0.7%
17	Louisiana	453	2.2%
38	Maine	104	0.5%
15	Maryland	466	2.2%
27	Massachusetts	214	1.0%
5	Michigan	872	4.2%
12	Minnesota	557	2.7%
28	Mississippi	212	1.0%
13	Missouri	532	2.6%
NA	Montana**	NA	NA
30	Nebraska	196	0.9%
29	Nevada	203	1.0%
44	New Hampshire	72	0.3%
14	New Jersey	483	2.3%
33	New Mexico	137	0.7%
8	New York	739	3.5%
10	North Carolina	655	3.1%
47	North Dakota	34	0.2%
9	Ohio	669	3.2%
19	Oklahoma	343	1.6%
22	Oregon	294	1.4%
4	Pennsylvania	1,267	6.1%
40	Rhode Island	94	0.5%
45	South Carolina	66	0.3%
46	South Dakota	57	0.3%
21	Tennessee	296	1.4%
1	Texas	2,177	10.4%
34	Utah	128	0.6%
42	Vermont	75	0.4%
20	Virginia	330	1.6%
7	Washington	756	3.6%
49	West Virginia	17	0.1%
6	Wisconsin	758	3.6%
48	Wyoming	29	0.1%

RANK	STATE	ARRESTS	% of USA
1	Texas	2,177	10.4%
2	Florida	2,157	10.3%
3	California	2,099	10.1%
4	Pennsylvania	1,267	6.1%
5	Michigan	872	4.2%
6	Wisconsin	758	3.6%
7	Washington	756	3.6%
8	New York	739	3.5%
9	Ohio	669	3.2%
10	North Carolina	655	3.1%
11	Illinois	561	2.7%
12	Minnesota	557	2.7%
13	Missouri	532	2.6%
14	New Jersey	483	2.3%
15	Maryland	466	2.2%
16	Alabama	457	2.2%
17	Louisiana	453	2.2%
18	Colorado	434	2.1%
19	Oklahoma	343	1.6%
20	Virginia	330	1.6%
21	Tennessee	296	1.4%
22	Oregon	294	1.4%
23	Georgia	286	1.4%
24	Connecticut	239	1.1%
25	Arizona	222	1.1%
26	Indiana	219	1.1%
27	Massachusetts	214	1.0%
28	Mississippi	212	1.0%
29	Nevada	203	1.0%
30	Nebraska	196	0.9%
31	Kansas	149	0.7%
32	Kentucky	143	0.7%
33	New Mexico	137	0.7%
34	Utah	128	0.6%
35	Iowa	123	0.6%
36	Arkansas	112	0.5%
37	Idaho	106	0.5%
38	Maine	104	0.5%
39	Delaware	101	0.5%
40	Rhode Island	94	0.5%
41	Alaska	82	0.4%
42	Vermont	75	0.4%
43	Hawaii	73	0.4%
44	New Hampshire	72	0.3%
45	South Carolina	66	0.3%
46	South Dakota	57	0.3%
47	North Dakota	34	0.2%
48	Wyoming	29	0.1%
49	West Virginia	17	0.1%
NA	Montana**	NA	NA
	District of Columbia**	NA	NA

Source: Federal Bureau of Investigation
   "Crime in the United States 2004" (Uniform Crime Reports, October 17, 2005)
*By law enforcement agencies submitting complete reports to the F.B.I. for 12 months in 2003. The F.B.I. estimates
26,173 reported and unreported arrests for rape occurred in 2003. Forcible rape is the carnal knowledge of a
female forcibly and against her will. Assaults or attempts to commit rape by force or threat of force are included.
See important note at beginning of this chapter. **Not available.

Reported Arrest Rate for Rape in 2004

National Rate = 9.2 Reported Arrests per 100,000 Population*

ALPHA ORDER

RANK	STATE	RATE
13	Alabama	11.4
9	Alaska	12.9
45	Arizona	4.0
32	Arkansas	7.6
37	California	6.3
15	Colorado	11.0
29	Connecticut	8.2
8	Delaware	13.4
10	Florida	12.4
21	Georgia	9.1
35	Hawaii	6.6
26	Idaho	8.4
NA	Illinois**	NA
43	Indiana	4.8
42	Iowa	4.9
31	Kansas	7.7
NA	Kentucky**	NA
4	Louisiana	14.4
30	Maine	7.9
26	Maryland	8.4
44	Massachusetts	4.7
20	Michigan	9.3
3	Minnesota	15.7
6	Mississippi	14.2
14	Missouri	11.2
NA	Montana**	NA
11	Nebraska	12.1
22	Nevada	9.0
34	New Hampshire	7.3
40	New Jersey	5.7
19	New Mexico	9.5
33	New York	7.5
16	North Carolina	10.8
35	North Dakota	6.6
24	Ohio	8.6
17	Oklahoma	10.1
24	Oregon	8.6
12	Pennsylvania	11.8
23	Rhode Island	8.7
NA	South Carolina**	NA
7	South Dakota	13.6
38	Tennessee	6.1
18	Texas	9.8
26	Utah	8.4
4	Vermont	14.4
41	Virginia	5.1
2	Washington	16.0
46	West Virginia	1.6
1	Wisconsin	16.7
39	Wyoming	5.9

RANK ORDER

RANK	STATE	RATE
1	Wisconsin	16.7
2	Washington	16.0
3	Minnesota	15.7
4	Louisiana	14.4
4	Vermont	14.4
6	Mississippi	14.2
7	South Dakota	13.6
8	Delaware	13.4
9	Alaska	12.9
10	Florida	12.4
11	Nebraska	12.1
12	Pennsylvania	11.8
13	Alabama	11.4
14	Missouri	11.2
15	Colorado	11.0
16	North Carolina	10.8
17	Oklahoma	10.1
18	Texas	9.8
19	New Mexico	9.5
20	Michigan	9.3
21	Georgia	9.1
22	Nevada	9.0
23	Rhode Island	8.7
24	Ohio	8.6
24	Oregon	8.6
26	Idaho	8.4
26	Maryland	8.4
26	Utah	8.4
29	Connecticut	8.2
30	Maine	7.9
31	Kansas	7.7
32	Arkansas	7.6
33	New York	7.5
34	New Hampshire	7.3
35	Hawaii	6.6
35	North Dakota	6.6
37	California	6.3
38	Tennessee	6.1
39	Wyoming	5.9
40	New Jersey	5.7
41	Virginia	5.1
42	Iowa	4.9
43	Indiana	4.8
44	Massachusetts	4.7
45	Arizona	4.0
46	West Virginia	1.6
NA	Illinois**	NA
NA	Kentucky**	NA
NA	Montana**	NA
NA	South Carolina**	NA

District of Columbia**   NA

Source: Morgan Quitno Press using data from Federal Bureau of Investigation
"Crime in the United States 2004" (Uniform Crime Reports, October 17, 2005)
*By law enforcement agencies submitting complete reports to the F.B.I. for 12 months in 2004. These rates based on population estimates for areas under the jurisdiction of those agencies reporting. Arrest rate based on the F.B.I. estimate of reported and unreported arrests for rape is 8.9 arrests per 100,000 population. See important note at beginning of this chapter. **Not available.

10

Reported Arrests for Robbery in 2004

National Total = 88,436 Reported Arrests*

ALPHA ORDER

RANK	STATE	ARRESTS	% of USA
19	Alabama	1,405	1.6%
42	Alaska	134	0.2%
18	Arizona	1,433	1.6%
30	Arkansas	449	0.5%
1	California	16,762	19.0%
26	Colorado	794	0.9%
22	Connecticut	1,282	1.4%
35	Delaware	305	0.3%
2	Florida	9,100	10.3%
14	Georgia	1,676	1.9%
37	Hawaii	292	0.3%
45	Idaho	89	0.1%
8	Illinois	2,914	3.3%
17	Indiana	1,496	1.7%
36	Iowa	298	0.3%
39	Kansas	247	0.3%
28	Kentucky	525	0.6%
23	Louisiana	1,202	1.4%
41	Maine	168	0.2%
7	Maryland	3,424	3.9%
25	Massachusetts	883	1.0%
11	Michigan	2,180	2.5%
33	Minnesota	341	0.4%
29	Mississippi	509	0.6%
13	Missouri	1,858	2.1%
NA	Montana**	NA	NA
34	Nebraska	317	0.4%
24	Nevada	1,192	1.3%
43	New Hampshire	112	0.1%
5	New Jersey	4,095	4.6%
32	New Mexico	369	0.4%
6	New York	3,619	4.1%
9	North Carolina	2,844	3.2%
48	North Dakota	16	0.0%
10	Ohio	2,650	3.0%
27	Oklahoma	631	0.7%
21	Oregon	1,386	1.6%
4	Pennsylvania	6,624	7.5%
38	Rhode Island	282	0.3%
40	South Carolina	185	0.2%
47	South Dakota	20	0.0%
12	Tennessee	2,005	2.3%
3	Texas	7,294	8.2%
31	Utah	403	0.5%
49	Vermont	4	0.0%
15	Virginia	1,552	1.8%
20	Washington	1,391	1.6%
44	West Virginia	93	0.1%
16	Wisconsin	1,525	1.7%
46	Wyoming	26	0.0%

RANK ORDER

RANK	STATE	ARRESTS	% of USA
1	California	16,762	19.0%
2	Florida	9,100	10.3%
3	Texas	7,294	8.2%
4	Pennsylvania	6,624	7.5%
5	New Jersey	4,095	4.6%
6	New York	3,619	4.1%
7	Maryland	3,424	3.9%
8	Illinois	2,914	3.3%
9	North Carolina	2,844	3.2%
10	Ohio	2,650	3.0%
11	Michigan	2,180	2.5%
12	Tennessee	2,005	2.3%
13	Missouri	1,858	2.1%
14	Georgia	1,676	1.9%
15	Virginia	1,552	1.8%
16	Wisconsin	1,525	1.7%
17	Indiana	1,496	1.7%
18	Arizona	1,433	1.6%
19	Alabama	1,405	1.6%
20	Washington	1,391	1.6%
21	Oregon	1,386	1.6%
22	Connecticut	1,282	1.4%
23	Louisiana	1,202	1.4%
24	Nevada	1,192	1.3%
25	Massachusetts	883	1.0%
26	Colorado	794	0.9%
27	Oklahoma	631	0.7%
28	Kentucky	525	0.6%
29	Mississippi	509	0.6%
30	Arkansas	449	0.5%
31	Utah	403	0.5%
32	New Mexico	369	0.4%
33	Minnesota	341	0.4%
34	Nebraska	317	0.4%
35	Delaware	305	0.3%
36	Iowa	298	0.3%
37	Hawaii	292	0.3%
38	Rhode Island	282	0.3%
39	Kansas	247	0.3%
40	South Carolina	185	0.2%
41	Maine	168	0.2%
42	Alaska	134	0.2%
43	New Hampshire	112	0.1%
44	West Virginia	93	0.1%
45	Idaho	89	0.1%
46	Wyoming	26	0.0%
47	South Dakota	20	0.0%
48	North Dakota	16	0.0%
49	Vermont	4	0.0%
NA	Montana**	NA	NA
	District of Columbia**	NA	NA

Source: Federal Bureau of Investigation
   "Crime in the United States 2004" (Uniform Crime Reports, October 17, 2005)
*By law enforcement agencies submitting complete reports to the F.B.I. for 12 months in 2004. The F.B.I. estimates 109,528 reported and unreported arrests for robbery occurred in 2004. Robbery is the taking or attempting to take anything of value by force or threat of force.   See important note at beginning of this chapter.
**Not available.

Reported Arrest Rate for Robbery in 2004

National Rate = 38.8 Reported Arrests per 100,000 Population*

ALPHA ORDER

RANK ORDER

RANK	STATE	RATE		RANK	STATE	RATE
16	Alabama	35.1		1	Pennsylvania	61.9
31	Alaska	21.0		2	Maryland	61.6
27	Arizona	25.6		3	Georgia	53.3
22	Arkansas	30.5		4	Nevada	52.9
6	California	49.9		5	Florida	52.3
32	Colorado	20.1		6	California	49.9
9	Connecticut	43.9		7	New Jersey	48.5
11	Delaware	40.5		8	North Carolina	47.0
5	Florida	52.3		9	Connecticut	43.9
3	Georgia	53.3		10	Tennessee	41.4
24	Hawaii	26.5		11	Delaware	40.5
42	Idaho	7.0		11	Oregon	40.5
NA	Illinois**	NA		13	Missouri	39.1
20	Indiana	32.7		14	Louisiana	38.2
38	Iowa	11.9		15	New York	36.9
37	Kansas	12.7		16	Alabama	35.1
NA	Kentucky**	NA		17	Mississippi	34.2
14	Louisiana	38.2		18	Ohio	33.9
36	Maine	12.8		19	Wisconsin	33.6
2	Maryland	61.6		20	Indiana	32.7
34	Massachusetts	19.2		20	Texas	32.7
30	Michigan	23.2		22	Arkansas	30.5
40	Minnesota	9.6		23	Washington	29.4
17	Mississippi	34.2		24	Hawaii	26.5
13	Missouri	39.1		25	Utah	26.3
NA	Montana**	NA		26	Rhode Island	26.1
33	Nebraska	19.5		27	Arizona	25.6
4	Nevada	52.9		27	New Mexico	25.6
39	New Hampshire	11.3		29	Virginia	23.9
7	New Jersey	48.5		30	Michigan	23.2
27	New Mexico	25.6		31	Alaska	21.0
15	New York	36.9		32	Colorado	20.1
8	North Carolina	47.0		33	Nebraska	19.5
45	North Dakota	3.1		34	Massachusetts	19.2
18	Ohio	33.9		35	Oklahoma	18.5
35	Oklahoma	18.5		36	Maine	12.8
11	Oregon	40.5		37	Kansas	12.7
1	Pennsylvania	61.9		38	Iowa	11.9
26	Rhode Island	26.1		39	New Hampshire	11.3
NA	South Carolina**	NA		40	Minnesota	9.6
44	South Dakota	4.8		41	West Virginia	8.8
10	Tennessee	41.4		42	Idaho	7.0
20	Texas	32.7		43	Wyoming	5.3
25	Utah	26.3		44	South Dakota	4.8
46	Vermont	0.8		45	North Dakota	3.1
29	Virginia	23.9		46	Vermont	0.8
23	Washington	29.4		NA	Illinois**	NA
41	West Virginia	8.8		NA	Kentucky**	NA
19	Wisconsin	33.6		NA	Montana**	NA
43	Wyoming	5.3		NA	South Carolina**	NA
					District of Columbia**	NA

Source: Morgan Quitno Press using data from Federal Bureau of Investigation
"Crime in the United States 2004" (Uniform Crime Reports, October 17, 2005)
*By law enforcement agencies submitting complete reports to the F.B.I. for 12 months in 2004. These rates based on population estimates for areas under the jurisdiction of those agencies reporting. Arrest rate based on the F.B.I. estimate of reported and unreported arrests for robbery is 37.3 arrests per 100,000 population. See important note at beginning of this chapter. **Not available.

Reported Arrests for Aggravated Assault in 2004

National Total = 355,524 Reported Arrests*

ALPHA ORDER

RANK	STATE	ARRESTS	% of USA
24	Alabama	3,926	1.1%
36	Alaska	1,238	0.3%
15	Arizona	7,110	2.0%
30	Arkansas	2,382	0.7%
1	California	97,105	27.3%
20	Colorado	4,770	1.3%
26	Connecticut	3,355	0.9%
33	Delaware	1,478	0.4%
2	Florida	38,888	10.9%
14	Georgia	7,183	2.0%
43	Hawaii	771	0.2%
37	Idaho	1,078	0.3%
18	Illinois	5,617	1.6%
11	Indiana	8,901	2.5%
27	Iowa	3,274	0.9%
32	Kansas	1,624	0.5%
38	Kentucky	1,068	0.3%
13	Louisiana	7,645	2.2%
44	Maine	584	0.2%
12	Maryland	7,954	2.2%
17	Massachusetts	5,858	1.6%
6	Michigan	10,790	3.0%
31	Minnesota	2,065	0.6%
34	Mississippi	1,372	0.4%
9	Missouri	9,758	2.7%
NA	Montana**	NA	NA
39	Nebraska	1,014	0.3%
25	Nevada	3,755	1.1%
46	New Hampshire	324	0.1%
7	New Jersey	10,005	2.8%
29	New Mexico	2,798	0.8%
10	New York	9,742	2.7%
5	North Carolina	12,387	3.5%
49	North Dakota	135	0.0%
23	Ohio	3,983	1.1%
21	Oklahoma	4,480	1.3%
28	Oregon	3,005	0.8%
4	Pennsylvania	15,149	4.3%
42	Rhode Island	862	0.2%
35	South Carolina	1,304	0.4%
47	South Dakota	235	0.1%
8	Tennessee	9,807	2.8%
3	Texas	23,148	6.5%
41	Utah	864	0.2%
48	Vermont	205	0.1%
22	Virginia	4,103	1.2%
19	Washington	4,851	1.4%
40	West Virginia	874	0.2%
16	Wisconsin	6,169	1.7%
45	Wyoming	480	0.1%

RANK ORDER

RANK	STATE	ARRESTS	% of USA
1	California	97,105	27.3%
2	Florida	38,888	10.9%
3	Texas	23,148	6.5%
4	Pennsylvania	15,149	4.3%
5	North Carolina	12,387	3.5%
6	Michigan	10,790	3.0%
7	New Jersey	10,005	2.8%
8	Tennessee	9,807	2.8%
9	Missouri	9,758	2.7%
10	New York	9,742	2.7%
11	Indiana	8,901	2.5%
12	Maryland	7,954	2.2%
13	Louisiana	7,645	2.2%
14	Georgia	7,183	2.0%
15	Arizona	7,110	2.0%
16	Wisconsin	6,169	1.7%
17	Massachusetts	5,858	1.6%
18	Illinois	5,617	1.6%
19	Washington	4,851	1.4%
20	Colorado	4,770	1.3%
21	Oklahoma	4,480	1.3%
22	Virginia	4,103	1.2%
23	Ohio	3,983	1.1%
24	Alabama	3,926	1.1%
25	Nevada	3,755	1.1%
26	Connecticut	3,355	0.9%
27	Iowa	3,274	0.9%
28	Oregon	3,005	0.8%
29	New Mexico	2,798	0.8%
30	Arkansas	2,382	0.7%
31	Minnesota	2,065	0.6%
32	Kansas	1,624	0.5%
33	Delaware	1,478	0.4%
34	Mississippi	1,372	0.4%
35	South Carolina	1,304	0.4%
36	Alaska	1,238	0.3%
37	Idaho	1,078	0.3%
38	Kentucky	1,068	0.3%
39	Nebraska	1,014	0.3%
40	West Virginia	874	0.2%
41	Utah	864	0.2%
42	Rhode Island	862	0.2%
43	Hawaii	771	0.2%
44	Maine	584	0.2%
45	Wyoming	480	0.1%
46	New Hampshire	324	0.1%
47	South Dakota	235	0.1%
48	Vermont	205	0.1%
49	North Dakota	135	0.0%
NA	Montana**	NA	NA
	District of Columbia**	NA	NA

Source: Federal Bureau of Investigation
"Crime in the United States 2004" (Uniform Crime Reports, October 17, 2005)
By law enforcement agencies submitting complete reports to the F.B.I. for 12 months in 2004. The F.B.I. estimates 440,553 reported and unreported arrests for aggravated assault occurred in 2004. Aggravated assault is an attack for the purpose of inflicting severe bodily injury. See important note at beginning of this chapter.
**Not available.*

13

Reported Arrest Rate for Aggravated Assault in 2004

National Rate = 156.2 Reported Arrests per 100,000 Population*

ALPHA ORDER

RANK	STATE	RATE
28	Alabama	98.1
10	Alaska	194.2
20	Arizona	127.1
13	Arkansas	162.1
1	California	289.3
21	Colorado	121.0
23	Connecticut	115.0
8	Delaware	196.5
4	Florida	223.6
3	Georgia	228.3
36	Hawaii	69.9
32	Idaho	85.3
NA	Illinois**	NA
9	Indiana	194.5
18	Iowa	130.3
33	Kansas	83.8
NA	Kentucky**	NA
2	Louisiana	243.1
43	Maine	44.4
14	Maryland	143.2
19	Massachusetts	127.5
24	Michigan	114.7
39	Minnesota	58.1
30	Mississippi	92.1
5	Missouri	205.5
NA	Montana**	NA
38	Nebraska	62.5
12	Nevada	166.6
45	New Hampshire	32.7
22	New Jersey	118.5
11	New Mexico	193.9
27	New York	99.3
6	North Carolina	204.5
46	North Dakota	26.4
42	Ohio	51.0
17	Oklahoma	131.5
31	Oregon	87.8
15	Pennsylvania	141.5
35	Rhode Island	79.8
NA	South Carolina**	NA
41	South Dakota	55.9
7	Tennessee	202.6
25	Texas	103.9
40	Utah	56.4
44	Vermont	39.4
37	Virginia	63.3
26	Washington	102.4
34	West Virginia	83.0
16	Wisconsin	135.9
29	Wyoming	97.4

RANK ORDER

RANK	STATE	RATE
1	California	289.3
2	Louisiana	243.1
3	Georgia	228.3
4	Florida	223.6
5	Missouri	205.5
6	North Carolina	204.5
7	Tennessee	202.6
8	Delaware	196.5
9	Indiana	194.5
10	Alaska	194.2
11	New Mexico	193.9
12	Nevada	166.6
13	Arkansas	162.1
14	Maryland	143.2
15	Pennsylvania	141.5
16	Wisconsin	135.9
17	Oklahoma	131.5
18	Iowa	130.3
19	Massachusetts	127.5
20	Arizona	127.1
21	Colorado	121.0
22	New Jersey	118.5
23	Connecticut	115.0
24	Michigan	114.7
25	Texas	103.9
26	Washington	102.4
27	New York	99.3
28	Alabama	98.1
29	Wyoming	97.4
30	Mississippi	92.1
31	Oregon	87.8
32	Idaho	85.3
33	Kansas	83.8
34	West Virginia	83.0
35	Rhode Island	79.8
36	Hawaii	69.9
37	Virginia	63.3
38	Nebraska	62.5
39	Minnesota	58.1
40	Utah	56.4
41	South Dakota	55.9
42	Ohio	51.0
43	Maine	44.4
44	Vermont	39.4
45	New Hampshire	32.7
46	North Dakota	26.4
NA	Illinois**	NA
NA	Kentucky**	NA
NA	Montana**	NA
NA	South Carolina**	NA

District of Columbia**   NA

Source: Morgan Quitno Press using data from Federal Bureau of Investigation
    "Crime in the United States 2004" (Uniform Crime Reports, October 17, 2005)
*By law enforcement agencies submitting complete reports to the F.B.I. for 12 months in 2004. These rates based
on population estimates for areas under the jurisdiction of those agencies reporting. Arrest rate based on the F.B.I.
estimate of reported and unreported arrests for aggravated assault is 150.0 arrests per 100,000 population.   See
important note at beginning of this chapter. **Not available.

Reported Arrests for Property Crime in 2004

National Total = 1,321,230 Reported Arrests*

ALPHA ORDER

RANK	STATE	ARRESTS	% of USA
23	Alabama	20,565	1.6%
42	Alaska	3,973	0.3%
7	Arizona	41,894	3.2%
33	Arkansas	9,945	0.8%
1	California	169,143	12.8%
17	Colorado	29,734	2.3%
27	Connecticut	15,353	1.2%
40	Delaware	4,795	0.4%
3	Florida	126,598	9.6%
21	Georgia	24,443	1.9%
39	Hawaii	5,199	0.4%
38	Idaho	6,524	0.5%
19	Illinois	26,615	2.0%
22	Indiana	23,803	1.8%
29	Iowa	12,349	0.9%
35	Kansas	8,632	0.7%
34	Kentucky	8,910	0.7%
18	Louisiana	28,677	2.2%
37	Maine	7,366	0.6%
9	Maryland	38,322	2.9%
30	Massachusetts	11,667	0.9%
14	Michigan	32,384	2.5%
25	Minnesota	17,865	1.4%
31	Mississippi	11,176	0.8%
11	Missouri	34,382	2.6%
NA	Montana**	NA	NA
32	Nebraska	10,202	0.8%
24	Nevada	19,157	1.4%
45	New Hampshire	2,639	0.2%
13	New Jersey	32,843	2.5%
36	New Mexico	7,412	0.6%
6	New York	47,689	3.6%
5	North Carolina	47,747	3.6%
47	North Dakota	2,121	0.2%
10	Ohio	35,714	2.7%
26	Oklahoma	17,469	1.3%
16	Oregon	30,610	2.3%
4	Pennsylvania	53,569	4.1%
41	Rhode Island	4,489	0.3%
44	South Carolina	3,483	0.3%
48	South Dakota	1,754	0.1%
15	Tennessee	32,024	2.4%
2	Texas	131,922	10.0%
28	Utah	14,005	1.1%
49	Vermont	1,069	0.1%
20	Virginia	25,583	1.9%
12	Washington	34,086	2.6%
43	West Virginia	3,540	0.3%
8	Wisconsin	39,111	3.0%
46	Wyoming	2,593	0.2%

RANK ORDER

RANK	STATE	ARRESTS	% of USA
1	California	169,143	12.8%
2	Texas	131,922	10.0%
3	Florida	126,598	9.6%
4	Pennsylvania	53,569	4.1%
5	North Carolina	47,747	3.6%
6	New York	47,689	3.6%
7	Arizona	41,894	3.2%
8	Wisconsin	39,111	3.0%
9	Maryland	38,322	2.9%
10	Ohio	35,714	2.7%
11	Missouri	34,382	2.6%
12	Washington	34,086	2.6%
13	New Jersey	32,843	2.5%
14	Michigan	32,384	2.5%
15	Tennessee	32,024	2.4%
16	Oregon	30,610	2.3%
17	Colorado	29,734	2.3%
18	Louisiana	28,677	2.2%
19	Illinois	26,615	2.0%
20	Virginia	25,583	1.9%
21	Georgia	24,443	1.9%
22	Indiana	23,803	1.8%
23	Alabama	20,565	1.6%
24	Nevada	19,157	1.4%
25	Minnesota	17,865	1.4%
26	Oklahoma	17,469	1.3%
27	Connecticut	15,353	1.2%
28	Utah	14,005	1.1%
29	Iowa	12,349	0.9%
30	Massachusetts	11,667	0.9%
31	Mississippi	11,176	0.8%
32	Nebraska	10,202	0.8%
33	Arkansas	9,945	0.8%
34	Kentucky	8,910	0.7%
35	Kansas	8,632	0.7%
36	New Mexico	7,412	0.6%
37	Maine	7,366	0.6%
38	Idaho	6,524	0.5%
39	Hawaii	5,199	0.4%
40	Delaware	4,795	0.4%
41	Rhode Island	4,489	0.3%
42	Alaska	3,973	0.3%
43	West Virginia	3,540	0.3%
44	South Carolina	3,483	0.3%
45	New Hampshire	2,639	0.2%
46	Wyoming	2,593	0.2%
47	North Dakota	2,121	0.2%
48	South Dakota	1,754	0.1%
49	Vermont	1,069	0.1%
NA	Montana**	NA	NA
	District of Columbia**	NA	NA

Source: Federal Bureau of Investigation
"Crime in the United States 2004" (Uniform Crime Reports, October 17, 2005)
*By law enforcement agencies submitting complete reports to the F.B.I. for 12 months in 2004. The F.B.I. estimates 1,649,825 reported and unreported arrests for property crime occurred in 2004. Property crimes are offenses of burglary, larceny-theft, motor vehicle theft and arson. See important note at beginning of this chapter.
**Not available.

Reported Arrest Rate for Property Crime in 2004

National Rate = 580.4 Reported Arrests per 100,000 Population*

ALPHA ORDER				RANK ORDER		
RANK	STATE	RATE		RANK	STATE	RATE
26	Alabama	514.1		1	Utah	914.0
19	Alaska	623.4		2	Louisiana	912.0
10	Arizona	748.9		3	Oregon	894.3
15	Arkansas	676.6		4	Wisconsin	861.3
29	California	504.0		5	Nevada	850.0
8	Colorado	754.3		6	North Carolina	788.3
23	Connecticut	526.2		7	Georgia	776.8
17	Delaware	637.4		8	Colorado	754.3
11	Florida	728.0		9	Mississippi	750.3
7	Georgia	776.8		10	Arizona	748.9
34	Hawaii	471.0		11	Florida	728.0
25	Idaho	516.1		12	Missouri	724.0
NA	Illinois**	NA		13	Washington	719.8
24	Indiana	520.1		14	Maryland	689.9
32	Iowa	491.4		15	Arkansas	676.6
36	Kansas	445.2		16	Tennessee	661.6
NA	Kentucky**	NA		17	Delaware	637.4
2	Louisiana	912.0		18	Nebraska	628.8
21	Maine	559.6		19	Alaska	623.4
14	Maryland	689.9		20	Texas	592.3
45	Massachusetts	254.0		21	Maine	559.6
42	Michigan	344.4		22	Wyoming	526.3
30	Minnesota	502.8		23	Connecticut	526.2
9	Mississippi	750.3		24	Indiana	520.1
12	Missouri	724.0		25	Idaho	516.1
NA	Montana**	NA		26	Alabama	514.1
18	Nebraska	628.8		27	New Mexico	513.6
5	Nevada	850.0		28	Oklahoma	512.8
44	New Hampshire	266.1		29	California	504.0
41	New Jersey	389.0		30	Minnesota	502.8
27	New Mexico	513.6		31	Pennsylvania	500.3
33	New York	486.3		32	Iowa	491.4
6	North Carolina	788.3		33	New York	486.3
39	North Dakota	414.8		34	Hawaii	471.0
35	Ohio	456.9		35	Ohio	456.9
28	Oklahoma	512.8		36	Kansas	445.2
3	Oregon	894.3		37	South Dakota	417.0
31	Pennsylvania	500.3		38	Rhode Island	415.4
38	Rhode Island	415.4		39	North Dakota	414.8
NA	South Carolina**	NA		40	Virginia	394.8
37	South Dakota	417.0		41	New Jersey	389.0
16	Tennessee	661.6		42	Michigan	344.4
20	Texas	592.3		43	West Virginia	336.1
1	Utah	914.0		44	New Hampshire	266.1
46	Vermont	205.6		45	Massachusetts	254.0
40	Virginia	394.8		46	Vermont	205.6
13	Washington	719.8		NA	Illinois**	NA
43	West Virginia	336.1		NA	Kentucky**	NA
4	Wisconsin	861.3		NA	Montana**	NA
22	Wyoming	526.3		NA	South Carolina**	NA
					District of Columbia**	NA

Source: Morgan Quitno Press using data from Federal Bureau of Investigation
  "Crime in the United States 2004" (Uniform Crime Reports, October 17, 2005)
*By law enforcement agencies submitting complete reports to the F.B.I. for 12 months in 2004. These rates based
on population estimates for areas under the jurisdiction of those agencies reporting. Arrest rate based on the F.B.I.
estimate of reported and unreported arrests for property crime is 561.8 arrests per 100,000 population. See
important note at beginning of this chapter. **Not available.

Reported Arrests for Burglary in 2004

National Total = 237,518 Reported Arrests*

ALPHA ORDER

RANK	STATE	ARRESTS	% of USA
19	Alabama	3,498	1.5%
42	Alaska	543	0.2%
13	Arizona	5,179	2.2%
31	Arkansas	1,653	0.7%
1	California	48,917	20.6%
25	Colorado	2,833	1.2%
26	Connecticut	2,415	1.0%
38	Delaware	909	0.4%
2	Florida	25,970	10.9%
21	Georgia	3,402	1.4%
43	Hawaii	530	0.2%
39	Idaho	867	0.4%
23	Illinois	2,988	1.3%
20	Indiana	3,477	1.5%
30	Iowa	1,857	0.8%
34	Kansas	1,260	0.5%
32	Kentucky	1,598	0.7%
11	Louisiana	5,438	2.3%
33	Maine	1,309	0.6%
7	Maryland	7,245	3.1%
28	Massachusetts	2,224	0.9%
12	Michigan	5,310	2.2%
27	Minnesota	2,338	1.0%
29	Mississippi	2,160	0.9%
14	Missouri	5,119	2.2%
NA	Montana**	NA	NA
37	Nebraska	988	0.4%
16	Nevada	4,767	2.0%
45	New Hampshire	364	0.2%
9	New Jersey	6,087	2.6%
35	New Mexico	1,222	0.5%
6	New York	7,522	3.2%
4	North Carolina	13,031	5.5%
49	North Dakota	174	0.1%
8	Ohio	6,664	2.8%
24	Oklahoma	2,983	1.3%
18	Oregon	3,611	1.5%
5	Pennsylvania	9,688	4.1%
40	Rhode Island	838	0.4%
41	South Carolina	690	0.3%
47	South Dakota	254	0.1%
15	Tennessee	5,047	2.1%
3	Texas	19,361	8.2%
36	Utah	1,161	0.5%
48	Vermont	229	0.1%
22	Virginia	3,340	1.4%
10	Washington	5,474	2.3%
44	West Virginia	508	0.2%
17	Wisconsin	4,126	1.7%
46	Wyoming	350	0.1%

RANK ORDER

RANK	STATE	ARRESTS	% of USA
1	California	48,917	20.6%
2	Florida	25,970	10.9%
3	Texas	19,361	8.2%
4	North Carolina	13,031	5.5%
5	Pennsylvania	9,688	4.1%
6	New York	7,522	3.2%
7	Maryland	7,245	3.1%
8	Ohio	6,664	2.8%
9	New Jersey	6,087	2.6%
10	Washington	5,474	2.3%
11	Louisiana	5,438	2.3%
12	Michigan	5,310	2.2%
13	Arizona	5,179	2.2%
14	Missouri	5,119	2.2%
15	Tennessee	5,047	2.1%
16	Nevada	4,767	2.0%
17	Wisconsin	4,126	1.7%
18	Oregon	3,611	1.5%
19	Alabama	3,498	1.5%
20	Indiana	3,477	1.5%
21	Georgia	3,402	1.4%
22	Virginia	3,340	1.4%
23	Illinois	2,988	1.3%
24	Oklahoma	2,983	1.3%
25	Colorado	2,833	1.2%
26	Connecticut	2,415	1.0%
27	Minnesota	2,338	1.0%
28	Massachusetts	2,224	0.9%
29	Mississippi	2,160	0.9%
30	Iowa	1,857	0.8%
31	Arkansas	1,653	0.7%
32	Kentucky	1,598	0.7%
33	Maine	1,309	0.6%
34	Kansas	1,260	0.5%
35	New Mexico	1,222	0.5%
36	Utah	1,161	0.5%
37	Nebraska	988	0.4%
38	Delaware	909	0.4%
39	Idaho	867	0.4%
40	Rhode Island	838	0.4%
41	South Carolina	690	0.3%
42	Alaska	543	0.2%
43	Hawaii	530	0.2%
44	West Virginia	508	0.2%
45	New Hampshire	364	0.2%
46	Wyoming	350	0.1%
47	South Dakota	254	0.1%
48	Vermont	229	0.1%
49	North Dakota	174	0.1%
NA	Montana**	NA	NA
	District of Columbia**	NA	NA

Source: Federal Bureau of Investigation
   "Crime in the United States 2004" (Uniform Crime Reports, October 17, 2005)
*By law enforcement agencies submitting complete reports to the F.B.I. for 12 months in 2004. The F.B.I. estimates
294,591 reported and unreported arrests for burglary occurred in 2004. Burglary is the unlawful entry of a structure
to commit a felony or theft. Attempts are included.   See important note at beginning of this chapter.
**Not available.

Reported Arrest Rate for Burglary in 2004

National Rate = 104.3 Reported Arrests per 100,000 Population*

ALPHA ORDER

RANK	STATE	RATE
20	Alabama	87.4
23	Alaska	85.2
16	Arizona	92.6
10	Arkansas	112.5
5	California	145.8
32	Colorado	71.9
25	Connecticut	82.8
8	Delaware	120.8
4	Florida	149.3
11	Georgia	108.1
43	Hawaii	48.0
34	Idaho	68.6
NA	Illinois**	NA
28	Indiana	76.0
30	Iowa	73.9
36	Kansas	65.0
NA	Kentucky**	NA
3	Louisiana	172.9
15	Maine	99.4
7	Maryland	130.4
41	Massachusetts	48.4
39	Michigan	56.5
35	Minnesota	65.8
6	Mississippi	145.0
12	Missouri	107.8
NA	Montana**	NA
37	Nebraska	60.9
2	Nevada	211.5
45	New Hampshire	36.7
31	New Jersey	72.1
24	New Mexico	84.7
27	New York	76.7
1	North Carolina	215.1
46	North Dakota	34.0
22	Ohio	85.3
19	Oklahoma	87.6
13	Oregon	105.5
18	Pennsylvania	90.5
26	Rhode Island	77.5
NA	South Carolina**	NA
38	South Dakota	60.4
14	Tennessee	104.3
21	Texas	86.9
29	Utah	75.8
44	Vermont	44.0
40	Virginia	51.5
9	Washington	115.6
42	West Virginia	48.2
17	Wisconsin	90.9
33	Wyoming	71.0

RANK ORDER

RANK	STATE	RATE
1	North Carolina	215.1
2	Nevada	211.5
3	Louisiana	172.9
4	Florida	149.3
5	California	145.8
6	Mississippi	145.0
7	Maryland	130.4
8	Delaware	120.8
9	Washington	115.6
10	Arkansas	112.5
11	Georgia	108.1
12	Missouri	107.8
13	Oregon	105.5
14	Tennessee	104.3
15	Maine	99.4
16	Arizona	92.6
17	Wisconsin	90.9
18	Pennsylvania	90.5
19	Oklahoma	87.6
20	Alabama	87.4
21	Texas	86.9
22	Ohio	85.3
23	Alaska	85.2
24	New Mexico	84.7
25	Connecticut	82.8
26	Rhode Island	77.5
27	New York	76.7
28	Indiana	76.0
29	Utah	75.8
30	Iowa	73.9
31	New Jersey	72.1
32	Colorado	71.9
33	Wyoming	71.0
34	Idaho	68.6
35	Minnesota	65.8
36	Kansas	65.0
37	Nebraska	60.9
38	South Dakota	60.4
39	Michigan	56.5
40	Virginia	51.5
41	Massachusetts	48.4
42	West Virginia	48.2
43	Hawaii	48.0
44	Vermont	44.0
45	New Hampshire	36.7
46	North Dakota	34.0
NA	Illinois**	NA
NA	Kentucky**	NA
NA	Montana**	NA
NA	South Carolina**	NA
	District of Columbia**	NA

*Source: Morgan Quitno Press using data from Federal Bureau of Investigation
"Crime in the United States 2004" (Uniform Crime Reports, October 17, 2005)*
*By law enforcement agencies submitting complete reports to the F.B.I. for 12 months in 2004. These rates based
on population estimates for areas under the jurisdiction of those agencies reporting. Arrest rate based on the F.B.I.
estimate of reported and unreported arrests for burglary is 100.3 arrests per 100,000 population. See important
note at beginning of this chapter. **Not available.*

Reported Arrests for Larceny and Theft in 2004

National Total = 954,482 Reported Arrests*

ALPHA ORDER

RANK ORDER

RANK	STATE	ARRESTS	% of USA		RANK	STATE	ARRESTS	% of USA
23	Alabama	15,773	1.7%		1	Texas	102,940	10.8%
42	Alaska	3,020	0.3%		2	California	89,261	9.4%
8	Arizona	31,272	3.3%		3	Florida	88,265	9.2%
33	Arkansas	7,863	0.8%		4	Pennsylvania	38,143	4.0%
2	California	89,261	9.4%		5	New York	37,127	3.9%
16	Colorado	23,998	2.5%		6	North Carolina	32,921	3.4%
28	Connecticut	11,764	1.2%		7	Wisconsin	32,852	3.4%
40	Delaware	3,709	0.4%		8	Arizona	31,272	3.3%
3	Florida	88,265	9.2%		9	Ohio	26,213	2.7%
20	Georgia	19,068	2.0%		10	Washington	26,187	2.7%
39	Hawaii	3,850	0.4%		11	Maryland	25,447	2.7%
38	Idaho	5,221	0.5%		12	New Jersey	25,221	2.6%
22	Illinois	16,080	1.7%		13	Missouri	25,066	2.6%
21	Indiana	18,316	1.9%		14	Michigan	24,930	2.6%
29	Iowa	9,771	1.0%		15	Tennessee	24,360	2.6%
35	Kansas	6,790	0.7%		16	Colorado	23,998	2.5%
34	Kentucky	6,893	0.7%		17	Oregon	23,541	2.5%
18	Louisiana	21,845	2.3%		18	Louisiana	21,845	2.3%
37	Maine	5,649	0.6%		19	Virginia	20,659	2.2%
11	Maryland	25,447	2.7%		20	Georgia	19,068	2.0%
31	Massachusetts	8,588	0.9%		21	Indiana	18,316	1.9%
14	Michigan	24,930	2.6%		22	Illinois	16,080	1.7%
24	Minnesota	14,384	1.5%		23	Alabama	15,773	1.7%
32	Mississippi	8,494	0.9%		24	Minnesota	14,384	1.5%
13	Missouri	25,066	2.6%		25	Oklahoma	13,180	1.4%
NA	Montana**	NA	NA		26	Nevada	12,281	1.3%
30	Nebraska	8,717	0.9%		27	Utah	12,223	1.3%
26	Nevada	12,281	1.3%		28	Connecticut	11,764	1.2%
45	New Hampshire	2,082	0.2%		29	Iowa	9,771	1.0%
12	New Jersey	25,221	2.6%		30	Nebraska	8,717	0.9%
36	New Mexico	5,764	0.6%		31	Massachusetts	8,588	0.9%
5	New York	37,127	3.9%		32	Mississippi	8,494	0.9%
6	North Carolina	32,921	3.4%		33	Arkansas	7,863	0.8%
47	North Dakota	1,774	0.2%		34	Kentucky	6,893	0.7%
9	Ohio	26,213	2.7%		35	Kansas	6,790	0.7%
25	Oklahoma	13,180	1.4%		36	New Mexico	5,764	0.6%
17	Oregon	23,541	2.5%		37	Maine	5,649	0.6%
4	Pennsylvania	38,143	4.0%		38	Idaho	5,221	0.5%
41	Rhode Island	3,305	0.3%		39	Hawaii	3,850	0.4%
44	South Carolina	2,630	0.3%		40	Delaware	3,709	0.4%
48	South Dakota	1,416	0.1%		41	Rhode Island	3,305	0.3%
15	Tennessee	24,360	2.6%		42	Alaska	3,020	0.3%
1	Texas	102,940	10.8%		43	West Virginia	2,784	0.3%
27	Utah	12,223	1.3%		44	South Carolina	2,630	0.3%
49	Vermont	739	0.1%		45	New Hampshire	2,082	0.2%
19	Virginia	20,659	2.2%		46	Wyoming	2,069	0.2%
10	Washington	26,187	2.7%		47	North Dakota	1,774	0.2%
43	West Virginia	2,784	0.3%		48	South Dakota	1,416	0.1%
7	Wisconsin	32,852	3.4%		49	Vermont	739	0.1%
46	Wyoming	2,069	0.2%		NA	Montana**	NA	NA
						District of Columbia**	NA	NA

Source: Federal Bureau of Investigation
   "Crime in the United States 2004" (Uniform Crime Reports, October 17, 2005)
*By law enforcement agencies submitting complete reports to the F.B.I. for 12 months in 2004. The F.B.I. estimates 1,191,945 reported and unreported arrests for larceny and theft occurred in 2004. Larceny and theft is the unlawful taking of property without use of force, violence or fraud. Attempts are included. Motor vehicle thefts are excluded. See important note at beginning of this chapter. **Not available.

Reported Arrest Rate for Larceny and Theft in 2004

National Rate = 419.3 Reported Arrests per 100,000 Population*

ALPHA ORDER

RANK	STATE	RATE
28	Alabama	394.3
18	Alaska	473.8
8	Arizona	559.1
13	Arkansas	535.0
41	California	266.0
5	Colorado	608.8
25	Connecticut	403.2
17	Delaware	493.0
15	Florida	507.6
6	Georgia	606.0
34	Hawaii	348.8
23	Idaho	413.0
NA	Illinois**	NA
26	Indiana	400.2
29	Iowa	388.8
33	Kansas	350.2
NA	Kentucky**	NA
3	Louisiana	694.7
21	Maine	429.2
20	Maryland	458.1
45	Massachusetts	187.0
42	Michigan	265.1
24	Minnesota	404.8
7	Mississippi	570.2
14	Missouri	527.8
NA	Montana**	NA
12	Nebraska	537.3
10	Nevada	544.9
44	New Hampshire	210.0
40	New Jersey	298.7
27	New Mexico	399.4
31	New York	378.6
11	North Carolina	543.5
35	North Dakota	346.9
37	Ohio	335.4
30	Oklahoma	386.9
4	Oregon	687.8
32	Pennsylvania	356.2
39	Rhode Island	305.8
NA	South Carolina**	NA
36	South Dakota	336.7
16	Tennessee	503.2
19	Texas	462.2
1	Utah	797.7
46	Vermont	142.1
38	Virginia	318.8
9	Washington	553.0
43	West Virginia	264.4
2	Wisconsin	723.5
22	Wyoming	419.9

RANK ORDER

RANK	STATE	RATE
1	Utah	797.7
2	Wisconsin	723.5
3	Louisiana	694.7
4	Oregon	687.8
5	Colorado	608.8
6	Georgia	606.0
7	Mississippi	570.2
8	Arizona	559.1
9	Washington	553.0
10	Nevada	544.9
11	North Carolina	543.5
12	Nebraska	537.3
13	Arkansas	535.0
14	Missouri	527.8
15	Florida	507.6
16	Tennessee	503.2
17	Delaware	493.0
18	Alaska	473.8
19	Texas	462.2
20	Maryland	458.1
21	Maine	429.2
22	Wyoming	419.9
23	Idaho	413.0
24	Minnesota	404.8
25	Connecticut	403.2
26	Indiana	400.2
27	New Mexico	399.4
28	Alabama	394.3
29	Iowa	388.8
30	Oklahoma	386.9
31	New York	378.6
32	Pennsylvania	356.2
33	Kansas	350.2
34	Hawaii	348.8
35	North Dakota	346.9
36	South Dakota	336.7
37	Ohio	335.4
38	Virginia	318.8
39	Rhode Island	305.8
40	New Jersey	298.7
41	California	266.0
42	Michigan	265.1
43	West Virginia	264.4
44	New Hampshire	210.0
45	Massachusetts	187.0
46	Vermont	142.1
NA	Illinois**	NA
NA	Kentucky**	NA
NA	Montana**	NA
NA	South Carolina**	NA

District of Columbia**   NA

Source: Morgan Quitno Press using data from Federal Bureau of Investigation
"Crime in the United States 2004" (Uniform Crime Reports, October 17, 2005)
*By law enforcement agencies submitting complete reports to the F.B.I. for 12 months in 2004. These rates based on population estimates for areas under the jurisdiction of those agencies reporting. Arrest rate based on the F.B.I. estimate of reported and unreported arrests for larceny and theft is 405.9 arrests per 100,000 population. See important note at beginning of this chapter. **Not available.

Reported Arrests for Motor Vehicle Theft in 2004

National Total = 117,544 Reported Arrests*

ALPHA ORDER

RANK	STATE	ARRESTS	% of USA
23	Alabama	1,173	1.0%
34	Alaska	395	0.3%
5	Arizona	5,180	4.4%
35	Arkansas	390	0.3%
1	California	29,346	25.0%
10	Colorado	2,688	2.3%
27	Connecticut	833	0.7%
46	Delaware	123	0.1%
2	Florida	11,798	10.0%
19	Georgia	1,668	1.4%
28	Hawaii	783	0.7%
40	Idaho	318	0.3%
4	Illinois	7,409	6.3%
18	Indiana	1,810	1.5%
30	Iowa	570	0.5%
32	Kansas	495	0.4%
37	Kentucky	382	0.3%
22	Louisiana	1,185	1.0%
39	Maine	362	0.3%
7	Maryland	4,904	4.2%
29	Massachusetts	750	0.6%
17	Michigan	1,812	1.5%
26	Minnesota	994	0.8%
33	Mississippi	441	0.4%
8	Missouri	3,815	3.2%
NA	Montana**	NA	NA
36	Nebraska	386	0.3%
15	Nevada	2,004	1.7%
43	New Hampshire	169	0.1%
24	New Jersey	1,157	1.0%
37	New Mexico	382	0.3%
11	New York	2,658	2.3%
20	North Carolina	1,523	1.3%
44	North Dakota	155	0.1%
12	Ohio	2,434	2.1%
25	Oklahoma	1,087	0.9%
9	Oregon	3,122	2.7%
6	Pennsylvania	5,010	4.3%
41	Rhode Island	257	0.2%
45	South Carolina	145	0.1%
49	South Dakota	69	0.1%
13	Tennessee	2,409	2.0%
3	Texas	8,754	7.4%
31	Utah	533	0.5%
48	Vermont	81	0.1%
21	Virginia	1,302	1.1%
14	Washington	2,044	1.7%
42	West Virginia	219	0.2%
16	Wisconsin	1,859	1.6%
47	Wyoming	113	0.1%

RANK ORDER

RANK	STATE	ARRESTS	% of USA
1	California	29,346	25.0%
2	Florida	11,798	10.0%
3	Texas	8,754	7.4%
4	Illinois	7,409	6.3%
5	Arizona	5,180	4.4%
6	Pennsylvania	5,010	4.3%
7	Maryland	4,904	4.2%
8	Missouri	3,815	3.2%
9	Oregon	3,122	2.7%
10	Colorado	2,688	2.3%
11	New York	2,658	2.3%
12	Ohio	2,434	2.1%
13	Tennessee	2,409	2.0%
14	Washington	2,044	1.7%
15	Nevada	2,004	1.7%
16	Wisconsin	1,859	1.6%
17	Michigan	1,812	1.5%
18	Indiana	1,810	1.5%
19	Georgia	1,668	1.4%
20	North Carolina	1,523	1.3%
21	Virginia	1,302	1.1%
22	Louisiana	1,185	1.0%
23	Alabama	1,173	1.0%
24	New Jersey	1,157	1.0%
25	Oklahoma	1,087	0.9%
26	Minnesota	994	0.8%
27	Connecticut	833	0.7%
28	Hawaii	783	0.7%
29	Massachusetts	750	0.6%
30	Iowa	570	0.5%
31	Utah	533	0.5%
32	Kansas	495	0.4%
33	Mississippi	441	0.4%
34	Alaska	395	0.3%
35	Arkansas	390	0.3%
36	Nebraska	386	0.3%
37	Kentucky	382	0.3%
37	New Mexico	382	0.3%
39	Maine	362	0.3%
40	Idaho	318	0.3%
41	Rhode Island	257	0.2%
42	West Virginia	219	0.2%
43	New Hampshire	169	0.1%
44	North Dakota	155	0.1%
45	South Carolina	145	0.1%
46	Delaware	123	0.1%
47	Wyoming	113	0.1%
48	Vermont	81	0.1%
49	South Dakota	69	0.1%
NA	Montana**	NA	NA
	District of Columbia**	NA	NA

Source: Federal Bureau of Investigation
  "Crime in the United States 2004" (Uniform Crime Reports, October 17, 2005)
*By law enforcement agencies submitting complete reports to the F.B.I. for 12 months in 2004. The F.B.I. estimates 147,732 reported and unreported arrests for motor vehicle theft occurred in 2004. Motor vehicle theft includes the theft or attempted theft of a self-propelled vehicle. Excludes motorboats, construction equipment, airplanes and farming equipment. See important note at beginning of this chapter. **Not available.

21

Reported Arrest Rate for Motor Vehicle Theft in 2004

National Rate = 51.6 Reported Arrests per 100,000 Population*

ALPHA ORDER

RANK	STATE	RATE
24	Alabama	29.3
10	Alaska	62.0
1	Arizona	92.6
29	Arkansas	26.5
5	California	87.4
8	Colorado	68.2
25	Connecticut	28.6
43	Delaware	16.3
9	Florida	67.8
11	Georgia	53.0
7	Hawaii	70.9
32	Idaho	25.2
NA	Illinois**	NA
16	Indiana	39.5
37	Iowa	22.7
31	Kansas	25.5
NA	Kentucky**	NA
18	Louisiana	37.7
27	Maine	27.5
4	Maryland	88.3
43	Massachusetts	16.3
40	Michigan	19.3
26	Minnesota	28.0
23	Mississippi	29.6
6	Missouri	80.3
NA	Montana**	NA
34	Nebraska	23.8
3	Nevada	88.9
41	New Hampshire	17.0
46	New Jersey	13.7
29	New Mexico	26.5
28	New York	27.1
33	North Carolina	25.1
22	North Dakota	30.3
21	Ohio	31.1
20	Oklahoma	31.9
2	Oregon	91.2
13	Pennsylvania	46.8
34	Rhode Island	23.8
NA	South Carolina**	NA
42	South Dakota	16.4
12	Tennessee	49.8
17	Texas	39.3
19	Utah	34.8
45	Vermont	15.6
39	Virginia	20.1
14	Washington	43.2
38	West Virginia	20.8
15	Wisconsin	40.9
36	Wyoming	22.9

RANK ORDER

RANK	STATE	RATE
1	Arizona	92.6
2	Oregon	91.2
3	Nevada	88.9
4	Maryland	88.3
5	California	87.4
6	Missouri	80.3
7	Hawaii	70.9
8	Colorado	68.2
9	Florida	67.8
10	Alaska	62.0
11	Georgia	53.0
12	Tennessee	49.8
13	Pennsylvania	46.8
14	Washington	43.2
15	Wisconsin	40.9
16	Indiana	39.5
17	Texas	39.3
18	Louisiana	37.7
19	Utah	34.8
20	Oklahoma	31.9
21	Ohio	31.1
22	North Dakota	30.3
23	Mississippi	29.6
24	Alabama	29.3
25	Connecticut	28.6
26	Minnesota	28.0
27	Maine	27.5
28	New York	27.1
29	Arkansas	26.5
29	New Mexico	26.5
31	Kansas	25.5
32	Idaho	25.2
33	North Carolina	25.1
34	Nebraska	23.8
34	Rhode Island	23.8
36	Wyoming	22.9
37	Iowa	22.7
38	West Virginia	20.8
39	Virginia	20.1
40	Michigan	19.3
41	New Hampshire	17.0
42	South Dakota	16.4
43	Delaware	16.3
43	Massachusetts	16.3
45	Vermont	15.6
46	New Jersey	13.7
NA	Illinois**	NA
NA	Kentucky**	NA
NA	Montana**	NA
NA	South Carolina**	NA

District of Columbia**   NA

Source: Morgan Quitno Press using data from Federal Bureau of Investigation
    "Crime in the United States 2004" (Uniform Crime Reports, October 17, 2005)
*By law enforcement agencies submitting complete reports to the F.B.I. for 12 months in 2004. These rates based on population estimates for areas under the jurisdiction of those agencies reporting. Arrest rate based on the F.B.I. estimate of reported and unreported arrests for motor vehicle theft is 50.3 arrests per 100,000 population. See important note at beginning of this chapter. **Not available.

Reported Arrests for Arson in 2004

National Total = 11,686 Reported Arrests*

RANK	STATE (ALPHA ORDER)	ARRESTS	% of USA	RANK	STATE (RANK ORDER)	ARRESTS	% of USA
27	Alabama	121	1.0%	1	California	1,619	13.9%
48	Alaska	15	0.1%	2	Texas	867	7.4%
18	Arizona	263	2.3%	3	Pennsylvania	728	6.2%
40	Arkansas	39	0.3%	4	Maryland	726	6.2%
1	California	1,619	13.9%	5	Florida	565	4.8%
20	Colorado	215	1.8%	6	Ohio	403	3.4%
11	Connecticut	341	2.9%	7	Missouri	382	3.3%
37	Delaware	54	0.5%	7	New York	382	3.3%
5	Florida	565	4.8%	9	Washington	381	3.3%
14	Georgia	305	2.6%	10	New Jersey	378	3.2%
42	Hawaii	36	0.3%	11	Connecticut	341	2.9%
28	Idaho	118	1.0%	12	Oregon	336	2.9%
26	Illinois	138	1.2%	13	Michigan	332	2.8%
23	Indiana	200	1.7%	14	Georgia	305	2.6%
24	Iowa	151	1.3%	15	Virginia	282	2.4%
34	Kansas	87	0.7%	16	Wisconsin	274	2.3%
41	Kentucky	37	0.3%	17	North Carolina	272	2.3%
21	Louisiana	209	1.8%	18	Arizona	263	2.3%
38	Maine	46	0.4%	19	Oklahoma	219	1.9%
4	Maryland	726	6.2%	20	Colorado	215	1.8%
30	Massachusetts	105	0.9%	21	Louisiana	209	1.8%
13	Michigan	332	2.8%	22	Tennessee	208	1.8%
25	Minnesota	149	1.3%	23	Indiana	200	1.7%
35	Mississippi	81	0.7%	24	Iowa	151	1.3%
7	Missouri	382	3.3%	25	Minnesota	149	1.3%
NA	Montana**	NA	NA	26	Illinois	138	1.2%
29	Nebraska	111	0.9%	27	Alabama	121	1.0%
30	Nevada	105	0.9%	28	Idaho	118	1.0%
44	New Hampshire	24	0.2%	29	Nebraska	111	0.9%
10	New Jersey	378	3.2%	30	Massachusetts	105	0.9%
39	New Mexico	44	0.4%	30	Nevada	105	0.9%
7	New York	382	3.3%	32	Rhode Island	89	0.8%
17	North Carolina	272	2.3%	33	Utah	88	0.8%
46	North Dakota	18	0.2%	34	Kansas	87	0.7%
6	Ohio	403	3.4%	35	Mississippi	81	0.7%
19	Oklahoma	219	1.9%	36	Wyoming	61	0.5%
12	Oregon	336	2.9%	37	Delaware	54	0.5%
3	Pennsylvania	728	6.2%	38	Maine	46	0.4%
32	Rhode Island	89	0.8%	39	New Mexico	44	0.4%
46	South Carolina	18	0.2%	40	Arkansas	39	0.3%
48	South Dakota	15	0.1%	41	Kentucky	37	0.3%
22	Tennessee	208	1.8%	42	Hawaii	36	0.3%
2	Texas	867	7.4%	43	West Virginia	29	0.2%
33	Utah	88	0.8%	44	New Hampshire	24	0.2%
45	Vermont	20	0.2%	45	Vermont	20	0.2%
15	Virginia	282	2.4%	46	North Dakota	18	0.2%
9	Washington	381	3.3%	46	South Carolina	18	0.2%
43	West Virginia	29	0.2%	48	Alaska	15	0.1%
16	Wisconsin	274	2.3%	48	South Dakota	15	0.1%
36	Wyoming	61	0.5%	NA	Montana**	NA	NA
					District of Columbia**	NA	NA

Source: Federal Bureau of Investigation
    "Crime in the United States 2004" (Uniform Crime Reports, October 17, 2005)
*By law enforcement agencies submitting complete reports to the F.B.I. for 12 months in 2004. The F.B.I. estimates
15,557 reported and unreported arrests for arson occurred in 2004. Arson is the willful burning of or attempt to burn
a building, vehicle or another's personal property. See important note at beginning of this chapter.
**Not available.

Reported Arrest Rate for Arson in 2004

National Rate = 5.1 Reported Arrests per 100,000 Population*

ALPHA ORDER

RANK	STATE	RATE
40	Alabama	3.0
44	Alaska	2.4
22	Arizona	4.7
43	Arkansas	2.7
21	California	4.8
18	Colorado	5.5
3	Connecticut	11.7
10	Delaware	7.2
39	Florida	3.2
5	Georgia	9.7
38	Hawaii	3.3
6	Idaho	9.3
NA	Illinois**	NA
27	Indiana	4.4
15	Iowa	6.0
24	Kansas	4.5
NA	Kentucky**	NA
13	Louisiana	6.6
35	Maine	3.5
1	Maryland	13.1
46	Massachusetts	2.3
35	Michigan	3.5
30	Minnesota	4.2
19	Mississippi	5.4
8	Missouri	8.0
NA	Montana**	NA
11	Nebraska	6.8
22	Nevada	4.7
44	New Hampshire	2.4
24	New Jersey	4.5
40	New Mexico	3.0
31	New York	3.9
24	North Carolina	4.5
35	North Dakota	3.5
20	Ohio	5.2
14	Oklahoma	6.4
4	Oregon	9.8
11	Pennsylvania	6.8
7	Rhode Island	8.2
NA	South Carolina**	NA
34	South Dakota	3.6
29	Tennessee	4.3
31	Texas	3.9
17	Utah	5.7
33	Vermont	3.8
27	Virginia	4.4
8	Washington	8.0
42	West Virginia	2.8
15	Wisconsin	6.0
2	Wyoming	12.4

RANK ORDER

RANK	STATE	RATE
1	Maryland	13.1
2	Wyoming	12.4
3	Connecticut	11.7
4	Oregon	9.8
5	Georgia	9.7
6	Idaho	9.3
7	Rhode Island	8.2
8	Missouri	8.0
8	Washington	8.0
10	Delaware	7.2
11	Nebraska	6.8
11	Pennsylvania	6.8
13	Louisiana	6.6
14	Oklahoma	6.4
15	Iowa	6.0
15	Wisconsin	6.0
17	Utah	5.7
18	Colorado	5.5
19	Mississippi	5.4
20	Ohio	5.2
21	California	4.8
22	Arizona	4.7
22	Nevada	4.7
24	Kansas	4.5
24	New Jersey	4.5
24	North Carolina	4.5
27	Indiana	4.4
27	Virginia	4.4
29	Tennessee	4.3
30	Minnesota	4.2
31	New York	3.9
31	Texas	3.9
33	Vermont	3.8
34	South Dakota	3.6
35	Maine	3.5
35	Michigan	3.5
35	North Dakota	3.5
38	Hawaii	3.3
39	Florida	3.2
40	Alabama	3.0
40	New Mexico	3.0
42	West Virginia	2.8
43	Arkansas	2.7
44	Alaska	2.4
44	New Hampshire	2.4
46	Massachusetts	2.3
NA	Illinois**	NA
NA	Kentucky**	NA
NA	Montana**	NA
NA	South Carolina**	NA
	District of Columbia**	NA

Source: Morgan Quitno Press using data from Federal Bureau of Investigation
"Crime in the United States 2004" (Uniform Crime Reports, October 17, 2005)
*By law enforcement agencies submitting complete reports to the F.B.I. for 12 months in 2004. These rates based on population estimates for areas under the jurisdiction of those agencies reporting. Arrest rate based on the F.B.I. estimate of reported and unreported arrests for arson is 5.3 arrests per 100,000 population. See important note at beginning of this chapter. **Not available.

Reported Arrests for Weapons Violations in 2004

National Total = 135,323 Reported Arrests*

ALPHA ORDER				RANK ORDER			
RANK	STATE	ARRESTS	% of USA	RANK	STATE	ARRESTS	% of USA
26	Alabama	1,215	0.9%	1	California	28,413	21.0%
39	Alaska	361	0.3%	2	Texas	13,019	9.6%
13	Arizona	3,331	2.5%	3	Florida	7,777	5.7%
29	Arkansas	978	0.7%	4	New Jersey	6,044	4.5%
1	California	28,413	21.0%	5	North Carolina	5,601	4.1%
19	Colorado	2,335	1.7%	6	Illinois	4,817	3.6%
25	Connecticut	1,270	0.9%	7	Michigan	4,763	3.5%
40	Delaware	333	0.2%	8	Pennsylvania	4,583	3.4%
3	Florida	7,777	5.7%	9	Wisconsin	4,361	3.2%
12	Georgia	3,698	2.7%	10	Maryland	4,135	3.1%
44	Hawaii	206	0.2%	11	New York	4,095	3.0%
35	Idaho	626	0.5%	12	Georgia	3,698	2.7%
6	Illinois	4,817	3.6%	13	Arizona	3,331	2.5%
24	Indiana	1,447	1.1%	14	Missouri	3,279	2.4%
38	Iowa	447	0.3%	15	Virginia	3,142	2.3%
34	Kansas	692	0.5%	16	Ohio	2,927	2.2%
37	Kentucky	574	0.4%	17	Tennessee	2,906	2.1%
22	Louisiana	1,655	1.2%	18	Washington	2,777	2.1%
42	Maine	315	0.2%	19	Colorado	2,335	1.7%
10	Maryland	4,135	3.1%	20	Oklahoma	2,281	1.7%
31	Massachusetts	773	0.6%	21	Oregon	2,206	1.6%
7	Michigan	4,763	3.5%	22	Louisiana	1,655	1.2%
30	Minnesota	878	0.6%	23	Nevada	1,589	1.2%
33	Mississippi	736	0.5%	24	Indiana	1,447	1.1%
14	Missouri	3,279	2.4%	25	Connecticut	1,270	0.9%
NA	Montana**	NA	NA	26	Alabama	1,215	0.9%
28	Nebraska	1,095	0.8%	27	Utah	1,171	0.9%
23	Nevada	1,589	1.2%	28	Nebraska	1,095	0.8%
47	New Hampshire	87	0.1%	29	Arkansas	978	0.7%
4	New Jersey	6,044	4.5%	30	Minnesota	878	0.6%
32	New Mexico	754	0.6%	31	Massachusetts	773	0.6%
11	New York	4,095	3.0%	32	New Mexico	754	0.6%
5	North Carolina	5,601	4.1%	33	Mississippi	736	0.5%
46	North Dakota	136	0.1%	34	Kansas	692	0.5%
16	Ohio	2,927	2.2%	35	Idaho	626	0.5%
20	Oklahoma	2,281	1.7%	36	Rhode Island	590	0.4%
21	Oregon	2,206	1.6%	37	Kentucky	574	0.4%
8	Pennsylvania	4,583	3.4%	38	Iowa	447	0.3%
36	Rhode Island	590	0.4%	39	Alaska	361	0.3%
41	South Carolina	331	0.2%	40	Delaware	333	0.2%
48	South Dakota	80	0.1%	41	South Carolina	331	0.2%
17	Tennessee	2,906	2.1%	42	Maine	315	0.2%
2	Texas	13,019	9.6%	43	West Virginia	305	0.2%
27	Utah	1,171	0.9%	44	Hawaii	206	0.2%
49	Vermont	16	0.0%	45	Wyoming	140	0.1%
15	Virginia	3,142	2.3%	46	North Dakota	136	0.1%
18	Washington	2,777	2.1%	47	New Hampshire	87	0.1%
43	West Virginia	305	0.2%	48	South Dakota	80	0.1%
9	Wisconsin	4,361	3.2%	49	Vermont	16	0.0%
45	Wyoming	140	0.1%	NA	Montana**	NA	NA
					District of Columbia**	NA	NA

Source: Federal Bureau of Investigation
       "Crime in the United States 2004" (Uniform Crime Reports, October 17, 2005)
*By law enforcement agencies submitting complete reports to the F.B.I. for 12 months in 2004. The F.B.I. estimates
177,330 reported and unreported arrests for weapons violations occurred in 2004. Weapons violations include
illegal carrying and possession. See important note at beginning of this chapter.
**Not available.

Reported Arrest Rate for Driving Under the Influence in 2004

National Rate = 470.0 Reported Arrests per 100,000 Population*

ALPHA ORDER

RANK	STATE	RATE
38	Alabama	339.5
7	Alaska	800.8
13	Arizona	676.0
28	Arkansas	470.0
23	California	528.6
22	Colorado	539.2
40	Connecticut	308.4
46	Delaware	22.6
39	Florida	320.9
27	Georgia	480.4
33	Hawaii	371.6
11	Idaho	721.3
NA	Illinois**	NA
17	Indiana	595.7
20	Iowa	555.1
12	Kansas	695.1
NA	Kentucky**	NA
36	Louisiana	356.0
21	Maine	548.0
30	Maryland	424.8
45	Massachusetts	204.2
26	Michigan	484.6
14	Minnesota	652.8
8	Mississippi	795.1
16	Missouri	616.2
NA	Montana**	NA
4	Nebraska	858.4
31	Nevada	405.2
18	New Hampshire	562.9
41	New Jersey	294.2
3	New Mexico	890.4
42	New York	276.5
5	North Carolina	821.4
9	North Dakota	789.7
43	Ohio	257.2
19	Oklahoma	555.2
25	Oregon	488.6
32	Pennsylvania	387.2
44	Rhode Island	219.0
NA	South Carolina**	NA
2	South Dakota	907.8
24	Tennessee	489.3
29	Texas	435.2
35	Utah	358.0
15	Vermont	623.8
37	Virginia	351.6
6	Washington	806.6
34	West Virginia	368.7
10	Wisconsin	774.5
1	Wyoming	953.7

RANK ORDER

RANK	STATE	RATE
1	Wyoming	953.7
2	South Dakota	907.8
3	New Mexico	890.4
4	Nebraska	858.4
5	North Carolina	821.4
6	Washington	806.6
7	Alaska	800.8
8	Mississippi	795.1
9	North Dakota	789.7
10	Wisconsin	774.5
11	Idaho	721.3
12	Kansas	695.1
13	Arizona	676.0
14	Minnesota	652.8
15	Vermont	623.8
16	Missouri	616.2
17	Indiana	595.7
18	New Hampshire	562.9
19	Oklahoma	555.2
20	Iowa	555.1
21	Maine	548.0
22	Colorado	539.2
23	California	528.6
24	Tennessee	489.3
25	Oregon	488.6
26	Michigan	484.6
27	Georgia	480.4
28	Arkansas	470.0
29	Texas	435.2
30	Maryland	424.8
31	Nevada	405.2
32	Pennsylvania	387.2
33	Hawaii	371.6
34	West Virginia	368.7
35	Utah	358.0
36	Louisiana	356.0
37	Virginia	351.6
38	Alabama	339.5
39	Florida	320.9
40	Connecticut	308.4
41	New Jersey	294.2
42	New York	276.5
43	Ohio	257.2
44	Rhode Island	219.0
45	Massachusetts	204.2
46	Delaware	22.6
NA	Illinois**	NA
NA	Kentucky**	NA
NA	Montana**	NA
NA	South Carolina**	NA
	District of Columbia**	NA

Source: Morgan Quitno Press using data from Federal Bureau of Investigation
    "Crime in the United States 2004" (Uniform Crime Reports, October 17, 2005)

*By law enforcement agencies submitting complete reports to the F.B.I. for 12 months in 2004. These rates based on population estimates for areas under the jurisdiction of those agencies reporting. Arrest rate based on the F.B.I. estimate of reported and unreported arrests for driving under the influence is 487.8 arrests per 100,000 population. See important note at beginning of this chapter. **Not available.

28

Reported Arrests for Drug Abuse Violations in 2004

National Total = 1,401,393 Reported Arrests*

ALPHA ORDER

RANK	STATE	ARRESTS	% of USA
23	Alabama	18,315	1.3%
46	Alaska	1,786	0.1%
9	Arizona	35,722	2.5%
35	Arkansas	7,313	0.5%
1	California	272,980	19.5%
24	Colorado	17,434	1.2%
25	Connecticut	14,904	1.1%
43	Delaware	3,243	0.2%
2	Florida	150,334	10.7%
15	Georgia	27,629	2.0%
45	Hawaii	2,529	0.2%
38	Idaho	5,393	0.4%
4	Illinois	59,054	4.2%
18	Indiana	22,648	1.6%
32	Iowa	9,355	0.7%
33	Kansas	8,490	0.6%
29	Kentucky	10,894	0.8%
16	Louisiana	25,884	1.8%
37	Maine	5,526	0.4%
6	Maryland	51,938	3.7%
28	Massachusetts	11,617	0.8%
14	Michigan	31,520	2.2%
27	Minnesota	11,841	0.8%
26	Mississippi	13,579	1.0%
10	Missouri	35,103	2.5%
NA	Montana**	NA	NA
30	Nebraska	10,732	0.8%
31	Nevada	9,832	0.7%
41	New Hampshire	3,389	0.2%
5	New Jersey	53,713	3.8%
34	New Mexico	7,429	0.5%
8	New York	50,313	3.6%
13	North Carolina	31,802	2.3%
48	North Dakota	1,538	0.1%
11	Ohio	33,164	2.4%
20	Oklahoma	21,840	1.6%
22	Oregon	21,390	1.5%
7	Pennsylvania	51,743	3.7%
39	Rhode Island	4,388	0.3%
40	South Carolina	3,634	0.3%
47	South Dakota	1,542	0.1%
12	Tennessee	32,402	2.3%
3	Texas	125,343	8.9%
36	Utah	6,702	0.5%
49	Vermont	1,332	0.1%
17	Virginia	24,011	1.7%
21	Washington	21,443	1.5%
42	West Virginia	3,259	0.2%
19	Wisconsin	22,303	1.6%
44	Wyoming	3,044	0.2%

RANK ORDER

RANK	STATE	ARRESTS	% of USA
1	California	272,980	19.5%
2	Florida	150,334	10.7%
3	Texas	125,343	8.9%
4	Illinois	59,054	4.2%
5	New Jersey	53,713	3.8%
6	Maryland	51,938	3.7%
7	Pennsylvania	51,743	3.7%
8	New York	50,313	3.6%
9	Arizona	35,722	2.5%
10	Missouri	35,103	2.5%
11	Ohio	33,164	2.4%
12	Tennessee	32,402	2.3%
13	North Carolina	31,802	2.3%
14	Michigan	31,520	2.2%
15	Georgia	27,629	2.0%
16	Louisiana	25,884	1.8%
17	Virginia	24,011	1.7%
18	Indiana	22,648	1.6%
19	Wisconsin	22,303	1.6%
20	Oklahoma	21,840	1.6%
21	Washington	21,443	1.5%
22	Oregon	21,390	1.5%
23	Alabama	18,315	1.3%
24	Colorado	17,434	1.2%
25	Connecticut	14,904	1.1%
26	Mississippi	13,579	1.0%
27	Minnesota	11,841	0.8%
28	Massachusetts	11,617	0.8%
29	Kentucky	10,894	0.8%
30	Nebraska	10,732	0.8%
31	Nevada	9,832	0.7%
32	Iowa	9,355	0.7%
33	Kansas	8,490	0.6%
34	New Mexico	7,429	0.5%
35	Arkansas	7,313	0.5%
36	Utah	6,702	0.5%
37	Maine	5,526	0.4%
38	Idaho	5,393	0.4%
39	Rhode Island	4,388	0.3%
40	South Carolina	3,634	0.3%
41	New Hampshire	3,389	0.2%
42	West Virginia	3,259	0.2%
43	Delaware	3,243	0.2%
44	Wyoming	3,044	0.2%
45	Hawaii	2,529	0.2%
46	Alaska	1,786	0.1%
47	South Dakota	1,542	0.1%
48	North Dakota	1,538	0.1%
49	Vermont	1,332	0.1%
NA	Montana**	NA	NA
	District of Columbia**	NA	NA

Source: Federal Bureau of Investigation
    "Crime in the United States 2004" (Uniform Crime Reports, October 17, 2005)
*By law enforcement agencies submitting complete reports to the F.B.I. for 12 months in 2004. The F.B.I. estimates
1,745,712 reported and unreported arrests for drug abuse violations occurred in 2004. Includes offenses relating to
possession, sale, use, growing and manufacturing of narcotic drugs. See important note at beginning of this chapter.
**Not available.

Reported Arrest Rate for Drug Abuse Violations in 2004

National Rate = 615.6 Reported Arrests per 100,000 Population*

ALPHA ORDER

RANK	STATE	RATE
24	Alabama	457.9
43	Alaska	280.2
11	Arizona	638.6
20	Arkansas	497.5
6	California	813.4
26	Colorado	442.3
19	Connecticut	510.8
30	Delaware	431.1
4	Florida	864.5
3	Georgia	878.1
46	Hawaii	229.1
31	Idaho	426.6
NA	Illinois**	NA
21	Indiana	494.8
35	Iowa	372.3
27	Kansas	437.9
NA	Kentucky**	NA
5	Louisiana	823.2
33	Maine	419.8
1	Maryland	935.1
45	Massachusetts	252.9
39	Michigan	335.2
40	Minnesota	333.3
2	Mississippi	911.6
7	Missouri	739.2
NA	Montana**	NA
9	Nebraska	661.4
29	Nevada	436.2
38	New Hampshire	341.8
12	New Jersey	636.2
17	New Mexico	514.8
18	New York	513.0
16	North Carolina	525.1
42	North Dakota	300.8
32	Ohio	424.3
10	Oklahoma	641.1
13	Oregon	624.9
23	Pennsylvania	483.2
34	Rhode Island	406.1
NA	South Carolina**	NA
37	South Dakota	366.6
8	Tennessee	669.4
15	Texas	562.8
28	Utah	437.4
44	Vermont	256.2
36	Virginia	370.5
25	Washington	452.8
41	West Virginia	309.5
22	Wisconsin	491.2
14	Wyoming	617.8

RANK ORDER

RANK	STATE	RATE
1	Maryland	935.1
2	Mississippi	911.6
3	Georgia	878.1
4	Florida	864.5
5	Louisiana	823.2
6	California	813.4
7	Missouri	739.2
8	Tennessee	669.4
9	Nebraska	661.4
10	Oklahoma	641.1
11	Arizona	638.6
12	New Jersey	636.2
13	Oregon	624.9
14	Wyoming	617.8
15	Texas	562.8
16	North Carolina	525.1
17	New Mexico	514.8
18	New York	513.0
19	Connecticut	510.8
20	Arkansas	497.5
21	Indiana	494.8
22	Wisconsin	491.2
23	Pennsylvania	483.2
24	Alabama	457.9
25	Washington	452.8
26	Colorado	442.3
27	Kansas	437.9
28	Utah	437.4
29	Nevada	436.2
30	Delaware	431.1
31	Idaho	426.6
32	Ohio	424.3
33	Maine	419.8
34	Rhode Island	406.1
35	Iowa	372.3
36	Virginia	370.5
37	South Dakota	366.6
38	New Hampshire	341.8
39	Michigan	335.2
40	Minnesota	333.3
41	West Virginia	309.5
42	North Dakota	300.8
43	Alaska	280.2
44	Vermont	256.2
45	Massachusetts	252.9
46	Hawaii	229.1
NA	Illinois**	NA
NA	Kentucky**	NA
NA	Montana**	NA
NA	South Carolina**	NA
	District of Columbia**	NA

Source: Morgan Quitno Press using data from Federal Bureau of Investigation
"Crime in the United States 2004" (Uniform Crime Reports, October 17, 2005)
*By law enforcement agencies submitting complete reports to the F.B.I. for 12 months in 2004. These rates based on population estimates for areas under the jurisdiction of those agencies reporting. Arrest rate based on the F.B.I. estimate of reported and unreported arrests for drug abuse violations is 594.5 arrests per 100,000 population. See important note at beginning of this chapter. **Not available.

Reported Arrests for Sex Offenses in 2004

National Total = 69,326 Reported Arrests*

ALPHA ORDER

RANK	STATE	ARRESTS	% of USA
29	Alabama	396	0.6%
39	Alaska	208	0.3%
10	Arizona	1,880	2.7%
38	Arkansas	209	0.3%
1	California	14,493	20.9%
17	Colorado	1,272	1.8%
27	Connecticut	615	0.9%
48	Delaware	54	0.1%
4	Florida	4,015	5.8%
6	Georgia	3,231	4.7%
35	Hawaii	276	0.4%
32	Idaho	335	0.5%
9	Illinois	2,144	3.1%
13	Indiana	1,479	2.1%
36	Iowa	266	0.4%
33	Kansas	306	0.4%
37	Kentucky	221	0.3%
19	Louisiana	1,245	1.8%
34	Maine	298	0.4%
15	Maryland	1,339	1.9%
30	Massachusetts	376	0.5%
14	Michigan	1,397	2.0%
22	Minnesota	953	1.4%
31	Mississippi	348	0.5%
8	Missouri	2,825	4.1%
NA	Montana**	NA	NA
28	Nebraska	608	0.9%
12	Nevada	1,553	2.2%
40	New Hampshire	159	0.2%
11	New Jersey	1,838	2.7%
42	New Mexico	144	0.2%
3	New York	4,402	6.3%
21	North Carolina	1,030	1.5%
46	North Dakota	91	0.1%
15	Ohio	1,339	1.9%
25	Oklahoma	819	1.2%
20	Oregon	1,216	1.8%
7	Pennsylvania	3,130	4.5%
45	Rhode Island	110	0.2%
41	South Carolina	145	0.2%
44	South Dakota	117	0.2%
26	Tennessee	623	0.9%
2	Texas	5,004	7.2%
24	Utah	844	1.2%
49	Vermont	51	0.1%
23	Virginia	942	1.4%
18	Washington	1,261	1.8%
47	West Virginia	88	0.1%
5	Wisconsin	3,505	5.1%
43	Wyoming	126	0.2%

RANK ORDER

RANK	STATE	ARRESTS	% of USA
1	California	14,493	20.9%
2	Texas	5,004	7.2%
3	New York	4,402	6.3%
4	Florida	4,015	5.8%
5	Wisconsin	3,505	5.1%
6	Georgia	3,231	4.7%
7	Pennsylvania	3,130	4.5%
8	Missouri	2,825	4.1%
9	Illinois	2,144	3.1%
10	Arizona	1,880	2.7%
11	New Jersey	1,838	2.7%
12	Nevada	1,553	2.2%
13	Indiana	1,479	2.1%
14	Michigan	1,397	2.0%
15	Maryland	1,339	1.9%
15	Ohio	1,339	1.9%
17	Colorado	1,272	1.8%
18	Washington	1,261	1.8%
19	Louisiana	1,245	1.8%
20	Oregon	1,216	1.8%
21	North Carolina	1,030	1.5%
22	Minnesota	953	1.4%
23	Virginia	942	1.4%
24	Utah	844	1.2%
25	Oklahoma	819	1.2%
26	Tennessee	623	0.9%
27	Connecticut	615	0.9%
28	Nebraska	608	0.9%
29	Alabama	396	0.6%
30	Massachusetts	376	0.5%
31	Mississippi	348	0.5%
32	Idaho	335	0.5%
33	Kansas	306	0.4%
34	Maine	298	0.4%
35	Hawaii	276	0.4%
36	Iowa	266	0.4%
37	Kentucky	221	0.3%
38	Arkansas	209	0.3%
39	Alaska	208	0.3%
40	New Hampshire	159	0.2%
41	South Carolina	145	0.2%
42	New Mexico	144	0.2%
43	Wyoming	126	0.2%
44	South Dakota	117	0.2%
45	Rhode Island	110	0.2%
46	North Dakota	91	0.1%
47	West Virginia	88	0.1%
48	Delaware	54	0.1%
49	Vermont	51	0.1%
NA	Montana**	NA	NA
	District of Columbia**	NA	NA

Source: Federal Bureau of Investigation
   "Crime in the United States 2004" (Uniform Crime Reports, October 17, 2005)
*By law enforcement agencies submitting complete reports to the F.B.I. for 12 months in 2004. The F.B.I. estimates 91,395 reported and unreported arrests for sex offenses occurred in 2004. Excludes forcible rape, prostitution and commercialized vice. Includes statutory rape and offenses against chastity, common decency, morals and the like. See important note at beginning of this chapter. **Not available.

Reported Arrest Rate for Sex Offenses in 2004

National Rate = 30.5 Reported Arrests per 100,000 Population*

ALPHA ORDER

RANK	STATE	RATE
42	Alabama	9.9
12	Alaska	32.6
11	Arizona	33.6
37	Arkansas	14.2
7	California	43.2
13	Colorado	32.3
29	Connecticut	21.1
46	Delaware	7.2
25	Florida	23.1
1	Georgia	102.7
21	Hawaii	25.0
19	Idaho	26.5
NA	Illinois**	NA
13	Indiana	32.3
39	Iowa	10.6
34	Kansas	15.8
NA	Kentucky**	NA
8	Louisiana	39.6
26	Maine	22.6
22	Maryland	24.1
45	Massachusetts	8.2
35	Michigan	14.9
17	Minnesota	26.8
24	Mississippi	23.4
4	Missouri	59.5
NA	Montana**	NA
9	Nebraska	37.5
3	Nevada	68.9
33	New Hampshire	16.0
28	New Jersey	21.8
41	New Mexico	10.0
6	New York	44.9
32	North Carolina	17.0
30	North Dakota	17.8
31	Ohio	17.1
23	Oklahoma	24.0
10	Oregon	35.5
15	Pennsylvania	29.2
40	Rhode Island	10.2
NA	South Carolina**	NA
16	South Dakota	27.8
38	Tennessee	12.9
27	Texas	22.5
5	Utah	55.1
43	Vermont	9.8
36	Virginia	14.5
18	Washington	26.6
44	West Virginia	8.4
2	Wisconsin	77.2
20	Wyoming	25.6

RANK ORDER

RANK	STATE	RATE
1	Georgia	102.7
2	Wisconsin	77.2
3	Nevada	68.9
4	Missouri	59.5
5	Utah	55.1
6	New York	44.9
7	California	43.2
8	Louisiana	39.6
9	Nebraska	37.5
10	Oregon	35.5
11	Arizona	33.6
12	Alaska	32.6
13	Colorado	32.3
13	Indiana	32.3
15	Pennsylvania	29.2
16	South Dakota	27.8
17	Minnesota	26.8
18	Washington	26.6
19	Idaho	26.5
20	Wyoming	25.6
21	Hawaii	25.0
22	Maryland	24.1
23	Oklahoma	24.0
24	Mississippi	23.4
25	Florida	23.1
26	Maine	22.6
27	Texas	22.5
28	New Jersey	21.8
29	Connecticut	21.1
30	North Dakota	17.8
31	Ohio	17.1
32	North Carolina	17.0
33	New Hampshire	16.0
34	Kansas	15.8
35	Michigan	14.9
36	Virginia	14.5
37	Arkansas	14.2
38	Tennessee	12.9
39	Iowa	10.6
40	Rhode Island	10.2
41	New Mexico	10.0
42	Alabama	9.9
43	Vermont	9.8
44	West Virginia	8.4
45	Massachusetts	8.2
46	Delaware	7.2
NA	Illinois**	NA
NA	Kentucky**	NA
NA	Montana**	NA
NA	South Carolina**	NA
	District of Columbia**	NA

Source: Morgan Quitno Press using data from Federal Bureau of Investigation
"Crime in the United States 2004" (Uniform Crime Reports, October 17, 2005)
*By law enforcement agencies submitting complete reports to the F.B.I. for 12 months in 2004. These rates based on population estimates for areas under the jurisdiction of those agencies reporting. Arrest rate based on the F.B.I. estimate of reported and unreported arrests for sex offenses is 31.1 arrests per 100,000 population. See important note at beginning of this chapter. **Not available.

Reported Arrests for Prostitution and Commercialized Vice in 2004

National Total = 71,369 Reported Arrests*

ALPHA ORDER

RANK	STATE	ARRESTS	% of USA
34	Alabama	173	0.2%
38	Alaska	102	0.1%
10	Arizona	2,115	3.0%
30	Arkansas	330	0.5%
1	California	14,134	19.8%
18	Colorado	864	1.2%
26	Connecticut	455	0.6%
37	Delaware	118	0.2%
2	Florida	6,583	9.2%
13	Georgia	1,651	2.3%
32	Hawaii	255	0.4%
47	Idaho	4	0.0%
4	Illinois	6,060	8.5%
15	Indiana	1,504	2.1%
35	Iowa	170	0.2%
36	Kansas	143	0.2%
29	Kentucky	334	0.5%
25	Louisiana	538	0.8%
45	Maine	30	0.0%
7	Maryland	2,637	3.7%
20	Massachusetts	809	1.1%
12	Michigan	1,791	2.5%
41	Minnesota	40	0.1%
39	Mississippi	91	0.1%
17	Missouri	1,060	1.5%
NA	Montana**	NA	NA
31	Nebraska	312	0.4%
5	Nevada	5,301	7.4%
41	New Hampshire	40	0.1%
9	New Jersey	2,408	3.4%
27	New Mexico	412	0.6%
11	New York	1,795	2.5%
22	North Carolina	693	1.0%
46	North Dakota	16	0.0%
16	Ohio	1,392	2.0%
24	Oklahoma	555	0.8%
19	Oregon	863	1.2%
6	Pennsylvania	2,952	4.1%
33	Rhode Island	215	0.3%
44	South Carolina	34	0.0%
49	South Dakota	1	0.0%
14	Tennessee	1,582	2.2%
3	Texas	6,575	9.2%
28	Utah	353	0.5%
48	Vermont	3	0.0%
21	Virginia	723	1.0%
23	Washington	574	0.8%
40	West Virginia	58	0.1%
8	Wisconsin	2,486	3.5%
43	Wyoming	35	0.0%

RANK ORDER

RANK	STATE	ARRESTS	% of USA
1	California	14,134	19.8%
2	Florida	6,583	9.2%
3	Texas	6,575	9.2%
4	Illinois	6,060	8.5%
5	Nevada	5,301	7.4%
6	Pennsylvania	2,952	4.1%
7	Maryland	2,637	3.7%
8	Wisconsin	2,486	3.5%
9	New Jersey	2,408	3.4%
10	Arizona	2,115	3.0%
11	New York	1,795	2.5%
12	Michigan	1,791	2.5%
13	Georgia	1,651	2.3%
14	Tennessee	1,582	2.2%
15	Indiana	1,504	2.1%
16	Ohio	1,392	2.0%
17	Missouri	1,060	1.5%
18	Colorado	864	1.2%
19	Oregon	863	1.2%
20	Massachusetts	809	1.1%
21	Virginia	723	1.0%
22	North Carolina	693	1.0%
23	Washington	574	0.8%
24	Oklahoma	555	0.8%
25	Louisiana	538	0.8%
26	Connecticut	455	0.6%
27	New Mexico	412	0.6%
28	Utah	353	0.5%
29	Kentucky	334	0.5%
30	Arkansas	330	0.5%
31	Nebraska	312	0.4%
32	Hawaii	255	0.4%
33	Rhode Island	215	0.3%
34	Alabama	173	0.2%
35	Iowa	170	0.2%
36	Kansas	143	0.2%
37	Delaware	118	0.2%
38	Alaska	102	0.1%
39	Mississippi	91	0.1%
40	West Virginia	58	0.1%
41	Minnesota	40	0.1%
41	New Hampshire	40	0.1%
43	Wyoming	35	0.0%
44	South Carolina	34	0.0%
45	Maine	30	0.0%
46	North Dakota	16	0.0%
47	Idaho	4	0.0%
48	Vermont	3	0.0%
49	South Dakota	1	0.0%
NA	Montana**	NA	NA
	District of Columbia**	NA	NA

Source: Federal Bureau of Investigation
   "Crime in the United States 2004" (Uniform Crime Reports, October 17, 2005)
*By law enforcement agencies submitting complete reports to the F.B.I. for 12 months in 2004. The F.B.I. estimates 90,231 reported and unreported arrests for prostitution and commercialized vice occurred in 2004. Includes keeping a bawdy house, procuring or transporting women for immoral purposes. Attempts are included. See important note at beginning of this chapter. **Not available.

Reported Arrest Rate for Prostitution and Commercialized Vice in 2004

National Rate = 31.3 Reported Arrests per 100,000 Population*

ALPHA ORDER

RANK	STATE	RATE
39	Alabama	4.3
28	Alaska	16.0
7	Arizona	37.8
17	Arkansas	22.5
5	California	42.1
19	Colorado	21.9
30	Connecticut	15.6
29	Delaware	15.7
6	Florida	37.9
3	Georgia	52.5
15	Hawaii	23.1
45	Idaho	0.3
NA	Illinois**	NA
8	Indiana	32.9
36	Iowa	6.8
34	Kansas	7.4
NA	Kentucky**	NA
26	Louisiana	17.1
42	Maine	2.3
4	Maryland	47.5
25	Massachusetts	17.6
22	Michigan	19.0
43	Minnesota	1.1
37	Mississippi	6.1
18	Missouri	22.3
NA	Montana**	NA
21	Nebraska	19.2
1	Nevada	235.2
40	New Hampshire	4.0
12	New Jersey	28.5
11	New Mexico	28.6
23	New York	18.3
32	North Carolina	11.4
41	North Dakota	3.1
24	Ohio	17.8
27	Oklahoma	16.3
14	Oregon	25.2
13	Pennsylvania	27.6
20	Rhode Island	19.9
NA	South Carolina**	NA
46	South Dakota	0.2
9	Tennessee	32.7
10	Texas	29.5
16	Utah	23.0
44	Vermont	0.6
33	Virginia	11.2
31	Washington	12.1
38	West Virginia	5.5
2	Wisconsin	54.7
35	Wyoming	7.1

RANK ORDER

RANK	STATE	RATE
1	Nevada	235.2
2	Wisconsin	54.7
3	Georgia	52.5
4	Maryland	47.5
5	California	42.1
6	Florida	37.9
7	Arizona	37.8
8	Indiana	32.9
9	Tennessee	32.7
10	Texas	29.5
11	New Mexico	28.6
12	New Jersey	28.5
13	Pennsylvania	27.6
14	Oregon	25.2
15	Hawaii	23.1
16	Utah	23.0
17	Arkansas	22.5
18	Missouri	22.3
19	Colorado	21.9
20	Rhode Island	19.9
21	Nebraska	19.2
22	Michigan	19.0
23	New York	18.3
24	Ohio	17.8
25	Massachusetts	17.6
26	Louisiana	17.1
27	Oklahoma	16.3
28	Alaska	16.0
29	Delaware	15.7
30	Connecticut	15.6
31	Washington	12.1
32	North Carolina	11.4
33	Virginia	11.2
34	Kansas	7.4
35	Wyoming	7.1
36	Iowa	6.8
37	Mississippi	6.1
38	West Virginia	5.5
39	Alabama	4.3
40	New Hampshire	4.0
41	North Dakota	3.1
42	Maine	2.3
43	Minnesota	1.1
44	Vermont	0.6
45	Idaho	0.3
46	South Dakota	0.2
NA	Illinois**	NA
NA	Kentucky**	NA
NA	Montana**	NA
NA	South Carolina**	NA
	District of Columbia**	NA

Source: Morgan Quitno Press using data from Federal Bureau of Investigation
    "Crime in the United States 2004" (Uniform Crime Reports, October 17, 2005)
*By law enforcement agencies submitting complete reports to the F.B.I. for 12 months in 2004. These rates based on population estimates for areas under the jurisdiction of those agencies reporting. Arrest rate based on the F.B.I. estimate of reported and unreported arrests for prostitution and commercialized vice is 30.7 arrests per 100,000 population. See important note at beginning of this chapter. **Not available.

Reported Arrests for Offenses Against Families and Children in 2004

National Total = 88,738 Reported Arrests*

ALPHA ORDER

RANK	STATE	ARRESTS	% of USA
22	Alabama	1,143	1.3%
31	Alaska	433	0.5%
6	Arizona	3,210	3.6%
39	Arkansas	255	0.3%
30	California	474	0.5%
7	Colorado	2,876	3.2%
18	Connecticut	1,224	1.4%
41	Delaware	214	0.2%
49	Florida	0	0.0%
14	Georgia	1,677	1.9%
46	Hawaii	108	0.1%
33	Idaho	392	0.4%
34	Illinois	336	0.4%
16	Indiana	1,650	1.9%
28	Iowa	702	0.8%
40	Kansas	239	0.3%
26	Kentucky	1,083	1.2%
13	Louisiana	2,021	2.3%
36	Maine	334	0.4%
12	Maryland	2,436	2.7%
17	Massachusetts	1,452	1.6%
8	Michigan	2,827	3.2%
32	Minnesota	393	0.4%
9	Mississippi	2,803	3.2%
5	Missouri	4,020	4.5%
NA	Montana**	NA	NA
15	Nebraska	1,668	1.9%
21	Nevada	1,166	1.3%
43	New Hampshire	176	0.2%
1	New Jersey	15,123	17.0%
24	New Mexico	1,117	1.3%
10	New York	2,721	3.1%
3	North Carolina	8,736	9.8%
42	North Dakota	206	0.2%
2	Ohio	10,934	12.3%
23	Oklahoma	1,135	1.3%
29	Oregon	590	0.7%
27	Pennsylvania	886	1.0%
45	Rhode Island	139	0.2%
48	South Carolina	58	0.1%
44	South Dakota	164	0.2%
20	Tennessee	1,172	1.3%
4	Texas	4,680	5.3%
19	Utah	1,200	1.4%
35	Vermont	335	0.4%
24	Virginia	1,117	1.3%
37	Washington	305	0.3%
47	West Virginia	82	0.1%
11	Wisconsin	2,467	2.8%
38	Wyoming	259	0.3%

RANK ORDER

RANK	STATE	ARRESTS	% of USA
1	New Jersey	15,123	17.0%
2	Ohio	10,934	12.3%
3	North Carolina	8,736	9.8%
4	Texas	4,680	5.3%
5	Missouri	4,020	4.5%
6	Arizona	3,210	3.6%
7	Colorado	2,876	3.2%
8	Michigan	2,827	3.2%
9	Mississippi	2,803	3.2%
10	New York	2,721	3.1%
11	Wisconsin	2,467	2.8%
12	Maryland	2,436	2.7%
13	Louisiana	2,021	2.3%
14	Georgia	1,677	1.9%
15	Nebraska	1,668	1.9%
16	Indiana	1,650	1.9%
17	Massachusetts	1,452	1.6%
18	Connecticut	1,224	1.4%
19	Utah	1,200	1.4%
20	Tennessee	1,172	1.3%
21	Nevada	1,166	1.3%
22	Alabama	1,143	1.3%
23	Oklahoma	1,135	1.3%
24	New Mexico	1,117	1.3%
24	Virginia	1,117	1.3%
26	Kentucky	1,083	1.2%
27	Pennsylvania	886	1.0%
28	Iowa	702	0.8%
29	Oregon	590	0.7%
30	California	474	0.5%
31	Alaska	433	0.5%
32	Minnesota	393	0.4%
33	Idaho	392	0.4%
34	Illinois	336	0.4%
35	Vermont	335	0.4%
36	Maine	334	0.4%
37	Washington	305	0.3%
38	Wyoming	259	0.3%
39	Arkansas	255	0.3%
40	Kansas	239	0.3%
41	Delaware	214	0.2%
42	North Dakota	206	0.2%
43	New Hampshire	176	0.2%
44	South Dakota	164	0.2%
45	Rhode Island	139	0.2%
46	Hawaii	108	0.1%
47	West Virginia	82	0.1%
48	South Carolina	58	0.1%
49	Florida	0	0.0%
NA	Montana**	NA	NA
	District of Columbia**	NA	NA

Source: Federal Bureau of Investigation
   "Crime in the United States 2004" (Uniform Crime Reports, October 17, 2005)
*By law enforcement agencies submitting complete reports to the F.B.I. for 12 months in 2004. The F.B.I. estimates
125,955 reported and unreported arrests for offenses against families and children occurred in 2004. Includes
nonsupport, neglect, desertion or abuse of family and children. See important note at beginning of this chapter.
**Not available.

Reported Arrest Rate for Offenses Against Families and Children in 2004

National Rate = 39.0 Reported Arrests per 100,000 Population*

ALPHA ORDER

RANK	STATE	RATE
27	Alabama	28.6
10	Alaska	67.9
13	Arizona	57.4
35	Arkansas	17.3
45	California	1.4
9	Colorado	73.0
19	Connecticut	42.0
28	Delaware	28.4
46	Florida	0.0
15	Georgia	53.3
41	Hawaii	9.8
25	Idaho	31.0
NA	Illinois**	NA
22	Indiana	36.1
29	Iowa	27.9
39	Kansas	12.3
NA	Kentucky**	NA
12	Louisiana	64.3
31	Maine	25.4
18	Maryland	43.9
24	Massachusetts	31.6
26	Michigan	30.1
40	Minnesota	11.1
1	Mississippi	188.2
6	Missouri	84.6
NA	Montana**	NA
5	Nebraska	102.8
17	Nevada	51.7
34	New Hampshire	17.7
2	New Jersey	179.1
8	New Mexico	77.4
30	New York	27.7
3	North Carolina	144.2
20	North Dakota	40.3
4	Ohio	139.9
23	Oklahoma	33.3
36	Oregon	17.2
42	Pennsylvania	8.3
38	Rhode Island	12.9
NA	South Carolina**	NA
21	South Dakota	39.0
32	Tennessee	24.2
33	Texas	21.0
7	Utah	78.3
11	Vermont	64.4
36	Virginia	17.2
44	Washington	6.4
43	West Virginia	7.8
14	Wisconsin	54.3
16	Wyoming	52.6

RANK ORDER

RANK	STATE	RATE
1	Mississippi	188.2
2	New Jersey	179.1
3	North Carolina	144.2
4	Ohio	139.9
5	Nebraska	102.8
6	Missouri	84.6
7	Utah	78.3
8	New Mexico	77.4
9	Colorado	73.0
10	Alaska	67.9
11	Vermont	64.4
12	Louisiana	64.3
13	Arizona	57.4
14	Wisconsin	54.3
15	Georgia	53.3
16	Wyoming	52.6
17	Nevada	51.7
18	Maryland	43.9
19	Connecticut	42.0
20	North Dakota	40.3
21	South Dakota	39.0
22	Indiana	36.1
23	Oklahoma	33.3
24	Massachusetts	31.6
25	Idaho	31.0
26	Michigan	30.1
27	Alabama	28.6
28	Delaware	28.4
29	Iowa	27.9
30	New York	27.7
31	Maine	25.4
32	Tennessee	24.2
33	Texas	21.0
34	New Hampshire	17.7
35	Arkansas	17.3
36	Oregon	17.2
36	Virginia	17.2
38	Rhode Island	12.9
39	Kansas	12.3
40	Minnesota	11.1
41	Hawaii	9.8
42	Pennsylvania	8.3
43	West Virginia	7.8
44	Washington	6.4
45	California	1.4
46	Florida	0.0
NA	Illinois**	NA
NA	Kentucky**	NA
NA	Montana**	NA
NA	South Carolina**	NA
	District of Columbia**	NA

Source: Morgan Quitno Press using data from Federal Bureau of Investigation
"Crime in the United States 2004" (Uniform Crime Reports, October 17, 2005)
*By law enforcement agencies submitting complete reports to the F.B.I. for 12 months in 2004. These rates based on population estimates for areas under the jurisdiction of those agencies reporting. Arrest rate based on the F.B.I. estimate of reported and unreported arrests for offenses against families and children is 42.9 arrests per 100,000 population. See important note at beginning of this chapter. **Not available.

Percent of Crimes Cleared in 2003

National Percent = 19.9% Cleared*

<table>
<tr><td colspan="3">ALPHA ORDER</td><td colspan="3">RANK ORDER</td></tr>
<tr><td>RANK</td><td>STATE</td><td>PERCENT</td><td>RANK</td><td>STATE</td><td>PERCENT</td></tr>
<tr><td>22</td><td>Alabama</td><td>19.5</td><td>1</td><td>New York</td><td>30.1</td></tr>
<tr><td>2</td><td>Alaska</td><td>27.8</td><td>2</td><td>Alaska</td><td>27.8</td></tr>
<tr><td>42</td><td>Arizona</td><td>15.9</td><td>3</td><td>Maine</td><td>27.7</td></tr>
<tr><td>18</td><td>Arkansas</td><td>21.6</td><td>4</td><td>Delaware</td><td>27.2</td></tr>
<tr><td>33</td><td>California</td><td>18.3</td><td>5</td><td>Pennsylvania</td><td>27.1</td></tr>
<tr><td>35</td><td>Colorado</td><td>18.2</td><td>6</td><td>South Dakota</td><td>26.9</td></tr>
<tr><td>28</td><td>Connecticut</td><td>18.7</td><td>7</td><td>Minnesota</td><td>25.0</td></tr>
<tr><td>4</td><td>Delaware</td><td>27.2</td><td>8</td><td>Wyoming</td><td>24.8</td></tr>
<tr><td>13</td><td>Florida</td><td>22.7</td><td>9</td><td>Wisconsin</td><td>24.4</td></tr>
<tr><td>23</td><td>Georgia</td><td>19.4</td><td>10</td><td>North Carolina</td><td>24.3</td></tr>
<tr><td>49</td><td>Hawaii</td><td>12.1</td><td>11</td><td>Louisiana</td><td>24.0</td></tr>
<tr><td>16</td><td>Idaho</td><td>21.9</td><td>12</td><td>Nebraska</td><td>23.2</td></tr>
<tr><td>NA</td><td>Illinois**</td><td>NA</td><td>13</td><td>Florida</td><td>22.7</td></tr>
<tr><td>30</td><td>Indiana</td><td>18.5</td><td>14</td><td>Kentucky</td><td>22.6</td></tr>
<tr><td>27</td><td>Iowa</td><td>18.9</td><td>15</td><td>Maryland</td><td>22.2</td></tr>
<tr><td>48</td><td>Kansas</td><td>12.6</td><td>16</td><td>Idaho</td><td>21.9</td></tr>
<tr><td>14</td><td>Kentucky</td><td>22.6</td><td>17</td><td>Missouri</td><td>21.8</td></tr>
<tr><td>11</td><td>Louisiana</td><td>24.0</td><td>18</td><td>Arkansas</td><td>21.6</td></tr>
<tr><td>3</td><td>Maine</td><td>27.7</td><td>19</td><td>Mississippi</td><td>21.5</td></tr>
<tr><td>15</td><td>Maryland</td><td>22.2</td><td>20</td><td>South Carolina</td><td>20.3</td></tr>
<tr><td>24</td><td>Massachusetts</td><td>19.2</td><td>21</td><td>New Mexico</td><td>19.6</td></tr>
<tr><td>45</td><td>Michigan</td><td>15.2</td><td>22</td><td>Alabama</td><td>19.5</td></tr>
<tr><td>7</td><td>Minnesota</td><td>25.0</td><td>23</td><td>Georgia</td><td>19.4</td></tr>
<tr><td>19</td><td>Mississippi</td><td>21.5</td><td>24</td><td>Massachusetts</td><td>19.2</td></tr>
<tr><td>17</td><td>Missouri</td><td>21.8</td><td>24</td><td>New Jersey</td><td>19.2</td></tr>
<tr><td>30</td><td>Montana</td><td>18.5</td><td>26</td><td>Utah</td><td>19.1</td></tr>
<tr><td>12</td><td>Nebraska</td><td>23.2</td><td>27</td><td>Iowa</td><td>18.9</td></tr>
<tr><td>36</td><td>Nevada</td><td>17.9</td><td>28</td><td>Connecticut</td><td>18.7</td></tr>
<tr><td>44</td><td>New Hampshire</td><td>15.4</td><td>28</td><td>Oregon</td><td>18.7</td></tr>
<tr><td>24</td><td>New Jersey</td><td>19.2</td><td>30</td><td>Indiana</td><td>18.5</td></tr>
<tr><td>21</td><td>New Mexico</td><td>19.6</td><td>30</td><td>Montana</td><td>18.5</td></tr>
<tr><td>1</td><td>New York</td><td>30.1</td><td>30</td><td>North Dakota</td><td>18.5</td></tr>
<tr><td>10</td><td>North Carolina</td><td>24.3</td><td>33</td><td>California</td><td>18.3</td></tr>
<tr><td>30</td><td>North Dakota</td><td>18.5</td><td>33</td><td>Texas</td><td>18.3</td></tr>
<tr><td>41</td><td>Ohio</td><td>16.1</td><td>35</td><td>Colorado</td><td>18.2</td></tr>
<tr><td>39</td><td>Oklahoma</td><td>17.3</td><td>36</td><td>Nevada</td><td>17.9</td></tr>
<tr><td>28</td><td>Oregon</td><td>18.7</td><td>37</td><td>Virginia</td><td>17.6</td></tr>
<tr><td>5</td><td>Pennsylvania</td><td>27.1</td><td>37</td><td>Washington</td><td>17.6</td></tr>
<tr><td>42</td><td>Rhode Island</td><td>15.9</td><td>39</td><td>Oklahoma</td><td>17.3</td></tr>
<tr><td>20</td><td>South Carolina</td><td>20.3</td><td>40</td><td>Tennessee</td><td>17.2</td></tr>
<tr><td>6</td><td>South Dakota</td><td>26.9</td><td>41</td><td>Ohio</td><td>16.1</td></tr>
<tr><td>40</td><td>Tennessee</td><td>17.2</td><td>42</td><td>Arizona</td><td>15.9</td></tr>
<tr><td>33</td><td>Texas</td><td>18.3</td><td>42</td><td>Rhode Island</td><td>15.9</td></tr>
<tr><td>26</td><td>Utah</td><td>19.1</td><td>44</td><td>New Hampshire</td><td>15.4</td></tr>
<tr><td>45</td><td>Vermont</td><td>15.2</td><td>45</td><td>Michigan</td><td>15.2</td></tr>
<tr><td>37</td><td>Virginia</td><td>17.6</td><td>45</td><td>Vermont</td><td>15.2</td></tr>
<tr><td>37</td><td>Washington</td><td>17.6</td><td>47</td><td>West Virginia</td><td>14.3</td></tr>
<tr><td>47</td><td>West Virginia</td><td>14.3</td><td>48</td><td>Kansas</td><td>12.6</td></tr>
<tr><td>9</td><td>Wisconsin</td><td>24.4</td><td>49</td><td>Hawaii</td><td>12.1</td></tr>
<tr><td>8</td><td>Wyoming</td><td>24.8</td><td>NA</td><td>Illinois**</td><td>NA</td></tr>
<tr><td></td><td></td><td></td><td></td><td>District of Columbia</td><td>10.7</td></tr>
</table>

Source: Federal Bureau of Investigation (unpublished data)
*Includes murder, rape, robbery, aggravated assault, burglary, larceny-theft and motor vehicle theft. A crime is considered cleared when at least one person is arrested, charged and turned over to the court for prosecution. Clearances recorded in 2003 may be for crimes which occurred in prior years. Several crimes may be cleared by the arrest of one person while the arrest of many persons may clear only one crime.
**Not available.

Percent of Violent Crimes Cleared in 2003

National Percent = 46.7% Cleared*

ALPHA ORDER

RANK	STATE	PERCENT
37	Alabama	42.6
4	Alaska	61.8
41	Arizona	41.0
22	Arkansas	50.2
26	California	48.0
17	Colorado	51.3
30	Connecticut	46.6
6	Delaware	61.0
25	Florida	49.3
44	Georgia	38.6
10	Hawaii	56.5
9	Idaho	57.5
NA	Illinois**	NA
31	Indiana	46.2
12	Iowa	54.4
45	Kansas	36.8
34	Kentucky	44.7
23	Louisiana	50.1
7	Maine	60.7
20	Maryland	51.0
29	Massachusetts	47.1
46	Michigan	36.1
3	Minnesota	63.1
48	Mississippi	33.3
17	Missouri	51.3
28	Montana	47.3
5	Nebraska	61.2
49	Nevada	30.6
43	New Hampshire	40.0
33	New Jersey	44.8
24	New Mexico	49.5
13	New York	53.7
11	North Carolina	55.4
27	North Dakota	47.8
47	Ohio	35.3
19	Oklahoma	51.1
40	Oregon	41.5
14	Pennsylvania	52.9
36	Rhode Island	43.1
21	South Carolina	50.3
8	South Dakota	59.6
39	Tennessee	41.9
35	Texas	43.3
32	Utah	45.2
1	Vermont	72.2
38	Virginia	42.2
15	Washington	52.2
41	West Virginia	41.0
16	Wisconsin	52.0
2	Wyoming	67.7

RANK ORDER

RANK	STATE	PERCENT
1	Vermont	72.2
2	Wyoming	67.7
3	Minnesota	63.1
4	Alaska	61.8
5	Nebraska	61.2
6	Delaware	61.0
7	Maine	60.7
8	South Dakota	59.6
9	Idaho	57.5
10	Hawaii	56.5
11	North Carolina	55.4
12	Iowa	54.4
13	New York	53.7
14	Pennsylvania	52.9
15	Washington	52.2
16	Wisconsin	52.0
17	Colorado	51.3
17	Missouri	51.3
19	Oklahoma	51.1
20	Maryland	51.0
21	South Carolina	50.3
22	Arkansas	50.2
23	Louisiana	50.1
24	New Mexico	49.5
25	Florida	49.3
26	California	48.0
27	North Dakota	47.8
28	Montana	47.3
29	Massachusetts	47.1
30	Connecticut	46.6
31	Indiana	46.2
32	Utah	45.2
33	New Jersey	44.8
34	Kentucky	44.7
35	Texas	43.3
36	Rhode Island	43.1
37	Alabama	42.6
38	Virginia	42.2
39	Tennessee	41.9
40	Oregon	41.5
41	Arizona	41.0
41	West Virginia	41.0
43	New Hampshire	40.0
44	Georgia	38.6
45	Kansas	36.8
46	Michigan	36.1
47	Ohio	35.3
48	Mississippi	33.3
49	Nevada	30.6
NA	Illinois**	NA

District of Columbia   29.6

Source: Federal Bureau of Investigation (unpublished data)
*Includes murder, rape, robbery and aggravated assault. A crime is considered cleared when at least one person is arrested, charged and turned over to the court for prosecution. Clearances recorded in 2003 may be for crimes which occurred in prior years. Several crimes may be cleared by the arrest of one person while the arrest of many persons may clear only one crime.
**Not available.

Percent of Murders Cleared in 2003

National Percent = 63.2% Cleared*

ALPHA ORDER				RANK ORDER		
RANK	STATE	PERCENT		RANK	STATE	PERCENT
9	Alabama	77.7		1	Hawaii	100.0
18	Alaska	71.8		1	North Dakota	100.0
45	Arizona	48.9		1	South Dakota	100.0
17	Arkansas	72.0		4	Wyoming	92.9
37	California	55.1		5	Nebraska	90.6
33	Colorado	59.8		6	Washington	87.7
16	Connecticut	72.5		7	Missouri	86.2
46	Delaware	47.6		8	North Carolina	78.8
27	Florida	64.5		9	Alabama	77.7
34	Georgia	59.6		10	Idaho	76.9
1	Hawaii	100.0		11	Wisconsin	75.1
10	Idaho	76.9		12	Maine	75.0
NA	Illinois**	NA		12	Pennsylvania	75.0
23	Indiana	69.9		14	South Carolina	74.5
26	Iowa	66.0		15	Vermont	73.3
25	Kansas	68.0		16	Connecticut	72.5
32	Kentucky	60.3		17	Arkansas	72.0
40	Louisiana	54.2		18	Alaska	71.8
12	Maine	75.0		19	Oklahoma	71.4
29	Maryland	63.2		20	New Jersey	71.2
35	Massachusetts	56.6		21	Tennessee	70.0
47	Michigan	46.2		21	Texas	70.0
28	Minnesota	63.8		23	Indiana	69.9
24	Mississippi	69.7		24	Mississippi	69.7
7	Missouri	86.2		25	Kansas	68.0
42	Montana	52.4		26	Iowa	66.0
5	Nebraska	90.6		27	Florida	64.5
48	Nevada	45.4		28	Minnesota	63.8
49	New Hampshire	27.3		29	Maryland	63.2
20	New Jersey	71.2		30	New Mexico	61.5
30	New Mexico	61.5		31	Oregon	60.7
38	New York	54.5		32	Kentucky	60.3
8	North Carolina	78.8		33	Colorado	59.8
1	North Dakota	100.0		34	Georgia	59.6
40	Ohio	54.2		35	Massachusetts	56.6
19	Oklahoma	71.4		36	Rhode Island	56.0
31	Oregon	60.7		37	California	55.1
12	Pennsylvania	75.0		38	New York	54.5
36	Rhode Island	56.0		38	Virginia	54.5
14	South Carolina	74.5		40	Louisiana	54.2
1	South Dakota	100.0		40	Ohio	54.2
21	Tennessee	70.0		42	Montana	52.4
21	Texas	70.0		43	Utah	50.9
43	Utah	50.9		44	West Virginia	50.8
15	Vermont	73.3		45	Arizona	48.9
38	Virginia	54.5		46	Delaware	47.6
6	Washington	87.7		47	Michigan	46.2
44	West Virginia	50.8		48	Nevada	45.4
11	Wisconsin	75.1		49	New Hampshire	27.3
4	Wyoming	92.9		NA	Illinois**	NA
					District of Columbia	60.6

Source: Federal Bureau of Investigation (unpublished data)
*Includes nonnegligent manslaughter. A crime is considered cleared when at least one person is arrested, charged and turned over to the court for prosecution. Clearances recorded in 2003 may be for crimes which occurred in prior years. Several crimes may be cleared by the arrest of one person while the arrest of many persons may clear only one crime.
**Not available.

Percent of Rapes Cleared in 2003

National Percent = 44.0% Cleared*

RANK	STATE	PERCENT
14	Alabama	48.4
33	Alaska	38.0
43	Arizona	29.5
17	Arkansas	47.0
18	California	46.6
21	Colorado	45.3
31	Connecticut	38.7
1	Delaware	68.9
7	Florida	52.5
28	Georgia	41.6
29	Hawaii	39.6
34	Idaho	36.5
NA	Illinois**	NA
32	Indiana	38.4
45	Iowa	27.6
46	Kansas	25.7
9	Kentucky	51.1
22	Louisiana	45.1
19	Maine	46.0
8	Maryland	51.7
26	Massachusetts	42.4
42	Michigan	30.1
5	Minnesota	55.7
39	Mississippi	32.0
12	Missouri	49.3
47	Montana	22.8
16	Nebraska	47.8
41	Nevada	31.3
48	New Hampshire	20.7
11	New Jersey	49.8
25	New Mexico	42.6
15	New York	48.2
3	North Carolina	63.5
36	North Dakota	34.0
35	Ohio	34.3
6	Oklahoma	53.4
44	Oregon	28.7
4	Pennsylvania	57.3
40	Rhode Island	31.7
23	South Carolina	44.2
27	South Dakota	42.1
38	Tennessee	32.3
20	Texas	45.9
37	Utah	32.8
10	Vermont	50.4
30	Virginia	39.5
24	Washington	43.9
49	West Virginia	14.0
2	Wisconsin	65.9
13	Wyoming	48.5

RANK	STATE	PERCENT
1	Delaware	68.9
2	Wisconsin	65.9
3	North Carolina	63.5
4	Pennsylvania	57.3
5	Minnesota	55.7
6	Oklahoma	53.4
7	Florida	52.5
8	Maryland	51.7
9	Kentucky	51.1
10	Vermont	50.4
11	New Jersey	49.8
12	Missouri	49.3
13	Wyoming	48.5
14	Alabama	48.4
15	New York	48.2
16	Nebraska	47.8
17	Arkansas	47.0
18	California	46.6
19	Maine	46.0
20	Texas	45.9
21	Colorado	45.3
22	Louisiana	45.1
23	South Carolina	44.2
24	Washington	43.9
25	New Mexico	42.6
26	Massachusetts	42.4
27	South Dakota	42.1
28	Georgia	41.6
29	Hawaii	39.6
30	Virginia	39.5
31	Connecticut	38.7
32	Indiana	38.4
33	Alaska	38.0
34	Idaho	36.5
35	Ohio	34.3
36	North Dakota	34.0
37	Utah	32.8
38	Tennessee	32.3
39	Mississippi	32.0
40	Rhode Island	31.7
41	Nevada	31.3
42	Michigan	30.1
43	Arizona	29.5
44	Oregon	28.7
45	Iowa	27.6
46	Kansas	25.7
47	Montana	22.8
48	New Hampshire	20.7
49	West Virginia	14.0
NA	Illinois**	NA

District of Columbia 38.0

Source: Federal Bureau of Investigation (unpublished data)
*Forcible rape including attempts. However, statutory rape without force and other sex offenses are excluded. A crime is considered cleared when at least one person is arrested, charged and turned over to the court for prosecution. Clearances recorded in 2003 may be for crimes which occurred in prior years. Several crimes may be cleared by the arrest of one person while the arrest of many persons may clear only one crime.
**Not available.

Percent of Robberies Cleared in 2003

National Percent = 26.3% Cleared*

ALPHA ORDER

RANK	STATE	PERCENT
16	Alabama	31.4
37	Alaska	24.9
40	Arizona	22.8
12	Arkansas	34.2
28	California	27.0
35	Colorado	25.6
29	Connecticut	26.7
18	Delaware	30.5
21	Florida	29.1
43	Georgia	19.9
1	Hawaii	57.8
7	Idaho	37.4
NA	Illinois**	NA
24	Indiana	28.7
26	Iowa	27.9
48	Kansas	17.4
29	Kentucky	26.7
25	Louisiana	28.1
3	Maine	45.7
33	Maryland	25.8
36	Massachusetts	25.0
49	Michigan	16.3
13	Minnesota	33.8
45	Mississippi	19.4
27	Missouri	27.6
8	Montana	36.0
5	Nebraska	38.1
43	Nevada	19.9
10	New Hampshire	35.3
32	New Jersey	26.3
38	New Mexico	24.8
9	New York	35.6
14	North Carolina	33.1
2	North Dakota	46.3
41	Ohio	22.6
19	Oklahoma	30.1
21	Oregon	29.1
15	Pennsylvania	32.8
20	Rhode Island	29.2
31	South Carolina	26.4
6	South Dakota	37.6
46	Tennessee	18.5
39	Texas	24.7
21	Utah	29.1
4	Vermont	41.7
42	Virginia	21.1
16	Washington	31.4
47	West Virginia	18.4
33	Wisconsin	25.8
11	Wyoming	34.9

RANK ORDER

RANK	STATE	PERCENT
1	Hawaii	57.8
2	North Dakota	46.3
3	Maine	45.7
4	Vermont	41.7
5	Nebraska	38.1
6	South Dakota	37.6
7	Idaho	37.4
8	Montana	36.0
9	New York	35.6
10	New Hampshire	35.3
11	Wyoming	34.9
12	Arkansas	34.2
13	Minnesota	33.8
14	North Carolina	33.1
15	Pennsylvania	32.8
16	Alabama	31.4
16	Washington	31.4
18	Delaware	30.5
19	Oklahoma	30.1
20	Rhode Island	29.2
21	Florida	29.1
21	Oregon	29.1
21	Utah	29.1
24	Indiana	28.7
25	Louisiana	28.1
26	Iowa	27.9
27	Missouri	27.6
28	California	27.0
29	Connecticut	26.7
29	Kentucky	26.7
31	South Carolina	26.4
32	New Jersey	26.3
33	Maryland	25.8
33	Wisconsin	25.8
35	Colorado	25.6
36	Massachusetts	25.0
37	Alaska	24.9
38	New Mexico	24.8
39	Texas	24.7
40	Arizona	22.8
41	Ohio	22.6
42	Virginia	21.1
43	Georgia	19.9
43	Nevada	19.9
45	Mississippi	19.4
46	Tennessee	18.5
47	West Virginia	18.4
48	Kansas	17.4
49	Michigan	16.3
NA	Illinois**	NA

District of Columbia 12.5

Source: Federal Bureau of Investigation (unpublished data)
*Robbery is the taking of anything of value by force or threat of force. Attempts are included. A crime is considered cleared when at least one person is arrested, charged and turned over to the court for prosecution. Clearances recorded in 2003 may be for crimes which occurred in prior years. Several crimes may be cleared by the arrest of one person while the arrest of many persons may clear only one crime.
**Not available.

Percent of Aggravated Assaults Cleared in 2003

National Percent = 56.1% Cleared*

ALPHA ORDER				RANK ORDER		
RANK	STATE	PERCENT		RANK	STATE	PERCENT
45	Alabama	46.0		1	Vermont	81.1
4	Alaska	72.8		2	Minnesota	73.9
41	Arizona	49.4		3	Maine	72.9
31	Arkansas	54.2		4	Alaska	72.8
23	California	58.4		5	Wyoming	72.4
18	Colorado	62.4		6	Delaware	72.2
15	Connecticut	63.2		7	Nebraska	70.8
6	Delaware	72.2		8	South Dakota	69.1
24	Florida	56.3		9	Wisconsin	67.3
40	Georgia	49.8		10	North Carolina	66.0
22	Hawaii	58.6		11	Pennsylvania	65.7
14	Idaho	63.6		12	Maryland	64.9
NA	Illinois**	NA		13	New York	64.7
29	Indiana	55.3		14	Idaho	63.6
17	Iowa	62.7		15	Connecticut	63.2
48	Kansas	41.8		16	Washington	62.9
34	Kentucky	53.9		17	Iowa	62.7
19	Louisiana	59.1		18	Colorado	62.4
3	Maine	72.9		19	Louisiana	59.1
12	Maryland	64.9		20	Missouri	59.0
27	Massachusetts	55.6		21	New Jersey	58.9
46	Michigan	43.4		22	Hawaii	58.6
2	Minnesota	73.9		23	California	58.4
47	Mississippi	42.8		24	Florida	56.3
20	Missouri	59.0		25	South Carolina	55.9
38	Montana	50.5		26	Oklahoma	55.8
7	Nebraska	70.8		27	Massachusetts	55.6
49	Nevada	37.7		28	New Mexico	55.5
35	New Hampshire	53.5		29	Indiana	55.3
21	New Jersey	58.9		30	Virginia	54.5
28	New Mexico	55.5		31	Arkansas	54.2
13	New York	64.7		32	North Dakota	54.1
10	North Carolina	66.0		32	Utah	54.1
32	North Dakota	54.1		34	Kentucky	53.9
43	Ohio	48.5		35	New Hampshire	53.5
26	Oklahoma	55.8		36	Rhode Island	53.1
41	Oregon	49.4		37	Texas	51.6
11	Pennsylvania	65.7		38	Montana	50.5
36	Rhode Island	53.1		39	Tennessee	50.0
25	South Carolina	55.9		40	Georgia	49.8
8	South Dakota	69.1		41	Arizona	49.4
39	Tennessee	50.0		41	Oregon	49.4
37	Texas	51.6		43	Ohio	48.5
32	Utah	54.1		44	West Virginia	47.7
1	Vermont	81.1		45	Alabama	46.0
30	Virginia	54.5		46	Michigan	43.4
16	Washington	62.9		47	Mississippi	42.8
44	West Virginia	47.7		48	Kansas	41.8
9	Wisconsin	67.3		49	Nevada	37.7
5	Wyoming	72.4		NA	Illinois**	NA
					District of Columbia	42.2

Source: Federal Bureau of Investigation (unpublished data)
*Aggravated assault is an attack for the purpose of inflicting severe bodily injury. A crime is considered cleared when at least one person is arrested, charged and turned over to the court for prosecution. Clearances recorded in 2003 may be for crimes which occurred in prior years. Several crimes may be cleared by the arrest of one person while the arrest of many persons may clear only one crime.
**Not available.

Percent of Property Crimes Cleared in 2003

National Percent = 16.4% Cleared*

<table>
<tr><td colspan="3">ALPHA ORDER</td><td colspan="3">RANK ORDER</td></tr>
<tr><th>RANK</th><th>STATE</th><th>PERCENT</th><th>RANK</th><th>STATE</th><th>PERCENT</th></tr>
<tr><td>22</td><td>Alabama</td><td>17.2</td><td>1</td><td>New York</td><td>27.3</td></tr>
<tr><td>6</td><td>Alaska</td><td>22.4</td><td>2</td><td>Maine</td><td>26.2</td></tr>
<tr><td>40</td><td>Arizona</td><td>13.6</td><td>3</td><td>South Dakota</td><td>24.0</td></tr>
<tr><td>18</td><td>Arkansas</td><td>18.0</td><td>4</td><td>Minnesota</td><td>23.0</td></tr>
<tr><td>41</td><td>California</td><td>13.3</td><td>5</td><td>Pennsylvania</td><td>22.7</td></tr>
<tr><td>32</td><td>Colorado</td><td>15.2</td><td>6</td><td>Alaska</td><td>22.4</td></tr>
<tr><td>28</td><td>Connecticut</td><td>15.5</td><td>7</td><td>Wisconsin</td><td>22.2</td></tr>
<tr><td>10</td><td>Delaware</td><td>20.5</td><td>8</td><td>Wyoming</td><td>21.4</td></tr>
<tr><td>16</td><td>Florida</td><td>18.3</td><td>9</td><td>North Carolina</td><td>20.9</td></tr>
<tr><td>21</td><td>Georgia</td><td>17.3</td><td>10</td><td>Delaware</td><td>20.5</td></tr>
<tr><td>49</td><td>Hawaii</td><td>10.0</td><td>10</td><td>Mississippi</td><td>20.5</td></tr>
<tr><td>15</td><td>Idaho</td><td>19.0</td><td>12</td><td>Louisiana</td><td>20.2</td></tr>
<tr><td>NA</td><td>Illinois**</td><td>NA</td><td>13</td><td>Kentucky</td><td>20.1</td></tr>
<tr><td>26</td><td>Indiana</td><td>15.6</td><td>13</td><td>Nebraska</td><td>20.1</td></tr>
<tr><td>26</td><td>Iowa</td><td>15.6</td><td>15</td><td>Idaho</td><td>19.0</td></tr>
<tr><td>48</td><td>Kansas</td><td>10.3</td><td>16</td><td>Florida</td><td>18.3</td></tr>
<tr><td>13</td><td>Kentucky</td><td>20.1</td><td>16</td><td>Missouri</td><td>18.3</td></tr>
<tr><td>12</td><td>Louisiana</td><td>20.2</td><td>18</td><td>Arkansas</td><td>18.0</td></tr>
<tr><td>2</td><td>Maine</td><td>26.2</td><td>19</td><td>Utah</td><td>17.6</td></tr>
<tr><td>24</td><td>Maryland</td><td>16.9</td><td>20</td><td>North Dakota</td><td>17.4</td></tr>
<tr><td>38</td><td>Massachusetts</td><td>13.8</td><td>21</td><td>Georgia</td><td>17.3</td></tr>
<tr><td>46</td><td>Michigan</td><td>11.9</td><td>22</td><td>Alabama</td><td>17.2</td></tr>
<tr><td>4</td><td>Minnesota</td><td>23.0</td><td>22</td><td>Oregon</td><td>17.2</td></tr>
<tr><td>10</td><td>Mississippi</td><td>20.5</td><td>24</td><td>Maryland</td><td>16.9</td></tr>
<tr><td>16</td><td>Missouri</td><td>18.3</td><td>25</td><td>Nevada</td><td>16.1</td></tr>
<tr><td>30</td><td>Montana</td><td>15.4</td><td>26</td><td>Indiana</td><td>15.6</td></tr>
<tr><td>13</td><td>Nebraska</td><td>20.1</td><td>26</td><td>Iowa</td><td>15.6</td></tr>
<tr><td>25</td><td>Nevada</td><td>16.1</td><td>28</td><td>Connecticut</td><td>15.5</td></tr>
<tr><td>39</td><td>New Hampshire</td><td>13.7</td><td>28</td><td>New Jersey</td><td>15.5</td></tr>
<tr><td>28</td><td>New Jersey</td><td>15.5</td><td>30</td><td>Montana</td><td>15.4</td></tr>
<tr><td>35</td><td>New Mexico</td><td>14.9</td><td>31</td><td>Texas</td><td>15.3</td></tr>
<tr><td>1</td><td>New York</td><td>27.3</td><td>32</td><td>Colorado</td><td>15.2</td></tr>
<tr><td>9</td><td>North Carolina</td><td>20.9</td><td>33</td><td>Virginia</td><td>15.1</td></tr>
<tr><td>20</td><td>North Dakota</td><td>17.4</td><td>33</td><td>Washington</td><td>15.1</td></tr>
<tr><td>37</td><td>Ohio</td><td>14.3</td><td>35</td><td>New Mexico</td><td>14.9</td></tr>
<tr><td>41</td><td>Oklahoma</td><td>13.3</td><td>35</td><td>South Carolina</td><td>14.9</td></tr>
<tr><td>22</td><td>Oregon</td><td>17.2</td><td>37</td><td>Ohio</td><td>14.3</td></tr>
<tr><td>5</td><td>Pennsylvania</td><td>22.7</td><td>38</td><td>Massachusetts</td><td>13.8</td></tr>
<tr><td>41</td><td>Rhode Island</td><td>13.3</td><td>39</td><td>New Hampshire</td><td>13.7</td></tr>
<tr><td>35</td><td>South Carolina</td><td>14.9</td><td>40</td><td>Arizona</td><td>13.6</td></tr>
<tr><td>3</td><td>South Dakota</td><td>24.0</td><td>41</td><td>California</td><td>13.3</td></tr>
<tr><td>41</td><td>Tennessee</td><td>13.3</td><td>41</td><td>Oklahoma</td><td>13.3</td></tr>
<tr><td>31</td><td>Texas</td><td>15.3</td><td>41</td><td>Rhode Island</td><td>13.3</td></tr>
<tr><td>19</td><td>Utah</td><td>17.6</td><td>41</td><td>Tennessee</td><td>13.3</td></tr>
<tr><td>45</td><td>Vermont</td><td>12.1</td><td>45</td><td>Vermont</td><td>12.1</td></tr>
<tr><td>33</td><td>Virginia</td><td>15.1</td><td>46</td><td>Michigan</td><td>11.9</td></tr>
<tr><td>33</td><td>Washington</td><td>15.1</td><td>47</td><td>West Virginia</td><td>11.3</td></tr>
<tr><td>47</td><td>West Virginia</td><td>11.3</td><td>48</td><td>Kansas</td><td>10.3</td></tr>
<tr><td>7</td><td>Wisconsin</td><td>22.2</td><td>49</td><td>Hawaii</td><td>10.0</td></tr>
<tr><td>8</td><td>Wyoming</td><td>21.4</td><td>NA</td><td>Illinois**</td><td>NA</td></tr>
<tr><td></td><td></td><td></td><td></td><td>District of Columbia</td><td>5.4</td></tr>
</table>

Source: Federal Bureau of Investigation (unpublished data)
*Property crimes are offenses of burglary, larceny-theft and motor vehicle theft. A crime is considered cleared when at least one person is arrested, charged and turned over to the court for prosecution. Clearances recorded in 2003 may be for crimes which occurred in prior years. Several crimes may be cleared by the arrest of one person while the arrest of many persons may clear only one crime.
**Not available.

Percent of Burglaries Cleared in 2003

National Percent = 13.1% Cleared*

ALPHA ORDER

RANK	STATE	PERCENT
26	Alabama	12.1
7	Alaska	17.7
47	Arizona	7.8
21	Arkansas	13.9
24	California	12.5
36	Colorado	10.5
23	Connecticut	12.6
4	Delaware	20.5
12	Florida	15.4
24	Georgia	12.5
42	Hawaii	9.8
22	Idaho	13.0
NA	Illinois**	NA
29	Indiana	12.0
43	Iowa	9.6
49	Kansas	6.1
18	Kentucky	14.1
14	Louisiana	15.2
5	Maine	20.2
9	Maryland	17.1
32	Massachusetts	11.3
44	Michigan	9.5
15	Minnesota	14.6
17	Mississippi	14.2
12	Missouri	15.4
41	Montana	9.9
16	Nebraska	14.3
1	Nevada	22.4
26	New Hampshire	12.1
18	New Jersey	14.1
34	New Mexico	10.9
2	New York	22.3
8	North Carolina	17.5
39	North Dakota	10.2
36	Ohio	10.5
31	Oklahoma	11.5
39	Oregon	10.2
3	Pennsylvania	20.8
26	Rhode Island	12.1
30	South Carolina	11.9
6	South Dakota	17.8
45	Tennessee	9.0
35	Texas	10.8
33	Utah	11.1
46	Vermont	8.6
18	Virginia	14.1
36	Washington	10.5
48	West Virginia	7.2
11	Wisconsin	15.7
10	Wyoming	16.8

RANK ORDER

RANK	STATE	PERCENT
1	Nevada	22.4
2	New York	22.3
3	Pennsylvania	20.8
4	Delaware	20.5
5	Maine	20.2
6	South Dakota	17.8
7	Alaska	17.7
8	North Carolina	17.5
9	Maryland	17.1
10	Wyoming	16.8
11	Wisconsin	15.7
12	Florida	15.4
12	Missouri	15.4
14	Louisiana	15.2
15	Minnesota	14.6
16	Nebraska	14.3
17	Mississippi	14.2
18	Kentucky	14.1
18	New Jersey	14.1
18	Virginia	14.1
21	Arkansas	13.9
22	Idaho	13.0
23	Connecticut	12.6
24	California	12.5
24	Georgia	12.5
26	Alabama	12.1
26	New Hampshire	12.1
26	Rhode Island	12.1
29	Indiana	12.0
30	South Carolina	11.9
31	Oklahoma	11.5
32	Massachusetts	11.3
33	Utah	11.1
34	New Mexico	10.9
35	Texas	10.8
36	Colorado	10.5
36	Ohio	10.5
36	Washington	10.5
39	North Dakota	10.2
39	Oregon	10.2
41	Montana	9.9
42	Hawaii	9.8
43	Iowa	9.6
44	Michigan	9.5
45	Tennessee	9.0
46	Vermont	8.6
47	Arizona	7.8
48	West Virginia	7.2
49	Kansas	6.1
NA	Illinois**	NA
	District of Columbia	11.0

Source: Federal Bureau of Investigation (unpublished data)
Burglary is the unlawful entry of a structure to commit a felony or theft. Attempts are included. A crime is considered cleared when at least one person is arrested, charged and turned over to the court for prosecution. Clearances recorded in 2003 may be for crimes which occurred in prior years. Several crimes may be cleared by the arrest of one person while the arrest of many persons may clear only one crime.
**Not available.*

Percent of Larcenies and Thefts Cleared in 2003

National Percent = 18.0% Cleared*

ALPHA ORDER

RANK	STATE	PERCENT
23	Alabama	18.6
6	Alaska	23.7
33	Arizona	16.2
18	Arkansas	19.4
41	California	14.9
30	Colorado	16.7
27	Connecticut	17.4
11	Delaware	22.4
17	Florida	19.5
21	Georgia	19.0
49	Hawaii	8.3
15	Idaho	20.4
NA	Illinois**	NA
31	Indiana	16.5
27	Iowa	17.4
48	Kansas	11.4
10	Kentucky	22.6
9	Louisiana	22.9
2	Maine	27.3
22	Maryland	18.7
37	Massachusetts	15.3
43	Michigan	13.6
4	Minnesota	24.4
8	Mississippi	23.5
16	Missouri	19.6
34	Montana	16.0
14	Nebraska	20.5
39	Nevada	15.1
43	New Hampshire	13.6
25	New Jersey	18.3
35	New Mexico	15.9
1	New York	28.7
12	North Carolina	22.0
24	North Dakota	18.4
36	Ohio	15.6
43	Oklahoma	13.6
18	Oregon	19.4
7	Pennsylvania	23.6
42	Rhode Island	14.8
32	South Carolina	16.3
3	South Dakota	25.2
39	Tennessee	15.1
29	Texas	16.8
18	Utah	19.4
46	Vermont	12.7
37	Virginia	15.3
26	Washington	17.5
47	West Virginia	12.6
5	Wisconsin	23.9
13	Wyoming	21.8

RANK ORDER

RANK	STATE	PERCENT
1	New York	28.7
2	Maine	27.3
3	South Dakota	25.2
4	Minnesota	24.4
5	Wisconsin	23.9
6	Alaska	23.7
7	Pennsylvania	23.6
8	Mississippi	23.5
9	Louisiana	22.9
10	Kentucky	22.6
11	Delaware	22.4
12	North Carolina	22.0
13	Wyoming	21.8
14	Nebraska	20.5
15	Idaho	20.4
16	Missouri	19.6
17	Florida	19.5
18	Arkansas	19.4
18	Oregon	19.4
18	Utah	19.4
21	Georgia	19.0
22	Maryland	18.7
23	Alabama	18.6
24	North Dakota	18.4
25	New Jersey	18.3
26	Washington	17.5
27	Connecticut	17.4
27	Iowa	17.4
29	Texas	16.8
30	Colorado	16.7
31	Indiana	16.5
32	South Carolina	16.3
33	Arizona	16.2
34	Montana	16.0
35	New Mexico	15.9
36	Ohio	15.6
37	Massachusetts	15.3
37	Virginia	15.3
39	Nevada	15.1
39	Tennessee	15.1
41	California	14.9
42	Rhode Island	14.8
43	Michigan	13.6
43	New Hampshire	13.6
43	Oklahoma	13.6
46	Vermont	12.7
47	West Virginia	12.6
48	Kansas	11.4
49	Hawaii	8.3
NA	Illinois**	NA

District of Columbia   5.2

Source: Federal Bureau of Investigation (unpublished data)
*Larceny and theft is the unlawful taking of property without use of force, violence or fraud. Attempts are included. Motor vehicle thefts are excluded. A crime is considered cleared when at least one person is arrested, charged and turned over to the court for prosecution. Clearances recorded in 2003 may be for crimes which occurred in prior years. Several crimes may be cleared by the arrest of one person while the arrest of many persons may clear only one crime. **Not available.

Percent of Motor Vehicle Thefts Cleared in 2003

National Percent = 13.1% Cleared*

ALPHA ORDER

RANK	STATE	PERCENT
9	Alabama	20.8
12	Alaska	20.4
41	Arizona	10.4
16	Arkansas	18.7
44	California	9.3
31	Colorado	14.0
47	Connecticut	8.5
46	Delaware	8.6
21	Florida	17.0
22	Georgia	16.1
7	Hawaii	25.4
13	Idaho	20.3
NA	Illinois**	NA
24	Indiana	15.6
28	Iowa	14.4
39	Kansas	10.8
26	Kentucky	15.4
29	Louisiana	14.2
1	Maine	35.8
42	Maryland	10.0
39	Massachusetts	10.8
45	Michigan	8.9
4	Minnesota	26.6
19	Mississippi	17.9
25	Missouri	15.5
18	Montana	18.2
5	Nebraska	26.5
38	Nevada	12.1
17	New Hampshire	18.3
49	New Jersey	5.6
20	New Mexico	17.5
6	New York	26.3
8	North Carolina	24.3
9	North Dakota	20.8
32	Ohio	13.8
23	Oklahoma	16.0
33	Oregon	13.6
14	Pennsylvania	20.1
48	Rhode Island	7.1
36	South Carolina	12.2
3	South Dakota	29.2
36	Tennessee	12.2
30	Texas	14.1
34	Utah	13.4
15	Vermont	19.3
27	Virginia	14.7
43	Washington	9.9
35	West Virginia	13.3
11	Wisconsin	20.6
2	Wyoming	30.4

RANK ORDER

RANK	STATE	PERCENT
1	Maine	35.8
2	Wyoming	30.4
3	South Dakota	29.2
4	Minnesota	26.6
5	Nebraska	26.5
6	New York	26.3
7	Hawaii	25.4
8	North Carolina	24.3
9	Alabama	20.8
9	North Dakota	20.8
11	Wisconsin	20.6
12	Alaska	20.4
13	Idaho	20.3
14	Pennsylvania	20.1
15	Vermont	19.3
16	Arkansas	18.7
17	New Hampshire	18.3
18	Montana	18.2
19	Mississippi	17.9
20	New Mexico	17.5
21	Florida	17.0
22	Georgia	16.1
23	Oklahoma	16.0
24	Indiana	15.6
25	Missouri	15.5
26	Kentucky	15.4
27	Virginia	14.7
28	Iowa	14.4
29	Louisiana	14.2
30	Texas	14.1
31	Colorado	14.0
32	Ohio	13.8
33	Oregon	13.6
34	Utah	13.4
35	West Virginia	13.3
36	South Carolina	12.2
36	Tennessee	12.2
38	Nevada	12.1
39	Kansas	10.8
39	Massachusetts	10.8
41	Arizona	10.4
42	Maryland	10.0
43	Washington	9.9
44	California	9.3
45	Michigan	8.9
46	Delaware	8.6
47	Connecticut	8.5
48	Rhode Island	7.1
49	New Jersey	5.6
NA	Illinois**	NA

District of Columbia 3.1

Source: Federal Bureau of Investigation (unpublished data)
*Motor vehicle theft includes the theft or attempted theft of a self-propelled vehicle. Excludes motorboats, construction equipment, airplanes and farming equipment. A crime is considered cleared when at least one person is arrested, charged and turned over to the court for prosecution. Clearances recorded in 2003 may be for crimes which occurred in prior years. Several crimes may be cleared by the arrest of one person while the arrest of many persons may clear only one crime. **Not available.

II. CORRECTIONS

Prisoners in State Correctional Institutions: Year End 2004

National Total = 1,316,301 State Prisoners*

ALPHA ORDER

RANK	STATE	PRISONERS	% of USA
16	Alabama	25,887	2.0%
41	Alaska	4,554	0.3%
13	Arizona	32,515	2.5%
28	Arkansas	13,807	1.0%
2	California	166,556	12.7%
24	Colorado	20,293	1.5%
25	Connecticut	19,497	1.5%
35	Delaware	6,927	0.5%
3	Florida	85,533	6.5%
5	Georgia	51,104	3.9%
39	Hawaii	5,960	0.5%
37	Idaho	6,375	0.5%
8	Illinois	44,054	3.3%
18	Indiana	24,008	1.8%
34	Iowa	8,525	0.6%
32	Kansas	8,966	0.7%
26	Kentucky	17,814	1.4%
10	Louisiana	36,939	2.8%
47	Maine	2,024	0.2%
21	Maryland	23,285	1.8%
31	Massachusetts	10,144	0.8%
6	Michigan	48,883	3.7%
33	Minnesota	8,758	0.7%
23	Mississippi	20,983	1.6%
14	Missouri	31,081	2.4%
43	Montana	3,877	0.3%
42	Nebraska	4,130	0.3%
30	Nevada	11,365	0.9%
46	New Hampshire	2,448	0.2%
15	New Jersey	26,757	2.0%
36	New Mexico	6,379	0.5%
4	New York	63,751	4.8%
12	North Carolina	35,434	2.7%
50	North Dakota	1,327	0.1%
7	Ohio	44,806	3.4%
20	Oklahoma	23,319	1.8%
29	Oregon	13,183	1.0%
9	Pennsylvania	40,963	3.1%
44	Rhode Island	3,430	0.3%
19	South Carolina	23,428	1.8%
45	South Dakota	3,095	0.2%
17	Tennessee	25,884	2.0%
1	Texas	168,105	12.8%
38	Utah	5,989	0.5%
49	Vermont	1,968	0.1%
11	Virginia	35,564	2.7%
27	Washington	16,614	1.3%
40	West Virginia	5,067	0.4%
22	Wisconsin	22,966	1.7%
48	Wyoming	1,980	0.2%

RANK ORDER

RANK	STATE	PRISONERS	% of USA
1	Texas	168,105	12.8%
2	California	166,556	12.7%
3	Florida	85,533	6.5%
4	New York	63,751	4.8%
5	Georgia	51,104	3.9%
6	Michigan	48,883	3.7%
7	Ohio	44,806	3.4%
8	Illinois	44,054	3.3%
9	Pennsylvania	40,963	3.1%
10	Louisiana	36,939	2.8%
11	Virginia	35,564	2.7%
12	North Carolina	35,434	2.7%
13	Arizona	32,515	2.5%
14	Missouri	31,081	2.4%
15	New Jersey	26,757	2.0%
16	Alabama	25,887	2.0%
17	Tennessee	25,884	2.0%
18	Indiana	24,008	1.8%
19	South Carolina	23,428	1.8%
20	Oklahoma	23,319	1.8%
21	Maryland	23,285	1.8%
22	Wisconsin	22,966	1.7%
23	Mississippi	20,983	1.6%
24	Colorado	20,293	1.5%
25	Connecticut	19,497	1.5%
26	Kentucky	17,814	1.4%
27	Washington	16,614	1.3%
28	Arkansas	13,807	1.0%
29	Oregon	13,183	1.0%
30	Nevada	11,365	0.9%
31	Massachusetts	10,144	0.8%
32	Kansas	8,966	0.7%
33	Minnesota	8,758	0.7%
34	Iowa	8,525	0.6%
35	Delaware	6,927	0.5%
36	New Mexico	6,379	0.5%
37	Idaho	6,375	0.5%
38	Utah	5,989	0.5%
39	Hawaii	5,960	0.5%
40	West Virginia	5,067	0.4%
41	Alaska	4,554	0.3%
42	Nebraska	4,130	0.3%
43	Montana	3,877	0.3%
44	Rhode Island	3,430	0.3%
45	South Dakota	3,095	0.2%
46	New Hampshire	2,448	0.2%
47	Maine	2,024	0.2%
48	Wyoming	1,980	0.2%
49	Vermont	1,968	0.1%
50	North Dakota	1,327	0.1%
	District of Columbia**	NA	NA

Source: U.S. Department of Justice, Bureau of Justice Statistics
    "Prisoners in 2004" (October 2005, NCJ-210677)
*Advance figures as of December 31, 2004. Totals reflect all prisoners, including those sentenced to a year or less and those unsentenced.   National total does not include 180,328 prisoners under federal jurisdiction. State and federal prisoners combined total 1,496,629.
**Responsibility for sentenced felons in D.C. was transferred to the Federal Bureau of Prisons in 2001.

Percent Change in Number of State Prisoners: 2003 to 2004

National Percent Change = 1.6% Increase*

ALPHA ORDER

RANK ORDER

RANK	STATE	PERCENT CHANGE	RANK	STATE	PERCENT CHANGE
50	Alabama	(7.3)	1	Minnesota	11.4
35	Alaska	0.6	2	Idaho	11.1
11	Arizona	4.3	3	Georgia	8.3
15	Arkansas	3.7	4	Nevada	7.8
32	California	1.3	5	Kentucky	7.2
17	Colorado	3.2	6	Montana	7.1
44	Connecticut	(1.8)	6	North Dakota	7.1
26	Delaware	2.0	8	West Virginia	6.5
11	Florida	4.3	9	Wyoming	5.8
3	Georgia	8.3	10	North Carolina	5.6
22	Hawaii	2.3	11	Arizona	4.3
2	Idaho	11.1	11	Florida	4.3
30	Illinois	1.5	13	Indiana	4.1
13	Indiana	4.1	14	Utah	3.9
40	Iowa	(0.2)	15	Arkansas	3.7
46	Kansas	(1.8)	15	Oregon	3.7
5	Kentucky	7.2	17	Colorado	3.2
20	Louisiana	2.5	18	Washington	2.9
37	Maine	0.5	19	Missouri	2.6
47	Maryland	(2.1)	20	Louisiana	2.5
41	Massachusetts	(0.9)	20	New Mexico	2.5
42	Michigan	(1.0)	22	Hawaii	2.3
1	Minnesota	11.4	22	South Dakota	2.3
27	Mississippi	1.9	24	Nebraska	2.2
19	Missouri	2.6	24	Oklahoma	2.2
6	Montana	7.1	26	Delaware	2.0
24	Nebraska	2.2	27	Mississippi	1.9
4	Nevada	7.8	27	Tennessee	1.9
35	New Hampshire	0.6	29	Wisconsin	1.6
45	New Jersey	(1.8)	30	Illinois	1.5
20	New Mexico	2.5	31	Virginia	1.4
48	New York	(2.2)	32	California	1.3
10	North Carolina	5.6	33	Vermont	1.2
6	North Dakota	7.1	34	Texas	0.7
39	Ohio	0.1	35	Alaska	0.6
24	Oklahoma	2.2	35	New Hampshire	0.6
15	Oregon	3.7	37	Maine	0.5
38	Pennsylvania	0.2	38	Pennsylvania	0.2
49	Rhode Island	(2.8)	39	Ohio	0.1
43	South Carolina	(1.2)	40	Iowa	(0.2)
22	South Dakota	2.3	41	Massachusetts	(0.9)
27	Tennessee	1.9	42	Michigan	(1.0)
34	Texas	0.7	43	South Carolina	(1.2)
14	Utah	3.9	44	Connecticut	(1.8)
33	Vermont	1.2	45	New Jersey	(1.8)
31	Virginia	1.4	46	Kansas	(1.8)
18	Washington	2.9	47	Maryland	(2.1)
8	West Virginia	6.5	48	New York	(2.2)
29	Wisconsin	1.6	49	Rhode Island	(2.8)
9	Wyoming	5.8	50	Alabama	(7.3)

District of Columbia**   NA

Source: U.S. Department of Justice, Bureau of Justice Statistics
   "Prisoners in 2004" (October 2005, NCJ-210677)
*From December 31, 2003 to December 31, 2004. Includes inmates sentenced to more than one year and those sentenced to a year or less or with no sentence. The percent change in number of prisoners under federal jurisdiction during the same period was an 4.2% increase. The combined state and federal increase was 1.9%.
**Responsibility for sentenced felons in D.C. was transferred to the Federal Bureau of Prisons in 2001.

State Prisoners Sentenced to More than One Year in 2004

National Total = 1,274,656 State Prisoners*

ALPHA ORDER

RANK	STATE	PRISONERS	% of USA
17	Alabama	25,257	2.0%
44	Alaska	2,632	0.2%
12	Arizona	31,106	2.4%
27	Arkansas	13,668	1.1%
1	California	164,933	12.9%
23	Colorado	20,293	1.6%
28	Connecticut	13,240	1.0%
40	Delaware	4,087	0.3%
3	Florida	85,530	6.7%
5	Georgia	51,089	4.0%
39	Hawaii	4,174	0.3%
35	Idaho	6,375	0.5%
8	Illinois	44,054	3.5%
18	Indiana	23,939	1.9%
34	Iowa	8,525	0.7%
31	Kansas	8,966	0.7%
25	Kentucky	17,140	1.3%
10	Louisiana	36,939	2.9%
47	Maine	1,961	0.2%
21	Maryland	22,696	1.8%
33	Massachusetts	8,688	0.7%
6	Michigan	48,883	3.8%
32	Minnesota	8,758	0.7%
24	Mississippi	19,469	1.5%
13	Missouri	31,061	2.4%
42	Montana	3,877	0.3%
41	Nebraska	4,038	0.3%
30	Nevada	11,280	0.9%
45	New Hampshire	2,448	0.2%
15	New Jersey	26,757	2.1%
36	New Mexico	6,111	0.5%
4	New York	63,751	5.0%
14	North Carolina	30,683	2.4%
50	North Dakota	1,238	0.1%
7	Ohio	44,806	3.5%
19	Oklahoma	22,913	1.8%
29	Oregon	13,167	1.0%
9	Pennsylvania	40,931	3.2%
48	Rhode Island	1,894	0.1%
20	South Carolina	22,730	1.8%
43	South Dakota	3,088	0.2%
16	Tennessee	25,884	2.0%
2	Texas	157,617	12.4%
37	Utah	5,916	0.5%
49	Vermont	1,451	0.1%
11	Virginia	35,564	2.8%
26	Washington	16,503	1.3%
38	West Virginia	5,026	0.4%
22	Wisconsin	21,540	1.7%
46	Wyoming	1,980	0.2%

RANK ORDER

RANK	STATE	PRISONERS	% of USA
1	California	164,933	12.9%
2	Texas	157,617	12.4%
3	Florida	85,530	6.7%
4	New York	63,751	5.0%
5	Georgia	51,089	4.0%
6	Michigan	48,883	3.8%
7	Ohio	44,806	3.5%
8	Illinois	44,054	3.5%
9	Pennsylvania	40,931	3.2%
10	Louisiana	36,939	2.9%
11	Virginia	35,564	2.8%
12	Arizona	31,106	2.4%
13	Missouri	31,061	2.4%
14	North Carolina	30,683	2.4%
15	New Jersey	26,757	2.1%
16	Tennessee	25,884	2.0%
17	Alabama	25,257	2.0%
18	Indiana	23,939	1.9%
19	Oklahoma	22,913	1.8%
20	South Carolina	22,730	1.8%
21	Maryland	22,696	1.8%
22	Wisconsin	21,540	1.7%
23	Colorado	20,293	1.6%
24	Mississippi	19,469	1.5%
25	Kentucky	17,140	1.3%
26	Washington	16,503	1.3%
27	Arkansas	13,668	1.1%
28	Connecticut	13,240	1.0%
29	Oregon	13,167	1.0%
30	Nevada	11,280	0.9%
31	Kansas	8,966	0.7%
32	Minnesota	8,758	0.7%
33	Massachusetts	8,688	0.7%
34	Iowa	8,525	0.7%
35	Idaho	6,375	0.5%
36	New Mexico	6,111	0.5%
37	Utah	5,916	0.5%
38	West Virginia	5,026	0.4%
39	Hawaii	4,174	0.3%
40	Delaware	4,087	0.3%
41	Nebraska	4,038	0.3%
42	Montana	3,877	0.3%
43	South Dakota	3,088	0.2%
44	Alaska	2,632	0.2%
45	New Hampshire	2,448	0.2%
46	Wyoming	1,980	0.2%
47	Maine	1,961	0.2%
48	Rhode Island	1,894	0.1%
49	Vermont	1,451	0.1%
50	North Dakota	1,238	0.1%
	District of Columbia**	NA	NA

Source: U.S. Department of Justice, Bureau of Justice Statistics
    "Prisoners in 2004" (October 2005, NCJ-210677)
*Advance figures as of December 31, 2004. Does not include 159,137 prisoners under federal jurisdiction
sentenced to more than one year. State and federal prisoners sentenced to more than one year total 1,433,793.
**Responsibility for sentenced felons in D.C. was transferred to the Federal Bureau of Prisons.

State Prisoner Incarceration Rate in 2004

National Rate = 432 State Prisoners per 100,000 Population*

ALPHA ORDER

RANK	STATE	RATE
6	Alabama	556
24	Alaska	398
9	Arizona	534
10	Arkansas	495
16	California	456
18	Colorado	438
29	Connecticut	377
11	Delaware	488
12	Florida	486
5	Georgia	574
34	Hawaii	329
17	Idaho	454
32	Illinois	346
28	Indiana	383
39	Iowa	288
36	Kansas	327
21	Kentucky	412
1	Louisiana	816
50	Maine	148
22	Maryland	406
44	Massachusetts	232
13	Michigan	483
49	Minnesota	171
3	Mississippi	669
8	Missouri	538
20	Montana	416
45	Nebraska	230
14	Nevada	474
47	New Hampshire	187
38	New Jersey	306
37	New Mexico	318
33	New York	331
31	North Carolina	357
46	North Dakota	195
25	Ohio	391
4	Oklahoma	649
30	Oregon	365
34	Pennsylvania	329
48	Rhode Island	175
7	South Carolina	539
23	South Dakota	399
19	Tennessee	437
2	Texas	694
42	Utah	246
43	Vermont	233
15	Virginia	473
41	Washington	264
40	West Virginia	277
26	Wisconsin	390
27	Wyoming	389

RANK ORDER

RANK	STATE	RATE
1	Louisiana	816
2	Texas	694
3	Mississippi	669
4	Oklahoma	649
5	Georgia	574
6	Alabama	556
7	South Carolina	539
8	Missouri	538
9	Arizona	534
10	Arkansas	495
11	Delaware	488
12	Florida	486
13	Michigan	483
14	Nevada	474
15	Virginia	473
16	California	456
17	Idaho	454
18	Colorado	438
19	Tennessee	437
20	Montana	416
21	Kentucky	412
22	Maryland	406
23	South Dakota	399
24	Alaska	398
25	Ohio	391
26	Wisconsin	390
27	Wyoming	389
28	Indiana	383
29	Connecticut	377
30	Oregon	365
31	North Carolina	357
32	Illinois	346
33	New York	331
34	Hawaii	329
34	Pennsylvania	329
36	Kansas	327
37	New Mexico	318
38	New Jersey	306
39	Iowa	288
40	West Virginia	277
41	Washington	264
42	Utah	246
43	Vermont	233
44	Massachusetts	232
45	Nebraska	230
46	North Dakota	195
47	New Hampshire	187
48	Rhode Island	175
49	Minnesota	171
50	Maine	148
	District of Columbia**	NA

Source: U.S. Department of Justice, Bureau of Justice Statistics
"Prisoners in 2004" (October 2005, NCJ-210677)

As of December 31, 2004. Includes only inmates sentenced to more than one year. Does not include federal incarceration rate of 54 prisoners per 100,000 population. State and federal combined incarceration rate is 486 prisoners per 100,000 population.

**Responsibility for sentenced felons in D.C. was transferred to the Federal Bureau of Prisons in 2001.*

Percent Change in State Prisoner Incarceration Rate: 2003 to 2004

National Percent Change = 0.5% Increase*

ALPHA ORDER
RANK ORDER

RANK	STATE	PERCENT CHANGE		RANK	STATE	PERCENT CHANGE
49	Alabama	(12.4)		1	Minnesota	10.3
36	Alaska	(0.7)		2	North Dakota	7.7
20	Arizona	1.7		3	Georgia	6.5
10	Arkansas	4.0		3	West Virginia	6.5
29	California	0.2		5	Idaho	6.3
18	Colorado	1.9		6	Montana	5.9
46	Connecticut	(3.1)		7	Kentucky	5.1
45	Delaware	(2.6)		8	Florida	5.0
8	Florida	5.0		9	Wyoming	4.6
3	Georgia	6.5		10	Arkansas	4.0
25	Hawaii	1.2		11	Indiana	3.5
5	Idaho	6.3		12	Oregon	3.1
25	Illinois	1.2		12	Vermont	3.1
11	Indiana	3.5		14	Nevada	2.6
36	Iowa	(0.7)		14	North Carolina	2.6
41	Kansas	(2.1)		16	Utah	2.5
7	Kentucky	5.1		17	Oklahoma	2.0
18	Louisiana	1.9		18	Colorado	1.9
36	Maine	(0.7)		18	Louisiana	1.9
47	Maryland	(3.3)		20	Arizona	1.7
33	Massachusetts	(0.4)		20	Missouri	1.7
40	Michigan	(1.2)		22	South Dakota	1.5
1	Minnesota	10.3		22	Washington	1.5
50	Mississippi	(12.9)		24	New Mexico	1.3
20	Missouri	1.7		25	Hawaii	1.2
6	Montana	5.9		25	Illinois	1.2
27	Nebraska	0.9		27	Nebraska	0.9
14	Nevada	2.6		27	Tennessee	0.9
34	New Hampshire	(0.5)		29	California	0.2
44	New Jersey	(2.5)		29	Virginia	0.2
24	New Mexico	1.3		31	Ohio	0.0
43	New York	(2.4)		32	Pennsylvania	(0.3)
14	North Carolina	2.6		33	Massachusetts	(0.4)
2	North Dakota	7.7		34	New Hampshire	(0.5)
31	Ohio	0.0		34	Wisconsin	(0.5)
17	Oklahoma	2.0		36	Alaska	(0.7)
12	Oregon	3.1		36	Iowa	(0.7)
32	Pennsylvania	(0.3)		36	Maine	(0.7)
48	Rhode Island	(4.9)		39	Texas	(1.1)
42	South Carolina	(2.2)		40	Michigan	(1.2)
22	South Dakota	1.5		41	Kansas	(2.1)
27	Tennessee	0.9		42	South Carolina	(2.2)
39	Texas	(1.1)		43	New York	(2.4)
16	Utah	2.5		44	New Jersey	(2.5)
12	Vermont	3.1		45	Delaware	(2.6)
29	Virginia	0.2		46	Connecticut	(3.1)
22	Washington	1.5		47	Maryland	(3.3)
3	West Virginia	6.5		48	Rhode Island	(4.9)
34	Wisconsin	(0.5)		49	Alabama	(12.4)
9	Wyoming	4.6		50	Mississippi	(12.9)

District of Columbia**   NA

Source: Morgan Quitno Press using data from U.S. Department of Justice, Bureau of Justice Statistics
    "Prisoners in 2004" (October 2005, NCJ-210677)
*From December 31, 2003 to December 31, 2004. Includes only inmates sentenced to more than one year. The percent change in rate of prisoners under federal jurisdiction during the same period was a 3.8% increase. The combined state and federal increase was 0.8%.
**Responsibility for sentenced felons in D.C. was transferred to the Federal Bureau of Prisons.

State Prison Population as a Percent of Highest Capacity in 2004

National Percent = 99% of Highest Capacity*

ALPHA ORDER

RANK	STATE	PERCENT		RANK	STATE	PERCENT
21	Alabama	101		1	Illinois	135
21	Alaska	101		2	Massachusetts	126
46	Arizona	82		3	Wisconsin	124
33	Arkansas	96		4	Montana	123
19	California	102		5	Colorado	119
5	Colorado	119		5	Ohio	119
NA	Connecticut**	NA		7	North Carolina	113
16	Delaware	103		8	Hawaii	112
26	Florida	98		9	Maine	111
16	Georgia	103		10	Washington	110
8	Hawaii	112		11	Iowa	109
48	Idaho	76		11	North Dakota	109
1	Illinois	135		13	Pennsylvania	107
39	Indiana	94		14	Nebraska	104
11	Iowa	109		14	New York	104
30	Kansas	97		16	Delaware	103
39	Kentucky	94		16	Georgia	103
25	Louisiana	99		16	Oregon	103
9	Maine	111		19	California	102
30	Maryland	97		19	Nevada	102
2	Massachusetts	126		21	Alabama	101
26	Michigan	98		21	Alaska	101
24	Minnesota	100		21	New Hampshire	101
49	Mississippi	74		24	Minnesota	100
36	Missouri	95		25	Louisiana	99
4	Montana	123		26	Florida	98
14	Nebraska	104		26	Michigan	98
19	Nevada	102		26	West Virginia	98
21	New Hampshire	101		26	Wyoming	98
44	New Jersey	88		30	Kansas	97
30	New Mexico	97		30	Maryland	97
14	New York	104		30	New Mexico	97
7	North Carolina	113		33	Arkansas	96
11	North Dakota	109		33	South Carolina	96
5	Ohio	119		33	Tennessee	96
36	Oklahoma	95		36	Missouri	95
16	Oregon	103		36	Oklahoma	95
13	Pennsylvania	107		36	South Dakota	95
47	Rhode Island	78		39	Indiana	94
33	South Carolina	96		39	Kentucky	94
36	South Dakota	95		39	Utah	94
33	Tennessee	96		39	Virginia	94
45	Texas	87		43	Vermont	89
39	Utah	94		44	New Jersey	88
43	Vermont	89		45	Texas	87
39	Virginia	94		46	Arizona	82
10	Washington	110		47	Rhode Island	78
26	West Virginia	98		48	Idaho	76
3	Wisconsin	124		49	Mississippi	74
26	Wyoming	98		NA	Connecticut**	NA
					District of Columbia**	NA

Source: U.S. Department of Justice, Bureau of Justice Statistics
   "Prisoners in 2004" (October 2005, NCJ-210677)
*As of December 31, 2004. Federal prison population is at 140% of highest rated capacity.
**Not available. Responsibility for sentenced felons in D.C. was transferred to the Federal Bureau of Prisons.

Female Prisoners in State Correctional Institutions in 2004

National Total = 92,684 Female State Prisoners*

ALPHA ORDER

RANK	STATE	PRISONERS	% of USA
20	Alabama	1,748	1.9%
42	Alaska	397	0.4%
7	Arizona	2,765	3.0%
29	Arkansas	962	1.0%
2	California	11,188	12.1%
16	Colorado	1,900	2.0%
23	Connecticut	1,488	1.6%
37	Delaware	557	0.6%
3	Florida	5,660	6.1%
4	Georgia	3,436	3.7%
33	Hawaii	699	0.8%
34	Idaho	647	0.7%
8	Illinois	2,750	3.0%
17	Indiana	1,892	2.0%
31	Iowa	757	0.8%
35	Kansas	620	0.7%
22	Kentucky	1,560	1.7%
12	Louisiana	2,386	2.6%
49	Maine	125	0.1%
27	Maryland	1,180	1.3%
32	Massachusetts	741	0.8%
14	Michigan	2,113	2.3%
38	Minnesota	544	0.6%
19	Mississippi	1,796	1.9%
10	Missouri	2,507	2.7%
40	Montana	473	0.5%
43	Nebraska	369	0.4%
30	Nevada	878	0.9%
50	New Hampshire	119	0.1%
24	New Jersey	1,470	1.6%
36	New Mexico	581	0.6%
6	New York	2,789	3.0%
11	North Carolina	2,430	2.6%
48	North Dakota	129	0.1%
5	Ohio	3,185	3.4%
13	Oklahoma	2,361	2.5%
28	Oregon	985	1.1%
18	Pennsylvania	1,827	2.0%
46	Rhode Island	208	0.2%
21	South Carolina	1,562	1.7%
44	South Dakota	292	0.3%
15	Tennessee	1,905	2.1%
1	Texas	13,958	15.1%
39	Utah	510	0.6%
47	Vermont	143	0.2%
9	Virginia	2,706	2.9%
26	Washington	1,330	1.4%
41	West Virginia	459	0.5%
25	Wisconsin	1,387	1.5%
45	Wyoming	210	0.2%

RANK ORDER

RANK	STATE	PRISONERS	% of USA
1	Texas	13,958	15.1%
2	California	11,188	12.1%
3	Florida	5,660	6.1%
4	Georgia	3,436	3.7%
5	Ohio	3,185	3.4%
6	New York	2,789	3.0%
7	Arizona	2,765	3.0%
8	Illinois	2,750	3.0%
9	Virginia	2,706	2.9%
10	Missouri	2,507	2.7%
11	North Carolina	2,430	2.6%
12	Louisiana	2,386	2.6%
13	Oklahoma	2,361	2.5%
14	Michigan	2,113	2.3%
15	Tennessee	1,905	2.1%
16	Colorado	1,900	2.0%
17	Indiana	1,892	2.0%
18	Pennsylvania	1,827	2.0%
19	Mississippi	1,796	1.9%
20	Alabama	1,748	1.9%
21	South Carolina	1,562	1.7%
22	Kentucky	1,560	1.7%
23	Connecticut	1,488	1.6%
24	New Jersey	1,470	1.6%
25	Wisconsin	1,387	1.5%
26	Washington	1,330	1.4%
27	Maryland	1,180	1.3%
28	Oregon	985	1.1%
29	Arkansas	962	1.0%
30	Nevada	878	0.9%
31	Iowa	757	0.8%
32	Massachusetts	741	0.8%
33	Hawaii	699	0.8%
34	Idaho	647	0.7%
35	Kansas	620	0.7%
36	New Mexico	581	0.6%
37	Delaware	557	0.6%
38	Minnesota	544	0.6%
39	Utah	510	0.6%
40	Montana	473	0.5%
41	West Virginia	459	0.5%
42	Alaska	397	0.4%
43	Nebraska	369	0.4%
44	South Dakota	292	0.3%
45	Wyoming	210	0.2%
46	Rhode Island	208	0.2%
47	Vermont	143	0.2%
48	North Dakota	129	0.1%
49	Maine	125	0.1%
50	New Hampshire	119	0.1%
	District of Columbia**	NA	NA

Source: U.S. Department of Justice, Bureau of Justice Statistics
    "Prisoners in 2004" (October 2005, NCJ-210677)
*As of December 31, 2004. Does not include 12,164 female prisoners under federal jurisdiction. State and federal female prisoners total 104,848.
**Responsibility for sentenced felons in D.C. was transferred to the Federal Bureau of Prisons.

Female State Prisoner Incarceration Rate in 2004

National Rate = 57 Female State Prisoners per 100,000 Female Population*

RANK	STATE	RATE		RANK	STATE	RATE
19	Alabama	63		1	Oklahoma	129
25	Alaska	54		2	Mississippi	107
7	Arizona	87		3	Louisiana	103
18	Arkansas	65		4	Montana	101
22	California	60		5	Texas	100
9	Colorado	83		6	Idaho	92
33	Connecticut	44		7	Arizona	87
28	Delaware	50		8	Missouri	85
19	Florida	63		9	Colorado	83
11	Georgia	76		9	Wyoming	83
15	Hawaii	69		11	Georgia	76
6	Idaho	92		12	Nevada	75
34	Illinois	42		13	South Dakota	74
23	Indiana	59		14	Virginia	71
28	Iowa	50		15	Hawaii	69
32	Kansas	45		16	Kentucky	68
16	Kentucky	68		17	South Carolina	66
3	Louisiana	103		18	Arkansas	65
47	Maine	18		19	Alabama	63
40	Maryland	39		19	Florida	63
49	Massachusetts	11		19	Tennessee	63
37	Michigan	41		22	California	60
46	Minnesota	21		23	Indiana	59
2	Mississippi	107		24	New Mexico	56
8	Missouri	85		25	Alaska	54
4	Montana	101		25	Ohio	54
40	Nebraska	39		25	Oregon	54
12	Nevada	75		28	Delaware	50
47	New Hampshire	18		28	Iowa	50
42	New Jersey	33		30	West Virginia	48
24	New Mexico	56		31	Wisconsin	47
43	New York	28		32	Kansas	45
39	North Carolina	40		33	Connecticut	44
37	North Dakota	41		34	Illinois	42
25	Ohio	54		34	Utah	42
1	Oklahoma	129		34	Washington	42
25	Oregon	54		37	Michigan	41
43	Pennsylvania	28		37	North Dakota	41
49	Rhode Island	11		39	North Carolina	40
17	South Carolina	66		40	Maryland	39
13	South Dakota	74		40	Nebraska	39
19	Tennessee	63		42	New Jersey	33
5	Texas	100		43	New York	28
34	Utah	42		43	Pennsylvania	28
45	Vermont	25		45	Vermont	25
14	Virginia	71		46	Minnesota	21
34	Washington	42		47	Maine	18
30	West Virginia	48		47	New Hampshire	18
31	Wisconsin	47		49	Massachusetts	11
9	Wyoming	83		49	Rhode Island	11
					District of Columbia**	NA

ALPHA ORDER — RANK ORDER

Source: U.S. Department of Justice, Bureau of Justice Statistics "Prisoners in 2004" (October 2005, NCJ-210677)

*As of December 31, 2004. Rate is for female prisoners sentenced to more than one year. National rate does not include federal female inmates. Federal female incarceration rate is seven federal female prisoners per 100,000 female population. The combined federal and state female incarceration rate is 64 female prisoners per 100,000 female population. **Responsibility for sentenced felons in D.C. was transferred to the Federal Bureau of Prisons.

Female Prisoners in State Correctional Institutions
As a Percent of All State Prisoners in 2004
National Percent = 7.0% of State Prisoners are Female*

ALPHA ORDER

RANK ORDER

RANK	STATE	PERCENT		RANK	STATE	PERCENT
34	Alabama	6.8		1	Montana	12.2
14	Alaska	8.7		2	Hawaii	11.7
16	Arizona	8.5		3	Wyoming	10.6
31	Arkansas	7.0		4	Idaho	10.1
35	California	6.7		4	Oklahoma	10.1
7	Colorado	9.4		6	North Dakota	9.7
24	Connecticut	7.6		7	Colorado	9.4
20	Delaware	8.0		7	South Dakota	9.4
38	Florida	6.6		9	New Mexico	9.1
35	Georgia	6.7		9	West Virginia	9.1
2	Hawaii	11.7		11	Iowa	8.9
4	Idaho	10.1		11	Nebraska	8.9
40	Illinois	6.2		13	Kentucky	8.8
22	Indiana	7.9		14	Alaska	8.7
11	Iowa	8.9		15	Mississippi	8.6
32	Kansas	6.9		16	Arizona	8.5
13	Kentucky	8.8		16	Utah	8.5
39	Louisiana	6.5		18	Texas	8.3
40	Maine	6.2		19	Missouri	8.1
46	Maryland	5.1		20	Delaware	8.0
28	Massachusetts	7.3		20	Washington	8.0
50	Michigan	4.3		22	Indiana	7.9
40	Minnesota	6.2		23	Nevada	7.7
15	Mississippi	8.6		24	Connecticut	7.6
19	Missouri	8.1		24	Virginia	7.6
1	Montana	12.2		26	Oregon	7.5
11	Nebraska	8.9		27	Tennessee	7.4
23	Nevada	7.7		28	Massachusetts	7.3
47	New Hampshire	4.9		28	Vermont	7.3
45	New Jersey	5.5		30	Ohio	7.1
9	New Mexico	9.1		31	Arkansas	7.0
49	New York	4.4		32	Kansas	6.9
32	North Carolina	6.9		32	North Carolina	6.9
6	North Dakota	9.7		34	Alabama	6.8
30	Ohio	7.1		35	California	6.7
4	Oklahoma	10.1		35	Georgia	6.7
26	Oregon	7.5		35	South Carolina	6.7
48	Pennsylvania	4.5		38	Florida	6.6
43	Rhode Island	6.1		39	Louisiana	6.5
35	South Carolina	6.7		40	Illinois	6.2
7	South Dakota	9.4		40	Maine	6.2
27	Tennessee	7.4		40	Minnesota	6.2
18	Texas	8.3		43	Rhode Island	6.1
16	Utah	8.5		44	Wisconsin	6.0
28	Vermont	7.3		45	New Jersey	5.5
24	Virginia	7.6		46	Maryland	5.1
20	Washington	8.0		47	New Hampshire	4.9
9	West Virginia	9.1		48	Pennsylvania	4.5
44	Wisconsin	6.0		49	New York	4.4
3	Wyoming	10.6		50	Michigan	4.3
					District of Columbia**	NA

Source: Morgan Quitno Press using data from U.S. Department of Justice, Bureau of Justice Statistics "Prisoners in 2004" (October 2005, NCJ-210677)

As of December 31, 2004. Rate does not include federal female inmates. Federal female inmates constitute 6.7% of federal inmates. The federal and state combined rate is 7.0%.

**Responsibility for sentenced felons in D.C. was transferred to the Federal Bureau of Prisons.*

Percent Change in Female State Prisoner Population: 2003 to 2004

National Percent Change = 3.9% Increase*

ALPHA ORDER

RANK	STATE	PERCENT CHANGE
50	Alabama	(12.7)
34	Alaska	1.3
26	Arizona	4.1
10	Arkansas	11.1
23	California	5.0
16	Colorado	9.4
45	Connecticut	(3.9)
13	Delaware	9.6
13	Florida	9.6
17	Georgia	9.3
30	Hawaii	2.0
15	Idaho	9.5
31	Illinois	1.9
20	Indiana	7.6
22	Iowa	5.7
43	Kansas	(1.4)
11	Kentucky	10.6
40	Louisiana	(0.8)
37	Maine	0.8
48	Maryland	(5.4)
24	Massachusetts	4.7
45	Michigan	(3.9)
1	Minnesota	25.1
29	Mississippi	2.3
8	Missouri	12.0
7	Montana	12.9
4	Nebraska	14.2
39	Nevada	(0.2)
33	New Hampshire	1.7
44	New Jersey	(3.1)
35	New Mexico	0.9
47	New York	(4.3)
19	North Carolina	7.7
4	North Dakota	14.2
12	Ohio	9.9
32	Oklahoma	1.8
9	Oregon	11.6
38	Pennsylvania	0.2
49	Rhode Island	(6.3)
41	South Carolina	(0.9)
18	South Dakota	8.6
25	Tennessee	4.3
27	Texas	3.5
3	Utah	19.4
21	Vermont	5.9
35	Virginia	0.9
28	Washington	3.3
6	West Virginia	13.3
42	Wisconsin	(1.3)
2	Wyoming	20.0

RANK ORDER

RANK	STATE	PERCENT CHANGE
1	Minnesota	25.1
2	Wyoming	20.0
3	Utah	19.4
4	Nebraska	14.2
4	North Dakota	14.2
6	West Virginia	13.3
7	Montana	12.9
8	Missouri	12.0
9	Oregon	11.6
10	Arkansas	11.1
11	Kentucky	10.6
12	Ohio	9.9
13	Delaware	9.6
13	Florida	9.6
15	Idaho	9.5
16	Colorado	9.4
17	Georgia	9.3
18	South Dakota	8.6
19	North Carolina	7.7
20	Indiana	7.6
21	Vermont	5.9
22	Iowa	5.7
23	California	5.0
24	Massachusetts	4.7
25	Tennessee	4.3
26	Arizona	4.1
27	Texas	3.5
28	Washington	3.3
29	Mississippi	2.3
30	Hawaii	2.0
31	Illinois	1.9
32	Oklahoma	1.8
33	New Hampshire	1.7
34	Alaska	1.3
35	New Mexico	0.9
35	Virginia	0.9
37	Maine	0.8
38	Pennsylvania	0.2
39	Nevada	(0.2)
40	Louisiana	(0.8)
41	South Carolina	(0.9)
42	Wisconsin	(1.3)
43	Kansas	(1.4)
44	New Jersey	(3.1)
45	Connecticut	(3.9)
45	Michigan	(3.9)
47	New York	(4.3)
48	Maryland	(5.4)
49	Rhode Island	(6.3)
50	Alabama	(12.7)
	District of Columbia**	NA

Source: U.S. Department of Justice, Bureau of Justice Statistics
"Prisoners in 2004" (October 2005, NCJ-210677)
*From December 31, 2003 to December 31, 2004. Does not include federal female inmates. The percent change in number of female prisoners under federal jurisdiction during the same period was a 4.5% increase. The combined state and federal increase was 4.0%.
**Responsibility for sentenced felons in D.C. was transferred to the Federal Bureau of Prisons.

Average Annual Percent Change in
Female State Prisoner Population: 1995 to 2004
National Average Percent Change = 4.7% Annual Increase*

ALPHA ORDER				RANK ORDER		
RANK	STATE	PERCENT CHANGE		RANK	STATE	PERCENT CHANGE
38	Alabama	3.4		1	North Dakota	18.0
30	Alaska	5.6		2	Montana	17.4
21	Arizona	7.6		3	West Virginia	15.1
22	Arkansas	7.0		4	Maine	14.8
42	California	2.3		5	Vermont	14.0
10	Colorado	11.5		6	Utah	13.7
34	Connecticut	4.8		7	Idaho	13.2
32	Delaware	5.0		8	Tennessee	12.9
32	Florida	5.0		9	Wisconsin	12.0
26	Georgia	6.0		10	Colorado	11.5
13	Hawaii	9.4		11	Minnesota	10.8
7	Idaho	13.2		12	Mississippi	9.5
41	Illinois	2.5		13	Hawaii	9.4
16	Indiana	8.7		14	South Dakota	9.0
23	Iowa	6.6		15	Missouri	8.8
36	Kansas	3.7		16	Indiana	8.7
16	Kentucky	8.7		16	Kentucky	8.7
27	Louisiana	5.9		16	Oregon	8.7
4	Maine	14.8		19	New Mexico	8.5
48	Maryland	1.0		20	Wyoming	7.9
46	Massachusetts	1.4		21	Arizona	7.6
44	Michigan	1.5		22	Arkansas	7.0
11	Minnesota	10.8		23	Iowa	6.6
12	Mississippi	9.5		24	Texas	6.5
15	Missouri	8.8		25	Nebraska	6.4
2	Montana	17.4		26	Georgia	6.0
25	Nebraska	6.4		27	Louisiana	5.9
29	Nevada	5.8		27	Washington	5.9
48	New Hampshire	1.0		29	Nevada	5.8
47	New Jersey	1.3		30	Alaska	5.6
19	New Mexico	8.5		30	Virginia	5.6
50	New York	(2.8)		32	Delaware	5.0
36	North Carolina	3.7		32	Florida	5.0
1	North Dakota	18.0		34	Connecticut	4.8
44	Ohio	1.5		35	South Carolina	4.6
40	Oklahoma	3.0		36	Kansas	3.7
16	Oregon	8.7		36	North Carolina	3.7
43	Pennsylvania	2.2		38	Alabama	3.4
39	Rhode Island	3.2		39	Rhode Island	3.2
35	South Carolina	4.6		40	Oklahoma	3.0
14	South Dakota	9.0		41	Illinois	2.5
8	Tennessee	12.9		42	California	2.3
24	Texas	6.5		43	Pennsylvania	2.2
6	Utah	13.7		44	Michigan	1.5
5	Vermont	14.0		44	Ohio	1.5
30	Virginia	5.6		46	Massachusetts	1.4
27	Washington	5.9		47	New Jersey	1.3
3	West Virginia	15.1		48	Maryland	1.0
9	Wisconsin	12.0		48	New Hampshire	1.0
20	Wyoming	7.9		50	New York	(2.8)
				District of Columbia**		NA

Source: U.S. Department of Justice, Bureau of Justice Statistics
   "Prisoners in 2004" (October 2005, NCJ-210677)
National rate does not include federal female inmates. Federal female inmates increased by an average annual
rate of 5.7%. The combined federal and state female prison population grew at an annual average rate of 4.8%.
***Responsibility for sentenced felons in D.C. was transferred to the Federal Bureau of Prisons.*

White State Prisoner Incarceration Rate in 2000

National Rate = 378 White State Prisoners per 100,000 White Population*

ALPHA ORDER

RANK	STATE	RATE
23	Alabama	373
33	Alaska	306
5	Arizona	607
11	Arkansas	468
10	California	487
15	Colorado	429
43	Connecticut	199
25	Delaware	361
7	Florida	502
6	Georgia	544
49	Hawaii	173
7	Idaho	502
40	Illinois	216
23	Indiana	373
34	Iowa	300
19	Kansas	397
12	Kentucky	466
16	Louisiana	421
41	Maine	207
35	Maryland	282
42	Massachusetts	204
27	Michigan	357
45	Minnesota	197
28	Mississippi	353
17	Missouri	402
26	Montana	358
39	Nebraska	226
4	Nevada	630
38	New Hampshire	242
48	New Jersey	175
32	New Mexico	311
47	New York	182
37	North Carolina	266
50	North Dakota	170
31	Ohio	333
3	Oklahoma	682
9	Oregon	488
36	Pennsylvania	281
43	Rhode Island	199
21	South Carolina	391
14	South Dakota	440
17	Tennessee	402
2	Texas	694
29	Utah	342
46	Vermont	183
13	Virginia	444
20	Washington	393
22	West Virginia	375
30	Wisconsin	341
1	Wyoming	740

RANK ORDER

RANK	STATE	RATE
1	Wyoming	740
2	Texas	694
3	Oklahoma	682
4	Nevada	630
5	Arizona	607
6	Georgia	544
7	Florida	502
7	Idaho	502
9	Oregon	488
10	California	487
11	Arkansas	468
12	Kentucky	466
13	Virginia	444
14	South Dakota	440
15	Colorado	429
16	Louisiana	421
17	Missouri	402
17	Tennessee	402
19	Kansas	397
20	Washington	393
21	South Carolina	391
22	West Virginia	375
23	Alabama	373
23	Indiana	373
25	Delaware	361
26	Montana	358
27	Michigan	357
28	Mississippi	353
29	Utah	342
30	Wisconsin	341
31	Ohio	333
32	New Mexico	311
33	Alaska	306
34	Iowa	300
35	Maryland	282
36	Pennsylvania	281
37	North Carolina	266
38	New Hampshire	242
39	Nebraska	226
40	Illinois	216
41	Maine	207
42	Massachusetts	204
43	Connecticut	199
43	Rhode Island	199
45	Minnesota	197
46	Vermont	183
47	New York	182
48	New Jersey	175
49	Hawaii	173
50	North Dakota	170

District of Columbia	46

Source: Human Rights Watch
"Incarceration Rates Reveal Striking Racial Disparities" (Press Release, 2/27/02)
(http://hrw.org/english/docs/2002/02/27/usdom3768.htm)
*Figures calculated on basis of U.S. Census Bureau data from Census 2000 on state residents and incarcerated population.

Black State Prisoner Incarceration Rate in 2000

National Rate = 2,489 Black State Prisoners per 100,000 Black Population*

ALPHA ORDER

RANK	STATE	RATE
43	Alabama	1,797
48	Alaska	1,606
8	Arizona	3,818
36	Arkansas	2,185
16	California	3,141
5	Colorado	4,023
19	Connecticut	2,991
29	Delaware	2,500
20	Florida	2,877
37	Georgia	2,153
50	Hawaii	577
35	Idaho	2,236
32	Illinois	2,273
26	Indiana	2,575
9	Iowa	3,775
11	Kansas	3,686
12	Kentucky	3,375
30	Louisiana	2,475
46	Maine	1,731
45	Maryland	1,749
42	Massachusetts	1,807
33	Michigan	2,256
22	Minnesota	2,811
44	Mississippi	1,762
31	Missouri	2,306
17	Montana	3,120
34	Nebraska	2,251
14	Nevada	3,206
28	New Hampshire	2,501
27	New Jersey	2,509
15	New Mexico	3,151
41	New York	1,951
47	North Carolina	1,640
49	North Dakota	1,277
25	Ohio	2,651
4	Oklahoma	4,077
7	Oregon	3,895
18	Pennsylvania	3,108
24	Rhode Island	2,735
40	South Carolina	1,979
2	South Dakota	6,510
39	Tennessee	2,021
10	Texas	3,734
13	Utah	3,256
38	Vermont	2,024
21	Virginia	2,842
23	Washington	2,757
3	West Virginia	6,400
6	Wisconsin	3,953
1	Wyoming	6,529

RANK ORDER

RANK	STATE	RATE
1	Wyoming	6,529
2	South Dakota	6,510
3	West Virginia	6,400
4	Oklahoma	4,077
5	Colorado	4,023
6	Wisconsin	3,953
7	Oregon	3,895
8	Arizona	3,818
9	Iowa	3,775
10	Texas	3,734
11	Kansas	3,686
12	Kentucky	3,375
13	Utah	3,256
14	Nevada	3,206
15	New Mexico	3,151
16	California	3,141
17	Montana	3,120
18	Pennsylvania	3,108
19	Connecticut	2,991
20	Florida	2,877
21	Virginia	2,842
22	Minnesota	2,811
23	Washington	2,757
24	Rhode Island	2,735
25	Ohio	2,651
26	Indiana	2,575
27	New Jersey	2,509
28	New Hampshire	2,501
29	Delaware	2,500
30	Louisiana	2,475
31	Missouri	2,306
32	Illinois	2,273
33	Michigan	2,256
34	Nebraska	2,251
35	Idaho	2,236
36	Arkansas	2,185
37	Georgia	2,153
38	Vermont	2,024
39	Tennessee	2,021
40	South Carolina	1,979
41	New York	1,951
42	Massachusetts	1,807
43	Alabama	1,797
44	Mississippi	1,762
45	Maryland	1,749
46	Maine	1,731
47	North Carolina	1,640
48	Alaska	1,606
49	North Dakota	1,277
50	Hawaii	577

| | District of Columbia | 768 |

Source: Human Rights Watch
"Incarceration Rates Reveal Striking Racial Disparities" (Press Release, 2/27/02)
(http://hrw.org/english/docs/2002/02/27/usdom3768.htm)
Figures calculated on basis of U.S. Census Bureau data from Census 2000 on state residents and incarcerated population.

Hispanic State Prisoner Incarceration Rate in 2000

National Rate = 922 Hispanic State Prisoners per 100,000 Hispanic Population*

ALPHA ORDER

RANK	STATE	RATE
24	Alabama	914
45	Alaska	549
12	Arizona	1,263
6	Arkansas	1,708
30	California	820
16	Colorado	1,131
7	Connecticut	1,669
49	Delaware	330
40	Florida	684
42	Georgia	620
44	Hawaii	587
17	Idaho	1,103
48	Illinois	426
43	Indiana	602
23	Iowa	923
37	Kansas	753
4	Kentucky	2,059
5	Louisiana	1,736
36	Maine	759
50	Maryland	230
9	Massachusetts	1,435
22	Michigan	951
18	Minnesota	1,031
1	Mississippi	3,131
38	Missouri	730
14	Montana	1,178
29	Nebraska	824
41	Nevada	676
10	New Hampshire	1,425
28	New Jersey	843
31	New Mexico	818
19	New York	1,002
47	North Carolina	440
21	North Dakota	976
26	Ohio	865
13	Oklahoma	1,223
35	Oregon	777
3	Pennsylvania	2,242
32	Rhode Island	817
25	South Carolina	871
8	South Dakota	1,486
34	Tennessee	790
15	Texas	1,152
20	Utah	998
33	Vermont	799
46	Virginia	508
39	Washington	717
2	West Virginia	2,834
27	Wisconsin	863
11	Wyoming	1,320

RANK ORDER

RANK	STATE	RATE
1	Mississippi	3,131
2	West Virginia	2,834
3	Pennsylvania	2,242
4	Kentucky	2,059
5	Louisiana	1,736
6	Arkansas	1,708
7	Connecticut	1,669
8	South Dakota	1,486
9	Massachusetts	1,435
10	New Hampshire	1,425
11	Wyoming	1,320
12	Arizona	1,263
13	Oklahoma	1,223
14	Montana	1,178
15	Texas	1,152
16	Colorado	1,131
17	Idaho	1,103
18	Minnesota	1,031
19	New York	1,002
20	Utah	998
21	North Dakota	976
22	Michigan	951
23	Iowa	923
24	Alabama	914
25	South Carolina	871
26	Ohio	865
27	Wisconsin	863
28	New Jersey	843
29	Nebraska	824
30	California	820
31	New Mexico	818
32	Rhode Island	817
33	Vermont	799
34	Tennessee	790
35	Oregon	777
36	Maine	759
37	Kansas	753
38	Missouri	730
39	Washington	717
40	Florida	684
41	Nevada	676
42	Georgia	620
43	Indiana	602
44	Hawaii	587
45	Alaska	549
46	Virginia	508
47	North Carolina	440
48	Illinois	426
49	Delaware	330
50	Maryland	230
	District of Columbia	260

Source: Human Rights Watch
"Incarceration Rates Reveal Striking Racial Disparities" (Press Release, 2/27/02)
(http://hrw.org/english/docs/2002/02/27/usdom3768.htm)
*Figures calculated on basis of U.S. Census Bureau data from Census 2000 on state residents and incarcerated population.

Prisoners Under Sentence of Death as of July 1, 2005

National Total = 3,378 State Prisoners*

ALPHA ORDER

RANK	STATE	PRISONERS	% of USA
7	Alabama	191	5.7%
NA	Alaska**	NA	NA
8	Arizona	128	3.8%
17	Arkansas	38	1.1%
1	California	648	19.2%
34	Colorado	3	0.1%
30	Connecticut	8	0.2%
23	Delaware	19	0.6%
3	Florida	388	11.5%
9	Georgia	112	3.3%
NA	Hawaii**	NA	NA
22	Idaho	21	0.6%
25	Illinois	10	0.3%
20	Indiana	30	0.9%
NA	Iowa**	NA	NA
31	Kansas	7	0.2%
18	Kentucky	37	1.1%
12	Louisiana	89	2.6%
NA	Maine**	NA	NA
29	Maryland	9	0.3%
NA	Massachusetts**	NA	NA
NA	Michigan**	NA	NA
NA	Minnesota**	NA	NA
15	Mississippi	70	2.1%
16	Missouri	55	1.6%
32	Montana	4	0.1%
25	Nebraska	10	0.3%
13	Nevada	85	2.5%
38	New Hampshire	0	0.0%
24	New Jersey	14	0.4%
35	New Mexico	2	0.1%
35	New York	2	0.1%
6	North Carolina	192	5.7%
NA	North Dakota**	NA	NA
5	Ohio	196	5.8%
11	Oklahoma	97	2.9%
19	Oregon	32	0.9%
4	Pennsylvania	233	6.9%
NA	Rhode Island**	NA	NA
14	South Carolina	77	2.3%
32	South Dakota	4	0.1%
10	Tennessee	108	3.2%
2	Texas	414	12.3%
25	Utah	10	0.3%
NA	Vermont**	NA	NA
21	Virginia	23	0.7%
25	Washington	10	0.3%
NA	West Virginia**	NA	NA
NA	Wisconsin**	NA	NA
35	Wyoming	2	0.1%

RANK ORDER

RANK	STATE	PRISONERS	% of USA
1	California	648	19.2%
2	Texas	414	12.3%
3	Florida	388	11.5%
4	Pennsylvania	233	6.9%
5	Ohio	196	5.8%
6	North Carolina	192	5.7%
7	Alabama	191	5.7%
8	Arizona	128	3.8%
9	Georgia	112	3.3%
10	Tennessee	108	3.2%
11	Oklahoma	97	2.9%
12	Louisiana	89	2.6%
13	Nevada	85	2.5%
14	South Carolina	77	2.3%
15	Mississippi	70	2.1%
16	Missouri	55	1.6%
17	Arkansas	38	1.1%
18	Kentucky	37	1.1%
19	Oregon	32	0.9%
20	Indiana	30	0.9%
21	Virginia	23	0.7%
22	Idaho	21	0.6%
23	Delaware	19	0.6%
24	New Jersey	14	0.4%
25	Illinois	10	0.3%
25	Nebraska	10	0.3%
25	Utah	10	0.3%
25	Washington	10	0.3%
29	Maryland	9	0.3%
30	Connecticut	8	0.2%
31	Kansas	7	0.2%
32	Montana	4	0.1%
32	South Dakota	4	0.1%
34	Colorado	3	0.1%
35	New Mexico	2	0.1%
35	New York	2	0.1%
35	Wyoming	2	0.1%
38	New Hampshire	0	0.0%
NA	Alaska**	NA	NA
NA	Hawaii**	NA	NA
NA	Iowa**	NA	NA
NA	Maine**	NA	NA
NA	Massachusetts**	NA	NA
NA	Michigan**	NA	NA
NA	Minnesota**	NA	NA
NA	North Dakota**	NA	NA
NA	Rhode Island**	NA	NA
NA	Vermont**	NA	NA
NA	West Virginia**	NA	NA
NA	Wisconsin**	NA	NA
	District of Columbia**	NA	NA

Source: NAACP Legal Defense and Educational Fund, Inc., Criminal Justice Project
    "Death Row 2005 USA, Summer 2005"
*Total does not include 36 federal prisoners or eight military prisoners under sentence of death.
**No death penalty as of 7/1/05.

Prisoners Under Sentence of Death in 2004

National Total = 3,282 State Prisoners*

ALPHA ORDER

RANK ORDER

RANK	STATE	PRISONERS	% of USA	RANK	STATE	PRISONERS	% of USA
6	Alabama	193	5.9%	1	California	637	19.4%
NA	Alaska**	NA	NA	2	Texas	446	13.6%
9	Arizona	105	3.2%	3	Florida	364	11.1%
17	Arkansas	39	1.2%	4	Pennsylvania	222	6.8%
1	California	637	19.4%	5	Ohio	201	6.1%
33	Colorado	3	0.1%	6	Alabama	193	5.9%
29	Connecticut	7	0.2%	7	North Carolina	181	5.5%
23	Delaware	17	0.5%	8	Georgia	109	3.3%
3	Florida	364	11.1%	9	Arizona	105	3.2%
8	Georgia	109	3.3%	10	Tennessee	99	3.0%
NA	Hawaii**	NA	NA	11	Oklahoma	91	2.8%
22	Idaho	22	0.7%	12	Louisiana	87	2.7%
30	Illinois	6	0.2%	13	Nevada	83	2.5%
20	Indiana	27	0.8%	14	South Carolina	71	2.2%
NA	Iowa**	NA	NA	15	Mississippi	70	2.1%
37	Kansas	0	0.0%	16	Missouri	52	1.6%
18	Kentucky	34	1.0%	17	Arkansas	39	1.2%
12	Louisiana	87	2.7%	18	Kentucky	34	1.0%
NA	Maine**	NA	NA	19	Oregon	30	0.9%
27	Maryland	9	0.3%	20	Indiana	27	0.8%
NA	Massachusetts**	NA	NA	21	Virginia	23	0.7%
NA	Michigan**	NA	NA	22	Idaho	22	0.7%
NA	Minnesota**	NA	NA	23	Delaware	17	0.5%
15	Mississippi	70	2.1%	24	New Jersey	11	0.3%
16	Missouri	52	1.6%	24	Washington	11	0.3%
31	Montana	4	0.1%	26	Utah	10	0.3%
28	Nebraska	8	0.2%	27	Maryland	9	0.3%
13	Nevada	83	2.5%	28	Nebraska	8	0.2%
37	New Hampshire	0	0.0%	29	Connecticut	7	0.2%
24	New Jersey	11	0.3%	30	Illinois	6	0.2%
34	New Mexico	2	0.1%	31	Montana	4	0.1%
34	New York	2	0.1%	31	South Dakota	4	0.1%
7	North Carolina	181	5.5%	33	Colorado	3	0.1%
NA	North Dakota**	NA	NA	34	New Mexico	2	0.1%
5	Ohio	201	6.1%	34	New York	2	0.1%
11	Oklahoma	91	2.8%	34	Wyoming	2	0.1%
19	Oregon	30	0.9%	37	Kansas	0	0.0%
4	Pennsylvania	222	6.8%	37	New Hampshire	0	0.0%
NA	Rhode Island**	NA	NA	NA	Alaska**	NA	NA
14	South Carolina	71	2.2%	NA	Hawaii**	NA	NA
31	South Dakota	4	0.1%	NA	Iowa**	NA	NA
10	Tennessee	99	3.0%	NA	Maine**	NA	NA
2	Texas	446	13.6%	NA	Massachusetts**	NA	NA
26	Utah	10	0.3%	NA	Michigan**	NA	NA
NA	Vermont**	NA	NA	NA	Minnesota**	NA	NA
21	Virginia	23	0.7%	NA	North Dakota**	NA	NA
24	Washington	11	0.3%	NA	Rhode Island**	NA	NA
NA	West Virginia**	NA	NA	NA	Vermont**	NA	NA
NA	Wisconsin**	NA	NA	NA	West Virginia**	NA	NA
34	Wyoming	2	0.1%	NA	Wisconsin**	NA	NA
				NA	District of Columbia**	NA	NA

Source: U.S. Department of Justice, Bureau of Justice Statistics
    "Capital Punishment 2004" (Bulletin, November 2005, NCJ-211349)
*As of December 31, 2004. Does not include 33 federal prisoners under sentence of death. There were 59
executions in 2004.
**No death penalty as of 12/31/04.

Average Number of Years Under Sentence of Death as of 2004

National Average = 10.2 Years*

ALPHA ORDER

RANK	STATE	YEARS
13	Alabama	9.7
NA	Alaska**	NA
6	Arizona	11.8
17	Arkansas	8.4
8	California	11.5
NA	Colorado***	NA
NA	Connecticut***	NA
25	Delaware	5.8
4	Florida	12.2
12	Georgia	11.0
NA	Hawaii**	NA
6	Idaho	11.8
NA	Illinois***	NA
2	Indiana	12.3
NA	Iowa**	NA
NA	Kansas***	NA
8	Kentucky	11.5
21	Louisiana	7.7
NA	Maine**	NA
NA	Maryland***	NA
NA	Massachusetts**	NA
NA	Michigan**	NA
NA	Minnesota**	NA
16	Mississippi	8.9
15	Missouri	9.1
NA	Montana***	NA
NA	Nebraska***	NA
2	Nevada	12.3
NA	New Hampshire***	NA
14	New Jersey	9.4
NA	New Mexico***	NA
NA	New York***	NA
18	North Carolina	8.3
NA	North Dakota**	NA
10	Ohio	11.3
22	Oklahoma	7.3
24	Oregon	6.9
11	Pennsylvania	11.2
NA	Rhode Island**	NA
20	South Carolina	7.9
NA	South Dakota***	NA
5	Tennessee	11.9
19	Texas	8.2
1	Utah	13.9
NA	Vermont**	NA
26	Virginia	3.5
23	Washington	7.1
NA	West Virginia**	NA
NA	Wisconsin**	NA
NA	Wyoming***	NA

RANK ORDER

RANK	STATE	YEARS
1	Utah	13.9
2	Indiana	12.3
2	Nevada	12.3
4	Florida	12.2
5	Tennessee	11.9
6	Arizona	11.8
6	Idaho	11.8
8	California	11.5
8	Kentucky	11.5
10	Ohio	11.3
11	Pennsylvania	11.2
12	Georgia	11.0
13	Alabama	9.7
14	New Jersey	9.4
15	Missouri	9.1
16	Mississippi	8.9
17	Arkansas	8.4
18	North Carolina	8.3
19	Texas	8.2
20	South Carolina	7.9
21	Louisiana	7.7
22	Oklahoma	7.3
23	Washington	7.1
24	Oregon	6.9
25	Delaware	5.8
26	Virginia	3.5
NA	Alaska**	NA
NA	Colorado***	NA
NA	Connecticut***	NA
NA	Hawaii**	NA
NA	Illinois***	NA
NA	Iowa**	NA
NA	Kansas***	NA
NA	Maine**	NA
NA	Maryland***	NA
NA	Massachusetts**	NA
NA	Michigan**	NA
NA	Minnesota**	NA
NA	Montana***	NA
NA	Nebraska***	NA
NA	New Hampshire***	NA
NA	New Mexico***	NA
NA	New York***	NA
NA	North Dakota**	NA
NA	Rhode Island**	NA
NA	South Dakota***	NA
NA	Vermont**	NA
NA	West Virginia**	NA
NA	Wisconsin**	NA
NA	Wyoming***	NA
	District of Columbia**	NA

Source: U.S. Department of Justice, Bureau of Justice Statistics
    "Capital Punishment 2004" (Bulletin, November 2005, NCJ-211349)
*As of December 31, 2004. Federal average is 3.8 years.
**No death penalty as of 12/31/04.
***Not available. These states had fewer than 10 prisoners under sentence of death. Averages were not calculated.

Male Prisoners Under Sentence of Death in 2004

National Total = 3,230 Male State Prisoners*

ALPHA ORDER

RANK ORDER

RANK	STATE	PRISONERS	% of USA
6	Alabama	190	5.9%
NA	Alaska**	NA	NA
9	Arizona	103	3.2%
17	Arkansas	39	1.2%
1	California	622	19.3%
33	Colorado	3	0.1%
29	Connecticut	7	0.2%
23	Delaware	16	0.5%
3	Florida	363	11.2%
8	Georgia	108	3.3%
NA	Hawaii**	NA	NA
22	Idaho	21	0.7%
30	Illinois	6	0.2%
20	Indiana	26	0.8%
NA	Iowa**	NA	NA
37	Kansas	0	0.0%
18	Kentucky	33	1.0%
12	Louisiana	86	2.7%
NA	Maine**	NA	NA
27	Maryland	9	0.3%
NA	Massachusetts**	NA	NA
NA	Michigan**	NA	NA
NA	Minnesota**	NA	NA
15	Mississippi	69	2.1%
16	Missouri	52	1.6%
31	Montana	4	0.1%
28	Nebraska	8	0.2%
13	Nevada	82	2.5%
37	New Hampshire	0	0.0%
24	New Jersey	11	0.3%
34	New Mexico	2	0.1%
34	New York	2	0.1%
7	North Carolina	177	5.5%
NA	North Dakota**	NA	NA
5	Ohio	200	6.2%
11	Oklahoma	90	2.8%
19	Oregon	30	0.9%
4	Pennsylvania	217	6.7%
NA	Rhode Island**	NA	NA
14	South Carolina	71	2.2%
31	South Dakota	4	0.1%
10	Tennessee	97	3.0%
2	Texas	437	13.5%
26	Utah	10	0.3%
NA	Vermont**	NA	NA
21	Virginia	22	0.7%
24	Washington	11	0.3%
NA	West Virginia**	NA	NA
NA	Wisconsin**	NA	NA
34	Wyoming	2	0.1%

RANK	STATE	PRISONERS	% of USA
1	California	622	19.3%
2	Texas	437	13.5%
3	Florida	363	11.2%
4	Pennsylvania	217	6.7%
5	Ohio	200	6.2%
6	Alabama	190	5.9%
7	North Carolina	177	5.5%
8	Georgia	108	3.3%
9	Arizona	103	3.2%
10	Tennessee	97	3.0%
11	Oklahoma	90	2.8%
12	Louisiana	86	2.7%
13	Nevada	82	2.5%
14	South Carolina	71	2.2%
15	Mississippi	69	2.1%
16	Missouri	52	1.6%
17	Arkansas	39	1.2%
18	Kentucky	33	1.0%
19	Oregon	30	0.9%
20	Indiana	26	0.8%
21	Virginia	22	0.7%
22	Idaho	21	0.7%
23	Delaware	16	0.5%
24	New Jersey	11	0.3%
24	Washington	11	0.3%
26	Utah	10	0.3%
27	Maryland	9	0.3%
28	Nebraska	8	0.2%
29	Connecticut	7	0.2%
30	Illinois	6	0.2%
31	Montana	4	0.1%
31	South Dakota	4	0.1%
33	Colorado	3	0.1%
34	New Mexico	2	0.1%
34	New York	2	0.1%
34	Wyoming	2	0.1%
37	Kansas	0	0.0%
37	New Hampshire	0	0.0%
NA	Alaska**	NA	NA
NA	Hawaii**	NA	NA
NA	Iowa**	NA	NA
NA	Maine**	NA	NA
NA	Massachusetts**	NA	NA
NA	Michigan**	NA	NA
NA	Minnesota**	NA	NA
NA	North Dakota**	NA	NA
NA	Rhode Island**	NA	NA
NA	Vermont**	NA	NA
NA	West Virginia**	NA	NA
NA	Wisconsin**	NA	NA

District of Columbia** NA NA

*Source: Morgan Quitno Press using data from U.S. Department of Justice, Bureau of Justice Statistics
    "Capital Punishment 2004" (Bulletin, November 2005, NCJ-211349)*
As of December 31, 2004. Does not include 33 male federal prisoners under sentence of death. There were 59 executions in 2004, all of whom were male.
**No death penalty as of 12/31/04.*

Female Prisoners Under Sentence of Death in 2004

National Total = 52 Female State Prisoners*

ALPHA ORDER

RANK	STATE	PRISONERS	% of USA
5	Alabama	3	5.8%
NA	Alaska**	NA	NA
6	Arizona	2	3.8%
20	Arkansas	0	0.0%
1	California	15	28.8%
20	Colorado	0	0.0%
20	Connecticut	0	0.0%
8	Delaware	1	1.9%
8	Florida	1	1.9%
8	Georgia	1	1.9%
NA	Hawaii**	NA	NA
8	Idaho	1	1.9%
20	Illinois	0	0.0%
8	Indiana	1	1.9%
NA	Iowa**	NA	NA
20	Kansas	0	0.0%
8	Kentucky	1	1.9%
8	Louisiana	1	1.9%
NA	Maine**	NA	NA
20	Maryland	0	0.0%
NA	Massachusetts**	NA	NA
NA	Michigan**	NA	NA
NA	Minnesota**	NA	NA
8	Mississippi	1	1.9%
20	Missouri	0	0.0%
20	Montana	0	0.0%
20	Nebraska	0	0.0%
8	Nevada	1	1.9%
20	New Hampshire	0	0.0%
20	New Jersey	0	0.0%
20	New Mexico	0	0.0%
20	New York	0	0.0%
4	North Carolina	4	7.7%
NA	North Dakota**	NA	NA
8	Ohio	1	1.9%
8	Oklahoma	1	1.9%
20	Oregon	0	0.0%
3	Pennsylvania	5	9.6%
NA	Rhode Island**	NA	NA
20	South Carolina	0	0.0%
20	South Dakota	0	0.0%
6	Tennessee	2	3.8%
2	Texas	9	17.3%
20	Utah	0	0.0%
NA	Vermont**	NA	NA
8	Virginia	1	1.9%
20	Washington	0	0.0%
NA	West Virginia**	NA	NA
NA	Wisconsin**	NA	NA
20	Wyoming	0	0.0%

RANK ORDER

RANK	STATE	PRISONERS	% of USA
1	California	15	28.8%
2	Texas	9	17.3%
3	Pennsylvania	5	9.6%
4	North Carolina	4	7.7%
5	Alabama	3	5.8%
6	Arizona	2	3.8%
6	Tennessee	2	3.8%
8	Delaware	1	1.9%
8	Florida	1	1.9%
8	Georgia	1	1.9%
8	Idaho	1	1.9%
8	Indiana	1	1.9%
8	Kentucky	1	1.9%
8	Louisiana	1	1.9%
8	Mississippi	1	1.9%
8	Nevada	1	1.9%
8	Ohio	1	1.9%
8	Oklahoma	1	1.9%
8	Virginia	1	1.9%
20	Arkansas	0	0.0%
20	Colorado	0	0.0%
20	Connecticut	0	0.0%
20	Illinois	0	0.0%
20	Kansas	0	0.0%
20	Maryland	0	0.0%
20	Missouri	0	0.0%
20	Montana	0	0.0%
20	Nebraska	0	0.0%
20	New Hampshire	0	0.0%
20	New Jersey	0	0.0%
20	New Mexico	0	0.0%
20	New York	0	0.0%
20	Oregon	0	0.0%
20	South Carolina	0	0.0%
20	South Dakota	0	0.0%
20	Utah	0	0.0%
20	Washington	0	0.0%
20	Wyoming	0	0.0%
NA	Alaska**	NA	NA
NA	Hawaii**	NA	NA
NA	Iowa**	NA	NA
NA	Maine**	NA	NA
NA	Massachusetts**	NA	NA
NA	Michigan**	NA	NA
NA	Minnesota**	NA	NA
NA	North Dakota**	NA	NA
NA	Rhode Island**	NA	NA
NA	Vermont**	NA	NA
NA	West Virginia**	NA	NA
NA	Wisconsin**	NA	NA
	District of Columbia**	NA	NA

Source: U.S. Department of Justice, Bureau of Justice Statistics
   "Capital Punishment 2004" (Bulletin, November 2005, NCJ-211349)
*As of December 31, 2004. There were no federal female prisoners under sentence of death. There were 59 executions in 2004, none of whom was female.
**No death penalty as of 12/31/04.

Percent of Prisoners Under Sentence of Death Who Are Female: 2004

National Percent = 1.6% of State Death Sentence Prisoners*

ALPHA ORDER

RANK	STATE	PERCENT
12	Alabama	1.6
NA	Alaska**	NA
11	Arizona	1.9
20	Arkansas	0.0
6	California	2.4
20	Colorado	0.0
20	Connecticut	0.0
1	Delaware	5.9
19	Florida	0.3
17	Georgia	0.9
NA	Hawaii**	NA
2	Idaho	4.5
20	Illinois	0.0
4	Indiana	3.7
NA	Iowa**	NA
20	Kansas	0.0
5	Kentucky	2.9
15	Louisiana	1.1
NA	Maine**	NA
20	Maryland	0.0
NA	Massachusetts**	NA
NA	Michigan**	NA
NA	Minnesota**	NA
13	Mississippi	1.4
20	Missouri	0.0
20	Montana	0.0
20	Nebraska	0.0
14	Nevada	1.2
20	New Hampshire	0.0
20	New Jersey	0.0
20	New Mexico	0.0
20	New York	0.0
8	North Carolina	2.2
NA	North Dakota**	NA
18	Ohio	0.5
15	Oklahoma	1.1
20	Oregon	0.0
7	Pennsylvania	2.3
NA	Rhode Island**	NA
20	South Carolina	0.0
20	South Dakota	0.0
9	Tennessee	2.0
9	Texas	2.0
20	Utah	0.0
NA	Vermont**	NA
3	Virginia	4.3
20	Washington	0.0
NA	West Virginia**	NA
NA	Wisconsin**	NA
20	Wyoming	0.0

RANK ORDER

RANK	STATE	PERCENT
1	Delaware	5.9
2	Idaho	4.5
3	Virginia	4.3
4	Indiana	3.7
5	Kentucky	2.9
6	California	2.4
7	Pennsylvania	2.3
8	North Carolina	2.2
9	Tennessee	2.0
9	Texas	2.0
11	Arizona	1.9
12	Alabama	1.6
13	Mississippi	1.4
14	Nevada	1.2
15	Louisiana	1.1
15	Oklahoma	1.1
17	Georgia	0.9
18	Ohio	0.5
19	Florida	0.3
20	Arkansas	0.0
20	Colorado	0.0
20	Connecticut	0.0
20	Illinois	0.0
20	Kansas	0.0
20	Maryland	0.0
20	Missouri	0.0
20	Montana	0.0
20	Nebraska	0.0
20	New Hampshire	0.0
20	New Jersey	0.0
20	New Mexico	0.0
20	New York	0.0
20	Oregon	0.0
20	South Carolina	0.0
20	South Dakota	0.0
20	Utah	0.0
20	Washington	0.0
20	Wyoming	0.0
NA	Alaska**	NA
NA	Hawaii**	NA
NA	Iowa**	NA
NA	Maine**	NA
NA	Massachusetts**	NA
NA	Michigan**	NA
NA	Minnesota**	NA
NA	North Dakota**	NA
NA	Rhode Island**	NA
NA	Vermont**	NA
NA	West Virginia**	NA
NA	Wisconsin**	NA
	District of Columbia**	NA

Source: Morgan Quitno Press using data from U.S. Department of Justice, Bureau of Justice Statistics
    "Capital Punishment 2004" (Bulletin, November 2005, NCJ-211349)
*As of December 31, 2004. There were no federal female prisoners under sentence of death. There were 59
executions in 2004, none of whom was female.
**No death penalty as of 12/31/04.

White Prisoners Under Sentence of Death in 2004

National Total = 1,839 White State Prisoners*

ALPHA ORDER

RANK	STATE	PRISONERS	% of USA
4	Alabama	101	5.5%
NA	Alaska**	NA	NA
6	Arizona	89	4.8%
21	Arkansas	17	0.9%
1	California	379	20.6%
35	Colorado	1	0.1%
28	Connecticut	4	0.2%
22	Delaware	13	0.7%
3	Florida	239	13.0%
10	Georgia	56	3.0%
NA	Hawaii**	NA	NA
19	Idaho	22	1.2%
27	Illinois	5	0.3%
20	Indiana	21	1.1%
NA	Iowa**	NA	NA
37	Kansas	0	0.0%
16	Kentucky	27	1.5%
15	Louisiana	30	1.6%
NA	Maine**	NA	NA
31	Maryland	3	0.2%
NA	Massachusetts**	NA	NA
NA	Michigan**	NA	NA
NA	Minnesota**	NA	NA
14	Mississippi	33	1.8%
16	Missouri	27	1.5%
31	Montana	3	0.2%
24	Nebraska	7	0.4%
11	Nevada	49	2.7%
37	New Hampshire	0	0.0%
28	New Jersey	4	0.2%
33	New Mexico	2	0.1%
35	New York	1	0.1%
8	North Carolina	72	3.9%
NA	North Dakota**	NA	NA
5	Ohio	97	5.3%
12	Oklahoma	47	2.6%
16	Oregon	27	1.5%
7	Pennsylvania	77	4.2%
NA	Rhode Island**	NA	NA
13	South Carolina	35	1.9%
28	South Dakota	4	0.2%
9	Tennessee	58	3.2%
2	Texas	264	14.4%
24	Utah	7	0.4%
NA	Vermont**	NA	NA
23	Virginia	10	0.5%
26	Washington	6	0.3%
NA	West Virginia**	NA	NA
NA	Wisconsin**	NA	NA
33	Wyoming	2	0.1%

RANK ORDER

RANK	STATE	PRISONERS	% of USA
1	California	379	20.6%
2	Texas	264	14.4%
3	Florida	239	13.0%
4	Alabama	101	5.5%
5	Ohio	97	5.3%
6	Arizona	89	4.8%
7	Pennsylvania	77	4.2%
8	North Carolina	72	3.9%
9	Tennessee	58	3.2%
10	Georgia	56	3.0%
11	Nevada	49	2.7%
12	Oklahoma	47	2.6%
13	South Carolina	35	1.9%
14	Mississippi	33	1.8%
15	Louisiana	30	1.6%
16	Kentucky	27	1.5%
16	Missouri	27	1.5%
16	Oregon	27	1.5%
19	Idaho	22	1.2%
20	Indiana	21	1.1%
21	Arkansas	17	0.9%
22	Delaware	13	0.7%
23	Virginia	10	0.5%
24	Nebraska	7	0.4%
24	Utah	7	0.4%
26	Washington	6	0.3%
27	Illinois	5	0.3%
28	Connecticut	4	0.2%
28	New Jersey	4	0.2%
28	South Dakota	4	0.2%
31	Maryland	3	0.2%
31	Montana	3	0.2%
33	New Mexico	2	0.1%
33	Wyoming	2	0.1%
35	Colorado	1	0.1%
35	New York	1	0.1%
37	Kansas	0	0.0%
37	New Hampshire	0	0.0%
NA	Alaska**	NA	NA
NA	Hawaii**	NA	NA
NA	Iowa**	NA	NA
NA	Maine**	NA	NA
NA	Massachusetts**	NA	NA
NA	Michigan**	NA	NA
NA	Minnesota**	NA	NA
NA	North Dakota**	NA	NA
NA	Rhode Island**	NA	NA
NA	Vermont**	NA	NA
NA	West Virginia**	NA	NA
NA	Wisconsin**	NA	NA
	District of Columbia**	NA	NA

Source: U.S. Department of Justice, Bureau of Justice Statistics
"Capital Punishment 2004" (Bulletin, November 2005, NCJ-211349)
As of December 31, 2004. Does not include 12 white federal prisoners under sentence of death. There were 59 executions in 2004, 36 of whom were white prisoners.
***No death penalty as of 12/31/04.*

Percent of Prisoners Under Sentence of Death Who Are White: 2004

National Percent = 56.0% of State Death Sentence Prisoners*

ALPHA ORDER

RANK	STATE	PERCENT
21	Alabama	52.3
NA	Alaska**	NA
7	Arizona	84.8
29	Arkansas	43.6
15	California	59.5
35	Colorado	33.3
19	Connecticut	57.1
11	Delaware	76.5
14	Florida	65.7
24	Georgia	51.4
NA	Hawaii**	NA
1	Idaho	100.0
8	Illinois	83.3
10	Indiana	77.8
NA	Iowa**	NA
37	Kansas	0.0
9	Kentucky	79.4
34	Louisiana	34.5
NA	Maine**	NA
35	Maryland	33.3
NA	Massachusetts**	NA
NA	Michigan**	NA
NA	Minnesota**	NA
28	Mississippi	47.1
22	Missouri	51.9
12	Montana	75.0
6	Nebraska	87.5
17	Nevada	59.0
37	New Hampshire	0.0
32	New Jersey	36.4
1	New Mexico	100.0
25	New York	50.0
31	North Carolina	39.8
NA	North Dakota**	NA
27	Ohio	48.3
23	Oklahoma	51.6
5	Oregon	90.0
33	Pennsylvania	34.7
NA	Rhode Island**	NA
26	South Carolina	49.3
1	South Dakota	100.0
18	Tennessee	58.6
16	Texas	59.2
13	Utah	70.0
NA	Vermont**	NA
30	Virginia	43.5
20	Washington	54.5
NA	West Virginia**	NA
NA	Wisconsin**	NA
1	Wyoming	100.0

RANK ORDER

RANK	STATE	PERCENT
1	Idaho	100.0
1	New Mexico	100.0
1	South Dakota	100.0
1	Wyoming	100.0
5	Oregon	90.0
6	Nebraska	87.5
7	Arizona	84.8
8	Illinois	83.3
9	Kentucky	79.4
10	Indiana	77.8
11	Delaware	76.5
12	Montana	75.0
13	Utah	70.0
14	Florida	65.7
15	California	59.5
16	Texas	59.2
17	Nevada	59.0
18	Tennessee	58.6
19	Connecticut	57.1
20	Washington	54.5
21	Alabama	52.3
22	Missouri	51.9
23	Oklahoma	51.6
24	Georgia	51.4
25	New York	50.0
26	South Carolina	49.3
27	Ohio	48.3
28	Mississippi	47.1
29	Arkansas	43.6
30	Virginia	43.5
31	North Carolina	39.8
32	New Jersey	36.4
33	Pennsylvania	34.7
34	Louisiana	34.5
35	Colorado	33.3
35	Maryland	33.3
37	Kansas	0.0
37	New Hampshire	0.0
NA	Alaska**	NA
NA	Hawaii**	NA
NA	Iowa**	NA
NA	Maine**	NA
NA	Massachusetts**	NA
NA	Michigan**	NA
NA	Minnesota**	NA
NA	North Dakota**	NA
NA	Rhode Island**	NA
NA	Vermont**	NA
NA	West Virginia**	NA
NA	Wisconsin**	NA
	District of Columbia**	NA

Source: Morgan Quitno Press using data from U.S. Department of Justice, Bureau of Justice Statistics
    "Capital Punishment 2004" (Bulletin, November 2005, NCJ-211349)
*As of December 31, 2004. Does not include federal prisoners under sentence of death, 36.4% of whom are white prisoners. Of the 59 executions in 2004, 61.0% were white prisoners.
**No death penalty as of 12/31/04.

Black Prisoners Under Sentence of Death in 2004

National Total = 1,370 Black State Prisoners*

ALPHA ORDER

RANK	STATE	PRISONERS	% of USA
7	Alabama	92	6.7%
NA	Alaska**	NA	NA
18	Arizona	10	0.7%
16	Arkansas	22	1.6%
1	California	232	16.9%
26	Colorado	2	0.1%
25	Connecticut	3	0.2%
24	Delaware	4	0.3%
4	Florida	125	9.1%
9	Georgia	52	3.8%
NA	Hawaii**	NA	NA
32	Idaho	0	0.0%
29	Illinois	1	0.1%
21	Indiana	6	0.4%
NA	Iowa**	NA	NA
32	Kansas	0	0.0%
19	Kentucky	7	0.5%
8	Louisiana	56	4.1%
NA	Maine**	NA	NA
21	Maryland	6	0.4%
NA	Massachusetts**	NA	NA
NA	Michigan**	NA	NA
NA	Minnesota**	NA	NA
12	Mississippi	36	2.6%
15	Missouri	25	1.8%
32	Montana	0	0.0%
29	Nebraska	1	0.1%
14	Nevada	33	2.4%
32	New Hampshire	0	0.0%
19	New Jersey	7	0.5%
32	New Mexico	0	0.0%
29	New York	1	0.1%
5	North Carolina	102	7.4%
NA	North Dakota**	NA	NA
6	Ohio	101	7.4%
11	Oklahoma	38	2.8%
26	Oregon	2	0.1%
3	Pennsylvania	134	9.8%
NA	Rhode Island**	NA	NA
12	South Carolina	36	2.6%
32	South Dakota	0	0.0%
10	Tennessee	39	2.8%
2	Texas	177	12.9%
26	Utah	2	0.1%
NA	Vermont**	NA	NA
17	Virginia	13	0.9%
23	Washington	5	0.4%
NA	West Virginia**	NA	NA
NA	Wisconsin**	NA	NA
32	Wyoming	0	0.0%

RANK ORDER

RANK	STATE	PRISONERS	% of USA
1	California	232	16.9%
2	Texas	177	12.9%
3	Pennsylvania	134	9.8%
4	Florida	125	9.1%
5	North Carolina	102	7.4%
6	Ohio	101	7.4%
7	Alabama	92	6.7%
8	Louisiana	56	4.1%
9	Georgia	52	3.8%
10	Tennessee	39	2.8%
11	Oklahoma	38	2.8%
12	Mississippi	36	2.6%
12	South Carolina	36	2.6%
14	Nevada	33	2.4%
15	Missouri	25	1.8%
16	Arkansas	22	1.6%
17	Virginia	13	0.9%
18	Arizona	10	0.7%
19	Kentucky	7	0.5%
19	New Jersey	7	0.5%
21	Indiana	6	0.4%
21	Maryland	6	0.4%
23	Washington	5	0.4%
24	Delaware	4	0.3%
25	Connecticut	3	0.2%
26	Colorado	2	0.1%
26	Oregon	2	0.1%
26	Utah	2	0.1%
29	Illinois	1	0.1%
29	Nebraska	1	0.1%
29	New York	1	0.1%
32	Idaho	0	0.0%
32	Kansas	0	0.0%
32	Montana	0	0.0%
32	New Hampshire	0	0.0%
32	New Mexico	0	0.0%
32	South Dakota	0	0.0%
32	Wyoming	0	0.0%
NA	Alaska**	NA	NA
NA	Hawaii**	NA	NA
NA	Iowa**	NA	NA
NA	Maine**	NA	NA
NA	Massachusetts**	NA	NA
NA	Michigan**	NA	NA
NA	Minnesota**	NA	NA
NA	North Dakota**	NA	NA
NA	Rhode Island**	NA	NA
NA	Vermont**	NA	NA
NA	West Virginia**	NA	NA
NA	Wisconsin**	NA	NA
	District of Columbia**	NA	NA

*Source: U.S. Department of Justice, Bureau of Justice Statistics
"Capital Punishment 2004" (Bulletin, November 2005, NCJ-211349)*
*As of December 31, 2004. Does not include 20 black federal prisoners under sentence of death. There were
59 executions in 2004, 19 of whom were black prisoners.
**No death penalty as of 12/31/04.*

Percent of Prisoners Under Sentence of Death Who Are Black: 2004

National Percent = 41.7% of State Death Sentence Prisoners*

ALPHA ORDER

RANK	STATE	PERCENT
14	Alabama	47.7
NA	Alaska**	NA
30	Arizona	9.5
7	Arkansas	56.4
22	California	36.4
1	Colorado	66.7
17	Connecticut	42.9
24	Delaware	23.5
23	Florida	34.3
14	Georgia	47.7
NA	Hawaii**	NA
32	Idaho	0.0
28	Illinois	16.7
25	Indiana	22.2
NA	Iowa**	NA
32	Kansas	0.0
26	Kentucky	20.6
3	Louisiana	64.4
NA	Maine**	NA
1	Maryland	66.7
NA	Massachusetts**	NA
NA	Michigan**	NA
NA	Minnesota**	NA
9	Mississippi	51.4
13	Missouri	48.1
32	Montana	0.0
29	Nebraska	12.5
19	Nevada	39.8
32	New Hampshire	0.0
4	New Jersey	63.6
32	New Mexico	0.0
12	New York	50.0
7	North Carolina	56.4
NA	North Dakota**	NA
11	Ohio	50.2
18	Oklahoma	41.8
31	Oregon	6.7
5	Pennsylvania	60.4
NA	Rhode Island**	NA
10	South Carolina	50.7
32	South Dakota	0.0
21	Tennessee	39.4
20	Texas	39.7
27	Utah	20.0
NA	Vermont**	NA
6	Virginia	56.5
16	Washington	45.5
NA	West Virginia**	NA
NA	Wisconsin**	NA
32	Wyoming	0.0

RANK ORDER

RANK	STATE	PERCENT
1	Colorado	66.7
1	Maryland	66.7
3	Louisiana	64.4
4	New Jersey	63.6
5	Pennsylvania	60.4
6	Virginia	56.5
7	Arkansas	56.4
7	North Carolina	56.4
9	Mississippi	51.4
10	South Carolina	50.7
11	Ohio	50.2
12	New York	50.0
13	Missouri	48.1
14	Alabama	47.7
14	Georgia	47.7
16	Washington	45.5
17	Connecticut	42.9
18	Oklahoma	41.8
19	Nevada	39.8
20	Texas	39.7
21	Tennessee	39.4
22	California	36.4
23	Florida	34.3
24	Delaware	23.5
25	Indiana	22.2
26	Kentucky	20.6
27	Utah	20.0
28	Illinois	16.7
29	Nebraska	12.5
30	Arizona	9.5
31	Oregon	6.7
32	Idaho	0.0
32	Kansas	0.0
32	Montana	0.0
32	New Hampshire	0.0
32	New Mexico	0.0
32	South Dakota	0.0
32	Wyoming	0.0
NA	Alaska**	NA
NA	Hawaii**	NA
NA	Iowa**	NA
NA	Maine**	NA
NA	Massachusetts**	NA
NA	Michigan**	NA
NA	Minnesota**	NA
NA	North Dakota**	NA
NA	Rhode Island**	NA
NA	Vermont**	NA
NA	West Virginia**	NA
NA	Wisconsin**	NA
	District of Columbia**	NA

Source: Morgan Quitno Press using data from U.S. Department of Justice, Bureau of Justice Statistics
    "Capital Punishment 2004" (Bulletin, November 2005, NCJ-211349)
*As of December 31, 2004. Does not include federal prisoners under sentence of death, 60.6% of whom are black prisoners. Of the 59 executions in 2004, 32.2% were black prisoners.
**No death penalty as of 12/31/04.

70

Hispanic Prisoners Under Sentence of Death in 2004

National Total = 365 Hispanic State Prisoners*

ALPHA ORDER

RANK	STATE	PRISONERS	% of USA
16	Alabama	1	0.3%
NA	Alaska**	NA	NA
5	Arizona	18	4.9%
24	Arkansas	0	0.0%
1	California	131	35.9%
16	Colorado	1	0.3%
16	Connecticut	1	0.3%
11	Delaware	2	0.5%
3	Florida	31	8.5%
8	Georgia	3	0.8%
NA	Hawaii**	NA	NA
24	Idaho	0	0.0%
11	Illinois	2	0.5%
16	Indiana	1	0.3%
NA	Iowa**	NA	NA
24	Kansas	0	0.0%
16	Kentucky	1	0.3%
16	Louisiana	1	0.3%
NA	Maine**	NA	NA
24	Maryland	0	0.0%
NA	Massachusetts**	NA	NA
NA	Michigan**	NA	NA
NA	Minnesota**	NA	NA
24	Mississippi	0	0.0%
24	Missouri	0	0.0%
24	Montana	0	0.0%
11	Nebraska	2	0.5%
6	Nevada	7	1.9%
24	New Hampshire	0	0.0%
24	New Jersey	0	0.0%
16	New Mexico	1	0.3%
24	New York	0	0.0%
8	North Carolina	3	0.8%
NA	North Dakota**	NA	NA
7	Ohio	5	1.4%
8	Oklahoma	3	0.8%
11	Oregon	2	0.5%
4	Pennsylvania	22	6.0%
NA	Rhode Island**	NA	NA
24	South Carolina	0	0.0%
24	South Dakota	0	0.0%
16	Tennessee	1	0.3%
2	Texas	124	34.0%
11	Utah	2	0.5%
NA	Vermont**	NA	NA
24	Virginia	0	0.0%
24	Washington	0	0.0%
NA	West Virginia**	NA	NA
NA	Wisconsin**	NA	NA
24	Wyoming	0	0.0%

RANK ORDER

RANK	STATE	PRISONERS	% of USA
1	California	131	35.9%
2	Texas	124	34.0%
3	Florida	31	8.5%
4	Pennsylvania	22	6.0%
5	Arizona	18	4.9%
6	Nevada	7	1.9%
7	Ohio	5	1.4%
8	Georgia	3	0.8%
8	North Carolina	3	0.8%
8	Oklahoma	3	0.8%
11	Delaware	2	0.5%
11	Illinois	2	0.5%
11	Nebraska	2	0.5%
11	Oregon	2	0.5%
11	Utah	2	0.5%
16	Alabama	1	0.3%
16	Colorado	1	0.3%
16	Connecticut	1	0.3%
16	Indiana	1	0.3%
16	Kentucky	1	0.3%
16	Louisiana	1	0.3%
16	New Mexico	1	0.3%
16	Tennessee	1	0.3%
24	Arkansas	0	0.0%
24	Idaho	0	0.0%
24	Kansas	0	0.0%
24	Maryland	0	0.0%
24	Mississippi	0	0.0%
24	Missouri	0	0.0%
24	Montana	0	0.0%
24	New Hampshire	0	0.0%
24	New Jersey	0	0.0%
24	New York	0	0.0%
24	South Carolina	0	0.0%
24	South Dakota	0	0.0%
24	Virginia	0	0.0%
24	Washington	0	0.0%
24	Wyoming	0	0.0%
NA	Alaska**	NA	NA
NA	Hawaii**	NA	NA
NA	Iowa**	NA	NA
NA	Maine**	NA	NA
NA	Massachusetts**	NA	NA
NA	Michigan**	NA	NA
NA	Minnesota**	NA	NA
NA	North Dakota**	NA	NA
NA	Rhode Island**	NA	NA
NA	Vermont**	NA	NA
NA	West Virginia**	NA	NA
NA	Wisconsin**	NA	NA
	District of Columbia**	NA	NA

*Source: U.S. Department of Justice, Bureau of Justice Statistics
"Capital Punishment 2004" (Bulletin, November 2005, NCJ-211349)*
*As of December 31, 2004. Does not include two Hispanic federal prisoners under sentence of death. There were 59 executions in 2004, three of whom were Hispanic prisoners. Hispanic can be of any race.
**No death penalty as of 12/31/04.

Percent of Prisoners Under Sentence of Death Who Are Hispanic: 2004

National Percent = 11.1% of State Death Sentence Prisoners*

<table>
<tr><td colspan="3">ALPHA ORDER</td><td colspan="3">RANK ORDER</td></tr>
<tr><td>RANK</td><td>STATE</td><td>PERCENT</td><td>RANK</td><td>STATE</td><td>PERCENT</td></tr>
<tr><td>23</td><td>Alabama</td><td>0.5</td><td>1</td><td>New Mexico</td><td>50.0</td></tr>
<tr><td>NA</td><td>Alaska**</td><td>NA</td><td>2</td><td>Colorado</td><td>33.3</td></tr>
<tr><td>8</td><td>Arizona</td><td>17.1</td><td>2</td><td>Illinois</td><td>33.3</td></tr>
<tr><td>24</td><td>Arkansas</td><td>0.0</td><td>4</td><td>Texas</td><td>27.8</td></tr>
<tr><td>6</td><td>California</td><td>20.6</td><td>5</td><td>Nebraska</td><td>25.0</td></tr>
<tr><td>2</td><td>Colorado</td><td>33.3</td><td>6</td><td>California</td><td>20.6</td></tr>
<tr><td>9</td><td>Connecticut</td><td>14.3</td><td>7</td><td>Utah</td><td>20.0</td></tr>
<tr><td>10</td><td>Delaware</td><td>11.8</td><td>8</td><td>Arizona</td><td>17.1</td></tr>
<tr><td>12</td><td>Florida</td><td>8.5</td><td>9</td><td>Connecticut</td><td>14.3</td></tr>
<tr><td>18</td><td>Georgia</td><td>2.8</td><td>10</td><td>Delaware</td><td>11.8</td></tr>
<tr><td>NA</td><td>Hawaii**</td><td>NA</td><td>11</td><td>Pennsylvania</td><td>9.9</td></tr>
<tr><td>24</td><td>Idaho</td><td>0.0</td><td>12</td><td>Florida</td><td>8.5</td></tr>
<tr><td>2</td><td>Illinois</td><td>33.3</td><td>13</td><td>Nevada</td><td>8.4</td></tr>
<tr><td>15</td><td>Indiana</td><td>3.7</td><td>14</td><td>Oregon</td><td>6.7</td></tr>
<tr><td>NA</td><td>Iowa**</td><td>NA</td><td>15</td><td>Indiana</td><td>3.7</td></tr>
<tr><td>24</td><td>Kansas</td><td>0.0</td><td>16</td><td>Oklahoma</td><td>3.3</td></tr>
<tr><td>17</td><td>Kentucky</td><td>2.9</td><td>17</td><td>Kentucky</td><td>2.9</td></tr>
<tr><td>21</td><td>Louisiana</td><td>1.1</td><td>18</td><td>Georgia</td><td>2.8</td></tr>
<tr><td>NA</td><td>Maine**</td><td>NA</td><td>19</td><td>Ohio</td><td>2.5</td></tr>
<tr><td>24</td><td>Maryland</td><td>0.0</td><td>20</td><td>North Carolina</td><td>1.7</td></tr>
<tr><td>NA</td><td>Massachusetts**</td><td>NA</td><td>21</td><td>Louisiana</td><td>1.1</td></tr>
<tr><td>NA</td><td>Michigan**</td><td>NA</td><td>22</td><td>Tennessee</td><td>1.0</td></tr>
<tr><td>NA</td><td>Minnesota**</td><td>NA</td><td>23</td><td>Alabama</td><td>0.5</td></tr>
<tr><td>24</td><td>Mississippi</td><td>0.0</td><td>24</td><td>Arkansas</td><td>0.0</td></tr>
<tr><td>24</td><td>Missouri</td><td>0.0</td><td>24</td><td>Idaho</td><td>0.0</td></tr>
<tr><td>24</td><td>Montana</td><td>0.0</td><td>24</td><td>Kansas</td><td>0.0</td></tr>
<tr><td>5</td><td>Nebraska</td><td>25.0</td><td>24</td><td>Maryland</td><td>0.0</td></tr>
<tr><td>13</td><td>Nevada</td><td>8.4</td><td>24</td><td>Mississippi</td><td>0.0</td></tr>
<tr><td>24</td><td>New Hampshire</td><td>0.0</td><td>24</td><td>Missouri</td><td>0.0</td></tr>
<tr><td>24</td><td>New Jersey</td><td>0.0</td><td>24</td><td>Montana</td><td>0.0</td></tr>
<tr><td>1</td><td>New Mexico</td><td>50.0</td><td>24</td><td>New Hampshire</td><td>0.0</td></tr>
<tr><td>24</td><td>New York</td><td>0.0</td><td>24</td><td>New Jersey</td><td>0.0</td></tr>
<tr><td>20</td><td>North Carolina</td><td>1.7</td><td>24</td><td>New York</td><td>0.0</td></tr>
<tr><td>NA</td><td>North Dakota**</td><td>NA</td><td>24</td><td>South Carolina</td><td>0.0</td></tr>
<tr><td>19</td><td>Ohio</td><td>2.5</td><td>24</td><td>South Dakota</td><td>0.0</td></tr>
<tr><td>16</td><td>Oklahoma</td><td>3.3</td><td>24</td><td>Virginia</td><td>0.0</td></tr>
<tr><td>14</td><td>Oregon</td><td>6.7</td><td>24</td><td>Washington</td><td>0.0</td></tr>
<tr><td>11</td><td>Pennsylvania</td><td>9.9</td><td>24</td><td>Wyoming</td><td>0.0</td></tr>
<tr><td>NA</td><td>Rhode Island**</td><td>NA</td><td>NA</td><td>Alaska**</td><td>NA</td></tr>
<tr><td>24</td><td>South Carolina</td><td>0.0</td><td>NA</td><td>Hawaii**</td><td>NA</td></tr>
<tr><td>24</td><td>South Dakota</td><td>0.0</td><td>NA</td><td>Iowa**</td><td>NA</td></tr>
<tr><td>22</td><td>Tennessee</td><td>1.0</td><td>NA</td><td>Maine**</td><td>NA</td></tr>
<tr><td>4</td><td>Texas</td><td>27.8</td><td>NA</td><td>Massachusetts**</td><td>NA</td></tr>
<tr><td>7</td><td>Utah</td><td>20.0</td><td>NA</td><td>Michigan**</td><td>NA</td></tr>
<tr><td>NA</td><td>Vermont**</td><td>NA</td><td>NA</td><td>Minnesota**</td><td>NA</td></tr>
<tr><td>24</td><td>Virginia</td><td>0.0</td><td>NA</td><td>North Dakota**</td><td>NA</td></tr>
<tr><td>24</td><td>Washington</td><td>0.0</td><td>NA</td><td>Rhode Island**</td><td>NA</td></tr>
<tr><td>NA</td><td>West Virginia**</td><td>NA</td><td>NA</td><td>Vermont**</td><td>NA</td></tr>
<tr><td>NA</td><td>Wisconsin**</td><td>NA</td><td>NA</td><td>West Virginia**</td><td>NA</td></tr>
<tr><td>24</td><td>Wyoming</td><td>0.0</td><td>NA</td><td>Wisconsin**</td><td>NA</td></tr>
<tr><td></td><td></td><td></td><td></td><td>District of Columbia**</td><td>NA</td></tr>
</table>

Source: Morgan Quitno Press using data from U.S. Department of Justice, Bureau of Justice Statistics
   "Capital Punishment 2004" (Bulletin, November 2005, NCJ-211349)
*As of December 31, 2004. Does not include federal prisoners under sentence of death, 6.1% of whom are
Hispanic prisoners. Of the 59 executions in 2004, 5.1% were Hispanic prisoners. Hispanic can be of any race.
**No death penalty as of 12/31/04.

Prisoners Executed: January through November 2005

National Total = 49 Prisoners*

ALPHA ORDER

RANK	STATE	EXECUTIONS	% of USA
4	Alabama	4	8.2%
NA	Alaska**	NA	NA
14	Arizona	0	0.0%
10	Arkansas	1	2.0%
14	California	0	0.0%
14	Colorado	0	0.0%
10	Connecticut	1	2.0%
10	Delaware	1	2.0%
10	Florida	1	2.0%
6	Georgia	3	6.1%
NA	Hawaii**	NA	NA
14	Idaho	0	0.0%
14	Illinois	0	0.0%
2	Indiana	5	10.2%
14	Iowa	0	0.0%
NA	Kansas**	NA	NA
14	Kentucky	0	0.0%
14	Louisiana	0	0.0%
14	Maine	0	0.0%
NA	Maryland**	NA	NA
NA	Massachusetts**	NA	NA
NA	Michigan**	NA	NA
NA	Minnesota**	NA	NA
14	Mississippi	0	0.0%
14	Missouri	0	0.0%
2	Montana	5	10.2%
14	Nebraska	0	0.0%
14	Nevada	0	0.0%
14	New Hampshire	0	0.0%
14	New Jersey	0	0.0%
14	New Mexico	0	0.0%
14	New York	0	0.0%
8	North Carolina	2	4.1%
NA	North Dakota**	NA	NA
6	Ohio	3	6.1%
4	Oklahoma	4	8.2%
14	Oregon	0	0.0%
14	Pennsylvania	0	0.0%
NA	Rhode Island**	NA	NA
8	South Carolina	2	4.1%
14	South Dakota	0	0.0%
14	Tennessee	0	0.0%
1	Texas	17	34.7%
14	Utah	0	0.0%
NA	Vermont**	NA	NA
14	Virginia	0	0.0%
14	Washington	0	0.0%
NA	West Virginia**	NA	NA
NA	Wisconsin**	NA	NA
14	Wyoming	0	0.0%

RANK ORDER

RANK	STATE	EXECUTIONS	% of USA
1	Texas	17	34.7%
2	Indiana	5	10.2%
2	Montana	5	10.2%
4	Alabama	4	8.2%
4	Oklahoma	4	8.2%
6	Georgia	3	6.1%
6	Ohio	3	6.1%
8	North Carolina	2	4.1%
8	South Carolina	2	4.1%
10	Arkansas	1	2.0%
10	Connecticut	1	2.0%
10	Delaware	1	2.0%
10	Florida	1	2.0%
14	Arizona	0	0.0%
14	California	0	0.0%
14	Colorado	0	0.0%
14	Idaho	0	0.0%
14	Illinois	0	0.0%
14	Iowa	0	0.0%
14	Kentucky	0	0.0%
14	Louisiana	0	0.0%
14	Maine	0	0.0%
14	Mississippi	0	0.0%
14	Missouri	0	0.0%
14	Nebraska	0	0.0%
14	Nevada	0	0.0%
14	New Hampshire	0	0.0%
14	New Jersey	0	0.0%
14	New Mexico	0	0.0%
14	New York	0	0.0%
14	Oregon	0	0.0%
14	Pennsylvania	0	0.0%
14	South Dakota	0	0.0%
14	Tennessee	0	0.0%
14	Utah	0	0.0%
14	Virginia	0	0.0%
14	Washington	0	0.0%
14	Wyoming	0	0.0%
NA	Alaska**	NA	NA
NA	Hawaii**	NA	NA
NA	Kansas**	NA	NA
NA	Maryland**	NA	NA
NA	Massachusetts**	NA	NA
NA	Michigan**	NA	NA
NA	Minnesota**	NA	NA
NA	North Dakota**	NA	NA
NA	Rhode Island**	NA	NA
NA	Vermont**	NA	NA
NA	West Virginia**	NA	NA
NA	Wisconsin**	NA	NA
	District of Columbia**	NA	NA

Source: U.S. Department of Justice, Bureau of Justice Statistics
    "Capital Punishment 2004" (Bulletin, November 2005, NCJ-211349)
*As of November 30, 2005.
**No death penalty as of 12/31/04.

Prisoners Executed in 2004

National Total = 59 Prisoners*

ALPHA ORDER

ALPHA ORDER

RANK	STATE	EXECUTIONS	% of USA
7	Alabama	2	3.4%
NA	Alaska**	NA	NA
13	Arizona	0	0.0%
11	Arkansas	1	1.7%
13	California	0	0.0%
13	Colorado	0	0.0%
13	Connecticut	0	0.0%
13	Delaware	0	0.0%
7	Florida	2	3.4%
7	Georgia	2	3.4%
NA	Hawaii**	NA	NA
13	Idaho	0	0.0%
13	Illinois	0	0.0%
NA	Indiana**	NA	NA
13	Iowa	0	0.0%
13	Kansas	0	0.0%
13	Kentucky	0	0.0%
13	Louisiana	0	0.0%
NA	Maine**	NA	NA
11	Maryland	1	1.7%
NA	Massachusetts**	NA	NA
NA	Michigan**	NA	NA
NA	Minnesota**	NA	NA
13	Mississippi	0	0.0%
13	Missouri	0	0.0%
13	Montana	0	0.0%
13	Nebraska	0	0.0%
7	Nevada	2	3.4%
13	New Hampshire	0	0.0%
13	New Jersey	0	0.0%
13	New Mexico	0	0.0%
13	New York	0	0.0%
5	North Carolina	4	6.8%
NA	North Dakota**	NA	NA
2	Ohio	7	11.9%
3	Oklahoma	6	10.2%
13	Oregon	0	0.0%
13	Pennsylvania	0	0.0%
NA	Rhode Island**	NA	NA
5	South Carolina	4	6.8%
13	South Dakota	0	0.0%
13	Tennessee	0	0.0%
1	Texas	23	39.0%
13	Utah	0	0.0%
NA	Vermont**	NA	NA
4	Virginia	5	8.5%
13	Washington	0	0.0%
NA	West Virginia**	NA	NA
NA	Wisconsin**	NA	NA
13	Wyoming	0	0.0%

RANK ORDER

RANK	STATE	EXECUTIONS	% of USA
1	Texas	23	39.0%
2	Ohio	7	11.9%
3	Oklahoma	6	10.2%
4	Virginia	5	8.5%
5	North Carolina	4	6.8%
5	South Carolina	4	6.8%
7	Alabama	2	3.4%
7	Florida	2	3.4%
7	Georgia	2	3.4%
7	Nevada	2	3.4%
11	Arkansas	1	1.7%
11	Maryland	1	1.7%
13	Arizona	0	0.0%
13	California	0	0.0%
13	Colorado	0	0.0%
13	Connecticut	0	0.0%
13	Delaware	0	0.0%
13	Idaho	0	0.0%
13	Illinois	0	0.0%
13	Iowa	0	0.0%
13	Kansas	0	0.0%
13	Kentucky	0	0.0%
13	Louisiana	0	0.0%
13	Mississippi	0	0.0%
13	Missouri	0	0.0%
13	Montana	0	0.0%
13	Nebraska	0	0.0%
13	New Hampshire	0	0.0%
13	New Jersey	0	0.0%
13	New Mexico	0	0.0%
13	New York	0	0.0%
13	Oregon	0	0.0%
13	Pennsylvania	0	0.0%
13	South Dakota	0	0.0%
13	Tennessee	0	0.0%
13	Utah	0	0.0%
13	Washington	0	0.0%
13	Wyoming	0	0.0%
NA	Alaska**	NA	NA
NA	Hawaii**	NA	NA
NA	Indiana**	NA	NA
NA	Maine**	NA	NA
NA	Massachusetts**	NA	NA
NA	Michigan**	NA	NA
NA	Minnesota**	NA	NA
NA	North Dakota**	NA	NA
NA	Rhode Island**	NA	NA
NA	Vermont**	NA	NA
NA	West Virginia**	NA	NA
NA	Wisconsin**	NA	NA
	District of Columbia**	NA	NA

Source: U.S. Department of Justice, Bureau of Justice Statistics
"Capital Punishment 2004" (Bulletin, November 2005, NCJ-211349)
There were no federal prisoners executed in 2004. Fifty-eight of the executions were by lethal injection. One was by electrocution.
***No death penalty as of 12/31/04.*

Prisoners Executed: 1930 to 2004

National Total = 4,803 Prisoners*

ALPHA ORDER

RANK	STATE	EXECUTIONS	% of USA
10	Alabama	165	3.4%
43	Alaska	0	0.0%
22	Arizona	60	1.2%
14	Arkansas	144	3.0%
4	California	302	6.3%
25	Colorado	48	1.0%
30	Connecticut	21	0.4%
29	Delaware	25	0.5%
6	Florida	229	4.8%
2	Georgia	402	8.4%
43	Hawaii	0	0.0%
39	Idaho	4	0.1%
18	Illinois	102	2.1%
23	Indiana	52	1.1%
33	Iowa	18	0.4%
34	Kansas	15	0.3%
17	Kentucky	105	2.2%
11	Louisiana	160	3.3%
43	Maine	0	0.0%
21	Maryland	72	1.5%
28	Massachusetts	27	0.6%
43	Michigan	0	0.0%
43	Minnesota	0	0.0%
11	Mississippi	160	3.3%
16	Missouri	123	2.6%
36	Montana	8	0.2%
38	Nebraska	7	0.1%
26	Nevada	40	0.8%
41	New Hampshire	1	0.0%
20	New Jersey	74	1.5%
35	New Mexico	9	0.2%
3	New York	329	6.8%
5	North Carolina	297	6.2%
43	North Dakota	0	0.0%
8	Ohio	187	3.9%
15	Oklahoma	135	2.8%
30	Oregon	21	0.4%
13	Pennsylvania	155	3.2%
43	Rhode Island	0	0.0%
7	South Carolina	194	4.0%
41	South Dakota	1	0.0%
19	Tennessee	94	2.0%
1	Texas	633	13.2%
32	Utah	19	0.4%
39	Vermont	4	0.1%
9	Virginia	186	3.9%
24	Washington	51	1.1%
26	West Virginia	40	0.8%
43	Wisconsin	0	0.0%
36	Wyoming	8	0.2%

RANK ORDER

RANK	STATE	EXECUTIONS	% of USA
1	Texas	633	13.2%
2	Georgia	402	8.4%
3	New York	329	6.8%
4	California	302	6.3%
5	North Carolina	297	6.2%
6	Florida	229	4.8%
7	South Carolina	194	4.0%
8	Ohio	187	3.9%
9	Virginia	186	3.9%
10	Alabama	165	3.4%
11	Louisiana	160	3.3%
11	Mississippi	160	3.3%
13	Pennsylvania	155	3.2%
14	Arkansas	144	3.0%
15	Oklahoma	135	2.8%
16	Missouri	123	2.6%
17	Kentucky	105	2.2%
18	Illinois	102	2.1%
19	Tennessee	94	2.0%
20	New Jersey	74	1.5%
21	Maryland	72	1.5%
22	Arizona	60	1.2%
23	Indiana	52	1.1%
24	Washington	51	1.1%
25	Colorado	48	1.0%
26	Nevada	40	0.8%
26	West Virginia	40	0.8%
28	Massachusetts	27	0.6%
29	Delaware	25	0.5%
30	Connecticut	21	0.4%
30	Oregon	21	0.4%
32	Utah	19	0.4%
33	Iowa	18	0.4%
34	Kansas	15	0.3%
35	New Mexico	9	0.2%
36	Montana	8	0.2%
36	Wyoming	8	0.2%
38	Nebraska	7	0.1%
39	Idaho	4	0.1%
39	Vermont	4	0.1%
41	New Hampshire	1	0.0%
41	South Dakota	1	0.0%
43	Alaska	0	0.0%
43	Hawaii	0	0.0%
43	Maine	0	0.0%
43	Michigan	0	0.0%
43	Minnesota	0	0.0%
43	North Dakota	0	0.0%
43	Rhode Island	0	0.0%
43	Wisconsin	0	0.0%
	District of Columbia	40	0.8%

Source: U.S. Department of Justice, Bureau of Justice Statistics
    "Capital Punishment 2004" (Bulletin, November 2005, NCJ-211349)
*Includes 36 executions by the federal government. Does not include 160 executions carried out under military authority from 1930 to 1961. There were no executions from 1968 to 1976.

Prisoners Executed: 1977 to 2004

National Total = 944 Prisoners*

RANK	STATE	EXECUTIONS	% of USA
9	Alabama	30	3.2%
33	Alaska	0	0.0%
12	Arizona	22	2.3%
11	Arkansas	26	2.8%
18	California	10	1.1%
28	Colorado	1	0.1%
33	Connecticut	0	0.0%
14	Delaware	13	1.4%
5	Florida	59	6.3%
6	Georgia	36	3.8%
33	Hawaii	0	0.0%
28	Idaho	1	0.1%
15	Illinois	12	1.3%
16	Indiana	11	1.2%
33	Iowa	0	0.0%
33	Kansas	0	0.0%
25	Kentucky	2	0.2%
10	Louisiana	27	2.9%
33	Maine	0	0.0%
21	Maryland	4	0.4%
33	Massachusetts	0	0.0%
33	Michigan	0	0.0%
33	Minnesota	0	0.0%
19	Mississippi	6	0.6%
4	Missouri	61	6.5%
25	Montana	2	0.2%
23	Nebraska	3	0.3%
16	Nevada	11	1.2%
33	New Hampshire	0	0.0%
33	New Jersey	0	0.0%
28	New Mexico	1	0.1%
33	New York	0	0.0%
7	North Carolina	34	3.6%
33	North Dakota	0	0.0%
13	Ohio	15	1.6%
3	Oklahoma	75	7.9%
25	Oregon	2	0.2%
23	Pennsylvania	3	0.3%
33	Rhode Island	0	0.0%
8	South Carolina	32	3.4%
33	South Dakota	0	0.0%
28	Tennessee	1	0.1%
1	Texas	336	35.6%
19	Utah	6	0.6%
33	Vermont	0	0.0%
2	Virginia	94	10.0%
21	Washington	4	0.4%
33	West Virginia	0	0.0%
33	Wisconsin	0	0.0%
28	Wyoming	1	0.1%

RANK	STATE	EXECUTIONS	% of USA
1	Texas	336	35.6%
2	Virginia	94	10.0%
3	Oklahoma	75	7.9%
4	Missouri	61	6.5%
5	Florida	59	6.3%
6	Georgia	36	3.8%
7	North Carolina	34	3.6%
8	South Carolina	32	3.4%
9	Alabama	30	3.2%
10	Louisiana	27	2.9%
11	Arkansas	26	2.8%
12	Arizona	22	2.3%
13	Ohio	15	1.6%
14	Delaware	13	1.4%
15	Illinois	12	1.3%
16	Indiana	11	1.2%
16	Nevada	11	1.2%
18	California	10	1.1%
19	Mississippi	6	0.6%
19	Utah	6	0.6%
21	Maryland	4	0.4%
21	Washington	4	0.4%
23	Nebraska	3	0.3%
23	Pennsylvania	3	0.3%
25	Kentucky	2	0.2%
25	Montana	2	0.2%
25	Oregon	2	0.2%
28	Colorado	1	0.1%
28	Idaho	1	0.1%
28	New Mexico	1	0.1%
28	Tennessee	1	0.1%
28	Wyoming	1	0.1%
33	Alaska	0	0.0%
33	Connecticut	0	0.0%
33	Hawaii	0	0.0%
33	Iowa	0	0.0%
33	Kansas	0	0.0%
33	Maine	0	0.0%
33	Massachusetts	0	0.0%
33	Michigan	0	0.0%
33	Minnesota	0	0.0%
33	New Hampshire	0	0.0%
33	New Jersey	0	0.0%
33	New York	0	0.0%
33	North Dakota	0	0.0%
33	Rhode Island	0	0.0%
33	South Dakota	0	0.0%
33	Vermont	0	0.0%
33	West Virginia	0	0.0%
33	Wisconsin	0	0.0%
	District of Columbia	0	0.0%

Source: U.S. Department of Justice, Bureau of Justice Statistics
   "Capital Punishment 2004" (Bulletin, November 2005, NCJ-211349)
*As of December 31, 2004. Includes three executions by the federal government. All executions since 1977 have been for murder. The most common method of executions was lethal injection (776) followed by electrocution (152), lethal gas (11), hanging (3) and firing squad (2).

Prisoners Sentenced to Death: 1973 to 2004

National Total = 7,486 State Death Sentences*

ALPHA ORDER					RANK ORDER			
RANK	STATE		SENTENCES	% of USA	RANK	STATE	SENTENCES	% of USA
7	Alabama		356	4.8%	1	Texas	979	13.1%
40	Alaska		0	0.0%	2	Florida	890	11.9%
11	Arizona		253	3.4%	3	California	828	11.1%
19	Arkansas		103	1.4%	4	North Carolina	511	6.8%
3	California		828	11.1%	5	Ohio	382	5.1%
31	Colorado		20	0.3%	6	Pennsylvania	365	4.9%
35	Connecticut		9	0.1%	7	Alabama	356	4.8%
24	Delaware		52	0.7%	8	Oklahoma	326	4.4%
2	Florida		890	11.9%	9	Georgia	304	4.1%
9	Georgia		304	4.1%	10	Illinois	297	4.0%
40	Hawaii		0	0.0%	11	Arizona	253	3.4%
26	Idaho		42	0.6%	12	Louisiana	224	3.0%
10	Illinois		297	4.0%	13	Tennessee	212	2.8%
20	Indiana		98	1.3%	14	South Carolina	187	2.5%
40	Iowa		0	0.0%	15	Mississippi	180	2.4%
36	Kansas		8	0.1%	16	Missouri	172	2.3%
21	Kentucky		76	1.0%	17	Virginia	144	1.9%
12	Louisiana		224	3.0%	18	Nevada	140	1.9%
40	Maine		0	0.0%	19	Arkansas	103	1.4%
23	Maryland		53	0.7%	20	Indiana	98	1.3%
38	Massachusetts		4	0.1%	21	Kentucky	76	1.0%
40	Michigan		0	0.0%	22	Oregon	55	0.7%
40	Minnesota		0	0.0%	23	Maryland	53	0.7%
15	Mississippi		180	2.4%	24	Delaware	52	0.7%
16	Missouri		172	2.3%	24	New Jersey	52	0.7%
32	Montana		15	0.2%	26	Idaho	42	0.6%
28	Nebraska		28	0.4%	27	Washington	38	0.5%
18	Nevada		140	1.9%	28	Nebraska	28	0.4%
40	New Hampshire		0	0.0%	28	New Mexico	28	0.4%
24	New Jersey		52	0.7%	30	Utah	26	0.3%
28	New Mexico		28	0.4%	31	Colorado	20	0.3%
34	New York		10	0.1%	32	Montana	15	0.2%
4	North Carolina		511	6.8%	33	Wyoming	12	0.2%
40	North Dakota		0	0.0%	34	New York	10	0.1%
5	Ohio		382	5.1%	35	Connecticut	9	0.1%
8	Oklahoma		326	4.4%	36	Kansas	8	0.1%
22	Oregon		55	0.7%	37	South Dakota	5	0.1%
6	Pennsylvania		365	4.9%	38	Massachusetts	4	0.1%
39	Rhode Island		2	0.0%	39	Rhode Island	2	0.0%
14	South Carolina		187	2.5%	40	Alaska	0	0.0%
37	South Dakota		5	0.1%	40	Hawaii	0	0.0%
13	Tennessee		212	2.8%	40	Iowa	0	0.0%
1	Texas		979	13.1%	40	Maine	0	0.0%
30	Utah		26	0.3%	40	Michigan	0	0.0%
40	Vermont		0	0.0%	40	Minnesota	0	0.0%
17	Virginia		144	1.9%	40	New Hampshire	0	0.0%
27	Washington		38	0.5%	40	North Dakota	0	0.0%
40	West Virginia		0	0.0%	40	Vermont	0	0.0%
40	Wisconsin		0	0.0%	40	West Virginia	0	0.0%
33	Wyoming		12	0.2%	40	Wisconsin	0	0.0%
						District of Columbia	0	0.0%

Source: U.S. Department of Justice, Bureau of Justice Statistics
    "Capital Punishment 2004" (Bulletin, November 2005, NCJ-211349)
*As of December 31, 2004. Does not include 43 federal prisoners sentenced to death. For those sentenced to
death more than once, the numbers are based on the most recent death sentence.

Death Sentences Overturned or Commuted: 1973 to 2004

National Total = 2,928 Sentences*

ALPHA ORDER

RANK	STATE	SENTENCES	% of USA
10	Alabama	115	3.9%
NA	Alaska**	NA	NA
11	Arizona	113	3.9%
19	Arkansas	36	1.2%
8	California	138	4.7%
29	Colorado	14	0.5%
37	Connecticut	2	0.1%
24	Delaware	22	0.8%
1	Florida	427	14.6%
7	Georgia	148	5.1%
NA	Hawaii**	NA	NA
28	Idaho	17	0.6%
3	Illinois	253	8.6%
16	Indiana	56	1.9%
NA	Iowa**	NA	NA
32	Kansas	8	0.3%
19	Kentucky	36	1.2%
12	Louisiana	104	3.6%
NA	Maine**	NA	NA
18	Maryland	38	1.3%
36	Massachusetts	4	0.1%
NA	Michigan**	NA	NA
NA	Minnesota**	NA	NA
13	Mississippi	98	3.3%
17	Missouri	50	1.7%
35	Montana	7	0.2%
29	Nebraska	14	0.5%
21	Nevada	35	1.2%
39	New Hampshire	0	0.0%
22	New Jersey	30	1.0%
23	New Mexico	24	0.8%
32	New York	8	0.3%
2	North Carolina	282	9.6%
NA	North Dakota**	NA	NA
5	Ohio	150	5.1%
6	Oklahoma	149	5.1%
24	Oregon	22	0.8%
9	Pennsylvania	125	4.3%
37	Rhode Island	2	0.1%
15	South Carolina	80	2.7%
39	South Dakota	0	0.0%
14	Tennessee	97	3.3%
4	Texas	165	5.6%
31	Utah	9	0.3%
NA	Vermont**	NA	NA
27	Virginia	20	0.7%
24	Washington	22	0.8%
NA	West Virginia**	NA	NA
NA	Wisconsin**	NA	NA
32	Wyoming	8	0.3%

RANK ORDER

RANK	STATE	SENTENCES	% of USA
1	Florida	427	14.6%
2	North Carolina	282	9.6%
3	Illinois	253	8.6%
4	Texas	165	5.6%
5	Ohio	150	5.1%
6	Oklahoma	149	5.1%
7	Georgia	148	5.1%
8	California	138	4.7%
9	Pennsylvania	125	4.3%
10	Alabama	115	3.9%
11	Arizona	113	3.9%
12	Louisiana	104	3.6%
13	Mississippi	98	3.3%
14	Tennessee	97	3.3%
15	South Carolina	80	2.7%
16	Indiana	56	1.9%
17	Missouri	50	1.7%
18	Maryland	38	1.3%
19	Arkansas	36	1.2%
19	Kentucky	36	1.2%
21	Nevada	35	1.2%
22	New Jersey	30	1.0%
23	New Mexico	24	0.8%
24	Delaware	22	0.8%
24	Oregon	22	0.8%
24	Washington	22	0.8%
27	Virginia	20	0.7%
28	Idaho	17	0.6%
29	Colorado	14	0.5%
29	Nebraska	14	0.5%
31	Utah	9	0.3%
32	Kansas	8	0.3%
32	New York	8	0.3%
32	Wyoming	8	0.3%
35	Montana	7	0.2%
36	Massachusetts	4	0.1%
37	Connecticut	2	0.1%
37	Rhode Island	2	0.1%
39	New Hampshire	0	0.0%
39	South Dakota	0	0.0%
NA	Alaska**	NA	NA
NA	Hawaii**	NA	NA
NA	Iowa**	NA	NA
NA	Maine**	NA	NA
NA	Michigan**	NA	NA
NA	Minnesota**	NA	NA
NA	North Dakota**	NA	NA
NA	Vermont**	NA	NA
NA	West Virginia**	NA	NA
NA	Wisconsin**	NA	NA
	District of Columbia**	NA	NA

*Source: Morgan Quitno Press using data from U.S. Department of Justice, Bureau of Justice Statistics
"Capital Punishment 2004" (Bulletin, November 2005, NCJ-211349)*
*As of December 31, 2004. Does not include seven federal prisoners whose sentences were overturned or commuted.
**Not applicable.

Percent of Death Penalty Sentences Overturned or Commuted: 1973 to 2004

National Percent = 39.1% of Sentences*

ALPHA ORDER

RANK	STATE	PERCENT
32	Alabama	32.3
NA	Alaska**	NA
23	Arizona	44.7
29	Arkansas	35.0
37	California	16.7
8	Colorado	70.0
35	Connecticut	22.2
25	Delaware	42.3
17	Florida	48.0
16	Georgia	48.7
NA	Hawaii**	NA
26	Idaho	40.5
5	Illinois	85.2
12	Indiana	57.1
NA	Iowa**	NA
1	Kansas	100.0
18	Kentucky	47.4
20	Louisiana	46.4
NA	Maine**	NA
7	Maryland	71.7
1	Massachusetts	100.0
NA	Michigan**	NA
NA	Minnesota**	NA
14	Mississippi	54.4
33	Missouri	29.1
19	Montana	46.7
15	Nebraska	50.0
34	Nevada	25.0
39	New Hampshire	0.0
11	New Jersey	57.7
4	New Mexico	85.7
6	New York	80.0
13	North Carolina	55.2
NA	North Dakota**	NA
28	Ohio	39.3
22	Oklahoma	45.7
27	Oregon	40.0
31	Pennsylvania	34.2
1	Rhode Island	100.0
24	South Carolina	42.8
39	South Dakota	0.0
21	Tennessee	45.8
36	Texas	16.9
30	Utah	34.6
NA	Vermont**	NA
38	Virginia	13.9
10	Washington	57.9
NA	West Virginia**	NA
NA	Wisconsin**	NA
9	Wyoming	66.7

RANK ORDER

RANK	STATE	PERCENT
1	Kansas	100.0
1	Massachusetts	100.0
1	Rhode Island	100.0
4	New Mexico	85.7
5	Illinois	85.2
6	New York	80.0
7	Maryland	71.7
8	Colorado	70.0
9	Wyoming	66.7
10	Washington	57.9
11	New Jersey	57.7
12	Indiana	57.1
13	North Carolina	55.2
14	Mississippi	54.4
15	Nebraska	50.0
16	Georgia	48.7
17	Florida	48.0
18	Kentucky	47.4
19	Montana	46.7
20	Louisiana	46.4
21	Tennessee	45.8
22	Oklahoma	45.7
23	Arizona	44.7
24	South Carolina	42.8
25	Delaware	42.3
26	Idaho	40.5
27	Oregon	40.0
28	Ohio	39.3
29	Arkansas	35.0
30	Utah	34.6
31	Pennsylvania	34.2
32	Alabama	32.3
33	Missouri	29.1
34	Nevada	25.0
35	Connecticut	22.2
36	Texas	16.9
37	California	16.7
38	Virginia	13.9
39	New Hampshire	0.0
39	South Dakota	0.0
NA	Alaska**	NA
NA	Hawaii**	NA
NA	Iowa**	NA
NA	Maine**	NA
NA	Michigan**	NA
NA	Minnesota**	NA
NA	North Dakota**	NA
NA	Vermont**	NA
NA	West Virginia**	NA
NA	Wisconsin**	NA

District of Columbia**   NA

Source: Morgan Quitno Press using data from U.S. Department of Justice, Bureau of Justice Statistics
   "Capital Punishment 2004" (Bulletin, November 2005, NCJ-211349)
*As of December 31, 2004. National percent does not include federal sentences or prisoners whose sentences
were overturned. Seven of 43 (16.3%) federal death penalty sentences have been overturned or commuted.
**Not applicable.

State Prisoner Deaths in 2003

National Total = 3,344 Deaths*

ALPHA ORDER

RANK	STATE	DEATHS	% of USA
9	Alabama	100	3.0%
47	Alaska	5	0.1%
14	Arizona	86	2.6%
26	Arkansas	39	1.2%
2	California	333	10.0%
24	Colorado	51	1.5%
27	Connecticut	36	1.1%
33	Delaware	19	0.6%
3	Florida	224	6.7%
6	Georgia	139	4.2%
43	Hawaii	8	0.2%
36	Idaho	13	0.4%
15	Illinois	81	2.4%
22	Indiana	60	1.8%
36	Iowa	13	0.4%
29	Kansas	32	1.0%
16	Kentucky	77	2.3%
13	Louisiana	87	2.6%
48	Maine	3	0.1%
19	Maryland	67	2.0%
30	Massachusetts	30	0.9%
7	Michigan	132	3.9%
35	Minnesota	14	0.4%
23	Mississippi	58	1.7%
18	Missouri	68	2.0%
36	Montana	13	0.4%
44	Nebraska	7	0.2%
32	Nevada	24	0.7%
45	New Hampshire	6	0.2%
20	New Jersey	63	1.9%
40	New Mexico	11	0.3%
4	New York	200	6.0%
17	North Carolina	76	2.3%
50	North Dakota	1	0.0%
8	Ohio	106	3.2%
11	Oklahoma	96	2.9%
31	Oregon	25	0.7%
5	Pennsylvania	147	4.4%
42	Rhode Island	9	0.3%
20	South Carolina	63	1.9%
39	South Dakota	12	0.4%
10	Tennessee	98	2.9%
1	Texas	407	12.2%
40	Utah	11	0.3%
45	Vermont	6	0.2%
11	Virginia	96	2.9%
28	Washington	34	1.0%
34	West Virginia	15	0.4%
25	Wisconsin	41	1.2%
49	Wyoming	2	0.1%

RANK ORDER

RANK	STATE	DEATHS	% of USA
1	Texas	407	12.2%
2	California	333	10.0%
3	Florida	224	6.7%
4	New York	200	6.0%
5	Pennsylvania	147	4.4%
6	Georgia	139	4.2%
7	Michigan	132	3.9%
8	Ohio	106	3.2%
9	Alabama	100	3.0%
10	Tennessee	98	2.9%
11	Oklahoma	96	2.9%
11	Virginia	96	2.9%
13	Louisiana	87	2.6%
14	Arizona	86	2.6%
15	Illinois	81	2.4%
16	Kentucky	77	2.3%
17	North Carolina	76	2.3%
18	Missouri	68	2.0%
19	Maryland	67	2.0%
20	New Jersey	63	1.9%
20	South Carolina	63	1.9%
22	Indiana	60	1.8%
23	Mississippi	58	1.7%
24	Colorado	51	1.5%
25	Wisconsin	41	1.2%
26	Arkansas	39	1.2%
27	Connecticut	36	1.1%
28	Washington	34	1.0%
29	Kansas	32	1.0%
30	Massachusetts	30	0.9%
31	Oregon	25	0.7%
32	Nevada	24	0.7%
33	Delaware	19	0.6%
34	West Virginia	15	0.4%
35	Minnesota	14	0.4%
36	Idaho	13	0.4%
36	Iowa	13	0.4%
36	Montana	13	0.4%
39	South Dakota	12	0.4%
40	New Mexico	11	0.3%
40	Utah	11	0.3%
42	Rhode Island	9	0.3%
43	Hawaii	8	0.2%
44	Nebraska	7	0.2%
45	New Hampshire	6	0.2%
45	Vermont	6	0.2%
47	Alaska	5	0.1%
48	Maine	3	0.1%
49	Wyoming	2	0.1%
50	North Dakota	1	0.0%
	District of Columbia**	NA	NA

Source: U.S. Department of Justice, Bureau of Justice Statistics
   "HIV in Prisons and Jails, 2003" (Bulletin, September 2005, NCJ 210344)
*Does not include deaths of federal prisoners.
**Not available.

Death Rate of State Prisoners in 2003

National Rate = 258 State Prisoner Deaths per 100,000 Inmates*

ALPHA ORDER				RANK ORDER		
RANK	STATE	RATE		RANK	STATE	RATE
8	Alabama	352		1	Kentucky	470
48	Alaska	113		2	Oklahoma	417
16	Arizona	280		3	South Dakota	392
10	Arkansas	315		4	Tennessee	386
36	California	204		5	Montana	378
21	Colorado	267		6	Pennsylvania	363
43	Connecticut	175		7	Kansas	355
19	Delaware	276		8	Alabama	352
17	Florida	279		9	West Virginia	319
13	Georgia	296		10	Arkansas	315
47	Hawaii	142		11	New York	303
32	Idaho	223		12	Vermont	302
39	Illinois	188		13	Georgia	296
23	Indiana	266		14	Massachusetts	285
45	Iowa	155		15	Mississippi	282
7	Kansas	355		16	Arizona	280
1	Kentucky	470		17	Florida	279
28	Louisiana	241		18	Maryland	277
46	Maine	149		19	Delaware	276
18	Maryland	277		19	Virginia	276
14	Massachusetts	285		21	Colorado	267
21	Michigan	267		21	Michigan	267
40	Minnesota	184		23	Indiana	266
15	Mississippi	282		24	South Carolina	260
34	Missouri	222		25	Rhode Island	252
5	Montana	378		26	Texas	243
44	Nebraska	171		27	New Hampshire	242
30	Nevada	228		28	Louisiana	241
27	New Hampshire	242		29	Ohio	231
32	New Jersey	223		30	Nevada	228
42	New Mexico	179		30	North Carolina	228
11	New York	303		32	Idaho	223
30	North Carolina	228		32	New Jersey	223
50	North Dakota	86		34	Missouri	222
29	Ohio	231		35	Washington	209
2	Oklahoma	417		36	California	204
37	Oregon	201		37	Oregon	201
6	Pennsylvania	363		38	Utah	196
25	Rhode Island	252		39	Illinois	188
24	South Carolina	260		40	Minnesota	184
3	South Dakota	392		41	Wisconsin	183
4	Tennessee	386		42	New Mexico	179
26	Texas	243		43	Connecticut	175
38	Utah	196		44	Nebraska	171
12	Vermont	302		45	Iowa	155
19	Virginia	276		46	Maine	149
35	Washington	209		47	Hawaii	142
9	West Virginia	319		48	Alaska	113
41	Wisconsin	183		49	Wyoming	111
49	Wyoming	111		50	North Dakota	86
				District of Columbia**		NA

Source: U.S. Department of Justice, Bureau of Justice Statistics
    "HIV in Prisons and Jails, 2003" (Bulletin, September 2005, NCJ 210344)
*Does not include deaths of federal prisoners.
**Not available.

AIDS-Related Deaths of State Prisoners in 2003

National Total = 268 Deaths

ALPHA ORDER

RANK	STATE	DEATHS	% of USA
11	Alabama	8	3.0%
33	Alaska	0	0.0%
20	Arizona	3	1.1%
20	Arkansas	3	1.1%
6	California	13	4.9%
24	Colorado	2	0.7%
11	Connecticut	8	3.0%
14	Delaware	6	2.2%
1	Florida	42	15.7%
4	Georgia	18	6.7%
33	Hawaii	0	0.0%
33	Idaho	0	0.0%
8	Illinois	12	4.5%
24	Indiana	2	0.7%
33	Iowa	0	0.0%
27	Kansas	1	0.4%
17	Kentucky	4	1.5%
8	Louisiana	12	4.5%
33	Maine	0	0.0%
6	Maryland	13	4.9%
33	Massachusetts	0	0.0%
20	Michigan	3	1.1%
33	Minnesota	0	0.0%
17	Mississippi	4	1.5%
27	Missouri	1	0.4%
33	Montana	0	0.0%
27	Nebraska	1	0.4%
33	Nevada	0	0.0%
33	New Hampshire	0	0.0%
10	New Jersey	10	3.7%
33	New Mexico	0	0.0%
2	New York	27	10.1%
17	North Carolina	4	1.5%
33	North Dakota	0	0.0%
11	Ohio	8	3.0%
24	Oklahoma	2	0.7%
33	Oregon	0	0.0%
5	Pennsylvania	17	6.3%
33	Rhode Island	0	0.0%
20	South Carolina	3	1.1%
33	South Dakota	0	0.0%
14	Tennessee	6	2.2%
2	Texas	27	10.1%
33	Utah	0	0.0%
27	Vermont	1	0.4%
16	Virginia	5	1.9%
27	Washington	1	0.4%
33	West Virginia	0	0.0%
27	Wisconsin	1	0.4%
33	Wyoming	0	0.0%

RANK ORDER

RANK	STATE	DEATHS	% of USA
1	Florida	42	15.7%
2	New York	27	10.1%
2	Texas	27	10.1%
4	Georgia	18	6.7%
5	Pennsylvania	17	6.3%
6	California	13	4.9%
6	Maryland	13	4.9%
8	Illinois	12	4.5%
8	Louisiana	12	4.5%
10	New Jersey	10	3.7%
11	Alabama	8	3.0%
11	Connecticut	8	3.0%
11	Ohio	8	3.0%
14	Delaware	6	2.2%
14	Tennessee	6	2.2%
16	Virginia	5	1.9%
17	Kentucky	4	1.5%
17	Mississippi	4	1.5%
17	North Carolina	4	1.5%
20	Arizona	3	1.1%
20	Arkansas	3	1.1%
20	Michigan	3	1.1%
20	South Carolina	3	1.1%
24	Colorado	2	0.7%
24	Indiana	2	0.7%
24	Oklahoma	2	0.7%
27	Kansas	1	0.4%
27	Missouri	1	0.4%
27	Nebraska	1	0.4%
27	Vermont	1	0.4%
27	Washington	1	0.4%
27	Wisconsin	1	0.4%
33	Alaska	0	0.0%
33	Hawaii	0	0.0%
33	Idaho	0	0.0%
33	Iowa	0	0.0%
33	Maine	0	0.0%
33	Massachusetts	0	0.0%
33	Minnesota	0	0.0%
33	Montana	0	0.0%
33	Nevada	0	0.0%
33	New Hampshire	0	0.0%
33	New Mexico	0	0.0%
33	North Dakota	0	0.0%
33	Oregon	0	0.0%
33	Rhode Island	0	0.0%
33	South Dakota	0	0.0%
33	Utah	0	0.0%
33	West Virginia	0	0.0%
33	Wyoming	0	0.0%
	District of Columbia**	NA	NA

Source: U.S. Department of Justice, Bureau of Justice Statistics
"HIV in Prisons and Jails, 2003" (Bulletin, September 2005, NCJ 210344)
*Not available.

AIDS-Related Death Rate for State Prisoners in 2003

National Rate = 21 State Prisoner Deaths per 100,000 Inmates

ALPHA ORDER			RANK ORDER		
RANK	STATE	RATE	RANK	STATE	RATE
11	Alabama	28	1	Delaware	87
33	Alaska	0	2	Maryland	54
24	Arizona	10	3	Florida	52
13	Arkansas	24	4	Vermont	50
28	California	8	5	Pennsylvania	42
24	Colorado	10	6	New York	41
7	Connecticut	39	7	Connecticut	39
1	Delaware	87	8	Georgia	38
3	Florida	52	9	New Jersey	35
8	Georgia	38	10	Louisiana	33
33	Hawaii	0	11	Alabama	28
33	Idaho	0	11	Illinois	28
11	Illinois	28	13	Arkansas	24
26	Indiana	9	13	Kentucky	24
33	Iowa	0	13	Nebraska	24
23	Kansas	11	13	Tennessee	24
13	Kentucky	24	17	Mississippi	19
10	Louisiana	33	18	Ohio	17
33	Maine	0	19	Texas	16
2	Maryland	54	20	Virginia	14
33	Massachusetts	0	21	North Carolina	12
29	Michigan	6	21	South Carolina	12
33	Minnesota	0	23	Kansas	11
17	Mississippi	19	24	Arizona	10
32	Missouri	3	24	Colorado	10
33	Montana	0	26	Indiana	9
13	Nebraska	24	26	Oklahoma	9
33	Nevada	0	28	California	8
33	New Hampshire	0	29	Michigan	6
9	New Jersey	35	29	Washington	6
33	New Mexico	0	31	Wisconsin	4
6	New York	41	32	Missouri	3
21	North Carolina	12	33	Alaska	0
33	North Dakota	0	33	Hawaii	0
18	Ohio	17	33	Idaho	0
26	Oklahoma	9	33	Iowa	0
33	Oregon	0	33	Maine	0
5	Pennsylvania	42	33	Massachusetts	0
33	Rhode Island	0	33	Minnesota	0
21	South Carolina	12	33	Montana	0
33	South Dakota	0	33	Nevada	0
13	Tennessee	24	33	New Hampshire	0
19	Texas	16	33	New Mexico	0
33	Utah	0	33	North Dakota	0
4	Vermont	50	33	Oregon	0
20	Virginia	14	33	Rhode Island	0
29	Washington	6	33	South Dakota	0
33	West Virginia	0	33	Utah	0
31	Wisconsin	4	33	West Virginia	0
33	Wyoming	0	33	Wyoming	0
				District of Columbia**	NA

Source: U.S. Department of Justice, Bureau of Justice Statistics
"HIV in Prisons and Jails, 2003" (Bulletin, September 2005, NCJ 210344)
*Not available.

AIDS-Related Deaths of State Prisoners
As a Percent of All Prison Deaths in 2003
National Percent = 8.0% of Deaths*

<table>
<tr><td colspan="3">ALPHA ORDER</td><td colspan="3">RANK ORDER</td></tr>
<tr><td>RANK</td><td>STATE</td><td>PERCENT</td><td>RANK</td><td>STATE</td><td>PERCENT</td></tr>
<tr><td>13</td><td>Alabama</td><td>8.0</td><td>1</td><td>Delaware</td><td>31.6</td></tr>
<tr><td>33</td><td>Alaska</td><td>0.0</td><td>2</td><td>Connecticut</td><td>22.2</td></tr>
<tr><td>25</td><td>Arizona</td><td>3.5</td><td>3</td><td>Maryland</td><td>19.4</td></tr>
<tr><td>14</td><td>Arkansas</td><td>7.7</td><td>4</td><td>Florida</td><td>18.8</td></tr>
<tr><td>23</td><td>California</td><td>3.9</td><td>5</td><td>Vermont</td><td>16.7</td></tr>
<tr><td>23</td><td>Colorado</td><td>3.9</td><td>6</td><td>New Jersey</td><td>15.9</td></tr>
<tr><td>2</td><td>Connecticut</td><td>22.2</td><td>7</td><td>Illinois</td><td>14.8</td></tr>
<tr><td>1</td><td>Delaware</td><td>31.6</td><td>8</td><td>Nebraska</td><td>14.3</td></tr>
<tr><td>4</td><td>Florida</td><td>18.8</td><td>9</td><td>Louisiana</td><td>13.8</td></tr>
<tr><td>11</td><td>Georgia</td><td>12.9</td><td>10</td><td>New York</td><td>13.5</td></tr>
<tr><td>33</td><td>Hawaii</td><td>0.0</td><td>11</td><td>Georgia</td><td>12.9</td></tr>
<tr><td>33</td><td>Idaho</td><td>0.0</td><td>12</td><td>Pennsylvania</td><td>11.6</td></tr>
<tr><td>7</td><td>Illinois</td><td>14.8</td><td>13</td><td>Alabama</td><td>8.0</td></tr>
<tr><td>26</td><td>Indiana</td><td>3.3</td><td>14</td><td>Arkansas</td><td>7.7</td></tr>
<tr><td>33</td><td>Iowa</td><td>0.0</td><td>15</td><td>Ohio</td><td>7.5</td></tr>
<tr><td>27</td><td>Kansas</td><td>3.1</td><td>16</td><td>Mississippi</td><td>6.9</td></tr>
<tr><td>20</td><td>Kentucky</td><td>5.2</td><td>17</td><td>Texas</td><td>6.6</td></tr>
<tr><td>9</td><td>Louisiana</td><td>13.8</td><td>18</td><td>Tennessee</td><td>6.1</td></tr>
<tr><td>33</td><td>Maine</td><td>0.0</td><td>19</td><td>North Carolina</td><td>5.3</td></tr>
<tr><td>3</td><td>Maryland</td><td>19.4</td><td>20</td><td>Kentucky</td><td>5.2</td></tr>
<tr><td>33</td><td>Massachusetts</td><td>0.0</td><td>20</td><td>Virginia</td><td>5.2</td></tr>
<tr><td>30</td><td>Michigan</td><td>2.3</td><td>22</td><td>South Carolina</td><td>4.8</td></tr>
<tr><td>33</td><td>Minnesota</td><td>0.0</td><td>23</td><td>California</td><td>3.9</td></tr>
<tr><td>16</td><td>Mississippi</td><td>6.9</td><td>23</td><td>Colorado</td><td>3.9</td></tr>
<tr><td>32</td><td>Missouri</td><td>1.5</td><td>25</td><td>Arizona</td><td>3.5</td></tr>
<tr><td>33</td><td>Montana</td><td>0.0</td><td>26</td><td>Indiana</td><td>3.3</td></tr>
<tr><td>8</td><td>Nebraska</td><td>14.3</td><td>27</td><td>Kansas</td><td>3.1</td></tr>
<tr><td>33</td><td>Nevada</td><td>0.0</td><td>28</td><td>Washington</td><td>2.9</td></tr>
<tr><td>33</td><td>New Hampshire</td><td>0.0</td><td>29</td><td>Wisconsin</td><td>2.4</td></tr>
<tr><td>6</td><td>New Jersey</td><td>15.9</td><td>30</td><td>Michigan</td><td>2.3</td></tr>
<tr><td>33</td><td>New Mexico</td><td>0.0</td><td>31</td><td>Oklahoma</td><td>2.1</td></tr>
<tr><td>10</td><td>New York</td><td>13.5</td><td>32</td><td>Missouri</td><td>1.5</td></tr>
<tr><td>19</td><td>North Carolina</td><td>5.3</td><td>33</td><td>Alaska</td><td>0.0</td></tr>
<tr><td>33</td><td>North Dakota</td><td>0.0</td><td>33</td><td>Hawaii</td><td>0.0</td></tr>
<tr><td>15</td><td>Ohio</td><td>7.5</td><td>33</td><td>Idaho</td><td>0.0</td></tr>
<tr><td>31</td><td>Oklahoma</td><td>2.1</td><td>33</td><td>Iowa</td><td>0.0</td></tr>
<tr><td>33</td><td>Oregon</td><td>0.0</td><td>33</td><td>Maine</td><td>0.0</td></tr>
<tr><td>12</td><td>Pennsylvania</td><td>11.6</td><td>33</td><td>Massachusetts</td><td>0.0</td></tr>
<tr><td>33</td><td>Rhode Island</td><td>0.0</td><td>33</td><td>Minnesota</td><td>0.0</td></tr>
<tr><td>22</td><td>South Carolina</td><td>4.8</td><td>33</td><td>Montana</td><td>0.0</td></tr>
<tr><td>33</td><td>South Dakota</td><td>0.0</td><td>33</td><td>Nevada</td><td>0.0</td></tr>
<tr><td>18</td><td>Tennessee</td><td>6.1</td><td>33</td><td>New Hampshire</td><td>0.0</td></tr>
<tr><td>17</td><td>Texas</td><td>6.6</td><td>33</td><td>New Mexico</td><td>0.0</td></tr>
<tr><td>33</td><td>Utah</td><td>0.0</td><td>33</td><td>North Dakota</td><td>0.0</td></tr>
<tr><td>5</td><td>Vermont</td><td>16.7</td><td>33</td><td>Oregon</td><td>0.0</td></tr>
<tr><td>20</td><td>Virginia</td><td>5.2</td><td>33</td><td>Rhode Island</td><td>0.0</td></tr>
<tr><td>28</td><td>Washington</td><td>2.9</td><td>33</td><td>South Dakota</td><td>0.0</td></tr>
<tr><td>33</td><td>West Virginia</td><td>0.0</td><td>33</td><td>Utah</td><td>0.0</td></tr>
<tr><td>29</td><td>Wisconsin</td><td>2.4</td><td>33</td><td>West Virginia</td><td>0.0</td></tr>
<tr><td>33</td><td>Wyoming</td><td>0.0</td><td>33</td><td>Wyoming</td><td>0.0</td></tr>
<tr><td></td><td></td><td></td><td></td><td>District of Columbia**</td><td>NA</td></tr>
</table>

Source: Morgan Quitno Press using data from U.S. Department of Justice, Bureau of Justice Statistics
"HIV in Prisons and Jails, 2003" (Bulletin, September 2005, NCJ 210344)
*Not available.

State Prisoners Known to be Positive for HIV Infection/AIDS in 2003

National Total = 22,028 Inmates*

ALPHA ORDER

RANK	STATE	INMATES	% of USA
17	Alabama	270	1.2%
NA	Alaska**	NA	NA
25	Arizona	123	0.6%
29	Arkansas	94	0.4%
4	California	1,196	5.4%
22	Colorado	162	0.7%
11	Connecticut	572	2.6%
28	Delaware	105	0.5%
2	Florida	3,112	14.1%
5	Georgia	1,095	5.0%
36	Hawaii	27	0.1%
37	Idaho	22	0.1%
12	Illinois	551	2.5%
NA	Indiana**	NA	NA
34	Iowa	31	0.1%
33	Kansas	32	0.1%
NA	Kentucky**	NA	NA
14	Louisiana	511	2.3%
42	Maine	10	0.0%
6	Maryland	988	4.5%
19	Massachusetts	230	1.0%
10	Michigan	579	2.6%
31	Minnesota	40	0.2%
21	Mississippi	200	0.9%
18	Missouri	268	1.2%
45	Montana	4	0.0%
38	Nebraska	21	0.1%
27	Nevada	107	0.5%
38	New Hampshire	21	0.1%
8	New Jersey	657	3.0%
35	New Mexico	29	0.1%
1	New York	5,000	22.7%
9	North Carolina	640	2.9%
46	North Dakota	2	0.0%
15	Ohio	416	1.9%
22	Oklahoma	162	0.7%
NA	Oregon**	NA	NA
7	Pennsylvania	775	3.5%
26	Rhode Island	120	0.5%
13	South Carolina	520	2.4%
41	South Dakota	11	0.0%
20	Tennessee	208	0.9%
3	Texas	2,460	11.2%
32	Utah	37	0.2%
43	Vermont	9	0.0%
16	Virginia	361	1.6%
30	Washington	93	0.4%
40	West Virginia	14	0.1%
24	Wisconsin	136	0.6%
44	Wyoming	7	0.0%

RANK ORDER

RANK	STATE	INMATES	% of USA
1	New York	5,000	22.7%
2	Florida	3,112	14.1%
3	Texas	2,460	11.2%
4	California	1,196	5.4%
5	Georgia	1,095	5.0%
6	Maryland	988	4.5%
7	Pennsylvania	775	3.5%
8	New Jersey	657	3.0%
9	North Carolina	640	2.9%
10	Michigan	579	2.6%
11	Connecticut	572	2.6%
12	Illinois	551	2.5%
13	South Carolina	520	2.4%
14	Louisiana	511	2.3%
15	Ohio	416	1.9%
16	Virginia	361	1.6%
17	Alabama	270	1.2%
18	Missouri	268	1.2%
19	Massachusetts	230	1.0%
20	Tennessee	208	0.9%
21	Mississippi	200	0.9%
22	Colorado	162	0.7%
22	Oklahoma	162	0.7%
24	Wisconsin	136	0.6%
25	Arizona	123	0.6%
26	Rhode Island	120	0.5%
27	Nevada	107	0.5%
28	Delaware	105	0.5%
29	Arkansas	94	0.4%
30	Washington	93	0.4%
31	Minnesota	40	0.2%
32	Utah	37	0.2%
33	Kansas	32	0.1%
34	Iowa	31	0.1%
35	New Mexico	29	0.1%
36	Hawaii	27	0.1%
37	Idaho	22	0.1%
38	Nebraska	21	0.1%
38	New Hampshire	21	0.1%
40	West Virginia	14	0.1%
41	South Dakota	11	0.0%
42	Maine	10	0.0%
43	Vermont	9	0.0%
44	Wyoming	7	0.0%
45	Montana	4	0.0%
46	North Dakota	2	0.0%
NA	Alaska**	NA	NA
NA	Indiana**	NA	NA
NA	Kentucky**	NA	NA
NA	Oregon**	NA	NA
	District of Columbia**	NA	NA

Source: U.S. Department of Justice, Bureau of Justice Statistics
   "HIV in Prisons and Jails, 2003" (Bulletin, September 2005, NCJ 210344)
*As of December 31, 2003. Does not include 1,631 positive federal inmates.
**Not available. The District of Columbia prisoners are included in the federal figures.

State Prisoners Known to be Positive for HIV Infection/AIDS
As a Percent of Total Prison Population in 2003
National Percent = 2.0% of State Prisoners*

ALPHA ORDER

RANK	STATE	PERCENT
20	Alabama	1.0
NA	Alaska**	NA
40	Arizona	0.4
28	Arkansas	0.7
28	California	0.7
20	Colorado	1.0
5	Connecticut	3.2
14	Delaware	1.6
3	Florida	3.9
8	Georgia	2.3
28	Hawaii	0.7
35	Idaho	0.5
17	Illinois	1.3
NA	Indiana**	NA
40	Iowa	0.4
44	Kansas	0.3
NA	Kentucky**	NA
7	Louisiana	2.6
35	Maine	0.5
2	Maryland	4.2
8	Massachusetts	2.3
18	Michigan	1.2
35	Minnesota	0.5
14	Mississippi	1.6
25	Missouri	0.9
45	Montana	0.2
35	Nebraska	0.5
20	Nevada	1.0
25	New Hampshire	0.9
6	New Jersey	2.8
35	New Mexico	0.5
1	New York	7.6
11	North Carolina	1.9
45	North Dakota	0.2
20	Ohio	1.0
20	Oklahoma	1.0
NA	Oregon**	NA
11	Pennsylvania	1.9
4	Rhode Island	3.4
8	South Carolina	2.3
40	South Dakota	0.4
16	Tennessee	1.5
13	Texas	1.8
27	Utah	0.8
32	Vermont	0.6
18	Virginia	1.2
32	Washington	0.6
40	West Virginia	0.4
28	Wisconsin	0.7
32	Wyoming	0.6

RANK ORDER

RANK	STATE	PERCENT
1	New York	7.6
2	Maryland	4.2
3	Florida	3.9
4	Rhode Island	3.4
5	Connecticut	3.2
6	New Jersey	2.8
7	Louisiana	2.6
8	Georgia	2.3
8	Massachusetts	2.3
8	South Carolina	2.3
11	North Carolina	1.9
11	Pennsylvania	1.9
13	Texas	1.8
14	Delaware	1.6
14	Mississippi	1.6
16	Tennessee	1.5
17	Illinois	1.3
18	Michigan	1.2
18	Virginia	1.2
20	Alabama	1.0
20	Colorado	1.0
20	Nevada	1.0
20	Ohio	1.0
20	Oklahoma	1.0
25	Missouri	0.9
25	New Hampshire	0.9
27	Utah	0.8
28	Arkansas	0.7
28	California	0.7
28	Hawaii	0.7
28	Wisconsin	0.7
32	Vermont	0.6
32	Washington	0.6
32	Wyoming	0.6
35	Idaho	0.5
35	Maine	0.5
35	Minnesota	0.5
35	Nebraska	0.5
35	New Mexico	0.5
40	Arizona	0.4
40	Iowa	0.4
40	South Dakota	0.4
40	West Virginia	0.4
44	Kansas	0.3
45	Montana	0.2
45	North Dakota	0.2
NA	Alaska**	NA
NA	Indiana**	NA
NA	Kentucky**	NA
NA	Oregon**	NA
	District of Columbia**	NA

Source: U.S. Department of Justice, Bureau of Justice Statistics
  "HIV in Prisons and Jails, 2003" (Bulletin, September 2005, NCJ 210344)
*Federal rate is 1.1%, combined state and federal rate is 1.9%.
**Not available.

Adults Under State Correctional Supervision in 2003

National Total = 6,607,000 Adults*

ALPHA ORDER

RANK	STATE	ADULTS	% of USA
26	Alabama	74,200	1.1%
47	Alaska	10,900	0.2%
17	Arizona	112,700	1.7%
30	Arkansas	59,600	0.9%
2	California	725,600	11.0%
23	Colorado	84,700	1.3%
27	Connecticut	74,100	1.1%
38	Delaware	26,200	0.4%
4	Florida	423,900	6.4%
3	Georgia	533,500	8.1%
40	Hawaii	25,200	0.4%
32	Idaho	43,600	0.7%
9	Illinois	244,400	3.7%
13	Indiana	155,300	2.4%
33	Iowa	36,200	0.5%
34	Kansas	34,400	0.5%
28	Kentucky	63,100	1.0%
19	Louisiana	106,600	1.6%
43	Maine	13,400	0.2%
15	Maryland	128,400	1.9%
14	Massachusetts	153,300	2.3%
8	Michigan	263,100	4.0%
16	Minnesota	127,900	1.9%
31	Mississippi	47,500	0.7%
18	Missouri	110,600	1.7%
44	Montana	12,500	0.2%
39	Nebraska	25,800	0.4%
35	Nevada	32,400	0.5%
48	New Hampshire	9,400	0.1%
11	New Jersey	183,600	2.8%
36	New Mexico	30,100	0.5%
7	New York	278,400	4.2%
12	North Carolina	165,500	2.5%
50	North Dakota	5,700	0.1%
6	Ohio	301,400	4.6%
29	Oklahoma	62,100	0.9%
24	Oregon	83,100	1.3%
5	Pennsylvania	315,000	4.8%
37	Rhode Island	27,700	0.4%
25	South Carolina	79,400	1.2%
46	South Dakota	11,600	0.2%
22	Tennessee	90,900	1.4%
1	Texas	738,000	11.2%
41	Utah	22,400	0.3%
45	Vermont	12,000	0.2%
20	Virginia	102,500	1.6%
10	Washington	199,500	3.0%
42	West Virginia	14,000	0.2%
21	Wisconsin	101,800	1.5%
49	Wyoming	8,100	0.1%

RANK ORDER

RANK	STATE	ADULTS	% of USA
1	Texas	738,000	11.2%
2	California	725,600	11.0%
3	Georgia	533,500	8.1%
4	Florida	423,900	6.4%
5	Pennsylvania	315,000	4.8%
6	Ohio	301,400	4.6%
7	New York	278,400	4.2%
8	Michigan	263,100	4.0%
9	Illinois	244,400	3.7%
10	Washington	199,500	3.0%
11	New Jersey	183,600	2.8%
12	North Carolina	165,500	2.5%
13	Indiana	155,300	2.4%
14	Massachusetts	153,300	2.3%
15	Maryland	128,400	1.9%
16	Minnesota	127,900	1.9%
17	Arizona	112,700	1.7%
18	Missouri	110,600	1.7%
19	Louisiana	106,600	1.6%
20	Virginia	102,500	1.6%
21	Wisconsin	101,800	1.5%
22	Tennessee	90,900	1.4%
23	Colorado	84,700	1.3%
24	Oregon	83,100	1.3%
25	South Carolina	79,400	1.2%
26	Alabama	74,200	1.1%
27	Connecticut	74,100	1.1%
28	Kentucky	63,100	1.0%
29	Oklahoma	62,100	0.9%
30	Arkansas	59,600	0.9%
31	Mississippi	47,500	0.7%
32	Idaho	43,600	0.7%
33	Iowa	36,200	0.5%
34	Kansas	34,400	0.5%
35	Nevada	32,400	0.5%
36	New Mexico	30,100	0.5%
37	Rhode Island	27,700	0.4%
38	Delaware	26,200	0.4%
39	Nebraska	25,800	0.4%
40	Hawaii	25,200	0.4%
41	Utah	22,400	0.3%
42	West Virginia	14,000	0.2%
43	Maine	13,400	0.2%
44	Montana	12,500	0.2%
45	Vermont	12,000	0.2%
46	South Dakota	11,600	0.2%
47	Alaska	10,900	0.2%
48	New Hampshire	9,400	0.1%
49	Wyoming	8,100	0.1%
50	North Dakota	5,700	0.1%
	District of Columbia	15,400	0.2%

Source: U.S. Department of Justice, Bureau of Justice Statistics
    "Probation and Parole in the United States, 2003" (July 2004, NCJ-205336)
*Includes adults in prison or jail, on probation or parole. Does not include 282,800 adults under federal correctional supervision. Figures are as of December 31, 2003 except for state prison and jail counts, which are as of June 30.

Rate of Adults Under State Correctional Supervision in 2003

National Rate = 3,042 Adults per 100,000 Adult Population*

RANK	STATE	RATE
32	Alabama	2,202
28	Alaska	2,382
19	Arizona	2,717
15	Arkansas	2,924
18	California	2,791
27	Colorado	2,486
17	Connecticut	2,815
3	Delaware	4,235
11	Florida	3,197
NA	Georgia**	NA
21	Hawaii	2,600
NA	Idaho**	NA
20	Illinois	2,609
7	Indiana	3,373
43	Iowa	1,638
42	Kansas	1,715
36	Kentucky	2,028
10	Louisiana	3,255
45	Maine	1,341
12	Maryland	3,117
12	Massachusetts	3,117
5	Michigan	3,527
6	Minnesota	3,411
30	Mississippi	2,264
22	Missouri	2,595
41	Montana	1,817
37	Nebraska	2,009
39	Nevada	1,909
48	New Hampshire	974
16	New Jersey	2,817
31	New Mexico	2,211
38	New York	1,925
23	North Carolina	2,589
46	North Dakota	1,189
4	Ohio	3,530
29	Oklahoma	2,372
14	Oregon	3,082
9	Pennsylvania	3,339
8	Rhode Island	3,357
25	South Carolina	2,547
34	South Dakota	2,069
35	Tennessee	2,054
1	Texas	4,609
44	Utah	1,397
24	Vermont	2,559
40	Virginia	1,827
2	Washington	4,350
47	West Virginia	991
26	Wisconsin	2,491
33	Wyoming	2,186

RANK	STATE	RATE
1	Texas	4,609
2	Washington	4,350
3	Delaware	4,235
4	Ohio	3,530
5	Michigan	3,527
6	Minnesota	3,411
7	Indiana	3,373
8	Rhode Island	3,357
9	Pennsylvania	3,339
10	Louisiana	3,255
11	Florida	3,197
12	Maryland	3,117
12	Massachusetts	3,117
14	Oregon	3,082
15	Arkansas	2,924
16	New Jersey	2,817
17	Connecticut	2,815
18	California	2,791
19	Arizona	2,717
20	Illinois	2,609
21	Hawaii	2,600
22	Missouri	2,595
23	North Carolina	2,589
24	Vermont	2,559
25	South Carolina	2,547
26	Wisconsin	2,491
27	Colorado	2,486
28	Alaska	2,382
29	Oklahoma	2,372
30	Mississippi	2,264
31	New Mexico	2,211
32	Alabama	2,202
33	Wyoming	2,186
34	South Dakota	2,069
35	Tennessee	2,054
36	Kentucky	2,028
37	Nebraska	2,009
38	New York	1,925
39	Nevada	1,909
40	Virginia	1,827
41	Montana	1,817
42	Kansas	1,715
43	Iowa	1,638
44	Utah	1,397
45	Maine	1,341
46	North Dakota	1,189
47	West Virginia	991
48	New Hampshire	974
NA	Georgia**	NA
NA	Idaho**	NA

	District of Columbia	3,440

Source: U.S. Department of Justice, Bureau of Justice Statistics
"Probation and Parole in the United States, 2003" (July 2004, NCJ-205336)
*Includes adults in prison or jail, on probation or parole. Figures are as of December 31, 2003 except for state jail counts, which are as of June 30. Does not include adults under federal correctional supervision. Federal rate is 130 per 100,000 adult population. The combined state and federal figure is 3,173 per 100,000 adult population.
**Not available.

Percent of Population Under State Correctional Supervision in 2003

National Percent = 6.3% of Adult Population*

ALPHA ORDER

RANK	STATE	PERCENT
32	Alabama	4.6
32	Alaska	4.6
20	Arizona	5.6
17	Arkansas	6.1
20	California	5.6
28	Colorado	5.0
18	Connecticut	5.9
3	Delaware	8.8
12	Florida	6.7
1	Georgia	17.1
25	Hawaii	5.3
3	Idaho	8.8
22	Illinois	5.4
8	Indiana	7.0
45	Iowa	3.3
44	Kansas	3.5
37	Kentucky	4.2
12	Louisiana	6.7
47	Maine	2.7
14	Maryland	6.5
14	Massachusetts	6.5
7	Michigan	7.2
11	Minnesota	6.8
31	Mississippi	4.7
22	Missouri	5.4
43	Montana	3.6
38	Nebraska	4.1
41	Nevada	3.8
50	New Hampshire	2.0
18	New Jersey	5.9
34	New Mexico	4.5
40	New York	4.0
22	North Carolina	5.4
48	North Dakota	2.4
6	Ohio	7.3
30	Oklahoma	4.8
16	Oregon	6.2
10	Pennsylvania	6.9
8	Rhode Island	7.0
25	South Carolina	5.3
38	South Dakota	4.1
35	Tennessee	4.3
2	Texas	9.4
46	Utah	2.8
27	Vermont	5.1
41	Virginia	3.8
5	Washington	8.7
49	West Virginia	2.1
28	Wisconsin	5.0
35	Wyoming	4.3

RANK ORDER

RANK	STATE	PERCENT
1	Georgia	17.1
2	Texas	9.4
3	Delaware	8.8
3	Idaho	8.8
5	Washington	8.7
6	Ohio	7.3
7	Michigan	7.2
8	Indiana	7.0
8	Rhode Island	7.0
10	Pennsylvania	6.9
11	Minnesota	6.8
12	Florida	6.7
12	Louisiana	6.7
14	Maryland	6.5
14	Massachusetts	6.5
16	Oregon	6.2
17	Arkansas	6.1
18	Connecticut	5.9
18	New Jersey	5.9
20	Arizona	5.6
20	California	5.6
22	Illinois	5.4
22	Missouri	5.4
22	North Carolina	5.4
25	Hawaii	5.3
25	South Carolina	5.3
27	Vermont	5.1
28	Colorado	5.0
28	Wisconsin	5.0
30	Oklahoma	4.8
31	Mississippi	4.7
32	Alabama	4.6
32	Alaska	4.6
34	New Mexico	4.5
35	Tennessee	4.3
35	Wyoming	4.3
37	Kentucky	4.2
38	Nebraska	4.1
38	South Dakota	4.1
40	New York	4.0
41	Nevada	3.8
41	Virginia	3.8
43	Montana	3.6
44	Kansas	3.5
45	Iowa	3.3
46	Utah	2.8
47	Maine	2.7
48	North Dakota	2.4
49	West Virginia	2.1
50	New Hampshire	2.0

District of Columbia 7.3

Source: Morgan Quitno Press using data from U.S. Department of Justice, Bureau of Justice Statistics "Probation and Parole in the United States, 2003" (July 2004, NCJ-205336)
*Population 18 years old and older. Includes adults in prison or jail, on probation or parole. Does not include adults under federal correctional supervision. Federal percent is 0.3%. The combined state and federal percent of adult population is under state or federal correctional supervision is 6.5%. Percents calculated using 2003 Census population estimates.

Percent of Adults Under State Correctional Supervision
Who are Incarcerated: 2003
National Percent = 29.0% Incarcerated*

ALPHA ORDER

RANK	STATE	PERCENT
15	Alabama	39.2
14	Alaska	41.7
18	Arizona	36.9
29	Arkansas	29.9
25	California	33.2
26	Colorado	33.0
35	Connecticut	26.0
36	Delaware	25.9
27	Florida	31.8
NA	Georgia**	NA
43	Hawaii	21.0
NA	Idaho**	NA
32	Illinois	26.6
40	Indiana	23.6
24	Iowa	33.7
7	Kansas	45.7
13	Kentucky	43.4
9	Louisiana	45.5
33	Maine	26.4
31	Maryland	28.6
44	Massachusetts	14.6
37	Michigan	25.6
48	Minnesota	10.6
1	Mississippi	56.0
19	Missouri	36.0
17	Montana	38.1
34	Nebraska	26.2
4	Nevada	49.7
11	New Hampshire	43.6
38	New Jersey	25.1
11	New Mexico	43.6
21	New York	35.3
28	North Carolina	30.0
22	North Dakota	34.0
42	Ohio	21.6
5	Oklahoma	47.9
41	Oregon	22.4
39	Pennsylvania	24.0
46	Rhode Island	12.8
9	South Carolina	45.5
16	South Dakota	38.2
8	Tennessee	45.6
30	Texas	29.0
6	Utah	46.9
47	Vermont	11.9
2	Virginia	54.6
45	Washington	14.5
3	West Virginia	50.5
23	Wisconsin	33.9
20	Wyoming	35.5

RANK ORDER

RANK	STATE	PERCENT
1	Mississippi	56.0
2	Virginia	54.6
3	West Virginia	50.5
4	Nevada	49.7
5	Oklahoma	47.9
6	Utah	46.9
7	Kansas	45.7
8	Tennessee	45.6
9	Louisiana	45.5
9	South Carolina	45.5
11	New Hampshire	43.6
11	New Mexico	43.6
13	Kentucky	43.4
14	Alaska	41.7
15	Alabama	39.2
16	South Dakota	38.2
17	Montana	38.1
18	Arizona	36.9
19	Missouri	36.0
20	Wyoming	35.5
21	New York	35.3
22	North Dakota	34.0
23	Wisconsin	33.9
24	Iowa	33.7
25	California	33.2
26	Colorado	33.0
27	Florida	31.8
28	North Carolina	30.0
29	Arkansas	29.9
30	Texas	29.0
31	Maryland	28.6
32	Illinois	26.6
33	Maine	26.4
34	Nebraska	26.2
35	Connecticut	26.0
36	Delaware	25.9
37	Michigan	25.6
38	New Jersey	25.1
39	Pennsylvania	24.0
40	Indiana	23.6
41	Oregon	22.4
42	Ohio	21.6
43	Hawaii	21.0
44	Massachusetts	14.6
45	Washington	14.5
46	Rhode Island	12.8
47	Vermont	11.9
48	Minnesota	10.6
NA	Georgia**	NA
NA	Idaho**	NA

District of Columbia 20.3

Source: U.S. Department of Justice, Bureau of Justice Statistics
"Probation and Parole in the United States, 2003" (July 2004, NCJ-205336)
*Includes adults in prison or jail, on probation or parole. Figures are as of December 31, 2003 except for state jail counts, which are as of June 30. Does not include adults under federal correctional supervision. Federal figure is 58.6% incarcerated. The combined state and federal figure is 30.2% incarcerated.
**Not available.

Adults on State Probation in 2004

National Total = 4,122,779 Adults*

ALPHA ORDER					RANK ORDER			
RANK	STATE	ADULTS	% of USA		RANK	STATE	ADULTS	% of USA
28	Alabama	36,795	0.9%		1	Texas	428,773	10.4%
46	Alaska	5,547	0.1%		2	Georgia	419,350	10.2%
17	Arizona	69,343	1.7%		3	California	384,852	9.3%
30	Arkansas	29,128	0.7%		4	Florida	281,170	6.8%
3	California	384,852	9.3%		5	Ohio	227,891	5.5%
18	Colorado	58,108	1.4%		6	Michigan	176,083	4.3%
21	Connecticut	52,092	1.3%		7	Pennsylvania	167,180	4.1%
36	Delaware	18,725	0.5%		8	Massachusetts	163,471	4.0%
4	Florida	281,170	6.8%		9	Illinois	143,871	3.5%
2	Georgia	419,350	10.2%		10	New Jersey	143,315	3.5%
34	Hawaii	21,446	0.5%		11	Washington	125,222	3.0%
23	Idaho	44,580	1.1%		12	New York	122,027	3.0%
9	Illinois	143,871	3.5%		13	Indiana	116,431	2.8%
13	Indiana	116,431	2.8%		14	Minnesota	114,226	2.8%
33	Iowa	22,832	0.6%		15	North Carolina	111,537	2.7%
39	Kansas	14,309	0.3%		16	Maryland	76,676	1.9%
29	Kentucky	33,286	0.8%		17	Arizona	69,343	1.7%
27	Louisiana	38,470	0.9%		18	Colorado	58,108	1.4%
43	Maine	9,322	0.2%		19	Wisconsin	54,970	1.3%
16	Maryland	76,676	1.9%		20	Missouri	53,832	1.3%
8	Massachusetts	163,471	4.0%		21	Connecticut	52,092	1.3%
6	Michigan	176,083	4.3%		22	Tennessee	47,392	1.1%
14	Minnesota	114,226	2.8%		23	Idaho	44,580	1.1%
35	Mississippi	21,324	0.5%		24	Oregon	44,435	1.1%
20	Missouri	53,832	1.3%		25	Virginia	43,470	1.1%
44	Montana	7,221	0.2%		26	South Carolina	38,856	0.9%
37	Nebraska	17,994	0.4%		27	Louisiana	38,470	0.9%
40	Nevada	12,521	0.3%		28	Alabama	36,795	0.9%
49	New Hampshire	4,285	0.1%		29	Kentucky	33,286	0.8%
10	New Jersey	143,315	3.5%		30	Arkansas	29,128	0.7%
38	New Mexico	17,725	0.4%		31	Oklahoma	28,435	0.7%
12	New York	122,027	3.0%		32	Rhode Island	26,085	0.6%
15	North Carolina	111,537	2.7%		33	Iowa	22,832	0.6%
50	North Dakota	3,687	0.1%		34	Hawaii	21,446	0.5%
5	Ohio	227,891	5.5%		35	Mississippi	21,324	0.5%
31	Oklahoma	28,435	0.7%		36	Delaware	18,725	0.5%
24	Oregon	44,435	1.1%		37	Nebraska	17,994	0.4%
7	Pennsylvania	167,180	4.1%		38	New Mexico	17,725	0.4%
32	Rhode Island	26,085	0.6%		39	Kansas	14,309	0.3%
26	South Carolina	38,856	0.9%		40	Nevada	12,521	0.3%
47	South Dakota	5,372	0.1%		41	Utah	10,244	0.2%
22	Tennessee	47,392	1.1%		42	Vermont	9,731	0.2%
1	Texas	428,773	10.4%		43	Maine	9,322	0.2%
41	Utah	10,244	0.2%		44	Montana	7,221	0.2%
42	Vermont	9,731	0.2%		45	West Virginia	6,977	0.2%
25	Virginia	43,470	1.1%		46	Alaska	5,547	0.1%
11	Washington	125,222	3.0%		47	South Dakota	5,372	0.1%
45	West Virginia	6,977	0.2%		48	Wyoming	4,418	0.1%
19	Wisconsin	54,970	1.3%		49	New Hampshire	4,285	0.1%
48	Wyoming	4,418	0.1%		50	North Dakota	3,687	0.1%
						District of Columbia	7,747	0.2%

Source: U.S. Department of Justice, Bureau of Justice Statistics
     "Probation and Parole in the United States, 2004" (November 2005, NCJ-210676)
*As of December 31, 2004. Does not include 28,346 adults on federal probation.

Rate of Adults on State Probation in 2004

National Rate = 1,871 Adults on State Probation per 100,000 Adult Population*

ALPHA ORDER

RANK	STATE	RATE
32	Alabama	1,071
29	Alaska	1,187
19	Arizona	1,652
23	Arkansas	1,403
22	California	1,463
18	Colorado	1,698
14	Connecticut	1,955
4	Delaware	2,940
12	Florida	2,099
NA	Georgia**	NA
10	Hawaii	2,224
NA	Idaho**	NA
21	Illinois	1,518
8	Indiana	2,511
37	Iowa	1,004
45	Kansas	697
34	Kentucky	1,051
30	Louisiana	1,148
40	Maine	901
15	Maryland	1,842
1	Massachusetts	3,301
9	Michigan	2,323
3	Minnesota	2,959
38	Mississippi	990
27	Missouri	1,232
36	Montana	1,005
24	Nebraska	1,371
44	Nevada	723
48	New Hampshire	431
11	New Jersey	2,190
26	New Mexico	1,256
41	New York	833
17	North Carolina	1,737
43	North Dakota	744
7	Ohio	2,626
33	Oklahoma	1,068
20	Oregon	1,620
16	Pennsylvania	1,747
2	Rhode Island	3,117
28	South Carolina	1,224
39	South Dakota	926
34	Tennessee	1,051
6	Texas	2,643
46	Utah	621
13	Vermont	2,000
42	Virginia	769
5	Washington	2,654
47	West Virginia	488
25	Wisconsin	1,308
31	Wyoming	1,134

RANK ORDER

RANK	STATE	RATE
1	Massachusetts	3,301
2	Rhode Island	3,117
3	Minnesota	2,959
4	Delaware	2,940
5	Washington	2,654
6	Texas	2,643
7	Ohio	2,626
8	Indiana	2,511
9	Michigan	2,323
10	Hawaii	2,224
11	New Jersey	2,190
12	Florida	2,099
13	Vermont	2,000
14	Connecticut	1,955
15	Maryland	1,842
16	Pennsylvania	1,747
17	North Carolina	1,737
18	Colorado	1,698
19	Arizona	1,652
20	Oregon	1,620
21	Illinois	1,518
22	California	1,463
23	Arkansas	1,403
24	Nebraska	1,371
25	Wisconsin	1,308
26	New Mexico	1,256
27	Missouri	1,232
28	South Carolina	1,224
29	Alaska	1,187
30	Louisiana	1,148
31	Wyoming	1,134
32	Alabama	1,071
33	Oklahoma	1,068
34	Kentucky	1,051
34	Tennessee	1,051
36	Montana	1,005
37	Iowa	1,004
38	Mississippi	990
39	South Dakota	926
40	Maine	901
41	New York	833
42	Virginia	769
43	North Dakota	744
44	Nevada	723
45	Kansas	697
46	Utah	621
47	West Virginia	488
48	New Hampshire	431
NA	Georgia**	NA
NA	Idaho**	NA

District of Columbia 1,745

Source: U.S. Department of Justice, Bureau of Justice Statistics
    "Probation and Parole in the United States, 2004" (November 2005, NCJ-210676)
*As of December 31, 2004. Federal rate is 13 adults on federal probation per 100,000 adult population.
**Not available.

Adults on State Parole in 2004

National Total = 675,534 Adults*

ALPHA ORDER			
RANK	STATE	ADULTS	% of USA
18	Alabama	7,745	1.1%
41	Alaska	951	0.1%
21	Arizona	5,671	0.8%
12	Arkansas	14,844	2.2%
1	California	110,261	16.3%
20	Colorado	7,383	1.1%
34	Connecticut	2,552	0.4%
46	Delaware	539	0.1%
22	Florida	4,888	0.7%
7	Georgia	23,344	3.5%
36	Hawaii	2,296	0.3%
35	Idaho	2,370	0.4%
5	Illinois	34,277	5.1%
19	Indiana	7,499	1.1%
29	Iowa	3,317	0.5%
23	Kansas	4,525	0.7%
17	Kentucky	8,006	1.2%
6	Louisiana	24,387	3.6%
50	Maine	32	0.0%
13	Maryland	14,351	2.1%
27	Massachusetts	3,854	0.6%
8	Michigan	20,924	3.1%
26	Minnesota	3,872	0.6%
38	Mississippi	1,979	0.3%
11	Missouri	17,400	2.6%
43	Montana	810	0.1%
44	Nebraska	805	0.1%
28	Nevada	3,610	0.5%
40	New Hampshire	1,212	0.2%
14	New Jersey	14,180	2.1%
33	New Mexico	2,676	0.4%
4	New York	54,524	8.1%
32	North Carolina	2,882	0.4%
48	North Dakota	239	0.0%
10	Ohio	18,882	2.8%
25	Oklahoma	4,329	0.6%
9	Oregon	20,858	3.1%
3	Pennsylvania	77,175	11.4%
47	Rhode Island	368	0.1%
31	South Carolina	3,292	0.5%
37	South Dakota	2,217	0.3%
16	Tennessee	8,410	1.2%
2	Texas	102,072	15.1%
30	Utah	3,312	0.5%
42	Vermont	922	0.1%
24	Virginia	4,392	0.7%
49	Washington	120	0.0%
39	West Virginia	1,216	0.2%
15	Wisconsin	13,883	2.1%
45	Wyoming	563	0.1%

RANK ORDER			
RANK	STATE	ADULTS	% of USA
1	California	110,261	16.3%
2	Texas	102,072	15.1%
3	Pennsylvania	77,175	11.4%
4	New York	54,524	8.1%
5	Illinois	34,277	5.1%
6	Louisiana	24,387	3.6%
7	Georgia	23,344	3.5%
8	Michigan	20,924	3.1%
9	Oregon	20,858	3.1%
10	Ohio	18,882	2.8%
11	Missouri	17,400	2.6%
12	Arkansas	14,844	2.2%
13	Maryland	14,351	2.1%
14	New Jersey	14,180	2.1%
15	Wisconsin	13,883	2.1%
16	Tennessee	8,410	1.2%
17	Kentucky	8,006	1.2%
18	Alabama	7,745	1.1%
19	Indiana	7,499	1.1%
20	Colorado	7,383	1.1%
21	Arizona	5,671	0.8%
22	Florida	4,888	0.7%
23	Kansas	4,525	0.7%
24	Virginia	4,392	0.7%
25	Oklahoma	4,329	0.6%
26	Minnesota	3,872	0.6%
27	Massachusetts	3,854	0.6%
28	Nevada	3,610	0.5%
29	Iowa	3,317	0.5%
30	Utah	3,312	0.5%
31	South Carolina	3,292	0.5%
32	North Carolina	2,882	0.4%
33	New Mexico	2,676	0.4%
34	Connecticut	2,552	0.4%
35	Idaho	2,370	0.4%
36	Hawaii	2,296	0.3%
37	South Dakota	2,217	0.3%
38	Mississippi	1,979	0.3%
39	West Virginia	1,216	0.2%
40	New Hampshire	1,212	0.2%
41	Alaska	951	0.1%
42	Vermont	922	0.1%
43	Montana	810	0.1%
44	Nebraska	805	0.1%
45	Wyoming	563	0.1%
46	Delaware	539	0.1%
47	Rhode Island	368	0.1%
48	North Dakota	239	0.0%
49	Washington	120	0.0%
50	Maine	32	0.0%
	District of Columbia	5,318	0.8%

Source: U.S. Department of Justice, Bureau of Justice Statistics
  "Probation and Parole in the United States, 2004" (November 2005, NCJ-210676)
*As of December 31, 2004. Does not include 89,821 adults on federal parole.

Rate of Adults on State Parole in 2004

National Rate = 307 Adults on State Parole per 100,000 Adult Population*

RANK	STATE (ALPHA ORDER)	RATE		RANK	STATE (RANK ORDER)	RATE
18	Alabama	225		1	Pennsylvania	806
24	Alaska	204		2	Oregon	761
33	Arizona	135		3	Louisiana	728
4	Arkansas	715		4	Arkansas	715
6	California	419		5	Texas	629
22	Colorado	216		6	California	419
38	Connecticut	96		7	Missouri	398
40	Delaware	85		8	South Dakota	382
48	Florida	36		9	New York	372
11	Georgia	359		10	Illinois	362
16	Hawaii	238		11	Georgia	359
17	Idaho	232		12	Maryland	345
10	Illinois	362		13	Wisconsin	330
30	Indiana	162		14	Michigan	276
31	Iowa	146		15	Kentucky	253
19	Kansas	221		16	Hawaii	238
15	Kentucky	253		17	Idaho	232
3	Louisiana	728		18	Alabama	225
49	Maine	3		19	Kansas	221
12	Maryland	345		20	Ohio	218
42	Massachusetts	78		21	New Jersey	217
14	Michigan	276		22	Colorado	216
37	Minnesota	100		23	Nevada	209
39	Mississippi	92		24	Alaska	204
7	Missouri	398		25	Utah	201
35	Montana	113		26	New Mexico	190
44	Nebraska	61		26	Vermont	190
23	Nevada	209		28	Tennessee	186
34	New Hampshire	122		29	Oklahoma	163
21	New Jersey	217		30	Indiana	162
26	New Mexico	190		31	Iowa	146
9	New York	372		32	Wyoming	145
46	North Carolina	45		33	Arizona	135
45	North Dakota	48		34	New Hampshire	122
20	Ohio	218		35	Montana	113
29	Oklahoma	163		36	South Carolina	104
2	Oregon	761		37	Minnesota	100
1	Pennsylvania	806		38	Connecticut	96
47	Rhode Island	44		39	Mississippi	92
36	South Carolina	104		40	Delaware	85
8	South Dakota	382		40	West Virginia	85
28	Tennessee	186		42	Massachusetts	78
5	Texas	629		42	Virginia	78
25	Utah	201		44	Nebraska	61
26	Vermont	190		45	North Dakota	48
42	Virginia	78		46	North Carolina	45
49	Washington	3		47	Rhode Island	44
40	West Virginia	85		48	Florida	36
13	Wisconsin	330		49	Maine	3
32	Wyoming	145		49	Washington	3
					District of Columbia	1,198

Source: U.S. Department of Justice, Bureau of Justice Statistics
"Probation and Parole in the United States, 2004" (November 2005, NCJ-210676)
As of December 31, 2004. Federal rate is 41 adults on federal parole per 100,000 adult population.

State Prison Expenditures in 2001

National Total = $29,491,268,000*

ALPHA ORDER

RANK	STATE	EXPENDITURES	% of USA
30	Alabama	$228,871,000	0.8%
36	Alaska	154,650,000	0.5%
15	Arizona	618,571,000	2.1%
32	Arkansas	199,003,000	0.7%
1	California	4,166,573,000	14.1%
20	Colorado	466,551,000	1.6%
16	Connecticut	523,960,000	1.8%
35	Delaware	166,327,000	0.6%
5	Florida	1,484,799,000	5.0%
9	Georgia	923,505,000	3.1%
41	Hawaii	117,101,000	0.4%
42	Idaho	95,494,000	0.3%
8	Illinois	1,011,311,000	3.4%
19	Indiana	477,628,000	1.6%
33	Iowa	188,391,000	0.6%
31	Kansas	199,843,000	0.7%
27	Kentucky	288,438,000	1.0%
18	Louisiana	479,260,000	1.6%
43	Maine	76,479,000	0.3%
14	Maryland	645,620,000	2.2%
23	Massachusetts	413,071,000	1.4%
4	Michigan	1,582,611,000	5.4%
29	Minnesota	253,385,000	0.9%
28	Mississippi	266,196,000	0.9%
21	Missouri	436,081,000	1.5%
44	Montana	71,994,000	0.2%
39	Nebraska	126,857,000	0.4%
34	Nevada	182,092,000	0.6%
45	New Hampshire	62,754,000	0.2%
11	New Jersey	799,560,000	2.7%
37	New Mexico	149,077,000	0.5%
2	New York	2,807,259,000	9.5%
10	North Carolina	863,892,000	2.9%
50	North Dakota	26,796,000	0.1%
6	Ohio	1,277,622,000	4.3%
26	Oklahoma	384,060,000	1.3%
25	Oregon	404,255,000	1.4%
7	Pennsylvania	1,203,219,000	4.1%
40	Rhode Island	124,333,000	0.4%
24	South Carolina	405,238,000	1.4%
49	South Dakota	37,529,000	0.1%
22	Tennessee	421,807,000	1.4%
3	Texas	2,315,899,000	7.9%
38	Utah	133,963,000	0.5%
48	Vermont	46,128,000	0.2%
12	Virginia	723,767,000	2.5%
17	Washington	488,314,000	1.7%
46	West Virginia	61,944,000	0.2%
13	Wisconsin	709,292,000	2.4%
47	Wyoming	56,199,000	0.2%

RANK ORDER

RANK	STATE	EXPENDITURES	% of USA
1	California	$4,166,573,000	14.1%
2	New York	2,807,259,000	9.5%
3	Texas	2,315,899,000	7.9%
4	Michigan	1,582,611,000	5.4%
5	Florida	1,484,799,000	5.0%
6	Ohio	1,277,622,000	4.3%
7	Pennsylvania	1,203,219,000	4.1%
8	Illinois	1,011,311,000	3.4%
9	Georgia	923,505,000	3.1%
10	North Carolina	863,892,000	2.9%
11	New Jersey	799,560,000	2.7%
12	Virginia	723,767,000	2.5%
13	Wisconsin	709,292,000	2.4%
14	Maryland	645,620,000	2.2%
15	Arizona	618,571,000	2.1%
16	Connecticut	523,960,000	1.8%
17	Washington	488,314,000	1.7%
18	Louisiana	479,260,000	1.6%
19	Indiana	477,628,000	1.6%
20	Colorado	466,551,000	1.6%
21	Missouri	436,081,000	1.5%
22	Tennessee	421,807,000	1.4%
23	Massachusetts	413,071,000	1.4%
24	South Carolina	405,238,000	1.4%
25	Oregon	404,255,000	1.4%
26	Oklahoma	384,060,000	1.3%
27	Kentucky	288,438,000	1.0%
28	Mississippi	266,196,000	0.9%
29	Minnesota	253,385,000	0.9%
30	Alabama	228,871,000	0.8%
31	Kansas	199,843,000	0.7%
32	Arkansas	199,003,000	0.7%
33	Iowa	188,391,000	0.6%
34	Nevada	182,092,000	0.6%
35	Delaware	166,327,000	0.6%
36	Alaska	154,650,000	0.5%
37	New Mexico	149,077,000	0.5%
38	Utah	133,963,000	0.5%
39	Nebraska	126,857,000	0.4%
40	Rhode Island	124,333,000	0.4%
41	Hawaii	117,101,000	0.4%
42	Idaho	95,494,000	0.3%
43	Maine	76,479,000	0.3%
44	Montana	71,994,000	0.2%
45	New Hampshire	62,754,000	0.2%
46	West Virginia	61,944,000	0.2%
47	Wyoming	56,199,000	0.2%
48	Vermont	46,128,000	0.2%
49	South Dakota	37,529,000	0.1%
50	North Dakota	26,796,000	0.1%
	District of Columbia	143,700,000	0.5%

Source: U.S. Department of Justice, Bureau of Justice Statistics
"State Prison Expenditures, 2001" (June 2004, NCJ-202949)
*Includes operating and capital outlay expenditures. Figures are net of amounts derived from revenue-generating activities such as farms. Does not include $8.7 billion in other correctional spending for programs such as juvenile correctional activities, adult parole boards and correctional empdministration not associated with specific penal institutions. Approximately 66 percent of operating expenditures are comprised of salaries and benefits.

Annual Operating Costs per State Prisoner in 2001

National Rate = $22,650 per Inmate*

RANK	STATE	PER INMATE		RANK	STATE	PER INMATE
50	Alabama	$8,128		1	Maine	$44,379
6	Alaska	36,730		2	Rhode Island	38,503
28	Arizona	22,476		3	Massachusetts	37,718
43	Arkansas	15,619		4	Minnesota	36,836
23	California	25,053		5	New York	36,835
20	Colorado	25,408		6	Alaska	36,730
16	Connecticut	26,856		7	Oregon	36,060
27	Delaware	22,802		8	Michigan	32,525
35	Florida	20,190		9	Pennsylvania	31,900
36	Georgia	19,860		10	Washington	30,168
33	Hawaii	21,637		11	Wyoming	28,845
41	Idaho	16,319		12	Wisconsin	28,622
31	Illinois	21,844		13	New Mexico	28,035
32	Indiana	21,841		14	New Jersey	27,347
25	Iowa	22,997		15	North Carolina	26,984
34	Kansas	21,381		16	Connecticut	26,856
38	Kentucky	17,818		17	Maryland	26,398
47	Louisiana	12,951		18	Ohio	26,295
1	Maine	44,379		19	New Hampshire	25,949
17	Maryland	26,398		20	Colorado	25,408
3	Massachusetts	37,718		21	Nebraska	25,321
8	Michigan	32,525		22	Vermont	25,178
4	Minnesota	36,836		23	California	25,053
49	Mississippi	12,795		24	Utah	24,574
48	Missouri	12,867		25	Iowa	22,997
30	Montana	21,898		26	Virginia	22,942
21	Nebraska	25,321		27	Delaware	22,802
39	Nevada	17,572		28	Arizona	22,476
19	New Hampshire	25,949		29	North Dakota	22,425
14	New Jersey	27,347		30	Montana	21,898
13	New Mexico	28,035		31	Illinois	21,844
5	New York	36,835		32	Indiana	21,841
15	North Carolina	26,984		33	Hawaii	21,637
29	North Dakota	22,425		34	Kansas	21,381
18	Ohio	26,295		35	Florida	20,190
42	Oklahoma	16,309		36	Georgia	19,860
7	Oregon	36,060		37	Tennessee	18,206
9	Pennsylvania	31,900		38	Kentucky	17,818
2	Rhode Island	38,503		39	Nevada	17,572
40	South Carolina	16,762		40	South Carolina	16,762
45	South Dakota	13,853		41	Idaho	16,319
37	Tennessee	18,206		42	Oklahoma	16,309
46	Texas	13,808		43	Arkansas	15,619
24	Utah	24,574		44	West Virginia	14,817
22	Vermont	25,178		45	South Dakota	13,853
26	Virginia	22,942		46	Texas	13,808
10	Washington	30,168		47	Louisiana	12,951
44	West Virginia	14,817		48	Missouri	12,867
12	Wisconsin	28,622		49	Mississippi	12,795
11	Wyoming	28,845		50	Alabama	8,128
					District of Columbia	26,670

ALPHA ORDER (left) / *RANK ORDER* (right)

Source: U.S. Department of Justice, Bureau of Justice Statistics
    "State Prison Expenditures, 2001" (June 2004, NCJ-202949)
*Figures are net of amounts derived from revenue-generating activities such as farms.

Per Capita Annual State Prison Operating Costs in 2001

National Per Capita = $100*

ALPHA ORDER

RANK	STATE	PER CAPITA
45	Alabama	$50
1	Alaska	243
8	Arizona	115
35	Arkansas	72
6	California	119
18	Colorado	98
4	Connecticut	148
2	Delaware	204
26	Florida	89
13	Georgia	107
21	Hawaii	96
36	Idaho	70
29	Illinois	80
32	Indiana	73
39	Iowa	64
37	Kansas	68
38	Kentucky	67
16	Louisiana	103
43	Maine	58
7	Maryland	118
41	Massachusetts	63
3	Michigan	157
47	Minnesota	48
23	Mississippi	93
39	Missouri	64
30	Montana	79
43	Nebraska	58
27	Nevada	86
47	New Hampshire	48
25	New Jersey	91
28	New Mexico	81
5	New York	134
16	North Carolina	103
49	North Dakota	38
14	Ohio	106
12	Oklahoma	109
8	Oregon	115
21	Pennsylvania	96
10	Rhode Island	114
24	South Carolina	92
46	South Dakota	49
32	Tennessee	73
14	Texas	106
42	Utah	59
32	Vermont	73
20	Virginia	97
31	Washington	77
50	West Virginia	34
11	Wisconsin	111
18	Wyoming	98

RANK ORDER

RANK	STATE	PER CAPITA
1	Alaska	$243
2	Delaware	204
3	Michigan	157
4	Connecticut	148
5	New York	134
6	California	119
7	Maryland	118
8	Arizona	115
8	Oregon	115
10	Rhode Island	114
11	Wisconsin	111
12	Oklahoma	109
13	Georgia	107
14	Ohio	106
14	Texas	106
16	Louisiana	103
16	North Carolina	103
18	Colorado	98
18	Wyoming	98
20	Virginia	97
21	Hawaii	96
21	Pennsylvania	96
23	Mississippi	93
24	South Carolina	92
25	New Jersey	91
26	Florida	89
27	Nevada	86
28	New Mexico	81
29	Illinois	80
30	Montana	79
31	Washington	77
32	Indiana	73
32	Tennessee	73
32	Vermont	73
35	Arkansas	72
36	Idaho	70
37	Kansas	68
38	Kentucky	67
39	Iowa	64
39	Missouri	64
41	Massachusetts	63
42	Utah	59
43	Maine	58
43	Nebraska	58
45	Alabama	50
46	South Dakota	49
47	Minnesota	48
47	New Hampshire	48
49	North Dakota	38
50	West Virginia	34

	District of Columbia	251

Source: U.S. Department of Justice, Bureau of Justice Statistics
  "State Prison Expenditures, 2001" (June 2004, NCJ-202949)
*Figures are net of amounts derived from revenue-generating activities such as farms.

Percent of State Prison Expenditures Used for Operating Costs in 2001

National Percent = 96.2%*

ALPHA ORDER

RANK	STATE	PERCENT
28	Alabama	96.9
2	Alaska	99.7
12	Arizona	98.6
29	Arkansas	96.8
12	California	98.6
40	Colorado	93.2
30	Connecticut	96.7
22	Delaware	97.6
21	Florida	97.9
22	Georgia	97.6
NA	Hawaii**	NA
27	Idaho	97.2
12	Illinois	98.6
38	Indiana	94.1
7	Iowa	98.9
42	Kansas	91.4
35	Kentucky	95.1
34	Louisiana	95.9
17	Maine	98.2
19	Maryland	98.0
19	Massachusetts	98.0
3	Michigan	99.4
36	Minnesota	94.7
3	Mississippi	99.4
47	Missouri	83.1
7	Montana	98.9
48	Nebraska	78.7
6	Nevada	99.3
32	New Hampshire	96.1
32	New Jersey	96.1
3	New Mexico	99.4
43	New York	90.7
25	North Carolina	97.3
44	North Dakota	90.4
39	Ohio	94.0
16	Oklahoma	98.3
9	Oregon	98.8
15	Pennsylvania	98.4
24	Rhode Island	97.5
41	South Carolina	92.1
11	South Dakota	98.7
NA	Tennessee**	NA
18	Texas	98.1
1	Utah	99.8
25	Vermont	97.3
31	Virginia	96.6
37	Washington	94.2
9	West Virginia	98.8
46	Wisconsin	84.5
45	Wyoming	86.2

RANK ORDER

RANK	STATE	PERCENT
1	Utah	99.8
2	Alaska	99.7
3	Michigan	99.4
3	Mississippi	99.4
3	New Mexico	99.4
6	Nevada	99.3
7	Iowa	98.9
7	Montana	98.9
9	Oregon	98.8
9	West Virginia	98.8
11	South Dakota	98.7
12	Arizona	98.6
12	California	98.6
12	Illinois	98.6
15	Pennsylvania	98.4
16	Oklahoma	98.3
17	Maine	98.2
18	Texas	98.1
19	Maryland	98.0
19	Massachusetts	98.0
21	Florida	97.9
22	Delaware	97.6
22	Georgia	97.6
24	Rhode Island	97.5
25	North Carolina	97.3
25	Vermont	97.3
27	Idaho	97.2
28	Alabama	96.9
29	Arkansas	96.8
30	Connecticut	96.7
31	Virginia	96.6
32	New Hampshire	96.1
32	New Jersey	96.1
34	Louisiana	95.9
35	Kentucky	95.1
36	Minnesota	94.7
37	Washington	94.2
38	Indiana	94.1
39	Ohio	94.0
40	Colorado	93.2
41	South Carolina	92.1
42	Kansas	91.4
43	New York	90.7
44	North Dakota	90.4
45	Wyoming	86.2
46	Wisconsin	84.5
47	Missouri	83.1
48	Nebraska	78.7
NA	Hawaii**	NA
NA	Tennessee**	NA
	District of Columbia**	NA

Source: Morgan Quitno Press using data from U.S. Department of Justice, Bureau of Justice Statistics
"State Prison Expenditures, 2001" (June 2004, NCJ-202949)

Figures are net of amounts derived from revenue-generating activities such as farms. Does not include other correctional spending for programs such as juvenile correctional activities, adult parole boards and correctional administration not associated with specific penal institutions.
***Not available.*

Percent of State Prison Expenditures Used for Capital Projects in 2001

National Percent = 3.8%*

ALPHA ORDER

RANK	STATE	PERCENT
21	Alabama	3.1
47	Alaska	0.3
35	Arizona	1.4
20	Arkansas	3.2
35	California	1.4
9	Colorado	6.8
19	Connecticut	3.3
26	Delaware	2.4
28	Florida	2.1
26	Georgia	2.4
NA	Hawaii**	NA
22	Idaho	2.8
35	Illinois	1.4
11	Indiana	5.9
41	Iowa	1.1
7	Kansas	8.6
14	Kentucky	4.9
15	Louisiana	4.1
32	Maine	1.8
29	Maryland	2.0
29	Massachusetts	2.0
44	Michigan	0.6
13	Minnesota	5.3
44	Mississippi	0.6
2	Missouri	16.9
41	Montana	1.1
1	Nebraska	21.3
43	Nevada	0.7
16	New Hampshire	3.9
16	New Jersey	3.9
44	New Mexico	0.6
6	New York	9.3
23	North Carolina	2.7
5	North Dakota	9.6
10	Ohio	6.0
33	Oklahoma	1.7
39	Oregon	1.2
34	Pennsylvania	1.6
25	Rhode Island	2.5
8	South Carolina	7.9
38	South Dakota	1.3
NA	Tennessee**	NA
31	Texas	1.9
48	Utah	0.2
23	Vermont	2.7
18	Virginia	3.4
12	Washington	5.8
39	West Virginia	1.2
3	Wisconsin	15.5
4	Wyoming	13.8

RANK ORDER

RANK	STATE	PERCENT
1	Nebraska	21.3
2	Missouri	16.9
3	Wisconsin	15.5
4	Wyoming	13.8
5	North Dakota	9.6
6	New York	9.3
7	Kansas	8.6
8	South Carolina	7.9
9	Colorado	6.8
10	Ohio	6.0
11	Indiana	5.9
12	Washington	5.8
13	Minnesota	5.3
14	Kentucky	4.9
15	Louisiana	4.1
16	New Hampshire	3.9
16	New Jersey	3.9
18	Virginia	3.4
19	Connecticut	3.3
20	Arkansas	3.2
21	Alabama	3.1
22	Idaho	2.8
23	North Carolina	2.7
23	Vermont	2.7
25	Rhode Island	2.5
26	Delaware	2.4
26	Georgia	2.4
28	Florida	2.1
29	Maryland	2.0
29	Massachusetts	2.0
31	Texas	1.9
32	Maine	1.8
33	Oklahoma	1.7
34	Pennsylvania	1.6
35	Arizona	1.4
35	California	1.4
35	Illinois	1.4
38	South Dakota	1.3
39	Oregon	1.2
39	West Virginia	1.2
41	Iowa	1.1
41	Montana	1.1
43	Nevada	0.7
44	Michigan	0.6
44	Mississippi	0.6
44	New Mexico	0.6
47	Alaska	0.3
48	Utah	0.2
NA	Hawaii**	NA
NA	Tennessee**	NA

District of Columbia**   NA

Source: Morgan Quitno Press using data from U.S. Department of Justice, Bureau of Justice Statistics
    "State Prison Expenditures, 2001" (June 2004, NCJ-202949)
*Figures are net of amounts derived from revenue-generating activities such as farms. Does not include other
correctional spending for programs such as juvenile correctional activities, adult parole boards and correctional
administration not associated with specific penal institutions.
**Not available.

Medical Costs per State Inmate in 2001

National Rate = $2,625 per Inmate*

<u>ALPHA ORDER</u>

RANK	STATE	PER INMATE
47	Alabama	$1,052
5	Alaska	4,047
21	Arizona	2,765
39	Arkansas	1,616
3	California	4,394
25	Colorado	2,541
10	Connecticut	3,620
29	Delaware	2,073
12	Florida	3,363
24	Georgia	2,588
35	Hawaii	1,809
37	Idaho	1,715
40	Illinois	1,605
34	Indiana	1,827
30	Iowa	2,063
23	Kansas	2,673
48	Kentucky	960
50	Louisiana	860
1	Maine	5,601
28	Maryland	2,177
4	Massachusetts	4,049
19	Michigan	2,841
6	Minnesota	3,908
46	Mississippi	1,255
36	Missouri	1,782
49	Montana	922
15	Nebraska	3,145
17	Nevada	2,871
38	New Hampshire	1,706
13	New Jersey	3,261
2	New Mexico	4,665
14	New York	3,177
42	North Carolina	1,463
22	North Dakota	2,678
26	Ohio	2,445
32	Oklahoma	2,008
45	Oregon	1,284
9	Pennsylvania	3,700
8	Rhode Island	3,756
44	South Carolina	1,290
31	South Dakota	2,044
41	Tennessee	1,551
33	Texas	2,001
43	Utah	1,343
16	Vermont	2,918
18	Virginia	2,866
11	Washington	3,412
20	West Virginia	2,797
27	Wisconsin	2,249
7	Wyoming	3,891

<u>RANK ORDER</u>

RANK	STATE	PER INMATE
1	Maine	$5,601
2	New Mexico	4,665
3	California	4,394
4	Massachusetts	4,049
5	Alaska	4,047
6	Minnesota	3,908
7	Wyoming	3,891
8	Rhode Island	3,756
9	Pennsylvania	3,700
10	Connecticut	3,620
11	Washington	3,412
12	Florida	3,363
13	New Jersey	3,261
14	New York	3,177
15	Nebraska	3,145
16	Vermont	2,918
17	Nevada	2,871
18	Virginia	2,866
19	Michigan	2,841
20	West Virginia	2,797
21	Arizona	2,765
22	North Dakota	2,678
23	Kansas	2,673
24	Georgia	2,588
25	Colorado	2,541
26	Ohio	2,445
27	Wisconsin	2,249
28	Maryland	2,177
29	Delaware	2,073
30	Iowa	2,063
31	South Dakota	2,044
32	Oklahoma	2,008
33	Texas	2,001
34	Indiana	1,827
35	Hawaii	1,809
36	Missouri	1,782
37	Idaho	1,715
38	New Hampshire	1,706
39	Arkansas	1,616
40	Illinois	1,605
41	Tennessee	1,551
42	North Carolina	1,463
43	Utah	1,343
44	South Carolina	1,290
45	Oregon	1,284
46	Mississippi	1,255
47	Alabama	1,052
48	Kentucky	960
49	Montana	922
50	Louisiana	860
	District of Columbia	1,935

Source: U.S. Department of Justice, Bureau of Justice Statistics
"State Prison Expenditures, 2001" (June 2004, NCJ-202949)
*Includes supplies and services of government staff and other providers. National average represents approximately 12 percent of operating expenditures.

Food Service Costs per State Inmate in 2001

National Rate = $955 per Inmate*

<table>
<tr><td colspan="3">ALPHA ORDER</td><td colspan="3">RANK ORDER</td></tr>
<tr><th>RANK</th><th>STATE</th><th>PER INMATE</th><th>RANK</th><th>STATE</th><th>PER INMATE</th></tr>
<tr><td>49</td><td>Alabama</td><td>$262</td><td>1</td><td>Pennsylvania</td><td>$2,077</td></tr>
<tr><td>17</td><td>Alaska</td><td>1,249</td><td>2</td><td>Washington</td><td>2,074</td></tr>
<tr><td>20</td><td>Arizona</td><td>1,196</td><td>3</td><td>Maine</td><td>1,835</td></tr>
<tr><td>46</td><td>Arkansas</td><td>424</td><td>4</td><td>Hawaii</td><td>1,777</td></tr>
<tr><td>35</td><td>California</td><td>859</td><td>5</td><td>Iowa</td><td>1,756</td></tr>
<tr><td>11</td><td>Colorado</td><td>1,425</td><td>6</td><td>North Dakota</td><td>1,670</td></tr>
<tr><td>18</td><td>Connecticut</td><td>1,242</td><td>7</td><td>Minnesota</td><td>1,665</td></tr>
<tr><td>14</td><td>Delaware</td><td>1,351</td><td>8</td><td>Ohio</td><td>1,651</td></tr>
<tr><td>25</td><td>Florida</td><td>1,090</td><td>9</td><td>South Dakota</td><td>1,561</td></tr>
<tr><td>21</td><td>Georgia</td><td>1,150</td><td>10</td><td>Nebraska</td><td>1,427</td></tr>
<tr><td>4</td><td>Hawaii</td><td>1,777</td><td>11</td><td>Colorado</td><td>1,425</td></tr>
<tr><td>40</td><td>Idaho</td><td>643</td><td>12</td><td>Kansas</td><td>1,402</td></tr>
<tr><td>21</td><td>Illinois</td><td>1,150</td><td>13</td><td>Nevada</td><td>1,401</td></tr>
<tr><td>30</td><td>Indiana</td><td>970</td><td>14</td><td>Delaware</td><td>1,351</td></tr>
<tr><td>5</td><td>Iowa</td><td>1,756</td><td>15</td><td>Virginia</td><td>1,308</td></tr>
<tr><td>12</td><td>Kansas</td><td>1,402</td><td>16</td><td>Rhode Island</td><td>1,305</td></tr>
<tr><td>43</td><td>Kentucky</td><td>564</td><td>17</td><td>Alaska</td><td>1,249</td></tr>
<tr><td>47</td><td>Louisiana</td><td>349</td><td>18</td><td>Connecticut</td><td>1,242</td></tr>
<tr><td>3</td><td>Maine</td><td>1,835</td><td>19</td><td>Wisconsin</td><td>1,200</td></tr>
<tr><td>41</td><td>Maryland</td><td>639</td><td>20</td><td>Arizona</td><td>1,196</td></tr>
<tr><td>33</td><td>Massachusetts</td><td>885</td><td>21</td><td>Georgia</td><td>1,150</td></tr>
<tr><td>28</td><td>Michigan</td><td>995</td><td>21</td><td>Illinois</td><td>1,150</td></tr>
<tr><td>7</td><td>Minnesota</td><td>1,665</td><td>23</td><td>Tennessee</td><td>1,103</td></tr>
<tr><td>48</td><td>Mississippi</td><td>297</td><td>24</td><td>West Virginia</td><td>1,102</td></tr>
<tr><td>38</td><td>Missouri</td><td>751</td><td>25</td><td>Florida</td><td>1,090</td></tr>
<tr><td>45</td><td>Montana</td><td>425</td><td>26</td><td>Wyoming</td><td>1,024</td></tr>
<tr><td>10</td><td>Nebraska</td><td>1,427</td><td>27</td><td>Oklahoma</td><td>1,011</td></tr>
<tr><td>13</td><td>Nevada</td><td>1,401</td><td>28</td><td>Michigan</td><td>995</td></tr>
<tr><td>34</td><td>New Hampshire</td><td>876</td><td>29</td><td>Vermont</td><td>977</td></tr>
<tr><td>37</td><td>New Jersey</td><td>810</td><td>30</td><td>Indiana</td><td>970</td></tr>
<tr><td>36</td><td>New Mexico</td><td>854</td><td>31</td><td>New York</td><td>963</td></tr>
<tr><td>31</td><td>New York</td><td>963</td><td>32</td><td>Utah</td><td>958</td></tr>
<tr><td>50</td><td>North Carolina</td><td>191</td><td>33</td><td>Massachusetts</td><td>885</td></tr>
<tr><td>6</td><td>North Dakota</td><td>1,670</td><td>34</td><td>New Hampshire</td><td>876</td></tr>
<tr><td>8</td><td>Ohio</td><td>1,651</td><td>35</td><td>California</td><td>859</td></tr>
<tr><td>27</td><td>Oklahoma</td><td>1,011</td><td>36</td><td>New Mexico</td><td>854</td></tr>
<tr><td>39</td><td>Oregon</td><td>664</td><td>37</td><td>New Jersey</td><td>810</td></tr>
<tr><td>1</td><td>Pennsylvania</td><td>2,077</td><td>38</td><td>Missouri</td><td>751</td></tr>
<tr><td>16</td><td>Rhode Island</td><td>1,305</td><td>39</td><td>Oregon</td><td>664</td></tr>
<tr><td>44</td><td>South Carolina</td><td>435</td><td>40</td><td>Idaho</td><td>643</td></tr>
<tr><td>9</td><td>South Dakota</td><td>1,561</td><td>41</td><td>Maryland</td><td>639</td></tr>
<tr><td>23</td><td>Tennessee</td><td>1,103</td><td>42</td><td>Texas</td><td>638</td></tr>
<tr><td>42</td><td>Texas</td><td>638</td><td>43</td><td>Kentucky</td><td>564</td></tr>
<tr><td>32</td><td>Utah</td><td>958</td><td>44</td><td>South Carolina</td><td>435</td></tr>
<tr><td>29</td><td>Vermont</td><td>977</td><td>45</td><td>Montana</td><td>425</td></tr>
<tr><td>15</td><td>Virginia</td><td>1,308</td><td>46</td><td>Arkansas</td><td>424</td></tr>
<tr><td>2</td><td>Washington</td><td>2,074</td><td>47</td><td>Louisiana</td><td>349</td></tr>
<tr><td>24</td><td>West Virginia</td><td>1,102</td><td>48</td><td>Mississippi</td><td>297</td></tr>
<tr><td>19</td><td>Wisconsin</td><td>1,200</td><td>49</td><td>Alabama</td><td>262</td></tr>
<tr><td>26</td><td>Wyoming</td><td>1,024</td><td>50</td><td>North Carolina</td><td>191</td></tr>
<tr><td></td><td></td><td></td><td></td><td>District of Columbia</td><td>549</td></tr>
</table>

Source: U.S. Department of Justice, Bureau of Justice Statistics
    "State Prison Expenditures, 2001" (June 2004, NCJ-202949)
*Costs are net of prisoner-operated farm and food processing operations. National average represents
approximately four percent of operating expenditures.

State and Local Government Employees in Corrections in 2004

National Total = 701,905 Employees*

RANK	STATE	EMPLOYEES	% of USA
26	Alabama	7,867	1.1%
44	Alaska	1,840	0.3%
15	Arizona	14,655	2.1%
30	Arkansas	6,321	0.9%
1	California	81,435	11.6%
22	Colorado	9,923	1.4%
28	Connecticut	7,473	1.1%
40	Delaware	2,839	0.4%
4	Florida	43,749	6.2%
6	Georgia	27,504	3.9%
41	Hawaii	2,376	0.3%
39	Idaho	2,846	0.4%
8	Illinois	24,415	3.5%
17	Indiana	13,498	1.9%
36	Iowa	4,473	0.6%
31	Kansas	6,097	0.9%
27	Kentucky	7,737	1.1%
18	Louisiana	13,438	1.9%
42	Maine	2,130	0.3%
13	Maryland	15,150	2.2%
23	Massachusetts	9,367	1.3%
10	Michigan	23,248	3.3%
24	Minnesota	8,662	1.2%
32	Mississippi	5,924	0.8%
14	Missouri	14,836	2.1%
46	Montana	1,695	0.2%
37	Nebraska	3,740	0.5%
34	Nevada	5,670	0.8%
43	New Hampshire	1,930	0.3%
12	New Jersey	16,803	2.4%
33	New Mexico	5,910	0.8%
3	New York	58,286	8.3%
9	North Carolina	23,606	3.4%
50	North Dakota	944	0.1%
7	Ohio	24,647	3.5%
29	Oklahoma	6,531	0.9%
25	Oregon	8,453	1.2%
5	Pennsylvania	29,559	4.2%
45	Rhode Island	1,716	0.2%
21	South Carolina	10,239	1.5%
48	South Dakota	1,292	0.2%
20	Tennessee	12,956	1.8%
2	Texas	70,241	10.0%
35	Utah	4,981	0.7%
49	Vermont	1,112	0.2%
11	Virginia	21,007	3.0%
16	Washington	13,604	1.9%
38	West Virginia	3,270	0.5%
19	Wisconsin	13,321	1.9%
47	Wyoming	1,499	0.2%

RANK	STATE	EMPLOYEES	% of USA
1	California	81,435	11.6%
2	Texas	70,241	10.0%
3	New York	58,286	8.3%
4	Florida	43,749	6.2%
5	Pennsylvania	29,559	4.2%
6	Georgia	27,504	3.9%
7	Ohio	24,647	3.5%
8	Illinois	24,415	3.5%
9	North Carolina	23,606	3.4%
10	Michigan	23,248	3.3%
11	Virginia	21,007	3.0%
12	New Jersey	16,803	2.4%
13	Maryland	15,150	2.2%
14	Missouri	14,836	2.1%
15	Arizona	14,655	2.1%
16	Washington	13,604	1.9%
17	Indiana	13,498	1.9%
18	Louisiana	13,438	1.9%
19	Wisconsin	13,321	1.9%
20	Tennessee	12,956	1.8%
21	South Carolina	10,239	1.5%
22	Colorado	9,923	1.4%
23	Massachusetts	9,367	1.3%
24	Minnesota	8,662	1.2%
25	Oregon	8,453	1.2%
26	Alabama	7,867	1.1%
27	Kentucky	7,737	1.1%
28	Connecticut	7,473	1.1%
29	Oklahoma	6,531	0.9%
30	Arkansas	6,321	0.9%
31	Kansas	6,097	0.9%
32	Mississippi	5,924	0.8%
33	New Mexico	5,910	0.8%
34	Nevada	5,670	0.8%
35	Utah	4,981	0.7%
36	Iowa	4,473	0.6%
37	Nebraska	3,740	0.5%
38	West Virginia	3,270	0.5%
39	Idaho	2,846	0.4%
40	Delaware	2,839	0.4%
41	Hawaii	2,376	0.3%
42	Maine	2,130	0.3%
43	New Hampshire	1,930	0.3%
44	Alaska	1,840	0.3%
45	Rhode Island	1,716	0.2%
46	Montana	1,695	0.2%
47	Wyoming	1,499	0.2%
48	South Dakota	1,292	0.2%
49	Vermont	1,112	0.2%
50	North Dakota	944	0.1%
	District of Columbia	1,090	0.2%

Source: U.S. Bureau of the Census, Governments Division
    "State and Local Employment and Payroll - March 2004" (http://www.census.gov/govs/www/apesstl04.html)
*Full-time equivalent as of March 2004.

State and Local Government Employees in Corrections as a Percent of All State and Local Government Employees in 2004
National Percent = 4.4% of Employees*

ALPHA ORDER

RANK	STATE	PERCENT		RANK	STATE	PERCENT
44	Alabama	2.9		1	Delaware	5.9
29	Alaska	3.6		1	Nevada	5.9
5	Arizona	5.4		3	Georgia	5.5
19	Arkansas	4.2		3	Texas	5.5
16	California	4.6		5	Arizona	5.4
25	Colorado	4.0		5	Maryland	5.4
22	Connecticut	4.1		7	Florida	5.3
1	Delaware	5.9		8	North Carolina	5.2
7	Florida	5.3		8	Pennsylvania	5.2
3	Georgia	5.5		10	Virginia	5.1
35	Hawaii	3.3		11	New York	4.9
29	Idaho	3.6		12	Louisiana	4.8
28	Illinois	3.8		12	Missouri	4.8
22	Indiana	4.1		14	New Mexico	4.7
49	Iowa	2.4		14	Oregon	4.7
31	Kansas	3.4		16	California	4.6
35	Kentucky	3.3		16	Michigan	4.6
12	Louisiana	4.8		16	Wisconsin	4.6
47	Maine	2.8		19	Arkansas	4.2
5	Maryland	5.4		19	South Carolina	4.2
44	Massachusetts	2.9		19	Washington	4.2
16	Michigan	4.6		22	Connecticut	4.1
40	Minnesota	3.1		22	Indiana	4.1
40	Mississippi	3.1		22	Tennessee	4.1
12	Missouri	4.8		25	Colorado	4.0
40	Montana	3.1		25	Ohio	4.0
35	Nebraska	3.3		27	Utah	3.9
1	Nevada	5.9		28	Illinois	3.8
47	New Hampshire	2.8		29	Alaska	3.6
31	New Jersey	3.4		29	Idaho	3.6
14	New Mexico	4.7		31	Kansas	3.4
11	New York	4.9		31	New Jersey	3.4
8	North Carolina	5.2		31	Rhode Island	3.4
50	North Dakota	2.3		31	Wyoming	3.4
25	Ohio	4.0		35	Hawaii	3.3
35	Oklahoma	3.3		35	Kentucky	3.3
14	Oregon	4.7		35	Nebraska	3.3
8	Pennsylvania	5.2		35	Oklahoma	3.3
31	Rhode Island	3.4		35	West Virginia	3.3
19	South Carolina	4.2		40	Minnesota	3.1
43	South Dakota	3.0		40	Mississippi	3.1
22	Tennessee	4.1		40	Montana	3.1
3	Texas	5.5		43	South Dakota	3.0
27	Utah	3.9		44	Alabama	2.9
44	Vermont	2.9		44	Massachusetts	2.9
10	Virginia	5.1		44	Vermont	2.9
19	Washington	4.2		47	Maine	2.8
35	West Virginia	3.3		47	New Hampshire	2.8
16	Wisconsin	4.6		49	Iowa	2.4
31	Wyoming	3.4		50	North Dakota	2.3
					District of Columbia	2.4

Source: Morgan Quitno Press using data from U.S. Bureau of the Census, Governments Division
"State and Local Employment and Payroll - March 2004" (http://www.census.gov/govs/www/apesstl04.html)
*Full-time equivalent as of March 2004.

Correctional Officers and Jailers in 2004

National Total = 416,490 Officers and Jailers*

ALPHA ORDER

RANK	STATE	EMPLOYEES	% of USA
24	Alabama	5,350	1.3%
46	Alaska	1,000	0.2%
15	Arizona	9,000	2.2%
31	Arkansas	4,150	1.0%
3	California	34,320	8.2%
22	Colorado	6,610	1.6%
30	Connecticut	4,230	1.0%
39	Delaware	1,460	0.4%
4	Florida	32,150	7.7%
6	Georgia	17,210	4.1%
40	Hawaii	1,380	0.3%
41	Idaho	1,280	0.3%
8	Illinois	13,850	3.3%
19	Indiana	6,930	1.7%
33	Iowa	3,790	0.9%
32	Kansas	4,070	1.0%
25	Kentucky	5,190	1.2%
13	Louisiana	9,530	2.3%
42	Maine	1,270	0.3%
12	Maryland	9,780	2.3%
23	Massachusetts	6,010	1.4%
16	Michigan	8,840	2.1%
26	Minnesota	4,910	1.2%
27	Mississippi	4,770	1.1%
14	Missouri	9,100	2.2%
43	Montana	1,190	0.3%
38	Nebraska	2,020	0.5%
37	Nevada	2,290	0.5%
47	New Hampshire	890	0.2%
10	New Jersey	13,150	3.2%
34	New Mexico	2,710	0.7%
2	New York	37,170	8.9%
7	North Carolina	14,370	3.5%
49	North Dakota	710	0.2%
8	Ohio	13,850	3.3%
28	Oklahoma	4,490	1.1%
29	Oregon	4,240	1.0%
5	Pennsylvania	17,740	4.3%
44	Rhode Island	1,080	0.3%
21	South Carolina	6,730	1.6%
45	South Dakota	1,010	0.2%
17	Tennessee	7,850	1.9%
1	Texas	45,780	11.0%
36	Utah	2,340	0.6%
NA	Vermont**	NA	NA
11	Virginia	11,560	2.8%
20	Washington	6,840	1.6%
35	West Virginia	2,660	0.6%
18	Wisconsin	6,990	1.7%
48	Wyoming	810	0.2%

RANK ORDER

RANK	STATE	EMPLOYEES	% of USA
1	Texas	45,780	11.0%
2	New York	37,170	8.9%
3	California	34,320	8.2%
4	Florida	32,150	7.7%
5	Pennsylvania	17,740	4.3%
6	Georgia	17,210	4.1%
7	North Carolina	14,370	3.5%
8	Illinois	13,850	3.3%
8	Ohio	13,850	3.3%
10	New Jersey	13,150	3.2%
11	Virginia	11,560	2.8%
12	Maryland	9,780	2.3%
13	Louisiana	9,530	2.3%
14	Missouri	9,100	2.2%
15	Arizona	9,000	2.2%
16	Michigan	8,840	2.1%
17	Tennessee	7,850	1.9%
18	Wisconsin	6,990	1.7%
19	Indiana	6,930	1.7%
20	Washington	6,840	1.6%
21	South Carolina	6,730	1.6%
22	Colorado	6,610	1.6%
23	Massachusetts	6,010	1.4%
24	Alabama	5,350	1.3%
25	Kentucky	5,190	1.2%
26	Minnesota	4,910	1.2%
27	Mississippi	4,770	1.1%
28	Oklahoma	4,490	1.1%
29	Oregon	4,240	1.0%
30	Connecticut	4,230	1.0%
31	Arkansas	4,150	1.0%
32	Kansas	4,070	1.0%
33	Iowa	3,790	0.9%
34	New Mexico	2,710	0.7%
35	West Virginia	2,660	0.6%
36	Utah	2,340	0.6%
37	Nevada	2,290	0.5%
38	Nebraska	2,020	0.5%
39	Delaware	1,460	0.4%
40	Hawaii	1,380	0.3%
41	Idaho	1,280	0.3%
42	Maine	1,270	0.3%
43	Montana	1,190	0.3%
44	Rhode Island	1,080	0.3%
45	South Dakota	1,010	0.2%
46	Alaska	1,000	0.2%
47	New Hampshire	890	0.2%
48	Wyoming	810	0.2%
49	North Dakota	710	0.2%
NA	Vermont**	NA	NA
	District of Columbia	1,260	0.3%

Source: U.S. Department of Labor, Bureau of Labor Statistics
"Occupational Employment and Wages, 2004" (http://www.bls.gov/oes/)
Does not include self-employed.
**Not available.*

104

Rate of Correctional Officers and Jailers in 2004

National Rate = 142 Officers and Jailers per 100,000 Population*

ALPHA ORDER			RANK ORDER		
RANK	STATE	RATE	RANK	STATE	RATE
32	Alabama	118	1	Louisiana	211
15	Alaska	152	2	Texas	204
13	Arizona	157	3	Georgia	193
16	Arkansas	151	3	New York	193
44	California	96	5	Florida	185
20	Colorado	144	6	Delaware	176
30	Connecticut	121	6	Maryland	176
6	Delaware	176	8	North Carolina	168
5	Florida	185	9	Mississippi	164
3	Georgia	193	10	South Carolina	160
38	Hawaii	109	10	Wyoming	160
47	Idaho	92	12	Missouri	158
38	Illinois	109	13	Arizona	157
36	Indiana	111	14	Virginia	155
25	Iowa	128	15	Alaska	152
18	Kansas	149	16	Arkansas	151
29	Kentucky	125	16	New Jersey	151
1	Louisiana	211	18	Kansas	149
42	Maine	97	19	West Virginia	147
6	Maryland	176	20	Colorado	144
46	Massachusetts	94	21	Pennsylvania	143
48	Michigan	87	22	New Mexico	142
44	Minnesota	96	23	Tennessee	133
9	Mississippi	164	24	South Dakota	131
12	Missouri	158	25	Iowa	128
25	Montana	128	25	Montana	128
34	Nebraska	116	27	Oklahoma	127
41	Nevada	98	27	Wisconsin	127
49	New Hampshire	69	29	Kentucky	125
16	New Jersey	151	30	Connecticut	121
22	New Mexico	142	30	Ohio	121
3	New York	193	32	Alabama	118
8	North Carolina	168	32	Oregon	118
35	North Dakota	112	34	Nebraska	116
30	Ohio	121	35	North Dakota	112
27	Oklahoma	127	36	Indiana	111
32	Oregon	118	37	Washington	110
21	Pennsylvania	143	38	Hawaii	109
40	Rhode Island	100	38	Illinois	109
10	South Carolina	160	40	Rhode Island	100
24	South Dakota	131	41	Nevada	98
23	Tennessee	133	42	Maine	97
2	Texas	204	42	Utah	97
42	Utah	97	44	California	96
NA	Vermont**	NA	44	Minnesota	96
14	Virginia	155	46	Massachusetts	94
37	Washington	110	47	Idaho	92
19	West Virginia	147	48	Michigan	87
27	Wisconsin	127	49	New Hampshire	69
10	Wyoming	160	NA	Vermont**	NA
				District of Columbia	227

Source: Morgan Quitno Press using data from U.S. Department of Labor, Bureau of Labor Statistics
"Occupational Employment and Wages, 2004" (http://www.bls.gov/oes/)
*Does not include self-employed.
**Not available.

Offenders in State Sex Offender Registries in 2005

National Total = 551,987 Offenders*

ALPHA ORDER					RANK ORDER			

RANK	STATE	OFFENDERS	% of USA
28	Alabama	5,616	1.0%
39	Alaska	2,873	0.5%
17	Arizona	9,221	1.7%
27	Arkansas	5,864	1.1%
1	California	102,616	18.6%
19	Colorado	8,381	1.5%
33	Connecticut	3,785	0.7%
38	Delaware	2,961	0.5%
4	Florida	33,990	6.2%
18	Georgia	8,958	1.6%
44	Hawaii	1,957	0.4%
40	Idaho	2,606	0.5%
9	Illinois	17,100	3.1%
23	Indiana	7,300	1.3%
26	Iowa	6,104	1.1%
34	Kansas	3,563	0.6%
30	Kentucky	4,898	0.9%
25	Louisiana	6,591	1.2%
48	Maine	1,553	0.3%
32	Maryland	4,253	0.8%
7	Massachusetts	18,000	3.3%
3	Michigan	36,233	6.6%
10	Minnesota	15,819	2.9%
36	Mississippi	3,300	0.6%
14	Missouri	10,719	1.9%
35	Montana	3,370	0.6%
43	Nebraska	2,041	0.4%
31	Nevada	4,734	0.9%
37	New Hampshire	3,100	0.6%
15	New Jersey	10,464	1.9%
45	New Mexico	1,864	0.3%
5	New York	20,969	3.8%
16	North Carolina	10,244	1.9%
50	North Dakota	801	0.1%
12	Ohio	13,485	2.4%
29	Oklahoma	5,507	1.0%
11	Oregon	15,259	2.8%
24	Pennsylvania	7,199	1.3%
47	Rhode Island	1,640	0.3%
20	South Carolina	8,049	1.5%
46	South Dakota	1,707	0.3%
22	Tennessee	7,873	1.4%
2	Texas	46,484	8.4%
21	Utah	8,000	1.4%
41	Vermont	2,226	0.4%
13	Virginia	13,211	2.4%
6	Washington	18,557	3.4%
42	West Virginia	2,220	0.4%
8	Wisconsin	17,169	3.1%
49	Wyoming	929	0.2%

RANK ORDER

RANK	STATE	OFFENDERS	% of USA
1	California	102,616	18.6%
2	Texas	46,484	8.4%
3	Michigan	36,233	6.6%
4	Florida	33,990	6.2%
5	New York	20,969	3.8%
6	Washington	18,557	3.4%
7	Massachusetts	18,000	3.3%
8	Wisconsin	17,169	3.1%
9	Illinois	17,100	3.1%
10	Minnesota	15,819	2.9%
11	Oregon	15,259	2.8%
12	Ohio	13,485	2.4%
13	Virginia	13,211	2.4%
14	Missouri	10,719	1.9%
15	New Jersey	10,464	1.9%
16	North Carolina	10,244	1.9%
17	Arizona	9,221	1.7%
18	Georgia	8,958	1.6%
19	Colorado	8,381	1.5%
20	South Carolina	8,049	1.5%
21	Utah	8,000	1.4%
22	Tennessee	7,873	1.4%
23	Indiana	7,300	1.3%
24	Pennsylvania	7,199	1.3%
25	Louisiana	6,591	1.2%
26	Iowa	6,104	1.1%
27	Arkansas	5,864	1.1%
28	Alabama	5,616	1.0%
29	Oklahoma	5,507	1.0%
30	Kentucky	4,898	0.9%
31	Nevada	4,734	0.9%
32	Maryland	4,253	0.8%
33	Connecticut	3,785	0.7%
34	Kansas	3,563	0.6%
35	Montana	3,370	0.6%
36	Mississippi	3,300	0.6%
37	New Hampshire	3,100	0.6%
38	Delaware	2,961	0.5%
39	Alaska	2,873	0.5%
40	Idaho	2,606	0.5%
41	Vermont	2,226	0.4%
42	West Virginia	2,220	0.4%
43	Nebraska	2,041	0.4%
44	Hawaii	1,957	0.4%
45	New Mexico	1,864	0.3%
46	South Dakota	1,707	0.3%
47	Rhode Island	1,640	0.3%
48	Maine	1,553	0.3%
49	Wyoming	929	0.2%
50	North Dakota	801	0.1%
	District of Columbia	624	0.1%

Source: Parents for Megan's Law
  "Megan's Law Report Card" (http://www.parentsformeganslaw.com/html/links.lasso)
As of April 22, 2005. Several factors in each state's authorizing legislation significantly influence the size of a state's registry. Among these factors are the number of different offenses requiring registration, the date that triggers the registration mandate and the duration of the registration requirement.

III. DRUGS AND ALCOHOL

Drug Laboratory Seizures in 2004

National Total = 17,159 Laboratories*

ALPHA ORDER

RANK	STATE	LABORATORIES	% of USA
14	Alabama	385	2.2%
35	Alaska	66	0.4%
28	Arizona	122	0.7%
7	Arkansas	800	4.7%
8	California	764	4.5%
22	Colorado	228	1.3%
48	Connecticut	0	0.0%
42	Delaware	3	0.0%
18	Florida	276	1.6%
20	Georgia	261	1.5%
41	Hawaii	20	0.1%
38	Idaho	42	0.2%
5	Illinois	1,058	6.2%
4	Indiana	1,074	6.3%
2	Iowa	1,335	7.8%
10	Kansas	584	3.4%
11	Kentucky	571	3.3%
27	Louisiana	123	0.7%
42	Maine	3	0.0%
45	Maryland	1	0.0%
45	Massachusetts	1	0.0%
16	Michigan	295	1.7%
25	Minnesota	168	1.0%
19	Mississippi	267	1.6%
1	Missouri	2,778	16.2%
36	Montana	65	0.4%
23	Nebraska	205	1.2%
31	Nevada	79	0.5%
44	New Hampshire	2	0.0%
48	New Jersey	0	0.0%
29	New Mexico	120	0.7%
37	New York	48	0.3%
15	North Carolina	318	1.9%
21	North Dakota	234	1.4%
17	Ohio	286	1.7%
9	Oklahoma	659	3.8%
12	Oregon	472	2.8%
30	Pennsylvania	106	0.6%
48	Rhode Island	0	0.0%
24	South Carolina	170	1.0%
39	South Dakota	31	0.2%
3	Tennessee	1,327	7.7%
13	Texas	452	2.6%
34	Utah	72	0.4%
45	Vermont	1	0.0%
33	Virginia	75	0.4%
6	Washington	947	5.5%
26	West Virginia	165	1.0%
32	Wisconsin	78	0.5%
40	Wyoming	21	0.1%

RANK ORDER

RANK	STATE	LABORATORIES	% of USA
1	Missouri	2,778	16.2%
2	Iowa	1,335	7.8%
3	Tennessee	1,327	7.7%
4	Indiana	1,074	6.3%
5	Illinois	1,058	6.2%
6	Washington	947	5.5%
7	Arkansas	800	4.7%
8	California	764	4.5%
9	Oklahoma	659	3.8%
10	Kansas	584	3.4%
11	Kentucky	571	3.3%
12	Oregon	472	2.8%
13	Texas	452	2.6%
14	Alabama	385	2.2%
15	North Carolina	318	1.9%
16	Michigan	295	1.7%
17	Ohio	286	1.7%
18	Florida	276	1.6%
19	Mississippi	267	1.6%
20	Georgia	261	1.5%
21	North Dakota	234	1.4%
22	Colorado	228	1.3%
23	Nebraska	205	1.2%
24	South Carolina	170	1.0%
25	Minnesota	168	1.0%
26	West Virginia	165	1.0%
27	Louisiana	123	0.7%
28	Arizona	122	0.7%
29	New Mexico	120	0.7%
30	Pennsylvania	106	0.6%
31	Nevada	79	0.5%
32	Wisconsin	78	0.5%
33	Virginia	75	0.4%
34	Utah	72	0.4%
35	Alaska	66	0.4%
36	Montana	65	0.4%
37	New York	48	0.3%
38	Idaho	42	0.2%
39	South Dakota	31	0.2%
40	Wyoming	21	0.1%
41	Hawaii	20	0.1%
42	Delaware	3	0.0%
42	Maine	3	0.0%
44	New Hampshire	2	0.0%
45	Maryland	1	0.0%
45	Massachusetts	1	0.0%
45	Vermont	1	0.0%
48	Connecticut	0	0.0%
48	New Jersey	0	0.0%
48	Rhode Island	0	0.0%
	District of Columbia	1	0.0%

Source: Drug Enforcement Administration
"State Fact Sheets 2004" (http://www.dea.gov/pubs/state_factsheets.html)
*Seizures by DEA, state and local authorities.

Federal Marijuana Seizures in 2004

National Total = 1,018,007.1 Kilograms

ALPHA ORDER

RANK	STATE	KILOGRAMS	% of USA
18	Alabama	1,075.5	0.1%
48	Alaska	3.2	0.0%
2	Arizona	312,663.5	30.7%
8	Arkansas	6,304.2	0.6%
3	California	131,871.5	13.0%
23	Colorado	774.6	0.1%
44	Connecticut	20.8	0.0%
46	Delaware	11.3	0.0%
5	Florida	11,335.0	1.1%
19	Georgia	1,045.0	0.1%
42	Hawaii	24.6	0.0%
15	Idaho	1,700.0	0.2%
9	Illinois	6,237.1	0.6%
20	Indiana	986.6	0.1%
29	Iowa	425.9	0.0%
11	Kansas	3,853.9	0.4%
28	Kentucky	429.9	0.0%
22	Louisiana	864.2	0.1%
30	Maine	280.4	0.0%
36	Maryland	106.4	0.0%
37	Massachusetts	84.7	0.0%
7	Michigan	6,535.0	0.6%
25	Minnesota	499.5	0.0%
13	Mississippi	2,394.1	0.2%
12	Missouri	2,621.6	0.3%
24	Montana	766.5	0.1%
49	Nebraska	0.9	0.0%
31	Nevada	243.1	0.0%
38	New Hampshire	70.6	0.0%
16	New Jersey	1,196.0	0.1%
4	New Mexico	42,666.2	4.2%
10	New York	6,073.4	0.6%
32	North Carolina	237.7	0.0%
47	North Dakota	5.9	0.0%
26	Ohio	439.1	0.0%
27	Oklahoma	433.8	0.0%
35	Oregon	123.7	0.0%
17	Pennsylvania	1,178.4	0.1%
45	Rhode Island	18.7	0.0%
34	South Carolina	132.0	0.0%
50	South Dakota	0.6	0.0%
14	Tennessee	2,034.3	0.2%
1	Texas	460,672.3	45.3%
33	Utah	150.6	0.0%
21	Vermont	874.2	0.1%
39	Virginia	59.4	0.0%
6	Washington	8,382.6	0.8%
41	West Virginia	36.9	0.0%
40	Wisconsin	37.8	0.0%
43	Wyoming	21.0	0.0%

RANK ORDER

RANK	STATE	KILOGRAMS	% of USA
1	Texas	460,672.3	45.3%
2	Arizona	312,663.5	30.7%
3	California	131,871.5	13.0%
4	New Mexico	42,666.2	4.2%
5	Florida	11,335.0	1.1%
6	Washington	8,382.6	0.8%
7	Michigan	6,535.0	0.6%
8	Arkansas	6,304.2	0.6%
9	Illinois	6,237.1	0.6%
10	New York	6,073.4	0.6%
11	Kansas	3,853.9	0.4%
12	Missouri	2,621.6	0.3%
13	Mississippi	2,394.1	0.2%
14	Tennessee	2,034.3	0.2%
15	Idaho	1,700.0	0.2%
16	New Jersey	1,196.0	0.1%
17	Pennsylvania	1,178.4	0.1%
18	Alabama	1,075.5	0.1%
19	Georgia	1,045.0	0.1%
20	Indiana	986.6	0.1%
21	Vermont	874.2	0.1%
22	Louisiana	864.2	0.1%
23	Colorado	774.6	0.1%
24	Montana	766.5	0.1%
25	Minnesota	499.5	0.0%
26	Ohio	439.1	0.0%
27	Oklahoma	433.8	0.0%
28	Kentucky	429.9	0.0%
29	Iowa	425.9	0.0%
30	Maine	280.4	0.0%
31	Nevada	243.1	0.0%
32	North Carolina	237.7	0.0%
33	Utah	150.6	0.0%
34	South Carolina	132.0	0.0%
35	Oregon	123.7	0.0%
36	Maryland	106.4	0.0%
37	Massachusetts	84.7	0.0%
38	New Hampshire	70.6	0.0%
39	Virginia	59.4	0.0%
40	Wisconsin	37.8	0.0%
41	West Virginia	36.9	0.0%
42	Hawaii	24.6	0.0%
43	Wyoming	21.0	0.0%
44	Connecticut	20.8	0.0%
45	Rhode Island	18.7	0.0%
46	Delaware	11.3	0.0%
47	North Dakota	5.9	0.0%
48	Alaska	3.2	0.0%
49	Nebraska	0.9	0.0%
50	South Dakota	0.6	0.0%
	District of Columbia	2.9	0.0%

Source: Drug Enforcement Administration
"State Fact Sheets 2004" (http://www.dea.gov/pubs/state_factsheets.html)

Federal Cocaine Seizures in 2004

National Total = 50,623.7 Kilograms

ALPHA ORDER

RANK	STATE	KILOGRAMS	% of USA
21	Alabama	220.7	0.4%
21	Alaska	220.7	0.4%
3	Arizona	3,577.8	7.1%
10	Arkansas	714.8	1.4%
4	California	3,186.6	6.3%
32	Colorado	36.0	0.1%
36	Connecticut	23.8	0.0%
34	Delaware	35.0	0.1%
2	Florida	14,329.7	28.3%
8	Georgia	1,308.1	2.6%
43	Hawaii	4.3	0.0%
38	Idaho	10.8	0.0%
5	Illinois	2,183.3	4.3%
27	Indiana	100.0	0.2%
28	Iowa	87.8	0.2%
20	Kansas	227.8	0.4%
13	Kentucky	442.9	0.9%
11	Louisiana	678.0	1.3%
42	Maine	4.6	0.0%
26	Maryland	111.2	0.2%
30	Massachusetts	46.9	0.1%
25	Michigan	124.6	0.2%
37	Minnesota	15.7	0.0%
17	Mississippi	268.6	0.5%
19	Missouri	253.0	0.5%
41	Montana	6.2	0.0%
33	Nebraska	35.7	0.1%
35	Nevada	26.6	0.1%
45	New Hampshire	2.4	0.0%
6	New Jersey	2,083.0	4.1%
9	New Mexico	913.6	1.8%
7	New York	1,921.4	3.8%
14	North Carolina	391.3	0.8%
49	North Dakota	0.1	0.0%
18	Ohio	257.1	0.5%
29	Oklahoma	83.7	0.2%
44	Oregon	2.8	0.0%
24	Pennsylvania	173.8	0.3%
46	Rhode Island	1.6	0.0%
15	South Carolina	313.1	0.6%
47	South Dakota	0.5	0.0%
12	Tennessee	571.0	1.1%
1	Texas	15,036.7	29.7%
23	Utah	176.3	0.3%
48	Vermont	0.4	0.0%
31	Virginia	39.3	0.1%
16	Washington	310.0	0.6%
40	West Virginia	7.4	0.0%
39	Wisconsin	7.9	0.0%
49	Wyoming	0.1	0.0%

RANK ORDER

RANK	STATE	KILOGRAMS	% of USA
1	Texas	15,036.7	29.7%
2	Florida	14,329.7	28.3%
3	Arizona	3,577.8	7.1%
4	California	3,186.6	6.3%
5	Illinois	2,183.3	4.3%
6	New Jersey	2,083.0	4.1%
7	New York	1,921.4	3.8%
8	Georgia	1,308.1	2.6%
9	New Mexico	913.6	1.8%
10	Arkansas	714.8	1.4%
11	Louisiana	678.0	1.3%
12	Tennessee	571.0	1.1%
13	Kentucky	442.9	0.9%
14	North Carolina	391.3	0.8%
15	South Carolina	313.1	0.6%
16	Washington	310.0	0.6%
17	Mississippi	268.6	0.5%
18	Ohio	257.1	0.5%
19	Missouri	253.0	0.5%
20	Kansas	227.8	0.4%
21	Alabama	220.7	0.4%
21	Alaska	220.7	0.4%
23	Utah	176.3	0.3%
24	Pennsylvania	173.8	0.3%
25	Michigan	124.6	0.2%
26	Maryland	111.2	0.2%
27	Indiana	100.0	0.2%
28	Iowa	87.8	0.2%
29	Oklahoma	83.7	0.2%
30	Massachusetts	46.9	0.1%
31	Virginia	39.3	0.1%
32	Colorado	36.0	0.1%
33	Nebraska	35.7	0.1%
34	Delaware	35.0	0.1%
35	Nevada	26.6	0.1%
36	Connecticut	23.8	0.0%
37	Minnesota	15.7	0.0%
38	Idaho	10.8	0.0%
39	Wisconsin	7.9	0.0%
40	West Virginia	7.4	0.0%
41	Montana	6.2	0.0%
42	Maine	4.6	0.0%
43	Hawaii	4.3	0.0%
44	Oregon	2.8	0.0%
45	New Hampshire	2.4	0.0%
46	Rhode Island	1.6	0.0%
47	South Dakota	0.5	0.0%
48	Vermont	0.4	0.0%
49	North Dakota	0.1	0.0%
49	Wyoming	0.1	0.0%
	District of Columbia	49.0	0.1%

Source: Drug Enforcement Administration
"State Fact Sheets 2004" (http://www.dea.gov/pubs/state_factsheets.html)

Federal Heroin Seizures in 2004

National Total = 1,715.9 Kilograms

ALPHA ORDER

RANK	STATE	KILOGRAMS	% of USA
25	Alabama	2.0	0.1%
25	Alaska	2.0	0.1%
6	Arizona	88.9	5.2%
35	Arkansas	0.2	0.0%
5	California	121.4	7.1%
18	Colorado	4.6	0.3%
16	Connecticut	7.8	0.5%
18	Delaware	4.6	0.3%
1	Florida	445.1	25.9%
9	Georgia	39.3	2.3%
30	Hawaii	1.1	0.1%
36	Idaho	0.1	0.0%
8	Illinois	48.3	2.8%
36	Indiana	0.1	0.0%
41	Iowa	0.0	0.0%
33	Kansas	0.5	0.0%
18	Kentucky	4.6	0.3%
31	Louisiana	0.7	0.0%
36	Maine	0.1	0.0%
13	Maryland	10.7	0.6%
17	Massachusetts	6.8	0.4%
14	Michigan	9.7	0.6%
12	Minnesota	11.7	0.7%
22	Mississippi	3.4	0.2%
21	Missouri	4.0	0.2%
41	Montana	0.0	0.0%
41	Nebraska	0.0	0.0%
33	Nevada	0.5	0.0%
41	New Hampshire	0.0	0.0%
4	New Jersey	184.0	10.7%
28	New Mexico	1.3	0.1%
2	New York	350.7	20.4%
23	North Carolina	3.1	0.2%
41	North Dakota	0.0	0.0%
15	Ohio	8.6	0.5%
41	Oklahoma	0.0	0.0%
29	Oregon	1.2	0.1%
11	Pennsylvania	14.3	0.8%
36	Rhode Island	0.1	0.0%
23	South Carolina	3.1	0.2%
41	South Dakota	0.0	0.0%
7	Tennessee	64.1	3.7%
3	Texas	207.0	12.1%
27	Utah	1.5	0.1%
41	Vermont	0.0	0.0%
31	Virginia	0.7	0.0%
10	Washington	24.1	1.4%
41	West Virginia	0.0	0.0%
36	Wisconsin	0.1	0.0%
41	Wyoming	0.0	0.0%

RANK ORDER

RANK	STATE	KILOGRAMS	% of USA
1	Florida	445.1	25.9%
2	New York	350.7	20.4%
3	Texas	207.0	12.1%
4	New Jersey	184.0	10.7%
5	California	121.4	7.1%
6	Arizona	88.9	5.2%
7	Tennessee	64.1	3.7%
8	Illinois	48.3	2.8%
9	Georgia	39.3	2.3%
10	Washington	24.1	1.4%
11	Pennsylvania	14.3	0.8%
12	Minnesota	11.7	0.7%
13	Maryland	10.7	0.6%
14	Michigan	9.7	0.6%
15	Ohio	8.6	0.5%
16	Connecticut	7.8	0.5%
17	Massachusetts	6.8	0.4%
18	Colorado	4.6	0.3%
18	Delaware	4.6	0.3%
18	Kentucky	4.6	0.3%
21	Missouri	4.0	0.2%
22	Mississippi	3.4	0.2%
23	North Carolina	3.1	0.2%
23	South Carolina	3.1	0.2%
25	Alabama	2.0	0.1%
25	Alaska	2.0	0.1%
27	Utah	1.5	0.1%
28	New Mexico	1.3	0.1%
29	Oregon	1.2	0.1%
30	Hawaii	1.1	0.1%
31	Louisiana	0.7	0.0%
31	Virginia	0.7	0.0%
33	Kansas	0.5	0.0%
33	Nevada	0.5	0.0%
35	Arkansas	0.2	0.0%
36	Idaho	0.1	0.0%
36	Indiana	0.1	0.0%
36	Maine	0.1	0.0%
36	Rhode Island	0.1	0.0%
36	Wisconsin	0.1	0.0%
41	Iowa	0.0	0.0%
41	Montana	0.0	0.0%
41	Nebraska	0.0	0.0%
41	New Hampshire	0.0	0.0%
41	North Dakota	0.0	0.0%
41	Oklahoma	0.0	0.0%
41	South Dakota	0.0	0.0%
41	Vermont	0.0	0.0%
41	West Virginia	0.0	0.0%
41	Wyoming	0.0	0.0%
	District of Columbia	33.8	2.0%

Source: Drug Enforcement Administration
"State Fact Sheets 2004" (http://www.dea.gov/pubs/state_factsheets.html)

Federal Methamphetamine Seizures in 2004

National Total = 2,799.9 Kilograms

ALPHA ORDER					RANK ORDER			
RANK	STATE	KILOGRAMS	% of USA		RANK	STATE	KILOGRAMS	% of USA
33	Alabama	3.8	0.1%		1	California	786.5	28.1%
39	Alaska	0.7	0.0%		2	Texas	673.5	24.1%
3	Arizona	523.1	18.7%		3	Arizona	523.1	18.7%
21	Arkansas	12.9	0.5%		4	Georgia	83.9	3.0%
1	California	786.5	28.1%		5	Louisiana	83.1	3.0%
13	Colorado	28.8	1.0%		6	Washington	73.0	2.6%
43	Connecticut	0.0	0.0%		7	Tennessee	70.4	2.5%
43	Delaware	0.0	0.0%		8	New Mexico	60.0	2.1%
11	Florida	36.9	1.3%		9	Nevada	51.5	1.8%
4	Georgia	83.9	3.0%		10	Iowa	39.1	1.4%
15	Hawaii	22.7	0.8%		11	Florida	36.9	1.3%
27	Idaho	6.9	0.2%		12	Oregon	35.2	1.3%
23	Illinois	12.4	0.4%		13	Colorado	28.8	1.0%
19	Indiana	17.5	0.6%		14	Minnesota	24.6	0.9%
10	Iowa	39.1	1.4%		15	Hawaii	22.7	0.8%
25	Kansas	10.0	0.4%		16	Kentucky	22.1	0.8%
16	Kentucky	22.1	0.8%		17	Missouri	21.2	0.8%
5	Louisiana	83.1	3.0%		18	Utah	18.1	0.6%
43	Maine	0.0	0.0%		19	Indiana	17.5	0.6%
43	Maryland	0.0	0.0%		20	Mississippi	15.6	0.6%
39	Massachusetts	0.7	0.0%		21	Arkansas	12.9	0.5%
36	Michigan	1.5	0.1%		22	North Carolina	12.7	0.5%
14	Minnesota	24.6	0.9%		23	Illinois	12.4	0.4%
20	Mississippi	15.6	0.6%		24	New York	10.7	0.4%
17	Missouri	21.2	0.8%		25	Kansas	10.0	0.4%
34	Montana	3.6	0.1%		26	Ohio	7.4	0.3%
28	Nebraska	6.3	0.2%		27	Idaho	6.9	0.2%
9	Nevada	51.5	1.8%		28	Nebraska	6.3	0.2%
43	New Hampshire	0.0	0.0%		28	Virginia	6.3	0.2%
38	New Jersey	0.8	0.0%		30	Oklahoma	4.8	0.2%
8	New Mexico	60.0	2.1%		31	South Carolina	4.2	0.2%
24	New York	10.7	0.4%		32	Pennsylvania	4.1	0.1%
22	North Carolina	12.7	0.5%		33	Alabama	3.8	0.1%
41	North Dakota	0.1	0.0%		34	Montana	3.6	0.1%
26	Ohio	7.4	0.3%		35	South Dakota	1.8	0.1%
30	Oklahoma	4.8	0.2%		36	Michigan	1.5	0.1%
12	Oregon	35.2	1.3%		37	Wyoming	1.0	0.0%
32	Pennsylvania	4.1	0.1%		38	New Jersey	0.8	0.0%
43	Rhode Island	0.0	0.0%		39	Alaska	0.7	0.0%
31	South Carolina	4.2	0.2%		39	Massachusetts	0.7	0.0%
35	South Dakota	1.8	0.1%		41	North Dakota	0.1	0.0%
7	Tennessee	70.4	2.5%		41	West Virginia	0.1	0.0%
2	Texas	673.5	24.1%		43	Connecticut	0.0	0.0%
18	Utah	18.1	0.6%		43	Delaware	0.0	0.0%
43	Vermont	0.0	0.0%		43	Maine	0.0	0.0%
28	Virginia	6.3	0.2%		43	Maryland	0.0	0.0%
6	Washington	73.0	2.6%		43	New Hampshire	0.0	0.0%
41	West Virginia	0.1	0.0%		43	Rhode Island	0.0	0.0%
43	Wisconsin	0.0	0.0%		43	Vermont	0.0	0.0%
37	Wyoming	1.0	0.0%		43	Wisconsin	0.0	0.0%
						District of Columbia	0.3	0.0%

Source: Drug Enforcement Administration
"State Fact Sheets 2004" (http://www.dea.gov/pubs/state_factsheets.html)

Federal Ecstasy Seizures in 2004

National Total = 1,154,520 Tablets

ALPHA ORDER

RANK	STATE	TABLETS	% of USA
42	Alabama	0	0.0%
37	Alaska	6	0.0%
25	Arizona	882	0.1%
30	Arkansas	271	0.0%
1	California	329,973	28.6%
42	Colorado	0	0.0%
35	Connecticut	49	0.0%
42	Delaware	0	0.0%
5	Florida	105,319	9.1%
11	Georgia	8,393	0.7%
42	Hawaii	0	0.0%
42	Idaho	0	0.0%
22	Illinois	1,826	0.2%
24	Indiana	958	0.1%
21	Iowa	2,205	0.2%
14	Kansas	5,507	0.5%
8	Kentucky	17,103	1.5%
6	Louisiana	22,475	1.9%
27	Maine	676	0.1%
34	Maryland	69	0.0%
38	Massachusetts	4	0.0%
15	Michigan	4,873	0.4%
29	Minnesota	624	0.1%
20	Mississippi	2,252	0.2%
23	Missouri	1,032	0.1%
40	Montana	2	0.0%
42	Nebraska	0	0.0%
26	Nevada	837	0.1%
19	New Hampshire	2,533	0.2%
9	New Jersey	12,902	1.1%
33	New Mexico	144	0.0%
2	New York	276,879	24.0%
13	North Carolina	5,921	0.5%
41	North Dakota	1	0.0%
12	Ohio	6,158	0.5%
16	Oklahoma	4,237	0.4%
32	Oregon	152	0.0%
7	Pennsylvania	20,373	1.8%
28	Rhode Island	657	0.1%
36	South Carolina	33	0.0%
39	South Dakota	3	0.0%
10	Tennessee	10,539	0.9%
4	Texas	137,752	11.9%
31	Utah	176	0.0%
17	Vermont	3,902	0.3%
18	Virginia	2,861	0.2%
3	Washington	162,661	14.1%
42	West Virginia	0	0.0%
42	Wisconsin	0	0.0%
42	Wyoming	0	0.0%

RANK ORDER

RANK	STATE	TABLETS	% of USA
1	California	329,973	28.6%
2	New York	276,879	24.0%
3	Washington	162,661	14.1%
4	Texas	137,752	11.9%
5	Florida	105,319	9.1%
6	Louisiana	22,475	1.9%
7	Pennsylvania	20,373	1.8%
8	Kentucky	17,103	1.5%
9	New Jersey	12,902	1.1%
10	Tennessee	10,539	0.9%
11	Georgia	8,393	0.7%
12	Ohio	6,158	0.5%
13	North Carolina	5,921	0.5%
14	Kansas	5,507	0.5%
15	Michigan	4,873	0.4%
16	Oklahoma	4,237	0.4%
17	Vermont	3,902	0.3%
18	Virginia	2,861	0.2%
19	New Hampshire	2,533	0.2%
20	Mississippi	2,252	0.2%
21	Iowa	2,205	0.2%
22	Illinois	1,826	0.2%
23	Missouri	1,032	0.1%
24	Indiana	958	0.1%
25	Arizona	882	0.1%
26	Nevada	837	0.1%
27	Maine	676	0.1%
28	Rhode Island	657	0.1%
29	Minnesota	624	0.1%
30	Arkansas	271	0.0%
31	Utah	176	0.0%
32	Oregon	152	0.0%
33	New Mexico	144	0.0%
34	Maryland	69	0.0%
35	Connecticut	49	0.0%
36	South Carolina	33	0.0%
37	Alaska	6	0.0%
38	Massachusetts	4	0.0%
39	South Dakota	3	0.0%
40	Montana	2	0.0%
41	North Dakota	1	0.0%
42	Alabama	0	0.0%
42	Colorado	0	0.0%
42	Delaware	0	0.0%
42	Hawaii	0	0.0%
42	Idaho	0	0.0%
42	Nebraska	0	0.0%
42	West Virginia	0	0.0%
42	Wisconsin	0	0.0%
42	Wyoming	0	0.0%
	District of Columbia	1,300	0.1%

Source: Drug Enforcement Administration
"State Fact Sheets 2004" (http://www.dea.gov/pubs/state_factsheets.html)

Percent of Population Who are Illicit Drug Users: 2003

National Percent = 8.3% of Population*

ALPHA ORDER				RANK ORDER		
RANK	STATE	PERCENT		RANK	STATE	PERCENT
46	Alabama	6.6		1	Alaska	12.0
1	Alaska	12.0		2	New Hampshire	11.2
16	Arizona	8.9		3	Colorado	11.1
28	Arkansas	7.8		4	Rhode Island	11.0
15	California	9.0		4	Vermont	11.0
3	Colorado	11.1		6	Oregon	10.8
19	Connecticut	8.8		7	Montana	10.6
20	Delaware	8.7		8	Nevada	10.3
20	Florida	8.7		9	New Mexico	10.0
33	Georgia	7.5		9	Washington	10.0
16	Hawaii	8.9		11	Maine	9.3
38	Idaho	7.2		11	Massachusetts	9.3
33	Illinois	7.5		13	Missouri	9.2
24	Indiana	8.1		14	Michigan	9.1
49	Iowa	6.5		15	California	9.0
44	Kansas	6.7		16	Arizona	8.9
23	Kentucky	8.3		16	Hawaii	8.9
24	Louisiana	8.1		16	New York	8.9
11	Maine	9.3		19	Connecticut	8.8
31	Maryland	7.6		20	Delaware	8.7
11	Massachusetts	9.3		20	Florida	8.7
14	Michigan	9.1		22	Oklahoma	8.6
31	Minnesota	7.6		23	Kentucky	8.3
46	Mississippi	6.6		24	Indiana	8.1
13	Missouri	9.2		24	Louisiana	8.1
7	Montana	10.6		26	Ohio	8.0
29	Nebraska	7.7		27	North Carolina	7.9
8	Nevada	10.3		28	Arkansas	7.8
2	New Hampshire	11.2		29	Nebraska	7.7
42	New Jersey	7.0		29	Virginia	7.7
9	New Mexico	10.0		31	Maryland	7.6
16	New York	8.9		31	Minnesota	7.6
27	North Carolina	7.9		33	Georgia	7.5
38	North Dakota	7.2		33	Illinois	7.5
26	Ohio	8.0		33	Pennsylvania	7.5
22	Oklahoma	8.6		33	Wisconsin	7.5
6	Oregon	10.8		33	Wyoming	7.5
33	Pennsylvania	7.5		38	Idaho	7.2
4	Rhode Island	11.0		38	North Dakota	7.2
38	South Carolina	7.2		38	South Carolina	7.2
38	South Dakota	7.2		38	South Dakota	7.2
44	Tennessee	6.7		42	New Jersey	7.0
42	Texas	7.0		42	Texas	7.0
50	Utah	6.3		44	Kansas	6.7
4	Vermont	11.0		44	Tennessee	6.7
29	Virginia	7.7		46	Alabama	6.6
9	Washington	10.0		46	Mississippi	6.6
46	West Virginia	6.6		46	West Virginia	6.6
33	Wisconsin	7.5		49	Iowa	6.5
33	Wyoming	7.5		50	Utah	6.3

District of Columbia   11.6

Source: U.S. Department of Health and Human Services, Substance Abuse and Mental Health Services Administration "2002/2003 National Survey on Drug Use and Health" (January 2005)
Population 12 years and older who used any illicit drug at least once within month of survey.

Percent of Population Who are Marijuana Users: 2003

National Percent = 6.2% of Population*

ALPHA ORDER

RANK ORDER

RANK	STATE	PERCENT		RANK	STATE	PERCENT
49	Alabama	4.3		1	New Hampshire	10.2
2	Alaska	9.8		2	Alaska	9.8
28	Arizona	5.7		2	Vermont	9.8
31	Arkansas	5.6		4	Rhode Island	9.6
20	California	6.5		5	Montana	9.2
7	Colorado	8.5		6	Oregon	8.9
16	Connecticut	6.9		7	Colorado	8.5
16	Delaware	6.9		8	Maine	8.0
19	Florida	6.6		9	Massachusetts	7.8
43	Georgia	4.9		10	Nevada	7.6
15	Hawaii	7.0		11	New Mexico	7.4
40	Idaho	5.1		11	Washington	7.4
31	Illinois	5.6		13	New York	7.3
23	Indiana	6.1		14	Michigan	7.2
43	Iowa	4.9		15	Hawaii	7.0
43	Kansas	4.9		16	Connecticut	6.9
31	Kentucky	5.6		16	Delaware	6.9
27	Louisiana	5.8		18	Missouri	6.8
8	Maine	8.0		19	Florida	6.6
28	Maryland	5.7		20	California	6.5
9	Massachusetts	7.8		20	Ohio	6.5
14	Michigan	7.2		22	Minnesota	6.4
22	Minnesota	6.4		23	Indiana	6.1
47	Mississippi	4.6		24	Nebraska	6.0
18	Missouri	6.8		24	Virginia	6.0
5	Montana	9.2		26	North Carolina	5.9
24	Nebraska	6.0		27	Louisiana	5.8
10	Nevada	7.6		28	Arizona	5.7
1	New Hampshire	10.2		28	Maryland	5.7
40	New Jersey	5.1		28	South Carolina	5.7
11	New Mexico	7.4		31	Arkansas	5.6
13	New York	7.3		31	Illinois	5.6
26	North Carolina	5.9		31	Kentucky	5.6
37	North Dakota	5.4		31	Oklahoma	5.6
20	Ohio	6.5		31	Pennsylvania	5.6
31	Oklahoma	5.6		36	Wyoming	5.5
6	Oregon	8.9		37	North Dakota	5.4
31	Pennsylvania	5.6		37	Wisconsin	5.4
4	Rhode Island	9.6		39	South Dakota	5.2
28	South Carolina	5.7		40	Idaho	5.1
39	South Dakota	5.2		40	New Jersey	5.1
47	Tennessee	4.6		40	West Virginia	5.1
46	Texas	4.8		43	Georgia	4.9
50	Utah	4.0		43	Iowa	4.9
2	Vermont	9.8		43	Kansas	4.9
24	Virginia	6.0		46	Texas	4.8
11	Washington	7.4		47	Mississippi	4.6
40	West Virginia	5.1		47	Tennessee	4.6
37	Wisconsin	5.4		49	Alabama	4.3
36	Wyoming	5.5		50	Utah	4.0
					District of Columbia	9.6

Source: U.S. Department of Health and Human Services, Substance Abuse and Mental Health Services Administration
"2002/2003 National Survey on Drug Use and Health" (January 2005)
*Population 12 years and older who used any marijuana at least once within month of survey.

Percent of Population Using Illicit Drugs Other Than Marijuana: 2003

National Percent = 3.7% of Population*

ALPHA ORDER

RANK	STATE	PERCENT
23	Alabama	3.7
13	Alaska	4.0
1	Arizona	4.7
16	Arkansas	3.9
16	California	3.9
1	Colorado	4.7
43	Connecticut	3.3
16	Delaware	3.9
23	Florida	3.7
13	Georgia	4.0
35	Hawaii	3.5
23	Idaho	3.7
43	Illinois	3.3
28	Indiana	3.6
47	Iowa	3.2
49	Kansas	3.1
6	Kentucky	4.4
9	Louisiana	4.2
21	Maine	3.8
38	Maryland	3.4
28	Massachusetts	3.6
28	Michigan	3.6
47	Minnesota	3.2
28	Mississippi	3.6
9	Missouri	4.2
21	Montana	3.8
38	Nebraska	3.4
5	Nevada	4.5
12	New Hampshire	4.1
38	New Jersey	3.4
3	New Mexico	4.6
49	New York	3.1
13	North Carolina	4.0
43	North Dakota	3.3
38	Ohio	3.4
6	Oklahoma	4.4
8	Oregon	4.3
38	Pennsylvania	3.4
3	Rhode Island	4.6
28	South Carolina	3.6
43	South Dakota	3.3
28	Tennessee	3.6
16	Texas	3.9
23	Utah	3.7
16	Vermont	3.9
35	Virginia	3.5
9	Washington	4.2
35	West Virginia	3.5
28	Wisconsin	3.6
23	Wyoming	3.7

RANK ORDER

RANK	STATE	PERCENT
1	Arizona	4.7
1	Colorado	4.7
3	New Mexico	4.6
3	Rhode Island	4.6
5	Nevada	4.5
6	Kentucky	4.4
6	Oklahoma	4.4
8	Oregon	4.3
9	Louisiana	4.2
9	Missouri	4.2
9	Washington	4.2
12	New Hampshire	4.1
13	Alaska	4.0
13	Georgia	4.0
13	North Carolina	4.0
16	Arkansas	3.9
16	California	3.9
16	Delaware	3.9
16	Texas	3.9
16	Vermont	3.9
21	Maine	3.8
21	Montana	3.8
23	Alabama	3.7
23	Florida	3.7
23	Idaho	3.7
23	Utah	3.7
23	Wyoming	3.7
28	Indiana	3.6
28	Massachusetts	3.6
28	Michigan	3.6
28	Mississippi	3.6
28	South Carolina	3.6
28	Tennessee	3.6
28	Wisconsin	3.6
35	Hawaii	3.5
35	Virginia	3.5
35	West Virginia	3.5
38	Maryland	3.4
38	Nebraska	3.4
38	New Jersey	3.4
38	Ohio	3.4
38	Pennsylvania	3.4
43	Connecticut	3.3
43	Illinois	3.3
43	North Dakota	3.3
43	South Dakota	3.3
47	Iowa	3.2
47	Minnesota	3.2
49	Kansas	3.1
49	New York	3.1

District of Columbia   4.1

Source: U.S. Department of Health and Human Services, Substance Abuse and Mental Health Services Administration "2002/2003 National Survey on Drug Use and Health" (January 2005)
Population 12 years and older who used any illicit drug except marijuana at least once within month of survey.

Percent of Population Who are Binge Drinkers: 2003

National Percent = 22.8% of Population*

ALPHA ORDER

RANK	STATE	PERCENT
48	Alabama	18.1
25	Alaska	23.1
17	Arizona	24.3
30	Arkansas	21.8
36	California	21.3
10	Colorado	25.8
25	Connecticut	23.1
23	Delaware	23.7
31	Florida	21.7
40	Georgia	20.7
23	Hawaii	23.7
37	Idaho	21.1
12	Illinois	25.2
29	Indiana	22.3
8	Iowa	26.3
31	Kansas	21.7
46	Kentucky	19.2
22	Louisiana	23.8
31	Maine	21.7
31	Maryland	21.7
6	Massachusetts	27.2
15	Michigan	24.5
3	Minnesota	28.1
43	Mississippi	19.7
14	Missouri	24.6
5	Montana	27.4
8	Nebraska	26.3
38	Nevada	20.9
19	New Hampshire	24.0
31	New Jersey	21.7
19	New Mexico	24.0
17	New York	24.3
44	North Carolina	19.3
1	North Dakota	31.4
16	Ohio	24.4
47	Oklahoma	19.0
41	Oregon	20.5
27	Pennsylvania	22.8
7	Rhode Island	27.0
28	South Carolina	22.5
3	South Dakota	28.1
49	Tennessee	16.6
21	Texas	23.9
50	Utah	15.9
11	Vermont	25.5
41	Virginia	20.5
38	Washington	20.9
44	West Virginia	19.3
2	Wisconsin	29.0
13	Wyoming	24.9

RANK ORDER

RANK	STATE	PERCENT
1	North Dakota	31.4
2	Wisconsin	29.0
3	Minnesota	28.1
3	South Dakota	28.1
5	Montana	27.4
6	Massachusetts	27.2
7	Rhode Island	27.0
8	Iowa	26.3
8	Nebraska	26.3
10	Colorado	25.8
11	Vermont	25.5
12	Illinois	25.2
13	Wyoming	24.9
14	Missouri	24.6
15	Michigan	24.5
16	Ohio	24.4
17	Arizona	24.3
17	New York	24.3
19	New Hampshire	24.0
19	New Mexico	24.0
21	Texas	23.9
22	Louisiana	23.8
23	Delaware	23.7
23	Hawaii	23.7
25	Alaska	23.1
25	Connecticut	23.1
27	Pennsylvania	22.8
28	South Carolina	22.5
29	Indiana	22.3
30	Arkansas	21.8
31	Florida	21.7
31	Kansas	21.7
31	Maine	21.7
31	Maryland	21.7
31	New Jersey	21.7
36	California	21.3
37	Idaho	21.1
38	Nevada	20.9
38	Washington	20.9
40	Georgia	20.7
41	Oregon	20.5
41	Virginia	20.5
43	Mississippi	19.7
44	North Carolina	19.3
44	West Virginia	19.3
46	Kentucky	19.2
47	Oklahoma	19.0
48	Alabama	18.1
49	Tennessee	16.6
50	Utah	15.9

| | District of Columbia | 25.3 |

Source: U.S. Department of Health and Human Services, Substance Abuse and Mental Health Services Administration "2002/2003 National Survey on Drug Use and Health" (January 2005)

*Population 12 years and older who reported binge alcohol use at least once within month of survey. "Binge" alcohol use is defined as drinking five or more drinks on the same occasion on at least one day in the past 30 days. By "occasion" is meant at the same time or within a couple of hours of each other.

Percent of Population Reporting Illicit Drug Dependence or Abuse: 2003

National Percent = 3.0% of Population*

ALPHA ORDER

RANK	STATE	PERCENT
42	Alabama	2.7
11	Alaska	3.1
5	Arizona	3.4
14	Arkansas	3.0
14	California	3.0
9	Colorado	3.2
24	Connecticut	2.9
14	Delaware	3.0
11	Florida	3.1
24	Georgia	2.9
34	Hawaii	2.8
24	Idaho	2.9
34	Illinois	2.8
34	Indiana	2.8
49	Iowa	2.5
49	Kansas	2.5
34	Kentucky	2.8
7	Louisiana	3.3
24	Maine	2.9
14	Maryland	3.0
3	Massachusetts	3.6
14	Michigan	3.0
34	Minnesota	2.8
24	Mississippi	2.9
14	Missouri	3.0
9	Montana	3.2
34	Nebraska	2.8
14	Nevada	3.0
5	New Hampshire	3.4
42	New Jersey	2.7
2	New Mexico	3.8
14	New York	3.0
24	North Carolina	2.9
34	North Dakota	2.8
24	Ohio	2.9
24	Oklahoma	2.9
11	Oregon	3.1
47	Pennsylvania	2.6
1	Rhode Island	3.9
24	South Carolina	2.9
42	South Dakota	2.7
34	Tennessee	2.8
42	Texas	2.7
24	Utah	2.9
3	Vermont	3.6
14	Virginia	3.0
7	Washington	3.3
14	West Virginia	3.0
42	Wisconsin	2.7
47	Wyoming	2.6

RANK ORDER

RANK	STATE	PERCENT
1	Rhode Island	3.9
2	New Mexico	3.8
3	Massachusetts	3.6
3	Vermont	3.6
5	Arizona	3.4
5	New Hampshire	3.4
7	Louisiana	3.3
7	Washington	3.3
9	Colorado	3.2
9	Montana	3.2
11	Alaska	3.1
11	Florida	3.1
11	Oregon	3.1
14	Arkansas	3.0
14	California	3.0
14	Delaware	3.0
14	Maryland	3.0
14	Michigan	3.0
14	Missouri	3.0
14	Nevada	3.0
14	New York	3.0
14	Virginia	3.0
14	West Virginia	3.0
24	Connecticut	2.9
24	Georgia	2.9
24	Idaho	2.9
24	Maine	2.9
24	Mississippi	2.9
24	North Carolina	2.9
24	Ohio	2.9
24	Oklahoma	2.9
24	South Carolina	2.9
24	Utah	2.9
34	Hawaii	2.8
34	Illinois	2.8
34	Indiana	2.8
34	Kentucky	2.8
34	Minnesota	2.8
34	Nebraska	2.8
34	North Dakota	2.8
34	Tennessee	2.8
42	Alabama	2.7
42	New Jersey	2.7
42	South Dakota	2.7
42	Texas	2.7
42	Wisconsin	2.7
47	Pennsylvania	2.6
47	Wyoming	2.6
49	Iowa	2.5
49	Kansas	2.5

| | District of Columbia | 4.0 |

Source: U.S. Department of Health and Human Services, Substance Abuse and Mental Health Services Administration "2002/2003 National Survey on Drug Use and Health" (January 2005)
Population 12 years and older reporting illicit drug dependence or abuse within one year of survey.

Percent of Population Needing But Not Receiving
Treatment for Illicit Drug Use: 2003
National Percent = 2.7% of Adults*

<table>
<thead>
<tr><th colspan="3">ALPHA ORDER</th><th colspan="3">RANK ORDER</th></tr>
<tr><th>RANK</th><th>STATE</th><th>PERCENT</th><th>RANK</th><th>STATE</th><th>PERCENT</th></tr>
</thead>
<tbody>
<tr><td>48</td><td>Alabama</td><td>2.2</td><td>1</td><td>New Mexico</td><td>3.5</td></tr>
<tr><td>5</td><td>Alaska</td><td>3.1</td><td>2</td><td>Vermont</td><td>3.4</td></tr>
<tr><td>3</td><td>Arizona</td><td>3.2</td><td>3</td><td>Arizona</td><td>3.2</td></tr>
<tr><td>19</td><td>Arkansas</td><td>2.7</td><td>3</td><td>Rhode Island</td><td>3.2</td></tr>
<tr><td>13</td><td>California</td><td>2.8</td><td>5</td><td>Alaska</td><td>3.1</td></tr>
<tr><td>8</td><td>Colorado</td><td>3.0</td><td>5</td><td>Massachusetts</td><td>3.1</td></tr>
<tr><td>13</td><td>Connecticut</td><td>2.8</td><td>5</td><td>Washington</td><td>3.1</td></tr>
<tr><td>26</td><td>Delaware</td><td>2.6</td><td>8</td><td>Colorado</td><td>3.0</td></tr>
<tr><td>13</td><td>Florida</td><td>2.8</td><td>8</td><td>New Hampshire</td><td>3.0</td></tr>
<tr><td>26</td><td>Georgia</td><td>2.6</td><td>10</td><td>Louisiana</td><td>2.9</td></tr>
<tr><td>26</td><td>Hawaii</td><td>2.6</td><td>10</td><td>Montana</td><td>2.9</td></tr>
<tr><td>13</td><td>Idaho</td><td>2.8</td><td>10</td><td>Oregon</td><td>2.9</td></tr>
<tr><td>36</td><td>Illinois</td><td>2.5</td><td>13</td><td>California</td><td>2.8</td></tr>
<tr><td>36</td><td>Indiana</td><td>2.5</td><td>13</td><td>Connecticut</td><td>2.8</td></tr>
<tr><td>43</td><td>Iowa</td><td>2.4</td><td>13</td><td>Florida</td><td>2.8</td></tr>
<tr><td>48</td><td>Kansas</td><td>2.2</td><td>13</td><td>Idaho</td><td>2.8</td></tr>
<tr><td>26</td><td>Kentucky</td><td>2.6</td><td>13</td><td>Maine</td><td>2.8</td></tr>
<tr><td>10</td><td>Louisiana</td><td>2.9</td><td>13</td><td>Missouri</td><td>2.8</td></tr>
<tr><td>13</td><td>Maine</td><td>2.8</td><td>19</td><td>Arkansas</td><td>2.7</td></tr>
<tr><td>19</td><td>Maryland</td><td>2.7</td><td>19</td><td>Maryland</td><td>2.7</td></tr>
<tr><td>5</td><td>Massachusetts</td><td>3.1</td><td>19</td><td>Nevada</td><td>2.7</td></tr>
<tr><td>26</td><td>Michigan</td><td>2.6</td><td>19</td><td>New York</td><td>2.7</td></tr>
<tr><td>26</td><td>Minnesota</td><td>2.6</td><td>19</td><td>Oklahoma</td><td>2.7</td></tr>
<tr><td>36</td><td>Mississippi</td><td>2.5</td><td>19</td><td>Utah</td><td>2.7</td></tr>
<tr><td>13</td><td>Missouri</td><td>2.8</td><td>19</td><td>Virginia</td><td>2.7</td></tr>
<tr><td>10</td><td>Montana</td><td>2.9</td><td>26</td><td>Delaware</td><td>2.6</td></tr>
<tr><td>26</td><td>Nebraska</td><td>2.6</td><td>26</td><td>Georgia</td><td>2.6</td></tr>
<tr><td>19</td><td>Nevada</td><td>2.7</td><td>26</td><td>Hawaii</td><td>2.6</td></tr>
<tr><td>8</td><td>New Hampshire</td><td>3.0</td><td>26</td><td>Kentucky</td><td>2.6</td></tr>
<tr><td>46</td><td>New Jersey</td><td>2.3</td><td>26</td><td>Michigan</td><td>2.6</td></tr>
<tr><td>1</td><td>New Mexico</td><td>3.5</td><td>26</td><td>Minnesota</td><td>2.6</td></tr>
<tr><td>19</td><td>New York</td><td>2.7</td><td>26</td><td>Nebraska</td><td>2.6</td></tr>
<tr><td>26</td><td>North Carolina</td><td>2.6</td><td>26</td><td>North Carolina</td><td>2.6</td></tr>
<tr><td>26</td><td>North Dakota</td><td>2.6</td><td>26</td><td>North Dakota</td><td>2.6</td></tr>
<tr><td>26</td><td>Ohio</td><td>2.6</td><td>26</td><td>Ohio</td><td>2.6</td></tr>
<tr><td>19</td><td>Oklahoma</td><td>2.7</td><td>36</td><td>Illinois</td><td>2.5</td></tr>
<tr><td>10</td><td>Oregon</td><td>2.9</td><td>36</td><td>Indiana</td><td>2.5</td></tr>
<tr><td>48</td><td>Pennsylvania</td><td>2.2</td><td>36</td><td>Mississippi</td><td>2.5</td></tr>
<tr><td>3</td><td>Rhode Island</td><td>3.2</td><td>36</td><td>Tennessee</td><td>2.5</td></tr>
<tr><td>43</td><td>South Carolina</td><td>2.4</td><td>36</td><td>Texas</td><td>2.5</td></tr>
<tr><td>43</td><td>South Dakota</td><td>2.4</td><td>36</td><td>West Virginia</td><td>2.5</td></tr>
<tr><td>36</td><td>Tennessee</td><td>2.5</td><td>36</td><td>Wyoming</td><td>2.5</td></tr>
<tr><td>36</td><td>Texas</td><td>2.5</td><td>43</td><td>Iowa</td><td>2.4</td></tr>
<tr><td>19</td><td>Utah</td><td>2.7</td><td>43</td><td>South Carolina</td><td>2.4</td></tr>
<tr><td>2</td><td>Vermont</td><td>3.4</td><td>43</td><td>South Dakota</td><td>2.4</td></tr>
<tr><td>19</td><td>Virginia</td><td>2.7</td><td>46</td><td>New Jersey</td><td>2.3</td></tr>
<tr><td>5</td><td>Washington</td><td>3.1</td><td>46</td><td>Wisconsin</td><td>2.3</td></tr>
<tr><td>36</td><td>West Virginia</td><td>2.5</td><td>48</td><td>Alabama</td><td>2.2</td></tr>
<tr><td>46</td><td>Wisconsin</td><td>2.3</td><td>48</td><td>Kansas</td><td>2.2</td></tr>
<tr><td>36</td><td>Wyoming</td><td>2.5</td><td>48</td><td>Pennsylvania</td><td>2.2</td></tr>
</tbody>
</table>

District of Columbia   3.0

Source: U.S. Department of Health and Human Services, Substance Abuse and Mental Health Services Administration
    "2002/2003 National Survey on Drug Use and Health" (January 2005)
*Percent of population 12 years and older needing but not receiving treatment within one year of survey.

Percent of Population Reporting Alcohol Dependence or Abuse: 2003

National Percent = 7.6% of Population*

<table>
<tr><td colspan="3">ALPHA ORDER</td><td colspan="3">RANK ORDER</td></tr>
<tr><td>RANK</td><td>STATE</td><td>PERCENT</td><td>RANK</td><td>STATE</td><td>PERCENT</td></tr>
<tr><td>49</td><td>Alabama</td><td>6.1</td><td>1</td><td>North Dakota</td><td>10.8</td></tr>
<tr><td>14</td><td>Alaska</td><td>8.6</td><td>1</td><td>South Dakota</td><td>10.8</td></tr>
<tr><td>8</td><td>Arizona</td><td>9.3</td><td>3</td><td>Montana</td><td>10.7</td></tr>
<tr><td>27</td><td>Arkansas</td><td>7.6</td><td>4</td><td>Nebraska</td><td>10.2</td></tr>
<tr><td>36</td><td>California</td><td>7.2</td><td>5</td><td>Rhode Island</td><td>10.1</td></tr>
<tr><td>9</td><td>Colorado</td><td>9.2</td><td>6</td><td>New Mexico</td><td>10.0</td></tr>
<tr><td>39</td><td>Connecticut</td><td>6.9</td><td>7</td><td>Wisconsin</td><td>9.5</td></tr>
<tr><td>26</td><td>Delaware</td><td>7.7</td><td>8</td><td>Arizona</td><td>9.3</td></tr>
<tr><td>39</td><td>Florida</td><td>6.9</td><td>9</td><td>Colorado</td><td>9.2</td></tr>
<tr><td>32</td><td>Georgia</td><td>7.4</td><td>9</td><td>Wyoming</td><td>9.2</td></tr>
<tr><td>30</td><td>Hawaii</td><td>7.5</td><td>11</td><td>New Hampshire</td><td>9.1</td></tr>
<tr><td>16</td><td>Idaho</td><td>8.5</td><td>12</td><td>Minnesota</td><td>9.0</td></tr>
<tr><td>13</td><td>Illinois</td><td>8.7</td><td>13</td><td>Illinois</td><td>8.7</td></tr>
<tr><td>21</td><td>Indiana</td><td>7.9</td><td>14</td><td>Alaska</td><td>8.6</td></tr>
<tr><td>18</td><td>Iowa</td><td>8.3</td><td>14</td><td>Massachusetts</td><td>8.6</td></tr>
<tr><td>38</td><td>Kansas</td><td>7.1</td><td>16</td><td>Idaho</td><td>8.5</td></tr>
<tr><td>48</td><td>Kentucky</td><td>6.2</td><td>16</td><td>Michigan</td><td>8.5</td></tr>
<tr><td>19</td><td>Louisiana</td><td>8.0</td><td>18</td><td>Iowa</td><td>8.3</td></tr>
<tr><td>34</td><td>Maine</td><td>7.3</td><td>19</td><td>Louisiana</td><td>8.0</td></tr>
<tr><td>27</td><td>Maryland</td><td>7.6</td><td>19</td><td>Nevada</td><td>8.0</td></tr>
<tr><td>14</td><td>Massachusetts</td><td>8.6</td><td>21</td><td>Indiana</td><td>7.9</td></tr>
<tr><td>16</td><td>Michigan</td><td>8.5</td><td>21</td><td>Missouri</td><td>7.9</td></tr>
<tr><td>12</td><td>Minnesota</td><td>9.0</td><td>21</td><td>Ohio</td><td>7.9</td></tr>
<tr><td>45</td><td>Mississippi</td><td>6.5</td><td>21</td><td>South Carolina</td><td>7.9</td></tr>
<tr><td>21</td><td>Missouri</td><td>7.9</td><td>25</td><td>Vermont</td><td>7.8</td></tr>
<tr><td>3</td><td>Montana</td><td>10.7</td><td>26</td><td>Delaware</td><td>7.7</td></tr>
<tr><td>4</td><td>Nebraska</td><td>10.2</td><td>27</td><td>Arkansas</td><td>7.6</td></tr>
<tr><td>19</td><td>Nevada</td><td>8.0</td><td>27</td><td>Maryland</td><td>7.6</td></tr>
<tr><td>11</td><td>New Hampshire</td><td>9.1</td><td>27</td><td>Texas</td><td>7.6</td></tr>
<tr><td>47</td><td>New Jersey</td><td>6.3</td><td>30</td><td>Hawaii</td><td>7.5</td></tr>
<tr><td>6</td><td>New Mexico</td><td>10.0</td><td>30</td><td>Washington</td><td>7.5</td></tr>
<tr><td>36</td><td>New York</td><td>7.2</td><td>32</td><td>Georgia</td><td>7.4</td></tr>
<tr><td>44</td><td>North Carolina</td><td>6.8</td><td>32</td><td>Oregon</td><td>7.4</td></tr>
<tr><td>1</td><td>North Dakota</td><td>10.8</td><td>34</td><td>Maine</td><td>7.3</td></tr>
<tr><td>21</td><td>Ohio</td><td>7.9</td><td>34</td><td>Virginia</td><td>7.3</td></tr>
<tr><td>39</td><td>Oklahoma</td><td>6.9</td><td>36</td><td>California</td><td>7.2</td></tr>
<tr><td>32</td><td>Oregon</td><td>7.4</td><td>36</td><td>New York</td><td>7.2</td></tr>
<tr><td>39</td><td>Pennsylvania</td><td>6.9</td><td>38</td><td>Kansas</td><td>7.1</td></tr>
<tr><td>5</td><td>Rhode Island</td><td>10.1</td><td>39</td><td>Connecticut</td><td>6.9</td></tr>
<tr><td>21</td><td>South Carolina</td><td>7.9</td><td>39</td><td>Florida</td><td>6.9</td></tr>
<tr><td>1</td><td>South Dakota</td><td>10.8</td><td>39</td><td>Oklahoma</td><td>6.9</td></tr>
<tr><td>50</td><td>Tennessee</td><td>6.0</td><td>39</td><td>Pennsylvania</td><td>6.9</td></tr>
<tr><td>27</td><td>Texas</td><td>7.6</td><td>39</td><td>Utah</td><td>6.9</td></tr>
<tr><td>39</td><td>Utah</td><td>6.9</td><td>44</td><td>North Carolina</td><td>6.8</td></tr>
<tr><td>25</td><td>Vermont</td><td>7.8</td><td>45</td><td>Mississippi</td><td>6.5</td></tr>
<tr><td>34</td><td>Virginia</td><td>7.3</td><td>45</td><td>West Virginia</td><td>6.5</td></tr>
<tr><td>30</td><td>Washington</td><td>7.5</td><td>47</td><td>New Jersey</td><td>6.3</td></tr>
<tr><td>45</td><td>West Virginia</td><td>6.5</td><td>48</td><td>Kentucky</td><td>6.2</td></tr>
<tr><td>7</td><td>Wisconsin</td><td>9.5</td><td>49</td><td>Alabama</td><td>6.1</td></tr>
<tr><td>9</td><td>Wyoming</td><td>9.2</td><td>50</td><td>Tennessee</td><td>6.0</td></tr>
<tr><td colspan="3"></td><td colspan="2">District of Columbia</td><td>9.2</td></tr>
</table>

Source: U.S. Department of Health and Human Services, Substance Abuse and Mental Health Services Administration
"2002/2003 National Survey on Drug Use and Health" (January 2005)
*Population 12 years and older reporting alcohol dependence or abuse within one year of survey.

Percent of Population Needing But Not Receiving
Treatment for Alcohol Use: 2002
National Percent = 7.2% of Adults*

ALPHA ORDER

RANK	STATE	PERCENT
48	Alabama	5.8
17	Alaska	7.8
6	Arizona	9.0
24	Arkansas	7.3
33	California	7.0
10	Colorado	8.6
42	Connecticut	6.4
29	Delaware	7.1
40	Florida	6.5
29	Georgia	7.1
24	Hawaii	7.3
13	Idaho	8.2
12	Illinois	8.3
28	Indiana	7.2
19	Iowa	7.6
35	Kansas	6.9
47	Kentucky	5.9
24	Louisiana	7.3
38	Maine	6.6
29	Maryland	7.1
16	Massachusetts	7.9
14	Michigan	8.1
14	Minnesota	8.1
45	Mississippi	6.2
19	Missouri	7.6
1	Montana	10.0
4	Nebraska	9.5
17	Nevada	7.8
10	New Hampshire	8.6
48	New Jersey	5.8
5	New Mexico	9.4
37	New York	6.8
43	North Carolina	6.3
2	North Dakota	9.9
21	Ohio	7.5
38	Oklahoma	6.6
35	Oregon	6.9
40	Pennsylvania	6.5
6	Rhode Island	9.0
22	South Carolina	7.4
3	South Dakota	9.6
50	Tennessee	5.7
22	Texas	7.4
43	Utah	6.3
24	Vermont	7.3
29	Virginia	7.1
33	Washington	7.0
45	West Virginia	6.2
8	Wisconsin	8.9
9	Wyoming	8.7

RANK ORDER

RANK	STATE	PERCENT
1	Montana	10.0
2	North Dakota	9.9
3	South Dakota	9.6
4	Nebraska	9.5
5	New Mexico	9.4
6	Arizona	9.0
6	Rhode Island	9.0
8	Wisconsin	8.9
9	Wyoming	8.7
10	Colorado	8.6
10	New Hampshire	8.6
12	Illinois	8.3
13	Idaho	8.2
14	Michigan	8.1
14	Minnesota	8.1
16	Massachusetts	7.9
17	Alaska	7.8
17	Nevada	7.8
19	Iowa	7.6
19	Missouri	7.6
21	Ohio	7.5
22	South Carolina	7.4
22	Texas	7.4
24	Arkansas	7.3
24	Hawaii	7.3
24	Louisiana	7.3
24	Vermont	7.3
28	Indiana	7.2
29	Delaware	7.1
29	Georgia	7.1
29	Maryland	7.1
29	Virginia	7.1
33	California	7.0
33	Washington	7.0
35	Kansas	6.9
35	Oregon	6.9
37	New York	6.8
38	Maine	6.6
38	Oklahoma	6.6
40	Florida	6.5
40	Pennsylvania	6.5
42	Connecticut	6.4
43	North Carolina	6.3
43	Utah	6.3
45	Mississippi	6.2
45	West Virginia	6.2
47	Kentucky	5.9
48	Alabama	5.8
48	New Jersey	5.8
50	Tennessee	5.7

District of Columbia	8.9

*Source: U.S. Department of Health and Human Services, Substance Abuse and Mental Health Services Administration
"2002/2003 National Survey on Drug Use and Health" (January 2005)*

*Percent of population 12 years and older needing but not receiving treatment within one year of survey.

Substance Abuse Treatment Admissions in 2004

National Total = 1,613,725 Admissions*

ALPHA ORDER

RANK	STATE	ADMISSIONS	% of USA
27	Alabama	14,765	0.9%
NA	Alaska**	NA	NA
17	Arizona	37,295	2.3%
28	Arkansas	13,716	0.8%
2	California	180,642	11.2%
4	Colorado	68,525	4.2%
NA	Connecticut**	NA	NA
34	Delaware	7,874	0.5%
5	Florida	66,927	4.1%
19	Georgia	31,219	1.9%
37	Hawaii	5,803	0.4%
NA	Idaho**	NA	NA
NA	Illinois**	NA	NA
16	Indiana	37,707	2.3%
20	Iowa	28,225	1.7%
26	Kansas	15,103	0.9%
NA	Kentucky**	NA	NA
21	Louisiana	28,189	1.7%
29	Maine	13,057	0.8%
6	Maryland	59,835	3.7%
9	Massachusetts	54,293	3.4%
12	Michigan	45,538	2.8%
13	Minnesota	45,323	2.8%
NA	Mississippi**	NA	NA
15	Missouri	40,072	2.5%
35	Montana	7,408	0.5%
25	Nebraska	15,127	0.9%
31	Nevada	11,523	0.7%
39	New Hampshire	5,544	0.3%
10	New Jersey	51,456	3.2%
NA	New Mexico**	NA	NA
1	New York	283,656	17.6%
NA	North Carolina**	NA	NA
NA	North Dakota**	NA	NA
11	Ohio	46,752	2.9%
24	Oklahoma	17,405	1.1%
14	Oregon	45,073	2.8%
3	Pennsylvania	85,511	5.3%
30	Rhode Island	12,784	0.8%
22	South Carolina	23,668	1.5%
33	South Dakota	9,380	0.6%
36	Tennessee	7,378	0.5%
18	Texas	37,037	2.3%
32	Utah	10,974	0.7%
38	Vermont	5,660	0.4%
8	Virginia	57,435	3.6%
7	Washington	58,047	3.6%
NA	West Virginia**	NA	NA
23	Wisconsin	22,823	1.4%
40	Wyoming	4,976	0.3%

RANK ORDER

RANK	STATE	ADMISSIONS	% of USA
1	New York	283,656	17.6%
2	California	180,642	11.2%
3	Pennsylvania	85,511	5.3%
4	Colorado	68,525	4.2%
5	Florida	66,927	4.1%
6	Maryland	59,835	3.7%
7	Washington	58,047	3.6%
8	Virginia	57,435	3.6%
9	Massachusetts	54,293	3.4%
10	New Jersey	51,456	3.2%
11	Ohio	46,752	2.9%
12	Michigan	45,538	2.8%
13	Minnesota	45,323	2.8%
14	Oregon	45,073	2.8%
15	Missouri	40,072	2.5%
16	Indiana	37,707	2.3%
17	Arizona	37,295	2.3%
18	Texas	37,037	2.3%
19	Georgia	31,219	1.9%
20	Iowa	28,225	1.7%
21	Louisiana	28,189	1.7%
22	South Carolina	23,668	1.5%
23	Wisconsin	22,823	1.4%
24	Oklahoma	17,405	1.1%
25	Nebraska	15,127	0.9%
26	Kansas	15,103	0.9%
27	Alabama	14,765	0.9%
28	Arkansas	13,716	0.8%
29	Maine	13,057	0.8%
30	Rhode Island	12,784	0.8%
31	Nevada	11,523	0.7%
32	Utah	10,974	0.7%
33	South Dakota	9,380	0.6%
34	Delaware	7,874	0.5%
35	Montana	7,408	0.5%
36	Tennessee	7,378	0.5%
37	Hawaii	5,803	0.4%
38	Vermont	5,660	0.4%
39	New Hampshire	5,544	0.3%
40	Wyoming	4,976	0.3%
NA	Alaska**	NA	NA
NA	Connecticut**	NA	NA
NA	Idaho**	NA	NA
NA	Illinois**	NA	NA
NA	Kentucky**	NA	NA
NA	Mississippi**	NA	NA
NA	New Mexico**	NA	NA
NA	North Carolina**	NA	NA
NA	North Dakota**	NA	NA
NA	West Virginia**	NA	NA
	District of Columbia**	NA	NA

Source: U.S. Department of Health and Human Services, Substance Abuse & Mental Health Services Administration "Treatment Episode Data Set" (http://wwwdasis.samhsa.gov/webt/NewMapv1.htm)
*Preliminary figures as of January 27, 2006.
**Not available.

Female Admissions to Substance Abuse Treatment Programs
As a Percent of All Admissions in 2004
National Percent = 32.8% of Admissions*

ALPHA ORDER

RANK	STATE	PERCENT
29	Alabama	30.2
NA	Alaska**	NA
1	Arizona	41.5
33	Arkansas	28.8
8	California	34.6
39	Colorado	22.2
NA	Connecticut**	NA
39	Delaware	22.2
10	Florida	34.3
3	Georgia	38.8
11	Hawaii	34.2
NA	Idaho**	NA
NA	Illinois**	NA
14	Indiana	33.5
15	Iowa	33.4
17	Kansas	32.8
NA	Kentucky**	NA
31	Louisiana	29.8
24	Maine	31.8
18	Maryland	32.7
32	Massachusetts	29.3
16	Michigan	33.0
21	Minnesota	32.3
NA	Mississippi**	NA
21	Missouri	32.3
25	Montana	31.7
36	Nebraska	27.8
7	Nevada	35.1
12	New Hampshire	33.6
27	New Jersey	30.4
NA	New Mexico**	NA
38	New York	24.9
NA	North Carolina**	NA
NA	North Dakota**	NA
4	Ohio	36.8
2	Oklahoma	40.9
19	Oregon	32.4
23	Pennsylvania	31.9
26	Rhode Island	30.7
35	South Carolina	28.5
37	South Dakota	27.3
30	Tennessee	29.9
5	Texas	36.5
9	Utah	34.5
12	Vermont	33.6
19	Virginia	32.4
5	Washington	36.5
NA	West Virginia**	NA
34	Wisconsin	28.7
28	Wyoming	30.3

RANK ORDER

RANK	STATE	PERCENT
1	Arizona	41.5
2	Oklahoma	40.9
3	Georgia	38.8
4	Ohio	36.8
5	Texas	36.5
5	Washington	36.5
7	Nevada	35.1
8	California	34.6
9	Utah	34.5
10	Florida	34.3
11	Hawaii	34.2
12	New Hampshire	33.6
12	Vermont	33.6
14	Indiana	33.5
15	Iowa	33.4
16	Michigan	33.0
17	Kansas	32.8
18	Maryland	32.7
19	Oregon	32.4
19	Virginia	32.4
21	Minnesota	32.3
21	Missouri	32.3
23	Pennsylvania	31.9
24	Maine	31.8
25	Montana	31.7
26	Rhode Island	30.7
27	New Jersey	30.4
28	Wyoming	30.3
29	Alabama	30.2
30	Tennessee	29.9
31	Louisiana	29.8
32	Massachusetts	29.3
33	Arkansas	28.8
34	Wisconsin	28.7
35	South Carolina	28.5
36	Nebraska	27.8
37	South Dakota	27.3
38	New York	24.9
39	Colorado	22.2
39	Delaware	22.2
NA	Alaska**	NA
NA	Connecticut**	NA
NA	Idaho**	NA
NA	Illinois**	NA
NA	Kentucky**	NA
NA	Mississippi**	NA
NA	New Mexico**	NA
NA	North Carolina**	NA
NA	North Dakota**	NA
NA	West Virginia**	NA

District of Columbia**   NA

Source: U.S. Department of Health and Human Services, Substance Abuse & Mental Health Services Administration "Treatment Episode Data Set" (http://wwwdasis.samhsa.gov/webt/NewMapv1.htm)
*Preliminary figures as of January 27, 2006. National figure is a weighted average of reporting states.
**Not available.

White Admissions to Substance Abuse Treatment Programs
As a Percent of All Admissions in 2004
National Percent = 63.7% of Admissions*

ALPHA ORDER

RANK ORDER

RANK	STATE	PERCENT	RANK	STATE	PERCENT
35	Alabama	59.0	1	New Hampshire	94.6
NA	Alaska**	NA	2	Maine	94.4
6	Arizona	85.4	3	Vermont	91.6
17	Arkansas	73.9	4	Iowa	91.3
37	California	46.9	5	Wyoming	86.3
8	Colorado	84.6	6	Arizona	85.4
NA	Connecticut**	NA	7	Wisconsin	85.1
31	Delaware	62.9	8	Colorado	84.6
17	Florida	73.9	9	Utah	81.8
34	Georgia	60.0	10	Montana	79.7
40	Hawaii	29.9	11	Oregon	78.5
NA	Idaho**	NA	12	Indiana	78.3
NA	Illinois**	NA	13	Rhode Island	77.6
12	Indiana	78.3	14	Pennsylvania	75.4
4	Iowa	91.3	15	Minnesota	75.3
21	Kansas	72.1	16	Nebraska	74.6
NA	Kentucky**	NA	17	Arkansas	73.9
32	Louisiana	60.4	17	Florida	73.9
2	Maine	94.4	17	Tennessee	73.9
36	Maryland	51.6	20	Massachusetts	72.9
20	Massachusetts	72.9	21	Kansas	72.1
26	Michigan	67.9	22	Oklahoma	70.6
15	Minnesota	75.3	22	Washington	70.6
NA	Mississippi**	NA	24	Ohio	69.6
25	Missouri	69.0	25	Missouri	69.0
10	Montana	79.7	26	Michigan	67.9
16	Nebraska	74.6	26	Nevada	67.9
26	Nevada	67.9	28	South Dakota	66.8
1	New Hampshire	94.6	29	New Jersey	66.1
29	New Jersey	66.1	30	South Carolina	63.3
NA	New Mexico**	NA	31	Delaware	62.9
39	New York	44.6	32	Louisiana	60.4
NA	North Carolina**	NA	33	Virginia	60.3
NA	North Dakota**	NA	34	Georgia	60.0
24	Ohio	69.6	35	Alabama	59.0
22	Oklahoma	70.6	36	Maryland	51.6
11	Oregon	78.5	37	California	46.9
14	Pennsylvania	75.4	38	Texas	46.4
13	Rhode Island	77.6	39	New York	44.6
30	South Carolina	63.3	40	Hawaii	29.9
28	South Dakota	66.8	NA	Alaska**	NA
17	Tennessee	73.9	NA	Connecticut**	NA
38	Texas	46.4	NA	Idaho**	NA
9	Utah	81.8	NA	Illinois**	NA
3	Vermont	91.6	NA	Kentucky**	NA
33	Virginia	60.3	NA	Mississippi**	NA
22	Washington	70.6	NA	New Mexico**	NA
NA	West Virginia**	NA	NA	North Carolina**	NA
7	Wisconsin	85.1	NA	North Dakota**	NA
5	Wyoming	86.3	NA	West Virginia**	NA
				District of Columbia**	NA

*Source: U.S. Department of Health and Human Services, Substance Abuse & Mental Health Services Administration
"Treatment Episode Data Set" (http://wwwdasis.samhsa.gov/webt/NewMapv1.htm)
*Preliminary figures as of January 27, 2006. National figure is a weighted average of reporting states.
**Not available.*

Black Admissions to Substance Abuse Treatment Programs
As a Percent of All Admissions in 2004
National Percent = 21.6% of Admissions*

ALPHA ORDER

RANK	STATE	PERCENT
2	Alabama	39.6
NA	Alaska**	NA
31	Arizona	6.4
14	Arkansas	23.7
18	California	16.9
29	Colorado	8.2
NA	Connecticut**	NA
7	Delaware	32.3
15	Florida	21.6
4	Georgia	36.0
35	Hawaii	2.2
NA	Idaho**	NA
NA	Illinois**	NA
18	Indiana	16.9
30	Iowa	6.9
20	Kansas	16.5
NA	Kentucky**	NA
3	Louisiana	37.8
36	Maine	2.0
1	Maryland	44.6
23	Massachusetts	11.7
12	Michigan	25.8
24	Minnesota	11.2
NA	Mississippi**	NA
10	Missouri	28.9
40	Montana	0.8
26	Nebraska	9.7
22	Nevada	12.2
38	New Hampshire	1.7
9	New Jersey	30.5
NA	New Mexico**	NA
5	New York	34.5
NA	North Carolina**	NA
NA	North Dakota**	NA
11	Ohio	27.7
21	Oklahoma	14.7
32	Oregon	4.3
17	Pennsylvania	19.4
27	Rhode Island	9.1
6	South Carolina	34.2
34	South Dakota	2.5
13	Tennessee	24.2
16	Texas	19.5
33	Utah	3.0
39	Vermont	1.4
8	Virginia	32.1
28	Washington	8.5
NA	West Virginia**	NA
24	Wisconsin	11.2
37	Wyoming	1.9

RANK ORDER

RANK	STATE	PERCENT
1	Maryland	44.6
2	Alabama	39.6
3	Louisiana	37.8
4	Georgia	36.0
5	New York	34.5
6	South Carolina	34.2
7	Delaware	32.3
8	Virginia	32.1
9	New Jersey	30.5
10	Missouri	28.9
11	Ohio	27.7
12	Michigan	25.8
13	Tennessee	24.2
14	Arkansas	23.7
15	Florida	21.6
16	Texas	19.5
17	Pennsylvania	19.4
18	California	16.9
18	Indiana	16.9
20	Kansas	16.5
21	Oklahoma	14.7
22	Nevada	12.2
23	Massachusetts	11.7
24	Minnesota	11.2
24	Wisconsin	11.2
26	Nebraska	9.7
27	Rhode Island	9.1
28	Washington	8.5
29	Colorado	8.2
30	Iowa	6.9
31	Arizona	6.4
32	Oregon	4.3
33	Utah	3.0
34	South Dakota	2.5
35	Hawaii	2.2
36	Maine	2.0
37	Wyoming	1.9
38	New Hampshire	1.7
39	Vermont	1.4
40	Montana	0.8
NA	Alaska**	NA
NA	Connecticut**	NA
NA	Idaho**	NA
NA	Illinois**	NA
NA	Kentucky**	NA
NA	Mississippi**	NA
NA	New Mexico**	NA
NA	North Carolina**	NA
NA	North Dakota**	NA
NA	West Virginia**	NA
	District of Columbia**	NA

Source: U.S. Department of Health and Human Services, Substance Abuse & Mental Health Services Administration "Treatment Episode Data Set" (http://wwwdasis.samhsa.gov/webt/NewMapv1.htm)
*Preliminary figures as of January 27, 2006. National figure is a weighted average of reporting states.
**Not available.

Hispanic Admissions to Substance Abuse Treatment Programs
As a Percent of All Admissions in 2004
National Percent = 14.1% of Admissions*

ALPHA ORDER

RANK	STATE	PERCENT
NA	Alabama**	NA
NA	Alaska**	NA
5	Arizona	18.8
27	Arkansas	2.6
1	California	33.1
3	Colorado	27.7
NA	Connecticut**	NA
17	Delaware	5.1
9	Florida	11.7
35	Georgia	1.1
20	Hawaii	4.4
NA	Idaho**	NA
NA	Illinois**	NA
20	Indiana	4.4
18	Iowa	4.6
13	Kansas	8.4
NA	Kentucky**	NA
29	Louisiana	1.9
32	Maine	1.8
23	Maryland	3.4
6	Massachusetts	15.3
24	Michigan	3.3
22	Minnesota	3.5
NA	Mississippi**	NA
29	Missouri	1.9
28	Montana	2.1
14	Nebraska	8.2
24	Nevada	3.3
26	New Hampshire	3.0
7	New Jersey	14.9
NA	New Mexico**	NA
4	New York	21.6
NA	North Carolina**	NA
NA	North Dakota**	NA
32	Ohio	1.8
29	Oklahoma	1.9
10	Oregon	10.2
15	Pennsylvania	6.2
NA	Rhode Island**	NA
34	South Carolina	1.7
NA	South Dakota**	NA
37	Tennessee	0.6
2	Texas	31.9
8	Utah	12.2
36	Vermont	1.0
16	Virginia	5.2
11	Washington	9.2
NA	West Virginia**	NA
19	Wisconsin	4.5
11	Wyoming	9.2

RANK ORDER

RANK	STATE	PERCENT
1	California	33.1
2	Texas	31.9
3	Colorado	27.7
4	New York	21.6
5	Arizona	18.8
6	Massachusetts	15.3
7	New Jersey	14.9
8	Utah	12.2
9	Florida	11.7
10	Oregon	10.2
11	Washington	9.2
11	Wyoming	9.2
13	Kansas	8.4
14	Nebraska	8.2
15	Pennsylvania	6.2
16	Virginia	5.2
17	Delaware	5.1
18	Iowa	4.6
19	Wisconsin	4.5
20	Hawaii	4.4
20	Indiana	4.4
22	Minnesota	3.5
23	Maryland	3.4
24	Michigan	3.3
24	Nevada	3.3
26	New Hampshire	3.0
27	Arkansas	2.6
28	Montana	2.1
29	Louisiana	1.9
29	Missouri	1.9
29	Oklahoma	1.9
32	Maine	1.8
32	Ohio	1.8
34	South Carolina	1.7
35	Georgia	1.1
36	Vermont	1.0
37	Tennessee	0.6
NA	Alabama**	NA
NA	Alaska**	NA
NA	Connecticut**	NA
NA	Idaho**	NA
NA	Illinois**	NA
NA	Kentucky**	NA
NA	Mississippi**	NA
NA	New Mexico**	NA
NA	North Carolina**	NA
NA	North Dakota**	NA
NA	Rhode Island**	NA
NA	South Dakota**	NA
NA	West Virginia**	NA
	District of Columbia**	NA

Source: U.S. Department of Health and Human Services, Substance Abuse & Mental Health Services Administration
  "Treatment Episode Data Set" (http://wwwdasis.samhsa.gov/webt/NewMapv1.htm)
*Preliminary figures as of January 27, 2006. National figure is a weighted average of reporting states. Hispanic
ethnic background can be of any race.
**Not available.

IV. FINANCE

Homeland Security Grants in 2005

National Total = $2,518,763,000*

ALPHA ORDER

RANK	STATE	GRANTS	% of USA
28	Alabama	$28,153,000	1.1%
46	Alaska	14,879,000	0.6%
17	Arizona	41,705,000	1.7%
36	Arkansas	21,561,000	0.9%
2	California	282,622,000	11.2%
21	Colorado	36,799,000	1.5%
30	Connecticut	24,080,000	1.0%
45	Delaware	14,984,000	0.6%
5	Florida	101,285,000	4.0%
11	Georgia	54,918,000	2.2%
32	Hawaii	23,130,000	0.9%
40	Idaho	16,805,000	0.7%
4	Illinois	102,593,000	4.1%
18	Indiana	38,996,000	1.5%
33	Iowa	22,291,000	0.9%
35	Kansas	21,784,000	0.9%
25	Kentucky	31,419,000	1.2%
15	Louisiana	42,670,000	1.7%
42	Maine	16,609,000	0.7%
16	Maryland	42,250,000	1.7%
9	Massachusetts	62,436,000	2.5%
8	Michigan	64,075,000	2.5%
22	Minnesota	35,311,000	1.4%
34	Mississippi	22,081,000	0.9%
12	Missouri	46,952,000	1.9%
44	Montana	15,318,000	0.6%
31	Nebraska	23,656,000	0.9%
27	Nevada	28,386,000	1.1%
41	New Hampshire	16,776,000	0.7%
10	New Jersey	60,811,000	2.4%
38	New Mexico	18,499,000	0.7%
1	New York	298,351,000	11.8%
13	North Carolina	46,609,000	1.9%
48	North Dakota	14,376,000	0.6%
7	Ohio	77,823,000	3.1%
26	Oklahoma	29,974,000	1.2%
23	Oregon	34,820,000	1.4%
6	Pennsylvania	87,671,000	3.5%
43	Rhode Island	16,074,000	0.6%
29	South Carolina	26,284,000	1.0%
47	South Dakota	14,809,000	0.6%
24	Tennessee	32,605,000	1.3%
3	Texas	138,570,000	5.5%
37	Utah	20,308,000	0.8%
49	Vermont	14,326,000	0.6%
19	Virginia	38,185,000	1.5%
14	Washington	45,330,000	1.8%
39	West Virginia	18,289,000	0.7%
20	Wisconsin	37,251,000	1.5%
50	Wyoming	13,934,000	0.6%

RANK ORDER

RANK	STATE	GRANTS	% of USA
1	New York	$298,351,000	11.8%
2	California	282,622,000	11.2%
3	Texas	138,570,000	5.5%
4	Illinois	102,593,000	4.1%
5	Florida	101,285,000	4.0%
6	Pennsylvania	87,671,000	3.5%
7	Ohio	77,823,000	3.1%
8	Michigan	64,075,000	2.5%
9	Massachusetts	62,436,000	2.5%
10	New Jersey	60,811,000	2.4%
11	Georgia	54,918,000	2.2%
12	Missouri	46,952,000	1.9%
13	North Carolina	46,609,000	1.9%
14	Washington	45,330,000	1.8%
15	Louisiana	42,670,000	1.7%
16	Maryland	42,250,000	1.7%
17	Arizona	41,705,000	1.7%
18	Indiana	38,996,000	1.5%
19	Virginia	38,185,000	1.5%
20	Wisconsin	37,251,000	1.5%
21	Colorado	36,799,000	1.5%
22	Minnesota	35,311,000	1.4%
23	Oregon	34,820,000	1.4%
24	Tennessee	32,605,000	1.3%
25	Kentucky	31,419,000	1.2%
26	Oklahoma	29,974,000	1.2%
27	Nevada	28,386,000	1.1%
28	Alabama	28,153,000	1.1%
29	South Carolina	26,284,000	1.0%
30	Connecticut	24,080,000	1.0%
31	Nebraska	23,656,000	0.9%
32	Hawaii	23,130,000	0.9%
33	Iowa	22,291,000	0.9%
34	Mississippi	22,081,000	0.9%
35	Kansas	21,784,000	0.9%
36	Arkansas	21,561,000	0.9%
37	Utah	20,308,000	0.8%
38	New Mexico	18,499,000	0.7%
39	West Virginia	18,289,000	0.7%
40	Idaho	16,805,000	0.7%
41	New Hampshire	16,776,000	0.7%
42	Maine	16,609,000	0.7%
43	Rhode Island	16,074,000	0.6%
44	Montana	15,318,000	0.6%
45	Delaware	14,984,000	0.6%
46	Alaska	14,879,000	0.6%
47	South Dakota	14,809,000	0.6%
48	North Dakota	14,376,000	0.6%
49	Vermont	14,326,000	0.6%
50	Wyoming	13,934,000	0.6%
	District of Columbia	96,144,000	3.8%

Source: U.S. Department of Homeland Security, State and Local Government Coordination and Preparedness
Unpublished data (reported in Census' Statistical Abstract of the United States: 2006)
*For fiscal year ending September 30. National total includes $43,199,000 in grants to U.S. territories. The Homeland Security Grant Program includes several sub-grant programs such as State Homeland Security, Urban Area Security Initiative, Law Enforcement Terrorism Prevention Program and Emergency Management Performance.

Per Capita Homeland Security Grants in 2005

National Per Capita = $8.35*

ALPHA ORDER

RANK	STATE	PER CAPITA
43	Alabama	$6.18
4	Alaska	22.42
35	Arizona	7.02
28	Arkansas	7.76
27	California	7.82
26	Colorado	7.89
38	Connecticut	6.86
7	Delaware	17.76
47	Florida	5.69
46	Georgia	6.05
6	Hawaii	18.14
14	Idaho	11.76
24	Illinois	8.04
42	Indiana	6.22
32	Iowa	7.51
25	Kansas	7.94
31	Kentucky	7.53
20	Louisiana	9.43
13	Maine	12.57
30	Maryland	7.54
17	Massachusetts	9.76
41	Michigan	6.33
37	Minnesota	6.88
29	Mississippi	7.56
23	Missouri	8.09
8	Montana	16.37
11	Nebraska	13.45
15	Nevada	11.75
12	New Hampshire	12.81
36	New Jersey	6.98
18	New Mexico	9.59
9	New York	15.50
49	North Carolina	5.37
3	North Dakota	22.58
39	Ohio	6.79
21	Oklahoma	8.45
19	Oregon	9.56
34	Pennsylvania	7.05
10	Rhode Island	14.94
43	South Carolina	6.18
5	South Dakota	19.09
48	Tennessee	5.47
45	Texas	6.06
22	Utah	8.22
2	Vermont	22.99
50	Virginia	5.05
33	Washington	7.21
16	West Virginia	10.07
40	Wisconsin	6.73
1	Wyoming	27.36

RANK ORDER

RANK	STATE	PER CAPITA
1	Wyoming	$27.36
2	Vermont	22.99
3	North Dakota	22.58
4	Alaska	22.42
5	South Dakota	19.09
6	Hawaii	18.14
7	Delaware	17.76
8	Montana	16.37
9	New York	15.50
10	Rhode Island	14.94
11	Nebraska	13.45
12	New Hampshire	12.81
13	Maine	12.57
14	Idaho	11.76
15	Nevada	11.75
16	West Virginia	10.07
17	Massachusetts	9.76
18	New Mexico	9.59
19	Oregon	9.56
20	Louisiana	9.43
21	Oklahoma	8.45
22	Utah	8.22
23	Missouri	8.09
24	Illinois	8.04
25	Kansas	7.94
26	Colorado	7.89
27	California	7.82
28	Arkansas	7.76
29	Mississippi	7.56
30	Maryland	7.54
31	Kentucky	7.53
32	Iowa	7.51
33	Washington	7.21
34	Pennsylvania	7.05
35	Arizona	7.02
36	New Jersey	6.98
37	Minnesota	6.88
38	Connecticut	6.86
39	Ohio	6.79
40	Wisconsin	6.73
41	Michigan	6.33
42	Indiana	6.22
43	Alabama	6.18
43	South Carolina	6.18
45	Texas	6.06
46	Georgia	6.05
47	Florida	5.69
48	Tennessee	5.47
49	North Carolina	5.37
50	Virginia	5.05

District of Columbia   174.64

Source: Morgan Quitno Press using data from U.S. Department of Homeland Security
    Unpublished data (reported in Census' Statistical Abstract of the United States: 2006)
*For fiscal year ending September 30. National per capita does not include grants to U.S. territories. The
Homeland Security Grant Program includes several sub-grant programs such as State Homeland Security, Urban
Area Security Initiative, Law Enforcement Terrorism Prevention Program and Emergency Management Performance.

Grants to Police Departments for Bulletproof Vests in 2005

National Total = $23,431,396*

ALPHA ORDER

RANK	STATE	GRANTS	% of USA
30	Alabama	$231,766	1.0%
48	Alaska	40,350	0.2%
23	Arizona	403,390	1.7%
32	Arkansas	184,770	0.8%
1	California	2,405,228	10.3%
15	Colorado	533,799	2.3%
24	Connecticut	361,077	1.5%
7	Delaware	868,249	3.7%
4	Florida	1,262,163	5.4%
11	Georgia	631,668	2.7%
50	Hawaii	20,953	0.1%
36	Idaho	152,853	0.7%
9	Illinois	736,595	3.1%
22	Indiana	423,878	1.8%
31	Iowa	218,046	0.9%
29	Kansas	253,030	1.1%
38	Kentucky	128,938	0.6%
18	Louisiana	481,190	2.1%
41	Maine	92,126	0.4%
19	Maryland	460,920	2.0%
14	Massachusetts	548,110	2.3%
12	Michigan	572,043	2.4%
27	Minnesota	298,491	1.3%
37	Mississippi	152,628	0.7%
25	Missouri	339,833	1.5%
49	Montana	39,878	0.2%
44	Nebraska	71,076	0.3%
39	Nevada	112,186	0.5%
40	New Hampshire	93,504	0.4%
2	New Jersey	1,773,134	7.6%
35	New Mexico	154,819	0.7%
3	New York	1,745,682	7.5%
10	North Carolina	725,155	3.1%
43	North Dakota	89,545	0.4%
8	Ohio	790,341	3.4%
13	Oklahoma	568,190	2.4%
26	Oregon	307,113	1.3%
6	Pennsylvania	1,006,813	4.3%
33	Rhode Island	171,457	0.7%
28	South Carolina	262,068	1.1%
45	South Dakota	62,760	0.3%
17	Tennessee	520,807	2.2%
5	Texas	1,172,777	5.0%
34	Utah	170,232	0.7%
42	Vermont	91,270	0.4%
16	Virginia	525,730	2.2%
21	Washington	455,328	1.9%
46	West Virginia	54,360	0.2%
20	Wisconsin	459,611	2.0%
47	Wyoming	53,842	0.2%

RANK ORDER

RANK	STATE	GRANTS	% of USA
1	California	$2,405,228	10.3%
2	New Jersey	1,773,134	7.6%
3	New York	1,745,682	7.5%
4	Florida	1,262,163	5.4%
5	Texas	1,172,777	5.0%
6	Pennsylvania	1,006,813	4.3%
7	Delaware	868,249	3.7%
8	Ohio	790,341	3.4%
9	Illinois	736,595	3.1%
10	North Carolina	725,155	3.1%
11	Georgia	631,668	2.7%
12	Michigan	572,043	2.4%
13	Oklahoma	568,190	2.4%
14	Massachusetts	548,110	2.3%
15	Colorado	533,799	2.3%
16	Virginia	525,730	2.2%
17	Tennessee	520,807	2.2%
18	Louisiana	481,190	2.1%
19	Maryland	460,920	2.0%
20	Wisconsin	459,611	2.0%
21	Washington	455,328	1.9%
22	Indiana	423,878	1.8%
23	Arizona	403,390	1.7%
24	Connecticut	361,077	1.5%
25	Missouri	339,833	1.5%
26	Oregon	307,113	1.3%
27	Minnesota	298,491	1.3%
28	South Carolina	262,068	1.1%
29	Kansas	253,030	1.1%
30	Alabama	231,766	1.0%
31	Iowa	218,046	0.9%
32	Arkansas	184,770	0.8%
33	Rhode Island	171,457	0.7%
34	Utah	170,232	0.7%
35	New Mexico	154,819	0.7%
36	Idaho	152,853	0.7%
37	Mississippi	152,628	0.7%
38	Kentucky	128,938	0.6%
39	Nevada	112,186	0.5%
40	New Hampshire	93,504	0.4%
41	Maine	92,126	0.4%
42	Vermont	91,270	0.4%
43	North Dakota	89,545	0.4%
44	Nebraska	71,076	0.3%
45	South Dakota	62,760	0.3%
46	West Virginia	54,360	0.2%
47	Wyoming	53,842	0.2%
48	Alaska	40,350	0.2%
49	Montana	39,878	0.2%
50	Hawaii	20,953	0.1%
	District of Columbia	151,621	0.6%

Source: U.S. Department of Justice, Office of Justice Programs
  "Bulletproof Vest Partnership Program" (http://www.ojp.usdoj.gov/bvpbasi/)
Does not include $161,173 in grants to U.S. territories.

State and Local Government Expenditures for Justice Activities in 2002

National Total = $150,414,874,000*

ALPHA ORDER

RANK	STATE	EXPENDITURES	% of USA
27	Alabama	$1,487,133,000	1.0%
40	Alaska	570,594,000	0.4%
15	Arizona	3,035,958,000	2.0%
35	Arkansas	967,933,000	0.6%
1	California	26,208,117,000	17.4%
18	Colorado	2,313,314,000	1.5%
25	Connecticut	1,902,173,000	1.3%
41	Delaware	542,389,000	0.4%
4	Florida	9,403,902,000	6.3%
10	Georgia	4,002,823,000	2.7%
38	Hawaii	625,776,000	0.4%
39	Idaho	593,029,000	0.4%
5	Illinois	6,212,482,000	4.1%
21	Indiana	2,120,127,000	1.4%
31	Iowa	1,076,379,000	0.7%
32	Kansas	1,074,566,000	0.7%
29	Kentucky	1,458,516,000	1.0%
22	Louisiana	2,107,569,000	1.4%
45	Maine	406,412,000	0.3%
14	Maryland	3,112,413,000	2.1%
12	Massachusetts	3,308,516,000	2.2%
8	Michigan	5,183,326,000	3.4%
20	Minnesota	2,189,440,000	1.5%
36	Mississippi	941,720,000	0.6%
19	Missouri	2,207,140,000	1.5%
46	Montana	368,512,000	0.2%
37	Nebraska	636,613,000	0.4%
28	Nevada	1,474,713,000	1.0%
44	New Hampshire	423,984,000	0.3%
9	New Jersey	5,108,651,000	3.4%
34	New Mexico	972,289,000	0.6%
2	New York	14,115,834,000	9.4%
13	North Carolina	3,229,175,000	2.1%
50	North Dakota	187,061,000	0.1%
7	Ohio	5,590,723,000	3.7%
30	Oklahoma	1,356,546,000	0.9%
24	Oregon	1,999,667,000	1.3%
6	Pennsylvania	6,042,329,000	4.0%
43	Rhode Island	499,682,000	0.3%
26	South Carolina	1,504,863,000	1.0%
48	South Dakota	242,075,000	0.2%
23	Tennessee	2,087,237,000	1.4%
3	Texas	9,750,308,000	6.5%
33	Utah	1,057,381,000	0.7%
49	Vermont	214,139,000	0.1%
11	Virginia	3,354,056,000	2.2%
17	Washington	2,807,823,000	1.9%
42	West Virginia	513,269,000	0.3%
16	Wisconsin	2,920,922,000	1.9%
47	Wyoming	288,163,000	0.2%

RANK ORDER

RANK	STATE	EXPENDITURES	% of USA
1	California	$26,208,117,000	17.4%
2	New York	14,115,834,000	9.4%
3	Texas	9,750,308,000	6.5%
4	Florida	9,403,902,000	6.3%
5	Illinois	6,212,482,000	4.1%
6	Pennsylvania	6,042,329,000	4.0%
7	Ohio	5,590,723,000	3.7%
8	Michigan	5,183,326,000	3.4%
9	New Jersey	5,108,651,000	3.4%
10	Georgia	4,002,823,000	2.7%
11	Virginia	3,354,056,000	2.2%
12	Massachusetts	3,308,516,000	2.2%
13	North Carolina	3,229,175,000	2.1%
14	Maryland	3,112,413,000	2.1%
15	Arizona	3,035,958,000	2.0%
16	Wisconsin	2,920,922,000	1.9%
17	Washington	2,807,823,000	1.9%
18	Colorado	2,313,314,000	1.5%
19	Missouri	2,207,140,000	1.5%
20	Minnesota	2,189,440,000	1.5%
21	Indiana	2,120,127,000	1.4%
22	Louisiana	2,107,569,000	1.4%
23	Tennessee	2,087,237,000	1.4%
24	Oregon	1,999,667,000	1.3%
25	Connecticut	1,902,173,000	1.3%
26	South Carolina	1,504,863,000	1.0%
27	Alabama	1,487,133,000	1.0%
28	Nevada	1,474,713,000	1.0%
29	Kentucky	1,458,516,000	1.0%
30	Oklahoma	1,356,546,000	0.9%
31	Iowa	1,076,379,000	0.7%
32	Kansas	1,074,566,000	0.7%
33	Utah	1,057,381,000	0.7%
34	New Mexico	972,289,000	0.6%
35	Arkansas	967,933,000	0.6%
36	Mississippi	941,720,000	0.6%
37	Nebraska	636,613,000	0.4%
38	Hawaii	625,776,000	0.4%
39	Idaho	593,029,000	0.4%
40	Alaska	570,594,000	0.4%
41	Delaware	542,389,000	0.4%
42	West Virginia	513,269,000	0.3%
43	Rhode Island	499,682,000	0.3%
44	New Hampshire	423,984,000	0.3%
45	Maine	406,412,000	0.3%
46	Montana	368,512,000	0.2%
47	Wyoming	288,163,000	0.2%
48	South Dakota	242,075,000	0.2%
49	Vermont	214,139,000	0.1%
50	North Dakota	187,061,000	0.1%
	District of Columbia	617,112,000	0.4%

Source: Morgan Quitno Press using data from U.S. Bureau of the Census, Governments Division
"State and Local Government Finances: 2002 Census" (http://www.census.gov/govs/www/estimate02.html)
*Direct general expenditures. Includes Police Protection, Corrections and Judicial and Legal Services.

Per Capita State & Local Government Expenditures for Justice Activities: 2002

National Per Capita = $522*

ALPHA ORDER

RANK	STATE	PER CAPITA
44	Alabama	$332
1	Alaska	890
11	Arizona	558
40	Arkansas	357
2	California	749
17	Colorado	514
12	Connecticut	550
5	Delaware	673
10	Florida	564
23	Georgia	469
18	Hawaii	507
29	Idaho	442
19	Illinois	494
43	Indiana	344
37	Iowa	367
32	Kansas	396
40	Kentucky	357
22	Louisiana	471
48	Maine	313
8	Maryland	572
15	Massachusetts	516
15	Michigan	516
30	Minnesota	436
46	Mississippi	328
33	Missouri	389
31	Montana	405
36	Nebraska	369
4	Nevada	680
44	New Hampshire	332
6	New Jersey	596
14	New Mexico	524
3	New York	737
33	North Carolina	389
49	North Dakota	295
20	Ohio	490
33	Oklahoma	389
9	Oregon	568
20	Pennsylvania	490
24	Rhode Island	467
37	South Carolina	367
47	South Dakota	318
39	Tennessee	360
28	Texas	449
27	Utah	456
42	Vermont	347
26	Virginia	461
25	Washington	463
50	West Virginia	284
13	Wisconsin	537
7	Wyoming	577

RANK ORDER

RANK	STATE	PER CAPITA
1	Alaska	$890
2	California	749
3	New York	737
4	Nevada	680
5	Delaware	673
6	New Jersey	596
7	Wyoming	577
8	Maryland	572
9	Oregon	568
10	Florida	564
11	Arizona	558
12	Connecticut	550
13	Wisconsin	537
14	New Mexico	524
15	Massachusetts	516
15	Michigan	516
17	Colorado	514
18	Hawaii	507
19	Illinois	494
20	Ohio	490
20	Pennsylvania	490
22	Louisiana	471
23	Georgia	469
24	Rhode Island	467
25	Washington	463
26	Virginia	461
27	Utah	456
28	Texas	449
29	Idaho	442
30	Minnesota	436
31	Montana	405
32	Kansas	396
33	Missouri	389
33	North Carolina	389
33	Oklahoma	389
36	Nebraska	369
37	Iowa	367
37	South Carolina	367
39	Tennessee	360
40	Arkansas	357
40	Kentucky	357
42	Vermont	347
43	Indiana	344
44	Alabama	332
44	New Hampshire	332
46	Mississippi	328
47	South Dakota	318
48	Maine	313
49	North Dakota	295
50	West Virginia	284

District of Columbia   1,093

Source: Morgan Quitno Press using data from U.S. Bureau of the Census, Governments Division
"State and Local Government Finances: 2002 Census" (http://www.census.gov/govs/www/estimate02.html)
*Direct general expenditures. Includes Police Protection, Corrections and Judicial and Legal Services.

State and Local Government Expenditures for Justice Activities
As a Percent of All Direct General Expenditures in 2002
National Percent = 8.7% of Direct General Expenditures*

ALPHA ORDER

RANK	STATE	PERCENT
46	Alabama	6.0
36	Alaska	6.8
2	Arizona	12.0
29	Arkansas	7.4
3	California	11.1
15	Colorado	8.5
23	Connecticut	7.9
5	Delaware	10.1
4	Florida	10.8
8	Georgia	8.9
26	Hawaii	7.5
10	Idaho	8.7
19	Illinois	8.4
39	Indiana	6.5
41	Iowa	6.3
34	Kansas	7.2
36	Kentucky	6.8
10	Louisiana	8.7
49	Maine	5.1
6	Maryland	9.8
24	Massachusetts	7.8
15	Michigan	8.5
41	Minnesota	6.3
45	Mississippi	6.1
25	Missouri	7.6
31	Montana	7.3
39	Nebraska	6.5
1	Nevada	12.5
38	New Hampshire	6.7
7	New Jersey	9.4
15	New Mexico	8.5
9	New York	8.8
31	North Carolina	7.3
50	North Dakota	4.8
20	Ohio	8.3
26	Oklahoma	7.5
10	Oregon	8.7
21	Pennsylvania	8.2
29	Rhode Island	7.4
41	South Carolina	6.3
44	South Dakota	6.2
34	Tennessee	7.2
10	Texas	8.7
21	Utah	8.2
47	Vermont	5.6
15	Virginia	8.5
31	Washington	7.3
48	West Virginia	5.2
14	Wisconsin	8.6
26	Wyoming	7.5

RANK ORDER

RANK	STATE	PERCENT
1	Nevada	12.5
2	Arizona	12.0
3	California	11.1
4	Florida	10.8
5	Delaware	10.1
6	Maryland	9.8
7	New Jersey	9.4
8	Georgia	8.9
9	New York	8.8
10	Idaho	8.7
10	Louisiana	8.7
10	Oregon	8.7
10	Texas	8.7
14	Wisconsin	8.6
15	Colorado	8.5
15	Michigan	8.5
15	New Mexico	8.5
15	Virginia	8.5
19	Illinois	8.4
20	Ohio	8.3
21	Pennsylvania	8.2
21	Utah	8.2
23	Connecticut	7.9
24	Massachusetts	7.8
25	Missouri	7.6
26	Hawaii	7.5
26	Oklahoma	7.5
26	Wyoming	7.5
29	Arkansas	7.4
29	Rhode Island	7.4
31	Montana	7.3
31	North Carolina	7.3
31	Washington	7.3
34	Kansas	7.2
34	Tennessee	7.2
36	Alaska	6.8
36	Kentucky	6.8
38	New Hampshire	6.7
39	Indiana	6.5
39	Nebraska	6.5
41	Iowa	6.3
41	Minnesota	6.3
41	South Carolina	6.3
44	South Dakota	6.2
45	Mississippi	6.1
46	Alabama	6.0
47	Vermont	5.6
48	West Virginia	5.2
49	Maine	5.1
50	North Dakota	4.8

District of Columbia	10.0

Source: Morgan Quitno Press using data from U.S. Bureau of the Census, Governments Division
   "State and Local Government Finances: 2002 Census" (http://www.census.gov/govs/www/estimate02.html)
*Includes Police Protection, Corrections and Judicial and Legal Services.

State Government Expenditures for Justice Activities in 2002

National Total = $60,295,061,000*

ALPHA ORDER

RANK	STATE	EXPENDITURES	% of USA
29	Alabama	$639,224,000	1.1%
37	Alaska	357,837,000	0.6%
19	Arizona	958,417,000	1.6%
33	Arkansas	488,753,000	0.8%
1	California	9,248,190,000	15.3%
20	Colorado	945,955,000	1.6%
15	Connecticut	1,249,227,000	2.1%
35	Delaware	411,750,000	0.7%
4	Florida	3,412,064,000	5.7%
12	Georgia	1,652,673,000	2.7%
39	Hawaii	337,978,000	0.6%
43	Idaho	272,850,000	0.5%
8	Illinois	1,962,152,000	3.3%
22	Indiana	912,424,000	1.5%
30	Iowa	542,324,000	0.9%
34	Kansas	470,920,000	0.8%
23	Kentucky	863,013,000	1.4%
24	Louisiana	816,436,000	1.4%
44	Maine	233,817,000	0.4%
13	Maryland	1,638,454,000	2.7%
9	Massachusetts	1,875,755,000	3.1%
7	Michigan	2,079,202,000	3.4%
26	Minnesota	754,065,000	1.3%
36	Mississippi	380,076,000	0.6%
18	Missouri	974,115,000	1.6%
47	Montana	165,123,000	0.3%
42	Nebraska	275,250,000	0.5%
38	Nevada	343,480,000	0.6%
45	New Hampshire	195,200,000	0.3%
6	New Jersey	2,114,329,000	3.5%
32	New Mexico	498,594,000	0.8%
2	New York	4,708,353,000	7.8%
11	North Carolina	1,691,149,000	2.8%
50	North Dakota	86,222,000	0.1%
10	Ohio	1,780,729,000	3.0%
25	Oklahoma	765,007,000	1.3%
21	Oregon	928,514,000	1.5%
5	Pennsylvania	2,673,448,000	4.4%
41	Rhode Island	296,740,000	0.5%
28	South Carolina	685,601,000	1.1%
49	South Dakota	112,892,000	0.2%
27	Tennessee	697,973,000	1.2%
3	Texas	3,929,491,000	6.5%
31	Utah	516,760,000	0.9%
46	Vermont	166,908,000	0.3%
14	Virginia	1,540,829,000	2.6%
17	Washington	989,156,000	1.6%
40	West Virginia	304,811,000	0.5%
16	Wisconsin	1,206,884,000	2.0%
48	Wyoming	143,947,000	0.2%

RANK ORDER

RANK	STATE	EXPENDITURES	% of USA
1	California	$9,248,190,000	15.3%
2	New York	4,708,353,000	7.8%
3	Texas	3,929,491,000	6.5%
4	Florida	3,412,064,000	5.7%
5	Pennsylvania	2,673,448,000	4.4%
6	New Jersey	2,114,329,000	3.5%
7	Michigan	2,079,202,000	3.4%
8	Illinois	1,962,152,000	3.3%
9	Massachusetts	1,875,755,000	3.1%
10	Ohio	1,780,729,000	3.0%
11	North Carolina	1,691,149,000	2.8%
12	Georgia	1,652,673,000	2.7%
13	Maryland	1,638,454,000	2.7%
14	Virginia	1,540,829,000	2.6%
15	Connecticut	1,249,227,000	2.1%
16	Wisconsin	1,206,884,000	2.0%
17	Washington	989,156,000	1.6%
18	Missouri	974,115,000	1.6%
19	Arizona	958,417,000	1.6%
20	Colorado	945,955,000	1.6%
21	Oregon	928,514,000	1.5%
22	Indiana	912,424,000	1.5%
23	Kentucky	863,013,000	1.4%
24	Louisiana	816,436,000	1.4%
25	Oklahoma	765,007,000	1.3%
26	Minnesota	754,065,000	1.3%
27	Tennessee	697,973,000	1.2%
28	South Carolina	685,601,000	1.1%
29	Alabama	639,224,000	1.1%
30	Iowa	542,324,000	0.9%
31	Utah	516,760,000	0.9%
32	New Mexico	498,594,000	0.8%
33	Arkansas	488,753,000	0.8%
34	Kansas	470,920,000	0.8%
35	Delaware	411,750,000	0.7%
36	Mississippi	380,076,000	0.6%
37	Alaska	357,837,000	0.6%
38	Nevada	343,480,000	0.6%
39	Hawaii	337,978,000	0.6%
40	West Virginia	304,811,000	0.5%
41	Rhode Island	296,740,000	0.5%
42	Nebraska	275,250,000	0.5%
43	Idaho	272,850,000	0.5%
44	Maine	233,817,000	0.4%
45	New Hampshire	195,200,000	0.3%
46	Vermont	166,908,000	0.3%
47	Montana	165,123,000	0.3%
48	Wyoming	143,947,000	0.2%
49	South Dakota	112,892,000	0.2%
50	North Dakota	86,222,000	0.1%
	District of Columbia**	NA	NA

Source: Morgan Quitno Press using data from U.S. Bureau of the Census, Governments Division
"State and Local Government Finances: 2002 Census" (http://www.census.gov/govs/www/estimate02.html)
*Direct general expenditures. Includes Police Protection, Corrections and Judicial and Legal Services.
**Not applicable.

Per Capita State Government Expenditures for Justice Activities in 2002

National Per Capita = $209*

ALPHA ORDER				RANK ORDER		
RANK	STATE	PER CAPITA		RANK	STATE	PER CAPITA
47	Alabama	$143		1	Alaska	$558
1	Alaska	558		2	Delaware	511
33	Arizona	176		3	Connecticut	361
29	Arkansas	181		4	Maryland	301
11	California	264		5	Massachusetts	293
21	Colorado	210		6	Wyoming	288
3	Connecticut	361		7	Rhode Island	278
2	Delaware	511		8	Hawaii	274
23	Florida	205		9	Vermont	271
26	Georgia	194		10	New Mexico	269
8	Hawaii	274		11	California	264
24	Idaho	203		11	Oregon	264
41	Illinois	156		13	New Jersey	247
45	Indiana	148		14	New York	246
27	Iowa	185		15	Utah	223
34	Kansas	174		16	Wisconsin	222
20	Kentucky	211		17	Oklahoma	219
28	Louisiana	182		18	Pennsylvania	217
32	Maine	180		19	Virginia	212
4	Maryland	301		20	Kentucky	211
5	Massachusetts	293		21	Colorado	210
22	Michigan	207		22	Michigan	207
44	Minnesota	150		23	Florida	205
49	Mississippi	133		24	Idaho	203
35	Missouri	172		24	North Carolina	203
29	Montana	181		26	Georgia	194
39	Nebraska	159		27	Iowa	185
40	Nevada	158		28	Louisiana	182
43	New Hampshire	153		29	Arkansas	181
13	New Jersey	247		29	Montana	181
10	New Mexico	269		29	Texas	181
14	New York	246		32	Maine	180
24	North Carolina	203		33	Arizona	176
48	North Dakota	136		34	Kansas	174
41	Ohio	156		35	Missouri	172
17	Oklahoma	219		36	West Virginia	169
11	Oregon	264		37	South Carolina	167
18	Pennsylvania	217		38	Washington	163
7	Rhode Island	278		39	Nebraska	159
37	South Carolina	167		40	Nevada	158
45	South Dakota	148		41	Illinois	156
50	Tennessee	121		41	Ohio	156
29	Texas	181		43	New Hampshire	153
15	Utah	223		44	Minnesota	150
9	Vermont	271		45	Indiana	148
19	Virginia	212		45	South Dakota	148
38	Washington	163		47	Alabama	143
36	West Virginia	169		48	North Dakota	136
16	Wisconsin	222		49	Mississippi	133
6	Wyoming	288		50	Tennessee	121
				District of Columbia**		NA

Source: Morgan Quitno Press using data from U.S. Bureau of the Census, Governments Division
   "State and Local Government Finances: 2002 Census" (http://www.census.gov/govs/www/estimate02.html)
*Direct general expenditures. Includes Police Protection, Corrections and Judicial and Legal Services.
**Not applicable.

State Government Expenditures for Justice Activities
As a Percent of All Direct General Expenditures in 2002
National Percent = 8.1% of Direct General Expenditures*

ALPHA ORDER

RANK ORDER

RANK	STATE	PERCENT		RANK	STATE	PERCENT
43	Alabama	5.3		1	Delaware	12.1
37	Alaska	6.3		2	California	11.1
4	Arizona	10.3		3	Maryland	10.6
33	Arkansas	6.5		4	Arizona	10.3
2	California	11.1		4	Florida	10.3
6	Colorado	9.1		6	Colorado	9.1
6	Connecticut	9.1		6	Connecticut	9.1
1	Delaware	12.1		8	Nevada	9.0
4	Florida	10.3		8	New Jersey	9.0
11	Georgia	8.9		8	Virginia	9.0
44	Hawaii	5.2		11	Georgia	8.9
16	Idaho	8.5		11	Wisconsin	8.9
32	Illinois	6.6		13	Wyoming	8.8
33	Indiana	6.5		14	Oregon	8.7
30	Iowa	6.7		14	Texas	8.7
26	Kansas	7.1		16	Idaho	8.5
30	Kentucky	6.7		16	Massachusetts	8.5
29	Louisiana	6.8		18	Michigan	8.4
45	Maine	5.0		18	North Carolina	8.4
3	Maryland	10.6		20	New York	8.2
16	Massachusetts	8.5		21	Oklahoma	8.0
18	Michigan	8.4		22	Pennsylvania	7.8
45	Minnesota	5.0		23	New Mexico	7.7
49	Mississippi	4.7		24	Utah	7.4
26	Missouri	7.1		25	Rhode Island	7.2
39	Montana	5.7		26	Kansas	7.1
37	Nebraska	6.3		26	Missouri	7.1
8	Nevada	9.0		28	Vermont	7.0
33	New Hampshire	6.5		29	Louisiana	6.8
8	New Jersey	9.0		30	Iowa	6.7
23	New Mexico	7.7		30	Kentucky	6.7
20	New York	8.2		32	Illinois	6.6
18	North Carolina	8.4		33	Arkansas	6.5
50	North Dakota	3.9		33	Indiana	6.5
33	Ohio	6.5		33	New Hampshire	6.5
21	Oklahoma	8.0		33	Ohio	6.5
14	Oregon	8.7		37	Alaska	6.3
22	Pennsylvania	7.8		37	Nebraska	6.3
25	Rhode Island	7.2		39	Montana	5.7
41	South Carolina	5.4		40	South Dakota	5.5
40	South Dakota	5.5		41	South Carolina	5.4
45	Tennessee	5.0		41	Washington	5.4
14	Texas	8.7		43	Alabama	5.3
24	Utah	7.4		44	Hawaii	5.2
28	Vermont	7.0		45	Maine	5.0
8	Virginia	9.0		45	Minnesota	5.0
41	Washington	5.4		45	Tennessee	5.0
45	West Virginia	5.0		45	West Virginia	5.0
11	Wisconsin	8.9		49	Mississippi	4.7
13	Wyoming	8.8		50	North Dakota	3.9

District of Columbia**   NA

Source: Morgan Quitno Press using data from U.S. Bureau of the Census, Governments Division
   "State and Local Government Finances: 2002 Census" (http://www.census.gov/govs/www/estimate02.html)
*Includes Police Protection, Corrections and Judicial and Legal Services.
**Not applicable.

Local Government Expenditures for Justice Activities in 2002

National Total = $90,119,813,000*

ALPHA ORDER

RANK	STATE	EXPENDITURES	% of USA
26	Alabama	$847,909,000	0.9%
41	Alaska	212,757,000	0.2%
11	Arizona	2,077,541,000	2.3%
35	Arkansas	479,180,000	0.5%
1	California	16,959,927,000	18.8%
20	Colorado	1,367,359,000	1.5%
28	Connecticut	652,946,000	0.7%
47	Delaware	130,639,000	0.1%
3	Florida	5,991,838,000	6.6%
10	Georgia	2,350,150,000	2.6%
39	Hawaii	287,798,000	0.3%
38	Idaho	320,179,000	0.4%
5	Illinois	4,250,330,000	4.7%
23	Indiana	1,207,703,000	1.3%
34	Iowa	534,055,000	0.6%
29	Kansas	603,646,000	0.7%
30	Kentucky	595,503,000	0.7%
21	Louisiana	1,291,133,000	1.4%
45	Maine	172,595,000	0.2%
16	Maryland	1,473,959,000	1.6%
18	Massachusetts	1,432,761,000	1.6%
8	Michigan	3,104,124,000	3.4%
17	Minnesota	1,435,375,000	1.6%
32	Mississippi	561,644,000	0.6%
22	Missouri	1,233,025,000	1.4%
43	Montana	203,389,000	0.2%
37	Nebraska	361,363,000	0.4%
24	Nevada	1,131,233,000	1.3%
40	New Hampshire	228,784,000	0.3%
9	New Jersey	2,994,322,000	3.3%
36	New Mexico	473,695,000	0.5%
2	New York	9,407,481,000	10.4%
15	North Carolina	1,538,026,000	1.7%
49	North Dakota	100,839,000	0.1%
6	Ohio	3,809,994,000	4.2%
31	Oklahoma	591,539,000	0.7%
25	Oregon	1,071,153,000	1.2%
7	Pennsylvania	3,368,881,000	3.7%
44	Rhode Island	202,942,000	0.2%
27	South Carolina	819,262,000	0.9%
48	South Dakota	129,183,000	0.1%
19	Tennessee	1,389,264,000	1.5%
4	Texas	5,820,817,000	6.5%
33	Utah	540,621,000	0.6%
50	Vermont	47,231,000	0.1%
13	Virginia	1,813,227,000	2.0%
12	Washington	1,818,667,000	2.0%
42	West Virginia	208,458,000	0.2%
14	Wisconsin	1,714,038,000	1.9%
46	Wyoming	144,216,000	0.2%

RANK ORDER

RANK	STATE	EXPENDITURES	% of USA
1	California	$16,959,927,000	18.8%
2	New York	9,407,481,000	10.4%
3	Florida	5,991,838,000	6.6%
4	Texas	5,820,817,000	6.5%
5	Illinois	4,250,330,000	4.7%
6	Ohio	3,809,994,000	4.2%
7	Pennsylvania	3,368,881,000	3.7%
8	Michigan	3,104,124,000	3.4%
9	New Jersey	2,994,322,000	3.3%
10	Georgia	2,350,150,000	2.6%
11	Arizona	2,077,541,000	2.3%
12	Washington	1,818,667,000	2.0%
13	Virginia	1,813,227,000	2.0%
14	Wisconsin	1,714,038,000	1.9%
15	North Carolina	1,538,026,000	1.7%
16	Maryland	1,473,959,000	1.6%
17	Minnesota	1,435,375,000	1.6%
18	Massachusetts	1,432,761,000	1.6%
19	Tennessee	1,389,264,000	1.5%
20	Colorado	1,367,359,000	1.5%
21	Louisiana	1,291,133,000	1.4%
22	Missouri	1,233,025,000	1.4%
23	Indiana	1,207,703,000	1.3%
24	Nevada	1,131,233,000	1.3%
25	Oregon	1,071,153,000	1.2%
26	Alabama	847,909,000	0.9%
27	South Carolina	819,262,000	0.9%
28	Connecticut	652,946,000	0.7%
29	Kansas	603,646,000	0.7%
30	Kentucky	595,503,000	0.7%
31	Oklahoma	591,539,000	0.7%
32	Mississippi	561,644,000	0.6%
33	Utah	540,621,000	0.6%
34	Iowa	534,055,000	0.6%
35	Arkansas	479,180,000	0.5%
36	New Mexico	473,695,000	0.5%
37	Nebraska	361,363,000	0.4%
38	Idaho	320,179,000	0.4%
39	Hawaii	287,798,000	0.3%
40	New Hampshire	228,784,000	0.3%
41	Alaska	212,757,000	0.2%
42	West Virginia	208,458,000	0.2%
43	Montana	203,389,000	0.2%
44	Rhode Island	202,942,000	0.2%
45	Maine	172,595,000	0.2%
46	Wyoming	144,216,000	0.2%
47	Delaware	130,639,000	0.1%
48	South Dakota	129,183,000	0.1%
49	North Dakota	100,839,000	0.1%
50	Vermont	47,231,000	0.1%
	District of Columbia	617,112,000	0.7%

Source: Morgan Quitno Press using data from U.S. Bureau of the Census, Governments Division
   "State and Local Government Finances: 2002 Census" (http://www.census.gov/govs/www/estimate02.html)
*Direct general expenditures. Includes Police Protection, Corrections and Judicial and Legal Services.

Per Capita Local Government Expenditures for Justice Activities in 2002

National Per Capita = $313*

ALPHA ORDER

RANK	STATE	PER CAPITA
37	Alabama	$189
9	Alaska	332
4	Arizona	382
42	Arkansas	177
3	California	485
12	Colorado	304
37	Connecticut	189
45	Delaware	162
5	Florida	359
18	Georgia	275
26	Hawaii	233
25	Idaho	238
7	Illinois	338
34	Indiana	196
40	Iowa	182
28	Kansas	223
47	Kentucky	146
16	Louisiana	288
48	Maine	133
20	Maryland	271
28	Massachusetts	223
11	Michigan	309
17	Minnesota	286
34	Mississippi	196
31	Missouri	217
28	Montana	223
32	Nebraska	209
1	Nevada	522
41	New Hampshire	179
6	New Jersey	349
22	New Mexico	255
2	New York	491
39	North Carolina	185
46	North Dakota	159
8	Ohio	334
43	Oklahoma	170
12	Oregon	304
19	Pennsylvania	273
36	Rhode Island	190
33	South Carolina	200
43	South Dakota	170
24	Tennessee	240
21	Texas	268
26	Utah	233
50	Vermont	77
23	Virginia	249
14	Washington	300
49	West Virginia	115
10	Wisconsin	315
15	Wyoming	289

RANK ORDER

RANK	STATE	PER CAPITA
1	Nevada	$522
2	New York	491
3	California	485
4	Arizona	382
5	Florida	359
6	New Jersey	349
7	Illinois	338
8	Ohio	334
9	Alaska	332
10	Wisconsin	315
11	Michigan	309
12	Colorado	304
12	Oregon	304
14	Washington	300
15	Wyoming	289
16	Louisiana	288
17	Minnesota	286
18	Georgia	275
19	Pennsylvania	273
20	Maryland	271
21	Texas	268
22	New Mexico	255
23	Virginia	249
24	Tennessee	240
25	Idaho	238
26	Hawaii	233
26	Utah	233
28	Kansas	223
28	Massachusetts	223
28	Montana	223
31	Missouri	217
32	Nebraska	209
33	South Carolina	200
34	Indiana	196
34	Mississippi	196
36	Rhode Island	190
37	Alabama	189
37	Connecticut	189
39	North Carolina	185
40	Iowa	182
41	New Hampshire	179
42	Arkansas	177
43	Oklahoma	170
43	South Dakota	170
45	Delaware	162
46	North Dakota	159
47	Kentucky	146
48	Maine	133
49	West Virginia	115
50	Vermont	77

District of Columbia	1,093

Source: Morgan Quitno Press using data from U.S. Bureau of the Census, Governments Division
"State and Local Government Finances: 2002 Census" (http://www.census.gov/govs/www/estimate02.html)
*Direct general expenditures. Includes Police Protection, Corrections and Judicial and Legal Services.

Local Government Expenditures for Justice Activities
As a Percent of All Direct General Expenditures in 2002
National Percent = 9.1% of Direct General Expenditures*

ALPHA ORDER

RANK	STATE	PERCENT
37	Alabama	6.8
28	Alaska	7.6
3	Arizona	13.0
20	Arkansas	8.7
4	California	11.2
25	Colorado	8.2
44	Connecticut	6.3
41	Delaware	6.7
5	Florida	11.1
17	Georgia	8.9
1	Hawaii	16.6
17	Idaho	8.9
8	Illinois	9.6
43	Indiana	6.4
47	Iowa	5.9
32	Kansas	7.3
37	Kentucky	6.8
6	Louisiana	10.5
49	Maine	5.3
15	Maryland	9.0
34	Massachusetts	7.1
22	Michigan	8.6
32	Minnesota	7.3
28	Mississippi	7.6
27	Missouri	8.0
11	Montana	9.3
37	Nebraska	6.8
2	Nevada	14.2
37	New Hampshire	6.8
7	New Jersey	9.7
10	New Mexico	9.5
14	New York	9.1
44	North Carolina	6.3
46	North Dakota	6.1
8	Ohio	9.6
36	Oklahoma	6.9
20	Oregon	8.7
22	Pennsylvania	8.6
28	Rhode Island	7.6
31	South Carolina	7.4
35	South Dakota	7.0
11	Tennessee	9.3
19	Texas	8.8
13	Utah	9.2
50	Vermont	3.3
25	Virginia	8.2
15	Washington	9.0
48	West Virginia	5.6
24	Wisconsin	8.4
42	Wyoming	6.5

RANK ORDER

RANK	STATE	PERCENT
1	Hawaii	16.6
2	Nevada	14.2
3	Arizona	13.0
4	California	11.2
5	Florida	11.1
6	Louisiana	10.5
7	New Jersey	9.7
8	Illinois	9.6
8	Ohio	9.6
10	New Mexico	9.5
11	Montana	9.3
11	Tennessee	9.3
13	Utah	9.2
14	New York	9.1
15	Maryland	9.0
15	Washington	9.0
17	Georgia	8.9
17	Idaho	8.9
19	Texas	8.8
20	Arkansas	8.7
20	Oregon	8.7
22	Michigan	8.6
22	Pennsylvania	8.6
24	Wisconsin	8.4
25	Colorado	8.2
25	Virginia	8.2
27	Missouri	8.0
28	Alaska	7.6
28	Mississippi	7.6
28	Rhode Island	7.6
31	South Carolina	7.4
32	Kansas	7.3
32	Minnesota	7.3
34	Massachusetts	7.1
35	South Dakota	7.0
36	Oklahoma	6.9
37	Alabama	6.8
37	Kentucky	6.8
37	Nebraska	6.8
37	New Hampshire	6.8
41	Delaware	6.7
42	Wyoming	6.5
43	Indiana	6.4
44	Connecticut	6.3
44	North Carolina	6.3
46	North Dakota	6.1
47	Iowa	5.9
48	West Virginia	5.6
49	Maine	5.3
50	Vermont	3.3

District of Columbia 10.0

Source: Morgan Quitno Press using data from U.S. Bureau of the Census, Governments Division
"State and Local Government Finances: 2002 Census" (http://www.census.gov/govs/www/estimate02.html)
*Includes Police Protection, Corrections and Judicial and Legal Services.

State and Local Government Expenditures for Police Protection in 2002

National Total = $64,491,894,000*

ALPHA ORDER

RANK	STATE	EXPENDITURES	% of USA
27	Alabama	$710,441,000	1.1%
38	Alaska	264,272,000	0.4%
16	Arizona	1,258,955,000	2.0%
36	Arkansas	403,229,000	0.6%
1	California	10,147,080,000	15.7%
18	Colorado	1,071,991,000	1.7%
24	Connecticut	780,782,000	1.2%
43	Delaware	190,774,000	0.3%
3	Florida	4,392,951,000	6.8%
10	Georgia	1,555,442,000	2.4%
39	Hawaii	254,636,000	0.4%
40	Idaho	240,794,000	0.4%
5	Illinois	3,226,031,000	5.0%
22	Indiana	895,372,000	1.4%
33	Iowa	458,397,000	0.7%
31	Kansas	477,726,000	0.7%
30	Kentucky	542,715,000	0.8%
23	Louisiana	889,447,000	1.4%
45	Maine	180,762,000	0.3%
13	Maryland	1,335,168,000	2.1%
12	Massachusetts	1,441,460,000	2.2%
9	Michigan	1,975,978,000	3.1%
19	Minnesota	1,018,638,000	1.6%
32	Mississippi	461,105,000	0.7%
20	Missouri	1,017,884,000	1.6%
46	Montana	170,135,000	0.3%
37	Nebraska	267,521,000	0.4%
28	Nevada	650,065,000	1.0%
42	New Hampshire	211,965,000	0.3%
7	New Jersey	2,419,342,000	3.8%
35	New Mexico	409,744,000	0.6%
2	New York	6,719,312,000	10.4%
11	North Carolina	1,504,076,000	2.3%
50	North Dakota	77,068,000	0.1%
8	Ohio	2,413,629,000	3.7%
29	Oklahoma	568,877,000	0.9%
25	Oregon	771,954,000	1.2%
6	Pennsylvania	2,447,631,000	3.8%
41	Rhode Island	238,841,000	0.4%
26	South Carolina	722,169,000	1.1%
48	South Dakota	105,443,000	0.2%
21	Tennessee	976,543,000	1.5%
4	Texas	3,727,574,000	5.8%
34	Utah	440,622,000	0.7%
49	Vermont	91,960,000	0.1%
14	Virginia	1,309,344,000	2.0%
17	Washington	1,091,514,000	1.7%
44	West Virginia	186,904,000	0.3%
15	Wisconsin	1,271,605,000	2.0%
47	Wyoming	121,336,000	0.2%

RANK ORDER

RANK	STATE	EXPENDITURES	% of USA
1	California	$10,147,080,000	15.7%
2	New York	6,719,312,000	10.4%
3	Florida	4,392,951,000	6.8%
4	Texas	3,727,574,000	5.8%
5	Illinois	3,226,031,000	5.0%
6	Pennsylvania	2,447,631,000	3.8%
7	New Jersey	2,419,342,000	3.8%
8	Ohio	2,413,629,000	3.7%
9	Michigan	1,975,978,000	3.1%
10	Georgia	1,555,442,000	2.4%
11	North Carolina	1,504,076,000	2.3%
12	Massachusetts	1,441,460,000	2.2%
13	Maryland	1,335,168,000	2.1%
14	Virginia	1,309,344,000	2.0%
15	Wisconsin	1,271,605,000	2.0%
16	Arizona	1,258,955,000	2.0%
17	Washington	1,091,514,000	1.7%
18	Colorado	1,071,991,000	1.7%
19	Minnesota	1,018,638,000	1.6%
20	Missouri	1,017,884,000	1.6%
21	Tennessee	976,543,000	1.5%
22	Indiana	895,372,000	1.4%
23	Louisiana	889,447,000	1.4%
24	Connecticut	780,782,000	1.2%
25	Oregon	771,954,000	1.2%
26	South Carolina	722,169,000	1.1%
27	Alabama	710,441,000	1.1%
28	Nevada	650,065,000	1.0%
29	Oklahoma	568,877,000	0.9%
30	Kentucky	542,715,000	0.8%
31	Kansas	477,726,000	0.7%
32	Mississippi	461,105,000	0.7%
33	Iowa	458,397,000	0.7%
34	Utah	440,622,000	0.7%
35	New Mexico	409,744,000	0.6%
36	Arkansas	403,229,000	0.6%
37	Nebraska	267,521,000	0.4%
38	Alaska	264,272,000	0.4%
39	Hawaii	254,636,000	0.4%
40	Idaho	240,794,000	0.4%
41	Rhode Island	238,841,000	0.4%
42	New Hampshire	211,965,000	0.3%
43	Delaware	190,774,000	0.3%
44	West Virginia	186,904,000	0.3%
45	Maine	180,762,000	0.3%
46	Montana	170,135,000	0.3%
47	Wyoming	121,336,000	0.2%
48	South Dakota	105,443,000	0.2%
49	Vermont	91,960,000	0.1%
50	North Dakota	77,068,000	0.1%
	District of Columbia	384,690,000	0.6%

Source: U.S. Bureau of the Census, Governments Division
   "State and Local Government Finances: 2002 Census" (http://www.census.gov/govs/www/estimate02.html)
Direct general expenditures.

Per Capita State & Local Government Expenditures for Police Protection: 2002

National Per Capita = $224*

ALPHA ORDER

RANK	STATE	PER CAPITA
40	Alabama	$159
1	Alaska	412
13	Arizona	231
43	Arkansas	149
4	California	290
10	Colorado	238
14	Connecticut	226
11	Delaware	237
6	Florida	263
27	Georgia	182
20	Hawaii	206
31	Idaho	179
7	Illinois	256
45	Indiana	145
41	Iowa	156
33	Kansas	176
48	Kentucky	133
22	Louisiana	199
46	Maine	139
8	Maryland	245
15	Massachusetts	225
24	Michigan	197
21	Minnesota	203
39	Mississippi	161
31	Missouri	179
26	Montana	187
42	Nebraska	155
3	Nevada	300
37	New Hampshire	166
5	New Jersey	282
17	New Mexico	221
2	New York	351
28	North Carolina	181
49	North Dakota	122
19	Ohio	212
38	Oklahoma	163
18	Oregon	219
22	Pennsylvania	199
16	Rhode Island	223
33	South Carolina	176
46	South Dakota	139
36	Tennessee	169
35	Texas	172
25	Utah	190
43	Vermont	149
29	Virginia	180
29	Washington	180
50	West Virginia	104
12	Wisconsin	234
9	Wyoming	243

RANK ORDER

RANK	STATE	PER CAPITA
1	Alaska	$412
2	New York	351
3	Nevada	300
4	California	290
5	New Jersey	282
6	Florida	263
7	Illinois	256
8	Maryland	245
9	Wyoming	243
10	Colorado	238
11	Delaware	237
12	Wisconsin	234
13	Arizona	231
14	Connecticut	226
15	Massachusetts	225
16	Rhode Island	223
17	New Mexico	221
18	Oregon	219
19	Ohio	212
20	Hawaii	206
21	Minnesota	203
22	Louisiana	199
22	Pennsylvania	199
24	Michigan	197
25	Utah	190
26	Montana	187
27	Georgia	182
28	North Carolina	181
29	Virginia	180
29	Washington	180
31	Idaho	179
31	Missouri	179
33	Kansas	176
33	South Carolina	176
35	Texas	172
36	Tennessee	169
37	New Hampshire	166
38	Oklahoma	163
39	Mississippi	161
40	Alabama	159
41	Iowa	156
42	Nebraska	155
43	Arkansas	149
43	Vermont	149
45	Indiana	145
46	Maine	139
46	South Dakota	139
48	Kentucky	133
49	North Dakota	122
50	West Virginia	104

	District of Columbia	681

Source: Morgan Quitno Press using data from U.S. Bureau of the Census, Governments Division
"State and Local Government Finances: 2002 Census" (http://www.census.gov/govs/www/estimate02.html)
*Direct general expenditures.

State and Local Government Expenditures for Police Protection
As a Percent of All Direct General Expenditures in 2002
National Percent = 3.7% of Direct General Expenditures

RANK	STATE	PERCENT
39	Alabama	2.9
32	Alaska	3.1
2	Arizona	5.0
32	Arkansas	3.1
6	California	4.3
9	Colorado	4.0
30	Connecticut	3.2
12	Delaware	3.6
2	Florida	5.0
15	Georgia	3.5
32	Hawaii	3.1
15	Idaho	3.5
4	Illinois	4.4
42	Indiana	2.7
42	Iowa	2.7
30	Kansas	3.2
46	Kentucky	2.5
10	Louisiana	3.7
48	Maine	2.3
7	Maryland	4.2
19	Massachusetts	3.4
25	Michigan	3.3
39	Minnesota	2.9
37	Mississippi	3.0
15	Missouri	3.5
19	Montana	3.4
42	Nebraska	2.7
1	Nevada	5.5
25	New Hampshire	3.3
4	New Jersey	4.4
12	New Mexico	3.6
7	New York	4.2
19	North Carolina	3.4
49	North Dakota	2.0
12	Ohio	3.6
32	Oklahoma	3.1
19	Oregon	3.4
25	Pennsylvania	3.3
15	Rhode Island	3.5
37	South Carolina	3.0
42	South Dakota	2.7
19	Tennessee	3.4
25	Texas	3.3
19	Utah	3.4
47	Vermont	2.4
25	Virginia	3.3
41	Washington	2.8
50	West Virginia	1.9
10	Wisconsin	3.7
32	Wyoming	3.1

RANK	STATE	PERCENT
1	Nevada	5.5
2	Arizona	5.0
2	Florida	5.0
4	Illinois	4.4
4	New Jersey	4.4
6	California	4.3
7	Maryland	4.2
7	New York	4.2
9	Colorado	4.0
10	Louisiana	3.7
10	Wisconsin	3.7
12	Delaware	3.6
12	New Mexico	3.6
12	Ohio	3.6
15	Georgia	3.5
15	Idaho	3.5
15	Missouri	3.5
15	Rhode Island	3.5
19	Massachusetts	3.4
19	Montana	3.4
19	North Carolina	3.4
19	Oregon	3.4
19	Tennessee	3.4
19	Utah	3.4
25	Michigan	3.3
25	New Hampshire	3.3
25	Pennsylvania	3.3
25	Texas	3.3
25	Virginia	3.3
30	Connecticut	3.2
30	Kansas	3.2
32	Alaska	3.1
32	Arkansas	3.1
32	Hawaii	3.1
32	Oklahoma	3.1
32	Wyoming	3.1
37	Mississippi	3.0
37	South Carolina	3.0
39	Alabama	2.9
39	Minnesota	2.9
41	Washington	2.8
42	Indiana	2.7
42	Iowa	2.7
42	Nebraska	2.7
42	South Dakota	2.7
46	Kentucky	2.5
47	Vermont	2.4
48	Maine	2.3
49	North Dakota	2.0
50	West Virginia	1.9

	District of Columbia	6.2

Source: Morgan Quitno Press using data from U.S. Bureau of the Census, Governments Division
"State and Local Government Finances: 2002 Census" (http://www.census.gov/govs/www/estimate02.html)

State Government Expenditures for Police Protection in 2002

National Total = $9,407,598,000*

ALPHA ORDER

RANK	STATE	EXPENDITURES	% of USA
27	Alabama	$100,402,000	1.1%
38	Alaska	63,170,000	0.7%
23	Arizona	151,152,000	1.6%
33	Arkansas	71,768,000	0.8%
1	California	1,132,235,000	12.0%
28	Colorado	99,690,000	1.1%
21	Connecticut	164,120,000	1.7%
34	Delaware	68,413,000	0.7%
4	Florida	424,501,000	4.5%
12	Georgia	255,475,000	2.7%
50	Hawaii	6,244,000	0.1%
44	Idaho	44,108,000	0.5%
6	Illinois	359,209,000	3.8%
17	Indiana	193,527,000	2.1%
32	Iowa	85,720,000	0.9%
37	Kansas	63,403,000	0.7%
22	Kentucky	163,317,000	1.7%
16	Louisiana	194,931,000	2.1%
39	Maine	59,165,000	0.6%
10	Maryland	296,897,000	3.2%
11	Massachusetts	286,952,000	3.1%
9	Michigan	306,612,000	3.3%
18	Minnesota	177,936,000	1.9%
35	Mississippi	66,609,000	0.7%
20	Missouri	172,082,000	1.8%
46	Montana	28,035,000	0.3%
40	Nebraska	51,632,000	0.5%
36	Nevada	63,653,000	0.7%
45	New Hampshire	36,800,000	0.4%
7	New Jersey	342,844,000	3.6%
31	New Mexico	88,817,000	0.9%
3	New York	567,888,000	6.0%
8	North Carolina	328,841,000	3.5%
49	North Dakota	13,805,000	0.1%
13	Ohio	233,180,000	2.5%
30	Oklahoma	91,636,000	1.0%
24	Oregon	141,259,000	1.5%
2	Pennsylvania	893,343,000	9.5%
43	Rhode Island	47,527,000	0.5%
15	South Carolina	204,655,000	2.2%
48	South Dakota	22,169,000	0.2%
25	Tennessee	125,377,000	1.3%
5	Texas	389,406,000	4.1%
26	Utah	103,937,000	1.1%
41	Vermont	48,332,000	0.5%
14	Virginia	231,914,000	2.5%
19	Washington	175,072,000	1.9%
42	West Virginia	47,790,000	0.5%
29	Wisconsin	96,662,000	1.0%
47	Wyoming	25,386,000	0.3%

RANK ORDER

RANK	STATE	EXPENDITURES	% of USA
1	California	$1,132,235,000	12.0%
2	Pennsylvania	893,343,000	9.5%
3	New York	567,888,000	6.0%
4	Florida	424,501,000	4.5%
5	Texas	389,406,000	4.1%
6	Illinois	359,209,000	3.8%
7	New Jersey	342,844,000	3.6%
8	North Carolina	328,841,000	3.5%
9	Michigan	306,612,000	3.3%
10	Maryland	296,897,000	3.2%
11	Massachusetts	286,952,000	3.1%
12	Georgia	255,475,000	2.7%
13	Ohio	233,180,000	2.5%
14	Virginia	231,914,000	2.5%
15	South Carolina	204,655,000	2.2%
16	Louisiana	194,931,000	2.1%
17	Indiana	193,527,000	2.1%
18	Minnesota	177,936,000	1.9%
19	Washington	175,072,000	1.9%
20	Missouri	172,082,000	1.8%
21	Connecticut	164,120,000	1.7%
22	Kentucky	163,317,000	1.7%
23	Arizona	151,152,000	1.6%
24	Oregon	141,259,000	1.5%
25	Tennessee	125,377,000	1.3%
26	Utah	103,937,000	1.1%
27	Alabama	100,402,000	1.1%
28	Colorado	99,690,000	1.1%
29	Wisconsin	96,662,000	1.0%
30	Oklahoma	91,636,000	1.0%
31	New Mexico	88,817,000	0.9%
32	Iowa	85,720,000	0.9%
33	Arkansas	71,768,000	0.8%
34	Delaware	68,413,000	0.7%
35	Mississippi	66,609,000	0.7%
36	Nevada	63,653,000	0.7%
37	Kansas	63,403,000	0.7%
38	Alaska	63,170,000	0.7%
39	Maine	59,165,000	0.6%
40	Nebraska	51,632,000	0.5%
41	Vermont	48,332,000	0.5%
42	West Virginia	47,790,000	0.5%
43	Rhode Island	47,527,000	0.5%
44	Idaho	44,108,000	0.5%
45	New Hampshire	36,800,000	0.4%
46	Montana	28,035,000	0.3%
47	Wyoming	25,386,000	0.3%
48	South Dakota	22,169,000	0.2%
49	North Dakota	13,805,000	0.1%
50	Hawaii	6,244,000	0.1%
	District of Columbia**	NA	NA

Source: U.S. Bureau of the Census, Governments Division
   "State and Local Government Finances: 2002 Census" (http://www.census.gov/govs/www/estimate02.html)
*Direct general expenditures.
**Not applicable.

Per Capita State Government Expenditures for Police Protection in 2002

National Per Capita = $32.67*

ALPHA ORDER

RANK	STATE	PER CAPITA
43	Alabama	$22.41
1	Alaska	98.57
36	Arizona	27.79
37	Arkansas	26.51
21	California	32.36
44	Colorado	22.16
9	Connecticut	47.45
2	Delaware	84.87
40	Florida	25.45
27	Georgia	29.92
50	Hawaii	5.06
20	Idaho	32.84
35	Illinois	28.54
23	Indiana	31.43
31	Iowa	29.21
41	Kansas	23.37
17	Kentucky	39.93
14	Louisiana	43.54
10	Maine	45.59
5	Maryland	54.56
12	Massachusetts	44.75
25	Michigan	30.53
19	Minnesota	35.41
42	Mississippi	23.23
26	Missouri	30.30
24	Montana	30.79
28	Nebraska	29.91
30	Nevada	29.36
34	New Hampshire	28.85
16	New Jersey	39.97
8	New Mexico	47.88
29	New York	29.65
18	North Carolina	39.56
45	North Dakota	21.78
47	Ohio	20.44
39	Oklahoma	26.27
15	Oregon	40.09
4	Pennsylvania	72.46
13	Rhode Island	44.46
7	South Carolina	49.84
32	South Dakota	29.15
46	Tennessee	21.65
48	Texas	17.93
11	Utah	44.81
3	Vermont	78.40
22	Virginia	31.88
33	Washington	28.86
38	West Virginia	26.47
49	Wisconsin	17.77
6	Wyoming	50.85

RANK ORDER

RANK	STATE	PER CAPITA
1	Alaska	$98.57
2	Delaware	84.87
3	Vermont	78.40
4	Pennsylvania	72.46
5	Maryland	54.56
6	Wyoming	50.85
7	South Carolina	49.84
8	New Mexico	47.88
9	Connecticut	47.45
10	Maine	45.59
11	Utah	44.81
12	Massachusetts	44.75
13	Rhode Island	44.46
14	Louisiana	43.54
15	Oregon	40.09
16	New Jersey	39.97
17	Kentucky	39.93
18	North Carolina	39.56
19	Minnesota	35.41
20	Idaho	32.84
21	California	32.36
22	Virginia	31.88
23	Indiana	31.43
24	Montana	30.79
25	Michigan	30.53
26	Missouri	30.30
27	Georgia	29.92
28	Nebraska	29.91
29	New York	29.65
30	Nevada	29.36
31	Iowa	29.21
32	South Dakota	29.15
33	Washington	28.86
34	New Hampshire	28.85
35	Illinois	28.54
36	Arizona	27.79
37	Arkansas	26.51
38	West Virginia	26.47
39	Oklahoma	26.27
40	Florida	25.45
41	Kansas	23.37
42	Mississippi	23.23
43	Alabama	22.41
44	Colorado	22.16
45	North Dakota	21.78
46	Tennessee	21.65
47	Ohio	20.44
48	Texas	17.93
49	Wisconsin	17.77
50	Hawaii	5.06

District of Columbia**   NA

Source: Morgan Quitno Press using data from U.S. Bureau of the Census, Governments Division
  "State and Local Government Finances: 2002 Census" (http://www.census.gov/govs/www/estimate02.html)
Direct general expenditures.
**Not applicable.*

State Government Expenditures for Police Protection
As a Percent of All Direct General Expenditures in 2002
National Percent = 1.3% of Direct General Expenditures

ALPHA ORDER

RANK	STATE	PERCENT
45	Alabama	0.8
32	Alaska	1.1
6	Arizona	1.6
41	Arkansas	0.9
13	California	1.4
35	Colorado	1.0
25	Connecticut	1.2
2	Delaware	2.0
19	Florida	1.3
13	Georgia	1.4
50	Hawaii	0.1
13	Idaho	1.4
25	Illinois	1.2
13	Indiana	1.4
32	Iowa	1.1
35	Kansas	1.0
19	Kentucky	1.3
6	Louisiana	1.6
19	Maine	1.3
4	Maryland	1.9
19	Massachusetts	1.3
25	Michigan	1.2
25	Minnesota	1.2
45	Mississippi	0.8
19	Missouri	1.3
35	Montana	1.0
25	Nebraska	1.2
5	Nevada	1.7
25	New Hampshire	1.2
11	New Jersey	1.5
13	New Mexico	1.4
35	New York	1.0
6	North Carolina	1.6
49	North Dakota	0.6
41	Ohio	0.9
35	Oklahoma	1.0
19	Oregon	1.3
1	Pennsylvania	2.6
25	Rhode Island	1.2
6	South Carolina	1.6
32	South Dakota	1.1
41	Tennessee	0.9
41	Texas	0.9
11	Utah	1.5
2	Vermont	2.0
13	Virginia	1.4
35	Washington	1.0
45	West Virginia	0.8
48	Wisconsin	0.7
6	Wyoming	1.6

RANK ORDER

RANK	STATE	PERCENT
1	Pennsylvania	2.6
2	Delaware	2.0
2	Vermont	2.0
4	Maryland	1.9
5	Nevada	1.7
6	Arizona	1.6
6	Louisiana	1.6
6	North Carolina	1.6
6	South Carolina	1.6
6	Wyoming	1.6
11	New Jersey	1.5
11	Utah	1.5
13	California	1.4
13	Georgia	1.4
13	Idaho	1.4
13	Indiana	1.4
13	New Mexico	1.4
13	Virginia	1.4
19	Florida	1.3
19	Kentucky	1.3
19	Maine	1.3
19	Massachusetts	1.3
19	Missouri	1.3
19	Oregon	1.3
25	Connecticut	1.2
25	Illinois	1.2
25	Michigan	1.2
25	Minnesota	1.2
25	Nebraska	1.2
25	New Hampshire	1.2
25	Rhode Island	1.2
32	Alaska	1.1
32	Iowa	1.1
32	South Dakota	1.1
35	Colorado	1.0
35	Kansas	1.0
35	Montana	1.0
35	New York	1.0
35	Oklahoma	1.0
35	Washington	1.0
41	Arkansas	0.9
41	Ohio	0.9
41	Tennessee	0.9
41	Texas	0.9
45	Alabama	0.8
45	Mississippi	0.8
45	West Virginia	0.8
48	Wisconsin	0.7
49	North Dakota	0.6
50	Hawaii	0.1

District of Columbia* — NA

Source: Morgan Quitno Press using data from U.S. Bureau of the Census, Governments Division
    "State and Local Government Finances: 2002 Census" (http://www.census.gov/govs/www/estimate02.html)
*Not applicable.

Local Government Expenditures for Police Protection in 2002

National Total = $55,084,296,000*

ALPHA ORDER

RANK	STATE	EXPENDITURES	% of USA
26	Alabama	$610,039,000	1.1%
39	Alaska	201,102,000	0.4%
14	Arizona	1,107,803,000	2.0%
35	Arkansas	331,461,000	0.6%
1	California	9,014,845,000	16.4%
17	Colorado	972,301,000	1.8%
25	Connecticut	616,662,000	1.1%
45	Delaware	122,361,000	0.2%
3	Florida	3,968,450,000	7.2%
10	Georgia	1,299,967,000	2.4%
37	Hawaii	248,392,000	0.5%
40	Idaho	196,686,000	0.4%
5	Illinois	2,866,822,000	5.2%
22	Indiana	701,845,000	1.3%
33	Iowa	372,677,000	0.7%
30	Kansas	414,323,000	0.8%
32	Kentucky	379,398,000	0.7%
23	Louisiana	694,516,000	1.3%
46	Maine	121,597,000	0.2%
16	Maryland	1,038,271,000	1.9%
13	Massachusetts	1,154,508,000	2.1%
8	Michigan	1,669,366,000	3.0%
21	Minnesota	840,702,000	1.5%
31	Mississippi	394,496,000	0.7%
20	Missouri	845,802,000	1.5%
43	Montana	142,100,000	0.3%
38	Nebraska	215,889,000	0.4%
27	Nevada	586,412,000	1.1%
42	New Hampshire	175,165,000	0.3%
7	New Jersey	2,076,498,000	3.8%
36	New Mexico	320,927,000	0.6%
2	New York	6,151,424,000	11.2%
11	North Carolina	1,175,235,000	2.1%
49	North Dakota	63,263,000	0.1%
6	Ohio	2,180,449,000	4.0%
29	Oklahoma	477,241,000	0.9%
24	Oregon	630,695,000	1.1%
9	Pennsylvania	1,554,288,000	2.8%
41	Rhode Island	191,314,000	0.3%
28	South Carolina	517,514,000	0.9%
48	South Dakota	83,274,000	0.2%
19	Tennessee	851,166,000	1.5%
4	Texas	3,338,168,000	6.1%
34	Utah	336,685,000	0.6%
50	Vermont	43,628,000	0.1%
15	Virginia	1,077,430,000	2.0%
18	Washington	916,442,000	1.7%
44	West Virginia	139,114,000	0.3%
12	Wisconsin	1,174,943,000	2.1%
47	Wyoming	95,950,000	0.2%

RANK ORDER

RANK	STATE	EXPENDITURES	% of USA
1	California	$9,014,845,000	16.4%
2	New York	6,151,424,000	11.2%
3	Florida	3,968,450,000	7.2%
4	Texas	3,338,168,000	6.1%
5	Illinois	2,866,822,000	5.2%
6	Ohio	2,180,449,000	4.0%
7	New Jersey	2,076,498,000	3.8%
8	Michigan	1,669,366,000	3.0%
9	Pennsylvania	1,554,288,000	2.8%
10	Georgia	1,299,967,000	2.4%
11	North Carolina	1,175,235,000	2.1%
12	Wisconsin	1,174,943,000	2.1%
13	Massachusetts	1,154,508,000	2.1%
14	Arizona	1,107,803,000	2.0%
15	Virginia	1,077,430,000	2.0%
16	Maryland	1,038,271,000	1.9%
17	Colorado	972,301,000	1.8%
18	Washington	916,442,000	1.7%
19	Tennessee	851,166,000	1.5%
20	Missouri	845,802,000	1.5%
21	Minnesota	840,702,000	1.5%
22	Indiana	701,845,000	1.3%
23	Louisiana	694,516,000	1.3%
24	Oregon	630,695,000	1.1%
25	Connecticut	616,662,000	1.1%
26	Alabama	610,039,000	1.1%
27	Nevada	586,412,000	1.1%
28	South Carolina	517,514,000	0.9%
29	Oklahoma	477,241,000	0.9%
30	Kansas	414,323,000	0.8%
31	Mississippi	394,496,000	0.7%
32	Kentucky	379,398,000	0.7%
33	Iowa	372,677,000	0.7%
34	Utah	336,685,000	0.6%
35	Arkansas	331,461,000	0.6%
36	New Mexico	320,927,000	0.6%
37	Hawaii	248,392,000	0.5%
38	Nebraska	215,889,000	0.4%
39	Alaska	201,102,000	0.4%
40	Idaho	196,686,000	0.4%
41	Rhode Island	191,314,000	0.3%
42	New Hampshire	175,165,000	0.3%
43	Montana	142,100,000	0.3%
44	West Virginia	139,114,000	0.3%
45	Delaware	122,361,000	0.2%
46	Maine	121,597,000	0.2%
47	Wyoming	95,950,000	0.2%
48	South Dakota	83,274,000	0.2%
49	North Dakota	63,263,000	0.1%
50	Vermont	43,628,000	0.1%
	District of Columbia	384,690,000	0.7%

Source: U.S. Bureau of the Census, Governments Division
"State and Local Government Finances: 2002 Census" (http://www.census.gov/govs/www/estimate02.html)
*Direct general expenditures.

Per Capita Local Government Expenditures for Police Protection in 2002

National Per Capita = $191*

ALPHA ORDER

RANK	STATE	PER CAPITA
38	Alabama	$136
2	Alaska	314
10	Arizona	204
43	Arkansas	122
4	California	258
8	Colorado	216
18	Connecticut	178
26	Delaware	152
6	Florida	238
26	Georgia	152
11	Hawaii	201
32	Idaho	146
7	Illinois	228
44	Indiana	114
39	Iowa	127
25	Kansas	153
48	Kentucky	93
23	Louisiana	155
47	Maine	94
13	Maryland	191
15	Massachusetts	180
21	Michigan	166
20	Minnesota	167
35	Mississippi	138
29	Missouri	149
22	Montana	156
42	Nebraska	125
3	Nevada	270
36	New Hampshire	137
5	New Jersey	242
19	New Mexico	173
1	New York	321
34	North Carolina	141
46	North Dakota	100
13	Ohio	191
36	Oklahoma	137
16	Oregon	179
40	Pennsylvania	126
16	Rhode Island	179
40	South Carolina	126
45	South Dakota	110
31	Tennessee	147
24	Texas	154
33	Utah	145
50	Vermont	71
30	Virginia	148
28	Washington	151
49	West Virginia	77
8	Wisconsin	216
12	Wyoming	192

RANK ORDER

RANK	STATE	PER CAPITA
1	New York	$321
2	Alaska	314
3	Nevada	270
4	California	258
5	New Jersey	242
6	Florida	238
7	Illinois	228
8	Colorado	216
8	Wisconsin	216
10	Arizona	204
11	Hawaii	201
12	Wyoming	192
13	Maryland	191
13	Ohio	191
15	Massachusetts	180
16	Oregon	179
16	Rhode Island	179
18	Connecticut	178
19	New Mexico	173
20	Minnesota	167
21	Michigan	166
22	Montana	156
23	Louisiana	155
24	Texas	154
25	Kansas	153
26	Delaware	152
26	Georgia	152
28	Washington	151
29	Missouri	149
30	Virginia	148
31	Tennessee	147
32	Idaho	146
33	Utah	145
34	North Carolina	141
35	Mississippi	138
36	New Hampshire	137
36	Oklahoma	137
38	Alabama	136
39	Iowa	127
40	Pennsylvania	126
40	South Carolina	126
42	Nebraska	125
43	Arkansas	122
44	Indiana	114
45	South Dakota	110
46	North Dakota	100
47	Maine	94
48	Kentucky	93
49	West Virginia	77
50	Vermont	71

District of Columbia   681

Source: Morgan Quitno Press using data from U.S. Bureau of the Census, Governments Division
    "State and Local Government Finances: 2002 Census" (http://www.census.gov/govs/www/estimate02.html)
*Direct general expenditures.

Local Government Expenditures for Police Protection
As a Percent of All Direct General Expenditures in 2002
National Percent = 5.6% of Direct General Expenditures

ALPHA ORDER

RANK	STATE	PERCENT
32	Alabama	4.9
4	Alaska	7.2
6	Arizona	6.9
13	Arkansas	6.0
14	California	5.9
17	Colorado	5.8
14	Connecticut	5.9
12	Delaware	6.3
2	Florida	7.4
32	Georgia	4.9
1	Hawaii	14.3
23	Idaho	5.5
8	Illinois	6.5
47	Indiana	3.7
43	Iowa	4.1
30	Kansas	5.0
40	Kentucky	4.3
22	Louisiana	5.6
47	Maine	3.7
10	Maryland	6.4
19	Massachusetts	5.7
37	Michigan	4.6
40	Minnesota	4.3
27	Mississippi	5.3
23	Missouri	5.5
8	Montana	6.5
44	Nebraska	4.0
2	Nevada	7.4
28	New Hampshire	5.2
7	New Jersey	6.7
10	New Mexico	6.4
14	New York	5.9
35	North Carolina	4.8
46	North Dakota	3.8
23	Ohio	5.5
23	Oklahoma	5.5
29	Oregon	5.1
44	Pennsylvania	4.0
4	Rhode Island	7.2
36	South Carolina	4.7
38	South Dakota	4.5
19	Tennessee	5.7
30	Texas	5.0
19	Utah	5.7
50	Vermont	3.0
32	Virginia	4.9
38	Washington	4.5
47	West Virginia	3.7
17	Wisconsin	5.8
40	Wyoming	4.3

RANK ORDER

RANK	STATE	PERCENT
1	Hawaii	14.3
2	Florida	7.4
2	Nevada	7.4
4	Alaska	7.2
4	Rhode Island	7.2
6	Arizona	6.9
7	New Jersey	6.7
8	Illinois	6.5
8	Montana	6.5
10	Maryland	6.4
10	New Mexico	6.4
12	Delaware	6.3
13	Arkansas	6.0
14	California	5.9
14	Connecticut	5.9
14	New York	5.9
17	Colorado	5.8
17	Wisconsin	5.8
19	Massachusetts	5.7
19	Tennessee	5.7
19	Utah	5.7
22	Louisiana	5.6
23	Idaho	5.5
23	Missouri	5.5
23	Ohio	5.5
23	Oklahoma	5.5
27	Mississippi	5.3
28	New Hampshire	5.2
29	Oregon	5.1
30	Kansas	5.0
30	Texas	5.0
32	Alabama	4.9
32	Georgia	4.9
32	Virginia	4.9
35	North Carolina	4.8
36	South Carolina	4.7
37	Michigan	4.6
38	South Dakota	4.5
38	Washington	4.5
40	Kentucky	4.3
40	Minnesota	4.3
40	Wyoming	4.3
43	Iowa	4.1
44	Nebraska	4.0
44	Pennsylvania	4.0
46	North Dakota	3.8
47	Indiana	3.7
47	Maine	3.7
47	West Virginia	3.7
50	Vermont	3.0

| District of Columbia | 6.2 |

Source: Morgan Quitno Press using data from U.S. Bureau of the Census, Governments Division
"State and Local Government Finances: 2002 Census" (http://www.census.gov/govs/www/estimate02.html)

State and Local Government Expenditures for Corrections in 2002

National Total = $54,687,169,000*

ALPHA ORDER

RANK	STATE	EXPENDITURES	% of USA
30	Alabama	$460,235,000	0.8%
41	Alaska	175,273,000	0.3%
17	Arizona	1,122,019,000	2.1%
33	Arkansas	369,445,000	0.7%
1	California	9,011,574,000	16.5%
18	Colorado	855,710,000	1.6%
25	Connecticut	637,897,000	1.2%
38	Delaware	245,203,000	0.4%
4	Florida	3,364,963,000	6.2%
9	Georgia	1,764,894,000	3.2%
43	Hawaii	157,286,000	0.3%
39	Idaho	229,177,000	0.4%
7	Illinois	1,879,410,000	3.4%
19	Indiana	840,770,000	1.5%
35	Iowa	329,721,000	0.6%
34	Kansas	361,276,000	0.7%
26	Kentucky	599,491,000	1.1%
22	Louisiana	774,344,000	1.4%
44	Maine	145,626,000	0.3%
12	Maryland	1,256,758,000	2.3%
16	Massachusetts	1,124,509,000	2.1%
6	Michigan	2,108,972,000	3.9%
24	Minnesota	648,684,000	1.2%
36	Mississippi	322,666,000	0.6%
21	Missouri	815,640,000	1.5%
45	Montana	121,909,000	0.2%
37	Nebraska	257,547,000	0.5%
29	Nevada	502,993,000	0.9%
46	New Hampshire	114,844,000	0.2%
10	New Jersey	1,606,822,000	2.9%
32	New Mexico	371,416,000	0.7%
2	New York	4,662,509,000	8.5%
14	North Carolina	1,171,635,000	2.1%
50	North Dakota	59,857,000	0.1%
8	Ohio	1,814,446,000	3.3%
28	Oklahoma	560,456,000	1.0%
20	Oregon	827,977,000	1.5%
5	Pennsylvania	2,451,080,000	4.5%
42	Rhode Island	157,531,000	0.3%
27	South Carolina	570,231,000	1.0%
48	South Dakota	93,320,000	0.2%
23	Tennessee	689,549,000	1.3%
3	Texas	4,400,979,000	8.0%
31	Utah	375,447,000	0.7%
49	Vermont	79,555,000	0.1%
11	Virginia	1,388,451,000	2.5%
15	Washington	1,145,962,000	2.1%
40	West Virginia	201,546,000	0.4%
13	Wisconsin	1,175,910,000	2.2%
47	Wyoming	109,836,000	0.2%

RANK ORDER

RANK	STATE	EXPENDITURES	% of USA
1	California	$9,011,574,000	16.5%
2	New York	4,662,509,000	8.5%
3	Texas	4,400,979,000	8.0%
4	Florida	3,364,963,000	6.2%
5	Pennsylvania	2,451,080,000	4.5%
6	Michigan	2,108,972,000	3.9%
7	Illinois	1,879,410,000	3.4%
8	Ohio	1,814,446,000	3.3%
9	Georgia	1,764,894,000	3.2%
10	New Jersey	1,606,822,000	2.9%
11	Virginia	1,388,451,000	2.5%
12	Maryland	1,256,758,000	2.3%
13	Wisconsin	1,175,910,000	2.2%
14	North Carolina	1,171,635,000	2.1%
15	Washington	1,145,962,000	2.1%
16	Massachusetts	1,124,509,000	2.1%
17	Arizona	1,122,019,000	2.1%
18	Colorado	855,710,000	1.6%
19	Indiana	840,770,000	1.5%
20	Oregon	827,977,000	1.5%
21	Missouri	815,640,000	1.5%
22	Louisiana	774,344,000	1.4%
23	Tennessee	689,549,000	1.3%
24	Minnesota	648,684,000	1.2%
25	Connecticut	637,897,000	1.2%
26	Kentucky	599,491,000	1.1%
27	South Carolina	570,231,000	1.0%
28	Oklahoma	560,456,000	1.0%
29	Nevada	502,993,000	0.9%
30	Alabama	460,235,000	0.8%
31	Utah	375,447,000	0.7%
32	New Mexico	371,416,000	0.7%
33	Arkansas	369,445,000	0.7%
34	Kansas	361,276,000	0.7%
35	Iowa	329,721,000	0.6%
36	Mississippi	322,666,000	0.6%
37	Nebraska	257,547,000	0.5%
38	Delaware	245,203,000	0.4%
39	Idaho	229,177,000	0.4%
40	West Virginia	201,546,000	0.4%
41	Alaska	175,273,000	0.3%
42	Rhode Island	157,531,000	0.3%
43	Hawaii	157,286,000	0.3%
44	Maine	145,626,000	0.3%
45	Montana	121,909,000	0.2%
46	New Hampshire	114,844,000	0.2%
47	Wyoming	109,836,000	0.2%
48	South Dakota	93,320,000	0.2%
49	Vermont	79,555,000	0.1%
50	North Dakota	59,857,000	0.1%
	District of Columbia	173,818,000	0.3%

Source: U.S. Bureau of the Census, Governments Division
    "State and Local Government Finances: 2002 Census" (http://www.census.gov/govs/www/estimate02.html)
*Direct general expenditures.

Per Capita State and Local Government Expenditures for Corrections in 2002

National Per Capita = $190*

ALPHA ORDER

RANK	STATE	PER CAPITA
48	Alabama	$103
2	Alaska	274
12	Arizona	206
36	Arkansas	136
3	California	258
18	Colorado	190
21	Connecticut	184
1	Delaware	304
14	Florida	202
11	Georgia	207
41	Hawaii	127
24	Idaho	171
28	Illinois	149
35	Indiana	137
45	Iowa	112
38	Kansas	133
30	Kentucky	147
23	Louisiana	173
45	Maine	112
7	Maryland	231
22	Massachusetts	175
10	Michigan	210
39	Minnesota	129
44	Mississippi	113
32	Missouri	144
37	Montana	134
28	Nebraska	149
6	Nevada	232
50	New Hampshire	90
20	New Jersey	187
15	New Mexico	200
4	New York	243
33	North Carolina	141
49	North Dakota	94
27	Ohio	159
26	Oklahoma	161
5	Oregon	235
16	Pennsylvania	199
30	Rhode Island	147
34	South Carolina	139
42	South Dakota	123
43	Tennessee	119
13	Texas	203
25	Utah	162
39	Vermont	129
17	Virginia	191
19	Washington	189
45	West Virginia	112
9	Wisconsin	216
8	Wyoming	220

RANK ORDER

RANK	STATE	PER CAPITA
1	Delaware	$304
2	Alaska	274
3	California	258
4	New York	243
5	Oregon	235
6	Nevada	232
7	Maryland	231
8	Wyoming	220
9	Wisconsin	216
10	Michigan	210
11	Georgia	207
12	Arizona	206
13	Texas	203
14	Florida	202
15	New Mexico	200
16	Pennsylvania	199
17	Virginia	191
18	Colorado	190
19	Washington	189
20	New Jersey	187
21	Connecticut	184
22	Massachusetts	175
23	Louisiana	173
24	Idaho	171
25	Utah	162
26	Oklahoma	161
27	Ohio	159
28	Illinois	149
28	Nebraska	149
30	Kentucky	147
30	Rhode Island	147
32	Missouri	144
33	North Carolina	141
34	South Carolina	139
35	Indiana	137
36	Arkansas	136
37	Montana	134
38	Kansas	133
39	Minnesota	129
39	Vermont	129
41	Hawaii	127
42	South Dakota	123
43	Tennessee	119
44	Mississippi	113
45	Iowa	112
45	Maine	112
45	West Virginia	112
48	Alabama	103
49	North Dakota	94
50	New Hampshire	90

District of Columbia	308

Source: Morgan Quitno Press using data from U.S. Bureau of the Census, Governments Division
"State and Local Government Finances: 2002 Census" (http://www.census.gov/govs/www/estimate02.html)
*Direct general expenditures.

State and Local Government Expenditures for Corrections
As a Percent of All Direct General Expenditures in 2002
National Percent = 3.2% of Direct General Expenditures

ALPHA ORDER

RANK	STATE	PERCENT
44	Alabama	1.9
40	Alaska	2.1
2	Arizona	4.4
24	Arkansas	2.8
8	California	3.8
15	Colorado	3.2
29	Connecticut	2.6
1	Delaware	4.6
5	Florida	3.9
5	Georgia	3.9
44	Hawaii	1.9
13	Idaho	3.4
33	Illinois	2.5
29	Indiana	2.6
44	Iowa	1.9
34	Kansas	2.4
24	Kentucky	2.8
15	Louisiana	3.2
48	Maine	1.8
4	Maryland	4.0
27	Massachusetts	2.7
10	Michigan	3.5
44	Minnesota	1.9
40	Mississippi	2.1
24	Missouri	2.8
34	Montana	2.4
29	Nebraska	2.6
3	Nevada	4.3
48	New Hampshire	1.8
19	New Jersey	3.0
15	New Mexico	3.2
21	New York	2.9
29	North Carolina	2.6
50	North Dakota	1.5
27	Ohio	2.7
18	Oklahoma	3.1
9	Oregon	3.6
14	Pennsylvania	3.3
39	Rhode Island	2.3
34	South Carolina	2.4
34	South Dakota	2.4
34	Tennessee	2.4
5	Texas	3.9
21	Utah	2.9
40	Vermont	2.1
10	Virginia	3.5
19	Washington	3.0
43	West Virginia	2.0
10	Wisconsin	3.5
21	Wyoming	2.9

RANK ORDER

RANK	STATE	PERCENT
1	Delaware	4.6
2	Arizona	4.4
3	Nevada	4.3
4	Maryland	4.0
5	Florida	3.9
5	Georgia	3.9
5	Texas	3.9
8	California	3.8
9	Oregon	3.6
10	Michigan	3.5
10	Virginia	3.5
10	Wisconsin	3.5
13	Idaho	3.4
14	Pennsylvania	3.3
15	Colorado	3.2
15	Louisiana	3.2
15	New Mexico	3.2
18	Oklahoma	3.1
19	New Jersey	3.0
19	Washington	3.0
21	New York	2.9
21	Utah	2.9
21	Wyoming	2.9
24	Arkansas	2.8
24	Kentucky	2.8
24	Missouri	2.8
27	Massachusetts	2.7
27	Ohio	2.7
29	Connecticut	2.6
29	Indiana	2.6
29	Nebraska	2.6
29	North Carolina	2.6
33	Illinois	2.5
34	Kansas	2.4
34	Montana	2.4
34	South Carolina	2.4
34	South Dakota	2.4
34	Tennessee	2.4
39	Rhode Island	2.3
40	Alaska	2.1
40	Mississippi	2.1
40	Vermont	2.1
43	West Virginia	2.0
44	Alabama	1.9
44	Hawaii	1.9
44	Iowa	1.9
44	Minnesota	1.9
48	Maine	1.8
48	New Hampshire	1.8
50	North Dakota	1.5

	District of Columbia	2.8

Source: Morgan Quitno Press using data from U.S. Bureau of the Census, Governments Division
"State and Local Government Finances: 2002 Census" (http://www.census.gov/govs/www/estimate02.html)

State Government Expenditures for Corrections in 2002

National Total = $36,471,670,000*

ALPHA ORDER

RANK	STATE	EXPENDITURES	% of USA
29	Alabama	$325,256,000	0.9%
39	Alaska	173,844,000	0.5%
17	Arizona	642,336,000	1.8%
30	Arkansas	284,256,000	0.8%
1	California	5,333,683,000	14.6%
18	Colorado	638,993,000	1.8%
19	Connecticut	637,897,000	1.7%
34	Delaware	245,203,000	0.7%
4	Florida	2,199,630,000	6.0%
9	Georgia	1,233,182,000	3.4%
43	Hawaii	157,286,000	0.4%
41	Idaho	170,029,000	0.5%
7	Illinois	1,300,005,000	3.6%
20	Indiana	614,959,000	1.7%
36	Iowa	233,012,000	0.6%
31	Kansas	267,757,000	0.7%
26	Kentucky	413,250,000	1.1%
24	Louisiana	479,744,000	1.3%
45	Maine	105,580,000	0.3%
11	Maryland	1,028,643,000	2.8%
14	Massachusetts	899,966,000	2.5%
5	Michigan	1,613,382,000	4.4%
28	Minnesota	335,289,000	0.9%
33	Mississippi	249,297,000	0.7%
21	Missouri	606,400,000	1.7%
44	Montana	106,311,000	0.3%
38	Nebraska	176,083,000	0.5%
37	Nevada	224,623,000	0.6%
48	New Hampshire	79,500,000	0.2%
10	New Jersey	1,138,972,000	3.1%
35	New Mexico	241,454,000	0.7%
3	New York	2,370,786,000	6.5%
13	North Carolina	913,713,000	2.5%
50	North Dakota	36,792,000	0.1%
8	Ohio	1,296,860,000	3.6%
22	Oklahoma	506,463,000	1.4%
23	Oregon	494,486,000	1.4%
6	Pennsylvania	1,456,084,000	4.0%
42	Rhode Island	157,531,000	0.4%
25	South Carolina	423,386,000	1.2%
49	South Dakota	66,903,000	0.2%
27	Tennessee	390,332,000	1.1%
2	Texas	3,035,815,000	8.3%
32	Utah	267,607,000	0.7%
47	Vermont	79,527,000	0.2%
12	Virginia	959,136,000	2.6%
16	Washington	734,604,000	2.0%
40	West Virginia	170,305,000	0.5%
15	Wisconsin	872,763,000	2.4%
46	Wyoming	82,755,000	0.2%

RANK ORDER

RANK	STATE	EXPENDITURES	% of USA
1	California	$5,333,683,000	14.6%
2	Texas	3,035,815,000	8.3%
3	New York	2,370,786,000	6.5%
4	Florida	2,199,630,000	6.0%
5	Michigan	1,613,382,000	4.4%
6	Pennsylvania	1,456,084,000	4.0%
7	Illinois	1,300,005,000	3.6%
8	Ohio	1,296,860,000	3.6%
9	Georgia	1,233,182,000	3.4%
10	New Jersey	1,138,972,000	3.1%
11	Maryland	1,028,643,000	2.8%
12	Virginia	959,136,000	2.6%
13	North Carolina	913,713,000	2.5%
14	Massachusetts	899,966,000	2.5%
15	Wisconsin	872,763,000	2.4%
16	Washington	734,604,000	2.0%
17	Arizona	642,336,000	1.8%
18	Colorado	638,993,000	1.8%
19	Connecticut	637,897,000	1.7%
20	Indiana	614,959,000	1.7%
21	Missouri	606,400,000	1.7%
22	Oklahoma	506,463,000	1.4%
23	Oregon	494,486,000	1.4%
24	Louisiana	479,744,000	1.3%
25	South Carolina	423,386,000	1.2%
26	Kentucky	413,250,000	1.1%
27	Tennessee	390,332,000	1.1%
28	Minnesota	335,289,000	0.9%
29	Alabama	325,256,000	0.9%
30	Arkansas	284,256,000	0.8%
31	Kansas	267,757,000	0.7%
32	Utah	267,607,000	0.7%
33	Mississippi	249,297,000	0.7%
34	Delaware	245,203,000	0.7%
35	New Mexico	241,454,000	0.7%
36	Iowa	233,012,000	0.6%
37	Nevada	224,623,000	0.6%
38	Nebraska	176,083,000	0.5%
39	Alaska	173,844,000	0.5%
40	West Virginia	170,305,000	0.5%
41	Idaho	170,029,000	0.5%
42	Rhode Island	157,531,000	0.4%
43	Hawaii	157,286,000	0.4%
44	Montana	106,311,000	0.3%
45	Maine	105,580,000	0.3%
46	Wyoming	82,755,000	0.2%
47	Vermont	79,527,000	0.2%
48	New Hampshire	79,500,000	0.2%
49	South Dakota	66,903,000	0.2%
50	North Dakota	36,792,000	0.1%
	District of Columbia**	NA	NA

Source: U.S. Bureau of the Census, Governments Division
    "State and Local Government Finances: 2002 Census" (http://www.census.gov/govs/www/estimate02.html)
Direct general expenditures.
**Not applicable.*

Per Capita State Government Expenditures for Corrections in 2002

National Per Capita = $127*

ALPHA ORDER

RANK	STATE	PER CAPITA
46	Alabama	$73
2	Alaska	271
25	Arizona	118
33	Arkansas	105
8	California	152
12	Colorado	142
4	Connecticut	184
1	Delaware	304
17	Florida	132
11	Georgia	144
21	Hawaii	127
21	Idaho	127
35	Illinois	103
39	Indiana	100
45	Iowa	79
40	Kansas	99
38	Kentucky	101
31	Louisiana	107
44	Maine	81
3	Maryland	189
13	Massachusetts	140
6	Michigan	161
47	Minnesota	67
43	Mississippi	87
31	Missouri	107
27	Montana	117
37	Nebraska	102
34	Nevada	104
49	New Hampshire	62
16	New Jersey	133
19	New Mexico	130
23	New York	124
30	North Carolina	110
50	North Dakota	58
29	Ohio	114
10	Oklahoma	145
13	Oregon	140
25	Pennsylvania	118
9	Rhode Island	147
35	South Carolina	103
42	South Dakota	88
47	Tennessee	67
13	Texas	140
28	Utah	115
20	Vermont	129
17	Virginia	132
24	Washington	121
41	West Virginia	94
7	Wisconsin	160
5	Wyoming	166

RANK ORDER

RANK	STATE	PER CAPITA
1	Delaware	$304
2	Alaska	271
3	Maryland	189
4	Connecticut	184
5	Wyoming	166
6	Michigan	161
7	Wisconsin	160
8	California	152
9	Rhode Island	147
10	Oklahoma	145
11	Georgia	144
12	Colorado	142
13	Massachusetts	140
13	Oregon	140
13	Texas	140
16	New Jersey	133
17	Florida	132
17	Virginia	132
19	New Mexico	130
20	Vermont	129
21	Hawaii	127
21	Idaho	127
23	New York	124
24	Washington	121
25	Arizona	118
25	Pennsylvania	118
27	Montana	117
28	Utah	115
29	Ohio	114
30	North Carolina	110
31	Louisiana	107
31	Missouri	107
33	Arkansas	105
34	Nevada	104
35	Illinois	103
35	South Carolina	103
37	Nebraska	102
38	Kentucky	101
39	Indiana	100
40	Kansas	99
41	West Virginia	94
42	South Dakota	88
43	Mississippi	87
44	Maine	81
45	Iowa	79
46	Alabama	73
47	Minnesota	67
47	Tennessee	67
49	New Hampshire	62
50	North Dakota	58

District of Columbia**   NA

Source: Morgan Quitno Press using data from U.S. Bureau of the Census, Governments Division
    "State and Local Government Finances: 2002 Census" (http://www.census.gov/govs/www/estimate02.html)
*Direct general expenditures.
**Not applicable.

State Government Expenditures for Corrections
As a Percent of All Direct General Expenditures in 2002
National Percent = 4.9% of Direct General Expenditures

ALPHA ORDER

RANK	STATE	PERCENT
45	Alabama	2.7
40	Alaska	3.1
2	Arizona	6.9
31	Arkansas	3.8
8	California	6.4
10	Colorado	6.2
18	Connecticut	4.6
1	Delaware	7.2
5	Florida	6.6
3	Georgia	6.7
47	Hawaii	2.4
13	Idaho	5.3
21	Illinois	4.4
21	Indiana	4.4
42	Iowa	2.9
27	Kansas	4.0
39	Kentucky	3.2
27	Louisiana	4.0
48	Maine	2.3
5	Maryland	6.6
25	Massachusetts	4.1
7	Michigan	6.5
49	Minnesota	2.2
40	Mississippi	3.1
21	Missouri	4.4
34	Montana	3.7
27	Nebraska	4.0
11	Nevada	5.9
45	New Hampshire	2.7
16	New Jersey	4.8
34	New Mexico	3.7
25	New York	4.1
20	North Carolina	4.5
50	North Dakota	1.7
17	Ohio	4.7
13	Oklahoma	5.3
18	Oregon	4.6
24	Pennsylvania	4.2
31	Rhode Island	3.8
37	South Carolina	3.3
37	South Dakota	3.3
43	Tennessee	2.8
3	Texas	6.7
31	Utah	3.8
36	Vermont	3.4
12	Virginia	5.6
27	Washington	4.0
43	West Virginia	2.8
8	Wisconsin	6.4
15	Wyoming	5.1

RANK ORDER

RANK	STATE	PERCENT
1	Delaware	7.2
2	Arizona	6.9
3	Georgia	6.7
3	Texas	6.7
5	Florida	6.6
5	Maryland	6.6
7	Michigan	6.5
8	California	6.4
8	Wisconsin	6.4
10	Colorado	6.2
11	Nevada	5.9
12	Virginia	5.6
13	Idaho	5.3
13	Oklahoma	5.3
15	Wyoming	5.1
16	New Jersey	4.8
17	Ohio	4.7
18	Connecticut	4.6
18	Oregon	4.6
20	North Carolina	4.5
21	Illinois	4.4
21	Indiana	4.4
21	Missouri	4.4
24	Pennsylvania	4.2
25	Massachusetts	4.1
25	New York	4.1
27	Kansas	4.0
27	Louisiana	4.0
27	Nebraska	4.0
27	Washington	4.0
31	Arkansas	3.8
31	Rhode Island	3.8
31	Utah	3.8
34	Montana	3.7
34	New Mexico	3.7
36	Vermont	3.4
37	South Carolina	3.3
37	South Dakota	3.3
39	Kentucky	3.2
40	Alaska	3.1
40	Mississippi	3.1
42	Iowa	2.9
43	Tennessee	2.8
43	West Virginia	2.8
45	Alabama	2.7
45	New Hampshire	2.7
47	Hawaii	2.4
48	Maine	2.3
49	Minnesota	2.2
50	North Dakota	1.7
	District of Columbia*	NA

Source: Morgan Quitno Press using data from U.S. Bureau of the Census, Governments Division
"State and Local Government Finances: 2002 Census" (http://www.census.gov/govs/www/estimate02.html)
*Not applicable.

Local Government Expenditures for Corrections in 2002

National Total = $18,215,499,000*

ALPHA ORDER

ALPHA ORDER

RANK	STATE	EXPENDITURES	% of USA
28	Alabama	$134,979,000	0.7%
45	Alaska	1,429,000	0.0%
10	Arizona	479,683,000	2.6%
33	Arkansas	85,189,000	0.5%
1	California	3,677,891,000	20.2%
24	Colorado	216,717,000	1.2%
47	Connecticut	0	0.0%
47	Delaware	0	0.0%
4	Florida	1,165,333,000	6.4%
7	Georgia	531,712,000	2.9%
47	Hawaii	0	0.0%
36	Idaho	59,148,000	0.3%
6	Illinois	579,405,000	3.2%
22	Indiana	225,811,000	1.2%
31	Iowa	96,709,000	0.5%
32	Kansas	93,519,000	0.5%
26	Kentucky	186,241,000	1.0%
18	Louisiana	294,600,000	1.6%
38	Maine	40,046,000	0.2%
21	Maryland	228,115,000	1.3%
23	Massachusetts	224,543,000	1.2%
9	Michigan	495,590,000	2.7%
15	Minnesota	313,395,000	1.7%
35	Mississippi	73,369,000	0.4%
25	Missouri	209,240,000	1.1%
44	Montana	15,598,000	0.1%
34	Nebraska	81,464,000	0.4%
19	Nevada	278,370,000	1.5%
39	New Hampshire	35,344,000	0.2%
11	New Jersey	467,850,000	2.6%
29	New Mexico	129,962,000	0.7%
2	New York	2,291,723,000	12.6%
20	North Carolina	257,922,000	1.4%
43	North Dakota	23,065,000	0.1%
8	Ohio	517,586,000	2.8%
37	Oklahoma	53,993,000	0.3%
14	Oregon	333,491,000	1.8%
5	Pennsylvania	994,996,000	5.5%
47	Rhode Island	0	0.0%
27	South Carolina	146,845,000	0.8%
42	South Dakota	26,417,000	0.1%
17	Tennessee	299,217,000	1.6%
3	Texas	1,365,164,000	7.5%
30	Utah	107,840,000	0.6%
46	Vermont	28,000	0.0%
12	Virginia	429,315,000	2.4%
13	Washington	411,358,000	2.3%
40	West Virginia	31,241,000	0.2%
16	Wisconsin	303,147,000	1.7%
41	Wyoming	27,081,000	0.1%

RANK ORDER

RANK	STATE	EXPENDITURES	% of USA
1	California	$3,677,891,000	20.2%
2	New York	2,291,723,000	12.6%
3	Texas	1,365,164,000	7.5%
4	Florida	1,165,333,000	6.4%
5	Pennsylvania	994,996,000	5.5%
6	Illinois	579,405,000	3.2%
7	Georgia	531,712,000	2.9%
8	Ohio	517,586,000	2.8%
9	Michigan	495,590,000	2.7%
10	Arizona	479,683,000	2.6%
11	New Jersey	467,850,000	2.6%
12	Virginia	429,315,000	2.4%
13	Washington	411,358,000	2.3%
14	Oregon	333,491,000	1.8%
15	Minnesota	313,395,000	1.7%
16	Wisconsin	303,147,000	1.7%
17	Tennessee	299,217,000	1.6%
18	Louisiana	294,600,000	1.6%
19	Nevada	278,370,000	1.5%
20	North Carolina	257,922,000	1.4%
21	Maryland	228,115,000	1.3%
22	Indiana	225,811,000	1.2%
23	Massachusetts	224,543,000	1.2%
24	Colorado	216,717,000	1.2%
25	Missouri	209,240,000	1.1%
26	Kentucky	186,241,000	1.0%
27	South Carolina	146,845,000	0.8%
28	Alabama	134,979,000	0.7%
29	New Mexico	129,962,000	0.7%
30	Utah	107,840,000	0.6%
31	Iowa	96,709,000	0.5%
32	Kansas	93,519,000	0.5%
33	Arkansas	85,189,000	0.5%
34	Nebraska	81,464,000	0.4%
35	Mississippi	73,369,000	0.4%
36	Idaho	59,148,000	0.3%
37	Oklahoma	53,993,000	0.3%
38	Maine	40,046,000	0.2%
39	New Hampshire	35,344,000	0.2%
40	West Virginia	31,241,000	0.2%
41	Wyoming	27,081,000	0.1%
42	South Dakota	26,417,000	0.1%
43	North Dakota	23,065,000	0.1%
44	Montana	15,598,000	0.1%
45	Alaska	1,429,000	0.0%
46	Vermont	28,000	0.0%
47	Connecticut	0	0.0%
47	Delaware	0	0.0%
47	Hawaii	0	0.0%
47	Rhode Island	0	0.0%
	District of Columbia	173,818,000	1.0%

Source: U.S. Bureau of the Census, Governments Division
    "State and Local Government Finances: 2002 Census" (http://www.census.gov/govs/www/estimate02.html)
*Direct general expenditures.

Per Capita Local Government Expenditures for Corrections in 2002

National Per Capita = $63.26*

ALPHA ORDER

RANK	STATE	PER CAPITA
39	Alabama	$30.12
45	Alaska	2.23
5	Arizona	88.19
36	Arkansas	31.46
3	California	105.12
20	Colorado	48.18
47	Connecticut	0.00
47	Delaware	0.00
8	Florida	69.86
13	Georgia	62.26
47	Hawaii	0.00
26	Idaho	44.04
23	Illinois	46.04
29	Indiana	36.67
35	Iowa	32.95
34	Kansas	34.47
24	Kentucky	45.54
10	Louisiana	65.80
38	Maine	30.86
27	Maryland	41.92
32	Massachusetts	35.02
19	Michigan	49.35
12	Minnesota	62.37
41	Mississippi	25.59
28	Missouri	36.84
43	Montana	17.13
21	Nebraska	47.19
1	Nevada	128.38
40	New Hampshire	27.71
16	New Jersey	54.55
7	New Mexico	70.05
2	New York	119.67
37	North Carolina	31.03
30	North Dakota	36.39
25	Ohio	45.36
44	Oklahoma	15.48
4	Oregon	94.65
6	Pennsylvania	80.71
47	Rhode Island	0.00
31	South Carolina	35.76
33	South Dakota	34.74
18	Tennessee	51.66
11	Texas	62.84
22	Utah	46.49
46	Vermont	0.05
14	Virginia	59.02
9	Washington	67.80
42	West Virginia	17.31
15	Wisconsin	55.72
17	Wyoming	54.25

RANK ORDER

RANK	STATE	PER CAPITA
1	Nevada	$128.38
2	New York	119.67
3	California	105.12
4	Oregon	94.65
5	Arizona	88.19
6	Pennsylvania	80.71
7	New Mexico	70.05
8	Florida	69.86
9	Washington	67.80
10	Louisiana	65.80
11	Texas	62.84
12	Minnesota	62.37
13	Georgia	62.26
14	Virginia	59.02
15	Wisconsin	55.72
16	New Jersey	54.55
17	Wyoming	54.25
18	Tennessee	51.66
19	Michigan	49.35
20	Colorado	48.18
21	Nebraska	47.19
22	Utah	46.49
23	Illinois	46.04
24	Kentucky	45.54
25	Ohio	45.36
26	Idaho	44.04
27	Maryland	41.92
28	Missouri	36.84
29	Indiana	36.67
30	North Dakota	36.39
31	South Carolina	35.76
32	Massachusetts	35.02
33	South Dakota	34.74
34	Kansas	34.47
35	Iowa	32.95
36	Arkansas	31.46
37	North Carolina	31.03
38	Maine	30.86
39	Alabama	30.12
40	New Hampshire	27.71
41	Mississippi	25.59
42	West Virginia	17.31
43	Montana	17.13
44	Oklahoma	15.48
45	Alaska	2.23
46	Vermont	0.05
47	Connecticut	0.00
47	Delaware	0.00
47	Hawaii	0.00
47	Rhode Island	0.00

District of Columbia   307.84

*Source: Morgan Quitno Press using data from U.S. Bureau of the Census, Governments Division
"State and Local Government Finances: 2002 Census" (http://www.census.gov/govs/www/estimate02.html)*
Direct general expenditures.

Local Government Expenditures for Corrections
As a Percent of All Direct General Expenditures in 2002
National Percent = 1.8% of Direct General Expenditures

ALPHA ORDER

RANK	STATE	PERCENT
35	Alabama	1.1
45	Alaska	0.1
2	Arizona	3.0
19	Arkansas	1.5
6	California	2.4
28	Colorado	1.3
46	Connecticut	0.0
46	Delaware	0.0
8	Florida	2.2
12	Georgia	2.0
46	Hawaii	0.0
17	Idaho	1.6
28	Illinois	1.3
32	Indiana	1.2
35	Iowa	1.1
35	Kansas	1.1
10	Kentucky	2.1
6	Louisiana	2.4
32	Maine	1.2
23	Maryland	1.4
35	Massachusetts	1.1
23	Michigan	1.4
17	Minnesota	1.6
41	Mississippi	1.0
23	Missouri	1.4
43	Montana	0.7
19	Nebraska	1.5
1	Nevada	3.5
35	New Hampshire	1.1
19	New Jersey	1.5
4	New Mexico	2.6
8	New York	2.2
35	North Carolina	1.1
23	North Dakota	1.4
28	Ohio	1.3
44	Oklahoma	0.6
3	Oregon	2.7
4	Pennsylvania	2.6
46	Rhode Island	0.0
28	South Carolina	1.3
23	South Dakota	1.4
12	Tennessee	2.0
10	Texas	2.1
16	Utah	1.8
46	Vermont	0.0
15	Virginia	1.9
12	Washington	2.0
42	West Virginia	0.8
19	Wisconsin	1.5
32	Wyoming	1.2

RANK ORDER

RANK	STATE	PERCENT
1	Nevada	3.5
2	Arizona	3.0
3	Oregon	2.7
4	New Mexico	2.6
4	Pennsylvania	2.6
6	California	2.4
6	Louisiana	2.4
8	Florida	2.2
8	New York	2.2
10	Kentucky	2.1
10	Texas	2.1
12	Georgia	2.0
12	Tennessee	2.0
12	Washington	2.0
15	Virginia	1.9
16	Utah	1.8
17	Idaho	1.6
17	Minnesota	1.6
19	Arkansas	1.5
19	Nebraska	1.5
19	New Jersey	1.5
19	Wisconsin	1.5
23	Maryland	1.4
23	Michigan	1.4
23	Missouri	1.4
23	North Dakota	1.4
23	South Dakota	1.4
28	Colorado	1.3
28	Illinois	1.3
28	Ohio	1.3
28	South Carolina	1.3
32	Indiana	1.2
32	Maine	1.2
32	Wyoming	1.2
35	Alabama	1.1
35	Iowa	1.1
35	Kansas	1.1
35	Massachusetts	1.1
35	New Hampshire	1.1
35	North Carolina	1.1
41	Mississippi	1.0
42	West Virginia	0.8
43	Montana	0.7
44	Oklahoma	0.6
45	Alaska	0.1
46	Connecticut	0.0
46	Delaware	0.0
46	Hawaii	0.0
46	Rhode Island	0.0
46	Vermont	0.0

| District of Columbia | 2.8 |

Source: Morgan Quitno Press using data from U.S. Bureau of the Census, Governments Division
"State and Local Government Finances: 2002 Census" (http://www.census.gov/govs/www/estimate02.html)

State and Local Government Expenditures for Judicial and Legal Services: 2002

National Total = $31,235,811,000*

ALPHA ORDER

RANK	STATE	EXPENDITURES	% of USA
27	Alabama	$316,457,000	1.0%
38	Alaska	131,049,000	0.4%
13	Arizona	654,984,000	2.1%
35	Arkansas	195,259,000	0.6%
1	California	7,049,463,000	22.6%
23	Colorado	385,613,000	1.2%
18	Connecticut	483,494,000	1.5%
42	Delaware	106,412,000	0.3%
3	Florida	1,645,988,000	5.3%
11	Georgia	682,487,000	2.2%
33	Hawaii	213,854,000	0.7%
40	Idaho	123,058,000	0.4%
7	Illinois	1,107,041,000	3.5%
24	Indiana	383,985,000	1.2%
29	Iowa	288,261,000	0.9%
31	Kansas	235,564,000	0.8%
28	Kentucky	316,310,000	1.0%
20	Louisiana	443,778,000	1.4%
45	Maine	80,024,000	0.3%
17	Maryland	520,487,000	1.7%
10	Massachusetts	742,547,000	2.4%
8	Michigan	1,098,376,000	3.5%
16	Minnesota	522,118,000	1.7%
37	Mississippi	157,949,000	0.5%
25	Missouri	373,616,000	1.2%
46	Montana	76,468,000	0.2%
41	Nebraska	111,545,000	0.4%
26	Nevada	321,655,000	1.0%
44	New Hampshire	97,175,000	0.3%
9	New Jersey	1,082,487,000	3.5%
36	New Mexico	191,129,000	0.6%
2	New York	2,734,013,000	8.8%
15	North Carolina	553,464,000	1.8%
48	North Dakota	50,136,000	0.2%
5	Ohio	1,362,648,000	4.4%
32	Oklahoma	227,213,000	0.7%
22	Oregon	399,736,000	1.3%
6	Pennsylvania	1,143,618,000	3.7%
43	Rhode Island	103,310,000	0.3%
34	South Carolina	212,463,000	0.7%
49	South Dakota	43,312,000	0.1%
21	Tennessee	421,145,000	1.3%
4	Texas	1,621,755,000	5.2%
30	Utah	241,312,000	0.8%
50	Vermont	42,624,000	0.1%
12	Virginia	656,261,000	2.1%
14	Washington	570,347,000	1.8%
39	West Virginia	124,819,000	0.4%
19	Wisconsin	473,407,000	1.5%
47	Wyoming	56,991,000	0.2%

RANK ORDER

RANK	STATE	EXPENDITURES	% of USA
1	California	$7,049,463,000	22.6%
2	New York	2,734,013,000	8.8%
3	Florida	1,645,988,000	5.3%
4	Texas	1,621,755,000	5.2%
5	Ohio	1,362,648,000	4.4%
6	Pennsylvania	1,143,618,000	3.7%
7	Illinois	1,107,041,000	3.5%
8	Michigan	1,098,376,000	3.5%
9	New Jersey	1,082,487,000	3.5%
10	Massachusetts	742,547,000	2.4%
11	Georgia	682,487,000	2.2%
12	Virginia	656,261,000	2.1%
13	Arizona	654,984,000	2.1%
14	Washington	570,347,000	1.8%
15	North Carolina	553,464,000	1.8%
16	Minnesota	522,118,000	1.7%
17	Maryland	520,487,000	1.7%
18	Connecticut	483,494,000	1.5%
19	Wisconsin	473,407,000	1.5%
20	Louisiana	443,778,000	1.4%
21	Tennessee	421,145,000	1.3%
22	Oregon	399,736,000	1.3%
23	Colorado	385,613,000	1.2%
24	Indiana	383,985,000	1.2%
25	Missouri	373,616,000	1.2%
26	Nevada	321,655,000	1.0%
27	Alabama	316,457,000	1.0%
28	Kentucky	316,310,000	1.0%
29	Iowa	288,261,000	0.9%
30	Utah	241,312,000	0.8%
31	Kansas	235,564,000	0.8%
32	Oklahoma	227,213,000	0.7%
33	Hawaii	213,854,000	0.7%
34	South Carolina	212,463,000	0.7%
35	Arkansas	195,259,000	0.6%
36	New Mexico	191,129,000	0.6%
37	Mississippi	157,949,000	0.5%
38	Alaska	131,049,000	0.4%
39	West Virginia	124,819,000	0.4%
40	Idaho	123,058,000	0.4%
41	Nebraska	111,545,000	0.4%
42	Delaware	106,412,000	0.3%
43	Rhode Island	103,310,000	0.3%
44	New Hampshire	97,175,000	0.3%
45	Maine	80,024,000	0.3%
46	Montana	76,468,000	0.2%
47	Wyoming	56,991,000	0.2%
48	North Dakota	50,136,000	0.2%
49	South Dakota	43,312,000	0.1%
50	Vermont	42,624,000	0.1%
	District of Columbia	58,604,000	0.2%

Source: U.S. Bureau of the Census, Governments Division
"State and Local Government Finances: 2002 Census" (http://www.census.gov/govs/www/estimate02.html)
*Direct general expenditures. Includes Courts, Prosecution and Legal Services and Public Defense.

Per Capita State and Local Government Expenditures for Judicial and Legal Services in 2002
National Per Capita = $108*

ALPHA ORDER

RANK	STATE	PER CAPITA
39	Alabama	$71
1	Alaska	204
9	Arizona	120
38	Arkansas	72
2	California	201
30	Colorado	86
6	Connecticut	140
7	Delaware	132
18	Florida	99
32	Georgia	80
3	Hawaii	173
25	Idaho	92
27	Illinois	88
46	Indiana	62
20	Iowa	98
28	Kansas	87
34	Kentucky	77
18	Louisiana	99
46	Maine	62
22	Maryland	96
11	Massachusetts	116
14	Michigan	109
15	Minnesota	104
49	Mississippi	55
43	Missouri	66
31	Montana	84
44	Nebraska	65
4	Nevada	148
35	New Hampshire	76
8	New Jersey	126
17	New Mexico	103
5	New York	143
42	North Carolina	67
33	North Dakota	79
10	Ohio	119
44	Oklahoma	65
13	Oregon	113
24	Pennsylvania	93
21	Rhode Island	97
50	South Carolina	52
48	South Dakota	57
37	Tennessee	73
36	Texas	75
15	Utah	104
40	Vermont	69
26	Virginia	90
23	Washington	94
40	West Virginia	69
28	Wisconsin	87
12	Wyoming	114

RANK ORDER

RANK	STATE	PER CAPITA
1	Alaska	$204
2	California	201
3	Hawaii	173
4	Nevada	148
5	New York	143
6	Connecticut	140
7	Delaware	132
8	New Jersey	126
9	Arizona	120
10	Ohio	119
11	Massachusetts	116
12	Wyoming	114
13	Oregon	113
14	Michigan	109
15	Minnesota	104
15	Utah	104
17	New Mexico	103
18	Florida	99
18	Louisiana	99
20	Iowa	98
21	Rhode Island	97
22	Maryland	96
23	Washington	94
24	Pennsylvania	93
25	Idaho	92
26	Virginia	90
27	Illinois	88
28	Kansas	87
28	Wisconsin	87
30	Colorado	86
31	Montana	84
32	Georgia	80
33	North Dakota	79
34	Kentucky	77
35	New Hampshire	76
36	Texas	75
37	Tennessee	73
38	Arkansas	72
39	Alabama	71
40	Vermont	69
40	West Virginia	69
42	North Carolina	67
43	Missouri	66
44	Nebraska	65
44	Oklahoma	65
46	Indiana	62
46	Maine	62
48	South Dakota	57
49	Mississippi	55
50	South Carolina	52

| | District of Columbia | 104 |

Source: Morgan Quitno Press using data from U.S. Bureau of the Census, Governments Division
"State and Local Government Finances: 2002 Census" (http://www.census.gov/govs/www/estimate02.html)
*Direct general expenditures. Includes Courts, Prosecution and Legal Services and Public Defense.

State and Local Government Expenditures for Judicial and Legal Services As a Percent of All Direct General Expenditures in 2002
National Percent = 1.8% of Direct General Expenditures*

ALPHA ORDER

RANK	STATE	PERCENT
38	Alabama	1.3
20	Alaska	1.6
3	Arizona	2.6
24	Arkansas	1.5
1	California	3.0
36	Colorado	1.4
5	Connecticut	2.0
5	Delaware	2.0
9	Florida	1.9
24	Georgia	1.5
3	Hawaii	2.6
11	Idaho	1.8
24	Illinois	1.5
43	Indiana	1.2
15	Iowa	1.7
20	Kansas	1.6
24	Kentucky	1.5
11	Louisiana	1.8
48	Maine	1.0
20	Maryland	1.6
11	Massachusetts	1.8
11	Michigan	1.8
24	Minnesota	1.5
48	Mississippi	1.0
38	Missouri	1.3
24	Montana	1.5
45	Nebraska	1.1
2	Nevada	2.7
24	New Hampshire	1.5
5	New Jersey	2.0
15	New Mexico	1.7
15	New York	1.7
43	North Carolina	1.2
38	North Dakota	1.3
5	Ohio	2.0
38	Oklahoma	1.3
15	Oregon	1.7
20	Pennsylvania	1.6
24	Rhode Island	1.5
50	South Carolina	0.9
45	South Dakota	1.1
24	Tennessee	1.5
24	Texas	1.5
9	Utah	1.9
45	Vermont	1.1
15	Virginia	1.7
24	Washington	1.5
38	West Virginia	1.3
36	Wisconsin	1.4
24	Wyoming	1.5

RANK ORDER

RANK	STATE	PERCENT
1	California	3.0
2	Nevada	2.7
3	Arizona	2.6
3	Hawaii	2.6
5	Connecticut	2.0
5	Delaware	2.0
5	New Jersey	2.0
5	Ohio	2.0
9	Florida	1.9
9	Utah	1.9
11	Idaho	1.8
11	Louisiana	1.8
11	Massachusetts	1.8
11	Michigan	1.8
15	Iowa	1.7
15	New Mexico	1.7
15	New York	1.7
15	Oregon	1.7
15	Virginia	1.7
20	Alaska	1.6
20	Kansas	1.6
20	Maryland	1.6
20	Pennsylvania	1.6
24	Arkansas	1.5
24	Georgia	1.5
24	Illinois	1.5
24	Kentucky	1.5
24	Minnesota	1.5
24	Montana	1.5
24	New Hampshire	1.5
24	Rhode Island	1.5
24	Tennessee	1.5
24	Texas	1.5
24	Washington	1.5
24	Wyoming	1.5
36	Colorado	1.4
36	Wisconsin	1.4
38	Alabama	1.3
38	Missouri	1.3
38	North Dakota	1.3
38	Oklahoma	1.3
38	West Virginia	1.3
43	Indiana	1.2
43	North Carolina	1.2
45	Nebraska	1.1
45	South Dakota	1.1
45	Vermont	1.1
48	Maine	1.0
48	Mississippi	1.0
50	South Carolina	0.9
	District of Columbia	0.9

Source: Morgan Quitno Press using data from U.S. Bureau of the Census, Governments Division
"State and Local Government Finances: 2002 Census" (http://www.census.gov/govs/www/estimate02.html)
*Includes Courts, Prosecution and Legal Services and Public Defense.

State Government Expenditures for Judicial and Legal Services in 2002

National Total = $14,415,793,000*

ALPHA ORDER

RANK	STATE	EXPENDITURES	% of USA
19	Alabama	$213,566,000	1.5%
33	Alaska	120,823,000	0.8%
26	Arizona	164,929,000	1.1%
32	Arkansas	132,729,000	0.9%
1	California	2,782,272,000	19.3%
20	Colorado	207,272,000	1.4%
8	Connecticut	447,210,000	3.1%
35	Delaware	98,134,000	0.7%
3	Florida	787,933,000	5.5%
27	Georgia	164,016,000	1.1%
23	Hawaii	174,448,000	1.2%
42	Idaho	58,713,000	0.4%
12	Illinois	302,938,000	2.1%
34	Indiana	103,938,000	0.7%
18	Iowa	223,592,000	1.6%
31	Kansas	139,760,000	1.0%
14	Kentucky	286,446,000	2.0%
30	Louisiana	141,761,000	1.0%
40	Maine	69,072,000	0.5%
11	Maryland	312,914,000	2.2%
4	Massachusetts	688,837,000	4.8%
28	Michigan	159,208,000	1.1%
16	Minnesota	240,840,000	1.7%
41	Mississippi	64,170,000	0.4%
21	Missouri	195,633,000	1.4%
49	Montana	30,777,000	0.2%
45	Nebraska	47,535,000	0.3%
44	Nevada	55,204,000	0.4%
39	New Hampshire	78,900,000	0.5%
5	New Jersey	632,513,000	4.4%
24	New Mexico	168,323,000	1.2%
2	New York	1,769,679,000	12.3%
7	North Carolina	448,595,000	3.1%
48	North Dakota	35,625,000	0.2%
15	Ohio	250,689,000	1.7%
25	Oklahoma	166,908,000	1.2%
13	Oregon	292,769,000	2.0%
10	Pennsylvania	324,021,000	2.2%
36	Rhode Island	91,682,000	0.6%
43	South Carolina	57,560,000	0.4%
50	South Dakota	23,820,000	0.2%
22	Tennessee	182,264,000	1.3%
6	Texas	504,270,000	3.5%
29	Utah	145,216,000	1.0%
46	Vermont	39,049,000	0.3%
9	Virginia	349,779,000	2.4%
38	Washington	79,480,000	0.6%
37	West Virginia	86,716,000	0.6%
17	Wisconsin	237,459,000	1.6%
47	Wyoming	35,806,000	0.2%

RANK ORDER

RANK	STATE	EXPENDITURES	% of USA
1	California	$2,782,272,000	19.3%
2	New York	1,769,679,000	12.3%
3	Florida	787,933,000	5.5%
4	Massachusetts	688,837,000	4.8%
5	New Jersey	632,513,000	4.4%
6	Texas	504,270,000	3.5%
7	North Carolina	448,595,000	3.1%
8	Connecticut	447,210,000	3.1%
9	Virginia	349,779,000	2.4%
10	Pennsylvania	324,021,000	2.2%
11	Maryland	312,914,000	2.2%
12	Illinois	302,938,000	2.1%
13	Oregon	292,769,000	2.0%
14	Kentucky	286,446,000	2.0%
15	Ohio	250,689,000	1.7%
16	Minnesota	240,840,000	1.7%
17	Wisconsin	237,459,000	1.6%
18	Iowa	223,592,000	1.6%
19	Alabama	213,566,000	1.5%
20	Colorado	207,272,000	1.4%
21	Missouri	195,633,000	1.4%
22	Tennessee	182,264,000	1.3%
23	Hawaii	174,448,000	1.2%
24	New Mexico	168,323,000	1.2%
25	Oklahoma	166,908,000	1.2%
26	Arizona	164,929,000	1.1%
27	Georgia	164,016,000	1.1%
28	Michigan	159,208,000	1.1%
29	Utah	145,216,000	1.0%
30	Louisiana	141,761,000	1.0%
31	Kansas	139,760,000	1.0%
32	Arkansas	132,729,000	0.9%
33	Alaska	120,823,000	0.8%
34	Indiana	103,938,000	0.7%
35	Delaware	98,134,000	0.7%
36	Rhode Island	91,682,000	0.6%
37	West Virginia	86,716,000	0.6%
38	Washington	79,480,000	0.6%
39	New Hampshire	78,900,000	0.5%
40	Maine	69,072,000	0.5%
41	Mississippi	64,170,000	0.4%
42	Idaho	58,713,000	0.4%
43	South Carolina	57,560,000	0.4%
44	Nevada	55,204,000	0.4%
45	Nebraska	47,535,000	0.3%
46	Vermont	39,049,000	0.3%
47	Wyoming	35,806,000	0.2%
48	North Dakota	35,625,000	0.2%
49	Montana	30,777,000	0.2%
50	South Dakota	23,820,000	0.2%
	District of Columbia**	NA	NA

Source: U.S. Bureau of the Census, Governments Division
    "State and Local Government Finances: 2002 Census" (http://www.census.gov/govs/www/estimate02.html)
*Direct general expenditures. Includes Courts, Prosecution and Legal Services and Public Defense.
**Not applicable.

Per Capita State Government Expenditures for Judicial and Legal Services: 2002

National Per Capita = $50.07*

ALPHA ORDER

RANK	STATE	PER CAPITA
28	Alabama	$47.66
1	Alaska	188.54
38	Arizona	30.32
23	Arkansas	49.02
10	California	79.52
30	Colorado	46.08
3	Connecticut	129.29
4	Delaware	121.74
29	Florida	47.23
46	Georgia	19.21
2	Hawaii	141.31
31	Idaho	43.71
42	Illinois	24.07
47	Indiana	16.88
11	Iowa	76.19
22	Kansas	51.52
14	Kentucky	70.04
35	Louisiana	31.66
21	Maine	53.22
18	Maryland	57.50
5	Massachusetts	107.42
48	Michigan	15.85
26	Minnesota	47.93
44	Mississippi	22.38
33	Missouri	34.44
34	Montana	33.80
39	Nebraska	27.53
41	Nevada	25.46
17	New Hampshire	61.85
12	New Jersey	73.74
7	New Mexico	90.73
6	New York	92.41
20	North Carolina	53.97
19	North Dakota	56.21
45	Ohio	21.97
27	Oklahoma	47.85
9	Oregon	83.10
40	Pennsylvania	26.28
8	Rhode Island	85.77
49	South Carolina	14.02
37	South Dakota	31.32
36	Tennessee	31.47
43	Texas	23.21
16	Utah	62.60
15	Vermont	63.34
24	Virginia	48.09
50	Washington	13.10
25	West Virginia	48.04
32	Wisconsin	43.65
13	Wyoming	71.73

RANK ORDER

RANK	STATE	PER CAPITA
1	Alaska	$188.54
2	Hawaii	141.31
3	Connecticut	129.29
4	Delaware	121.74
5	Massachusetts	107.42
6	New York	92.41
7	New Mexico	90.73
8	Rhode Island	85.77
9	Oregon	83.10
10	California	79.52
11	Iowa	76.19
12	New Jersey	73.74
13	Wyoming	71.73
14	Kentucky	70.04
15	Vermont	63.34
16	Utah	62.60
17	New Hampshire	61.85
18	Maryland	57.50
19	North Dakota	56.21
20	North Carolina	53.97
21	Maine	53.22
22	Kansas	51.52
23	Arkansas	49.02
24	Virginia	48.09
25	West Virginia	48.04
26	Minnesota	47.93
27	Oklahoma	47.85
28	Alabama	47.66
29	Florida	47.23
30	Colorado	46.08
31	Idaho	43.71
32	Wisconsin	43.65
33	Missouri	34.44
34	Montana	33.80
35	Louisiana	31.66
36	Tennessee	31.47
37	South Dakota	31.32
38	Arizona	30.32
39	Nebraska	27.53
40	Pennsylvania	26.28
41	Nevada	25.46
42	Illinois	24.07
43	Texas	23.21
44	Mississippi	22.38
45	Ohio	21.97
46	Georgia	19.21
47	Indiana	16.88
48	Michigan	15.85
49	South Carolina	14.02
50	Washington	13.10

District of Columbia**   NA

Source: Morgan Quitno Press using data from U.S. Bureau of the Census, Governments Division
"State and Local Government Finances: 2002 Census" (http://www.census.gov/govs/www/estimate02.html)
Direct general expenditures. Includes Courts, Prosecution and Legal Services and Public Defense.
**Not applicable.*

State Government Expenditures for Judicial and Legal Services
As a Percent of All Direct General Expenditures in 2002
National Percent = 1.9% of Direct General Expenditures*

ALPHA ORDER

RANK	STATE	PERCENT
23	Alabama	1.8
17	Alaska	2.1
23	Arizona	1.8
23	Arkansas	1.8
1	California	3.3
20	Colorado	2.0
2	Connecticut	3.2
5	Delaware	2.9
12	Florida	2.4
43	Georgia	0.9
7	Hawaii	2.7
23	Idaho	1.8
42	Illinois	1.0
47	Indiana	0.7
6	Iowa	2.8
17	Kansas	2.1
13	Kentucky	2.2
37	Louisiana	1.2
32	Maine	1.5
20	Maryland	2.0
3	Massachusetts	3.1
48	Michigan	0.6
29	Minnesota	1.6
46	Mississippi	0.8
33	Missouri	1.4
39	Montana	1.1
39	Nebraska	1.1
33	Nevada	1.4
10	New Hampshire	2.6
7	New Jersey	2.7
10	New Mexico	2.6
3	New York	3.1
13	North Carolina	2.2
29	North Dakota	1.6
43	Ohio	0.9
23	Oklahoma	1.8
7	Oregon	2.7
43	Pennsylvania	0.9
13	Rhode Island	2.2
49	South Carolina	0.4
37	South Dakota	1.2
36	Tennessee	1.3
39	Texas	1.1
17	Utah	2.1
29	Vermont	1.6
20	Virginia	2.0
49	Washington	0.4
33	West Virginia	1.4
28	Wisconsin	1.7
13	Wyoming	2.2

RANK ORDER

RANK	STATE	PERCENT
1	California	3.3
2	Connecticut	3.2
3	Massachusetts	3.1
3	New York	3.1
5	Delaware	2.9
6	Iowa	2.8
7	Hawaii	2.7
7	New Jersey	2.7
7	Oregon	2.7
10	New Hampshire	2.6
10	New Mexico	2.6
12	Florida	2.4
13	Kentucky	2.2
13	North Carolina	2.2
13	Rhode Island	2.2
13	Wyoming	2.2
17	Alaska	2.1
17	Kansas	2.1
17	Utah	2.1
20	Colorado	2.0
20	Maryland	2.0
20	Virginia	2.0
23	Alabama	1.8
23	Arizona	1.8
23	Arkansas	1.8
23	Idaho	1.8
23	Oklahoma	1.8
28	Wisconsin	1.7
29	Minnesota	1.6
29	North Dakota	1.6
29	Vermont	1.6
32	Maine	1.5
33	Missouri	1.4
33	Nevada	1.4
33	West Virginia	1.4
36	Tennessee	1.3
37	Louisiana	1.2
37	South Dakota	1.2
39	Montana	1.1
39	Nebraska	1.1
39	Texas	1.1
42	Illinois	1.0
43	Georgia	0.9
43	Ohio	0.9
43	Pennsylvania	0.9
46	Mississippi	0.8
47	Indiana	0.7
48	Michigan	0.6
49	South Carolina	0.4
49	Washington	0.4

District of Columbia**   NA

Source: Morgan Quitno Press using data from U.S. Bureau of the Census, Governments Division
"State and Local Government Finances: 2002 Census" (http://www.census.gov/govs/www/estimate02.html)
*Includes Courts, Prosecution and Legal Services and Public Defense.
**Not applicable.

Local Government Expenditures for Judicial and Legal Services in 2002

National Total = $16,820,018,000*

ALPHA ORDER

RANK	STATE	EXPENDITURES	% of USA	RANK	STATE	EXPENDITURES	% of USA
26	Alabama	$102,891,000	0.6%	1	California	$4,267,191,000	25.4%
48	Alaska	10,226,000	0.1%	2	Texas	1,117,485,000	6.6%
11	Arizona	490,055,000	2.9%	3	Ohio	1,111,959,000	6.6%
33	Arkansas	62,530,000	0.4%	4	New York	964,334,000	5.7%
1	California	4,267,191,000	25.4%	5	Michigan	939,168,000	5.6%
21	Colorado	178,341,000	1.1%	6	Florida	858,055,000	5.1%
39	Connecticut	36,284,000	0.2%	7	Pennsylvania	819,597,000	4.9%
49	Delaware	8,278,000	0.0%	8	Illinois	804,103,000	4.8%
6	Florida	858,055,000	5.1%	9	Georgia	518,471,000	3.1%
9	Georgia	518,471,000	3.1%	10	Washington	490,867,000	2.9%
37	Hawaii	39,406,000	0.2%	11	Arizona	490,055,000	2.9%
31	Idaho	64,345,000	0.4%	12	New Jersey	449,974,000	2.7%
8	Illinois	804,103,000	4.8%	13	Virginia	306,482,000	1.8%
16	Indiana	280,047,000	1.7%	14	Louisiana	302,017,000	1.8%
30	Iowa	64,669,000	0.4%	15	Minnesota	281,278,000	1.7%
28	Kansas	95,804,000	0.6%	16	Indiana	280,047,000	1.7%
40	Kentucky	29,864,000	0.2%	17	Nevada	266,451,000	1.6%
14	Louisiana	302,017,000	1.8%	18	Tennessee	238,881,000	1.4%
47	Maine	10,952,000	0.1%	19	Wisconsin	235,948,000	1.4%
20	Maryland	207,573,000	1.2%	20	Maryland	207,573,000	1.2%
35	Massachusetts	53,710,000	0.3%	21	Colorado	178,341,000	1.1%
5	Michigan	939,168,000	5.6%	22	Missouri	177,983,000	1.1%
15	Minnesota	281,278,000	1.7%	23	South Carolina	154,903,000	0.9%
29	Mississippi	93,779,000	0.6%	24	Oregon	106,967,000	0.6%
22	Missouri	177,983,000	1.1%	25	North Carolina	104,869,000	0.6%
36	Montana	45,691,000	0.3%	26	Alabama	102,891,000	0.6%
32	Nebraska	64,010,000	0.4%	27	Utah	96,096,000	0.6%
17	Nevada	266,451,000	1.6%	28	Kansas	95,804,000	0.6%
44	New Hampshire	18,275,000	0.1%	29	Mississippi	93,779,000	0.6%
12	New Jersey	449,974,000	2.7%	30	Iowa	64,669,000	0.4%
41	New Mexico	22,806,000	0.1%	31	Idaho	64,345,000	0.4%
4	New York	964,334,000	5.7%	32	Nebraska	64,010,000	0.4%
25	North Carolina	104,869,000	0.6%	33	Arkansas	62,530,000	0.4%
45	North Dakota	14,511,000	0.1%	34	Oklahoma	60,305,000	0.4%
3	Ohio	1,111,959,000	6.6%	35	Massachusetts	53,710,000	0.3%
34	Oklahoma	60,305,000	0.4%	36	Montana	45,691,000	0.3%
24	Oregon	106,967,000	0.6%	37	Hawaii	39,406,000	0.2%
7	Pennsylvania	819,597,000	4.9%	38	West Virginia	38,103,000	0.2%
46	Rhode Island	11,628,000	0.1%	39	Connecticut	36,284,000	0.2%
23	South Carolina	154,903,000	0.9%	40	Kentucky	29,864,000	0.2%
43	South Dakota	19,492,000	0.1%	41	New Mexico	22,806,000	0.1%
18	Tennessee	238,881,000	1.4%	42	Wyoming	21,185,000	0.1%
2	Texas	1,117,485,000	6.6%	43	South Dakota	19,492,000	0.1%
27	Utah	96,096,000	0.6%	44	New Hampshire	18,275,000	0.1%
50	Vermont	3,575,000	0.0%	45	North Dakota	14,511,000	0.1%
13	Virginia	306,482,000	1.8%	46	Rhode Island	11,628,000	0.1%
10	Washington	490,867,000	2.9%	47	Maine	10,952,000	0.1%
38	West Virginia	38,103,000	0.2%	48	Alaska	10,226,000	0.1%
19	Wisconsin	235,948,000	1.4%	49	Delaware	8,278,000	0.0%
42	Wyoming	21,185,000	0.1%	50	Vermont	3,575,000	0.0%
					District of Columbia	58,604,000	0.3%

Source: U.S. Bureau of the Census, Governments Division
"State and Local Government Finances: 2002 Census" (http://www.census.gov/govs/www/estimate02.html)
*Direct general expenditures. Includes Courts, Prosecution and Legal Services and Public Defense.

Per Capita Local Government Expenditures for Judicial & Legal Services: 2002

National Per Capita = $58.41*

ALPHA ORDER

RANK	STATE	PER CAPITA
35	Alabama	$22.96
40	Alaska	15.96
5	Arizona	90.10
34	Arkansas	23.10
2	California	121.96
24	Colorado	39.65
45	Connecticut	10.49
46	Delaware	10.27
13	Florida	51.44
10	Georgia	60.71
30	Hawaii	31.92
17	Idaho	47.90
9	Illinois	63.89
18	Indiana	45.47
37	Iowa	22.04
28	Kansas	35.31
49	Kentucky	7.30
7	Louisiana	67.46
47	Maine	8.44
25	Maryland	38.15
48	Massachusetts	8.38
4	Michigan	93.52
11	Minnesota	55.97
29	Mississippi	32.70
31	Missouri	31.34
16	Montana	50.17
27	Nebraska	37.08
1	Nevada	122.88
41	New Hampshire	14.33
12	New Jersey	52.46
43	New Mexico	12.29
15	New York	50.35
42	North Carolina	12.62
36	North Dakota	22.90
3	Ohio	97.45
39	Oklahoma	17.29
32	Oregon	30.36
8	Pennsylvania	66.48
44	Rhode Island	10.88
26	South Carolina	37.73
33	South Dakota	25.63
23	Tennessee	41.24
13	Texas	51.44
22	Utah	41.43
50	Vermont	5.80
21	Virginia	42.14
6	Washington	80.91
38	West Virginia	21.11
19	Wisconsin	43.37
20	Wyoming	42.44

RANK ORDER

RANK	STATE	PER CAPITA
1	Nevada	$122.88
2	California	121.96
3	Ohio	97.45
4	Michigan	93.52
5	Arizona	90.10
6	Washington	80.91
7	Louisiana	67.46
8	Pennsylvania	66.48
9	Illinois	63.89
10	Georgia	60.71
11	Minnesota	55.97
12	New Jersey	52.46
13	Florida	51.44
13	Texas	51.44
15	New York	50.35
16	Montana	50.17
17	Idaho	47.90
18	Indiana	45.47
19	Wisconsin	43.37
20	Wyoming	42.44
21	Virginia	42.14
22	Utah	41.43
23	Tennessee	41.24
24	Colorado	39.65
25	Maryland	38.15
26	South Carolina	37.73
27	Nebraska	37.08
28	Kansas	35.31
29	Mississippi	32.70
30	Hawaii	31.92
31	Missouri	31.34
32	Oregon	30.36
33	South Dakota	25.63
34	Arkansas	23.10
35	Alabama	22.96
36	North Dakota	22.90
37	Iowa	22.04
38	West Virginia	21.11
39	Oklahoma	17.29
40	Alaska	15.96
41	New Hampshire	14.33
42	North Carolina	12.62
43	New Mexico	12.29
44	Rhode Island	10.88
45	Connecticut	10.49
46	Delaware	10.27
47	Maine	8.44
48	Massachusetts	8.38
49	Kentucky	7.30
50	Vermont	5.80

District of Columbia 103.79

Source: Morgan Quitno Press using data from U.S. Bureau of the Census, Governments Division
"State and Local Government Finances: 2002 Census" (http://www.census.gov/govs/www/estimate02.html)
*Direct general expenditures. Includes Courts, Prosecution and Legal Services and Public Defense.

Local Government Expenditures for Judicial and Legal Services
As a Percent of All Direct General Expenditures in 2002
National Percent = 1.7% of Direct General Expenditures*

ALPHA ORDER

RANK	STATE	PERCENT
37	Alabama	0.8
42	Alaska	0.4
2	Arizona	3.1
29	Arkansas	1.1
3	California	2.8
29	Colorado	1.1
46	Connecticut	0.3
42	Delaware	0.4
15	Florida	1.6
11	Georgia	2.0
8	Hawaii	2.3
12	Idaho	1.8
12	Illinois	1.8
18	Indiana	1.5
38	Iowa	0.7
25	Kansas	1.2
46	Kentucky	0.3
6	Louisiana	2.5
46	Maine	0.3
23	Maryland	1.3
46	Massachusetts	0.3
5	Michigan	2.6
20	Minnesota	1.4
23	Mississippi	1.3
25	Missouri	1.2
9	Montana	2.1
25	Nebraska	1.2
1	Nevada	3.3
40	New Hampshire	0.5
18	New Jersey	1.5
40	New Mexico	0.5
34	New York	0.9
42	North Carolina	0.4
34	North Dakota	0.9
3	Ohio	2.8
38	Oklahoma	0.7
34	Oregon	0.9
9	Pennsylvania	2.1
42	Rhode Island	0.4
20	South Carolina	1.4
29	South Dakota	1.1
15	Tennessee	1.6
14	Texas	1.7
15	Utah	1.6
50	Vermont	0.2
20	Virginia	1.4
7	Washington	2.4
32	West Virginia	1.0
25	Wisconsin	1.2
32	Wyoming	1.0

RANK ORDER

RANK	STATE	PERCENT
1	Nevada	3.3
2	Arizona	3.1
3	California	2.8
3	Ohio	2.8
5	Michigan	2.6
6	Louisiana	2.5
7	Washington	2.4
8	Hawaii	2.3
9	Montana	2.1
9	Pennsylvania	2.1
11	Georgia	2.0
12	Idaho	1.8
12	Illinois	1.8
14	Texas	1.7
15	Florida	1.6
15	Tennessee	1.6
15	Utah	1.6
18	Indiana	1.5
18	New Jersey	1.5
20	Minnesota	1.4
20	South Carolina	1.4
20	Virginia	1.4
23	Maryland	1.3
23	Mississippi	1.3
25	Kansas	1.2
25	Missouri	1.2
25	Nebraska	1.2
25	Wisconsin	1.2
29	Arkansas	1.1
29	Colorado	1.1
29	South Dakota	1.1
32	West Virginia	1.0
32	Wyoming	1.0
34	New York	0.9
34	North Dakota	0.9
34	Oregon	0.9
37	Alabama	0.8
38	Iowa	0.7
38	Oklahoma	0.7
40	New Hampshire	0.5
40	New Mexico	0.5
42	Alaska	0.4
42	Delaware	0.4
42	North Carolina	0.4
42	Rhode Island	0.4
46	Connecticut	0.3
46	Kentucky	0.3
46	Maine	0.3
46	Massachusetts	0.3
50	Vermont	0.2

District of Columbia   0.9

Source: Morgan Quitno Press using data from U.S. Bureau of the Census, Governments Division
"State and Local Government Finances: 2002 Census" (http://www.census.gov/govs/www/estimate02.html)
*Includes Courts, Prosecution and Legal Services and Public Defense.

State and Local Government Judicial and Legal Payroll in 2004

National Total = $19,891,950,228*

ALPHA ORDER

RANK	STATE	PAYROLL	% of USA
26	Alabama	$202,245,708	1.0%
40	Alaska	71,176,464	0.4%
12	Arizona	408,470,904	2.1%
37	Arkansas	92,209,824	0.5%
1	California	3,431,936,784	17.3%
20	Colorado	300,464,484	1.5%
25	Connecticut	223,057,740	1.1%
42	Delaware	66,333,720	0.3%
3	Florida	1,358,001,012	6.8%
10	Georgia	500,405,040	2.5%
33	Hawaii	129,867,408	0.7%
41	Idaho	71,035,500	0.4%
6	Illinois	839,359,116	4.2%
21	Indiana	266,482,944	1.3%
29	Iowa	167,508,984	0.8%
32	Kansas	144,669,552	0.7%
24	Kentucky	249,442,152	1.3%
22	Louisiana	253,935,888	1.3%
46	Maine	42,878,460	0.2%
16	Maryland	332,126,940	1.7%
11	Massachusetts	489,587,292	2.5%
9	Michigan	574,095,972	2.9%
15	Minnesota	337,125,228	1.7%
36	Mississippi	102,129,384	0.5%
17	Missouri	310,980,960	1.6%
45	Montana	47,887,368	0.2%
39	Nebraska	81,016,380	0.4%
28	Nevada	192,729,768	1.0%
44	New Hampshire	52,550,016	0.3%
4	New Jersey	1,218,379,248	6.1%
34	New Mexico	123,009,300	0.6%
2	New York	1,979,437,872	10.0%
19	North Carolina	301,675,392	1.5%
49	North Dakota	32,228,628	0.2%
7	Ohio	793,846,692	4.0%
30	Oklahoma	161,593,356	0.8%
27	Oregon	196,827,468	1.0%
8	Pennsylvania	710,056,860	3.6%
43	Rhode Island	66,240,120	0.3%
31	South Carolina	152,417,304	0.8%
48	South Dakota	34,841,028	0.2%
23	Tennessee	253,824,420	1.3%
5	Texas	1,022,979,240	5.1%
35	Utah	117,521,052	0.6%
50	Vermont	30,026,868	0.2%
14	Virginia	364,880,016	1.8%
13	Washington	408,184,536	2.1%
38	West Virginia	84,051,900	0.4%
18	Wisconsin	305,927,124	1.5%
47	Wyoming	36,636,876	0.2%

RANK ORDER

RANK	STATE	PAYROLL	% of USA
1	California	$3,431,936,784	17.3%
2	New York	1,979,437,872	10.0%
3	Florida	1,358,001,012	6.8%
4	New Jersey	1,218,379,248	6.1%
5	Texas	1,022,979,240	5.1%
6	Illinois	839,359,116	4.2%
7	Ohio	793,846,692	4.0%
8	Pennsylvania	710,056,860	3.6%
9	Michigan	574,095,972	2.9%
10	Georgia	500,405,040	2.5%
11	Massachusetts	489,587,292	2.5%
12	Arizona	408,470,904	2.1%
13	Washington	408,184,536	2.1%
14	Virginia	364,880,016	1.8%
15	Minnesota	337,125,228	1.7%
16	Maryland	332,126,940	1.7%
17	Missouri	310,980,960	1.6%
18	Wisconsin	305,927,124	1.5%
19	North Carolina	301,675,392	1.5%
20	Colorado	300,464,484	1.5%
21	Indiana	266,482,944	1.3%
22	Louisiana	253,935,888	1.3%
23	Tennessee	253,824,420	1.3%
24	Kentucky	249,442,152	1.3%
25	Connecticut	223,057,740	1.1%
26	Alabama	202,245,708	1.0%
27	Oregon	196,827,468	1.0%
28	Nevada	192,729,768	1.0%
29	Iowa	167,508,984	0.8%
30	Oklahoma	161,593,356	0.8%
31	South Carolina	152,417,304	0.8%
32	Kansas	144,669,552	0.7%
33	Hawaii	129,867,408	0.7%
34	New Mexico	123,009,300	0.6%
35	Utah	117,521,052	0.6%
36	Mississippi	102,129,384	0.5%
37	Arkansas	92,209,824	0.5%
38	West Virginia	84,051,900	0.4%
39	Nebraska	81,016,380	0.4%
40	Alaska	71,176,464	0.4%
41	Idaho	71,035,500	0.4%
42	Delaware	66,333,720	0.3%
43	Rhode Island	66,240,120	0.3%
44	New Hampshire	52,550,016	0.3%
45	Montana	47,887,368	0.2%
46	Maine	42,878,460	0.2%
47	Wyoming	36,636,876	0.2%
48	South Dakota	34,841,028	0.2%
49	North Dakota	32,228,628	0.2%
50	Vermont	30,026,868	0.2%
	District of Columbia	157,653,936	0.8%

Source: Morgan Quitno Press using data from U.S. Bureau of the Census, Governments Division
"State and Local Employment and Payroll - March 2004" (http://www.census.gov/govs/www/apesstl04.html)
*Twelve times the March 2004 total payroll. Includes court and court related activities (except probation and parole which are part of corrections), court activities of sheriffs' offices, prosecuting attorneys' and public defenders' offices, legal departments and attorneys providing government-wide legal service.

State and Local Government Police Protection Payroll in 2004

National Total = $45,558,144,348*

ALPHA ORDER

RANK	STATE	PAYROLL	% of USA
25	Alabama	$468,699,852	1.0%
45	Alaska	98,420,724	0.2%
12	Arizona	945,013,824	2.1%
34	Arkansas	246,353,208	0.5%
1	California	6,978,290,952	15.3%
18	Colorado	721,435,800	1.6%
22	Connecticut	633,118,356	1.4%
43	Delaware	131,185,164	0.3%
3	Florida	2,983,731,312	6.5%
11	Georgia	952,986,576	2.1%
38	Hawaii	192,908,880	0.4%
41	Idaho	148,710,744	0.3%
6	Illinois	2,207,321,172	4.8%
20	Indiana	683,000,088	1.5%
32	Iowa	334,125,396	0.7%
31	Kansas	354,914,724	0.8%
29	Kentucky	407,682,240	0.9%
24	Louisiana	529,644,972	1.2%
42	Maine	132,405,168	0.3%
14	Maryland	903,726,780	2.0%
9	Massachusetts	1,344,033,756	3.0%
10	Michigan	1,276,019,652	2.8%
23	Minnesota	557,716,968	1.2%
33	Mississippi	263,573,088	0.6%
19	Missouri	705,236,304	1.5%
46	Montana	92,415,576	0.2%
37	Nebraska	204,064,368	0.4%
28	Nevada	417,574,608	0.9%
39	New Hampshire	174,891,756	0.4%
5	New Jersey	2,330,597,736	5.1%
35	New Mexico	229,849,860	0.5%
2	New York	5,679,216,312	12.5%
15	North Carolina	889,612,992	2.0%
50	North Dakota	53,655,024	0.1%
8	Ohio	1,589,281,596	3.5%
30	Oklahoma	389,298,948	0.9%
27	Oregon	449,085,288	1.0%
7	Pennsylvania	1,589,283,864	3.5%
40	Rhode Island	160,145,568	0.4%
26	South Carolina	464,019,252	1.0%
48	South Dakota	67,535,304	0.1%
21	Tennessee	642,321,108	1.4%
4	Texas	2,687,925,636	5.9%
36	Utah	229,371,552	0.5%
49	Vermont	57,786,216	0.1%
13	Virginia	913,719,864	2.0%
16	Washington	847,850,436	1.9%
44	West Virginia	117,310,320	0.3%
17	Wisconsin	735,649,356	1.6%
47	Wyoming	74,423,940	0.2%

RANK ORDER

RANK	STATE	PAYROLL	% of USA
1	California	$6,978,290,952	15.3%
2	New York	5,679,216,312	12.5%
3	Florida	2,983,731,312	6.5%
4	Texas	2,687,925,636	5.9%
5	New Jersey	2,330,597,736	5.1%
6	Illinois	2,207,321,172	4.8%
7	Pennsylvania	1,589,283,864	3.5%
8	Ohio	1,589,281,596	3.5%
9	Massachusetts	1,344,033,756	3.0%
10	Michigan	1,276,019,652	2.8%
11	Georgia	952,986,576	2.1%
12	Arizona	945,013,824	2.1%
13	Virginia	913,719,864	2.0%
14	Maryland	903,726,780	2.0%
15	North Carolina	889,612,992	2.0%
16	Washington	847,850,436	1.9%
17	Wisconsin	735,649,356	1.6%
18	Colorado	721,435,800	1.6%
19	Missouri	705,236,304	1.5%
20	Indiana	683,000,088	1.5%
21	Tennessee	642,321,108	1.4%
22	Connecticut	633,118,356	1.4%
23	Minnesota	557,716,968	1.2%
24	Louisiana	529,644,972	1.2%
25	Alabama	468,699,852	1.0%
26	South Carolina	464,019,252	1.0%
27	Oregon	449,085,288	1.0%
28	Nevada	417,574,608	0.9%
29	Kentucky	407,682,240	0.9%
30	Oklahoma	389,298,948	0.9%
31	Kansas	354,914,724	0.8%
32	Iowa	334,125,396	0.7%
33	Mississippi	263,573,088	0.6%
34	Arkansas	246,353,208	0.5%
35	New Mexico	229,849,860	0.5%
36	Utah	229,371,552	0.5%
37	Nebraska	204,064,368	0.4%
38	Hawaii	192,908,880	0.4%
39	New Hampshire	174,891,756	0.4%
40	Rhode Island	160,145,568	0.4%
41	Idaho	148,710,744	0.3%
42	Maine	132,405,168	0.3%
43	Delaware	131,185,164	0.3%
44	West Virginia	117,310,320	0.3%
45	Alaska	98,420,724	0.2%
46	Montana	92,415,576	0.2%
47	Wyoming	74,423,940	0.2%
48	South Dakota	67,535,304	0.1%
49	Vermont	57,786,216	0.1%
50	North Dakota	53,655,024	0.1%
	District of Columbia	271,002,168	0.6%

Source: Morgan Quitno Press using data from U.S. Bureau of the Census, Governments Division
"State and Local Employment and Payroll - March 2004" (http://www.census.gov/govs/www/apesstl04.html)
*Twelve times the March 2004 total payroll. Includes all activities concerned with the enforcement of law and order, including coroners' offices, police training academies, investigation bureaus and local jails.

State and Local Government Corrections Payroll in 2004

National Total = $28,863,303,300*

ALPHA ORDER

RANK	STATE	PAYROLL	% of USA
28	Alabama	$272,508,588	0.9%
42	Alaska	89,028,144	0.3%
16	Arizona	509,604,972	1.8%
35	Arkansas	171,764,412	0.6%
1	California	4,563,221,604	15.8%
18	Colorado	456,278,940	1.6%
22	Connecticut	406,350,348	1.4%
38	Delaware	112,267,956	0.4%
4	Florida	1,614,202,584	5.6%
10	Georgia	863,506,632	3.0%
39	Hawaii	103,818,072	0.4%
41	Idaho	92,874,804	0.3%
6	Illinois	1,115,674,020	3.9%
20	Indiana	427,376,304	1.5%
33	Iowa	186,685,164	0.6%
32	Kansas	202,450,800	0.7%
29	Kentucky	236,628,816	0.8%
19	Louisiana	450,084,588	1.6%
44	Maine	78,699,540	0.3%
13	Maryland	616,457,328	2.1%
17	Massachusetts	485,113,380	1.7%
7	Michigan	1,054,667,004	3.7%
24	Minnesota	397,479,780	1.4%
36	Mississippi	147,022,608	0.5%
23	Missouri	405,891,636	1.4%
46	Montana	54,196,224	0.2%
37	Nebraska	122,206,140	0.4%
27	Nevada	286,268,952	1.0%
45	New Hampshire	76,953,204	0.3%
9	New Jersey	941,183,400	3.3%
31	New Mexico	206,805,336	0.7%
2	New York	3,182,568,816	11.0%
11	North Carolina	741,618,864	2.6%
50	North Dakota	28,530,888	0.1%
8	Ohio	1,044,479,304	3.6%
30	Oklahoma	212,339,688	0.7%
25	Oregon	367,584,468	1.3%
5	Pennsylvania	1,215,580,200	4.2%
40	Rhode Island	95,395,536	0.3%
26	South Carolina	301,141,536	1.0%
49	South Dakota	39,256,236	0.1%
21	Tennessee	411,189,312	1.4%
3	Texas	2,202,937,548	7.6%
34	Utah	175,366,644	0.6%
48	Vermont	44,288,352	0.2%
12	Virginia	728,057,916	2.5%
14	Washington	587,665,884	2.0%
43	West Virginia	82,496,304	0.3%
15	Wisconsin	550,133,100	1.9%
47	Wyoming	47,726,220	0.2%

RANK ORDER

RANK	STATE	PAYROLL	% of USA
1	California	$4,563,221,604	15.8%
2	New York	3,182,568,816	11.0%
3	Texas	2,202,937,548	7.6%
4	Florida	1,614,202,584	5.6%
5	Pennsylvania	1,215,580,200	4.2%
6	Illinois	1,115,674,020	3.9%
7	Michigan	1,054,667,004	3.7%
8	Ohio	1,044,479,304	3.6%
9	New Jersey	941,183,400	3.3%
10	Georgia	863,506,632	3.0%
11	North Carolina	741,618,864	2.6%
12	Virginia	728,057,916	2.5%
13	Maryland	616,457,328	2.1%
14	Washington	587,665,884	2.0%
15	Wisconsin	550,133,100	1.9%
16	Arizona	509,604,972	1.8%
17	Massachusetts	485,113,380	1.7%
18	Colorado	456,278,940	1.6%
19	Louisiana	450,084,588	1.6%
20	Indiana	427,376,304	1.5%
21	Tennessee	411,189,312	1.4%
22	Connecticut	406,350,348	1.4%
23	Missouri	405,891,636	1.4%
24	Minnesota	397,479,780	1.4%
25	Oregon	367,584,468	1.3%
26	South Carolina	301,141,536	1.0%
27	Nevada	286,268,952	1.0%
28	Alabama	272,508,588	0.9%
29	Kentucky	236,628,816	0.8%
30	Oklahoma	212,339,688	0.7%
31	New Mexico	206,805,336	0.7%
32	Kansas	202,450,800	0.7%
33	Iowa	186,685,164	0.6%
34	Utah	175,366,644	0.6%
35	Arkansas	171,764,412	0.6%
36	Mississippi	147,022,608	0.5%
37	Nebraska	122,206,140	0.4%
38	Delaware	112,267,956	0.4%
39	Hawaii	103,818,072	0.4%
40	Rhode Island	95,395,536	0.3%
41	Idaho	92,874,804	0.3%
42	Alaska	89,028,144	0.3%
43	West Virginia	82,496,304	0.3%
44	Maine	78,699,540	0.3%
45	New Hampshire	76,953,204	0.3%
46	Montana	54,196,224	0.2%
47	Wyoming	47,726,220	0.2%
48	Vermont	44,288,352	0.2%
49	South Dakota	39,256,236	0.1%
50	North Dakota	28,530,888	0.1%
	District of Columbia	57,675,204	0.2%

Source: Morgan Quitno Press using data from U.S. Bureau of the Census, Governments Division
"State and Local Employment and Payroll - March 2004" (http://www.census.gov/govs/www/apesstl04.html)
*Twelve times the March 2004 total payroll. Includes all activities pertaining to the confinement and correction of
adults and minors accused or convicted of criminal offenses. Includes any pardon, probation or parole activity.

Average Annual Wages of Correctional Officers and Jailers in 2004

National Average = $36,160*

ALPHA ORDER

RANK	STATE	WAGES
28	Alabama	$28,870
6	Alaska	44,480
25	Arizona	31,080
45	Arkansas	25,820
1	California	53,590
11	Colorado	39,890
5	Connecticut	45,550
24	Delaware	31,770
21	Florida	34,540
40	Georgia	26,480
17	Hawaii	36,490
39	Idaho	26,520
8	Illinois	42,690
35	Indiana	27,590
18	Iowa	36,060
32	Kansas	27,930
46	Kentucky	25,740
47	Louisiana	24,880
38	Maine	27,180
16	Maryland	37,500
3	Massachusetts	50,230
12	Michigan	38,960
13	Minnesota	38,630
49	Mississippi	22,220
43	Missouri	26,110
37	Montana	27,260
30	Nebraska	28,770
7	Nevada	43,530
23	New Hampshire	32,820
2	New Jersey	52,350
41	New Mexico	26,440
4	New York	47,570
34	North Carolina	27,760
48	North Dakota	23,110
19	Ohio	34,930
44	Oklahoma	25,880
10	Oregon	40,650
15	Pennsylvania	38,610
9	Rhode Island	42,210
42	South Carolina	26,180
27	South Dakota	28,910
36	Tennessee	27,300
31	Texas	28,450
22	Utah	33,520
NA	Vermont**	NA
26	Virginia	31,010
14	Washington	38,620
33	West Virginia	27,800
20	Wisconsin	34,650
29	Wyoming	28,800

RANK ORDER

RANK	STATE	WAGES
1	California	$53,590
2	New Jersey	52,350
3	Massachusetts	50,230
4	New York	47,570
5	Connecticut	45,550
6	Alaska	44,480
7	Nevada	43,530
8	Illinois	42,690
9	Rhode Island	42,210
10	Oregon	40,650
11	Colorado	39,890
12	Michigan	38,960
13	Minnesota	38,630
14	Washington	38,620
15	Pennsylvania	38,610
16	Maryland	37,500
17	Hawaii	36,490
18	Iowa	36,060
19	Ohio	34,930
20	Wisconsin	34,650
21	Florida	34,540
22	Utah	33,520
23	New Hampshire	32,820
24	Delaware	31,770
25	Arizona	31,080
26	Virginia	31,010
27	South Dakota	28,910
28	Alabama	28,870
29	Wyoming	28,800
30	Nebraska	28,770
31	Texas	28,450
32	Kansas	27,930
33	West Virginia	27,800
34	North Carolina	27,760
35	Indiana	27,590
36	Tennessee	27,300
37	Montana	27,260
38	Maine	27,180
39	Idaho	26,520
40	Georgia	26,480
41	New Mexico	26,440
42	South Carolina	26,180
43	Missouri	26,110
44	Oklahoma	25,880
45	Arkansas	25,820
46	Kentucky	25,740
47	Louisiana	24,880
48	North Dakota	23,110
49	Mississippi	22,220
NA	Vermont**	NA

District of Columbia 40,270

Source: U.S. Department of Labor, Bureau of Labor Statistics
"Occupational Employment and Wages, 2004" (http://www.bls.gov/oes/)
Does not include self-employed.
**Not available.*

Average Annual Wages of Police and Sheriff Patrol Officers in 2004

National Average = $46,600*

ALPHA ORDER

RANK	STATE	WAGES
44	Alabama	$33,810
7	Alaska	51,740
16	Arizona	46,540
47	Arkansas	31,520
2	California	62,780
8	Colorado	50,790
9	Connecticut	50,660
11	Delaware	48,420
19	Florida	44,700
41	Georgia	34,800
23	Hawaii	42,200
30	Idaho	38,050
6	Illinois	53,010
27	Indiana	39,500
25	Iowa	40,710
39	Kansas	35,160
43	Kentucky	33,910
49	Louisiana	28,600
35	Maine	35,750
18	Maryland	45,110
14	Massachusetts	47,060
17	Michigan	46,500
15	Minnesota	46,590
50	Mississippi	27,210
29	Missouri	38,380
32	Montana	37,650
34	Nebraska	35,850
5	Nevada	53,630
26	New Hampshire	39,760
1	New Jersey	64,190
40	New Mexico	34,890
4	New York	54,390
33	North Carolina	36,540
36	North Dakota	35,720
22	Ohio	42,410
42	Oklahoma	34,630
10	Oregon	48,850
13	Pennsylvania	47,090
12	Rhode Island	47,550
45	South Carolina	32,770
46	South Dakota	32,620
38	Tennessee	35,340
21	Texas	42,810
28	Utah	38,850
37	Vermont	35,390
24	Virginia	40,840
3	Washington	55,540
48	West Virginia	30,960
20	Wisconsin	44,130
31	Wyoming	37,970

RANK ORDER

RANK	STATE	WAGES
1	New Jersey	$64,190
2	California	62,780
3	Washington	55,540
4	New York	54,390
5	Nevada	53,630
6	Illinois	53,010
7	Alaska	51,740
8	Colorado	50,790
9	Connecticut	50,660
10	Oregon	48,850
11	Delaware	48,420
12	Rhode Island	47,550
13	Pennsylvania	47,090
14	Massachusetts	47,060
15	Minnesota	46,590
16	Arizona	46,540
17	Michigan	46,500
18	Maryland	45,110
19	Florida	44,700
20	Wisconsin	44,130
21	Texas	42,810
22	Ohio	42,410
23	Hawaii	42,200
24	Virginia	40,840
25	Iowa	40,710
26	New Hampshire	39,760
27	Indiana	39,500
28	Utah	38,850
29	Missouri	38,380
30	Idaho	38,050
31	Wyoming	37,970
32	Montana	37,650
33	North Carolina	36,540
34	Nebraska	35,850
35	Maine	35,750
36	North Dakota	35,720
37	Vermont	35,390
38	Tennessee	35,340
39	Kansas	35,160
40	New Mexico	34,890
41	Georgia	34,800
42	Oklahoma	34,630
43	Kentucky	33,910
44	Alabama	33,810
45	South Carolina	32,770
46	South Dakota	32,620
47	Arkansas	31,520
48	West Virginia	30,960
49	Louisiana	28,600
50	Mississippi	27,210

| | District of Columbia | 55,130 |

Source: U.S. Department of Labor, Bureau of Labor Statistics
"Occupational Employment and Wages, 2004" (http://www.bls.gov/oes/)
*Does not include self-employed.

Average Annual Wages of Detectives and Criminal Investigators in 2004

National Average = $56,890*

ALPHA ORDER

RANK	STATE	WAGES
46	Alabama	$41,450
7	Alaska	64,270
22	Arizona	53,260
50	Arkansas	32,780
1	California	71,440
10	Colorado	62,290
13	Connecticut	59,990
26	Delaware	51,500
20	Florida	53,860
36	Georgia	47,010
3	Hawaii	65,550
34	Idaho	49,100
6	Illinois	64,990
43	Indiana	44,950
25	Iowa	51,660
35	Kansas	47,210
32	Kentucky	49,580
48	Louisiana	39,930
38	Maine	46,130
8	Maryland	63,640
4	Massachusetts	65,170
15	Michigan	58,340
14	Minnesota	59,190
49	Mississippi	39,720
39	Missouri	46,050
27	Montana	51,260
24	Nebraska	51,760
11	Nevada	61,420
33	New Hampshire	49,450
2	New Jersey	70,150
37	New Mexico	46,520
12	New York	60,580
45	North Carolina	43,030
30	North Dakota	49,760
23	Ohio	52,540
42	Oklahoma	45,000
19	Oregon	56,010
16	Pennsylvania	58,220
17	Rhode Island	58,080
47	South Carolina	40,600
40	South Dakota	45,860
41	Tennessee	45,820
28	Texas	51,000
29	Utah	50,690
18	Vermont	57,520
5	Virginia	65,160
9	Washington	63,480
44	West Virginia	43,430
21	Wisconsin	53,390
31	Wyoming	49,590

RANK ORDER

RANK	STATE	WAGES
1	California	$71,440
2	New Jersey	70,150
3	Hawaii	65,550
4	Massachusetts	65,170
5	Virginia	65,160
6	Illinois	64,990
7	Alaska	64,270
8	Maryland	63,640
9	Washington	63,480
10	Colorado	62,290
11	Nevada	61,420
12	New York	60,580
13	Connecticut	59,990
14	Minnesota	59,190
15	Michigan	58,340
16	Pennsylvania	58,220
17	Rhode Island	58,080
18	Vermont	57,520
19	Oregon	56,010
20	Florida	53,860
21	Wisconsin	53,390
22	Arizona	53,260
23	Ohio	52,540
24	Nebraska	51,760
25	Iowa	51,660
26	Delaware	51,500
27	Montana	51,260
28	Texas	51,000
29	Utah	50,690
30	North Dakota	49,760
31	Wyoming	49,590
32	Kentucky	49,580
33	New Hampshire	49,450
34	Idaho	49,100
35	Kansas	47,210
36	Georgia	47,010
37	New Mexico	46,520
38	Maine	46,130
39	Missouri	46,050
40	South Dakota	45,860
41	Tennessee	45,820
42	Oklahoma	45,000
43	Indiana	44,950
44	West Virginia	43,430
45	North Carolina	43,030
46	Alabama	41,450
47	South Carolina	40,600
48	Louisiana	39,930
49	Mississippi	39,720
50	Arkansas	32,780
	District of Columbia	79,210

Source: U.S. Department of Labor, Bureau of Labor Statistics
"Occupational Employment and Wages, 2004" (http://www.bls.gov/oes/)
*Does not include self-employed.

Average Annual Wages of Private Detectives and Investigators in 2004

National Average = $36,970*

ALPHA ORDER

RANK	STATE	WAGES
27	Alabama	$33,530
42	Alaska	27,290
1	Arizona	48,980
37	Arkansas	30,220
5	California	42,760
20	Colorado	35,200
8	Connecticut	41,210
26	Delaware	33,710
18	Florida	35,840
30	Georgia	32,680
NA	Hawaii**	NA
21	Idaho	35,140
6	Illinois	42,340
33	Indiana	32,040
23	Iowa	34,240
40	Kansas	28,750
45	Kentucky	26,170
19	Louisiana	35,380
25	Maine	34,080
14	Maryland	37,020
34	Massachusetts	31,200
11	Michigan	38,670
15	Minnesota	36,770
47	Mississippi	20,290
24	Missouri	34,120
43	Montana	27,100
39	Nebraska	28,950
12	Nevada	37,800
44	New Hampshire	26,840
9	New Jersey	40,120
2	New Mexico	48,590
3	New York	45,070
10	North Carolina	38,920
4	North Dakota	43,590
31	Ohio	32,610
13	Oklahoma	37,500
29	Oregon	32,750
36	Pennsylvania	30,670
35	Rhode Island	31,110
38	South Carolina	30,200
46	South Dakota	22,940
NA	Tennessee**	NA
17	Texas	35,850
41	Utah	27,580
NA	Vermont**	NA
16	Virginia	36,690
7	Washington	41,410
22	West Virginia	34,290
28	Wisconsin	32,940
32	Wyoming	32,220

RANK ORDER

RANK	STATE	WAGES
1	Arizona	$48,980
2	New Mexico	48,590
3	New York	45,070
4	North Dakota	43,590
5	California	42,760
6	Illinois	42,340
7	Washington	41,410
8	Connecticut	41,210
9	New Jersey	40,120
10	North Carolina	38,920
11	Michigan	38,670
12	Nevada	37,800
13	Oklahoma	37,500
14	Maryland	37,020
15	Minnesota	36,770
16	Virginia	36,690
17	Texas	35,850
18	Florida	35,840
19	Louisiana	35,380
20	Colorado	35,200
21	Idaho	35,140
22	West Virginia	34,290
23	Iowa	34,240
24	Missouri	34,120
25	Maine	34,080
26	Delaware	33,710
27	Alabama	33,530
28	Wisconsin	32,940
29	Oregon	32,750
30	Georgia	32,680
31	Ohio	32,610
32	Wyoming	32,220
33	Indiana	32,040
34	Massachusetts	31,200
35	Rhode Island	31,110
36	Pennsylvania	30,670
37	Arkansas	30,220
38	South Carolina	30,200
39	Nebraska	28,950
40	Kansas	28,750
41	Utah	27,580
42	Alaska	27,290
43	Montana	27,100
44	New Hampshire	26,840
45	Kentucky	26,170
46	South Dakota	22,940
47	Mississippi	20,290
NA	Hawaii**	NA
NA	Tennessee**	NA
NA	Vermont**	NA
	District of Columbia**	NA

Source: U.S. Department of Labor, Bureau of Labor Statistics
    "Occupational Employment and Wages, 2004" (http://www.bls.gov/oes/)
*Does not include self-employed.
**Not available.

Average Annual Wages of Security Guards in 2004

National Average = $22,380*

ALPHA ORDER

RANK	STATE	WAGES
48	Alabama	$18,600
1	Alaska	27,060
38	Arizona	21,420
47	Arkansas	18,960
22	California	22,810
6	Colorado	24,940
14	Connecticut	23,750
32	Delaware	21,870
42	Florida	19,780
37	Georgia	21,430
27	Hawaii	22,120
13	Idaho	23,810
18	Illinois	23,150
36	Indiana	21,640
31	Iowa	21,890
23	Kansas	22,390
44	Kentucky	19,560
45	Louisiana	19,220
26	Maine	22,230
5	Maryland	24,960
7	Massachusetts	24,560
17	Michigan	23,220
3	Minnesota	25,070
50	Mississippi	17,430
16	Missouri	23,370
45	Montana	19,220
20	Nebraska	22,970
21	Nevada	22,880
12	New Hampshire	24,060
11	New Jersey	24,080
10	New Mexico	24,200
19	New York	23,010
30	North Carolina	21,960
40	North Dakota	20,650
28	Ohio	22,080
25	Oklahoma	22,240
24	Oregon	22,340
41	Pennsylvania	20,570
9	Rhode Island	24,270
29	South Carolina	21,970
39	South Dakota	20,760
43	Tennessee	19,620
33	Texas	21,680
15	Utah	23,560
8	Vermont	24,520
4	Virginia	24,970
2	Washington	26,020
49	West Virginia	17,510
34	Wisconsin	21,650
34	Wyoming	21,650

RANK ORDER

RANK	STATE	WAGES
1	Alaska	$27,060
2	Washington	26,020
3	Minnesota	25,070
4	Virginia	24,970
5	Maryland	24,960
6	Colorado	24,940
7	Massachusetts	24,560
8	Vermont	24,520
9	Rhode Island	24,270
10	New Mexico	24,200
11	New Jersey	24,080
12	New Hampshire	24,060
13	Idaho	23,810
14	Connecticut	23,750
15	Utah	23,560
16	Missouri	23,370
17	Michigan	23,220
18	Illinois	23,150
19	New York	23,010
20	Nebraska	22,970
21	Nevada	22,880
22	California	22,810
23	Kansas	22,390
24	Oregon	22,340
25	Oklahoma	22,240
26	Maine	22,230
27	Hawaii	22,120
28	Ohio	22,080
29	South Carolina	21,970
30	North Carolina	21,960
31	Iowa	21,890
32	Delaware	21,870
33	Texas	21,680
34	Wisconsin	21,650
34	Wyoming	21,650
36	Indiana	21,640
37	Georgia	21,430
38	Arizona	21,420
39	South Dakota	20,760
40	North Dakota	20,650
41	Pennsylvania	20,570
42	Florida	19,780
43	Tennessee	19,620
44	Kentucky	19,560
45	Louisiana	19,220
45	Montana	19,220
47	Arkansas	18,960
48	Alabama	18,600
49	West Virginia	17,510
50	Mississippi	17,430

| | District of Columbia | 26,740 |

Source: U.S. Department of Labor, Bureau of Labor Statistics
"Occupational Employment and Wages, 2004" (http://www.bls.gov/oes/)
*Does not include self-employed.

Base Salary for Justices of States' Highest Courts in 2005

National Average = $130,328

ALPHA ORDER

RANK	STATE	SALARY
9	Alabama	$152,027
35	Alaska	117,900
25	Arizona	126,525
20	Arkansas	128,669
1	California	182,071
36	Colorado	116,251
11	Connecticut	146,016
2	Delaware	179,670
7	Florida	155,150
8	Georgia	153,086
37	Hawaii	115,547
48	Idaho	104,168
3	Illinois	173,261
16	Indiana	133,600
21	Iowa	128,000
34	Kansas	118,212
22	Kentucky	127,224
32	Louisiana	118,301
47	Maine	104,929
18	Maryland	132,352
23	Massachusetts	126,943
5	Michigan	164,610
15	Minnesota	135,567
42	Mississippi	112,530
29	Missouri	123,000
50	Montana	95,493
31	Nebraska	119,276
13	Nevada	140,000
26	New Hampshire	124,593
6	New Jersey	158,500
44	New Mexico	106,960
10	New York	151,200
33	North Carolina	118,219
49	North Dakota	99,122
19	Ohio	131,500
40	Oklahoma	113,531
46	Oregon	105,200
4	Pennsylvania	171,800
17	Rhode Island	132,816
28	South Carolina	123,095
45	South Dakota	105,765
24	Tennessee	126,528
41	Texas	113,000
38	Utah	115,250
39	Vermont	114,689
12	Virginia	142,416
14	Washington	137,276
30	West Virginia	121,000
27	Wisconsin	123,876
43	Wyoming	108,200

RANK ORDER

RANK	STATE	SALARY
1	California	$182,071
2	Delaware	179,670
3	Illinois	173,261
4	Pennsylvania	171,800
5	Michigan	164,610
6	New Jersey	158,500
7	Florida	155,150
8	Georgia	153,086
9	Alabama	152,027
10	New York	151,200
11	Connecticut	146,016
12	Virginia	142,416
13	Nevada	140,000
14	Washington	137,276
15	Minnesota	135,567
16	Indiana	133,600
17	Rhode Island	132,816
18	Maryland	132,352
19	Ohio	131,500
20	Arkansas	128,669
21	Iowa	128,000
22	Kentucky	127,224
23	Massachusetts	126,943
24	Tennessee	126,528
25	Arizona	126,525
26	New Hampshire	124,593
27	Wisconsin	123,876
28	South Carolina	123,095
29	Missouri	123,000
30	West Virginia	121,000
31	Nebraska	119,276
32	Louisiana	118,301
33	North Carolina	118,219
34	Kansas	118,212
35	Alaska	117,900
36	Colorado	116,251
37	Hawaii	115,547
38	Utah	115,250
39	Vermont	114,689
40	Oklahoma	113,531
41	Texas	113,000
42	Mississippi	112,530
43	Wyoming	108,200
44	New Mexico	106,960
45	South Dakota	105,765
46	Oregon	105,200
47	Maine	104,929
48	Idaho	104,168
49	North Dakota	99,122
50	Montana	95,493
	District of Columbia	171,800

Source: National Center for State Courts
"Survey of Judicial Salaries-April 2005" (Volume 30, Number 1)
(http://www.ncsconline.org/D_KIS/Salary_Survey/Index.html)

Base Salary for Judges of Intermediate Appellate Courts in 2005

National Average = $125,745

ALPHA ORDER				RANK ORDER		
RANK	STATE	SALARY		RANK	STATE	SALARY
6	Alabama	$151,027		1	California	$170,694
31	Alaska	111,384		2	Illinois	163,070
17	Arizona	123,900		3	Pennsylvania	162,100
15	Arkansas	124,652		4	Georgia	152,139
1	California	170,694		5	Michigan	151,441
30	Colorado	111,647		6	Alabama	151,027
10	Connecticut	137,137		7	New Jersey	150,000
NA	Delaware*	NA		8	New York	144,000
9	Florida	143,363		9	Florida	143,363
4	Georgia	152,139		10	Connecticut	137,137
32	Hawaii	110,618		11	Virginia	135,295
37	Idaho	103,168		12	Washington	130,678
2	Illinois	163,070		13	Indiana	129,800
13	Indiana	129,800		14	Minnesota	127,740
18	Iowa	123,120		15	Arkansas	124,652
26	Kansas	114,118		16	Maryland	124,552
20	Kentucky	122,085		17	Arizona	123,900
29	Louisiana	112,041		18	Iowa	123,120
NA	Maine*	NA		19	Ohio	122,550
16	Maryland	124,552		20	Kentucky	122,085
23	Massachusetts	117,467		21	Tennessee	120,636
5	Michigan	151,441		22	South Carolina	120,017
14	Minnesota	127,740		23	Massachusetts	117,467
36	Mississippi	105,050		24	Wisconsin	116,865
25	Missouri	115,000		25	Missouri	115,000
NA	Montana*	NA		26	Kansas	114,118
27	Nebraska	113,312		27	Nebraska	113,312
NA	Nevada*	NA		28	North Carolina	113,293
NA	New Hampshire*	NA		29	Louisiana	112,041
7	New Jersey	150,000		30	Colorado	111,647
39	New Mexico	101,612		31	Alaska	111,384
8	New York	144,000		32	Hawaii	110,618
28	North Carolina	113,293		33	Utah	110,000
NA	North Dakota*	NA		34	Oklahoma	108,336
19	Ohio	122,550		35	Texas	107,350
34	Oklahoma	108,336		36	Mississippi	105,050
38	Oregon	102,800		37	Idaho	103,168
3	Pennsylvania	162,100		38	Oregon	102,800
NA	Rhode Island*	NA		39	New Mexico	101,612
22	South Carolina	120,017		NA	Delaware*	NA
NA	South Dakota*	NA		NA	Maine*	NA
21	Tennessee	120,636		NA	Montana*	NA
35	Texas	107,350		NA	Nevada*	NA
33	Utah	110,000		NA	New Hampshire*	NA
NA	Vermont*	NA		NA	North Dakota*	NA
11	Virginia	135,295		NA	Rhode Island*	NA
12	Washington	130,678		NA	South Dakota*	NA
NA	West Virginia*	NA		NA	Vermont*	NA
24	Wisconsin	116,865		NA	West Virginia*	NA
NA	Wyoming*	NA		NA	Wyoming*	NA
				District of Columbia*		NA

Source: National Center for State Courts
"Survey of Judicial Salaries-April 2005" (Volume 30, Number 1
(http://www.ncsconline.org/D_KIS/Salary_Survey/Index.html)
*No intermediate court.

Base Salary for Judges of General Trial Courts in 2005

National Average = $117,328

ALPHA ORDER

RANK	STATE	SALARY
27	Alabama	$111,973
32	Alaska	109,032
14	Arizona	120,750
15	Arkansas	120,632
3	California	149,160
36	Colorado	107,044
10	Connecticut	131,875
1	Delaware	163,850
8	Florida	134,650
13	Georgia	121,938
37	Hawaii	106,922
46	Idaho	97,632
2	Illinois	149,638
29	Indiana	110,500
19	Iowa	117,040
41	Kansas	103,232
21	Kentucky	116,934
38	Louisiana	105,780
45	Maine	98,377
16	Maryland	120,352
25	Massachusetts	112,777
6	Michigan	139,919
17	Minnesota	119,913
40	Mississippi	104,170
34	Missouri	108,000
50	Montana	88,164
30	Nebraska	110,330
11	Nevada	130,000
22	New Hampshire	116,806
5	New Jersey	141,000
47	New Mexico	96,531
7	New York	136,700
35	North Carolina	107,136
49	North Dakota	90,671
26	Ohio	112,700
43	Oklahoma	102,529
48	Oregon	95,800
4	Pennsylvania	149,132
18	Rhode Island	119,579
20	South Carolina	116,940
44	South Dakota	98,787
24	Tennessee	115,428
28	Texas	111,700
39	Utah	104,700
33	Vermont	109,030
9	Virginia	132,211
12	Washington	124,411
23	West Virginia	116,000
31	Wisconsin	110,250
42	Wyoming	103,000

RANK ORDER

RANK	STATE	SALARY
1	Delaware	$163,850
2	Illinois	149,638
3	California	149,160
4	Pennsylvania	149,132
5	New Jersey	141,000
6	Michigan	139,919
7	New York	136,700
8	Florida	134,650
9	Virginia	132,211
10	Connecticut	131,875
11	Nevada	130,000
12	Washington	124,411
13	Georgia	121,938
14	Arizona	120,750
15	Arkansas	120,632
16	Maryland	120,352
17	Minnesota	119,913
18	Rhode Island	119,579
19	Iowa	117,040
20	South Carolina	116,940
21	Kentucky	116,934
22	New Hampshire	116,806
23	West Virginia	116,000
24	Tennessee	115,428
25	Massachusetts	112,777
26	Ohio	112,700
27	Alabama	111,973
28	Texas	111,700
29	Indiana	110,500
30	Nebraska	110,330
31	Wisconsin	110,250
32	Alaska	109,032
33	Vermont	109,030
34	Missouri	108,000
35	North Carolina	107,136
36	Colorado	107,044
37	Hawaii	106,922
38	Louisiana	105,780
39	Utah	104,700
40	Mississippi	104,170
41	Kansas	103,232
42	Wyoming	103,000
43	Oklahoma	102,529
44	South Dakota	98,787
45	Maine	98,377
46	Idaho	97,632
47	New Mexico	96,531
48	Oregon	95,800
49	North Dakota	90,671
50	Montana	88,164
	District of Columbia	162,100

Source: National Center for State Courts
"Survey of Judicial Salaries-April 2005" (Volume 30, Number 1)
(http://www.ncsconline.org/D_KIS/Salary_Survey/Index.html)

V. JUVENILES

V. JUVENILES (continued)

Important Note Regarding Juvenile Arrest Rates

The juvenile arrest rates shown in tables 176 to 229 were calculated by the editors as follows:

     The state arrest numbers reported by the FBI are only from those law enforcement agencies that submitted complete arrests reports for 12 months in 2004. Included in the FBI report are population totals of these reporting jurisdictions by state. Using these FBI population figures, we first determined what percentage the FBI numbers represented of each state's total resident population. Next, using 2004 Census state estimates for 10 to 17-year-olds we multiplied the percentages derived from the FBI population figures into the Census Bureau's total juvenile population counts. The resulting juvenile population is the base that was used to determine juvenile arrests per 100,000 juvenile population. The national rate was calculated in the same manner.

     Reports from law enforcement agencies in Illinois, Georgia, Kentucky and South Carolina represented 35% or less of their state populations and rates were not calculated. Reports from Arkansas, Mississippi, New York, South Dakota and West Virginia represented just over half of their state population. Rates for these states should be interpreted with caution. No arrest data were available for Montana or the District of Columbia.

Reported Arrests of Juveniles in 2004

National Total = 1,719,052 Reported Arrests*

ALPHA ORDER

RANK	STATE	ARRESTS	% of USA
32	Alabama	13,596	0.8%
46	Alaska	4,520	0.3%
7	Arizona	52,893	3.1%
37	Arkansas	9,358	0.5%
1	California	204,602	11.9%
11	Colorado	43,373	2.5%
26	Connecticut	19,671	1.1%
42	Delaware	6,767	0.4%
3	Florida	121,143	7.0%
23	Georgia	24,054	1.4%
36	Hawaii	9,542	0.6%
29	Idaho	15,567	0.9%
15	Illinois	36,581	2.1%
19	Indiana	34,024	2.0%
27	Iowa	18,872	1.1%
34	Kansas	12,426	0.7%
39	Kentucky	7,829	0.5%
17	Louisiana	35,055	2.0%
38	Maine	8,580	0.5%
8	Maryland	52,191	3.0%
31	Massachusetts	14,460	0.8%
12	Michigan	39,224	2.3%
21	Minnesota	30,905	1.8%
33	Mississippi	12,514	0.7%
14	Missouri	36,935	2.1%
NA	Montana**	NA	NA
30	Nebraska	14,577	0.8%
28	Nevada	17,722	1.0%
40	New Hampshire	7,812	0.5%
6	New Jersey	60,443	3.5%
35	New Mexico	10,994	0.6%
10	New York	47,820	2.8%
13	North Carolina	37,870	2.2%
44	North Dakota	6,396	0.4%
9	Ohio	47,954	2.8%
24	Oklahoma	23,128	1.3%
22	Oregon	30,109	1.8%
4	Pennsylvania	104,140	6.1%
41	Rhode Island	7,195	0.4%
47	South Carolina	2,866	0.2%
45	South Dakota	4,734	0.3%
18	Tennessee	34,434	2.0%
2	Texas	194,033	11.3%
25	Utah	21,687	1.3%
49	Vermont	1,401	0.1%
20	Virginia	33,881	2.0%
16	Washington	35,285	2.1%
48	West Virginia	1,940	0.1%
5	Wisconsin	101,245	5.9%
43	Wyoming	6,704	0.4%

RANK ORDER

RANK	STATE	ARRESTS	% of USA
1	California	204,602	11.9%
2	Texas	194,033	11.3%
3	Florida	121,143	7.0%
4	Pennsylvania	104,140	6.1%
5	Wisconsin	101,245	5.9%
6	New Jersey	60,443	3.5%
7	Arizona	52,893	3.1%
8	Maryland	52,191	3.0%
9	Ohio	47,954	2.8%
10	New York	47,820	2.8%
11	Colorado	43,373	2.5%
12	Michigan	39,224	2.3%
13	North Carolina	37,870	2.2%
14	Missouri	36,935	2.1%
15	Illinois	36,581	2.1%
16	Washington	35,285	2.1%
17	Louisiana	35,055	2.0%
18	Tennessee	34,434	2.0%
19	Indiana	34,024	2.0%
20	Virginia	33,881	2.0%
21	Minnesota	30,905	1.8%
22	Oregon	30,109	1.8%
23	Georgia	24,054	1.4%
24	Oklahoma	23,128	1.3%
25	Utah	21,687	1.3%
26	Connecticut	19,671	1.1%
27	Iowa	18,872	1.1%
28	Nevada	17,722	1.0%
29	Idaho	15,567	0.9%
30	Nebraska	14,577	0.8%
31	Massachusetts	14,460	0.8%
32	Alabama	13,596	0.8%
33	Mississippi	12,514	0.7%
34	Kansas	12,426	0.7%
35	New Mexico	10,994	0.6%
36	Hawaii	9,542	0.6%
37	Arkansas	9,358	0.5%
38	Maine	8,580	0.5%
39	Kentucky	7,829	0.5%
40	New Hampshire	7,812	0.5%
41	Rhode Island	7,195	0.4%
42	Delaware	6,767	0.4%
43	Wyoming	6,704	0.4%
44	North Dakota	6,396	0.4%
45	South Dakota	4,734	0.3%
46	Alaska	4,520	0.3%
47	South Carolina	2,866	0.2%
48	West Virginia	1,940	0.1%
49	Vermont	1,401	0.1%
NA	Montana**	NA	NA
	District of Columbia**	NA	NA

Source: Federal Bureau of Investigation
   "Crime in the United States 2004" (Uniform Crime Reports, October 17, 2005)
*Arrests of youths 17 years and younger by law enforcement agencies submitting complete reports to the F.B.I. for 12 months in 2004. See important note at beginning of this chapter.
**Not available.

Reported Juvenile Arrest Rate in 2004

National Rate = 6,566.3 Reported Arrests per 100,000 Juvenile Population*

ALPHA ORDER				RANK ORDER		
RANK	STATE	RATE		RANK	STATE	RATE
42	Alabama	3,034.7		1	Wisconsin	19,558.5
37	Alaska	5,176.5		2	Wyoming	12,258.4
13	Arizona	8,013.4		3	North Dakota	11,799.9
33	Arkansas	5,684.5		4	Utah	11,144.3
38	California	4,997.1		5	Idaho	10,176.8
7	Colorado	9,651.7		6	South Dakota	9,703.0
32	Connecticut	5,966.4		7	Colorado	9,651.7
10	Delaware	8,406.3		8	Louisiana	9,448.0
25	Florida	6,571.8		9	Pennsylvania	8,761.9
NA	Georgia**	NA		10	Delaware	8,406.3
11	Hawaii	8,233.3		11	Hawaii	8,233.3
5	Idaho	10,176.8		12	Maryland	8,031.2
NA	Illinois**	NA		13	Arizona	8,013.4
26	Indiana	6,353.8		14	Oregon	7,997.0
19	Iowa	6,953.7		15	Nebraska	7,950.6
35	Kansas	5,621.7		16	Minnesota	7,629.8
NA	Kentucky**	NA		17	Texas	7,140.7
8	Louisiana	9,448.0		18	Mississippi	7,119.7
31	Maine	6,035.6		19	Iowa	6,953.7
12	Maryland	8,031.2		20	Missouri	6,944.0
43	Massachusetts	2,969.9		21	Nevada	6,897.7
41	Michigan	3,505.3		22	New Hampshire	6,733.7
16	Minnesota	7,629.8		23	Tennessee	6,648.1
18	Mississippi	7,119.7		24	Washington	6,593.9
20	Missouri	6,944.0		25	Florida	6,571.8
NA	Montana**	NA		26	Indiana	6,353.8
15	Nebraska	7,950.6		27	New Mexico	6,296.2
21	Nevada	6,897.7		28	New Jersey	6,280.1
22	New Hampshire	6,733.7		29	Oklahoma	6,171.5
28	New Jersey	6,280.1		30	Rhode Island	6,165.0
27	New Mexico	6,296.2		31	Maine	6,035.6
40	New York	4,432.8		32	Connecticut	5,966.4
34	North Carolina	5,632.8		33	Arkansas	5,684.5
3	North Dakota	11,799.9		34	North Carolina	5,632.8
36	Ohio	5,381.6		35	Kansas	5,621.7
29	Oklahoma	6,171.5		36	Ohio	5,381.6
14	Oregon	7,997.0		37	Alaska	5,176.5
9	Pennsylvania	8,761.9		38	California	4,997.1
30	Rhode Island	6,165.0		39	Virginia	4,710.2
NA	South Carolina**	NA		40	New York	4,432.8
6	South Dakota	9,703.0		41	Michigan	3,505.3
23	Tennessee	6,648.1		42	Alabama	3,034.7
17	Texas	7,140.7		43	Massachusetts	2,969.9
4	Utah	11,144.3		44	Vermont	2,427.7
44	Vermont	2,427.7		45	West Virginia	1,842.1
39	Virginia	4,710.2		NA	Georgia**	NA
24	Washington	6,593.9		NA	Illinois**	NA
45	West Virginia	1,842.1		NA	Kentucky**	NA
1	Wisconsin	19,558.5		NA	Montana**	NA
2	Wyoming	12,258.4		NA	South Carolina**	NA
					District of Columbia**	NA

Source: Morgan Quitno Press using data from Federal Bureau of Investigation
    "Crime in the United States 2004" (Uniform Crime Reports, October 17; 2005)
*By law enforcement agencies submitting complete reports to the F.B.I. for 12 months in 2004. Arrests of youths 17
years and younger divided into population of 10 to 17 year olds. See important note at beginning of this chapter.
**Not available.

Reported Arrests of Juveniles as a Percent of All Arrests in 2004

National Percent = 15.5% of Reported Arrests*

ALPHA ORDER

RANK	STATE	PERCENT
48	Alabama	6.5
36	Alaska	12.3
19	Arizona	16.8
47	Arkansas	9.5
30	California	14.5
11	Colorado	18.9
19	Connecticut	16.8
6	Delaware	21.8
39	Florida	11.8
41	Georgia	11.7
9	Hawaii	19.3
7	Idaho	21.6
13	Illinois	18.2
24	Indiana	15.8
17	Iowa	17.1
26	Kansas	15.5
43	Kentucky	11.3
28	Louisiana	15.1
26	Maine	15.5
18	Maryland	16.9
32	Massachusetts	14.3
39	Michigan	11.8
5	Minnesota	23.4
44	Mississippi	11.0
33	Missouri	13.5
NA	Montana**	NA
25	Nebraska	15.7
37	Nevada	11.9
14	New Hampshire	17.8
23	New Jersey	15.9
37	New Mexico	11.9
28	New York	15.1
46	North Carolina	9.6
2	North Dakota	24.6
15	Ohio	17.6
30	Oklahoma	14.5
8	Oregon	19.4
4	Pennsylvania	23.6
21	Rhode Island	16.5
45	South Carolina	10.8
9	South Dakota	19.3
34	Tennessee	12.8
16	Texas	17.4
3	Utah	23.9
42	Vermont	11.6
35	Virginia	12.7
22	Washington	16.3
49	West Virginia	6.4
1	Wisconsin	26.4
12	Wyoming	18.7

RANK ORDER

RANK	STATE	PERCENT
1	Wisconsin	26.4
2	North Dakota	24.6
3	Utah	23.9
4	Pennsylvania	23.6
5	Minnesota	23.4
6	Delaware	21.8
7	Idaho	21.6
8	Oregon	19.4
9	Hawaii	19.3
9	South Dakota	19.3
11	Colorado	18.9
12	Wyoming	18.7
13	Illinois	18.2
14	New Hampshire	17.8
15	Ohio	17.6
16	Texas	17.4
17	Iowa	17.1
18	Maryland	16.9
19	Arizona	16.8
19	Connecticut	16.8
21	Rhode Island	16.5
22	Washington	16.3
23	New Jersey	15.9
24	Indiana	15.8
25	Nebraska	15.7
26	Kansas	15.5
26	Maine	15.5
28	Louisiana	15.1
28	New York	15.1
30	California	14.5
30	Oklahoma	14.5
32	Massachusetts	14.3
33	Missouri	13.5
34	Tennessee	12.8
35	Virginia	12.7
36	Alaska	12.3
37	Nevada	11.9
37	New Mexico	11.9
39	Florida	11.8
39	Michigan	11.8
41	Georgia	11.7
42	Vermont	11.6
43	Kentucky	11.3
44	Mississippi	11.0
45	South Carolina	10.8
46	North Carolina	9.6
47	Arkansas	9.5
48	Alabama	6.5
49	West Virginia	6.4
NA	Montana**	NA
	District of Columbia**	NA

Source: Morgan Quitno Press using data from Federal Bureau of Investigation
  "Crime in the United States 2004" (Uniform Crime Reports, October 17, 2005)
*Arrests of youths 17 years and younger by law enforcement agencies submitting complete reports to the F.B.I. for 12 months in 2004.
**Not available.

Reported Arrests of Juveniles for Crime Index Offenses in 2004

National Total = 439,692 Reported Arrests*

ALPHA ORDER

RANK ORDER

RANK	STATE	ARRESTS	% of USA	RANK	STATE	ARRESTS	% of USA
29	Alabama	3,949	0.9%	1	California	59,591	13.6%
42	Alaska	1,573	0.4%	2	Florida	44,744	10.2%
8	Arizona	13,392	3.0%	3	Texas	41,230	9.4%
35	Arkansas	2,670	0.6%	4	Pennsylvania	18,908	4.3%
1	California	59,591	13.6%	5	Wisconsin	17,916	4.1%
15	Colorado	10,065	2.3%	6	Maryland	16,124	3.7%
28	Connecticut	4,923	1.1%	7	New York	14,838	3.4%
41	Delaware	1,813	0.4%	8	Arizona	13,392	3.0%
2	Florida	44,744	10.2%	9	New Jersey	11,943	2.7%
22	Georgia	6,901	1.6%	10	Washington	11,763	2.7%
39	Hawaii	1,869	0.4%	11	Michigan	11,740	2.7%
32	Idaho	3,133	0.7%	12	North Carolina	10,791	2.5%
16	Illinois	9,471	2.2%	13	Ohio	10,760	2.4%
18	Indiana	8,628	2.0%	14	Missouri	10,142	2.3%
25	Iowa	5,653	1.3%	15	Colorado	10,065	2.3%
33	Kansas	2,976	0.7%	16	Illinois	9,471	2.2%
38	Kentucky	2,572	0.6%	17	Louisiana	8,834	2.0%
17	Louisiana	8,834	2.0%	18	Indiana	8,628	2.0%
36	Maine	2,626	0.6%	19	Oregon	8,472	1.9%
6	Maryland	16,124	3.7%	20	Minnesota	7,578	1.7%
31	Massachusetts	3,789	0.9%	21	Tennessee	7,332	1.7%
11	Michigan	11,740	2.7%	22	Georgia	6,901	1.6%
20	Minnesota	7,578	1.7%	23	Oklahoma	6,790	1.5%
34	Mississippi	2,878	0.7%	24	Virginia	6,692	1.5%
14	Missouri	10,142	2.3%	25	Iowa	5,653	1.3%
NA	Montana**	NA	NA	26	Utah	5,461	1.2%
30	Nebraska	3,790	0.9%	27	Nevada	5,033	1.1%
27	Nevada	5,033	1.1%	28	Connecticut	4,923	1.1%
45	New Hampshire	1,013	0.2%	29	Alabama	3,949	0.9%
9	New Jersey	11,943	2.7%	30	Nebraska	3,790	0.9%
37	New Mexico	2,615	0.6%	31	Massachusetts	3,789	0.9%
7	New York	14,838	3.4%	32	Idaho	3,133	0.7%
12	North Carolina	10,791	2.5%	33	Kansas	2,976	0.7%
43	North Dakota	1,039	0.2%	34	Mississippi	2,878	0.7%
13	Ohio	10,760	2.4%	35	Arkansas	2,670	0.6%
23	Oklahoma	6,790	1.5%	36	Maine	2,626	0.6%
19	Oregon	8,472	1.9%	37	New Mexico	2,615	0.6%
4	Pennsylvania	18,908	4.3%	38	Kentucky	2,572	0.6%
40	Rhode Island	1,825	0.4%	39	Hawaii	1,869	0.4%
44	South Carolina	1,030	0.2%	40	Rhode Island	1,825	0.4%
47	South Dakota	812	0.2%	41	Delaware	1,813	0.4%
21	Tennessee	7,332	1.7%	42	Alaska	1,573	0.4%
3	Texas	41,230	9.4%	43	North Dakota	1,039	0.2%
26	Utah	5,461	1.2%	44	South Carolina	1,030	0.2%
49	Vermont	318	0.1%	45	New Hampshire	1,013	0.2%
24	Virginia	6,692	1.5%	46	Wyoming	993	0.2%
10	Washington	11,763	2.7%	47	South Dakota	812	0.2%
48	West Virginia	694	0.2%	48	West Virginia	694	0.2%
5	Wisconsin	17,916	4.1%	49	Vermont	318	0.1%
46	Wyoming	993	0.2%	NA	Montana**	NA	NA
					District of Columbia**	NA	NA

Source: Morgan Quitno Press using data from Federal Bureau of Investigation
   "Crime in the United States 2004" (Uniform Crime Reports, October 17, 2005)
*Arrests of youths 17 years and younger by law enforcement agencies submitting complete reports to the F.B.I. for
12 months in 2004. Crime index offenses consist of murder, forcible rape, robbery, aggravated assault, burglary,
larceny-theft, motor vehicle theft and arson. See important note at beginning of this chapter.
**Not available.

Reported Juvenile Arrest Rate for Crime Index Offenses in 2004

National Rate = 1,679.5 Reported Arrests per 100,000 Juvenile Population*

ALPHA ORDER

RANK	STATE	RATE
41	Alabama	881.4
21	Alaska	1,801.5
13	Arizona	2,028.9
24	Arkansas	1,621.9
33	California	1,455.4
8	Colorado	2,239.8
32	Connecticut	1,493.2
6	Delaware	2,252.2
4	Florida	2,427.3
NA	Georgia**	NA
25	Hawaii	1,612.7
12	Idaho	2,048.2
NA	Illinois**	NA
26	Indiana	1,611.2
10	Iowa	2,082.9
36	Kansas	1,346.4
NA	Kentucky**	NA
5	Louisiana	2,380.9
18	Maine	1,847.3
3	Maryland	2,481.2
43	Massachusetts	778.2
39	Michigan	1,049.1
17	Minnesota	1,870.9
23	Mississippi	1,637.4
16	Missouri	1,906.8
NA	Montana**	NA
11	Nebraska	2,067.1
14	Nevada	1,958.9
42	New Hampshire	873.2
37	New Jersey	1,240.9
31	New Mexico	1,497.6
35	New York	1,375.4
27	North Carolina	1,605.1
15	North Dakota	1,916.8
38	Ohio	1,207.5
20	Oklahoma	1,811.9
7	Oregon	2,250.2
28	Pennsylvania	1,590.8
29	Rhode Island	1,563.7
NA	South Carolina**	NA
22	South Dakota	1,664.3
34	Tennessee	1,415.6
30	Texas	1,517.3
2	Utah	2,806.2
45	Vermont	551.0
40	Virginia	930.3
9	Washington	2,198.2
44	West Virginia	659.0
1	Wisconsin	3,461.0
19	Wyoming	1,815.7

RANK ORDER

RANK	STATE	RATE
1	Wisconsin	3,461.0
2	Utah	2,806.2
3	Maryland	2,481.2
4	Florida	2,427.3
5	Louisiana	2,380.9
6	Delaware	2,252.2
7	Oregon	2,250.2
8	Colorado	2,239.8
9	Washington	2,198.2
10	Iowa	2,082.9
11	Nebraska	2,067.1
12	Idaho	2,048.2
13	Arizona	2,028.9
14	Nevada	1,958.9
15	North Dakota	1,916.8
16	Missouri	1,906.8
17	Minnesota	1,870.9
18	Maine	1,847.3
19	Wyoming	1,815.7
20	Oklahoma	1,811.9
21	Alaska	1,801.5
22	South Dakota	1,664.3
23	Mississippi	1,637.4
24	Arkansas	1,621.9
25	Hawaii	1,612.7
26	Indiana	1,611.2
27	North Carolina	1,605.1
28	Pennsylvania	1,590.8
29	Rhode Island	1,563.7
30	Texas	1,517.3
31	New Mexico	1,497.6
32	Connecticut	1,493.2
33	California	1,455.4
34	Tennessee	1,415.6
35	New York	1,375.4
36	Kansas	1,346.4
37	New Jersey	1,240.9
38	Ohio	1,207.5
39	Michigan	1,049.1
40	Virginia	930.3
41	Alabama	881.4
42	New Hampshire	873.2
43	Massachusetts	778.2
44	West Virginia	659.0
45	Vermont	551.0
NA	Georgia**	NA
NA	Illinois**	NA
NA	Kentucky**	NA
NA	Montana**	NA
NA	South Carolina**	NA

District of Columbia**   NA

Source: Morgan Quitno Press using data from Federal Bureau of Investigation
   "Crime in the United States 2004" (Uniform Crime Reports, October 17, 2005)
*By law enforcement agencies submitting complete reports to the F.B.I. for 12 months in 2004. Arrests of youths 17 years and younger divided into population of 10 to 17 year olds. See important note at beginning of this chapter. Crime index offenses consist of murder, forcible rape, robbery, aggravated assault, burglary, larceny-theft, motor vehicle theft and arson.   **Not available.

Reported Arrests of Juveniles for Crime Index Offenses
As a Percent of All Such Arrests in 2004
National Percent = 24.5% of Reported Crime Index Offense Arrests*

ALPHA ORDER

RANK ORDER

RANK	STATE	PERCENT		RANK	STATE	PERCENT
49	Alabama	14.8		1	North Dakota	44.9
16	Alaska	28.8		2	Idaho	40.1
21	Arizona	26.3		3	South Dakota	39.2
41	Arkansas	20.7		4	Wisconsin	37.2
40	California	20.8		5	Minnesota	36.3
18	Colorado	28.1		6	Utah	35.4
30	Connecticut	24.2		7	Iowa	35.1
20	Delaware	27.1		8	Nebraska	32.2
23	Florida	25.2		9	New Hampshire	32.1
43	Georgia	20.4		10	Maryland	32.0
15	Hawaii	29.3		11	Maine	31.9
2	Idaho	40.1		12	Rhode Island	31.8
22	Illinois	26.2		13	Wyoming	31.6
26	Indiana	24.9		14	Oklahoma	29.4
7	Iowa	35.1		15	Hawaii	29.3
19	Kansas	27.8		16	Alaska	28.8
32	Kentucky	24.0		17	Washington	28.5
36	Louisiana	23.1		18	Colorado	28.1
11	Maine	31.9		19	Kansas	27.8
10	Maryland	32.0		20	Delaware	27.1
44	Massachusetts	20.3		21	Arizona	26.3
23	Michigan	25.2		22	Illinois	26.2
5	Minnesota	36.3		23	Florida	25.2
38	Mississippi	21.4		23	Michigan	25.2
37	Missouri	21.6		25	New Jersey	25.0
NA	Montana**	NA		26	Indiana	24.9
8	Nebraska	32.2		26	Ohio	24.9
42	Nevada	20.6		26	Texas	24.9
9	New Hampshire	32.1		29	Pennsylvania	24.5
25	New Jersey	25.0		30	Connecticut	24.2
30	New Mexico	24.2		30	New Mexico	24.2
33	New York	23.9		32	Kentucky	24.0
46	North Carolina	16.8		33	New York	23.9
1	North Dakota	44.9		33	Oregon	23.9
26	Ohio	24.9		35	Vermont	23.4
14	Oklahoma	29.4		36	Louisiana	23.1
33	Oregon	23.9		37	Missouri	21.6
29	Pennsylvania	24.5		38	Mississippi	21.4
12	Rhode Island	31.8		39	Virginia	21.0
44	South Carolina	20.3		40	California	20.8
3	South Dakota	39.2		41	Arkansas	20.7
47	Tennessee	16.5		42	Nevada	20.6
26	Texas	24.9		43	Georgia	20.4
6	Utah	35.4		44	Massachusetts	20.3
35	Vermont	23.4		44	South Carolina	20.3
39	Virginia	21.0		46	North Carolina	16.8
17	Washington	28.5		47	Tennessee	16.5
48	West Virginia	15.3		48	West Virginia	15.3
4	Wisconsin	37.2		49	Alabama	14.8
13	Wyoming	31.6		NA	Montana**	NA
					District of Columbia**	NA

Source: Morgan Quitno Press using data from Federal Bureau of Investigation
   "Crime in the United States 2004" (Uniform Crime Reports, October 17, 2005)
*Arrests of youths 17 years and younger by law enforcement agencies submitting complete reports to the F.B.I. for
12 months in 2004. Crime index offenses consist of murder, forcible rape, robbery, aggravated assault, burglary,
larceny-theft, motor vehicle theft and arson.
**Not available.

Reported Arrests of Juveniles for Violent Crime in 2004

National Total = 74,889 Reported Arrests*

ALPHA ORDER

RANK	STATE	ARRESTS	% of USA
29	Alabama	557	0.7%
42	Alaska	178	0.2%
13	Arizona	1,553	2.1%
38	Arkansas	234	0.3%
1	California	14,205	19.0%
21	Colorado	1,025	1.4%
22	Connecticut	974	1.3%
31	Delaware	395	0.5%
2	Florida	8,662	11.6%
19	Georgia	1,232	1.6%
34	Hawaii	276	0.4%
37	Idaho	249	0.3%
7	Illinois	3,283	4.4%
10	Indiana	1,733	2.3%
28	Iowa	668	0.9%
32	Kansas	346	0.5%
35	Kentucky	274	0.4%
15	Louisiana	1,489	2.0%
43	Maine	143	0.2%
6	Maryland	3,327	4.4%
16	Massachusetts	1,314	1.8%
11	Michigan	1,646	2.2%
27	Minnesota	690	0.9%
39	Mississippi	219	0.3%
14	Missouri	1,542	2.1%
NA	Montana**	NA	NA
39	Nebraska	219	0.3%
26	Nevada	697	0.9%
44	New Hampshire	84	0.1%
5	New Jersey	3,457	4.6%
30	New Mexico	463	0.6%
8	New York	2,798	3.7%
12	North Carolina	1,637	2.2%
49	North Dakota	32	0.0%
17	Ohio	1,311	1.8%
25	Oklahoma	736	1.0%
24	Oregon	830	1.1%
4	Pennsylvania	4,962	6.6%
36	Rhode Island	259	0.3%
41	South Carolina	215	0.3%
47	South Dakota	44	0.1%
20	Tennessee	1,230	1.6%
3	Texas	5,160	6.9%
33	Utah	340	0.5%
48	Vermont	38	0.1%
23	Virginia	858	1.1%
18	Washington	1,259	1.7%
46	West Virginia	61	0.1%
9	Wisconsin	1,916	2.6%
45	Wyoming	69	0.1%

RANK ORDER

RANK	STATE	ARRESTS	% of USA
1	California	14,205	19.0%
2	Florida	8,662	11.6%
3	Texas	5,160	6.9%
4	Pennsylvania	4,962	6.6%
5	New Jersey	3,457	4.6%
6	Maryland	3,327	4.4%
7	Illinois	3,283	4.4%
8	New York	2,798	3.7%
9	Wisconsin	1,916	2.6%
10	Indiana	1,733	2.3%
11	Michigan	1,646	2.2%
12	North Carolina	1,637	2.2%
13	Arizona	1,553	2.1%
14	Missouri	1,542	2.1%
15	Louisiana	1,489	2.0%
16	Massachusetts	1,314	1.8%
17	Ohio	1,311	1.8%
18	Washington	1,259	1.7%
19	Georgia	1,232	1.6%
20	Tennessee	1,230	1.6%
21	Colorado	1,025	1.4%
22	Connecticut	974	1.3%
23	Virginia	858	1.1%
24	Oregon	830	1.1%
25	Oklahoma	736	1.0%
26	Nevada	697	0.9%
27	Minnesota	690	0.9%
28	Iowa	668	0.9%
29	Alabama	557	0.7%
30	New Mexico	463	0.6%
31	Delaware	395	0.5%
32	Kansas	346	0.5%
33	Utah	340	0.5%
34	Hawaii	276	0.4%
35	Kentucky	274	0.4%
36	Rhode Island	259	0.3%
37	Idaho	249	0.3%
38	Arkansas	234	0.3%
39	Mississippi	219	0.3%
39	Nebraska	219	0.3%
41	South Carolina	215	0.3%
42	Alaska	178	0.2%
43	Maine	143	0.2%
44	New Hampshire	84	0.1%
45	Wyoming	69	0.1%
46	West Virginia	61	0.1%
47	South Dakota	44	0.1%
48	Vermont	38	0.1%
49	North Dakota	32	0.0%
NA	Montana**	NA	NA
	District of Columbia**	NA	NA

Source: Federal Bureau of Investigation
"Crime in the United States 2004" (Uniform Crime Reports, October 17, 2005)
*Arrests of youths 17 years and younger by law enforcement agencies submitting complete reports to the F.B.I. for 12 months in 2004. Violent crimes are offenses of murder, forcible rape, robbery and aggravated assault. See important note at beginning of this chapter.
**Not available.

Reported Juvenile Arrest Rate for Violent Crime in 2004

National Rate = 286.1 Reported Arrests per 100,000 Juvenile Population*

ALPHA ORDER

RANK ORDER

RANK	STATE	RATE		RANK	STATE	RATE
37	Alabama	124.3		1	Maryland	512.0
25	Alaska	203.9		2	Delaware	490.7
20	Arizona	235.3		3	Florida	469.9
34	Arkansas	142.1		4	Pennsylvania	417.5
8	California	346.9		5	Louisiana	401.3
22	Colorado	228.1		6	Wisconsin	370.1
10	Connecticut	295.4		7	New Jersey	359.2
2	Delaware	490.7		8	California	346.9
3	Florida	469.9		9	Indiana	323.6
NA	Georgia**	NA		10	Connecticut	295.4
18	Hawaii	238.1		11	Missouri	289.9
30	Idaho	162.8		12	Nevada	271.3
NA	Illinois**	NA		13	Massachusetts	269.9
9	Indiana	323.6		14	New Mexico	265.2
16	Iowa	246.1		15	New York	259.4
31	Kansas	156.5		16	Iowa	246.1
NA	Kentucky**	NA		17	North Carolina	243.5
5	Louisiana	401.3		18	Hawaii	238.1
40	Maine	100.6		19	Tennessee	237.5
1	Maryland	512.0		20	Arizona	235.3
13	Massachusetts	269.9		20	Washington	235.3
32	Michigan	147.1		22	Colorado	228.1
29	Minnesota	170.3		23	Rhode Island	221.9
36	Mississippi	124.6		24	Oregon	220.4
11	Missouri	289.9		25	Alaska	203.9
NA	Montana**	NA		26	Oklahoma	196.4
38	Nebraska	119.4		27	Texas	189.9
12	Nevada	271.3		28	Utah	174.7
42	New Hampshire	72.4		29	Minnesota	170.3
7	New Jersey	359.2		30	Idaho	162.8
14	New Mexico	265.2		31	Kansas	156.5
15	New York	259.4		32	Michigan	147.1
17	North Carolina	243.5		32	Ohio	147.1
44	North Dakota	59.0		34	Arkansas	142.1
32	Ohio	147.1		35	Wyoming	126.2
26	Oklahoma	196.4		36	Mississippi	124.6
24	Oregon	220.4		37	Alabama	124.3
4	Pennsylvania	417.5		38	Nebraska	119.4
23	Rhode Island	221.9		39	Virginia	119.3
NA	South Carolina**	NA		40	Maine	100.6
41	South Dakota	90.2		41	South Dakota	90.2
19	Tennessee	237.5		42	New Hampshire	72.4
27	Texas	189.9		43	Vermont	65.8
28	Utah	174.7		44	North Dakota	59.0
43	Vermont	65.8		45	West Virginia	57.9
39	Virginia	119.3		NA	Georgia**	NA
20	Washington	235.3		NA	Illinois**	NA
45	West Virginia	57.9		NA	Kentucky**	NA
6	Wisconsin	370.1		NA	Montana**	NA
35	Wyoming	126.2		NA	South Carolina**	NA
					District of Columbia**	NA

Source: Morgan Quitno Press using data from Federal Bureau of Investigation
    "Crime in the United States 2004" (Uniform Crime Reports, October 17, 2005)
*By law enforcement agencies submitting complete reports to the F.B.I. for 12 months in 2004. Arrests of youths 17 years and younger divided into population of 10 to 17 year olds. See important note at beginning of this chapter. Violent crimes are offenses of murder, forcible rape, robbery and aggravated assault.
**Not available.

Reported Arrests of Juveniles for Violent Crime
As a Percent of All Such Arrests in 2004
National Percent = 15.8% of Reported Violent Crime Arrests*

ALPHA ORDER

RANK	STATE	PERCENT
47	Alabama	9.2
42	Alaska	12.0
19	Arizona	17.2
48	Arkansas	7.9
41	California	12.1
22	Colorado	16.7
11	Connecticut	19.6
9	Delaware	20.9
20	Florida	17.0
36	Georgia	13.1
4	Hawaii	23.5
13	Idaho	19.2
1	Illinois	34.5
26	Indiana	16.0
15	Iowa	17.9
21	Kansas	16.8
29	Kentucky	15.3
27	Louisiana	15.5
24	Maine	16.6
2	Maryland	27.4
14	Massachusetts	18.7
43	Michigan	11.6
6	Minnesota	23.0
46	Mississippi	9.7
40	Missouri	12.4
NA	Montana**	NA
30	Nebraska	14.0
35	Nevada	13.2
25	New Hampshire	16.3
5	New Jersey	23.3
33	New Mexico	13.6
12	New York	19.5
44	North Carolina	10.0
22	North Dakota	16.7
17	Ohio	17.4
36	Oklahoma	13.1
18	Oregon	17.3
8	Pennsylvania	21.0
10	Rhode Island	20.6
34	South Carolina	13.5
31	South Dakota	13.8
45	Tennessee	9.9
28	Texas	15.4
3	Utah	23.6
36	Vermont	13.1
32	Virginia	13.7
16	Washington	17.7
49	West Virginia	6.0
7	Wisconsin	21.3
39	Wyoming	12.6

RANK ORDER

RANK	STATE	PERCENT
1	Illinois	34.5
2	Maryland	27.4
3	Utah	23.6
4	Hawaii	23.5
5	New Jersey	23.3
6	Minnesota	23.0
7	Wisconsin	21.3
8	Pennsylvania	21.0
9	Delaware	20.9
10	Rhode Island	20.6
11	Connecticut	19.6
12	New York	19.5
13	Idaho	19.2
14	Massachusetts	18.7
15	Iowa	17.9
16	Washington	17.7
17	Ohio	17.4
18	Oregon	17.3
19	Arizona	17.2
20	Florida	17.0
21	Kansas	16.8
22	Colorado	16.7
22	North Dakota	16.7
24	Maine	16.6
25	New Hampshire	16.3
26	Indiana	16.0
27	Louisiana	15.5
28	Texas	15.4
29	Kentucky	15.3
30	Nebraska	14.0
31	South Dakota	13.8
32	Virginia	13.7
33	New Mexico	13.6
34	South Carolina	13.5
35	Nevada	13.2
36	Georgia	13.1
36	Oklahoma	13.1
36	Vermont	13.1
39	Wyoming	12.6
40	Missouri	12.4
41	California	12.1
42	Alaska	12.0
43	Michigan	11.6
44	North Carolina	10.0
45	Tennessee	9.9
46	Mississippi	9.7
47	Alabama	9.2
48	Arkansas	7.9
49	West Virginia	6.0
NA	Montana**	NA

District of Columbia**   NA

Source: Morgan Quitno Press using data from Federal Bureau of Investigation
    "Crime in the United States 2004" (Uniform Crime Reports, October 17, 2005)
*Arrests of youths 17 years and younger by law enforcement agencies submitting complete reports to the F.B.I. for
12 months in 2004. Violent crimes are offenses of murder, forcible rape, robbery and aggravated assault.
**Not available.

Reported Arrests of Juveniles for Murder in 2004

National Total = 1,119 Reported Arrests*

ALPHA ORDER

RANK	STATE	ARRESTS	% of USA
17	Alabama	16	1.4%
32	Alaska	4	0.4%
18	Arizona	14	1.3%
38	Arkansas	2	0.2%
2	California	180	16.1%
26	Colorado	8	0.7%
29	Connecticut	6	0.5%
38	Delaware	2	0.2%
4	Florida	54	4.8%
11	Georgia	23	2.1%
35	Hawaii	3	0.3%
40	Idaho	1	0.1%
5	Illinois	46	4.1%
23	Indiana	10	0.9%
29	Iowa	6	0.5%
41	Kansas	0	0.0%
35	Kentucky	3	0.3%
14	Louisiana	20	1.8%
41	Maine	0	0.0%
9	Maryland	32	2.9%
29	Massachusetts	6	0.5%
19	Michigan	13	1.2%
32	Minnesota	4	0.4%
26	Mississippi	8	0.7%
7	Missouri	42	3.8%
NA	Montana**	NA	NA
32	Nebraska	4	0.4%
11	Nevada	23	2.1%
41	New Hampshire	0	0.0%
10	New Jersey	24	2.1%
22	New Mexico	11	1.0%
16	New York	17	1.5%
8	North Carolina	37	3.3%
41	North Dakota	0	0.0%
19	Ohio	13	1.2%
23	Oklahoma	10	0.9%
13	Oregon	21	1.9%
5	Pennsylvania	46	4.1%
41	Rhode Island	0	0.0%
26	South Carolina	8	0.7%
41	South Dakota	0	0.0%
15	Tennessee	19	1.7%
3	Texas	71	6.3%
35	Utah	3	0.3%
41	Vermont	0	0.0%
21	Virginia	12	1.1%
23	Washington	10	0.9%
41	West Virginia	0	0.0%
1	Wisconsin	287	25.6%
41	Wyoming	0	0.0%

RANK ORDER

RANK	STATE	ARRESTS	% of USA
1	Wisconsin	287	25.6%
2	California	180	16.1%
3	Texas	71	6.3%
4	Florida	54	4.8%
5	Illinois	46	4.1%
5	Pennsylvania	46	4.1%
7	Missouri	42	3.8%
8	North Carolina	37	3.3%
9	Maryland	32	2.9%
10	New Jersey	24	2.1%
11	Georgia	23	2.1%
11	Nevada	23	2.1%
13	Oregon	21	1.9%
14	Louisiana	20	1.8%
15	Tennessee	19	1.7%
16	New York	17	1.5%
17	Alabama	16	1.4%
18	Arizona	14	1.3%
19	Michigan	13	1.2%
19	Ohio	13	1.2%
21	Virginia	12	1.1%
22	New Mexico	11	1.0%
23	Indiana	10	0.9%
23	Oklahoma	10	0.9%
23	Washington	10	0.9%
26	Colorado	8	0.7%
26	Mississippi	8	0.7%
26	South Carolina	8	0.7%
29	Connecticut	6	0.5%
29	Iowa	6	0.5%
29	Massachusetts	6	0.5%
32	Alaska	4	0.4%
32	Minnesota	4	0.4%
32	Nebraska	4	0.4%
35	Hawaii	3	0.3%
35	Kentucky	3	0.3%
35	Utah	3	0.3%
38	Arkansas	2	0.2%
38	Delaware	2	0.2%
40	Idaho	1	0.1%
41	Kansas	0	0.0%
41	Maine	0	0.0%
41	New Hampshire	0	0.0%
41	North Dakota	0	0.0%
41	Rhode Island	0	0.0%
41	South Dakota	0	0.0%
41	Vermont	0	0.0%
41	West Virginia	0	0.0%
41	Wyoming	0	0.0%
NA	Montana**	NA	NA
	District of Columbia**	NA	NA

Source: Federal Bureau of Investigation
   "Crime in the United States 2004" (Uniform Crime Reports, October 17, 2005)
*Arrests of youths 17 years and younger by law enforcement agencies submitting complete reports to the F.B.I. for 12 months in 2004. Includes nonnegligent manslaughter. See important note at beginning of this chapter.
**Not available.

Reported Juvenile Arrest Rate for Murder in 2004

National Rate = 4.3 Reported Arrests per 100,000 Juvenile Population*

ALPHA ORDER

RANK	STATE	RATE
14	Alabama	3.6
9	Alaska	4.6
23	Arizona	2.1
32	Arkansas	1.2
11	California	4.4
26	Colorado	1.8
26	Connecticut	1.8
19	Delaware	2.5
15	Florida	2.9
NA	Georgia**	NA
17	Hawaii	2.6
36	Idaho	0.7
NA	Illinois**	NA
24	Indiana	1.9
21	Iowa	2.2
37	Kansas	0.0
NA	Kentucky**	NA
7	Louisiana	5.4
37	Maine	0.0
8	Maryland	4.9
32	Massachusetts	1.2
32	Michigan	1.2
35	Minnesota	1.0
9	Mississippi	4.6
3	Missouri	7.9
NA	Montana**	NA
21	Nebraska	2.2
2	Nevada	9.0
37	New Hampshire	0.0
19	New Jersey	2.5
4	New Mexico	6.3
29	New York	1.6
6	North Carolina	5.5
37	North Dakota	0.0
30	Ohio	1.5
16	Oklahoma	2.7
5	Oregon	5.6
12	Pennsylvania	3.9
37	Rhode Island	0.0
NA	South Carolina**	NA
37	South Dakota	0.0
13	Tennessee	3.7
17	Texas	2.6
30	Utah	1.5
37	Vermont	0.0
28	Virginia	1.7
24	Washington	1.9
37	West Virginia	0.0
1	Wisconsin	55.4
37	Wyoming	0.0

RANK ORDER

RANK	STATE	RATE
1	Wisconsin	55.4
2	Nevada	9.0
3	Missouri	7.9
4	New Mexico	6.3
5	Oregon	5.6
6	North Carolina	5.5
7	Louisiana	5.4
8	Maryland	4.9
9	Alaska	4.6
9	Mississippi	4.6
11	California	4.4
12	Pennsylvania	3.9
13	Tennessee	3.7
14	Alabama	3.6
15	Florida	2.9
16	Oklahoma	2.7
17	Hawaii	2.6
17	Texas	2.6
19	Delaware	2.5
19	New Jersey	2.5
21	Iowa	2.2
21	Nebraska	2.2
23	Arizona	2.1
24	Indiana	1.9
24	Washington	1.9
26	Colorado	1.8
26	Connecticut	1.8
28	Virginia	1.7
29	New York	1.6
30	Ohio	1.5
30	Utah	1.5
32	Arkansas	1.2
32	Massachusetts	1.2
32	Michigan	1.2
35	Minnesota	1.0
36	Idaho	0.7
37	Kansas	0.0
37	Maine	0.0
37	New Hampshire	0.0
37	North Dakota	0.0
37	Rhode Island	0.0
37	South Dakota	0.0
37	Vermont	0.0
37	West Virginia	0.0
37	Wyoming	0.0
NA	Georgia**	NA
NA	Illinois**	NA
NA	Kentucky**	NA
NA	Montana**	NA
NA	South Carolina**	NA
	District of Columbia**	NA

Source: Morgan Quitno Press using data from Federal Bureau of Investigation
"Crime in the United States 2004" (Uniform Crime Reports, October 17, 2005)
*By law enforcement agencies submitting complete reports to the F.B.I. for 12 months in 2004. Includes nonnegligent manslaughter. Arrests of youths 17 years and younger divided into population of 10 to 17 year olds. See important note at beginning of this chapter.
**Not available.

Reported Arrests of Juveniles for Murder
As a Percent of All Such Arrests in 2004
National Percent = 10.5% of Reported Murder Arrests*

ALPHA ORDER

RANK	STATE	PERCENT
32	Alabama	5.7
8	Alaska	12.9
33	Arizona	5.6
29	Arkansas	6.1
15	California	9.5
34	Colorado	5.5
24	Connecticut	6.8
3	Delaware	20.0
21	Florida	7.8
16	Georgia	9.3
22	Hawaii	7.5
39	Idaho	4.2
13	Illinois	10.6
37	Indiana	4.3
6	Iowa	15.0
41	Kansas	0.0
34	Kentucky	5.5
26	Louisiana	6.6
41	Maine	0.0
12	Maryland	10.8
10	Massachusetts	11.1
40	Michigan	3.6
14	Minnesota	10.5
36	Mississippi	5.1
7	Missouri	13.1
NA	Montana**	NA
10	Nebraska	11.1
5	Nevada	16.1
41	New Hampshire	0.0
17	New Jersey	8.9
9	New Mexico	12.0
28	New York	6.5
23	North Carolina	6.9
41	North Dakota	0.0
29	Ohio	6.1
31	Oklahoma	5.8
4	Oregon	16.8
18	Pennsylvania	8.6
41	Rhode Island	0.0
2	South Carolina	20.5
41	South Dakota	0.0
26	Tennessee	6.6
19	Texas	8.5
25	Utah	6.7
41	Vermont	0.0
37	Virginia	4.3
20	Washington	8.1
41	West Virginia	0.0
1	Wisconsin	53.3
41	Wyoming	0.0

RANK ORDER

RANK	STATE	PERCENT
1	Wisconsin	53.3
2	South Carolina	20.5
3	Delaware	20.0
4	Oregon	16.8
5	Nevada	16.1
6	Iowa	15.0
7	Missouri	13.1
8	Alaska	12.9
9	New Mexico	12.0
10	Massachusetts	11.1
10	Nebraska	11.1
12	Maryland	10.8
13	Illinois	10.6
14	Minnesota	10.5
15	California	9.5
16	Georgia	9.3
17	New Jersey	8.9
18	Pennsylvania	8.6
19	Texas	8.5
20	Washington	8.1
21	Florida	7.8
22	Hawaii	7.5
23	North Carolina	6.9
24	Connecticut	6.8
25	Utah	6.7
26	Louisiana	6.6
26	Tennessee	6.6
28	New York	6.5
29	Arkansas	6.1
29	Ohio	6.1
31	Oklahoma	5.8
32	Alabama	5.7
33	Arizona	5.6
34	Colorado	5.5
34	Kentucky	5.5
36	Mississippi	5.1
37	Indiana	4.3
37	Virginia	4.3
39	Idaho	4.2
40	Michigan	3.6
41	Kansas	0.0
41	Maine	0.0
41	New Hampshire	0.0
41	North Dakota	0.0
41	Rhode Island	0.0
41	South Dakota	0.0
41	Vermont	0.0
41	West Virginia	0.0
41	Wyoming	0.0
NA	Montana**	NA
	District of Columbia**	NA

Source: Morgan Quitno Press using data from Federal Bureau of Investigation
    "Crime in the United States 2004" (Uniform Crime Reports, October 17, 2005)
*Arrests of youths 17 years and younger by law enforcement agencies submitting complete reports to the F.B.I. for 12 months in 2004. Includes nonnegligent manslaughter.
**Not available.

Reported Arrests of Juveniles for Rape in 2004

National Total = 3,385 Reported Arrests*

ALPHA ORDER

RANK	STATE	ARRESTS	% of USA
23	Alabama	36	1.1%
42	Alaska	13	0.4%
23	Arizona	36	1.1%
40	Arkansas	14	0.4%
3	California	297	8.8%
17	Colorado	63	1.9%
22	Connecticut	44	1.3%
38	Delaware	19	0.6%
2	Florida	347	10.3%
28	Georgia	28	0.8%
45	Hawaii	8	0.2%
36	Idaho	22	0.6%
13	Illinois	78	2.3%
29	Indiana	27	0.8%
31	Iowa	26	0.8%
29	Kansas	27	0.8%
21	Kentucky	45	1.3%
10	Louisiana	106	3.1%
37	Maine	21	0.6%
15	Maryland	71	2.1%
35	Massachusetts	23	0.7%
6	Michigan	154	4.5%
9	Minnesota	110	3.2%
31	Mississippi	26	0.8%
11	Missouri	99	2.9%
NA	Montana**	NA	NA
39	Nebraska	16	0.5%
23	Nevada	36	1.1%
43	New Hampshire	12	0.4%
14	New Jersey	72	2.1%
33	New Mexico	25	0.7%
12	New York	88	2.6%
16	North Carolina	68	2.0%
47	North Dakota	7	0.2%
7	Ohio	140	4.1%
20	Oklahoma	46	1.4%
27	Oregon	29	0.9%
4	Pennsylvania	240	7.1%
34	Rhode Island	24	0.7%
40	South Carolina	14	0.4%
45	South Dakota	8	0.2%
19	Tennessee	50	1.5%
1	Texas	348	10.3%
26	Utah	33	1.0%
43	Vermont	12	0.4%
18	Virginia	53	1.6%
8	Washington	113	3.3%
49	West Virginia	0	0.0%
5	Wisconsin	210	6.2%
48	Wyoming	1	0.0%

RANK ORDER

RANK	STATE	ARRESTS	% of USA
1	Texas	348	10.3%
2	Florida	347	10.3%
3	California	297	8.8%
4	Pennsylvania	240	7.1%
5	Wisconsin	210	6.2%
6	Michigan	154	4.5%
7	Ohio	140	4.1%
8	Washington	113	3.3%
9	Minnesota	110	3.2%
10	Louisiana	106	3.1%
11	Missouri	99	2.9%
12	New York	88	2.6%
13	Illinois	78	2.3%
14	New Jersey	72	2.1%
15	Maryland	71	2.1%
16	North Carolina	68	2.0%
17	Colorado	63	1.9%
18	Virginia	53	1.6%
19	Tennessee	50	1.5%
20	Oklahoma	46	1.4%
21	Kentucky	45	1.3%
22	Connecticut	44	1.3%
23	Alabama	36	1.1%
23	Arizona	36	1.1%
23	Nevada	36	1.1%
26	Utah	33	1.0%
27	Oregon	29	0.9%
28	Georgia	28	0.8%
29	Indiana	27	0.8%
29	Kansas	27	0.8%
31	Iowa	26	0.8%
31	Mississippi	26	0.8%
33	New Mexico	25	0.7%
34	Rhode Island	24	0.7%
35	Massachusetts	23	0.7%
36	Idaho	22	0.6%
37	Maine	21	0.6%
38	Delaware	19	0.6%
39	Nebraska	16	0.5%
40	Arkansas	14	0.4%
40	South Carolina	14	0.4%
42	Alaska	13	0.4%
43	New Hampshire	12	0.4%
43	Vermont	12	0.4%
45	Hawaii	8	0.2%
45	South Dakota	8	0.2%
47	North Dakota	7	0.2%
48	Wyoming	1	0.0%
49	West Virginia	0	0.0%
NA	Montana**	NA	NA
	District of Columbia**	NA	NA

Source: Federal Bureau of Investigation
"Crime in the United States 2004" (Uniform Crime Reports, October 17, 2005)
*Arrests of youths 17 years and younger by law enforcement agencies submitting complete reports to the F.B.I. for 12 months in 2004. Forcible rape is the carnal knowledge of a female forcibly and against her will. Assaults or attempts to commit rape by force or threat of force are included. However, statutory rape without force and other sex offenses are excluded. See important note at beginning of this chapter. **Not available.

Reported Juvenile Arrest Rate for Rape in 2004

National Rate = 12.9 Reported Arrests per 100,000 Juvenile Population*

ALPHA ORDER

RANK ORDER

RANK	STATE	RATE	RANK	STATE	RATE
35	Alabama	8.0	1	Wisconsin	40.6
14	Alaska	14.9	2	Louisiana	28.6
41	Arizona	5.5	3	Minnesota	27.2
33	Arkansas	8.5	4	Delaware	23.6
39	California	7.3	5	Washington	21.1
19	Colorado	14.0	6	Vermont	20.8
22	Connecticut	13.3	7	Rhode Island	20.6
4	Delaware	23.6	8	Pennsylvania	20.2
9	Florida	18.8	9	Florida	18.8
NA	Georgia**	NA	10	Missouri	18.6
40	Hawaii	6.9	11	Utah	17.0
17	Idaho	14.4	12	South Dakota	16.4
NA	Illinois**	NA	13	Ohio	15.7
42	Indiana	5.0	14	Alaska	14.9
31	Iowa	9.6	15	Maine	14.8
26	Kansas	12.2	15	Mississippi	14.8
NA	Kentucky**	NA	17	Idaho	14.4
2	Louisiana	28.6	18	New Mexico	14.3
15	Maine	14.8	19	Colorado	14.0
27	Maryland	10.9	19	Nevada	14.0
43	Massachusetts	4.7	21	Michigan	13.8
21	Michigan	13.8	22	Connecticut	13.3
3	Minnesota	27.2	23	North Dakota	12.9
15	Mississippi	14.8	24	Texas	12.8
10	Missouri	18.6	25	Oklahoma	12.3
NA	Montana**	NA	26	Kansas	12.2
32	Nebraska	8.7	27	Maryland	10.9
19	Nevada	14.0	28	New Hampshire	10.3
28	New Hampshire	10.3	29	North Carolina	10.1
37	New Jersey	7.5	30	Tennessee	9.7
18	New Mexico	14.3	31	Iowa	9.6
34	New York	8.2	32	Nebraska	8.7
29	North Carolina	10.1	33	Arkansas	8.5
23	North Dakota	12.9	34	New York	8.2
13	Ohio	15.7	35	Alabama	8.0
25	Oklahoma	12.3	36	Oregon	7.7
36	Oregon	7.7	37	New Jersey	7.5
8	Pennsylvania	20.2	38	Virginia	7.4
7	Rhode Island	20.6	39	California	7.3
NA	South Carolina**	NA	40	Hawaii	6.9
12	South Dakota	16.4	41	Arizona	5.5
30	Tennessee	9.7	42	Indiana	5.0
24	Texas	12.8	43	Massachusetts	4.7
11	Utah	17.0	44	Wyoming	1.8
6	Vermont	20.8	45	West Virginia	0.0
38	Virginia	7.4	NA	Georgia**	NA
5	Washington	21.1	NA	Illinois**	NA
45	West Virginia	0.0	NA	Kentucky**	NA
1	Wisconsin	40.6	NA	Montana**	NA
44	Wyoming	1.8	NA	South Carolina**	NA
				District of Columbia**	NA

Source: Morgan Quitno Press using data from Federal Bureau of Investigation
    "Crime in the United States 2004" (Uniform Crime Reports, October 17, 2005)
*By law enforcement agencies submitting complete reports to the F.B.I. for 12 months in 2004. Arrests of youths 17
years and younger divided into population of 10 to 17 year olds. See important note at beginning of this chapter.
Forcible rape is the carnal knowledge of a female forcibly and against her will. Assaults or attempts to commit rape
by force or threat of force are included. **Not available.

Reported Arrests of Juveniles for Rape
As a Percent of All Such Arrests in 2004
National Percent = 16.2% of Reported Rape Arrests*

Source: Morgan Quitno Press using data from Federal Bureau of Investigation

ALPHA ORDER

RANK	STATE	PERCENT
47	Alabama	7.9
28	Alaska	15.9
23	Arizona	16.2
37	Arkansas	12.5
33	California	14.1
32	Colorado	14.5
16	Connecticut	18.4
14	Delaware	18.8
24	Florida	16.1
45	Georgia	9.8
41	Hawaii	11.0
9	Idaho	20.8
35	Illinois	13.9
38	Indiana	12.3
7	Iowa	21.1
18	Kansas	18.1
1	Kentucky	31.5
5	Louisiana	23.4
11	Maine	20.2
29	Maryland	15.2
42	Massachusetts	10.7
19	Michigan	17.7
12	Minnesota	19.7
38	Mississippi	12.3
15	Missouri	18.6
NA	Montana**	NA
46	Nebraska	8.2
19	Nevada	17.7
22	New Hampshire	16.7
30	New Jersey	14.9
17	New Mexico	18.2
40	New York	11.9
43	North Carolina	10.4
10	North Dakota	20.6
8	Ohio	20.9
36	Oklahoma	13.4
44	Oregon	9.9
13	Pennsylvania	18.9
4	Rhode Island	25.5
6	South Carolina	21.2
34	South Dakota	14.0
21	Tennessee	16.9
26	Texas	16.0
3	Utah	25.8
26	Vermont	16.0
24	Virginia	16.1
30	Washington	14.9
49	West Virginia	0.0
2	Wisconsin	27.7
48	Wyoming	3.4

RANK ORDER

RANK	STATE	PERCENT
1	Kentucky	31.5
2	Wisconsin	27.7
3	Utah	25.8
4	Rhode Island	25.5
5	Louisiana	23.4
6	South Carolina	21.2
7	Iowa	21.1
8	Ohio	20.9
9	Idaho	20.8
10	North Dakota	20.6
11	Maine	20.2
12	Minnesota	19.7
13	Pennsylvania	18.9
14	Delaware	18.8
15	Missouri	18.6
16	Connecticut	18.4
17	New Mexico	18.2
18	Kansas	18.1
19	Michigan	17.7
19	Nevada	17.7
21	Tennessee	16.9
22	New Hampshire	16.7
23	Arizona	16.2
24	Florida	16.1
24	Virginia	16.1
26	Texas	16.0
26	Vermont	16.0
28	Alaska	15.9
29	Maryland	15.2
30	New Jersey	14.9
30	Washington	14.9
32	Colorado	14.5
33	California	14.1
34	South Dakota	14.0
35	Illinois	13.9
36	Oklahoma	13.4
37	Arkansas	12.5
38	Indiana	12.3
38	Mississippi	12.3
40	New York	11.9
41	Hawaii	11.0
42	Massachusetts	10.7
43	North Carolina	10.4
44	Oregon	9.9
45	Georgia	9.8
46	Nebraska	8.2
47	Alabama	7.9
48	Wyoming	3.4
49	West Virginia	0.0
NA	Montana**	NA
	District of Columbia**	NA

Source: Morgan Quitno Press using data from Federal Bureau of Investigation
   "Crime in the United States 2004" (Uniform Crime Reports, October 17, 2005)
*Arrests of youths 17 years and younger by law enforcement agencies submitting complete reports to the F.B.I. for
12 months in 2004. Forcible rape is the carnal knowledge of a female forcibly and against her will. Assaults or
attempts to commit rape by force or threat of force are included. However, statutory rape without force and other sex
offenses are excluded. **Not available.

Reported Arrests of Juveniles for Robbery in 2004

National Total = 20,550 Reported Arrests*

RANK	STATE	ARRESTS	% of USA		RANK	STATE	ARRESTS	% of USA
23	Alabama	199	1.0%		1	California	4,482	21.8%
41	Alaska	26	0.1%		2	Florida	2,017	9.8%
20	Arizona	265	1.3%		3	Pennsylvania	1,628	7.9%
39	Arkansas	42	0.2%		4	Texas	1,374	6.7%
1	California	4,482	21.8%		5	New Jersey	1,249	6.1%
25	Colorado	176	0.9%		6	Illinois	1,173	5.7%
15	Connecticut	301	1.5%		7	Maryland	1,169	5.7%
30	Delaware	82	0.4%		8	New York	1,073	5.2%
2	Florida	2,017	9.8%		9	Wisconsin	535	2.6%
17	Georgia	285	1.4%		10	Ohio	501	2.4%
28	Hawaii	105	0.5%		11	North Carolina	389	1.9%
46	Idaho	7	0.0%		12	Missouri	349	1.7%
6	Illinois	1,173	5.7%		13	Michigan	313	1.5%
22	Indiana	235	1.1%		14	Tennessee	311	1.5%
33	Iowa	71	0.3%		15	Connecticut	301	1.5%
36	Kansas	57	0.3%		16	Washington	299	1.5%
34	Kentucky	69	0.3%		17	Georgia	285	1.4%
21	Louisiana	243	1.2%		18	Virginia	281	1.4%
40	Maine	32	0.2%		19	Oregon	273	1.3%
7	Maryland	1,169	5.7%		20	Arizona	265	1.3%
24	Massachusetts	179	0.9%		21	Louisiana	243	1.2%
13	Michigan	313	1.5%		22	Indiana	235	1.1%
29	Minnesota	93	0.5%		23	Alabama	199	1.0%
32	Mississippi	73	0.4%		24	Massachusetts	179	0.9%
12	Missouri	349	1.7%		25	Colorado	176	0.9%
NA	Montana**	NA	NA		26	Nevada	173	0.8%
34	Nebraska	69	0.3%		27	Oklahoma	107	0.5%
26	Nevada	173	0.8%		28	Hawaii	105	0.5%
43	New Hampshire	19	0.1%		29	Minnesota	93	0.5%
5	New Jersey	1,249	6.1%		30	Delaware	82	0.4%
38	New Mexico	46	0.2%		31	Rhode Island	79	0.4%
8	New York	1,073	5.2%		32	Mississippi	73	0.4%
11	North Carolina	389	1.9%		33	Iowa	71	0.3%
45	North Dakota	9	0.0%		34	Kentucky	69	0.3%
10	Ohio	501	2.4%		34	Nebraska	69	0.3%
27	Oklahoma	107	0.5%		36	Kansas	57	0.3%
19	Oregon	273	1.3%		36	Utah	57	0.3%
3	Pennsylvania	1,628	7.9%		38	New Mexico	46	0.2%
31	Rhode Island	79	0.4%		39	Arkansas	42	0.2%
42	South Carolina	24	0.1%		40	Maine	32	0.2%
48	South Dakota	0	0.0%		41	Alaska	26	0.1%
14	Tennessee	311	1.5%		42	South Carolina	24	0.1%
4	Texas	1,374	6.7%		43	New Hampshire	19	0.1%
36	Utah	57	0.3%		44	West Virginia	10	0.0%
48	Vermont	0	0.0%		45	North Dakota	9	0.0%
18	Virginia	281	1.4%		46	Idaho	7	0.0%
16	Washington	299	1.5%		47	Wyoming	1	0.0%
44	West Virginia	10	0.0%		48	South Dakota	0	0.0%
9	Wisconsin	535	2.6%		48	Vermont	0	0.0%
47	Wyoming	1	0.0%		NA	Montana**	NA	NA
						District of Columbia**	NA	NA

Source: Federal Bureau of Investigation
    "Crime in the United States 2004" (Uniform Crime Reports, October 17, 2005)
*Arrests of youths 17 years and younger by law enforcement agencies submitting complete reports to the F.B.I. for 12 months in 2004. Robbery is the taking or attempting to take anything of value by force or threat of force. See important note at beginning of this chapter. **Not available.*

Reported Juvenile Arrest Rate for Robbery in 2004

National Rate = 78.5 Reported Arrests per 100,000 Juvenile Population*

ALPHA ORDER				RANK ORDER		
RANK	STATE	RATE		RANK	STATE	RATE
21	Alabama	44.4		1	Maryland	179.9
29	Alaska	29.8		2	Pennsylvania	137.0
24	Arizona	40.1		3	New Jersey	129.8
36	Arkansas	25.5		4	California	109.5
4	California	109.5		5	Florida	109.4
25	Colorado	39.2		6	Wisconsin	103.4
9	Connecticut	91.3		7	Delaware	101.9
7	Delaware	101.9		8	New York	99.5
5	Florida	109.4		9	Connecticut	91.3
NA	Georgia**	NA		10	Hawaii	90.6
10	Hawaii	90.6		11	Oregon	72.5
42	Idaho	4.6		12	Rhode Island	67.7
NA	Illinois**	NA		13	Nevada	67.3
22	Indiana	43.9		14	Missouri	65.6
34	Iowa	26.2		15	Louisiana	65.5
35	Kansas	25.8		16	Tennessee	60.0
NA	Kentucky**	NA		17	North Carolina	57.9
15	Louisiana	65.5		18	Ohio	56.2
38	Maine	22.5		19	Washington	55.9
1	Maryland	179.9		20	Texas	50.6
28	Massachusetts	36.8		21	Alabama	44.4
32	Michigan	28.0		22	Indiana	43.9
37	Minnesota	23.0		23	Mississippi	41.5
23	Mississippi	41.5		24	Arizona	40.1
14	Missouri	65.6		25	Colorado	39.2
NA	Montana**	NA		26	Virginia	39.1
27	Nebraska	37.6		27	Nebraska	37.6
13	Nevada	67.3		28	Massachusetts	36.8
40	New Hampshire	16.4		29	Alaska	29.8
3	New Jersey	129.8		30	Utah	29.3
33	New Mexico	26.3		31	Oklahoma	28.6
8	New York	99.5		32	Michigan	28.0
17	North Carolina	57.9		33	New Mexico	26.3
39	North Dakota	16.6		34	Iowa	26.2
18	Ohio	56.2		35	Kansas	25.8
31	Oklahoma	28.6		36	Arkansas	25.5
11	Oregon	72.5		37	Minnesota	23.0
2	Pennsylvania	137.0		38	Maine	22.5
12	Rhode Island	67.7		39	North Dakota	16.6
NA	South Carolina**	NA		40	New Hampshire	16.4
44	South Dakota	0.0		41	West Virginia	9.5
16	Tennessee	60.0		42	Idaho	4.6
20	Texas	50.6		43	Wyoming	1.8
30	Utah	29.3		44	South Dakota	0.0
44	Vermont	0.0		44	Vermont	0.0
26	Virginia	39.1		NA	Georgia**	NA
19	Washington	55.9		NA	Illinois**	NA
41	West Virginia	9.5		NA	Kentucky**	NA
6	Wisconsin	103.4		NA	Montana**	NA
43	Wyoming	1.8		NA	South Carolina**	NA
					District of Columbia**	NA

Source: Morgan Quitno Press using data from Federal Bureau of Investigation
   "Crime in the United States 2004" (Uniform Crime Reports, October 17, 2005)
*By law enforcement agencies submitting complete reports to the F.B.I. for 12 months in 2004. Arrests of youths 17
years and younger divided into population of 10 to 17 year olds. See important note at beginning of this chapter.
Robbery is the taking or attempting to take anything of value by force or threat of force.*
***Not available.*

Reported Arrests of Juveniles for Robbery
As a Percent of All Such Arrests in 2004
National Percent = 23.2% of Reported Robbery Arrests*

ALPHA ORDER

RANK	STATE	PERCENT
38	Alabama	14.2
23	Alaska	19.4
28	Arizona	18.5
45	Arkansas	9.4
11	California	26.7
16	Colorado	22.2
14	Connecticut	23.5
10	Delaware	26.9
16	Florida	22.2
30	Georgia	17.0
3	Hawaii	36.0
46	Idaho	7.9
2	Illinois	40.3
33	Indiana	15.7
13	Iowa	23.8
15	Kansas	23.1
41	Kentucky	13.1
21	Louisiana	20.2
24	Maine	19.0
5	Maryland	34.1
20	Massachusetts	20.3
36	Michigan	14.4
9	Minnesota	27.3
37	Mississippi	14.3
26	Missouri	18.8
NA	Montana**	NA
18	Nebraska	21.8
35	Nevada	14.5
30	New Hampshire	17.0
6	New Jersey	30.5
43	New Mexico	12.5
7	New York	29.6
40	North Carolina	13.7
1	North Dakota	56.3
25	Ohio	18.9
30	Oklahoma	17.0
22	Oregon	19.7
12	Pennsylvania	24.6
8	Rhode Island	28.0
42	South Carolina	13.0
48	South Dakota	0.0
34	Tennessee	15.5
26	Texas	18.8
39	Utah	14.1
48	Vermont	0.0
29	Virginia	18.1
19	Washington	21.5
44	West Virginia	10.8
4	Wisconsin	35.1
47	Wyoming	3.8

RANK ORDER

RANK	STATE	PERCENT
1	North Dakota	56.3
2	Illinois	40.3
3	Hawaii	36.0
4	Wisconsin	35.1
5	Maryland	34.1
6	New Jersey	30.5
7	New York	29.6
8	Rhode Island	28.0
9	Minnesota	27.3
10	Delaware	26.9
11	California	26.7
12	Pennsylvania	24.6
13	Iowa	23.8
14	Connecticut	23.5
15	Kansas	23.1
16	Colorado	22.2
16	Florida	22.2
18	Nebraska	21.8
19	Washington	21.5
20	Massachusetts	20.3
21	Louisiana	20.2
22	Oregon	19.7
23	Alaska	19.4
24	Maine	19.0
25	Ohio	18.9
26	Missouri	18.8
26	Texas	18.8
28	Arizona	18.5
29	Virginia	18.1
30	Georgia	17.0
30	New Hampshire	17.0
30	Oklahoma	17.0
33	Indiana	15.7
34	Tennessee	15.5
35	Nevada	14.5
36	Michigan	14.4
37	Mississippi	14.3
38	Alabama	14.2
39	Utah	14.1
40	North Carolina	13.7
41	Kentucky	13.1
42	South Carolina	13.0
43	New Mexico	12.5
44	West Virginia	10.8
45	Arkansas	9.4
46	Idaho	7.9
47	Wyoming	3.8
48	South Dakota	0.0
48	Vermont	0.0
NA	Montana**	NA
	District of Columbia**	NA

Source: Morgan Quitno Press using data from Federal Bureau of Investigation
"Crime in the United States 2004" (Uniform Crime Reports, October 17, 2005)
*Arrests of youths 17 years and younger by law enforcement agencies submitting complete reports to the F.B.I. for
12 months in 2004. Robbery is the taking or attempting to take anything of value by force or threat of force.
**Not available.

Reported Arrests of Juveniles for Aggravated Assault in 2004

National Total = 49,835 Reported Arrests*

ALPHA ORDER

RANK	STATE	ARRESTS	% of USA
30	Alabama	306	0.6%
40	Alaska	135	0.3%
10	Arizona	1,238	2.5%
35	Arkansas	176	0.4%
1	California	9,246	18.6%
20	Colorado	778	1.6%
22	Connecticut	623	1.3%
31	Delaware	292	0.6%
2	Florida	6,244	12.5%
16	Georgia	896	1.8%
37	Hawaii	160	0.3%
34	Idaho	219	0.4%
7	Illinois	1,986	4.0%
9	Indiana	1,461	2.9%
24	Iowa	565	1.1%
32	Kansas	262	0.5%
38	Kentucky	157	0.3%
13	Louisiana	1,120	2.2%
43	Maine	90	0.2%
6	Maryland	2,055	4.1%
14	Massachusetts	1,106	2.2%
11	Michigan	1,166	2.3%
27	Minnesota	483	1.0%
42	Mississippi	112	0.2%
15	Missouri	1,052	2.1%
NA	Montana**	NA	NA
41	Nebraska	130	0.3%
28	Nevada	465	0.9%
45	New Hampshire	53	0.1%
5	New Jersey	2,112	4.2%
29	New Mexico	381	0.8%
8	New York	1,620	3.3%
12	North Carolina	1,143	2.3%
49	North Dakota	16	0.0%
21	Ohio	657	1.3%
23	Oklahoma	573	1.1%
26	Oregon	507	1.0%
4	Pennsylvania	3,048	6.1%
39	Rhode Island	156	0.3%
36	South Carolina	169	0.3%
47	South Dakota	36	0.1%
18	Tennessee	850	1.7%
3	Texas	3,367	6.8%
33	Utah	247	0.5%
48	Vermont	26	0.1%
25	Virginia	512	1.0%
19	Washington	837	1.7%
46	West Virginia	51	0.1%
17	Wisconsin	884	1.8%
44	Wyoming	67	0.1%

RANK ORDER

RANK	STATE	ARRESTS	% of USA
1	California	9,246	18.6%
2	Florida	6,244	12.5%
3	Texas	3,367	6.8%
4	Pennsylvania	3,048	6.1%
5	New Jersey	2,112	4.2%
6	Maryland	2,055	4.1%
7	Illinois	1,986	4.0%
8	New York	1,620	3.3%
9	Indiana	1,461	2.9%
10	Arizona	1,238	2.5%
11	Michigan	1,166	2.3%
12	North Carolina	1,143	2.3%
13	Louisiana	1,120	2.2%
14	Massachusetts	1,106	2.2%
15	Missouri	1,052	2.1%
16	Georgia	896	1.8%
17	Wisconsin	884	1.8%
18	Tennessee	850	1.7%
19	Washington	837	1.7%
20	Colorado	778	1.6%
21	Ohio	657	1.3%
22	Connecticut	623	1.3%
23	Oklahoma	573	1.1%
24	Iowa	565	1.1%
25	Virginia	512	1.0%
26	Oregon	507	1.0%
27	Minnesota	483	1.0%
28	Nevada	465	0.9%
29	New Mexico	381	0.8%
30	Alabama	306	0.6%
31	Delaware	292	0.6%
32	Kansas	262	0.5%
33	Utah	247	0.5%
34	Idaho	219	0.4%
35	Arkansas	176	0.4%
36	South Carolina	169	0.3%
37	Hawaii	160	0.3%
38	Kentucky	157	0.3%
39	Rhode Island	156	0.3%
40	Alaska	135	0.3%
41	Nebraska	130	0.3%
42	Mississippi	112	0.2%
43	Maine	90	0.2%
44	Wyoming	67	0.1%
45	New Hampshire	53	0.1%
46	West Virginia	51	0.1%
47	South Dakota	36	0.1%
48	Vermont	26	0.1%
49	North Dakota	16	0.0%
NA	Montana**	NA	NA
	District of Columbia**	NA	NA

Source: Federal Bureau of Investigation
  "Crime in the United States 2004" (Uniform Crime Reports, October 17, 2005)
*Arrests of youths 17 years and younger by law enforcement agencies submitting complete reports to the F.B.I. for 12 months in 2004. Aggravated assault is an attack for the purpose of inflicting severe bodily injury. See important note at beginning of this chapter.
**Not available.

Reported Juvenile Arrest Rate for Aggravated Assault in 2004

National Rate = 190.4 Reported Arrests per 100,000 Juvenile Population*

ALPHA ORDER

RANK ORDER

RANK	STATE	RATE		RANK	STATE	RATE
39	Alabama	68.3		1	Delaware	362.7
21	Alaska	154.6		2	Florida	338.7
14	Arizona	187.6		3	Maryland	316.2
33	Arkansas	106.9		4	Louisiana	301.9
8	California	225.8		5	Indiana	272.8
16	Colorado	173.1		6	Pennsylvania	256.4
13	Connecticut	189.0		7	Massachusetts	227.2
1	Delaware	362.7		8	California	225.8
2	Florida	338.7		9	New Jersey	219.4
NA	Georgia**	NA		10	New Mexico	218.2
25	Hawaii	138.1		11	Iowa	208.2
24	Idaho	143.2		12	Missouri	197.8
NA	Illinois**	NA		13	Connecticut	189.0
5	Indiana	272.8		14	Arizona	187.6
11	Iowa	208.2		15	Nevada	181.0
32	Kansas	118.5		16	Colorado	173.1
NA	Kentucky**	NA		17	Wisconsin	170.8
4	Louisiana	301.9		18	North Carolina	170.0
41	Maine	63.3		19	Tennessee	164.1
3	Maryland	316.2		20	Washington	156.4
7	Massachusetts	227.2		21	Alaska	154.6
34	Michigan	104.2		22	Oklahoma	152.9
31	Minnesota	119.2		23	New York	150.2
40	Mississippi	63.7		24	Idaho	143.2
12	Missouri	197.8		25	Hawaii	138.1
NA	Montana**	NA		26	Oregon	134.7
38	Nebraska	70.9		27	Rhode Island	133.7
15	Nevada	181.0		28	Utah	126.9
43	New Hampshire	45.7		29	Texas	123.9
9	New Jersey	219.4		30	Wyoming	122.5
10	New Mexico	218.2		31	Minnesota	119.2
23	New York	150.2		32	Kansas	118.5
18	North Carolina	170.0		33	Arkansas	106.9
45	North Dakota	29.5		34	Michigan	104.2
36	Ohio	73.7		35	South Dakota	73.8
22	Oklahoma	152.9		36	Ohio	73.7
26	Oregon	134.7		37	Virginia	71.2
6	Pennsylvania	256.4		38	Nebraska	70.9
27	Rhode Island	133.7		39	Alabama	68.3
NA	South Carolina**	NA		40	Mississippi	63.7
35	South Dakota	73.8		41	Maine	63.3
19	Tennessee	164.1		42	West Virginia	48.4
29	Texas	123.9		43	New Hampshire	45.7
28	Utah	126.9		44	Vermont	45.1
44	Vermont	45.1		45	North Dakota	29.5
37	Virginia	71.2		NA	Georgia**	NA
20	Washington	156.4		NA	Illinois**	NA
42	West Virginia	48.4		NA	Kentucky**	NA
17	Wisconsin	170.8		NA	Montana**	NA
30	Wyoming	122.5		NA	South Carolina**	NA
					District of Columbia**	NA

Source: Morgan Quitno Press using data from Federal Bureau of Investigation
  "Crime in the United States 2004" (Uniform Crime Reports, October 17, 2005)
*By law enforcement agencies submitting complete reports to the F.B.I. for 12 months in 2004. Arrests of youths 17 years and younger divided into population of 10 to 17 year olds. See important note at beginning of this chapter. Aggravated assault is an attack for the purpose of inflicting severe bodily injury.
**Not available.

195

Reported Arrests of Juveniles for Aggravated Assault
As a Percent of All Such Arrests in 2004
National Percent = 14.0% of Reported Aggravated Assault Arrests*

ALPHA ORDER

RANK	STATE	PERCENT
47	Alabama	7.8
40	Alaska	10.9
13	Arizona	17.4
48	Arkansas	7.4
43	California	9.5
21	Colorado	16.3
11	Connecticut	18.6
9	Delaware	19.8
22	Florida	16.1
36	Georgia	12.5
6	Hawaii	20.8
7	Idaho	20.3
1	Illinois	35.4
19	Indiana	16.4
14	Iowa	17.3
22	Kansas	16.1
26	Kentucky	14.7
26	Louisiana	14.7
24	Maine	15.4
3	Maryland	25.8
10	Massachusetts	18.9
41	Michigan	10.8
4	Minnesota	23.4
46	Mississippi	8.2
41	Missouri	10.8
NA	Montana**	NA
33	Nebraska	12.8
38	Nevada	12.4
19	New Hampshire	16.4
5	New Jersey	21.1
31	New Mexico	13.6
17	New York	16.6
44	North Carolina	9.2
39	North Dakota	11.9
18	Ohio	16.5
33	Oklahoma	12.8
16	Oregon	16.9
8	Pennsylvania	20.1
12	Rhode Island	18.1
32	South Carolina	13.0
25	South Dakota	15.3
45	Tennessee	8.7
28	Texas	14.5
2	Utah	28.6
35	Vermont	12.7
36	Virginia	12.5
14	Washington	17.3
49	West Virginia	5.8
29	Wisconsin	14.3
30	Wyoming	14.0

RANK ORDER

RANK	STATE	PERCENT
1	Illinois	35.4
2	Utah	28.6
3	Maryland	25.8
4	Minnesota	23.4
5	New Jersey	21.1
6	Hawaii	20.8
7	Idaho	20.3
8	Pennsylvania	20.1
9	Delaware	19.8
10	Massachusetts	18.9
11	Connecticut	18.6
12	Rhode Island	18.1
13	Arizona	17.4
14	Iowa	17.3
14	Washington	17.3
16	Oregon	16.9
17	New York	16.6
18	Ohio	16.5
19	Indiana	16.4
19	New Hampshire	16.4
21	Colorado	16.3
22	Florida	16.1
22	Kansas	16.1
24	Maine	15.4
25	South Dakota	15.3
26	Kentucky	14.7
26	Louisiana	14.7
28	Texas	14.5
29	Wisconsin	14.3
30	Wyoming	14.0
31	New Mexico	13.6
32	South Carolina	13.0
33	Nebraska	12.8
33	Oklahoma	12.8
35	Vermont	12.7
36	Georgia	12.5
36	Virginia	12.5
38	Nevada	12.4
39	North Dakota	11.9
40	Alaska	10.9
41	Michigan	10.8
41	Missouri	10.8
43	California	9.5
44	North Carolina	9.2
45	Tennessee	8.7
46	Mississippi	8.2
47	Alabama	7.8
48	Arkansas	7.4
49	West Virginia	5.8
NA	Montana**	NA
	District of Columbia**	NA

Source: Morgan Quitno Press using data from Federal Bureau of Investigation
    "Crime in the United States 2004" (Uniform Crime Reports, October 17, 2005)
*Arrests of youths 17 years and younger by law enforcement agencies submitting complete reports to the F.B.I. for 12 months in 2004. Aggravated assault is an attack for the purpose of inflicting severe bodily injury.
**Not available.

Reported Arrests of Juveniles for Property Crime in 2004

National Total = 364,803 Reported Arrests*

ALPHA ORDER

RANK	STATE	ARRESTS	% of USA
30	Alabama	3,392	0.9%
42	Alaska	1,395	0.4%
8	Arizona	11,839	3.2%
36	Arkansas	2,436	0.7%
1	California	45,386	12.4%
13	Colorado	9,040	2.5%
28	Connecticut	3,949	1.1%
41	Delaware	1,418	0.4%
2	Florida	36,082	9.9%
24	Georgia	5,669	1.6%
39	Hawaii	1,593	0.4%
31	Idaho	2,884	0.8%
20	Illinois	6,188	1.7%
18	Indiana	6,895	1.9%
26	Iowa	4,985	1.4%
33	Kansas	2,630	0.7%
37	Kentucky	2,298	0.6%
17	Louisiana	7,345	2.0%
34	Maine	2,483	0.7%
6	Maryland	12,797	3.5%
35	Massachusetts	2,475	0.7%
10	Michigan	10,094	2.8%
19	Minnesota	6,888	1.9%
32	Mississippi	2,659	0.7%
14	Missouri	8,600	2.4%
NA	Montana**	NA	NA
29	Nebraska	3,571	1.0%
27	Nevada	4,336	1.2%
44	New Hampshire	929	0.3%
15	New Jersey	8,486	2.3%
38	New Mexico	2,152	0.6%
7	New York	12,040	3.3%
12	North Carolina	9,154	2.5%
43	North Dakota	1,007	0.3%
11	Ohio	9,449	2.6%
22	Oklahoma	6,054	1.7%
16	Oregon	7,642	2.1%
5	Pennsylvania	13,946	3.8%
40	Rhode Island	1,566	0.4%
46	South Carolina	815	0.2%
47	South Dakota	768	0.2%
21	Tennessee	6,102	1.7%
3	Texas	36,070	9.9%
25	Utah	5,121	1.4%
49	Vermont	280	0.1%
23	Virginia	5,834	1.6%
9	Washington	10,504	2.9%
48	West Virginia	633	0.2%
4	Wisconsin	16,000	4.4%
45	Wyoming	924	0.3%

RANK ORDER

RANK	STATE	ARRESTS	% of USA
1	California	45,386	12.4%
2	Florida	36,082	9.9%
3	Texas	36,070	9.9%
4	Wisconsin	16,000	4.4%
5	Pennsylvania	13,946	3.8%
6	Maryland	12,797	3.5%
7	New York	12,040	3.3%
8	Arizona	11,839	3.2%
9	Washington	10,504	2.9%
10	Michigan	10,094	2.8%
11	Ohio	9,449	2.6%
12	North Carolina	9,154	2.5%
13	Colorado	9,040	2.5%
14	Missouri	8,600	2.4%
15	New Jersey	8,486	2.3%
16	Oregon	7,642	2.1%
17	Louisiana	7,345	2.0%
18	Indiana	6,895	1.9%
19	Minnesota	6,888	1.9%
20	Illinois	6,188	1.7%
21	Tennessee	6,102	1.7%
22	Oklahoma	6,054	1.7%
23	Virginia	5,834	1.6%
24	Georgia	5,669	1.6%
25	Utah	5,121	1.4%
26	Iowa	4,985	1.4%
27	Nevada	4,336	1.2%
28	Connecticut	3,949	1.1%
29	Nebraska	3,571	1.0%
30	Alabama	3,392	0.9%
31	Idaho	2,884	0.8%
32	Mississippi	2,659	0.7%
33	Kansas	2,630	0.7%
34	Maine	2,483	0.7%
35	Massachusetts	2,475	0.7%
36	Arkansas	2,436	0.7%
37	Kentucky	2,298	0.6%
38	New Mexico	2,152	0.6%
39	Hawaii	1,593	0.4%
40	Rhode Island	1,566	0.4%
41	Delaware	1,418	0.4%
42	Alaska	1,395	0.4%
43	North Dakota	1,007	0.3%
44	New Hampshire	929	0.3%
45	Wyoming	924	0.3%
46	South Carolina	815	0.2%
47	South Dakota	768	0.2%
48	West Virginia	633	0.2%
49	Vermont	280	0.1%
NA	Montana**	NA	NA
	District of Columbia**	NA	NA

Source: Federal Bureau of Investigation
"Crime in the United States 2004" (Uniform Crime Reports, October 17, 2005)
*Arrests of youths 17 years and younger by law enforcement agencies submitting complete reports to the F.B.I. for 12 months in 2004. Property crimes are offenses of burglary, larceny-theft, motor vehicle theft and arson. See important note at beginning of this chapter.
**Not available.

Reported Juvenile Arrest Rate for Property Crime in 2004

National Rate = 1,393.4 Reported Arrests per 100,000 Juvenile Population*

ALPHA ORDER

RANK	STATE	RATE
42	Alabama	757.1
21	Alaska	1,597.6
13	Arizona	1,793.6
24	Arkansas	1,479.8
36	California	1,108.5
4	Colorado	2,011.7
31	Connecticut	1,197.8
14	Delaware	1,761.5
8	Florida	1,957.4
NA	Georgia**	NA
25	Hawaii	1,374.5
10	Idaho	1,885.4
NA	Illinois**	NA
29	Indiana	1,287.6
12	Iowa	1,836.8
32	Kansas	1,189.8
NA	Kentucky**	NA
5	Louisiana	1,979.6
15	Maine	1,746.7
6	Maryland	1,969.2
44	Massachusetts	508.3
38	Michigan	902.1
16	Minnesota	1,700.5
23	Mississippi	1,512.8
19	Missouri	1,616.9
NA	Montana**	NA
9	Nebraska	1,947.7
18	Nevada	1,687.6
41	New Hampshire	800.8
39	New Jersey	881.7
30	New Mexico	1,232.4
35	New York	1,116.1
26	North Carolina	1,361.6
11	North Dakota	1,857.8
37	Ohio	1,060.4
20	Oklahoma	1,615.5
3	Oregon	2,029.7
34	Pennsylvania	1,173.4
27	Rhode Island	1,341.8
NA	South Carolina**	NA
22	South Dakota	1,574.1
33	Tennessee	1,178.1
28	Texas	1,327.4
2	Utah	2,631.5
45	Vermont	485.2
40	Virginia	811.1
7	Washington	1,962.9
43	West Virginia	601.1
1	Wisconsin	3,090.9
17	Wyoming	1,689.6

RANK ORDER

RANK	STATE	RATE
1	Wisconsin	3,090.9
2	Utah	2,631.5
3	Oregon	2,029.7
4	Colorado	2,011.7
5	Louisiana	1,979.6
6	Maryland	1,969.2
7	Washington	1,962.9
8	Florida	1,957.4
9	Nebraska	1,947.7
10	Idaho	1,885.4
11	North Dakota	1,857.8
12	Iowa	1,836.8
13	Arizona	1,793.6
14	Delaware	1,761.5
15	Maine	1,746.7
16	Minnesota	1,700.5
17	Wyoming	1,689.6
18	Nevada	1,687.6
19	Missouri	1,616.9
20	Oklahoma	1,615.5
21	Alaska	1,597.6
22	South Dakota	1,574.1
23	Mississippi	1,512.8
24	Arkansas	1,479.8
25	Hawaii	1,374.5
26	North Carolina	1,361.6
27	Rhode Island	1,341.8
28	Texas	1,327.4
29	Indiana	1,287.6
30	New Mexico	1,232.4
31	Connecticut	1,197.8
32	Kansas	1,189.8
33	Tennessee	1,178.1
34	Pennsylvania	1,173.4
35	New York	1,116.1
36	California	1,108.5
37	Ohio	1,060.4
38	Michigan	902.1
39	New Jersey	881.7
40	Virginia	811.1
41	New Hampshire	800.8
42	Alabama	757.1
43	West Virginia	601.1
44	Massachusetts	508.3
45	Vermont	485.2
NA	Georgia**	NA
NA	Illinois**	NA
NA	Kentucky**	NA
NA	Montana**	NA
NA	South Carolina**	NA
	District of Columbia**	NA

Source: Morgan Quitno Press using data from Federal Bureau of Investigation
"Crime in the United States 2004" (Uniform Crime Reports, October 17, 2005)
*By law enforcement agencies submitting complete reports to the F.B.I. for 12 months in 2004. Arrests of youths 17 years and younger divided into population of 10 to 17 year olds. See important note at beginning of this chapter. Property crimes are offenses of burglary, larceny-theft, motor vehicle theft and arson.
**Not available.

Reported Arrests of Juveniles for Property Crime
As a Percent of All Such Arrests in 2004
National Percent = 27.6% of Reported Property Crime Arrests*

ALPHA ORDER

RANK	STATE	PERCENT
49	Alabama	16.5
10	Alaska	35.1
25	Arizona	28.3
38	Arkansas	24.5
27	California	26.8
20	Colorado	30.4
33	Connecticut	25.7
21	Delaware	29.6
24	Florida	28.5
42	Georgia	23.2
18	Hawaii	30.6
2	Idaho	44.2
41	Illinois	23.3
22	Indiana	29.0
5	Iowa	40.4
19	Kansas	30.5
31	Kentucky	25.8
34	Louisiana	25.6
14	Maine	33.7
15	Maryland	33.4
45	Massachusetts	21.2
16	Michigan	31.2
6	Minnesota	38.6
39	Mississippi	23.8
36	Missouri	25.0
NA	Montana**	NA
11	Nebraska	35.0
44	Nevada	22.6
9	New Hampshire	35.2
31	New Jersey	25.8
22	New Mexico	29.0
35	New York	25.2
46	North Carolina	19.2
1	North Dakota	47.5
28	Ohio	26.5
13	Oklahoma	34.7
36	Oregon	25.0
30	Pennsylvania	26.0
12	Rhode Island	34.9
40	South Carolina	23.4
3	South Dakota	43.8
47	Tennessee	19.1
26	Texas	27.3
7	Utah	36.6
29	Vermont	26.2
43	Virginia	22.8
17	Washington	30.8
48	West Virginia	17.9
4	Wisconsin	40.9
8	Wyoming	35.6

RANK ORDER

RANK	STATE	PERCENT
1	North Dakota	47.5
2	Idaho	44.2
3	South Dakota	43.8
4	Wisconsin	40.9
5	Iowa	40.4
6	Minnesota	38.6
7	Utah	36.6
8	Wyoming	35.6
9	New Hampshire	35.2
10	Alaska	35.1
11	Nebraska	35.0
12	Rhode Island	34.9
13	Oklahoma	34.7
14	Maine	33.7
15	Maryland	33.4
16	Michigan	31.2
17	Washington	30.8
18	Hawaii	30.6
19	Kansas	30.5
20	Colorado	30.4
21	Delaware	29.6
22	Indiana	29.0
22	New Mexico	29.0
24	Florida	28.5
25	Arizona	28.3
26	Texas	27.3
27	California	26.8
28	Ohio	26.5
29	Vermont	26.2
30	Pennsylvania	26.0
31	Kentucky	25.8
31	New Jersey	25.8
33	Connecticut	25.7
34	Louisiana	25.6
35	New York	25.2
36	Missouri	25.0
36	Oregon	25.0
38	Arkansas	24.5
39	Mississippi	23.8
40	South Carolina	23.4
41	Illinois	23.3
42	Georgia	23.2
43	Virginia	22.8
44	Nevada	22.6
45	Massachusetts	21.2
46	North Carolina	19.2
47	Tennessee	19.1
48	West Virginia	17.9
49	Alabama	16.5
NA	Montana**	NA
	District of Columbia**	NA

Source: Morgan Quitno Press using data from Federal Bureau of Investigation
    "Crime in the United States 2004" (Uniform Crime Reports, October 17, 2005)
*Arrests of youths 17 years and younger by law enforcement agencies submitting complete reports to the F.B.I. for
12 months in 2004. Property crimes are offenses of burglary, larceny-theft, motor vehicle theft and arson.
**Not available.

Reported Arrests of Juveniles for Burglary in 2004

National Total = 67,376 Reported Arrests*

ALPHA ORDER

RANK	STATE	ARRESTS	% of USA
27	Alabama	646	1.0%
41	Alaska	233	0.3%
11	Arizona	1,587	2.4%
33	Arkansas	429	0.6%
1	California	12,460	18.5%
21	Colorado	907	1.3%
26	Connecticut	685	1.0%
37	Delaware	324	0.5%
2	Florida	8,715	12.9%
18	Georgia	999	1.5%
43	Hawaii	144	0.2%
35	Idaho	340	0.5%
19	Illinois	972	1.4%
23	Indiana	896	1.3%
25	Iowa	733	1.1%
34	Kansas	401	0.6%
31	Kentucky	463	0.7%
13	Louisiana	1,540	2.3%
32	Maine	455	0.7%
5	Maryland	2,524	3.7%
29	Massachusetts	555	0.8%
14	Michigan	1,405	2.1%
24	Minnesota	853	1.3%
30	Mississippi	529	0.8%
15	Missouri	1,340	2.0%
NA	Montana**	NA	NA
36	Nebraska	336	0.5%
28	Nevada	597	0.9%
44	New Hampshire	119	0.2%
12	New Jersey	1,573	2.3%
39	New Mexico	313	0.5%
6	New York	2,494	3.7%
7	North Carolina	2,336	3.5%
46	North Dakota	98	0.1%
8	Ohio	1,955	2.9%
20	Oklahoma	929	1.4%
17	Oregon	1,031	1.5%
4	Pennsylvania	2,572	3.8%
40	Rhode Island	294	0.4%
42	South Carolina	203	0.3%
45	South Dakota	101	0.1%
16	Tennessee	1,123	1.7%
3	Texas	6,241	9.3%
38	Utah	321	0.5%
48	Vermont	76	0.1%
22	Virginia	906	1.3%
9	Washington	1,736	2.6%
47	West Virginia	83	0.1%
10	Wisconsin	1,732	2.6%
49	Wyoming	72	0.1%

RANK ORDER

RANK	STATE	ARRESTS	% of USA
1	California	12,460	18.5%
2	Florida	8,715	12.9%
3	Texas	6,241	9.3%
4	Pennsylvania	2,572	3.8%
5	Maryland	2,524	3.7%
6	New York	2,494	3.7%
7	North Carolina	2,336	3.5%
8	Ohio	1,955	2.9%
9	Washington	1,736	2.6%
10	Wisconsin	1,732	2.6%
11	Arizona	1,587	2.4%
12	New Jersey	1,573	2.3%
13	Louisiana	1,540	2.3%
14	Michigan	1,405	2.1%
15	Missouri	1,340	2.0%
16	Tennessee	1,123	1.7%
17	Oregon	1,031	1.5%
18	Georgia	999	1.5%
19	Illinois	972	1.4%
20	Oklahoma	929	1.4%
21	Colorado	907	1.3%
22	Virginia	906	1.3%
23	Indiana	896	1.3%
24	Minnesota	853	1.3%
25	Iowa	733	1.1%
26	Connecticut	685	1.0%
27	Alabama	646	1.0%
28	Nevada	597	0.9%
29	Massachusetts	555	0.8%
30	Mississippi	529	0.8%
31	Kentucky	463	0.7%
32	Maine	455	0.7%
33	Arkansas	429	0.6%
34	Kansas	401	0.6%
35	Idaho	340	0.5%
36	Nebraska	336	0.5%
37	Delaware	324	0.5%
38	Utah	321	0.5%
39	New Mexico	313	0.5%
40	Rhode Island	294	0.4%
41	Alaska	233	0.3%
42	South Carolina	203	0.3%
43	Hawaii	144	0.2%
44	New Hampshire	119	0.2%
45	South Dakota	101	0.1%
46	North Dakota	98	0.1%
47	West Virginia	83	0.1%
48	Vermont	76	0.1%
49	Wyoming	72	0.1%
NA	Montana**	NA	NA
	District of Columbia**	NA	NA

Source: Federal Bureau of Investigation
"Crime in the United States 2004" (Uniform Crime Reports, October 17, 2005)
*Arrests of youths 17 years and younger by law enforcement agencies submitting complete reports to the F.B.I. for 12 months in 2004. Burglary is the unlawful entry of a structure to commit a felony or theft. Attempts are included. See important note at beginning of this chapter.
**Not available.

Reported Juvenile Arrest Rate for Burglary in 2004

National Rate = 257.4 Reported Arrests per 100,000 Juvenile Population*

ALPHA ORDER

RANK	STATE	RATE
37	Alabama	144.2
13	Alaska	266.8
18	Arizona	240.4
14	Arkansas	260.6
9	California	304.3
29	Colorado	201.8
27	Connecticut	207.8
3	Delaware	402.5
1	Florida	472.8
NA	Georgia**	NA
42	Hawaii	124.3
22	Idaho	222.3
NA	Illinois**	NA
34	Indiana	167.3
12	Iowa	270.1
31	Kansas	181.4
NA	Kentucky**	NA
2	Louisiana	415.1
8	Maine	320.1
4	Maryland	388.4
43	Massachusetts	114.0
41	Michigan	125.6
26	Minnesota	210.6
10	Mississippi	301.0
15	Missouri	251.9
NA	Montana**	NA
30	Nebraska	183.3
19	Nevada	232.4
44	New Hampshire	102.6
36	New Jersey	163.4
33	New Mexico	179.3
20	New York	231.2
5	North Carolina	347.5
32	North Dakota	180.8
23	Ohio	219.4
17	Oklahoma	247.9
11	Oregon	273.8
25	Pennsylvania	216.4
15	Rhode Island	251.9
NA	South Carolina**	NA
28	South Dakota	207.0
24	Tennessee	216.8
21	Texas	229.7
35	Utah	165.0
38	Vermont	131.7
40	Virginia	126.0
7	Washington	324.4
45	West Virginia	78.8
6	Wisconsin	334.6
38	Wyoming	131.7

RANK ORDER

RANK	STATE	RATE
1	Florida	472.8
2	Louisiana	415.1
3	Delaware	402.5
4	Maryland	388.4
5	North Carolina	347.5
6	Wisconsin	334.6
7	Washington	324.4
8	Maine	320.1
9	California	304.3
10	Mississippi	301.0
11	Oregon	273.8
12	Iowa	270.1
13	Alaska	266.8
14	Arkansas	260.6
15	Missouri	251.9
15	Rhode Island	251.9
17	Oklahoma	247.9
18	Arizona	240.4
19	Nevada	232.4
20	New York	231.2
21	Texas	229.7
22	Idaho	222.3
23	Ohio	219.4
24	Tennessee	216.8
25	Pennsylvania	216.4
26	Minnesota	210.6
27	Connecticut	207.8
28	South Dakota	207.0
29	Colorado	201.8
30	Nebraska	183.3
31	Kansas	181.4
32	North Dakota	180.8
33	New Mexico	179.3
34	Indiana	167.3
35	Utah	165.0
36	New Jersey	163.4
37	Alabama	144.2
38	Vermont	131.7
38	Wyoming	131.7
40	Virginia	126.0
41	Michigan	125.6
42	Hawaii	124.3
43	Massachusetts	114.0
44	New Hampshire	102.6
45	West Virginia	78.8
NA	Georgia**	NA
NA	Illinois**	NA
NA	Kentucky**	NA
NA	Montana**	NA
NA	South Carolina**	NA

District of Columbia**   NA

Source: Morgan Quitno Press using data from Federal Bureau of Investigation
"Crime in the United States 2004" (Uniform Crime Reports, October 17, 2005)
*By law enforcement agencies submitting complete reports to the F.B.I. for 12 months in 2004. Arrests of youths 17 years and younger divided into population of 10 to 17 year olds. See important note at beginning of this chapter. Burglary is the unlawful entry of a structure to commit a felony or theft. Attempts are included.
**Not available.

Reported Arrests of Juveniles for Burglary
As a Percent of All Such Arrests in 2004
National Percent = 28.4% of Reported Burglary Arrests*

ALPHA ORDER

RANK	STATE	PERCENT
46	Alabama	18.5
2	Alaska	42.9
23	Arizona	30.6
37	Arkansas	26.0
41	California	25.5
19	Colorado	32.0
29	Connecticut	28.4
8	Delaware	35.6
13	Florida	33.6
24	Georgia	29.4
32	Hawaii	27.2
6	Idaho	39.2
17	Illinois	32.5
38	Indiana	25.8
5	Iowa	39.5
20	Kansas	31.8
27	Kentucky	29.0
30	Louisiana	28.3
10	Maine	34.8
10	Maryland	34.8
42	Massachusetts	25.0
34	Michigan	26.5
7	Minnesota	36.5
43	Mississippi	24.5
36	Missouri	26.2
NA	Montana**	NA
12	Nebraska	34.0
49	Nevada	12.5
16	New Hampshire	32.7
38	New Jersey	25.8
40	New Mexico	25.6
14	New York	33.2
47	North Carolina	17.9
1	North Dakota	56.3
26	Ohio	29.3
22	Oklahoma	31.1
28	Oregon	28.6
34	Pennsylvania	26.5
9	Rhode Island	35.1
24	South Carolina	29.4
4	South Dakota	39.8
44	Tennessee	22.3
18	Texas	32.2
31	Utah	27.6
14	Vermont	33.2
33	Virginia	27.1
21	Washington	31.7
48	West Virginia	16.3
3	Wisconsin	42.0
45	Wyoming	20.6

RANK ORDER

RANK	STATE	PERCENT
1	North Dakota	56.3
2	Alaska	42.9
3	Wisconsin	42.0
4	South Dakota	39.8
5	Iowa	39.5
6	Idaho	39.2
7	Minnesota	36.5
8	Delaware	35.6
9	Rhode Island	35.1
10	Maine	34.8
10	Maryland	34.8
12	Nebraska	34.0
13	Florida	33.6
14	New York	33.2
14	Vermont	33.2
16	New Hampshire	32.7
17	Illinois	32.5
18	Texas	32.2
19	Colorado	32.0
20	Kansas	31.8
21	Washington	31.7
22	Oklahoma	31.1
23	Arizona	30.6
24	Georgia	29.4
24	South Carolina	29.4
26	Ohio	29.3
27	Kentucky	29.0
28	Oregon	28.6
29	Connecticut	28.4
30	Louisiana	28.3
31	Utah	27.6
32	Hawaii	27.2
33	Virginia	27.1
34	Michigan	26.5
34	Pennsylvania	26.5
36	Missouri	26.2
37	Arkansas	26.0
38	Indiana	25.8
38	New Jersey	25.8
40	New Mexico	25.6
41	California	25.5
42	Massachusetts	25.0
43	Mississippi	24.5
44	Tennessee	22.3
45	Wyoming	20.6
46	Alabama	18.5
47	North Carolina	17.9
48	West Virginia	16.3
49	Nevada	12.5
NA	Montana**	NA
	District of Columbia**	NA

Source: Morgan Quitno Press using data from Federal Bureau of Investigation
    "Crime in the United States 2004" (Uniform Crime Reports, October 17, 2005)
*Arrests of youths 17 years and younger by law enforcement agencies submitting complete reports to the F.B.I. for 12 months in 2004. Burglary is the unlawful entry of a structure to commit a felony or theft. Attempts are included.
**Not available.

Reported Arrests of Juveniles for Larceny and Theft in 2004

National Total = 259,978 Reported Arrests*

ALPHA ORDER

RANK	STATE	ARRESTS	% of USA
30	Alabama	2,545	1.0%
42	Alaska	999	0.4%
6	Arizona	8,818	3.4%
34	Arkansas	1,939	0.7%
2	California	26,217	10.1%
11	Colorado	7,147	2.7%
28	Connecticut	2,856	1.1%
41	Delaware	1,003	0.4%
3	Florida	23,508	9.0%
24	Georgia	4,120	1.6%
39	Hawaii	1,287	0.5%
31	Idaho	2,327	0.9%
29	Illinois	2,722	1.0%
19	Indiana	5,383	2.1%
25	Iowa	3,906	1.5%
32	Kansas	2,032	0.8%
37	Kentucky	1,664	0.6%
18	Louisiana	5,400	2.1%
35	Maine	1,847	0.7%
10	Maryland	7,853	3.0%
38	Massachusetts	1,639	0.6%
8	Michigan	7,941	3.1%
17	Minnesota	5,599	2.2%
33	Mississippi	2,021	0.8%
15	Missouri	6,158	2.4%
NA	Montana**	NA	NA
27	Nebraska	3,029	1.2%
26	Nevada	3,376	1.3%
45	New Hampshire	720	0.3%
14	New Jersey	6,294	2.4%
36	New Mexico	1,735	0.7%
7	New York	8,619	3.3%
12	North Carolina	6,476	2.5%
43	North Dakota	827	0.3%
13	Ohio	6,444	2.5%
20	Oklahoma	4,676	1.8%
16	Oregon	5,772	2.2%
5	Pennsylvania	9,371	3.6%
40	Rhode Island	1,097	0.4%
47	South Carolina	572	0.2%
46	South Dakota	637	0.2%
22	Tennessee	4,400	1.7%
1	Texas	27,498	10.6%
21	Utah	4,542	1.7%
49	Vermont	161	0.1%
23	Virginia	4,385	1.7%
9	Washington	7,901	3.0%
48	West Virginia	499	0.2%
4	Wisconsin	13,202	5.1%
44	Wyoming	814	0.3%

RANK ORDER

RANK	STATE	ARRESTS	% of USA
1	Texas	27,498	10.6%
2	California	26,217	10.1%
3	Florida	23,508	9.0%
4	Wisconsin	13,202	5.1%
5	Pennsylvania	9,371	3.6%
6	Arizona	8,818	3.4%
7	New York	8,619	3.3%
8	Michigan	7,941	3.1%
9	Washington	7,901	3.0%
10	Maryland	7,853	3.0%
11	Colorado	7,147	2.7%
12	North Carolina	6,476	2.5%
13	Ohio	6,444	2.5%
14	New Jersey	6,294	2.4%
15	Missouri	6,158	2.4%
16	Oregon	5,772	2.2%
17	Minnesota	5,599	2.2%
18	Louisiana	5,400	2.1%
19	Indiana	5,383	2.1%
20	Oklahoma	4,676	1.8%
21	Utah	4,542	1.7%
22	Tennessee	4,400	1.7%
23	Virginia	4,385	1.7%
24	Georgia	4,120	1.6%
25	Iowa	3,906	1.5%
26	Nevada	3,376	1.3%
27	Nebraska	3,029	1.2%
28	Connecticut	2,856	1.1%
29	Illinois	2,722	1.0%
30	Alabama	2,545	1.0%
31	Idaho	2,327	0.9%
32	Kansas	2,032	0.8%
33	Mississippi	2,021	0.8%
34	Arkansas	1,939	0.7%
35	Maine	1,847	0.7%
36	New Mexico	1,735	0.7%
37	Kentucky	1,664	0.6%
38	Massachusetts	1,639	0.6%
39	Hawaii	1,287	0.5%
40	Rhode Island	1,097	0.4%
41	Delaware	1,003	0.4%
42	Alaska	999	0.4%
43	North Dakota	827	0.3%
44	Wyoming	814	0.3%
45	New Hampshire	720	0.3%
46	South Dakota	637	0.2%
47	South Carolina	572	0.2%
48	West Virginia	499	0.2%
49	Vermont	161	0.1%
NA	Montana**	NA	NA
	District of Columbia**	NA	NA

Source: Federal Bureau of Investigation
   "Crime in the United States 2004" (Uniform Crime Reports, October 17, 2005)
*Arrests of youths 17 years and younger by law enforcement agencies submitting complete reports to the F.B.I. for 12 months in 2004. Larceny and theft is the unlawful taking of property without use of force, violence or fraud. Attempts are included. Motor vehicle thefts are excluded. See important note at beginning of this chapter.
**Not available.

Reported Juvenile Arrest Rate for Larceny and Theft in 2004

National Rate = 993.0 Reported Arrests per 100,000 Juvenile Population*

ALPHA ORDER

RANK	STATE	RATE
42	Alabama	568.1
24	Alaska	1,144.1
13	Arizona	1,335.9
21	Arkansas	1,177.8
39	California	640.3
4	Colorado	1,590.4
32	Connecticut	866.2
19	Delaware	1,246.0
17	Florida	1,275.3
NA	Georgia**	NA
25	Hawaii	1,110.5
7	Idaho	1,521.3
NA	Illinois**	NA
27	Indiana	1,005.2
11	Iowa	1,439.2
31	Kansas	919.3
NA	Kentucky**	NA
10	Louisiana	1,455.4
16	Maine	1,299.3
20	Maryland	1,208.4
44	Massachusetts	336.6
37	Michigan	709.7
12	Minnesota	1,382.3
23	Mississippi	1,149.8
22	Missouri	1,157.7
NA	Montana**	NA
3	Nebraska	1,652.1
14	Nevada	1,314.0
40	New Hampshire	620.6
38	New Jersey	654.0
28	New Mexico	993.6
34	New York	799.0
29	North Carolina	963.2
6	North Dakota	1,525.7
36	Ohio	723.2
18	Oklahoma	1,247.7
5	Oregon	1,533.1
35	Pennsylvania	788.4
30	Rhode Island	940.0
NA	South Carolina**	NA
15	South Dakota	1,305.6
33	Tennessee	849.5
26	Texas	1,012.0
2	Utah	2,334.0
45	Vermont	279.0
41	Virginia	609.6
9	Washington	1,476.5
43	West Virginia	473.8
1	Wisconsin	2,550.4
8	Wyoming	1,488.4

RANK ORDER

RANK	STATE	RATE
1	Wisconsin	2,550.4
2	Utah	2,334.0
3	Nebraska	1,652.1
4	Colorado	1,590.4
5	Oregon	1,533.1
6	North Dakota	1,525.7
7	Idaho	1,521.3
8	Wyoming	1,488.4
9	Washington	1,476.5
10	Louisiana	1,455.4
11	Iowa	1,439.2
12	Minnesota	1,382.3
13	Arizona	1,335.9
14	Nevada	1,314.0
15	South Dakota	1,305.6
16	Maine	1,299.3
17	Florida	1,275.3
18	Oklahoma	1,247.7
19	Delaware	1,246.0
20	Maryland	1,208.4
21	Arkansas	1,177.8
22	Missouri	1,157.7
23	Mississippi	1,149.8
24	Alaska	1,144.1
25	Hawaii	1,110.5
26	Texas	1,012.0
27	Indiana	1,005.2
28	New Mexico	993.6
29	North Carolina	963.2
30	Rhode Island	940.0
31	Kansas	919.3
32	Connecticut	866.2
33	Tennessee	849.5
34	New York	799.0
35	Pennsylvania	788.4
36	Ohio	723.2
37	Michigan	709.7
38	New Jersey	654.0
39	California	640.3
40	New Hampshire	620.6
41	Virginia	609.6
42	Alabama	568.1
43	West Virginia	473.8
44	Massachusetts	336.6
45	Vermont	279.0
NA	Georgia**	NA
NA	Illinois**	NA
NA	Kentucky**	NA
NA	Montana**	NA
NA	South Carolina**	NA

District of Columbia**   NA

Source: Morgan Quitno Press using data from Federal Bureau of Investigation
    "Crime in the United States 2004" (Uniform Crime Reports, October 17, 2005)
*By law enforcement agencies submitting complete reports to the F.B.I. for 12 months in 2004. Arrests of youths 17 years and younger divided into population of 10 to 17 year olds. See important note at beginning of this chapter. Larceny and theft is the unlawful taking of property without use of force, violence or fraud. Attempts are included. Motor vehicle thefts are excluded. **Not available.

Reported Arrests of Juveniles for Larceny and Theft
As a Percent of All Such Arrests in 2004
National Percent = 27.2% of Reported Larceny and Theft Arrests*

ALPHA ORDER

RANK	STATE	PERCENT
49	Alabama	16.1
14	Alaska	33.1
24	Arizona	28.2
30	Arkansas	24.7
22	California	29.4
21	Colorado	29.8
36	Connecticut	24.3
26	Delaware	27.0
28	Florida	26.6
42	Georgia	21.6
12	Hawaii	33.4
3	Idaho	44.6
48	Illinois	16.9
22	Indiana	29.4
5	Iowa	40.0
20	Kansas	29.9
37	Kentucky	24.1
30	Louisiana	24.7
15	Maine	32.7
17	Maryland	30.9
45	Massachusetts	19.1
16	Michigan	31.9
7	Minnesota	38.9
38	Mississippi	23.8
32	Missouri	24.6
NA	Montana**	NA
10	Nebraska	34.7
25	Nevada	27.5
11	New Hampshire	34.6
29	New Jersey	25.0
19	New Mexico	30.1
39	New York	23.2
44	North Carolina	19.7
1	North Dakota	46.6
32	Ohio	24.6
9	Oklahoma	35.5
35	Oregon	24.5
32	Pennsylvania	24.6
13	Rhode Island	33.2
41	South Carolina	21.7
2	South Dakota	45.0
46	Tennessee	18.1
27	Texas	26.7
8	Utah	37.2
40	Vermont	21.8
43	Virginia	21.2
18	Washington	30.2
47	West Virginia	17.9
4	Wisconsin	40.2
6	Wyoming	39.3

RANK ORDER

RANK	STATE	PERCENT
1	North Dakota	46.6
2	South Dakota	45.0
3	Idaho	44.6
4	Wisconsin	40.2
5	Iowa	40.0
6	Wyoming	39.3
7	Minnesota	38.9
8	Utah	37.2
9	Oklahoma	35.5
10	Nebraska	34.7
11	New Hampshire	34.6
12	Hawaii	33.4
13	Rhode Island	33.2
14	Alaska	33.1
15	Maine	32.7
16	Michigan	31.9
17	Maryland	30.9
18	Washington	30.2
19	New Mexico	30.1
20	Kansas	29.9
21	Colorado	29.8
22	California	29.4
22	Indiana	29.4
24	Arizona	28.2
25	Nevada	27.5
26	Delaware	27.0
27	Texas	26.7
28	Florida	26.6
29	New Jersey	25.0
30	Arkansas	24.7
30	Louisiana	24.7
32	Missouri	24.6
32	Ohio	24.6
32	Pennsylvania	24.6
35	Oregon	24.5
36	Connecticut	24.3
37	Kentucky	24.1
38	Mississippi	23.8
39	New York	23.2
40	Vermont	21.8
41	South Carolina	21.7
42	Georgia	21.6
43	Virginia	21.2
44	North Carolina	19.7
45	Massachusetts	19.1
46	Tennessee	18.1
47	West Virginia	17.9
48	Illinois	16.9
49	Alabama	16.1
NA	Montana**	NA
	District of Columbia**	NA

Source: Morgan Quitno Press using data from Federal Bureau of Investigation
   "Crime in the United States 2004" (Uniform Crime Reports, October 17, 2005)
*Arrests of youths 17 years and younger by law enforcement agencies submitting complete reports to the F.B.I. for 12 months in 2004. Larceny and theft is the unlawful taking of property without use of force, violence or fraud. Attempts are included. Motor vehicle thefts are excluded.
**Not available.

Reported Arrests of Juveniles for Motor Vehicle Theft in 2004

National Total = 31,585 Reported Arrests*

ALPHA ORDER

RANK	STATE	ARRESTS	% of USA
30	Alabama	178	0.6%
31	Alaska	155	0.5%
7	Arizona	1,262	4.0%
43	Arkansas	65	0.2%
1	California	5,805	18.4%
11	Colorado	852	2.7%
25	Connecticut	263	0.8%
44	Delaware	61	0.2%
2	Florida	3,574	11.3%
18	Georgia	475	1.5%
35	Hawaii	145	0.5%
36	Idaho	137	0.4%
3	Illinois	2,441	7.7%
16	Indiana	523	1.7%
27	Iowa	248	0.8%
33	Kansas	148	0.5%
34	Kentucky	146	0.5%
23	Louisiana	315	1.0%
32	Maine	152	0.5%
4	Maryland	1,965	6.2%
28	Massachusetts	220	0.7%
14	Michigan	619	2.0%
22	Minnesota	346	1.1%
40	Mississippi	91	0.3%
8	Missouri	947	3.0%
NA	Montana**	NA	NA
37	Nebraska	133	0.4%
24	Nevada	307	1.0%
41	New Hampshire	75	0.2%
19	New Jersey	391	1.2%
39	New Mexico	92	0.3%
12	New York	741	2.3%
26	North Carolina	251	0.8%
42	North Dakota	70	0.2%
10	Ohio	855	2.7%
21	Oklahoma	366	1.2%
15	Oregon	616	2.0%
6	Pennsylvania	1,676	5.3%
38	Rhode Island	109	0.3%
47	South Carolina	33	0.1%
49	South Dakota	17	0.1%
17	Tennessee	501	1.6%
5	Texas	1,957	6.2%
29	Utah	205	0.6%
46	Vermont	38	0.1%
20	Virginia	386	1.2%
13	Washington	657	2.1%
45	West Virginia	47	0.1%
9	Wisconsin	904	2.9%
48	Wyoming	25	0.1%

RANK ORDER

RANK	STATE	ARRESTS	% of USA
1	California	5,805	18.4%
2	Florida	3,574	11.3%
3	Illinois	2,441	7.7%
4	Maryland	1,965	6.2%
5	Texas	1,957	6.2%
6	Pennsylvania	1,676	5.3%
7	Arizona	1,262	4.0%
8	Missouri	947	3.0%
9	Wisconsin	904	2.9%
10	Ohio	855	2.7%
11	Colorado	852	2.7%
12	New York	741	2.3%
13	Washington	657	2.1%
14	Michigan	619	2.0%
15	Oregon	616	2.0%
16	Indiana	523	1.7%
17	Tennessee	501	1.6%
18	Georgia	475	1.5%
19	New Jersey	391	1.2%
20	Virginia	386	1.2%
21	Oklahoma	366	1.2%
22	Minnesota	346	1.1%
23	Louisiana	315	1.0%
24	Nevada	307	1.0%
25	Connecticut	263	0.8%
26	North Carolina	251	0.8%
27	Iowa	248	0.8%
28	Massachusetts	220	0.7%
29	Utah	205	0.6%
30	Alabama	178	0.6%
31	Alaska	155	0.5%
32	Maine	152	0.5%
33	Kansas	148	0.5%
34	Kentucky	146	0.5%
35	Hawaii	145	0.5%
36	Idaho	137	0.4%
37	Nebraska	133	0.4%
38	Rhode Island	109	0.3%
39	New Mexico	92	0.3%
40	Mississippi	91	0.3%
41	New Hampshire	75	0.2%
42	North Dakota	70	0.2%
43	Arkansas	65	0.2%
44	Delaware	61	0.2%
45	West Virginia	47	0.1%
46	Vermont	38	0.1%
47	South Carolina	33	0.1%
48	Wyoming	25	0.1%
49	South Dakota	17	0.1%
NA	Montana**	NA	NA
	District of Columbia**	NA	NA

Source: Morgan Quitno Press using data from Federal Bureau of Investigation
   "Crime in the United States 2004" (Uniform Crime Reports, October 17, 2005)
*Arrests of youths 17 years and younger by law enforcement agencies submitting complete reports to the F.B.I. for 12 months in 2004. Motor vehicle theft includes the theft or attempted theft of a self-propelled vehicle. Excludes motorboats, construction equipment, airplanes and farming equipment. See important note at beginning of this chapter. **Not available.

Reported Juvenile Arrest Rate for Motor Vehicle Theft in 2004

National Rate = 120.6 Reported Arrests per 100,000 Juvenile Population*

ALPHA ORDER

RANK ORDER

RANK	STATE	RATE		RANK	STATE	RATE
42	Alabama	39.7		1	Maryland	302.4
6	Alaska	177.5		2	Florida	193.9
3	Arizona	191.2		3	Arizona	191.2
43	Arkansas	39.5		4	Colorado	189.6
9	California	141.8		5	Missouri	178.0
4	Colorado	189.6		6	Alaska	177.5
26	Connecticut	79.8		7	Wisconsin	174.6
27	Delaware	75.8		8	Oregon	163.6
2	Florida	193.9		9	California	141.8
NA	Georgia**	NA		10	Pennsylvania	141.0
12	Hawaii	125.1		11	North Dakota	129.1
23	Idaho	89.6		12	Hawaii	125.1
NA	Illinois**	NA		13	Washington	122.8
17	Indiana	97.7		14	Nevada	119.5
22	Iowa	91.4		15	Maine	106.9
31	Kansas	67.0		16	Utah	105.3
NA	Kentucky**	NA		17	Indiana	97.7
25	Louisiana	84.9		17	Oklahoma	97.7
15	Maine	106.9		19	Tennessee	96.7
1	Maryland	302.4		20	Ohio	96.0
39	Massachusetts	45.2		21	Rhode Island	93.4
34	Michigan	55.3		22	Iowa	91.4
24	Minnesota	85.4		23	Idaho	89.6
37	Mississippi	51.8		24	Minnesota	85.4
5	Missouri	178.0		25	Louisiana	84.9
NA	Montana**	NA		26	Connecticut	79.8
28	Nebraska	72.5		27	Delaware	75.8
14	Nevada	119.5		28	Nebraska	72.5
33	New Hampshire	64.6		29	Texas	72.0
41	New Jersey	40.6		30	New York	68.7
36	New Mexico	52.7		31	Kansas	67.0
30	New York	68.7		32	Vermont	65.8
44	North Carolina	37.3		33	New Hampshire	64.6
11	North Dakota	129.1		34	Michigan	55.3
20	Ohio	96.0		35	Virginia	53.7
17	Oklahoma	97.7		36	New Mexico	52.7
8	Oregon	163.6		37	Mississippi	51.8
10	Pennsylvania	141.0		38	Wyoming	45.7
21	Rhode Island	93.4		39	Massachusetts	45.2
NA	South Carolina**	NA		40	West Virginia	44.6
45	South Dakota	34.8		41	New Jersey	40.6
19	Tennessee	96.7		42	Alabama	39.7
29	Texas	72.0		43	Arkansas	39.5
16	Utah	105.3		44	North Carolina	37.3
32	Vermont	65.8		45	South Dakota	34.8
35	Virginia	53.7		NA	Georgia**	NA
13	Washington	122.8		NA	Illinois**	NA
40	West Virginia	44.6		NA	Kentucky**	NA
7	Wisconsin	174.6		NA	Montana**	NA
38	Wyoming	45.7		NA	South Carolina**	NA
					District of Columbia**	NA

Source: Morgan Quitno Press using data from Federal Bureau of Investigation
  "Crime in the United States 2004" (Uniform Crime Reports, October 17, 2005)
*By law enforcement agencies submitting complete reports to the F.B.I. for 12 months in 2004. Arrests of youths 17 years and younger divided into population of 10 to 17 year olds. See important note at beginning of this chapter. Motor vehicle theft includes the theft or attempted theft of a self-propelled vehicle. Excludes motorboats, construction equipment, airplanes and farming equipment. **Not available.

Reported Arrests of Juveniles for Motor Vehicle Theft
As a Percent of All Such Arrests in 2004
National Percent = 26.9% of Reported Motor Vehicle Theft Arrests*

ALPHA ORDER

RANK	STATE	PERCENT
49	Alabama	15.2
11	Alaska	39.2
35	Arizona	24.4
46	Arkansas	16.7
43	California	19.8
23	Colorado	31.7
24	Connecticut	31.6
1	Delaware	49.6
25	Florida	30.3
30	Georgia	28.5
45	Hawaii	18.5
7	Idaho	43.1
21	Illinois	32.9
29	Indiana	28.9
6	Iowa	43.5
26	Kansas	29.9
13	Kentucky	38.2
32	Louisiana	26.6
9	Maine	42.0
10	Maryland	40.1
28	Massachusetts	29.3
17	Michigan	34.2
15	Minnesota	34.8
42	Mississippi	20.6
33	Missouri	24.8
NA	Montana**	NA
16	Nebraska	34.5
48	Nevada	15.3
5	New Hampshire	44.4
18	New Jersey	33.8
36	New Mexico	24.1
31	New York	27.9
47	North Carolina	16.5
4	North Dakota	45.2
14	Ohio	35.1
19	Oklahoma	33.7
44	Oregon	19.7
20	Pennsylvania	33.5
8	Rhode Island	42.4
37	South Carolina	22.8
34	South Dakota	24.6
41	Tennessee	20.8
38	Texas	22.4
12	Utah	38.5
3	Vermont	.46.9
27	Virginia	29.6
22	Washington	32.1
40	West Virginia	21.5
2	Wisconsin	48.6
39	Wyoming	22.1

RANK ORDER

RANK	STATE	PERCENT
1	Delaware	49.6
2	Wisconsin	48.6
3	Vermont	46.9
4	North Dakota	45.2
5	New Hampshire	44.4
6	Iowa	43.5
7	Idaho	43.1
8	Rhode Island	42.4
9	Maine	42.0
10	Maryland	40.1
11	Alaska	39.2
12	Utah	38.5
13	Kentucky	38.2
14	Ohio	35.1
15	Minnesota	34.8
16	Nebraska	34.5
17	Michigan	34.2
18	New Jersey	33.8
19	Oklahoma	33.7
20	Pennsylvania	33.5
21	Illinois	32.9
22	Washington	32.1
23	Colorado	31.7
24	Connecticut	31.6
25	Florida	30.3
26	Kansas	29.9
27	Virginia	29.6
28	Massachusetts	29.3
29	Indiana	28.9
30	Georgia	28.5
31	New York	27.9
32	Louisiana	26.6
33	Missouri	24.8
34	South Dakota	24.6
35	Arizona	24.4
36	New Mexico	24.1
37	South Carolina	22.8
38	Texas	22.4
39	Wyoming	22.1
40	West Virginia	21.5
41	Tennessee	20.8
42	Mississippi	20.6
43	California	19.8
44	Oregon	19.7
45	Hawaii	18.5
46	Arkansas	16.7
47	North Carolina	16.5
48	Nevada	15.3
49	Alabama	15.2
NA	Montana**	NA
	District of Columbia**	NA

Source: Morgan Quitno Press using data from Federal Bureau of Investigation
   "Crime in the United States 2004" (Uniform Crime Reports, October 17, 2005)
*Arrests of youths 17 years and younger by law enforcement agencies submitting complete reports to the F.B.I. for 12 months in 2004. Motor vehicle theft includes the theft or attempted theft of a self-propelled vehicle. Excludes motorboats, construction equipment, airplanes and farming equipment.
**Not available.

Reported Arrests of Juveniles for Arson in 2004

National Total = 5,864 Reported Arrests*

ALPHA ORDER

RANK	STATE	ARRESTS	% of USA
37	Alabama	23	0.4%
45	Alaska	8	0.1%
11	Arizona	172	2.9%
49	Arkansas	3	0.1%
1	California	904	15.4%
16	Colorado	134	2.3%
15	Connecticut	145	2.5%
34	Delaware	30	0.5%
5	Florida	285	4.9%
26	Georgia	75	1.3%
39	Hawaii	17	0.3%
24	Idaho	80	1.4%
31	Illinois	53	0.9%
19	Indiana	93	1.6%
18	Iowa	98	1.7%
33	Kansas	49	0.8%
36	Kentucky	25	0.4%
21	Louisiana	90	1.5%
35	Maine	29	0.5%
2	Maryland	455	7.8%
29	Massachusetts	61	1.0%
17	Michigan	129	2.2%
21	Minnesota	90	1.5%
38	Mississippi	18	0.3%
14	Missouri	155	2.6%
NA	Montana**	NA	NA
27	Nebraska	73	1.2%
30	Nevada	56	1.0%
40	New Hampshire	15	0.3%
6	New Jersey	228	3.9%
43	New Mexico	12	0.2%
10	New York	186	3.2%
20	North Carolina	91	1.6%
43	North Dakota	12	0.2%
9	Ohio	195	3.3%
23	Oklahoma	83	1.4%
7	Oregon	223	3.8%
4	Pennsylvania	327	5.6%
28	Rhode Island	66	1.1%
46	South Carolina	7	0.1%
41	South Dakota	13	0.2%
25	Tennessee	78	1.3%
3	Texas	374	6.4%
31	Utah	53	0.9%
47	Vermont	5	0.1%
13	Virginia	157	2.7%
8	Washington	210	3.6%
48	West Virginia	4	0.1%
12	Wisconsin	162	2.8%
41	Wyoming	13	0.2%

RANK ORDER

RANK	STATE	ARRESTS	% of USA
1	California	904	15.4%
2	Maryland	455	7.8%
3	Texas	374	6.4%
4	Pennsylvania	327	5.6%
5	Florida	285	4.9%
6	New Jersey	228	3.9%
7	Oregon	223	3.8%
8	Washington	210	3.6%
9	Ohio	195	3.3%
10	New York	186	3.2%
11	Arizona	172	2.9%
12	Wisconsin	162	2.8%
13	Virginia	157	2.7%
14	Missouri	155	2.6%
15	Connecticut	145	2.5%
16	Colorado	134	2.3%
17	Michigan	129	2.2%
18	Iowa	98	1.7%
19	Indiana	93	1.6%
20	North Carolina	91	1.6%
21	Louisiana	90	1.5%
21	Minnesota	90	1.5%
23	Oklahoma	83	1.4%
24	Idaho	80	1.4%
25	Tennessee	78	1.3%
26	Georgia	75	1.3%
27	Nebraska	73	1.2%
28	Rhode Island	66	1.1%
29	Massachusetts	61	1.0%
30	Nevada	56	1.0%
31	Illinois	53	0.9%
31	Utah	53	0.9%
33	Kansas	49	0.8%
34	Delaware	30	0.5%
35	Maine	29	0.5%
36	Kentucky	25	0.4%
37	Alabama	23	0.4%
38	Mississippi	18	0.3%
39	Hawaii	17	0.3%
40	New Hampshire	15	0.3%
41	South Dakota	13	0.2%
41	Wyoming	13	0.2%
43	New Mexico	12	0.2%
43	North Dakota	12	0.2%
45	Alaska	8	0.1%
46	South Carolina	7	0.1%
47	Vermont	5	0.1%
48	West Virginia	4	0.1%
49	Arkansas	3	0.1%
NA	Montana**	NA	NA
	District of Columbia**	NA	NA

Source: Federal Bureau of Investigation
    "Crime in the United States 2004" (Uniform Crime Reports, October 17, 2005)
*Arrests of youths 17 years and younger by law enforcement agencies submitting complete reports to the F.B.I. for 12 months in 2004. Arson is the willful burning of or attempt to burn a building, vehicle or another's personal property. See important note at beginning of this chapter.
**Not available.

Reported Juvenile Arrest Rate for Arson in 2004

National Rate = 22.4 Reported Arrests per 100,000 Juvenile Population*

ALPHA ORDER

RANK	STATE	RATE
43	Alabama	5.1
40	Alaska	9.2
16	Arizona	26.1
45	Arkansas	1.8
22	California	22.1
11	Colorado	29.8
5	Connecticut	44.0
8	Delaware	37.3
31	Florida	15.5
NA	Georgia**	NA
33	Hawaii	14.7
4	Idaho	52.3
NA	Illinois**	NA
29	Indiana	17.4
9	Iowa	36.1
20	Kansas	22.2
NA	Kentucky**	NA
17	Louisiana	24.3
28	Maine	20.4
1	Maryland	70.0
37	Massachusetts	12.5
38	Michigan	11.5
20	Minnesota	22.2
39	Mississippi	10.2
12	Missouri	29.1
NA	Montana**	NA
6	Nebraska	39.8
26	Nevada	21.8
36	New Hampshire	12.9
19	New Jersey	23.7
42	New Mexico	6.9
30	New York	17.2
35	North Carolina	13.5
22	North Dakota	22.1
25	Ohio	21.9
22	Oklahoma	22.1
2	Oregon	59.2
13	Pennsylvania	27.5
3	Rhode Island	56.6
NA	South Carolina**	NA
15	South Dakota	26.6
32	Tennessee	15.1
34	Texas	13.8
14	Utah	27.2
41	Vermont	8.7
26	Virginia	21.8
7	Washington	39.2
44	West Virginia	3.8
10	Wisconsin	31.3
18	Wyoming	23.8

RANK ORDER

RANK	STATE	RATE
1	Maryland	70.0
2	Oregon	59.2
3	Rhode Island	56.6
4	Idaho	52.3
5	Connecticut	44.0
6	Nebraska	39.8
7	Washington	39.2
8	Delaware	37.3
9	Iowa	36.1
10	Wisconsin	31.3
11	Colorado	29.8
12	Missouri	29.1
13	Pennsylvania	27.5
14	Utah	27.2
15	South Dakota	26.6
16	Arizona	26.1
17	Louisiana	24.3
18	Wyoming	23.8
19	New Jersey	23.7
20	Kansas	22.2
20	Minnesota	22.2
22	California	22.1
22	North Dakota	22.1
22	Oklahoma	22.1
25	Ohio	21.9
26	Nevada	21.8
26	Virginia	21.8
28	Maine	20.4
29	Indiana	17.4
30	New York	17.2
31	Florida	15.5
32	Tennessee	15.1
33	Hawaii	14.7
34	Texas	13.8
35	North Carolina	13.5
36	New Hampshire	12.9
37	Massachusetts	12.5
38	Michigan	11.5
39	Mississippi	10.2
40	Alaska	9.2
41	Vermont	8.7
42	New Mexico	6.9
43	Alabama	5.1
44	West Virginia	3.8
45	Arkansas	1.8
NA	Georgia**	NA
NA	Illinois**	NA
NA	Kentucky**	NA
NA	Montana**	NA
NA	South Carolina**	NA
	District of Columbia**	NA

Source: Morgan Quitno Press using data from Federal Bureau of Investigation
    "Crime in the United States 2004" (Uniform Crime Reports, October 17, 2005)

*By law enforcement agencies submitting complete reports to the F.B.I. for 12 months in 2004. Arrests of youths 17 years and younger divided into population of 10 to 17 year olds. See important note at beginning of this chapter. Arson is the willful burning of or attempt to burn a building, vehicle or another's personal property.
**Not available.

Reported Arrests of Juveniles for Arson
As a Percent of All Such Arrests in 2004
National Percent = 50.2% of Reported Arson Arrests*

ALPHA ORDER

RANK	STATE	PERCENT
47	Alabama	19.0
24	Alaska	53.3
8	Arizona	65.4
49	Arkansas	7.7
20	California	55.8
13	Colorado	62.3
34	Connecticut	42.5
22	Delaware	55.6
26	Florida	50.4
44	Georgia	24.6
29	Hawaii	47.2
3	Idaho	67.8
38	Illinois	38.4
30	Indiana	46.5
9	Iowa	64.9
19	Kansas	56.3
4	Kentucky	67.6
32	Louisiana	43.1
10	Maine	63.0
11	Maryland	62.7
18	Massachusetts	58.1
36	Michigan	38.9
14	Minnesota	60.4
45	Mississippi	22.2
35	Missouri	40.6
NA	Montana**	NA
7	Nebraska	65.8
24	Nevada	53.3
12	New Hampshire	62.5
15	New Jersey	60.3
42	New Mexico	27.3
27	New York	48.7
41	North Carolina	33.5
5	North Dakota	66.7
28	Ohio	48.4
39	Oklahoma	37.9
6	Oregon	66.4
31	Pennsylvania	44.9
2	Rhode Island	74.2
36	South Carolina	38.9
1	South Dakota	86.7
40	Tennessee	37.5
32	Texas	43.1
16	Utah	60.2
43	Vermont	25.0
21	Virginia	55.7
23	Washington	55.1
48	West Virginia	13.8
17	Wisconsin	59.1
46	Wyoming	21.3

RANK ORDER

RANK	STATE	PERCENT
1	South Dakota	86.7
2	Rhode Island	74.2
3	Idaho	67.8
4	Kentucky	67.6
5	North Dakota	66.7
6	Oregon	66.4
7	Nebraska	65.8
8	Arizona	65.4
9	Iowa	64.9
10	Maine	63.0
11	Maryland	62.7
12	New Hampshire	62.5
13	Colorado	62.3
14	Minnesota	60.4
15	New Jersey	60.3
16	Utah	60.2
17	Wisconsin	59.1
18	Massachusetts	58.1
19	Kansas	56.3
20	California	55.8
21	Virginia	55.7
22	Delaware	55.6
23	Washington	55.1
24	Alaska	53.3
24	Nevada	53.3
26	Florida	50.4
27	New York	48.7
28	Ohio	48.4
29	Hawaii	47.2
30	Indiana	46.5
31	Pennsylvania	44.9
32	Louisiana	43.1
32	Texas	43.1
34	Connecticut	42.5
35	Missouri	40.6
36	Michigan	38.9
36	South Carolina	38.9
38	Illinois	38.4
39	Oklahoma	37.9
40	Tennessee	37.5
41	North Carolina	33.5
42	New Mexico	27.3
43	Vermont	25.0
44	Georgia	24.6
45	Mississippi	22.2
46	Wyoming	21.3
47	Alabama	19.0
48	West Virginia	13.8
49	Arkansas	7.7
NA	Montana**	NA
	District of Columbia**	NA

Source: Morgan Quitno Press using data from Federal Bureau of Investigation
    "Crime in the United States 2004" (Uniform Crime Reports, October 17, 2005)
*Arrests of youths 17 years and younger by law enforcement agencies submitting complete reports to the F.B.I. for 12 months in 2004. Arson is the willful burning of or attempt to burn a building, vehicle or another's personal property.
**Not available.

211

Reported Arrests of Juveniles for Weapons Violations in 2004

National Total = 32,150 Reported Arrests*

ALPHA ORDER

RANK	STATE	ARRESTS	% of USA
36	Alabama	134	0.4%
43	Alaska	45	0.1%
18	Arizona	522	1.6%
37	Arkansas	103	0.3%
1	California	7,729	24.0%
11	Colorado	665	2.1%
22	Connecticut	321	1.0%
35	Delaware	139	0.4%
2	Florida	2,712	8.4%
15	Georgia	608	1.9%
44	Hawaii	41	0.1%
27	Idaho	205	0.6%
8	Illinois	1,282	4.0%
33	Indiana	155	0.5%
39	Iowa	85	0.3%
34	Kansas	141	0.4%
38	Kentucky	90	0.3%
25	Louisiana	281	0.9%
42	Maine	47	0.1%
6	Maryland	1,525	4.7%
28	Massachusetts	193	0.6%
13	Michigan	632	2.0%
20	Minnesota	379	1.2%
32	Mississippi	176	0.5%
19	Missouri	512	1.6%
NA	Montana**	NA	NA
31	Nebraska	182	0.6%
30	Nevada	184	0.6%
48	New Hampshire	13	0.0%
3	New Jersey	2,086	6.5%
26	New Mexico	258	0.8%
10	New York	889	2.8%
9	North Carolina	1,201	3.7%
45	North Dakota	39	0.1%
17	Ohio	575	1.8%
23	Oklahoma	307	1.0%
24	Oregon	284	0.9%
5	Pennsylvania	1,575	4.9%
29	Rhode Island	188	0.6%
40	South Carolina	67	0.2%
46	South Dakota	33	0.1%
16	Tennessee	584	1.8%
4	Texas	1,820	5.7%
21	Utah	333	1.0%
49	Vermont	11	0.0%
14	Virginia	628	2.0%
12	Washington	662	2.1%
47	West Virginia	26	0.1%
7	Wisconsin	1,429	4.4%
41	Wyoming	54	0.2%

RANK ORDER

RANK	STATE	ARRESTS	% of USA
1	California	7,729	24.0%
2	Florida	2,712	8.4%
3	New Jersey	2,086	6.5%
4	Texas	1,820	5.7%
5	Pennsylvania	1,575	4.9%
6	Maryland	1,525	4.7%
7	Wisconsin	1,429	4.4%
8	Illinois	1,282	4.0%
9	North Carolina	1,201	3.7%
10	New York	889	2.8%
11	Colorado	665	2.1%
12	Washington	662	2.1%
13	Michigan	632	2.0%
14	Virginia	628	2.0%
15	Georgia	608	1.9%
16	Tennessee	584	1.8%
17	Ohio	575	1.8%
18	Arizona	522	1.6%
19	Missouri	512	1.6%
20	Minnesota	379	1.2%
21	Utah	333	1.0%
22	Connecticut	321	1.0%
23	Oklahoma	307	1.0%
24	Oregon	284	0.9%
25	Louisiana	281	0.9%
26	New Mexico	258	0.8%
27	Idaho	205	0.6%
28	Massachusetts	193	0.6%
29	Rhode Island	188	0.6%
30	Nevada	184	0.6%
31	Nebraska	182	0.6%
32	Mississippi	176	0.5%
33	Indiana	155	0.5%
34	Kansas	141	0.4%
35	Delaware	139	0.4%
36	Alabama	134	0.4%
37	Arkansas	103	0.3%
38	Kentucky	90	0.3%
39	Iowa	85	0.3%
40	South Carolina	67	0.2%
41	Wyoming	54	0.2%
42	Maine	47	0.1%
43	Alaska	45	0.1%
44	Hawaii	41	0.1%
45	North Dakota	39	0.1%
46	South Dakota	33	0.1%
47	West Virginia	26	0.1%
48	New Hampshire	13	0.0%
49	Vermont	11	0.0%
NA	Montana**	NA	NA
	District of Columbia**	NA	NA

Source: Federal Bureau of Investigation
   "Crime in the United States 2004" (Uniform Crime Reports, October 17, 2005)
*Arrests of youths 17 years and younger by law enforcement agencies submitting complete reports to the F.B.I. for 12 months in 2004. Weapons violations include illegal carrying and possession. See important note at beginning of this chapter.
**Not available.

Reported Juvenile Arrest Rate for Weapons Violations in 2004

National Rate = 122.8 Reported Arrests per 100,000 Juvenile Population*

ALPHA ORDER

RANK	STATE	RATE
41	Alabama	29.9
36	Alaska	51.5
25	Arizona	79.1
34	Arkansas	62.6
4	California	188.8
9	Colorado	148.0
19	Connecticut	97.4
6	Delaware	172.7
11	Florida	147.1
NA	Georgia**	NA
38	Hawaii	35.4
12	Idaho	134.0
NA	Illinois**	NA
42	Indiana	28.9
40	Iowa	31.3
33	Kansas	63.8
NA	Kentucky**	NA
26	Louisiana	75.7
39	Maine	33.1
2	Maryland	234.7
37	Massachusetts	39.6
35	Michigan	56.5
21	Minnesota	93.6
16	Mississippi	100.1
20	Missouri	96.3
NA	Montana**	NA
17	Nebraska	99.3
29	Nevada	71.6
45	New Hampshire	11.2
3	New Jersey	216.7
10	New Mexico	147.8
23	New York	82.4
5	North Carolina	178.6
28	North Dakota	72.0
32	Ohio	64.5
24	Oklahoma	81.9
27	Oregon	75.4
13	Pennsylvania	132.5
8	Rhode Island	161.1
NA	South Carolina**	NA
30	South Dakota	67.6
15	Tennessee	112.8
31	Texas	67.0
7	Utah	171.1
44	Vermont	19.1
22	Virginia	87.3
14	Washington	123.7
43	West Virginia	24.7
1	Wisconsin	276.1
18	Wyoming	98.7

RANK ORDER

RANK	STATE	RATE
1	Wisconsin	276.1
2	Maryland	234.7
3	New Jersey	216.7
4	California	188.8
5	North Carolina	178.6
6	Delaware	172.7
7	Utah	171.1
8	Rhode Island	161.1
9	Colorado	148.0
10	New Mexico	147.8
11	Florida	147.1
12	Idaho	134.0
13	Pennsylvania	132.5
14	Washington	123.7
15	Tennessee	112.8
16	Mississippi	100.1
17	Nebraska	99.3
18	Wyoming	98.7
19	Connecticut	97.4
20	Missouri	96.3
21	Minnesota	93.6
22	Virginia	87.3
23	New York	82.4
24	Oklahoma	81.9
25	Arizona	79.1
26	Louisiana	75.7
27	Oregon	75.4
28	North Dakota	72.0
29	Nevada	71.6
30	South Dakota	67.6
31	Texas	67.0
32	Ohio	64.5
33	Kansas	63.8
34	Arkansas	62.6
35	Michigan	56.5
36	Alaska	51.5
37	Massachusetts	39.6
38	Hawaii	35.4
39	Maine	33.1
40	Iowa	31.3
41	Alabama	29.9
42	Indiana	28.9
43	West Virginia	24.7
44	Vermont	19.1
45	New Hampshire	11.2
NA	Georgia**	NA
NA	Illinois**	NA
NA	Kentucky**	NA
NA	Montana**	NA
NA	South Carolina**	NA
	District of Columbia**	NA

Source: Morgan Quitno Press using data from Federal Bureau of Investigation
    "Crime in the United States 2004" (Uniform Crime Reports, October 17, 2005)
*By law enforcement agencies submitting complete reports to the F.B.I. for 12 months in 2004. Arrests of youths 17 years and younger divided into population of 10 to 17 year olds. See important note at beginning of this chapter. Weapons violations include illegal carrying and possession.
**Not available.

Reported Arrests of Juveniles for Weapons Violations
As a Percent of All Such Arrests in 2004
National Percent = 23.8% of Reported Weapons Violations Arrests*

ALPHA ORDER

RANK ORDER

RANK	STATE	PERCENT
46	Alabama	11.0
44	Alaska	12.5
35	Arizona	15.7
48	Arkansas	10.5
17	California	27.2
15	Colorado	28.5
19	Connecticut	25.3
3	Delaware	41.7
7	Florida	34.9
34	Georgia	16.4
29	Hawaii	19.9
12	Idaho	32.7
18	Illinois	26.6
47	Indiana	10.7
31	Iowa	19.0
25	Kansas	20.4
35	Kentucky	15.7
32	Louisiana	17.0
38	Maine	14.9
6	Maryland	36.9
20	Massachusetts	25.0
42	Michigan	13.3
2	Minnesota	43.2
21	Mississippi	23.9
37	Missouri	15.6
NA	Montana**	NA
33	Nebraska	16.6
45	Nevada	11.6
38	New Hampshire	14.9
8	New Jersey	34.5
10	New Mexico	34.2
23	New York	21.7
24	North Carolina	21.4
14	North Dakota	28.7
30	Ohio	19.6
41	Oklahoma	13.5
43	Oregon	12.9
9	Pennsylvania	34.4
13	Rhode Island	31.9
26	South Carolina	20.2
4	South Dakota	41.3
27	Tennessee	20.1
40	Texas	14.0
16	Utah	28.4
1	Vermont	68.8
28	Virginia	20.0
22	Washington	23.8
49	West Virginia	8.5
11	Wisconsin	32.8
5	Wyoming	38.6

RANK	STATE	PERCENT
1	Vermont	68.8
2	Minnesota	43.2
3	Delaware	41.7
4	South Dakota	41.3
5	Wyoming	38.6
6	Maryland	36.9
7	Florida	34.9
8	New Jersey	34.5
9	Pennsylvania	34.4
10	New Mexico	34.2
11	Wisconsin	32.8
12	Idaho	32.7
13	Rhode Island	31.9
14	North Dakota	28.7
15	Colorado	28.5
16	Utah	28.4
17	California	27.2
18	Illinois	26.6
19	Connecticut	25.3
20	Massachusetts	25.0
21	Mississippi	23.9
22	Washington	23.8
23	New York	21.7
24	North Carolina	21.4
25	Kansas	20.4
26	South Carolina	20.2
27	Tennessee	20.1
28	Virginia	20.0
29	Hawaii	19.9
30	Ohio	19.6
31	Iowa	19.0
32	Louisiana	17.0
33	Nebraska	16.6
34	Georgia	16.4
35	Arizona	15.7
35	Kentucky	15.7
37	Missouri	15.6
38	Maine	14.9
38	New Hampshire	14.9
40	Texas	14.0
41	Oklahoma	13.5
42	Michigan	13.3
43	Oregon	12.9
44	Alaska	12.5
45	Nevada	11.6
46	Alabama	11.0
47	Indiana	10.7
48	Arkansas	10.5
49	West Virginia	8.5
NA	Montana**	NA
	District of Columbia**	NA

Source: Morgan Quitno Press using data from Federal Bureau of Investigation
"Crime in the United States 2004" (Uniform Crime Reports, October 17, 2005)
*Arrests of youths 17 years and younger by law enforcement agencies submitting complete reports to the F.B.I. for 12 months in 2004. Weapons violations include illegal carrying and possession.
**Not available.

Reported Arrests of Juveniles for Driving Under the Influence in 2004

National Total = 14,533 Reported Arrests*

ALPHA ORDER

RANK	STATE	ARRESTS	% of USA
33	Alabama	133	0.9%
37	Alaska	98	0.7%
6	Arizona	588	4.0%
38	Arkansas	95	0.7%
1	California	1,456	10.0%
12	Colorado	454	3.1%
32	Connecticut	134	0.9%
49	Delaware	0	0.0%
11	Florida	480	3.3%
27	Georgia	178	1.2%
41	Hawaii	68	0.5%
26	Idaho	189	1.3%
44	Illinois	52	0.4%
21	Indiana	231	1.6%
15	Iowa	321	2.2%
19	Kansas	287	2.0%
43	Kentucky	62	0.4%
28	Louisiana	154	1.1%
31	Maine	138	0.9%
17	Maryland	313	2.2%
35	Massachusetts	119	0.8%
3	Michigan	812	5.6%
4	Minnesota	687	4.7%
30	Mississippi	144	1.0%
10	Missouri	524	3.6%
NA	Montana**	NA	NA
14	Nebraska	338	2.3%
39	Nevada	90	0.6%
34	New Hampshire	120	0.8%
13	New Jersey	344	2.4%
22	New Mexico	225	1.5%
18	New York	298	2.1%
8	North Carolina	572	3.9%
42	North Dakota	66	0.5%
20	Ohio	257	1.8%
16	Oklahoma	316	2.2%
25	Oregon	197	1.4%
7	Pennsylvania	583	4.0%
46	Rhode Island	36	0.2%
48	South Carolina	10	0.1%
36	South Dakota	111	0.8%
24	Tennessee	203	1.4%
2	Texas	1,313	9.0%
29	Utah	146	1.0%
47	Vermont	34	0.2%
23	Virginia	214	1.5%
9	Washington	557	3.8%
45	West Virginia	41	0.3%
5	Wisconsin	662	4.6%
40	Wyoming	83	0.6%

RANK ORDER

RANK	STATE	ARRESTS	% of USA
1	California	1,456	10.0%
2	Texas	1,313	9.0%
3	Michigan	812	5.6%
4	Minnesota	687	4.7%
5	Wisconsin	662	4.6%
6	Arizona	588	4.0%
7	Pennsylvania	583	4.0%
8	North Carolina	572	3.9%
9	Washington	557	3.8%
10	Missouri	524	3.6%
11	Florida	480	3.3%
12	Colorado	454	3.1%
13	New Jersey	344	2.4%
14	Nebraska	338	2.3%
15	Iowa	321	2.2%
16	Oklahoma	316	2.2%
17	Maryland	313	2.2%
18	New York	298	2.1%
19	Kansas	287	2.0%
20	Ohio	257	1.8%
21	Indiana	231	1.6%
22	New Mexico	225	1.5%
23	Virginia	214	1.5%
24	Tennessee	203	1.4%
25	Oregon	197	1.4%
26	Idaho	189	1.3%
27	Georgia	178	1.2%
28	Louisiana	154	1.1%
29	Utah	146	1.0%
30	Mississippi	144	1.0%
31	Maine	138	0.9%
32	Connecticut	134	0.9%
33	Alabama	133	0.9%
34	New Hampshire	120	0.8%
35	Massachusetts	119	0.8%
36	South Dakota	111	0.8%
37	Alaska	98	0.7%
38	Arkansas	95	0.7%
39	Nevada	90	0.6%
40	Wyoming	83	0.6%
41	Hawaii	68	0.5%
42	North Dakota	66	0.5%
43	Kentucky	62	0.4%
44	Illinois	52	0.4%
45	West Virginia	41	0.3%
46	Rhode Island	36	0.2%
47	Vermont	34	0.2%
48	South Carolina	10	0.1%
49	Delaware	0	0.0%
NA	Montana**	NA	NA
	District of Columbia**	NA	NA

Source: Federal Bureau of Investigation
   "Crime in the United States 2004" (Uniform Crime Reports, October 17, 2005)
*Arrests of youths 17 years and younger by law enforcement agencies submitting complete reports to the F.B.I. for 12 months in 2004. Includes driving any vehicle while drunk or under the influence of liquor or narcotics. See important note at beginning of this chapter.
**Not available.

Reported Juvenile Arrest Rate for Driving Under the Influence in 2004

National Rate = 55.5 Reported Arrests per 100,000 Juvenile Population*

ALPHA ORDER

RANK	STATE	RATE
40	Alabama	29.7
11	Alaska	112.2
17	Arizona	89.1
25	Arkansas	57.7
36	California	35.6
14	Colorado	101.0
32	Connecticut	40.6
45	Delaware	0.0
43	Florida	26.0
NA	Georgia**	NA
24	Hawaii	58.7
8	Idaho	123.6
NA	Illinois**	NA
30	Indiana	43.1
10	Iowa	118.3
5	Kansas	129.8
NA	Kentucky**	NA
31	Louisiana	41.5
16	Maine	97.1
29	Maryland	48.2
44	Massachusetts	24.4
22	Michigan	72.6
3	Minnesota	169.6
20	Mississippi	81.9
15	Missouri	98.5
NA	Montana**	NA
2	Nebraska	184.4
37	Nevada	35.0
13	New Hampshire	103.4
35	New Jersey	35.7
6	New Mexico	128.9
42	New York	27.6
18	North Carolina	85.1
9	North Dakota	121.8
41	Ohio	28.8
19	Oklahoma	84.3
26	Oregon	52.3
27	Pennsylvania	49.1
38	Rhode Island	30.8
NA	South Carolina**	NA
1	South Dakota	227.5
33	Tennessee	39.2
28	Texas	48.3
21	Utah	75.0
23	Vermont	58.9
39	Virginia	29.8
12	Washington	104.1
34	West Virginia	38.9
7	Wisconsin	127.9
4	Wyoming	151.8

RANK ORDER

RANK	STATE	RATE
1	South Dakota	227.5
2	Nebraska	184.4
3	Minnesota	169.6
4	Wyoming	151.8
5	Kansas	129.8
6	New Mexico	128.9
7	Wisconsin	127.9
8	Idaho	123.6
9	North Dakota	121.8
10	Iowa	118.3
11	Alaska	112.2
12	Washington	104.1
13	New Hampshire	103.4
14	Colorado	101.0
15	Missouri	98.5
16	Maine	97.1
17	Arizona	89.1
18	North Carolina	85.1
19	Oklahoma	84.3
20	Mississippi	81.9
21	Utah	75.0
22	Michigan	72.6
23	Vermont	58.9
24	Hawaii	58.7
25	Arkansas	57.7
26	Oregon	52.3
27	Pennsylvania	49.1
28	Texas	48.3
29	Maryland	48.2
30	Indiana	43.1
31	Louisiana	41.5
32	Connecticut	40.6
33	Tennessee	39.2
34	West Virginia	38.9
35	New Jersey	35.7
36	California	35.6
37	Nevada	35.0
38	Rhode Island	30.8
39	Virginia	29.8
40	Alabama	29.7
41	Ohio	28.8
42	New York	27.6
43	Florida	26.0
44	Massachusetts	24.4
45	Delaware	0.0
NA	Georgia**	NA
NA	Illinois**	NA
NA	Kentucky**	NA
NA	Montana**	NA
NA	South Carolina**	NA
	District of Columbia**	NA

Source: Morgan Quitno Press using data from Federal Bureau of Investigation
    "Crime in the United States 2004" (Uniform Crime Reports, October 17, 2005)
*By law enforcement agencies submitting complete reports to the F.B.I. for 12 months in 2004. Arrests of youths 17 years and younger divided into population of 10 to 17 year olds. See important note at beginning of this chapter. Includes driving any vehicle while drunk or under the influence of liquor or narcotics.
**Not available.

Reported Arrests of Juveniles for Driving Under the Influence
As a Percent of All Such Arrests in 2004
National Percent = 1.4% of Reported Driving Under the Influence Arrests*

ALPHA ORDER

RANK	STATE	PERCENT
39	Alabama	1.0
10	Alaska	1.9
19	Arizona	1.6
24	Arkansas	1.4
46	California	0.8
6	Colorado	2.1
21	Connecticut	1.5
49	Delaware	0.0
42	Florida	0.9
32	Georgia	1.2
17	Hawaii	1.7
6	Idaho	2.1
42	Illinois	0.9
46	Indiana	0.8
5	Iowa	2.3
6	Kansas	2.1
35	Kentucky	1.1
24	Louisiana	1.4
10	Maine	1.9
29	Maryland	1.3
29	Massachusetts	1.3
13	Michigan	1.8
1	Minnesota	3.0
32	Mississippi	1.2
13	Missouri	1.8
NA	Montana**	NA
4	Nebraska	2.4
39	Nevada	1.0
6	New Hampshire	2.1
24	New Jersey	1.4
13	New Mexico	1.8
35	New York	1.1
35	North Carolina	1.1
19	North Dakota	1.6
29	Ohio	1.3
17	Oklahoma	1.7
32	Oregon	1.2
24	Pennsylvania	1.4
21	Rhode Island	1.5
48	South Carolina	0.4
2	South Dakota	2.9
42	Tennessee	0.9
24	Texas	1.4
3	Utah	2.7
39	Vermont	1.0
42	Virginia	0.9
21	Washington	1.5
35	West Virginia	1.1
10	Wisconsin	1.9
13	Wyoming	1.8

RANK ORDER

RANK	STATE	PERCENT
1	Minnesota	3.0
2	South Dakota	2.9
3	Utah	2.7
4	Nebraska	2.4
5	Iowa	2.3
6	Colorado	2.1
6	Idaho	2.1
6	Kansas	2.1
6	New Hampshire	2.1
10	Alaska	1.9
10	Maine	1.9
10	Wisconsin	1.9
13	Michigan	1.8
13	Missouri	1.8
13	New Mexico	1.8
13	Wyoming	1.8
17	Hawaii	1.7
17	Oklahoma	1.7
19	Arizona	1.6
19	North Dakota	1.6
21	Connecticut	1.5
21	Rhode Island	1.5
21	Washington	1.5
24	Arkansas	1.4
24	Louisiana	1.4
24	New Jersey	1.4
24	Pennsylvania	1.4
24	Texas	1.4
29	Maryland	1.3
29	Massachusetts	1.3
29	Ohio	1.3
32	Georgia	1.2
32	Mississippi	1.2
32	Oregon	1.2
35	Kentucky	1.1
35	New York	1.1
35	North Carolina	1.1
35	West Virginia	1.1
39	Alabama	1.0
39	Nevada	1.0
39	Vermont	1.0
42	Florida	0.9
42	Illinois	0.9
42	Tennessee	0.9
42	Virginia	0.9
46	California	0.8
46	Indiana	0.8
48	South Carolina	0.4
49	Delaware	0.0
NA	Montana**	NA
	District of Columbia**	NA

Source: Morgan Quitno Press using data from Federal Bureau of Investigation
"Crime in the United States 2004" (Uniform Crime Reports, October 17, 2005)
*Arrests of youths 17 years and younger by law enforcement agencies submitting complete reports to the F.B.I. for
12 months in 2004. Includes driving any vehicle while drunk or under the influence of liquor or narcotics.
**Not available.

Reported Arrests of Juveniles for Drug Abuse Violations in 2004

National Total = 153,298 Reported Arrests*

ALPHA ORDER

RANK	STATE	ARRESTS	% of USA
31	Alabama	1,096	0.7%
45	Alaska	327	0.2%
9	Arizona	5,491	3.6%
40	Arkansas	630	0.4%
1	California	20,267	13.2%
14	Colorado	3,178	2.1%
24	Connecticut	1,867	1.2%
42	Delaware	532	0.3%
3	Florida	14,134	9.2%
22	Georgia	2,230	1.5%
43	Hawaii	432	0.3%
36	Idaho	813	0.5%
4	Illinois	8,441	5.5%
19	Indiana	2,406	1.6%
32	Iowa	1,028	0.7%
28	Kansas	1,133	0.7%
34	Kentucky	984	0.6%
23	Louisiana	2,217	1.4%
37	Maine	803	0.5%
5	Maryland	8,110	5.3%
26	Massachusetts	1,728	1.1%
11	Michigan	3,500	2.3%
18	Minnesota	2,409	1.6%
33	Mississippi	1,003	0.7%
13	Missouri	3,317	2.2%
NA	Montana**	NA	NA
29	Nebraska	1,130	0.7%
35	Nevada	843	0.5%
38	New Hampshire	695	0.5%
7	New Jersey	6,351	4.1%
30	New Mexico	1,104	0.7%
8	New York	5,697	3.7%
15	North Carolina	2,843	1.9%
46	North Dakota	208	0.1%
12	Ohio	3,365	2.2%
25	Oklahoma	1,826	1.2%
20	Oregon	2,340	1.5%
6	Pennsylvania	6,634	4.3%
39	Rhode Island	658	0.4%
44	South Carolina	331	0.2%
47	South Dakota	203	0.1%
16	Tennessee	2,812	1.8%
2	Texas	16,515	10.8%
27	Utah	1,167	0.8%
49	Vermont	148	0.1%
21	Virginia	2,263	1.5%
17	Washington	2,527	1.6%
48	West Virginia	173	0.1%
10	Wisconsin	4,821	3.1%
41	Wyoming	568	0.4%

RANK ORDER

RANK	STATE	ARRESTS	% of USA
1	California	20,267	13.2%
2	Texas	16,515	10.8%
3	Florida	14,134	9.2%
4	Illinois	8,441	5.5%
5	Maryland	8,110	5.3%
6	Pennsylvania	6,634	4.3%
7	New Jersey	6,351	4.1%
8	New York	5,697	3.7%
9	Arizona	5,491	3.6%
10	Wisconsin	4,821	3.1%
11	Michigan	3,500	2.3%
12	Ohio	3,365	2.2%
13	Missouri	3,317	2.2%
14	Colorado	3,178	2.1%
15	North Carolina	2,843	1.9%
16	Tennessee	2,812	1.8%
17	Washington	2,527	1.6%
18	Minnesota	2,409	1.6%
19	Indiana	2,406	1.6%
20	Oregon	2,340	1.5%
21	Virginia	2,263	1.5%
22	Georgia	2,230	1.5%
23	Louisiana	2,217	1.4%
24	Connecticut	1,867	1.2%
25	Oklahoma	1,826	1.2%
26	Massachusetts	1,728	1.1%
27	Utah	1,167	0.8%
28	Kansas	1,133	0.7%
29	Nebraska	1,130	0.7%
30	New Mexico	1,104	0.7%
31	Alabama	1,096	0.7%
32	Iowa	1,028	0.7%
33	Mississippi	1,003	0.7%
34	Kentucky	984	0.6%
35	Nevada	843	0.5%
36	Idaho	813	0.5%
37	Maine	803	0.5%
38	New Hampshire	695	0.5%
39	Rhode Island	658	0.4%
40	Arkansas	630	0.4%
41	Wyoming	568	0.4%
42	Delaware	532	0.3%
43	Hawaii	432	0.3%
44	South Carolina	331	0.2%
45	Alaska	327	0.2%
46	North Dakota	208	0.1%
47	South Dakota	203	0.1%
48	West Virginia	173	0.1%
49	Vermont	148	0.1%
NA	Montana**	NA	NA
	District of Columbia**	NA	NA

Source: Federal Bureau of Investigation
   "Crime in the United States 2004" (Uniform Crime Reports, October 17, 2005)
*Arrests of youths 17 years and younger by law enforcement agencies submitting complete reports to the F.B.I. for 12 months in 2004. Includes offenses relating to possession, sale, use, growing and manufacturing of narcotic drugs. See important note at beginning of this chapter.
**Not available.

Reported Juvenile Arrest Rate for Drug Abuse Violations in 2004

National Rate = 585.6 Reported Arrests per 100,000 Juvenile Population*

ALPHA ORDER

RANK ORDER

RANK	STATE	RATE		RANK	STATE	RATE
44	Alabama	244.6		1	Maryland	1,248.0
37	Alaska	374.5		2	Wyoming	1,038.6
4	Arizona	831.9		3	Wisconsin	931.3
34	Arkansas	382.7		4	Arizona	831.9
27	California	495.0		5	Florida	766.7
6	Colorado	707.2		6	Colorado	707.2
19	Connecticut	566.3		7	Delaware	660.9
7	Delaware	660.9		8	New Jersey	659.9
5	Florida	766.7		9	New Mexico	632.3
NA	Georgia**	NA		10	Missouri	623.6
38	Hawaii	372.8		11	Oregon	621.5
24	Idaho	531.5		12	Nebraska	616.3
NA	Illinois**	NA		13	Texas	607.8
30	Indiana	449.3		14	Utah	599.7
35	Iowa	378.8		15	New Hampshire	599.1
26	Kansas	512.6		16	Louisiana	597.5
NA	Kentucky**	NA		17	Minnesota	594.7
16	Louisiana	597.5		18	Mississippi	570.6
20	Maine	564.9		19	Connecticut	566.3
1	Maryland	1,248.0		20	Maine	564.9
39	Massachusetts	354.9		21	Rhode Island	563.8
42	Michigan	312.8		22	Pennsylvania	558.2
17	Minnesota	594.7		23	Tennessee	542.9
18	Mississippi	570.6		24	Idaho	531.5
10	Missouri	623.6		25	New York	528.1
NA	Montana**	NA		26	Kansas	512.6
12	Nebraska	616.3		27	California	495.0
40	Nevada	328.1		28	Oklahoma	487.3
15	New Hampshire	599.1		29	Washington	472.2
8	New Jersey	659.9		30	Indiana	449.3
9	New Mexico	632.3		31	North Carolina	422.9
25	New York	528.1		32	South Dakota	416.1
31	North Carolina	422.9		33	North Dakota	383.7
33	North Dakota	383.7		34	Arkansas	382.7
36	Ohio	377.6		35	Iowa	378.8
28	Oklahoma	487.3		36	Ohio	377.6
11	Oregon	621.5		37	Alaska	374.5
22	Pennsylvania	558.2		38	Hawaii	372.8
21	Rhode Island	563.8		39	Massachusetts	354.9
NA	South Carolina**	NA		40	Nevada	328.1
32	South Dakota	416.1		41	Virginia	314.6
23	Tennessee	542.9		42	Michigan	312.8
13	Texas	607.8		43	Vermont	256.5
14	Utah	599.7		44	Alabama	244.6
43	Vermont	256.5		45	West Virginia	164.3
41	Virginia	314.6		NA	Georgia**	NA
29	Washington	472.2		NA	Illinois**	NA
45	West Virginia	164.3		NA	Kentucky**	NA
3	Wisconsin	931.3		NA	Montana**	NA
2	Wyoming	1,038.6		NA	South Carolina**	NA
					District of Columbia**	NA

Source: Morgan Quitno Press using data from Federal Bureau of Investigation
    "Crime in the United States 2004" (Uniform Crime Reports, October 17, 2005)
*By law enforcement agencies submitting complete reports to the F.B.I. for 12 months in 2004. Arrests of youths 17
years and younger divided into population of 10 to 17 year olds. See important note at beginning of this chapter.
Includes offenses relating to possession, sale, use, growing and manufacturing of narcotic drugs.
**Not available.

Reported Arrests of Juveniles for Drug Abuse Violations
As a Percent of All Such Arrests in 2004
National Percent = 10.9% of Reported Drug Abuse Violations Arrests*

ALPHA ORDER

RANK	STATE	PERCENT
48	Alabama	6.0
5	Alaska	18.3
11	Arizona	15.4
41	Arkansas	8.6
46	California	7.4
6	Colorado	18.2
23	Connecticut	12.5
9	Delaware	16.4
34	Florida	9.4
45	Georgia	8.1
8	Hawaii	17.1
12	Idaho	15.1
17	Illinois	14.3
31	Indiana	10.6
29	Iowa	11.0
19	Kansas	13.3
38	Kentucky	9.0
41	Louisiana	8.6
16	Maine	14.5
10	Maryland	15.6
14	Massachusetts	14.9
27	Michigan	11.1
3	Minnesota	20.3
46	Mississippi	7.4
34	Missouri	9.4
NA	Montana**	NA
32	Nebraska	10.5
41	Nevada	8.6
2	New Hampshire	20.5
24	New Jersey	11.8
14	New Mexico	14.9
26	New York	11.3
39	North Carolina	8.9
18	North Dakota	13.5
33	Ohio	10.1
44	Oklahoma	8.4
30	Oregon	10.9
22	Pennsylvania	12.8
13	Rhode Island	15.0
37	South Carolina	9.1
20	South Dakota	13.2
40	Tennessee	8.7
20	Texas	13.2
7	Utah	17.4
27	Vermont	11.1
34	Virginia	9.4
24	Washington	11.8
49	West Virginia	5.3
1	Wisconsin	21.6
4	Wyoming	18.7

RANK ORDER

RANK	STATE	PERCENT
1	Wisconsin	21.6
2	New Hampshire	20.5
3	Minnesota	20.3
4	Wyoming	18.7
5	Alaska	18.3
6	Colorado	18.2
7	Utah	17.4
8	Hawaii	17.1
9	Delaware	16.4
10	Maryland	15.6
11	Arizona	15.4
12	Idaho	15.1
13	Rhode Island	15.0
14	Massachusetts	14.9
14	New Mexico	14.9
16	Maine	14.5
17	Illinois	14.3
18	North Dakota	13.5
19	Kansas	13.3
20	South Dakota	13.2
20	Texas	13.2
22	Pennsylvania	12.8
23	Connecticut	12.5
24	New Jersey	11.8
24	Washington	11.8
26	New York	11.3
27	Michigan	11.1
27	Vermont	11.1
29	Iowa	11.0
30	Oregon	10.9
31	Indiana	10.6
32	Nebraska	10.5
33	Ohio	10.1
34	Florida	9.4
34	Missouri	9.4
34	Virginia	9.4
37	South Carolina	9.1
38	Kentucky	9.0
39	North Carolina	8.9
40	Tennessee	8.7
41	Arkansas	8.6
41	Louisiana	8.6
41	Nevada	8.6
44	Oklahoma	8.4
45	Georgia	8.1
46	California	7.4
46	Mississippi	7.4
48	Alabama	6.0
49	West Virginia	5.3
NA	Montana**	NA
	District of Columbia**	NA

Source: Morgan Quitno Press using data from Federal Bureau of Investigation
    "Crime in the United States 2004" (Uniform Crime Reports, October 17, 2005)
*Arrests of youths 17 years and younger by law enforcement agencies submitting complete reports to the F.B.I. for 12 months in 2004. Includes offenses relating to possession, sale, use, growing and manufacturing of narcotic drugs.
**Not available.

Reported Arrests of Juveniles for Sex Offenses in 2004

National Total = 13,563 Reported Arrests*

ALPHA ORDER

RANK ORDER

RANK	STATE	ARRESTS	% of USA		RANK	STATE	ARRESTS	% of USA
45	Alabama	22	0.2%		1	California	2,370	17.5%
40	Alaska	33	0.2%		2	Wisconsin	1,452	10.7%
9	Arizona	406	3.0%		3	Texas	1,013	7.5%
36	Arkansas	45	0.3%		4	New York	891	6.6%
1	California	2,370	17.5%		5	Pennsylvania	694	5.1%
10	Colorado	399	2.9%		6	Florida	482	3.6%
22	Connecticut	163	1.2%		7	Missouri	472	3.5%
47	Delaware	12	0.1%		8	Utah	407	3.0%
6	Florida	482	3.6%		9	Arizona	406	3.0%
14	Georgia	344	2.5%		10	Colorado	399	2.9%
32	Hawaii	79	0.6%		11	New Jersey	383	2.8%
26	Idaho	111	0.8%		12	Maryland	366	2.7%
23	Illinois	135	1.0%		13	Michigan	350	2.6%
16	Indiana	276	2.0%		14	Georgia	344	2.5%
33	Iowa	73	0.5%		15	Ohio	321	2.4%
27	Kansas	110	0.8%		16	Indiana	276	2.0%
29	Kentucky	90	0.7%		17	Washington	254	1.9%
18	Louisiana	227	1.7%		18	Louisiana	227	1.7%
35	Maine	61	0.4%		19	Oregon	225	1.7%
12	Maryland	366	2.7%		20	Minnesota	224	1.7%
31	Massachusetts	81	0.6%		21	Virginia	220	1.6%
13	Michigan	350	2.6%		22	Connecticut	163	1.2%
20	Minnesota	224	1.7%		23	Illinois	135	1.0%
37	Mississippi	42	0.3%		24	Tennessee	132	1.0%
7	Missouri	472	3.5%		25	North Carolina	112	0.8%
NA	Montana**	NA	NA		26	Idaho	111	0.8%
27	Nebraska	110	0.8%		27	Kansas	110	0.8%
30	Nevada	85	0.6%		27	Nebraska	110	0.8%
38	New Hampshire	35	0.3%		29	Kentucky	90	0.7%
11	New Jersey	383	2.8%		30	Nevada	85	0.6%
44	New Mexico	25	0.2%		31	Massachusetts	81	0.6%
4	New York	891	6.6%		32	Hawaii	79	0.6%
25	North Carolina	112	0.8%		33	Iowa	73	0.5%
38	North Dakota	35	0.3%		34	Oklahoma	71	0.5%
15	Ohio	321	2.4%		35	Maine	61	0.4%
34	Oklahoma	71	0.5%		36	Arkansas	45	0.3%
19	Oregon	225	1.7%		37	Mississippi	42	0.3%
5	Pennsylvania	694	5.1%		38	New Hampshire	35	0.3%
42	Rhode Island	31	0.2%		38	North Dakota	35	0.3%
41	South Carolina	32	0.2%		40	Alaska	33	0.2%
43	South Dakota	30	0.2%		41	South Carolina	32	0.2%
24	Tennessee	132	1.0%		42	Rhode Island	31	0.2%
3	Texas	1,013	7.5%		43	South Dakota	30	0.2%
8	Utah	407	3.0%		44	New Mexico	25	0.2%
48	Vermont	8	0.1%		45	Alabama	22	0.2%
21	Virginia	220	1.6%		46	Wyoming	19	0.1%
17	Washington	254	1.9%		47	Delaware	12	0.1%
49	West Virginia	5	0.0%		48	Vermont	8	0.1%
2	Wisconsin	1,452	10.7%		49	West Virginia	5	0.0%
46	Wyoming	19	0.1%		NA	Montana**	NA	NA
						District of Columbia**	NA	NA

Source: Federal Bureau of Investigation
   "Crime in the United States 2004" (Uniform Crime Reports, October 17, 2005)
*Arrests of youths 17 years and younger by law enforcement agencies submitting complete reports to the F.B.I. for 12 months in 2004. Excludes forcible rape, prostitution and commercialized vice. Includes statutory rape and offenses against chastity, common decency, morals and the like. See important note at beginning of this chapter.
**Not available.

Reported Juvenile Arrest Rate for Sex Offenses in 2004

National Rate = 51.8 Reported Arrests per 100,000 Juvenile Population*

ALPHA ORDER

RANK	STATE	RATE
44	Alabama	4.9
24	Alaska	37.8
9	Arizona	61.5
32	Arkansas	27.3
15	California	57.9
3	Colorado	88.8
20	Connecticut	49.4
41	Delaware	14.9
35	Florida	26.1
NA	Georgia**	NA
7	Hawaii	68.2
6	Idaho	72.6
NA	Illinois**	NA
18	Indiana	51.5
33	Iowa	26.9
19	Kansas	49.8
NA	Kentucky**	NA
11	Louisiana	61.2
22	Maine	42.9
16	Maryland	56.3
40	Massachusetts	16.6
29	Michigan	31.3
17	Minnesota	55.3
37	Mississippi	23.9
4	Missouri	88.7
NA	Montana**	NA
12	Nebraska	60.0
28	Nevada	33.1
31	New Hampshire	30.2
23	New Jersey	39.8
42	New Mexico	14.3
5	New York	82.6
39	North Carolina	16.7
8	North Dakota	64.6
26	Ohio	36.0
38	Oklahoma	18.9
13	Oregon	59.8
14	Pennsylvania	58.4
34	Rhode Island	26.6
NA	South Carolina**	NA
9	South Dakota	61.5
36	Tennessee	25.5
25	Texas	37.3
2	Utah	209.1
43	Vermont	13.9
30	Virginia	30.6
21	Washington	47.5
45	West Virginia	4.7
1	Wisconsin	280.5
27	Wyoming	34.7

RANK ORDER

RANK	STATE	RATE
1	Wisconsin	280.5
2	Utah	209.1
3	Colorado	88.8
4	Missouri	88.7
5	New York	82.6
6	Idaho	72.6
7	Hawaii	68.2
8	North Dakota	64.6
9	Arizona	61.5
9	South Dakota	61.5
11	Louisiana	61.2
12	Nebraska	60.0
13	Oregon	59.8
14	Pennsylvania	58.4
15	California	57.9
16	Maryland	56.3
17	Minnesota	55.3
18	Indiana	51.5
19	Kansas	49.8
20	Connecticut	49.4
21	Washington	47.5
22	Maine	42.9
23	New Jersey	39.8
24	Alaska	37.8
25	Texas	37.3
26	Ohio	36.0
27	Wyoming	34.7
28	Nevada	33.1
29	Michigan	31.3
30	Virginia	30.6
31	New Hampshire	30.2
32	Arkansas	27.3
33	Iowa	26.9
34	Rhode Island	26.6
35	Florida	26.1
36	Tennessee	25.5
37	Mississippi	23.9
38	Oklahoma	18.9
39	North Carolina	16.7
40	Massachusetts	16.6
41	Delaware	14.9
42	New Mexico	14.3
43	Vermont	13.9
44	Alabama	4.9
45	West Virginia	4.7
NA	Georgia**	NA
NA	Illinois**	NA
NA	Kentucky**	NA
NA	Montana**	NA
NA	South Carolina**	NA
	District of Columbia**	NA

Source: Morgan Quitno Press using data from Federal Bureau of Investigation
    "Crime in the United States 2004" (Uniform Crime Reports, October 17, 2005)
*By law enforcement agencies submitting complete reports to the F.B.I. for 12 months in 2004. Arrests of youths 17 years and younger divided into population of 10 to 17 year olds. See important note at beginning of this chapter. Excludes forcible rape, prostitution and commercialized vice. Includes statutory rape and offenses against chastity, common decency, morals and the like. **Not available.

Reported Arrests of Juveniles for Sex Offenses
As a Percent of All Such Arrests in 2004
National Percent = 19.6% of Reported Sex Offense Arrests*

ALPHA ORDER

RANK ORDER

RANK	STATE	PERCENT
48	Alabama	5.6
38	Alaska	15.9
22	Arizona	21.6
23	Arkansas	21.5
37	California	16.4
7	Colorado	31.4
12	Connecticut	26.5
18	Delaware	22.2
42	Florida	12.0
44	Georgia	10.6
8	Hawaii	28.6
6	Idaho	33.1
46	Illinois	6.3
31	Indiana	18.7
10	Iowa	27.4
5	Kansas	35.9
3	Kentucky	40.7
33	Louisiana	18.2
27	Maine	20.5
11	Maryland	27.3
23	Massachusetts	21.5
14	Michigan	25.1
16	Minnesota	23.5
41	Mississippi	12.1
36	Missouri	16.7
NA	Montana**	NA
34	Nebraska	18.1
49	Nevada	5.5
21	New Hampshire	22.0
26	New Jersey	20.8
35	New Mexico	17.4
28	New York	20.2
43	North Carolina	10.9
4	North Dakota	38.5
15	Ohio	24.0
45	Oklahoma	8.7
32	Oregon	18.5
18	Pennsylvania	22.2
9	Rhode Island	28.2
20	South Carolina	22.1
13	South Dakota	25.6
25	Tennessee	21.2
28	Texas	20.2
1	Utah	48.2
39	Vermont	15.7
17	Virginia	23.4
30	Washington	20.1
47	West Virginia	5.7
2	Wisconsin	41.4
40	Wyoming	15.1

RANK	STATE	PERCENT
1	Utah	48.2
2	Wisconsin	41.4
3	Kentucky	40.7
4	North Dakota	38.5
5	Kansas	35.9
6	Idaho	33.1
7	Colorado	31.4
8	Hawaii	28.6
9	Rhode Island	28.2
10	Iowa	27.4
11	Maryland	27.3
12	Connecticut	26.5
13	South Dakota	25.6
14	Michigan	25.1
15	Ohio	24.0
16	Minnesota	23.5
17	Virginia	23.4
18	Delaware	22.2
18	Pennsylvania	22.2
20	South Carolina	22.1
21	New Hampshire	22.0
22	Arizona	21.6
23	Arkansas	21.5
23	Massachusetts	21.5
25	Tennessee	21.2
26	New Jersey	20.8
27	Maine	20.5
28	New York	20.2
28	Texas	20.2
30	Washington	20.1
31	Indiana	18.7
32	Oregon	18.5
33	Louisiana	18.2
34	Nebraska	18.1
35	New Mexico	17.4
36	Missouri	16.7
37	California	16.4
38	Alaska	15.9
39	Vermont	15.7
40	Wyoming	15.1
41	Mississippi	12.1
42	Florida	12.0
43	North Carolina	10.9
44	Georgia	10.6
45	Oklahoma	8.7
46	Illinois	6.3
47	West Virginia	5.7
48	Alabama	5.6
49	Nevada	5.5
NA	Montana**	NA
	District of Columbia**	NA

Source: Morgan Quitno Press using data from Federal Bureau of Investigation
   "Crime in the United States 2004" (Uniform Crime Reports, October 17, 2005)
*Arrests of youths 17 years and younger by law enforcement agencies submitting complete reports to the F.B.I. for 12 months in 2004. Excludes forcible rape, prostitution and commercialized vice. Includes statutory rape and offenses against chastity, common decency, morals and the like.
**Not available.

Reported Arrests of Juveniles for Prostitution and Commercialized Vice in 2004

National Total = 1,385 Reported Arrests*

ALPHA ORDER

RANK	STATE	ARRESTS	% of USA
37	Alabama	1	0.1%
40	Alaska	0	0.0%
7	Arizona	48	3.5%
31	Arkansas	3	0.2%
1	California	482	34.8%
22	Colorado	7	0.5%
28	Connecticut	4	0.3%
37	Delaware	1	0.1%
5	Florida	76	5.5%
11	Georgia	28	2.0%
27	Hawaii	5	0.4%
40	Idaho	0	0.0%
4	Illinois	84	6.1%
20	Indiana	10	0.7%
37	Iowa	1	0.1%
40	Kansas	0	0.0%
34	Kentucky	2	0.1%
22	Louisiana	7	0.5%
28	Maine	4	0.3%
8	Maryland	42	3.0%
16	Massachusetts	15	1.1%
18	Michigan	12	0.9%
34	Minnesota	2	0.1%
40	Mississippi	0	0.0%
26	Missouri	6	0.4%
NA	Montana**	NA	NA
31	Nebraska	3	0.2%
2	Nevada	143	10.3%
40	New Hampshire	0	0.0%
9	New Jersey	35	2.5%
31	New Mexico	3	0.2%
15	New York	17	1.2%
16	North Carolina	15	1.1%
20	North Dakota	10	0.7%
19	Ohio	11	0.8%
22	Oklahoma	7	0.5%
10	Oregon	29	2.1%
12	Pennsylvania	25	1.8%
40	Rhode Island	0	0.0%
40	South Carolina	0	0.0%
40	South Dakota	0	0.0%
13	Tennessee	22	1.6%
3	Texas	120	8.7%
22	Utah	7	0.5%
40	Vermont	0	0.0%
28	Virginia	4	0.3%
14	Washington	21	1.5%
40	West Virginia	0	0.0%
6	Wisconsin	71	5.1%
34	Wyoming	2	0.1%

RANK ORDER

RANK	STATE	ARRESTS	% of USA
1	California	482	34.8%
2	Nevada	143	10.3%
3	Texas	120	8.7%
4	Illinois	84	6.1%
5	Florida	76	5.5%
6	Wisconsin	71	5.1%
7	Arizona	48	3.5%
8	Maryland	42	3.0%
9	New Jersey	35	2.5%
10	Oregon	29	2.1%
11	Georgia	28	2.0%
12	Pennsylvania	25	1.8%
13	Tennessee	22	1.6%
14	Washington	21	1.5%
15	New York	17	1.2%
16	Massachusetts	15	1.1%
16	North Carolina	15	1.1%
18	Michigan	12	0.9%
19	Ohio	11	0.8%
20	Indiana	10	0.7%
20	North Dakota	10	0.7%
22	Colorado	7	0.5%
22	Louisiana	7	0.5%
22	Oklahoma	7	0.5%
22	Utah	7	0.5%
26	Missouri	6	0.4%
27	Hawaii	5	0.4%
28	Connecticut	4	0.3%
28	Maine	4	0.3%
28	Virginia	4	0.3%
31	Arkansas	3	0.2%
31	Nebraska	3	0.2%
31	New Mexico	3	0.2%
34	Kentucky	2	0.1%
34	Minnesota	2	0.1%
34	Wyoming	2	0.1%
37	Alabama	1	0.1%
37	Delaware	1	0.1%
37	Iowa	1	0.1%
40	Alaska	0	0.0%
40	Idaho	0	0.0%
40	Kansas	0	0.0%
40	Mississippi	0	0.0%
40	New Hampshire	0	0.0%
40	Rhode Island	0	0.0%
40	South Carolina	0	0.0%
40	South Dakota	0	0.0%
40	Vermont	0	0.0%
40	West Virginia	0	0.0%
NA	Montana**	NA	NA
	District of Columbia**	NA	NA

Source: Federal Bureau of Investigation
    "Crime in the United States 2004" (Uniform Crime Reports, October 17, 2005)
*Arrests of youths 17 years and younger by law enforcement agencies submitting complete reports to the F.B.I. for
12 months in 2004. Includes keeping a bawdy house, procuring or transporting women for immoral purposes.
Attempts are included. See important note at beginning of this chapter.
**Not available.

Reported Juvenile Arrest Rate for Prostitution and Commercialized Vice in 2004

National Rate = 5.3 Reported Arrests per 100,000 Juvenile Population*

ALPHA ORDER

RANK	STATE	RATE
36	Alabama	0.2
37	Alaska	0.0
6	Arizona	7.3
23	Arkansas	1.8
4	California	11.8
25	Colorado	1.6
28	Connecticut	1.2
28	Delaware	1.2
11	Florida	4.1
NA	Georgia**	NA
9	Hawaii	4.3
37	Idaho	0.0
NA	Illinois**	NA
20	Indiana	1.9
35	Iowa	0.4
37	Kansas	0.0
NA	Kentucky**	NA
20	Louisiana	1.9
17	Maine	2.8
7	Maryland	6.5
16	Massachusetts	3.1
31	Michigan	1.1
34	Minnesota	0.5
37	Mississippi	0.0
31	Missouri	1.1
NA	Montana**	NA
25	Nebraska	1.6
1	Nevada	55.7
37	New Hampshire	0.0
14	New Jersey	3.6
24	New Mexico	1.7
25	New York	1.6
18	North Carolina	2.2
2	North Dakota	18.4
28	Ohio	1.2
20	Oklahoma	1.9
5	Oregon	7.7
19	Pennsylvania	2.1
37	Rhode Island	0.0
NA	South Carolina**	NA
37	South Dakota	0.0
10	Tennessee	4.2
8	Texas	4.4
14	Utah	3.6
37	Vermont	0.0
33	Virginia	0.6
12	Washington	3.9
37	West Virginia	0.0
3	Wisconsin	13.7
13	Wyoming	3.7

RANK ORDER

RANK	STATE	RATE
1	Nevada	55.7
2	North Dakota	18.4
3	Wisconsin	13.7
4	California	11.8
5	Oregon	7.7
6	Arizona	7.3
7	Maryland	6.5
8	Texas	4.4
9	Hawaii	4.3
10	Tennessee	4.2
11	Florida	4.1
12	Washington	3.9
13	Wyoming	3.7
14	New Jersey	3.6
14	Utah	3.6
16	Massachusetts	3.1
17	Maine	2.8
18	North Carolina	2.2
19	Pennsylvania	2.1
20	Indiana	1.9
20	Louisiana	1.9
20	Oklahoma	1.9
23	Arkansas	1.8
24	New Mexico	1.7
25	Colorado	1.6
25	Nebraska	1.6
25	New York	1.6
28	Connecticut	1.2
28	Delaware	1.2
28	Ohio	1.2
31	Michigan	1.1
31	Missouri	1.1
33	Virginia	0.6
34	Minnesota	0.5
35	Iowa	0.4
36	Alabama	0.2
37	Alaska	0.0
37	Idaho	0.0
37	Kansas	0.0
37	Mississippi	0.0
37	New Hampshire	0.0
37	Rhode Island	0.0
37	South Dakota	0.0
37	Vermont	0.0
37	West Virginia	0.0
NA	Georgia**	NA
NA	Illinois**	NA
NA	Kentucky**	NA
NA	Montana**	NA
NA	South Carolina**	NA

District of Columbia**   NA

Source: Morgan Quitno Press using data from Federal Bureau of Investigation
   "Crime in the United States 2004" (Uniform Crime Reports, October 17, 2005)
*By law enforcement agencies submitting complete reports to the F.B.I. for 12 months in 2004. Arrests of youths 17
years and younger divided into population of 10 to 17 year olds. See important note at beginning of this chapter.
Includes keeping a bawdy house, procuring or transporting women for immoral purposes. Attempts are included.
**Not available.

Reported Arrests of Juveniles for Prostitution and Commercialized Vice
As a Percent of All Such Arrests in 2004
National Percent = 1.9% of Reported Prostitution/Commercialized Vice Arrests*

ALPHA ORDER

RANK	STATE	PERCENT
35	Alabama	0.6
40	Alaska	0.0
10	Arizona	2.3
25	Arkansas	0.9
6	California	3.4
28	Colorado	0.8
25	Connecticut	0.9
28	Delaware	0.8
23	Florida	1.2
16	Georgia	1.7
12	Hawaii	2.0
40	Idaho	0.0
19	Illinois	1.4
32	Indiana	0.7
35	Iowa	0.6
40	Kansas	0.0
35	Kentucky	0.6
21	Louisiana	1.3
2	Maine	13.3
17	Maryland	1.6
14	Massachusetts	1.9
32	Michigan	0.7
4	Minnesota	5.0
40	Mississippi	0.0
35	Missouri	0.6
NA	Montana**	NA
24	Nebraska	1.0
9	Nevada	2.7
40	New Hampshire	0.0
18	New Jersey	1.5
32	New Mexico	0.7
25	New York	0.9
11	North Carolina	2.2
1	North Dakota	62.5
28	Ohio	0.8
21	Oklahoma	1.3
6	Oregon	3.4
28	Pennsylvania	0.8
40	Rhode Island	0.0
40	South Carolina	0.0
40	South Dakota	0.0
19	Tennessee	1.4
15	Texas	1.8
12	Utah	2.0
40	Vermont	0.0
35	Virginia	0.6
5	Washington	3.7
40	West Virginia	0.0
8	Wisconsin	2.9
3	Wyoming	5.7

RANK ORDER

RANK	STATE	PERCENT
1	North Dakota	62.5
2	Maine	13.3
3	Wyoming	5.7
4	Minnesota	5.0
5	Washington	3.7
6	California	3.4
6	Oregon	3.4
8	Wisconsin	2.9
9	Nevada	2.7
10	Arizona	2.3
11	North Carolina	2.2
12	Hawaii	2.0
12	Utah	2.0
14	Massachusetts	1.9
15	Texas	1.8
16	Georgia	1.7
17	Maryland	1.6
18	New Jersey	1.5
19	Illinois	1.4
19	Tennessee	1.4
21	Louisiana	1.3
21	Oklahoma	1.3
23	Florida	1.2
24	Nebraska	1.0
25	Arkansas	0.9
25	Connecticut	0.9
25	New York	0.9
28	Colorado	0.8
28	Delaware	0.8
28	Ohio	0.8
28	Pennsylvania	0.8
32	Indiana	0.7
32	Michigan	0.7
32	New Mexico	0.7
35	Alabama	0.6
35	Iowa	0.6
35	Kentucky	0.6
35	Missouri	0.6
35	Virginia	0.6
40	Alaska	0.0
40	Idaho	0.0
40	Kansas	0.0
40	Mississippi	0.0
40	New Hampshire	0.0
40	Rhode Island	0.0
40	South Carolina	0.0
40	South Dakota	0.0
40	Vermont	0.0
40	West Virginia	0.0
NA	Montana**	NA
	District of Columbia**	NA

Source: Morgan Quitno Press using data from Federal Bureau of Investigation
   "Crime in the United States 2004" (Uniform Crime Reports, October 17, 2005)
*Arrests of youths 17 years and younger by law enforcement agencies submitting complete reports to the F.B.I. for
12 months in 2004. Includes keeping a bawdy house, procuring or transporting women for immoral purposes.
Attempts are included.*
**Not available.*

Reported Arrests of Juveniles for Offenses Against Families & Children in 2004

National Total = 4,142 Reported Arrests*

ALPHA ORDER

RANK	STATE	ARRESTS	% of USA
36	Alabama	7	0.2%
24	Alaska	18	0.4%
2	Arizona	449	10.8%
43	Arkansas	5	0.1%
36	California	7	0.2%
18	Colorado	56	1.4%
11	Connecticut	84	2.0%
47	Delaware	2	0.0%
48	Florida	0	0.0%
17	Georgia	57	1.4%
43	Hawaii	5	0.1%
26	Idaho	15	0.4%
33	Illinois	9	0.2%
3	Indiana	340	8.2%
38	Iowa	6	0.1%
22	Kansas	27	0.7%
38	Kentucky	6	0.1%
5	Louisiana	204	4.9%
38	Maine	6	0.1%
16	Maryland	60	1.4%
13	Massachusetts	80	1.9%
29	Michigan	14	0.3%
38	Minnesota	6	0.1%
9	Mississippi	98	2.4%
6	Missouri	179	4.3%
NA	Montana**	NA	NA
21	Nebraska	28	0.7%
26	Nevada	15	0.4%
35	New Hampshire	8	0.2%
13	New Jersey	80	1.9%
33	New Mexico	9	0.2%
4	New York	276	6.7%
9	North Carolina	98	2.4%
12	North Dakota	81	2.0%
1	Ohio	1,277	30.8%
23	Oklahoma	23	0.6%
26	Oregon	15	0.4%
20	Pennsylvania	37	0.9%
15	Rhode Island	61	1.5%
43	South Carolina	5	0.1%
38	South Dakota	6	0.1%
19	Tennessee	41	1.0%
8	Texas	124	3.0%
25	Utah	17	0.4%
43	Vermont	5	0.1%
29	Virginia	14	0.3%
31	Washington	13	0.3%
48	West Virginia	0	0.0%
7	Wisconsin	158	3.8%
32	Wyoming	11	0.3%

RANK ORDER

RANK	STATE	ARRESTS	% of USA
1	Ohio	1,277	30.8%
2	Arizona	449	10.8%
3	Indiana	340	8.2%
4	New York	276	6.7%
5	Louisiana	204	4.9%
6	Missouri	179	4.3%
7	Wisconsin	158	3.8%
8	Texas	124	3.0%
9	Mississippi	98	2.4%
9	North Carolina	98	2.4%
11	Connecticut	84	2.0%
12	North Dakota	81	2.0%
13	Massachusetts	80	1.9%
13	New Jersey	80	1.9%
15	Rhode Island	61	1.5%
16	Maryland	60	1.4%
17	Georgia	57	1.4%
18	Colorado	56	1.4%
19	Tennessee	41	1.0%
20	Pennsylvania	37	0.9%
21	Nebraska	28	0.7%
22	Kansas	27	0.7%
23	Oklahoma	23	0.6%
24	Alaska	18	0.4%
25	Utah	17	0.4%
26	Idaho	15	0.4%
26	Nevada	15	0.4%
26	Oregon	15	0.4%
29	Michigan	14	0.3%
29	Virginia	14	0.3%
31	Washington	13	0.3%
32	Wyoming	11	0.3%
33	Illinois	9	0.2%
33	New Mexico	9	0.2%
35	New Hampshire	8	0.2%
36	Alabama	7	0.2%
36	California	7	0.2%
38	Iowa	6	0.1%
38	Kentucky	6	0.1%
38	Maine	6	0.1%
38	Minnesota	6	0.1%
38	South Dakota	6	0.1%
43	Arkansas	5	0.1%
43	Hawaii	5	0.1%
43	South Carolina	5	0.1%
43	Vermont	5	0.1%
47	Delaware	2	0.0%
48	Florida	0	0.0%
48	West Virginia	0	0.0%
NA	Montana**	NA	NA
	District of Columbia**	NA	NA

Source: Federal Bureau of Investigation
   "Crime in the United States 2004" (Uniform Crime Reports, October 17, 2005)
*Arrests of youths 17 years and younger by law enforcement agencies submitting complete reports to the F.B.I. for 12 months in 2004. Includes nonsupport, neglect, desertion or abuse of family and children. See important note at beginning of this chapter.
**Not available.

Reported Juvenile Arrest Rate for Offenses Against Families & Children in 2004

National Rate = 15.8 Reported Arrests per 100,000 Juvenile Population*

ALPHA ORDER

RANK	STATE	RATE
40	Alabama	1.6
12	Alaska	20.6
3	Arizona	68.0
35	Arkansas	3.0
43	California	0.2
17	Colorado	12.5
11	Connecticut	25.5
36	Delaware	2.5
44	Florida	0.0
NA	Georgia**	NA
31	Hawaii	4.3
20	Idaho	9.8
NA	Illinois**	NA
4	Indiana	63.5
38	Iowa	2.2
19	Kansas	12.2
NA	Kentucky**	NA
6	Louisiana	55.0
32	Maine	4.2
21	Maryland	9.2
14	Massachusetts	16.4
42	Michigan	1.3
41	Minnesota	1.5
5	Mississippi	55.8
8	Missouri	33.7
NA	Montana**	NA
15	Nebraska	15.3
28	Nevada	5.8
26	New Hampshire	6.9
24	New Jersey	8.3
29	New Mexico	5.2
10	New York	25.6
16	North Carolina	14.6
1	North Dakota	149.4
2	Ohio	143.3
27	Oklahoma	6.1
33	Oregon	4.0
34	Pennsylvania	3.1
7	Rhode Island	52.3
NA	South Carolina**	NA
18	South Dakota	12.3
25	Tennessee	7.9
30	Texas	4.6
22	Utah	8.7
22	Vermont	8.7
39	Virginia	1.9
37	Washington	2.4
44	West Virginia	0.0
9	Wisconsin	30.5
13	Wyoming	20.1

RANK ORDER

RANK	STATE	RATE
1	North Dakota	149.4
2	Ohio	143.3
3	Arizona	68.0
4	Indiana	63.5
5	Mississippi	55.8
6	Louisiana	55.0
7	Rhode Island	52.3
8	Missouri	33.7
9	Wisconsin	30.5
10	New York	25.6
11	Connecticut	25.5
12	Alaska	20.6
13	Wyoming	20.1
14	Massachusetts	16.4
15	Nebraska	15.3
16	North Carolina	14.6
17	Colorado	12.5
18	South Dakota	12.3
19	Kansas	12.2
20	Idaho	9.8
21	Maryland	9.2
22	Utah	8.7
22	Vermont	8.7
24	New Jersey	8.3
25	Tennessee	7.9
26	New Hampshire	6.9
27	Oklahoma	6.1
28	Nevada	5.8
29	New Mexico	5.2
30	Texas	4.6
31	Hawaii	4.3
32	Maine	4.2
33	Oregon	4.0
34	Pennsylvania	3.1
35	Arkansas	3.0
36	Delaware	2.5
37	Washington	2.4
38	Iowa	2.2
39	Virginia	1.9
40	Alabama	1.6
41	Minnesota	1.5
42	Michigan	1.3
43	California	0.2
44	Florida	0.0
44	West Virginia	0.0
NA	Georgia**	NA
NA	Illinois**	NA
NA	Kentucky**	NA
NA	Montana**	NA
NA	South Carolina**	NA
	District of Columbia**	NA

Source: Morgan Quitno Press using data from Federal Bureau of Investigation
"Crime in the United States 2004" (Uniform Crime Reports, October 17, 2005)
By law enforcement agencies submitting complete reports to the F.B.I. for 12 months in 2004. Arrests of youths 17 years and younger divided into population of 10 to 17 year olds. See important note at beginning of this chapter. Includes nonsupport, neglect, desertion or abuse of family and children.
**Not available.*

Reported Arrests of Juveniles for Offenses Against Families and Children As a Percent of All Such Arrests in 2004
National Percent = 4.7% of Offenses Against Families and Children Arrests*

ALPHA ORDER

RANK	STATE	PERCENT
44	Alabama	0.6
17	Alaska	4.2
4	Arizona	14.0
29	Arkansas	2.0
34	California	1.5
31	Colorado	1.9
10	Connecticut	6.9
41	Delaware	0.9
NA	Florida**	NA
24	Georgia	3.4
13	Hawaii	4.6
20	Idaho	3.8
25	Illinois	2.7
3	Indiana	20.6
41	Iowa	0.9
6	Kansas	11.3
44	Kentucky	0.6
7	Louisiana	10.1
32	Maine	1.8
27	Maryland	2.5
12	Massachusetts	5.5
46	Michigan	0.5
34	Minnesota	1.5
22	Mississippi	3.5
14	Missouri	4.5
NA	Montana**	NA
33	Nebraska	1.7
38	Nevada	1.3
14	New Hampshire	4.5
46	New Jersey	0.5
43	New Mexico	0.8
7	New York	10.1
40	North Carolina	1.1
2	North Dakota	39.3
5	Ohio	11.7
29	Oklahoma	2.0
27	Oregon	2.5
17	Pennsylvania	4.2
1	Rhode Island	43.9
9	South Carolina	8.6
21	South Dakota	3.7
22	Tennessee	3.5
26	Texas	2.6
37	Utah	1.4
34	Vermont	1.5
38	Virginia	1.3
16	Washington	4.3
48	West Virginia	0.0
11	Wisconsin	6.4
17	Wyoming	4.2

RANK ORDER

RANK	STATE	PERCENT
1	Rhode Island	43.9
2	North Dakota	39.3
3	Indiana	20.6
4	Arizona	14.0
5	Ohio	11.7
6	Kansas	11.3
7	Louisiana	10.1
7	New York	10.1
9	South Carolina	8.6
10	Connecticut	6.9
11	Wisconsin	6.4
12	Massachusetts	5.5
13	Hawaii	4.6
14	Missouri	4.5
14	New Hampshire	4.5
16	Washington	4.3
17	Alaska	4.2
17	Pennsylvania	4.2
17	Wyoming	4.2
20	Idaho	3.8
21	South Dakota	3.7
22	Mississippi	3.5
22	Tennessee	3.5
24	Georgia	3.4
25	Illinois	2.7
26	Texas	2.6
27	Maryland	2.5
27	Oregon	2.5
29	Arkansas	2.0
29	Oklahoma	2.0
31	Colorado	1.9
32	Maine	1.8
33	Nebraska	1.7
34	California	1.5
34	Minnesota	1.5
34	Vermont	1.5
37	Utah	1.4
38	Nevada	1.3
38	Virginia	1.3
40	North Carolina	1.1
41	Delaware	0.9
41	Iowa	0.9
43	New Mexico	0.8
44	Alabama	0.6
44	Kentucky	0.6
46	Michigan	0.5
46	New Jersey	0.5
48	West Virginia	0.0
NA	Florida**	NA
NA	Montana**	NA
	District of Columbia**	NA

Source: Morgan Quitno Press using data from Federal Bureau of Investigation
   "Crime in the United States 2004" (Uniform Crime Reports, October 17, 2005)
*Arrests of youths 17 years and younger by law enforcement agencies submitting complete reports to the F.B.I. for
12 months in 2004. Includes nonsupport, neglect, desertion or abuse of family and children.
**Not available.

Juveniles in Residential Custody in 2003

National Total = 96,655 Juveniles*

ALPHA ORDER

RANK	STATE	JUVENILES	% of USA
15	Alabama	1,794	1.9%
43	Alaska	336	0.3%
13	Arizona	1,890	2.0%
33	Arkansas	675	0.7%
1	California	16,782	17.4%
16	Colorado	1,776	1.8%
35	Connecticut	627	0.6%
44	Delaware	333	0.3%
2	Florida	8,208	8.5%
10	Georgia	2,451	2.5%
49	Hawaii	129	0.1%
40	Idaho	489	0.5%
8	Illinois	2,715	2.8%
7	Indiana	3,045	3.2%
29	Iowa	975	1.0%
27	Kansas	1,071	1.1%
32	Kentucky	837	0.9%
14	Louisiana	1,821	1.9%
47	Maine	222	0.2%
26	Maryland	1,167	1.2%
23	Massachusetts	1,302	1.3%
9	Michigan	2,706	2.8%
18	Minnesota	1,527	1.6%
37	Mississippi	528	0.5%
22	Missouri	1,413	1.5%
45	Montana	261	0.3%
34	Nebraska	672	0.7%
31	Nevada	921	1.0%
48	New Hampshire	198	0.2%
12	New Jersey	1,941	2.0%
36	New Mexico	606	0.6%
5	New York	4,308	4.5%
25	North Carolina	1,203	1.2%
46	North Dakota	246	0.3%
6	Ohio	4,176	4.3%
28	Oklahoma	1,059	1.1%
24	Oregon	1,275	1.3%
4	Pennsylvania	4,341	4.5%
42	Rhode Island	342	0.4%
20	South Carolina	1,443	1.5%
38	South Dakota	522	0.5%
21	Tennessee	1,434	1.5%
3	Texas	7,662	7.9%
30	Utah	954	1.0%
50	Vermont	51	0.1%
11	Virginia	2,376	2.5%
17	Washington	1,656	1.7%
39	West Virginia	498	0.5%
19	Wisconsin	1,524	1.6%
41	Wyoming	357	0.4%

RANK ORDER

RANK	STATE	JUVENILES	% of USA
1	California	16,782	17.4%
2	Florida	8,208	8.5%
3	Texas	7,662	7.9%
4	Pennsylvania	4,341	4.5%
5	New York	4,308	4.5%
6	Ohio	4,176	4.3%
7	Indiana	3,045	3.2%
8	Illinois	2,715	2.8%
9	Michigan	2,706	2.8%
10	Georgia	2,451	2.5%
11	Virginia	2,376	2.5%
12	New Jersey	1,941	2.0%
13	Arizona	1,890	2.0%
14	Louisiana	1,821	1.9%
15	Alabama	1,794	1.9%
16	Colorado	1,776	1.8%
17	Washington	1,656	1.7%
18	Minnesota	1,527	1.6%
19	Wisconsin	1,524	1.6%
20	South Carolina	1,443	1.5%
21	Tennessee	1,434	1.5%
22	Missouri	1,413	1.5%
23	Massachusetts	1,302	1.3%
24	Oregon	1,275	1.3%
25	North Carolina	1,203	1.2%
26	Maryland	1,167	1.2%
27	Kansas	1,071	1.1%
28	Oklahoma	1,059	1.1%
29	Iowa	975	1.0%
30	Utah	954	1.0%
31	Nevada	921	1.0%
32	Kentucky	837	0.9%
33	Arkansas	675	0.7%
34	Nebraska	672	0.7%
35	Connecticut	627	0.6%
36	New Mexico	606	0.6%
37	Mississippi	528	0.5%
38	South Dakota	522	0.5%
39	West Virginia	498	0.5%
40	Idaho	489	0.5%
41	Wyoming	357	0.4%
42	Rhode Island	342	0.4%
43	Alaska	336	0.3%
44	Delaware	333	0.3%
45	Montana	261	0.3%
46	North Dakota	246	0.3%
47	Maine	222	0.2%
48	New Hampshire	198	0.2%
49	Hawaii	129	0.1%
50	Vermont	51	0.1%
	District of Columbia	285	0.3%

Source: U.S. Department of Justice, Office of Juvenile Justice and Delinquency Prevention
"Census of Juveniles in Residential Placement Databook" (http://www.ojjdp.ncjrs.org/ojstatbb/cjrp/)
*Based on state of offense. Includes 1,398 juveniles not shown by state and 123 juveniles in tribal facilities.

Percent of Juveniles in Residential Custody Who are Female: 2003

National Percent = 15.1%

ALPHA ORDER

RANK	STATE	PERCENT
11	Alabama	19.9
46	Alaska	10.7
19	Arizona	17.9
23	Arkansas	16.9
34	California	12.7
47	Colorado	10.0
8	Connecticut	21.1
44	Delaware	10.8
15	Florida	18.6
26	Georgia	15.1
3	Hawaii	25.6
21	Idaho	17.2
42	Illinois	11.0
6	Indiana	23.4
7	Iowa	21.2
28	Kansas	14.8
26	Kentucky	15.1
25	Louisiana	16.5
44	Maine	10.8
49	Maryland	8.2
40	Massachusetts	11.5
13	Michigan	19.4
29	Minnesota	14.5
14	Mississippi	19.3
32	Missouri	13.6
16	Montana	18.4
2	Nebraska	32.1
10	Nevada	20.5
17	New Hampshire	18.2
48	New Jersey	8.3
38	New Mexico	11.9
9	New York	21.0
17	North Carolina	18.2
3	North Dakota	25.6
36	Ohio	12.5
22	Oklahoma	17.0
37	Oregon	12.0
41	Pennsylvania	11.1
50	Rhode Island	7.0
24	South Carolina	16.8
5	South Dakota	24.7
43	Tennessee	10.9
34	Texas	12.7
12	Utah	19.8
39	Vermont	11.8
30	Virginia	14.4
33	Washington	12.9
20	West Virginia	17.5
31	Wisconsin	14.2
1	Wyoming	39.5

RANK ORDER

RANK	STATE	PERCENT
1	Wyoming	39.5
2	Nebraska	32.1
3	Hawaii	25.6
3	North Dakota	25.6
5	South Dakota	24.7
6	Indiana	23.4
7	Iowa	21.2
8	Connecticut	21.1
9	New York	21.0
10	Nevada	20.5
11	Alabama	19.9
12	Utah	19.8
13	Michigan	19.4
14	Mississippi	19.3
15	Florida	18.6
16	Montana	18.4
17	New Hampshire	18.2
17	North Carolina	18.2
19	Arizona	17.9
20	West Virginia	17.5
21	Idaho	17.2
22	Oklahoma	17.0
23	Arkansas	16.9
24	South Carolina	16.8
25	Louisiana	16.5
26	Georgia	15.1
26	Kentucky	15.1
28	Kansas	14.8
29	Minnesota	14.5
30	Virginia	14.4
31	Wisconsin	14.2
32	Missouri	13.6
33	Washington	12.9
34	California	12.7
34	Texas	12.7
36	Ohio	12.5
37	Oregon	12.0
38	New Mexico	11.9
39	Vermont	11.8
40	Massachusetts	11.5
41	Pennsylvania	11.1
42	Illinois	11.0
43	Tennessee	10.9
44	Delaware	10.8
44	Maine	10.8
46	Alaska	10.7
47	Colorado	10.0
48	New Jersey	8.3
49	Maryland	8.2
50	Rhode Island	7.0

District of Columbia   10.5

Source: Morgan Quitno Press using data from U.S. Dept of Justice, Office of Juvenile Justice and Delinquency Prevention
"Census of Juveniles in Residential Placement Databook" (http://www.ojjdp.ncjrs.org/ojstatbb/cjrp/)
*Based on state of offense. Includes juveniles not shown by state and juveniles in tribal facilities.

Percent of Juveniles in Residential Custody Who are White: 2003

National Percent = 38.6%

RANK	STATE	PERCENT
29	Alabama	42.8
40	Alaska	30.4
31	Arizona	40.5
24	Arkansas	47.6
47	California	20.8
16	Colorado	53.4
34	Connecticut	35.4
46	Delaware	23.4
28	Florida	43.9
41	Georgia	29.4
50	Hawaii	14.0
5	Idaho	74.2
36	Illinois	34.3
12	Indiana	63.4
6	Iowa	73.2
21	Kansas	50.1
13	Kentucky	63.1
42	Louisiana	28.7
2	Maine	93.2
39	Maryland	31.4
33	Massachusetts	39.4
23	Michigan	48.6
20	Minnesota	50.5
45	Mississippi	25.6
18	Missouri	51.6
10	Montana	65.5
15	Nebraska	54.0
26	Nevada	45.9
3	New Hampshire	90.9
49	New Jersey	15.6
48	New Mexico	20.3
43	New York	27.9
32	North Carolina	39.9
14	North Dakota	59.8
17	Ohio	52.4
19	Oklahoma	51.0
8	Oregon	71.8
35	Pennsylvania	34.7
22	Rhode Island	49.1
37	South Carolina	33.7
27	South Dakota	44.8
25	Tennessee	47.1
44	Texas	26.7
9	Utah	70.4
1	Vermont	94.1
38	Virginia	32.4
11	Washington	63.9
4	West Virginia	80.1
30	Wisconsin	42.7
7	Wyoming	72.3

RANK	STATE	PERCENT
1	Vermont	94.1
2	Maine	93.2
3	New Hampshire	90.9
4	West Virginia	80.1
5	Idaho	74.2
6	Iowa	73.2
7	Wyoming	72.3
8	Oregon	71.8
9	Utah	70.4
10	Montana	65.5
11	Washington	63.9
12	Indiana	63.4
13	Kentucky	63.1
14	North Dakota	59.8
15	Nebraska	54.0
16	Colorado	53.4
17	Ohio	52.4
18	Missouri	51.6
19	Oklahoma	51.0
20	Minnesota	50.5
21	Kansas	50.1
22	Rhode Island	49.1
23	Michigan	48.6
24	Arkansas	47.6
25	Tennessee	47.1
26	Nevada	45.9
27	South Dakota	44.8
28	Florida	43.9
29	Alabama	42.8
30	Wisconsin	42.7
31	Arizona	40.5
32	North Carolina	39.9
33	Massachusetts	39.4
34	Connecticut	35.4
35	Pennsylvania	34.7
36	Illinois	34.3
37	South Carolina	33.7
38	Virginia	32.4
39	Maryland	31.4
40	Alaska	30.4
41	Georgia	29.4
42	Louisiana	28.7
43	New York	27.9
44	Texas	26.7
45	Mississippi	25.6
46	Delaware	23.4
47	California	20.8
48	New Mexico	20.3
49	New Jersey	15.6
50	Hawaii	14.0

District of Columbia 7.4

Source: Morgan Quitno Press using data from U.S. Dept of Justice, Office of Juvenile Justice and Delinquency Prevention "Census of Juveniles in Residential Placement Databook" (http://www.ojjdp.ncjrs.org/ojstatbb/cjrp/)
Based on state of offense. Includes juveniles not shown by state and juveniles in tribal facilities.

Percent of Juveniles in Residential Custody Who are Black: 2003

National Percent = 38.0%

ALPHA ORDER

ALPHA ORDER

RANK	STATE	PERCENT
10	Alabama	54.5
44	Alaska	4.5
38	Arizona	8.3
17	Arkansas	46.2
31	California	25.5
33	Colorado	17.6
21	Connecticut	39.2
2	Delaware	69.4
15	Florida	47.4
5	Georgia	64.5
40	Hawaii	7.0
47	Idaho	1.8
11	Illinois	54.0
25	Indiana	31.5
35	Iowa	16.0
26	Kansas	31.1
22	Kentucky	34.4
3	Louisiana	69.2
48	Maine	1.4
8	Maryland	57.6
27	Massachusetts	30.4
18	Michigan	44.6
30	Minnesota	26.3
1	Mississippi	73.3
20	Missouri	43.9
49	Montana	1.1
28	Nebraska	27.7
32	Nevada	24.1
44	New Hampshire	4.5
4	New Jersey	66.6
41	New Mexico	6.9
13	New York	50.6
9	North Carolina	54.6
43	North Dakota	4.9
19	Ohio	44.2
29	Oklahoma	26.9
37	Oregon	9.2
12	Pennsylvania	52.1
23	Rhode Island	34.2
6	South Carolina	62.4
39	South Dakota	7.5
14	Tennessee	49.4
24	Texas	31.6
46	Utah	3.8
50	Vermont	0.0
7	Virginia	60.7
34	Washington	16.5
36	West Virginia	15.1
16	Wisconsin	46.5
42	Wyoming	5.9

RANK ORDER

RANK	STATE	PERCENT
1	Mississippi	73.3
2	Delaware	69.4
3	Louisiana	69.2
4	New Jersey	66.6
5	Georgia	64.5
6	South Carolina	62.4
7	Virginia	60.7
8	Maryland	57.6
9	North Carolina	54.6
10	Alabama	54.5
11	Illinois	54.0
12	Pennsylvania	52.1
13	New York	50.6
14	Tennessee	49.4
15	Florida	47.4
16	Wisconsin	46.5
17	Arkansas	46.2
18	Michigan	44.6
19	Ohio	44.2
20	Missouri	43.9
21	Connecticut	39.2
22	Kentucky	34.4
23	Rhode Island	34.2
24	Texas	31.6
25	Indiana	31.5
26	Kansas	31.1
27	Massachusetts	30.4
28	Nebraska	27.7
29	Oklahoma	26.9
30	Minnesota	26.3
31	California	25.5
32	Nevada	24.1
33	Colorado	17.6
34	Washington	16.5
35	Iowa	16.0
36	West Virginia	15.1
37	Oregon	9.2
38	Arizona	8.3
39	South Dakota	7.5
40	Hawaii	7.0
41	New Mexico	6.9
42	Wyoming	5.9
43	North Dakota	4.9
44	Alaska	4.5
44	New Hampshire	4.5
46	Utah	3.8
47	Idaho	1.8
48	Maine	1.4
49	Montana	1.1
50	Vermont	0.0

District of Columbia	81.1

Source: Morgan Quitno Press using data from U.S. Dept of Justice, Office of Juvenile Justice and Delinquency Prevention
"Census of Juveniles in Residential Placement Databook" (http://www.ojjdp.ncjrs.org/ojstatbb/cjrp/)
*Based on state of offense. Includes juveniles not shown by state and juveniles in tribal facilities.

Percent of Juveniles in Residential Custody Who are Hispanic: 2003

National Percent = 19.1%

ALPHA ORDER

RANK	STATE	PERCENT
44	Alabama	2.2
50	Alaska	0.0
2	Arizona	45.4
34	Arkansas	4.0
1	California	48.9
4	Colorado	26.0
7	Connecticut	20.6
23	Delaware	7.2
22	Florida	8.2
31	Georgia	5.0
32	Hawaii	4.7
11	Idaho	18.4
15	Illinois	11.2
36	Indiana	3.9
24	Iowa	7.1
16	Kansas	10.6
47	Kentucky	1.1
48	Louisiana	1.0
46	Maine	1.4
20	Maryland	9.0
5	Massachusetts	25.8
34	Michigan	4.0
26	Minnesota	5.9
49	Mississippi	0.6
39	Missouri	3.2
28	Montana	5.7
17	Nebraska	10.3
6	Nevada	25.1
40	New Hampshire	3.0
12	New Jersey	16.5
8	New Mexico	20.3
10	New York	18.7
42	North Carolina	2.5
37	North Dakota	3.7
43	Ohio	2.4
25	Oklahoma	6.5
14	Oregon	11.5
18	Pennsylvania	9.7
21	Rhode Island	8.8
38	South Carolina	3.3
30	South Dakota	5.2
41	Tennessee	2.7
3	Texas	41.5
9	Utah	19.5
26	Vermont	5.9
29	Virginia	5.3
19	Washington	9.6
45	West Virginia	1.8
33	Wisconsin	4.1
13	Wyoming	13.4

RANK ORDER

RANK	STATE	PERCENT
1	California	48.9
2	Arizona	45.4
3	Texas	41.5
4	Colorado	26.0
5	Massachusetts	25.8
6	Nevada	25.1
7	Connecticut	20.6
8	New Mexico	20.3
9	Utah	19.5
10	New York	18.7
11	Idaho	18.4
12	New Jersey	16.5
13	Wyoming	13.4
14	Oregon	11.5
15	Illinois	11.2
16	Kansas	10.6
17	Nebraska	10.3
18	Pennsylvania	9.7
19	Washington	9.6
20	Maryland	9.0
21	Rhode Island	8.8
22	Florida	8.2
23	Delaware	7.2
24	Iowa	7.1
25	Oklahoma	6.5
26	Minnesota	5.9
26	Vermont	5.9
28	Montana	5.7
29	Virginia	5.3
30	South Dakota	5.2
31	Georgia	5.0
32	Hawaii	4.7
33	Wisconsin	4.1
34	Arkansas	4.0
34	Michigan	4.0
36	Indiana	3.9
37	North Dakota	3.7
38	South Carolina	3.3
39	Missouri	3.2
40	New Hampshire	3.0
41	Tennessee	2.7
42	North Carolina	2.5
43	Ohio	2.4
44	Alabama	2.2
45	West Virginia	1.8
46	Maine	1.4
47	Kentucky	1.1
48	Louisiana	1.0
49	Mississippi	0.6
50	Alaska	0.0

District of Columbia 11.6

Source: Morgan Quitno Press using data from U.S. Dept of Justice, Office of Juvenile Justice and Delinquency Prevention "Census of Juveniles in Residential Placement Databook" (http://www.ojjdp.ncjrs.org/ojstatbb/cjrp/)
*Based on state of offense. Includes juveniles not shown by state and juveniles in tribal facilities. The "Hispanic" category includes persons of Latin American or other Spanish culture or origin regardless of race. These persons are not included in the other race/ethnicity categories.

Public High School Drop Out Rate in 2001

National Median = 4.2%*

ALPHA ORDER

RANK	STATE	RATE
27	Alabama	4.1
3	Alaska	8.2
1	Arizona	10.9
11	Arkansas	5.3
NA	California**	NA
NA	Colorado**	NA
41	Connecticut	3.0
22	Delaware	4.2
20	Florida	4.4
4	Georgia	7.2
8	Hawaii	5.7
9	Idaho	5.6
7	Illinois	6.0
NA	Indiana**	NA
43	Iowa	2.7
39	Kansas	3.2
18	Kentucky	4.6
2	Louisiana	8.3
40	Maine	3.1
27	Maryland	4.1
37	Massachusetts	3.4
NA	Michigan**	NA
29	Minnesota	4.0
18	Mississippi	4.6
22	Missouri	4.2
22	Montana	4.2
29	Nebraska	4.0
14	Nevada	5.2
10	New Hampshire	5.4
42	New Jersey	2.8
11	New Mexico	5.3
33	New York	3.8
6	North Carolina	6.3
45	North Dakota	2.2
31	Ohio	3.9
14	Oklahoma	5.2
11	Oregon	5.3
35	Pennsylvania	3.6
16	Rhode Island	5.0
38	South Carolina	3.3
31	South Dakota	3.9
21	Tennessee	4.3
22	Texas	4.2
34	Utah	3.7
17	Vermont	4.7
36	Virginia	3.5
NA	Washington**	NA
22	West Virginia	4.2
44	Wisconsin	2.3
5	Wyoming	6.4

RANK ORDER

RANK	STATE	RATE
1	Arizona	10.9
2	Louisiana	8.3
3	Alaska	8.2
4	Georgia	7.2
5	Wyoming	6.4
6	North Carolina	6.3
7	Illinois	6.0
8	Hawaii	5.7
9	Idaho	5.6
10	New Hampshire	5.4
11	Arkansas	5.3
11	New Mexico	5.3
11	Oregon	5.3
14	Nevada	5.2
14	Oklahoma	5.2
16	Rhode Island	5.0
17	Vermont	4.7
18	Kentucky	4.6
18	Mississippi	4.6
20	Florida	4.4
21	Tennessee	4.3
22	Delaware	4.2
22	Missouri	4.2
22	Montana	4.2
22	Texas	4.2
22	West Virginia	4.2
27	Alabama	4.1
27	Maryland	4.1
29	Minnesota	4.0
29	Nebraska	4.0
31	Ohio	3.9
31	South Dakota	3.9
33	New York	3.8
34	Utah	3.7
35	Pennsylvania	3.6
36	Virginia	3.5
37	Massachusetts	3.4
38	South Carolina	3.3
39	Kansas	3.2
40	Maine	3.1
41	Connecticut	3.0
42	New Jersey	2.8
43	Iowa	2.7
44	Wisconsin	2.3
45	North Dakota	2.2
NA	California**	NA
NA	Colorado**	NA
NA	Indiana**	NA
NA	Michigan**	NA
NA	Washington**	NA

District of Columbia**   NA

Source: U.S. Department of Education, National Center for Educational Statistics
    "Dropout Rates in the United States: 2001" (NCES 2005-046, October 2004)
*"Event" dropout rates showing the number of 9-12th grade dropouts divided by the number of students enrolled at
the beginning of the school year in those grades. National rate is the median of reporting states.
**Not available.

Percent of High School Students Who Carried a Weapon on School Property in 2003
National Percent = 6.1%*

ALPHA ORDER

RANK	STATE	PERCENT
6	Alabama	7.3
8	Alaska	7.1
30	Arizona	4.9
NA	Arkansas**	NA
NA	California**	NA
NA	Colorado**	NA
NA	Connecticut**	NA
26	Delaware	5.0
22	Florida	5.3
26	Georgia	5.0
NA	Hawaii**	NA
4	Idaho	7.7
NA	Illinois**	NA
14	Indiana	6.2
NA	Iowa**	NA
NA	Kansas**	NA
5	Kentucky	7.4
NA	Louisiana**	NA
10	Maine	6.6
NA	Maryland**	NA
26	Massachusetts	5.0
25	Michigan	5.1
NA	Minnesota**	NA
23	Mississippi	5.2
20	Missouri	5.5
7	Montana	7.2
26	Nebraska	5.0
12	Nevada	6.3
16	New Hampshire	5.8
NA	New Jersey**	NA
NA	New Mexico**	NA
23	New York	5.2
12	North Carolina	6.3
18	North Dakota	5.7
31	Ohio	3.6
3	Oklahoma	8.0
NA	Oregon**	NA
NA	Pennsylvania**	NA
15	Rhode Island	5.9
NA	South Carolina**	NA
8	South Dakota	7.1
21	Tennessee	5.4
16	Texas	5.8
19	Utah	5.6
2	Vermont	8.3
NA	Virginia**	NA
NA	Washington**	NA
10	West Virginia	6.6
32	Wisconsin	3.2
1	Wyoming	10.1

RANK ORDER

RANK	STATE	PERCENT
1	Wyoming	10.1
2	Vermont	8.3
3	Oklahoma	8.0
4	Idaho	7.7
5	Kentucky	7.4
6	Alabama	7.3
7	Montana	7.2
8	Alaska	7.1
8	South Dakota	7.1
10	Maine	6.6
10	West Virginia	6.6
12	Nevada	6.3
12	North Carolina	6.3
14	Indiana	6.2
15	Rhode Island	5.9
16	New Hampshire	5.8
16	Texas	5.8
18	North Dakota	5.7
19	Utah	5.6
20	Missouri	5.5
21	Tennessee	5.4
22	Florida	5.3
23	Mississippi	5.2
23	New York	5.2
25	Michigan	5.1
26	Delaware	5.0
26	Georgia	5.0
26	Massachusetts	5.0
26	Nebraska	5.0
30	Arizona	4.9
31	Ohio	3.6
32	Wisconsin	3.2
NA	Arkansas**	NA
NA	California**	NA
NA	Colorado**	NA
NA	Connecticut**	NA
NA	Hawaii**	NA
NA	Illinois**	NA
NA	Iowa**	NA
NA	Kansas**	NA
NA	Louisiana**	NA
NA	Maryland**	NA
NA	Minnesota**	NA
NA	New Jersey**	NA
NA	New Mexico**	NA
NA	Oregon**	NA
NA	Pennsylvania**	NA
NA	South Carolina**	NA
NA	Virginia**	NA
NA	Washington**	NA

District of Columbia   10.6

Source: U.S. Department of Health and Human Services, Centers for Disease Control and Prevention
     "Youth Risk Behavior Surveillance--U.S., 2003" (Morbidity Mortality Weekly Report, Vol. 53, No. SS-2, 5/21/04)
*Weapons include guns, knives, clubs or other instrument. National percent includes nonreporting states.
**Not available.

Percent of High School Students Who Were Threatened or Injured With a Weapon on School Property in 2003
National Percent = 9.2%*

ALPHA ORDER

RANK	STATE	PERCENT
21	Alabama	7.2
12	Alaska	8.1
4	Arizona	9.2
NA	Arkansas**	NA
NA	California**	NA
NA	Colorado**	NA
NA	Connecticut**	NA
13	Delaware	7.7
8	Florida	8.4
10	Georgia	8.2
NA	Hawaii**	NA
3	Idaho	9.4
NA	Illinois**	NA
25	Indiana	6.7
NA	Iowa**	NA
NA	Kansas**	NA
32	Kentucky	5.2
NA	Louisiana**	NA
6	Maine	8.5
NA	Maryland**	NA
28	Massachusetts	6.3
1	Michigan	9.7
NA	Minnesota**	NA
26	Mississippi	6.6
16	Missouri	7.5
24	Montana	7.1
5	Nebraska	8.8
29	Nevada	6.0
16	New Hampshire	7.5
NA	New Jersey**	NA
NA	New Mexico**	NA
21	New York	7.2
21	North Carolina	7.2
30	North Dakota	5.9
13	Ohio	7.7
18	Oklahoma	7.4
NA	Oregon**	NA
NA	Pennsylvania**	NA
10	Rhode Island	8.2
NA	South Carolina**	NA
27	South Dakota	6.5
8	Tennessee	8.4
13	Texas	7.7
19	Utah	7.3
19	Vermont	7.3
NA	Virginia**	NA
NA	Washington**	NA
6	West Virginia	8.5
31	Wisconsin	5.5
1	Wyoming	9.7

RANK ORDER

RANK	STATE	PERCENT
1	Michigan	9.7
1	Wyoming	9.7
3	Idaho	9.4
4	Arizona	9.2
5	Nebraska	8.8
6	Maine	8.5
6	West Virginia	8.5
8	Florida	8.4
8	Tennessee	8.4
10	Georgia	8.2
10	Rhode Island	8.2
12	Alaska	8.1
13	Delaware	7.7
13	Ohio	7.7
13	Texas	7.7
16	Missouri	7.5
16	New Hampshire	7.5
18	Oklahoma	7.4
19	Utah	7.3
19	Vermont	7.3
21	Alabama	7.2
21	New York	7.2
21	North Carolina	7.2
24	Montana	7.1
25	Indiana	6.7
26	Mississippi	6.6
27	South Dakota	6.5
28	Massachusetts	6.3
29	Nevada	6.0
30	North Dakota	5.9
31	Wisconsin	5.5
32	Kentucky	5.2
NA	Arkansas**	NA
NA	California**	NA
NA	Colorado**	NA
NA	Connecticut**	NA
NA	Hawaii**	NA
NA	Illinois**	NA
NA	Iowa**	NA
NA	Kansas**	NA
NA	Louisiana**	NA
NA	Maryland**	NA
NA	Minnesota**	NA
NA	New Jersey**	NA
NA	New Mexico**	NA
NA	Oregon**	NA
NA	Pennsylvania**	NA
NA	South Carolina**	NA
NA	Virginia**	NA
NA	Washington**	NA

District of Columbia   12.7

Source: U.S. Department of Health and Human Services, Centers for Disease Control and Prevention
"Youth Risk Behavior Surveillance--U.S., 2003" (Morbidity Mortality Weekly Report, Vol. 53, No. SS-2, 5/21/04)
*One or more times during the 12 months preceding the survey. National percent includes nonreporting states.
**Not available.

Percent of High School Students Who Drink Alcohol: 2003

National Percent = 44.9%*

ALPHA ORDER

RANK	STATE	PERCENT
27	Alabama	40.2
29	Alaska	38.7
2	Arizona	50.9
NA	Arkansas**	NA
NA	California**	NA
NA	Colorado**	NA
NA	Connecticut**	NA
12	Delaware	45.4
22	Florida	42.7
30	Georgia	37.7
NA	Hawaii**	NA
31	Idaho	34.8
NA	Illinois**	NA
14	Indiana	44.9
NA	Iowa**	NA
NA	Kansas**	NA
13	Kentucky	45.1
NA	Louisiana**	NA
23	Maine	42.2
NA	Maryland**	NA
11	Massachusetts	45.7
18	Michigan	44.0
NA	Minnesota**	NA
25	Mississippi	41.8
5	Missouri	49.2
4	Montana	49.5
10	Nebraska	46.5
20	Nevada	43.4
9	New Hampshire	47.1
NA	New Jersey**	NA
NA	New Mexico**	NA
17	New York	44.2
28	North Carolina	39.4
1	North Dakota	54.2
23	Ohio	42.2
7	Oklahoma	47.8
NA	Oregon**	NA
NA	Pennsylvania**	NA
15	Rhode Island	44.5
NA	South Carolina**	NA
3	South Dakota	50.2
26	Tennessee	41.1
21	Texas	43.0
32	Utah	21.3
19	Vermont	43.5
NA	Virginia**	NA
NA	Washington**	NA
16	West Virginia	44.4
8	Wisconsin	47.3
6	Wyoming	49.0

RANK ORDER

RANK	STATE	PERCENT
1	North Dakota	54.2
2	Arizona	50.9
3	South Dakota	50.2
4	Montana	49.5
5	Missouri	49.2
6	Wyoming	49.0
7	Oklahoma	47.8
8	Wisconsin	47.3
9	New Hampshire	47.1
10	Nebraska	46.5
11	Massachusetts	45.7
12	Delaware	45.4
13	Kentucky	45.1
14	Indiana	44.9
15	Rhode Island	44.5
16	West Virginia	44.4
17	New York	44.2
18	Michigan	44.0
19	Vermont	43.5
20	Nevada	43.4
21	Texas	43.0
22	Florida	42.7
23	Maine	42.2
23	Ohio	42.2
25	Mississippi	41.8
26	Tennessee	41.1
27	Alabama	40.2
28	North Carolina	39.4
29	Alaska	38.7
30	Georgia	37.7
31	Idaho	34.8
32	Utah	21.3
NA	Arkansas**	NA
NA	California**	NA
NA	Colorado**	NA
NA	Connecticut**	NA
NA	Hawaii**	NA
NA	Illinois**	NA
NA	Iowa**	NA
NA	Kansas**	NA
NA	Louisiana**	NA
NA	Maryland**	NA
NA	Minnesota**	NA
NA	New Jersey**	NA
NA	New Mexico**	NA
NA	Oregon**	NA
NA	Pennsylvania**	NA
NA	South Carolina**	NA
NA	Virginia**	NA
NA	Washington**	NA

	District of Columbia	33.8

Source: U.S. Department of Health and Human Services, Centers for Disease Control and Prevention
"Youth Risk Behavior Surveillance--U.S., 2003" (Morbidity Mortality Weekly Report, Vol. 53, No. SS-2, 5/21/04)
*Drank alcohol on one or more of the 30 days preceding the survey. National percent includes nonreporting states.
**Not available.

Percent of High School Students Who Use Marijuana: 2003

National Percent = 22.4%*

ALPHA ORDER			RANK ORDER		
RANK	STATE	PERCENT	RANK	STATE	PERCENT
30	Alabama	17.7	1	New Hampshire	30.6
9	Alaska	23.9	2	Vermont	28.2
10	Arizona	23.7	3	Massachusetts	27.7
NA	Arkansas**	NA	4	Rhode Island	27.6
NA	California**	NA	5	Delaware	27.3
NA	Colorado**	NA	6	Maine	26.4
NA	Connecticut**	NA	7	North Carolina	24.3
5	Delaware	27.3	8	Michigan	24.0
20	Florida	21.4	9	Alaska	23.9
28	Georgia	19.5	10	Arizona	23.7
NA	Hawaii**	NA	11	Tennessee	23.6
31	Idaho	14.7	12	Montana	23.1
NA	Illinois**	NA	12	West Virginia	23.1
15	Indiana	22.1	14	Nevada	22.3
NA	Iowa**	NA	15	Indiana	22.1
NA	Kansas**	NA	16	Oklahoma	22.0
22	Kentucky	21.1	17	Missouri	21.8
NA	Louisiana**	NA	17	Wisconsin	21.8
6	Maine	26.4	19	South Dakota	21.5
NA	Maryland**	NA	20	Florida	21.4
3	Massachusetts	27.7	20	Ohio	21.4
8	Michigan	24.0	22	Kentucky	21.1
NA	Minnesota**	NA	23	New York	20.7
24	Mississippi	20.6	24	Mississippi	20.6
17	Missouri	21.8	24	North Dakota	20.6
12	Montana	23.1	26	Texas	20.4
29	Nebraska	18.3	26	Wyoming	20.4
14	Nevada	22.3	28	Georgia	19.5
1	New Hampshire	30.6	29	Nebraska	18.3
NA	New Jersey**	NA	30	Alabama	17.7
NA	New Mexico**	NA	31	Idaho	14.7
23	New York	20.7	32	Utah	11.4
7	North Carolina	24.3	NA	Arkansas**	NA
24	North Dakota	20.6	NA	California**	NA
20	Ohio	21.4	NA	Colorado**	NA
16	Oklahoma	22.0	NA	Connecticut**	NA
NA	Oregon**	NA	NA	Hawaii**	NA
NA	Pennsylvania**	NA	NA	Illinois**	NA
4	Rhode Island	27.6	NA	Iowa**	NA
NA	South Carolina**	NA	NA	Kansas**	NA
19	South Dakota	21.5	NA	Louisiana**	NA
11	Tennessee	23.6	NA	Maryland**	NA
26	Texas	20.4	NA	Minnesota**	NA
32	Utah	11.4	NA	New Jersey**	NA
2	Vermont	28.2	NA	New Mexico**	NA
NA	Virginia**	NA	NA	Oregon**	NA
NA	Washington**	NA	NA	Pennsylvania**	NA
12	West Virginia	23.1	NA	South Carolina**	NA
17	Wisconsin	21.8	NA	Virginia**	NA
26	Wyoming	20.4	NA	Washington**	NA

District of Columbia   23.5

Source: U.S. Department of Health and Human Services, Centers for Disease Control and Prevention
    "Youth Risk Behavior Surveillance--U.S., 2003" (Morbidity Mortality Weekly Report, Vol. 53, No. SS-2, 5/21/04)
*Used marijuana one or more times in the 30 days preceding the survey. National percent includes nonreporting states.
**Not available.

Admissions of Juveniles to Substance Abuse Treatment Programs
As a Percent of All Admissions in 2004
National Percent = 10.0% of Admissions*

ALPHA ORDER

RANK	STATE	PERCENT
21	Alabama	9.5
NA	Alaska**	NA
5	Arizona	16.1
29	Arkansas	7.7
19	California	9.7
35	Colorado	4.6
NA	Connecticut**	NA
40	Delaware	0.0
2	Florida	21.6
31	Georgia	6.6
1	Hawaii	23.5
NA	Idaho**	NA
NA	Illinois**	NA
35	Indiana	4.6
14	Iowa	11.5
4	Kansas	16.7
NA	Kentucky**	NA
27	Louisiana	8.1
21	Maine	9.5
24	Maryland	8.8
26	Massachusetts	8.4
37	Michigan	4.3
8	Minnesota	12.4
NA	Mississippi**	NA
25	Missouri	8.5
12	Montana	12.1
39	Nebraska	0.7
3	Nevada	17.5
23	New Hampshire	9.4
34	New Jersey	4.7
NA	New Mexico**	NA
33	New York	4.9
NA	North Carolina**	NA
NA	North Dakota**	NA
17	Ohio	10.0
27	Oklahoma	8.1
16	Oregon	11.2
30	Pennsylvania	7.4
32	Rhode Island	5.7
13	South Carolina	11.8
15	South Dakota	11.4
8	Tennessee	12.4
6	Texas	13.7
11	Utah	12.2
20	Vermont	9.6
18	Virginia	9.9
7	Washington	12.7
NA	West Virginia**	NA
38	Wisconsin	3.0
10	Wyoming	12.3

RANK ORDER

RANK	STATE	PERCENT
1	Hawaii	23.5
2	Florida	21.6
3	Nevada	17.5
4	Kansas	16.7
5	Arizona	16.1
6	Texas	13.7
7	Washington	12.7
8	Minnesota	12.4
8	Tennessee	12.4
10	Wyoming	12.3
11	Utah	12.2
12	Montana	12.1
13	South Carolina	11.8
14	Iowa	11.5
15	South Dakota	11.4
16	Oregon	11.2
17	Ohio	10.0
18	Virginia	9.9
19	California	9.7
20	Vermont	9.6
21	Alabama	9.5
21	Maine	9.5
23	New Hampshire	9.4
24	Maryland	8.8
25	Missouri	8.5
26	Massachusetts	8.4
27	Louisiana	8.1
27	Oklahoma	8.1
29	Arkansas	7.7
30	Pennsylvania	7.4
31	Georgia	6.6
32	Rhode Island	5.7
33	New York	4.9
34	New Jersey	4.7
35	Colorado	4.6
35	Indiana	4.6
37	Michigan	4.3
38	Wisconsin	3.0
39	Nebraska	0.7
40	Delaware	0.0
NA	Alaska**	NA
NA	Connecticut**	NA
NA	Idaho**	NA
NA	Illinois**	NA
NA	Kentucky**	NA
NA	Mississippi**	NA
NA	New Mexico**	NA
NA	North Carolina**	NA
NA	North Dakota**	NA
NA	West Virginia**	NA
	District of Columbia**	NA

*Source: U.S. Department of Health and Human Services, Substance Abuse & Mental Health Services Administration
"Treatment Episode Data Set" (http://wwwdasis.samhsa.gov/webt/NewMapv1.htm)*
*Preliminary figures as of January 27, 2006. National figure is a weighted average of reporting states. Admissions of those 17 or younger.
**Not available.

Victims of Child Abuse and Neglect in 2003

National Total = 787,156 Children*

ALPHA ORDER

RANK	STATE	CHILDREN	% of USA
23	Alabama	9,290	1.2%
28	Alaska	7,996	1.0%
35	Arizona	4,838	0.6%
29	Arkansas	7,232	0.9%
NA	California**	NA	NA
26	Colorado	8,137	1.0%
16	Connecticut	12,256	1.6%
46	Delaware	1,236	0.2%
1	Florida	138,499	17.6%
5	Georgia	43,923	5.6%
40	Hawaii	4,046	0.5%
44	Idaho	1,527	0.2%
9	Illinois	28,344	3.6%
10	Indiana	21,205	2.7%
13	Iowa	13,303	1.7%
34	Kansas	5,682	0.7%
11	Kentucky	18,178	2.3%
17	Louisiana	11,432	1.5%
36	Maine	4,719	0.6%
12	Maryland	16,688	2.1%
6	Massachusetts	36,558	4.6%
8	Michigan	28,690	3.6%
24	Minnesota	9,230	1.2%
33	Mississippi	5,940	0.8%
20	Missouri	10,183	1.3%
43	Montana	1,951	0.2%
41	Nebraska	3,875	0.5%
37	Nevada	4,578	0.6%
48	New Hampshire	1,043	0.1%
27	New Jersey	8,123	1.0%
31	New Mexico	6,238	0.8%
2	New York	75,784	9.6%
7	North Carolina	32,847	4.2%
45	North Dakota	1,494	0.2%
4	Ohio	47,444	6.0%
14	Oklahoma	12,529	1.6%
19	Oregon	10,368	1.3%
38	Pennsylvania	4,571	0.6%
42	Rhode Island	3,290	0.4%
18	South Carolina	11,143	1.4%
39	South Dakota	4,346	0.6%
22	Tennessee	9,421	1.2%
3	Texas	50,522	6.4%
15	Utah	12,366	1.6%
47	Vermont	1,233	0.2%
30	Virginia	6,485	0.8%
32	Washington	6,020	0.8%
25	West Virginia	8,875	1.1%
21	Wisconsin	10,174	1.3%
49	Wyoming	786	0.1%

RANK ORDER

RANK	STATE	CHILDREN	% of USA
1	Florida	138,499	17.6%
2	New York	75,784	9.6%
3	Texas	50,522	6.4%
4	Ohio	47,444	6.0%
5	Georgia	43,923	5.6%
6	Massachusetts	36,558	4.6%
7	North Carolina	32,847	4.2%
8	Michigan	28,690	3.6%
9	Illinois	28,344	3.6%
10	Indiana	21,205	2.7%
11	Kentucky	18,178	2.3%
12	Maryland	16,688	2.1%
13	Iowa	13,303	1.7%
14	Oklahoma	12,529	1.6%
15	Utah	12,366	1.6%
16	Connecticut	12,256	1.6%
17	Louisiana	11,432	1.5%
18	South Carolina	11,143	1.4%
19	Oregon	10,368	1.3%
20	Missouri	10,183	1.3%
21	Wisconsin	10,174	1.3%
22	Tennessee	9,421	1.2%
23	Alabama	9,290	1.2%
24	Minnesota	9,230	1.2%
25	West Virginia	8,875	1.1%
26	Colorado	8,137	1.0%
27	New Jersey	8,123	1.0%
28	Alaska	7,996	1.0%
29	Arkansas	7,232	0.9%
30	Virginia	6,485	0.8%
31	New Mexico	6,238	0.8%
32	Washington	6,020	0.8%
33	Mississippi	5,940	0.8%
34	Kansas	5,682	0.7%
35	Arizona	4,838	0.6%
36	Maine	4,719	0.6%
37	Nevada	4,578	0.6%
38	Pennsylvania	4,571	0.6%
39	South Dakota	4,346	0.6%
40	Hawaii	4,046	0.5%
41	Nebraska	3,875	0.5%
42	Rhode Island	3,290	0.4%
43	Montana	1,951	0.2%
44	Idaho	1,527	0.2%
45	North Dakota	1,494	0.2%
46	Delaware	1,236	0.2%
47	Vermont	1,233	0.2%
48	New Hampshire	1,043	0.1%
49	Wyoming	786	0.1%
NA	California**	NA	NA
	District of Columbia	2,518	0.3%

Source: U.S. Department of Health and Human Services, Children's Bureau
  "Child Maltreatment 2003"

*State-substantiated or indicated incidents. Some children may be counted twice if they were victims of multiple types of abuse. Sixty-one percent of maltreated children suffered neglect, 18.9% physical abuse, 9.9% sexual abuse, and the remainder suffered emotional maltreatment, medical neglect or other forms of maltreatment.
**Not available.

Rate of Child Abuse and Neglect in 2003

National Rate = 12.4 Abused Children per 1,000 Population Under 18*

ALPHA ORDER

RANK	STATE	RATE
31	Alabama	8.4
1	Alaska	42.2
48	Arizona	3.2
24	Arkansas	10.6
NA	California**	NA
39	Colorado	7.1
14	Connecticut	14.7
42	Delaware	6.2
2	Florida	35.3
7	Georgia	19.1
16	Hawaii	13.6
43	Idaho	4.1
29	Illinois	8.8
18	Indiana	13.2
6	Iowa	19.2
32	Kansas	8.2
8	Kentucky	18.3
26	Louisiana	9.7
12	Maine	16.5
21	Maryland	12.1
3	Massachusetts	24.6
22	Michigan	11.3
37	Minnesota	7.4
35	Mississippi	7.8
38	Missouri	7.2
27	Montana	9.0
29	Nebraska	8.8
34	Nevada	7.9
47	New Hampshire	3.4
45	New Jersey	3.8
19	New Mexico	12.4
10	New York	16.7
13	North Carolina	15.7
25	North Dakota	10.2
9	Ohio	16.9
15	Oklahoma	14.3
20	Oregon	12.2
49	Pennsylvania	1.6
17	Rhode Island	13.5
23	South Carolina	10.9
5	South Dakota	22.2
40	Tennessee	6.8
33	Texas	8.1
11	Utah	16.6
27	Vermont	9.0
46	Virginia	3.6
44	Washington	4.0
4	West Virginia	22.7
36	Wisconsin	7.6
41	Wyoming	6.5

RANK ORDER

RANK	STATE	RATE
1	Alaska	42.2
2	Florida	35.3
3	Massachusetts	24.6
4	West Virginia	22.7
5	South Dakota	22.2
6	Iowa	19.2
7	Georgia	19.1
8	Kentucky	18.3
9	Ohio	16.9
10	New York	16.7
11	Utah	16.6
12	Maine	16.5
13	North Carolina	15.7
14	Connecticut	14.7
15	Oklahoma	14.3
16	Hawaii	13.6
17	Rhode Island	13.5
18	Indiana	13.2
19	New Mexico	12.4
20	Oregon	12.2
21	Maryland	12.1
22	Michigan	11.3
23	South Carolina	10.9
24	Arkansas	10.6
25	North Dakota	10.2
26	Louisiana	9.7
27	Montana	9.0
27	Vermont	9.0
29	Illinois	8.8
29	Nebraska	8.8
31	Alabama	8.4
32	Kansas	8.2
33	Texas	8.1
34	Nevada	7.9
35	Mississippi	7.8
36	Wisconsin	7.6
37	Minnesota	7.4
38	Missouri	7.2
39	Colorado	7.1
40	Tennessee	6.8
41	Wyoming	6.5
42	Delaware	6.2
43	Idaho	4.1
44	Washington	4.0
45	New Jersey	3.8
46	Virginia	3.6
47	New Hampshire	3.4
48	Arizona	3.2
49	Pennsylvania	1.6
NA	California**	NA

District of Columbia 23.2

Source: U.S. Department of Health and Human Services, Children's Bureau
"Child Maltreatment 2003"
State-substantiated or indicated incidents.
**Not available.*

Physically Abused Children in 2003

National Total = 148,877 Children*

ALPHA ORDER

RANK	STATE	CHILDREN	% of USA
12	Alabama	3,586	2.4%
25	Alaska	1,742	1.2%
37	Arizona	1,074	0.7%
31	Arkansas	1,369	0.9%
NA	California**	NA	NA
24	Colorado	1,752	1.2%
29	Connecticut	1,414	0.9%
46	Delaware	310	0.2%
1	Florida	19,205	12.9%
9	Georgia	4,364	2.9%
44	Hawaii	482	0.3%
47	Idaho	258	0.2%
4	Illinois	9,867	6.6%
11	Indiana	3,734	2.5%
20	Iowa	2,063	1.4%
28	Kansas	1,458	1.0%
13	Kentucky	3,187	2.1%
17	Louisiana	2,511	1.7%
33	Maine	1,284	0.9%
8	Maryland	5,334	3.6%
6	Massachusetts	5,940	4.0%
7	Michigan	5,758	3.9%
22	Minnesota	1,819	1.2%
32	Mississippi	1,353	0.9%
16	Missouri	2,837	1.9%
35	Montana	1,154	0.8%
40	Nebraska	821	0.6%
41	Nevada	734	0.5%
48	New Hampshire	202	0.1%
19	New Jersey	2,076	1.4%
21	New Mexico	2,007	1.3%
5	New York	9,715	6.5%
38	North Carolina	1,016	0.7%
45	North Dakota	330	0.2%
3	Ohio	10,875	7.3%
18	Oklahoma	2,352	1.6%
36	Oregon	1,151	0.8%
26	Pennsylvania	1,671	1.1%
43	Rhode Island	590	0.4%
10	South Carolina	3,865	2.6%
39	South Dakota	903	0.6%
14	Tennessee	3,082	2.1%
2	Texas	13,600	9.1%
23	Utah	1,756	1.2%
42	Vermont	651	0.4%
27	Virginia	1,588	1.1%
34	Washington	1,192	0.8%
15	West Virginia	2,838	1.9%
30	Wisconsin	1,400	0.9%
49	Wyoming	116	0.1%

RANK ORDER

RANK	STATE	CHILDREN	% of USA
1	Florida	19,205	12.9%
2	Texas	13,600	9.1%
3	Ohio	10,875	7.3%
4	Illinois	9,867	6.6%
5	New York	9,715	6.5%
6	Massachusetts	5,940	4.0%
7	Michigan	5,758	3.9%
8	Maryland	5,334	3.6%
9	Georgia	4,364	2.9%
10	South Carolina	3,865	2.6%
11	Indiana	3,734	2.5%
12	Alabama	3,586	2.4%
13	Kentucky	3,187	2.1%
14	Tennessee	3,082	2.1%
15	West Virginia	2,838	1.9%
16	Missouri	2,837	1.9%
17	Louisiana	2,511	1.7%
18	Oklahoma	2,352	1.6%
19	New Jersey	2,076	1.4%
20	Iowa	2,063	1.4%
21	New Mexico	2,007	1.3%
22	Minnesota	1,819	1.2%
23	Utah	1,756	1.2%
24	Colorado	1,752	1.2%
25	Alaska	1,742	1.2%
26	Pennsylvania	1,671	1.1%
27	Virginia	1,588	1.1%
28	Kansas	1,458	1.0%
29	Connecticut	1,414	0.9%
30	Wisconsin	1,400	0.9%
31	Arkansas	1,369	0.9%
32	Mississippi	1,353	0.9%
33	Maine	1,284	0.9%
34	Washington	1,192	0.8%
35	Montana	1,154	0.8%
36	Oregon	1,151	0.8%
37	Arizona	1,074	0.7%
38	North Carolina	1,016	0.7%
39	South Dakota	903	0.6%
40	Nebraska	821	0.6%
41	Nevada	734	0.5%
42	Vermont	651	0.4%
43	Rhode Island	590	0.4%
44	Hawaii	482	0.3%
45	North Dakota	330	0.2%
46	Delaware	310	0.2%
47	Idaho	258	0.2%
48	New Hampshire	202	0.1%
49	Wyoming	116	0.1%
NA	California**	NA	NA
	District of Columbia	491	0.3%

Source: U.S. Department of Health and Human Services, Children's Bureau
   "Child Maltreatment 2003"
*State-substantiated or indicated incidents. Some children may be counted twice if they were victims of multiple types of abuse. Sixty-one percent of maltreated children suffered neglect, 18.9% physical abuse, 9.9% sexual abuse, and the remainder suffered emotional maltreatment, medical neglect or other forms of maltreatment.
**Not available.

Rate of Physically Abused Children in 2003

National Rate = 2.3 Physically Abused Children per 1,000 Population Under 18*

ALPHA ORDER

RANK	STATE	RATE
13	Alabama	3.2
1	Alaska	9.2
45	Arizona	0.7
28	Arkansas	2.0
NA	California**	NA
36	Colorado	1.5
33	Connecticut	1.7
34	Delaware	1.6
4	Florida	4.9
30	Georgia	1.9
34	Hawaii	1.6
45	Idaho	0.7
15	Illinois	3.1
20	Indiana	2.3
16	Iowa	3.0
25	Kansas	2.1
13	Kentucky	3.2
25	Louisiana	2.1
7	Maine	4.5
10	Maryland	3.9
8	Massachusetts	4.0
20	Michigan	2.3
36	Minnesota	1.5
32	Mississippi	1.8
28	Missouri	2.0
3	Montana	5.3
30	Nebraska	1.9
39	Nevada	1.3
45	New Hampshire	0.7
41	New Jersey	1.0
8	New Mexico	4.0
25	New York	2.1
49	North Carolina	0.5
22	North Dakota	2.2
10	Ohio	3.9
17	Oklahoma	2.7
38	Oregon	1.4
48	Pennsylvania	0.6
18	Rhode Island	2.4
12	South Carolina	3.8
6	South Dakota	4.6
22	Tennessee	2.2
22	Texas	2.2
18	Utah	2.4
5	Vermont	4.7
43	Virginia	0.9
44	Washington	0.8
2	West Virginia	7.3
40	Wisconsin	1.1
41	Wyoming	1.0

RANK ORDER

RANK	STATE	RATE
1	Alaska	9.2
2	West Virginia	7.3
3	Montana	5.3
4	Florida	4.9
5	Vermont	4.7
6	South Dakota	4.6
7	Maine	4.5
8	Massachusetts	4.0
8	New Mexico	4.0
10	Maryland	3.9
10	Ohio	3.9
12	South Carolina	3.8
13	Alabama	3.2
13	Kentucky	3.2
15	Illinois	3.1
16	Iowa	3.0
17	Oklahoma	2.7
18	Rhode Island	2.4
18	Utah	2.4
20	Indiana	2.3
20	Michigan	2.3
22	North Dakota	2.2
22	Tennessee	2.2
22	Texas	2.2
25	Kansas	2.1
25	Louisiana	2.1
25	New York	2.1
28	Arkansas	2.0
28	Missouri	2.0
30	Georgia	1.9
30	Nebraska	1.9
32	Mississippi	1.8
33	Connecticut	1.7
34	Delaware	1.6
34	Hawaii	1.6
36	Colorado	1.5
36	Minnesota	1.5
38	Oregon	1.4
39	Nevada	1.3
40	Wisconsin	1.1
41	New Jersey	1.0
41	Wyoming	1.0
43	Virginia	0.9
44	Washington	0.8
45	Arizona	0.7
45	Idaho	0.7
45	New Hampshire	0.7
48	Pennsylvania	0.6
49	North Carolina	0.5
NA	California**	NA

District of Columbia   4.5

Source: Morgan Quitno Press using data from U.S. Department of Health and Human Services, Children's Bureau "Child Maltreatment 2003"

*State-substantiated or indicated incidents. Some children may be counted twice if they were victims of multiple types of abuse. Sixty-one percent of maltreated children suffered neglect, 18.9% physical abuse, 9.9% sexual abuse, and the remainder suffered emotional maltreatment, medical neglect or other forms of maltreatment.
**Not available.

Sexually Abused Children in 2003

National Total = 78,188 Children*

RANK	STATE	CHILDREN	% of USA
ALPHA ORDER			
12	Alabama	2,294	2.9%
33	Alaska	575	0.7%
39	Arizona	289	0.4%
14	Arkansas	2,110	2.7%
NA	California**	NA	NA
23	Colorado	935	1.2%
34	Connecticut	550	0.7%
47	Delaware	153	0.2%
3	Florida	6,228	8.0%
13	Georgia	2,214	2.8%
40	Hawaii	230	0.3%
48	Idaho	117	0.1%
4	Illinois	5,454	7.0%
5	Indiana	4,311	5.5%
26	Iowa	890	1.1%
28	Kansas	861	1.1%
21	Kentucky	1,069	1.4%
29	Louisiana	843	1.1%
31	Maine	676	0.9%
15	Maryland	2,079	2.7%
18	Massachusetts	1,126	1.4%
16	Michigan	1,588	2.0%
22	Minnesota	949	1.2%
25	Mississippi	894	1.1%
8	Missouri	2,845	3.6%
46	Montana	170	0.2%
37	Nebraska	389	0.5%
45	Nevada	175	0.2%
42	New Hampshire	217	0.3%
30	New Jersey	753	1.0%
38	New Mexico	384	0.5%
7	New York	3,018	3.9%
17	North Carolina	1,188	1.5%
44	North Dakota	176	0.2%
2	Ohio	7,335	9.4%
24	Oklahoma	926	1.2%
19	Oregon	1,111	1.4%
9	Pennsylvania	2,616	3.3%
41	Rhode Island	224	0.3%
27	South Carolina	868	1.1%
43	South Dakota	181	0.2%
11	Tennessee	2,317	3.0%
1	Texas	7,370	9.4%
10	Utah	2,418	3.1%
35	Vermont	519	0.7%
20	Virginia	1,080	1.4%
36	Washington	460	0.6%
32	West Virginia	588	0.8%
6	Wisconsin	4,213	5.4%
49	Wyoming	89	0.1%

RANK	STATE	CHILDREN	% of USA
RANK ORDER			
1	Texas	7,370	9.4%
2	Ohio	7,335	9.4%
3	Florida	6,228	8.0%
4	Illinois	5,454	7.0%
5	Indiana	4,311	5.5%
6	Wisconsin	4,213	5.4%
7	New York	3,018	3.9%
8	Missouri	2,845	3.6%
9	Pennsylvania	2,616	3.3%
10	Utah	2,418	3.1%
11	Tennessee	2,317	3.0%
12	Alabama	2,294	2.9%
13	Georgia	2,214	2.8%
14	Arkansas	2,110	2.7%
15	Maryland	2,079	2.7%
16	Michigan	1,588	2.0%
17	North Carolina	1,188	1.5%
18	Massachusetts	1,126	1.4%
19	Oregon	1,111	1.4%
20	Virginia	1,080	1.4%
21	Kentucky	1,069	1.4%
22	Minnesota	949	1.2%
23	Colorado	935	1.2%
24	Oklahoma	926	1.2%
25	Mississippi	894	1.1%
26	Iowa	890	1.1%
27	South Carolina	868	1.1%
28	Kansas	861	1.1%
29	Louisiana	843	1.1%
30	New Jersey	753	1.0%
31	Maine	676	0.9%
32	West Virginia	588	0.8%
33	Alaska	575	0.7%
34	Connecticut	550	0.7%
35	Vermont	519	0.7%
36	Washington	460	0.6%
37	Nebraska	389	0.5%
38	New Mexico	384	0.5%
39	Arizona	289	0.4%
40	Hawaii	230	0.3%
41	Rhode Island	224	0.3%
42	New Hampshire	217	0.3%
43	South Dakota	181	0.2%
44	North Dakota	176	0.2%
45	Nevada	175	0.2%
46	Montana	170	0.2%
47	Delaware	153	0.2%
48	Idaho	117	0.1%
49	Wyoming	89	0.1%
NA	California**	NA	NA
	District of Columbia	123	0.2%

Source: U.S. Department of Health and Human Services, Children's Bureau
    "Child Maltreatment 2003"
*State-substantiated or indicated incidents. Some children may be counted twice if they were victims of multiple types of abuse. Sixty-one percent of maltreated children suffered neglect, 18.9% physical abuse, 9.9% sexual abuse, and the remainder suffered emotional maltreatment, medical neglect or other forms of maltreatment.
**Not available.

Rate of Sexually Abused Children in 2003

National Rate = 1.2 Sexually Abused Children per 1,000 Population Under 18*

ALPHA ORDER

RANK	STATE	RATE
9	Alabama	2.1
5	Alaska	3.0
49	Arizona	0.2
4	Arkansas	3.1
NA	California**	NA
29	Colorado	0.8
37	Connecticut	0.7
29	Delaware	0.8
13	Florida	1.6
24	Georgia	1.0
29	Hawaii	0.8
46	Idaho	0.3
11	Illinois	1.7
6	Indiana	2.7
16	Iowa	1.3
18	Kansas	1.2
22	Kentucky	1.1
37	Louisiana	0.7
8	Maine	2.4
14	Maryland	1.5
29	Massachusetts	0.8
42	Michigan	0.6
29	Minnesota	0.8
18	Mississippi	1.2
10	Missouri	2.0
29	Montana	0.8
25	Nebraska	0.9
46	Nevada	0.3
37	New Hampshire	0.7
45	New Jersey	0.4
29	New Mexico	0.8
37	New York	0.7
42	North Carolina	0.6
18	North Dakota	1.2
7	Ohio	2.6
22	Oklahoma	1.1
16	Oregon	1.3
25	Pennsylvania	0.9
25	Rhode Island	0.9
29	South Carolina	0.8
25	South Dakota	0.9
11	Tennessee	1.7
18	Texas	1.2
2	Utah	3.3
1	Vermont	3.8
42	Virginia	0.6
46	Washington	0.3
14	West Virginia	1.5
3	Wisconsin	3.2
37	Wyoming	0.7

RANK ORDER

RANK	STATE	RATE
1	Vermont	3.8
2	Utah	3.3
3	Wisconsin	3.2
4	Arkansas	3.1
5	Alaska	3.0
6	Indiana	2.7
7	Ohio	2.6
8	Maine	2.4
9	Alabama	2.1
10	Missouri	2.0
11	Illinois	1.7
11	Tennessee	1.7
13	Florida	1.6
14	Maryland	1.5
14	West Virginia	1.5
16	Iowa	1.3
16	Oregon	1.3
18	Kansas	1.2
18	Mississippi	1.2
18	North Dakota	1.2
18	Texas	1.2
22	Kentucky	1.1
22	Oklahoma	1.1
24	Georgia	1.0
25	Nebraska	0.9
25	Pennsylvania	0.9
25	Rhode Island	0.9
25	South Dakota	0.9
29	Colorado	0.8
29	Delaware	0.8
29	Hawaii	0.8
29	Massachusetts	0.8
29	Minnesota	0.8
29	Montana	0.8
29	New Mexico	0.8
29	South Carolina	0.8
37	Connecticut	0.7
37	Louisiana	0.7
37	New Hampshire	0.7
37	New York	0.7
37	Wyoming	0.7
42	Michigan	0.6
42	North Carolina	0.6
42	Virginia	0.6
45	New Jersey	0.4
46	Idaho	0.3
46	Nevada	0.3
46	Washington	0.3
49	Arizona	0.2
NA	California**	NA

	District of Columbia	1.1

Source: Morgan Quitno Press using data from U.S. Department of Health and Human Services, Children's Bureau
   "Child Maltreatment 2003"

*State-substantiated or indicated incidents. Some children may be counted twice if they were victims of multiple
types of abuse. Sixty-one percent of maltreated children suffered neglect, 18.9% physical abuse, 9.9% sexual
abuse, and the remainder suffered emotional maltreatment, medical neglect or other forms of maltreatment.
**Not available.

Emotionally Abused Children in 2003

National Total = 38,603 Children*

ALPHA ORDER

RANK	STATE	CHILDREN	% of USA
31	Alabama	120	0.3%
11	Alaska	901	2.3%
43	Arizona	45	0.1%
36	Arkansas	78	0.2%
NA	California**	NA	NA
19	Colorado	404	1.0%
3	Connecticut	4,123	10.7%
26	Delaware	279	0.7%
4	Florida	3,277	8.5%
7	Georgia	1,521	3.9%
34	Hawaii	100	0.3%
47	Idaho	7	0.0%
42	Illinois	46	0.1%
NA	Indiana**	NA	NA
28	Iowa	171	0.4%
10	Kansas	1,034	2.7%
27	Kentucky	206	0.5%
18	Louisiana	446	1.2%
5	Maine	2,735	7.1%
41	Maryland	48	0.1%
33	Massachusetts	104	0.3%
8	Michigan	1,176	3.0%
37	Minnesota	74	0.2%
17	Mississippi	554	1.4%
15	Missouri	625	1.6%
25	Montana	303	0.8%
23	Nebraska	310	0.8%
23	Nevada	310	0.8%
45	New Hampshire	16	0.0%
21	New Jersey	343	0.9%
22	New Mexico	341	0.9%
14	New York	710	1.8%
30	North Carolina	126	0.3%
12	North Dakota	792	2.1%
1	Ohio	6,613	17.1%
16	Oklahoma	555	1.4%
19	Oregon	404	1.0%
39	Pennsylvania	65	0.2%
48	Rhode Island	6	0.0%
29	South Carolina	141	0.4%
13	South Dakota	768	2.0%
40	Tennessee	53	0.1%
9	Texas	1,060	2.7%
2	Utah	5,440	14.1%
46	Vermont	15	0.0%
32	Virginia	111	0.3%
38	Washington	66	0.2%
6	West Virginia	1,865	4.8%
44	Wisconsin	35	0.1%
35	Wyoming	81	0.2%

RANK ORDER

RANK	STATE	CHILDREN	% of USA
1	Ohio	6,613	17.1%
2	Utah	5,440	14.1%
3	Connecticut	4,123	10.7%
4	Florida	3,277	8.5%
5	Maine	2,735	7.1%
6	West Virginia	1,865	4.8%
7	Georgia	1,521	3.9%
8	Michigan	1,176	3.0%
9	Texas	1,060	2.7%
10	Kansas	1,034	2.7%
11	Alaska	901	2.3%
12	North Dakota	792	2.1%
13	South Dakota	768	2.0%
14	New York	710	1.8%
15	Missouri	625	1.6%
16	Oklahoma	555	1.4%
17	Mississippi	554	1.4%
18	Louisiana	446	1.2%
19	Colorado	404	1.0%
19	Oregon	404	1.0%
21	New Jersey	343	0.9%
22	New Mexico	341	0.9%
23	Nebraska	310	0.8%
23	Nevada	310	0.8%
25	Montana	303	0.8%
26	Delaware	279	0.7%
27	Kentucky	206	0.5%
28	Iowa	171	0.4%
29	South Carolina	141	0.4%
30	North Carolina	126	0.3%
31	Alabama	120	0.3%
32	Virginia	111	0.3%
33	Massachusetts	104	0.3%
34	Hawaii	100	0.3%
35	Wyoming	81	0.2%
36	Arkansas	78	0.2%
37	Minnesota	74	0.2%
38	Washington	66	0.2%
39	Pennsylvania	65	0.2%
40	Tennessee	53	0.1%
41	Maryland	48	0.1%
42	Illinois	46	0.1%
43	Arizona	45	0.1%
44	Wisconsin	35	0.1%
45	New Hampshire	16	0.0%
46	Vermont	15	0.0%
47	Idaho	7	0.0%
48	Rhode Island	6	0.0%
NA	California**	NA	NA
NA	Indiana**	NA	NA
	District of Columbia**	NA	NA

Source: U.S. Department of Health and Human Services, Children's Bureau
"Child Maltreatment 2003"

*State-substantiated or indicated incidents. Also called psychological maltreatment. Some children may be counted twice if they were victims of multiple types of abuse. Sixty-one percent of maltreated children suffered neglect, 18.9% physical abuse, 9.9% sexual abuse, and the remainder suffered emotional maltreatment, medical neglect or other forms of maltreatment. **Not available.

Rate of Emotionally Abused Children in 2003

National Rate = 0.6 Emotionally Abused Children per 1,000 Population*

ALPHA ORDER

RANK	STATE	RATE
31	Alabama	0.1
5	Alaska	4.8
40	Arizona	0.0
31	Arkansas	0.1
NA	California**	NA
22	Colorado	0.4
4	Connecticut	4.9
10	Delaware	1.4
12	Florida	0.8
13	Georgia	0.7
25	Hawaii	0.3
40	Idaho	0.0
40	Illinois	0.0
NA	Indiana**	NA
26	Iowa	0.2
9	Kansas	1.5
26	Kentucky	0.2
22	Louisiana	0.4
1	Maine	9.5
40	Maryland	0.0
31	Massachusetts	0.1
19	Michigan	0.5
31	Minnesota	0.1
13	Mississippi	0.7
22	Missouri	0.4
10	Montana	1.4
13	Nebraska	0.7
19	Nevada	0.5
31	New Hampshire	0.1
26	New Jersey	0.2
13	New Mexico	0.7
26	New York	0.2
31	North Carolina	0.1
3	North Dakota	5.4
8	Ohio	2.3
18	Oklahoma	0.6
19	Oregon	0.5
40	Pennsylvania	0.0
40	Rhode Island	0.0
31	South Carolina	0.1
7	South Dakota	3.9
40	Tennessee	0.0
26	Texas	0.2
2	Utah	7.3
31	Vermont	0.1
31	Virginia	0.1
40	Washington	0.0
5	West Virginia	4.8
40	Wisconsin	0.0
13	Wyoming	0.7

RANK ORDER

RANK	STATE	RATE
1	Maine	9.5
2	Utah	7.3
3	North Dakota	5.4
4	Connecticut	4.9
5	Alaska	4.8
5	West Virginia	4.8
7	South Dakota	3.9
8	Ohio	2.3
9	Kansas	1.5
10	Delaware	1.4
10	Montana	1.4
12	Florida	0.8
13	Georgia	0.7
13	Mississippi	0.7
13	Nebraska	0.7
13	New Mexico	0.7
13	Wyoming	0.7
18	Oklahoma	0.6
19	Michigan	0.5
19	Nevada	0.5
19	Oregon	0.5
22	Colorado	0.4
22	Louisiana	0.4
22	Missouri	0.4
25	Hawaii	0.3
26	Iowa	0.2
26	Kentucky	0.2
26	New Jersey	0.2
26	New York	0.2
26	Texas	0.2
31	Alabama	0.1
31	Arkansas	0.1
31	Massachusetts	0.1
31	Minnesota	0.1
31	New Hampshire	0.1
31	North Carolina	0.1
31	South Carolina	0.1
31	Vermont	0.1
31	Virginia	0.1
40	Arizona	0.0
40	Idaho	0.0
40	Illinois	0.0
40	Maryland	0.0
40	Pennsylvania	0.0
40	Rhode Island	0.0
40	Tennessee	0.0
40	Washington	0.0
40	Wisconsin	0.0
NA	California**	NA
NA	Indiana**	NA
	District of Columbia**	NA

Source: Morgan Quitno Press using data from U.S. Department of Health and Human Services, Children's Bureau "Child Maltreatment 2003"

*State-substantiated or indicated incidents. Also called psychological maltreatment. Some children may be counted twice if they were victims of multiple types of abuse. Sixty-one percent of maltreated children suffered neglect, 18.9% physical abuse, 9.9% sexual abuse, and the remainder suffered emotional maltreatment, medical neglect or other forms of maltreatment. **Not available.*

Neglected Children in 2003

National Total = 479,567 Children*

ALPHA ORDER					RANK ORDER			
RANK	STATE	CHILDREN	% of USA		RANK	STATE	CHILDREN	% of USA
30	Alabama	3,679	0.8%		1	New York	68,539	14.3%
20	Alaska	4,778	1.0%		2	Florida	41,826	8.7%
31	Arizona	3,599	0.8%		3	Georgia	34,982	7.3%
26	Arkansas	3,939	0.8%		4	Massachusetts	32,822	6.8%
NA	California**	NA	NA		5	Texas	32,250	6.7%
28	Colorado	3,794	0.8%		6	North Carolina	29,653	6.2%
16	Connecticut	8,350	1.7%		7	Ohio	25,410	5.3%
47	Delaware	451	0.1%		8	Michigan	20,214	4.2%
2	Florida	41,826	8.7%		9	Illinois	16,521	3.4%
3	Georgia	34,982	7.3%		10	Kentucky	14,392	3.0%
44	Hawaii	683	0.1%		11	Indiana	14,190	3.0%
42	Idaho	1,070	0.2%		12	Oklahoma	10,835	2.3%
9	Illinois	16,521	3.4%		13	Iowa	9,843	2.1%
11	Indiana	14,190	3.0%		14	Maryland	9,602	2.0%
13	Iowa	9,843	2.1%		15	Louisiana	8,796	1.8%
40	Kansas	1,508	0.3%		16	Connecticut	8,350	1.7%
10	Kentucky	14,392	3.0%		17	South Carolina	7,226	1.5%
15	Louisiana	8,796	1.8%		18	Minnesota	6,717	1.4%
32	Maine	3,394	0.7%		19	Missouri	5,137	1.1%
14	Maryland	9,602	2.0%		20	Alaska	4,778	1.0%
4	Massachusetts	32,822	6.8%		21	West Virginia	4,762	1.0%
8	Michigan	20,214	4.2%		22	Washington	4,708	1.0%
18	Minnesota	6,717	1.4%		23	Tennessee	4,642	1.0%
33	Mississippi	3,265	0.7%		24	New Mexico	4,219	0.9%
19	Missouri	5,137	1.1%		25	New Jersey	4,216	0.9%
43	Montana	755	0.2%		26	Arkansas	3,939	0.8%
35	Nebraska	2,819	0.6%		27	Virginia	3,884	0.8%
29	Nevada	3,758	0.8%		28	Colorado	3,794	0.8%
45	New Hampshire	656	0.1%		29	Nevada	3,758	0.8%
25	New Jersey	4,216	0.9%		30	Alabama	3,679	0.8%
24	New Mexico	4,219	0.9%		31	Arizona	3,599	0.8%
1	New York	68,539	14.3%		32	Maine	3,394	0.7%
6	North Carolina	29,653	6.2%		33	Mississippi	3,265	0.7%
41	North Dakota	1,318	0.3%		34	South Dakota	3,179	0.7%
7	Ohio	25,410	5.3%		35	Nebraska	2,819	0.6%
12	Oklahoma	10,835	2.3%		36	Oregon	2,653	0.6%
36	Oregon	2,653	0.6%		37	Utah	2,584	0.5%
48	Pennsylvania	178	0.0%		38	Rhode Island	2,582	0.5%
38	Rhode Island	2,582	0.5%		39	Wisconsin	2,547	0.5%
17	South Carolina	7,226	1.5%		40	Kansas	1,508	0.3%
34	South Dakota	3,179	0.7%		41	North Dakota	1,318	0.3%
23	Tennessee	4,642	1.0%		42	Idaho	1,070	0.2%
5	Texas	32,250	6.7%		43	Montana	755	0.2%
37	Utah	2,584	0.5%		44	Hawaii	683	0.1%
49	Vermont	59	0.0%		45	New Hampshire	656	0.1%
27	Virginia	3,884	0.8%		46	Wyoming	511	0.1%
22	Washington	4,708	1.0%		47	Delaware	451	0.1%
21	West Virginia	4,762	1.0%		48	Pennsylvania	178	0.0%
39	Wisconsin	2,547	0.5%		49	Vermont	59	0.0%
46	Wyoming	511	0.1%		NA	California**	NA	NA
						District of Columbia	2,072	0.4%

Source: U.S. Department of Health and Human Services, Children's Bureau
    "Child Maltreatment 2003"
*State-substantiated or indicated incidents. Some children may be counted twice if they were victims of multiple
types of abuse. Sixty-one percent of maltreated children suffered neglect, 18.9% physical abuse, 9.9% sexual
abuse, and the remainder suffered emotional maltreatment, medical neglect or other forms of maltreatment.
**Not available.

249

Rate of Neglected Children in 2003

National Rate = 7.5 Neglected Children per 1,000 Population Under 18*

ALPHA ORDER

RANK	STATE	RATE
34	Alabama	3.3
1	Alaska	25.2
40	Arizona	2.4
25	Arkansas	5.8
NA	California**	NA
34	Colorado	3.3
14	Connecticut	10.0
41	Delaware	2.3
12	Florida	10.7
4	Georgia	15.2
41	Hawaii	2.3
39	Idaho	2.9
28	Illinois	5.1
17	Indiana	8.8
7	Iowa	14.2
43	Kansas	2.2
6	Kentucky	14.5
20	Louisiana	7.5
11	Maine	11.8
22	Maryland	7.0
2	Massachusetts	22.1
19	Michigan	8.0
26	Minnesota	5.4
29	Mississippi	4.3
31	Missouri	3.7
32	Montana	3.5
24	Nebraska	6.4
23	Nevada	6.5
45	New Hampshire	2.1
46	New Jersey	2.0
18	New Mexico	8.4
5	New York	15.1
7	North Carolina	14.2
15	North Dakota	9.0
15	Ohio	9.0
9	Oklahoma	12.3
37	Oregon	3.1
49	Pennsylvania	0.1
13	Rhode Island	10.6
21	South Carolina	7.1
3	South Dakota	16.3
34	Tennessee	3.3
27	Texas	5.2
32	Utah	3.5
48	Vermont	0.4
43	Virginia	2.2
37	Washington	3.1
10	West Virginia	12.2
47	Wisconsin	1.9
30	Wyoming	4.2

RANK ORDER

RANK	STATE	RATE
1	Alaska	25.2
2	Massachusetts	22.1
3	South Dakota	16.3
4	Georgia	15.2
5	New York	15.1
6	Kentucky	14.5
7	Iowa	14.2
7	North Carolina	14.2
9	Oklahoma	12.3
10	West Virginia	12.2
11	Maine	11.8
12	Florida	10.7
13	Rhode Island	10.6
14	Connecticut	10.0
15	North Dakota	9.0
15	Ohio	9.0
17	Indiana	8.8
18	New Mexico	8.4
19	Michigan	8.0
20	Louisiana	7.5
21	South Carolina	7.1
22	Maryland	7.0
23	Nevada	6.5
24	Nebraska	6.4
25	Arkansas	5.8
26	Minnesota	5.4
27	Texas	5.2
28	Illinois	5.1
29	Mississippi	4.3
30	Wyoming	4.2
31	Missouri	3.7
32	Montana	3.5
32	Utah	3.5
34	Alabama	3.3
34	Colorado	3.3
34	Tennessee	3.3
37	Oregon	3.1
37	Washington	3.1
39	Idaho	2.9
40	Arizona	2.4
41	Delaware	2.3
41	Hawaii	2.3
43	Kansas	2.2
43	Virginia	2.2
45	New Hampshire	2.1
46	New Jersey	2.0
47	Wisconsin	1.9
48	Vermont	0.4
49	Pennsylvania	0.1
NA	California**	NA

District of Columbia 19.1

Source: Morgan Quitno Press using data from U.S. Department of Health and Human Services, Children's Bureau "Child Maltreatment 2003"

State-substantiated or indicated incidents. Some children may be counted twice if they were victims of multiple types of abuse. Sixty-one percent of maltreated children suffered neglect, 18.9% physical abuse, 9.9% sexual abuse, and the remainder suffered emotional maltreatment, medical neglect or other forms of maltreatment.
*Not available.

Child Abuse and Neglect Fatalities in 2003

National Total = 1,177 Fatalities*

<table>
<tr><td colspan="4">ALPHA ORDER</td><td colspan="4">RANK ORDER</td></tr>
<tr><th>RANK</th><th>STATE</th><th>FATALITIES</th><th>% of USA</th><th>RANK</th><th>STATE</th><th>FATALITIES</th><th>% of USA</th></tr>
<tr><td>18</td><td>Alabama</td><td>22</td><td>1.9%</td><td>1</td><td>Texas</td><td>203</td><td>17.2%</td></tr>
<tr><td>42</td><td>Alaska</td><td>2</td><td>0.2%</td><td>2</td><td>Florida</td><td>101</td><td>8.6%</td></tr>
<tr><td>23</td><td>Arizona</td><td>14</td><td>1.2%</td><td>3</td><td>Ohio</td><td>68</td><td>5.8%</td></tr>
<tr><td>28</td><td>Arkansas</td><td>10</td><td>0.8%</td><td>4</td><td>New York</td><td>62</td><td>5.3%</td></tr>
<tr><td>NA</td><td>California**</td><td>NA</td><td>NA</td><td>5</td><td>Illinois</td><td>61</td><td>5.2%</td></tr>
<tr><td>15</td><td>Colorado</td><td>27</td><td>2.3%</td><td>6</td><td>Georgia</td><td>49</td><td>4.2%</td></tr>
<tr><td>32</td><td>Connecticut</td><td>6</td><td>0.5%</td><td>6</td><td>Indiana</td><td>49</td><td>4.2%</td></tr>
<tr><td>46</td><td>Delaware</td><td>0</td><td>0.0%</td><td>8</td><td>Pennsylvania</td><td>46</td><td>3.9%</td></tr>
<tr><td>2</td><td>Florida</td><td>101</td><td>8.6%</td><td>9</td><td>Missouri</td><td>45</td><td>3.8%</td></tr>
<tr><td>6</td><td>Georgia</td><td>49</td><td>4.2%</td><td>10</td><td>Louisiana</td><td>43</td><td>3.7%</td></tr>
<tr><td>32</td><td>Hawaii</td><td>6</td><td>0.5%</td><td>11</td><td>New Jersey</td><td>34</td><td>2.9%</td></tr>
<tr><td>42</td><td>Idaho</td><td>2</td><td>0.2%</td><td>12</td><td>Virginia</td><td>31</td><td>2.6%</td></tr>
<tr><td>5</td><td>Illinois</td><td>61</td><td>5.2%</td><td>13</td><td>West Virginia</td><td>30</td><td>2.5%</td></tr>
<tr><td>6</td><td>Indiana</td><td>49</td><td>4.2%</td><td>14</td><td>Oklahoma</td><td>29</td><td>2.5%</td></tr>
<tr><td>20</td><td>Iowa</td><td>16</td><td>1.4%</td><td>15</td><td>Colorado</td><td>27</td><td>2.3%</td></tr>
<tr><td>35</td><td>Kansas</td><td>5</td><td>0.4%</td><td>15</td><td>Maryland</td><td>27</td><td>2.3%</td></tr>
<tr><td>32</td><td>Kentucky</td><td>6</td><td>0.5%</td><td>17</td><td>Tennessee</td><td>24</td><td>2.0%</td></tr>
<tr><td>10</td><td>Louisiana</td><td>43</td><td>3.7%</td><td>18</td><td>Alabama</td><td>22</td><td>1.9%</td></tr>
<tr><td>38</td><td>Maine</td><td>3</td><td>0.3%</td><td>19</td><td>South Carolina</td><td>20</td><td>1.7%</td></tr>
<tr><td>15</td><td>Maryland</td><td>27</td><td>2.3%</td><td>20</td><td>Iowa</td><td>16</td><td>1.4%</td></tr>
<tr><td>23</td><td>Massachusetts</td><td>14</td><td>1.2%</td><td>20</td><td>Nebraska</td><td>16</td><td>1.4%</td></tr>
<tr><td>NA</td><td>Michigan**</td><td>NA</td><td>NA</td><td>22</td><td>Minnesota</td><td>15</td><td>1.3%</td></tr>
<tr><td>22</td><td>Minnesota</td><td>15</td><td>1.3%</td><td>23</td><td>Arizona</td><td>14</td><td>1.2%</td></tr>
<tr><td>26</td><td>Mississippi</td><td>13</td><td>1.1%</td><td>23</td><td>Massachusetts</td><td>14</td><td>1.2%</td></tr>
<tr><td>9</td><td>Missouri</td><td>45</td><td>3.8%</td><td>23</td><td>Oregon</td><td>14</td><td>1.2%</td></tr>
<tr><td>38</td><td>Montana</td><td>3</td><td>0.3%</td><td>26</td><td>Mississippi</td><td>13</td><td>1.1%</td></tr>
<tr><td>20</td><td>Nebraska</td><td>16</td><td>1.4%</td><td>27</td><td>Wisconsin</td><td>12</td><td>1.0%</td></tr>
<tr><td>38</td><td>Nevada</td><td>3</td><td>0.3%</td><td>28</td><td>Arkansas</td><td>10</td><td>0.8%</td></tr>
<tr><td>38</td><td>New Hampshire</td><td>3</td><td>0.3%</td><td>29</td><td>Utah</td><td>9</td><td>0.8%</td></tr>
<tr><td>11</td><td>New Jersey</td><td>34</td><td>2.9%</td><td>29</td><td>Washington</td><td>9</td><td>0.8%</td></tr>
<tr><td>37</td><td>New Mexico</td><td>4</td><td>0.3%</td><td>31</td><td>Wyoming</td><td>8</td><td>0.7%</td></tr>
<tr><td>4</td><td>New York</td><td>62</td><td>5.3%</td><td>32</td><td>Connecticut</td><td>6</td><td>0.5%</td></tr>
<tr><td>NA</td><td>North Carolina**</td><td>NA</td><td>NA</td><td>32</td><td>Hawaii</td><td>6</td><td>0.5%</td></tr>
<tr><td>46</td><td>North Dakota</td><td>0</td><td>0.0%</td><td>32</td><td>Kentucky</td><td>6</td><td>0.5%</td></tr>
<tr><td>3</td><td>Ohio</td><td>68</td><td>5.8%</td><td>35</td><td>Kansas</td><td>5</td><td>0.4%</td></tr>
<tr><td>14</td><td>Oklahoma</td><td>29</td><td>2.5%</td><td>35</td><td>South Dakota</td><td>5</td><td>0.4%</td></tr>
<tr><td>23</td><td>Oregon</td><td>14</td><td>1.2%</td><td>37</td><td>New Mexico</td><td>4</td><td>0.3%</td></tr>
<tr><td>8</td><td>Pennsylvania</td><td>46</td><td>3.9%</td><td>38</td><td>Maine</td><td>3</td><td>0.3%</td></tr>
<tr><td>44</td><td>Rhode Island</td><td>1</td><td>0.1%</td><td>38</td><td>Montana</td><td>3</td><td>0.3%</td></tr>
<tr><td>19</td><td>South Carolina</td><td>20</td><td>1.7%</td><td>38</td><td>Nevada</td><td>3</td><td>0.3%</td></tr>
<tr><td>35</td><td>South Dakota</td><td>5</td><td>0.4%</td><td>38</td><td>New Hampshire</td><td>3</td><td>0.3%</td></tr>
<tr><td>17</td><td>Tennessee</td><td>24</td><td>2.0%</td><td>42</td><td>Alaska</td><td>2</td><td>0.2%</td></tr>
<tr><td>1</td><td>Texas</td><td>203</td><td>17.2%</td><td>42</td><td>Idaho</td><td>2</td><td>0.2%</td></tr>
<tr><td>29</td><td>Utah</td><td>9</td><td>0.8%</td><td>44</td><td>Rhode Island</td><td>1</td><td>0.1%</td></tr>
<tr><td>44</td><td>Vermont</td><td>1</td><td>0.1%</td><td>44</td><td>Vermont</td><td>1</td><td>0.1%</td></tr>
<tr><td>12</td><td>Virginia</td><td>31</td><td>2.6%</td><td>46</td><td>Delaware</td><td>0</td><td>0.0%</td></tr>
<tr><td>29</td><td>Washington</td><td>9</td><td>0.8%</td><td>46</td><td>North Dakota</td><td>0</td><td>0.0%</td></tr>
<tr><td>13</td><td>West Virginia</td><td>30</td><td>2.5%</td><td>NA</td><td>California**</td><td>NA</td><td>NA</td></tr>
<tr><td>27</td><td>Wisconsin</td><td>12</td><td>1.0%</td><td>NA</td><td>Michigan**</td><td>NA</td><td>NA</td></tr>
<tr><td>31</td><td>Wyoming</td><td>8</td><td>0.7%</td><td>NA</td><td>North Carolina**</td><td>NA</td><td>NA</td></tr>
<tr><td></td><td></td><td></td><td></td><td></td><td>District of Columbia</td><td>6</td><td>0.5%</td></tr>
</table>

Source: U.S. Department of Health and Human Services, Children's Bureau
"Child Maltreatment 2003"

*State-substantiated or indicated incidents. Some children may be counted twice if they were victims of multiple types of abuse. Sixty-one percent of maltreated children suffered neglect, 18.9% physical abuse, 9.9% sexual abuse, and the remainder suffered emotional maltreatment, medical neglect or other forms of maltreatment.
**Not available.

Rate of Child Abuse and Neglect Fatalities in 2003

National Rate = 2.00 Fatalities per 100,000 Population Under 18*

ALPHA ORDER

RANK	STATE	RATE
16	Alabama	1.99
31	Alaska	1.06
35	Arizona	0.92
26	Arkansas	1.47
NA	California**	NA
12	Colorado	2.34
39	Connecticut	0.72
46	Delaware	0.00
9	Florida	2.57
14	Georgia	2.13
15	Hawaii	2.02
43	Idaho	0.54
19	Illinois	1.89
8	Indiana	3.06
13	Iowa	2.31
39	Kansas	0.72
41	Kentucky	0.60
3	Louisiana	3.65
32	Maine	1.05
17	Maryland	1.96
34	Massachusetts	0.94
NA	Michigan**	NA
30	Minnesota	1.20
22	Mississippi	1.71
7	Missouri	3.20
27	Montana	1.39
4	Nebraska	3.63
44	Nevada	0.52
33	New Hampshire	0.98
25	New Jersey	1.60
37	New Mexico	0.80
28	New York	1.37
NA	North Carolina**	NA
46	North Dakota	0.00
11	Ohio	2.42
5	Oklahoma	3.30
23	Oregon	1.65
24	Pennsylvania	1.63
45	Rhode Island	0.41
18	South Carolina	1.95
10	South Dakota	2.56
20	Tennessee	1.72
6	Texas	3.25
29	Utah	1.21
38	Vermont	0.73
20	Virginia	1.72
41	Washington	0.60
1	West Virginia	7.67
36	Wisconsin	0.90
2	Wyoming	6.61

RANK ORDER

RANK	STATE	RATE
1	West Virginia	7.67
2	Wyoming	6.61
3	Louisiana	3.65
4	Nebraska	3.63
5	Oklahoma	3.30
6	Texas	3.25
7	Missouri	3.20
8	Indiana	3.06
9	Florida	2.57
10	South Dakota	2.56
11	Ohio	2.42
12	Colorado	2.34
13	Iowa	2.31
14	Georgia	2.13
15	Hawaii	2.02
16	Alabama	1.99
17	Maryland	1.96
18	South Carolina	1.95
19	Illinois	1.89
20	Tennessee	1.72
20	Virginia	1.72
22	Mississippi	1.71
23	Oregon	1.65
24	Pennsylvania	1.63
25	New Jersey	1.60
26	Arkansas	1.47
27	Montana	1.39
28	New York	1.37
29	Utah	1.21
30	Minnesota	1.20
31	Alaska	1.06
32	Maine	1.05
33	New Hampshire	0.98
34	Massachusetts	0.94
35	Arizona	0.92
36	Wisconsin	0.90
37	New Mexico	0.80
38	Vermont	0.73
39	Connecticut	0.72
39	Kansas	0.72
41	Kentucky	0.60
41	Washington	0.60
43	Idaho	0.54
44	Nevada	0.52
45	Rhode Island	0.41
46	Delaware	0.00
46	North Dakota	0.00
NA	California**	NA
NA	Michigan**	NA
NA	North Carolina**	NA

District of Columbia   5.53

Source: U.S. Department of Health and Human Services, Children's Bureau
    "Child Maltreatment 2003"
*State-substantiated or indicated incidents. Some children may be counted twice if they were victims of multiple types of abuse. Sixty-one percent of maltreated children suffered neglect, 18.9% physical abuse, 9.9% sexual abuse, and the remainder suffered emotional maltreatment, medical neglect or other forms of maltreatment.
**Not available.

252

VI. LAW ENFORCEMENT

Federal Law Enforcement Officers in 2002

National Total = 93,446 Officers*

ALPHA ORDER

RANK	STATE	OFFICERS	% of USA
26	Alabama	687	0.7%
39	Alaska	377	0.4%
5	Arizona	4,292	4.6%
33	Arkansas	486	0.5%
2	California	12,315	13.2%
14	Colorado	1,462	1.6%
37	Connecticut	420	0.4%
49	Delaware	95	0.1%
4	Florida	5,963	6.4%
9	Georgia	2,298	2.5%
29	Hawaii	666	0.7%
43	Idaho	289	0.3%
8	Illinois	2,766	3.0%
28	Indiana	668	0.7%
46	Iowa	158	0.2%
35	Kansas	459	0.5%
23	Kentucky	963	1.0%
15	Louisiana	1,460	1.6%
40	Maine	364	0.4%
17	Maryland	1,353	1.4%
16	Massachusetts	1,382	1.5%
11	Michigan	1,699	1.8%
22	Minnesota	976	1.0%
32	Mississippi	500	0.5%
18	Missouri	1,250	1.3%
38	Montana	391	0.4%
42	Nebraska	309	0.3%
31	Nevada	507	0.5%
50	New Hampshire	77	0.1%
10	New Jersey	2,285	2.4%
13	New Mexico	1,473	1.6%
3	New York	7,202	7.7%
20	North Carolina	1,196	1.3%
44	North Dakota	252	0.3%
19	Ohio	1,216	1.3%
25	Oklahoma	751	0.8%
27	Oregon	669	0.7%
6	Pennsylvania	3,282	3.5%
47	Rhode Island	113	0.1%
24	South Carolina	813	0.9%
45	South Dakota	210	0.2%
21	Tennessee	1,038	1.1%
1	Texas	13,374	14.3%
34	Utah	477	0.5%
41	Vermont	323	0.3%
7	Virginia	3,271	3.5%
12	Washington	1,614	1.7%
30	West Virginia	597	0.6%
36	Wisconsin	433	0.5%
48	Wyoming	109	0.1%

RANK ORDER

RANK	STATE	OFFICERS	% of USA
1	Texas	13,374	14.3%
2	California	12,315	13.2%
3	New York	7,202	7.7%
4	Florida	5,963	6.4%
5	Arizona	4,292	4.6%
6	Pennsylvania	3,282	3.5%
7	Virginia	3,271	3.5%
8	Illinois	2,766	3.0%
9	Georgia	2,298	2.5%
10	New Jersey	2,285	2.4%
11	Michigan	1,699	1.8%
12	Washington	1,614	1.7%
13	New Mexico	1,473	1.6%
14	Colorado	1,462	1.6%
15	Louisiana	1,460	1.6%
16	Massachusetts	1,382	1.5%
17	Maryland	1,353	1.4%
18	Missouri	1,250	1.3%
19	Ohio	1,216	1.3%
20	North Carolina	1,196	1.3%
21	Tennessee	1,038	1.1%
22	Minnesota	976	1.0%
23	Kentucky	963	1.0%
24	South Carolina	813	0.9%
25	Oklahoma	751	0.8%
26	Alabama	687	0.7%
27	Oregon	669	0.7%
28	Indiana	668	0.7%
29	Hawaii	666	0.7%
30	West Virginia	597	0.6%
31	Nevada	507	0.5%
32	Mississippi	500	0.5%
33	Arkansas	486	0.5%
34	Utah	477	0.5%
35	Kansas	459	0.5%
36	Wisconsin	433	0.5%
37	Connecticut	420	0.4%
38	Montana	391	0.4%
39	Alaska	377	0.4%
40	Maine	364	0.4%
41	Vermont	323	0.3%
42	Nebraska	309	0.3%
43	Idaho	289	0.3%
44	North Dakota	252	0.3%
45	South Dakota	210	0.2%
46	Iowa	158	0.2%
47	Rhode Island	113	0.1%
48	Wyoming	109	0.1%
49	Delaware	95	0.1%
50	New Hampshire	77	0.1%
	District of Columbia	8,114	8.7%

Source: U.S. Department of Justice, Bureau of Justice Statistics
"Federal Law Enforcement Officers, 2002" (August 2003, NCJ 199995)
*Full-time officers authorized to carry firearms and make arrests. Includes F.B.I., Customs Service, Immigration and Naturalization Service, I.R.S., Postal Inspection, Drug Enforcement Administration, Secret Service, National Park Service, Bureau of Alcohol, Tobacco and Firearms, Capitol Police, U.S. Courts, Federal Bureau of Prisons, Tennessee Valley Authority, and U.S. Forest Service.

Rate of Federal Law Enforcement Officers in 2002

National Rate = 32 Officers per 100,000 Population*

ALPHA ORDER			RANK ORDER		
RANK	STATE	RATE	RANK	STATE	RATE
41	Alabama	15	1	Arizona	79
4	Alaska	59	1	New Mexico	79
1	Arizona	79	3	Texas	61
35	Arkansas	18	4	Alaska	59
12	California	35	5	Hawaii	54
15	Colorado	32	6	Vermont	52
43	Connecticut	12	7	Virginia	45
43	Delaware	12	8	Montana	43
11	Florida	36	9	North Dakota	40
18	Georgia	27	10	New York	38
5	Hawaii	54	11	Florida	36
25	Idaho	22	12	California	35
25	Illinois	22	13	Louisiana	33
45	Indiana	11	13	West Virginia	33
50	Iowa	5	15	Colorado	32
38	Kansas	17	16	Maine	28
23	Kentucky	24	16	South Dakota	28
13	Louisiana	33	18	Georgia	27
16	Maine	28	18	New Jersey	27
22	Maryland	25	18	Pennsylvania	27
25	Massachusetts	22	18	Washington	27
38	Michigan	17	22	Maryland	25
33	Minnesota	19	23	Kentucky	24
38	Mississippi	17	24	Nevada	23
25	Missouri	22	25	Idaho	22
8	Montana	43	25	Illinois	22
35	Nebraska	18	25	Massachusetts	22
24	Nevada	23	25	Missouri	22
49	New Hampshire	6	25	Wyoming	22
18	New Jersey	27	30	Oklahoma	21
1	New Mexico	79	30	Utah	21
10	New York	38	32	South Carolina	20
42	North Carolina	14	33	Minnesota	19
9	North Dakota	40	33	Oregon	19
45	Ohio	11	35	Arkansas	18
30	Oklahoma	21	35	Nebraska	18
33	Oregon	19	35	Tennessee	18
18	Pennsylvania	27	38	Kansas	17
45	Rhode Island	11	38	Michigan	17
32	South Carolina	20	38	Mississippi	17
16	South Dakota	28	41	Alabama	15
35	Tennessee	18	42	North Carolina	14
3	Texas	61	43	Connecticut	12
30	Utah	21	43	Delaware	12
6	Vermont	52	45	Indiana	11
7	Virginia	45	45	Ohio	11
18	Washington	27	45	Rhode Island	11
13	West Virginia	33	48	Wisconsin	8
48	Wisconsin	8	49	New Hampshire	6
25	Wyoming	22	50	Iowa	5

District of Columbia   1,421

Source: U.S. Department of Justice, Bureau of Justice Statistics
    "Federal Law Enforcement Officers, 2002" (August 2003, NCJ 199995)
*Full-time officers authorized to carry firearms and make arrests. Includes F.B.I., Customs Service, Immigration and
Naturalization Service, I.R.S., Postal Inspection, Drug Enforcement Administration, Secret Service, National Park
Service, Bureau of Alcohol, Tobacco and Firearms, Capitol Police, U.S. Courts, Federal Bureau of Prisons,
Tennessee Valley Authority, and U.S. Forest Service.

State and Local Justice System Employees in 2004

National Total = 2,004,275 Employees*

ALPHA ORDER				RANK ORDER			
RANK	STATE	EMPLOYEES	% of USA	RANK	STATE	EMPLOYEES	% of USA
24	Alabama	25,200	1.3%	1	California	233,084	11.6%
46	Alaska	4,813	0.2%	2	New York	178,735	8.9%
13	Arizona	42,191	2.1%	3	Texas	156,350	7.8%
32	Arkansas	16,931	0.8%	4	Florida	137,111	6.8%
1	California	233,084	11.6%	5	Illinois	87,441	4.4%
22	Colorado	29,052	1.4%	6	Pennsylvania	78,466	3.9%
27	Connecticut	22,903	1.1%	7	Ohio	78,413	3.9%
41	Delaware	6,898	0.3%	8	New Jersey	75,023	3.7%
4	Florida	137,111	6.8%	9	Georgia	64,524	3.2%
9	Georgia	64,524	3.2%	10	Michigan	59,844	3.0%
39	Hawaii	8,871	0.4%	11	North Carolina	53,633	2.7%
40	Idaho	8,207	0.4%	12	Virginia	48,869	2.4%
5	Illinois	87,441	4.4%	13	Arizona	42,191	2.1%
17	Indiana	38,064	1.9%	14	Massachusetts	41,704	2.1%
34	Iowa	15,584	0.8%	15	Missouri	41,445	2.1%
30	Kansas	18,484	0.9%	16	Maryland	39,478	2.0%
26	Kentucky	24,391	1.2%	17	Indiana	38,064	1.9%
19	Louisiana	37,278	1.9%	18	Tennessee	37,509	1.9%
43	Maine	6,162	0.3%	19	Louisiana	37,278	1.9%
16	Maryland	39,478	2.0%	20	Washington	35,297	1.8%
14	Massachusetts	41,704	2.1%	21	Wisconsin	35,148	1.8%
10	Michigan	59,844	3.0%	22	Colorado	29,052	1.4%
25	Minnesota	25,184	1.3%	23	South Carolina	28,167	1.4%
31	Mississippi	17,209	0.9%	24	Alabama	25,200	1.3%
15	Missouri	41,445	2.1%	25	Minnesota	25,184	1.3%
45	Montana	5,392	0.3%	26	Kentucky	24,391	1.2%
37	Nebraska	10,402	0.5%	27	Connecticut	22,903	1.1%
33	Nevada	15,895	0.8%	28	Oklahoma	21,868	1.1%
42	New Hampshire	6,820	0.3%	29	Oregon	21,583	1.1%
8	New Jersey	75,023	3.7%	30	Kansas	18,484	0.9%
35	New Mexico	14,709	0.7%	31	Mississippi	17,209	0.9%
2	New York	178,735	8.9%	32	Arkansas	16,931	0.8%
11	North Carolina	53,633	2.7%	33	Nevada	15,895	0.8%
49	North Dakota	3,200	0.2%	34	Iowa	15,584	0.8%
7	Ohio	78,413	3.9%	35	New Mexico	14,709	0.7%
28	Oklahoma	21,868	1.1%	36	Utah	13,260	0.7%
29	Oregon	21,583	1.1%	37	Nebraska	10,402	0.5%
6	Pennsylvania	78,466	3.9%	38	West Virginia	9,322	0.5%
44	Rhode Island	5,950	0.3%	39	Hawaii	8,871	0.4%
23	South Carolina	28,167	1.4%	40	Idaho	8,207	0.4%
48	South Dakota	3,916	0.2%	41	Delaware	6,898	0.3%
18	Tennessee	37,509	1.9%	42	New Hampshire	6,820	0.3%
3	Texas	156,350	7.8%	43	Maine	6,162	0.3%
36	Utah	13,260	0.7%	44	Rhode Island	5,950	0.3%
50	Vermont	2,994	0.1%	45	Montana	5,392	0.3%
12	Virginia	48,869	2.4%	46	Alaska	4,813	0.2%
20	Washington	35,297	1.8%	47	Wyoming	4,191	0.2%
38	West Virginia	9,322	0.5%	48	South Dakota	3,916	0.2%
21	Wisconsin	35,148	1.8%	49	North Dakota	3,200	0.2%
47	Wyoming	4,191	0.2%	50	Vermont	2,994	0.1%
					District of Columbia	7,110	0.4%

Source: Morgan Quitno Press using data from U.S. Bureau of the Census, Governments Division
"State and Local Employment and Payroll - March 2004" (http://www.census.gov/govs/www/apesstl04.html)
*Full-time equivalent as of March 2004. Includes police, courts, prosecution, public defense and corrections.

Rate of State and Local Justice System Employment in 2004

National Rate = 68.3 Employees per 10,000 Population*

ALPHA ORDER

RANK	STATE	RATE
40	Alabama	55.7
9	Alaska	73.2
8	Arizona	73.5
30	Arkansas	61.6
23	California	65.0
27	Colorado	63.1
20	Connecticut	65.5
3	Delaware	83.1
6	Florida	78.9
10	Georgia	72.4
13	Hawaii	70.3
37	Idaho	58.8
15	Illinois	68.8
31	Indiana	61.1
43	Iowa	52.8
18	Kansas	67.6
36	Kentucky	58.9
5	Louisiana	82.7
50	Maine	46.9
12	Maryland	71.0
22	Massachusetts	65.1
35	Michigan	59.2
48	Minnesota	49.4
34	Mississippi	59.3
11	Missouri	72.0
38	Montana	58.2
33	Nebraska	59.5
17	Nevada	68.1
44	New Hampshire	52.5
2	New Jersey	86.4
7	New Mexico	77.3
1	New York	92.7
28	North Carolina	62.8
47	North Dakota	50.3
16	Ohio	68.5
29	Oklahoma	62.1
32	Oregon	60.1
26	Pennsylvania	63.3
41	Rhode Island	55.1
19	South Carolina	67.1
46	South Dakota	50.8
25	Tennessee	63.6
14	Texas	69.6
42	Utah	54.8
49	Vermont	48.2
21	Virginia	65.3
39	Washington	56.9
45	West Virginia	51.4
24	Wisconsin	63.9
4	Wyoming	82.8

RANK ORDER

RANK	STATE	RATE
1	New York	92.7
2	New Jersey	86.4
3	Delaware	83.1
4	Wyoming	82.8
5	Louisiana	82.7
6	Florida	78.9
7	New Mexico	77.3
8	Arizona	73.5
9	Alaska	73.2
10	Georgia	72.4
11	Missouri	72.0
12	Maryland	71.0
13	Hawaii	70.3
14	Texas	69.6
15	Illinois	68.8
16	Ohio	68.5
17	Nevada	68.1
18	Kansas	67.6
19	South Carolina	67.1
20	Connecticut	65.5
21	Virginia	65.3
22	Massachusetts	65.1
23	California	65.0
24	Wisconsin	63.9
25	Tennessee	63.6
26	Pennsylvania	63.3
27	Colorado	63.1
28	North Carolina	62.8
29	Oklahoma	62.1
30	Arkansas	61.6
31	Indiana	61.1
32	Oregon	60.1
33	Nebraska	59.5
34	Mississippi	59.3
35	Michigan	59.2
36	Kentucky	58.9
37	Idaho	58.8
38	Montana	58.2
39	Washington	56.9
40	Alabama	55.7
41	Rhode Island	55.1
42	Utah	54.8
43	Iowa	52.8
44	New Hampshire	52.5
45	West Virginia	51.4
46	South Dakota	50.8
47	North Dakota	50.3
48	Minnesota	49.4
49	Vermont	48.2
50	Maine	46.9

District of Columbia	128.3

Source: Morgan Quitno Press using data from U.S. Bureau of the Census, Governments Division
"State and Local Employment and Payroll - March 2004" (http://www.census.gov/govs/www/apesstl04.html)
*Full-time equivalent as of March 2004. Includes police, courts, prosecution, public defense and corrections.

State and Local Judicial and Legal Employment in 2004

National Total = 409,944 Employees*

ALPHA ORDER

RANK	STATE	EMPLOYEES	% of USA
25	Alabama	4,627	1.1%
42	Alaska	1,313	0.3%
12	Arizona	9,096	2.2%
33	Arkansas	3,057	0.7%
1	California	52,413	12.8%
24	Colorado	5,757	1.4%
27	Connecticut	4,519	1.1%
41	Delaware	1,591	0.4%
3	Florida	31,384	7.7%
10	Georgia	11,515	2.8%
35	Hawaii	2,834	0.7%
40	Idaho	1,644	0.4%
8	Illinois	16,933	4.1%
18	Indiana	7,273	1.8%
31	Iowa	3,474	0.8%
30	Kansas	3,627	0.9%
21	Kentucky	6,330	1.5%
16	Louisiana	7,694	1.9%
46	Maine	984	0.2%
15	Maryland	7,716	1.9%
11	Massachusetts	9,185	2.2%
9	Michigan	12,082	2.9%
22	Minnesota	6,079	1.5%
37	Mississippi	2,657	0.6%
13	Missouri	8,094	2.0%
43	Montana	1,262	0.3%
39	Nebraska	1,932	0.5%
32	Nevada	3,365	0.8%
45	New Hampshire	1,235	0.3%
5	New Jersey	22,210	5.4%
34	New Mexico	3,015	0.7%
2	New York	34,636	8.4%
19	North Carolina	6,720	1.6%
49	North Dakota	819	0.2%
6	Ohio	20,175	4.9%
29	Oklahoma	4,085	1.0%
26	Oregon	4,535	1.1%
7	Pennsylvania	17,750	4.3%
44	Rhode Island	1,246	0.3%
28	South Carolina	4,245	1.0%
48	South Dakota	844	0.2%
20	Tennessee	6,371	1.6%
4	Texas	24,053	5.9%
36	Utah	2,759	0.7%
50	Vermont	661	0.2%
14	Virginia	7,732	1.9%
17	Washington	7,477	1.8%
38	West Virginia	2,423	0.6%
23	Wisconsin	6,056	1.5%
47	Wyoming	850	0.2%

RANK ORDER

RANK	STATE	EMPLOYEES	% of USA
1	California	52,413	12.8%
2	New York	34,636	8.4%
3	Florida	31,384	7.7%
4	Texas	24,053	5.9%
5	New Jersey	22,210	5.4%
6	Ohio	20,175	4.9%
7	Pennsylvania	17,750	4.3%
8	Illinois	16,933	4.1%
9	Michigan	12,082	2.9%
10	Georgia	11,515	2.8%
11	Massachusetts	9,185	2.2%
12	Arizona	9,096	2.2%
13	Missouri	8,094	2.0%
14	Virginia	7,732	1.9%
15	Maryland	7,716	1.9%
16	Louisiana	7,694	1.9%
17	Washington	7,477	1.8%
18	Indiana	7,273	1.8%
19	North Carolina	6,720	1.6%
20	Tennessee	6,371	1.6%
21	Kentucky	6,330	1.5%
22	Minnesota	6,079	1.5%
23	Wisconsin	6,056	1.5%
24	Colorado	5,757	1.4%
25	Alabama	4,627	1.1%
26	Oregon	4,535	1.1%
27	Connecticut	4,519	1.1%
28	South Carolina	4,245	1.0%
29	Oklahoma	4,085	1.0%
30	Kansas	3,627	0.9%
31	Iowa	3,474	0.8%
32	Nevada	3,365	0.8%
33	Arkansas	3,057	0.7%
34	New Mexico	3,015	0.7%
35	Hawaii	2,834	0.7%
36	Utah	2,759	0.7%
37	Mississippi	2,657	0.6%
38	West Virginia	2,423	0.6%
39	Nebraska	1,932	0.5%
40	Idaho	1,644	0.4%
41	Delaware	1,591	0.4%
42	Alaska	1,313	0.3%
43	Montana	1,262	0.3%
44	Rhode Island	1,246	0.3%
45	New Hampshire	1,235	0.3%
46	Maine	984	0.2%
47	Wyoming	850	0.2%
48	South Dakota	844	0.2%
49	North Dakota	819	0.2%
50	Vermont	661	0.2%
	District of Columbia	1,610	0.4%

Source: U.S. Bureau of the Census, Governments Division
    "State and Local Employment and Payroll - March 2004" (http://www.census.gov/govs/www/apesstl04.html)
*Full-time equivalent as of March 2004. Includes courts, prosecution and public defense.

Rate of State and Local Judicial and Legal Employment in 2004

National Rate = 14.0 Employees per 10,000 Population*

ALPHA ORDER

RANK	STATE	RATE
45	Alabama	10.2
3	Alaska	20.0
10	Arizona	15.8
37	Arkansas	11.1
13	California	14.6
27	Colorado	12.5
23	Connecticut	12.9
4	Delaware	19.2
5	Florida	18.1
23	Georgia	12.9
2	Hawaii	22.5
31	Idaho	11.8
21	Illinois	13.3
33	Indiana	11.7
31	Iowa	11.8
21	Kansas	13.3
12	Kentucky	15.3
8	Louisiana	17.1
50	Maine	7.5
18	Maryland	13.9
15	Massachusetts	14.3
28	Michigan	12.0
30	Minnesota	11.9
48	Mississippi	9.2
17	Missouri	14.1
19	Montana	13.6
37	Nebraska	11.1
14	Nevada	14.4
47	New Hampshire	9.5
1	New Jersey	25.6
10	New Mexico	15.8
6	New York	18.0
49	North Carolina	7.9
23	North Dakota	12.9
7	Ohio	17.6
34	Oklahoma	11.6
26	Oregon	12.6
15	Pennsylvania	14.3
35	Rhode Island	11.5
46	South Carolina	10.1
39	South Dakota	11.0
41	Tennessee	10.8
42	Texas	10.7
36	Utah	11.4
43	Vermont	10.6
44	Virginia	10.3
28	Washington	12.0
20	West Virginia	13.4
39	Wisconsin	11.0
9	Wyoming	16.8

RANK ORDER

RANK	STATE	RATE
1	New Jersey	25.6
2	Hawaii	22.5
3	Alaska	20.0
4	Delaware	19.2
5	Florida	18.1
6	New York	18.0
7	Ohio	17.6
8	Louisiana	17.1
9	Wyoming	16.8
10	Arizona	15.8
10	New Mexico	15.8
12	Kentucky	15.3
13	California	14.6
14	Nevada	14.4
15	Massachusetts	14.3
15	Pennsylvania	14.3
17	Missouri	14.1
18	Maryland	13.9
19	Montana	13.6
20	West Virginia	13.4
21	Illinois	13.3
21	Kansas	13.3
23	Connecticut	12.9
23	Georgia	12.9
23	North Dakota	12.9
26	Oregon	12.6
27	Colorado	12.5
28	Michigan	12.0
28	Washington	12.0
30	Minnesota	11.9
31	Idaho	11.8
31	Iowa	11.8
33	Indiana	11.7
34	Oklahoma	11.6
35	Rhode Island	11.5
36	Utah	11.4
37	Arkansas	11.1
37	Nebraska	11.1
39	South Dakota	11.0
39	Wisconsin	11.0
41	Tennessee	10.8
42	Texas	10.7
43	Vermont	10.6
44	Virginia	10.3
45	Alabama	10.2
46	South Carolina	10.1
47	New Hampshire	9.5
48	Mississippi	9.2
49	North Carolina	7.9
50	Maine	7.5

District of Columbia — 29.0

Source: Morgan Quitno Press using data from U.S. Bureau of the Census, Governments Division
"State and Local Employment and Payroll - March 2004" (http://www.census.gov/govs/www/apesstl04.html)
*Full-time equivalent as of March 2004. Includes courts, prosecution and public defense.

State and Local Police Officers in 2004

National Total = 663,986 Officers*

ALPHA ORDER				RANK ORDER			
RANK	STATE	EMPLOYEES	% of USA	RANK	STATE	EMPLOYEES	% of USA
23	Alabama	9,674	1.5%	1	New York	73,427	11.1%
49	Alaska	1,076	0.2%	2	California	65,953	9.9%
14	Arizona	13,520	2.0%	3	Texas	45,948	6.9%
32	Arkansas	5,717	0.9%	4	Florida	39,867	6.0%
2	California	65,953	9.9%	5	Illinois	36,661	5.5%
24	Colorado	9,649	1.5%	6	New Jersey	26,394	4.0%
25	Connecticut	8,568	1.3%	7	Pennsylvania	25,496	3.8%
44	Delaware	1,754	0.3%	8	Ohio	24,882	3.7%
4	Florida	39,867	6.0%	9	Georgia	20,156	3.0%
9	Georgia	20,156	3.0%	10	Massachusetts	19,325	2.9%
40	Hawaii	2,807	0.4%	11	Michigan	19,275	2.9%
41	Idaho	2,610	0.4%	12	North Carolina	18,536	2.8%
5	Illinois	36,661	5.5%	13	Virginia	15,396	2.3%
18	Indiana	12,160	1.8%	14	Arizona	13,520	2.0%
33	Iowa	5,654	0.9%	15	Tennessee	13,408	2.0%
30	Kansas	6,169	0.9%	16	Missouri	13,157	2.0%
28	Kentucky	7,480	1.1%	17	Louisiana	12,292	1.9%
17	Louisiana	12,292	1.9%	18	Indiana	12,160	1.8%
42	Maine	2,272	0.3%	19	Wisconsin	11,965	1.8%
20	Maryland	11,917	1.8%	20	Maryland	11,917	1.8%
10	Massachusetts	19,325	2.9%	21	South Carolina	9,935	1.5%
11	Michigan	19,275	2.9%	22	Washington	9,792	1.5%
26	Minnesota	7,597	1.1%	23	Alabama	9,674	1.5%
29	Mississippi	6,211	0.9%	24	Colorado	9,649	1.5%
16	Missouri	13,157	2.0%	25	Connecticut	8,568	1.3%
45	Montana	1,631	0.2%	26	Minnesota	7,597	1.1%
37	Nebraska	3,587	0.5%	27	Oklahoma	7,580	1.1%
34	Nevada	4,257	0.6%	28	Kentucky	7,480	1.1%
38	New Hampshire	2,832	0.4%	29	Mississippi	6,211	0.9%
6	New Jersey	26,394	4.0%	30	Kansas	6,169	0.9%
35	New Mexico	4,227	0.6%	31	Oregon	5,969	0.9%
1	New York	73,427	11.1%	32	Arkansas	5,717	0.9%
12	North Carolina	18,536	2.8%	33	Iowa	5,654	0.9%
48	North Dakota	1,134	0.2%	34	Nevada	4,257	0.6%
8	Ohio	24,882	3.7%	35	New Mexico	4,227	0.6%
27	Oklahoma	7,580	1.1%	36	Utah	3,886	0.6%
31	Oregon	5,969	0.9%	37	Nebraska	3,587	0.5%
7	Pennsylvania	25,496	3.8%	38	New Hampshire	2,832	0.4%
43	Rhode Island	2,166	0.3%	39	West Virginia	2,827	0.4%
21	South Carolina	9,935	1.5%	40	Hawaii	2,807	0.4%
46	South Dakota	1,329	0.2%	41	Idaho	2,610	0.4%
15	Tennessee	13,408	2.0%	42	Maine	2,272	0.3%
3	Texas	45,948	6.9%	43	Rhode Island	2,166	0.3%
36	Utah	3,886	0.6%	44	Delaware	1,754	0.3%
50	Vermont	937	0.1%	45	Montana	1,631	0.2%
13	Virginia	15,396	2.3%	46	South Dakota	1,329	0.2%
22	Washington	9,792	1.5%	47	Wyoming	1,277	0.2%
39	West Virginia	2,827	0.4%	48	North Dakota	1,134	0.2%
19	Wisconsin	11,965	1.8%	49	Alaska	1,076	0.2%
47	Wyoming	1,277	0.2%	50	Vermont	937	0.1%
					District of Columbia	3,647	0.5%

Source: U.S. Bureau of the Census, Governments Division
"State and Local Employment and Payroll - March 2004" (http://www.census.gov/govs/www/apesstl04.html)
*Full-time equivalent as of March 2004. Does not include employees of police departments who are not officers.

Rate of State and Local Police Officers in 2004

National Rate = 22.6 Officers per 10,000 Population*

ALPHA ORDER				RANK ORDER		
RANK	STATE	RATE		RANK	STATE	RATE
22	Alabama	21.4		1	New York	38.1
45	Alaska	16.4		2	New Jersey	30.4
9	Arizona	23.6		3	Massachusetts	30.2
27	Arkansas	20.8		4	Illinois	28.8
37	California	18.4		5	Louisiana	27.3
26	Colorado	21.0		6	Wyoming	25.2
7	Connecticut	24.5		7	Connecticut	24.5
25	Delaware	21.1		8	South Carolina	23.7
10	Florida	22.9		9	Arizona	23.6
13	Georgia	22.6		10	Florida	22.9
15	Hawaii	22.2		11	Missouri	22.8
36	Idaho	18.7		11	Tennessee	22.8
4	Illinois	28.8		13	Georgia	22.6
33	Indiana	19.5		13	Kansas	22.6
34	Iowa	19.1		15	Hawaii	22.2
13	Kansas	22.6		15	New Mexico	22.2
39	Kentucky	18.1		17	New Hampshire	21.8
5	Louisiana	27.3		18	North Carolina	21.7
42	Maine	17.3		18	Ohio	21.7
22	Maryland	21.4		18	Wisconsin	21.7
3	Massachusetts	30.2		21	Oklahoma	21.5
34	Michigan	19.1		22	Alabama	21.4
50	Minnesota	14.9		22	Maryland	21.4
22	Mississippi	21.4		22	Mississippi	21.4
11	Missouri	22.8		25	Delaware	21.1
41	Montana	17.6		26	Colorado	21.0
30	Nebraska	20.5		27	Arkansas	20.8
38	Nevada	18.2		28	Pennsylvania	20.6
17	New Hampshire	21.8		28	Virginia	20.6
2	New Jersey	30.4		30	Nebraska	20.5
15	New Mexico	22.2		31	Texas	20.4
1	New York	38.1		32	Rhode Island	20.1
18	North Carolina	21.7		33	Indiana	19.5
40	North Dakota	17.8		34	Iowa	19.1
18	Ohio	21.7		34	Michigan	19.1
21	Oklahoma	21.5		36	Idaho	18.7
44	Oregon	16.6		37	California	18.4
28	Pennsylvania	20.6		38	Nevada	18.2
32	Rhode Island	20.1		39	Kentucky	18.1
8	South Carolina	23.7		40	North Dakota	17.8
43	South Dakota	17.2		41	Montana	17.6
11	Tennessee	22.8		42	Maine	17.3
31	Texas	20.4		43	South Dakota	17.2
46	Utah	16.1		44	Oregon	16.6
49	Vermont	15.1		45	Alaska	16.4
28	Virginia	20.6		46	Utah	16.1
47	Washington	15.8		47	Washington	15.8
48	West Virginia	15.6		48	West Virginia	15.6
18	Wisconsin	21.7		49	Vermont	15.1
6	Wyoming	25.2		50	Minnesota	14.9
					District of Columbia	65.8

Source: Morgan Quitno Press using data from U.S. Bureau of the Census, Governments Division
"State and Local Employment and Payroll - March 2004" (http://www.census.gov/govs/www/apesstl04.html)
*Full-time equivalent as of March 2004. Does not include employees of police departments who are not officers.

Law Enforcement Agencies in 2000

National Total = 17,784 Agencies*

ALPHA ORDER

RANK	STATE	AGENCIES	% of USA
16	Alabama	424	2.4%
44	Alaska	95	0.5%
37	Arizona	135	0.8%
21	Arkansas	356	2.0%
9	California	517	2.9%
29	Colorado	248	1.4%
42	Connecticut	125	0.7%
49	Delaware	43	0.2%
18	Florida	383	2.2%
7	Georgia	561	3.2%
50	Hawaii	7	0.0%
43	Idaho	122	0.7%
3	Illinois	886	5.0%
12	Indiana	495	2.8%
17	Iowa	400	2.2%
22	Kansas	353	2.0%
19	Kentucky	382	2.1%
24	Louisiana	343	1.9%
36	Maine	139	0.8%
35	Maryland	146	0.8%
23	Massachusetts	351	2.0%
6	Michigan	565	3.2%
14	Minnesota	460	2.6%
25	Mississippi	333	1.9%
5	Missouri	586	3.3%
41	Montana	126	0.7%
30	Nebraska	237	1.3%
47	Nevada	62	0.3%
32	New Hampshire	195	1.1%
8	New Jersey	551	3.1%
37	New Mexico	135	0.8%
9	New York	517	2.9%
13	North Carolina	491	2.8%
39	North Dakota	129	0.7%
4	Ohio	845	4.8%
15	Oklahoma	449	2.5%
33	Oregon	178	1.0%
2	Pennsylvania	1,166	6.6%
48	Rhode Island	51	0.3%
27	South Carolina	258	1.5%
34	South Dakota	170	1.0%
20	Tennessee	367	2.1%
1	Texas	1,800	10.1%
39	Utah	129	0.7%
46	Vermont	65	0.4%
26	Virginia	327	1.8%
28	Washington	256	1.4%
31	West Virginia	229	1.3%
11	Wisconsin	512	2.9%
45	Wyoming	81	0.5%

RANK ORDER

RANK	STATE	AGENCIES	% of USA
1	Texas	1,800	10.1%
2	Pennsylvania	1,166	6.6%
3	Illinois	886	5.0%
4	Ohio	845	4.8%
5	Missouri	586	3.3%
6	Michigan	565	3.2%
7	Georgia	561	3.2%
8	New Jersey	551	3.1%
9	California	517	2.9%
9	New York	517	2.9%
11	Wisconsin	512	2.9%
12	Indiana	495	2.8%
13	North Carolina	491	2.8%
14	Minnesota	460	2.6%
15	Oklahoma	449	2.5%
16	Alabama	424	2.4%
17	Iowa	400	2.2%
18	Florida	383	2.2%
19	Kentucky	382	2.1%
20	Tennessee	367	2.1%
21	Arkansas	356	2.0%
22	Kansas	353	2.0%
23	Massachusetts	351	2.0%
24	Louisiana	343	1.9%
25	Mississippi	333	1.9%
26	Virginia	327	1.8%
27	South Carolina	258	1.5%
28	Washington	256	1.4%
29	Colorado	248	1.4%
30	Nebraska	237	1.3%
31	West Virginia	229	1.3%
32	New Hampshire	195	1.1%
33	Oregon	178	1.0%
34	South Dakota	170	1.0%
35	Maryland	146	0.8%
36	Maine	139	0.8%
37	Arizona	135	0.8%
37	New Mexico	135	0.8%
39	North Dakota	129	0.7%
39	Utah	129	0.7%
41	Montana	126	0.7%
42	Connecticut	125	0.7%
43	Idaho	122	0.7%
44	Alaska	95	0.5%
45	Wyoming	81	0.5%
46	Vermont	65	0.4%
47	Nevada	62	0.3%
48	Rhode Island	51	0.3%
49	Delaware	43	0.2%
50	Hawaii	7	0.0%
	District of Columbia	3	0.0%

Source: U.S. Department of Justice, Bureau of Justice Statistics
    "Census of State and Local Law Enforcement Agencies, 2000" (Bulletin, October 2002, NCJ 194066)
*Includes state and local police, sheriffs' departments and special police agencies.

Population per Law Enforcement Agency in 2000

National Rate = 15,870 Population per Agency*

ALPHA ORDER

RANK	STATE	RATE
33	Alabama	10,500
46	Alaska	6,607
4	Arizona	38,275
42	Arkansas	7,524
2	California	65,784
16	Colorado	17,447
8	Connecticut	27,296
13	Delaware	18,291
3	Florida	41,910
22	Georgia	14,678
1	Hawaii	173,239
30	Idaho	10,653
23	Illinois	14,042
27	Indiana	12,307
43	Iowa	7,322
41	Kansas	7,628
31	Kentucky	10,599
26	Louisiana	13,031
37	Maine	9,189
6	Maryland	36,387
14	Massachusetts	18,125
15	Michigan	17,621
29	Minnesota	10,727
38	Mississippi	8,555
35	Missouri	9,565
45	Montana	7,170
44	Nebraska	7,229
7	Nevada	32,562
47	New Hampshire	6,361
21	New Jersey	15,305
24	New Mexico	13,495
5	New York	36,750
18	North Carolina	16,461
49	North Dakota	4,970
25	Ohio	13,448
40	Oklahoma	7,694
12	Oregon	19,276
32	Pennsylvania	10,537
11	Rhode Island	20,602
19	South Carolina	15,596
50	South Dakota	4,446
20	Tennessee	15,540
28	Texas	11,642
17	Utah	17,391
36	Vermont	9,384
10	Virginia	21,731
9	Washington	23,093
39	West Virginia	7,892
34	Wisconsin	10,497
48	Wyoming	6,100

RANK ORDER

RANK	STATE	RATE
1	Hawaii	173,239
2	California	65,784
3	Florida	41,910
4	Arizona	38,275
5	New York	36,750
6	Maryland	36,387
7	Nevada	32,562
8	Connecticut	27,296
9	Washington	23,093
10	Virginia	21,731
11	Rhode Island	20,602
12	Oregon	19,276
13	Delaware	18,291
14	Massachusetts	18,125
15	Michigan	17,621
16	Colorado	17,447
17	Utah	17,391
18	North Carolina	16,461
19	South Carolina	15,596
20	Tennessee	15,540
21	New Jersey	15,305
22	Georgia	14,678
23	Illinois	14,042
24	New Mexico	13,495
25	Ohio	13,448
26	Louisiana	13,031
27	Indiana	12,307
28	Texas	11,642
29	Minnesota	10,727
30	Idaho	10,653
31	Kentucky	10,599
32	Pennsylvania	10,537
33	Alabama	10,500
34	Wisconsin	10,497
35	Missouri	9,565
36	Vermont	9,384
37	Maine	9,189
38	Mississippi	8,555
39	West Virginia	7,892
40	Oklahoma	7,694
41	Kansas	7,628
42	Arkansas	7,524
43	Iowa	7,322
44	Nebraska	7,229
45	Montana	7,170
46	Alaska	6,607
47	New Hampshire	6,361
48	Wyoming	6,100
49	North Dakota	4,970
50	South Dakota	4,446

	District of Columbia	190,547

Source: Morgan Quitno Press using data from U.S. Department of Justice, Bureau of Justice Statistics
"Census of State and Local Law Enforcement Agencies, 2000" (Bulletin, October 2002, NCJ 194066)
*Includes state and local police, sheriffs' departments and special police agencies.

Law Enforcement Agencies per 1,000 Square Miles in 2000

National Rate = 4.8 Agencies per 1,000 Square Miles*

ALPHA ORDER				RANK ORDER		
RANK	STATE	RATE		RANK	STATE	RATE
20	Alabama	8.1		1	New Jersey	67.1
50	Alaska	0.2		2	Rhode Island	41.4
44	Arizona	1.2		3	Massachusetts	38.0
27	Arkansas	6.7		4	Pennsylvania	25.3
36	California	3.3		5	Connecticut	22.5
38	Colorado	2.4		6	New Hampshire	21.0
5	Connecticut	22.5		7	Ohio	18.8
8	Delaware	17.9		8	Delaware	17.9
29	Florida	6.4		9	Illinois	15.3
13	Georgia	9.5		10	Indiana	13.6
45	Hawaii	1.1		11	Maryland	11.9
42	Idaho	1.5		12	New York	9.6
9	Illinois	15.3		13	Georgia	9.5
10	Indiana	13.6		13	Kentucky	9.5
23	Iowa	7.1		13	West Virginia	9.5
33	Kansas	4.3		16	North Carolina	9.3
13	Kentucky	9.5		17	Tennessee	8.7
24	Louisiana	6.9		18	Missouri	8.4
34	Maine	4.1		19	South Carolina	8.3
11	Maryland	11.9		20	Alabama	8.1
3	Massachusetts	38.0		21	Wisconsin	7.8
31	Michigan	5.8		22	Virginia	7.7
32	Minnesota	5.3		23	Iowa	7.1
24	Mississippi	6.9		24	Louisiana	6.9
18	Missouri	8.4		24	Mississippi	6.9
47	Montana	0.9		26	Vermont	6.8
37	Nebraska	3.1		27	Arkansas	6.7
49	Nevada	0.6		27	Texas	6.7
6	New Hampshire	21.0		29	Florida	6.4
1	New Jersey	67.1		29	Oklahoma	6.4
45	New Mexico	1.1		31	Michigan	5.8
12	New York	9.6		32	Minnesota	5.3
16	North Carolina	9.3		33	Kansas	4.3
40	North Dakota	1.8		34	Maine	4.1
7	Ohio	18.8		35	Washington	3.6
29	Oklahoma	6.4		36	California	3.3
40	Oregon	1.8		37	Nebraska	3.1
4	Pennsylvania	25.3		38	Colorado	2.4
2	Rhode Island	41.4		39	South Dakota	2.2
19	South Carolina	8.3		40	North Dakota	1.8
39	South Dakota	2.2		40	Oregon	1.8
17	Tennessee	8.7		42	Idaho	1.5
27	Texas	6.7		42	Utah	1.5
42	Utah	1.5		44	Arizona	1.2
26	Vermont	6.8		45	Hawaii	1.1
22	Virginia	7.7		45	New Mexico	1.1
35	Washington	3.6		47	Montana	0.9
13	West Virginia	9.5		48	Wyoming	0.8
21	Wisconsin	7.8		49	Nevada	0.6
48	Wyoming	0.8		50	Alaska	0.2
					District of Columbia**	NA

Source: Morgan Quitno Press using data from U.S. Department of Justice, Bureau of Justice Statistics
   "Census of State and Local Law Enforcement Agencies, 2000" (Bulletin, October 2002, NCJ 194066)
*Includes state and local police, sheriffs' departments and special police agencies.
**The District of Columbia has three agencies for its 68 square miles.

Full-Time Sworn Officers in Law Enforcement Agencies in 2000

National Total = 708,022 Officers*

ALPHA ORDER

RANK	STATE	OFFICERS	% of USA
21	Alabama	10,655	1.5%
48	Alaska	1,348	0.2%
20	Arizona	11,533	1.6%
32	Arkansas	6,157	0.9%
1	California	73,662	10.4%
22	Colorado	10,309	1.5%
26	Connecticut	8,327	1.2%
44	Delaware	1,774	0.3%
5	Florida	39,452	5.6%
10	Georgia	21,173	3.0%
39	Hawaii	2,914	0.4%
40	Idaho	2,749	0.4%
4	Illinois	39,847	5.6%
19	Indiana	11,900	1.7%
33	Iowa	5,333	0.8%
29	Kansas	6,563	0.9%
28	Kentucky	7,144	1.0%
13	Louisiana	18,548	2.6%
43	Maine	2,367	0.3%
15	Maryland	15,221	2.1%
14	Massachusetts	18,082	2.6%
9	Michigan	21,673	3.1%
25	Minnesota	8,606	1.2%
30	Mississippi	6,562	0.9%
17	Missouri	13,630	1.9%
45	Montana	1,760	0.2%
37	Nebraska	3,486	0.5%
34	Nevada	5,252	0.7%
42	New Hampshire	2,542	0.4%
6	New Jersey	29,062	4.1%
35	New Mexico	4,456	0.6%
2	New York	72,853	10.3%
12	North Carolina	18,903	2.7%
49	North Dakota	1,293	0.2%
8	Ohio	25,082	3.5%
27	Oklahoma	7,622	1.1%
31	Oregon	6,496	0.9%
7	Pennsylvania	26,373	3.7%
41	Rhode Island	2,688	0.4%
24	South Carolina	9,741	1.4%
46	South Dakota	1,708	0.2%
16	Tennessee	14,494	2.0%
3	Texas	51,478	7.3%
36	Utah	4,179	0.6%
50	Vermont	1,034	0.1%
11	Virginia	20,254	2.9%
23	Washington	9,910	1.4%
38	West Virginia	3,150	0.4%
18	Wisconsin	13,237	1.9%
47	Wyoming	1,477	0.2%

RANK ORDER

RANK	STATE	OFFICERS	% of USA
1	California	73,662	10.4%
2	New York	72,853	10.3%
3	Texas	51,478	7.3%
4	Illinois	39,847	5.6%
5	Florida	39,452	5.6%
6	New Jersey	29,062	4.1%
7	Pennsylvania	26,373	3.7%
8	Ohio	25,082	3.5%
9	Michigan	21,673	3.1%
10	Georgia	21,173	3.0%
11	Virginia	20,254	2.9%
12	North Carolina	18,903	2.7%
13	Louisiana	18,548	2.6%
14	Massachusetts	18,082	2.6%
15	Maryland	15,221	2.1%
16	Tennessee	14,494	2.0%
17	Missouri	13,630	1.9%
18	Wisconsin	13,237	1.9%
19	Indiana	11,900	1.7%
20	Arizona	11,533	1.6%
21	Alabama	10,655	1.5%
22	Colorado	10,309	1.5%
23	Washington	9,910	1.4%
24	South Carolina	9,741	1.4%
25	Minnesota	8,606	1.2%
26	Connecticut	8,327	1.2%
27	Oklahoma	7,622	1.1%
28	Kentucky	7,144	1.0%
29	Kansas	6,563	0.9%
30	Mississippi	6,562	0.9%
31	Oregon	6,496	0.9%
32	Arkansas	6,157	0.9%
33	Iowa	5,333	0.8%
34	Nevada	5,252	0.7%
35	New Mexico	4,456	0.6%
36	Utah	4,179	0.6%
37	Nebraska	3,486	0.5%
38	West Virginia	3,150	0.4%
39	Hawaii	2,914	0.4%
40	Idaho	2,749	0.4%
41	Rhode Island	2,688	0.4%
42	New Hampshire	2,542	0.4%
43	Maine	2,367	0.3%
44	Delaware	1,774	0.3%
45	Montana	1,760	0.2%
46	South Dakota	1,708	0.2%
47	Wyoming	1,477	0.2%
48	Alaska	1,348	0.2%
49	North Dakota	1,293	0.2%
50	Vermont	1,034	0.1%
	District of Columbia	3,963	0.6%

Source: U.S. Department of Justice, Bureau of Justice Statistics
"Census of State and Local Law Enforcement Agencies, 2000" (Bulletin, October 2002, NCJ 194066)
*Includes state and local police, sheriffs' departments and special police agencies.

Percent of Full-Time Law Enforcement Agency Employees
Who are Sworn Officers: 2000
National Percent = 69.4% of Employees*

ALPHA ORDER

RANK ORDER

RANK	STATE	PERCENT	RANK	STATE	PERCENT
33	Alabama	66.3	1	Connecticut	81.0
45	Alaska	62.7	2	Rhode Island	79.3
50	Arizona	56.0	3	Pennsylvania	78.9
31	Arkansas	66.9	4	Louisiana	78.7
43	California	63.6	5	Delaware	78.6
28	Colorado	67.7	6	Virginia	78.4
1	Connecticut	81.0	7	Hawaii	78.1
5	Delaware	78.6	8	New Hampshire	77.8
49	Florida	57.9	9	New Jersey	77.7
28	Georgia	67.7	10	New York	76.8
7	Hawaii	78.1	11	Massachusetts	76.6
46	Idaho	60.8	12	West Virginia	75.9
13	Illinois	75.5	13	Illinois	75.5
35	Indiana	66.2	14	Maryland	75.1
24	Iowa	70.2	15	South Carolina	74.7
44	Kansas	63.5	16	Kentucky	74.5
16	Kentucky	74.5	17	North Dakota	73.7
4	Louisiana	78.7	18	Wisconsin	73.5
38	Maine	65.1	19	Michigan	73.1
14	Maryland	75.1	20	Nebraska	73.0
11	Massachusetts	76.6	21	North Carolina	72.4
19	Michigan	73.1	22	Vermont	70.9
27	Minnesota	67.9	23	New Mexico	70.5
39	Mississippi	64.6	24	Iowa	70.2
32	Missouri	66.6	25	South Dakota	69.2
48	Montana	59.5	26	Ohio	68.0
20	Nebraska	73.0	27	Minnesota	67.9
33	Nevada	66.3	28	Colorado	67.7
8	New Hampshire	77.8	28	Georgia	67.7
9	New Jersey	77.7	30	Oklahoma	67.0
23	New Mexico	70.5	31	Arkansas	66.9
10	New York	76.8	32	Missouri	66.6
21	North Carolina	72.4	33	Alabama	66.3
17	North Dakota	73.7	33	Nevada	66.3
26	Ohio	68.0	35	Indiana	66.2
30	Oklahoma	67.0	36	Utah	65.9
46	Oregon	60.8	37	Tennessee	65.4
3	Pennsylvania	78.9	38	Maine	65.1
2	Rhode Island	79.3	39	Mississippi	64.6
15	South Carolina	74.7	39	Wyoming	64.6
25	South Dakota	69.2	41	Texas	63.9
37	Tennessee	65.4	41	Washington	63.9
41	Texas	63.9	43	California	63.6
36	Utah	65.9	44	Kansas	63.5
22	Vermont	70.9	45	Alaska	62.7
6	Virginia	78.4	46	Idaho	60.8
41	Washington	63.9	46	Oregon	60.8
12	West Virginia	75.9	48	Montana	59.5
18	Wisconsin	73.5	49	Florida	57.9
39	Wyoming	64.6	50	Arizona	56.0

District of Columbia   80.6

*Source: Morgan Quitno Press using data from U.S. Department of Justice, Bureau of Justice Statistics
    "Census of State and Local Law Enforcement Agencies, 2000" (Bulletin, October 2002, NCJ 194066)*
Includes state and local police, sheriffs' departments and special police agencies.

Rate of Full-Time Sworn Officers in Law Enforcement Agencies in 2000

National Rate = 252 Officers per 100,000 Population*

ALPHA ORDER

RANK ORDER

RANK	STATE	RATE
22	Alabama	240
34	Alaska	215
29	Arizona	225
26	Arkansas	230
33	California	217
22	Colorado	240
16	Connecticut	245
27	Delaware	226
13	Florida	247
10	Georgia	259
21	Hawaii	241
36	Idaho	212
4	Illinois	321
40	Indiana	196
45	Iowa	182
18	Kansas	244
46	Kentucky	177
1	Louisiana	415
44	Maine	186
6	Maryland	287
8	Massachusetts	285
32	Michigan	218
47	Minnesota	175
25	Mississippi	231
18	Missouri	244
41	Montana	195
38	Nebraska	204
9	Nevada	263
37	New Hampshire	206
3	New Jersey	345
16	New Mexico	245
2	New York	384
24	North Carolina	235
39	North Dakota	201
30	Ohio	221
30	Oklahoma	221
42	Oregon	190
34	Pennsylvania	215
11	Rhode Island	256
20	South Carolina	243
27	South Dakota	226
12	Tennessee	255
13	Texas	247
43	Utah	187
49	Vermont	170
7	Virginia	286
50	Washington	168
48	West Virginia	174
13	Wisconsin	247
5	Wyoming	299

RANK	STATE	RATE
1	Louisiana	415
2	New York	384
3	New Jersey	345
4	Illinois	321
5	Wyoming	299
6	Maryland	287
7	Virginia	286
8	Massachusetts	285
9	Nevada	263
10	Georgia	259
11	Rhode Island	256
12	Tennessee	255
13	Florida	247
13	Texas	247
13	Wisconsin	247
16	Connecticut	245
16	New Mexico	245
18	Kansas	244
18	Missouri	244
20	South Carolina	243
21	Hawaii	241
22	Alabama	240
22	Colorado	240
24	North Carolina	235
25	Mississippi	231
26	Arkansas	230
27	Delaware	226
27	South Dakota	226
29	Arizona	225
30	Ohio	221
30	Oklahoma	221
32	Michigan	218
33	California	217
34	Alaska	215
34	Pennsylvania	215
36	Idaho	212
37	New Hampshire	206
38	Nebraska	204
39	North Dakota	201
40	Indiana	196
41	Montana	195
42	Oregon	190
43	Utah	187
44	Maine	186
45	Iowa	182
46	Kentucky	177
47	Minnesota	175
48	West Virginia	174
49	Vermont	170
50	Washington	168

	District of Columbia	693

Source: U.S. Department of Justice, Bureau of Justice Statistics
"Census of State and Local Law Enforcement Agencies, 2000" (Bulletin, October 2002, NCJ 194066)
*Includes state and local police, sheriffs' departments and special police agencies.

Full-Time Sworn Law Enforcement Officers per 1,000 Square Miles in 2000

National Rate = 190 Officers per 1,000 Square Miles*

ALPHA ORDER

RANK	STATE	RATE
23	Alabama	204
50	Alaska	2
34	Arizona	101
31	Arkansas	116
13	California	464
35	Colorado	99
4	Connecticut	1,502
7	Delaware	740
9	Florida	658
16	Georgia	359
14	Hawaii	451
45	Idaho	33
8	Illinois	688
19	Indiana	327
37	Iowa	95
38	Kansas	80
27	Kentucky	177
15	Louisiana	374
39	Maine	70
6	Maryland	1,238
3	Massachusetts	1,957
22	Michigan	224
35	Minnesota	99
29	Mississippi	136
25	Missouri	196
49	Montana	12
43	Nebraska	45
42	Nevada	48
21	New Hampshire	274
1	New Jersey	3,538
44	New Mexico	37
5	New York	1,349
16	North Carolina	359
47	North Dakota	18
11	Ohio	560
32	Oklahoma	109
40	Oregon	67
10	Pennsylvania	573
2	Rhode Island	2,184
20	South Carolina	312
46	South Dakota	22
18	Tennessee	344
26	Texas	193
41	Utah	49
33	Vermont	108
12	Virginia	479
28	Washington	140
30	West Virginia	130
24	Wisconsin	202
48	Wyoming	15

RANK ORDER

RANK	STATE	RATE
1	New Jersey	3,538
2	Rhode Island	2,184
3	Massachusetts	1,957
4	Connecticut	1,502
5	New York	1,349
6	Maryland	1,238
7	Delaware	740
8	Illinois	688
9	Florida	658
10	Pennsylvania	573
11	Ohio	560
12	Virginia	479
13	California	464
14	Hawaii	451
15	Louisiana	374
16	Georgia	359
16	North Carolina	359
18	Tennessee	344
19	Indiana	327
20	South Carolina	312
21	New Hampshire	274
22	Michigan	224
23	Alabama	204
24	Wisconsin	202
25	Missouri	196
26	Texas	193
27	Kentucky	177
28	Washington	140
29	Mississippi	136
30	West Virginia	130
31	Arkansas	116
32	Oklahoma	109
33	Vermont	108
34	Arizona	101
35	Colorado	99
35	Minnesota	99
37	Iowa	95
38	Kansas	80
39	Maine	70
40	Oregon	67
41	Utah	49
42	Nevada	48
43	Nebraska	45
44	New Mexico	37
45	Idaho	33
46	South Dakota	22
47	North Dakota	18
48	Wyoming	15
49	Montana	12
50	Alaska	2
	District of Columbia**	NA

Source: Morgan Quitno Press using data from U.S. Department of Justice, Bureau of Justice Statistics
   "Census of State and Local Law Enforcement Agencies, 2000" (Bulletin, October 2002, NCJ 194066)
*Includes state and local police, sheriffs' departments and special police agencies.
**The District of Columbia has 3,963 sworn officers for its 68 square miles.

Full-Time Employees in Law Enforcement Agencies in 2000

National Total = 1,019,496 Employees*

<table>
<tr><td colspan="4">ALPHA ORDER</td><td colspan="4">RANK ORDER</td></tr>
<tr><th>RANK</th><th>STATE</th><th>EMPLOYEES</th><th>% of USA</th><th>RANK</th><th>STATE</th><th>EMPLOYEES</th><th>% of USA</th></tr>
<tr><td>21</td><td>Alabama</td><td>16,062</td><td>1.6%</td><td>1</td><td>California</td><td>115,906</td><td>11.4%</td></tr>
<tr><td>48</td><td>Alaska</td><td>2,151</td><td>0.2%</td><td>2</td><td>New York</td><td>94,863</td><td>9.3%</td></tr>
<tr><td>16</td><td>Arizona</td><td>20,595</td><td>2.0%</td><td>3</td><td>Texas</td><td>80,535</td><td>7.9%</td></tr>
<tr><td>32</td><td>Arkansas</td><td>9,207</td><td>0.9%</td><td>4</td><td>Florida</td><td>68,165</td><td>6.7%</td></tr>
<tr><td>1</td><td>California</td><td>115,906</td><td>11.4%</td><td>5</td><td>Illinois</td><td>52,769</td><td>5.2%</td></tr>
<tr><td>23</td><td>Colorado</td><td>15,237</td><td>1.5%</td><td>6</td><td>New Jersey</td><td>37,387</td><td>3.7%</td></tr>
<tr><td>29</td><td>Connecticut</td><td>10,277</td><td>1.0%</td><td>7</td><td>Ohio</td><td>36,863</td><td>3.6%</td></tr>
<tr><td>47</td><td>Delaware</td><td>2,257</td><td>0.2%</td><td>8</td><td>Pennsylvania</td><td>33,427</td><td>3.3%</td></tr>
<tr><td>4</td><td>Florida</td><td>68,165</td><td>6.7%</td><td>9</td><td>Georgia</td><td>31,282</td><td>3.1%</td></tr>
<tr><td>9</td><td>Georgia</td><td>31,282</td><td>3.1%</td><td>10</td><td>Michigan</td><td>29,654</td><td>2.9%</td></tr>
<tr><td>40</td><td>Hawaii</td><td>3,731</td><td>0.4%</td><td>11</td><td>North Carolina</td><td>26,101</td><td>2.6%</td></tr>
<tr><td>38</td><td>Idaho</td><td>4,522</td><td>0.4%</td><td>12</td><td>Virginia</td><td>25,842</td><td>2.5%</td></tr>
<tr><td>5</td><td>Illinois</td><td>52,769</td><td>5.2%</td><td>13</td><td>Massachusetts</td><td>23,593</td><td>2.3%</td></tr>
<tr><td>20</td><td>Indiana</td><td>17,969</td><td>1.8%</td><td>14</td><td>Louisiana</td><td>23,573</td><td>2.3%</td></tr>
<tr><td>34</td><td>Iowa</td><td>7,600</td><td>0.7%</td><td>15</td><td>Tennessee</td><td>22,148</td><td>2.2%</td></tr>
<tr><td>28</td><td>Kansas</td><td>10,343</td><td>1.0%</td><td>16</td><td>Arizona</td><td>20,595</td><td>2.0%</td></tr>
<tr><td>31</td><td>Kentucky</td><td>9,589</td><td>0.9%</td><td>17</td><td>Missouri</td><td>20,459</td><td>2.0%</td></tr>
<tr><td>14</td><td>Louisiana</td><td>23,573</td><td>2.3%</td><td>18</td><td>Maryland</td><td>20,272</td><td>2.0%</td></tr>
<tr><td>41</td><td>Maine</td><td>3,638</td><td>0.4%</td><td>19</td><td>Wisconsin</td><td>18,010</td><td>1.8%</td></tr>
<tr><td>18</td><td>Maryland</td><td>20,272</td><td>2.0%</td><td>20</td><td>Indiana</td><td>17,969</td><td>1.8%</td></tr>
<tr><td>13</td><td>Massachusetts</td><td>23,593</td><td>2.3%</td><td>21</td><td>Alabama</td><td>16,062</td><td>1.6%</td></tr>
<tr><td>10</td><td>Michigan</td><td>29,654</td><td>2.9%</td><td>22</td><td>Washington</td><td>15,513</td><td>1.5%</td></tr>
<tr><td>25</td><td>Minnesota</td><td>12,677</td><td>1.2%</td><td>23</td><td>Colorado</td><td>15,237</td><td>1.5%</td></tr>
<tr><td>30</td><td>Mississippi</td><td>10,163</td><td>1.0%</td><td>24</td><td>South Carolina</td><td>13,046</td><td>1.3%</td></tr>
<tr><td>17</td><td>Missouri</td><td>20,459</td><td>2.0%</td><td>25</td><td>Minnesota</td><td>12,677</td><td>1.2%</td></tr>
<tr><td>44</td><td>Montana</td><td>2,958</td><td>0.3%</td><td>26</td><td>Oklahoma</td><td>11,376</td><td>1.1%</td></tr>
<tr><td>37</td><td>Nebraska</td><td>4,776</td><td>0.5%</td><td>27</td><td>Oregon</td><td>10,683</td><td>1.0%</td></tr>
<tr><td>33</td><td>Nevada</td><td>7,918</td><td>0.8%</td><td>28</td><td>Kansas</td><td>10,343</td><td>1.0%</td></tr>
<tr><td>43</td><td>New Hampshire</td><td>3,268</td><td>0.3%</td><td>29</td><td>Connecticut</td><td>10,277</td><td>1.0%</td></tr>
<tr><td>6</td><td>New Jersey</td><td>37,387</td><td>3.7%</td><td>30</td><td>Mississippi</td><td>10,163</td><td>1.0%</td></tr>
<tr><td>36</td><td>New Mexico</td><td>6,324</td><td>0.6%</td><td>31</td><td>Kentucky</td><td>9,589</td><td>0.9%</td></tr>
<tr><td>2</td><td>New York</td><td>94,863</td><td>9.3%</td><td>32</td><td>Arkansas</td><td>9,207</td><td>0.9%</td></tr>
<tr><td>11</td><td>North Carolina</td><td>26,101</td><td>2.6%</td><td>33</td><td>Nevada</td><td>7,918</td><td>0.8%</td></tr>
<tr><td>49</td><td>North Dakota</td><td>1,755</td><td>0.2%</td><td>34</td><td>Iowa</td><td>7,600</td><td>0.7%</td></tr>
<tr><td>7</td><td>Ohio</td><td>36,863</td><td>3.6%</td><td>35</td><td>Utah</td><td>6,346</td><td>0.6%</td></tr>
<tr><td>26</td><td>Oklahoma</td><td>11,376</td><td>1.1%</td><td>36</td><td>New Mexico</td><td>6,324</td><td>0.6%</td></tr>
<tr><td>27</td><td>Oregon</td><td>10,683</td><td>1.0%</td><td>37</td><td>Nebraska</td><td>4,776</td><td>0.5%</td></tr>
<tr><td>8</td><td>Pennsylvania</td><td>33,427</td><td>3.3%</td><td>38</td><td>Idaho</td><td>4,522</td><td>0.4%</td></tr>
<tr><td>42</td><td>Rhode Island</td><td>3,390</td><td>0.3%</td><td>39</td><td>West Virginia</td><td>4,148</td><td>0.4%</td></tr>
<tr><td>24</td><td>South Carolina</td><td>13,046</td><td>1.3%</td><td>40</td><td>Hawaii</td><td>3,731</td><td>0.4%</td></tr>
<tr><td>45</td><td>South Dakota</td><td>2,468</td><td>0.2%</td><td>41</td><td>Maine</td><td>3,638</td><td>0.4%</td></tr>
<tr><td>15</td><td>Tennessee</td><td>22,148</td><td>2.2%</td><td>42</td><td>Rhode Island</td><td>3,390</td><td>0.3%</td></tr>
<tr><td>3</td><td>Texas</td><td>80,535</td><td>7.9%</td><td>43</td><td>New Hampshire</td><td>3,268</td><td>0.3%</td></tr>
<tr><td>35</td><td>Utah</td><td>6,346</td><td>0.6%</td><td>44</td><td>Montana</td><td>2,958</td><td>0.3%</td></tr>
<tr><td>50</td><td>Vermont</td><td>1,459</td><td>0.1%</td><td>45</td><td>South Dakota</td><td>2,468</td><td>0.2%</td></tr>
<tr><td>12</td><td>Virginia</td><td>25,842</td><td>2.5%</td><td>46</td><td>Wyoming</td><td>2,287</td><td>0.2%</td></tr>
<tr><td>22</td><td>Washington</td><td>15,513</td><td>1.5%</td><td>47</td><td>Delaware</td><td>2,257</td><td>0.2%</td></tr>
<tr><td>39</td><td>West Virginia</td><td>4,148</td><td>0.4%</td><td>48</td><td>Alaska</td><td>2,151</td><td>0.2%</td></tr>
<tr><td>19</td><td>Wisconsin</td><td>18,010</td><td>1.8%</td><td>49</td><td>North Dakota</td><td>1,755</td><td>0.2%</td></tr>
<tr><td>46</td><td>Wyoming</td><td>2,287</td><td>0.2%</td><td>50</td><td>Vermont</td><td>1,459</td><td>0.1%</td></tr>
<tr><td></td><td></td><td></td><td></td><td></td><td>District of Columbia</td><td>4,914</td><td>0.5%</td></tr>
</table>

Source: U.S. Department of Justice, Bureau of Justice Statistics
"Census of State and Local Law Enforcement Agencies, 2000" (Bulletin, October 2002, NCJ 194066)
*Includes state and local police, sheriffs' departments and special police agencies.

Rate of Full-Time Employees in Law Enforcement Agencies in 2000

National Rate = 362 Employees per 100,000 Population*

ALPHA ORDER

RANK	STATE	RATE
17	Alabama	361
23	Alaska	343
7	Arizona	401
22	Arkansas	344
24	California	342
19	Colorado	354
35	Connecticut	302
38	Delaware	288
5	Florida	427
13	Georgia	382
34	Hawaii	308
20	Idaho	349
6	Illinois	425
37	Indiana	296
46	Iowa	260
11	Kansas	385
49	Kentucky	237
1	Louisiana	527
39	Maine	285
12	Maryland	383
14	Massachusetts	372
36	Michigan	298
47	Minnesota	258
18	Mississippi	357
15	Missouri	366
27	Montana	328
41	Nebraska	279
8	Nevada	396
44	New Hampshire	264
4	New Jersey	444
21	New Mexico	348
2	New York	500
31	North Carolina	324
42	North Dakota	273
29	Ohio	325
26	Oklahoma	330
33	Oregon	312
43	Pennsylvania	272
32	Rhode Island	323
29	South Carolina	325
28	South Dakota	327
9	Tennessee	389
10	Texas	386
40	Utah	284
48	Vermont	240
16	Virginia	365
45	Washington	263
50	West Virginia	229
25	Wisconsin	336
3	Wyoming	463

RANK ORDER

RANK	STATE	RATE
1	Louisiana	527
2	New York	500
3	Wyoming	463
4	New Jersey	444
5	Florida	427
6	Illinois	425
7	Arizona	401
8	Nevada	396
9	Tennessee	389
10	Texas	386
11	Kansas	385
12	Maryland	383
13	Georgia	382
14	Massachusetts	372
15	Missouri	366
16	Virginia	365
17	Alabama	361
18	Mississippi	357
19	Colorado	354
20	Idaho	349
21	New Mexico	348
22	Arkansas	344
23	Alaska	343
24	California	342
25	Wisconsin	336
26	Oklahoma	330
27	Montana	328
28	South Dakota	327
29	Ohio	325
29	South Carolina	325
31	North Carolina	324
32	Rhode Island	323
33	Oregon	312
34	Hawaii	308
35	Connecticut	302
36	Michigan	298
37	Indiana	296
38	Delaware	288
39	Maine	285
40	Utah	284
41	Nebraska	279
42	North Dakota	273
43	Pennsylvania	272
44	New Hampshire	264
45	Washington	263
46	Iowa	260
47	Minnesota	258
48	Vermont	240
49	Kentucky	237
50	West Virginia	229

District of Columbia   859

Source: U.S. Department of Justice, Bureau of Justice Statistics
"Census of State and Local Law Enforcement Agencies, 2000" (Bulletin, October 2002, NCJ 194066)
*Includes state and local police, sheriffs' departments and special police agencies.

Full-Time Sworn Officers in State Police Departments in 2000

National Total = 56,348 Officers*

ALPHA ORDER

RANK	STATE	OFFICERS	% of USA
28	Alabama	628	1.1%
44	Alaska	232	0.4%
17	Arizona	1,050	1.9%
30	Arkansas	559	1.0%
1	California	6,678	11.9%
27	Colorado	654	1.2%
15	Connecticut	1,135	2.0%
29	Delaware	580	1.0%
10	Florida	1,658	2.9%
24	Georgia	786	1.4%
50	Hawaii	0	0.0%
43	Idaho	292	0.5%
8	Illinois	2,089	3.7%
14	Indiana	1,278	2.3%
37	Iowa	455	0.8%
36	Kansas	457	0.8%
20	Kentucky	937	1.7%
21	Louisiana	934	1.7%
40	Maine	325	0.6%
11	Maryland	1,575	2.8%
6	Massachusetts	2,221	3.9%
7	Michigan	2,102	3.7%
31	Minnesota	548	1.0%
32	Mississippi	532	0.9%
16	Missouri	1,080	1.9%
46	Montana	205	0.4%
35	Nebraska	462	0.8%
38	Nevada	414	0.7%
41	New Hampshire	315	0.6%
5	New Jersey	2,569	4.6%
33	New Mexico	525	0.9%
3	New York	4,112	7.3%
12	North Carolina	1,416	2.5%
49	North Dakota	126	0.2%
13	Ohio	1,382	2.5%
25	Oklahoma	782	1.4%
23	Oregon	826	1.5%
2	Pennsylvania	4,152	7.4%
45	Rhode Island	221	0.4%
19	South Carolina	977	1.7%
47	South Dakota	153	0.3%
22	Tennessee	899	1.6%
4	Texas	3,119	5.5%
39	Utah	397	0.7%
42	Vermont	304	0.5%
9	Virginia	1,883	3.3%
18	Washington	987	1.8%
26	West Virginia	681	1.2%
34	Wisconsin	508	0.9%
48	Wyoming	148	0.3%

RANK ORDER

RANK	STATE	OFFICERS	% of USA
1	California	6,678	11.9%
2	Pennsylvania	4,152	7.4%
3	New York	4,112	7.3%
4	Texas	3,119	5.5%
5	New Jersey	2,569	4.6%
6	Massachusetts	2,221	3.9%
7	Michigan	2,102	3.7%
8	Illinois	2,089	3.7%
9	Virginia	1,883	3.3%
10	Florida	1,658	2.9%
11	Maryland	1,575	2.8%
12	North Carolina	1,416	2.5%
13	Ohio	1,382	2.5%
14	Indiana	1,278	2.3%
15	Connecticut	1,135	2.0%
16	Missouri	1,080	1.9%
17	Arizona	1,050	1.9%
18	Washington	987	1.8%
19	South Carolina	977	1.7%
20	Kentucky	937	1.7%
21	Louisiana	934	1.7%
22	Tennessee	899	1.6%
23	Oregon	826	1.5%
24	Georgia	786	1.4%
25	Oklahoma	782	1.4%
26	West Virginia	681	1.2%
27	Colorado	654	1.2%
28	Alabama	628	1.1%
29	Delaware	580	1.0%
30	Arkansas	559	1.0%
31	Minnesota	548	1.0%
32	Mississippi	532	0.9%
33	New Mexico	525	0.9%
34	Wisconsin	508	0.9%
35	Nebraska	462	0.8%
36	Kansas	457	0.8%
37	Iowa	455	0.8%
38	Nevada	414	0.7%
39	Utah	397	0.7%
40	Maine	325	0.6%
41	New Hampshire	315	0.6%
42	Vermont	304	0.5%
43	Idaho	292	0.5%
44	Alaska	232	0.4%
45	Rhode Island	221	0.4%
46	Montana	205	0.4%
47	South Dakota	153	0.3%
48	Wyoming	148	0.3%
49	North Dakota	126	0.2%
50	Hawaii	0	0.0%
	District of Columbia	0	0.0%

Source: U.S. Department of Justice, Bureau of Justice Statistics
"Census of State and Local Law Enforcement Agencies, 2000" (Bulletin, October 2002, NCJ 194066)
All states except Hawaii and the District of Columbia have a state police department.

Percent of Full-Time State Police Department Employees
Who are Sworn Officers: 2000
National Percent = 64.7% of Employees*

ALPHA ORDER

RANK	STATE	PERCENT
43	Alabama	52.3
36	Alaska	56.7
37	Arizona	56.1
32	Arkansas	61.2
21	California	68.8
16	Colorado	71.9
23	Connecticut	67.1
17	Delaware	70.1
9	Florida	77.5
49	Georgia	44.0
NA	Hawaii**	NA
35	Idaho	57.3
39	Illinois	55.1
26	Indiana	65.8
11	Iowa	76.0
24	Kansas	65.9
37	Kentucky	56.1
31	Louisiana	65.0
27	Maine	65.7
22	Maryland	67.7
2	Massachusetts	85.8
24	Michigan	65.9
19	Minnesota	69.3
44	Mississippi	51.6
46	Missouri	49.8
13	Montana	73.2
15	Nebraska	72.2
19	Nevada	69.3
5	New Hampshire	81.0
18	New Jersey	69.8
6	New Mexico	80.9
3	New York	83.1
8	North Carolina	78.2
29	North Dakota	65.3
41	Ohio	54.2
39	Oklahoma	55.1
34	Oregon	58.6
14	Pennsylvania	72.9
4	Rhode Island	82.5
7	South Carolina	80.1
27	South Dakota	65.7
42	Tennessee	52.4
48	Texas	44.4
1	Utah	90.0
33	Vermont	59.3
12	Virginia	75.0
47	Washington	46.0
30	West Virginia	65.2
10	Wisconsin	76.4
45	Wyoming	50.2

RANK ORDER

RANK	STATE	PERCENT
1	Utah	90.0
2	Massachusetts	85.8
3	New York	83.1
4	Rhode Island	82.5
5	New Hampshire	81.0
6	New Mexico	80.9
7	South Carolina	80.1
8	North Carolina	78.2
9	Florida	77.5
10	Wisconsin	76.4
11	Iowa	76.0
12	Virginia	75.0
13	Montana	73.2
14	Pennsylvania	72.9
15	Nebraska	72.2
16	Colorado	71.9
17	Delaware	70.1
18	New Jersey	69.8
19	Minnesota	69.3
19	Nevada	69.3
21	California	68.8
22	Maryland	67.7
23	Connecticut	67.1
24	Kansas	65.9
24	Michigan	65.9
26	Indiana	65.8
27	Maine	65.7
27	South Dakota	65.7
29	North Dakota	65.3
30	West Virginia	65.2
31	Louisiana	65.0
32	Arkansas	61.2
33	Vermont	59.3
34	Oregon	58.6
35	Idaho	57.3
36	Alaska	56.7
37	Arizona	56.1
37	Kentucky	56.1
39	Illinois	55.1
39	Oklahoma	55.1
41	Ohio	54.2
42	Tennessee	52.4
43	Alabama	52.3
44	Mississippi	51.6
45	Wyoming	50.2
46	Missouri	49.8
47	Washington	46.0
48	Texas	44.4
49	Georgia	44.0
NA	Hawaii**	NA
	District of Columbia**	NA

Source: Morgan Quitno Press using data from U.S. Department of Justice, Bureau of Justice Statistics
"Census of State and Local Law Enforcement Agencies, 2000" (Bulletin, October 2002, NCJ 194066)
*All states except Hawaii and the District of Columbia have a state police department.
**Not applicable.

Rate of Full-Time Sworn Officers in State Police Departments in 2000

National Rate = 20 Officers per 100,000 Population*

ALPHA ORDER

RANK	STATE	RATE
44	Alabama	14
4	Alaska	37
29	Arizona	20
23	Arkansas	21
29	California	20
42	Colorado	15
7	Connecticut	33
1	Delaware	74
47	Florida	10
47	Georgia	10
50	Hawaii*	0
18	Idaho	23
37	Illinois	17
23	Indiana	21
40	Iowa	16
37	Kansas	17
18	Kentucky	23
23	Louisiana	21
14	Maine	25
9	Maryland	30
5	Massachusetts	35
23	Michigan	21
46	Minnesota	11
33	Mississippi	19
33	Missouri	19
18	Montana	23
12	Nebraska	27
23	Nevada	21
14	New Hampshire	25
8	New Jersey	31
11	New Mexico	29
22	New York	22
35	North Carolina	18
29	North Dakota	20
45	Ohio	12
18	Oklahoma	23
16	Oregon	24
6	Pennsylvania	34
23	Rhode Island	21
16	South Carolina	24
29	South Dakota	20
40	Tennessee	16
42	Texas	15
35	Utah	18
2	Vermont	50
12	Virginia	27
37	Washington	17
3	West Virginia	38
49	Wisconsin	9
9	Wyoming	30

RANK ORDER

RANK	STATE	RATE
1	Delaware	74
2	Vermont	50
3	West Virginia	38
4	Alaska	37
5	Massachusetts	35
6	Pennsylvania	34
7	Connecticut	33
8	New Jersey	31
9	Maryland	30
9	Wyoming	30
11	New Mexico	29
12	Nebraska	27
12	Virginia	27
14	Maine	25
14	New Hampshire	25
16	Oregon	24
16	South Carolina	24
18	Idaho	23
18	Kentucky	23
18	Montana	23
18	Oklahoma	23
22	New York	22
23	Arkansas	21
23	Indiana	21
23	Louisiana	21
23	Michigan	21
23	Nevada	21
23	Rhode Island	21
29	Arizona	20
29	California	20
29	North Dakota	20
29	South Dakota	20
33	Mississippi	19
33	Missouri	19
35	North Carolina	18
35	Utah	18
37	Illinois	17
37	Kansas	17
37	Washington	17
40	Iowa	16
40	Tennessee	16
42	Colorado	15
42	Texas	15
44	Alabama	14
45	Ohio	12
46	Minnesota	11
47	Florida	10
47	Georgia	10
49	Wisconsin	9
50	Hawaii*	0
	District of Columbia*	0

Source: U.S. Department of Justice, Bureau of Justice Statistics
    "Census of State and Local Law Enforcement Agencies, 2000" (Bulletin, October 2002, NCJ 194066)
*All states except Hawaii and the District of Columbia have a state police department.

State Government Law Enforcement Officers in 2004

National Total = 71,286 Officers*

ALPHA ORDER

RANK	STATE	OFFICERS	% of USA
26	Alabama	845	1.2%
39	Alaska	353	0.5%
21	Arizona	1,164	1.6%
NA	Arkansas**	NA	NA
1	California	7,975	11.2%
30	Colorado	683	1.0%
20	Connecticut	1,236	1.7%
24	Delaware	999	1.4%
6	Florida	3,118	4.4%
17	Georgia	1,390	1.9%
49	Hawaii	0	0.0%
43	Idaho	242	0.3%
9	Illinois	2,278	3.2%
22	Indiana	1,162	1.6%
34	Iowa	559	0.8%
28	Kansas	731	1.0%
18	Kentucky	1,339	1.9%
19	Louisiana	1,244	1.7%
41	Maine	331	0.5%
7	Maryland	2,561	3.6%
10	Massachusetts	2,199	3.1%
14	Michigan	1,591	2.2%
35	Minnesota	545	0.8%
32	Mississippi	576	0.8%
15	Missouri	1,486	2.1%
45	Montana	221	0.3%
37	Nebraska	498	0.7%
38	Nevada	367	0.5%
42	New Hampshire	287	0.4%
4	New Jersey	4,624	6.5%
33	New Mexico	565	0.8%
2	New York	6,491	9.1%
8	North Carolina	2,522	3.5%
48	North Dakota	134	0.2%
16	Ohio	1,481	2.1%
25	Oklahoma	854	1.2%
31	Oregon	610	0.9%
3	Pennsylvania	4,780	6.7%
44	Rhode Island	223	0.3%
12	South Carolina	2,062	2.9%
46	South Dakota	188	0.3%
13	Tennessee	1,597	2.2%
5	Texas	3,407	4.8%
36	Utah	527	0.7%
40	Vermont	342	0.5%
11	Virginia	2,155	3.0%
23	Washington	1,054	1.5%
27	West Virginia	788	1.1%
29	Wisconsin	728	1.0%
47	Wyoming	174	0.2%

RANK ORDER

RANK	STATE	OFFICERS	% of USA
1	California	7,975	11.2%
2	New York	6,491	9.1%
3	Pennsylvania	4,780	6.7%
4	New Jersey	4,624	6.5%
5	Texas	3,407	4.8%
6	Florida	3,118	4.4%
7	Maryland	2,561	3.6%
8	North Carolina	2,522	3.5%
9	Illinois	2,278	3.2%
10	Massachusetts	2,199	3.1%
11	Virginia	2,155	3.0%
12	South Carolina	2,062	2.9%
13	Tennessee	1,597	2.2%
14	Michigan	1,591	2.2%
15	Missouri	1,486	2.1%
16	Ohio	1,481	2.1%
17	Georgia	1,390	1.9%
18	Kentucky	1,339	1.9%
19	Louisiana	1,244	1.7%
20	Connecticut	1,236	1.7%
21	Arizona	1,164	1.6%
22	Indiana	1,162	1.6%
23	Washington	1,054	1.5%
24	Delaware	999	1.4%
25	Oklahoma	854	1.2%
26	Alabama	845	1.2%
27	West Virginia	788	1.1%
28	Kansas	731	1.0%
29	Wisconsin	728	1.0%
30	Colorado	683	1.0%
31	Oregon	610	0.9%
32	Mississippi	576	0.8%
33	New Mexico	565	0.8%
34	Iowa	559	0.8%
35	Minnesota	545	0.8%
36	Utah	527	0.7%
37	Nebraska	498	0.7%
38	Nevada	367	0.5%
39	Alaska	353	0.5%
40	Vermont	342	0.5%
41	Maine	331	0.5%
42	New Hampshire	287	0.4%
43	Idaho	242	0.3%
44	Rhode Island	223	0.3%
45	Montana	221	0.3%
46	South Dakota	188	0.3%
47	Wyoming	174	0.2%
48	North Dakota	134	0.2%
49	Hawaii	0	0.0%
NA	Arkansas**	NA	NA
	District of Columbia	0	0.0%

Source: Morgan Quitno Press using data from Federal Bureau of Investigation
    "Crime in the United States 2004" (Uniform Crime Reports, October 17, 2005)
*Includes state police agencies and other agencies with law enforcement powers. Hawaii and the District of
Columbia do not have a state police agency.
**Not available.

Female State Government Law Enforcement Officers in 2004

National Total = 5,473 Female Officers*

ALPHA ORDER

RANK	STATE	OFFICERS	% of USA
35	Alabama	22	0.4%
39	Alaska	19	0.3%
21	Arizona	77	1.4%
NA	Arkansas**	NA	NA
1	California	869	15.9%
27	Colorado	42	0.8%
19	Connecticut	80	1.5%
13	Delaware	165	3.0%
3	Florida	354	6.5%
19	Georgia	80	1.5%
49	Hawaii	0	0.0%
44	Idaho	13	0.2%
7	Illinois	229	4.2%
22	Indiana	65	1.2%
29	Iowa	34	0.6%
31	Kansas	24	0.4%
27	Kentucky	42	0.8%
25	Louisiana	50	0.9%
33	Maine	23	0.4%
4	Maryland	287	5.2%
9	Massachusetts	204	3.7%
9	Michigan	204	3.7%
26	Minnesota	48	0.9%
43	Mississippi	16	0.3%
23	Missouri	63	1.2%
45	Montana	7	0.1%
33	Nebraska	23	0.4%
40	Nevada	18	0.3%
30	New Hampshire	25	0.5%
5	New Jersey	263	4.8%
31	New Mexico	24	0.4%
2	New York	541	9.9%
11	North Carolina	186	3.4%
47	North Dakota	5	0.1%
14	Ohio	143	2.6%
38	Oklahoma	20	0.4%
24	Oregon	61	1.1%
6	Pennsylvania	246	4.5%
37	Rhode Island	21	0.4%
12	South Carolina	172	3.1%
47	South Dakota	5	0.1%
15	Tennessee	133	2.4%
8	Texas	209	3.8%
42	Utah	17	0.3%
35	Vermont	22	0.4%
16	Virginia	131	2.4%
17	Washington	83	1.5%
40	West Virginia	18	0.3%
17	Wisconsin	83	1.5%
45	Wyoming	7	0.1%

RANK ORDER

RANK	STATE	OFFICERS	% of USA
1	California	869	15.9%
2	New York	541	9.9%
3	Florida	354	6.5%
4	Maryland	287	5.2%
5	New Jersey	263	4.8%
6	Pennsylvania	246	4.5%
7	Illinois	229	4.2%
8	Texas	209	3.8%
9	Massachusetts	204	3.7%
9	Michigan	204	3.7%
11	North Carolina	186	3.4%
12	South Carolina	172	3.1%
13	Delaware	165	3.0%
14	Ohio	143	2.6%
15	Tennessee	133	2.4%
16	Virginia	131	2.4%
17	Washington	83	1.5%
17	Wisconsin	83	1.5%
19	Connecticut	80	1.5%
19	Georgia	80	1.5%
21	Arizona	77	1.4%
22	Indiana	65	1.2%
23	Missouri	63	1.2%
24	Oregon	61	1.1%
25	Louisiana	50	0.9%
26	Minnesota	48	0.9%
27	Colorado	42	0.8%
27	Kentucky	42	0.8%
29	Iowa	34	0.6%
30	New Hampshire	25	0.5%
31	Kansas	24	0.4%
31	New Mexico	24	0.4%
33	Maine	23	0.4%
33	Nebraska	23	0.4%
35	Alabama	22	0.4%
35	Vermont	22	0.4%
37	Rhode Island	21	0.4%
38	Oklahoma	20	0.4%
39	Alaska	19	0.3%
40	Nevada	18	0.3%
40	West Virginia	18	0.3%
42	Utah	17	0.3%
43	Mississippi	16	0.3%
44	Idaho	13	0.2%
45	Montana	7	0.1%
45	Wyoming	7	0.1%
47	North Dakota	5	0.1%
47	South Dakota	5	0.1%
49	Hawaii	0	0.0%
NA	Arkansas**	NA	NA
	District of Columbia	0	0.0%

Source: Morgan Quitno Press using data from Federal Bureau of Investigation
    "Crime in the United States 2004" (Uniform Crime Reports, October 17, 2005)
*Includes state police agencies and other agencies with law enforcement powers. Hawaii and the District of Columbia do not have a state police agency.
**Not available.

Female State Government Law Enforcement Officers
As a Percent of All Officers in 2004
National Percent = 7.7% of Officers*

ALPHA ORDER

RANK	STATE	PERCENT
46	Alabama	2.6
30	Alaska	5.4
20	Arizona	6.6
NA	Arkansas**	NA
6	California	10.9
23	Colorado	6.1
21	Connecticut	6.5
1	Delaware	16.5
3	Florida	11.4
27	Georgia	5.8
NA	Hawaii**	NA
30	Idaho	5.4
7	Illinois	10.1
29	Indiana	5.6
23	Iowa	6.1
40	Kansas	3.3
43	Kentucky	3.1
37	Louisiana	4.0
19	Maine	6.9
5	Maryland	11.2
11	Massachusetts	9.3
2	Michigan	12.8
12	Minnesota	8.8
44	Mississippi	2.8
35	Missouri	4.2
41	Montana	3.2
34	Nebraska	4.6
33	Nevada	4.9
13	New Hampshire	8.7
28	New Jersey	5.7
35	New Mexico	4.2
14	New York	8.3
18	North Carolina	7.4
39	North Dakota	3.7
9	Ohio	9.7
47	Oklahoma	2.3
8	Oregon	10.0
32	Pennsylvania	5.1
10	Rhode Island	9.4
14	South Carolina	8.3
45	South Dakota	2.7
14	Tennessee	8.3
23	Texas	6.1
41	Utah	3.2
22	Vermont	6.4
23	Virginia	6.1
17	Washington	7.9
47	West Virginia	2.3
3	Wisconsin	11.4
37	Wyoming	4.0

RANK ORDER

RANK	STATE	PERCENT
1	Delaware	16.5
2	Michigan	12.8
3	Florida	11.4
3	Wisconsin	11.4
5	Maryland	11.2
6	California	10.9
7	Illinois	10.1
8	Oregon	10.0
9	Ohio	9.7
10	Rhode Island	9.4
11	Massachusetts	9.3
12	Minnesota	8.8
13	New Hampshire	8.7
14	New York	8.3
14	South Carolina	8.3
14	Tennessee	8.3
17	Washington	7.9
18	North Carolina	7.4
19	Maine	6.9
20	Arizona	6.6
21	Connecticut	6.5
22	Vermont	6.4
23	Colorado	6.1
23	Iowa	6.1
23	Texas	6.1
23	Virginia	6.1
27	Georgia	5.8
28	New Jersey	5.7
29	Indiana	5.6
30	Alaska	5.4
30	Idaho	5.4
32	Pennsylvania	5.1
33	Nevada	4.9
34	Nebraska	4.6
35	Missouri	4.2
35	New Mexico	4.2
37	Louisiana	4.0
37	Wyoming	4.0
39	North Dakota	3.7
40	Kansas	3.3
41	Montana	3.2
41	Utah	3.2
43	Kentucky	3.1
44	Mississippi	2.8
45	South Dakota	2.7
46	Alabama	2.6
47	Oklahoma	2.3
47	West Virginia	2.3
NA	Arkansas**	NA
NA	Hawaii**	NA

District of Columbia**   NA

Source: Morgan Quitno Press using data from Federal Bureau of Investigation
    "Crime in the United States 2004" (Uniform Crime Reports, October 17, 2005)
*Includes state police agencies and other agencies with law enforcement powers.
**Hawaii and the District of Columbia do not have a state police agency. Arkansas' information is not available.

Local Police Departments in 2000

National Total = 12,666 Departments*

<table>
<tr><td colspan="4">ALPHA ORDER</td><td colspan="4">RANK ORDER</td></tr>
<tr><td>RANK</td><td>STATE</td><td>DEPARTMENTS</td><td>% of USA</td><td>RANK</td><td>STATE</td><td>DEPARTMENTS</td><td>% of USA</td></tr>
<tr><td>16</td><td>Alabama</td><td>324</td><td>2.6%</td><td>1</td><td>Pennsylvania</td><td>1,015</td><td>8.0%</td></tr>
<tr><td>39</td><td>Alaska</td><td>87</td><td>0.7%</td><td>2</td><td>Texas</td><td>737</td><td>5.8%</td></tr>
<tr><td>37</td><td>Arizona</td><td>93</td><td>0.7%</td><td>3</td><td>Illinois</td><td>729</td><td>5.8%</td></tr>
<tr><td>20</td><td>Arkansas</td><td>258</td><td>2.0%</td><td>4</td><td>Ohio</td><td>712</td><td>5.6%</td></tr>
<tr><td>14</td><td>California</td><td>341</td><td>2.7%</td><td>5</td><td>New Jersey</td><td>484</td><td>3.8%</td></tr>
<tr><td>29</td><td>Colorado</td><td>167</td><td>1.3%</td><td>6</td><td>Michigan</td><td>450</td><td>3.6%</td></tr>
<tr><td>35</td><td>Connecticut</td><td>106</td><td>0.8%</td><td>7</td><td>Missouri</td><td>449</td><td>3.5%</td></tr>
<tr><td>48</td><td>Delaware</td><td>33</td><td>0.3%</td><td>8</td><td>Wisconsin</td><td>417</td><td>3.3%</td></tr>
<tr><td>19</td><td>Florida</td><td>287</td><td>2.3%</td><td>9</td><td>New York</td><td>393</td><td>3.1%</td></tr>
<tr><td>13</td><td>Georgia</td><td>356</td><td>2.8%</td><td>10</td><td>Indiana</td><td>379</td><td>3.0%</td></tr>
<tr><td>50</td><td>Hawaii</td><td>4</td><td>0.0%</td><td>11</td><td>Minnesota</td><td>358</td><td>2.8%</td></tr>
<tr><td>42</td><td>Idaho</td><td>74</td><td>0.6%</td><td>12</td><td>North Carolina</td><td>357</td><td>2.8%</td></tr>
<tr><td>3</td><td>Illinois</td><td>729</td><td>5.8%</td><td>13</td><td>Georgia</td><td>356</td><td>2.8%</td></tr>
<tr><td>10</td><td>Indiana</td><td>379</td><td>3.0%</td><td>14</td><td>California</td><td>341</td><td>2.7%</td></tr>
<tr><td>18</td><td>Iowa</td><td>292</td><td>2.3%</td><td>15</td><td>Oklahoma</td><td>340</td><td>2.7%</td></tr>
<tr><td>24</td><td>Kansas</td><td>227</td><td>1.8%</td><td>16</td><td>Alabama</td><td>324</td><td>2.6%</td></tr>
<tr><td>23</td><td>Kentucky</td><td>245</td><td>1.9%</td><td>17</td><td>Massachusetts</td><td>308</td><td>2.4%</td></tr>
<tr><td>22</td><td>Louisiana</td><td>246</td><td>1.9%</td><td>18</td><td>Iowa</td><td>292</td><td>2.3%</td></tr>
<tr><td>34</td><td>Maine</td><td>115</td><td>0.9%</td><td>19</td><td>Florida</td><td>287</td><td>2.3%</td></tr>
<tr><td>41</td><td>Maryland</td><td>77</td><td>0.6%</td><td>20</td><td>Arkansas</td><td>258</td><td>2.0%</td></tr>
<tr><td>17</td><td>Massachusetts</td><td>308</td><td>2.4%</td><td>21</td><td>Tennessee</td><td>248</td><td>2.0%</td></tr>
<tr><td>6</td><td>Michigan</td><td>450</td><td>3.6%</td><td>22</td><td>Louisiana</td><td>246</td><td>1.9%</td></tr>
<tr><td>11</td><td>Minnesota</td><td>358</td><td>2.8%</td><td>23</td><td>Kentucky</td><td>245</td><td>1.9%</td></tr>
<tr><td>25</td><td>Mississippi</td><td>217</td><td>1.7%</td><td>24</td><td>Kansas</td><td>227</td><td>1.8%</td></tr>
<tr><td>7</td><td>Missouri</td><td>449</td><td>3.5%</td><td>25</td><td>Mississippi</td><td>217</td><td>1.7%</td></tr>
<tr><td>44</td><td>Montana</td><td>62</td><td>0.5%</td><td>26</td><td>Washington</td><td>204</td><td>1.6%</td></tr>
<tr><td>32</td><td>Nebraska</td><td>141</td><td>1.1%</td><td>27</td><td>South Carolina</td><td>186</td><td>1.5%</td></tr>
<tr><td>49</td><td>Nevada</td><td>28</td><td>0.2%</td><td>28</td><td>New Hampshire</td><td>181</td><td>1.4%</td></tr>
<tr><td>28</td><td>New Hampshire</td><td>181</td><td>1.4%</td><td>29</td><td>Colorado</td><td>167</td><td>1.3%</td></tr>
<tr><td>5</td><td>New Jersey</td><td>484</td><td>3.8%</td><td>30</td><td>Virginia</td><td>165</td><td>1.3%</td></tr>
<tr><td>38</td><td>New Mexico</td><td>89</td><td>0.7%</td><td>31</td><td>West Virginia</td><td>158</td><td>1.2%</td></tr>
<tr><td>9</td><td>New York</td><td>393</td><td>3.1%</td><td>32</td><td>Nebraska</td><td>141</td><td>1.1%</td></tr>
<tr><td>12</td><td>North Carolina</td><td>357</td><td>2.8%</td><td>33</td><td>Oregon</td><td>135</td><td>1.1%</td></tr>
<tr><td>43</td><td>North Dakota</td><td>69</td><td>0.5%</td><td>34</td><td>Maine</td><td>115</td><td>0.9%</td></tr>
<tr><td>4</td><td>Ohio</td><td>712</td><td>5.6%</td><td>35</td><td>Connecticut</td><td>106</td><td>0.8%</td></tr>
<tr><td>15</td><td>Oklahoma</td><td>340</td><td>2.7%</td><td>36</td><td>South Dakota</td><td>100</td><td>0.8%</td></tr>
<tr><td>33</td><td>Oregon</td><td>135</td><td>1.1%</td><td>37</td><td>Arizona</td><td>93</td><td>0.7%</td></tr>
<tr><td>1</td><td>Pennsylvania</td><td>1,015</td><td>8.0%</td><td>38</td><td>New Mexico</td><td>89</td><td>0.7%</td></tr>
<tr><td>47</td><td>Rhode Island</td><td>39</td><td>0.3%</td><td>39</td><td>Alaska</td><td>87</td><td>0.7%</td></tr>
<tr><td>27</td><td>South Carolina</td><td>186</td><td>1.5%</td><td>40</td><td>Utah</td><td>83</td><td>0.7%</td></tr>
<tr><td>36</td><td>South Dakota</td><td>100</td><td>0.8%</td><td>41</td><td>Maryland</td><td>77</td><td>0.6%</td></tr>
<tr><td>21</td><td>Tennessee</td><td>248</td><td>2.0%</td><td>42</td><td>Idaho</td><td>74</td><td>0.6%</td></tr>
<tr><td>2</td><td>Texas</td><td>737</td><td>5.8%</td><td>43</td><td>North Dakota</td><td>69</td><td>0.5%</td></tr>
<tr><td>40</td><td>Utah</td><td>83</td><td>0.7%</td><td>44</td><td>Montana</td><td>62</td><td>0.5%</td></tr>
<tr><td>46</td><td>Vermont</td><td>48</td><td>0.4%</td><td>45</td><td>Wyoming</td><td>52</td><td>0.4%</td></tr>
<tr><td>30</td><td>Virginia</td><td>165</td><td>1.3%</td><td>46</td><td>Vermont</td><td>48</td><td>0.4%</td></tr>
<tr><td>26</td><td>Washington</td><td>204</td><td>1.6%</td><td>47</td><td>Rhode Island</td><td>39</td><td>0.3%</td></tr>
<tr><td>31</td><td>West Virginia</td><td>158</td><td>1.2%</td><td>48</td><td>Delaware</td><td>33</td><td>0.3%</td></tr>
<tr><td>8</td><td>Wisconsin</td><td>417</td><td>3.3%</td><td>49</td><td>Nevada</td><td>28</td><td>0.2%</td></tr>
<tr><td>45</td><td>Wyoming</td><td>52</td><td>0.4%</td><td>50</td><td>Hawaii</td><td>4</td><td>0.0%</td></tr>
<tr><td></td><td></td><td></td><td></td><td></td><td>District of Columbia</td><td>1</td><td>0.0%</td></tr>
</table>

Source: U.S. Department of Justice, Bureau of Justice Statistics
    "Census of State and Local Law Enforcement Agencies, 2000" (Bulletin, October 2002, NCJ 194066)
*Includes consolidated police-sheriffs' departments.

Full-Time Officers in Local Police Departments in 2000

National Total = 440,920 Officers*

ALPHA ORDER

RANK	STATE	OFFICERS	% of USA
19	Alabama	7,089	1.6%
45	Alaska	899	0.2%
17	Arizona	8,159	1.9%
31	Arkansas	3,675	0.8%
2	California	37,674	8.5%
23	Colorado	6,028	1.4%
21	Connecticut	6,592	1.5%
44	Delaware	992	0.2%
6	Florida	21,035	4.8%
11	Georgia	10,992	2.5%
35	Hawaii	2,605	0.6%
43	Idaho	1,279	0.3%
4	Illinois	27,452	6.2%
20	Indiana	7,016	1.6%
34	Iowa	3,175	0.7%
29	Kansas	3,870	0.9%
27	Kentucky	4,518	1.0%
22	Louisiana	6,339	1.4%
41	Maine	1,503	0.3%
13	Maryland	9,680	2.2%
10	Massachusetts	13,826	3.1%
9	Michigan	14,044	3.2%
25	Minnesota	5,347	1.2%
30	Mississippi	3,764	0.9%
15	Missouri	9,372	2.1%
47	Montana	765	0.2%
39	Nebraska	2,040	0.5%
33	Nevada	3,216	0.7%
40	New Hampshire	2,031	0.5%
5	New Jersey	21,046	4.8%
36	New Mexico	2,539	0.6%
1	New York	58,588	13.3%
12	North Carolina	10,473	2.4%
48	North Dakota	681	0.2%
8	Ohio	16,956	3.8%
26	Oklahoma	5,246	1.2%
32	Oregon	3,465	0.8%
7	Pennsylvania	18,913	4.3%
38	Rhode Island	2,153	0.5%
28	South Carolina	4,383	1.0%
46	South Dakota	896	0.2%
16	Tennessee	8,408	1.9%
3	Texas	30,525	6.9%
37	Utah	2,181	0.5%
50	Vermont	571	0.1%
14	Virginia	9,604	2.2%
24	Washington	5,766	1.3%
42	West Virginia	1,404	0.3%
18	Wisconsin	7,879	1.8%
49	Wyoming	654	0.1%

RANK ORDER

RANK	STATE	OFFICERS	% of USA
1	New York	58,588	13.3%
2	California	37,674	8.5%
3	Texas	30,525	6.9%
4	Illinois	27,452	6.2%
5	New Jersey	21,046	4.8%
6	Florida	21,035	4.8%
7	Pennsylvania	18,913	4.3%
8	Ohio	16,956	3.8%
9	Michigan	14,044	3.2%
10	Massachusetts	13,826	3.1%
11	Georgia	10,992	2.5%
12	North Carolina	10,473	2.4%
13	Maryland	9,680	2.2%
14	Virginia	9,604	2.2%
15	Missouri	9,372	2.1%
16	Tennessee	8,408	1.9%
17	Arizona	8,159	1.9%
18	Wisconsin	7,879	1.8%
19	Alabama	7,089	1.6%
20	Indiana	7,016	1.6%
21	Connecticut	6,592	1.5%
22	Louisiana	6,339	1.4%
23	Colorado	6,028	1.4%
24	Washington	5,766	1.3%
25	Minnesota	5,347	1.2%
26	Oklahoma	5,246	1.2%
27	Kentucky	4,518	1.0%
28	South Carolina	4,383	1.0%
29	Kansas	3,870	0.9%
30	Mississippi	3,764	0.9%
31	Arkansas	3,675	0.8%
32	Oregon	3,465	0.8%
33	Nevada	3,216	0.7%
34	Iowa	3,175	0.7%
35	Hawaii	2,605	0.6%
36	New Mexico	2,539	0.6%
37	Utah	2,181	0.5%
38	Rhode Island	2,153	0.5%
39	Nebraska	2,040	0.5%
40	New Hampshire	2,031	0.5%
41	Maine	1,503	0.3%
42	West Virginia	1,404	0.3%
43	Idaho	1,279	0.3%
44	Delaware	992	0.2%
45	Alaska	899	0.2%
46	South Dakota	896	0.2%
47	Montana	765	0.2%
48	North Dakota	681	0.2%
49	Wyoming	654	0.1%
50	Vermont	571	0.1%
	District of Columbia	3,612	0.8%

Source: U.S. Department of Justice, Bureau of Justice Statistics
    "Census of State and Local Law Enforcement Agencies, 2000" (Bulletin, October 2002, NCJ 194066)
*Includes consolidated police-sheriffs' departments.

Percent of Full-Time Local Police Department Employees
Who are Sworn Officers: 2000
National Percent = 77.9% of Employees*

<table>
<tr><td colspan="3">ALPHA ORDER</td><td colspan="3">RANK ORDER</td></tr>
<tr><td>RANK</td><td>STATE</td><td>PERCENT</td><td>RANK</td><td>STATE</td><td>PERCENT</td></tr>
<tr><td>38</td><td>Alabama</td><td>75.0</td><td>1</td><td>Pennsylvania</td><td>87.8</td></tr>
<tr><td>50</td><td>Alaska</td><td>66.2</td><td>2</td><td>West Virginia</td><td>87.5</td></tr>
<tr><td>46</td><td>Arizona</td><td>70.5</td><td>3</td><td>Delaware</td><td>86.9</td></tr>
<tr><td>22</td><td>Arkansas</td><td>78.6</td><td>4</td><td>Michigan</td><td>84.0</td></tr>
<tr><td>45</td><td>California</td><td>71.7</td><td>5</td><td>New Jersey</td><td>83.8</td></tr>
<tr><td>42</td><td>Colorado</td><td>73.5</td><td>6</td><td>Connecticut</td><td>83.5</td></tr>
<tr><td>6</td><td>Connecticut</td><td>83.5</td><td>7</td><td>Massachusetts</td><td>82.7</td></tr>
<tr><td>3</td><td>Delaware</td><td>86.9</td><td>8</td><td>North Carolina</td><td>82.4</td></tr>
<tr><td>47</td><td>Florida</td><td>70.3</td><td>9</td><td>Iowa</td><td>81.9</td></tr>
<tr><td>21</td><td>Georgia</td><td>79.0</td><td>10</td><td>Wisconsin</td><td>81.7</td></tr>
<tr><td>28</td><td>Hawaii</td><td>77.9</td><td>11</td><td>South Carolina</td><td>81.2</td></tr>
<tr><td>26</td><td>Idaho</td><td>78.3</td><td>12</td><td>Maryland</td><td>80.7</td></tr>
<tr><td>18</td><td>Illinois</td><td>79.8</td><td>12</td><td>North Dakota</td><td>80.7</td></tr>
<tr><td>17</td><td>Indiana</td><td>79.9</td><td>14</td><td>Loulsiana</td><td>80.6</td></tr>
<tr><td>9</td><td>Iowa</td><td>81.9</td><td>15</td><td>Minnesota</td><td>80.4</td></tr>
<tr><td>40</td><td>Kansas</td><td>73.7</td><td>15</td><td>Ohio</td><td>80.4</td></tr>
<tr><td>23</td><td>Kentucky</td><td>78.4</td><td>17</td><td>Indiana</td><td>79.9</td></tr>
<tr><td>14</td><td>Louisiana</td><td>80.6</td><td>18</td><td>Illinois</td><td>79.8</td></tr>
<tr><td>26</td><td>Maine</td><td>78.3</td><td>18</td><td>Nebraska</td><td>79.8</td></tr>
<tr><td>12</td><td>Maryland</td><td>80.7</td><td>20</td><td>New Hampshire</td><td>79.3</td></tr>
<tr><td>7</td><td>Massachusetts</td><td>82.7</td><td>21</td><td>Georgia</td><td>79.0</td></tr>
<tr><td>4</td><td>Michigan</td><td>84.0</td><td>22</td><td>Arkansas</td><td>78.6</td></tr>
<tr><td>15</td><td>Minnesota</td><td>80.4</td><td>23</td><td>Kentucky</td><td>78.4</td></tr>
<tr><td>38</td><td>Mississippi</td><td>75.0</td><td>23</td><td>New York</td><td>78.4</td></tr>
<tr><td>35</td><td>Missouri</td><td>76.2</td><td>23</td><td>Rhode Island</td><td>78.4</td></tr>
<tr><td>30</td><td>Montana</td><td>77.8</td><td>26</td><td>Idaho</td><td>78.3</td></tr>
<tr><td>18</td><td>Nebraska</td><td>79.8</td><td>26</td><td>Maine</td><td>78.3</td></tr>
<tr><td>49</td><td>Nevada</td><td>67.7</td><td>28</td><td>Hawaii</td><td>77.9</td></tr>
<tr><td>20</td><td>New Hampshire</td><td>79.3</td><td>28</td><td>Utah</td><td>77.9</td></tr>
<tr><td>5</td><td>New Jersey</td><td>83.8</td><td>30</td><td>Montana</td><td>77.8</td></tr>
<tr><td>48</td><td>New Mexico</td><td>69.5</td><td>30</td><td>Oklahoma</td><td>77.8</td></tr>
<tr><td>23</td><td>New York</td><td>78.4</td><td>32</td><td>Vermont</td><td>77.7</td></tr>
<tr><td>8</td><td>North Carolina</td><td>82.4</td><td>33</td><td>Virginia</td><td>77.2</td></tr>
<tr><td>12</td><td>North Dakota</td><td>80.7</td><td>34</td><td>Tennessee</td><td>77.0</td></tr>
<tr><td>15</td><td>Ohio</td><td>80.4</td><td>35</td><td>Missouri</td><td>76.2</td></tr>
<tr><td>30</td><td>Oklahoma</td><td>77.8</td><td>36</td><td>South Dakota</td><td>75.7</td></tr>
<tr><td>43</td><td>Oregon</td><td>73.3</td><td>36</td><td>Texas</td><td>75.7</td></tr>
<tr><td>1</td><td>Pennsylvania</td><td>87.8</td><td>38</td><td>Alabama</td><td>75.0</td></tr>
<tr><td>23</td><td>Rhode Island</td><td>78.4</td><td>38</td><td>Mississippi</td><td>75.0</td></tr>
<tr><td>11</td><td>South Carolina</td><td>81.2</td><td>40</td><td>Kansas</td><td>73.7</td></tr>
<tr><td>36</td><td>South Dakota</td><td>75.7</td><td>41</td><td>Washington</td><td>73.6</td></tr>
<tr><td>34</td><td>Tennessee</td><td>77.0</td><td>42</td><td>Colorado</td><td>73.5</td></tr>
<tr><td>36</td><td>Texas</td><td>75.7</td><td>43</td><td>Oregon</td><td>73.3</td></tr>
<tr><td>28</td><td>Utah</td><td>77.9</td><td>44</td><td>Wyoming</td><td>72.1</td></tr>
<tr><td>32</td><td>Vermont</td><td>77.7</td><td>45</td><td>California</td><td>71.7</td></tr>
<tr><td>33</td><td>Virginia</td><td>77.2</td><td>46</td><td>Arizona</td><td>70.5</td></tr>
<tr><td>41</td><td>Washington</td><td>73.6</td><td>47</td><td>Florida</td><td>70.3</td></tr>
<tr><td>2</td><td>West Virginia</td><td>87.5</td><td>48</td><td>New Mexico</td><td>69.5</td></tr>
<tr><td>10</td><td>Wisconsin</td><td>81.7</td><td>49</td><td>Nevada</td><td>67.7</td></tr>
<tr><td>44</td><td>Wyoming</td><td>72.1</td><td>50</td><td>Alaska</td><td>66.2</td></tr>
<tr><td></td><td></td><td></td><td></td><td>District of Columbia</td><td>80.8</td></tr>
</table>

Source: Morgan Quitno Press using data from U.S. Department of Justice, Bureau of Justice Statistics
   "Census of State and Local Law Enforcement Agencies, 2000" (Bulletin, October 2002, NCJ 194066)
*Includes consolidated police-sheriffs' departments.

Rate of Full-Time Sworn Officers in Local Police Departments in 2000

National Rate = 157 Officers per 100,000 Population*

ALPHA ORDER

RANK	STATE	RATE
12	Alabama	159
21	Alaska	143
12	Arizona	159
26	Arkansas	137
39	California	111
24	Colorado	140
7	Connecticut	194
33	Delaware	127
29	Florida	132
28	Georgia	134
5	Hawaii	215
45	Idaho	99
3	Illinois	221
37	Indiana	115
42	Iowa	108
20	Kansas	144
38	Kentucky	112
22	Louisiana	142
36	Maine	118
8	Maryland	183
4	Massachusetts	218
23	Michigan	141
40	Minnesota	109
29	Mississippi	132
9	Missouri	168
49	Montana	85
34	Nebraska	119
11	Nevada	161
10	New Hampshire	164
2	New Jersey	250
24	New Mexico	140
1	New York	309
32	North Carolina	130
43	North Dakota	106
16	Ohio	149
15	Oklahoma	152
44	Oregon	101
14	Pennsylvania	154
6	Rhode Island	205
40	South Carolina	109
34	South Dakota	119
17	Tennessee	148
19	Texas	146
46	Utah	98
48	Vermont	94
27	Virginia	136
46	Washington	98
50	West Virginia	78
18	Wisconsin	147
29	Wyoming	132

RANK ORDER

RANK	STATE	RATE
1	New York	309
2	New Jersey	250
3	Illinois	221
4	Massachusetts	218
5	Hawaii	215
6	Rhode Island	205
7	Connecticut	194
8	Maryland	183
9	Missouri	168
10	New Hampshire	164
11	Nevada	161
12	Alabama	159
12	Arizona	159
14	Pennsylvania	154
15	Oklahoma	152
16	Ohio	149
17	Tennessee	148
18	Wisconsin	147
19	Texas	146
20	Kansas	144
21	Alaska	143
22	Louisiana	142
23	Michigan	141
24	Colorado	140
24	New Mexico	140
26	Arkansas	137
27	Virginia	136
28	Georgia	134
29	Florida	132
29	Mississippi	132
29	Wyoming	132
32	North Carolina	130
33	Delaware	127
34	Nebraska	119
34	South Dakota	119
36	Maine	118
37	Indiana	115
38	Kentucky	112
39	California	111
40	Minnesota	109
40	South Carolina	109
42	Iowa	108
43	North Dakota	106
44	Oregon	101
45	Idaho	99
46	Utah	98
46	Washington	98
48	Vermont	94
49	Montana	85
50	West Virginia	78
	District of Columbia	631

Source: U.S. Department of Justice, Bureau of Justice Statistics
"Census of State and Local Law Enforcement Agencies, 2000" (Bulletin, October 2002, NCJ 194066)
Includes consolidated police-sheriffs' departments.

Full-Time Employees in Local Police Departments in 2000

National Total = 565,915 Employees*

ALPHA ORDER

RANK	STATE	EMPLOYEES	% of USA
19	Alabama	9,456	1.7%
44	Alaska	1,357	0.2%
16	Arizona	11,569	2.0%
33	Arkansas	4,677	0.8%
2	California	52,541	9.3%
21	Colorado	8,205	1.4%
22	Connecticut	7,890	1.4%
46	Delaware	1,142	0.2%
5	Florida	29,922	5.3%
11	Georgia	13,918	2.5%
36	Hawaii	3,346	0.6%
42	Idaho	1,634	0.3%
4	Illinois	34,382	6.1%
20	Indiana	8,779	1.6%
34	Iowa	3,875	0.7%
29	Kansas	5,254	0.9%
27	Kentucky	5,763	1.0%
23	Louisiana	7,866	1.4%
41	Maine	1,920	0.3%
15	Maryland	11,998	2.1%
10	Massachusetts	16,718	3.0%
9	Michigan	16,727	3.0%
26	Minnesota	6,651	1.2%
30	Mississippi	5,016	0.9%
14	Missouri	12,294	2.2%
47	Montana	983	0.2%
40	Nebraska	2,556	0.5%
31	Nevada	4,753	0.8%
39	New Hampshire	2,562	0.5%
6	New Jersey	25,114	4.4%
35	New Mexico	3,651	0.6%
1	New York	74,737	13.2%
12	North Carolina	12,717	2.2%
49	North Dakota	844	0.1%
8	Ohio	21,086	3.7%
25	Oklahoma	6,746	1.2%
32	Oregon	4,726	0.8%
7	Pennsylvania	21,545	3.8%
38	Rhode Island	2,745	0.5%
28	South Carolina	5,399	1.0%
45	South Dakota	1,184	0.2%
17	Tennessee	10,919	1.9%
3	Texas	40,321	7.1%
37	Utah	2,798	0.5%
50	Vermont	735	0.1%
13	Virginia	12,439	2.2%
24	Washington	7,837	1.4%
43	West Virginia	1,604	0.3%
18	Wisconsin	9,639	1.7%
48	Wyoming	907	0.2%

RANK ORDER

RANK	STATE	EMPLOYEES	% of USA
1	New York	74,737	13.2%
2	California	52,541	9.3%
3	Texas	40,321	7.1%
4	Illinois	34,382	6.1%
5	Florida	29,922	5.3%
6	New Jersey	25,114	4.4%
7	Pennsylvania	21,545	3.8%
8	Ohio	21,086	3.7%
9	Michigan	16,727	3.0%
10	Massachusetts	16,718	3.0%
11	Georgia	13,918	2.5%
12	North Carolina	12,717	2.2%
13	Virginia	12,439	2.2%
14	Missouri	12,294	2.2%
15	Maryland	11,998	2.1%
16	Arizona	11,569	2.0%
17	Tennessee	10,919	1.9%
18	Wisconsin	9,639	1.7%
19	Alabama	9,456	1.7%
20	Indiana	8,779	1.6%
21	Colorado	8,205	1.4%
22	Connecticut	7,890	1.4%
23	Louisiana	7,866	1.4%
24	Washington	7,837	1.4%
25	Oklahoma	6,746	1.2%
26	Minnesota	6,651	1.2%
27	Kentucky	5,763	1.0%
28	South Carolina	5,399	1.0%
29	Kansas	5,254	0.9%
30	Mississippi	5,016	0.9%
31	Nevada	4,753	0.8%
32	Oregon	4,726	0.8%
33	Arkansas	4,677	0.8%
34	Iowa	3,875	0.7%
35	New Mexico	3,651	0.6%
36	Hawaii	3,346	0.6%
37	Utah	2,798	0.5%
38	Rhode Island	2,745	0.5%
39	New Hampshire	2,562	0.5%
40	Nebraska	2,556	0.5%
41	Maine	1,920	0.3%
42	Idaho	1,634	0.3%
43	West Virginia	1,604	0.3%
44	Alaska	1,357	0.2%
45	South Dakota	1,184	0.2%
46	Delaware	1,142	0.2%
47	Montana	983	0.2%
48	Wyoming	907	0.2%
49	North Dakota	844	0.1%
50	Vermont	735	0.1%
	District of Columbia	4,468	0.8%

Source: U.S. Department of Justice, Bureau of Justice Statistics
   "Census of State and Local Law Enforcement Agencies, 2000" (Bulletin, October 2002, NCJ 194066)
*Includes consolidated police-sheriffs' departments.

Sheriffs' Departments in 2000

National Total = 3,070 Departments*

ALPHA ORDER

RANK	STATE	DEPARTMENTS	% of USA
20	Alabama	67	2.2%
49	Alaska	0	0.0%
42	Arizona	15	0.5%
18	Arkansas	75	2.4%
26	California	58	1.9%
25	Colorado	62	2.0%
47	Connecticut	4	0.1%
48	Delaware	3	0.1%
21	Florida	65	2.1%
2	Georgia	158	5.1%
49	Hawaii	0	0.0%
32	Idaho	44	1.4%
7	Illinois	102	3.3%
11	Indiana	92	3.0%
9	Iowa	99	3.2%
6	Kansas	104	3.4%
4	Kentucky	120	3.9%
23	Louisiana	64	2.1%
40	Maine	16	0.5%
37	Maryland	24	0.8%
44	Massachusetts	10	0.3%
15	Michigan	83	2.7%
14	Minnesota	87	2.8%
16	Mississippi	82	2.7%
5	Missouri	114	3.7%
28	Montana	55	1.8%
11	Nebraska	92	3.0%
40	Nevada	16	0.5%
44	New Hampshire	10	0.3%
39	New Jersey	21	0.7%
35	New Mexico	32	1.0%
27	New York	57	1.9%
8	North Carolina	100	3.3%
30	North Dakota	53	1.7%
13	Ohio	88	2.9%
17	Oklahoma	77	2.5%
34	Oregon	36	1.2%
21	Pennsylvania	65	2.1%
46	Rhode Island	5	0.2%
31	South Carolina	46	1.5%
23	South Dakota	64	2.1%
10	Tennessee	94	3.1%
1	Texas	254	8.3%
36	Utah	29	0.9%
43	Vermont	14	0.5%
3	Virginia	125	4.1%
33	Washington	39	1.3%
28	West Virginia	55	1.8%
19	Wisconsin	72	2.3%
38	Wyoming	23	0.7%

RANK ORDER

RANK	STATE	DEPARTMENTS	% of USA
1	Texas	254	8.3%
2	Georgia	158	5.1%
3	Virginia	125	4.1%
4	Kentucky	120	3.9%
5	Missouri	114	3.7%
6	Kansas	104	3.4%
7	Illinois	102	3.3%
8	North Carolina	100	3.3%
9	Iowa	99	3.2%
10	Tennessee	94	3.1%
11	Indiana	92	3.0%
11	Nebraska	92	3.0%
13	Ohio	88	2.9%
14	Minnesota	87	2.8%
15	Michigan	83	2.7%
16	Mississippi	82	2.7%
17	Oklahoma	77	2.5%
18	Arkansas	75	2.4%
19	Wisconsin	72	2.3%
20	Alabama	67	2.2%
21	Florida	65	2.1%
21	Pennsylvania	65	2.1%
23	Louisiana	64	2.1%
23	South Dakota	64	2.1%
25	Colorado	62	2.0%
26	California	58	1.9%
27	New York	57	1.9%
28	Montana	55	1.8%
28	West Virginia	55	1.8%
30	North Dakota	53	1.7%
31	South Carolina	46	1.5%
32	Idaho	44	1.4%
33	Washington	39	1.3%
34	Oregon	36	1.2%
35	New Mexico	32	1.0%
36	Utah	29	0.9%
37	Maryland	24	0.8%
38	Wyoming	23	0.7%
39	New Jersey	21	0.7%
40	Maine	16	0.5%
40	Nevada	16	0.5%
42	Arizona	15	0.5%
43	Vermont	14	0.5%
44	Massachusetts	10	0.3%
44	New Hampshire	10	0.3%
46	Rhode Island	5	0.2%
47	Connecticut	4	0.1%
48	Delaware	3	0.1%
49	Alaska	0	0.0%
49	Hawaii	0	0.0%
	District of Columbia	0	0.0%

Source: U.S. Department of Justice, Bureau of Justice Statistics
   "Census of State and Local Law Enforcement Agencies, 2000" (Bulletin, October 2002, NCJ 194066)
*Sheriffs' departments generally operate at the county level.

Full-Time Officers in Sheriffs' Departments in 2000

National Total = 164,711 Officers*

ALPHA ORDER

RANK	STATE	OFFICERS	% of USA
21	Alabama	2,210	1.3%
49	Alaska	0	0.0%
24	Arizona	1,764	1.1%
31	Arkansas	1,285	0.8%
1	California	25,361	15.4%
16	Colorado	3,072	1.9%
43	Connecticut	336	0.2%
48	Delaware	20	0.0%
2	Florida	14,770	9.0%
6	Georgia	7,703	4.7%
49	Hawaii	0	0.0%
35	Idaho	1,024	0.6%
5	Illinois	9,073	5.5%
17	Indiana	2,883	1.8%
27	Iowa	1,458	0.9%
23	Kansas	1,803	1.1%
29	Kentucky	1,406	0.9%
4	Louisiana	10,329	6.3%
44	Maine	309	0.2%
25	Maryland	1,711	1.0%
32	Massachusetts	1,208	0.7%
11	Michigan	4,641	2.8%
20	Minnesota	2,287	1.4%
26	Mississippi	1,698	1.0%
19	Missouri	2,423	1.5%
39	Montana	629	0.4%
37	Nebraska	901	0.5%
36	Nevada	1,008	0.6%
46	New Hampshire	120	0.1%
15	New Jersey	3,200	1.9%
34	New Mexico	1,038	0.6%
9	New York	6,018	3.7%
8	North Carolina	6,140	3.7%
42	North Dakota	384	0.2%
10	Ohio	5,366	3.3%
33	Oklahoma	1,092	0.7%
22	Oregon	2,113	1.3%
28	Pennsylvania	1,428	0.9%
45	Rhode Island	159	0.1%
14	South Carolina	3,569	2.2%
41	South Dakota	388	0.2%
12	Tennessee	4,242	2.6%
3	Texas	11,133	6.8%
30	Utah	1,311	0.8%
47	Vermont	104	0.1%
7	Virginia	7,382	4.5%
18	Washington	2,753	1.7%
38	West Virginia	814	0.5%
13	Wisconsin	4,069	2.5%
40	Wyoming	576	0.3%

RANK ORDER

RANK	STATE	OFFICERS	% of USA
1	California	25,361	15.4%
2	Florida	14,770	9.0%
3	Texas	11,133	6.8%
4	Louisiana	10,329	6.3%
5	Illinois	9,073	5.5%
6	Georgia	7,703	4.7%
7	Virginia	7,382	4.5%
8	North Carolina	6,140	3.7%
9	New York	6,018	3.7%
10	Ohio	5,366	3.3%
11	Michigan	4,641	2.8%
12	Tennessee	4,242	2.6%
13	Wisconsin	4,069	2.5%
14	South Carolina	3,569	2.2%
15	New Jersey	3,200	1.9%
16	Colorado	3,072	1.9%
17	Indiana	2,883	1.8%
18	Washington	2,753	1.7%
19	Missouri	2,423	1.5%
20	Minnesota	2,287	1.4%
21	Alabama	2,210	1.3%
22	Oregon	2,113	1.3%
23	Kansas	1,803	1.1%
24	Arizona	1,764	1.1%
25	Maryland	1,711	1.0%
26	Mississippi	1,698	1.0%
27	Iowa	1,458	0.9%
28	Pennsylvania	1,428	0.9%
29	Kentucky	1,406	0.9%
30	Utah	1,311	0.8%
31	Arkansas	1,285	0.8%
32	Massachusetts	1,208	0.7%
33	Oklahoma	1,092	0.7%
34	New Mexico	1,038	0.6%
35	Idaho	1,024	0.6%
36	Nevada	1,008	0.6%
37	Nebraska	901	0.5%
38	West Virginia	814	0.5%
39	Montana	629	0.4%
40	Wyoming	576	0.3%
41	South Dakota	388	0.2%
42	North Dakota	384	0.2%
43	Connecticut	336	0.2%
44	Maine	309	0.2%
45	Rhode Island	159	0.1%
46	New Hampshire	120	0.1%
47	Vermont	104	0.1%
48	Delaware	20	0.0%
49	Alaska	0	0.0%
49	Hawaii	0	0.0%
	District of Columbia	0	0.0%

Source: U.S. Department of Justice, Bureau of Justice Statistics
"Census of State and Local Law Enforcement Agencies, 2000" (Bulletin, October 2002, NCJ 194066)
*Sheriffs' departments generally operate at the county level.

Percent of Full-Time Sheriffs' Department Employees
Who are Sworn Officers: 2000
National Percent = 56.1% of Employees*

ALPHA ORDER

RANK	STATE	PERCENT
34	Alabama	50.5
NA	Alaska**	NA
48	Arizona	32.1
43	Arkansas	44.6
27	California	55.5
23	Colorado	58.7
2	Connecticut	93.9
15	Delaware	64.5
44	Florida	44.4
21	Georgia	59.3
NA	Hawaii**	NA
40	Idaho	46.2
12	Illinois	69.5
42	Indiana	45.1
32	Iowa	52.0
35	Kansas	49.7
3	Kentucky	83.8
6	Louisiana	81.0
47	Maine	32.6
17	Maryland	63.5
46	Massachusetts	37.5
26	Michigan	55.6
36	Minnesota	48.6
33	Mississippi	51.6
15	Missouri	64.5
45	Montana	43.1
18	Nebraska	61.5
10	Nevada	69.8
28	New Hampshire	54.8
7	New Jersey	76.1
8	New Mexico	74.6
22	New York	59.0
23	North Carolina	58.7
10	North Dakota	69.8
30	Ohio	52.6
41	Oklahoma	45.2
38	Oregon	47.6
4	Pennsylvania	83.1
1	Rhode Island	97.5
14	South Carolina	65.6
25	South Dakota	57.1
31	Tennessee	52.2
39	Texas	47.1
37	Utah	48.1
9	Vermont	72.7
5	Virginia	82.8
28	Washington	54.8
13	West Virginia	66.7
19	Wisconsin	60.0
20	Wyoming	59.4

RANK ORDER

RANK	STATE	PERCENT
1	Rhode Island	97.5
2	Connecticut	93.9
3	Kentucky	83.8
4	Pennsylvania	83.1
5	Virginia	82.8
6	Louisiana	81.0
7	New Jersey	76.1
8	New Mexico	74.6
9	Vermont	72.7
10	Nevada	69.8
10	North Dakota	69.8
12	Illinois	69.5
13	West Virginia	66.7
14	South Carolina	65.6
15	Delaware	64.5
15	Missouri	64.5
17	Maryland	63.5
18	Nebraska	61.5
19	Wisconsin	60.0
20	Wyoming	59.4
21	Georgia	59.3
22	New York	59.0
23	Colorado	58.7
23	North Carolina	58.7
25	South Dakota	57.1
26	Michigan	55.6
27	California	55.5
28	New Hampshire	54.8
28	Washington	54.8
30	Ohio	52.6
31	Tennessee	52.2
32	Iowa	52.0
33	Mississippi	51.6
34	Alabama	50.5
35	Kansas	49.7
36	Minnesota	48.6
37	Utah	48.1
38	Oregon	47.6
39	Texas	47.1
40	Idaho	46.2
41	Oklahoma	45.2
42	Indiana	45.1
43	Arkansas	44.6
44	Florida	44.4
45	Montana	43.1
46	Massachusetts	37.5
47	Maine	32.6
48	Arizona	32.1
NA	Alaska**	NA
NA	Hawaii**	NA
	District of Columbia**	NA

Source: Morgan Quitno Press using data from U.S. Department of Justice, Bureau of Justice Statistics
    "Census of State and Local Law Enforcement Agencies, 2000" (Bulletin, October 2002, NCJ 194066)
*Sheriffs' departments generally operate at the county level.
**Not applicable.

Rate of Full-Time Sworn Officers in Sheriffs' Departments in 2000

National Rate = 59 Officers per 100,000 Population*

ALPHA ORDER				RANK ORDER		
RANK	STATE	RATE		RANK	STATE	RATE
24	Alabama	50		1	Louisiana	231
49	Alaska	0		2	Wyoming	117
36	Arizona	35		3	Virginia	104
27	Arkansas	48		4	Georgia	94
10	California	75		5	Florida	92
13	Colorado	71		6	South Carolina	89
46	Connecticut	10		7	Idaho	79
48	Delaware	3		8	North Carolina	76
5	Florida	92		8	Wisconsin	76
4	Georgia	94		10	California	75
49	Hawaii	0		10	Tennessee	75
7	Idaho	79		12	Illinois	73
12	Illinois	73		13	Colorado	71
28	Indiana	47		14	Montana	70
24	Iowa	50		15	Kansas	67
15	Kansas	67		16	Oregon	62
36	Kentucky	35		17	Mississippi	60
1	Louisiana	231		17	North Dakota	60
41	Maine	24		19	Utah	59
38	Maryland	32		20	New Mexico	57
42	Massachusetts	19		21	Nebraska	53
28	Michigan	47		21	Texas	53
32	Minnesota	46		23	South Dakota	51
17	Mississippi	60		24	Alabama	50
34	Missouri	43		24	Iowa	50
14	Montana	70		24	Nevada	50
21	Nebraska	53		27	Arkansas	48
24	Nevada	50		28	Indiana	47
46	New Hampshire	10		28	Michigan	47
35	New Jersey	38		28	Ohio	47
20	New Mexico	57		28	Washington	47
38	New York	32		32	Minnesota	46
8	North Carolina	76		33	West Virginia	45
17	North Dakota	60		34	Missouri	43
28	Ohio	47		35	New Jersey	38
38	Oklahoma	32		36	Arizona	35
16	Oregon	62		36	Kentucky	35
45	Pennsylvania	12		38	Maryland	32
44	Rhode Island	15		38	New York	32
6	South Carolina	89		38	Oklahoma	32
23	South Dakota	51		41	Maine	24
10	Tennessee	75		42	Massachusetts	19
21	Texas	53		43	Vermont	17
19	Utah	59		44	Rhode Island	15
43	Vermont	17		45	Pennsylvania	12
3	Virginia	104		46	Connecticut	10
28	Washington	47		46	New Hampshire	10
33	West Virginia	45		48	Delaware	3
8	Wisconsin	76		49	Alaska	0
2	Wyoming	117		49	Hawaii	0
					District of Columbia	0

Source: U.S. Department of Justice, Bureau of Justice Statistics
Source: U.S. Department of Justice, Bureau of Justice Statistics
"Census of State and Local Law Enforcement Agencies, 2000" (Bulletin, October 2002, NCJ 194066)
*Sheriffs' departments generally operate at the county level.

Full-Time Employees in Sheriffs' Departments in 2000

National Total = 293,823 Employees*

ALPHA ORDER

RANK	STATE	EMPLOYEES	% of USA
21	Alabama	4,379	1.5%
49	Alaska	0	0.0%
15	Arizona	5,490	1.9%
27	Arkansas	2,882	1.0%
1	California	45,706	15.6%
17	Colorado	5,229	1.8%
44	Connecticut	358	0.1%
48	Delaware	31	0.0%
2	Florida	33,303	11.3%
5	Georgia	12,990	4.4%
49	Hawaii	0	0.0%
32	Idaho	2,217	0.8%
4	Illinois	13,051	4.4%
14	Indiana	6,388	2.2%
28	Iowa	2,805	1.0%
24	Kansas	3,627	1.2%
34	Kentucky	1,677	0.6%
6	Louisiana	12,745	4.3%
41	Maine	947	0.3%
30	Maryland	2,696	0.9%
26	Massachusetts	3,219	1.1%
11	Michigan	8,351	2.8%
19	Minnesota	4,704	1.6%
25	Mississippi	3,291	1.1%
23	Missouri	3,756	1.3%
36	Montana	1,458	0.5%
35	Nebraska	1,465	0.5%
37	Nevada	1,444	0.5%
45	New Hampshire	219	0.1%
22	New Jersey	4,206	1.4%
38	New Mexico	1,392	0.5%
8	New York	10,208	3.5%
7	North Carolina	10,457	3.6%
43	North Dakota	550	0.2%
9	Ohio	10,199	3.5%
31	Oklahoma	2,415	0.8%
20	Oregon	4,437	1.5%
33	Pennsylvania	1,719	0.6%
46	Rhode Island	163	0.1%
16	South Carolina	5,439	1.9%
42	South Dakota	679	0.2%
12	Tennessee	8,126	2.8%
3	Texas	23,621	8.0%
29	Utah	2,728	0.9%
47	Vermont	143	0.0%
10	Virginia	8,914	3.0%
18	Washington	5,028	1.7%
39	West Virginia	1,220	0.4%
13	Wisconsin	6,782	2.3%
40	Wyoming	969	0.3%

RANK ORDER

RANK	STATE	EMPLOYEES	% of USA
1	California	45,706	15.6%
2	Florida	33,303	11.3%
3	Texas	23,621	8.0%
4	Illinois	13,051	4.4%
5	Georgia	12,990	4.4%
6	Louisiana	12,745	4.3%
7	North Carolina	10,457	3.6%
8	New York	10,208	3.5%
9	Ohio	10,199	3.5%
10	Virginia	8,914	3.0%
11	Michigan	8,351	2.8%
12	Tennessee	8,126	2.8%
13	Wisconsin	6,782	2.3%
14	Indiana	6,388	2.2%
15	Arizona	5,490	1.9%
16	South Carolina	5,439	1.9%
17	Colorado	5,229	1.8%
18	Washington	5,028	1.7%
19	Minnesota	4,704	1.6%
20	Oregon	4,437	1.5%
21	Alabama	4,379	1.5%
22	New Jersey	4,206	1.4%
23	Missouri	3,756	1.3%
24	Kansas	3,627	1.2%
25	Mississippi	3,291	1.1%
26	Massachusetts	3,219	1.1%
27	Arkansas	2,882	1.0%
28	Iowa	2,805	1.0%
29	Utah	2,728	0.9%
30	Maryland	2,696	0.9%
31	Oklahoma	2,415	0.8%
32	Idaho	2,217	0.8%
33	Pennsylvania	1,719	0.6%
34	Kentucky	1,677	0.6%
35	Nebraska	1,465	0.5%
36	Montana	1,458	0.5%
37	Nevada	1,444	0.5%
38	New Mexico	1,392	0.5%
39	West Virginia	1,220	0.4%
40	Wyoming	969	0.3%
41	Maine	947	0.3%
42	South Dakota	679	0.2%
43	North Dakota	550	0.2%
44	Connecticut	358	0.1%
45	New Hampshire	219	0.1%
46	Rhode Island	163	0.1%
47	Vermont	143	0.0%
48	Delaware	31	0.0%
49	Alaska	0	0.0%
49	Hawaii	0	0.0%
	District of Columbia	0	0.0%

Source: U.S. Department of Justice, Bureau of Justice Statistics
    "Census of State and Local Law Enforcement Agencies, 2000" (Bulletin, October 2002, NCJ 194066)
*Sheriffs' departments generally operate at the county level.

Special Police Agencies in 2000

National Total = 1,376 Agencies*

ALPHA ORDER

RANK	STATE	AGENCIES	% of USA
13	Alabama	32	2.3%
38	Alaska	7	0.5%
19	Arizona	26	1.9%
23	Arkansas	22	1.6%
2	California	117	8.5%
27	Colorado	18	1.3%
32	Connecticut	14	1.0%
40	Delaware	6	0.4%
18	Florida	30	2.2%
6	Georgia	46	3.3%
46	Hawaii	3	0.2%
46	Idaho	3	0.2%
5	Illinois	54	3.9%
22	Indiana	23	1.7%
36	Iowa	8	0.6%
26	Kansas	21	1.5%
29	Kentucky	16	1.2%
13	Louisiana	32	2.3%
38	Maine	7	0.5%
8	Maryland	44	3.2%
13	Massachusetts	32	2.3%
16	Michigan	31	2.3%
32	Minnesota	14	1.0%
11	Mississippi	33	2.4%
23	Missouri	22	1.6%
36	Montana	8	0.6%
46	Nebraska	3	0.2%
28	Nevada	17	1.2%
46	New Hampshire	3	0.2%
7	New Jersey	45	3.3%
34	New Mexico	13	0.9%
4	New York	66	4.8%
11	North Carolina	33	2.4%
40	North Dakota	6	0.4%
8	Ohio	44	3.2%
16	Oklahoma	31	2.3%
40	Oregon	6	0.4%
3	Pennsylvania	85	6.2%
40	Rhode Island	6	0.4%
20	South Carolina	25	1.8%
44	South Dakota	5	0.4%
21	Tennessee	24	1.7%
1	Texas	185	13.4%
29	Utah	16	1.2%
50	Vermont	2	0.1%
10	Virginia	36	2.6%
35	Washington	12	0.9%
31	West Virginia	15	1.1%
23	Wisconsin	22	1.6%
44	Wyoming	5	0.4%

RANK ORDER

RANK	STATE	AGENCIES	% of USA
1	Texas	185	13.4%
2	California	117	8.5%
3	Pennsylvania	85	6.2%
4	New York	66	4.8%
5	Illinois	54	3.9%
6	Georgia	46	3.3%
7	New Jersey	45	3.3%
8	Maryland	44	3.2%
8	Ohio	44	3.2%
10	Virginia	36	2.6%
11	Mississippi	33	2.4%
11	North Carolina	33	2.4%
13	Alabama	32	2.3%
13	Louisiana	32	2.3%
13	Massachusetts	32	2.3%
16	Michigan	31	2.3%
16	Oklahoma	31	2.3%
18	Florida	30	2.2%
19	Arizona	26	1.9%
20	South Carolina	25	1.8%
21	Tennessee	24	1.7%
22	Indiana	23	1.7%
23	Arkansas	22	1.6%
23	Missouri	22	1.6%
23	Wisconsin	22	1.6%
26	Kansas	21	1.5%
27	Colorado	18	1.3%
28	Nevada	17	1.2%
29	Kentucky	16	1.2%
29	Utah	16	1.2%
31	West Virginia	15	1.1%
32	Connecticut	14	1.0%
32	Minnesota	14	1.0%
34	New Mexico	13	0.9%
35	Washington	12	0.9%
36	Iowa	8	0.6%
36	Montana	8	0.6%
38	Alaska	7	0.5%
38	Maine	7	0.5%
40	Delaware	6	0.4%
40	North Dakota	6	0.4%
40	Oregon	6	0.4%
40	Rhode Island	6	0.4%
44	South Dakota	5	0.4%
44	Wyoming	5	0.4%
46	Hawaii	3	0.2%
46	Idaho	3	0.2%
46	Nebraska	3	0.2%
46	New Hampshire	3	0.2%
50	Vermont	2	0.1%
	District of Columbia	2	0.1%

Source: U.S. Department of Justice, Bureau of Justice Statistics
"Census of State and Local Law Enforcement Agencies, 2000" (Bulletin, October 2002, NCJ 194066)
*Agencies with special jurisdictions or special enforcement responsibilities.

Full-Time Sworn Officers in Special Police Departments in 2000

National Total = 43,413 Officers*

ALPHA ORDER

RANK	STATE	OFFICERS	% of USA
20	Alabama	728	1.7%
40	Alaska	217	0.5%
25	Arizona	560	1.3%
22	Arkansas	638	1.5%
3	California	3,949	9.1%
26	Colorado	555	1.3%
36	Connecticut	264	0.6%
41	Delaware	182	0.4%
6	Florida	1,989	4.6%
8	Georgia	1,692	3.9%
32	Hawaii	309	0.7%
44	Idaho	154	0.4%
11	Illinois	1,233	2.8%
21	Indiana	723	1.7%
38	Iowa	245	0.6%
28	Kansas	433	1.0%
34	Kentucky	283	0.7%
12	Louisiana	946	2.2%
39	Maine	230	0.5%
4	Maryland	2,255	5.2%
16	Massachusetts	827	1.9%
14	Michigan	886	2.0%
29	Minnesota	424	1.0%
24	Mississippi	568	1.3%
19	Missouri	755	1.7%
42	Montana	161	0.4%
48	Nebraska	83	0.2%
23	Nevada	614	1.4%
49	New Hampshire	76	0.2%
5	New Jersey	2,247	5.2%
31	New Mexico	354	0.8%
1	New York	4,135	9.5%
15	North Carolina	874	2.0%
45	North Dakota	102	0.2%
10	Ohio	1,378	3.2%
27	Oklahoma	502	1.2%
47	Oregon	92	0.2%
7	Pennsylvania	1,880	4.3%
43	Rhode Island	155	0.4%
17	South Carolina	812	1.9%
35	South Dakota	271	0.6%
13	Tennessee	945	2.2%
2	Texas	4,071	9.4%
33	Utah	290	0.7%
50	Vermont	55	0.1%
9	Virginia	1,385	3.2%
30	Washington	404	0.9%
37	West Virginia	251	0.6%
18	Wisconsin	781	1.8%
46	Wyoming	99	0.2%

RANK ORDER

RANK	STATE	OFFICERS	% of USA
1	New York	4,135	9.5%
2	Texas	4,071	9.4%
3	California	3,949	9.1%
4	Maryland	2,255	5.2%
5	New Jersey	2,247	5.2%
6	Florida	1,989	4.6%
7	Pennsylvania	1,880	4.3%
8	Georgia	1,692	3.9%
9	Virginia	1,385	3.2%
10	Ohio	1,378	3.2%
11	Illinois	1,233	2.8%
12	Louisiana	946	2.2%
13	Tennessee	945	2.2%
14	Michigan	886	2.0%
15	North Carolina	874	2.0%
16	Massachusetts	827	1.9%
17	South Carolina	812	1.9%
18	Wisconsin	781	1.8%
19	Missouri	755	1.7%
20	Alabama	728	1.7%
21	Indiana	723	1.7%
22	Arkansas	638	1.5%
23	Nevada	614	1.4%
24	Mississippi	568	1.3%
25	Arizona	560	1.3%
26	Colorado	555	1.3%
27	Oklahoma	502	1.2%
28	Kansas	433	1.0%
29	Minnesota	424	1.0%
30	Washington	404	0.9%
31	New Mexico	354	0.8%
32	Hawaii	309	0.7%
33	Utah	290	0.7%
34	Kentucky	283	0.7%
35	South Dakota	271	0.6%
36	Connecticut	264	0.6%
37	West Virginia	251	0.6%
38	Iowa	245	0.6%
39	Maine	230	0.5%
40	Alaska	217	0.5%
41	Delaware	182	0.4%
42	Montana	161	0.4%
43	Rhode Island	155	0.4%
44	Idaho	154	0.4%
45	North Dakota	102	0.2%
46	Wyoming	99	0.2%
47	Oregon	92	0.2%
48	Nebraska	83	0.2%
49	New Hampshire	76	0.2%
50	Vermont	55	0.1%
	District of Columbia	351	0.8%

Source: U.S. Department of Justice, Bureau of Justice Statistics
"Census of State and Local Law Enforcement Agencies, 2000" (Bulletin, October 2002, NCJ 194066)
*Agencies with special jurisdictions or special enforcement responsibilities.

Percent of Full-Time Special Police Department Employees
Who are Sworn Officers: 2000
National Percent = 62.3% of Employees*

ALPHA ORDER

RANK	STATE	PERCENT
25	Alabama	71.0
41	Alaska	56.4
49	Arizona	33.7
3	Arkansas	86.8
46	California	49.7
37	Colorado	62.1
16	Connecticut	78.3
27	Delaware	70.8
25	Florida	71.0
33	Georgia	65.4
12	Hawaii	80.3
1	Idaho	95.7
14	Illinois	79.9
6	Indiana	84.0
21	Iowa	76.3
41	Kansas	56.4
40	Kentucky	59.1
37	Louisiana	62.1
7	Maine	83.3
29	Maryland	69.4
18	Massachusetts	77.6
34	Michigan	63.9
15	Minnesota	79.8
30	Mississippi	68.8
49	Missouri	33.7
32	Montana	67.9
24	Nebraska	72.2
44	Nevada	54.6
18	New Hampshire	77.6
45	New Jersey	51.2
43	New Mexico	56.0
8	New York	83.2
17	North Carolina	78.2
39	North Dakota	60.7
47	Ohio	45.5
35	Oklahoma	63.1
9	Oregon	82.9
48	Pennsylvania	42.1
23	Rhode Island	72.4
10	South Carolina	82.2
22	South Dakota	72.8
31	Tennessee	68.1
36	Texas	62.7
20	Utah	76.5
11	Vermont	80.9
28	Virginia	70.0
12	Washington	80.3
2	West Virginia	89.6
5	Wisconsin	84.5
4	Wyoming	85.3

RANK ORDER

RANK	STATE	PERCENT
1	Idaho	95.7
2	West Virginia	89.6
3	Arkansas	86.8
4	Wyoming	85.3
5	Wisconsin	84.5
6	Indiana	84.0
7	Maine	83.3
8	New York	83.2
9	Oregon	82.9
10	South Carolina	82.2
11	Vermont	80.9
12	Hawaii	80.3
12	Washington	80.3
14	Illinois	79.9
15	Minnesota	79.8
16	Connecticut	78.3
17	North Carolina	78.2
18	Massachusetts	77.6
18	New Hampshire	77.6
20	Utah	76.5
21	Iowa	76.3
22	South Dakota	72.8
23	Rhode Island	72.4
24	Nebraska	72.2
25	Alabama	71.0
25	Florida	71.0
27	Delaware	70.8
28	Virginia	70.0
29	Maryland	69.4
30	Mississippi	68.8
31	Tennessee	68.1
32	Montana	67.9
33	Georgia	65.4
34	Michigan	63.9
35	Oklahoma	63.1
36	Texas	62.7
37	Colorado	62.1
37	Louisiana	62.1
39	North Dakota	60.7
40	Kentucky	59.1
41	Alaska	56.4
41	Kansas	56.4
43	New Mexico	56.0
44	Nevada	54.6
45	New Jersey	51.2
46	California	49.7
47	Ohio	45.5
48	Pennsylvania	42.1
49	Arizona	33.7
49	Missouri	33.7

District of Columbia	78.7

*Source: Morgan Quitno Press using data from U.S. Department of Justice, Bureau of Justice Statistics
"Census of State and Local Law Enforcement Agencies, 2000" (Bulletin, October 2002, NCJ 194066)
Agencies with special jurisdictions or special enforcement responsibilities.

Rate of Full-Time Sworn Officers in Special Police Departments in 2000

National Rate = 15 Officers per 100,000 Population*

ALPHA ORDER				RANK ORDER		
RANK	STATE	RATE		RANK	STATE	RATE
21	Alabama	16		1	Maryland	43
3	Alaska	35		2	South Dakota	36
38	Arizona	11		3	Alaska	35
7	Arkansas	24		4	Nevada	31
33	California	12		5	New Jersey	27
29	Colorado	13		6	Hawaii	26
44	Connecticut	8		7	Arkansas	24
8	Delaware	23		8	Delaware	23
33	Florida	12		8	Wyoming	23
11	Georgia	21		10	New York	22
6	Hawaii	26		11	Georgia	21
33	Idaho	12		11	Louisiana	21
40	Illinois	10		13	Mississippi	20
33	Indiana	12		13	South Carolina	20
44	Iowa	8		13	Texas	20
21	Kansas	16		13	Virginia	20
46	Kentucky	7		17	New Mexico	19
11	Louisiana	21		18	Maine	18
18	Maine	18		18	Montana	18
1	Maryland	43		20	Tennessee	17
29	Massachusetts	13		21	Alabama	16
41	Michigan	9		21	Kansas	16
41	Minnesota	9		21	North Dakota	16
13	Mississippi	20		24	Oklahoma	15
29	Missouri	13		24	Pennsylvania	15
18	Montana	18		24	Rhode Island	15
49	Nebraska	5		24	Wisconsin	15
4	Nevada	31		28	West Virginia	14
48	New Hampshire	6		29	Colorado	13
5	New Jersey	27		29	Massachusetts	13
17	New Mexico	19		29	Missouri	13
10	New York	22		29	Utah	13
38	North Carolina	11		33	California	12
21	North Dakota	16		33	Florida	12
33	Ohio	12		33	Idaho	12
24	Oklahoma	15		33	Indiana	12
50	Oregon	3		33	Ohio	12
24	Pennsylvania	15		38	Arizona	11
24	Rhode Island	15		38	North Carolina	11
13	South Carolina	20		40	Illinois	10
2	South Dakota	36		41	Michigan	9
20	Tennessee	17		41	Minnesota	9
13	Texas	20		41	Vermont	9
29	Utah	13		44	Connecticut	8
41	Vermont	9		44	Iowa	8
13	Virginia	20		46	Kentucky	7
46	Washington	7		46	Washington	7
28	West Virginia	14		48	New Hampshire	6
24	Wisconsin	15		49	Nebraska	5
8	Wyoming	23		50	Oregon	3

District of Columbia   61

Source: U.S. Department of Justice, Bureau of Justice Statistics
    "Census of State and Local Law Enforcement Agencies, 2000" (Bulletin, October 2002, NCJ 194066)
*Agencies with special jurisdictions or special enforcement responsibilities.

Full-Time Employees in Special Police Departments in 2000

National Total = 69,650 Employees*

ALPHA ORDER

RANK	STATE	EMPLOYEES	% of USA
20	Alabama	1,026	1.5%
33	Alaska	385	0.6%
12	Arizona	1,664	2.4%
28	Arkansas	735	1.1%
1	California	7,953	11.4%
23	Colorado	894	1.3%
37	Connecticut	337	0.5%
41	Delaware	257	0.4%
8	Florida	2,802	4.0%
9	Georgia	2,589	3.7%
33	Hawaii	385	0.6%
45	Idaho	161	0.2%
13	Illinois	1,544	2.2%
24	Indiana	861	1.2%
38	Iowa	321	0.5%
27	Kansas	768	1.1%
32	Kentucky	479	0.7%
14	Louisiana	1,524	2.2%
40	Maine	276	0.4%
6	Maryland	3,250	4.7%
19	Massachusetts	1,066	1.5%
16	Michigan	1,387	2.0%
30	Minnesota	531	0.8%
25	Mississippi	825	1.2%
10	Missouri	2,239	3.2%
42	Montana	237	0.3%
47	Nebraska	115	0.2%
17	Nevada	1,124	1.6%
49	New Hampshire	98	0.1%
5	New Jersey	4,385	6.3%
29	New Mexico	632	0.9%
3	New York	4,970	7.1%
18	North Carolina	1,117	1.6%
44	North Dakota	168	0.2%
7	Ohio	3,026	4.3%
26	Oklahoma	795	1.1%
48	Oregon	111	0.2%
4	Pennsylvania	4,469	6.4%
43	Rhode Island	214	0.3%
21	South Carolina	988	1.4%
36	South Dakota	372	0.5%
15	Tennessee	1,388	2.0%
2	Texas	6,488	9.3%
35	Utah	379	0.5%
50	Vermont	68	0.1%
11	Virginia	1,978	2.8%
31	Washington	503	0.7%
39	West Virginia	280	0.4%
22	Wisconsin	924	1.3%
46	Wyoming	116	0.2%

RANK ORDER

RANK	STATE	EMPLOYEES	% of USA
1	California	7,953	11.4%
2	Texas	6,488	9.3%
3	New York	4,970	7.1%
4	Pennsylvania	4,469	6.4%
5	New Jersey	4,385	6.3%
6	Maryland	3,250	4.7%
7	Ohio	3,026	4.3%
8	Florida	2,802	4.0%
9	Georgia	2,589	3.7%
10	Missouri	2,239	3.2%
11	Virginia	1,978	2.8%
12	Arizona	1,664	2.4%
13	Illinois	1,544	2.2%
14	Louisiana	1,524	2.2%
15	Tennessee	1,388	2.0%
16	Michigan	1,387	2.0%
17	Nevada	1,124	1.6%
18	North Carolina	1,117	1.6%
19	Massachusetts	1,066	1.5%
20	Alabama	1,026	1.5%
21	South Carolina	988	1.4%
22	Wisconsin	924	1.3%
23	Colorado	894	1.3%
24	Indiana	861	1.2%
25	Mississippi	825	1.2%
26	Oklahoma	795	1.1%
27	Kansas	768	1.1%
28	Arkansas	735	1.1%
29	New Mexico	632	0.9%
30	Minnesota	531	0.8%
31	Washington	503	0.7%
32	Kentucky	479	0.7%
33	Alaska	385	0.6%
33	Hawaii	385	0.6%
35	Utah	379	0.5%
36	South Dakota	372	0.5%
37	Connecticut	337	0.5%
38	Iowa	321	0.5%
39	West Virginia	280	0.4%
40	Maine	276	0.4%
41	Delaware	257	0.4%
42	Montana	237	0.3%
43	Rhode Island	214	0.3%
44	North Dakota	168	0.2%
45	Idaho	161	0.2%
46	Wyoming	116	0.2%
47	Nebraska	115	0.2%
48	Oregon	111	0.2%
49	New Hampshire	98	0.1%
50	Vermont	68	0.1%
	District of Columbia	446	0.6%

Source: U.S. Department of Justice, Bureau of Justice Statistics
"Census of State and Local Law Enforcement Agencies, 2000" (Bulletin, October 2002, NCJ 194066)
*Agencies with special jurisdictions or special enforcement responsibilities.

Law Enforcement Officers Feloniously Killed in 2004

National Total = 54 Officers*

ALPHA ORDER

RANK	STATE	OFFICERS	% of USA
2	Alabama	5	9.3%
23	Alaska	0	0.0%
11	Arizona	2	3.7%
23	Arkansas	0	0.0%
2	California	5	9.3%
23	Colorado	0	0.0%
13	Connecticut	1	1.9%
23	Delaware	0	0.0%
6	Florida	3	5.6%
13	Georgia	1	1.9%
23	Hawaii	0	0.0%
23	Idaho	0	0.0%
13	Illinois	1	1.9%
11	Indiana	2	3.7%
23	Iowa	0	0.0%
23	Kansas	0	0.0%
23	Kentucky	0	0.0%
1	Louisiana	6	11.1%
23	Maine	0	0.0%
13	Maryland	1	1.9%
23	Massachusetts	0	0.0%
4	Michigan	4	7.4%
23	Minnesota	0	0.0%
23	Mississippi	0	0.0%
13	Missouri	1	1.9%
23	Montana	0	0.0%
23	Nebraska	0	0.0%
23	Nevada	0	0.0%
23	New Hampshire	0	0.0%
23	New Jersey	0	0.0%
13	New Mexico	1	1.9%
4	New York	4	7.4%
6	North Carolina	3	5.6%
23	North Dakota	0	0.0%
13	Ohio	1	1.9%
23	Oklahoma	0	0.0%
23	Oregon	0	0.0%
6	Pennsylvania	3	5.6%
23	Rhode Island	0	0.0%
13	South Carolina	1	1.9%
23	South Dakota	0	0.0%
6	Tennessee	3	5.6%
6	Texas	3	5.6%
23	Utah	0	0.0%
23	Vermont	0	0.0%
23	Virginia	0	0.0%
13	Washington	1	1.9%
23	West Virginia	0	0.0%
13	Wisconsin	1	1.9%
23	Wyoming	0	0.0%

RANK ORDER

RANK	STATE	OFFICERS	% of USA
1	Louisiana	6	11.1%
2	Alabama	5	9.3%
2	California	5	9.3%
4	Michigan	4	7.4%
4	New York	4	7.4%
6	Florida	3	5.6%
6	North Carolina	3	5.6%
6	Pennsylvania	3	5.6%
6	Tennessee	3	5.6%
6	Texas	3	5.6%
11	Arizona	2	3.7%
11	Indiana	2	3.7%
13	Connecticut	1	1.9%
13	Georgia	1	1.9%
13	Illinois	1	1.9%
13	Maryland	1	1.9%
13	Missouri	1	1.9%
13	New Mexico	1	1.9%
13	Ohio	1	1.9%
13	South Carolina	1	1.9%
13	Washington	1	1.9%
13	Wisconsin	1	1.9%
23	Alaska	0	0.0%
23	Arkansas	0	0.0%
23	Colorado	0	0.0%
23	Delaware	0	0.0%
23	Hawaii	0	0.0%
23	Idaho	0	0.0%
23	Iowa	0	0.0%
23	Kansas	0	0.0%
23	Kentucky	0	0.0%
23	Maine	0	0.0%
23	Massachusetts	0	0.0%
23	Minnesota	0	0.0%
23	Mississippi	0	0.0%
23	Montana	0	0.0%
23	Nebraska	0	0.0%
23	Nevada	0	0.0%
23	New Hampshire	0	0.0%
23	New Jersey	0	0.0%
23	North Dakota	0	0.0%
23	Oklahoma	0	0.0%
23	Oregon	0	0.0%
23	Rhode Island	0	0.0%
23	South Dakota	0	0.0%
23	Utah	0	0.0%
23	Vermont	0	0.0%
23	Virginia	0	0.0%
23	West Virginia	0	0.0%
23	Wyoming	0	0.0%
	District of Columbia	1	1.9%

Source: Federal Bureau of Investigation
    "Law Enforcement Officers Killed and Assaulted 2004" (http://www.fbi.gov/ucr/killed/2004/table1.htm)
*Total does not include two officers killed in Puerto Rico or one killed in the U.S. Virgin Islands.

Law Enforcement Officers Feloniously Killed: 1995 to 2004

National Total = 559 Officers*

ALPHA ORDER

RANK	STATE	OFFICERS	% of USA
13	Alabama	17	3.0%
28	Alaska	7	1.3%
13	Arizona	17	3.0%
22	Arkansas	10	1.8%
1	California	56	10.0%
29	Colorado	6	1.1%
38	Connecticut	2	0.4%
45	Delaware	0	0.0%
8	Florida	20	3.6%
3	Georgia	25	4.5%
38	Hawaii	2	0.4%
33	Idaho	4	0.7%
10	Illinois	18	3.2%
15	Indiana	16	2.9%
45	Iowa	0	0.0%
26	Kansas	8	1.4%
26	Kentucky	8	1.4%
5	Louisiana	22	3.9%
45	Maine	0	0.0%
18	Maryland	13	2.3%
35	Massachusetts	3	0.5%
10	Michigan	18	3.2%
30	Minnesota	5	0.9%
16	Mississippi	14	2.5%
24	Missouri	9	1.6%
42	Montana	1	0.2%
38	Nebraska	2	0.4%
30	Nevada	5	0.9%
35	New Hampshire	3	0.5%
24	New Jersey	9	1.6%
30	New Mexico	5	0.9%
5	New York	22	3.9%
3	North Carolina	25	4.5%
42	North Dakota	1	0.2%
9	Ohio	19	3.4%
18	Oklahoma	13	2.3%
35	Oregon	3	0.5%
16	Pennsylvania	14	2.5%
45	Rhode Island	0	0.0%
10	South Carolina	18	3.2%
45	South Dakota	0	0.0%
7	Tennessee	21	3.8%
2	Texas	48	8.6%
33	Utah	4	0.7%
45	Vermont	0	0.0%
18	Virginia	13	2.3%
22	Washington	10	1.8%
38	West Virginia	2	0.4%
21	Wisconsin	11	2.0%
42	Wyoming	1	0.2%

RANK ORDER

RANK	STATE	OFFICERS	% of USA
1	California	56	10.0%
2	Texas	48	8.6%
3	Georgia	25	4.5%
3	North Carolina	25	4.5%
5	Louisiana	22	3.9%
5	New York	22	3.9%
7	Tennessee	21	3.8%
8	Florida	20	3.6%
9	Ohio	19	3.4%
10	Illinois	18	3.2%
10	Michigan	18	3.2%
10	South Carolina	18	3.2%
13	Alabama	17	3.0%
13	Arizona	17	3.0%
15	Indiana	16	2.9%
16	Mississippi	14	2.5%
16	Pennsylvania	14	2.5%
18	Maryland	13	2.3%
18	Oklahoma	13	2.3%
18	Virginia	13	2.3%
21	Wisconsin	11	2.0%
22	Arkansas	10	1.8%
22	Washington	10	1.8%
24	Missouri	9	1.6%
24	New Jersey	9	1.6%
26	Kansas	8	1.4%
26	Kentucky	8	1.4%
28	Alaska	7	1.3%
29	Colorado	6	1.1%
30	Minnesota	5	0.9%
30	Nevada	5	0.9%
30	New Mexico	5	0.9%
33	Idaho	4	0.7%
33	Utah	4	0.7%
35	Massachusetts	3	0.5%
35	New Hampshire	3	0.5%
35	Oregon	3	0.5%
38	Connecticut	2	0.4%
38	Hawaii	2	0.4%
38	Nebraska	2	0.4%
38	West Virginia	2	0.4%
42	Montana	1	0.2%
42	North Dakota	1	0.2%
42	Wyoming	1	0.2%
45	Delaware	0	0.0%
45	Iowa	0	0.0%
45	Maine	0	0.0%
45	Rhode Island	0	0.0%
45	South Dakota	0	0.0%
45	Vermont	0	0.0%
	District of Columbia	9	1.6%

Source: Federal Bureau of Investigation
"Law Enforcement Officers Killed and Assaulted 2004" (http://www.fbi.gov/ucr/killed/2004/table1.htm)
Total does not include 35 officers killed in U.S. territories (33 officers killed in Puerto Rico, one in the Mariana Islands and one in U.S. Virgin Islands). Total also does not include the 72 deaths that resulted from the events of September 11, 2001.

Law Enforcement Officers Assaulted in 2004

National Total = 59,373 Officers*

ALPHA ORDER

RANK	STATE	OFFICERS	% of USA
30	Alabama	345	0.6%
38	Alaska	217	0.4%
9	Arizona	2,067	3.5%
42	Arkansas	138	0.2%
2	California	7,330	12.3%
20	Colorado	815	1.4%
29	Connecticut	400	0.7%
31	Delaware	330	0.6%
1	Florida	8,717	14.7%
21	Georgia	791	1.3%
32	Hawaii	324	0.5%
36	Idaho	282	0.5%
NA	Illinois**	NA	NA
14	Indiana	1,198	2.0%
26	Iowa	484	0.8%
15	Kansas	1,118	1.9%
23	Kentucky	733	1.2%
10	Louisiana	1,907	3.2%
35	Maine	285	0.5%
4	Maryland	3,864	6.5%
41	Massachusetts	172	0.3%
13	Michigan	1,229	2.1%
43	Minnesota	65	0.1%
34	Mississippi	310	0.5%
7	Missouri	2,353	4.0%
44	Montana	63	0.1%
40	Nebraska	180	0.3%
28	Nevada	458	0.8%
39	New Hampshire	204	0.3%
5	New Jersey	2,968	5.0%
25	New Mexico	672	1.1%
24	New York	705	1.2%
11	North Carolina	1,741	2.9%
46	North Dakota	52	0.1%
22	Ohio	742	1.2%
18	Oklahoma	898	1.5%
33	Oregon	322	0.5%
6	Pennsylvania	2,622	4.4%
27	Rhode Island	465	0.8%
17	South Carolina	981	1.7%
47	South Dakota	42	0.1%
8	Tennessee	2,245	3.8%
3	Texas	4,844	8.2%
37	Utah	254	0.4%
NA	Vermont**	NA	NA
12	Virginia	1,358	2.3%
16	Washington	1,101	1.9%
NA	West Virginia**	NA	NA
19	Wisconsin	883	1.5%
45	Wyoming	57	0.1%

RANK ORDER

RANK	STATE	OFFICERS	% of USA
1	Florida	8,717	14.7%
2	California	7,330	12.3%
3	Texas	4,844	8.2%
4	Maryland	3,864	6.5%
5	New Jersey	2,968	5.0%
6	Pennsylvania	2,622	4.4%
7	Missouri	2,353	4.0%
8	Tennessee	2,245	3.8%
9	Arizona	2,067	3.5%
10	Louisiana	1,907	3.2%
11	North Carolina	1,741	2.9%
12	Virginia	1,358	2.3%
13	Michigan	1,229	2.1%
14	Indiana	1,198	2.0%
15	Kansas	1,118	1.9%
16	Washington	1,101	1.9%
17	South Carolina	981	1.7%
18	Oklahoma	898	1.5%
19	Wisconsin	883	1.5%
20	Colorado	815	1.4%
21	Georgia	791	1.3%
22	Ohio	742	1.2%
23	Kentucky	733	1.2%
24	New York	705	1.2%
25	New Mexico	672	1.1%
26	Iowa	484	0.8%
27	Rhode Island	465	0.8%
28	Nevada	458	0.8%
29	Connecticut	400	0.7%
30	Alabama	345	0.6%
31	Delaware	330	0.6%
32	Hawaii	324	0.5%
33	Oregon	322	0.5%
34	Mississippi	310	0.5%
35	Maine	285	0.5%
36	Idaho	282	0.5%
37	Utah	254	0.4%
38	Alaska	217	0.4%
39	New Hampshire	204	0.3%
40	Nebraska	180	0.3%
41	Massachusetts	172	0.3%
42	Arkansas	138	0.2%
43	Minnesota	65	0.1%
44	Montana	63	0.1%
45	Wyoming	57	0.1%
46	North Dakota	52	0.1%
47	South Dakota	42	0.1%
NA	Illinois**	NA	NA
NA	Vermont**	NA	NA
NA	West Virginia**	NA	NA
	District of Columbia**	NA	NA

Source: Federal Bureau of Investigation
   "Law Enforcement Officers Killed and Assaulted 2004" (http://www.fbi.gov/ucr/killed/2004/table69.htm)
*Figures based on reporting agencies for each state. Assaulted includes by firearm, knife, other dangerous weapons or personal weapons (e.g. fists).
**Not available.

Rate of Law Enforcement Officers Assaulted in 2004

National Rate = 26.3 Officers Assaulted per 100,000 Population*

ALPHA ORDER

RANK	STATE	RATE
44	Alabama	8.7
13	Alaska	33.9
10	Arizona	38.0
34	Arkansas	16.1
20	California	23.5
26	Colorado	19.1
39	Connecticut	11.5
7	Delaware	43.8
4	Florida	50.1
28	Georgia	18.5
14	Hawaii	29.4
24	Idaho	20.4
NA	Illinois**	NA
17	Indiana	24.0
33	Iowa	16.6
3	Kansas	54.0
18	Kentucky	23.8
2	Louisiana	54.6
22	Maine	21.7
1	Maryland	69.6
35	Massachusetts	14.4
36	Michigan	12.7
47	Minnesota	1.5
31	Mississippi	17.3
5	Missouri	47.3
42	Montana	10.0
40	Nebraska	11.3
25	Nevada	19.7
21	New Hampshire	22.3
11	New Jersey	35.6
6	New Mexico	45.0
45	New York	7.4
15	North Carolina	26.9
43	North Dakota	8.9
30	Ohio	17.4
16	Oklahoma	25.5
41	Oregon	10.6
12	Pennsylvania	34.5
8	Rhode Island	43.3
19	South Carolina	23.7
46	South Dakota	7.2
9	Tennessee	38.4
22	Texas	21.7
37	Utah	11.6
NA	Vermont**	NA
27	Virginia	18.6
29	Washington	18.0
NA	West Virginia**	NA
32	Wisconsin	17.2
37	Wyoming	11.6

RANK ORDER

RANK	STATE	RATE
1	Maryland	69.6
2	Louisiana	54.6
3	Kansas	54.0
4	Florida	50.1
5	Missouri	47.3
6	New Mexico	45.0
7	Delaware	43.8
8	Rhode Island	43.3
9	Tennessee	38.4
10	Arizona	38.0
11	New Jersey	35.6
12	Pennsylvania	34.5
13	Alaska	33.9
14	Hawaii	29.4
15	North Carolina	26.9
16	Oklahoma	25.5
17	Indiana	24.0
18	Kentucky	23.8
19	South Carolina	23.7
20	California	23.5
21	New Hampshire	22.3
22	Maine	21.7
22	Texas	21.7
24	Idaho	20.4
25	Nevada	19.7
26	Colorado	19.1
27	Virginia	18.6
28	Georgia	18.5
29	Washington	18.0
30	Ohio	17.4
31	Mississippi	17.3
32	Wisconsin	17.2
33	Iowa	16.6
34	Arkansas	16.1
35	Massachusetts	14.4
36	Michigan	12.7
37	Utah	11.6
37	Wyoming	11.6
39	Connecticut	11.5
40	Nebraska	11.3
41	Oregon	10.6
42	Montana	10.0
43	North Dakota	8.9
44	Alabama	8.7
45	New York	7.4
46	South Dakota	7.2
47	Minnesota	1.5
NA	Illinois**	NA
NA	Vermont**	NA
NA	West Virginia**	NA
	District of Columbia**	NA

Source: Morgan Quitno Press using data from Federal Bureau of Investigation
"Law Enforcement Officers Killed and Assaulted 2004" (http://www.fbi.gov/ucr/killed/2004/table69.htm)
*Figures based on reporting agencies and the population for those agencies for each state. Assaulted includes by firearm, knife, other dangerous weapons or personal weapons (e.g. fists).
**Not available.

Percent of Law Enforcement Officers Assaulted in 2004

National Percent = 11.9% of Officers Assaulted*

ALPHA ORDER

RANK	STATE	PERCENT
45	Alabama	4.2
8	Alaska	18.6
5	Arizona	18.9
35	Arkansas	6.7
26	California	10.1
30	Colorado	8.0
42	Connecticut	5.1
9	Delaware	16.6
3	Florida	20.6
37	Georgia	6.3
16	Hawaii	13.9
20	Idaho	11.6
NA	Illinois**	NA
15	Indiana	14.4
23	Iowa	11.1
4	Kansas	20.2
19	Kentucky	12.0
10	Louisiana	15.8
11	Maine	15.1
1	Maryland	25.9
43	Massachusetts	4.7
38	Michigan	6.2
47	Minnesota	1.0
30	Mississippi	8.0
2	Missouri	21.8
36	Montana	6.4
39	Nebraska	5.5
25	Nevada	10.5
18	New Hampshire	12.4
17	New Jersey	13.1
7	New Mexico	18.7
46	New York	3.0
21	North Carolina	11.4
40	North Dakota	5.3
28	Ohio	9.8
13	Oklahoma	14.5
33	Oregon	7.6
12	Pennsylvania	14.9
6	Rhode Island	18.8
26	South Carolina	10.1
44	South Dakota	4.4
13	Tennessee	14.5
24	Texas	10.7
34	Utah	7.2
NA	Vermont**	NA
29	Virginia	9.3
21	Washington	11.4
NA	West Virginia**	NA
32	Wisconsin	7.9
40	Wyoming	5.3

RANK ORDER

RANK	STATE	PERCENT
1	Maryland	25.9
2	Missouri	21.8
3	Florida	20.6
4	Kansas	20.2
5	Arizona	18.9
6	Rhode Island	18.8
7	New Mexico	18.7
8	Alaska	18.6
9	Delaware	16.6
10	Louisiana	15.8
11	Maine	15.1
12	Pennsylvania	14.9
13	Oklahoma	14.5
13	Tennessee	14.5
15	Indiana	14.4
16	Hawaii	13.9
17	New Jersey	13.1
18	New Hampshire	12.4
19	Kentucky	12.0
20	Idaho	11.6
21	North Carolina	11.4
21	Washington	11.4
23	Iowa	11.1
24	Texas	10.7
25	Nevada	10.5
26	California	10.1
26	South Carolina	10.1
28	Ohio	9.8
29	Virginia	9.3
30	Colorado	8.0
30	Mississippi	8.0
32	Wisconsin	7.9
33	Oregon	7.6
34	Utah	7.2
35	Arkansas	6.7
36	Montana	6.4
37	Georgia	6.3
38	Michigan	6.2
39	Nebraska	5.5
40	North Dakota	5.3
40	Wyoming	5.3
42	Connecticut	5.1
43	Massachusetts	4.7
44	South Dakota	4.4
45	Alabama	4.2
46	New York	3.0
47	Minnesota	1.0
NA	Illinois**	NA
NA	Vermont**	NA
NA	West Virginia**	NA
	District of Columbia**	NA

Source: Morgan Quitno Press using data from Federal Bureau of Investigation
"Law Enforcement Officers Killed and Assaulted 2004" (http://www.fbi.gov/ucr/killed/2004/table69.htm)
*Figures based on reporting agencies and the number of officers for those agencies for each state. Assaulted includes by firearm, knife, other dangerous weapons or personal weapons (e.g. fists).
**Not available.

Detectives and Criminal Investigators in 2004

National Total = 87,730 Detectives and Investigators*

ALPHA ORDER

RANK	STATE	EMPLOYEES	% of USA
25	Alabama	1,030	1.2%
46	Alaska	180	0.2%
15	Arizona	1,680	1.9%
26	Arkansas	910	1.0%
1	California	8,980	10.2%
16	Colorado	1,670	1.9%
24	Connecticut	1,110	1.3%
41	Delaware	290	0.3%
4	Florida	6,620	7.5%
6	Georgia	3,620	4.1%
35	Hawaii	460	0.5%
39	Idaho	390	0.4%
7	Illinois	3,530	4.0%
20	Indiana	1,140	1.3%
37	Iowa	400	0.5%
31	Kansas	740	0.8%
33	Kentucky	520	0.6%
14	Louisiana	1,780	2.0%
40	Maine	330	0.4%
20	Maryland	1,140	1.3%
22	Massachusetts	1,130	1.3%
13	Michigan	2,170	2.5%
28	Minnesota	870	1.0%
27	Mississippi	880	1.0%
16	Missouri	1,670	1.9%
44	Montana	250	0.3%
41	Nebraska	290	0.3%
34	Nevada	510	0.6%
41	New Hampshire	290	0.3%
5	New Jersey	3,860	4.4%
32	New Mexico	630	0.7%
2	New York	7,710	8.8%
10	North Carolina	2,450	2.8%
48	North Dakota	160	0.2%
12	Ohio	2,180	2.5%
30	Oklahoma	750	0.9%
29	Oregon	770	0.9%
8	Pennsylvania	3,300	3.8%
NA	Rhode Island**	NA	NA
19	South Carolina	1,260	1.4%
45	South Dakota	240	0.3%
11	Tennessee	2,320	2.6%
3	Texas	7,670	8.7%
36	Utah	420	0.5%
49	Vermont	130	0.1%
9	Virginia	2,680	3.1%
22	Washington	1,130	1.3%
37	West Virginia	400	0.5%
18	Wisconsin	1,580	1.8%
46	Wyoming	180	0.2%

RANK ORDER

RANK	STATE	EMPLOYEES	% of USA
1	California	8,980	10.2%
2	New York	7,710	8.8%
3	Texas	7,670	8.7%
4	Florida	6,620	7.5%
5	New Jersey	3,860	4.4%
6	Georgia	3,620	4.1%
7	Illinois	3,530	4.0%
8	Pennsylvania	3,300	3.8%
9	Virginia	2,680	3.1%
10	North Carolina	2,450	2.8%
11	Tennessee	2,320	2.6%
12	Ohio	2,180	2.5%
13	Michigan	2,170	2.5%
14	Louisiana	1,780	2.0%
15	Arizona	1,680	1.9%
16	Colorado	1,670	1.9%
16	Missouri	1,670	1.9%
18	Wisconsin	1,580	1.8%
19	South Carolina	1,260	1.4%
20	Indiana	1,140	1.3%
20	Maryland	1,140	1.3%
22	Massachusetts	1,130	1.3%
22	Washington	1,130	1.3%
24	Connecticut	1,110	1.3%
25	Alabama	1,030	1.2%
26	Arkansas	910	1.0%
27	Mississippi	880	1.0%
28	Minnesota	870	1.0%
29	Oregon	770	0.9%
30	Oklahoma	750	0.9%
31	Kansas	740	0.8%
32	New Mexico	630	0.7%
33	Kentucky	520	0.6%
34	Nevada	510	0.6%
35	Hawaii	460	0.5%
36	Utah	420	0.5%
37	Iowa	400	0.5%
37	West Virginia	400	0.5%
39	Idaho	390	0.4%
40	Maine	330	0.4%
41	Delaware	290	0.3%
41	Nebraska	290	0.3%
41	New Hampshire	290	0.3%
44	Montana	250	0.3%
45	South Dakota	240	0.3%
46	Alaska	180	0.2%
46	Wyoming	180	0.2%
48	North Dakota	160	0.2%
49	Vermont	130	0.1%
NA	Rhode Island**	NA	NA
	District of Columbia	2,550	2.9%

Source: U.S. Department of Labor, Bureau of Labor Statistics
 "Occupational Employment and Wages, 2004" (http://www.bls.gov/oes/)
*Does not include self-employed.
**Not available.

Rate of Detectives and Criminal Investigators in 2004

National Rate = 30 Detectives and Investigators per 100,000 Population*

ALPHA ORDER

RANK	STATE	RATE
32	Alabama	23
25	Alaska	27
19	Arizona	29
13	Arkansas	33
29	California	25
7	Colorado	36
15	Connecticut	32
11	Delaware	35
6	Florida	38
2	Georgia	41
7	Hawaii	36
23	Idaho	28
23	Illinois	28
42	Indiana	18
48	Iowa	14
25	Kansas	27
49	Kentucky	13
4	Louisiana	39
29	Maine	25
40	Maryland	20
42	Massachusetts	18
36	Michigan	21
45	Minnesota	17
17	Mississippi	30
19	Missouri	29
25	Montana	27
45	Nebraska	17
33	Nevada	22
33	New Hampshire	22
1	New Jersey	44
13	New Mexico	33
3	New York	40
19	North Carolina	29
29	North Dakota	25
41	Ohio	19
36	Oklahoma	21
36	Oregon	21
25	Pennsylvania	27
NA	Rhode Island**	NA
17	South Carolina	30
16	South Dakota	31
4	Tennessee	39
12	Texas	34
45	Utah	17
36	Vermont	21
7	Virginia	36
42	Washington	18
33	West Virginia	22
19	Wisconsin	29
7	Wyoming	36

RANK ORDER

RANK	STATE	RATE
1	New Jersey	44
2	Georgia	41
3	New York	40
4	Louisiana	39
4	Tennessee	39
6	Florida	38
7	Colorado	36
7	Hawaii	36
7	Virginia	36
7	Wyoming	36
11	Delaware	35
12	Texas	34
13	Arkansas	33
13	New Mexico	33
15	Connecticut	32
16	South Dakota	31
17	Mississippi	30
17	South Carolina	30
19	Arizona	29
19	Missouri	29
19	North Carolina	29
19	Wisconsin	29
23	Idaho	28
23	Illinois	28
25	Alaska	27
25	Kansas	27
25	Montana	27
25	Pennsylvania	27
29	California	25
29	Maine	25
29	North Dakota	25
32	Alabama	23
33	Nevada	22
33	New Hampshire	22
33	West Virginia	22
36	Michigan	21
36	Oklahoma	21
36	Oregon	21
36	Vermont	21
40	Maryland	20
41	Ohio	19
42	Indiana	18
42	Massachusetts	18
42	Washington	18
45	Minnesota	17
45	Nebraska	17
45	Utah	17
48	Iowa	14
49	Kentucky	13
NA	Rhode Island**	NA

District of Columbia   460

Source: Morgan Quitno Press using data from U.S. Department of Labor, Bureau of Labor Statistics
    "Occupational Employment and Wages, 2004" (http://www.bls.gov/oes/)
*Does not include self-employed.
**Not available.

Private Detectives and Investigators in 2004

National Total = 34,940 Private Detectives and Investigators

ALPHA ORDER					RANK ORDER			
RANK	STATE		EMPLOYEES	% of USA	RANK	STATE		EMPLOYEES	% of USA
18	Alabama		450	1.3%	1	Texas		4,190	12.0%
NA	Alaska*		NA	NA	2	California		3,370	9.6%
14	Arizona		570	1.6%	3	Florida		2,900	8.3%
35	Arkansas		160	0.5%	4	New York		1,790	5.1%
2	California		3,370	9.6%	5	Pennsylvania		1,480	4.2%
29	Colorado		240	0.7%	6	Ohio		1,150	3.3%
32	Connecticut		190	0.5%	7	Michigan		980	2.8%
42	Delaware		70	0.2%	8	New Jersey		810	2.3%
3	Florida		2,900	8.3%	9	Georgia		780	2.2%
9	Georgia		780	2.2%	10	Maryland		720	2.1%
NA	Hawaii*		NA	NA	11	North Carolina		680	1.9%
40	Idaho		120	0.3%	11	Virginia		680	1.9%
NA	Illinois*		NA	NA	13	Oklahoma		670	1.9%
21	Indiana		370	1.1%	14	Arizona		570	1.6%
30	Iowa		220	0.6%	15	New Hampshire		500	1.4%
35	Kansas		160	0.5%	16	Mississippi		460	1.3%
26	Kentucky		300	0.9%	16	Washington		460	1.3%
27	Louisiana		280	0.8%	18	Alabama		450	1.3%
35	Maine		160	0.5%	18	Missouri		450	1.3%
10	Maryland		720	2.1%	20	Nevada		380	1.1%
22	Massachusetts		350	1.0%	21	Indiana		370	1.1%
7	Michigan		980	2.8%	22	Massachusetts		350	1.0%
22	Minnesota		350	1.0%	22	Minnesota		350	1.0%
16	Mississippi		460	1.3%	22	South Carolina		350	1.0%
18	Missouri		450	1.3%	25	Wisconsin		320	0.9%
38	Montana		140	0.4%	26	Kentucky		300	0.9%
38	Nebraska		140	0.4%	27	Louisiana		280	0.8%
20	Nevada		380	1.1%	28	Oregon		260	0.7%
15	New Hampshire		500	1.4%	29	Colorado		240	0.7%
8	New Jersey		810	2.3%	30	Iowa		220	0.6%
31	New Mexico		210	0.6%	31	New Mexico		210	0.6%
4	New York		1,790	5.1%	32	Connecticut		190	0.5%
11	North Carolina		680	1.9%	32	Utah		190	0.5%
NA	North Dakota*		NA	NA	34	West Virginia		180	0.5%
6	Ohio		1,150	3.3%	35	Arkansas		160	0.5%
13	Oklahoma		670	1.9%	35	Kansas		160	0.5%
28	Oregon		260	0.7%	35	Maine		160	0.5%
5	Pennsylvania		1,480	4.2%	38	Montana		140	0.4%
41	Rhode Island		80	0.2%	38	Nebraska		140	0.4%
22	South Carolina		350	1.0%	40	Idaho		120	0.3%
NA	South Dakota*		NA	NA	41	Rhode Island		80	0.2%
NA	Tennessee*		NA	NA	42	Delaware		70	0.2%
1	Texas		4,190	12.0%	NA	Alaska*		NA	NA
32	Utah		190	0.5%	NA	Hawaii*		NA	NA
NA	Vermont*		NA	NA	NA	Illinois*		NA	NA
11	Virginia		680	1.9%	NA	North Dakota*		NA	NA
16	Washington		460	1.3%	NA	South Dakota*		NA	NA
34	West Virginia		180	0.5%	NA	Tennessee*		NA	NA
25	Wisconsin		320	0.9%	NA	Vermont*		NA	NA
NA	Wyoming*		NA	NA	NA	Wyoming*		NA	NA
						District of Columbia*		NA	NA

Source: U.S. Department of Labor, Bureau of Labor Statistics
"Occupational Employment and Wages, 2004" (http://www.bls.gov/oes/)
*Not available.

Rate of Private Detectives and Investigators in 2004

National Rate = 12 Private Detectives and Investigators per 100,000 Population

ALPHA ORDER

RANK	STATE	RATE
12	Alabama	10
NA	Alaska*	NA
12	Arizona	10
35	Arkansas	6
17	California	9
40	Colorado	5
40	Connecticut	5
23	Delaware	8
4	Florida	17
17	Georgia	9
NA	Hawaii*	NA
17	Idaho	9
NA	Illinois*	NA
35	Indiana	6
29	Iowa	7
35	Kansas	6
29	Kentucky	7
35	Louisiana	6
9	Maine	12
8	Maryland	13
40	Massachusetts	5
12	Michigan	10
29	Minnesota	7
5	Mississippi	16
23	Missouri	8
7	Montana	15
23	Nebraska	8
5	Nevada	16
1	New Hampshire	38
17	New Jersey	9
11	New Mexico	11
17	New York	9
23	North Carolina	8
NA	North Dakota*	NA
12	Ohio	10
2	Oklahoma	19
29	Oregon	7
9	Pennsylvania	12
29	Rhode Island	7
23	South Carolina	8
NA	South Dakota*	NA
NA	Tennessee*	NA
2	Texas	19
23	Utah	8
NA	Vermont*	NA
17	Virginia	9
29	Washington	7
12	West Virginia	10
35	Wisconsin	6
NA	Wyoming*	NA

RANK ORDER

RANK	STATE	RATE
1	New Hampshire	38
2	Oklahoma	19
2	Texas	19
4	Florida	17
5	Mississippi	16
5	Nevada	16
7	Montana	15
8	Maryland	13
9	Maine	12
9	Pennsylvania	12
11	New Mexico	11
12	Alabama	10
12	Arizona	10
12	Michigan	10
12	Ohio	10
12	West Virginia	10
17	California	9
17	Georgia	9
17	Idaho	9
17	New Jersey	9
17	New York	9
17	Virginia	9
23	Delaware	8
23	Missouri	8
23	Nebraska	8
23	North Carolina	8
23	South Carolina	8
23	Utah	8
29	Iowa	7
29	Kentucky	7
29	Minnesota	7
29	Oregon	7
29	Rhode Island	7
29	Washington	7
35	Arkansas	6
35	Indiana	6
35	Kansas	6
35	Louisiana	6
35	Wisconsin	6
40	Colorado	5
40	Connecticut	5
40	Massachusetts	5
NA	Alaska*	NA
NA	Hawaii*	NA
NA	Illinois*	NA
NA	North Dakota*	NA
NA	South Dakota*	NA
NA	Tennessee*	NA
NA	Vermont*	NA
NA	Wyoming*	NA
	District of Columbia*	NA

Source: Morgan Quitno Press using data from U.S. Department of Labor, Bureau of Labor Statistics
    "Occupational Employment and Wages, 2004" (http://www.bls.gov/oes/)
*Not available.

Security Guards in 2004

National Total = 992,180 Guards*

ALPHA ORDER

RANK	STATE	EMPLOYEES	% of USA
23	Alabama	13,000	1.3%
45	Alaska	2,040	0.2%
15	Arizona	20,560	2.1%
34	Arkansas	6,320	0.6%
1	California	137,280	13.8%
26	Colorado	12,360	1.2%
25	Connecticut	12,460	1.3%
40	Delaware	3,240	0.3%
3	Florida	69,460	7.0%
11	Georgia	25,840	2.6%
31	Hawaii	7,520	0.8%
42	Idaho	2,770	0.3%
5	Illinois	43,310	4.4%
18	Indiana	17,560	1.8%
35	Iowa	6,290	0.6%
37	Kansas	5,160	0.5%
28	Kentucky	10,690	1.1%
19	Louisiana	17,130	1.7%
43	Maine	2,380	0.2%
12	Maryland	22,900	2.3%
14	Massachusetts	22,220	2.2%
9	Michigan	29,300	3.0%
22	Minnesota	13,400	1.4%
29	Mississippi	9,020	0.9%
17	Missouri	18,880	1.9%
46	Montana	1,440	0.1%
39	Nebraska	3,790	0.4%
20	Nevada	17,060	1.7%
44	New Hampshire	2,050	0.2%
6	New Jersey	40,740	4.1%
32	New Mexico	7,400	0.7%
2	New York	98,240	9.9%
13	North Carolina	22,580	2.3%
47	North Dakota	1,300	0.1%
8	Ohio	30,800	3.1%
30	Oklahoma	8,280	0.8%
33	Oregon	6,950	0.7%
7	Pennsylvania	38,350	3.9%
41	Rhode Island	3,210	0.3%
24	South Carolina	12,580	1.3%
48	South Dakota	1,040	0.1%
16	Tennessee	20,410	2.1%
4	Texas	69,080	7.0%
36	Utah	5,600	0.6%
49	Vermont	940	0.1%
10	Virginia	27,420	2.8%
21	Washington	15,380	1.6%
38	West Virginia	4,810	0.5%
27	Wisconsin	10,840	1.1%
50	Wyoming	920	0.1%

RANK ORDER

RANK	STATE	EMPLOYEES	% of USA
1	California	137,280	13.8%
2	New York	98,240	9.9%
3	Florida	69,460	7.0%
4	Texas	69,080	7.0%
5	Illinois	43,310	4.4%
6	New Jersey	40,740	4.1%
7	Pennsylvania	38,350	3.9%
8	Ohio	30,800	3.1%
9	Michigan	29,300	3.0%
10	Virginia	27,420	2.8%
11	Georgia	25,840	2.6%
12	Maryland	22,900	2.3%
13	North Carolina	22,580	2.3%
14	Massachusetts	22,220	2.2%
15	Arizona	20,560	2.1%
16	Tennessee	20,410	2.1%
17	Missouri	18,880	1.9%
18	Indiana	17,560	1.8%
19	Louisiana	17,130	1.7%
20	Nevada	17,060	1.7%
21	Washington	15,380	1.6%
22	Minnesota	13,400	1.4%
23	Alabama	13,000	1.3%
24	South Carolina	12,580	1.3%
25	Connecticut	12,460	1.3%
26	Colorado	12,360	1.2%
27	Wisconsin	10,840	1.1%
28	Kentucky	10,690	1.1%
29	Mississippi	9,020	0.9%
30	Oklahoma	8,280	0.8%
31	Hawaii	7,520	0.8%
32	New Mexico	7,400	0.7%
33	Oregon	6,950	0.7%
34	Arkansas	6,320	0.6%
35	Iowa	6,290	0.6%
36	Utah	5,600	0.6%
37	Kansas	5,160	0.5%
38	West Virginia	4,810	0.5%
39	Nebraska	3,790	0.4%
40	Delaware	3,240	0.3%
41	Rhode Island	3,210	0.3%
42	Idaho	2,770	0.3%
43	Maine	2,380	0.2%
44	New Hampshire	2,050	0.2%
45	Alaska	2,040	0.2%
46	Montana	1,440	0.1%
47	North Dakota	1,300	0.1%
48	South Dakota	1,040	0.1%
49	Vermont	940	0.1%
50	Wyoming	920	0.1%
	District of Columbia	9,850	1.0%

Source: U.S. Department of Labor, Bureau of Labor Statistics
"Occupational Employment and Wages, 2004" (http://www.bls.gov/oes/)
*Does not include self-employed.

Rate of Security Guards in 2004

National Rate = 338 Guards per 100,000 Population*

<table>
<tr><td colspan="3">ALPHA ORDER</td><td colspan="3">RANK ORDER</td></tr>
<tr><td>RANK</td><td>STATE</td><td>RATE</td><td>RANK</td><td>STATE</td><td>RATE</td></tr>
<tr><td>26</td><td>Alabama</td><td>287</td><td>1</td><td>Nevada</td><td>731</td></tr>
<tr><td>19</td><td>Alaska</td><td>310</td><td>2</td><td>Hawaii</td><td>596</td></tr>
<tr><td>12</td><td>Arizona</td><td>358</td><td>3</td><td>New York</td><td>510</td></tr>
<tr><td>37</td><td>Arkansas</td><td>230</td><td>4</td><td>New Jersey</td><td>469</td></tr>
<tr><td>9</td><td>California</td><td>383</td><td>5</td><td>Maryland</td><td>412</td></tr>
<tr><td>28</td><td>Colorado</td><td>269</td><td>6</td><td>Florida</td><td>400</td></tr>
<tr><td>13</td><td>Connecticut</td><td>356</td><td>7</td><td>Delaware</td><td>390</td></tr>
<tr><td>7</td><td>Delaware</td><td>390</td><td>8</td><td>New Mexico</td><td>389</td></tr>
<tr><td>6</td><td>Florida</td><td>400</td><td>9</td><td>California</td><td>383</td></tr>
<tr><td>24</td><td>Georgia</td><td>290</td><td>10</td><td>Louisiana</td><td>380</td></tr>
<tr><td>2</td><td>Hawaii</td><td>596</td><td>11</td><td>Virginia</td><td>367</td></tr>
<tr><td>41</td><td>Idaho</td><td>199</td><td>12</td><td>Arizona</td><td>358</td></tr>
<tr><td>16</td><td>Illinois</td><td>341</td><td>13</td><td>Connecticut</td><td>356</td></tr>
<tr><td>27</td><td>Indiana</td><td>282</td><td>14</td><td>Massachusetts</td><td>347</td></tr>
<tr><td>39</td><td>Iowa</td><td>213</td><td>15</td><td>Tennessee</td><td>346</td></tr>
<tr><td>44</td><td>Kansas</td><td>189</td><td>16</td><td>Illinois</td><td>341</td></tr>
<tr><td>33</td><td>Kentucky</td><td>258</td><td>17</td><td>Missouri</td><td>328</td></tr>
<tr><td>10</td><td>Louisiana</td><td>380</td><td>18</td><td>Mississippi</td><td>311</td></tr>
<tr><td>46</td><td>Maine</td><td>181</td><td>19</td><td>Alaska</td><td>310</td></tr>
<tr><td>5</td><td>Maryland</td><td>412</td><td>20</td><td>Pennsylvania</td><td>309</td></tr>
<tr><td>14</td><td>Massachusetts</td><td>347</td><td>21</td><td>Texas</td><td>307</td></tr>
<tr><td>24</td><td>Michigan</td><td>290</td><td>22</td><td>South Carolina</td><td>300</td></tr>
<tr><td>32</td><td>Minnesota</td><td>263</td><td>23</td><td>Rhode Island</td><td>297</td></tr>
<tr><td>18</td><td>Mississippi</td><td>311</td><td>24</td><td>Georgia</td><td>290</td></tr>
<tr><td>17</td><td>Missouri</td><td>328</td><td>24</td><td>Michigan</td><td>290</td></tr>
<tr><td>48</td><td>Montana</td><td>155</td><td>26</td><td>Alabama</td><td>287</td></tr>
<tr><td>38</td><td>Nebraska</td><td>217</td><td>27</td><td>Indiana</td><td>282</td></tr>
<tr><td>1</td><td>Nevada</td><td>731</td><td>28</td><td>Colorado</td><td>269</td></tr>
<tr><td>47</td><td>New Hampshire</td><td>158</td><td>28</td><td>Ohio</td><td>269</td></tr>
<tr><td>4</td><td>New Jersey</td><td>469</td><td>30</td><td>West Virginia</td><td>265</td></tr>
<tr><td>8</td><td>New Mexico</td><td>389</td><td>31</td><td>North Carolina</td><td>264</td></tr>
<tr><td>3</td><td>New York</td><td>510</td><td>32</td><td>Minnesota</td><td>263</td></tr>
<tr><td>31</td><td>North Carolina</td><td>264</td><td>33</td><td>Kentucky</td><td>258</td></tr>
<tr><td>40</td><td>North Dakota</td><td>204</td><td>34</td><td>Washington</td><td>248</td></tr>
<tr><td>28</td><td>Ohio</td><td>269</td><td>35</td><td>Oklahoma</td><td>235</td></tr>
<tr><td>35</td><td>Oklahoma</td><td>235</td><td>36</td><td>Utah</td><td>231</td></tr>
<tr><td>43</td><td>Oregon</td><td>194</td><td>37</td><td>Arkansas</td><td>230</td></tr>
<tr><td>20</td><td>Pennsylvania</td><td>309</td><td>38</td><td>Nebraska</td><td>217</td></tr>
<tr><td>23</td><td>Rhode Island</td><td>297</td><td>39</td><td>Iowa</td><td>213</td></tr>
<tr><td>22</td><td>South Carolina</td><td>300</td><td>40</td><td>North Dakota</td><td>204</td></tr>
<tr><td>50</td><td>South Dakota</td><td>135</td><td>41</td><td>Idaho</td><td>199</td></tr>
<tr><td>15</td><td>Tennessee</td><td>346</td><td>42</td><td>Wisconsin</td><td>197</td></tr>
<tr><td>21</td><td>Texas</td><td>307</td><td>43</td><td>Oregon</td><td>194</td></tr>
<tr><td>36</td><td>Utah</td><td>231</td><td>44</td><td>Kansas</td><td>189</td></tr>
<tr><td>49</td><td>Vermont</td><td>151</td><td>45</td><td>Wyoming</td><td>182</td></tr>
<tr><td>11</td><td>Virginia</td><td>367</td><td>46</td><td>Maine</td><td>181</td></tr>
<tr><td>34</td><td>Washington</td><td>248</td><td>47</td><td>New Hampshire</td><td>158</td></tr>
<tr><td>30</td><td>West Virginia</td><td>265</td><td>48</td><td>Montana</td><td>155</td></tr>
<tr><td>42</td><td>Wisconsin</td><td>197</td><td>49</td><td>Vermont</td><td>151</td></tr>
<tr><td>45</td><td>Wyoming</td><td>182</td><td>50</td><td>South Dakota</td><td>135</td></tr>
<tr><td></td><td></td><td></td><td></td><td>District of Columbia</td><td>1,777</td></tr>
</table>

Source: Morgan Quitno Press using data from U.S. Department of Labor, Bureau of Labor Statistics
   "Occupational Employment and Wages, 2004" (http://www.bls.gov/oes/)
*Does not include self-employed.

U.S. District Court Judges in 2004

National Total = 679 Judges*

ALPHA ORDER					RANK ORDER			
RANK	STATE		JUDGES	% of USA	RANK	STATE	JUDGES	% of USA
13	Alabama		14	2.1%	1	California	62	9.1%
40	Alaska		3	0.4%	2	New York	52	7.7%
16	Arizona		13	1.9%	2	Texas	52	7.7%
26	Arkansas		8	1.2%	4	Pennsylvania	38	5.6%
1	California		62	9.1%	5	Florida	37	5.4%
29	Colorado		7	1.0%	6	Illinois	30	4.4%
26	Connecticut		8	1.2%	7	Louisiana	22	3.2%
38	Delaware		4	0.6%	8	Ohio	20	2.9%
5	Florida		37	5.4%	9	Michigan	19	2.8%
10	Georgia		18	2.7%	10	Georgia	18	2.7%
38	Hawaii		4	0.6%	11	New Jersey	17	2.5%
48	Idaho		2	0.3%	12	Virginia	15	2.2%
6	Illinois		30	4.4%	13	Alabama	14	2.1%
21	Indiana		10	1.5%	13	Missouri	14	2.1%
36	Iowa		5	0.7%	13	Tennessee	14	2.1%
34	Kansas		6	0.9%	16	Arizona	13	1.9%
21	Kentucky		10	1.5%	16	Massachusetts	13	1.9%
7	Louisiana		22	3.2%	16	North Carolina	13	1.9%
40	Maine		3	0.4%	19	Oklahoma	11	1.6%
21	Maryland		10	1.5%	19	Washington	11	1.6%
16	Massachusetts		13	1.9%	21	Indiana	10	1.5%
9	Michigan		19	2.8%	21	Kentucky	10	1.5%
29	Minnesota		7	1.0%	21	Maryland	10	1.5%
25	Mississippi		9	1.3%	21	South Carolina	10	1.5%
13	Missouri		14	2.1%	25	Mississippi	9	1.3%
40	Montana		3	0.4%	26	Arkansas	8	1.2%
40	Nebraska		3	0.4%	26	Connecticut	8	1.2%
29	Nevada		7	1.0%	26	West Virginia	8	1.2%
40	New Hampshire		3	0.4%	29	Colorado	7	1.0%
11	New Jersey		17	2.5%	29	Minnesota	7	1.0%
29	New Mexico		7	1.0%	29	Nevada	7	1.0%
2	New York		52	7.7%	29	New Mexico	7	1.0%
16	North Carolina		13	1.9%	29	Wisconsin	7	1.0%
48	North Dakota		2	0.3%	34	Kansas	6	0.9%
8	Ohio		20	2.9%	34	Oregon	6	0.9%
19	Oklahoma		11	1.6%	36	Iowa	5	0.7%
34	Oregon		6	0.9%	36	Utah	5	0.7%
4	Pennsylvania		38	5.6%	38	Delaware	4	0.6%
40	Rhode Island		3	0.4%	38	Hawaii	4	0.6%
21	South Carolina		10	1.5%	40	Alaska	3	0.4%
40	South Dakota		3	0.4%	40	Maine	3	0.4%
13	Tennessee		14	2.1%	40	Montana	3	0.4%
2	Texas		52	7.7%	40	Nebraska	3	0.4%
36	Utah		5	0.7%	40	New Hampshire	3	0.4%
48	Vermont		2	0.3%	40	Rhode Island	3	0.4%
12	Virginia		15	2.2%	40	South Dakota	3	0.4%
19	Washington		11	1.6%	40	Wyoming	3	0.4%
26	West Virginia		8	1.2%	48	Idaho	2	0.3%
29	Wisconsin		7	1.0%	48	North Dakota	2	0.3%
40	Wyoming		3	0.4%	48	Vermont	2	0.3%
						District of Columbia	15	2.2%

Source: Administrative Office of the United States Courts
"2004 Federal Court Management Statistics" (www.uscourts.gov/cgi-bin/cmsd2004.pl)
*Total includes 11 judgeships in U.S. territories.

Population per U.S. District Court Judge in 2004

National Rate = 439,606 People per U.S. District Judge*

RANK	STATE	RATE		RANK	STATE	RATE
37	Alabama	323,241		1	Wisconsin	786,219
47	Alaska	219,252		2	Minnesota	728,078
22	Arizona	441,529		3	Idaho	697,570
34	Arkansas	343,750		4	Colorado	657,403
10	California	578,097		5	North Carolina	656,959
4	Colorado	657,403		6	Indiana	622,654
24	Connecticut	437,371		7	Oregon	598,561
48	Delaware	207,517		8	Iowa	590,581
20	Florida	469,876		9	Nebraska	582,568
17	Georgia	495,452		10	California	578,097
41	Hawaii	315,531		11	Ohio	572,507
3	Idaho	697,570		12	Washington	564,277
27	Illinois	423,734		13	Maryland	556,133
6	Indiana	622,654		14	Michigan	531,800
8	Iowa	590,581		15	New Jersey	510,892
21	Kansas	455,616		16	Virginia	498,755
30	Kentucky	414,184		17	Georgia	495,452
49	Louisiana	204,849		18	Massachusetts	492,876
23	Maine	438,328		19	Utah	484,142
13	Maryland	556,133		20	Florida	469,876
18	Massachusetts	492,876		21	Kansas	455,616
14	Michigan	531,800		22	Arizona	441,529
2	Minnesota	728,078		23	Maine	438,328
38	Mississippi	322,308		24	Connecticut	437,371
31	Missouri	411,395		25	New Hampshire	433,056
43	Montana	308,973		26	Texas	432,145
9	Nebraska	582,568		27	Illinois	423,734
35	Nevada	333,271		28	Tennessee	420,950
25	New Hampshire	433,056		29	South Carolina	419,789
15	New Jersey	510,892		30	Kentucky	414,184
44	New Mexico	271,858		31	Missouri	411,395
32	New York	370,783		32	New York	370,783
5	North Carolina	656,959		33	Rhode Island	359,972
40	North Dakota	318,154		34	Arkansas	343,750
11	Ohio	572,507		35	Nevada	333,271
39	Oklahoma	320,322		36	Pennsylvania	326,170
7	Oregon	598,561		37	Alabama	323,241
36	Pennsylvania	326,170		38	Mississippi	322,308
33	Rhode Island	359,972		39	Oklahoma	320,322
29	South Carolina	419,789		40	North Dakota	318,154
45	South Dakota	256,874		41	Hawaii	315,531
28	Tennessee	420,950		42	Vermont	310,617
26	Texas	432,145		43	Montana	308,973
19	Utah	484,142		44	New Mexico	271,858
42	Vermont	310,617		45	South Dakota	256,874
16	Virginia	498,755		46	West Virginia	226,569
12	Washington	564,277		47	Alaska	219,252
46	West Virginia	226,569		48	Delaware	207,517
1	Wisconsin	786,219		49	Louisiana	204,849
50	Wyoming	168,629		50	Wyoming	168,629
					District of Columbia	36,949

Source: Morgan Quitno Press using data from Administrative Office of the United States Courts
"2004 Federal Court Management Statistics" (www.uscourts.gov/cgi-bin/cmsd2004.pl)
*National rate does not include judgeships or population in U.S. territories.

ALPHA ORDER

RANK ORDER

Authorized Wiretaps in 2004

National Total = 980 Wiretaps*

ALPHA ORDER

RANK	STATE	WIRETAPS	% of USA
NA	Alabama**	NA	NA
20	Alaska	0	0.0%
13	Arizona	10	1.0%
NA	Arkansas**	NA	NA
2	California	180	18.4%
20	Colorado	0	0.0%
20	Connecticut	0	0.0%
15	Delaware	4	0.4%
4	Florida	72	7.3%
7	Georgia	33	3.4%
20	Hawaii	0	0.0%
20	Idaho	0	0.0%
10	Illinois	21	2.1%
20	Indiana	0	0.0%
20	Iowa	0	0.0%
20	Kansas	0	0.0%
NA	Kentucky**	NA	NA
20	Louisiana	0	0.0%
20	Maine	0	0.0%
6	Maryland	34	3.5%
9	Massachusetts	23	2.3%
NA	Michigan**	NA	NA
18	Minnesota	1	0.1%
16	Mississippi	3	0.3%
20	Missouri	0	0.0%
NA	Montana**	NA	NA
20	Nebraska	0	0.0%
14	Nevada	8	0.8%
12	New Hampshire	13	1.3%
3	New Jersey	144	14.7%
20	New Mexico	0	0.0%
1	New York	347	35.4%
20	North Carolina	0	0.0%
20	North Dakota	0	0.0%
18	Ohio	1	0.1%
11	Oklahoma	16	1.6%
20	Oregon	0	0.0%
8	Pennsylvania	32	3.3%
20	Rhode Island	0	0.0%
20	South Carolina	0	0.0%
20	South Dakota	0	0.0%
5	Tennessee	36	3.7%
20	Texas	0	0.0%
20	Utah	0	0.0%
NA	Vermont**	NA	NA
20	Virginia	0	0.0%
20	Washington	0	0.0%
20	West Virginia	0	0.0%
17	Wisconsin	2	0.2%
20	Wyoming	0	0.0%

RANK ORDER

RANK	STATE	WIRETAPS	% of USA
1	New York	347	35.4%
2	California	180	18.4%
3	New Jersey	144	14.7%
4	Florida	72	7.3%
5	Tennessee	36	3.7%
6	Maryland	34	3.5%
7	Georgia	33	3.4%
8	Pennsylvania	32	3.3%
9	Massachusetts	23	2.3%
10	Illinois	21	2.1%
11	Oklahoma	16	1.6%
12	New Hampshire	13	1.3%
13	Arizona	10	1.0%
14	Nevada	8	0.8%
15	Delaware	4	0.4%
16	Mississippi	3	0.3%
17	Wisconsin	2	0.2%
18	Minnesota	1	0.1%
18	Ohio	1	0.1%
20	Alaska	0	0.0%
20	Colorado	0	0.0%
20	Connecticut	0	0.0%
20	Hawaii	0	0.0%
20	Idaho	0	0.0%
20	Indiana	0	0.0%
20	Iowa	0	0.0%
20	Kansas	0	0.0%
20	Louisiana	0	0.0%
20	Maine	0	0.0%
20	Missouri	0	0.0%
20	Nebraska	0	0.0%
20	New Mexico	0	0.0%
20	North Carolina	0	0.0%
20	North Dakota	0	0.0%
20	Oregon	0	0.0%
20	Rhode Island	0	0.0%
20	South Carolina	0	0.0%
20	South Dakota	0	0.0%
20	Texas	0	0.0%
20	Utah	0	0.0%
20	Virginia	0	0.0%
20	Washington	0	0.0%
20	West Virginia	0	0.0%
20	Wyoming	0	0.0%
NA	Alabama**	NA	NA
NA	Arkansas**	NA	NA
NA	Kentucky**	NA	NA
NA	Michigan**	NA	NA
NA	Montana**	NA	NA
NA	Vermont**	NA	NA
	District of Columbia	0	0.0%

Source: Administrative Office of the United States Courts
"2004 Wiretap Report" (2005) (www.uscourts.gov/wiretap04/contents.html)
*Total does not include 730 wiretaps authorized under federal statute.
**No state statute authorizing wiretaps.

VII. OFFENSES

VII. OFFENSES (continued)

Urban/Rural Crime

VII. OFFENSES (continued)

VII. OFFENSES (continued)

Crimes in 2004

National Total = 11,695,264 Crimes*

ALPHA ORDER					RANK ORDER			
RANK	STATE	CRIMES	% of USA		RANK	STATE	CRIMES	% of USA
21	Alabama	201,664	1.7%		1	California	1,425,264	12.2%
46	Alaska	26,331	0.2%		2	Texas	1,132,256	9.7%
11	Arizona	335,699	2.9%		3	Florida	850,895	7.3%
28	Arkansas	124,201	1.1%		4	New York	507,648	4.3%
1	California	1,425,264	12.2%		5	Illinois	474,096	4.1%
22	Colorado	197,527	1.7%		6	Ohio	460,073	3.9%
34	Connecticut	102,078	0.9%		7	Georgia	416,873	3.6%
43	Delaware	30,992	0.3%		8	North Carolina	393,572	3.4%
3	Florida	850,895	7.3%		9	Michigan	358,785	3.1%
7	Georgia	416,873	3.6%		10	Pennsylvania	350,609	3.0%
38	Hawaii	63,738	0.5%		11	Arizona	335,699	2.9%
40	Idaho	42,345	0.4%		12	Washington	322,167	2.8%
5	Illinois	474,096	4.1%		13	Tennessee	295,147	2.5%
17	Indiana	232,223	2.0%		14	Missouri	252,855	2.2%
35	Iowa	93,839	0.8%		15	New Jersey	242,256	2.1%
29	Kansas	118,939	1.0%		16	Maryland	241,258	2.1%
30	Kentucky	115,361	1.0%		17	Indiana	232,223	2.0%
18	Louisiana	227,997	1.9%		18	Louisiana	227,997	1.9%
42	Maine	33,104	0.3%		19	South Carolina	222,035	1.9%
16	Maryland	241,258	2.1%		20	Virginia	220,227	1.9%
23	Massachusetts	187,262	1.6%		21	Alabama	201,664	1.7%
9	Michigan	358,785	3.1%		22	Colorado	197,527	1.7%
25	Minnesota	168,770	1.4%		23	Massachusetts	187,262	1.6%
32	Mississippi	109,548	0.9%		24	Oregon	177,199	1.5%
14	Missouri	252,855	2.2%		25	Minnesota	168,770	1.4%
44	Montana	29,938	0.3%		26	Oklahoma	167,107	1.4%
37	Nebraska	66,905	0.6%		27	Wisconsin	158,258	1.4%
31	Nevada	112,594	1.0%		28	Arkansas	124,201	1.1%
45	New Hampshire	28,681	0.2%		29	Kansas	118,939	1.0%
15	New Jersey	242,256	2.1%		30	Kentucky	115,361	1.0%
36	New Mexico	92,976	0.8%		31	Nevada	112,594	1.0%
4	New York	507,648	4.3%		32	Mississippi	109,548	0.9%
8	North Carolina	393,572	3.4%		33	Utah	103,246	0.9%
50	North Dakota	12,662	0.1%		34	Connecticut	102,078	0.9%
6	Ohio	460,073	3.9%		35	Iowa	93,839	0.8%
26	Oklahoma	167,107	1.4%		36	New Mexico	92,976	0.8%
24	Oregon	177,199	1.5%		37	Nebraska	66,905	0.6%
10	Pennsylvania	350,609	3.0%		38	Hawaii	63,738	0.5%
41	Rhode Island	33,839	0.3%		39	West Virginia	50,421	0.4%
19	South Carolina	222,035	1.9%		40	Idaho	42,345	0.4%
48	South Dakota	16,227	0.1%		41	Rhode Island	33,839	0.3%
13	Tennessee	295,147	2.5%		42	Maine	33,104	0.3%
2	Texas	1,132,256	9.7%		43	Delaware	30,992	0.3%
33	Utah	103,246	0.9%		44	Montana	29,938	0.3%
49	Vermont	15,039	0.1%		45	New Hampshire	28,681	0.2%
20	Virginia	220,227	1.9%		46	Alaska	26,331	0.2%
12	Washington	322,167	2.8%		47	Wyoming	18,052	0.2%
39	West Virginia	50,421	0.4%		48	South Dakota	16,227	0.1%
27	Wisconsin	158,258	1.4%		49	Vermont	15,039	0.1%
47	Wyoming	18,052	0.2%		50	North Dakota	12,662	0.1%
						District of Columbia	34,486	0.3%

Source: Morgan Quitno Press using data from Federal Bureau of Investigation
    "Crime in the United States 2004" (Uniform Crime Reports, October 17, 2005)
*Includes murder, rape, robbery, aggravated assault, burglary, larceny-theft and motor vehicle theft.

Average Time Between Crimes in 2004

National Rate = A Crime Occurs Every 2.7 Seconds*

ALPHA ORDER			RANK ORDER		
RANK	STATE	MINUTES.SECONDS	RANK	STATE	MINUTES.SECONDS
30	Alabama	2.37	1	North Dakota	41.37
5	Alaska	20.01	2	Vermont	35.02
40	Arizona	1.34	3	South Dakota	32.29
23	Arkansas	4.14	4	Wyoming	29.12
50	California	0.22	5	Alaska	20.01
29	Colorado	2.40	6	New Hampshire	18.23
17	Connecticut	5.10	7	Montana	17.36
8	Delaware	17.01	8	Delaware	17.01
48	Florida	0.37	9	Maine	15.55
44	Georgia	1.16	10	Rhode Island	15.35
13	Hawaii	8.16	11	Idaho	12.27
11	Idaho	12.27	12	West Virginia	10.27
46	Illinois	1.07	13	Hawaii	8.16
34	Indiana	2.16	14	Nebraska	7.53
16	Iowa	5.37	15	New Mexico	5.40
22	Kansas	4.26	16	Iowa	5.37
21	Kentucky	4.34	17	Connecticut	5.10
33	Louisiana	2.19	18	Utah	5.06
9	Maine	15.55	19	Mississippi	4.49
35	Maryland	2.11	20	Nevada	4.41
28	Massachusetts	2.49	21	Kentucky	4.34
42	Michigan	1.28	22	Kansas	4.26
26	Minnesota	3.07	23	Arkansas	4.14
19	Mississippi	4.49	24	Wisconsin	3.20
37	Missouri	2.05	25	Oklahoma	3.09
7	Montana	17.36	26	Minnesota	3.07
14	Nebraska	7.53	27	Oregon	2.58
20	Nevada	4.41	28	Massachusetts	2.49
6	New Hampshire	18.23	29	Colorado	2.40
35	New Jersey	2.11	30	Alabama	2.37
15	New Mexico	5.40	31	Virginia	2.23
47	New York	1.02	32	South Carolina	2.22
43	North Carolina	1.20	33	Louisiana	2.19
1	North Dakota	41.37	34	Indiana	2.16
45	Ohio	1.09	35	Maryland	2.11
25	Oklahoma	3.09	35	New Jersey	2.11
27	Oregon	2.58	37	Missouri	2.05
41	Pennsylvania	1.30	38	Tennessee	1.47
10	Rhode Island	15.35	39	Washington	1.38
32	South Carolina	2.22	40	Arizona	1.34
3	South Dakota	32.29	41	Pennsylvania	1.30
38	Tennessee	1.47	42	Michigan	1.28
49	Texas	0.28	43	North Carolina	1.20
18	Utah	5.06	44	Georgia	1.16
2	Vermont	35.02	45	Ohio	1.09
31	Virginia	2.23	46	Illinois	1.07
39	Washington	1.38	47	New York	1.02
12	West Virginia	10.27	48	Florida	0.37
24	Wisconsin	3.20	49	Texas	0.28
4	Wyoming	29.12	50	California	0.22
				District of Columbia	15.17

Source: Morgan Quitno Press using data from Federal Bureau of Investigation
"Crime in the United States 2004" (Uniform Crime Reports, October 17, 2005)
*Includes murder, rape, robbery, aggravated assault, burglary, larceny-theft and motor vehicle theft.

Crimes per Square Mile in 2004

National Rate = 3.1 Crimes per Square Mile*

ALPHA ORDER				RANK ORDER		
RANK	STATE	RATE		RANK	STATE	RATE
23	Alabama	3.8		1	New Jersey	27.8
50	Alaska	0.0		2	Rhode Island	21.9
27	Arizona	2.9		3	Maryland	19.4
31	Arkansas	2.3		4	Connecticut	18.4
10	California	8.7		5	Massachusetts	17.7
34	Colorado	1.9		6	Florida	12.9
4	Connecticut	18.4		7	Delaware	12.5
7	Delaware	12.5		8	Ohio	10.3
6	Florida	12.9		9	New York	9.3
14	Georgia	7.0		10	California	8.7
18	Hawaii	5.8		11	Illinois	8.2
45	Idaho	0.5		12	Pennsylvania	7.6
11	Illinois	8.2		13	North Carolina	7.3
17	Indiana	6.4		14	Georgia	7.0
37	Iowa	1.7		14	Tennessee	7.0
39	Kansas	1.4		16	South Carolina	6.9
27	Kentucky	2.9		17	Indiana	6.4
21	Louisiana	4.4		18	Hawaii	5.8
42	Maine	0.9		19	Virginia	5.1
3	Maryland	19.4		20	Washington	4.5
5	Massachusetts	17.7		21	Louisiana	4.4
24	Michigan	3.7		22	Texas	4.2
34	Minnesota	1.9		23	Alabama	3.8
31	Mississippi	2.3		24	Michigan	3.7
25	Missouri	3.6		25	Missouri	3.6
46	Montana	0.2		26	New Hampshire	3.1
42	Nebraska	0.9		27	Arizona	2.9
41	Nevada	1.0		27	Kentucky	2.9
26	New Hampshire	3.1		29	Oklahoma	2.4
1	New Jersey	27.8		29	Wisconsin	2.4
44	New Mexico	0.8		31	Arkansas	2.3
9	New York	9.3		31	Mississippi	2.3
13	North Carolina	7.3		33	West Virginia	2.1
46	North Dakota	0.2		34	Colorado	1.9
8	Ohio	10.3		34	Minnesota	1.9
29	Oklahoma	2.4		36	Oregon	1.8
36	Oregon	1.8		37	Iowa	1.7
12	Pennsylvania	7.6		38	Vermont	1.6
2	Rhode Island	21.9		39	Kansas	1.4
16	South Carolina	6.9		40	Utah	1.2
46	South Dakota	0.2		41	Nevada	1.0
14	Tennessee	7.0		42	Maine	0.9
22	Texas	4.2		42	Nebraska	0.9
40	Utah	1.2		44	New Mexico	0.8
38	Vermont	1.6		45	Idaho	0.5
19	Virginia	5.1		46	Montana	0.2
20	Washington	4.5		46	North Dakota	0.2
33	West Virginia	2.1		46	South Dakota	0.2
29	Wisconsin	2.4		46	Wyoming	0.2
46	Wyoming	0.2		50	Alaska	0.0

District of Columbia   507.1

Source: Morgan Quitno Press using data from Federal Bureau of Investigation
     "Crime in the United States 2004" (Uniform Crime Reports, October 17, 2005)
*Includes murder, rape, robbery, aggravated assault, burglary, larceny-theft and motor vehicle theft. "Square miles"
includes total land and water area.

Percent Change in Number of Crimes: 2003 to 2004

National Percent Change = 1.1% Decrease*

ALPHA ORDER

RANK	STATE	PERCENT CHANGE
18	Alabama	0.0
46	Alaska	(6.8)
30	Arizona	(2.1)
1	Arkansas	11.4
16	California	0.3
10	Colorado	1.1
28	Connecticut	(1.9)
48	Delaware	(7.4)
38	Florida	(3.5)
8	Georgia	1.9
49	Hawaii	(8.0)
31	Idaho	(2.4)
32	Illinois	(2.5)
11	Indiana	1.0
29	Iowa	(2.0)
22	Kansas	(1.0)
9	Kentucky	1.5
6	Louisiana	2.6
25	Maine	(1.2)
36	Maryland	(2.8)
40	Massachusetts	(3.9)
45	Michigan	(6.1)
26	Minnesota	(1.3)
43	Mississippi	(5.7)
37	Missouri	(3.4)
44	Montana	(5.8)
42	Nebraska	(4.8)
7	Nevada	2.4
11	New Hampshire	1.0
39	New Jersey	(3.8)
3	New Mexico	4.1
35	New York	(2.7)
23	North Carolina	(1.1)
50	North Dakota	(8.7)
11	Ohio	1.0
23	Oklahoma	(1.1)
27	Oregon	(1.8)
17	Pennsylvania	0.2
41	Rhode Island	(4.2)
15	South Carolina	0.4
33	South Dakota	(2.6)
20	Tennessee	(0.6)
20	Texas	(0.6)
33	Utah	(2.6)
4	Vermont	3.6
19	Virginia	(0.3)
5	Washington	3.0
2	West Virginia	7.3
46	Wisconsin	(6.8)
14	Wyoming	0.5

RANK ORDER

RANK	STATE	PERCENT CHANGE
1	Arkansas	11.4
2	West Virginia	7.3
3	New Mexico	4.1
4	Vermont	3.6
5	Washington	3.0
6	Louisiana	2.6
7	Nevada	2.4
8	Georgia	1.9
9	Kentucky	1.5
10	Colorado	1.1
11	Indiana	1.0
11	New Hampshire	1.0
11	Ohio	1.0
14	Wyoming	0.5
15	South Carolina	0.4
16	California	0.3
17	Pennsylvania	0.2
18	Alabama	0.0
19	Virginia	(0.3)
20	Tennessee	(0.6)
20	Texas	(0.6)
22	Kansas	(1.0)
23	North Carolina	(1.1)
23	Oklahoma	(1.1)
25	Maine	(1.2)
26	Minnesota	(1.3)
27	Oregon	(1.8)
28	Connecticut	(1.9)
29	Iowa	(2.0)
30	Arizona	(2.1)
31	Idaho	(2.4)
32	Illinois	(2.5)
33	South Dakota	(2.6)
33	Utah	(2.6)
35	New York	(2.7)
36	Maryland	(2.8)
37	Missouri	(3.4)
38	Florida	(3.5)
39	New Jersey	(3.8)
40	Massachusetts	(3.9)
41	Rhode Island	(4.2)
42	Nebraska	(4.8)
43	Mississippi	(5.7)
44	Montana	(5.8)
45	Michigan	(6.1)
46	Alaska	(6.8)
46	Wisconsin	(6.8)
48	Delaware	(7.4)
49	Hawaii	(8.0)
50	North Dakota	(8.7)

	District of Columbia	(17.4)

Source: Morgan Quitno Press using data from Federal Bureau of Investigation
    "Crime in the United States 2004" (Uniform Crime Reports, October 17, 2005)
*Includes murder, rape, robbery, aggravated assault, burglary, larceny-theft and motor vehicle theft.

Crime Rate in 2004

National Rate = 3,982.6 Crimes per 100,000 Population*

ALPHA ORDER

RANK STATE

RANK	STATE	RATE
16	Alabama	4,451.6
22	Alaska	4,017.3
1	Arizona	5,844.6
15	Arkansas	4,512.1
24	California	3,970.8
21	Colorado	4,292.8
39	Connecticut	2,913.5
27	Delaware	3,732.3
9	Florida	4,891.0
13	Georgia	4,721.4
5	Hawaii	5,047.2
36	Idaho	3,039.3
28	Illinois	3,729.0
29	Indiana	3,723.0
34	Iowa	3,176.2
18	Kansas	4,348.0
43	Kentucky	2,782.6
4	Louisiana	5,048.9
46	Maine	2,513.1
19	Maryland	4,340.7
38	Massachusetts	2,918.5
31	Michigan	3,547.8
32	Minnesota	3,308.6
26	Mississippi	3,773.6
17	Missouri	4,394.0
33	Montana	3,230.0
25	Nebraska	3,829.3
11	Nevada	4,822.5
48	New Hampshire	2,207.1
42	New Jersey	2,784.9
10	New Mexico	4,885.0
45	New York	2,640.2
14	North Carolina	4,608.0
50	North Dakota	1,996.0
23	Ohio	4,015.0
12	Oklahoma	4,742.6
8	Oregon	4,929.6
41	Pennsylvania	2,826.1
35	Rhode Island	3,131.5
2	South Carolina	5,289.0
49	South Dakota	2,105.0
7	Tennessee	5,001.7
6	Texas	5,034.5
20	Utah	4,321.6
47	Vermont	2,420.2
37	Virginia	2,952.2
3	Washington	5,193.0
44	West Virginia	2,777.4
40	Wisconsin	2,872.7
30	Wyoming	3,563.9

RANK ORDER

RANK STATE

RANK	STATE	RATE
1	Arizona	5,844.6
2	South Carolina	5,289.0
3	Washington	5,193.0
4	Louisiana	5,048.9
5	Hawaii	5,047.2
6	Texas	5,034.5
7	Tennessee	5,001.7
8	Oregon	4,929.6
9	Florida	4,891.0
10	New Mexico	4,885.0
11	Nevada	4,822.5
12	Oklahoma	4,742.6
13	Georgia	4,721.4
14	North Carolina	4,608.0
15	Arkansas	4,512.1
16	Alabama	4,451.6
17	Missouri	4,394.0
18	Kansas	4,348.0
19	Maryland	4,340.7
20	Utah	4,321.6
21	Colorado	4,292.8
22	Alaska	4,017.3
23	Ohio	4,015.0
24	California	3,970.8
25	Nebraska	3,829.3
26	Mississippi	3,773.6
27	Delaware	3,732.3
28	Illinois	3,729.0
29	Indiana	3,723.0
30	Wyoming	3,563.9
31	Michigan	3,547.8
32	Minnesota	3,308.6
33	Montana	3,230.0
34	Iowa	3,176.2
35	Rhode Island	3,131.5
36	Idaho	3,039.3
37	Virginia	2,952.2
38	Massachusetts	2,918.5
39	Connecticut	2,913.5
40	Wisconsin	2,872.7
41	Pennsylvania	2,826.1
42	New Jersey	2,784.9
43	Kentucky	2,782.6
44	West Virginia	2,777.4
45	New York	2,640.2
46	Maine	2,513.1
47	Vermont	2,420.2
48	New Hampshire	2,207.1
49	South Dakota	2,105.0
50	North Dakota	1,996.0
	District of Columbia	6,230.3

Source: Morgan Quitno Press using data from Federal Bureau of Investigation
    "Crime in the United States 2004" (Uniform Crime Reports, October 17, 2005)
*Includes murder, rape, robbery, aggravated assault, burglary, larceny-theft and motor vehicle theft.

Percent Change in Crime Rate: 2003 to 2004

National Percent Change = 2.1% Decrease*

ALPHA ORDER

RANK	STATE	PERCENT CHANGE
15	Alabama	(0.5)
47	Alaska	(7.9)
40	Arizona	(4.9)
1	Arkansas	10.4
17	California	(0.9)
12	Colorado	(0.1)
25	Connecticut	(2.3)
48	Delaware	(8.8)
42	Florida	(5.7)
10	Georgia	0.2
50	Hawaii	(9.0)
37	Idaho	(4.3)
31	Illinois	(3.0)
9	Indiana	0.4
27	Iowa	(2.4)
18	Kansas	(1.4)
7	Kentucky	0.9
5	Louisiana	2.1
23	Maine	(1.8)
33	Maryland	(3.6)
34	Massachusetts	(3.9)
43	Michigan	(6.4)
24	Minnesota	(2.0)
43	Mississippi	(6.4)
34	Missouri	(3.9)
45	Montana	(6.7)
41	Nebraska	(5.3)
19	Nevada	(1.6)
10	New Hampshire	0.2
38	New Jersey	(4.4)
4	New Mexico	2.7
30	New York	(2.7)
28	North Carolina	(2.5)
49	North Dakota	(8.9)
8	Ohio	0.8
19	Oklahoma	(1.6)
29	Oregon	(2.6)
12	Pennsylvania	(0.1)
39	Rhode Island	(4.6)
16	South Carolina	(0.7)
32	South Dakota	(3.3)
19	Tennessee	(1.6)
25	Texas	(2.3)
36	Utah	(4.1)
3	Vermont	3.3
19	Virginia	(1.6)
6	Washington	1.8
2	West Virginia	7.1
46	Wisconsin	(7.4)
14	Wyoming	(0.4)

RANK ORDER

RANK	STATE	PERCENT CHANGE
1	Arkansas	10.4
2	West Virginia	7.1
3	Vermont	3.3
4	New Mexico	2.7
5	Louisiana	2.1
6	Washington	1.8
7	Kentucky	0.9
8	Ohio	0.8
9	Indiana	0.4
10	Georgia	0.2
10	New Hampshire	0.2
12	Colorado	(0.1)
12	Pennsylvania	(0.1)
14	Wyoming	(0.4)
15	Alabama	(0.5)
16	South Carolina	(0.7)
17	California	(0.9)
18	Kansas	(1.4)
19	Nevada	(1.6)
19	Oklahoma	(1.6)
19	Tennessee	(1.6)
19	Virginia	(1.6)
23	Maine	(1.8)
24	Minnesota	(2.0)
25	Connecticut	(2.3)
25	Texas	(2.3)
27	Iowa	(2.4)
28	North Carolina	(2.5)
29	Oregon	(2.6)
30	New York	(2.7)
31	Illinois	(3.0)
32	South Dakota	(3.3)
33	Maryland	(3.6)
34	Massachusetts	(3.9)
34	Missouri	(3.9)
36	Utah	(4.1)
37	Idaho	(4.3)
38	New Jersey	(4.4)
39	Rhode Island	(4.6)
40	Arizona	(4.9)
41	Nebraska	(5.3)
42	Florida	(5.7)
43	Michigan	(6.4)
43	Mississippi	(6.4)
45	Montana	(6.7)
46	Wisconsin	(7.4)
47	Alaska	(7.9)
48	Delaware	(8.8)
49	North Dakota	(8.9)
50	Hawaii	(9.0)

District of Columbia (16.8)

Source: Morgan Quitno Press using data from Federal Bureau of Investigation
"Crime in the United States 2004" (Uniform Crime Reports, October 17, 2005)
*Includes murder, rape, robbery, aggravated assault, burglary, larceny-theft and motor vehicle theft.

Violent Crimes in 2004

National Total = 1,367,009 Violent Crimes*

ALPHA ORDER

RANK	STATE	CRIMES	% of USA
22	Alabama	19,324	1.4%
40	Alaska	4,159	0.3%
16	Arizona	28,952	2.1%
27	Arkansas	13,737	1.0%
1	California	198,070	14.5%
24	Colorado	17,185	1.3%
33	Connecticut	10,032	0.7%
39	Delaware	4,720	0.3%
2	Florida	123,754	9.1%
9	Georgia	40,217	2.9%
42	Hawaii	3,213	0.2%
41	Idaho	3,412	0.2%
5	Illinois	69,026	5.0%
21	Indiana	20,294	1.5%
35	Iowa	8,003	0.6%
31	Kansas	10,245	0.7%
32	Kentucky	10,152	0.7%
17	Louisiana	28,844	2.1%
46	Maine	1,364	0.1%
11	Maryland	38,932	2.8%
15	Massachusetts	29,437	2.2%
7	Michigan	49,577	3.6%
26	Minnesota	13,751	1.0%
34	Mississippi	8,568	0.6%
18	Missouri	28,226	2.1%
43	Montana	2,723	0.2%
37	Nebraska	5,393	0.4%
25	Nevada	14,379	1.1%
45	New Hampshire	2,170	0.2%
14	New Jersey	30,943	2.3%
28	New Mexico	13,081	1.0%
4	New York	84,914	6.2%
12	North Carolina	38,244	2.8%
50	North Dakota	504	0.0%
10	Ohio	39,163	2.9%
23	Oklahoma	17,635	1.3%
30	Oregon	10,724	0.8%
6	Pennsylvania	50,998	3.7%
44	Rhode Island	2,673	0.2%
13	South Carolina	32,922	2.4%
47	South Dakota	1,322	0.1%
8	Tennessee	41,024	3.0%
3	Texas	121,554	8.9%
36	Utah	5,639	0.4%
49	Vermont	696	0.1%
20	Virginia	20,559	1.5%
19	Washington	21,330	1.6%
38	West Virginia	4,924	0.4%
29	Wisconsin	11,548	0.8%
48	Wyoming	1,163	0.1%

RANK ORDER

RANK	STATE	CRIMES	% of USA
1	California	198,070	14.5%
2	Florida	123,754	9.1%
3	Texas	121,554	8.9%
4	New York	84,914	6.2%
5	Illinois	69,026	5.0%
6	Pennsylvania	50,998	3.7%
7	Michigan	49,577	3.6%
8	Tennessee	41,024	3.0%
9	Georgia	40,217	2.9%
10	Ohio	39,163	2.9%
11	Maryland	38,932	2.8%
12	North Carolina	38,244	2.8%
13	South Carolina	32,922	2.4%
14	New Jersey	30,943	2.3%
15	Massachusetts	29,437	2.2%
16	Arizona	28,952	2.1%
17	Louisiana	28,844	2.1%
18	Missouri	28,226	2.1%
19	Washington	21,330	1.6%
20	Virginia	20,559	1.5%
21	Indiana	20,294	1.5%
22	Alabama	19,324	1.4%
23	Oklahoma	17,635	1.3%
24	Colorado	17,185	1.3%
25	Nevada	14,379	1.1%
26	Minnesota	13,751	1.0%
27	Arkansas	13,737	1.0%
28	New Mexico	13,081	1.0%
29	Wisconsin	11,548	0.8%
30	Oregon	10,724	0.8%
31	Kansas	10,245	0.7%
32	Kentucky	10,152	0.7%
33	Connecticut	10,032	0.7%
34	Mississippi	8,568	0.6%
35	Iowa	8,003	0.6%
36	Utah	5,639	0.4%
37	Nebraska	5,393	0.4%
38	West Virginia	4,924	0.4%
39	Delaware	4,720	0.3%
40	Alaska	4,159	0.3%
41	Idaho	3,412	0.2%
42	Hawaii	3,213	0.2%
43	Montana	2,723	0.2%
44	Rhode Island	2,673	0.2%
45	New Hampshire	2,170	0.2%
46	Maine	1,364	0.1%
47	South Dakota	1,322	0.1%
48	Wyoming	1,163	0.1%
49	Vermont	696	0.1%
50	North Dakota	504	0.0%
	District of Columbia	7,590	0.6%

Source: Federal Bureau of Investigation
"Crime in the United States 2004" (Uniform Crime Reports, October 17, 2005)
Violent crimes are offenses of murder, forcible rape, robbery and aggravated assault.

Average Time Between Violent Crimes in 2004

National Rate = A Violent Crime Occurs Every 23 Seconds*

ALPHA ORDER				RANK ORDER		
RANK	STATE	MINUTES.SECONDS		RANK	STATE	MINUTES.SECONDS
29	Alabama	27.16		1	North Dakota	1,045.43
11	Alaska	126.43		2	Vermont	757.14
35	Arizona	18.12		3	Wyoming	453.10
24	Arkansas	38.22		4	South Dakota	398.40
50	California	2.40		5	Maine	386.23
27	Colorado	30.40		6	New Hampshire	242.53
18	Connecticut	52.32		7	Rhode Island	197.10
12	Delaware	111.40		8	Montana	193.33
49	Florida	4.16		9	Hawaii	164.02
42	Georgia	13.06		10	Idaho	154.28
9	Hawaii	164.02		11	Alaska	126.43
10	Idaho	154.28		12	Delaware	111.40
46	Illinois	7.38		13	West Virginia	107.02
30	Indiana	25.58		14	Nebraska	97.44
16	Iowa	65.52		15	Utah	93.28
20	Kansas	51.26		16	Iowa	65.52
19	Kentucky	51.55		17	Mississippi	61.31
34	Louisiana	18.16		18	Connecticut	52.32
5	Maine	386.23		19	Kentucky	51.55
40	Maryland	13.32		20	Kansas	51.26
36	Massachusetts	17.54		21	Oregon	49.09
44	Michigan	10.38		22	Wisconsin	45.38
25	Minnesota	38.20		23	New Mexico	40.17
17	Mississippi	61.31		24	Arkansas	38.22
33	Missouri	18.40		25	Minnesota	38.20
8	Montana	193.33		26	Nevada	36.39
14	Nebraska	97.44		27	Colorado	30.40
26	Nevada	36.39		28	Oklahoma	29.53
6	New Hampshire	242.53		29	Alabama	27.16
37	New Jersey	17.02		30	Indiana	25.58
23	New Mexico	40.17		31	Virginia	25.38
47	New York	6.13		32	Washington	24.43
39	North Carolina	13.47		33	Missouri	18.40
1	North Dakota	1,045.43		34	Louisiana	18.16
41	Ohio	13.28		35	Arizona	18.12
28	Oklahoma	29.53		36	Massachusetts	17.54
21	Oregon	49.09		37	New Jersey	17.02
45	Pennsylvania	10.20		38	South Carolina	16.01
7	Rhode Island	197.10		39	North Carolina	13.47
38	South Carolina	16.01		40	Maryland	13.32
4	South Dakota	398.40		41	Ohio	13.28
43	Tennessee	12.51		42	Georgia	13.06
48	Texas	4.20		43	Tennessee	12.51
15	Utah	93.28		44	Michigan	10.38
2	Vermont	757.14		45	Pennsylvania	10.20
31	Virginia	25.38		46	Illinois	7.38
32	Washington	24.43		47	New York	6.13
13	West Virginia	107.02		48	Texas	4.20
22	Wisconsin	45.38		49	Florida	4.16
3	Wyoming	453.10		50	California	2.40
					District of Columbia	69.26

Source: Morgan Quitno Press using data from Federal Bureau of Investigation
   "Crime in the United States 2004" (Uniform Crime Reports, October 17, 2005)
*Violent crimes are offenses of murder, forcible rape, robbery and aggravated assault.

Violent Crimes per Square Mile in 2004

National Rate = 0.36 Violent Crimes per Square Mile*

ALPHA ORDER

RANK	STATE	RATE
23	Alabama	0.37
48	Alaska	0.01
27	Arizona	0.25
26	Arkansas	0.26
9	California	1.21
34	Colorado	0.17
6	Connecticut	1.81
4	Delaware	1.90
5	Florida	1.88
16	Georgia	0.68
25	Hawaii	0.29
44	Idaho	0.04
10	Illinois	1.19
17	Indiana	0.56
36	Iowa	0.14
38	Kansas	0.12
27	Kentucky	0.25
17	Louisiana	0.56
44	Maine	0.04
2	Maryland	3.14
3	Massachusetts	2.79
19	Michigan	0.51
35	Minnesota	0.16
32	Mississippi	0.18
22	Missouri	0.40
46	Montana	0.02
41	Nebraska	0.07
37	Nevada	0.13
30	New Hampshire	0.23
1	New Jersey	3.55
39	New Mexico	0.11
8	New York	1.56
15	North Carolina	0.71
48	North Dakota	0.01
14	Ohio	0.87
27	Oklahoma	0.25
39	Oregon	0.11
11	Pennsylvania	1.11
7	Rhode Island	1.73
12	South Carolina	1.03
46	South Dakota	0.02
13	Tennessee	0.97
21	Texas	0.45
41	Utah	0.07
41	Vermont	0.07
20	Virginia	0.48
24	Washington	0.30
31	West Virginia	0.20
32	Wisconsin	0.18
48	Wyoming	0.01

RANK ORDER

RANK	STATE	RATE
1	New Jersey	3.55
2	Maryland	3.14
3	Massachusetts	2.79
4	Delaware	1.90
5	Florida	1.88
6	Connecticut	1.81
7	Rhode Island	1.73
8	New York	1.56
9	California	1.21
10	Illinois	1.19
11	Pennsylvania	1.11
12	South Carolina	1.03
13	Tennessee	0.97
14	Ohio	0.87
15	North Carolina	0.71
16	Georgia	0.68
17	Indiana	0.56
17	Louisiana	0.56
19	Michigan	0.51
20	Virginia	0.48
21	Texas	0.45
22	Missouri	0.40
23	Alabama	0.37
24	Washington	0.30
25	Hawaii	0.29
26	Arkansas	0.26
27	Arizona	0.25
27	Kentucky	0.25
27	Oklahoma	0.25
30	New Hampshire	0.23
31	West Virginia	0.20
32	Mississippi	0.18
32	Wisconsin	0.18
34	Colorado	0.17
35	Minnesota	0.16
36	Iowa	0.14
37	Nevada	0.13
38	Kansas	0.12
39	New Mexico	0.11
39	Oregon	0.11
41	Nebraska	0.07
41	Utah	0.07
41	Vermont	0.07
44	Idaho	0.04
44	Maine	0.04
46	Montana	0.02
46	South Dakota	0.02
48	Alaska	0.01
48	North Dakota	0.01
48	Wyoming	0.01

District of Columbia   111.62

Source: Morgan Quitno Press using data from Federal Bureau of Investigation
"Crime in the United States 2004" (Uniform Crime Reports, October 17, 2005)
*Violent crimes are offenses of murder, forcible rape, robbery and aggravated assault. "Square miles" includes total land and water area.

Percent Change in Number of Violent Crimes: 2003 to 2004

National Percent Change = 1.2% Decrease*

RANK	STATE (ALPHA ORDER)	PERCENT CHANGE		RANK	STATE (RANK ORDER)	PERCENT CHANGE
22	Alabama	0.0		1	New Hampshire	12.0
4	Alaska	7.3		2	Arkansas	10.3
16	Arizona	1.1		3	Colorado	9.1
2	Arkansas	10.3		4	Alaska	7.3
36	California	(3.6)		5	West Virginia	6.4
3	Colorado	9.1		6	Nebraska	5.6
46	Connecticut	(9.2)		7	New Mexico	4.4
49	Delaware	(14.6)		8	Nevada	4.1
24	Florida	(0.4)		9	Pennsylvania	3.6
13	Georgia	2.0		10	Minnesota	3.3
43	Hawaii	(5.5)		11	Ohio	2.6
14	Idaho	1.5		12	Oregon	2.1
33	Illinois	(1.9)		13	Georgia	2.0
44	Indiana	(7.1)		14	Idaho	1.5
34	Iowa	(2.1)		14	Tennessee	1.5
42	Kansas	(5.4)		16	Arizona	1.1
28	Kentucky	(0.8)		17	Louisiana	0.8
17	Louisiana	0.8		18	Missouri	0.6
38	Maine	(4.1)		19	Maryland	0.4
19	Maryland	0.4		20	Virginia	0.3
35	Massachusetts	(3.1)		20	Washington	0.3
37	Michigan	(3.8)		22	Alabama	0.0
10	Minnesota	3.3		22	North Carolina	0.0
45	Mississippi	(8.2)		24	Florida	(0.4)
18	Missouri	0.6		25	South Dakota	(0.5)
50	Montana	(18.7)		26	Texas	(0.6)
6	Nebraska	5.6		27	Oklahoma	(0.7)
8	Nevada	4.1		28	Kentucky	(0.8)
1	New Hampshire	12.0		28	North Dakota	(0.8)
32	New Jersey	(1.7)		30	South Carolina	(1.6)
7	New Mexico	4.4		30	Vermont	(1.6)
41	New York	(5.1)		32	New Jersey	(1.7)
22	North Carolina	0.0		33	Illinois	(1.9)
28	North Dakota	(0.8)		34	Iowa	(2.1)
11	Ohio	2.6		35	Massachusetts	(3.1)
27	Oklahoma	(0.7)		36	California	(3.6)
12	Oregon	2.1		37	Michigan	(3.8)
9	Pennsylvania	3.6		38	Maine	(4.1)
48	Rhode Island	(13.0)		39	Utah	(4.2)
30	South Carolina	(1.6)		40	Wisconsin	(4.6)
25	South Dakota	(0.5)		41	New York	(5.1)
14	Tennessee	1.5		42	Kansas	(5.4)
26	Texas	(0.6)		43	Hawaii	(5.5)
39	Utah	(4.2)		44	Indiana	(7.1)
30	Vermont	(1.6)		45	Mississippi	(8.2)
20	Virginia	0.3		46	Connecticut	(9.2)
20	Washington	0.3		47	Wyoming	(11.5)
5	West Virginia	6.4		48	Rhode Island	(13.0)
40	Wisconsin	(4.6)		49	Delaware	(14.6)
47	Wyoming	(11.5)		50	Montana	(18.7)
					District of Columbia	(16.2)

Source: Morgan Quitno Press using data from Federal Bureau of Investigation
   "Crime in the United States 2004" (Uniform Crime Reports, October 17, 2005)
*Violent crimes are offenses of murder, forcible rape, robbery and aggravated assault.

Violent Crime Rate in 2004

National Rate = 465.5 Violent Crimes per 100,000 Population*

ALPHA ORDER

RANK	STATE	RATE
22	Alabama	426.6
7	Alaska	634.5
13	Arizona	504.1
15	Arkansas	499.1
10	California	551.8
25	Colorado	373.5
34	Connecticut	286.3
9	Delaware	568.4
2	Florida	711.3
19	Georgia	455.5
39	Hawaii	254.4
41	Idaho	244.9
11	Illinois	542.9
29	Indiana	325.4
37	Iowa	270.9
24	Kansas	374.5
41	Kentucky	244.9
6	Louisiana	638.7
49	Maine	103.5
3	Maryland	700.5
18	Massachusetts	458.8
17	Michigan	490.2
38	Minnesota	269.6
32	Mississippi	295.1
16	Missouri	490.5
33	Montana	293.8
30	Nebraska	308.7
8	Nevada	615.9
47	New Hampshire	167.0
26	New Jersey	355.7
5	New Mexico	687.3
21	New York	441.6
20	North Carolina	447.8
50	North Dakota	79.4
28	Ohio	341.8
14	Oklahoma	500.5
31	Oregon	298.3
23	Pennsylvania	411.1
40	Rhode Island	247.4
1	South Carolina	784.2
46	South Dakota	171.5
4	Tennessee	695.2
12	Texas	540.5
43	Utah	236.0
48	Vermont	112.0
35	Virginia	275.6
27	Washington	343.8
36	West Virginia	271.2
45	Wisconsin	209.6
44	Wyoming	229.6

RANK ORDER

RANK	STATE	RATE
1	South Carolina	784.2
2	Florida	711.3
3	Maryland	700.5
4	Tennessee	695.2
5	New Mexico	687.3
6	Louisiana	638.7
7	Alaska	634.5
8	Nevada	615.9
9	Delaware	568.4
10	California	551.8
11	Illinois	542.9
12	Texas	540.5
13	Arizona	504.1
14	Oklahoma	500.5
15	Arkansas	499.1
16	Missouri	490.5
17	Michigan	490.2
18	Massachusetts	458.8
19	Georgia	455.5
20	North Carolina	447.8
21	New York	441.6
22	Alabama	426.6
23	Pennsylvania	411.1
24	Kansas	374.5
25	Colorado	373.5
26	New Jersey	355.7
27	Washington	343.8
28	Ohio	341.8
29	Indiana	325.4
30	Nebraska	308.7
31	Oregon	298.3
32	Mississippi	295.1
33	Montana	293.8
34	Connecticut	286.3
35	Virginia	275.6
36	West Virginia	271.2
37	Iowa	270.9
38	Minnesota	269.6
39	Hawaii	254.4
40	Rhode Island	247.4
41	Idaho	244.9
41	Kentucky	244.9
43	Utah	236.0
44	Wyoming	229.6
45	Wisconsin	209.6
46	South Dakota	171.5
47	New Hampshire	167.0
48	Vermont	112.0
49	Maine	103.5
50	North Dakota	79.4

District of Columbia 1,371.2

Source: Federal Bureau of Investigation
    "Crime in the United States 2004" (Uniform Crime Reports, October 17, 2005)
*Violent crimes are offenses of murder, forcible rape, robbery and aggravated assault.

Percent Change in Violent Crime Rate: 2003 to 2004

National Percent Change = 2.2% Decrease*

ALPHA ORDER

RANK	STATE	PERCENT CHANGE
19	Alabama	(0.6)
5	Alaska	6.1
27	Arizona	(1.8)
2	Arkansas	9.3
38	California	(4.8)
3	Colorado	7.8
46	Connecticut	(9.6)
49	Delaware	(15.8)
33	Florida	(2.7)
14	Georgia	0.2
43	Hawaii	(6.6)
17	Idaho	(0.4)
30	Illinois	(2.4)
44	Indiana	(7.7)
32	Iowa	(2.5)
42	Kansas	(5.8)
25	Kentucky	(1.4)
13	Louisiana	0.3
37	Maine	(4.7)
17	Maryland	(0.4)
35	Massachusetts	(3.0)
36	Michigan	(4.1)
9	Minnesota	2.5
45	Mississippi	(8.9)
16	Missouri	(0.1)
50	Montana	(19.5)
6	Nebraska	5.1
15	Nevada	0.0
1	New Hampshire	11.1
30	New Jersey	(2.4)
8	New Mexico	3.0
39	New York	(5.2)
25	North Carolina	(1.4)
20	North Dakota	(0.9)
10	Ohio	2.4
23	Oklahoma	(1.2)
11	Oregon	1.2
7	Pennsylvania	3.3
48	Rhode Island	(13.4)
33	South Carolina	(2.7)
24	South Dakota	(1.3)
12	Tennessee	0.6
29	Texas	(2.3)
41	Utah	(5.7)
28	Vermont	(1.9)
20	Virginia	(0.9)
20	Washington	(0.9)
4	West Virginia	6.2
39	Wisconsin	(5.2)
47	Wyoming	(12.3)

RANK ORDER

RANK	STATE	PERCENT CHANGE
1	New Hampshire	11.1
2	Arkansas	9.3
3	Colorado	7.8
4	West Virginia	6.2
5	Alaska	6.1
6	Nebraska	5.1
7	Pennsylvania	3.3
8	New Mexico	3.0
9	Minnesota	2.5
10	Ohio	2.4
11	Oregon	1.2
12	Tennessee	0.6
13	Louisiana	0.3
14	Georgia	0.2
15	Nevada	0.0
16	Missouri	(0.1)
17	Idaho	(0.4)
17	Maryland	(0.4)
19	Alabama	(0.6)
20	North Dakota	(0.9)
20	Virginia	(0.9)
20	Washington	(0.9)
23	Oklahoma	(1.2)
24	South Dakota	(1.3)
25	Kentucky	(1.4)
25	North Carolina	(1.4)
27	Arizona	(1.8)
28	Vermont	(1.9)
29	Texas	(2.3)
30	Illinois	(2.4)
30	New Jersey	(2.4)
32	Iowa	(2.5)
33	Florida	(2.7)
33	South Carolina	(2.7)
35	Massachusetts	(3.0)
36	Michigan	(4.1)
37	Maine	(4.7)
38	California	(4.8)
39	New York	(5.2)
39	Wisconsin	(5.2)
41	Utah	(5.7)
42	Kansas	(5.8)
43	Hawaii	(6.6)
44	Indiana	(7.7)
45	Mississippi	(8.9)
46	Connecticut	(9.6)
47	Wyoming	(12.3)
48	Rhode Island	(13.4)
49	Delaware	(15.8)
50	Montana	(19.5)

District of Columbia   (15.6)

Source: Morgan Quitno Press using data from Federal Bureau of Investigation
"Crime in the United States 2004" (Uniform Crime Reports, October 17, 2005)
*Violent crimes are offenses of murder, forcible rape, robbery and aggravated assault.

Violent Crimes with Firearms in 2004

National Total = 277,868 Violent Crimes*

ALPHA ORDER				RANK ORDER			
RANK	STATE	CRIMES	% of USA	RANK	STATE	CRIMES	% of USA
22	Alabama	3,412	1.2%	1	California	44,450	16.0%
38	Alaska	624	0.2%	2	Texas	32,773	11.8%
6	Arizona	9,066	3.3%	3	Tennessee	13,850	5.0%
24	Arkansas	3,108	1.1%	4	Pennsylvania	13,379	4.8%
1	California	44,450	16.0%	5	Michigan	12,817	4.6%
21	Colorado	3,558	1.3%	6	Arizona	9,066	3.3%
30	Connecticut	1,574	0.6%	7	Ohio	8,899	3.2%
33	Delaware	973	0.4%	8	Georgia	8,860	3.2%
NA	Florida**	NA	NA	9	South Carolina	8,520	3.1%
8	Georgia	8,860	3.2%	10	Louisiana	8,464	3.0%
41	Hawaii	293	0.1%	11	North Carolina	7,766	2.8%
39	Idaho	606	0.2%	12	Missouri	7,385	2.7%
NA	Illinois**	NA	NA	13	Maryland	6,937	2.5%
15	Indiana	4,632	1.7%	14	New Jersey	6,855	2.5%
36	Iowa	825	0.3%	15	Indiana	4,632	1.7%
29	Kansas	1,821	0.7%	16	New York	4,586	1.7%
27	Kentucky	2,158	0.8%	17	Virginia	4,324	1.6%
10	Louisiana	8,464	3.0%	18	Nevada	3,781	1.4%
45	Maine	105	0.0%	19	Oklahoma	3,618	1.3%
13	Maryland	6,937	2.5%	20	Massachusetts	3,571	1.3%
20	Massachusetts	3,571	1.3%	21	Colorado	3,558	1.3%
5	Michigan	12,817	4.6%	22	Alabama	3,412	1.2%
35	Minnesota	854	0.3%	23	Wisconsin	3,109	1.1%
28	Mississippi	2,082	0.7%	24	Arkansas	3,108	1.1%
12	Missouri	7,385	2.7%	25	Washington	2,684	1.0%
43	Montana	211	0.1%	26	New Mexico	2,527	0.9%
32	Nebraska	1,035	0.4%	27	Kentucky	2,158	0.8%
18	Nevada	3,781	1.4%	28	Mississippi	2,082	0.7%
42	New Hampshire	223	0.1%	29	Kansas	1,821	0.7%
14	New Jersey	6,855	2.5%	30	Connecticut	1,574	0.6%
26	New Mexico	2,527	0.9%	31	Oregon	1,377	0.5%
16	New York	4,586	1.7%	32	Nebraska	1,035	0.4%
11	North Carolina	7,766	2.8%	33	Delaware	973	0.4%
48	North Dakota	24	0.0%	34	Utah	860	0.3%
7	Ohio	8,899	3.2%	35	Minnesota	854	0.3%
19	Oklahoma	3,618	1.3%	36	Iowa	825	0.3%
31	Oregon	1,377	0.5%	37	West Virginia	739	0.3%
4	Pennsylvania	13,379	4.8%	38	Alaska	624	0.2%
40	Rhode Island	534	0.2%	39	Idaho	606	0.2%
9	South Carolina	8,520	3.1%	40	Rhode Island	534	0.2%
46	South Dakota	99	0.0%	41	Hawaii	293	0.1%
3	Tennessee	13,850	5.0%	42	New Hampshire	223	0.1%
2	Texas	32,773	11.8%	43	Montana	211	0.1%
34	Utah	860	0.3%	44	Wyoming	151	0.1%
47	Vermont	75	0.0%	45	Maine	105	0.0%
17	Virginia	4,324	1.6%	46	South Dakota	99	0.0%
25	Washington	2,684	1.0%	47	Vermont	75	0.0%
37	West Virginia	739	0.3%	48	North Dakota	24	0.0%
23	Wisconsin	3,109	1.1%	NA	Florida**	NA	NA
44	Wyoming	151	0.1%	NA	Illinois**	NA	NA
					District of Columbia**	NA	NA

Source: Morgan Quitno Press using data from Federal Bureau of Investigation
 "Crime in the United States 2004" (Uniform Crime Reports, October 17, 2005)
Includes murder, robbery and aggravated assault. Does not include rape. National total reflects only those violent crimes for which the type of weapon was known and reported. There were an additional 221,578 violent crimes (excluding rape) for which the type of weapon was not reported to the F.B.I.
**Not available.*

Violent Crime Rate with Firearms in 2004

National Rate = 113.7 Violent Crimes per 100,000 Population*

ALPHA ORDER				RANK ORDER		
RANK	STATE	RATE		RANK	STATE	RATE
18	Alabama	102.8		1	Tennessee	238.1
21	Alaska	97.6		2	South Carolina	216.4
6	Arizona	161.8		3	Louisiana	215.1
9	Arkansas	145.5		4	Georgia	196.0
14	California	124.4		5	Nevada	161.9
24	Colorado	89.0		6	Arizona	161.8
32	Connecticut	58.7		7	New Mexico	152.1
16	Delaware	117.4		8	Texas	146.8
NA	Florida**	NA		9	Arkansas	145.5
4	Georgia	196.0		10	Maryland	141.0
42	Hawaii	26.5		11	Missouri	137.0
36	Idaho	43.6		12	Michigan	133.2
NA	Illinois**	NA		13	Pennsylvania	124.7
23	Indiana	93.6		14	California	124.4
41	Iowa	30.4		15	North Carolina	120.0
22	Kansas	95.3		16	Delaware	117.4
26	Kentucky	67.0		17	Mississippi	110.8
3	Louisiana	215.1		18	Alabama	102.8
47	Maine	8.0		19	Oklahoma	102.7
10	Maryland	141.0		20	Ohio	101.0
30	Massachusetts	64.7		21	Alaska	97.6
12	Michigan	133.2		22	Kansas	95.3
44	Minnesota	19.7		23	Indiana	93.6
17	Mississippi	110.8		24	Colorado	89.0
11	Missouri	137.0		25	New Jersey	79.0
39	Montana	32.1		26	Kentucky	67.0
27	Nebraska	66.5		27	Nebraska	66.5
5	Nevada	161.9		28	West Virginia	65.1
43	New Hampshire	22.5		29	Virginia	65.0
25	New Jersey	79.0		30	Massachusetts	64.7
7	New Mexico	152.1		31	Wisconsin	59.7
35	New York	45.5		32	Connecticut	58.7
15	North Carolina	120.0		33	Rhode Island	49.4
48	North Dakota	4.7		34	Washington	48.6
20	Ohio	101.0		35	New York	45.5
19	Oklahoma	102.7		36	Idaho	43.6
37	Oregon	41.0		37	Oregon	41.0
13	Pennsylvania	124.7		38	Utah	40.7
33	Rhode Island	49.4		39	Montana	32.1
2	South Carolina	216.4		40	Wyoming	30.6
45	South Dakota	17.1		41	Iowa	30.4
1	Tennessee	238.1		42	Hawaii	26.5
8	Texas	146.8		43	New Hampshire	22.5
38	Utah	40.7		44	Minnesota	19.7
46	Vermont	12.8		45	South Dakota	17.1
29	Virginia	65.0		46	Vermont	12.8
34	Washington	48.6		47	Maine	8.0
28	West Virginia	65.1		48	North Dakota	4.7
31	Wisconsin	59.7		NA	Florida**	NA
40	Wyoming	30.6		NA	Illinois**	NA
					District of Columbia**	NA

Source: Morgan Quitno Press using data from Federal Bureau of Investigation
    "Crime in the United States 2004" (Uniform Crime Reports, October 17, 2005)
*Based only on population of reporting jurisdictions. Includes murder, robbery and aggravated assault. Does not include rape. National rate reflects only those violent crimes for which the type of weapon was known and reported.
**Not available.

Percent of Violent Crimes Involving Firearms in 2004

National Percent = 26.4% of Violent Crimes*

ALPHA ORDER

RANK	STATE	PERCENT
7	Alabama	32.9
36	Alaska	17.7
5	Arizona	34.2
12	Arkansas	29.4
25	California	23.8
23	Colorado	25.2
29	Connecticut	22.5
24	Delaware	24.2
NA	Florida**	NA
2	Georgia	37.6
46	Hawaii	10.8
32	Idaho	21.4
NA	Illinois**	NA
20	Indiana	27.6
45	Iowa	11.6
16	Kansas	28.5
21	Kentucky	27.3
4	Louisiana	35.3
47	Maine	10.0
22	Maryland	26.3
42	Massachusetts	14.3
11	Michigan	29.7
38	Minnesota	16.9
1	Mississippi	38.3
14	Missouri	28.7
43	Montana	12.9
29	Nebraska	22.5
18	Nevada	28.2
33	New Hampshire	20.0
26	New Jersey	23.2
27	New Mexico	23.1
35	New York	18.7
6	North Carolina	33.1
48	North Dakota	7.7
17	Ohio	28.4
29	Oklahoma	22.5
39	Oregon	16.5
8	Pennsylvania	30.8
28	Rhode Island	22.7
15	South Carolina	28.6
44	South Dakota	12.3
3	Tennessee	35.9
13	Texas	29.2
33	Utah	20.0
40	Vermont	14.9
10	Virginia	30.2
36	Washington	17.7
19	West Virginia	27.7
9	Wisconsin	30.6
41	Wyoming	14.7

RANK ORDER

RANK	STATE	PERCENT
1	Mississippi	38.3
2	Georgia	37.6
3	Tennessee	35.9
4	Louisiana	35.3
5	Arizona	34.2
6	North Carolina	33.1
7	Alabama	32.9
8	Pennsylvania	30.8
9	Wisconsin	30.6
10	Virginia	30.2
11	Michigan	29.7
12	Arkansas	29.4
13	Texas	29.2
14	Missouri	28.7
15	South Carolina	28.6
16	Kansas	28.5
17	Ohio	28.4
18	Nevada	28.2
19	West Virginia	27.7
20	Indiana	27.6
21	Kentucky	27.3
22	Maryland	26.3
23	Colorado	25.2
24	Delaware	24.2
25	California	23.8
26	New Jersey	23.2
27	New Mexico	23.1
28	Rhode Island	22.7
29	Connecticut	22.5
29	Nebraska	22.5
29	Oklahoma	22.5
32	Idaho	21.4
33	New Hampshire	20.0
33	Utah	20.0
35	New York	18.7
36	Alaska	17.7
36	Washington	17.7
38	Minnesota	16.9
39	Oregon	16.5
40	Vermont	14.9
41	Wyoming	14.7
42	Massachusetts	14.3
43	Montana	12.9
44	South Dakota	12.3
45	Iowa	11.6
46	Hawaii	10.8
47	Maine	10.0
48	North Dakota	7.7
NA	Florida**	NA
NA	Illinois**	NA

District of Columbia** NA

Source: Morgan Quitno Press using data from Federal Bureau of Investigation
 "Crime in the United States 2004" (Uniform Crime Reports, October 17, 2005)
*Includes murder, robbery and aggravated assault. Does not include rape. National percent reflects only those violent crimes for which the type of weapon was known and reported. There were an additional 221,578 violent crimes (excluding rape) for which the type of weapon was not reported to the F.B.I.
**Not available.

Murders in 2004

National Total = 16,137 Murders*

RANK	STATE	MURDERS	% of USA
20	Alabama	254	1.6%
39	Alaska	37	0.2%
13	Arizona	414	2.6%
26	Arkansas	176	1.1%
1	California	2,392	14.8%
23	Colorado	203	1.3%
33	Connecticut	91	0.6%
47	Delaware	17	0.1%
3	Florida	946	5.9%
8	Georgia	613	3.8%
40	Hawaii	33	0.2%
41	Idaho	30	0.2%
5	Illinois	776	4.8%
18	Indiana	316	2.0%
36	Iowa	46	0.3%
31	Kansas	123	0.8%
21	Kentucky	236	1.5%
9	Louisiana	574	3.6%
44	Maine	18	0.1%
11	Maryland	521	3.2%
28	Massachusetts	169	1.0%
7	Michigan	643	4.0%
32	Minnesota	113	0.7%
22	Mississippi	227	1.4%
16	Missouri	354	2.2%
41	Montana	30	0.2%
38	Nebraska	40	0.2%
27	Nevada	172	1.1%
44	New Hampshire	18	0.1%
14	New Jersey	392	2.4%
28	New Mexico	169	1.0%
4	New York	889	5.5%
10	North Carolina	532	3.3%
50	North Dakota	9	0.1%
12	Ohio	517	3.2%
25	Oklahoma	186	1.2%
34	Oregon	90	0.6%
6	Pennsylvania	650	4.0%
43	Rhode Island	26	0.2%
19	South Carolina	288	1.8%
44	South Dakota	18	0.1%
17	Tennessee	351	2.2%
2	Texas	1,364	8.5%
36	Utah	46	0.3%
48	Vermont	16	0.1%
15	Virginia	391	2.4%
24	Washington	190	1.2%
35	West Virginia	68	0.4%
30	Wisconsin	154	1.0%
49	Wyoming	11	0.1%

RANK	STATE	MURDERS	% of USA
1	California	2,392	14.8%
2	Texas	1,364	8.5%
3	Florida	946	5.9%
4	New York	889	5.5%
5	Illinois	776	4.8%
6	Pennsylvania	650	4.0%
7	Michigan	643	4.0%
8	Georgia	613	3.8%
9	Louisiana	574	3.6%
10	North Carolina	532	3.3%
11	Maryland	521	3.2%
12	Ohio	517	3.2%
13	Arizona	414	2.6%
14	New Jersey	392	2.4%
15	Virginia	391	2.4%
16	Missouri	354	2.2%
17	Tennessee	351	2.2%
18	Indiana	316	2.0%
19	South Carolina	288	1.8%
20	Alabama	254	1.6%
21	Kentucky	236	1.5%
22	Mississippi	227	1.4%
23	Colorado	203	1.3%
24	Washington	190	1.2%
25	Oklahoma	186	1.2%
26	Arkansas	176	1.1%
27	Nevada	172	1.1%
28	Massachusetts	169	1.0%
28	New Mexico	169	1.0%
30	Wisconsin	154	1.0%
31	Kansas	123	0.8%
32	Minnesota	113	0.7%
33	Connecticut	91	0.6%
34	Oregon	90	0.6%
35	West Virginia	68	0.4%
36	Iowa	46	0.3%
36	Utah	46	0.3%
38	Nebraska	40	0.2%
39	Alaska	37	0.2%
40	Hawaii	33	0.2%
41	Idaho	30	0.2%
41	Montana	30	0.2%
43	Rhode Island	26	0.2%
44	Maine	18	0.1%
44	New Hampshire	18	0.1%
44	South Dakota	18	0.1%
47	Delaware	17	0.1%
48	Vermont	16	0.1%
49	Wyoming	11	0.1%
50	North Dakota	9	0.1%
	District of Columbia	198	1.2%

Source: Federal Bureau of Investigation
"Crime in the United States 2004" (Uniform Crime Reports, October 17, 2005)
Includes nonnegligent manslaughter.

Average Time Between Murders in 2004

National Rate = A Murder Occurs Every 32 Minutes*

ALPHA ORDER

RANK	STATE	HOURS.MINUTES
31	Alabama	34.35
12	Alaska	237.25
38	Arizona	21.13
25	Arkansas	49.55
50	California	3.40
28	Colorado	43.16
18	Connecticut	96.32
4	Delaware	516.43
48	Florida	9.17
43	Georgia	14.20
11	Hawaii	266.11
9	Idaho	292.48
46	Illinois	11.19
33	Indiana	27.48
14	Iowa	190.58
20	Kansas	71.25
30	Kentucky	37.13
42	Louisiana	15.18
5	Maine	488.00
40	Maryland	16.52
22	Massachusetts	51.59
44	Michigan	13.40
19	Minnesota	77.44
29	Mississippi	38.42
35	Missouri	24.49
9	Montana	292.48
13	Nebraska	219.36
24	Nevada	51.04
5	New Hampshire	488.00
37	New Jersey	22.25
22	New Mexico	51.59
47	New York	9.53
41	North Carolina	16.31
1	North Dakota	976.00
39	Ohio	16.59
26	Oklahoma	47.14
17	Oregon	97.36
45	Pennsylvania	13.31
8	Rhode Island	337.51
32	South Carolina	30.30
5	South Dakota	488.00
34	Tennessee	25.02
49	Texas	6.26
14	Utah	190.58
3	Vermont	549.00
36	Virginia	22.28
27	Washington	46.14
16	West Virginia	129.11
21	Wisconsin	57.02
2	Wyoming	798.33

RANK ORDER

RANK	STATE	HOURS.MINUTES
1	North Dakota	976.00
2	Wyoming	798.33
3	Vermont	549.00
4	Delaware	516.43
5	Maine	488.00
5	New Hampshire	488.00
5	South Dakota	488.00
8	Rhode Island	337.51
9	Idaho	292.48
9	Montana	292.48
11	Hawaii	266.11
12	Alaska	237.25
13	Nebraska	219.36
14	Iowa	190.58
14	Utah	190.58
16	West Virginia	129.11
17	Oregon	97.36
18	Connecticut	96.32
19	Minnesota	77.44
20	Kansas	71.25
21	Wisconsin	57.02
22	Massachusetts	51.59
22	New Mexico	51.59
24	Nevada	51.04
25	Arkansas	49.55
26	Oklahoma	47.14
27	Washington	46.14
28	Colorado	43.16
29	Mississippi	38.42
30	Kentucky	37.13
31	Alabama	34.35
32	South Carolina	30.30
33	Indiana	27.48
34	Tennessee	25.02
35	Missouri	24.49
36	Virginia	22.28
37	New Jersey	22.25
38	Arizona	21.13
39	Ohio	16.59
40	Maryland	16.52
41	North Carolina	16.31
42	Louisiana	15.18
43	Georgia	14.20
44	Michigan	13.40
45	Pennsylvania	13.31
46	Illinois	11.19
47	New York	9.53
48	Florida	9.17
49	Texas	6.26
50	California	3.40
	District of Columbia	44.22

Source: Morgan Quitno Press using data from Federal Bureau of Investigation
"Crime in the United States 2004" (Uniform Crime Reports, October 17, 2005)
*Includes nonnegligent manslaughter.

Percent Change in Number of Murders: 2003 to 2004

National Percent Change = 2.4% Decrease*

ALPHA ORDER

RANK ORDER

RANK	STATE	PERCENT CHANGE		RANK	STATE	PERCENT CHANGE
44	Alabama	(15.1)		1	South Dakota	80.0
31	Alaska	(5.1)		2	Hawaii	50.0
33	Arizona	(6.1)		3	New Mexico	45.7
26	Arkansas	(2.2)		4	Oregon	32.4
21	California	(0.6)		5	Kentucky	30.4
10	Colorado	9.7		6	Missouri	22.5
46	Connecticut	(18.8)		7	Massachusetts	20.7
47	Delaware	(19.0)		8	Idaho	15.4
17	Florida	2.4		9	Maine	12.5
35	Georgia	(6.7)		10	Colorado	9.7
2	Hawaii	50.0		11	Vermont	6.7
8	Idaho	15.4		12	New Hampshire	5.9
42	Illinois	(13.3)		13	Michigan	5.1
34	Indiana	(6.5)		13	North Carolina	5.1
37	Iowa	(8.0)		15	Washington	4.4
23	Kansas	(1.6)		16	Rhode Island	4.0
5	Kentucky	30.4		17	Florida	2.4
24	Louisiana	(1.7)		18	Pennsylvania	0.5
9	Maine	12.5		19	Montana	0.0
22	Maryland	(0.8)		19	North Dakota	0.0
7	Massachusetts	20.7		21	California	(0.6)
13	Michigan	5.1		22	Maryland	(0.8)
39	Minnesota	(11.0)		23	Kansas	(1.6)
43	Mississippi	(15.0)		24	Louisiana	(1.7)
6	Missouri	22.5		24	Ohio	(1.7)
19	Montana	0.0		26	Arkansas	(2.2)
50	Nebraska	(28.6)		27	New Jersey	(3.4)
41	Nevada	(12.7)		28	Texas	(4.1)
12	New Hampshire	5.9		29	New York	(4.8)
27	New Jersey	(3.4)		30	South Carolina	(5.0)
3	New Mexico	45.7		31	Alaska	(5.1)
29	New York	(4.8)		32	Virginia	(6.0)
13	North Carolina	5.1		33	Arizona	(6.1)
19	North Dakota	0.0		34	Indiana	(6.5)
24	Ohio	(1.7)		35	Georgia	(6.7)
38	Oklahoma	(9.7)		36	West Virginia	(6.8)
4	Oregon	32.4		37	Iowa	(8.0)
18	Pennsylvania	0.5		38	Oklahoma	(9.7)
16	Rhode Island	4.0		39	Minnesota	(11.0)
30	South Carolina	(5.0)		40	Tennessee	(11.4)
1	South Dakota	80.0		41	Nevada	(12.7)
40	Tennessee	(11.4)		42	Illinois	(13.3)
28	Texas	(4.1)		43	Mississippi	(15.0)
49	Utah	(23.3)		44	Alabama	(15.1)
11	Vermont	6.7		45	Wisconsin	(15.8)
32	Virginia	(6.0)		46	Connecticut	(18.8)
15	Washington	4.4		47	Delaware	(19.0)
36	West Virginia	(6.8)		48	Wyoming	(21.4)
45	Wisconsin	(15.8)		49	Utah	(23.3)
48	Wyoming	(21.4)		50	Nebraska	(28.6)
					District of Columbia	(20.5)

Source: Federal Bureau of Investigation
    "Crime in the United States 2004" (Uniform Crime Reports, October 17, 2005)
*Includes nonnegligent manslaughter.

Murder Rate in 2004

National Rate = 5.5 Murders per 100,000 Population*

ALPHA ORDER

RANK	STATE	RATE
18	Alabama	5.6
18	Alaska	5.6
6	Arizona	7.2
10	Arkansas	6.4
9	California	6.7
29	Colorado	4.4
34	Connecticut	2.6
45	Delaware	2.0
20	Florida	5.4
7	Georgia	6.9
34	Hawaii	2.6
42	Idaho	2.2
14	Illinois	6.1
24	Indiana	5.1
47	Iowa	1.6
26	Kansas	4.5
17	Kentucky	5.7
1	Louisiana	12.7
48	Maine	1.4
2	Maryland	9.4
34	Massachusetts	2.6
10	Michigan	6.4
42	Minnesota	2.2
4	Mississippi	7.8
12	Missouri	6.2
31	Montana	3.2
40	Nebraska	2.3
5	Nevada	7.4
48	New Hampshire	1.4
26	New Jersey	4.5
3	New Mexico	8.9
25	New York	4.6
12	North Carolina	6.2
48	North Dakota	1.4
26	Ohio	4.5
21	Oklahoma	5.3
38	Oregon	2.5
22	Pennsylvania	5.2
39	Rhode Island	2.4
7	South Carolina	6.9
40	South Dakota	2.3
16	Tennessee	5.9
14	Texas	6.1
46	Utah	1.9
34	Vermont	2.6
22	Virginia	5.2
32	Washington	3.1
30	West Virginia	3.7
33	Wisconsin	2.8
42	Wyoming	2.2

RANK ORDER

RANK	STATE	RATE
1	Louisiana	12.7
2	Maryland	9.4
3	New Mexico	8.9
4	Mississippi	7.8
5	Nevada	7.4
6	Arizona	7.2
7	Georgia	6.9
7	South Carolina	6.9
9	California	6.7
10	Arkansas	6.4
10	Michigan	6.4
12	Missouri	6.2
12	North Carolina	6.2
14	Illinois	6.1
14	Texas	6.1
16	Tennessee	5.9
17	Kentucky	5.7
18	Alabama	5.6
18	Alaska	5.6
20	Florida	5.4
21	Oklahoma	5.3
22	Pennsylvania	5.2
22	Virginia	5.2
24	Indiana	5.1
25	New York	4.6
26	Kansas	4.5
26	New Jersey	4.5
26	Ohio	4.5
29	Colorado	4.4
30	West Virginia	3.7
31	Montana	3.2
32	Washington	3.1
33	Wisconsin	2.8
34	Connecticut	2.6
34	Hawaii	2.6
34	Massachusetts	2.6
34	Vermont	2.6
38	Oregon	2.5
39	Rhode Island	2.4
40	Nebraska	2.3
40	South Dakota	2.3
42	Idaho	2.2
42	Minnesota	2.2
42	Wyoming	2.2
45	Delaware	2.0
46	Utah	1.9
47	Iowa	1.6
48	Maine	1.4
48	New Hampshire	1.4
48	North Dakota	1.4

District of Columbia	35.8

Source: Federal Bureau of Investigation
    "Crime in the United States 2004" (Uniform Crime Reports, October 17, 2005)
*Includes nonnegligent manslaughter.

Percent Change in Murder Rate: 2003 to 2004

National Percent Change = 3.3% Decrease*

<table>
<tr><td colspan="3">ALPHA ORDER</td><td colspan="3">RANK ORDER</td></tr>
<tr><td>RANK</td><td>STATE</td><td>PERCENT CHANGE</td><td>RANK</td><td>STATE</td><td>PERCENT CHANGE</td></tr>
<tr><td>42</td><td>Alabama</td><td>(15.5)</td><td>1</td><td>South Dakota</td><td>78.6</td></tr>
<tr><td>31</td><td>Alaska</td><td>(6.2)</td><td>2</td><td>Hawaii</td><td>48.3</td></tr>
<tr><td>37</td><td>Arizona</td><td>(8.8)</td><td>3</td><td>New Mexico</td><td>43.8</td></tr>
<tr><td>26</td><td>Arkansas</td><td>(3.1)</td><td>4</td><td>Oregon</td><td>31.2</td></tr>
<tr><td>22</td><td>California</td><td>(1.8)</td><td>5</td><td>Kentucky</td><td>29.5</td></tr>
<tr><td>10</td><td>Colorado</td><td>8.4</td><td>6</td><td>Missouri</td><td>21.7</td></tr>
<tr><td>46</td><td>Connecticut</td><td>(19.1)</td><td>7</td><td>Massachusetts</td><td>20.8</td></tr>
<tr><td>47</td><td>Delaware</td><td>(20.2)</td><td>8</td><td>Idaho</td><td>13.2</td></tr>
<tr><td>18</td><td>Florida</td><td>0.0</td><td>9</td><td>Maine</td><td>11.8</td></tr>
<tr><td>35</td><td>Georgia</td><td>(8.3)</td><td>10</td><td>Colorado</td><td>8.4</td></tr>
<tr><td>2</td><td>Hawaii</td><td>48.3</td><td>11</td><td>Vermont</td><td>6.3</td></tr>
<tr><td>8</td><td>Idaho</td><td>13.2</td><td>12</td><td>New Hampshire</td><td>5.0</td></tr>
<tr><td>41</td><td>Illinois</td><td>(13.7)</td><td>13</td><td>Michigan</td><td>4.8</td></tr>
<tr><td>32</td><td>Indiana</td><td>(7.1)</td><td>14</td><td>North Carolina</td><td>3.7</td></tr>
<tr><td>36</td><td>Iowa</td><td>(8.4)</td><td>15</td><td>Rhode Island</td><td>3.6</td></tr>
<tr><td>24</td><td>Kansas</td><td>(2.0)</td><td>16</td><td>Washington</td><td>3.2</td></tr>
<tr><td>5</td><td>Kentucky</td><td>29.5</td><td>17</td><td>Pennsylvania</td><td>0.2</td></tr>
<tr><td>25</td><td>Louisiana</td><td>(2.2)</td><td>18</td><td>Florida</td><td>0.0</td></tr>
<tr><td>9</td><td>Maine</td><td>11.8</td><td>19</td><td>North Dakota</td><td>(0.2)</td></tr>
<tr><td>21</td><td>Maryland</td><td>(1.6)</td><td>20</td><td>Montana</td><td>(0.9)</td></tr>
<tr><td>7</td><td>Massachusetts</td><td>20.8</td><td>21</td><td>Maryland</td><td>(1.6)</td></tr>
<tr><td>13</td><td>Michigan</td><td>4.8</td><td>22</td><td>California</td><td>(1.8)</td></tr>
<tr><td>39</td><td>Minnesota</td><td>(11.7)</td><td>23</td><td>Ohio</td><td>(1.9)</td></tr>
<tr><td>43</td><td>Mississippi</td><td>(15.6)</td><td>24</td><td>Kansas</td><td>(2.0)</td></tr>
<tr><td>6</td><td>Missouri</td><td>21.7</td><td>25</td><td>Louisiana</td><td>(2.2)</td></tr>
<tr><td>20</td><td>Montana</td><td>(0.9)</td><td>26</td><td>Arkansas</td><td>(3.1)</td></tr>
<tr><td>50</td><td>Nebraska</td><td>(29.0)</td><td>27</td><td>New Jersey</td><td>(4.1)</td></tr>
<tr><td>44</td><td>Nevada</td><td>(16.2)</td><td>28</td><td>New York</td><td>(4.9)</td></tr>
<tr><td>12</td><td>New Hampshire</td><td>5.0</td><td>29</td><td>Texas</td><td>(5.7)</td></tr>
<tr><td>27</td><td>New Jersey</td><td>(4.1)</td><td>30</td><td>South Carolina</td><td>(6.1)</td></tr>
<tr><td>3</td><td>New Mexico</td><td>43.8</td><td>31</td><td>Alaska</td><td>(6.2)</td></tr>
<tr><td>28</td><td>New York</td><td>(4.9)</td><td>32</td><td>Indiana</td><td>(7.1)</td></tr>
<tr><td>14</td><td>North Carolina</td><td>3.7</td><td>32</td><td>West Virginia</td><td>(7.1)</td></tr>
<tr><td>19</td><td>North Dakota</td><td>(0.2)</td><td>34</td><td>Virginia</td><td>(7.2)</td></tr>
<tr><td>23</td><td>Ohio</td><td>(1.9)</td><td>35</td><td>Georgia</td><td>(8.3)</td></tr>
<tr><td>38</td><td>Oklahoma</td><td>(10.1)</td><td>36</td><td>Iowa</td><td>(8.4)</td></tr>
<tr><td>4</td><td>Oregon</td><td>31.2</td><td>37</td><td>Arizona</td><td>(8.8)</td></tr>
<tr><td>17</td><td>Pennsylvania</td><td>0.2</td><td>38</td><td>Oklahoma</td><td>(10.1)</td></tr>
<tr><td>15</td><td>Rhode Island</td><td>3.6</td><td>39</td><td>Minnesota</td><td>(11.7)</td></tr>
<tr><td>30</td><td>South Carolina</td><td>(6.1)</td><td>40</td><td>Tennessee</td><td>(12.2)</td></tr>
<tr><td>1</td><td>South Dakota</td><td>78.6</td><td>41</td><td>Illinois</td><td>(13.7)</td></tr>
<tr><td>40</td><td>Tennessee</td><td>(12.2)</td><td>42</td><td>Alabama</td><td>(15.5)</td></tr>
<tr><td>29</td><td>Texas</td><td>(5.7)</td><td>43</td><td>Mississippi</td><td>(15.6)</td></tr>
<tr><td>49</td><td>Utah</td><td>(24.5)</td><td>44</td><td>Nevada</td><td>(16.2)</td></tr>
<tr><td>11</td><td>Vermont</td><td>6.3</td><td>45</td><td>Wisconsin</td><td>(16.4)</td></tr>
<tr><td>34</td><td>Virginia</td><td>(7.2)</td><td>46</td><td>Connecticut</td><td>(19.1)</td></tr>
<tr><td>16</td><td>Washington</td><td>3.2</td><td>47</td><td>Delaware</td><td>(20.2)</td></tr>
<tr><td>32</td><td>West Virginia</td><td>(7.1)</td><td>48</td><td>Wyoming</td><td>(22.1)</td></tr>
<tr><td>45</td><td>Wisconsin</td><td>(16.4)</td><td>49</td><td>Utah</td><td>(24.5)</td></tr>
<tr><td>48</td><td>Wyoming</td><td>(22.1)</td><td>50</td><td>Nebraska</td><td>(29.0)</td></tr>
<tr><td></td><td></td><td></td><td></td><td>District of Columbia</td><td>(19.9)</td></tr>
</table>

Source: Federal Bureau of Investigation
    "Crime in the United States 2004" (Uniform Crime Reports, October 17, 2005)
*Includes nonnegligent manslaughter.

Murders with Firearms in 2004

National Total = 9,326 Murders*

ALPHA ORDER

RANK	STATE	MURDERS	% of USA
19	Alabama	158	1.7%
36	Alaska	17	0.2%
10	Arizona	295	3.2%
28	Arkansas	95	1.0%
1	California	1,724	18.5%
22	Colorado	116	1.2%
32	Connecticut	47	0.5%
42	Delaware	9	0.1%
NA	Florida**	NA	NA
8	Georgia	342	3.7%
44	Hawaii	6	0.1%
36	Idaho	17	0.2%
9	Illinois*	337	3.6%
17	Indiana	208	2.2%
35	Iowa	19	0.2%
33	Kansas	45	0.5%
20	Kentucky	136	1.5%
6	Louisiana	442	4.7%
42	Maine	9	0.1%
7	Maryland	386	4.1%
27	Massachusetts	97	1.0%
4	Michigan	456	4.9%
30	Minnesota	73	0.8%
21	Mississippi	124	1.3%
14	Missouri	243	2.6%
41	Montana	11	0.1%
36	Nebraska	17	0.2%
23	Nevada	110	1.2%
46	New Hampshire	4	0.0%
15	New Jersey	230	2.5%
29	New Mexico	75	0.8%
3	New York	500	5.4%
11	North Carolina	284	3.0%
46	North Dakota	4	0.0%
13	Ohio	245	2.6%
24	Oklahoma	106	1.1%
31	Oregon	48	0.5%
5	Pennsylvania	449	4.8%
39	Rhode Island	16	0.2%
18	South Carolina	194	2.1%
45	South Dakota	5	0.1%
16	Tennessee	221	2.4%
2	Texas	882	9.5%
40	Utah	12	0.1%
48	Vermont	3	0.0%
12	Virginia	270	2.9%
24	Washington	106	1.1%
34	West Virginia	31	0.3%
26	Wisconsin	99	1.1%
48	Wyoming	3	0.0%

RANK ORDER

RANK	STATE	MURDERS	% of USA
1	California	1,724	18.5%
2	Texas	882	9.5%
3	New York	500	5.4%
4	Michigan	456	4.9%
5	Pennsylvania	449	4.8%
6	Louisiana	442	4.7%
7	Maryland	386	4.1%
8	Georgia	342	3.7%
9	Illinois*	337	3.6%
10	Arizona	295	3.2%
11	North Carolina	284	3.0%
12	Virginia	270	2.9%
13	Ohio	245	2.6%
14	Missouri	243	2.6%
15	New Jersey	230	2.5%
16	Tennessee	221	2.4%
17	Indiana	208	2.2%
18	South Carolina	194	2.1%
19	Alabama	158	1.7%
20	Kentucky	136	1.5%
21	Mississippi	124	1.3%
22	Colorado	116	1.2%
23	Nevada	110	1.2%
24	Oklahoma	106	1.1%
24	Washington	106	1.1%
26	Wisconsin	99	1.1%
27	Massachusetts	97	1.0%
28	Arkansas	95	1.0%
29	New Mexico	75	0.8%
30	Minnesota	73	0.8%
31	Oregon	48	0.5%
32	Connecticut	47	0.5%
33	Kansas	45	0.5%
34	West Virginia	31	0.3%
35	Iowa	19	0.2%
36	Alaska	17	0.2%
36	Idaho	17	0.2%
36	Nebraska	17	0.2%
39	Rhode Island	16	0.2%
40	Utah	12	0.1%
41	Montana	11	0.1%
42	Delaware	9	0.1%
42	Maine	9	0.1%
44	Hawaii	6	0.1%
45	South Dakota	5	0.1%
46	New Hampshire	4	0.0%
46	North Dakota	4	0.0%
48	Vermont	3	0.0%
48	Wyoming	3	0.0%
NA	Florida**	NA	NA
	District of Columbia**	NA	NA

Source: Federal Bureau of Investigation
    "Crime in the United States 2004" (Uniform Crime Reports, October 17, 2005)

*Of the 14,121 murders in 2004 for which supplemental data were received by the F.B.I. There were an additional
2,016 murders for which the type of murder weapon was not reported to the F.B.I. Includes nonnegligent
manslaughter. Numbers are for reporting jurisdictions only. Illinois' figure is for Chicago only.
**Not available.

Murder Rate with Firearms in 2004

National Rate = 4.1 Murders per 100,000 Population*

ALPHA ORDER

RANK	STATE	RATE
9	Alabama	4.8
26	Alaska	2.7
6	Arizona	5.3
15	Arkansas	4.4
9	California	4.8
24	Colorado	2.9
32	Connecticut	1.8
39	Delaware	1.1
NA	Florida**	NA
4	Georgia	7.6
47	Hawaii	0.5
38	Idaho	1.2
1	Illinois*	11.7
17	Indiana	4.2
43	Iowa	0.7
29	Kansas	2.4
17	Kentucky	4.2
2	Louisiana	11.2
43	Maine	0.7
3	Maryland	7.8
32	Massachusetts	1.8
11	Michigan	4.7
34	Minnesota	1.7
5	Mississippi	6.6
13	Missouri	4.5
34	Montana	1.7
39	Nebraska	1.1
11	Nevada	4.7
49	New Hampshire	0.4
26	New Jersey	2.7
13	New Mexico	4.5
7	New York	5.0
15	North Carolina	4.4
42	North Dakota	0.8
25	Ohio	2.8
23	Oklahoma	3.0
37	Oregon	1.4
17	Pennsylvania	4.2
36	Rhode Island	1.5
8	South Carolina	4.9
41	South Dakota	0.9
22	Tennessee	3.8
21	Texas	4.0
45	Utah	0.6
47	Vermont	0.5
20	Virginia	4.1
30	Washington	1.9
26	West Virginia	2.7
30	Wisconsin	1.9
45	Wyoming	0.6

RANK ORDER

RANK	STATE	RATE
1	Illinois*	11.7
2	Louisiana	11.2
3	Maryland	7.8
4	Georgia	7.6
5	Mississippi	6.6
6	Arizona	5.3
7	New York	5.0
8	South Carolina	4.9
9	Alabama	4.8
9	California	4.8
11	Michigan	4.7
11	Nevada	4.7
13	Missouri	4.5
13	New Mexico	4.5
15	Arkansas	4.4
15	North Carolina	4.4
17	Indiana	4.2
17	Kentucky	4.2
17	Pennsylvania	4.2
20	Virginia	4.1
21	Texas	4.0
22	Tennessee	3.8
23	Oklahoma	3.0
24	Colorado	2.9
25	Ohio	2.8
26	Alaska	2.7
26	New Jersey	2.7
26	West Virginia	2.7
29	Kansas	2.4
30	Washington	1.9
30	Wisconsin	1.9
32	Connecticut	1.8
32	Massachusetts	1.8
34	Minnesota	1.7
34	Montana	1.7
36	Rhode Island	1.5
37	Oregon	1.4
38	Idaho	1.2
39	Delaware	1.1
39	Nebraska	1.1
41	South Dakota	0.9
42	North Dakota	0.8
43	Iowa	0.7
43	Maine	0.7
45	Utah	0.6
45	Wyoming	0.6
47	Hawaii	0.5
47	Vermont	0.5
49	New Hampshire	0.4
NA	Florida**	NA
	District of Columbia**	NA

Source: Morgan Quitno Press using data from Federal Bureau of Investigation
  "Crime in the United States 2004" (Uniform Crime Reports, October 17, 2005)
*Of the 14,121 murders in 2004 for which supplemental data were received by the F.B.I. There were an additional
2,016 murders for which the type of murder weapon was not reported to the F.B.I. Includes nonnegligent
manslaughter. National and state rates based on population for reporting jurisdictions only. Illinois' rate is for
Chicago only. **Not available.

Percent of Murders Involving Firearms in 2004

National Percent = 66.0% of Murders*

ALPHA ORDER

RANK	STATE	PERCENT
18	Alabama	64.0
44	Alaska	45.9
4	Arizona	72.1
23	Arkansas	62.5
4	California	72.1
28	Colorado	58.3
35	Connecticut	54.7
16	Delaware	64.3
NA	Florida**	NA
14	Georgia	64.8
48	Hawaii	19.4
33	Idaho	56.7
2	Illinois*	75.2
9	Indiana	69.6
43	Iowa	47.5
25	Kansas	60.0
22	Kentucky	62.7
1	Louisiana	79.4
37	Maine	52.9
3	Maryland	74.2
29	Massachusetts	58.1
6	Michigan	71.5
13	Minnesota	66.4
8	Mississippi	70.9
11	Missouri	68.8
42	Montana	47.8
21	Nebraska	63.0
18	Nevada	64.0
46	New Hampshire	30.8
27	New Jersey	58.8
39	New Mexico	50.0
30	New York	57.9
26	North Carolina	59.5
39	North Dakota	50.0
38	Ohio	52.8
32	Oklahoma	57.0
36	Oregon	53.3
7	Pennsylvania	71.0
24	Rhode Island	61.5
12	South Carolina	67.6
45	South Dakota	31.3
20	Tennessee	63.1
14	Texas	64.8
31	Utah	57.1
49	Vermont	18.8
10	Virginia	69.2
34	Washington	56.1
39	West Virginia	50.0
16	Wisconsin	64.3
47	Wyoming	27.3

RANK ORDER

RANK	STATE	PERCENT
1	Louisiana	79.4
2	Illinois*	75.2
3	Maryland	74.2
4	Arizona	72.1
4	California	72.1
6	Michigan	71.5
7	Pennsylvania	71.0
8	Mississippi	70.9
9	Indiana	69.6
10	Virginia	69.2
11	Missouri	68.8
12	South Carolina	67.6
13	Minnesota	66.4
14	Georgia	64.8
14	Texas	64.8
16	Delaware	64.3
16	Wisconsin	64.3
18	Alabama	64.0
18	Nevada	64.0
20	Tennessee	63.1
21	Nebraska	63.0
22	Kentucky	62.7
23	Arkansas	62.5
24	Rhode Island	61.5
25	Kansas	60.0
26	North Carolina	59.5
27	New Jersey	58.8
28	Colorado	58.3
29	Massachusetts	58.1
30	New York	57.9
31	Utah	57.1
32	Oklahoma	57.0
33	Idaho	56.7
34	Washington	56.1
35	Connecticut	54.7
36	Oregon	53.3
37	Maine	52.9
38	Ohio	52.8
39	New Mexico	50.0
39	North Dakota	50.0
39	West Virginia	50.0
42	Montana	47.8
43	Iowa	47.5
44	Alaska	45.9
45	South Dakota	31.3
46	New Hampshire	30.8
47	Wyoming	27.3
48	Hawaii	19.4
49	Vermont	18.8
NA	Florida**	NA
	District of Columbia**	NA

Source: Morgan Quitno Press using data from Federal Bureau of Investigation
    "Crime in the United States 2004" (Uniform Crime Reports, October 17, 2005)
*Of the 14,121 murders in 2004 for which supplemental data were received by the F.B.I. There were an additional 2,016 murders for which the type of murder weapon was not reported to the F.B.I. Includes nonnegligent manslaughter. National and state rates based on population for reporting jurisdictions only. Illinois' rate is for Chicago only. **Not available.

Murders with Handguns in 2004

National Total = 7,265 Murders*

ALPHA ORDER

RANK	STATE	MURDERS	% of USA
17	Alabama	137	1.9%
34	Alaska	16	0.2%
10	Arizona	244	3.4%
26	Arkansas	69	0.9%
1	California	1,442	19.8%
22	Colorado	85	1.2%
31	Connecticut	39	0.5%
41	Delaware	7	0.1%
NA	Florida**	NA	NA
9	Georgia	283	3.9%
45	Hawaii	3	0.0%
41	Idaho	7	0.1%
8	Illinois*	313	4.3%
15	Indiana	144	2.0%
37	Iowa	11	0.2%
32	Kansas	31	0.4%
20	Kentucky	99	1.4%
4	Louisiana	369	5.1%
43	Maine	6	0.1%
6	Maryland	362	5.0%
27	Massachusetts	67	0.9%
5	Michigan	364	5.0%
29	Minnesota	63	0.9%
19	Mississippi	104	1.4%
21	Missouri	97	1.3%
40	Montana	8	0.1%
36	Nebraska	13	0.2%
25	Nevada	71	1.0%
44	New Hampshire	4	0.1%
11	New Jersey	225	3.1%
28	New Mexico	66	0.9%
3	New York	419	5.8%
12	North Carolina	199	2.7%
48	North Dakota	1	0.0%
13	Ohio	160	2.2%
24	Oklahoma	78	1.1%
33	Oregon	19	0.3%
7	Pennsylvania	359	4.9%
37	Rhode Island	11	0.2%
14	South Carolina	151	2.1%
47	South Dakota	2	0.0%
16	Tennessee	142	2.0%
2	Texas	688	9.5%
39	Utah	10	0.1%
45	Vermont	3	0.0%
18	Virginia	122	1.7%
23	Washington	82	1.1%
35	West Virginia	15	0.2%
30	Wisconsin	54	0.7%
48	Wyoming	1	0.0%

RANK ORDER

RANK	STATE	MURDERS	% of USA
1	California	1,442	19.8%
2	Texas	688	9.5%
3	New York	419	5.8%
4	Louisiana	369	5.1%
5	Michigan	364	5.0%
6	Maryland	362	5.0%
7	Pennsylvania	359	4.9%
8	Illinois*	313	4.3%
9	Georgia	283	3.9%
10	Arizona	244	3.4%
11	New Jersey	225	3.1%
12	North Carolina	199	2.7%
13	Ohio	160	2.2%
14	South Carolina	151	2.1%
15	Indiana	144	2.0%
16	Tennessee	142	2.0%
17	Alabama	137	1.9%
18	Virginia	122	1.7%
19	Mississippi	104	1.4%
20	Kentucky	99	1.4%
21	Missouri	97	1.3%
22	Colorado	85	1.2%
23	Washington	82	1.1%
24	Oklahoma	78	1.1%
25	Nevada	71	1.0%
26	Arkansas	69	0.9%
27	Massachusetts	67	0.9%
28	New Mexico	66	0.9%
29	Minnesota	63	0.9%
30	Wisconsin	54	0.7%
31	Connecticut	39	0.5%
32	Kansas	31	0.4%
33	Oregon	19	0.3%
34	Alaska	16	0.2%
35	West Virginia	15	0.2%
36	Nebraska	13	0.2%
37	Iowa	11	0.2%
37	Rhode Island	11	0.2%
39	Utah	10	0.1%
40	Montana	8	0.1%
41	Delaware	7	0.1%
41	Idaho	7	0.1%
43	Maine	6	0.1%
44	New Hampshire	4	0.1%
45	Hawaii	3	0.0%
45	Vermont	3	0.0%
47	South Dakota	2	0.0%
48	North Dakota	1	0.0%
48	Wyoming	1	0.0%
NA	Florida**	NA	NA
	District of Columbia**	NA	NA

Source: Federal Bureau of Investigation
    "Crime in the United States 2003" (Uniform Crime Reports, October 25, 2004)
*Of the 14,121 murders in 2004 for which supplemental data were received by the F.B.I. There were an additional 2,016 murders for which the type of murder weapon was not reported to the F.B.I. There were also 1,161 murders that were reported as murders by "firearms, type unknown." Murder includes nonnegligent manslaughter. Numbers are for reporting jurisdictions only. Illinois' figure is for Chicago only. **Not available.*

Murder Rate with Handguns in 2004

National Rate = 3.2 Murders per 100,000 Population*

ALPHA ORDER

RANK	STATE	RATE
8	Alabama	4.1
21	Alaska	2.5
6	Arizona	4.4
14	Arkansas	3.2
9	California	4.0
24	Colorado	2.1
29	Connecticut	1.5
37	Delaware	0.8
NA	Florida**	NA
4	Georgia	6.3
46	Hawaii	0.3
40	Idaho	0.5
1	Illinois*	10.9
19	Indiana	2.9
44	Iowa	0.4
28	Kansas	1.6
15	Kentucky	3.1
2	Louisiana	9.4
40	Maine	0.5
3	Maryland	7.4
33	Massachusetts	1.2
11	Michigan	3.8
29	Minnesota	1.5
5	Mississippi	5.5
25	Missouri	1.8
33	Montana	1.2
37	Nebraska	0.8
18	Nevada	3.0
44	New Hampshire	0.4
20	New Jersey	2.6
9	New Mexico	4.0
7	New York	4.2
15	North Carolina	3.1
48	North Dakota	0.2
25	Ohio	1.8
23	Oklahoma	2.2
39	Oregon	0.6
13	Pennsylvania	3.3
35	Rhode Island	1.0
11	South Carolina	3.8
46	South Dakota	0.3
22	Tennessee	2.4
15	Texas	3.1
40	Utah	0.5
40	Vermont	0.5
25	Virginia	1.8
29	Washington	1.5
32	West Virginia	1.3
35	Wisconsin	1.0
48	Wyoming	0.2

RANK ORDER

RANK	STATE	RATE
1	Illinois*	10.9
2	Louisiana	9.4
3	Maryland	7.4
4	Georgia	6.3
5	Mississippi	5.5
6	Arizona	4.4
7	New York	4.2
8	Alabama	4.1
9	California	4.0
9	New Mexico	4.0
11	Michigan	3.8
11	South Carolina	3.8
13	Pennsylvania	3.3
14	Arkansas	3.2
15	Kentucky	3.1
15	North Carolina	3.1
15	Texas	3.1
18	Nevada	3.0
19	Indiana	2.9
20	New Jersey	2.6
21	Alaska	2.5
22	Tennessee	2.4
23	Oklahoma	2.2
24	Colorado	2.1
25	Missouri	1.8
25	Ohio	1.8
25	Virginia	1.8
28	Kansas	1.6
29	Connecticut	1.5
29	Minnesota	1.5
29	Washington	1.5
32	West Virginia	1.3
33	Massachusetts	1.2
33	Montana	1.2
35	Rhode Island	1.0
35	Wisconsin	1.0
37	Delaware	0.8
37	Nebraska	0.8
39	Oregon	0.6
40	Idaho	0.5
40	Maine	0.5
40	Utah	0.5
40	Vermont	0.5
44	Iowa	0.4
44	New Hampshire	0.4
46	Hawaii	0.3
46	South Dakota	0.3
48	North Dakota	0.2
48	Wyoming	0.2
NA	Florida**	NA
	District of Columbia**	NA

Source: Morgan Quitno Press using data from Federal Bureau of Investigation
      "Crime in the United States 2003" (Uniform Crime Reports, October 25, 2004)
*Of the 14,121 murders in 2004 for which supplemental data were received by the F.B.I. There were an additional 2,016 murders for which the type of murder weapon was not reported to the F.B.I. There were also 1,161 murders that were reported as murders by "firearms, type unknown." Murder includes nonnegligent manslaughter. Numbers are for reporting jurisdictions only. Illinois' figure is for Chicago only. **Not available.

Percent of Murders Involving Handguns in 2004

National Percent = 51.4% of Murders*

ALPHA ORDER

RANK	STATE	PERCENT
11	Alabama	55.5
25	Alaska	43.2
5	Arizona	59.7
21	Arkansas	45.4
4	California	60.3
26	Colorado	42.7
22	Connecticut	45.3
15	Delaware	50.0
NA	Florida**	NA
12	Georgia	53.6
48	Hawaii	9.7
43	Idaho	23.3
1	Illinois*	69.9
17	Indiana	48.2
40	Iowa	27.5
30	Kansas	41.3
20	Kentucky	45.6
3	Louisiana	66.2
34	Maine	35.3
2	Maryland	69.6
33	Massachusetts	40.1
9	Michigan	57.1
8	Minnesota	57.3
6	Mississippi	59.4
40	Missouri	27.5
36	Montana	34.8
18	Nebraska	48.1
30	Nevada	41.3
39	New Hampshire	30.8
7	New Jersey	57.5
23	New Mexico	44.0
16	New York	48.5
29	North Carolina	41.7
46	North Dakota	12.5
37	Ohio	34.5
28	Oklahoma	41.9
44	Oregon	21.1
10	Pennsylvania	56.8
27	Rhode Island	42.3
13	South Carolina	52.6
46	South Dakota	12.5
32	Tennessee	40.6
14	Texas	50.5
19	Utah	47.6
45	Vermont	18.8
38	Virginia	31.3
24	Washington	43.4
42	West Virginia	24.2
35	Wisconsin	35.1
49	Wyoming	9.1

RANK ORDER

RANK	STATE	PERCENT
1	Illinois*	69.9
2	Maryland	69.6
3	Louisiana	66.2
4	California	60.3
5	Arizona	59.7
6	Mississippi	59.4
7	New Jersey	57.5
8	Minnesota	57.3
9	Michigan	57.1
10	Pennsylvania	56.8
11	Alabama	55.5
12	Georgia	53.6
13	South Carolina	52.6
14	Texas	50.5
15	Delaware	50.0
16	New York	48.5
17	Indiana	48.2
18	Nebraska	48.1
19	Utah	47.6
20	Kentucky	45.6
21	Arkansas	45.4
22	Connecticut	45.3
23	New Mexico	44.0
24	Washington	43.4
25	Alaska	43.2
26	Colorado	42.7
27	Rhode Island	42.3
28	Oklahoma	41.9
29	North Carolina	41.7
30	Kansas	41.3
30	Nevada	41.3
32	Tennessee	40.6
33	Massachusetts	40.1
34	Maine	35.3
35	Wisconsin	35.1
36	Montana	34.8
37	Ohio	34.5
38	Virginia	31.3
39	New Hampshire	30.8
40	Iowa	27.5
40	Missouri	27.5
42	West Virginia	24.2
43	Idaho	23.3
44	Oregon	21.1
45	Vermont	18.8
46	North Dakota	12.5
46	South Dakota	12.5
48	Hawaii	9.7
49	Wyoming	9.1
NA	Florida**	NA
	District of Columbia**	NA

Source: Morgan Quitno Press using data from Federal Bureau of Investigation
  "Crime in the United States 2003" (Uniform Crime Reports, October 25, 2004)
*Of the 14,121 murders in 2004 for which supplemental data were received by the F.B.I. There were an additional
2,016 murders for which the type of murder weapon was not reported to the F.B.I. There were also 1,161 murders that
were reported as murders by "firearms, type unknown." Murder includes nonnegligent manslaughter. Numbers are
for reporting jurisdictions only. Illinois' figure is for Chicago only. **Not available.

Murders with Rifles in 2004

National Total = 393 Murders*

<table>
<tr><td colspan="4">ALPHA ORDER</td><td colspan="4">RANK ORDER</td></tr>
<tr><td>RANK</td><td>STATE</td><td>MURDERS</td><td>% of USA</td><td>RANK</td><td>STATE</td><td>MURDERS</td><td>% of USA</td></tr>
<tr><td>37</td><td>Alabama</td><td>0</td><td>0.0%</td><td>1</td><td>California</td><td>75</td><td>19.1%</td></tr>
<tr><td>37</td><td>Alaska</td><td>0</td><td>0.0%</td><td>2</td><td>Texas</td><td>49</td><td>12.5%</td></tr>
<tr><td>4</td><td>Arizona</td><td>30</td><td>7.6%</td><td>3</td><td>Louisiana</td><td>34</td><td>8.7%</td></tr>
<tr><td>23</td><td>Arkansas</td><td>3</td><td>0.8%</td><td>4</td><td>Arizona</td><td>30</td><td>7.6%</td></tr>
<tr><td>1</td><td>California</td><td>75</td><td>19.1%</td><td>5</td><td>Missouri</td><td>19</td><td>4.8%</td></tr>
<tr><td>19</td><td>Colorado</td><td>5</td><td>1.3%</td><td>6</td><td>Michigan</td><td>18</td><td>4.6%</td></tr>
<tr><td>37</td><td>Connecticut</td><td>0</td><td>0.0%</td><td>7</td><td>South Carolina</td><td>15</td><td>3.8%</td></tr>
<tr><td>37</td><td>Delaware</td><td>0</td><td>0.0%</td><td>8</td><td>Georgia</td><td>14</td><td>3.6%</td></tr>
<tr><td>NA</td><td>Florida**</td><td>NA</td><td>NA</td><td>8</td><td>North Carolina</td><td>14</td><td>3.6%</td></tr>
<tr><td>8</td><td>Georgia</td><td>14</td><td>3.6%</td><td>10</td><td>Kentucky</td><td>11</td><td>2.8%</td></tr>
<tr><td>37</td><td>Hawaii</td><td>0</td><td>0.0%</td><td>11</td><td>New York</td><td>10</td><td>2.5%</td></tr>
<tr><td>23</td><td>Idaho</td><td>3</td><td>0.8%</td><td>11</td><td>Ohio</td><td>10</td><td>2.5%</td></tr>
<tr><td>22</td><td>Illinois*</td><td>4</td><td>1.0%</td><td>11</td><td>Tennessee</td><td>10</td><td>2.5%</td></tr>
<tr><td>19</td><td>Indiana</td><td>5</td><td>1.3%</td><td>14</td><td>Pennsylvania</td><td>8</td><td>2.0%</td></tr>
<tr><td>33</td><td>Iowa</td><td>1</td><td>0.3%</td><td>14</td><td>Virginia</td><td>8</td><td>2.0%</td></tr>
<tr><td>33</td><td>Kansas</td><td>1</td><td>0.3%</td><td>16</td><td>Washington</td><td>7</td><td>1.8%</td></tr>
<tr><td>10</td><td>Kentucky</td><td>11</td><td>2.8%</td><td>16</td><td>Wisconsin</td><td>7</td><td>1.8%</td></tr>
<tr><td>3</td><td>Louisiana</td><td>34</td><td>8.7%</td><td>18</td><td>Minnesota</td><td>6</td><td>1.5%</td></tr>
<tr><td>37</td><td>Maine</td><td>0</td><td>0.0%</td><td>19</td><td>Colorado</td><td>5</td><td>1.3%</td></tr>
<tr><td>28</td><td>Maryland</td><td>2</td><td>0.5%</td><td>19</td><td>Indiana</td><td>5</td><td>1.3%</td></tr>
<tr><td>33</td><td>Massachusetts</td><td>1</td><td>0.3%</td><td>19</td><td>Oklahoma</td><td>5</td><td>1.3%</td></tr>
<tr><td>6</td><td>Michigan</td><td>18</td><td>4.6%</td><td>22</td><td>Illinois*</td><td>4</td><td>1.0%</td></tr>
<tr><td>18</td><td>Minnesota</td><td>6</td><td>1.5%</td><td>23</td><td>Arkansas</td><td>3</td><td>0.8%</td></tr>
<tr><td>28</td><td>Mississippi</td><td>2</td><td>0.5%</td><td>23</td><td>Idaho</td><td>3</td><td>0.8%</td></tr>
<tr><td>5</td><td>Missouri</td><td>19</td><td>4.8%</td><td>23</td><td>New Mexico</td><td>3</td><td>0.8%</td></tr>
<tr><td>37</td><td>Montana</td><td>0</td><td>0.0%</td><td>23</td><td>Oregon</td><td>3</td><td>0.8%</td></tr>
<tr><td>37</td><td>Nebraska</td><td>0</td><td>0.0%</td><td>23</td><td>West Virginia</td><td>3</td><td>0.8%</td></tr>
<tr><td>28</td><td>Nevada</td><td>2</td><td>0.5%</td><td>28</td><td>Maryland</td><td>2</td><td>0.5%</td></tr>
<tr><td>37</td><td>New Hampshire</td><td>0</td><td>0.0%</td><td>28</td><td>Mississippi</td><td>2</td><td>0.5%</td></tr>
<tr><td>28</td><td>New Jersey</td><td>2</td><td>0.5%</td><td>28</td><td>Nevada</td><td>2</td><td>0.5%</td></tr>
<tr><td>23</td><td>New Mexico</td><td>3</td><td>0.8%</td><td>28</td><td>New Jersey</td><td>2</td><td>0.5%</td></tr>
<tr><td>11</td><td>New York</td><td>10</td><td>2.5%</td><td>28</td><td>North Dakota</td><td>2</td><td>0.5%</td></tr>
<tr><td>8</td><td>North Carolina</td><td>14</td><td>3.6%</td><td>33</td><td>Iowa</td><td>1</td><td>0.3%</td></tr>
<tr><td>28</td><td>North Dakota</td><td>2</td><td>0.5%</td><td>33</td><td>Kansas</td><td>1</td><td>0.3%</td></tr>
<tr><td>11</td><td>Ohio</td><td>10</td><td>2.5%</td><td>33</td><td>Massachusetts</td><td>1</td><td>0.3%</td></tr>
<tr><td>19</td><td>Oklahoma</td><td>5</td><td>1.3%</td><td>33</td><td>South Dakota</td><td>1</td><td>0.3%</td></tr>
<tr><td>23</td><td>Oregon</td><td>3</td><td>0.8%</td><td>37</td><td>Alabama</td><td>0</td><td>0.0%</td></tr>
<tr><td>14</td><td>Pennsylvania</td><td>8</td><td>2.0%</td><td>37</td><td>Alaska</td><td>0</td><td>0.0%</td></tr>
<tr><td>37</td><td>Rhode Island</td><td>0</td><td>0.0%</td><td>37</td><td>Connecticut</td><td>0</td><td>0.0%</td></tr>
<tr><td>7</td><td>South Carolina</td><td>15</td><td>3.8%</td><td>37</td><td>Delaware</td><td>0</td><td>0.0%</td></tr>
<tr><td>33</td><td>South Dakota</td><td>1</td><td>0.3%</td><td>37</td><td>Hawaii</td><td>0</td><td>0.0%</td></tr>
<tr><td>11</td><td>Tennessee</td><td>10</td><td>2.5%</td><td>37</td><td>Maine</td><td>0</td><td>0.0%</td></tr>
<tr><td>2</td><td>Texas</td><td>49</td><td>12.5%</td><td>37</td><td>Montana</td><td>0</td><td>0.0%</td></tr>
<tr><td>37</td><td>Utah</td><td>0</td><td>0.0%</td><td>37</td><td>Nebraska</td><td>0</td><td>0.0%</td></tr>
<tr><td>37</td><td>Vermont</td><td>0</td><td>0.0%</td><td>37</td><td>New Hampshire</td><td>0</td><td>0.0%</td></tr>
<tr><td>14</td><td>Virginia</td><td>8</td><td>2.0%</td><td>37</td><td>Rhode Island</td><td>0</td><td>0.0%</td></tr>
<tr><td>16</td><td>Washington</td><td>7</td><td>1.8%</td><td>37</td><td>Utah</td><td>0</td><td>0.0%</td></tr>
<tr><td>23</td><td>West Virginia</td><td>3</td><td>0.8%</td><td>37</td><td>Vermont</td><td>0</td><td>0.0%</td></tr>
<tr><td>16</td><td>Wisconsin</td><td>7</td><td>1.8%</td><td>37</td><td>Wyoming</td><td>0</td><td>0.0%</td></tr>
<tr><td>37</td><td>Wyoming</td><td>0</td><td>0.0%</td><td>NA</td><td>Florida**</td><td>NA</td><td>NA</td></tr>
<tr><td></td><td></td><td></td><td></td><td></td><td>District of Columbia**</td><td>NA</td><td>NA</td></tr>
</table>

Source: Federal Bureau of Investigation
"Crime in the United States 2003" (Uniform Crime Reports, October 25, 2004)
*Of the 14,121 murders in 2004 for which supplemental data were received by the F.B.I. There were an additional 2,016 murders for which the type of murder weapon was not reported to the F.B.I. There were also 1,161 murders that were reported as murders by "firearms, type unknown." Murder includes nonnegligent manslaughter. Numbers are for reporting jurisdictions only. Illinois' figure is for Chicago only. **Not available.

Percent of Murders Involving Rifles in 2004

National Percent = 2.8% of Murders*

RANK	STATE	PERCENT
37	Alabama	0.0
37	Alaska	0.0
3	Arizona	7.3
25	Arkansas	2.0
15	California	3.1
21	Colorado	2.5
37	Connecticut	0.0
37	Delaware	0.0
NA	Florida**	NA
19	Georgia	2.7
37	Hawaii	0.0
2	Idaho	10.0
33	Illinois*	0.9
27	Indiana	1.7
21	Iowa	2.5
28	Kansas	1.3
9	Kentucky	5.1
5	Louisiana	6.1
37	Maine	0.0
36	Maryland	0.4
34	Massachusetts	0.6
18	Michigan	2.8
6	Minnesota	5.5
32	Mississippi	1.1
7	Missouri	5.4
37	Montana	0.0
37	Nebraska	0.0
30	Nevada	1.2
37	New Hampshire	0.0
35	New Jersey	0.5
25	New Mexico	2.0
30	New York	1.2
16	North Carolina	2.9
1	North Dakota	25.0
23	Ohio	2.2
19	Oklahoma	2.7
14	Oregon	3.3
28	Pennsylvania	1.3
37	Rhode Island	0.0
8	South Carolina	5.2
4	South Dakota	6.3
16	Tennessee	2.9
13	Texas	3.6
37	Utah	0.0
37	Vermont	0.0
24	Virginia	2.1
12	Washington	3.7
10	West Virginia	4.8
11	Wisconsin	4.5
37	Wyoming	0.0

RANK	STATE	PERCENT
1	North Dakota	25.0
2	Idaho	10.0
3	Arizona	7.3
4	South Dakota	6.3
5	Louisiana	6.1
6	Minnesota	5.5
7	Missouri	5.4
8	South Carolina	5.2
9	Kentucky	5.1
10	West Virginia	4.8
11	Wisconsin	4.5
12	Washington	3.7
13	Texas	3.6
14	Oregon	3.3
15	California	3.1
16	North Carolina	2.9
16	Tennessee	2.9
18	Michigan	2.8
19	Georgia	2.7
19	Oklahoma	2.7
21	Colorado	2.5
21	Iowa	2.5
23	Ohio	2.2
24	Virginia	2.1
25	Arkansas	2.0
25	New Mexico	2.0
27	Indiana	1.7
28	Kansas	1.3
28	Pennsylvania	1.3
30	Nevada	1.2
30	New York	1.2
32	Mississippi	1.1
33	Illinois*	0.9
34	Massachusetts	0.6
35	New Jersey	0.5
36	Maryland	0.4
37	Alabama	0.0
37	Alaska	0.0
37	Connecticut	0.0
37	Delaware	0.0
37	Hawaii	0.0
37	Maine	0.0
37	Montana	0.0
37	Nebraska	0.0
37	New Hampshire	0.0
37	Rhode Island	0.0
37	Utah	0.0
37	Vermont	0.0
37	Wyoming	0.0
NA	Florida**	NA
	District of Columbia**	NA

Source: Morgan Quitno Press using data from Federal Bureau of Investigation
"Crime in the United States 2003" (Uniform Crime Reports, October 25, 2004)
*Of the 14,121 murders in 2004 for which supplemental data were received by the F.B.I. There were an additional 2,016 murders for which the type of murder weapon was not reported to the F.B.I. There were also 1,161 murders that were reported as murders by "firearms, type unknown." Murder includes nonnegligent manslaughter. Numbers are for reporting jurisdictions only. Illinois' figure is for Chicago only. **Not available.*

Murders with Shotguns in 2004

National Total = 507 Murders*

ALPHA ORDER

RANK	STATE	MURDERS	% of USA
6	Alabama	20	3.9%
37	Alaska	1	0.2%
13	Arizona	14	2.8%
24	Arkansas	6	1.2%
2	California	69	13.6%
22	Colorado	8	1.6%
32	Connecticut	2	0.4%
43	Delaware	0	0.0%
NA	Florida**	NA	NA
10	Georgia	16	3.2%
32	Hawaii	2	0.4%
37	Idaho	1	0.2%
43	Illinois*	0	0.0%
18	Indiana	11	2.2%
26	Iowa	4	0.8%
29	Kansas	3	0.6%
13	Kentucky	14	2.8%
13	Louisiana	14	2.8%
29	Maine	3	0.6%
8	Maryland	17	3.4%
29	Massachusetts	3	0.6%
3	Michigan	27	5.3%
26	Minnesota	4	0.8%
19	Mississippi	10	2.0%
19	Missouri	10	2.0%
43	Montana	0	0.0%
43	Nebraska	0	0.0%
21	Nevada	9	1.8%
43	New Hampshire	0	0.0%
32	New Jersey	2	0.4%
32	New Mexico	2	0.4%
4	New York	25	4.9%
5	North Carolina	24	4.7%
37	North Dakota	1	0.2%
12	Ohio	15	3.0%
8	Oklahoma	17	3.4%
37	Oregon	1	0.2%
13	Pennsylvania	14	2.8%
37	Rhode Island	1	0.2%
17	South Carolina	13	2.6%
32	South Dakota	2	0.4%
7	Tennessee	18	3.6%
1	Texas	70	13.8%
43	Utah	0	0.0%
43	Vermont	0	0.0%
10	Virginia	16	3.2%
23	Washington	7	1.4%
26	West Virginia	4	0.8%
24	Wisconsin	6	1.2%
37	Wyoming	1	0.2%

RANK ORDER

RANK	STATE	MURDERS	% of USA
1	Texas	70	13.8%
2	California	69	13.6%
3	Michigan	27	5.3%
4	New York	25	4.9%
5	North Carolina	24	4.7%
6	Alabama	20	3.9%
7	Tennessee	18	3.6%
8	Maryland	17	3.4%
8	Oklahoma	17	3.4%
10	Georgia	16	3.2%
10	Virginia	16	3.2%
12	Ohio	15	3.0%
13	Arizona	14	2.8%
13	Kentucky	14	2.8%
13	Louisiana	14	2.8%
13	Pennsylvania	14	2.8%
17	South Carolina	13	2.6%
18	Indiana	11	2.2%
19	Mississippi	10	2.0%
19	Missouri	10	2.0%
21	Nevada	9	1.8%
22	Colorado	8	1.6%
23	Washington	7	1.4%
24	Arkansas	6	1.2%
24	Wisconsin	6	1.2%
26	Iowa	4	0.8%
26	Minnesota	4	0.8%
26	West Virginia	4	0.8%
29	Kansas	3	0.6%
29	Maine	3	0.6%
29	Massachusetts	3	0.6%
32	Connecticut	2	0.4%
32	Hawaii	2	0.4%
32	New Jersey	2	0.4%
32	New Mexico	2	0.4%
32	South Dakota	2	0.4%
37	Alaska	1	0.2%
37	Idaho	1	0.2%
37	North Dakota	1	0.2%
37	Oregon	1	0.2%
37	Rhode Island	1	0.2%
37	Wyoming	1	0.2%
43	Delaware	0	0.0%
43	Illinois*	0	0.0%
43	Montana	0	0.0%
43	Nebraska	0	0.0%
43	New Hampshire	0	0.0%
43	Utah	0	0.0%
43	Vermont	0	0.0%
NA	Florida**	NA	NA
	District of Columbia**	NA	NA

Source: Federal Bureau of Investigation
   "Crime in the United States 2003" (Uniform Crime Reports, October 25, 2004)
*Of the 14,121 murders in 2004 for which supplemental data were received by the F.B.I. There were an additional
2,016 murders for which the type of murder weapon was not reported to the F.B.I. There were also 1,161 murders that
were reported as murders by "firearms, type unknown." Murder includes nonnegligent manslaughter. Numbers are
for reporting jurisdictions only. Illinois' figure is for Chicago only. **Not available.

Percent of Murders Involving Shotguns in 2004

National Percent = 3.6% of Murders*

ALPHA ORDER

<table>
<tr><td colspan="3">ALPHA ORDER</td><td colspan="3">RANK ORDER</td></tr>
<tr><td>RANK</td><td>STATE</td><td>PERCENT</td><td>RANK</td><td>STATE</td><td>PERCENT</td></tr>
<tr><td>7</td><td>Alabama</td><td>8.1</td><td>1</td><td>Maine</td><td>17.6</td></tr>
<tr><td>35</td><td>Alaska</td><td>2.7</td><td>2</td><td>North Dakota</td><td>12.5</td></tr>
<tr><td>27</td><td>Arizona</td><td>3.4</td><td>2</td><td>South Dakota</td><td>12.5</td></tr>
<tr><td>21</td><td>Arkansas</td><td>3.9</td><td>4</td><td>Iowa</td><td>10.0</td></tr>
<tr><td>32</td><td>California</td><td>2.9</td><td>5</td><td>Oklahoma</td><td>9.1</td></tr>
<tr><td>19</td><td>Colorado</td><td>4.0</td><td>5</td><td>Wyoming</td><td>9.1</td></tr>
<tr><td>37</td><td>Connecticut</td><td>2.3</td><td>7</td><td>Alabama</td><td>8.1</td></tr>
<tr><td>43</td><td>Delaware</td><td>0.0</td><td>8</td><td>Hawaii</td><td>6.5</td></tr>
<tr><td>NA</td><td>Florida**</td><td>NA</td><td>8</td><td>Kentucky</td><td>6.5</td></tr>
<tr><td>31</td><td>Georgia</td><td>3.0</td><td>8</td><td>West Virginia</td><td>6.5</td></tr>
<tr><td>8</td><td>Hawaii</td><td>6.5</td><td>11</td><td>Mississippi</td><td>5.7</td></tr>
<tr><td>28</td><td>Idaho</td><td>3.3</td><td>12</td><td>Nevada</td><td>5.2</td></tr>
<tr><td>43</td><td>Illinois*</td><td>0.0</td><td>13</td><td>Tennessee</td><td>5.1</td></tr>
<tr><td>24</td><td>Indiana</td><td>3.7</td><td>13</td><td>Texas</td><td>5.1</td></tr>
<tr><td>4</td><td>Iowa</td><td>10.0</td><td>15</td><td>North Carolina</td><td>5.0</td></tr>
<tr><td>19</td><td>Kansas</td><td>4.0</td><td>16</td><td>South Carolina</td><td>4.5</td></tr>
<tr><td>8</td><td>Kentucky</td><td>6.5</td><td>17</td><td>Michigan</td><td>4.2</td></tr>
<tr><td>36</td><td>Louisiana</td><td>2.5</td><td>18</td><td>Virginia</td><td>4.1</td></tr>
<tr><td>1</td><td>Maine</td><td>17.6</td><td>19</td><td>Colorado</td><td>4.0</td></tr>
<tr><td>28</td><td>Maryland</td><td>3.3</td><td>19</td><td>Kansas</td><td>4.0</td></tr>
<tr><td>39</td><td>Massachusetts</td><td>1.8</td><td>21</td><td>Arkansas</td><td>3.9</td></tr>
<tr><td>17</td><td>Michigan</td><td>4.2</td><td>21</td><td>Wisconsin</td><td>3.9</td></tr>
<tr><td>26</td><td>Minnesota</td><td>3.6</td><td>23</td><td>Rhode Island</td><td>3.8</td></tr>
<tr><td>11</td><td>Mississippi</td><td>5.7</td><td>24</td><td>Indiana</td><td>3.7</td></tr>
<tr><td>34</td><td>Missouri</td><td>2.8</td><td>24</td><td>Washington</td><td>3.7</td></tr>
<tr><td>43</td><td>Montana</td><td>0.0</td><td>26</td><td>Minnesota</td><td>3.6</td></tr>
<tr><td>43</td><td>Nebraska</td><td>0.0</td><td>27</td><td>Arizona</td><td>3.4</td></tr>
<tr><td>12</td><td>Nevada</td><td>5.2</td><td>28</td><td>Idaho</td><td>3.3</td></tr>
<tr><td>43</td><td>New Hampshire</td><td>0.0</td><td>28</td><td>Maryland</td><td>3.3</td></tr>
<tr><td>42</td><td>New Jersey</td><td>0.5</td><td>30</td><td>Ohio</td><td>3.2</td></tr>
<tr><td>40</td><td>New Mexico</td><td>1.3</td><td>31</td><td>Georgia</td><td>3.0</td></tr>
<tr><td>32</td><td>New York</td><td>2.9</td><td>32</td><td>California</td><td>2.9</td></tr>
<tr><td>15</td><td>North Carolina</td><td>5.0</td><td>32</td><td>New York</td><td>2.9</td></tr>
<tr><td>2</td><td>North Dakota</td><td>12.5</td><td>34</td><td>Missouri</td><td>2.8</td></tr>
<tr><td>30</td><td>Ohio</td><td>3.2</td><td>35</td><td>Alaska</td><td>2.7</td></tr>
<tr><td>5</td><td>Oklahoma</td><td>9.1</td><td>36</td><td>Louisiana</td><td>2.5</td></tr>
<tr><td>41</td><td>Oregon</td><td>1.1</td><td>37</td><td>Connecticut</td><td>2.3</td></tr>
<tr><td>38</td><td>Pennsylvania</td><td>2.2</td><td>38</td><td>Pennsylvania</td><td>2.2</td></tr>
<tr><td>23</td><td>Rhode Island</td><td>3.8</td><td>39</td><td>Massachusetts</td><td>1.8</td></tr>
<tr><td>16</td><td>South Carolina</td><td>4.5</td><td>40</td><td>New Mexico</td><td>1.3</td></tr>
<tr><td>2</td><td>South Dakota</td><td>12.5</td><td>41</td><td>Oregon</td><td>1.1</td></tr>
<tr><td>13</td><td>Tennessee</td><td>5.1</td><td>42</td><td>New Jersey</td><td>0.5</td></tr>
<tr><td>13</td><td>Texas</td><td>5.1</td><td>43</td><td>Delaware</td><td>0.0</td></tr>
<tr><td>43</td><td>Utah</td><td>0.0</td><td>43</td><td>Illinois*</td><td>0.0</td></tr>
<tr><td>43</td><td>Vermont</td><td>0.0</td><td>43</td><td>Montana</td><td>0.0</td></tr>
<tr><td>18</td><td>Virginia</td><td>4.1</td><td>43</td><td>Nebraska</td><td>0.0</td></tr>
<tr><td>24</td><td>Washington</td><td>3.7</td><td>43</td><td>New Hampshire</td><td>0.0</td></tr>
<tr><td>8</td><td>West Virginia</td><td>6.5</td><td>43</td><td>Utah</td><td>0.0</td></tr>
<tr><td>21</td><td>Wisconsin</td><td>3.9</td><td>43</td><td>Vermont</td><td>0.0</td></tr>
<tr><td>5</td><td>Wyoming</td><td>9.1</td><td>NA</td><td>Florida**</td><td>NA</td></tr>
<tr><td></td><td></td><td></td><td></td><td>District of Columbia**</td><td>NA</td></tr>
</table>

Source: Morgan Quitno Press using data from Federal Bureau of Investigation
   "Crime in the United States 2003" (Uniform Crime Reports, October 25, 2004)
*Of the 14,121 murders in 2004 for which supplemental data were received by the F.B.I. There were an additional
2,016 murders for which the type of murder weapon was not reported to the F.B.I. There were also 1,161 murders that
were reported as murders by "firearms, type unknown." Murder includes nonnegligent manslaughter. Numbers are
for reporting jurisdictions only. Illinois' figure is for Chicago only. **Not available.

Murders with Knives or Cutting Instruments in 2004

National Total = 1,866 Murders*

ALPHA ORDER

RANK	STATE	MURDERS	% of USA
25	Alabama	24	1.3%
40	Alaska	4	0.2%
12	Arizona	44	2.4%
29	Arkansas	19	1.0%
1	California	281	15.1%
20	Colorado	32	1.7%
32	Connecticut	16	0.9%
43	Delaware	3	0.2%
NA	Florida**	NA	NA
4	Georgia	70	3.8%
33	Hawaii	13	0.7%
39	Idaho	5	0.3%
16	Illinois*	37	2.0%
16	Indiana	37	2.0%
34	Iowa	9	0.5%
38	Kansas	6	0.3%
24	Kentucky	25	1.3%
12	Louisiana	44	2.4%
40	Maine	4	0.2%
8	Maryland	57	3.1%
16	Massachusetts	37	2.0%
6	Michigan	68	3.6%
29	Minnesota	19	1.0%
27	Mississippi	22	1.2%
16	Missouri	37	2.0%
36	Montana	7	0.4%
43	Nebraska	3	0.2%
25	Nevada	24	1.3%
43	New Hampshire	3	0.2%
5	New Jersey	69	3.7%
23	New Mexico	28	1.5%
3	New York	173	9.3%
7	North Carolina	67	3.6%
49	North Dakota	0	0.0%
8	Ohio	57	3.1%
20	Oklahoma	32	1.7%
29	Oregon	19	1.0%
10	Pennsylvania	54	2.9%
43	Rhode Island	3	0.2%
15	South Carolina	38	2.0%
40	South Dakota	4	0.2%
11	Tennessee	48	2.6%
2	Texas	211	11.3%
48	Utah	2	0.1%
36	Vermont	7	0.4%
12	Virginia	44	2.4%
22	Washington	29	1.6%
35	West Virginia	8	0.4%
28	Wisconsin	20	1.1%
43	Wyoming	3	0.2%

RANK ORDER

RANK	STATE	MURDERS	% of USA
1	California	281	15.1%
2	Texas	211	11.3%
3	New York	173	9.3%
4	Georgia	70	3.8%
5	New Jersey	69	3.7%
6	Michigan	68	3.6%
7	North Carolina	67	3.6%
8	Maryland	57	3.1%
8	Ohio	57	3.1%
10	Pennsylvania	54	2.9%
11	Tennessee	48	2.6%
12	Arizona	44	2.4%
12	Louisiana	44	2.4%
12	Virginia	44	2.4%
15	South Carolina	38	2.0%
16	Illinois*	37	2.0%
16	Indiana	37	2.0%
16	Massachusetts	37	2.0%
16	Missouri	37	2.0%
20	Colorado	32	1.7%
20	Oklahoma	32	1.7%
22	Washington	29	1.6%
23	New Mexico	28	1.5%
24	Kentucky	25	1.3%
25	Alabama	24	1.3%
25	Nevada	24	1.3%
27	Mississippi	22	1.2%
28	Wisconsin	20	1.1%
29	Arkansas	19	1.0%
29	Minnesota	19	1.0%
29	Oregon	19	1.0%
32	Connecticut	16	0.9%
33	Hawaii	13	0.7%
34	Iowa	9	0.5%
35	West Virginia	8	0.4%
36	Montana	7	0.4%
36	Vermont	7	0.4%
38	Kansas	6	0.3%
39	Idaho	5	0.3%
40	Alaska	4	0.2%
40	Maine	4	0.2%
40	South Dakota	4	0.2%
43	Delaware	3	0.2%
43	Nebraska	3	0.2%
43	New Hampshire	3	0.2%
43	Rhode Island	3	0.2%
43	Wyoming	3	0.2%
48	Utah	2	0.1%
49	North Dakota	0	0.0%
NA	Florida**	NA	NA
	District of Columbia**	NA	NA

Source: Federal Bureau of Investigation
   "Crime in the United States 2003" (Uniform Crime Reports, October 25, 2004)

*Of the 14,121 murders in 2004 for which supplemental data were received by the F.B.I. There were an additional 2,016 murders for which the type of murder weapon was not reported to the F.B.I. There were also 1,161 murders that were reported as murders by "firearms, type unknown." Murder includes nonnegligent manslaughter. Numbers are for reporting jurisdictions only. Illinois' figure is for Chicago only. **Not available.

Percent of Murders Involving Knives or Cutting Instruments in 2004

National Percent = 13.2% of Murders*

<table>
<tr><td colspan="3">ALPHA ORDER</td><td colspan="3">RANK ORDER</td></tr>
<tr><td>RANK</td><td>STATE</td><td>PERCENT</td><td>RANK</td><td>STATE</td><td>PERCENT</td></tr>
<tr><td>43</td><td>Alabama</td><td>9.7</td><td>1</td><td>Vermont</td><td>43.8</td></tr>
<tr><td>39</td><td>Alaska</td><td>10.8</td><td>2</td><td>Hawaii</td><td>41.9</td></tr>
<tr><td>39</td><td>Arizona</td><td>10.8</td><td>3</td><td>Montana</td><td>30.4</td></tr>
<tr><td>30</td><td>Arkansas</td><td>12.5</td><td>4</td><td>Wyoming</td><td>27.3</td></tr>
<tr><td>33</td><td>California</td><td>11.8</td><td>5</td><td>South Dakota</td><td>25.0</td></tr>
<tr><td>19</td><td>Colorado</td><td>16.1</td><td>6</td><td>Maine</td><td>23.5</td></tr>
<tr><td>14</td><td>Connecticut</td><td>18.6</td><td>7</td><td>New Hampshire</td><td>23.1</td></tr>
<tr><td>10</td><td>Delaware</td><td>21.4</td><td>8</td><td>Iowa</td><td>22.5</td></tr>
<tr><td>NA</td><td>Florida**</td><td>NA</td><td>9</td><td>Massachusetts</td><td>22.2</td></tr>
<tr><td>25</td><td>Georgia</td><td>13.3</td><td>10</td><td>Delaware</td><td>21.4</td></tr>
<tr><td>2</td><td>Hawaii</td><td>41.9</td><td>11</td><td>Oregon</td><td>21.1</td></tr>
<tr><td>18</td><td>Idaho</td><td>16.7</td><td>12</td><td>New York</td><td>20.0</td></tr>
<tr><td>46</td><td>Illinois*</td><td>8.3</td><td>13</td><td>New Mexico</td><td>18.7</td></tr>
<tr><td>31</td><td>Indiana</td><td>12.4</td><td>14</td><td>Connecticut</td><td>18.6</td></tr>
<tr><td>8</td><td>Iowa</td><td>22.5</td><td>15</td><td>New Jersey</td><td>17.6</td></tr>
<tr><td>47</td><td>Kansas</td><td>8.0</td><td>16</td><td>Minnesota</td><td>17.3</td></tr>
<tr><td>34</td><td>Kentucky</td><td>11.5</td><td>17</td><td>Oklahoma</td><td>17.2</td></tr>
<tr><td>48</td><td>Louisiana</td><td>7.9</td><td>18</td><td>Idaho</td><td>16.7</td></tr>
<tr><td>6</td><td>Maine</td><td>23.5</td><td>19</td><td>Colorado</td><td>16.1</td></tr>
<tr><td>38</td><td>Maryland</td><td>11.0</td><td>20</td><td>Texas</td><td>15.5</td></tr>
<tr><td>9</td><td>Massachusetts</td><td>22.2</td><td>21</td><td>Washington</td><td>15.3</td></tr>
<tr><td>41</td><td>Michigan</td><td>10.7</td><td>22</td><td>Nevada</td><td>14.0</td></tr>
<tr><td>16</td><td>Minnesota</td><td>17.3</td><td>22</td><td>North Carolina</td><td>14.0</td></tr>
<tr><td>29</td><td>Mississippi</td><td>12.6</td><td>24</td><td>Tennessee</td><td>13.7</td></tr>
<tr><td>42</td><td>Missouri</td><td>10.5</td><td>25</td><td>Georgia</td><td>13.3</td></tr>
<tr><td>3</td><td>Montana</td><td>30.4</td><td>26</td><td>South Carolina</td><td>13.2</td></tr>
<tr><td>37</td><td>Nebraska</td><td>11.1</td><td>27</td><td>Wisconsin</td><td>13.0</td></tr>
<tr><td>22</td><td>Nevada</td><td>14.0</td><td>28</td><td>West Virginia</td><td>12.9</td></tr>
<tr><td>7</td><td>New Hampshire</td><td>23.1</td><td>29</td><td>Mississippi</td><td>12.6</td></tr>
<tr><td>15</td><td>New Jersey</td><td>17.6</td><td>30</td><td>Arkansas</td><td>12.5</td></tr>
<tr><td>13</td><td>New Mexico</td><td>18.7</td><td>31</td><td>Indiana</td><td>12.4</td></tr>
<tr><td>12</td><td>New York</td><td>20.0</td><td>32</td><td>Ohio</td><td>12.3</td></tr>
<tr><td>22</td><td>North Carolina</td><td>14.0</td><td>33</td><td>California</td><td>11.8</td></tr>
<tr><td>49</td><td>North Dakota</td><td>0.0</td><td>34</td><td>Kentucky</td><td>11.5</td></tr>
<tr><td>32</td><td>Ohio</td><td>12.3</td><td>34</td><td>Rhode Island</td><td>11.5</td></tr>
<tr><td>17</td><td>Oklahoma</td><td>17.2</td><td>36</td><td>Virginia</td><td>11.3</td></tr>
<tr><td>11</td><td>Oregon</td><td>21.1</td><td>37</td><td>Nebraska</td><td>11.1</td></tr>
<tr><td>45</td><td>Pennsylvania</td><td>8.5</td><td>38</td><td>Maryland</td><td>11.0</td></tr>
<tr><td>34</td><td>Rhode Island</td><td>11.5</td><td>39</td><td>Alaska</td><td>10.8</td></tr>
<tr><td>26</td><td>South Carolina</td><td>13.2</td><td>39</td><td>Arizona</td><td>10.8</td></tr>
<tr><td>5</td><td>South Dakota</td><td>25.0</td><td>41</td><td>Michigan</td><td>10.7</td></tr>
<tr><td>24</td><td>Tennessee</td><td>13.7</td><td>42</td><td>Missouri</td><td>10.5</td></tr>
<tr><td>20</td><td>Texas</td><td>15.5</td><td>43</td><td>Alabama</td><td>9.7</td></tr>
<tr><td>44</td><td>Utah</td><td>9.5</td><td>44</td><td>Utah</td><td>9.5</td></tr>
<tr><td>1</td><td>Vermont</td><td>43.8</td><td>45</td><td>Pennsylvania</td><td>8.5</td></tr>
<tr><td>36</td><td>Virginia</td><td>11.3</td><td>46</td><td>Illinois*</td><td>8.3</td></tr>
<tr><td>21</td><td>Washington</td><td>15.3</td><td>47</td><td>Kansas</td><td>8.0</td></tr>
<tr><td>28</td><td>West Virginia</td><td>12.9</td><td>48</td><td>Louisiana</td><td>7.9</td></tr>
<tr><td>27</td><td>Wisconsin</td><td>13.0</td><td>49</td><td>North Dakota</td><td>0.0</td></tr>
<tr><td>4</td><td>Wyoming</td><td>27.3</td><td>NA</td><td>Florida**</td><td>NA</td></tr>
<tr><td></td><td></td><td></td><td></td><td>District of Columbia**</td><td>NA</td></tr>
</table>

Source: Morgan Quitno Press using data from Federal Bureau of Investigation
    "Crime in the United States 2003" (Uniform Crime Reports, October 25, 2004)
*Of the 14,121 murders in 2004 for which supplemental data were received by the F.B.I. There were an additional 2,016 murders for which the type of murder weapon was not reported to the F.B.I. There were also 1,161 murders that were reported as murders by "firearms, type unknown." Murder includes nonnegligent manslaughter. Numbers are for reporting jurisdictions only. Illinois' figure is for Chicago only. **Not available.

Murders by Hands, Fists or Feet in 2004

National Total = 933 Murders*

ALPHA ORDER

RANK	STATE	MURDERS	% of USA
13	Alabama	21	2.3%
35	Alaska	4	0.4%
12	Arizona	25	2.7%
27	Arkansas	7	0.8%
1	California	144	15.4%
9	Colorado	34	3.6%
32	Connecticut	5	0.5%
44	Delaware	1	0.1%
NA	Florida**	NA	NA
5	Georgia	47	5.0%
27	Hawaii	7	0.8%
41	Idaho	2	0.2%
25	Illinois*	10	1.1%
21	Indiana	15	1.6%
27	Iowa	7	0.8%
41	Kansas	2	0.2%
23	Kentucky	13	1.4%
13	Louisiana	21	2.3%
39	Maine	3	0.3%
10	Maryland	30	3.2%
31	Massachusetts	6	0.6%
8	Michigan	35	3.8%
24	Minnesota	11	1.2%
27	Mississippi	7	0.8%
32	Missouri	5	0.5%
35	Montana	4	0.4%
39	Nebraska	3	0.3%
26	Nevada	8	0.9%
41	New Hampshire	2	0.2%
7	New Jersey	36	3.9%
17	New Mexico	18	1.9%
3	New York	68	7.3%
6	North Carolina	42	4.5%
44	North Dakota	1	0.1%
4	Ohio	49	5.3%
13	Oklahoma	21	2.3%
35	Oregon	4	0.4%
17	Pennsylvania	18	1.9%
35	Rhode Island	4	0.4%
19	South Carolina	17	1.8%
48	South Dakota	0	0.0%
11	Tennessee	28	3.0%
2	Texas	90	9.6%
44	Utah	1	0.1%
48	Vermont	0	0.0%
21	Virginia	15	1.6%
16	Washington	19	2.0%
32	West Virginia	5	0.5%
19	Wisconsin	17	1.8%
44	Wyoming	1	0.1%

RANK ORDER

RANK	STATE	MURDERS	% of USA
1	California	144	15.4%
2	Texas	90	9.6%
3	New York	68	7.3%
4	Ohio	49	5.3%
5	Georgia	47	5.0%
6	North Carolina	42	4.5%
7	New Jersey	36	3.9%
8	Michigan	35	3.8%
9	Colorado	34	3.6%
10	Maryland	30	3.2%
11	Tennessee	28	3.0%
12	Arizona	25	2.7%
13	Alabama	21	2.3%
13	Louisiana	21	2.3%
13	Oklahoma	21	2.3%
16	Washington	19	2.0%
17	New Mexico	18	1.9%
17	Pennsylvania	18	1.9%
19	South Carolina	17	1.8%
19	Wisconsin	17	1.8%
21	Indiana	15	1.6%
21	Virginia	15	1.6%
23	Kentucky	13	1.4%
24	Minnesota	11	1.2%
25	Illinois*	10	1.1%
26	Nevada	8	0.9%
27	Arkansas	7	0.8%
27	Hawaii	7	0.8%
27	Iowa	7	0.8%
27	Mississippi	7	0.8%
31	Massachusetts	6	0.6%
32	Connecticut	5	0.5%
32	Missouri	5	0.5%
32	West Virginia	5	0.5%
35	Alaska	4	0.4%
35	Montana	4	0.4%
35	Oregon	4	0.4%
35	Rhode Island	4	0.4%
39	Maine	3	0.3%
39	Nebraska	3	0.3%
41	Idaho	2	0.2%
41	Kansas	2	0.2%
41	New Hampshire	2	0.2%
44	Delaware	1	0.1%
44	North Dakota	1	0.1%
44	Utah	1	0.1%
44	Wyoming	1	0.1%
48	South Dakota	0	0.0%
48	Vermont	0	0.0%
NA	Florida**	NA	NA
	District of Columbia**	NA	NA

Source: Federal Bureau of Investigation
   "Crime in the United States 2003" (Uniform Crime Reports, October 25, 2004)

*Of the 14,121 murders in 2004 for which supplemental data were received by the F.B.I. There were an additional 2,016 murders for which the type of murder weapon was not reported to the F.B.I. There were also 1,161 murders that were reported as murders by "firearms, type unknown." Murder includes nonnegligent manslaughter. Numbers are for reporting jurisdictions only. Illinois' figure is for Chicago only. **Not available.

Percent of Murders Involving Hands, Fists or Feet in 2004

National Percent = 6.6% of Murders*

<table>
<tr><td colspan="3">ALPHA ORDER</td><td colspan="3">RANK ORDER</td></tr>
<tr><td>RANK</td><td>STATE</td><td>PERCENT</td><td>RANK</td><td>STATE</td><td>PERCENT</td></tr>
<tr><td>21</td><td>Alabama</td><td>8.5</td><td>1</td><td>Hawaii</td><td>22.6</td></tr>
<tr><td>13</td><td>Alaska</td><td>10.8</td><td>2</td><td>Maine</td><td>17.6</td></tr>
<tr><td>28</td><td>Arizona</td><td>6.1</td><td>3</td><td>Iowa</td><td>17.5</td></tr>
<tr><td>38</td><td>Arkansas</td><td>4.6</td><td>4</td><td>Montana</td><td>17.4</td></tr>
<tr><td>29</td><td>California</td><td>6.0</td><td>5</td><td>Colorado</td><td>17.1</td></tr>
<tr><td>5</td><td>Colorado</td><td>17.1</td><td>6</td><td>New Hampshire</td><td>15.4</td></tr>
<tr><td>32</td><td>Connecticut</td><td>5.8</td><td>6</td><td>Rhode Island</td><td>15.4</td></tr>
<tr><td>25</td><td>Delaware</td><td>7.1</td><td>8</td><td>North Dakota</td><td>12.5</td></tr>
<tr><td>NA</td><td>Florida**</td><td>NA</td><td>9</td><td>New Mexico</td><td>12.0</td></tr>
<tr><td>19</td><td>Georgia</td><td>8.9</td><td>10</td><td>Oklahoma</td><td>11.3</td></tr>
<tr><td>1</td><td>Hawaii</td><td>22.6</td><td>11</td><td>Nebraska</td><td>11.1</td></tr>
<tr><td>26</td><td>Idaho</td><td>6.7</td><td>12</td><td>Wisconsin</td><td>11.0</td></tr>
<tr><td>46</td><td>Illinois*</td><td>2.2</td><td>13</td><td>Alaska</td><td>10.8</td></tr>
<tr><td>35</td><td>Indiana</td><td>5.0</td><td>14</td><td>Ohio</td><td>10.6</td></tr>
<tr><td>3</td><td>Iowa</td><td>17.5</td><td>15</td><td>Washington</td><td>10.1</td></tr>
<tr><td>45</td><td>Kansas</td><td>2.7</td><td>16</td><td>Minnesota</td><td>10.0</td></tr>
<tr><td>29</td><td>Kentucky</td><td>6.0</td><td>17</td><td>New Jersey</td><td>9.2</td></tr>
<tr><td>41</td><td>Louisiana</td><td>3.8</td><td>18</td><td>Wyoming</td><td>9.1</td></tr>
<tr><td>2</td><td>Maine</td><td>17.6</td><td>19</td><td>Georgia</td><td>8.9</td></tr>
<tr><td>32</td><td>Maryland</td><td>5.8</td><td>20</td><td>North Carolina</td><td>8.8</td></tr>
<tr><td>43</td><td>Massachusetts</td><td>3.6</td><td>21</td><td>Alabama</td><td>8.5</td></tr>
<tr><td>34</td><td>Michigan</td><td>5.5</td><td>22</td><td>West Virginia</td><td>8.1</td></tr>
<tr><td>16</td><td>Minnesota</td><td>10.0</td><td>23</td><td>Tennessee</td><td>8.0</td></tr>
<tr><td>40</td><td>Mississippi</td><td>4.0</td><td>24</td><td>New York</td><td>7.9</td></tr>
<tr><td>47</td><td>Missouri</td><td>1.4</td><td>25</td><td>Delaware</td><td>7.1</td></tr>
<tr><td>4</td><td>Montana</td><td>17.4</td><td>26</td><td>Idaho</td><td>6.7</td></tr>
<tr><td>11</td><td>Nebraska</td><td>11.1</td><td>27</td><td>Texas</td><td>6.6</td></tr>
<tr><td>37</td><td>Nevada</td><td>4.7</td><td>28</td><td>Arizona</td><td>6.1</td></tr>
<tr><td>6</td><td>New Hampshire</td><td>15.4</td><td>29</td><td>California</td><td>6.0</td></tr>
<tr><td>17</td><td>New Jersey</td><td>9.2</td><td>29</td><td>Kentucky</td><td>6.0</td></tr>
<tr><td>9</td><td>New Mexico</td><td>12.0</td><td>31</td><td>South Carolina</td><td>5.9</td></tr>
<tr><td>24</td><td>New York</td><td>7.9</td><td>32</td><td>Connecticut</td><td>5.8</td></tr>
<tr><td>20</td><td>North Carolina</td><td>8.8</td><td>32</td><td>Maryland</td><td>5.8</td></tr>
<tr><td>8</td><td>North Dakota</td><td>12.5</td><td>34</td><td>Michigan</td><td>5.5</td></tr>
<tr><td>14</td><td>Ohio</td><td>10.6</td><td>35</td><td>Indiana</td><td>5.0</td></tr>
<tr><td>10</td><td>Oklahoma</td><td>11.3</td><td>36</td><td>Utah</td><td>4.8</td></tr>
<tr><td>39</td><td>Oregon</td><td>4.4</td><td>37</td><td>Nevada</td><td>4.7</td></tr>
<tr><td>44</td><td>Pennsylvania</td><td>2.8</td><td>38</td><td>Arkansas</td><td>4.6</td></tr>
<tr><td>6</td><td>Rhode Island</td><td>15.4</td><td>39</td><td>Oregon</td><td>4.4</td></tr>
<tr><td>31</td><td>South Carolina</td><td>5.9</td><td>40</td><td>Mississippi</td><td>4.0</td></tr>
<tr><td>48</td><td>South Dakota</td><td>0.0</td><td>41</td><td>Louisiana</td><td>3.8</td></tr>
<tr><td>23</td><td>Tennessee</td><td>8.0</td><td>41</td><td>Virginia</td><td>3.8</td></tr>
<tr><td>27</td><td>Texas</td><td>6.6</td><td>43</td><td>Massachusetts</td><td>3.6</td></tr>
<tr><td>36</td><td>Utah</td><td>4.8</td><td>44</td><td>Pennsylvania</td><td>2.8</td></tr>
<tr><td>48</td><td>Vermont</td><td>0.0</td><td>45</td><td>Kansas</td><td>2.7</td></tr>
<tr><td>41</td><td>Virginia</td><td>3.8</td><td>46</td><td>Illinois*</td><td>2.2</td></tr>
<tr><td>15</td><td>Washington</td><td>10.1</td><td>47</td><td>Missouri</td><td>1.4</td></tr>
<tr><td>22</td><td>West Virginia</td><td>8.1</td><td>48</td><td>South Dakota</td><td>0.0</td></tr>
<tr><td>12</td><td>Wisconsin</td><td>11.0</td><td>48</td><td>Vermont</td><td>0.0</td></tr>
<tr><td>18</td><td>Wyoming</td><td>9.1</td><td>NA</td><td>Florida**</td><td>NA</td></tr>
<tr><td></td><td></td><td></td><td></td><td>District of Columbia**</td><td>NA</td></tr>
</table>

Source: Morgan Quitno Press using data from Federal Bureau of Investigation
   "Crime in the United States 2003" (Uniform Crime Reports, October 25, 2004)
*Of the 14,121 murders in 2004 for which supplemental data were received by the F.B.I. There were an additional 2,016 murders for which the type of murder weapon was not reported to the F.B.I. There were also 1,161 murders that were reported as murders by "firearms, type unknown." Murder includes nonnegligent manslaughter. Numbers are for reporting jurisdictions only. Illinois' figure is for Chicago only. **Not available.

Rapes in 2004

National Total = 94,635 Rapes*

ALPHA ORDER

RANK	STATE	RAPES	% of USA
19	Alabama	1,742	1.8%
39	Alaska	558	0.6%
15	Arizona	1,896	2.0%
28	Arkansas	1,166	1.2%
1	California	9,615	10.2%
14	Colorado	1,956	2.1%
36	Connecticut	724	0.8%
41	Delaware	345	0.4%
3	Florida	6,612	7.0%
10	Georgia	2,387	2.5%
43	Hawaii	333	0.4%
38	Idaho	570	0.6%
6	Illinois	4,216	4.5%
16	Indiana	1,803	1.9%
35	Iowa	790	0.8%
31	Kansas	1,104	1.2%
27	Kentucky	1,238	1.3%
21	Louisiana	1,616	1.7%
46	Maine	315	0.3%
25	Maryland	1,316	1.4%
17	Massachusetts	1,799	1.9%
4	Michigan	5,486	5.8%
13	Minnesota	2,123	2.2%
29	Mississippi	1,161	1.2%
23	Missouri	1,479	1.6%
47	Montana	273	0.3%
37	Nebraska	620	0.7%
33	Nevada	954	1.0%
40	New Hampshire	459	0.5%
24	New Jersey	1,331	1.4%
32	New Mexico	1,039	1.1%
7	New York	3,608	3.8%
11	North Carolina	2,339	2.5%
48	North Dakota	159	0.2%
5	Ohio	4,646	4.9%
22	Oklahoma	1,557	1.6%
26	Oregon	1,283	1.4%
8	Pennsylvania	3,535	3.7%
44	Rhode Island	320	0.3%
20	South Carolina	1,718	1.8%
42	South Dakota	338	0.4%
12	Tennessee	2,220	2.3%
2	Texas	8,388	8.9%
34	Utah	933	1.0%
49	Vermont	152	0.2%
18	Virginia	1,766	1.9%
9	Washington	2,857	3.0%
44	West Virginia	320	0.3%
30	Wisconsin	1,136	1.2%
50	Wyoming	112	0.1%

RANK ORDER

RANK	STATE	RAPES	% of USA
1	California	9,615	10.2%
2	Texas	8,388	8.9%
3	Florida	6,612	7.0%
4	Michigan	5,486	5.8%
5	Ohio	4,646	4.9%
6	Illinois	4,216	4.5%
7	New York	3,608	3.8%
8	Pennsylvania	3,535	3.7%
9	Washington	2,857	3.0%
10	Georgia	2,387	2.5%
11	North Carolina	2,339	2.5%
12	Tennessee	2,220	2.3%
13	Minnesota	2,123	2.2%
14	Colorado	1,956	2.1%
15	Arizona	1,896	2.0%
16	Indiana	1,803	1.9%
17	Massachusetts	1,799	1.9%
18	Virginia	1,766	1.9%
19	Alabama	1,742	1.8%
20	South Carolina	1,718	1.8%
21	Louisiana	1,616	1.7%
22	Oklahoma	1,557	1.6%
23	Missouri	1,479	1.6%
24	New Jersey	1,331	1.4%
25	Maryland	1,316	1.4%
26	Oregon	1,283	1.4%
27	Kentucky	1,238	1.3%
28	Arkansas	1,166	1.2%
29	Mississippi	1,161	1.2%
30	Wisconsin	1,136	1.2%
31	Kansas	1,104	1.2%
32	New Mexico	1,039	1.1%
33	Nevada	954	1.0%
34	Utah	933	1.0%
35	Iowa	790	0.8%
36	Connecticut	724	0.8%
37	Nebraska	620	0.7%
38	Idaho	570	0.6%
39	Alaska	558	0.6%
40	New Hampshire	459	0.5%
41	Delaware	345	0.4%
42	South Dakota	338	0.4%
43	Hawaii	333	0.4%
44	Rhode Island	320	0.3%
44	West Virginia	320	0.3%
46	Maine	315	0.3%
47	Montana	273	0.3%
48	North Dakota	159	0.2%
49	Vermont	152	0.2%
50	Wyoming	112	0.1%
	District of Columbia	222	0.2%

Source: Federal Bureau of Investigation
   "Crime in the United States 2004" (Uniform Crime Reports, October 17, 2005)
*Forcible rape is the carnal knowledge of a female forcibly and against her will. Assaults or attempts to commit rape by force or threat of force are included. However, statutory rape without force and other sex offenses are excluded.

Average Time Between Rapes in 2004

National Rate = A Rape Occurs Every 6 Minutes*

ALPHA ORDER				RANK ORDER		
RANK	STATE	HOURS.MINUTES		RANK	STATE	HOURS.MINUTES
32	Alabama	5.02		1	Wyoming	78.26
12	Alaska	15.44		2	Vermont	57.47
36	Arizona	4.38		3	North Dakota	55.15
23	Arkansas	7.32		4	Montana	32.11
50	California	0.55		5	Maine	27.53
37	Colorado	4.29		6	Rhode Island	27.27
15	Connecticut	12.08		6	West Virginia	27.27
10	Delaware	25.28		8	Hawaii	26.23
48	Florida	1.20		9	South Dakota	25.59
41	Georgia	3.41		10	Delaware	25.28
8	Hawaii	26.23		11	New Hampshire	19.08
13	Idaho	15.25		12	Alaska	15.44
45	Illinois	2.05		13	Idaho	15.25
35	Indiana	4.52		14	Nebraska	14.10
16	Iowa	11.07		15	Connecticut	12.08
20	Kansas	7.58		16	Iowa	11.07
24	Kentucky	7.06		17	Utah	9.25
30	Louisiana	5.26		18	Nevada	9.13
5	Maine	27.53		19	New Mexico	8.27
26	Maryland	6.40		20	Kansas	7.58
34	Massachusetts	4.53		21	Wisconsin	7.44
47	Michigan	1.36		22	Mississippi	7.34
38	Minnesota	4.08		23	Arkansas	7.32
22	Mississippi	7.34		24	Kentucky	7.06
28	Missouri	5.56		25	Oregon	6.51
4	Montana	32.11		26	Maryland	6.40
14	Nebraska	14.10		27	New Jersey	6.36
18	Nevada	9.13		28	Missouri	5.56
11	New Hampshire	19.08		29	Oklahoma	5.38
27	New Jersey	6.36		30	Louisiana	5.26
19	New Mexico	8.27		31	South Carolina	5.07
44	New York	2.26		32	Alabama	5.02
40	North Carolina	3.46		33	Virginia	4.58
3	North Dakota	55.15		34	Massachusetts	4.53
46	Ohio	1.53		35	Indiana	4.52
29	Oklahoma	5.38		36	Arizona	4.38
25	Oregon	6.51		37	Colorado	4.29
43	Pennsylvania	2.29		38	Minnesota	4.08
6	Rhode Island	27.27		39	Tennessee	3.58
31	South Carolina	5.07		40	North Carolina	3.46
9	South Dakota	25.59		41	Georgia	3.41
39	Tennessee	3.58		42	Washington	3.04
49	Texas	1.03		43	Pennsylvania	2.29
17	Utah	9.25		44	New York	2.26
2	Vermont	57.47		45	Illinois	2.05
33	Virginia	4.58		46	Ohio	1.53
42	Washington	3.04		47	Michigan	1.36
6	West Virginia	27.27		48	Florida	1.20
21	Wisconsin	7.44		49	Texas	1.03
1	Wyoming	78.26		50	California	0.55
					District of Columbia	39.34

Source: Morgan Quitno Press using data from Federal Bureau of Investigation
   "Crime in the United States 2004" (Uniform Crime Reports, October 17, 2005)
*Forcible rape is the carnal knowledge of a female forcibly and against her will. Assaults or attempts to commit rape by force or threat of force are included. However, statutory rape without force and other sex offenses are excluded.

Percent Change in Number of Rapes: 2003 to 2004

National Percent Change = 0.8% Increase*

ALPHA ORDER				RANK ORDER		
RANK	STATE	PERCENT CHANGE		RANK	STATE	PERCENT CHANGE
14	Alabama	5.2		1	Arkansas	28.0
45	Alaska	(7.8)		2	Nebraska	23.0
23	Arizona	2.2		3	Vermont	20.6
1	Arkansas	28.0		4	Montana	11.0
40	California	(3.8)		5	New Mexico	10.5
23	Colorado	2.2		6	Kentucky	10.1
19	Connecticut	3.7		7	Nevada	9.5
44	Delaware	(6.8)		8	North Carolina	9.4
36	Florida	(1.7)		9	Mississippi	7.6
10	Georgia	6.8		10	Georgia	6.8
46	Hawaii	(9.3)		11	Idaho	6.5
11	Idaho	6.5		12	Missouri	5.6
29	Illinois	0.6		13	Oregon	5.3
15	Indiana	4.8		14	Alabama	5.2
35	Iowa	(0.8)		15	Indiana	4.8
25	Kansas	1.8		15	New Hampshire	4.8
6	Kentucky	10.1		17	Texas	4.5
28	Louisiana	0.9		18	Tennessee	4.3
47	Maine	(11.0)		19	Connecticut	3.7
39	Maryland	(3.1)		19	Oklahoma	3.7
38	Massachusetts	(2.7)		21	New Jersey	3.3
30	Michigan	0.3		22	West Virginia	2.9
26	Minnesota	1.5		23	Arizona	2.2
9	Mississippi	7.6		23	Colorado	2.2
12	Missouri	5.6		25	Kansas	1.8
4	Montana	11.0		26	Minnesota	1.5
2	Nebraska	23.0		26	Utah	1.5
7	Nevada	9.5		28	Louisiana	0.9
15	New Hampshire	4.8		29	Illinois	0.6
21	New Jersey	3.3		30	Michigan	0.3
5	New Mexico	10.5		31	Washington	(0.2)
41	New York	(4.4)		32	Ohio	(0.3)
8	North Carolina	9.4		33	North Dakota	(0.6)
33	North Dakota	(0.6)		33	Pennsylvania	(0.6)
32	Ohio	(0.3)		35	Iowa	(0.8)
19	Oklahoma	3.7		36	Florida	(1.7)
13	Oregon	5.3		37	Virginia	(2.3)
33	Pennsylvania	(0.6)		38	Massachusetts	(2.7)
50	Rhode Island	(36.6)		39	Maryland	(3.1)
48	South Carolina	(12.0)		40	California	(3.8)
42	South Dakota	(5.1)		41	New York	(4.4)
18	Tennessee	4.3		42	South Dakota	(5.1)
17	Texas	4.5		43	Wisconsin	(5.5)
26	Utah	1.5		44	Delaware	(6.8)
3	Vermont	20.6		45	Alaska	(7.8)
37	Virginia	(2.3)		46	Hawaii	(9.3)
31	Washington	(0.2)		47	Maine	(11.0)
22	West Virginia	2.9		48	South Carolina	(12.0)
43	Wisconsin	(5.5)		49	Wyoming	(17.6)
49	Wyoming	(17.6)		50	Rhode Island	(36.6)
					District of Columbia	(19.0)

Source: Federal Bureau of Investigation
     "Crime in the United States 2004" (Uniform Crime Reports, October 17, 2005)
*Forcible rape is the carnal knowledge of a female forcibly and against her will. Assaults or attempts to commit rape by force or threat of force are included. However, statutory rape without force and other sex offenses are excluded.

Rape Rate in 2004

National Rate = 32.2 Rapes per 100,000 Population*

ALPHA ORDER

RANK	STATE	RATE
18	Alabama	38.5
1	Alaska	85.1
27	Arizona	33.0
8	Arkansas	42.4
36	California	26.8
7	Colorado	42.5
46	Connecticut	20.7
10	Delaware	41.5
19	Florida	38.0
35	Georgia	27.0
38	Hawaii	26.4
11	Idaho	40.9
26	Illinois	33.2
31	Indiana	28.9
37	Iowa	26.7
15	Kansas	40.4
28	Kentucky	29.9
22	Louisiana	35.8
42	Maine	23.9
43	Maryland	23.7
33	Massachusetts	28.0
3	Michigan	54.2
9	Minnesota	41.6
16	Mississippi	40.0
39	Missouri	25.7
30	Montana	29.5
24	Nebraska	35.5
11	Nevada	40.9
25	New Hampshire	35.3
50	New Jersey	15.3
2	New Mexico	54.6
48	New York	18.8
34	North Carolina	27.4
40	North Dakota	25.1
14	Ohio	40.5
5	Oklahoma	44.2
23	Oregon	35.7
32	Pennsylvania	28.5
29	Rhode Island	29.6
11	South Carolina	40.9
6	South Dakota	43.8
20	Tennessee	37.6
21	Texas	37.3
17	Utah	39.1
41	Vermont	24.5
43	Virginia	23.7
4	Washington	46.1
49	West Virginia	17.6
47	Wisconsin	20.6
45	Wyoming	22.1

RANK ORDER

RANK	STATE	RATE
1	Alaska	85.1
2	New Mexico	54.6
3	Michigan	54.2
4	Washington	46.1
5	Oklahoma	44.2
6	South Dakota	43.8
7	Colorado	42.5
8	Arkansas	42.4
9	Minnesota	41.6
10	Delaware	41.5
11	Idaho	40.9
11	Nevada	40.9
11	South Carolina	40.9
14	Ohio	40.5
15	Kansas	40.4
16	Mississippi	40.0
17	Utah	39.1
18	Alabama	38.5
19	Florida	38.0
20	Tennessee	37.6
21	Texas	37.3
22	Louisiana	35.8
23	Oregon	35.7
24	Nebraska	35.5
25	New Hampshire	35.3
26	Illinois	33.2
27	Arizona	33.0
28	Kentucky	29.9
29	Rhode Island	29.6
30	Montana	29.5
31	Indiana	28.9
32	Pennsylvania	28.5
33	Massachusetts	28.0
34	North Carolina	27.4
35	Georgia	27.0
36	California	26.8
37	Iowa	26.7
38	Hawaii	26.4
39	Missouri	25.7
40	North Dakota	25.1
41	Vermont	24.5
42	Maine	23.9
43	Maryland	23.7
43	Virginia	23.7
45	Wyoming	22.1
46	Connecticut	20.7
47	Wisconsin	20.6
48	New York	18.8
49	West Virginia	17.6
50	New Jersey	15.3

	District of Columbia	40.1

Source: Federal Bureau of Investigation
    "Crime in the United States 2004" (Uniform Crime Reports, October 17, 2005)
*Forcible rape is the carnal knowledge of a female forcibly and against her will. Assaults or attempts to commit rape by force or threat of force are included. However, statutory rape without force and other sex offenses are excluded.

Percent Change in Rape Rate: 2003 to 2004

National Percent Change = 0.2% Decrease*

ALPHA ORDER				RANK ORDER		
RANK	**STATE**	**PERCENT CHANGE**		**RANK**	**STATE**	**PERCENT CHANGE**
12	Alabama	4.6		1	Arkansas	26.8
45	Alaska	(8.8)		2	Nebraska	22.3
31	Arizona	(0.8)		3	Vermont	20.2
1	Arkansas	26.8		4	Montana	9.9
41	California	(4.9)		5	Kentucky	9.4
24	Colorado	1.1		6	New Mexico	9.1
18	Connecticut	3.2		7	North Carolina	7.8
44	Delaware	(8.1)		8	Mississippi	6.8
39	Florida	(4.0)		9	Nevada	5.2
10	Georgia	5.0		10	Georgia	5.0
46	Hawaii	(10.3)		10	Missouri	5.0
13	Idaho	4.5		12	Alabama	4.6
27	Illinois	0.1		13	Idaho	4.5
15	Indiana	4.2		14	Oregon	4.4
34	Iowa	(1.2)		15	Indiana	4.2
23	Kansas	1.4		16	New Hampshire	3.9
5	Kentucky	9.4		17	Tennessee	3.3
26	Louisiana	0.4		18	Connecticut	3.2
47	Maine	(11.6)		18	Oklahoma	3.2
38	Maryland	(3.9)		20	New Jersey	2.7
36	Massachusetts	(2.6)		20	Texas	2.7
28	Michigan	0.0		20	West Virginia	2.7
25	Minnesota	0.7		23	Kansas	1.4
8	Mississippi	6.8		24	Colorado	1.1
10	Missouri	5.0		25	Minnesota	0.7
4	Montana	9.9		26	Louisiana	0.4
2	Nebraska	22.3		27	Illinois	0.1
9	Nevada	5.2		28	Michigan	0.0
16	New Hampshire	3.9		28	Utah	0.0
20	New Jersey	2.7		30	Ohio	(0.5)
6	New Mexico	9.1		31	Arizona	(0.8)
40	New York	(4.5)		31	North Dakota	(0.8)
7	North Carolina	7.8		33	Pennsylvania	(0.9)
31	North Dakota	(0.8)		34	Iowa	(1.2)
30	Ohio	(0.5)		35	Washington	(1.4)
18	Oklahoma	3.2		36	Massachusetts	(2.6)
14	Oregon	4.4		37	Virginia	(3.5)
33	Pennsylvania	(0.9)		38	Maryland	(3.9)
50	Rhode Island	(36.9)		39	Florida	(4.0)
48	South Carolina	(13.0)		40	New York	(4.5)
42	South Dakota	(5.8)		41	California	(4.9)
17	Tennessee	3.3		42	South Dakota	(5.8)
20	Texas	2.7		43	Wisconsin	(6.1)
28	Utah	0.0		44	Delaware	(8.1)
3	Vermont	20.2		45	Alaska	(8.8)
37	Virginia	(3.5)		46	Hawaii	(10.3)
35	Washington	(1.4)		47	Maine	(11.6)
20	West Virginia	2.7		48	South Carolina	(13.0)
43	Wisconsin	(6.1)		49	Wyoming	(18.4)
49	Wyoming	(18.4)		50	Rhode Island	(36.9)
					District of Columbia	(18.4)

Source: Federal Bureau of Investigation
   "Crime in the United States 2004" (Uniform Crime Reports, October 17, 2005)
*Forcible rape is the carnal knowledge of a female forcibly and against her will. Assaults or attempts to commit rape by force or threat of force are included. However, statutory rape without force and other sex offenses are excluded.

Rape Rate per 100,000 Female Population in 2004

National Rate = 63.5 Rapes per 100,000 Female Population*

ALPHA ORDER				RANK ORDER		
RANK	STATE	RATE		RANK	STATE	RATE
18	Alabama	74.6		1	Alaska	176.3
1	Alaska	176.3		2	New Mexico	107.4
26	Arizona	66.1		3	Michigan	106.6
9	Arkansas	83.1		4	Washington	91.9
35	California	53.5		5	Oklahoma	87.3
7	Colorado	85.8		6	South Dakota	87.2
47	Connecticut	40.1		7	Colorado	85.8
12	Delaware	81.0		8	Nevada	83.2
19	Florida	74.5		9	Arkansas	83.1
35	Georgia	53.5		10	Minnesota	82.6
38	Hawaii	52.6		11	Idaho	82.1
11	Idaho	82.1		12	Delaware	81.0
27	Illinois	65.2		13	Kansas	80.2
31	Indiana	56.9		14	South Carolina	79.8
37	Iowa	52.7		15	Ohio	79.0
13	Kansas	80.2		16	Utah	78.4
29	Kentucky	58.6		17	Mississippi	77.7
25	Louisiana	69.6		18	Alabama	74.6
42	Maine	46.7		19	Florida	74.5
44	Maryland	45.9		20	Texas	74.3
33	Massachusetts	54.3		21	Tennessee	73.6
3	Michigan	106.6		22	Oregon	71.0
10	Minnesota	82.6		23	Nebraska	70.2
17	Mississippi	77.7		24	New Hampshire	69.7
39	Missouri	50.2		25	Louisiana	69.6
28	Montana	58.8		26	Arizona	66.1
23	Nebraska	70.2		27	Illinois	65.2
8	Nevada	83.2		28	Montana	58.8
24	New Hampshire	69.7		29	Kentucky	58.6
50	New Jersey	29.8		30	Rhode Island	57.2
2	New Mexico	107.4		31	Indiana	56.9
48	New York	36.4		32	Pennsylvania	55.3
34	North Carolina	53.9		33	Massachusetts	54.3
40	North Dakota	50.0		34	North Carolina	53.9
15	Ohio	79.0		35	California	53.5
5	Oklahoma	87.3		35	Georgia	53.5
22	Oregon	71.0		37	Iowa	52.7
32	Pennsylvania	55.3		38	Hawaii	52.6
30	Rhode Island	57.2		39	Missouri	50.2
14	South Carolina	79.8		40	North Dakota	50.0
6	South Dakota	87.2		41	Vermont	48.2
21	Tennessee	73.6		42	Maine	46.7
20	Texas	74.3		43	Virginia	46.6
16	Utah	78.4		44	Maryland	45.9
41	Vermont	48.2		45	Wyoming	44.5
43	Virginia	46.6		46	Wisconsin	40.8
4	Washington	91.9		47	Connecticut	40.1
49	West Virginia	34.5		48	New York	36.4
46	Wisconsin	40.8		49	West Virginia	34.5
45	Wyoming	44.5		50	New Jersey	29.8
					District of Columbia	76.1

Source: Morgan Quitno Press using data from Federal Bureau of Investigation
"Crime in the United States 2004" (Uniform Crime Reports, October 17, 2005)
*Forcible rape is the carnal knowledge of a female forcibly and against her will. Assaults or attempts to commit rape by force or threat of force are included. However, statutory rape without force and other sex offenses are excluded. Calculated with 2004 female population.

Robberies in 2004

National Total = 401,326 Robberies*

ALPHA ORDER

RANK	STATE	ROBBERIES	% of USA
20	Alabama	6,042	1.5%
43	Alaska	447	0.1%
14	Arizona	7,721	1.9%
32	Arkansas	2,372	0.6%
1	California	61,768	15.4%
27	Colorado	3,750	0.9%
24	Connecticut	4,222	1.1%
36	Delaware	1,218	0.3%
4	Florida	29,997	7.5%
8	Georgia	13,656	3.4%
39	Hawaii	944	0.2%
45	Idaho	240	0.1%
5	Illinois	22,532	5.6%
19	Indiana	6,373	1.6%
38	Iowa	1,124	0.3%
34	Kansas	1,813	0.5%
28	Kentucky	3,268	0.8%
18	Louisiana	6,564	1.6%
44	Maine	289	0.1%
10	Maryland	12,761	3.2%
15	Massachusetts	7,467	1.9%
12	Michigan	11,320	2.8%
25	Minnesota	4,070	1.0%
31	Mississippi	2,503	0.6%
17	Missouri	6,630	1.7%
46	Montana	233	0.1%
37	Nebraska	1,138	0.3%
23	Nevada	4,905	1.2%
42	New Hampshire	500	0.1%
9	New Jersey	13,076	3.3%
33	New Mexico	2,062	0.5%
3	New York	33,506	8.3%
11	North Carolina	11,782	2.9%
50	North Dakota	39	0.0%
7	Ohio	17,543	4.4%
29	Oklahoma	3,090	0.8%
30	Oregon	2,751	0.7%
6	Pennsylvania	18,474	4.6%
41	Rhode Island	731	0.2%
22	South Carolina	5,446	1.4%
47	South Dakota	114	0.0%
13	Tennessee	8,840	2.2%
2	Texas	35,817	8.9%
35	Utah	1,236	0.3%
48	Vermont	76	0.0%
16	Virginia	6,906	1.7%
21	Washington	5,866	1.5%
40	West Virginia	768	0.2%
26	Wisconsin	4,067	1.0%
49	Wyoming	67	0.0%

RANK ORDER

RANK	STATE	ROBBERIES	% of USA
1	California	61,768	15.4%
2	Texas	35,817	8.9%
3	New York	33,506	8.3%
4	Florida	29,997	7.5%
5	Illinois	22,532	5.6%
6	Pennsylvania	18,474	4.6%
7	Ohio	17,543	4.4%
8	Georgia	13,656	3.4%
9	New Jersey	13,076	3.3%
10	Maryland	12,761	3.2%
11	North Carolina	11,782	2.9%
12	Michigan	11,320	2.8%
13	Tennessee	8,840	2.2%
14	Arizona	7,721	1.9%
15	Massachusetts	7,467	1.9%
16	Virginia	6,906	1.7%
17	Missouri	6,630	1.7%
18	Louisiana	6,564	1.6%
19	Indiana	6,373	1.6%
20	Alabama	6,042	1.5%
21	Washington	5,866	1.5%
22	South Carolina	5,446	1.4%
23	Nevada	4,905	1.2%
24	Connecticut	4,222	1.1%
25	Minnesota	4,070	1.0%
26	Wisconsin	4,067	1.0%
27	Colorado	3,750	0.9%
28	Kentucky	3,268	0.8%
29	Oklahoma	3,090	0.8%
30	Oregon	2,751	0.7%
31	Mississippi	2,503	0.6%
32	Arkansas	2,372	0.6%
33	New Mexico	2,062	0.5%
34	Kansas	1,813	0.5%
35	Utah	1,236	0.3%
36	Delaware	1,218	0.3%
37	Nebraska	1,138	0.3%
38	Iowa	1,124	0.3%
39	Hawaii	944	0.2%
40	West Virginia	768	0.2%
41	Rhode Island	731	0.2%
42	New Hampshire	500	0.1%
43	Alaska	447	0.1%
44	Maine	289	0.1%
45	Idaho	240	0.1%
46	Montana	233	0.1%
47	South Dakota	114	0.0%
48	Vermont	76	0.0%
49	Wyoming	67	0.0%
50	North Dakota	39	0.0%
	District of Columbia	3,202	0.8%

Source: Federal Bureau of Investigation
   "Crime in the United States 2004" (Uniform Crime Reports, October 17, 2005)
*Robbery is the taking or attempting to take anything of value by force or threat of force.

Average Time Between Robberies in 2004

National Rate = A Robbery Occurs Every 1 Minute*

ALPHA ORDER				RANK ORDER		
RANK	STATE	HOURS.MINUTES		RANK	STATE	HOURS.MINUTES
31	Alabama	1.27		1	North Dakota	225.14
8	Alaska	19.39		2	Wyoming	131.06
37	Arizona	1.08		3	Vermont	115.35
19	Arkansas	3.42		4	South Dakota	77.03
50	California	0.08		5	Montana	37.42
24	Colorado	2.20		6	Idaho	36.36
27	Connecticut	2.05		7	Maine	30.23
15	Delaware	7.13		8	Alaska	19.39
47	Florida	0.17		9	New Hampshire	17.34
43	Georgia	0.38		10	Rhode Island	12.01
12	Hawaii	9.19		11	West Virginia	11.26
6	Idaho	36.36		12	Hawaii	9.19
46	Illinois	0.23		13	Iowa	7.49
32	Indiana	1.23		14	Nebraska	7.43
13	Iowa	7.49		15	Delaware	7.13
17	Kansas	4.51		16	Utah	7.07
23	Kentucky	2.41		17	Kansas	4.51
33	Louisiana	1.20		18	New Mexico	4.16
7	Maine	30.23		19	Arkansas	3.42
41	Maryland	0.41		20	Mississippi	3.31
36	Massachusetts	1.11		21	Oregon	3.11
39	Michigan	0.47		22	Oklahoma	2.50
25	Minnesota	2.10		23	Kentucky	2.41
20	Mississippi	3.31		24	Colorado	2.20
34	Missouri	1.19		25	Minnesota	2.10
5	Montana	37.42		25	Wisconsin	2.10
14	Nebraska	7.43		27	Connecticut	2.05
28	Nevada	1.47		28	Nevada	1.47
9	New Hampshire	17.34		29	South Carolina	1.37
42	New Jersey	0.40		30	Washington	1.30
18	New Mexico	4.16		31	Alabama	1.27
48	New York	0.16		32	Indiana	1.23
40	North Carolina	0.45		33	Louisiana	1.20
1	North Dakota	225.14		34	Missouri	1.19
44	Ohio	0.30		35	Virginia	1.16
22	Oklahoma	2.50		36	Massachusetts	1.11
21	Oregon	3.11		37	Arizona	1.08
45	Pennsylvania	0.29		38	Tennessee	0.59
10	Rhode Island	12.01		39	Michigan	0.47
29	South Carolina	1.37		40	North Carolina	0.45
4	South Dakota	77.03		41	Maryland	0.41
38	Tennessee	0.59		42	New Jersey	0.40
49	Texas	0.15		43	Georgia	0.38
16	Utah	7.07		44	Ohio	0.30
3	Vermont	115.35		45	Pennsylvania	0.29
35	Virginia	1.16		46	Illinois	0.23
30	Washington	1.30		47	Florida	0.17
11	West Virginia	11.26		48	New York	0.16
25	Wisconsin	2.10		49	Texas	0.15
2	Wyoming	131.06		50	California	0.08
					District of Columbia	2.44

*Source: Morgan Quitno Press using data from Federal Bureau of Investigation
"Crime in the United States 2004" (Uniform Crime Reports, October 17, 2005)*
*Robbery is the taking or attempting to take anything of value by force or threat of force.

Percent Change in Number of Robberies: 2003 to 2004

National Percent Change = 3.1% Decrease*

ALPHA ORDER			RANK ORDER		
RANK	STATE	PERCENT CHANGE	RANK	STATE	PERCENT CHANGE
18	Alabama	0.1	1	Vermont	22.6
16	Alaska	0.2	2	South Dakota	9.6
13	Arizona	1.3	2	West Virginia	9.6
4	Arkansas	6.5	4	Arkansas	6.5
28	California	(3.1)	4	New Mexico	6.5
15	Colorado	0.3	6	Minnesota	4.2
16	Connecticut	0.2	6	New Hampshire	4.2
44	Delaware	(15.5)	8	Ohio	3.8
34	Florida	(4.8)	9	Virginia	2.9
27	Georgia	(2.8)	10	Pennsylvania	2.7
46	Hawaii	(19.2)	11	Washington	2.6
24	Idaho	(2.0)	12	Kentucky	1.4
35	Illinois	(5.3)	13	Arizona	1.3
20	Indiana	(0.4)	14	Michigan	0.6
21	Iowa	(0.6)	15	Colorado	0.3
47	Kansas	(19.3)	16	Alaska	0.2
12	Kentucky	1.4	16	Connecticut	0.2
39	Louisiana	(6.3)	18	Alabama	0.1
19	Maine	0.0	19	Maine	0.0
32	Maryland	(4.1)	20	Indiana	(0.4)
41	Massachusetts	(6.8)	21	Iowa	(0.6)
14	Michigan	0.6	22	Missouri	(0.8)
6	Minnesota	4.2	23	Utah	(1.7)
45	Mississippi	(17.0)	24	Idaho	(2.0)
22	Missouri	(0.8)	24	New Jersey	(2.0)
49	Montana	(21.8)	26	Nebraska	(2.3)
26	Nebraska	(2.3)	27	Georgia	(2.8)
36	Nevada	(6.1)	28	California	(3.1)
6	New Hampshire	4.2	29	Texas	(3.2)
24	New Jersey	(2.0)	30	Oregon	(3.4)
4	New Mexico	6.5	31	North Carolina	(3.7)
40	New York	(6.4)	32	Maryland	(4.1)
31	North Carolina	(3.7)	33	Oklahoma	(4.2)
50	North Dakota	(26.4)	34	Florida	(4.8)
8	Ohio	3.8	35	Illinois	(5.3)
33	Oklahoma	(4.2)	36	Nevada	(6.1)
30	Oregon	(3 4)	36	South Carolina	(6.1)
10	Pennsylvania	2.7	36	Tennessee	(6.1)
43	Rhode Island	(11.9)	39	Louisiana	(6.3)
36	South Carolina	(6.1)	40	New York	(6.4)
2	South Dakota	9.6	41	Massachusetts	(6.8)
36	Tennessee	(6.1)	42	Wisconsin	(7.5)
29	Texas	(3.2)	43	Rhode Island	(11.9)
23	Utah	(1.7)	44	Delaware	(15.5)
1	Vermont	22.6	45	Mississippi	(17.0)
9	Virginia	2.9	46	Hawaii	(19.2)
11	Washington	2.6	47	Kansas	(19.3)
2	West Virginia	9.6	48	Wyoming	(20.2)
42	Wisconsin	(7.5)	49	Montana	(21.8)
48	Wyoming	(20.2)	50	North Dakota	(26.4)
				District of Columbia	(18.8)

Source: Federal Bureau of Investigation
"Crime in the United States 2004" (Uniform Crime Reports, October 17, 2005)
Robbery is the taking or attempting to take anything of value by force or threat of force.

Robbery Rate in 2004

National Rate = 136.7 Robberies per 100,000 Population*

ALPHA ORDER

RANK	STATE	RATE
17	Alabama	133.4
36	Alaska	68.2
16	Arizona	134.4
28	Arkansas	86.2
6	California	172.1
30	Colorado	81.5
19	Connecticut	120.5
13	Delaware	146.7
5	Florida	172.4
8	Georgia	154.7
34	Hawaii	74.8
46	Idaho	17.2
3	Illinois	177.2
24	Indiana	102.2
43	Iowa	38.0
38	Kansas	66.3
32	Kentucky	78.8
14	Louisiana	145.4
45	Maine	21.9
1	Maryland	229.6
20	Massachusetts	116.4
22	Michigan	111.9
31	Minnesota	79.8
28	Mississippi	86.2
21	Missouri	115.2
44	Montana	25.1
39	Nebraska	65.1
2	Nevada	210.1
42	New Hampshire	38.5
10	New Jersey	150.3
23	New Mexico	108.3
4	New York	174.3
15	North Carolina	137.9
50	North Dakota	6.1
9	Ohio	153.1
27	Oklahoma	87.7
33	Oregon	76.5
12	Pennsylvania	148.9
37	Rhode Island	67.6
18	South Carolina	129.7
47	South Dakota	14.8
11	Tennessee	149.8
7	Texas	159.3
40	Utah	51.7
49	Vermont	12.2
26	Virginia	92.6
25	Washington	94.6
41	West Virginia	42.3
35	Wisconsin	73.8
48	Wyoming	13.2

RANK ORDER

RANK	STATE	RATE
1	Maryland	229.6
2	Nevada	210.1
3	Illinois	177.2
4	New York	174.3
5	Florida	172.4
6	California	172.1
7	Texas	159.3
8	Georgia	154.7
9	Ohio	153.1
10	New Jersey	150.3
11	Tennessee	149.8
12	Pennsylvania	148.9
13	Delaware	146.7
14	Louisiana	145.4
15	North Carolina	137.9
16	Arizona	134.4
17	Alabama	133.4
18	South Carolina	129.7
19	Connecticut	120.5
20	Massachusetts	116.4
21	Missouri	115.2
22	Michigan	111.9
23	New Mexico	108.3
24	Indiana	102.2
25	Washington	94.6
26	Virginia	92.6
27	Oklahoma	87.7
28	Arkansas	86.2
28	Mississippi	86.2
30	Colorado	81.5
31	Minnesota	79.8
32	Kentucky	78.8
33	Oregon	76.5
34	Hawaii	74.8
35	Wisconsin	73.8
36	Alaska	68.2
37	Rhode Island	67.6
38	Kansas	66.3
39	Nebraska	65.1
40	Utah	51.7
41	West Virginia	42.3
42	New Hampshire	38.5
43	Iowa	38.0
44	Montana	25.1
45	Maine	21.9
46	Idaho	17.2
47	South Dakota	14.8
48	Wyoming	13.2
49	Vermont	12.2
50	North Dakota	6.1

	District of Columbia	578.5

Source: Federal Bureau of Investigation
        "Crime in the United States 2004" (Uniform Crime Reports, October 17, 2005)
*Robbery is the taking or attempting to take anything of value by force or threat of force.

348

Percent Change in Robbery Rate: 2003 to 2004

National Percent Change = 4.1% Decrease*

ALPHA ORDER

RANK	STATE	PERCENT CHANGE
15	Alabama	(0.5)
17	Alaska	(0.9)
22	Arizona	(1.6)
4	Arkansas	5.5
28	California	(4.3)
17	Colorado	(0.9)
14	Connecticut	(0.2)
44	Delaware	(16.7)
38	Florida	(7.0)
29	Georgia	(4.4)
47	Hawaii	(20.1)
26	Idaho	(3.9)
34	Illinois	(5.8)
19	Indiana	(1.0)
19	Iowa	(1.0)
46	Kansas	(19.6)
12	Kentucky	0.7
37	Louisiana	(6.8)
16	Maine	(0.6)
31	Maryland	(4.9)
36	Massachusetts	(6.7)
13	Michigan	0.3
7	Minnesota	3.4
45	Mississippi	(17.6)
21	Missouri	(1.4)
49	Montana	(22.5)
24	Nebraska	(2.9)
42	Nevada	(9.8)
8	New Hampshire	3.3
23	New Jersey	(2.6)
5	New Mexico	5.1
35	New York	(6.5)
33	North Carolina	(5.0)
50	North Dakota	(26.5)
6	Ohio	3.6
30	Oklahoma	(4.6)
27	Oregon	(4.2)
9	Pennsylvania	2.5
43	Rhode Island	(12.3)
40	South Carolina	(7.2)
3	South Dakota	8.8
38	Tennessee	(7.0)
31	Texas	(4.9)
25	Utah	(3.3)
1	Vermont	22.2
10	Virginia	1.6
11	Washington	1.4
2	West Virginia	9.3
41	Wisconsin	(8.1)
48	Wyoming	(20.9)

RANK ORDER

RANK	STATE	PERCENT CHANGE
1	Vermont	22.2
2	West Virginia	9.3
3	South Dakota	8.8
4	Arkansas	5.5
5	New Mexico	5.1
6	Ohio	3.6
7	Minnesota	3.4
8	New Hampshire	3.3
9	Pennsylvania	2.5
10	Virginia	1.6
11	Washington	1.4
12	Kentucky	0.7
13	Michigan	0.3
14	Connecticut	(0.2)
15	Alabama	(0.5)
16	Maine	(0.6)
17	Alaska	(0.9)
17	Colorado	(0.9)
19	Indiana	(1.0)
19	Iowa	(1.0)
21	Missouri	(1.4)
22	Arizona	(1.6)
23	New Jersey	(2.6)
24	Nebraska	(2.9)
25	Utah	(3.3)
26	Idaho	(3.9)
27	Oregon	(4.2)
28	California	(4.3)
29	Georgia	(4.4)
30	Oklahoma	(4.6)
31	Maryland	(4.9)
31	Texas	(4.9)
33	North Carolina	(5.0)
34	Illinois	(5.8)
35	New York	(6.5)
36	Massachusetts	(6.7)
37	Louisiana	(6.8)
38	Florida	(7.0)
38	Tennessee	(7.0)
40	South Carolina	(7.2)
41	Wisconsin	(8.1)
42	Nevada	(9.8)
43	Rhode Island	(12.3)
44	Delaware	(16.7)
45	Mississippi	(17.6)
46	Kansas	(19.6)
47	Hawaii	(20.1)
48	Wyoming	(20.9)
49	Montana	(22.5)
50	North Dakota	(26.5)

	District of Columbia	(18.2)

Source: Federal Bureau of Investigation
"Crime in the United States 2004" (Uniform Crime Reports, October 17, 2005)
*Robbery is the taking or attempting to take anything of value by force or threat of force.

Robberies with Firearms in 2004

National Total = 130,554 Robberies*

ALPHA ORDER

RANK	STATE	ROBBERIES	% of USA
22	Alabama	1,516	1.2%
40	Alaska	148	0.1%
11	Arizona	3,855	3.0%
29	Arkansas	1,005	0.8%
1	California	20,529	15.7%
25	Colorado	1,346	1.0%
27	Connecticut	1,111	0.9%
33	Delaware	452	0.3%
3	Florida	11,504	8.8%
7	Georgia	4,917	3.8%
42	Hawaii	112	0.1%
43	Idaho	72	0.1%
NA	Illinois**	NA	NA
14	Indiana	2,913	2.2%
37	Iowa	259	0.2%
34	Kansas	356	0.3%
23	Kentucky	1,442	1.1%
12	Louisiana	3,577	2.7%
44	Maine	61	0.0%
9	Maryland	4,273	3.3%
21	Massachusetts	1,777	1.4%
6	Michigan	5,262	4.0%
35	Minnesota	339	0.3%
28	Mississippi	1,091	0.8%
15	Missouri	2,843	2.2%
46	Montana	21	0.0%
32	Nebraska	515	0.4%
20	Nevada	2,019	1.5%
41	New Hampshire	113	0.1%
10	New Jersey	4,251	3.3%
30	New Mexico	769	0.6%
18	New York	2,395	1.8%
13	North Carolina	3,278	2.5%
49	North Dakota	9	0.0%
5	Ohio	5,500	4.2%
24	Oklahoma	1,353	1.0%
31	Oregon	648	0.5%
4	Pennsylvania	7,485	5.7%
38	Rhode Island	212	0.2%
16	South Carolina	2,635	2.0%
47	South Dakota	19	0.0%
8	Tennessee	4,820	3.7%
2	Texas	15,784	12.1%
36	Utah	338	0.3%
48	Vermont	10	0.0%
17	Virginia	2,475	1.9%
26	Washington	1,240	0.9%
39	West Virginia	150	0.1%
19	Wisconsin	2,204	1.7%
45	Wyoming	26	0.0%

RANK ORDER

RANK	STATE	ROBBERIES	% of USA
1	California	20,529	15.7%
2	Texas	15,784	12.1%
3	Florida	11,504	8.8%
4	Pennsylvania	7,485	5.7%
5	Ohio	5,500	4.2%
6	Michigan	5,262	4.0%
7	Georgia	4,917	3.8%
8	Tennessee	4,820	3.7%
9	Maryland	4,273	3.3%
10	New Jersey	4,251	3.3%
11	Arizona	3,855	3.0%
12	Louisiana	3,577	2.7%
13	North Carolina	3,278	2.5%
14	Indiana	2,913	2.2%
15	Missouri	2,843	2.2%
16	South Carolina	2,635	2.0%
17	Virginia	2,475	1.9%
18	New York	2,395	1.8%
19	Wisconsin	2,204	1.7%
20	Nevada	2,019	1.5%
21	Massachusetts	1,777	1.4%
22	Alabama	1,516	1.2%
23	Kentucky	1,442	1.1%
24	Oklahoma	1,353	1.0%
25	Colorado	1,346	1.0%
26	Washington	1,240	0.9%
27	Connecticut	1,111	0.9%
28	Mississippi	1,091	0.8%
29	Arkansas	1,005	0.8%
30	New Mexico	769	0.6%
31	Oregon	648	0.5%
32	Nebraska	515	0.4%
33	Delaware	452	0.3%
34	Kansas	356	0.3%
35	Minnesota	339	0.3%
36	Utah	338	0.3%
37	Iowa	259	0.2%
38	Rhode Island	212	0.2%
39	West Virginia	150	0.1%
40	Alaska	148	0.1%
41	New Hampshire	113	0.1%
42	Hawaii	112	0.1%
43	Idaho	72	0.1%
44	Maine	61	0.0%
45	Wyoming	26	0.0%
46	Montana	21	0.0%
47	South Dakota	19	0.0%
48	Vermont	10	0.0%
49	North Dakota	9	0.0%
NA	Illinois**	NA	NA
	District of Columbia	1,525	1.2%

Source: Federal Bureau of Investigation
"Crime in the United States 2004" (Uniform Crime Reports, October 17, 2005)
*Of the 321,299 robberies in 2004 for which supplemental data were received by the F.B.I. There were an additional 80,027 robberies for which the type of weapon was not reported to the F.B.I. Robbery is the taking or attempting to take anything of value by force or threat of force. Numbers are for reporting jurisdictions only.
**Not available.

Robbery Rate with Firearms in 2004

National Rate = 53.4 Robberies per 100,000 Population*

ALPHA ORDER

RANK	STATE	RATE
22	Alabama	45.7
32	Alaska	23.2
8	Arizona	68.8
20	Arkansas	47.1
14	California	57.4
28	Colorado	33.7
25	Connecticut	41.4
16	Delaware	54.6
10	Florida	66.2
1	Georgia	108.8
40	Hawaii	10.1
44	Idaho	5.2
NA	Illinois**	NA
12	Indiana	58.9
41	Iowa	9.6
36	Kansas	18.6
23	Kentucky	44.8
2	Louisiana	90.9
45	Maine	4.6
3	Maryland	86.8
30	Massachusetts	32.2
15	Michigan	54.7
42	Minnesota	7.8
13	Mississippi	58.1
17	Missouri	52.7
47	Montana	3.2
29	Nebraska	33.1
4	Nevada	86.5
39	New Hampshire	11.4
19	New Jersey	49.0
21	New Mexico	46.3
31	New York	23.7
18	North Carolina	50.6
48	North Dakota	1.7
11	Ohio	62.4
26	Oklahoma	38.4
35	Oregon	19.3
7	Pennsylvania	69.8
34	Rhode Island	19.6
9	South Carolina	66.9
46	South Dakota	3.3
5	Tennessee	82.8
6	Texas	70.7
37	Utah	16.0
48	Vermont	1.7
27	Virginia	37.2
33	Washington	22.4
38	West Virginia	13.2
24	Wisconsin	42.3
43	Wyoming	5.3

RANK ORDER

RANK	STATE	RATE
1	Georgia	108.8
2	Louisiana	90.9
3	Maryland	86.8
4	Nevada	86.5
5	Tennessee	82.8
6	Texas	70.7
7	Pennsylvania	69.8
8	Arizona	68.8
9	South Carolina	66.9
10	Florida	66.2
11	Ohio	62.4
12	Indiana	58.9
13	Mississippi	58.1
14	California	57.4
15	Michigan	54.7
16	Delaware	54.6
17	Missouri	52.7
18	North Carolina	50.6
19	New Jersey	49.0
20	Arkansas	47.1
21	New Mexico	46.3
22	Alabama	45.7
23	Kentucky	44.8
24	Wisconsin	42.3
25	Connecticut	41.4
26	Oklahoma	38.4
27	Virginia	37.2
28	Colorado	33.7
29	Nebraska	33.1
30	Massachusetts	32.2
31	New York	23.7
32	Alaska	23.2
33	Washington	22.4
34	Rhode Island	19.6
35	Oregon	19.3
36	Kansas	18.6
37	Utah	16.0
38	West Virginia	13.2
39	New Hampshire	11.4
40	Hawaii	10.1
41	Iowa	9.6
42	Minnesota	7.8
43	Wyoming	5.3
44	Idaho	5.2
45	Maine	4.6
46	South Dakota	3.3
47	Montana	3.2
48	North Dakota	1.7
48	Vermont	1.7
NA	Illinois**	NA

District of Columbia   275.5

Source: Morgan Quitno Press using data from Federal Bureau of Investigation
"Crime in the United States 2004" (Uniform Crime Reports, October 17, 2005)
*Based only on population of reporting jurisdictions. Robbery is the taking or attempting to take anything of value by force or threat of force. National rate reflects only those robberies for which the type of weapon was known and reported.
**Not available.

351

Percent of Robberies Involving Firearms in 2004

National Percent = 40.6% of Robberies*

ALPHA ORDER

RANK	STATE	PERCENT
2	Alabama	55.1
33	Alaska	33.4
7	Arizona	50.5
14	Arkansas	47.0
32	California	33.5
26	Colorado	38.2
28	Connecticut	34.5
21	Delaware	42.4
25	Florida	38.4
2	Georgia	55.1
49	Hawaii	12.3
36	Idaho	30.0
NA	Illinois**	NA
12	Indiana	48.6
44	Iowa	24.7
29	Kansas	34.1
11	Kentucky	48.7
1	Louisiana	58.5
45	Maine	21.1
9	Maryland	49.1
40	Massachusetts	26.6
13	Michigan	47.7
35	Minnesota	30.4
6	Mississippi	52.3
18	Missouri	44.1
46	Montana	18.1
16	Nebraska	45.7
22	Nevada	41.2
30	New Hampshire	33.8
34	New Jersey	32.5
24	New Mexico	39.2
37	New York	29.4
15	North Carolina	46.8
43	North Dakota	25.0
31	Ohio	33.6
19	Oklahoma	43.8
42	Oregon	25.4
20	Pennsylvania	42.6
38	Rhode Island	29.0
8	South Carolina	50.3
47	South Dakota	17.8
4	Tennessee	54.6
17	Texas	44.3
39	Utah	28.1
48	Vermont	14.5
10	Virginia	48.8
41	Washington	25.9
27	West Virginia	35.7
5	Wisconsin	54.5
23	Wyoming	39.4

RANK ORDER

RANK	STATE	PERCENT
1	Louisiana	58.5
2	Alabama	55.1
2	Georgia	55.1
4	Tennessee	54.6
5	Wisconsin	54.5
6	Mississippi	52.3
7	Arizona	50.5
8	South Carolina	50.3
9	Maryland	49.1
10	Virginia	48.8
11	Kentucky	48.7
12	Indiana	48.6
13	Michigan	47.7
14	Arkansas	47.0
15	North Carolina	46.8
16	Nebraska	45.7
17	Texas	44.3
18	Missouri	44.1
19	Oklahoma	43.8
20	Pennsylvania	42.6
21	Delaware	42.4
22	Nevada	41.2
23	Wyoming	39.4
24	New Mexico	39.2
25	Florida	38.4
26	Colorado	38.2
27	West Virginia	35.7
28	Connecticut	34.5
29	Kansas	34.1
30	New Hampshire	33.8
31	Ohio	33.6
32	California	33.5
33	Alaska	33.4
34	New Jersey	32.5
35	Minnesota	30.4
36	Idaho	30.0
37	New York	29.4
38	Rhode Island	29.0
39	Utah	28.1
40	Massachusetts	26.6
41	Washington	25.9
42	Oregon	25.4
43	North Dakota	25.0
44	Iowa	24.7
45	Maine	21.1
46	Montana	18.1
47	South Dakota	17.8
48	Vermont	14.5
49	Hawaii	12.3
NA	Illinois**	NA
	District of Columbia	47.7

Source: Morgan Quitno Press using data from Federal Bureau of Investigation
   "Crime in the United States 2004" (Uniform Crime Reports, October 17, 2005)
*Of the 321,299 robberies in 2004 for which supplemental data were received by the F.B.I. There were an additional 80,027 robberies for which the type of weapon was not reported to the F.B.I. Robbery is the taking or attempting to take anything of value by force or threat of force. Numbers are for reporting jurisdictions only.
**Not available.

Robberies with Knives or Cutting Instruments in 2004

National Total = 28,624 Robberies*

ALPHA ORDER					RANK ORDER			
RANK	STATE	ROBBERIES	% of USA		RANK	STATE	ROBBERIES	% of USA
29	Alabama	199	0.7%		1	California	6,099	21.3%
42	Alaska	45	0.2%		2	Texas	3,571	12.5%
11	Arizona	721	2.5%		3	Florida	2,262	7.9%
31	Arkansas	128	0.4%		4	New Jersey	1,359	4.7%
1	California	6,099	21.3%		5	Massachusetts	1,348	4.7%
22	Colorado	367	1.3%		6	Pennsylvania	1,335	4.7%
20	Connecticut	391	1.4%		7	New York	951	3.3%
35	Delaware	92	0.3%		8	Maryland	884	3.1%
3	Florida	2,262	7.9%		9	Ohio	805	2.8%
15	Georgia	477	1.7%		10	Tennessee	735	2.6%
38	Hawaii	85	0.3%		11	Arizona	721	2.5%
44	Idaho	38	0.1%		12	North Carolina	660	2.3%
NA	Illinois**	NA	NA		13	Michigan	644	2.2%
19	Indiana	394	1.4%		14	Nevada	494	1.7%
34	Iowa	106	0.4%		15	Georgia	477	1.7%
40	Kansas	48	0.2%		16	Missouri	476	1.7%
28	Kentucky	213	0.7%		17	Washington	472	1.6%
21	Louisiana	380	1.3%		18	South Carolina	453	1.6%
41	Maine	47	0.2%		19	Indiana	394	1.4%
8	Maryland	884	3.1%		20	Connecticut	391	1.4%
5	Massachusetts	1,348	4.7%		21	Louisiana	380	1.3%
13	Michigan	644	2.2%		22	Colorado	367	1.3%
36	Minnesota	91	0.3%		23	Virginia	360	1.3%
31	Mississippi	128	0.4%		24	Oklahoma	296	1.0%
16	Missouri	476	1.7%		25	Oregon	280	1.0%
46	Montana	16	0.1%		26	New Mexico	272	1.0%
33	Nebraska	113	0.4%		27	Wisconsin	256	0.9%
14	Nevada	494	1.7%		28	Kentucky	213	0.7%
43	New Hampshire	40	0.1%		29	Alabama	199	0.7%
4	New Jersey	1,359	4.7%		30	Utah	132	0.5%
26	New Mexico	272	1.0%		31	Arkansas	128	0.4%
7	New York	951	3.3%		31	Mississippi	128	0.4%
12	North Carolina	660	2.3%		33	Nebraska	113	0.4%
49	North Dakota	3	0.0%		34	Iowa	106	0.4%
9	Ohio	805	2.8%		35	Delaware	92	0.3%
24	Oklahoma	296	1.0%		36	Minnesota	91	0.3%
25	Oregon	280	1.0%		37	Rhode Island	90	0.3%
6	Pennsylvania	1,335	4.7%		38	Hawaii	85	0.3%
37	Rhode Island	90	0.3%		39	West Virginia	58	0.2%
18	South Carolina	453	1.6%		40	Kansas	48	0.2%
45	South Dakota	19	0.1%		41	Maine	47	0.2%
10	Tennessee	735	2.6%		42	Alaska	45	0.2%
2	Texas	3,571	12.5%		43	New Hampshire	40	0.1%
30	Utah	132	0.5%		44	Idaho	38	0.1%
47	Vermont	11	0.0%		45	South Dakota	19	0.1%
23	Virginia	360	1.3%		46	Montana	16	0.1%
17	Washington	472	1.6%		47	Vermont	11	0.0%
39	West Virginia	58	0.2%		48	Wyoming	4	0.0%
27	Wisconsin	256	0.9%		49	North Dakota	3	0.0%
48	Wyoming	4	0.0%		NA	Illinois**	NA	NA
						District of Columbia	176	0.6%

Source: Federal Bureau of Investigation
    "Crime in the United States 2004" (Uniform Crime Reports, October 17, 2005)
*Of the 321,299 robberies in 2004 for which supplemental data were received by the F.B.I. There were an additional 80,027 robberies for which the type of weapon was not reported to the F.B.I. Robbery is the taking or attempting to take anything of value by force or threat of force. Numbers are for reporting jurisdictions only.
**Not available.

Percent of Robberies Involving Knives or Cutting Instruments in 2004

National Percent = 8.9% of Robberies*

ALPHA ORDER

RANK	STATE	PERCENT
37	Alabama	7.2
17	Alaska	10.2
26	Arizona	9.4
45	Arkansas	6.0
21	California	10.0
15	Colorado	10.4
10	Connecticut	12.2
29	Delaware	8.6
35	Florida	7.5
47	Georgia	5.3
28	Hawaii	9.3
5	Idaho	15.8
NA	Illinois**	NA
40	Indiana	6.6
18	Iowa	10.1
49	Kansas	4.6
37	Kentucky	7.2
42	Louisiana	6.2
3	Maine	16.3
18	Maryland	10.1
1	Massachusetts	20.2
46	Michigan	5.8
33	Minnesota	8.2
43	Mississippi	6.1
36	Missouri	7.4
7	Montana	13.8
21	Nebraska	10.0
18	Nevada	10.1
11	New Hampshire	12.0
15	New Jersey	10.4
6	New Mexico	13.9
12	New York	11.7
26	North Carolina	9.4
31	North Dakota	8.3
48	Ohio	4.9
25	Oklahoma	9.6
13	Oregon	11.0
34	Pennsylvania	7.6
9	Rhode Island	12.3
29	South Carolina	8.6
2	South Dakota	17.8
31	Tennessee	8.3
21	Texas	10.0
13	Utah	11.0
4	Vermont	15.9
39	Virginia	7.1
24	Washington	9.9
7	West Virginia	13.8
41	Wisconsin	6.3
43	Wyoming	6.1

RANK ORDER

RANK	STATE	PERCENT
1	Massachusetts	20.2
2	South Dakota	17.8
3	Maine	16.3
4	Vermont	15.9
5	Idaho	15.8
6	New Mexico	13.9
7	Montana	13.8
7	West Virginia	13.8
9	Rhode Island	12.3
10	Connecticut	12.2
11	New Hampshire	12.0
12	New York	11.7
13	Oregon	11.0
13	Utah	11.0
15	Colorado	10.4
15	New Jersey	10.4
17	Alaska	10.2
18	Iowa	10.1
18	Maryland	10.1
18	Nevada	10.1
21	California	10.0
21	Nebraska	10.0
21	Texas	10.0
24	Washington	9.9
25	Oklahoma	9.6
26	Arizona	9.4
26	North Carolina	9.4
28	Hawaii	9.3
29	Delaware	8.6
29	South Carolina	8.6
31	North Dakota	8.3
31	Tennessee	8.3
33	Minnesota	8.2
34	Pennsylvania	7.6
35	Florida	7.5
36	Missouri	7.4
37	Alabama	7.2
37	Kentucky	7.2
39	Virginia	7.1
40	Indiana	6.6
41	Wisconsin	6.3
42	Louisiana	6.2
43	Mississippi	6.1
43	Wyoming	6.1
45	Arkansas	6.0
46	Michigan	5.8
47	Georgia	5.3
48	Ohio	4.9
49	Kansas	4.6
NA	Illinois**	NA
	District of Columbia	5.5

Source: Morgan Quitno Press using data from Federal Bureau of Investigation
    "Crime in the United States 2004" (Uniform Crime Reports, October 17, 2005)
*Of the 321,299 robberies in 2004 for which supplemental data were received by the F.B.I. There were an additional 80,027 robberies for which the type of weapon was not reported to the F.B.I. Robbery is the taking or attempting to take anything of value by force or threat of force. Numbers are for reporting jurisdictions only.
**Not available.

Robberies with Blunt Objects and Other Dangerous Weapons in 2004

National Total = 30,163 Robberies*

ALPHA ORDER					RANK ORDER			
RANK	STATE	ROBBERIES	% of USA		RANK	STATE	ROBBERIES	% of USA
33	Alabama	167	0.6%		1	California	5,495	18.2%
44	Alaska	34	0.1%		2	Texas	3,350	11.1%
13	Arizona	701	2.3%		3	Florida	3,211	10.6%
30	Arkansas	215	0.7%		4	Ohio	1,946	6.5%
1	California	5,495	18.2%		5	Michigan	1,180	3.9%
22	Colorado	376	1.2%		6	Pennsylvania	1,159	3.8%
26	Connecticut	276	0.9%		7	Tennessee	973	3.2%
37	Delaware	80	0.3%		8	New Jersey	966	3.2%
3	Florida	3,211	10.6%		9	New York	912	3.0%
11	Georgia	761	2.5%		10	Massachusetts	838	2.8%
38	Hawaii	78	0.3%		11	Georgia	761	2.5%
42	Idaho	41	0.1%		12	North Carolina	742	2.5%
NA	Illinois**	NA	NA		13	Arizona	701	2.3%
19	Indiana	411	1.4%		14	Virginia	636	2.1%
34	Iowa	150	0.5%		15	Missouri	563	1.9%
31	Kansas	192	0.6%		16	Maryland	500	1.7%
24	Kentucky	301	1.0%		17	South Carolina	486	1.6%
21	Louisiana	395	1.3%		18	Washington	479	1.6%
45	Maine	22	0.1%		19	Indiana	411	1.4%
16	Maryland	500	1.7%		20	Nevada	398	1.3%
10	Massachusetts	838	2.8%		21	Louisiana	395	1.3%
5	Michigan	1,180	3.9%		22	Colorado	376	1.2%
23	Minnesota	325	1.1%		23	Minnesota	325	1.1%
25	Mississippi	297	1.0%		24	Kentucky	301	1.0%
15	Missouri	563	1.9%		25	Mississippi	297	1.0%
41	Montana	43	0.1%		26	Connecticut	276	0.9%
36	Nebraska	103	0.3%		27	Oregon	258	0.9%
20	Nevada	398	1.3%		28	Wisconsin	227	0.8%
42	New Hampshire	41	0.1%		29	Oklahoma	223	0.7%
8	New Jersey	966	3.2%		30	Arkansas	215	0.7%
34	New Mexico	150	0.5%		31	Kansas	192	0.6%
9	New York	912	3.0%		32	Utah	170	0.6%
12	North Carolina	742	2.5%		33	Alabama	167	0.6%
49	North Dakota	3	0.0%		34	Iowa	150	0.5%
4	Ohio	1,946	6.5%		34	New Mexico	150	0.5%
29	Oklahoma	223	0.7%		36	Nebraska	103	0.3%
27	Oregon	258	0.9%		37	Delaware	80	0.3%
6	Pennsylvania	1,159	3.8%		38	Hawaii	78	0.3%
39	Rhode Island	73	0.2%		39	Rhode Island	73	0.2%
17	South Carolina	486	1.6%		40	West Virginia	46	0.2%
46	South Dakota	17	0.1%		41	Montana	43	0.1%
7	Tennessee	973	3.2%		42	Idaho	41	0.1%
2	Texas	3,350	11.1%		42	New Hampshire	41	0.1%
32	Utah	170	0.6%		44	Alaska	34	0.1%
47	Vermont	15	0.0%		45	Maine	22	0.1%
14	Virginia	636	2.1%		46	South Dakota	17	0.1%
18	Washington	479	1.6%		47	Vermont	15	0.0%
40	West Virginia	46	0.2%		48	Wyoming	7	0.0%
28	Wisconsin	227	0.8%		49	North Dakota	3	0.0%
48	Wyoming	7	0.0%		NA	Illinois**	NA	NA
						District of Columbia	131	0.4%

Source: Federal Bureau of Investigation
   "Crime in the United States 2004" (Uniform Crime Reports, October 17, 2005)
Of the 321,299 robberies in 2004 for which supplemental data were received by the F.B.I. There were an additional 80,027 robberies for which the type of weapon was not reported to the F.B.I. Robbery is the taking or attempting to take anything of value by force or threat of force. Numbers are for reporting jurisdictions only.
**Not available.*

Percent of Robberies Involving Blunt Objects and
Other Dangerous Weapons in 2004
National Percent = 9.4% of Robberies*

ALPHA ORDER

ALPHA ORDER

RANK	STATE	PERCENT
47	Alabama	6.1
38	Alaska	7.7
29	Arizona	9.2
23	Arkansas	10.1
31	California	9.0
17	Colorado	10.7
33	Connecticut	8.6
41	Delaware	7.5
17	Florida	10.7
35	Georgia	8.5
33	Hawaii	8.6
5	Idaho	17.1
NA	Illinois**	NA
44	Indiana	6.9
7	Iowa	14.3
4	Kansas	18.4
22	Kentucky	10.2
46	Louisiana	6.5
39	Maine	7.6
48	Maryland	5.7
10	Massachusetts	12.6
17	Michigan	10.7
2	Minnesota	29.1
8	Mississippi	14.2
32	Missouri	8.7
1	Montana	37.1
30	Nebraska	9.1
37	Nevada	8.1
12	New Hampshire	12.3
42	New Jersey	7.4
39	New Mexico	7.6
14	New York	11.2
20	North Carolina	10.6
36	North Dakota	8.3
13	Ohio	11.9
43	Oklahoma	7.2
23	Oregon	10.1
45	Pennsylvania	6.6
25	Rhode Island	10.0
28	South Carolina	9.3
6	South Dakota	15.9
15	Tennessee	11.0
27	Texas	9.4
9	Utah	14.1
3	Vermont	21.7
11	Virginia	12.5
25	Washington	10.0
15	West Virginia	11.0
49	Wisconsin	5.6
20	Wyoming	10.6

RANK ORDER

RANK	STATE	PERCENT
1	Montana	37.1
2	Minnesota	29.1
3	Vermont	21.7
4	Kansas	18.4
5	Idaho	17.1
6	South Dakota	15.9
7	Iowa	14.3
8	Mississippi	14.2
9	Utah	14.1
10	Massachusetts	12.6
11	Virginia	12.5
12	New Hampshire	12.3
13	Ohio	11.9
14	New York	11.2
15	Tennessee	11.0
15	West Virginia	11.0
17	Colorado	10.7
17	Florida	10.7
17	Michigan	10.7
20	North Carolina	10.6
20	Wyoming	10.6
22	Kentucky	10.2
23	Arkansas	10.1
23	Oregon	10.1
25	Rhode Island	10.0
25	Washington	10.0
27	Texas	9.4
28	South Carolina	9.3
29	Arizona	9.2
30	Nebraska	9.1
31	California	9.0
32	Missouri	8.7
33	Connecticut	8.6
33	Hawaii	8.6
35	Georgia	8.5
36	North Dakota	8.3
37	Nevada	8.1
38	Alaska	7.7
39	Maine	7.6
39	New Mexico	7.6
41	Delaware	7.5
42	New Jersey	7.4
43	Oklahoma	7.2
44	Indiana	6.9
45	Pennsylvania	6.6
46	Louisiana	6.5
47	Alabama	6.1
48	Maryland	5.7
49	Wisconsin	5.6
NA	Illinois**	NA

	District of Columbia	4.1

Source: Morgan Quitno Press using data from Federal Bureau of Investigation
    "Crime in the United States 2004" (Uniform Crime Reports, October 17, 2005)
*Of the 321,299 robberies in 2004 for which supplemental data were received by the F.B.I. There were an
additional 80,027 robberies for which the type of weapon was not reported to the F.B.I. Robbery is the taking or
attempting to take anything of value by force or threat of force. Numbers are for reporting jurisdictions only.
**Not available.

Robberies Committed with Hands, Fists or Feet in 2004

National Total = 131,958 Robberies*

ALPHA ORDER

RANK	STATE	ROBBERIES	% of USA
28	Alabama	867	0.7%
40	Alaska	216	0.2%
14	Arizona	2,355	1.8%
29	Arkansas	789	0.6%
1	California	29,129	22.1%
23	Colorado	1,435	1.1%
22	Connecticut	1,438	1.1%
36	Delaware	442	0.3%
2	Florida	13,007	9.9%
10	Georgia	2,766	2.1%
31	Hawaii	635	0.5%
44	Idaho	89	0.1%
NA	Illinois**	NA	NA
17	Indiana	2,279	1.7%
34	Iowa	532	0.4%
35	Kansas	449	0.3%
27	Kentucky	1,004	0.8%
19	Louisiana	1,759	1.3%
42	Maine	159	0.1%
9	Maryland	3,053	2.3%
11	Massachusetts	2,712	2.1%
7	Michigan	3,949	3.0%
38	Minnesota	361	0.3%
32	Mississippi	570	0.4%
13	Missouri	2,559	1.9%
46	Montana	36	0.0%
37	Nebraska	396	0.3%
18	Nevada	1,994	1.5%
43	New Hampshire	140	0.1%
6	New Jersey	6,484	4.9%
30	New Mexico	770	0.6%
8	New York	3,899	3.0%
15	North Carolina	2,320	1.8%
49	North Dakota	21	0.0%
4	Ohio	8,135	6.2%
26	Oklahoma	1,218	0.9%
24	Oregon	1,370	1.0%
5	Pennsylvania	7,572	5.7%
39	Rhode Island	356	0.3%
20	South Carolina	1,664	1.3%
45	South Dakota	52	0.0%
16	Tennessee	2,307	1.7%
3	Texas	12,952	9.8%
33	Utah	563	0.4%
47	Vermont	33	0.0%
21	Virginia	1,605	1.2%
12	Washington	2,599	2.0%
41	West Virginia	166	0.1%
25	Wisconsin	1,355	1.0%
48	Wyoming	29	0.0%

RANK ORDER

RANK	STATE	ROBBERIES	% of USA
1	California	29,129	22.1%
2	Florida	13,007	9.9%
3	Texas	12,952	9.8%
4	Ohio	8,135	6.2%
5	Pennsylvania	7,572	5.7%
6	New Jersey	6,484	4.9%
7	Michigan	3,949	3.0%
8	New York	3,899	3.0%
9	Maryland	3,053	2.3%
10	Georgia	2,766	2.1%
11	Massachusetts	2,712	2.1%
12	Washington	2,599	2.0%
13	Missouri	2,559	1.9%
14	Arizona	2,355	1.8%
15	North Carolina	2,320	1.8%
16	Tennessee	2,307	1.7%
17	Indiana	2,279	1.7%
18	Nevada	1,994	1.5%
19	Louisiana	1,759	1.3%
20	South Carolina	1,664	1.3%
21	Virginia	1,605	1.2%
22	Connecticut	1,438	1.1%
23	Colorado	1,435	1.1%
24	Oregon	1,370	1.0%
25	Wisconsin	1,355	1.0%
26	Oklahoma	1,218	0.9%
27	Kentucky	1,004	0.8%
28	Alabama	867	0.7%
29	Arkansas	789	0.6%
30	New Mexico	770	0.6%
31	Hawaii	635	0.5%
32	Mississippi	570	0.4%
33	Utah	563	0.4%
34	Iowa	532	0.4%
35	Kansas	449	0.3%
36	Delaware	442	0.3%
37	Nebraska	396	0.3%
38	Minnesota	361	0.3%
39	Rhode Island	356	0.3%
40	Alaska	216	0.2%
41	West Virginia	166	0.1%
42	Maine	159	0.1%
43	New Hampshire	140	0.1%
44	Idaho	89	0.1%
45	South Dakota	52	0.0%
46	Montana	36	0.0%
47	Vermont	33	0.0%
48	Wyoming	29	0.0%
49	North Dakota	21	0.0%
NA	Illinois**	NA	NA
	District of Columbia	1,368	1.0%

Source: Federal Bureau of Investigation
   "Crime in the United States 2004" (Uniform Crime Reports, October 17, 2005)
*Also called strong-armed robberies. Of the 321,299 robberies in 2004 for which supplemental data were received
by the F.B.I. There were an additional 80,027 robberies for which the type of weapon was not reported to the
F.B.I. Robbery is the taking or attempting to take anything of value by force or threat of force. Numbers are for
reporting jurisdictions only. **Not available.

Percent of Robberies Committed with Hands, Fists or Feet in 2004

National Percent = 41.1% of Robberies*

ALPHA ORDER

RANK	STATE	PERCENT
43	Alabama	31.5
9	Alaska	48.8
46	Arizona	30.9
32	Arkansas	36.9
14	California	47.6
23	Colorado	40.7
16	Connecticut	44.7
22	Delaware	41.5
18	Florida	43.4
44	Georgia	31.0
1	Hawaii	69.8
31	Idaho	37.1
NA	Illinois**	NA
30	Indiana	38.0
6	Iowa	50.8
20	Kansas	43.0
37	Kentucky	33.9
47	Louisiana	28.8
3	Maine	55.0
35	Maryland	35.1
25	Massachusetts	40.6
34	Michigan	35.8
40	Minnesota	32.3
48	Mississippi	27.3
26	Missouri	39.7
44	Montana	31.0
35	Nebraska	35.1
23	Nevada	40.7
21	New Hampshire	41.9
7	New Jersey	49.6
29	New Mexico	39.3
12	New York	47.8
39	North Carolina	33.1
2	North Dakota	58.3
7	Ohio	49.6
28	Oklahoma	39.4
5	Oregon	53.6
19	Pennsylvania	43.1
10	Rhode Island	48.7
41	South Carolina	31.8
11	South Dakota	48.6
49	Tennessee	26.1
33	Texas	36.3
15	Utah	46.8
12	Vermont	47.8
42	Virginia	31.6
4	Washington	54.3
27	West Virginia	39.5
38	Wisconsin	33.5
17	Wyoming	43.9

RANK ORDER

RANK	STATE	PERCENT
1	Hawaii	69.8
2	North Dakota	58.3
3	Maine	55.0
4	Washington	54.3
5	Oregon	53.6
6	Iowa	50.8
7	New Jersey	49.6
7	Ohio	49.6
9	Alaska	48.8
10	Rhode Island	48.7
11	South Dakota	48.6
12	New York	47.8
12	Vermont	47.8
14	California	47.6
15	Utah	46.8
16	Connecticut	44.7
17	Wyoming	43.9
18	Florida	43.4
19	Pennsylvania	43.1
20	Kansas	43.0
21	New Hampshire	41.9
22	Delaware	41.5
23	Colorado	40.7
23	Nevada	40.7
25	Massachusetts	40.6
26	Missouri	39.7
27	West Virginia	39.5
28	Oklahoma	39.4
29	New Mexico	39.3
30	Indiana	38.0
31	Idaho	37.1
32	Arkansas	36.9
33	Texas	36.3
34	Michigan	35.8
35	Maryland	35.1
35	Nebraska	35.1
37	Kentucky	33.9
38	Wisconsin	33.5
39	North Carolina	33.1
40	Minnesota	32.3
41	South Carolina	31.8
42	Virginia	31.6
43	Alabama	31.5
44	Georgia	31.0
44	Montana	31.0
46	Arizona	30.9
47	Louisiana	28.8
48	Mississippi	27.3
49	Tennessee	26.1
NA	Illinois**	NA
	District of Columbia	42.8

Source: Morgan Quitno Press using data from Federal Bureau of Investigation
    "Crime in the United States 2004" (Uniform Crime Reports, October 17, 2005)
*Also called strong-armed robberies. Of the 321,299 robberies in 2004 for which supplemental data were received by the F.B.I. There were an additional 80,027 robberies for which the type of weapon was not reported to the F.B.I. Robbery is the taking or attempting to take anything of value by force or threat of force. Numbers are for reporting jurisdictions only. **Not available.

Bank Robberies in 2004

National Total = 7,533 Robberies*

ALPHA ORDER					RANK ORDER			
RANK	STATE	ROBBERIES	% of USA		RANK	STATE	ROBBERIES	% of USA
27	Alabama	78	1.0%		1	California	1,013	13.4%
44	Alaska	13	0.2%		2	Florida	471	6.3%
18	Arizona	161	2.1%		3	Michigan	454	6.0%
36	Arkansas	39	0.5%		4	Ohio	451	6.0%
1	California	1,013	13.4%		5	Pennsylvania	434	5.8%
19	Colorado	147	2.0%		6	Texas	371	4.9%
25	Connecticut	89	1.2%		7	New York	335	4.4%
34	Delaware	50	0.7%		8	Maryland	292	3.9%
2	Florida	471	6.3%		9	North Carolina	251	3.3%
13	Georgia	222	2.9%		10	Massachusetts	238	3.2%
41	Hawaii	22	0.3%		11	Washington	234	3.1%
43	Idaho	15	0.2%		12	Illinois	232	3.1%
12	Illinois	232	3.1%		13	Georgia	222	2.9%
20	Indiana	126	1.7%		14	Oregon	191	2.5%
32	Iowa	54	0.7%		15	New Jersey	173	2.3%
39	Kansas	32	0.4%		16	Virginia	170	2.3%
29	Kentucky	75	1.0%		17	Nevada	166	2.2%
30	Louisiana	67	0.9%		18	Arizona	161	2.1%
45	Maine	3	0.0%		19	Colorado	147	2.0%
8	Maryland	292	3.9%		20	Indiana	126	1.7%
10	Massachusetts	238	3.2%		21	Minnesota	107	1.4%
3	Michigan	454	6.0%		21	Tennessee	107	1.4%
21	Minnesota	107	1.4%		23	South Carolina	95	1.3%
37	Mississippi	37	0.5%		24	Missouri	92	1.2%
24	Missouri	92	1.2%		25	Connecticut	89	1.2%
50	Montana	0	0.0%		26	Wisconsin	85	1.1%
38	Nebraska	35	0.5%		27	Alabama	78	1.0%
17	Nevada	166	2.2%		28	Utah	76	1.0%
40	New Hampshire	26	0.3%		29	Kentucky	75	1.0%
15	New Jersey	173	2.3%		30	Louisiana	67	0.9%
31	New Mexico	55	0.7%		31	New Mexico	55	0.7%
7	New York	335	4.4%		32	Iowa	54	0.7%
9	North Carolina	251	3.3%		33	Oklahoma	53	0.7%
45	North Dakota	3	0.0%		34	Delaware	50	0.7%
4	Ohio	451	6.0%		35	Rhode Island	44	0.6%
33	Oklahoma	53	0.7%		36	Arkansas	39	0.5%
14	Oregon	191	2.5%		37	Mississippi	37	0.5%
5	Pennsylvania	434	5.8%		38	Nebraska	35	0.5%
35	Rhode Island	44	0.6%		39	Kansas	32	0.4%
23	South Carolina	95	1.3%		40	New Hampshire	26	0.3%
48	South Dakota	2	0.0%		41	Hawaii	22	0.3%
21	Tennessee	107	1.4%		42	West Virginia	19	0.3%
6	Texas	371	4.9%		43	Idaho	15	0.2%
28	Utah	76	1.0%		44	Alaska	13	0.2%
45	Vermont	3	0.0%		45	Maine	3	0.0%
16	Virginia	170	2.3%		45	North Dakota	3	0.0%
11	Washington	234	3.1%		45	Vermont	3	0.0%
42	West Virginia	19	0.3%		48	South Dakota	2	0.0%
26	Wisconsin	85	1.1%		48	Wyoming	2	0.0%
48	Wyoming	2	0.0%		50	Montana	0	0.0%
						District of Columbia	23	0.3%

Source: Federal Bureau of Investigation
"Bank Crime Statistics, Federally Insured Financial Institutions, January 1, 2004 - December 31, 2004"
*Does not include 23 robberies in Puerto Rico. In addition, there were 134 bank burglaries, 30 bank larcenies and 29 bank extortions. During these 7,759 bank crimes, 20 people were killed (13 of them the perpetrator), 146 were injured (20 of them the perpetrator) and 74 were taken hostage.

Aggravated Assaults in 2004

National Total = 854,911 Aggravated Assaults*

ALPHA ORDER					RANK ORDER			
RANK	STATE		ASSAULTS	% of USA	RANK	STATE	ASSAULTS	% of USA
23	Alabama		11,286	1.3%	1	California	124,295	14.5%
40	Alaska		3,117	0.4%	2	Florida	86,199	10.1%
16	Arizona		18,921	2.2%	3	Texas	75,985	8.9%
25	Arkansas		10,023	1.2%	4	New York	46,911	5.5%
1	California		124,295	14.5%	5	Illinois	41,502	4.9%
24	Colorado		11,276	1.3%	6	Michigan	32,128	3.8%
34	Connecticut		4,995	0.6%	7	Tennessee	29,613	3.5%
39	Delaware		3,140	0.4%	8	Pennsylvania	28,339	3.3%
2	Florida		86,199	10.1%	9	South Carolina	25,470	3.0%
12	Georgia		23,561	2.8%	10	Maryland	24,334	2.8%
43	Hawaii		1,903	0.2%	11	North Carolina	23,591	2.8%
41	Idaho		2,572	0.3%	12	Georgia	23,561	2.8%
5	Illinois		41,502	4.9%	13	Louisiana	20,090	2.3%
21	Indiana		11,802	1.4%	14	Massachusetts	20,002	2.3%
32	Iowa		6,043	0.7%	15	Missouri	19,763	2.3%
29	Kansas		7,205	0.8%	16	Arizona	18,921	2.2%
33	Kentucky		5,410	0.6%	17	Ohio	16,457	1.9%
13	Louisiana		20,090	2.3%	18	New Jersey	16,144	1.9%
48	Maine		742	0.1%	19	Oklahoma	12,802	1.5%
10	Maryland		24,334	2.8%	20	Washington	12,417	1.5%
14	Massachusetts		20,002	2.3%	21	Indiana	11,802	1.4%
6	Michigan		32,128	3.8%	22	Virginia	11,496	1.3%
28	Minnesota		7,445	0.9%	23	Alabama	11,286	1.3%
35	Mississippi		4,677	0.5%	24	Colorado	11,276	1.3%
15	Missouri		19,763	2.3%	25	Arkansas	10,023	1.2%
42	Montana		2,187	0.3%	26	New Mexico	9,811	1.1%
37	Nebraska		3,595	0.4%	27	Nevada	8,348	1.0%
27	Nevada		8,348	1.0%	28	Minnesota	7,445	0.9%
45	New Hampshire		1,193	0.1%	29	Kansas	7,205	0.8%
18	New Jersey		16,144	1.9%	30	Oregon	6,600	0.8%
26	New Mexico		9,811	1.1%	31	Wisconsin	6,191	0.7%
4	New York		46,911	5.5%	32	Iowa	6,043	0.7%
11	North Carolina		23,591	2.8%	33	Kentucky	5,410	0.6%
50	North Dakota		297	0.0%	34	Connecticut	4,995	0.6%
17	Ohio		16,457	1.9%	35	Mississippi	4,677	0.5%
19	Oklahoma		12,802	1.5%	36	West Virginia	3,768	0.4%
30	Oregon		6,600	0.8%	37	Nebraska	3,595	0.4%
8	Pennsylvania		28,339	3.3%	38	Utah	3,424	0.4%
44	Rhode Island		1,596	0.2%	39	Delaware	3,140	0.4%
9	South Carolina		25,470	3.0%	40	Alaska	3,117	0.4%
47	South Dakota		852	0.1%	41	Idaho	2,572	0.3%
7	Tennessee		29,613	3.5%	42	Montana	2,187	0.3%
3	Texas		75,985	8.9%	43	Hawaii	1,903	0.2%
38	Utah		3,424	0.4%	44	Rhode Island	1,596	0.2%
49	Vermont		452	0.1%	45	New Hampshire	1,193	0.1%
22	Virginia		11,496	1.3%	46	Wyoming	973	0.1%
20	Washington		12,417	1.5%	47	South Dakota	852	0.1%
36	West Virginia		3,768	0.4%	48	Maine	742	0.1%
31	Wisconsin		6,191	0.7%	49	Vermont	452	0.1%
46	Wyoming		973	0.1%	50	North Dakota	297	0.0%
						District of Columbia	3,968	0.5%

Source: Federal Bureau of Investigation
   "Crime in the United States 2004" (Uniform Crime Reports, October 17, 2005)
*Aggravated assault is an attack for the purpose of inflicting severe bodily injury.

Average Time Between Aggravated Assaults in 2004

National Rate = An Aggravated Assault Occurs Every 37 Seconds*

ALPHA ORDER

RANK	STATE	HOURS.MINUTES
27	Alabama	0.47
11	Alaska	2.49
35	Arizona	0.28
26	Arkansas	0.53
50	California	0.04
27	Colorado	0.47
17	Connecticut	1.46
12	Delaware	2.48
49	Florida	0.06
39	Georgia	0.22
8	Hawaii	4.37
10	Idaho	3.25
46	Illinois	0.13
30	Indiana	0.44
19	Iowa	1.27
22	Kansas	1.13
18	Kentucky	1.37
36	Louisiana	0.26
3	Maine	11.50
39	Maryland	0.22
36	Massachusetts	0.26
45	Michigan	0.16
23	Minnesota	1.11
16	Mississippi	1.53
36	Missouri	0.26
9	Montana	4.01
14	Nebraska	2.26
24	Nevada	1.03
6	New Hampshire	7.22
33	New Jersey	0.32
25	New Mexico	0.54
47	New York	0.11
39	North Carolina	0.22
1	North Dakota	29.35
33	Ohio	0.32
32	Oklahoma	0.41
21	Oregon	1.20
43	Pennsylvania	0.19
7	Rhode Island	5.30
42	South Carolina	0.20
4	South Dakota	10.19
44	Tennessee	0.18
48	Texas	0.07
13	Utah	2.34
2	Vermont	19.26
29	Virginia	0.46
31	Washington	0.43
15	West Virginia	2.20
20	Wisconsin	1.25
5	Wyoming	9.02

RANK ORDER

RANK	STATE	HOURS.MINUTES
1	North Dakota	29.35
2	Vermont	19.26
3	Maine	11.50
4	South Dakota	10.19
5	Wyoming	9.02
6	New Hampshire	7.22
7	Rhode Island	5.30
8	Hawaii	4.37
9	Montana	4.01
10	Idaho	3.25
11	Alaska	2.49
12	Delaware	2.48
13	Utah	2.34
14	Nebraska	2.26
15	West Virginia	2.20
16	Mississippi	1.53
17	Connecticut	1.46
18	Kentucky	1.37
19	Iowa	1.27
20	Wisconsin	1.25
21	Oregon	1.20
22	Kansas	1.13
23	Minnesota	1.11
24	Nevada	1.03
25	New Mexico	0.54
26	Arkansas	0.53
27	Alabama	0.47
27	Colorado	0.47
29	Virginia	0.46
30	Indiana	0.44
31	Washington	0.43
32	Oklahoma	0.41
33	New Jersey	0.32
33	Ohio	0.32
35	Arizona	0.28
36	Louisiana	0.26
36	Massachusetts	0.26
36	Missouri	0.26
39	Georgia	0.22
39	Maryland	0.22
39	North Carolina	0.22
42	South Carolina	0.20
43	Pennsylvania	0.19
44	Tennessee	0.18
45	Michigan	0.16
46	Illinois	0.13
47	New York	0.11
48	Texas	0.07
49	Florida	0.06
50	California	0.04

District of Columbia 2.13

Source: Morgan Quitno Press using data from Federal Bureau of Investigation
    "Crime in the United States 2004" (Uniform Crime Reports, October 17, 2005)
*Aggravated assault is an attack for the purpose of inflicting severe bodily injury.

Percent Change in Number of Aggravated Assaults: 2003 to 2004

National Percent Change = 0.5% Decrease*

<table>
<tr><td colspan="3">ALPHA ORDER</td><td colspan="3">RANK ORDER</td></tr>
<tr><th>RANK</th><th>STATE</th><th>PERCENT CHANGE</th><th>RANK</th><th>STATE</th><th>PERCENT CHANGE</th></tr>
<tr><td>28</td><td>Alabama</td><td>(0.5)</td><td>1</td><td>New Hampshire</td><td>19.1</td></tr>
<tr><td>3</td><td>Alaska</td><td>11.8</td><td>2</td><td>Colorado</td><td>13.7</td></tr>
<tr><td>20</td><td>Arizona</td><td>1.1</td><td>3</td><td>Alaska</td><td>11.8</td></tr>
<tr><td>5</td><td>Arkansas</td><td>9.8</td><td>4</td><td>Nevada</td><td>11.0</td></tr>
<tr><td>38</td><td>California</td><td>(3.9)</td><td>5</td><td>Arkansas</td><td>9.8</td></tr>
<tr><td>2</td><td>Colorado</td><td>13.7</td><td>6</td><td>Nebraska</td><td>6.4</td></tr>
<tr><td>49</td><td>Connecticut</td><td>(17.1)</td><td>6</td><td>West Virginia</td><td>6.4</td></tr>
<tr><td>48</td><td>Delaware</td><td>(15.0)</td><td>8</td><td>Pennsylvania</td><td>4.9</td></tr>
<tr><td>19</td><td>Florida</td><td>1.3</td><td>9</td><td>Georgia</td><td>4.7</td></tr>
<tr><td>9</td><td>Georgia</td><td>4.7</td><td>10</td><td>Tennessee</td><td>4.0</td></tr>
<tr><td>15</td><td>Hawaii</td><td>3.3</td><td>11</td><td>North Dakota</td><td>3.8</td></tr>
<tr><td>22</td><td>Idaho</td><td>0.6</td><td>12</td><td>Oregon</td><td>3.6</td></tr>
<tr><td>26</td><td>Illinois</td><td>0.0</td><td>13</td><td>Minnesota</td><td>3.5</td></tr>
<tr><td>47</td><td>Indiana</td><td>(11.8)</td><td>14</td><td>Louisiana</td><td>3.4</td></tr>
<tr><td>36</td><td>Iowa</td><td>(2.5)</td><td>15</td><td>Hawaii</td><td>3.3</td></tr>
<tr><td>35</td><td>Kansas</td><td>(2.3)</td><td>16</td><td>Maryland</td><td>3.1</td></tr>
<tr><td>40</td><td>Kentucky</td><td>(5.1)</td><td>17</td><td>New Mexico</td><td>2.8</td></tr>
<tr><td>14</td><td>Louisiana</td><td>3.4</td><td>18</td><td>Ohio</td><td>2.2</td></tr>
<tr><td>37</td><td>Maine</td><td>(2.8)</td><td>19</td><td>Florida</td><td>1.3</td></tr>
<tr><td>16</td><td>Maryland</td><td>3.1</td><td>20</td><td>Arizona</td><td>1.1</td></tr>
<tr><td>32</td><td>Massachusetts</td><td>(1.8)</td><td>21</td><td>North Carolina</td><td>0.9</td></tr>
<tr><td>42</td><td>Michigan</td><td>(6.1)</td><td>22</td><td>Idaho</td><td>0.6</td></tr>
<tr><td>13</td><td>Minnesota</td><td>3.5</td><td>23</td><td>Missouri</td><td>0.4</td></tr>
<tr><td>41</td><td>Mississippi</td><td>(6.0)</td><td>24</td><td>South Carolina</td><td>0.3</td></tr>
<tr><td>23</td><td>Missouri</td><td>0.4</td><td>24</td><td>Texas</td><td>0.3</td></tr>
<tr><td>50</td><td>Montana</td><td>(21.2)</td><td>26</td><td>Illinois</td><td>0.0</td></tr>
<tr><td>6</td><td>Nebraska</td><td>6.4</td><td>27</td><td>Oklahoma</td><td>(0.2)</td></tr>
<tr><td>4</td><td>Nevada</td><td>11.0</td><td>28</td><td>Alabama</td><td>(0.5)</td></tr>
<tr><td>1</td><td>New Hampshire</td><td>19.1</td><td>28</td><td>Virginia</td><td>(0.5)</td></tr>
<tr><td>33</td><td>New Jersey</td><td>(1.9)</td><td>30</td><td>Washington</td><td>(0.7)</td></tr>
<tr><td>17</td><td>New Mexico</td><td>2.8</td><td>31</td><td>South Dakota</td><td>(0.8)</td></tr>
<tr><td>39</td><td>New York</td><td>(4.2)</td><td>32</td><td>Massachusetts</td><td>(1.8)</td></tr>
<tr><td>21</td><td>North Carolina</td><td>0.9</td><td>33</td><td>New Jersey</td><td>(1.9)</td></tr>
<tr><td>11</td><td>North Dakota</td><td>3.8</td><td>34</td><td>Wisconsin</td><td>(2.1)</td></tr>
<tr><td>18</td><td>Ohio</td><td>2.2</td><td>35</td><td>Kansas</td><td>(2.3)</td></tr>
<tr><td>27</td><td>Oklahoma</td><td>(0.2)</td><td>36</td><td>Iowa</td><td>(2.5)</td></tr>
<tr><td>12</td><td>Oregon</td><td>3.6</td><td>37</td><td>Maine</td><td>(2.8)</td></tr>
<tr><td>8</td><td>Pennsylvania</td><td>4.9</td><td>38</td><td>California</td><td>(3.9)</td></tr>
<tr><td>44</td><td>Rhode Island</td><td>(6.9)</td><td>39</td><td>New York</td><td>(4.2)</td></tr>
<tr><td>24</td><td>South Carolina</td><td>0.3</td><td>40</td><td>Kentucky</td><td>(5.1)</td></tr>
<tr><td>31</td><td>South Dakota</td><td>(0.8)</td><td>41</td><td>Mississippi</td><td>(6.0)</td></tr>
<tr><td>10</td><td>Tennessee</td><td>4.0</td><td>42</td><td>Michigan</td><td>(6.1)</td></tr>
<tr><td>24</td><td>Texas</td><td>0.3</td><td>43</td><td>Utah</td><td>(6.2)</td></tr>
<tr><td>43</td><td>Utah</td><td>(6.2)</td><td>44</td><td>Rhode Island</td><td>(6.9)</td></tr>
<tr><td>46</td><td>Vermont</td><td>(10.3)</td><td>45</td><td>Wyoming</td><td>(9.9)</td></tr>
<tr><td>28</td><td>Virginia</td><td>(0.5)</td><td>46</td><td>Vermont</td><td>(10.3)</td></tr>
<tr><td>30</td><td>Washington</td><td>(0.7)</td><td>47</td><td>Indiana</td><td>(11.8)</td></tr>
<tr><td>6</td><td>West Virginia</td><td>6.4</td><td>48</td><td>Delaware</td><td>(15.0)</td></tr>
<tr><td>34</td><td>Wisconsin</td><td>(2.1)</td><td>49</td><td>Connecticut</td><td>(17.1)</td></tr>
<tr><td>45</td><td>Wyoming</td><td>(9.9)</td><td>50</td><td>Montana</td><td>(21.2)</td></tr>
<tr><td></td><td></td><td></td><td></td><td>District of Columbia</td><td>(13.7)</td></tr>
</table>

Source: Federal Bureau of Investigation
    "Crime in the United States 2004" (Uniform Crime Reports, October 17, 2005)
*Aggravated assault is an attack for the purpose of inflicting severe bodily injury.

Aggravated Assault Rate in 2004

National Rate = 291.1 Aggravated Assaults per 100,000 Population*

ALPHA ORDER

RANK	STATE	RATE
22	Alabama	249.1
5	Alaska	475.6
15	Arizona	329.4
9	Arkansas	364.1
12	California	346.3
23	Colorado	245.1
43	Connecticut	142.6
8	Delaware	378.1
4	Florida	495.5
20	Georgia	266.8
38	Hawaii	150.7
34	Idaho	184.6
16	Illinois	326.4
32	Indiana	189.2
29	Iowa	204.5
21	Kansas	263.4
44	Kentucky	130.5
6	Louisiana	444.9
49	Maine	56.3
7	Maryland	437.8
18	Massachusetts	311.7
17	Michigan	317.7
40	Minnesota	146.0
36	Mississippi	161.1
13	Missouri	343.4
25	Montana	236.0
28	Nebraska	205.8
11	Nevada	357.6
47	New Hampshire	91.8
33	New Jersey	185.6
2	New Mexico	515.5
24	New York	244.0
19	North Carolina	276.2
50	North Dakota	46.8
41	Ohio	143.6
10	Oklahoma	363.3
35	Oregon	183.6
26	Pennsylvania	228.4
39	Rhode Island	147.7
1	South Carolina	606.7
46	South Dakota	110.5
3	Tennessee	501.8
14	Texas	337.9
42	Utah	143.3
48	Vermont	72.7
37	Virginia	154.1
30	Washington	200.2
27	West Virginia	207.6
45	Wisconsin	112.4
31	Wyoming	192.1

RANK ORDER

RANK	STATE	RATE
1	South Carolina	606.7
2	New Mexico	515.5
3	Tennessee	501.8
4	Florida	495.5
5	Alaska	475.6
6	Louisiana	444.9
7	Maryland	437.8
8	Delaware	378.1
9	Arkansas	364.1
10	Oklahoma	363.3
11	Nevada	357.6
12	California	346.3
13	Missouri	343.4
14	Texas	337.9
15	Arizona	329.4
16	Illinois	326.4
17	Michigan	317.7
18	Massachusetts	311.7
19	North Carolina	276.2
20	Georgia	266.8
21	Kansas	263.4
22	Alabama	249.1
23	Colorado	245.1
24	New York	244.0
25	Montana	236.0
26	Pennsylvania	228.4
27	West Virginia	207.6
28	Nebraska	205.8
29	Iowa	204.5
30	Washington	200.2
31	Wyoming	192.1
32	Indiana	189.2
33	New Jersey	185.6
34	Idaho	184.6
35	Oregon	183.6
36	Mississippi	161.1
37	Virginia	154.1
38	Hawaii	150.7
39	Rhode Island	147.7
40	Minnesota	146.0
41	Ohio	143.6
42	Utah	143.3
43	Connecticut	142.6
44	Kentucky	130.5
45	Wisconsin	112.4
46	South Dakota	110.5
47	New Hampshire	91.8
48	Vermont	72.7
49	Maine	56.3
50	North Dakota	46.8

District of Columbia 716.9

Source: Federal Bureau of Investigation
"Crime in the United States 2004" (Uniform Crime Reports, October 17, 2005)
*Aggravated assault is an attack for the purpose of inflicting severe bodily injury.

Percent Change in Aggravated Assault Rate: 2003 to 2004

National Percent Change = 1.5% Decrease*

ALPHA ORDER

RANK	STATE	PERCENT CHANGE
24	Alabama	(1.0)
3	Alaska	10.6
29	Arizona	(1.8)
4	Arkansas	8.8
39	California	(5.1)
2	Colorado	12.3
49	Connecticut	(17.5)
48	Delaware	(16.2)
24	Florida	(1.0)
11	Georgia	2.9
16	Hawaii	2.1
26	Idaho	(1.3)
20	Illinois	(0.5)
47	Indiana	(12.4)
36	Iowa	(2.9)
34	Kansas	(2.7)
40	Kentucky	(5.8)
11	Louisiana	2.9
37	Maine	(3.3)
15	Maryland	2.3
29	Massachusetts	(1.8)
41	Michigan	(6.4)
13	Minnesota	2.8
42	Mississippi	(6.6)
19	Missouri	(0.3)
50	Montana	(22.0)
7	Nebraska	5.8
5	Nevada	6.6
1	New Hampshire	18.1
33	New Jersey	(2.5)
18	New Mexico	1.5
38	New York	(4.3)
20	North Carolina	(0.5)
9	North Dakota	3.7
17	Ohio	2.0
22	Oklahoma	(0.7)
14	Oregon	2.7
8	Pennsylvania	4.6
43	Rhode Island	(7.3)
23	South Carolina	(0.9)
28	South Dakota	(1.6)
10	Tennessee	3.0
27	Texas	(1.5)
44	Utah	(7.7)
45	Vermont	(10.6)
29	Virginia	(1.8)
32	Washington	(1.9)
6	West Virginia	6.2
34	Wisconsin	(2.7)
46	Wyoming	(10.7)

RANK ORDER

RANK	STATE	PERCENT CHANGE
1	New Hampshire	18.1
2	Colorado	12.3
3	Alaska	10.6
4	Arkansas	8.8
5	Nevada	6.6
6	West Virginia	6.2
7	Nebraska	5.8
8	Pennsylvania	4.6
9	North Dakota	3.7
10	Tennessee	3.0
11	Georgia	2.9
11	Louisiana	2.9
13	Minnesota	2.8
14	Oregon	2.7
15	Maryland	2.3
16	Hawaii	2.1
17	Ohio	2.0
18	New Mexico	1.5
19	Missouri	(0.3)
20	Illinois	(0.5)
20	North Carolina	(0.5)
22	Oklahoma	(0.7)
23	South Carolina	(0.9)
24	Alabama	(1.0)
24	Florida	(1.0)
26	Idaho	(1.3)
27	Texas	(1.5)
28	South Dakota	(1.6)
29	Arizona	(1.8)
29	Massachusetts	(1.8)
29	Virginia	(1.8)
32	Washington	(1.9)
33	New Jersey	(2.5)
34	Kansas	(2.7)
34	Wisconsin	(2.7)
36	Iowa	(2.9)
37	Maine	(3.3)
38	New York	(4.3)
39	California	(5.1)
40	Kentucky	(5.8)
41	Michigan	(6.4)
42	Mississippi	(6.6)
43	Rhode Island	(7.3)
44	Utah	(7.7)
45	Vermont	(10.6)
46	Wyoming	(10.7)
47	Indiana	(12.4)
48	Delaware	(16.2)
49	Connecticut	(17.5)
50	Montana	(22.0)
	District of Columbia	(13.0)

Source: Federal Bureau of Investigation
"Crime in the United States 2004" (Uniform Crime Reports, October 17, 2005)
*Aggravated assault is an attack for the purpose of inflicting severe bodily injury.

Aggravated Assaults with Firearms in 2004

National Total = 137,988 Aggravated Assaults*

ALPHA ORDER

RANK	STATE	ASSAULTS	% of USA
19	Alabama	1,738	1.3%
38	Alaska	459	0.3%
8	Arizona	4,916	3.6%
18	Arkansas	2,008	1.5%
1	California	22,197	16.1%
17	Colorado	2,096	1.5%
40	Connecticut	416	0.3%
35	Delaware	512	0.4%
3	Florida	13,539	9.8%
12	Georgia	3,601	2.6%
43	Hawaii	175	0.1%
34	Idaho	517	0.4%
NA	Illinois**	NA	NA
25	Indiana	1,511	1.1%
33	Iowa	547	0.4%
26	Kansas	1,420	1.0%
31	Kentucky	580	0.4%
9	Louisiana	4,445	3.2%
48	Maine	35	0.0%
15	Maryland	2,278	1.7%
20	Massachusetts	1,697	1.2%
5	Michigan	7,099	5.1%
39	Minnesota	442	0.3%
28	Mississippi	867	0.6%
10	Missouri	4,299	3.1%
42	Montana	179	0.1%
37	Nebraska	503	0.4%
23	Nevada	1,652	1.2%
45	New Hampshire	106	0.1%
14	New Jersey	2,374	1.7%
22	New Mexico	1,683	1.2%
21	New York	1,691	1.2%
11	North Carolina	4,204	3.0%
49	North Dakota	11	0.0%
13	Ohio	3,154	2.3%
16	Oklahoma	2,159	1.6%
30	Oregon	681	0.5%
7	Pennsylvania	5,445	3.9%
41	Rhode Island	306	0.2%
6	South Carolina	5,691	4.1%
46	South Dakota	75	0.1%
4	Tennessee	8,809	6.4%
2	Texas	16,107	11.7%
36	Utah	510	0.4%
47	Vermont	62	0.0%
24	Virginia	1,579	1.1%
27	Washington	1,338	1.0%
32	West Virginia	558	0.4%
29	Wisconsin	806	0.6%
44	Wyoming	122	0.1%

RANK ORDER

RANK	STATE	ASSAULTS	% of USA
1	California	22,197	16.1%
2	Texas	16,107	11.7%
3	Florida	13,539	9.8%
4	Tennessee	8,809	6.4%
5	Michigan	7,099	5.1%
6	South Carolina	5,691	4.1%
7	Pennsylvania	5,445	3.9%
8	Arizona	4,916	3.6%
9	Louisiana	4,445	3.2%
10	Missouri	4,299	3.1%
11	North Carolina	4,204	3.0%
12	Georgia	3,601	2.6%
13	Ohio	3,154	2.3%
14	New Jersey	2,374	1.7%
15	Maryland	2,278	1.7%
16	Oklahoma	2,159	1.6%
17	Colorado	2,096	1.5%
18	Arkansas	2,008	1.5%
19	Alabama	1,738	1.3%
20	Massachusetts	1,697	1.2%
21	New York	1,691	1.2%
22	New Mexico	1,683	1.2%
23	Nevada	1,652	1.2%
24	Virginia	1,579	1.1%
25	Indiana	1,511	1.1%
26	Kansas	1,420	1.0%
27	Washington	1,338	1.0%
28	Mississippi	867	0.6%
29	Wisconsin	806	0.6%
30	Oregon	681	0.5%
31	Kentucky	580	0.4%
32	West Virginia	558	0.4%
33	Iowa	547	0.4%
34	Idaho	517	0.4%
35	Delaware	512	0.4%
36	Utah	510	0.4%
37	Nebraska	503	0.4%
38	Alaska	459	0.3%
39	Minnesota	442	0.3%
40	Connecticut	416	0.3%
41	Rhode Island	306	0.2%
42	Montana	179	0.1%
43	Hawaii	175	0.1%
44	Wyoming	122	0.1%
45	New Hampshire	106	0.1%
46	South Dakota	75	0.1%
47	Vermont	62	0.0%
48	Maine	35	0.0%
49	North Dakota	11	0.0%
NA	Illinois**	NA	NA
	District of Columbia	789	0.6%

Source: Federal Bureau of Investigation
    "Crime in the United States 2004" (Uniform Crime Reports, October 17, 2005)
*Of the 715,376 aggravated assaults in 2004 for which supplemental data were received by the F.B.I. There were an additional 139,535 aggravated assaults for which the type of weapon was not reported to the F.B.I. Aggravated assault is an attack for the purpose of inflicting severe bodily injury. Numbers are for reporting jurisdictions only.
**Not available.

Aggravated Assault Rate with Firearms in 2004

National Rate = 56.5 Aggravated Assaults per 100,000 Population*

ALPHA ORDER				RANK ORDER		
RANK	STATE	RATE		RANK	STATE	RATE
20	Alabama	52.3		1	Tennessee	151.4
13	Alaska	71.8		2	South Carolina	144.6
6	Arizona	87.7		3	Louisiana	112.9
5	Arkansas	94.0		4	New Mexico	101.3
16	California	62.1		5	Arkansas	94.0
19	Colorado	52.4		6	Arizona	87.7
42	Connecticut	15.5		7	Georgia	79.7
17	Delaware	61.8		7	Missouri	79.7
9	Florida	77.9		9	Florida	77.9
7	Georgia	79.7		10	Kansas	74.3
41	Hawaii	15.9		11	Michigan	73.8
25	Idaho	37.2		12	Texas	72.2
NA	Illinois**	NA		13	Alaska	71.8
29	Indiana	30.5		14	Nevada	70.8
38	Iowa	20.2		15	North Carolina	64.9
10	Kansas	74.3		16	California	62.1
39	Kentucky	18.0		17	Delaware	61.8
3	Louisiana	112.9		18	Oklahoma	61.3
48	Maine	2.7		19	Colorado	52.4
23	Maryland	46.3		20	Alabama	52.3
28	Massachusetts	30.7		21	Pennsylvania	50.8
11	Michigan	73.8		22	West Virginia	49.1
47	Minnesota	10.2		23	Maryland	46.3
24	Mississippi	46.1		24	Mississippi	46.1
7	Missouri	79.7		25	Idaho	37.2
32	Montana	27.2		26	Ohio	35.8
27	Nebraska	32.3		27	Nebraska	32.3
14	Nevada	70.8		28	Massachusetts	30.7
45	New Hampshire	10.7		29	Indiana	30.5
31	New Jersey	27.4		30	Rhode Island	28.3
4	New Mexico	101.3		31	New Jersey	27.4
40	New York	16.8		32	Montana	27.2
15	North Carolina	64.9		33	Wyoming	24.8
49	North Dakota	2.1		34	Washington	24.2
26	Ohio	35.8		35	Utah	24.1
18	Oklahoma	61.3		36	Virginia	23.8
37	Oregon	20.3		37	Oregon	20.3
21	Pennsylvania	50.8		38	Iowa	20.2
30	Rhode Island	28.3		39	Kentucky	18.0
2	South Carolina	144.6		40	New York	16.8
44	South Dakota	13.0		41	Hawaii	15.9
1	Tennessee	151.4		42	Connecticut	15.5
12	Texas	72.2		42	Wisconsin	15.5
35	Utah	24.1		44	South Dakota	13.0
46	Vermont	10.6		45	New Hampshire	10.7
36	Virginia	23.8		46	Vermont	10.6
34	Washington	24.2		47	Minnesota	10.2
22	West Virginia	49.1		48	Maine	2.7
42	Wisconsin	15.5		49	North Dakota	2.1
33	Wyoming	24.8		NA	Illinois**	NA

District of Columbia   142.5

Source: Morgan Quitno Press using data from Federal Bureau of Investigation
    "Crime in the United States 2004" (Uniform Crime Reports, October 17, 2005)
*Based only on population of reporting jurisdictions. Aggravated assault is an attack for the purpose of inflicting severe bodily injury. National rate reflects only those robberies for which the type of weapon was known and reported.
**Not available.

Percent of Aggravated Assaults Involving Firearms in 2004

National Percent = 19.3% of Aggravated Assaults*

ALPHA ORDER			RANK ORDER		
RANK	STATE	PERCENT	RANK	STATE	PERCENT
10	Alabama	23.5	1	Tennessee	30.0
28	Alaska	15.1	2	Mississippi	27.3
4	Arizona	26.6	3	Kansas	26.9
9	Arkansas	24.3	4	Arizona	26.6
22	California	18.0	5	North Carolina	26.3
17	Colorado	20.2	6	Louisiana	25.7
42	Connecticut	11.2	7	Georgia	25.5
24	Delaware	17.4	7	West Virginia	25.5
27	Florida	15.7	9	Arkansas	24.3
7	Georgia	25.5	10	Alabama	23.5
45	Hawaii	9.9	10	South Carolina	23.5
18	Idaho	20.1	12	Missouri	22.7
NA	Illinois**	NA	13	Michigan	22.6
32	Indiana	14.4	14	Ohio	21.8
47	Iowa	9.1	15	Pennsylvania	21.5
3	Kansas	26.9	16	Texas	21.4
38	Kentucky	12.3	17	Colorado	20.2
6	Louisiana	25.7	18	Idaho	20.1
48	Maine	4.7	19	Nevada	19.8
35	Maryland	13.3	20	Rhode Island	19.2
46	Massachusetts	9.3	21	New Mexico	19.0
13	Michigan	22.6	22	California	18.0
41	Minnesota	11.5	23	Virginia	17.8
2	Mississippi	27.3	24	Delaware	17.4
12	Missouri	22.7	25	Oklahoma	16.9
39	Montana	12.0	26	Utah	16.6
31	Nebraska	14.6	27	Florida	15.7
19	Nevada	19.8	28	Alaska	15.1
33	New Hampshire	13.8	29	Vermont	14.8
30	New Jersey	14.7	30	New Jersey	14.7
21	New Mexico	19.0	31	Nebraska	14.6
44	New York	10.9	32	Indiana	14.4
5	North Carolina	26.3	33	New Hampshire	13.8
49	North Dakota	4.1	34	Wisconsin	13.6
14	Ohio	21.8	35	Maryland	13.3
25	Oklahoma	16.9	36	Washington	13.2
40	Oregon	11.9	37	Wyoming	12.9
15	Pennsylvania	21.5	38	Kentucky	12.3
20	Rhode Island	19.2	39	Montana	12.0
10	South Carolina	23.5	40	Oregon	11.9
43	South Dakota	11.0	41	Minnesota	11.5
1	Tennessee	30.0	42	Connecticut	11.2
16	Texas	21.4	43	South Dakota	11.0
26	Utah	16.6	44	New York	10.9
29	Vermont	14.8	45	Hawaii	9.9
23	Virginia	17.8	46	Massachusetts	9.3
36	Washington	13.2	47	Iowa	9.1
7	West Virginia	25.5	48	Maine	4.7
34	Wisconsin	13.6	49	North Dakota	4.1
37	Wyoming	12.9	NA	Illinois**	NA
				District of Columbia	19.9

Source: Morgan Quitno Press using data from Federal Bureau of Investigation
    "Crime in the United States 2004" (Uniform Crime Reports, October 17, 2005)
*Of the 715,376 aggravated assaults in 2004 for which supplemental data were received by the F.B.I. There were
an additional 139,535 aggravated assaults for which the type of weapon was not reported to the F.B.I. Aggravated
assault is an attack for the purpose of inflicting severe bodily injury. Numbers are for reporting jurisdictions only.
**Not available.

Aggravated Assaults with Knives or Cutting Instruments in 2004

National Total = 132,814 Aggravated Assaults*

ALPHA ORDER

RANK	STATE	ASSAULTS	% of USA
27	Alabama	998	0.8%
35	Alaska	668	0.5%
15	Arizona	3,034	2.3%
25	Arkansas	1,296	1.0%
1	California	18,570	14.0%
18	Colorado	2,322	1.7%
31	Connecticut	792	0.6%
36	Delaware	642	0.5%
3	Florida	15,277	11.5%
14	Georgia	3,134	2.4%
40	Hawaii	445	0.3%
38	Idaho	587	0.4%
NA	Illinois**	NA	NA
24	Indiana	1,387	1.0%
28	Iowa	964	0.7%
32	Kansas	747	0.6%
34	Kentucky	675	0.5%
11	Louisiana	3,429	2.6%
47	Maine	137	0.1%
10	Maryland	3,538	2.7%
7	Massachusetts	3,928	3.0%
5	Michigan	6,319	4.8%
29	Minnesota	942	0.7%
39	Mississippi	541	0.4%
16	Missouri	2,746	2.1%
44	Montana	212	0.2%
37	Nebraska	636	0.5%
21	Nevada	1,828	1.4%
43	New Hampshire	230	0.2%
12	New Jersey	3,365	2.5%
23	New Mexico	1,651	1.2%
9	New York	3,577	2.7%
13	North Carolina	3,346	2.5%
49	North Dakota	38	0.0%
17	Ohio	2,649	2.0%
19	Oklahoma	2,127	1.6%
26	Oregon	1,027	0.8%
8	Pennsylvania	3,866	2.9%
41	Rhode Island	375	0.3%
6	South Carolina	4,507	3.4%
45	South Dakota	191	0.1%
4	Tennessee	6,324	4.8%
2	Texas	16,796	12.6%
33	Utah	715	0.5%
48	Vermont	73	0.1%
22	Virginia	1,793	1.4%
20	Washington	1,965	1.5%
42	West Virginia	344	0.3%
30	Wisconsin	875	0.7%
46	Wyoming	159	0.1%

RANK ORDER

RANK	STATE	ASSAULTS	% of USA
1	California	18,570	14.0%
2	Texas	16,796	12.6%
3	Florida	15,277	11.5%
4	Tennessee	6,324	4.8%
5	Michigan	6,319	4.8%
6	South Carolina	4,507	3.4%
7	Massachusetts	3,928	3.0%
8	Pennsylvania	3,866	2.9%
9	New York	3,577	2.7%
10	Maryland	3,538	2.7%
11	Louisiana	3,429	2.6%
12	New Jersey	3,365	2.5%
13	North Carolina	3,346	2.5%
14	Georgia	3,134	2.4%
15	Arizona	3,034	2.3%
16	Missouri	2,746	2.1%
17	Ohio	2,649	2.0%
18	Colorado	2,322	1.7%
19	Oklahoma	2,127	1.6%
20	Washington	1,965	1.5%
21	Nevada	1,828	1.4%
22	Virginia	1,793	1.4%
23	New Mexico	1,651	1.2%
24	Indiana	1,387	1.0%
25	Arkansas	1,296	1.0%
26	Oregon	1,027	0.8%
27	Alabama	998	0.8%
28	Iowa	964	0.7%
29	Minnesota	942	0.7%
30	Wisconsin	875	0.7%
31	Connecticut	792	0.6%
32	Kansas	747	0.6%
33	Utah	715	0.5%
34	Kentucky	675	0.5%
35	Alaska	668	0.5%
36	Delaware	642	0.5%
37	Nebraska	636	0.5%
38	Idaho	587	0.4%
39	Mississippi	541	0.4%
40	Hawaii	445	0.3%
41	Rhode Island	375	0.3%
42	West Virginia	344	0.3%
43	New Hampshire	230	0.2%
44	Montana	212	0.2%
45	South Dakota	191	0.1%
46	Wyoming	159	0.1%
47	Maine	137	0.1%
48	Vermont	73	0.1%
49	North Dakota	38	0.0%
NA	Illinois**	NA	NA
	District of Columbia	1,027	0.8%

Source: Federal Bureau of Investigation
"Crime in the United States 2004" (Uniform Crime Reports, October 17, 2005)
Of the 715,376 aggravated assaults in 2004 for which supplemental data were received by the F.B.I. There were an additional 139,535 aggravated assaults for which the type of weapon was not reported to the F.B.I. Aggravated assault is an attack for the purpose of inflicting severe bodily injury. Numbers are for reporting jurisdictions only.
***Not available.*

Percent of Aggravated Assaults Involving Knives or Cutting Instruments in 2004

National Percent = 18.6% of Aggravated Assaults*

ALPHA ORDER				RANK ORDER		
RANK	STATE	PERCENT		RANK	STATE	PERCENT
48	Alabama	13.5		1	New Hampshire	29.9
12	Alaska	21.9		2	South Dakota	28.0
36	Arizona	16.4		3	Hawaii	25.2
39	Arkansas	15.7		4	Minnesota	24.6
41	California	15.0		5	Rhode Island	23.5
9	Colorado	22.4		6	Utah	23.3
17	Connecticut	21.4		7	New York	23.1
12	Delaware	21.9		8	Idaho	22.9
31	Florida	17.7		9	Colorado	22.4
11	Georgia	22.2		10	Texas	22.3
3	Hawaii	25.2		11	Georgia	22.2
8	Idaho	22.9		12	Alaska	21.9
NA	Illinois**	NA		12	Delaware	21.9
49	Indiana	13.2		12	Nevada	21.9
37	Iowa	16.0		15	Massachusetts	21.6
45	Kansas	14.2		16	Tennessee	21.5
44	Kentucky	14.3		17	Connecticut	21.4
23	Louisiana	19.8		18	New Jersey	20.9
27	Maine	18.5		18	North Carolina	20.9
20	Maryland	20.6		20	Maryland	20.6
15	Massachusetts	21.6		21	Virginia	20.2
22	Michigan	20.1		22	Michigan	20.1
4	Minnesota	24.6		23	Louisiana	19.8
33	Mississippi	17.0		24	Washington	19.3
43	Missouri	14.5		25	New Mexico	18.7
45	Montana	14.2		26	South Carolina	18.6
27	Nebraska	18.5		27	Maine	18.5
12	Nevada	21.9		27	Nebraska	18.5
1	New Hampshire	29.9		29	Ohio	18.3
18	New Jersey	20.9		30	Oregon	18.0
25	New Mexico	18.7		31	Florida	17.7
7	New York	23.1		32	Vermont	17.4
18	North Carolina	20.9		33	Mississippi	17.0
45	North Dakota	14.2		34	Wyoming	16.8
29	Ohio	18.3		35	Oklahoma	16.6
35	Oklahoma	16.6		36	Arizona	16.4
30	Oregon	18.0		37	Iowa	16.0
40	Pennsylvania	15.3		38	West Virginia	15.8
5	Rhode Island	23.5		39	Arkansas	15.7
26	South Carolina	18.6		40	Pennsylvania	15.3
2	South Dakota	28.0		41	California	15.0
16	Tennessee	21.5		42	Wisconsin	14.7
10	Texas	22.3		43	Missouri	14.5
6	Utah	23.3		44	Kentucky	14.3
32	Vermont	17.4		45	Kansas	14.2
21	Virginia	20.2		45	Montana	14.2
24	Washington	19.3		45	North Dakota	14.2
38	West Virginia	15.8		48	Alabama	13.5
42	Wisconsin	14.7		49	Indiana	13.2
34	Wyoming	16.8		NA	Illinois**	NA
				District of Columbia		25.9

Source: Morgan Quitno Press using data from Federal Bureau of Investigation
    "Crime in the United States 2004" (Uniform Crime Reports, October 17, 2005)
*Of the 715,376 aggravated assaults in 2004 for which supplemental data were received by the F.B.I. There were
an additional 139,535 aggravated assaults for which the type of weapon was not reported to the F.B.I. Aggravated
assault is an attack for the purpose of inflicting severe bodily injury. Numbers are for reporting jurisdictions only.
**Not available.

Aggravated Assaults with Blunt Objects and Other Dangerous Weapons in 2004

National Total = 254,356 Aggravated Assaults*

ALPHA ORDER

RANK	STATE	ASSAULTS	% of USA
28	Alabama	1,673	0.7%
39	Alaska	720	0.3%
12	Arizona	5,525	2.2%
25	Arkansas	2,511	1.0%
1	California	41,547	16.3%
22	Colorado	2,849	1.1%
33	Connecticut	1,448	0.6%
32	Delaware	1,536	0.6%
2	Florida	39,951	15.7%
16	Georgia	4,597	1.8%
40	Hawaii	675	0.3%
37	Idaho	1,017	0.4%
NA	Illinois**	NA	NA
23	Indiana	2,653	1.0%
31	Iowa	1,577	0.6%
26	Kansas	2,432	1.0%
30	Kentucky	1,604	0.6%
11	Louisiana	5,548	2.2%
47	Maine	213	0.1%
7	Maryland	7,558	3.0%
6	Massachusetts	9,121	3.6%
4	Michigan	12,281	4.8%
34	Minnesota	1,353	0.5%
38	Mississippi	840	0.3%
10	Missouri	5,954	2.3%
42	Montana	587	0.2%
29	Nebraska	1,637	0.6%
19	Nevada	3,728	1.5%
46	New Hampshire	234	0.1%
13	New Jersey	5,173	2.0%
24	New Mexico	2,649	1.0%
14	New York	4,858	1.9%
18	North Carolina	4,437	1.7%
49	North Dakota	65	0.0%
17	Ohio	4,515	1.8%
15	Oklahoma	4,835	1.9%
27	Oregon	2,010	0.8%
9	Pennsylvania	6,489	2.6%
41	Rhode Island	633	0.2%
8	South Carolina	7,278	2.9%
45	South Dakota	237	0.1%
5	Tennessee	10,812	4.3%
3	Texas	27,892	11.0%
36	Utah	1,025	0.4%
48	Vermont	100	0.0%
21	Virginia	2,985	1.2%
20	Washington	3,388	1.3%
43	West Virginia	405	0.2%
35	Wisconsin	1,287	0.5%
44	Wyoming	305	0.1%

RANK ORDER

RANK	STATE	ASSAULTS	% of USA
1	California	41,547	16.3%
2	Florida	39,951	15.7%
3	Texas	27,892	11.0%
4	Michigan	12,281	4.8%
5	Tennessee	10,812	4.3%
6	Massachusetts	9,121	3.6%
7	Maryland	7,558	3.0%
8	South Carolina	7,278	2.9%
9	Pennsylvania	6,489	2.6%
10	Missouri	5,954	2.3%
11	Louisiana	5,548	2.2%
12	Arizona	5,525	2.2%
13	New Jersey	5,173	2.0%
14	New York	4,858	1.9%
15	Oklahoma	4,835	1.9%
16	Georgia	4,597	1.8%
17	Ohio	4,515	1.8%
18	North Carolina	4,437	1.7%
19	Nevada	3,728	1.5%
20	Washington	3,388	1.3%
21	Virginia	2,985	1.2%
22	Colorado	2,849	1.1%
23	Indiana	2,653	1.0%
24	New Mexico	2,649	1.0%
25	Arkansas	2,511	1.0%
26	Kansas	2,432	1.0%
27	Oregon	2,010	0.8%
28	Alabama	1,673	0.7%
29	Nebraska	1,637	0.6%
30	Kentucky	1,604	0.6%
31	Iowa	1,577	0.6%
32	Delaware	1,536	0.6%
33	Connecticut	1,448	0.6%
34	Minnesota	1,353	0.5%
35	Wisconsin	1,287	0.5%
36	Utah	1,025	0.4%
37	Idaho	1,017	0.4%
38	Mississippi	840	0.3%
39	Alaska	720	0.3%
40	Hawaii	675	0.3%
41	Rhode Island	633	0.2%
42	Montana	587	0.2%
43	West Virginia	405	0.2%
44	Wyoming	305	0.1%
45	South Dakota	237	0.1%
46	New Hampshire	234	0.1%
47	Maine	213	0.1%
48	Vermont	100	0.0%
49	North Dakota	65	0.0%
NA	Illinois**	NA	NA
	District of Columbia	1,609	0.6%

Source: Federal Bureau of Investigation
    "Crime in the United States 2004" (Uniform Crime Reports, October 17, 2005)
*Of the 715,376 aggravated assaults in 2004 for which supplemental data were received by the F.B.I. There were an additional 139,535 aggravated assaults for which the type of weapon was not reported to the F.B.I. Aggravated assault is an attack for the purpose of inflicting severe bodily injury. Numbers are for reporting jurisdictions only.
**Not available.

Percent of Aggravated Assaults Involving Blunt Objects and Other Dangerous Weapons in 2004
National Percent = 35.6% of Aggravated Assaults*

ALPHA ORDER

RANK	STATE	PERCENT
47	Alabama	22.7
46	Alaska	23.6
36	Arizona	29.9
33	Arkansas	30.4
21	California	33.7
39	Colorado	27.4
11	Connecticut	39.1
1	Delaware	52.3
4	Florida	46.4
25	Georgia	32.6
13	Hawaii	38.2
9	Idaho	39.6
NA	Illinois**	NA
43	Indiana	25.3
41	Iowa	26.1
5	Kansas	46.1
20	Kentucky	34.0
26	Louisiana	32.1
37	Maine	28.7
7	Maryland	44.0
2	Massachusetts	50.2
11	Michigan	39.1
17	Minnesota	35.3
40	Mississippi	26.4
29	Missouri	31.5
10	Montana	39.3
3	Nebraska	47.6
6	Nevada	44.7
32	New Hampshire	30.5
26	New Jersey	32.1
34	New Mexico	30.0
30	New York	31.4
38	North Carolina	27.8
44	North Dakota	24.3
31	Ohio	31.2
14	Oklahoma	37.8
18	Oregon	35.2
42	Pennsylvania	25.6
8	Rhode Island	39.7
34	South Carolina	30.0
19	South Dakota	34.7
16	Tennessee	36.8
15	Texas	37.0
23	Utah	33.4
45	Vermont	23.8
21	Virginia	33.7
23	Washington	33.4
49	West Virginia	18.5
48	Wisconsin	21.6
26	Wyoming	32.1

RANK ORDER

RANK	STATE	PERCENT
1	Delaware	52.3
2	Massachusetts	50.2
3	Nebraska	47.6
4	Florida	46.4
5	Kansas	46.1
6	Nevada	44.7
7	Maryland	44.0
8	Rhode Island	39.7
9	Idaho	39.6
10	Montana	39.3
11	Connecticut	39.1
11	Michigan	39.1
13	Hawaii	38.2
14	Oklahoma	37.8
15	Texas	37.0
16	Tennessee	36.8
17	Minnesota	35.3
18	Oregon	35.2
19	South Dakota	34.7
20	Kentucky	34.0
21	California	33.7
21	Virginia	33.7
23	Utah	33.4
23	Washington	33.4
25	Georgia	32.6
26	Louisiana	32.1
26	New Jersey	32.1
26	Wyoming	32.1
29	Missouri	31.5
30	New York	31.4
31	Ohio	31.2
32	New Hampshire	30.5
33	Arkansas	30.4
34	New Mexico	30.0
34	South Carolina	30.0
36	Arizona	29.9
37	Maine	28.7
38	North Carolina	27.8
39	Colorado	27.4
40	Mississippi	26.4
41	Iowa	26.1
42	Pennsylvania	25.6
43	Indiana	25.3
44	North Dakota	24.3
45	Vermont	23.8
46	Alaska	23.6
47	Alabama	22.7
48	Wisconsin	21.6
49	West Virginia	18.5
NA	Illinois**	NA

District of Columbia   40.5

Source: Morgan Quitno Press using data from Federal Bureau of Investigation
    "Crime in the United States 2004" (Uniform Crime Reports, October 17, 2005)
*Of the 715,376 aggravated assaults in 2004 for which supplemental data were received by the F.B.I. There were an additional 139,535 aggravated assaults for which the type of weapon was not reported to the F.B.I. Aggravated assault is an attack for the purpose of inflicting severe bodily injury. Numbers are for reporting jurisdictions only.
**Not available.

Aggravated Assaults Committed with Hands, Fists or Feet in 2004

National Total = 190,218 Aggravated Assaults*

RANK	STATE	ASSAULTS	% of USA
22	Alabama	2,977	1.6%
30	Alaska	1,201	0.6%
10	Arizona	5,008	2.6%
27	Arkansas	2,453	1.3%
1	California	41,100	21.6%
20	Colorado	3,122	1.6%
33	Connecticut	1,048	0.6%
45	Delaware	245	0.1%
2	Florida	17,389	9.1%
25	Georgia	2,785	1.5%
40	Hawaii	474	0.2%
41	Idaho	447	0.2%
NA	Illinois**	NA	NA
11	Indiana	4,953	2.6%
23	Iowa	2,949	1.6%
37	Kansas	677	0.4%
29	Kentucky	1,858	1.0%
14	Louisiana	3,859	2.0%
43	Maine	357	0.2%
15	Maryland	3,798	2.0%
19	Massachusetts	3,432	1.8%
7	Michigan	5,743	3.0%
32	Minnesota	1,092	0.6%
34	Mississippi	928	0.5%
6	Missouri	5,907	3.1%
39	Montana	514	0.3%
38	Nebraska	664	0.3%
31	Nevada	1,140	0.6%
46	New Hampshire	198	0.1%
9	New Jersey	5,211	2.7%
24	New Mexico	2,857	1.5%
8	New York	5,369	2.8%
13	North Carolina	3,988	2.1%
49	North Dakota	153	0.1%
12	Ohio	4,147	2.2%
16	Oklahoma	3,681	1.9%
28	Oregon	1,990	1.0%
4	Pennsylvania	9,517	5.0%
44	Rhode Island	282	0.1%
5	South Carolina	6,789	3.6%
48	South Dakota	180	0.1%
18	Tennessee	3,438	1.8%
3	Texas	14,556	7.7%
36	Utah	820	0.4%
47	Vermont	185	0.1%
26	Virginia	2,508	1.3%
17	Washington	3,466	1.8%
35	West Virginia	877	0.5%
21	Wisconsin	2,980	1.6%
42	Wyoming	363	0.2%

RANK	STATE	ASSAULTS	% of USA
1	California	41,100	21.6%
2	Florida	17,389	9.1%
3	Texas	14,556	7.7%
4	Pennsylvania	9,517	5.0%
5	South Carolina	6,789	3.6%
6	Missouri	5,907	3.1%
7	Michigan	5,743	3.0%
8	New York	5,369	2.8%
9	New Jersey	5,211	2.7%
10	Arizona	5,008	2.6%
11	Indiana	4,953	2.6%
12	Ohio	4,147	2.2%
13	North Carolina	3,988	2.1%
14	Louisiana	3,859	2.0%
15	Maryland	3,798	2.0%
16	Oklahoma	3,681	1.9%
17	Washington	3,466	1.8%
18	Tennessee	3,438	1.8%
19	Massachusetts	3,432	1.8%
20	Colorado	3,122	1.6%
21	Wisconsin	2,980	1.6%
22	Alabama	2,977	1.6%
23	Iowa	2,949	1.6%
24	New Mexico	2,857	1.5%
25	Georgia	2,785	1.5%
26	Virginia	2,508	1.3%
27	Arkansas	2,453	1.3%
28	Oregon	1,990	1.0%
29	Kentucky	1,858	1.0%
30	Alaska	1,201	0.6%
31	Nevada	1,140	0.6%
32	Minnesota	1,092	0.6%
33	Connecticut	1,048	0.6%
34	Mississippi	928	0.5%
35	West Virginia	877	0.5%
36	Utah	820	0.4%
37	Kansas	677	0.4%
38	Nebraska	664	0.3%
39	Montana	514	0.3%
40	Hawaii	474	0.2%
41	Idaho	447	0.2%
42	Wyoming	363	0.2%
43	Maine	357	0.2%
44	Rhode Island	282	0.1%
45	Delaware	245	0.1%
46	New Hampshire	198	0.1%
47	Vermont	185	0.1%
48	South Dakota	180	0.1%
49	North Dakota	153	0.1%
NA	Illinois**	NA	NA
	District of Columbia	543	0.3%

Source: Federal Bureau of Investigation
  "Crime in the United States 2004" (Uniform Crime Reports, October 17, 2005)
*Of the 715,376 aggravated assaults in 2004 for which supplemental data were received by the F.B.I. There were an additional 139,535 aggravated assaults for which the type of weapon was not reported to the F.B.I. Aggravated assault is an attack for the purpose of inflicting severe bodily injury. Numbers are for reporting jurisdictions only.
**Not available.

Percent of Aggravated Assaults Committed with Hands, Fists or Feet in 2004

National Percent = 26.6% of Aggravated Assaults*

ALPHA ORDER				RANK ORDER		
RANK	STATE	PERCENT		RANK	STATE	PERCENT
7	Alabama	40.3		1	North Dakota	57.3
9	Alaska	39.4		2	Wisconsin	50.1
30	Arizona	27.1		3	Iowa	48.8
22	Arkansas	29.7		4	Maine	48.1
17	California	33.3		5	Indiana	47.2
21	Colorado	30.1		6	Vermont	44.0
27	Connecticut	28.3		7	Alabama	40.3
49	Delaware	8.3		8	West Virginia	40.2
38	Florida	20.2		9	Alaska	39.4
39	Georgia	19.7		9	Kentucky	39.4
31	Hawaii	26.8		11	Wyoming	38.3
45	Idaho	17.4		12	Pennsylvania	37.6
NA	Illinois**	NA		13	Oregon	34.9
5	Indiana	47.2		14	New York	34.6
3	Iowa	48.8		15	Montana	34.5
47	Kansas	12.8		16	Washington	34.1
9	Kentucky	39.4		17	California	33.3
36	Louisiana	22.3		18	New Jersey	32.3
4	Maine	48.1		18	New Mexico	32.3
37	Maryland	22.1		20	Missouri	31.2
42	Massachusetts	18.9		21	Colorado	30.1
43	Michigan	18.3		22	Arkansas	29.7
26	Minnesota	28.5		23	Mississippi	29.2
23	Mississippi	29.2		24	Oklahoma	28.8
20	Missouri	31.2		25	Ohio	28.7
15	Montana	34.5		26	Minnesota	28.5
40	Nebraska	19.3		27	Connecticut	28.3
46	Nevada	13.7		27	Virginia	28.3
34	New Hampshire	25.8		29	South Carolina	28.0
18	New Jersey	32.3		30	Arizona	27.1
18	New Mexico	32.3		31	Hawaii	26.8
14	New York	34.6		32	Utah	26.7
35	North Carolina	25.0		33	South Dakota	26.4
1	North Dakota	57.3		34	New Hampshire	25.8
25	Ohio	28.7		35	North Carolina	25.0
24	Oklahoma	28.8		36	Louisiana	22.3
13	Oregon	34.9		37	Maryland	22.1
12	Pennsylvania	37.6		38	Florida	20.2
44	Rhode Island	17.7		39	Georgia	19.7
29	South Carolina	28.0		40	Nebraska	19.3
33	South Dakota	26.4		40	Texas	19.3
48	Tennessee	11.7		42	Massachusetts	18.9
40	Texas	19.3		43	Michigan	18.3
32	Utah	26.7		44	Rhode Island	17.7
6	Vermont	44.0		45	Idaho	17.4
27	Virginia	28.3		46	Nevada	13.7
16	Washington	34.1		47	Kansas	12.8
8	West Virginia	40.2		48	Tennessee	11.7
2	Wisconsin	50.1		49	Delaware	8.3
11	Wyoming	38.3		NA	Illinois**	NA
					District of Columbia	13.7

Source: Morgan Quitno Press using data from Federal Bureau of Investigation
   "Crime in the United States 2004" (Uniform Crime Reports, October 17, 2005)
*Of the 715,376 aggravated assaults in 2004 for which supplemental data were received by the F.B.I. There were
an additional 139,535 aggravated assaults for which the type of weapon was not reported to the F.B.I. Aggravated
assault is an attack for the purpose of inflicting severe bodily injury. Numbers are for reporting jurisdictions only.
**Not available.

Property Crimes in 2004

National Total = 10,328,255 Property Crimes*

ALPHA ORDER

RANK	STATE	CRIMES	% of USA
21	Alabama	182,340	1.8%
46	Alaska	22,172	0.2%
10	Arizona	306,747	3.0%
28	Arkansas	110,464	1.1%
1	California	1,227,194	11.9%
22	Colorado	180,342	1.7%
34	Connecticut	92,046	0.9%
45	Delaware	26,272	0.3%
3	Florida	727,141	7.0%
7	Georgia	376,656	3.6%
38	Hawaii	60,525	0.6%
40	Idaho	38,933	0.4%
6	Illinois	405,070	3.9%
15	Indiana	211,929	2.1%
35	Iowa	85,836	0.8%
29	Kansas	108,694	1.1%
30	Kentucky	105,209	1.0%
19	Louisiana	199,153	1.9%
41	Maine	31,740	0.3%
17	Maryland	202,326	2.0%
24	Massachusetts	157,825	1.5%
9	Michigan	309,208	3.0%
25	Minnesota	155,019	1.5%
31	Mississippi	100,980	1.0%
14	Missouri	224,629	2.2%
43	Montana	27,215	0.3%
37	Nebraska	61,512	0.6%
32	Nevada	98,215	1.0%
44	New Hampshire	26,511	0.3%
16	New Jersey	211,313	2.0%
36	New Mexico	79,895	0.8%
4	New York	422,734	4.1%
8	North Carolina	355,328	3.4%
50	North Dakota	12,158	0.1%
5	Ohio	420,910	4.1%
26	Oklahoma	149,472	1.4%
23	Oregon	166,475	1.6%
12	Pennsylvania	299,611	2.9%
42	Rhode Island	31,166	0.3%
20	South Carolina	189,113	1.8%
48	South Dakota	14,905	0.1%
13	Tennessee	254,123	2.5%
2	Texas	1,010,702	9.8%
33	Utah	97,607	0.9%
49	Vermont	14,343	0.1%
18	Virginia	199,668	1.9%
11	Washington	300,837	2.9%
39	West Virginia	45,497	0.4%
27	Wisconsin	146,710	1.4%
47	Wyoming	16,889	0.2%

RANK ORDER

RANK	STATE	CRIMES	% of USA
1	California	1,227,194	11.9%
2	Texas	1,010,702	9.8%
3	Florida	727,141	7.0%
4	New York	422,734	4.1%
5	Ohio	420,910	4.1%
6	Illinois	405,070	3.9%
7	Georgia	376,656	3.6%
8	North Carolina	355,328	3.4%
9	Michigan	309,208	3.0%
10	Arizona	306,747	3.0%
11	Washington	300,837	2.9%
12	Pennsylvania	299,611	2.9%
13	Tennessee	254,123	2.5%
14	Missouri	224,629	2.2%
15	Indiana	211,929	2.1%
16	New Jersey	211,313	2.0%
17	Maryland	202,326	2.0%
18	Virginia	199,668	1.9%
19	Louisiana	199,153	1.9%
20	South Carolina	189,113	1.8%
21	Alabama	182,340	1.8%
22	Colorado	180,342	1.7%
23	Oregon	166,475	1.6%
24	Massachusetts	157,825	1.5%
25	Minnesota	155,019	1.5%
26	Oklahoma	149,472	1.4%
27	Wisconsin	146,710	1.4%
28	Arkansas	110,464	1.1%
29	Kansas	108,694	1.1%
30	Kentucky	105,209	1.0%
31	Mississippi	100,980	1.0%
32	Nevada	98,215	1.0%
33	Utah	97,607	0.9%
34	Connecticut	92,046	0.9%
35	Iowa	85,836	0.8%
36	New Mexico	79,895	0.8%
37	Nebraska	61,512	0.6%
38	Hawaii	60,525	0.6%
39	West Virginia	45,497	0.4%
40	Idaho	38,933	0.4%
41	Maine	31,740	0.3%
42	Rhode Island	31,166	0.3%
43	Montana	27,215	0.3%
44	New Hampshire	26,511	0.3%
45	Delaware	26,272	0.3%
46	Alaska	22,172	0.2%
47	Wyoming	16,889	0.2%
48	South Dakota	14,905	0.1%
49	Vermont	14,343	0.1%
50	North Dakota	12,158	0.1%
	District of Columbia	26,896	0.3%

Source: Federal Bureau of Investigation
  "Crime in the United States 2004" (Uniform Crime Reports, October 17, 2005)
*Property crimes are offenses of burglary, larceny-theft and motor vehicle theft.

Average Time Between Property Crimes in 2004

National Rate = A Property Crime Occurs Every 3 Seconds*

ALPHA ORDER				RANK ORDER		
RANK	STATE	MINUTES.SECONDS		RANK	STATE	MINUTES.SECONDS
30	Alabama	2.53		1	North Dakota	43.21
5	Alaska	23.46		2	Vermont	36.45
41	Arizona	1.43		3	South Dakota	35.22
23	Arkansas	4.46		4	Wyoming	31.13
50	California	0.26		5	Alaska	23.46
29	Colorado	2.55		6	Delaware	20.04
17	Connecticut	5.44		7	New Hampshire	19.53
6	Delaware	20.04		8	Montana	19.22
48	Florida	0.43		9	Rhode Island	16.55
44	Georgia	1.24		10	Maine	16.36
13	Hawaii	8.43		11	Idaho	13.32
11	Idaho	13.32		12	West Virginia	11.35
45	Illinois	1.18		13	Hawaii	8.43
35	Indiana	2.29		14	Nebraska	8.34
16	Iowa	6.08		15	New Mexico	6.36
22	Kansas	4.51		16	Iowa	6.08
21	Kentucky	5.01		17	Connecticut	5.44
32	Louisiana	2.39		18	Utah	5.24
10	Maine	16.36		19	Nevada	5.22
34	Maryland	2.36		20	Mississippi	5.13
27	Massachusetts	3.20		21	Kentucky	5.01
42	Michigan	1.42		22	Kansas	4.51
26	Minnesota	3.24		23	Arkansas	4.46
20	Mississippi	5.13		24	Wisconsin	3.35
37	Missouri	2.21		25	Oklahoma	3.32
8	Montana	19.22		26	Minnesota	3.24
14	Nebraska	8.34		27	Massachusetts	3.20
19	Nevada	5.22		28	Oregon	3.10
7	New Hampshire	19.53		29	Colorado	2.55
35	New Jersey	2.29		30	Alabama	2.53
15	New Mexico	6.36		31	South Carolina	2.47
46	New York	1.15		32	Louisiana	2.39
43	North Carolina	1.29		33	Virginia	2.38
1	North Dakota	43.21		34	Maryland	2.36
46	Ohio	1.15		35	Indiana	2.29
25	Oklahoma	3.32		35	New Jersey	2.29
28	Oregon	3.10		37	Missouri	2.21
39	Pennsylvania	1.46		38	Tennessee	2.04
9	Rhode Island	16.55		39	Pennsylvania	1.46
31	South Carolina	2.47		40	Washington	1.45
3	South Dakota	35.22		41	Arizona	1.43
38	Tennessee	2.04		42	Michigan	1.42
49	Texas	0.31		43	North Carolina	1.29
18	Utah	5.24		44	Georgia	1.24
2	Vermont	36.45		45	Illinois	1.18
33	Virginia	2.38		46	New York	1.15
40	Washington	1.45		46	Ohio	1.15
12	West Virginia	11.35		48	Florida	0.43
24	Wisconsin	3.35		49	Texas	0.31
4	Wyoming	31.13		50	California	0.26
				District of Columbia		19.36

Source: Morgan Quitno Press using data from Federal Bureau of Investigation
    "Crime in the United States 2004" (Uniform Crime Reports, October 17, 2005)
*Property crimes are offenses of burglary, larceny-theft and motor vehicle theft.

Property Crimes per Square Mile in 2004

National Rate = 2.7 Property Crimes per Square Mile*

ALPHA ORDER

RANK	STATE	RATE
23	Alabama	3.5
50	Alaska	0.0
27	Arizona	2.7
30	Arkansas	2.1
10	California	7.5
35	Colorado	1.7
3	Connecticut	16.6
7	Delaware	10.6
6	Florida	11.1
14	Georgia	6.3
18	Hawaii	5.5
45	Idaho	0.5
11	Illinois	7.0
17	Indiana	5.8
37	Iowa	1.5
39	Kansas	1.3
28	Kentucky	2.6
21	Louisiana	3.8
41	Maine	0.9
4	Maryland	16.3
5	Massachusetts	15.0
24	Michigan	3.2
34	Minnesota	1.8
30	Mississippi	2.1
24	Missouri	3.2
46	Montana	0.2
43	Nebraska	0.8
41	Nevada	0.9
26	New Hampshire	2.8
1	New Jersey	24.2
44	New Mexico	0.7
9	New York	7.7
12	North Carolina	6.6
46	North Dakota	0.2
8	Ohio	9.4
30	Oklahoma	2.1
35	Oregon	1.7
13	Pennsylvania	6.5
2	Rhode Island	20.2
16	South Carolina	5.9
46	South Dakota	0.2
15	Tennessee	6.0
21	Texas	3.8
40	Utah	1.1
37	Vermont	1.5
19	Virginia	4.7
20	Washington	4.2
33	West Virginia	1.9
29	Wisconsin	2.2
46	Wyoming	0.2

RANK ORDER

RANK	STATE	RATE
1	New Jersey	24.2
2	Rhode Island	20.2
3	Connecticut	16.6
4	Maryland	16.3
5	Massachusetts	15.0
6	Florida	11.1
7	Delaware	10.6
8	Ohio	9.4
9	New York	7.7
10	California	7.5
11	Illinois	7.0
12	North Carolina	6.6
13	Pennsylvania	6.5
14	Georgia	6.3
15	Tennessee	6.0
16	South Carolina	5.9
17	Indiana	5.8
18	Hawaii	5.5
19	Virginia	4.7
20	Washington	4.2
21	Louisiana	3.8
21	Texas	3.8
23	Alabama	3.5
24	Michigan	3.2
24	Missouri	3.2
26	New Hampshire	2.8
27	Arizona	2.7
28	Kentucky	2.6
29	Wisconsin	2.2
30	Arkansas	2.1
30	Mississippi	2.1
30	Oklahoma	2.1
33	West Virginia	1.9
34	Minnesota	1.8
35	Colorado	1.7
35	Oregon	1.7
37	Iowa	1.5
37	Vermont	1.5
39	Kansas	1.3
40	Utah	1.1
41	Maine	0.9
41	Nevada	0.9
43	Nebraska	0.8
44	New Mexico	0.7
45	Idaho	0.5
46	Montana	0.2
46	North Dakota	0.2
46	South Dakota	0.2
46	Wyoming	0.2
50	Alaska	0.0

District of Columbia	395.5

Source: Morgan Quitno Press using data from Federal Bureau of Investigation
    "Crime in the United States 2004" (Uniform Crime Reports, October 17, 2005)
*Property crimes are offenses of burglary, larceny-theft and motor vehicle theft. "Square miles" includes total land and water area.

Percent Change in Number of Property Crimes: 2003 to 2004

National Percent Change = 1.1% Decrease*

ALPHA ORDER				RANK ORDER		
RANK	STATE	PERCENT CHANGE		RANK	STATE	PERCENT CHANGE
17	Alabama	0.1		1	Arkansas	11.5
50	Alaska	(9.1)		2	West Virginia	7.4
31	Arizona	(2.4)		3	New Mexico	4.0
1	Arkansas	11.5		4	Vermont	3.9
12	California	1.0		5	Washington	3.2
15	Colorado	0.4		6	Louisiana	2.8
22	Connecticut	(1.0)		7	Nevada	2.2
45	Delaware	(6.0)		8	Georgia	1.9
39	Florida	(4.0)		8	Indiana	1.9
8	Georgia	1.9		10	Kentucky	1.8
48	Hawaii	(8.1)		11	Wyoming	1.4
35	Idaho	(2.8)		12	California	1.0
33	Illinois	(2.6)		13	Ohio	0.8
8	Indiana	1.9		13	South Carolina	0.8
28	Iowa	(2.0)		15	Colorado	0.4
20	Kansas	(0.5)		16	New Hampshire	0.2
10	Kentucky	1.8		17	Alabama	0.1
6	Louisiana	2.8		18	Pennsylvania	(0.3)
24	Maine	(1.1)		19	Virginia	(0.4)
37	Maryland	(3.4)		20	Kansas	(0.5)
40	Massachusetts	(4.1)		21	Texas	(0.6)
46	Michigan	(6.5)		22	Connecticut	(1.0)
27	Minnesota	(1.7)		22	Tennessee	(1.0)
43	Mississippi	(5.5)		24	Maine	(1.1)
38	Missouri	(3.8)		24	Oklahoma	(1.1)
42	Montana	(4.3)		26	North Carolina	(1.2)
44	Nebraska	(5.6)		27	Minnesota	(1.7)
7	Nevada	2.2		28	Iowa	(2.0)
16	New Hampshire	0.2		28	Oregon	(2.0)
40	New Jersey	(4.1)		30	New York	(2.2)
3	New Mexico	4.0		31	Arizona	(2.4)
30	New York	(2.2)		32	Utah	(2.5)
26	North Carolina	(1.2)		33	Illinois	(2.6)
49	North Dakota	(9.0)		34	South Dakota	(2.7)
13	Ohio	0.8		35	Idaho	(2.8)
24	Oklahoma	(1.1)		36	Rhode Island	(3.3)
28	Oregon	(2.0)		37	Maryland	(3.4)
18	Pennsylvania	(0.3)		38	Missouri	(3.8)
36	Rhode Island	(3.3)		39	Florida	(4.0)
13	South Carolina	0.8		40	Massachusetts	(4.1)
34	South Dakota	(2.7)		40	New Jersey	(4.1)
22	Tennessee	(1.0)		42	Montana	(4.3)
21	Texas	(0.6)		43	Mississippi	(5.5)
32	Utah	(2.5)		44	Nebraska	(5.6)
4	Vermont	3.9		45	Delaware	(6.0)
19	Virginia	(0.4)		46	Michigan	(6.5)
5	Washington	3.2		47	Wisconsin	(7.0)
2	West Virginia	7.4		48	Hawaii	(8.1)
47	Wisconsin	(7.0)		49	North Dakota	(9.0)
11	Wyoming	1.4		50	Alaska	(9.1)
					District of Columbia	(17.7)

Source: Federal Bureau of Investigation
"Crime in the United States 2004" (Uniform Crime Reports, October 17, 2005)
*Property crimes are offenses of burglary, larceny-theft and motor vehicle theft.

Property Crime Rate in 2004

National Rate = 3,517.1 Property Crimes per 100,000 Population*

ALPHA ORDER

RANK	STATE	RATE
16	Alabama	4,025.0
27	Alaska	3,382.8
1	Arizona	5,340.5
17	Arkansas	4,013.0
25	California	3,419.0
19	Colorado	3,919.3
39	Connecticut	2,627.2
30	Delaware	3,163.9
13	Florida	4,179.7
9	Georgia	4,265.9
3	Hawaii	4,792.8
36	Idaho	2,794.4
29	Illinois	3,186.1
26	Indiana	3,397.6
34	Iowa	2,905.3
18	Kansas	3,973.5
40	Kentucky	2,537.7
7	Louisiana	4,410.2
45	Maine	2,409.6
22	Maryland	3,640.2
42	Massachusetts	2,459.7
31	Michigan	3,057.6
32	Minnesota	3,039.0
24	Mississippi	3,478.5
20	Missouri	3,903.5
33	Montana	2,936.2
23	Nebraska	3,520.6
11	Nevada	4,206.6
48	New Hampshire	2,040.1
43	New Jersey	2,429.2
12	New Mexico	4,197.7
47	New York	2,198.6
14	North Carolina	4,160.2
50	North Dakota	1,916.6
21	Ohio	3,673.2
10	Oklahoma	4,242.1
4	Oregon	4,631.3
44	Pennsylvania	2,415.0
35	Rhode Island	2,884.1
5	South Carolina	4,504.8
49	South Dakota	1,933.5
8	Tennessee	4,306.5
6	Texas	4,494.0
15	Utah	4,085.6
46	Vermont	2,308.2
37	Virginia	2,676.6
2	Washington	4,849.2
41	West Virginia	2,506.2
38	Wisconsin	2,663.1
28	Wyoming	3,334.3

RANK ORDER

RANK	STATE	RATE
1	Arizona	5,340.5
2	Washington	4,849.2
3	Hawaii	4,792.8
4	Oregon	4,631.3
5	South Carolina	4,504.8
6	Texas	4,494.0
7	Louisiana	4,410.2
8	Tennessee	4,306.5
9	Georgia	4,265.9
10	Oklahoma	4,242.1
11	Nevada	4,206.6
12	New Mexico	4,197.7
13	Florida	4,179.7
14	North Carolina	4,160.2
15	Utah	4,085.6
16	Alabama	4,025.0
17	Arkansas	4,013.0
18	Kansas	3,973.5
19	Colorado	3,919.3
20	Missouri	3,903.5
21	Ohio	3,673.2
22	Maryland	3,640.2
23	Nebraska	3,520.6
24	Mississippi	3,478.5
25	California	3,419.0
26	Indiana	3,397.6
27	Alaska	3,382.8
28	Wyoming	3,334.3
29	Illinois	3,186.1
30	Delaware	3,163.9
31	Michigan	3,057.6
32	Minnesota	3,039.0
33	Montana	2,936.2
34	Iowa	2,905.3
35	Rhode Island	2,884.1
36	Idaho	2,794.4
37	Virginia	2,676.6
38	Wisconsin	2,663.1
39	Connecticut	2,627.2
40	Kentucky	2,537.7
41	West Virginia	2,506.2
42	Massachusetts	2,459.7
43	New Jersey	2,429.2
44	Pennsylvania	2,415.0
45	Maine	2,409.6
46	Vermont	2,308.2
47	New York	2,198.6
48	New Hampshire	2,040.1
49	South Dakota	1,933.5
50	North Dakota	1,916.6
	District of Columbia	4,859.1

Source: Federal Bureau of Investigation
   "Crime in the United States 2004" (Uniform Crime Reports, October 17, 2005)
*Property crimes are offenses of burglary, larceny-theft and motor vehicle theft.

Percent Change in Property Crime Rate: 2003 to 2004

National Percent Change = 2.1% Decrease*

ALPHA ORDER

RANK	STATE	PERCENT CHANGE
14	Alabama	(0.5)
50	Alaska	(10.1)
40	Arizona	(5.2)
1	Arkansas	10.5
12	California	(0.2)
17	Colorado	(0.8)
19	Connecticut	(1.5)
46	Delaware	(7.4)
42	Florida	(6.2)
11	Georgia	0.1
48	Hawaii	(9.1)
38	Idaho	(4.6)
31	Illinois	(3.1)
7	Indiana	1.2
27	Iowa	(2.4)
18	Kansas	(0.9)
8	Kentucky	1.1
5	Louisiana	2.3
21	Maine	(1.7)
36	Maryland	(4.2)
34	Massachusetts	(4.0)
45	Michigan	(6.7)
27	Minnesota	(2.4)
42	Mississippi	(6.2)
37	Missouri	(4.4)
40	Montana	(5.2)
42	Nebraska	(6.2)
23	Nevada	(1.9)
15	New Hampshire	(0.6)
39	New Jersey	(4.7)
4	New Mexico	2.7
25	New York	(2.2)
29	North Carolina	(2.6)
49	North Dakota	(9.2)
9	Ohio	0.6
20	Oklahoma	(1.6)
30	Oregon	(2.8)
15	Pennsylvania	(0.6)
33	Rhode Island	(3.7)
13	South Carolina	(0.4)
32	South Dakota	(3.5)
23	Tennessee	(1.9)
26	Texas	(2.3)
34	Utah	(4.0)
3	Vermont	3.6
21	Virginia	(1.7)
6	Washington	2.0
2	West Virginia	7.1
47	Wisconsin	(7.5)
9	Wyoming	0.6

RANK ORDER

RANK	STATE	PERCENT CHANGE
1	Arkansas	10.5
2	West Virginia	7.1
3	Vermont	3.6
4	New Mexico	2.7
5	Louisiana	2.3
6	Washington	2.0
7	Indiana	1.2
8	Kentucky	1.1
9	Ohio	0.6
9	Wyoming	0.6
11	Georgia	0.1
12	California	(0.2)
13	South Carolina	(0.4)
14	Alabama	(0.5)
15	New Hampshire	(0.6)
15	Pennsylvania	(0.6)
17	Colorado	(0.8)
18	Kansas	(0.9)
19	Connecticut	(1.5)
20	Oklahoma	(1.6)
21	Maine	(1.7)
21	Virginia	(1.7)
23	Nevada	(1.9)
23	Tennessee	(1.9)
25	New York	(2.2)
26	Texas	(2.3)
27	Iowa	(2.4)
27	Minnesota	(2.4)
29	North Carolina	(2.6)
30	Oregon	(2.8)
31	Illinois	(3.1)
32	South Dakota	(3.5)
33	Rhode Island	(3.7)
34	Massachusetts	(4.0)
34	Utah	(4.0)
36	Maryland	(4.2)
37	Missouri	(4.4)
38	Idaho	(4.6)
39	New Jersey	(4.7)
40	Arizona	(5.2)
40	Montana	(5.2)
42	Florida	(6.2)
42	Mississippi	(6.2)
42	Nebraska	(6.2)
45	Michigan	(6.7)
46	Delaware	(7.4)
47	Wisconsin	(7.5)
48	Hawaii	(9.1)
49	North Dakota	(9.2)
50	Alaska	(10.1)
	District of Columbia	(17.1)

Source: Federal Bureau of Investigation
    "Crime in the United States 2004" (Uniform Crime Reports, October 17, 2005)
*Property crimes are offenses of burglary, larceny-theft and motor vehicle theft.

Burglaries in 2004

National Total = 2,143,456 Burglaries*

ALPHA ORDER

RANK	STATE	BURGLARIES	% of USA
15	Alabama	44,666	2.1%
45	Alaska	3,773	0.2%
12	Arizona	56,885	2.7%
24	Arkansas	30,099	1.4%
1	California	245,903	11.5%
23	Colorado	33,008	1.5%
35	Connecticut	15,570	0.7%
43	Delaware	5,383	0.3%
3	Florida	166,332	7.8%
6	Georgia	82,992	3.9%
38	Hawaii	10,827	0.5%
40	Idaho	7,626	0.4%
7	Illinois	75,944	3.5%
17	Indiana	42,168	2.0%
34	Iowa	18,174	0.8%
32	Kansas	19,999	0.9%
29	Kentucky	25,902	1.2%
14	Louisiana	45,359	2.1%
41	Maine	6,341	0.3%
20	Maryland	36,682	1.7%
22	Massachusetts	34,469	1.6%
9	Michigan	64,394	3.0%
27	Minnesota	28,048	1.3%
28	Mississippi	27,661	1.3%
19	Missouri	40,472	1.9%
46	Montana	3,515	0.2%
39	Nebraska	9,826	0.5%
31	Nevada	23,142	1.1%
44	New Hampshire	4,966	0.2%
18	New Jersey	41,030	1.9%
33	New Mexico	19,924	0.9%
8	New York	70,696	3.3%
4	North Carolina	101,193	4.7%
50	North Dakota	1,910	0.1%
5	Ohio	96,954	4.5%
21	Oklahoma	35,244	1.6%
25	Oregon	30,072	1.4%
13	Pennsylvania	54,443	2.5%
42	Rhode Island	5,465	0.3%
16	South Carolina	43,425	2.0%
48	South Dakota	3,149	0.1%
11	Tennessee	60,205	2.8%
2	Texas	220,118	10.3%
36	Utah	15,221	0.7%
47	Vermont	3,386	0.2%
26	Virginia	28,793	1.3%
10	Washington	60,632	2.8%
37	West Virginia	10,932	0.5%
30	Wisconsin	23,854	1.1%
49	Wyoming	2,738	0.1%

RANK ORDER

RANK	STATE	BURGLARIES	% of USA
1	California	245,903	11.5%
2	Texas	220,118	10.3%
3	Florida	166,332	7.8%
4	North Carolina	101,193	4.7%
5	Ohio	96,954	4.5%
6	Georgia	82,992	3.9%
7	Illinois	75,944	3.5%
8	New York	70,696	3.3%
9	Michigan	64,394	3.0%
10	Washington	60,632	2.8%
11	Tennessee	60,205	2.8%
12	Arizona	56,885	2.7%
13	Pennsylvania	54,443	2.5%
14	Louisiana	45,359	2.1%
15	Alabama	44,666	2.1%
16	South Carolina	43,425	2.0%
17	Indiana	42,168	2.0%
18	New Jersey	41,030	1.9%
19	Missouri	40,472	1.9%
20	Maryland	36,682	1.7%
21	Oklahoma	35,244	1.6%
22	Massachusetts	34,469	1.6%
23	Colorado	33,008	1.5%
24	Arkansas	30,099	1.4%
25	Oregon	30,072	1.4%
26	Virginia	28,793	1.3%
27	Minnesota	28,048	1.3%
28	Mississippi	27,661	1.3%
29	Kentucky	25,902	1.2%
30	Wisconsin	23,854	1.1%
31	Nevada	23,142	1.1%
32	Kansas	19,999	0.9%
33	New Mexico	19,924	0.9%
34	Iowa	18,174	0.8%
35	Connecticut	15,570	0.7%
36	Utah	15,221	0.7%
37	West Virginia	10,932	0.5%
38	Hawaii	10,827	0.5%
39	Nebraska	9,826	0.5%
40	Idaho	7,626	0.4%
41	Maine	6,341	0.3%
42	Rhode Island	5,465	0.3%
43	Delaware	5,383	0.3%
44	New Hampshire	4,966	0.2%
45	Alaska	3,773	0.2%
46	Montana	3,515	0.2%
47	Vermont	3,386	0.2%
48	South Dakota	3,149	0.1%
49	Wyoming	2,738	0.1%
50	North Dakota	1,910	0.1%
	District of Columbia	3,946	0.2%

Source: Federal Bureau of Investigation
   "Crime in the United States 2004" (Uniform Crime Reports, October 17, 2005)
*Burglary is the unlawful entry of a structure to commit a felony or theft. Attempts are included.

Average Time Between Burglaries in 2004

National Rate = A Burglary Occurs Every 15 Seconds*

ALPHA ORDER

RANK	STATE	MINUTES.SECONDS
36	Alabama	11.48
6	Alaska	139.41
39	Arizona	9.16
27	Arkansas	17.31
50	California	2.08
28	Colorado	15.58
16	Connecticut	33.51
8	Delaware	97.55
48	Florida	3.10
45	Georgia	6.21
13	Hawaii	48.41
11	Idaho	69.07
44	Illinois	6.56
34	Indiana	12.30
17	Iowa	29.00
19	Kansas	26.21
22	Kentucky	20.21
37	Louisiana	11.37
10	Maine	83.07
31	Maryland	14.22
29	Massachusetts	15.17
42	Michigan	8.11
24	Minnesota	18.47
23	Mississippi	19.03
32	Missouri	13.01
5	Montana	149.56
12	Nebraska	53.38
20	Nevada	22.46
7	New Hampshire	106.08
33	New Jersey	12.51
18	New Mexico	26.27
43	New York	7.28
47	North Carolina	5.13
1	North Dakota	275.56
46	Ohio	5.26
30	Oklahoma	14.57
26	Oregon	17.32
38	Pennsylvania	9.41
9	Rhode Island	96.26
35	South Carolina	12.08
3	South Dakota	167.22
40	Tennessee	8.45
49	Texas	2.23
15	Utah	34.38
4	Vermont	155.39
25	Virginia	18.18
41	Washington	8.41
14	West Virginia	48.13
21	Wisconsin	22.05
2	Wyoming	192.29

RANK ORDER

RANK	STATE	MINUTES.SECONDS
1	North Dakota	275.56
2	Wyoming	192.29
3	South Dakota	167.22
4	Vermont	155.39
5	Montana	149.56
6	Alaska	139.41
7	New Hampshire	106.08
8	Delaware	97.55
9	Rhode Island	96.26
10	Maine	83.07
11	Idaho	69.07
12	Nebraska	53.38
13	Hawaii	48.41
14	West Virginia	48.13
15	Utah	34.38
16	Connecticut	33.51
17	Iowa	29.00
18	New Mexico	26.27
19	Kansas	26.21
20	Nevada	22.46
21	Wisconsin	22.05
22	Kentucky	20.21
23	Mississippi	19.03
24	Minnesota	18.47
25	Virginia	18.18
26	Oregon	17.32
27	Arkansas	17.31
28	Colorado	15.58
29	Massachusetts	15.17
30	Oklahoma	14.57
31	Maryland	14.22
32	Missouri	13.01
33	New Jersey	12.51
34	Indiana	12.30
35	South Carolina	12.08
36	Alabama	11.48
37	Louisiana	11.37
38	Pennsylvania	9.41
39	Arizona	9.16
40	Tennessee	8.45
41	Washington	8.41
42	Michigan	8.11
43	New York	7.28
44	Illinois	6.56
45	Georgia	6.21
46	Ohio	5.26
47	North Carolina	5.13
48	Florida	3.10
49	Texas	2.23
50	California	2.08

| | District of Columbia | 133.34 |

Source: Morgan Quitno Press using data from Federal Bureau of Investigation
    "Crime in the United States 2004" (Uniform Crime Reports, October 17, 2005)
*Burglary is the unlawful entry of a structure to commit a felony or theft. Attempts are included.

Percent Change in Number of Burglaries: 2003 to 2004

National Percent Change = 0.5% Decrease*

ALPHA ORDER				RANK ORDER		
RANK	STATE	PERCENT CHANGE		RANK	STATE	PERCENT CHANGE
13	Alabama	3.3		1	Arkansas	20.3
31	Alaska	(2.6)		2	Vermont	12.2
33	Arizona	(2.9)		3	South Dakota	9.4
1	Arkansas	20.3		4	New Hampshire	8.2
17	California	1.5		5	Nevada	5.4
15	Colorado	1.9		6	Oregon	5.3
33	Connecticut	(2.9)		7	Georgia	5.1
50	Delaware	(11.3)		8	New Mexico	4.9
29	Florida	(2.5)		8	Wyoming	4.9
7	Georgia	5.1		10	Washington	4.1
40	Hawaii	(5.1)		10	West Virginia	4.1
32	Idaho	(2.7)		12	Iowa	3.8
36	Illinois	(3.1)		13	Alabama	3.3
18	Indiana	1.4		14	Ohio	2.0
12	Iowa	3.8		15	Colorado	1.9
47	Kansas	(9.0)		16	Louisiana	1.8
24	Kentucky	(0.5)		17	California	1.5
16	Louisiana	1.8		18	Indiana	1.4
37	Maine	(3.6)		19	Minnesota	1.3
40	Maryland	(5.1)		20	Oklahoma	1.1
28	Massachusetts	(1.4)		21	Pennsylvania	1.0
44	Michigan	(5.7)		22	North Carolina	0.5
19	Minnesota	1.3		23	Texas	0.1
46	Mississippi	(6.4)		24	Kentucky	(0.5)
37	Missouri	(3.6)		25	Rhode Island	(1.1)
42	Montana	(5.6)		25	Virginia	(1.1)
35	Nebraska	(3.0)		27	South Carolina	(1.3)
5	Nevada	5.4		28	Massachusetts	(1.4)
4	New Hampshire	8.2		29	Florida	(2.5)
42	New Jersey	(5.6)		29	North Dakota	(2.5)
8	New Mexico	4.9		31	Alaska	(2.6)
45	New York	(6.3)		32	Idaho	(2.7)
22	North Carolina	0.5		33	Arizona	(2.9)
29	North Dakota	(2.5)		33	Connecticut	(2.9)
14	Ohio	2.0		35	Nebraska	(3.0)
20	Oklahoma	1.1		36	Illinois	(3.1)
6	Oregon	5.3		37	Maine	(3.6)
21	Pennsylvania	1.0		37	Missouri	(3.6)
25	Rhode Island	(1.1)		39	Tennessee	(4.9)
27	South Carolina	(1.3)		40	Hawaii	(5.1)
3	South Dakota	9.4		40	Maryland	(5.1)
39	Tennessee	(4.9)		42	Montana	(5.6)
23	Texas	0.1		42	New Jersey	(5.6)
49	Utah	(10.3)		44	Michigan	(5.7)
2	Vermont	12.2		45	New York	(6.3)
25	Virginia	(1.1)		46	Mississippi	(6.4)
10	Washington	4.1		47	Kansas	(9.0)
10	West Virginia	4.1		48	Wisconsin	(10.1)
48	Wisconsin	(10.1)		49	Utah	(10.3)
8	Wyoming	4.9		50	Delaware	(11.3)
					District of Columbia	(15.5)

Source: Federal Bureau of Investigation
"Crime in the United States 2004" (Uniform Crime Reports, October 17, 2005)
*Burglary is the unlawful entry of a structure to commit a felony or theft. Attempts are included.

Burglary Rate in 2004

National Rate = 729.9 Burglaries per 100,000 Population*

ALPHA ORDER

RANK	STATE	RATE
10	Alabama	986.0
32	Alaska	575.6
9	Arizona	990.4
2	Arkansas	1,093.5
22	California	685.1
20	Colorado	717.3
42	Connecticut	444.4
25	Delaware	648.3
13	Florida	956.1
15	Georgia	940.0
16	Hawaii	857.4
35	Idaho	547.3
31	Illinois	597.3
23	Indiana	676.0
29	Iowa	615.1
19	Kansas	731.1
28	Kentucky	624.8
6	Louisiana	1,004.5
40	Maine	481.4
24	Maryland	660.0
38	Massachusetts	537.2
27	Michigan	636.8
34	Minnesota	549.9
14	Mississippi	952.9
21	Missouri	703.3
48	Montana	379.2
33	Nebraska	562.4
8	Nevada	991.2
47	New Hampshire	382.1
41	New Jersey	471.7
3	New Mexico	1,046.8
49	New York	367.7
1	North Carolina	1,184.8
50	North Dakota	301.1
17	Ohio	846.1
7	Oklahoma	1,000.2
18	Oregon	836.6
43	Pennsylvania	438.8
39	Rhode Island	505.7
4	South Carolina	1,034.4
45	South Dakota	408.5
5	Tennessee	1,020.3
11	Texas	978.7
26	Utah	637.1
36	Vermont	544.9
46	Virginia	386.0
12	Washington	977.3
30	West Virginia	602.2
44	Wisconsin	433.0
37	Wyoming	540.5

RANK ORDER

RANK	STATE	RATE
1	North Carolina	1,184.8
2	Arkansas	1,093.5
3	New Mexico	1,046.8
4	South Carolina	1,034.4
5	Tennessee	1,020.3
6	Louisiana	1,004.5
7	Oklahoma	1,000.2
8	Nevada	991.2
9	Arizona	990.4
10	Alabama	986.0
11	Texas	978.7
12	Washington	977.3
13	Florida	956.1
14	Mississippi	952.9
15	Georgia	940.0
16	Hawaii	857.4
17	Ohio	846.1
18	Oregon	836.6
19	Kansas	731.1
20	Colorado	717.3
21	Missouri	703.3
22	California	685.1
23	Indiana	676.0
24	Maryland	660.0
25	Delaware	648.3
26	Utah	637.1
27	Michigan	636.8
28	Kentucky	624.8
29	Iowa	615.1
30	West Virginia	602.2
31	Illinois	597.3
32	Alaska	575.6
33	Nebraska	562.4
34	Minnesota	549.9
35	Idaho	547.3
36	Vermont	544.9
37	Wyoming	540.5
38	Massachusetts	537.2
39	Rhode Island	505.7
40	Maine	481.4
41	New Jersey	471.7
42	Connecticut	444.4
43	Pennsylvania	438.8
44	Wisconsin	433.0
45	South Dakota	408.5
46	Virginia	386.0
47	New Hampshire	382.1
48	Montana	379.2
49	New York	367.7
50	North Dakota	301.1
	District of Columbia	712.9

Source: Federal Bureau of Investigation
"Crime in the United States 2004" (Uniform Crime Reports, October 17, 2005)
*Burglary is the unlawful entry of a structure to commit a felony or theft. Attempts are included.

Percent Change in Burglary Rate: 2003 to 2004

National Percent Change = 1.5% Decrease*

ALPHA ORDER

RANK	STATE	PERCENT CHANGE
12	Alabama	2.7
33	Alaska	(3.7)
38	Arizona	(5.7)
1	Arkansas	19.2
21	California	0.3
17	Colorado	0.7
30	Connecticut	(3.4)
50	Delaware	(12.6)
37	Florida	(4.8)
10	Georgia	3.2
42	Hawaii	(6.2)
36	Idaho	(4.5)
31	Illinois	(3.6)
16	Indiana	0.8
9	Iowa	3.3
47	Kansas	(9.3)
23	Kentucky	(1.2)
14	Louisiana	1.3
34	Maine	(4.2)
40	Maryland	(5.9)
24	Massachusetts	(1.4)
41	Michigan	(6.0)
20	Minnesota	0.5
46	Mississippi	(7.1)
34	Missouri	(4.2)
44	Montana	(6.4)
31	Nebraska	(3.6)
15	Nevada	1.2
4	New Hampshire	7.3
42	New Jersey	(6.2)
8	New Mexico	3.5
44	New York	(6.4)
22	North Carolina	(0.9)
29	North Dakota	(2.6)
13	Ohio	1.8
17	Oklahoma	0.7
5	Oregon	4.4
17	Pennsylvania	0.7
25	Rhode Island	(1.5)
28	South Carolina	(2.5)
3	South Dakota	8.6
39	Tennessee	(5.8)
26	Texas	(1.6)
49	Utah	(11.6)
2	Vermont	11.9
27	Virginia	(2.3)
11	Washington	2.8
6	West Virginia	3.9
48	Wisconsin	(10.7)
6	Wyoming	3.9

RANK ORDER

RANK	STATE	PERCENT CHANGE
1	Arkansas	19.2
2	Vermont	11.9
3	South Dakota	8.6
4	New Hampshire	7.3
5	Oregon	4.4
6	West Virginia	3.9
6	Wyoming	3.9
8	New Mexico	3.5
9	Iowa	3.3
10	Georgia	3.2
11	Washington	2.8
12	Alabama	2.7
13	Ohio	1.8
14	Louisiana	1.3
15	Nevada	1.2
16	Indiana	0.8
17	Colorado	0.7
17	Oklahoma	0.7
17	Pennsylvania	0.7
20	Minnesota	0.5
21	California	0.3
22	North Carolina	(0.9)
23	Kentucky	(1.2)
24	Massachusetts	(1.4)
25	Rhode Island	(1.5)
26	Texas	(1.6)
27	Virginia	(2.3)
28	South Carolina	(2.5)
29	North Dakota	(2.6)
30	Connecticut	(3.4)
31	Illinois	(3.6)
31	Nebraska	(3.6)
33	Alaska	(3.7)
34	Maine	(4.2)
34	Missouri	(4.2)
36	Idaho	(4.5)
37	Florida	(4.8)
38	Arizona	(5.7)
39	Tennessee	(5.8)
40	Maryland	(5.9)
41	Michigan	(6.0)
42	Hawaii	(6.2)
42	New Jersey	(6.2)
44	Montana	(6.4)
44	New York	(6.4)
46	Mississippi	(7.1)
47	Kansas	(9.3)
48	Wisconsin	(10.7)
49	Utah	(11.6)
50	Delaware	(12.6)
	District of Columbia	(14.9)

Source: Federal Bureau of Investigation
"Crime in the United States 2004" (Uniform Crime Reports, October 17, 2005)
*Burglary is the unlawful entry of a structure to commit a felony or theft. Attempts are included.

384

Larcenies and Thefts in 2004

National Total = 6,947,685 Larcenies and Thefts*

ALPHA ORDER

RANK	STATE	THEFTS	% of USA
21	Alabama	123,650	1.8%
46	Alaska	16,159	0.2%
11	Arizona	194,556	2.8%
30	Arkansas	73,874	1.1%
1	California	728,687	10.5%
22	Colorado	123,271	1.8%
32	Connecticut	65,451	0.9%
45	Delaware	18,742	0.3%
3	Florida	482,484	6.9%
7	Georgia	249,426	3.6%
38	Hawaii	41,078	0.6%
40	Idaho	28,583	0.4%
5	Illinois	288,771	4.2%
16	Indiana	148,670	2.1%
34	Iowa	62,258	0.9%
28	Kansas	80,260	1.2%
31	Kentucky	70,535	1.0%
18	Louisiana	134,080	1.9%
41	Maine	24,096	0.3%
20	Maryland	129,786	1.9%
26	Massachusetts	101,303	1.5%
12	Michigan	194,259	2.8%
24	Minnesota	113,453	1.6%
33	Mississippi	65,440	0.9%
14	Missouri	158,264	2.3%
42	Montana	22,082	0.3%
37	Nebraska	46,399	0.7%
35	Nevada	52,438	0.8%
44	New Hampshire	19,603	0.3%
17	New Jersey	139,977	2.0%
36	New Mexico	52,069	0.7%
4	New York	311,036	4.5%
8	North Carolina	227,147	3.3%
50	North Dakota	9,342	0.1%
6	Ohio	283,103	4.1%
27	Oklahoma	101,271	1.5%
23	Oregon	117,868	1.7%
9	Pennsylvania	214,199	3.1%
43	Rhode Island	21,623	0.3%
19	South Carolina	130,051	1.9%
48	South Dakota	10,910	0.2%
13	Tennessee	169,169	2.4%
2	Texas	696,507	10.0%
29	Utah	74,735	1.1%
49	Vermont	10,382	0.1%
15	Virginia	153,464	2.2%
10	Washington	196,972	2.8%
39	West Virginia	30,826	0.4%
25	Wisconsin	111,482	1.6%
47	Wyoming	13,352	0.2%

RANK ORDER

RANK	STATE	THEFTS	% of USA
1	California	728,687	10.5%
2	Texas	696,507	10.0%
3	Florida	482,484	6.9%
4	New York	311,036	4.5%
5	Illinois	288,771	4.2%
6	Ohio	283,103	4.1%
7	Georgia	249,426	3.6%
8	North Carolina	227,147	3.3%
9	Pennsylvania	214,199	3.1%
10	Washington	196,972	2.8%
11	Arizona	194,556	2.8%
12	Michigan	194,259	2.8%
13	Tennessee	169,169	2.4%
14	Missouri	158,264	2.3%
15	Virginia	153,464	2.2%
16	Indiana	148,670	2.1%
17	New Jersey	139,977	2.0%
18	Louisiana	134,080	1.9%
19	South Carolina	130,051	1.9%
20	Maryland	129,786	1.9%
21	Alabama	123,650	1.8%
22	Colorado	123,271	1.8%
23	Oregon	117,868	1.7%
24	Minnesota	113,453	1.6%
25	Wisconsin	111,482	1.6%
26	Massachusetts	101,303	1.5%
27	Oklahoma	101,271	1.5%
28	Kansas	80,260	1.2%
29	Utah	74,735	1.1%
30	Arkansas	73,874	1.1%
31	Kentucky	70,535	1.0%
32	Connecticut	65,451	0.9%
33	Mississippi	65,440	0.9%
34	Iowa	62,258	0.9%
35	Nevada	52,438	0.8%
36	New Mexico	52,069	0.7%
37	Nebraska	46,399	0.7%
38	Hawaii	41,078	0.6%
39	West Virginia	30,826	0.4%
40	Idaho	28,583	0.4%
41	Maine	24,096	0.3%
42	Montana	22,082	0.3%
43	Rhode Island	21,623	0.3%
44	New Hampshire	19,603	0.3%
45	Delaware	18,742	0.3%
46	Alaska	16,159	0.2%
47	Wyoming	13,352	0.2%
48	South Dakota	10,910	0.2%
49	Vermont	10,382	0.1%
50	North Dakota	9,342	0.1%
	District of Columbia	14,542	0.2%

Source: Federal Bureau of Investigation
   "Crime in the United States 2004" (Uniform Crime Reports, October 17, 2005)
*Larceny and theft is the unlawful taking of property without use of force, violence or fraud. Attempts are included.
Motor vehicle thefts are excluded.

Average Time Between Larcenies and Thefts in 2004

National Rate = A Larceny Occurs Every 5 Seconds*

ALPHA ORDER

RANK	STATE	MINUTES.SECONDS
30	Alabama	4.16
5	Alaska	32.37
39	Arizona	2.43
21	Arkansas	7.08
50	California	0.43
29	Colorado	4.17
18	Connecticut	8.03
6	Delaware	28.07
48	Florida	1.05
44	Georgia	2.07
13	Hawaii	12.50
11	Idaho	18.26
46	Illinois	1.50
35	Indiana	3.33
17	Iowa	8.28
23	Kansas	6.34
20	Kentucky	7.28
33	Louisiana	3.56
10	Maine	21.52
31	Maryland	4.04
24	Massachusetts	5.12
39	Michigan	2.43
27	Minnesota	4.39
18	Mississippi	8.03
37	Missouri	3.20
9	Montana	23.52
14	Nebraska	11.22
16	Nevada	10.03
7	New Hampshire	26.53
34	New Jersey	3.46
15	New Mexico	10.07
47	New York	1.41
43	North Carolina	2.19
1	North Dakota	56.25
45	Ohio	1.52
24	Oklahoma	5.12
28	Oregon	4.28
42	Pennsylvania	2.28
8	Rhode Island	24.22
32	South Carolina	4.03
3	South Dakota	48.19
38	Tennessee	3.07
49	Texas	0.46
22	Utah	7.03
2	Vermont	50.46
36	Virginia	3.26
41	Washington	2.41
12	West Virginia	17.06
26	Wisconsin	4.44
4	Wyoming	39.28

RANK ORDER

RANK	STATE	MINUTES.SECONDS
1	North Dakota	56.25
2	Vermont	50.46
3	South Dakota	48.19
4	Wyoming	39.28
5	Alaska	32.37
6	Delaware	28.07
7	New Hampshire	26.53
8	Rhode Island	24.22
9	Montana	23.52
10	Maine	21.52
11	Idaho	18.26
12	West Virginia	17.06
13	Hawaii	12.50
14	Nebraska	11.22
15	New Mexico	10.07
16	Nevada	10.03
17	Iowa	8.28
18	Connecticut	8.03
18	Mississippi	8.03
20	Kentucky	7.28
21	Arkansas	7.08
22	Utah	7.03
23	Kansas	6.34
24	Massachusetts	5.12
24	Oklahoma	5.12
26	Wisconsin	4.44
27	Minnesota	4.39
28	Oregon	4.28
29	Colorado	4.17
30	Alabama	4.16
31	Maryland	4.04
32	South Carolina	4.03
33	Louisiana	3.56
34	New Jersey	3.46
35	Indiana	3.33
36	Virginia	3.26
37	Missouri	3.20
38	Tennessee	3.07
39	Arizona	2.43
39	Michigan	2.43
41	Washington	2.41
42	Pennsylvania	2.28
43	North Carolina	2.19
44	Georgia	2.07
45	Ohio	1.52
46	Illinois	1.50
47	New York	1.41
48	Florida	1.05
49	Texas	0.46
50	California	0.43

District of Columbia 36.14

Source: Morgan Quitno Press using data from Federal Bureau of Investigation
"Crime in the United States 2004" (Uniform Crime Reports, October 17, 2005)
*Larceny and theft is the unlawful taking of property without use of force, violence or fraud. Attempts are included.
Motor vehicle thefts are excluded.

Percent Change in Number of Larcenies and Thefts: 2003 to 2004

National Percent Change = 1.1% Decrease*

ALPHA ORDER			RANK ORDER		
RANK	STATE	PERCENT CHANGE	RANK	STATE	PERCENT CHANGE
20	Alabama	(0.3)	1	Arkansas	8.5
50	Alaska	(10.5)	1	West Virginia	8.5
29	Arizona	(2.1)	3	Louisiana	3.6
1	Arkansas	8.5	4	New Mexico	2.9
22	California	(0.4)	5	Vermont	2.5
24	Colorado	(1.0)	6	Washington	2.2
19	Connecticut	(0.2)	7	Kentucky	2.1
24	Delaware	(1.0)	8	Indiana	2.0
43	Florida	(4.6)	9	South Carolina	1.8
12	Georgia	0.9	10	Tennessee	1.4
48	Hawaii	(8.3)	11	Kansas	1.0
38	Idaho	(3.3)	12	Georgia	0.9
33	Illinois	(2.4)	12	Wyoming	0.9
8	Indiana	2.0	14	Ohio	0.6
38	Iowa	(3.3)	15	Pennsylvania	0.4
11	Kansas	1.0	16	Maine	0.2
7	Kentucky	2.1	17	Virginia	0.1
3	Louisiana	3.6	18	New York	(0.1)
16	Maine	0.2	19	Connecticut	(0.2)
40	Maryland	(3.4)	20	Alabama	(0.3)
35	Massachusetts	(2.7)	20	Texas	(0.3)
47	Michigan	(6.8)	22	California	(0.4)
33	Minnesota	(2.4)	23	Utah	(0.8)
42	Mississippi	(4.2)	24	Colorado	(1.0)
29	Missouri	(2.1)	24	Delaware	(1.0)
36	Montana	(3.1)	26	New Jersey	(1.6)
44	Nebraska	(5.2)	27	Nevada	(1.7)
27	Nevada	(1.7)	27	New Hampshire	(1.7)
27	New Hampshire	(1.7)	29	Arizona	(2.1)
26	New Jersey	(1.6)	29	Missouri	(2.1)
4	New Mexico	2.9	29	North Carolina	(2.1)
18	New York	(0.1)	29	Oklahoma	(2.1)
29	North Carolina	(2.1)	33	Illinois	(2.4)
49	North Dakota	(9.5)	33	Minnesota	(2.4)
14	Ohio	0.6	35	Massachusetts	(2.7)
29	Oklahoma	(2.1)	36	Montana	(3.1)
41	Oregon	(3.6)	36	Rhode Island	(3.1)
15	Pennsylvania	0.4	38	Idaho	(3.3)
36	Rhode Island	(3.1)	38	Iowa	(3.3)
9	South Carolina	1.8	40	Maryland	(3.4)
45	South Dakota	(5.7)	41	Oregon	(3.6)
10	Tennessee	1.4	42	Mississippi	(4.2)
20	Texas	(0.3)	43	Florida	(4.6)
23	Utah	(0.8)	44	Nebraska	(5.2)
5	Vermont	2.5	45	South Dakota	(5.7)
17	Virginia	0.1	46	Wisconsin	(6.1)
6	Washington	2.2	47	Michigan	(6.8)
1	West Virginia	8.5	48	Hawaii	(8.3)
46	Wisconsin	(6.1)	49	North Dakota	(9.5)
12	Wyoming	0.9	50	Alaska	(10.5)

District of Columbia (19.7)

Source: Federal Bureau of Investigation
   "Crime in the United States 2004" (Uniform Crime Reports, October 17, 2005)
*Larceny and theft is the unlawful taking of property without use of force, violence or fraud. Attempts are included.
Motor vehicle thefts are excluded.

Larceny and Theft Rate in 2004

National Rate = 2,365.9 Larcenies and Thefts per 100,000 Population*

ALPHA ORDER

RANK	STATE	RATE
16	Alabama	2,729.5
23	Alaska	2,465.4
1	Arizona	3,387.2
17	Arkansas	2,683.8
35	California	2,030.1
18	Colorado	2,679.0
39	Connecticut	1,868.1
28	Delaware	2,257.1
13	Florida	2,773.3
12	Georgia	2,825.0
3	Hawaii	3,252.8
34	Idaho	2,051.5
27	Illinois	2,271.3
24	Indiana	2,383.5
32	Iowa	2,107.3
9	Kansas	2,934.0
42	Kentucky	1,701.3
8	Louisiana	2,969.2
40	Maine	1,829.3
26	Maryland	2,335.1
47	Massachusetts	1,578.8
38	Michigan	1,921.0
31	Minnesota	2,224.2
29	Mississippi	2,254.2
14	Missouri	2,750.2
25	Montana	2,382.4
20	Nebraska	2,655.6
30	Nevada	2,246.0
48	New Hampshire	1,508.5
46	New Jersey	1,609.1
15	New Mexico	2,735.7
45	New York	1,617.7
19	North Carolina	2,659.4
49	North Dakota	1,472.7
22	Ohio	2,470.6
10	Oklahoma	2,874.1
2	Oregon	3,279.0
41	Pennsylvania	1,726.5
37	Rhode Island	2,001.0
6	South Carolina	3,097.9
50	South Dakota	1,415.3
11	Tennessee	2,866.8
7	Texas	3,097.0
5	Utah	3,128.2
44	Vermont	1,670.8
33	Virginia	2,057.2
4	Washington	3,175.0
43	West Virginia	1,698.1
36	Wisconsin	2,023.6
21	Wyoming	2,636.0

RANK ORDER

RANK	STATE	RATE
1	Arizona	3,387.2
2	Oregon	3,279.0
3	Hawaii	3,252.8
4	Washington	3,175.0
5	Utah	3,128.2
6	South Carolina	3,097.9
7	Texas	3,097.0
8	Louisiana	2,969.2
9	Kansas	2,934.0
10	Oklahoma	2,874.1
11	Tennessee	2,866.8
12	Georgia	2,825.0
13	Florida	2,773.3
14	Missouri	2,750.2
15	New Mexico	2,735.7
16	Alabama	2,729.5
17	Arkansas	2,683.8
18	Colorado	2,679.0
19	North Carolina	2,659.4
20	Nebraska	2,655.6
21	Wyoming	2,636.0
22	Ohio	2,470.6
23	Alaska	2,465.4
24	Indiana	2,383.5
25	Montana	2,382.4
26	Maryland	2,335.1
27	Illinois	2,271.3
28	Delaware	2,257.1
29	Mississippi	2,254.2
30	Nevada	2,246.0
31	Minnesota	2,224.2
32	Iowa	2,107.3
33	Virginia	2,057.2
34	Idaho	2,051.5
35	California	2,030.1
36	Wisconsin	2,023.6
37	Rhode Island	2,001.0
38	Michigan	1,921.0
39	Connecticut	1,868.1
40	Maine	1,829.3
41	Pennsylvania	1,726.5
42	Kentucky	1,701.3
43	West Virginia	1,698.1
44	Vermont	1,670.8
45	New York	1,617.7
46	New Jersey	1,609.1
47	Massachusetts	1,578.8
48	New Hampshire	1,508.5
49	North Dakota	1,472.7
50	South Dakota	1,415.3

District of Columbia	2,627.2

Source: Federal Bureau of Investigation
"Crime in the United States 2004" (Uniform Crime Reports, October 17, 2005)
*Larceny and theft is the unlawful taking of property without use of force, violence or fraud. Attempts are included. Motor vehicle thefts are excluded.

Percent Change in Larceny and Theft Rate: 2003 to 2004

National Percent Change = 2.1% Decrease*

RANK	STATE	PERCENT CHANGE
19	Alabama	(0.9)
50	Alaska	(11.5)
39	Arizona	(4.9)
2	Arkansas	7.6
21	California	(1.6)
23	Colorado	(2.1)
17	Connecticut	(0.7)
26	Delaware	(2.5)
45	Florida	(6.7)
18	Georgia	(0.8)
48	Hawaii	(9.3)
41	Idaho	(5.1)
31	Illinois	(2.9)
6	Indiana	1.4
35	Iowa	(3.7)
9	Kansas	0.6
6	Kentucky	1.4
3	Louisiana	3.1
16	Maine	(0.4)
37	Maryland	(4.2)
29	Massachusetts	(2.6)
47	Michigan	(7.1)
32	Minnesota	(3.1)
39	Mississippi	(4.9)
30	Missouri	(2.7)
36	Montana	(4.1)
43	Nebraska	(5.7)
42	Nevada	(5.6)
26	New Hampshire	(2.5)
24	New Jersey	(2.3)
5	New Mexico	1.6
15	New York	(0.2)
33	North Carolina	(3.5)
49	North Dakota	(9.7)
12	Ohio	0.4
26	Oklahoma	(2.5)
38	Oregon	(4.5)
13	Pennsylvania	0.1
33	Rhode Island	(3.5)
9	South Carolina	0.6
44	South Dakota	(6.5)
11	Tennessee	0.5
22	Texas	(2.0)
24	Utah	(2.3)
4	Vermont	2.1
20	Virginia	(1.2)
8	Washington	1.0
1	West Virginia	8.3
45	Wisconsin	(6.7)
14	Wyoming	0.0

RANK	STATE	PERCENT CHANGE
1	West Virginia	8.3
2	Arkansas	7.6
3	Louisiana	3.1
4	Vermont	2.1
5	New Mexico	1.6
6	Indiana	1.4
6	Kentucky	1.4
8	Washington	1.0
9	Kansas	0.6
9	South Carolina	0.6
11	Tennessee	0.5
12	Ohio	0.4
13	Pennsylvania	0.1
14	Wyoming	0.0
15	New York	(0.2)
16	Maine	(0.4)
17	Connecticut	(0.7)
18	Georgia	(0.8)
19	Alabama	(0.9)
20	Virginia	(1.2)
21	California	(1.6)
22	Texas	(2.0)
23	Colorado	(2.1)
24	New Jersey	(2.3)
24	Utah	(2.3)
26	Delaware	(2.5)
26	New Hampshire	(2.5)
26	Oklahoma	(2.5)
29	Massachusetts	(2.6)
30	Missouri	(2.7)
31	Illinois	(2.9)
32	Minnesota	(3.1)
33	North Carolina	(3.5)
33	Rhode Island	(3.5)
35	Iowa	(3.7)
36	Montana	(4.1)
37	Maryland	(4.2)
38	Oregon	(4.5)
39	Arizona	(4.9)
39	Mississippi	(4.9)
41	Idaho	(5.1)
42	Nevada	(5.6)
43	Nebraska	(5.7)
44	South Dakota	(6.5)
45	Florida	(6.7)
45	Wisconsin	(6.7)
47	Michigan	(7.1)
48	Hawaii	(9.3)
49	North Dakota	(9.7)
50	Alaska	(11.5)

District of Columbia (19.1)

Source: Federal Bureau of Investigation
    "Crime in the United States 2004" (Uniform Crime Reports, October 17, 2005)
*Larceny and theft is the unlawful taking of property without use of force, violence or fraud. Attempts are included.
Motor vehicle thefts are excluded.

Motor Vehicle Thefts in 2004

National Total = 1,237,114 Motor Vehicle Thefts*

RANK	STATE	THEFTS	% of USA
25	Alabama	14,024	1.1%
42	Alaska	2,240	0.2%
4	Arizona	55,306	4.5%
36	Arkansas	6,491	0.5%
1	California	252,604	20.4%
17	Colorado	24,063	1.9%
29	Connecticut	11,025	0.9%
43	Delaware	2,147	0.2%
3	Florida	78,325	6.3%
6	Georgia	44,238	3.6%
31	Hawaii	8,620	0.7%
41	Idaho	2,724	0.2%
10	Illinois	40,355	3.3%
20	Indiana	21,091	1.7%
37	Iowa	5,404	0.4%
32	Kansas	8,435	0.7%
30	Kentucky	8,772	0.7%
21	Louisiana	19,714	1.6%
46	Maine	1,303	0.1%
11	Maryland	35,858	2.9%
19	Massachusetts	22,053	1.8%
5	Michigan	50,555	4.1%
26	Minnesota	13,518	1.1%
34	Mississippi	7,879	0.6%
15	Missouri	25,893	2.1%
45	Montana	1,618	0.1%
38	Nebraska	5,287	0.4%
18	Nevada	22,635	1.8%
44	New Hampshire	1,942	0.2%
13	New Jersey	30,306	2.4%
33	New Mexico	7,902	0.6%
8	New York	41,002	3.3%
14	North Carolina	26,988	2.2%
47	North Dakota	906	0.1%
9	Ohio	40,853	3.3%
27	Oklahoma	12,957	1.0%
22	Oregon	18,535	1.5%
12	Pennsylvania	30,969	2.5%
39	Rhode Island	4,078	0.3%
24	South Carolina	15,637	1.3%
48	South Dakota	846	0.1%
16	Tennessee	24,749	2.0%
2	Texas	94,077	7.6%
35	Utah	7,651	0.6%
50	Vermont	575	0.0%
23	Virginia	17,411	1.4%
7	Washington	43,233	3.5%
40	West Virginia	3,739	0.3%
28	Wisconsin	11,374	0.9%
49	Wyoming	799	0.1%

RANK	STATE	THEFTS	% of USA
1	California	252,604	20.4%
2	Texas	94,077	7.6%
3	Florida	78,325	6.3%
4	Arizona	55,306	4.5%
5	Michigan	50,555	4.1%
6	Georgia	44,238	3.6%
7	Washington	43,233	3.5%
8	New York	41,002	3.3%
9	Ohio	40,853	3.3%
10	Illinois	40,355	3.3%
11	Maryland	35,858	2.9%
12	Pennsylvania	30,969	2.5%
13	New Jersey	30,306	2.4%
14	North Carolina	26,988	2.2%
15	Missouri	25,893	2.1%
16	Tennessee	24,749	2.0%
17	Colorado	24,063	1.9%
18	Nevada	22,635	1.8%
19	Massachusetts	22,053	1.8%
20	Indiana	21,091	1.7%
21	Louisiana	19,714	1.6%
22	Oregon	18,535	1.5%
23	Virginia	17,411	1.4%
24	South Carolina	15,637	1.3%
25	Alabama	14,024	1.1%
26	Minnesota	13,518	1.1%
27	Oklahoma	12,957	1.0%
28	Wisconsin	11,374	0.9%
29	Connecticut	11,025	0.9%
30	Kentucky	8,772	0.7%
31	Hawaii	8,620	0.7%
32	Kansas	8,435	0.7%
33	New Mexico	7,902	0.6%
34	Mississippi	7,879	0.6%
35	Utah	7,651	0.6%
36	Arkansas	6,491	0.5%
37	Iowa	5,404	0.4%
38	Nebraska	5,287	0.4%
39	Rhode Island	4,078	0.3%
40	West Virginia	3,739	0.3%
41	Idaho	2,724	0.2%
42	Alaska	2,240	0.2%
43	Delaware	2,147	0.2%
44	New Hampshire	1,942	0.2%
45	Montana	1,618	0.1%
46	Maine	1,303	0.1%
47	North Dakota	906	0.1%
48	South Dakota	846	0.1%
49	Wyoming	799	0.1%
50	Vermont	575	0.0%
	District of Columbia	8,408	0.7%

Source: Federal Bureau of Investigation
"Crime in the United States 2004" (Uniform Crime Reports, October 17, 2005)
*Includes the theft or attempted theft of a self-propelled vehicle. Excludes motorboats, construction equipment, airplanes and farming equipment.

Average Time Between Motor Vehicle Thefts in 2004

National Rate = A Motor Vehicle Theft Occurs Every 26 Seconds*

ALPHA ORDER

RANK	STATE	MINUTES.SECONDS
26	Alabama	37.35
9	Alaska	235.17
47	Arizona	9.32
15	Arkansas	81.12
50	California	2.05
34	Colorado	21.54
22	Connecticut	47.48
8	Delaware	245.29
48	Florida	6.44
45	Georgia	11.55
20	Hawaii	61.08
10	Idaho	193.29
41	Illinois	13.04
31	Indiana	24.59
14	Iowa	97.32
19	Kansas	62.29
21	Kentucky	60.05
30	Louisiana	26.44
5	Maine	404.29
40	Maryland	14.42
32	Massachusetts	23.54
46	Michigan	10.26
25	Minnesota	38.59
17	Mississippi	66.53
36	Missouri	20.21
6	Montana	325.44
13	Nebraska	99.41
33	Nevada	23.17
7	New Hampshire	271.23
38	New Jersey	17.23
18	New Mexico	66.42
43	New York	12.51
37	North Carolina	19.32
4	North Dakota	581.43
42	Ohio	12.54
24	Oklahoma	40.41
29	Oregon	28.26
39	Pennsylvania	17.01
12	Rhode Island	129.14
27	South Carolina	33.42
3	South Dakota	622.59
35	Tennessee	21.18
49	Texas	5.36
16	Utah	68.53
1	Vermont	916.35
28	Virginia	30.16
44	Washington	12.11
11	West Virginia	140.58
23	Wisconsin	46.20
2	Wyoming	659.37

RANK ORDER

RANK	STATE	MINUTES.SECONDS
1	Vermont	916.35
2	Wyoming	659.37
3	South Dakota	622.59
4	North Dakota	581.43
5	Maine	404.29
6	Montana	325.44
7	New Hampshire	271.23
8	Delaware	245.29
9	Alaska	235.17
10	Idaho	193.29
11	West Virginia	140.58
12	Rhode Island	129.14
13	Nebraska	99.41
14	Iowa	97.32
15	Arkansas	81.12
16	Utah	68.53
17	Mississippi	66.53
18	New Mexico	66.42
19	Kansas	62.29
20	Hawaii	61.08
21	Kentucky	60.05
22	Connecticut	47.48
23	Wisconsin	46.20
24	Oklahoma	40.41
25	Minnesota	38.59
26	Alabama	37.35
27	South Carolina	33.42
28	Virginia	30.16
29	Oregon	28.26
30	Louisiana	26.44
31	Indiana	24.59
32	Massachusetts	23.54
33	Nevada	23.17
34	Colorado	21.54
35	Tennessee	21.18
36	Missouri	20.21
37	North Carolina	19.32
38	New Jersey	17.23
39	Pennsylvania	17.01
40	Maryland	14.42
41	Illinois	13.04
42	Ohio	12.54
43	New York	12.51
44	Washington	12.11
45	Georgia	11.55
46	Michigan	10.26
47	Arizona	9.32
48	Florida	6.44
49	Texas	5.36
50	California	2.05

District of Columbia 62.41

Source: Morgan Quitno Press using data from Federal Bureau of Investigation
"Crime in the United States 2004" (Uniform Crime Reports, October 17, 2005)
*Includes the theft or attempted theft of a self-propelled vehicle. Excludes motorboats, construction equipment, airplanes and farming equipment.

Percent Change in Number of Motor Vehicle Thefts: 2003 to 2004

National Percent Change = 1.9% Decrease*

ALPHA ORDER

RANK	STATE	PERCENT CHANGE
33	Alabama	(6.2)
38	Alaska	(9.0)
24	Arizona	(3.0)
3	Arkansas	8.1
9	California	4.7
8	Colorado	5.5
24	Connecticut	(3.0)
50	Delaware	(27.1)
29	Florida	(4.0)
11	Georgia	1.9
41	Hawaii	(10.7)
10	Idaho	2.9
26	Illinois	(3.1)
12	Indiana	1.5
30	Iowa	(4.2)
5	Kansas	7.7
7	Kentucky	6.3
15	Louisiana	0.3
40	Maine	(10.5)
20	Maryland	(1.5)
46	Massachusetts	(13.6)
32	Michigan	(5.9)
21	Minnesota	(1.7)
43	Mississippi	(12.4)
45	Missouri	(13.5)
48	Montana	(15.1)
47	Nebraska	(13.8)
2	Nevada	8.6
13	New Hampshire	0.5
43	New Jersey	(12.4)
1	New Mexico	9.4
39	New York	(9.3)
14	North Carolina	0.4
49	North Dakota	(16.0)
18	Ohio	(0.4)
17	Oklahoma	0.0
23	Oregon	(2.3)
36	Pennsylvania	(7.4)
35	Rhode Island	(7.0)
19	South Carolina	(1.0)
28	South Dakota	(3.2)
34	Tennessee	(6.5)
30	Texas	(4.2)
22	Utah	(1.9)
42	Vermont	(12.1)
26	Virginia	(3.1)
6	Washington	6.4
4	West Virginia	8.0
37	Wisconsin	(8.0)
16	Wyoming	0.1

RANK ORDER

RANK	STATE	PERCENT CHANGE
1	New Mexico	9.4
2	Nevada	8.6
3	Arkansas	8.1
4	West Virginia	8.0
5	Kansas	7.7
6	Washington	6.4
7	Kentucky	6.3
8	Colorado	5.5
9	California	4.7
10	Idaho	2.9
11	Georgia	1.9
12	Indiana	1.5
13	New Hampshire	0.5
14	North Carolina	0.4
15	Louisiana	0.3
16	Wyoming	0.1
17	Oklahoma	0.0
18	Ohio	(0.4)
19	South Carolina	(1.0)
20	Maryland	(1.5)
21	Minnesota	(1.7)
22	Utah	(1.9)
23	Oregon	(2.3)
24	Arizona	(3.0)
24	Connecticut	(3.0)
26	Illinois	(3.1)
26	Virginia	(3.1)
28	South Dakota	(3.2)
29	Florida	(4.0)
30	Iowa	(4.2)
30	Texas	(4.2)
32	Michigan	(5.9)
33	Alabama	(6.2)
34	Tennessee	(6.5)
35	Rhode Island	(7.0)
36	Pennsylvania	(7.4)
37	Wisconsin	(8.0)
38	Alaska	(9.0)
39	New York	(9.3)
40	Maine	(10.5)
41	Hawaii	(10.7)
42	Vermont	(12.1)
43	Mississippi	(12.4)
43	New Jersey	(12.4)
45	Missouri	(13.5)
46	Massachusetts	(13.6)
47	Nebraska	(13.8)
48	Montana	(15.1)
49	North Dakota	(16.0)
50	Delaware	(27.1)

District of Columbia   (15.1)

Source: Federal Bureau of Investigation
"Crime in the United States 2004" (Uniform Crime Reports, October 17, 2005)
Includes the theft or attempted theft of a self-propelled vehicle. Excludes motorboats, construction equipment, airplanes and farming equipment.

Motor Vehicle Theft Rate in 2004

National Rate = 421.3 Motor Vehicle Thefts per 100,000 Population*

ALPHA ORDER

RANK	STATE	RATE
29	Alabama	309.6
23	Alaska	341.8
2	Arizona	962.9
36	Arkansas	235.8
3	California	703.8
7	Colorado	522.9
28	Connecticut	314.7
34	Delaware	258.6
11	Florida	450.2
9	Georgia	501.0
5	Hawaii	682.6
42	Idaho	195.5
26	Illinois	317.4
24	Indiana	338.1
43	Iowa	182.9
30	Kansas	308.4
39	Kentucky	211.6
13	Louisiana	436.6
49	Maine	98.9
6	Maryland	645.2
22	Massachusetts	343.7
10	Michigan	499.9
33	Minnesota	265.0
32	Mississippi	271.4
12	Missouri	450.0
44	Montana	174.6
31	Nebraska	302.6
1	Nevada	969.5
46	New Hampshire	149.4
21	New Jersey	348.4
16	New Mexico	415.2
38	New York	213.3
27	North Carolina	316.0
47	North Dakota	142.8
20	Ohio	356.5
19	Oklahoma	367.7
8	Oregon	515.6
35	Pennsylvania	249.6
17	Rhode Island	377.4
18	South Carolina	372.5
48	South Dakota	109.7
14	Tennessee	419.4
15	Texas	418.3
25	Utah	320.3
50	Vermont	92.5
37	Virginia	233.4
4	Washington	696.9
41	West Virginia	206.0
40	Wisconsin	206.5
45	Wyoming	157.7

RANK ORDER

RANK	STATE	RATE
1	Nevada	969.5
2	Arizona	962.9
3	California	703.8
4	Washington	696.9
5	Hawaii	682.6
6	Maryland	645.2
7	Colorado	522.9
8	Oregon	515.6
9	Georgia	501.0
10	Michigan	499.9
11	Florida	450.2
12	Missouri	450.0
13	Louisiana	436.6
14	Tennessee	419.4
15	Texas	418.3
16	New Mexico	415.2
17	Rhode Island	377.4
18	South Carolina	372.5
19	Oklahoma	367.7
20	Ohio	356.5
21	New Jersey	348.4
22	Massachusetts	343.7
23	Alaska	341.8
24	Indiana	338.1
25	Utah	320.3
26	Illinois	317.4
27	North Carolina	316.0
28	Connecticut	314.7
29	Alabama	309.6
30	Kansas	308.4
31	Nebraska	302.6
32	Mississippi	271.4
33	Minnesota	265.0
34	Delaware	258.6
35	Pennsylvania	249.6
36	Arkansas	235.8
37	Virginia	233.4
38	New York	213.3
39	Kentucky	211.6
40	Wisconsin	206.5
41	West Virginia	206.0
42	Idaho	195.5
43	Iowa	182.9
44	Montana	174.6
45	Wyoming	157.7
46	New Hampshire	149.4
47	North Dakota	142.8
48	South Dakota	109.7
49	Maine	98.9
50	Vermont	92.5
	District of Columbia	1,519.0

Source: Federal Bureau of Investigation
"Crime in the United States 2004" (Uniform Crime Reports, October 17, 2005)
*Includes the theft or attempted theft of a self-propelled vehicle. Excludes motorboats, construction equipment, airplanes and farming equipment.

Percent Change in Motor Vehicle Theft Rate: 2003 to 2004

National Percent Change = 2.9% Decrease*

<table>
<tr><td colspan="3">ALPHA ORDER</td><td colspan="3">RANK ORDER</td></tr>
<tr><td>RANK</td><td>STATE</td><td>PERCENT CHANGE</td><td>RANK</td><td>STATE</td><td>PERCENT CHANGE</td></tr>
<tr><td>33</td><td>Alabama</td><td>(6.8)</td><td>1</td><td>New Mexico</td><td>8.0</td></tr>
<tr><td>39</td><td>Alaska</td><td>(10.0)</td><td>2</td><td>West Virginia</td><td>7.7</td></tr>
<tr><td>29</td><td>Arizona</td><td>(5.7)</td><td>3</td><td>Kansas</td><td>7.3</td></tr>
<tr><td>4</td><td>Arkansas</td><td>7.1</td><td>4</td><td>Arkansas</td><td>7.1</td></tr>
<tr><td>9</td><td>California</td><td>3.4</td><td>5</td><td>Kentucky</td><td>5.6</td></tr>
<tr><td>8</td><td>Colorado</td><td>4.2</td><td>6</td><td>Washington</td><td>5.2</td></tr>
<tr><td>23</td><td>Connecticut</td><td>(3.5)</td><td>7</td><td>Nevada</td><td>4.3</td></tr>
<tr><td>50</td><td>Delaware</td><td>(28.1)</td><td>8</td><td>Colorado</td><td>4.2</td></tr>
<tr><td>31</td><td>Florida</td><td>(6.2)</td><td>9</td><td>California</td><td>3.4</td></tr>
<tr><td>12</td><td>Georgia</td><td>0.2</td><td>10</td><td>Idaho</td><td>1.0</td></tr>
<tr><td>41</td><td>Hawaii</td><td>(11.7)</td><td>11</td><td>Indiana</td><td>0.9</td></tr>
<tr><td>10</td><td>Idaho</td><td>1.0</td><td>12</td><td>Georgia</td><td>0.2</td></tr>
<tr><td>25</td><td>Illinois</td><td>(3.6)</td><td>13</td><td>Louisiana</td><td>(0.2)</td></tr>
<tr><td>11</td><td>Indiana</td><td>0.9</td><td>14</td><td>New Hampshire</td><td>(0.4)</td></tr>
<tr><td>28</td><td>Iowa</td><td>(4.6)</td><td>15</td><td>Oklahoma</td><td>(0.5)</td></tr>
<tr><td>3</td><td>Kansas</td><td>7.3</td><td>16</td><td>Ohio</td><td>(0.6)</td></tr>
<tr><td>5</td><td>Kentucky</td><td>5.6</td><td>17</td><td>Wyoming</td><td>(0.7)</td></tr>
<tr><td>13</td><td>Louisiana</td><td>(0.2)</td><td>18</td><td>North Carolina</td><td>(1.1)</td></tr>
<tr><td>40</td><td>Maine</td><td>(11.1)</td><td>19</td><td>South Carolina</td><td>(2.1)</td></tr>
<tr><td>20</td><td>Maryland</td><td>(2.3)</td><td>20</td><td>Maryland</td><td>(2.3)</td></tr>
<tr><td>45</td><td>Massachusetts</td><td>(13.5)</td><td>21</td><td>Minnesota</td><td>(2.4)</td></tr>
<tr><td>31</td><td>Michigan</td><td>(6.2)</td><td>22</td><td>Oregon</td><td>(3.1)</td></tr>
<tr><td>21</td><td>Minnesota</td><td>(2.4)</td><td>23</td><td>Connecticut</td><td>(3.5)</td></tr>
<tr><td>43</td><td>Mississippi</td><td>(13.0)</td><td>23</td><td>Utah</td><td>(3.5)</td></tr>
<tr><td>46</td><td>Missouri</td><td>(14.1)</td><td>25</td><td>Illinois</td><td>(3.6)</td></tr>
<tr><td>48</td><td>Montana</td><td>(15.9)</td><td>26</td><td>South Dakota</td><td>(4.0)</td></tr>
<tr><td>47</td><td>Nebraska</td><td>(14.3)</td><td>27</td><td>Virginia</td><td>(4.4)</td></tr>
<tr><td>7</td><td>Nevada</td><td>4.3</td><td>28</td><td>Iowa</td><td>(4.6)</td></tr>
<tr><td>14</td><td>New Hampshire</td><td>(0.4)</td><td>29</td><td>Arizona</td><td>(5.7)</td></tr>
<tr><td>43</td><td>New Jersey</td><td>(13.0)</td><td>30</td><td>Texas</td><td>(5.9)</td></tr>
<tr><td>1</td><td>New Mexico</td><td>8.0</td><td>31</td><td>Florida</td><td>(6.2)</td></tr>
<tr><td>38</td><td>New York</td><td>(9.4)</td><td>31</td><td>Michigan</td><td>(6.2)</td></tr>
<tr><td>18</td><td>North Carolina</td><td>(1.1)</td><td>33</td><td>Alabama</td><td>(6.8)</td></tr>
<tr><td>49</td><td>North Dakota</td><td>(16.1)</td><td>34</td><td>Rhode Island</td><td>(7.4)</td></tr>
<tr><td>16</td><td>Ohio</td><td>(0.6)</td><td>34</td><td>Tennessee</td><td>(7.4)</td></tr>
<tr><td>15</td><td>Oklahoma</td><td>(0.5)</td><td>36</td><td>Pennsylvania</td><td>(7.7)</td></tr>
<tr><td>22</td><td>Oregon</td><td>(3.1)</td><td>37</td><td>Wisconsin</td><td>(8.6)</td></tr>
<tr><td>36</td><td>Pennsylvania</td><td>(7.7)</td><td>38</td><td>New York</td><td>(9.4)</td></tr>
<tr><td>34</td><td>Rhode Island</td><td>(7.4)</td><td>39</td><td>Alaska</td><td>(10.0)</td></tr>
<tr><td>19</td><td>South Carolina</td><td>(2.1)</td><td>40</td><td>Maine</td><td>(11.1)</td></tr>
<tr><td>26</td><td>South Dakota</td><td>(4.0)</td><td>41</td><td>Hawaii</td><td>(11.7)</td></tr>
<tr><td>34</td><td>Tennessee</td><td>(7.4)</td><td>42</td><td>Vermont</td><td>(12.4)</td></tr>
<tr><td>30</td><td>Texas</td><td>(5.9)</td><td>43</td><td>Mississippi</td><td>(13.0)</td></tr>
<tr><td>23</td><td>Utah</td><td>(3.5)</td><td>43</td><td>New Jersey</td><td>(13.0)</td></tr>
<tr><td>42</td><td>Vermont</td><td>(12.4)</td><td>45</td><td>Massachusetts</td><td>(13.5)</td></tr>
<tr><td>27</td><td>Virginia</td><td>(4.4)</td><td>46</td><td>Missouri</td><td>(14.1)</td></tr>
<tr><td>6</td><td>Washington</td><td>5.2</td><td>47</td><td>Nebraska</td><td>(14.3)</td></tr>
<tr><td>2</td><td>West Virginia</td><td>7.7</td><td>48</td><td>Montana</td><td>(15.9)</td></tr>
<tr><td>37</td><td>Wisconsin</td><td>(8.6)</td><td>49</td><td>North Dakota</td><td>(16.1)</td></tr>
<tr><td>17</td><td>Wyoming</td><td>(0.7)</td><td>50</td><td>Delaware</td><td>(28.1)</td></tr>
<tr><td></td><td></td><td></td><td colspan="2">District of Columbia</td><td>(14.5)</td></tr>
</table>

Source: Federal Bureau of Investigation
  "Crime in the United States 2004" (Uniform Crime Reports, October 17, 2005)
*Includes the theft or attempted theft of a self-propelled vehicle. Excludes motorboats, construction equipment, airplanes and farming equipment.

Crimes in Urban Areas in 2004

National Urban Total = 11,119,511 Crimes*

ALPHA ORDER				RANK ORDER			
RANK	STATE	CRIMES	% of USA	RANK	STATE	CRIMES	% of USA
21	Alabama	191,082	1.7%	1	California	1,412,473	12.7%
45	Alaska	21,017	0.2%	2	Texas	1,102,477	9.9%
10	Arizona	327,715	2.9%	3	Florida	827,062	7.4%
27	Arkansas	113,743	1.0%	4	New York	490,986	4.4%
1	California	1,412,473	12.7%	5	Ohio	437,124	3.9%
19	Colorado	192,494	1.7%	6	Georgia	390,184	3.5%
31	Connecticut	96,899	0.9%	7	North Carolina	345,286	3.1%
43	Delaware	27,534	0.2%	8	Michigan	335,713	3.0%
3	Florida	827,062	7.4%	9	Pennsylvania	334,024	3.0%
6	Georgia	390,184	3.5%	10	Arizona	327,715	2.9%
37	Hawaii	46,628	0.4%	11	Washington	309,264	2.8%
39	Idaho	37,666	0.3%	12	Tennessee	271,395	2.4%
NA	Illinois**	NA	NA	13	New Jersey	242,256	2.2%
16	Indiana	219,356	2.0%	14	Missouri	237,500	2.1%
34	Iowa	87,844	0.8%	15	Maryland	236,930	2.1%
28	Kansas	110,743	1.0%	16	Indiana	219,356	2.0%
32	Kentucky	95,921	0.9%	17	Louisiana	211,365	1.9%
17	Louisiana	211,365	1.9%	18	Virginia	207,209	1.9%
41	Maine	29,027	0.3%	19	Colorado	192,494	1.7%
15	Maryland	236,930	2.1%	20	South Carolina	191,574	1.7%
22	Massachusetts	187,262	1.7%	21	Alabama	191,082	1.7%
8	Michigan	335,713	3.0%	22	Massachusetts	187,262	1.7%
25	Minnesota	154,289	1.4%	23	Oregon	166,780	1.5%
33	Mississippi	91,742	0.8%	24	Oklahoma	157,355	1.4%
14	Missouri	237,500	2.1%	25	Minnesota	154,289	1.4%
44	Montana	22,406	0.2%	26	Wisconsin	146,540	1.3%
36	Nebraska	62,476	0.6%	27	Arkansas	113,743	1.0%
29	Nevada	107,699	1.0%	28	Kansas	110,743	1.0%
42	New Hampshire	28,373	0.3%	29	Nevada	107,699	1.0%
13	New Jersey	242,256	2.2%	30	Utah	100,635	0.9%
35	New Mexico	86,056	0.8%	31	Connecticut	96,899	0.9%
4	New York	490,986	4.4%	32	Kentucky	95,921	0.9%
7	North Carolina	345,286	3.1%	33	Mississippi	91,742	0.8%
49	North Dakota	11,151	0.1%	34	Iowa	87,844	0.8%
5	Ohio	437,124	3.9%	35	New Mexico	86,056	0.8%
24	Oklahoma	157,355	1.4%	36	Nebraska	62,476	0.6%
23	Oregon	166,780	1.5%	37	Hawaii	46,628	0.4%
9	Pennsylvania	334,024	3.0%	38	West Virginia	40,594	0.4%
40	Rhode Island	33,792	0.3%	39	Idaho	37,666	0.3%
20	South Carolina	191,574	1.7%	40	Rhode Island	33,792	0.3%
47	South Dakota	14,961	0.1%	41	Maine	29,027	0.3%
12	Tennessee	271,395	2.4%	42	New Hampshire	28,373	0.3%
2	Texas	1,102,477	9.9%	43	Delaware	27,534	0.2%
30	Utah	100,635	0.9%	44	Montana	22,406	0.2%
48	Vermont	11,833	0.1%	45	Alaska	21,017	0.2%
18	Virginia	207,209	1.9%	46	Wyoming	15,470	0.1%
11	Washington	309,264	2.8%	47	South Dakota	14,961	0.1%
38	West Virginia	40,594	0.4%	48	Vermont	11,833	0.1%
26	Wisconsin	146,540	1.3%	49	North Dakota	11,151	0.1%
46	Wyoming	15,470	0.1%	NA	Illinois**	NA	NA
					District of Columbia	34,486	0.3%

Source: Morgan Quitno Press using data from Federal Bureau of Investigation
"Crime in the United States 2004" (Uniform Crime Reports, October 17, 2005)
**Estimated totals for urban areas, defined by the F.B.I. as Metropolitan Statistical Areas and other cities outside
such areas. National total includes those states listed as not available. Includes murder, rape, robbery,
aggravated assault, burglary, larceny-theft and motor vehicle theft.*
**Not available.

Urban Crime Rate in 2004

National Urban Rate = 4,224.4 Crimes per 100,000 Population*

ALPHA ORDER				RANK ORDER		
RANK	STATE	RATE		RANK	STATE	RATE
13	Alabama	5,061.5		1	Arizona	6,047.6
20	Alaska	4,746.6		2	South Carolina	5,599.5
1	Arizona	6,047.6		3	Tennessee	5,575.1
5	Arkansas	5,469.6		4	Louisiana	5,552.7
29	California	3,998.4		5	Arkansas	5,469.6
21	Colorado	4,537.6		6	Oklahoma	5,390.8
37	Connecticut	3,248.1		7	Washington	5,374.5
31	Delaware	3,939.2		8	Oregon	5,304.5
16	Florida	5,012.4		9	New Mexico	5,297.7
15	Georgia	5,041.9		10	Texas	5,280.4
12	Hawaii	5,143.2		11	North Carolina	5,154.3
34	Idaho	3,414.9		12	Hawaii	5,143.2
NA	Illinois**	NA		13	Alabama	5,061.5
28	Indiana	4,109.4		14	Nevada	5,046.5
30	Iowa	3,989.9		15	Georgia	5,041.9
19	Kansas	4,782.5		16	Florida	5,012.4
35	Kentucky	3,358.5		17	Mississippi	4,959.6
4	Louisiana	5,552.7		18	Missouri	4,874.6
45	Maine	2,782.9		19	Kansas	4,782.5
24	Maryland	4,435.7		20	Alaska	4,746.6
43	Massachusetts	2,918.9		21	Colorado	4,537.6
32	Michigan	3,778.5		22	Nebraska	4,524.5
33	Minnesota	3,635.3		23	Utah	4,486.3
17	Mississippi	4,959.6		24	Maryland	4,435.7
18	Missouri	4,874.6		25	Montana	4,388.3
25	Montana	4,388.3		26	Ohio	4,340.7
22	Nebraska	4,524.5		27	Wyoming	4,249.7
14	Nevada	5,046.5		28	Indiana	4,109.4
49	New Hampshire	2,282.4		29	California	3,998.4
44	New Jersey	2,784.9		30	Iowa	3,989.9
9	New Mexico	5,297.7		31	Delaware	3,939.2
47	New York	2,691.6		32	Michigan	3,778.5
11	North Carolina	5,154.3		33	Minnesota	3,635.3
48	North Dakota	2,596.5		34	Idaho	3,414.9
26	Ohio	4,340.7		35	Kentucky	3,358.5
6	Oklahoma	5,390.8		36	West Virginia	3,326.3
8	Oregon	5,304.5		37	Connecticut	3,248.1
41	Pennsylvania	2,959.4		38	Wisconsin	3,188.3
39	Rhode Island	3,127.1		39	Rhode Island	3,127.1
2	South Carolina	5,599.5		40	Virginia	3,124.3
46	South Dakota	2,770.2		41	Pennsylvania	2,959.4
3	Tennessee	5,575.1		42	Vermont	2,945.1
10	Texas	5,280.4		43	Massachusetts	2,918.9
23	Utah	4,486.3		44	New Jersey	2,784.9
42	Vermont	2,945.1		45	Maine	2,782.9
40	Virginia	3,124.3		46	South Dakota	2,770.2
7	Washington	5,374.5		47	New York	2,691.6
36	West Virginia	3,326.3		48	North Dakota	2,596.5
38	Wisconsin	3,188.3		49	New Hampshire	2,282.4
27	Wyoming	4,249.7		NA	Illinois**	NA
					District of Columbia	6,230.3

Source: Morgan Quitno Press using data from Federal Bureau of Investigation
   "Crime in the United States 2004" (Uniform Crime Reports, October 17, 2005)
*Estimated rates for urban areas, defined by the F.B.I. as Metropolitan Statistical Areas and other cities outside
such areas. National rate includes those states listed as not available. Includes murder, rape, robbery,
aggravated assault, burglary, larceny-theft and motor vehicle theft.
**Not available.

Percent of Crimes Occurring in Urban Areas in 2004

National Percent = 95.1% of Crimes*

ALPHA ORDER

RANK	STATE	PERCENT
18	Alabama	94.8
46	Alaska	79.8
7	Arizona	97.6
34	Arkansas	91.6
4	California	99.1
8	Colorado	97.5
17	Connecticut	94.9
37	Delaware	88.8
11	Florida	97.2
24	Georgia	93.6
49	Hawaii	73.2
36	Idaho	89.0
NA	Illinois**	NA
19	Indiana	94.5
24	Iowa	93.6
28	Kansas	93.1
44	Kentucky	83.1
29	Louisiana	92.7
39	Maine	87.7
6	Maryland	98.2
1	Massachusetts	100.0
24	Michigan	93.6
35	Minnesota	91.4
43	Mississippi	83.7
23	Missouri	93.9
48	Montana	74.8
27	Nebraska	93.4
14	Nevada	95.7
5	New Hampshire	98.9
1	New Jersey	100.0
30	New Mexico	92.6
12	New York	96.7
39	North Carolina	87.7
38	North Dakota	88.1
16	Ohio	95.0
20	Oklahoma	94.2
21	Oregon	94.1
15	Pennsylvania	95.3
3	Rhode Island	99.9
41	South Carolina	86.3
32	South Dakota	92.2
33	Tennessee	92.0
10	Texas	97.4
8	Utah	97.5
47	Vermont	78.7
21	Virginia	94.1
13	Washington	96.0
45	West Virginia	80.5
30	Wisconsin	92.6
42	Wyoming	85.7

RANK ORDER

RANK	STATE	PERCENT
1	Massachusetts	100.0
1	New Jersey	100.0
3	Rhode Island	99.9
4	California	99.1
5	New Hampshire	98.9
6	Maryland	98.2
7	Arizona	97.6
8	Colorado	97.5
8	Utah	97.5
10	Texas	97.4
11	Florida	97.2
12	New York	96.7
13	Washington	96.0
14	Nevada	95.7
15	Pennsylvania	95.3
16	Ohio	95.0
17	Connecticut	94.9
18	Alabama	94.8
19	Indiana	94.5
20	Oklahoma	94.2
21	Oregon	94.1
21	Virginia	94.1
23	Missouri	93.9
24	Georgia	93.6
24	Iowa	93.6
24	Michigan	93.6
27	Nebraska	93.4
28	Kansas	93.1
29	Louisiana	92.7
30	New Mexico	92.6
30	Wisconsin	92.6
32	South Dakota	92.2
33	Tennessee	92.0
34	Arkansas	91.6
35	Minnesota	91.4
36	Idaho	89.0
37	Delaware	88.8
38	North Dakota	88.1
39	Maine	87.7
39	North Carolina	87.7
41	South Carolina	86.3
42	Wyoming	85.7
43	Mississippi	83.7
44	Kentucky	83.1
45	West Virginia	80.5
46	Alaska	79.8
47	Vermont	78.7
48	Montana	74.8
49	Hawaii	73.2
NA	Illinois**	NA

| | District of Columbia | 100.0 |

Source: Morgan Quitno Press using data from Federal Bureau of Investigation
   "Crime in the United States 2004" (Uniform Crime Reports, October 17, 2005)
*Estimated percentages for urban areas, defined by the F.B.I. as Metropolitan Statistical Areas and other cities
outside such areas. National percent includes those states listed as not available. Includes murder, rape, robbery,
aggravated assault, burglary, larceny-theft and motor vehicle theft.
**Not available.

Crimes in Rural Areas in 2004

National Rural Total = 575,753 Crimes*

ALPHA ORDER

RANK	STATE	CRIMES	% of USA
22	Alabama	10,582	1.8%
32	Alaska	5,314	0.9%
28	Arizona	7,984	1.4%
23	Arkansas	10,458	1.8%
20	California	12,791	2.2%
34	Colorado	5,033	0.9%
33	Connecticut	5,179	0.9%
40	Delaware	3,458	0.6%
5	Florida	23,833	4.1%
4	Georgia	26,689	4.6%
11	Hawaii	17,110	3.0%
36	Idaho	4,679	0.8%
NA	Illinois**	NA	NA
19	Indiana	12,867	2.2%
31	Iowa	5,995	1.0%
27	Kansas	8,196	1.4%
9	Kentucky	19,440	3.4%
13	Louisiana	16,632	2.9%
39	Maine	4,077	0.7%
38	Maryland	4,328	0.8%
48	Massachusetts	0	0.0%
7	Michigan	23,072	4.0%
16	Minnesota	14,481	2.5%
10	Mississippi	17,806	3.1%
15	Missouri	15,355	2.7%
29	Montana	7,532	1.3%
37	Nebraska	4,429	0.8%
35	Nevada	4,895	0.9%
46	New Hampshire	308	0.1%
48	New Jersey	0	0.0%
30	New Mexico	6,920	1.2%
12	New York	16,662	2.9%
1	North Carolina	48,286	8.4%
44	North Dakota	1,511	0.3%
8	Ohio	22,949	4.0%
26	Oklahoma	9,752	1.7%
24	Oregon	10,419	1.8%
14	Pennsylvania	16,585	2.9%
47	Rhode Island	47	0.0%
2	South Carolina	30,461	5.3%
45	South Dakota	1,266	0.2%
6	Tennessee	23,752	4.1%
3	Texas	29,779	5.2%
42	Utah	2,611	0.5%
41	Vermont	3,206	0.6%
17	Virginia	13,018	2.3%
18	Washington	12,903	2.2%
25	West Virginia	9,827	1.7%
21	Wisconsin	11,718	2.0%
43	Wyoming	2,582	0.4%

RANK ORDER

RANK	STATE	CRIMES	% of USA
1	North Carolina	48,286	8.4%
2	South Carolina	30,461	5.3%
3	Texas	29,779	5.2%
4	Georgia	26,689	4.6%
5	Florida	23,833	4.1%
6	Tennessee	23,752	4.1%
7	Michigan	23,072	4.0%
8	Ohio	22,949	4.0%
9	Kentucky	19,440	3.4%
10	Mississippi	17,806	3.1%
11	Hawaii	17,110	3.0%
12	New York	16,662	2.9%
13	Louisiana	16,632	2.9%
14	Pennsylvania	16,585	2.9%
15	Missouri	15,355	2.7%
16	Minnesota	14,481	2.5%
17	Virginia	13,018	2.3%
18	Washington	12,903	2.2%
19	Indiana	12,867	2.2%
20	California	12,791	2.2%
21	Wisconsin	11,718	2.0%
22	Alabama	10,582	1.8%
23	Arkansas	10,458	1.8%
24	Oregon	10,419	1.8%
25	West Virginia	9,827	1.7%
26	Oklahoma	9,752	1.7%
27	Kansas	8,196	1.4%
28	Arizona	7,984	1.4%
29	Montana	7,532	1.3%
30	New Mexico	6,920	1.2%
31	Iowa	5,995	1.0%
32	Alaska	5,314	0.9%
33	Connecticut	5,179	0.9%
34	Colorado	5,033	0.9%
35	Nevada	4,895	0.9%
36	Idaho	4,679	0.8%
37	Nebraska	4,429	0.8%
38	Maryland	4,328	0.8%
39	Maine	4,077	0.7%
40	Delaware	3,458	0.6%
41	Vermont	3,206	0.6%
42	Utah	2,611	0.5%
43	Wyoming	2,582	0.4%
44	North Dakota	1,511	0.3%
45	South Dakota	1,266	0.2%
46	New Hampshire	308	0.1%
47	Rhode Island	47	0.0%
48	Massachusetts	0	0.0%
48	New Jersey	0	0.0%
NA	Illinois**	NA	NA
	District of Columbia	0	0.0%

Source: Morgan Quitno Press using data from Federal Bureau of Investigation
    "Crime in the United States 2004" (Uniform Crime Reports, October 17, 2005)
*Estimated totals for nonmetropolitan areas, defined by the F.B.I. as other than Metropolitan Statistical Areas and other cities outside such areas. National total includes those states listed as not available. Includes murder, rape, robbery, aggravated assault, burglary, larceny-theft and motor vehicle theft.
**Not available.

Rural Crime Rate in 2004

National Rural Rate = 1,891.9 Crimes per 100,000 Population*

ALPHA ORDER

RANK	STATE	RATE
38	Alabama	1,401.6
7	Alaska	2,498.9
9	Arizona	2,457.6
32	Arkansas	1,553.8
15	California	2,252.9
39	Colorado	1,401.2
42	Connecticut	995.3
5	Delaware	2,632.0
4	Florida	2,657.4
10	Georgia	2,447.1
1	Hawaii	4,802.8
30	Idaho	1,611.9
NA	Illinois**	NA
37	Indiana	1,430.2
43	Iowa	796.3
17	Kansas	1,951.9
33	Kentucky	1,507.1
12	Louisiana	2,345.0
34	Maine	1,486.7
16	Maryland	1,997.9
47	Massachusetts	0.0
18	Michigan	1,879.0
26	Minnesota	1,690.2
24	Mississippi	1,690.7
23	Missouri	1,740.0
21	Montana	1,809.4
41	Nebraska	1,208.9
11	Nevada	2,439.6
46	New Hampshire	546.2
47	New Jersey	0.0
8	New Mexico	2,481.3
25	New York	1,690.3
6	North Carolina	2,621.0
44	North Dakota	737.4
27	Ohio	1,652.7
29	Oklahoma	1,613.0
13	Oregon	2,312.8
35	Pennsylvania	1,481.4
47	Rhode Island	0.0
2	South Carolina	3,921.4
45	South Dakota	548.5
14	Tennessee	2,299.4
19	Texas	1,848.3
22	Utah	1,789.9
36	Vermont	1,459.8
31	Virginia	1,573.1
3	Washington	2,870.3
28	West Virginia	1,651.7
40	Wisconsin	1,283.6
20	Wyoming	1,811.9

RANK ORDER

RANK	STATE	RATE
1	Hawaii	4,802.8
2	South Carolina	3,921.4
3	Washington	2,870.3
4	Florida	2,657.4
5	Delaware	2,632.0
6	North Carolina	2,621.0
7	Alaska	2,498.9
8	New Mexico	2,481.3
9	Arizona	2,457.6
10	Georgia	2,447.1
11	Nevada	2,439.6
12	Louisiana	2,345.0
13	Oregon	2,312.8
14	Tennessee	2,299.4
15	California	2,252.9
16	Maryland	1,997.9
17	Kansas	1,951.9
18	Michigan	1,879.0
19	Texas	1,848.3
20	Wyoming	1,811.9
21	Montana	1,809.4
22	Utah	1,789.9
23	Missouri	1,740.0
24	Mississippi	1,690.7
25	New York	1,690.3
26	Minnesota	1,690.2
27	Ohio	1,652.7
28	West Virginia	1,651.7
29	Oklahoma	1,613.0
30	Idaho	1,611.9
31	Virginia	1,573.1
32	Arkansas	1,553.8
33	Kentucky	1,507.1
34	Maine	1,486.7
35	Pennsylvania	1,481.4
36	Vermont	1,459.8
37	Indiana	1,430.2
38	Alabama	1,401.6
39	Colorado	1,401.2
40	Wisconsin	1,283.6
41	Nebraska	1,208.9
42	Connecticut	995.3
43	Iowa	796.3
44	North Dakota	737.4
45	South Dakota	548.5
46	New Hampshire	546.2
47	Massachusetts	0.0
47	New Jersey	0.0
47	Rhode Island	0.0
NA	Illinois**	NA

District of Columbia 0.0

Source: Morgan Quitno Press using data from Federal Bureau of Investigation
    "Crime in the United States 2004" (Uniform Crime Reports, October 17, 2005)
*Estimated rates for nonmetropolitan areas, defined by the F.B.I. as other than Metropolitan Statistical Areas and
other cities outside such areas. National rate includes those states listed as not available. Includes murder, rape,
robbery, aggravated assault, burglary, larceny-theft and motor vehicle theft.
**Not available.

Percent of Crimes Occurring in Rural Areas in 2004

National Percent = 4.9% of Crimes*

ALPHA ORDER

RANK	STATE	PERCENT
32	Alabama	5.2
4	Alaska	20.2
43	Arizona	2.4
16	Arkansas	8.4
46	California	0.9
41	Colorado	2.5
33	Connecticut	5.1
13	Delaware	11.2
39	Florida	2.8
24	Georgia	6.4
1	Hawaii	26.8
14	Idaho	11.0
NA	Illinois**	NA
31	Indiana	5.5
24	Iowa	6.4
22	Kansas	6.9
6	Kentucky	16.9
21	Louisiana	7.3
10	Maine	12.3
44	Maryland	1.8
48	Massachusetts	0.0
24	Michigan	6.4
15	Minnesota	8.6
7	Mississippi	16.3
27	Missouri	6.1
2	Montana	25.2
23	Nebraska	6.6
36	Nevada	4.3
45	New Hampshire	1.1
48	New Jersey	0.0
19	New Mexico	7.4
38	New York	3.3
10	North Carolina	12.3
12	North Dakota	11.9
34	Ohio	5.0
30	Oklahoma	5.8
28	Oregon	5.9
35	Pennsylvania	4.7
47	Rhode Island	0.1
9	South Carolina	13.7
18	South Dakota	7.8
17	Tennessee	8.0
40	Texas	2.6
41	Utah	2.5
3	Vermont	21.3
28	Virginia	5.9
37	Washington	4.0
5	West Virginia	19.5
19	Wisconsin	7.4
8	Wyoming	14.3

RANK ORDER

RANK	STATE	PERCENT
1	Hawaii	26.8
2	Montana	25.2
3	Vermont	21.3
4	Alaska	20.2
5	West Virginia	19.5
6	Kentucky	16.9
7	Mississippi	16.3
8	Wyoming	14.3
9	South Carolina	13.7
10	Maine	12.3
10	North Carolina	12.3
12	North Dakota	11.9
13	Delaware	11.2
14	Idaho	11.0
15	Minnesota	8.6
16	Arkansas	8.4
17	Tennessee	8.0
18	South Dakota	7.8
19	New Mexico	7.4
19	Wisconsin	7.4
21	Louisiana	7.3
22	Kansas	6.9
23	Nebraska	6.6
24	Georgia	6.4
24	Iowa	6.4
24	Michigan	6.4
27	Missouri	6.1
28	Oregon	5.9
28	Virginia	5.9
30	Oklahoma	5.8
31	Indiana	5.5
32	Alabama	5.2
33	Connecticut	5.1
34	Ohio	5.0
35	Pennsylvania	4.7
36	Nevada	4.3
37	Washington	4.0
38	New York	3.3
39	Florida	2.8
40	Texas	2.6
41	Colorado	2.5
41	Utah	2.5
43	Arizona	2.4
44	Maryland	1.8
45	New Hampshire	1.1
46	California	0.9
47	Rhode Island	0.1
48	Massachusetts	0.0
48	New Jersey	0.0
NA	Illinois**	NA
	District of Columbia	0.0

Source: Morgan Quitno Press using data from Federal Bureau of Investigation
    "Crime in the United States 2004" (Uniform Crime Reports, October 17, 2005)
*Estimated percentages for nonmetropolitan areas, defined by the F.B.I. as other than Metropolitan Statistical Areas
and other cities outside such areas. National percent includes those states listed as not available. Includes
murder, rape, robbery, aggravated assault, burglary, larceny-theft and motor vehicle theft.
**Not available.

Violent Crimes in Urban Areas in 2004

National Urban Total = 1,305,700 Violent Crimes*

<table>
<tr><td colspan="4">ALPHA ORDER</td><td colspan="4">RANK ORDER</td></tr>
<tr><th>RANK</th><th>STATE</th><th>CRIMES</th><th>% of USA</th><th>RANK</th><th>STATE</th><th>CRIMES</th><th>% of USA</th></tr>
<tr><td>21</td><td>Alabama</td><td>18,209</td><td>1.4%</td><td>1</td><td>California</td><td>196,242</td><td>15.0%</td></tr>
<tr><td>39</td><td>Alaska</td><td>3,202</td><td>0.2%</td><td>2</td><td>Florida</td><td>119,787</td><td>9.2%</td></tr>
<tr><td>15</td><td>Arizona</td><td>27,808</td><td>2.1%</td><td>3</td><td>Texas</td><td>117,858</td><td>9.0%</td></tr>
<tr><td>26</td><td>Arkansas</td><td>12,570</td><td>1.0%</td><td>4</td><td>New York</td><td>83,152</td><td>6.4%</td></tr>
<tr><td>1</td><td>California</td><td>196,242</td><td>15.0%</td><td>5</td><td>Pennsylvania</td><td>49,559</td><td>3.8%</td></tr>
<tr><td>22</td><td>Colorado</td><td>16,675</td><td>1.3%</td><td>6</td><td>Michigan</td><td>46,977</td><td>3.6%</td></tr>
<tr><td>30</td><td>Connecticut</td><td>9,639</td><td>0.7%</td><td>7</td><td>Maryland</td><td>38,275</td><td>2.9%</td></tr>
<tr><td>37</td><td>Delaware</td><td>4,143</td><td>0.3%</td><td>8</td><td>Ohio</td><td>38,069</td><td>2.9%</td></tr>
<tr><td>2</td><td>Florida</td><td>119,787</td><td>9.2%</td><td>9</td><td>Georgia</td><td>38,037</td><td>2.9%</td></tr>
<tr><td>9</td><td>Georgia</td><td>38,037</td><td>2.9%</td><td>10</td><td>Tennessee</td><td>37,844</td><td>2.9%</td></tr>
<tr><td>42</td><td>Hawaii</td><td>2,507</td><td>0.2%</td><td>11</td><td>North Carolina</td><td>33,720</td><td>2.6%</td></tr>
<tr><td>40</td><td>Idaho</td><td>2,914</td><td>0.2%</td><td>12</td><td>New Jersey</td><td>30,943</td><td>2.4%</td></tr>
<tr><td>NA</td><td>Illinois**</td><td>NA</td><td>NA</td><td>13</td><td>Massachusetts</td><td>29,437</td><td>2.3%</td></tr>
<tr><td>20</td><td>Indiana</td><td>19,183</td><td>1.5%</td><td>14</td><td>South Carolina</td><td>28,053</td><td>2.1%</td></tr>
<tr><td>33</td><td>Iowa</td><td>7,497</td><td>0.6%</td><td>15</td><td>Arizona</td><td>27,808</td><td>2.1%</td></tr>
<tr><td>31</td><td>Kansas</td><td>9,400</td><td>0.7%</td><td>16</td><td>Louisiana</td><td>26,094</td><td>2.0%</td></tr>
<tr><td>32</td><td>Kentucky</td><td>8,359</td><td>0.6%</td><td>17</td><td>Missouri</td><td>25,995</td><td>2.0%</td></tr>
<tr><td>16</td><td>Louisiana</td><td>26,094</td><td>2.0%</td><td>18</td><td>Washington</td><td>20,558</td><td>1.6%</td></tr>
<tr><td>45</td><td>Maine</td><td>1,210</td><td>0.1%</td><td>19</td><td>Virginia</td><td>19,354</td><td>1.5%</td></tr>
<tr><td>7</td><td>Maryland</td><td>38,275</td><td>2.9%</td><td>20</td><td>Indiana</td><td>19,183</td><td>1.5%</td></tr>
<tr><td>13</td><td>Massachusetts</td><td>29,437</td><td>2.3%</td><td>21</td><td>Alabama</td><td>18,209</td><td>1.4%</td></tr>
<tr><td>6</td><td>Michigan</td><td>46,977</td><td>3.6%</td><td>22</td><td>Colorado</td><td>16,675</td><td>1.3%</td></tr>
<tr><td>25</td><td>Minnesota</td><td>12,842</td><td>1.0%</td><td>23</td><td>Oklahoma</td><td>16,187</td><td>1.2%</td></tr>
<tr><td>34</td><td>Mississippi</td><td>6,635</td><td>0.5%</td><td>24</td><td>Nevada</td><td>13,857</td><td>1.1%</td></tr>
<tr><td>17</td><td>Missouri</td><td>25,995</td><td>2.0%</td><td>25</td><td>Minnesota</td><td>12,842</td><td>1.0%</td></tr>
<tr><td>44</td><td>Montana</td><td>1,679</td><td>0.1%</td><td>26</td><td>Arkansas</td><td>12,570</td><td>1.0%</td></tr>
<tr><td>36</td><td>Nebraska</td><td>5,073</td><td>0.4%</td><td>27</td><td>New Mexico</td><td>12,217</td><td>0.9%</td></tr>
<tr><td>24</td><td>Nevada</td><td>13,857</td><td>1.1%</td><td>28</td><td>Wisconsin</td><td>10,825</td><td>0.8%</td></tr>
<tr><td>43</td><td>New Hampshire</td><td>2,119</td><td>0.2%</td><td>29</td><td>Oregon</td><td>10,013</td><td>0.8%</td></tr>
<tr><td>12</td><td>New Jersey</td><td>30,943</td><td>2.4%</td><td>30</td><td>Connecticut</td><td>9,639</td><td>0.7%</td></tr>
<tr><td>27</td><td>New Mexico</td><td>12,217</td><td>0.9%</td><td>31</td><td>Kansas</td><td>9,400</td><td>0.7%</td></tr>
<tr><td>4</td><td>New York</td><td>83,152</td><td>6.4%</td><td>32</td><td>Kentucky</td><td>8,359</td><td>0.6%</td></tr>
<tr><td>11</td><td>North Carolina</td><td>33,720</td><td>2.6%</td><td>33</td><td>Iowa</td><td>7,497</td><td>0.6%</td></tr>
<tr><td>49</td><td>North Dakota</td><td>444</td><td>0.0%</td><td>34</td><td>Mississippi</td><td>6,635</td><td>0.5%</td></tr>
<tr><td>8</td><td>Ohio</td><td>38,069</td><td>2.9%</td><td>35</td><td>Utah</td><td>5,452</td><td>0.4%</td></tr>
<tr><td>23</td><td>Oklahoma</td><td>16,187</td><td>1.2%</td><td>36</td><td>Nebraska</td><td>5,073</td><td>0.4%</td></tr>
<tr><td>29</td><td>Oregon</td><td>10,013</td><td>0.8%</td><td>37</td><td>Delaware</td><td>4,143</td><td>0.3%</td></tr>
<tr><td>5</td><td>Pennsylvania</td><td>49,559</td><td>3.8%</td><td>38</td><td>West Virginia</td><td>3,896</td><td>0.3%</td></tr>
<tr><td>41</td><td>Rhode Island</td><td>2,660</td><td>0.2%</td><td>39</td><td>Alaska</td><td>3,202</td><td>0.2%</td></tr>
<tr><td>14</td><td>South Carolina</td><td>28,053</td><td>2.1%</td><td>40</td><td>Idaho</td><td>2,914</td><td>0.2%</td></tr>
<tr><td>46</td><td>South Dakota</td><td>1,166</td><td>0.1%</td><td>41</td><td>Rhode Island</td><td>2,660</td><td>0.2%</td></tr>
<tr><td>10</td><td>Tennessee</td><td>37,844</td><td>2.9%</td><td>42</td><td>Hawaii</td><td>2,507</td><td>0.2%</td></tr>
<tr><td>3</td><td>Texas</td><td>117,858</td><td>9.0%</td><td>43</td><td>New Hampshire</td><td>2,119</td><td>0.2%</td></tr>
<tr><td>35</td><td>Utah</td><td>5,452</td><td>0.4%</td><td>44</td><td>Montana</td><td>1,679</td><td>0.1%</td></tr>
<tr><td>48</td><td>Vermont</td><td>552</td><td>0.0%</td><td>45</td><td>Maine</td><td>1,210</td><td>0.1%</td></tr>
<tr><td>19</td><td>Virginia</td><td>19,354</td><td>1.5%</td><td>46</td><td>South Dakota</td><td>1,166</td><td>0.1%</td></tr>
<tr><td>18</td><td>Washington</td><td>20,558</td><td>1.6%</td><td>47</td><td>Wyoming</td><td>903</td><td>0.1%</td></tr>
<tr><td>38</td><td>West Virginia</td><td>3,896</td><td>0.3%</td><td>48</td><td>Vermont</td><td>552</td><td>0.0%</td></tr>
<tr><td>28</td><td>Wisconsin</td><td>10,825</td><td>0.8%</td><td>49</td><td>North Dakota</td><td>444</td><td>0.0%</td></tr>
<tr><td>47</td><td>Wyoming</td><td>903</td><td>0.1%</td><td>NA</td><td>Illinois**</td><td>NA</td><td>NA</td></tr>
<tr><td></td><td></td><td></td><td></td><td></td><td>District of Columbia</td><td>7,590</td><td>0.6%</td></tr>
</table>

Source: Morgan Quitno Press using data from Federal Bureau of Investigation
   "Crime in the United States 2004" (Uniform Crime Reports, October 17, 2005)
*Estimated totals for urban areas, defined by the F.B.I. as Metropolitan Statistical Areas and other cities outside such areas. National total includes those states listed as not available. Violent crimes are offenses of murder, forcible rape, robbery and aggravated assault.
**Not available.

Urban Violent Crime Rate in 2004

National Urban Rate = 496.0 Violent Crimes per 100,000 Population*

ALPHA ORDER

RANK	STATE	RATE
19	Alabama	482.3
5	Alaska	723.2
16	Arizona	513.2
9	Arkansas	604.5
12	California	555.5
24	Colorado	393.1
33	Connecticut	323.1
10	Delaware	592.7
4	Florida	726.0
18	Georgia	491.5
39	Hawaii	276.5
40	Idaho	264.2
NA	Illinois**	NA
27	Indiana	359.4
31	Iowa	340.5
23	Kansas	405.9
37	Kentucky	292.7
7	Louisiana	685.5
48	Maine	116.0
6	Maryland	716.6
20	Massachusetts	458.8
15	Michigan	528.7
36	Minnesota	302.6
28	Mississippi	358.7
14	Missouri	533.5
32	Montana	328.8
26	Nebraska	367.4
8	Nevada	649.3
46	New Hampshire	170.5
30	New Jersey	355.7
3	New Mexico	752.1
21	New York	455.8
17	North Carolina	503.4
49	North Dakota	103.4
25	Ohio	378.0
13	Oklahoma	554.5
35	Oregon	318.5
22	Pennsylvania	439.1
42	Rhode Island	246.2
1	South Carolina	820.0
45	South Dakota	215.9
2	Tennessee	777.4
11	Texas	564.5
43	Utah	243.0
47	Vermont	137.4
38	Virginia	291.8
29	Washington	357.3
34	West Virginia	319.2
44	Wisconsin	235.5
41	Wyoming	248.1

RANK ORDER

RANK	STATE	RATE
1	South Carolina	820.0
2	Tennessee	777.4
3	New Mexico	752.1
4	Florida	726.0
5	Alaska	723.2
6	Maryland	716.6
7	Louisiana	685.5
8	Nevada	649.3
9	Arkansas	604.5
10	Delaware	592.7
11	Texas	564.5
12	California	555.5
13	Oklahoma	554.5
14	Missouri	533.5
15	Michigan	528.7
16	Arizona	513.2
17	North Carolina	503.4
18	Georgia	491.5
19	Alabama	482.3
20	Massachusetts	458.8
21	New York	455.8
22	Pennsylvania	439.1
23	Kansas	405.9
24	Colorado	393.1
25	Ohio	378.0
26	Nebraska	367.4
27	Indiana	359.4
28	Mississippi	358.7
29	Washington	357.3
30	New Jersey	355.7
31	Iowa	340.5
32	Montana	328.8
33	Connecticut	323.1
34	West Virginia	319.2
35	Oregon	318.5
36	Minnesota	302.6
37	Kentucky	292.7
38	Virginia	291.8
39	Hawaii	276.5
40	Idaho	264.2
41	Wyoming	248.1
42	Rhode Island	246.2
43	Utah	243.0
44	Wisconsin	235.5
45	South Dakota	215.9
46	New Hampshire	170.5
47	Vermont	137.4
48	Maine	116.0
49	North Dakota	103.4
NA	Illinois**	NA

District of Columbia   1,371.2

Source: Morgan Quitno Press using data from Federal Bureau of Investigation
"Crime in the United States 2004" (Uniform Crime Reports, October 17, 2005)
*Estimated rates for urban areas, defined by the F.B.I. as Metropolitan Statistical Areas and other cities outside such areas. National rate includes those states listed as not available. Violent crimes are offenses of murder, forcible rape, robbery and aggravated assault.
**Not available.

Percent of Violent Crimes Occurring in Urban Areas in 2004

National Percent = 95.5% of Violent Crimes*

ALPHA ORDER

RANK	STATE	PERCENT
21	Alabama	94.2
48	Alaska	77.0
17	Arizona	96.0
33	Arkansas	91.5
4	California	99.1
10	Colorado	97.0
16	Connecticut	96.1
39	Delaware	87.8
12	Florida	96.8
19	Georgia	94.6
45	Hawaii	78.0
40	Idaho	85.4
NA	Illinois**	NA
20	Indiana	94.5
24	Iowa	93.7
31	Kansas	91.8
42	Kentucky	82.3
34	Louisiana	90.5
35	Maine	88.7
5	Maryland	98.3
1	Massachusetts	100.0
18	Michigan	94.8
26	Minnesota	93.4
47	Mississippi	77.4
30	Missouri	92.1
49	Montana	61.7
22	Nebraska	94.1
14	Nevada	96.4
7	New Hampshire	97.6
1	New Jersey	100.0
26	New Mexico	93.4
6	New York	97.9
36	North Carolina	88.2
38	North Dakota	88.1
8	Ohio	97.2
31	Oklahoma	91.8
26	Oregon	93.4
8	Pennsylvania	97.2
3	Rhode Island	99.5
41	South Carolina	85.2
36	South Dakota	88.2
29	Tennessee	92.2
10	Texas	97.0
13	Utah	96.7
43	Vermont	79.3
22	Virginia	94.1
14	Washington	96.4
44	West Virginia	79.1
24	Wisconsin	93.7
46	Wyoming	77.6

RANK ORDER

RANK	STATE	PERCENT
1	Massachusetts	100.0
1	New Jersey	100.0
3	Rhode Island	99.5
4	California	99.1
5	Maryland	98.3
6	New York	97.9
7	New Hampshire	97.6
8	Ohio	97.2
8	Pennsylvania	97.2
10	Colorado	97.0
10	Texas	97.0
12	Florida	96.8
13	Utah	96.7
14	Nevada	96.4
14	Washington	96.4
16	Connecticut	96.1
17	Arizona	96.0
18	Michigan	94.8
19	Georgia	94.6
20	Indiana	94.5
21	Alabama	94.2
22	Nebraska	94.1
22	Virginia	94.1
24	Iowa	93.7
24	Wisconsin	93.7
26	Minnesota	93.4
26	New Mexico	93.4
26	Oregon	93.4
29	Tennessee	92.2
30	Missouri	92.1
31	Kansas	91.8
31	Oklahoma	91.8
33	Arkansas	91.5
34	Louisiana	90.5
35	Maine	88.7
36	North Carolina	88.2
36	South Dakota	88.2
38	North Dakota	88.1
39	Delaware	87.8
40	Idaho	85.4
41	South Carolina	85.2
42	Kentucky	82.3
43	Vermont	79.3
44	West Virginia	79.1
45	Hawaii	78.0
46	Wyoming	77.6
47	Mississippi	77.4
48	Alaska	77.0
49	Montana	61.7
NA	Illinois**	NA
	District of Columbia	100.0

Source: Morgan Quitno Press using data from Federal Bureau of Investigation
    "Crime in the United States 2004" (Uniform Crime Reports, October 17, 2005)
*Estimated percentages for urban areas, defined by the F.B.I. as Metropolitan Statistical Areas and other cities
outside such areas. National percent includes those states listed as not available. Violent crimes are offenses of
murder, forcible rape, robbery and aggravated assault.
**Not available.

Violent Crimes in Rural Areas in 2004

National Rural Total = 61,309 Violent Crimes*

RANK	STATE	CRIMES	% of USA
19	Alabama	1,115	1.8%
24	Alaska	957	1.6%
18	Arizona	1,144	1.9%
17	Arkansas	1,167	1.9%
11	California	1,828	3.0%
35	Colorado	510	0.8%
38	Connecticut	393	0.6%
33	Delaware	577	0.9%
3	Florida	3,967	6.5%
9	Georgia	2,180	3.6%
31	Hawaii	706	1.2%
37	Idaho	498	0.8%
NA	Illinois**	NA	NA
20	Indiana	1,111	1.8%
36	Iowa	506	0.8%
27	Kansas	845	1.4%
12	Kentucky	1,793	2.9%
6	Louisiana	2,750	4.5%
43	Maine	154	0.3%
32	Maryland	657	1.1%
48	Massachusetts	0	0.0%
7	Michigan	2,600	4.2%
25	Minnesota	909	1.5%
10	Mississippi	1,933	3.2%
8	Missouri	2,231	3.6%
22	Montana	1,044	1.7%
39	Nebraska	320	0.5%
34	Nevada	522	0.9%
46	New Hampshire	51	0.1%
48	New Jersey	0	0.0%
26	New Mexico	864	1.4%
13	New York	1,762	2.9%
2	North Carolina	4,524	7.4%
45	North Dakota	60	0.1%
21	Ohio	1,094	1.8%
14	Oklahoma	1,448	2.4%
30	Oregon	711	1.2%
15	Pennsylvania	1,439	2.3%
47	Rhode Island	13	0.0%
1	South Carolina	4,869	7.9%
42	South Dakota	156	0.3%
5	Tennessee	3,180	5.2%
4	Texas	3,696	6.0%
41	Utah	187	0.3%
44	Vermont	144	0.2%
16	Virginia	1,205	2.0%
28	Washington	772	1.3%
23	West Virginia	1,028	1.7%
29	Wisconsin	723	1.2%
40	Wyoming	260	0.4%

RANK	STATE	CRIMES	% of USA
1	South Carolina	4,869	7.9%
2	North Carolina	4,524	7.4%
3	Florida	3,967	6.5%
4	Texas	3,696	6.0%
5	Tennessee	3,180	5.2%
6	Louisiana	2,750	4.5%
7	Michigan	2,600	4.2%
8	Missouri	2,231	3.6%
9	Georgia	2,180	3.6%
10	Mississippi	1,933	3.2%
11	California	1,828	3.0%
12	Kentucky	1,793	2.9%
13	New York	1,762	2.9%
14	Oklahoma	1,448	2.4%
15	Pennsylvania	1,439	2.3%
16	Virginia	1,205	2.0%
17	Arkansas	1,167	1.9%
18	Arizona	1,144	1.9%
19	Alabama	1,115	1.8%
20	Indiana	1,111	1.8%
21	Ohio	1,094	1.8%
22	Montana	1,044	1.7%
23	West Virginia	1,028	1.7%
24	Alaska	957	1.6%
25	Minnesota	909	1.5%
26	New Mexico	864	1.4%
27	Kansas	845	1.4%
28	Washington	772	1.3%
29	Wisconsin	723	1.2%
30	Oregon	711	1.2%
31	Hawaii	706	1.2%
32	Maryland	657	1.1%
33	Delaware	577	0.9%
34	Nevada	522	0.9%
35	Colorado	510	0.8%
36	Iowa	506	0.8%
37	Idaho	498	0.8%
38	Connecticut	393	0.6%
39	Nebraska	320	0.5%
40	Wyoming	260	0.4%
41	Utah	187	0.3%
42	South Dakota	156	0.3%
43	Maine	154	0.3%
44	Vermont	144	0.2%
45	North Dakota	60	0.1%
46	New Hampshire	51	0.1%
47	Rhode Island	13	0.0%
48	Massachusetts	0	0.0%
48	New Jersey	0	0.0%
NA	Illinois**	NA	NA
	District of Columbia	0	0.0%

Source: Federal Bureau of Investigation
   "Crime in the United States 2004" (Uniform Crime Reports, October 17, 2005)
*Estimated totals for nonmetropolitan areas, defined by the F.B.I. as other than Metropolitan Statistical Areas and other cities outside such areas. National total includes those states listed as not available. Violent crimes are offenses of murder, forcible rape, robbery and aggravated assault.
**Not available.

Rural Violent Crime Rate in 2004

National Rural Rate = 201.5 Violent Crimes per 100,000 Population*

RANK	STATE	RATE		RANK	STATE	RATE
29	Alabama	147.7		1	South Carolina	626.8
2	Alaska	450.0		2	Alaska	450.0
6	Arizona	352.1		3	Florida	442.3
24	Arkansas	173.4		4	Delaware	439.2
7	California	322.0		5	Louisiana	387.7
31	Colorado	142.0		6	Arizona	352.1
41	Connecticut	75.5		7	California	322.0
4	Delaware	439.2		8	New Mexico	309.8
3	Florida	442.3		9	Tennessee	307.9
19	Georgia	199.9		10	Maryland	303.3
20	Hawaii	198.2		11	Nevada	260.2
27	Idaho	171.6		12	Missouri	252.8
NA	Illinois**	NA		13	Montana	250.8
35	Indiana	123.5		14	North Carolina	245.6
43	Iowa	67.2		15	Oklahoma	239.5
18	Kansas	201.2		16	Texas	229.4
32	Kentucky	139.0		17	Michigan	211.7
5	Louisiana	387.7		18	Kansas	201.2
45	Maine	56.2		19	Georgia	199.9
10	Maryland	303.3		20	Hawaii	198.2
47	Massachusetts	0.0		21	Mississippi	183.5
17	Michigan	211.7		22	Wyoming	182.4
36	Minnesota	106.1		23	New York	178.7
21	Mississippi	183.5		24	Arkansas	173.4
12	Missouri	252.8		25	West Virginia	172.8
13	Montana	250.8		26	Washington	171.7
38	Nebraska	87.3		27	Idaho	171.6
11	Nevada	260.2		28	Oregon	157.8
37	New Hampshire	90.4		29	Alabama	147.7
47	New Jersey	0.0		30	Virginia	145.6
8	New Mexico	309.8		31	Colorado	142.0
23	New York	178.7		32	Kentucky	139.0
14	North Carolina	245.6		33	Pennsylvania	128.5
46	North Dakota	29.3		34	Utah	128.2
40	Ohio	78.8		35	Indiana	123.5
15	Oklahoma	239.5		36	Minnesota	106.1
28	Oregon	157.8		37	New Hampshire	90.4
33	Pennsylvania	128.5		38	Nebraska	87.3
47	Rhode Island	0.0		39	Wisconsin	79.2
1	South Carolina	626.8		40	Ohio	78.8
42	South Dakota	67.6		41	Connecticut	75.5
9	Tennessee	307.9		42	South Dakota	67.6
16	Texas	229.4		43	Iowa	67.2
34	Utah	128.2		44	Vermont	65.6
44	Vermont	65.6		45	Maine	56.2
30	Virginia	145.6		46	North Dakota	29.3
26	Washington	171.7		47	Massachusetts	0.0
25	West Virginia	172.8		47	New Jersey	0.0
39	Wisconsin	79.2		47	Rhode Island	0.0
22	Wyoming	182.4		NA	Illinois**	NA
					District of Columbia	0.0

Source: Morgan Quitno Press using data from Federal Bureau of Investigation
    "Crime in the United States 2004" (Uniform Crime Reports, October 17, 2005)
*Estimated rates for nonmetropolitan areas, defined by the F.B.I. as other than Metropolitan Statistical Areas and other cities outside such areas. National rate includes those states listed as not available. Violent crimes are offenses of murder, forcible rape, robbery and aggravated assault.
**Not available.

Percent of Violent Crimes Occurring in Rural Areas in 2004

National Percent = 4.9% of Violent Crimes*

ALPHA ORDER

RANK	STATE	PERCENT
29	Alabama	5.8
2	Alaska	23.0
33	Arizona	4.0
17	Arkansas	8.5
46	California	0.9
39	Colorado	3.0
34	Connecticut	3.9
11	Delaware	12.2
38	Florida	3.2
31	Georgia	5.4
5	Hawaii	22.0
10	Idaho	14.6
NA	Illinois**	NA
30	Indiana	5.5
25	Iowa	6.3
18	Kansas	8.2
8	Kentucky	17.7
16	Louisiana	9.5
15	Maine	11.3
45	Maryland	1.7
48	Massachusetts	0.0
32	Michigan	5.2
22	Minnesota	6.6
3	Mississippi	22.6
20	Missouri	7.9
1	Montana	38.3
27	Nebraska	5.9
35	Nevada	3.6
43	New Hampshire	2.4
48	New Jersey	0.0
22	New Mexico	6.6
44	New York	2.1
13	North Carolina	11.8
12	North Dakota	11.9
41	Ohio	2.8
18	Oklahoma	8.2
22	Oregon	6.6
41	Pennsylvania	2.8
47	Rhode Island	0.5
9	South Carolina	14.8
13	South Dakota	11.8
21	Tennessee	7.8
39	Texas	3.0
37	Utah	3.3
7	Vermont	20.7
27	Virginia	5.9
35	Washington	3.6
6	West Virginia	20.9
25	Wisconsin	6.3
4	Wyoming	22.4

RANK ORDER

RANK	STATE	PERCENT
1	Montana	38.3
2	Alaska	23.0
3	Mississippi	22.6
4	Wyoming	22.4
5	Hawaii	22.0
6	West Virginia	20.9
7	Vermont	20.7
8	Kentucky	17.7
9	South Carolina	14.8
10	Idaho	14.6
11	Delaware	12.2
12	North Dakota	11.9
13	North Carolina	11.8
13	South Dakota	11.8
15	Maine	11.3
16	Louisiana	9.5
17	Arkansas	8.5
18	Kansas	8.2
18	Oklahoma	8.2
20	Missouri	7.9
21	Tennessee	7.8
22	Minnesota	6.6
22	New Mexico	6.6
22	Oregon	6.6
25	Iowa	6.3
25	Wisconsin	6.3
27	Nebraska	5.9
27	Virginia	5.9
29	Alabama	5.8
30	Indiana	5.5
31	Georgia	5.4
32	Michigan	5.2
33	Arizona	4.0
34	Connecticut	3.9
35	Nevada	3.6
35	Washington	3.6
37	Utah	3.3
38	Florida	3.2
39	Colorado	3.0
39	Texas	3.0
41	Ohio	2.8
41	Pennsylvania	2.8
43	New Hampshire	2.4
44	New York	2.1
45	Maryland	1.7
46	California	0.9
47	Rhode Island	0.5
48	Massachusetts	0.0
48	New Jersey	0.0
NA	Illinois**	NA

District of Columbia   0.0

Source: Morgan Quitno Press using data from Federal Bureau of Investigation

Source: Morgan Quitno Press using data from Federal Bureau of Investigation
    "Crime in the United States 2004" (Uniform Crime Reports, October 17, 2005)
*Estimated percentages for nonmetropolitan areas, defined by the F.B.I. as other than Metropolitan Statistical Areas and other cities outside such areas. National percent includes those states listed as not available. Violent crimes are offenses of murder, forcible rape, robbery and aggravated assault.
**Not available.

Murders in Urban Areas in 2004

National Urban Total = 15,038 Murders*

ALPHA ORDER

RANK	STATE	MURDERS	% of USA
18	Alabama	238	1.6%
40	Alaska	22	0.1%
12	Arizona	399	2.7%
26	Arkansas	149	1.0%
1	California	2,368	15.7%
20	Colorado	197	1.3%
32	Connecticut	79	0.5%
44	Delaware	17	0.1%
3	Florida	918	6.1%
7	Georgia	565	3.8%
38	Hawaii	26	0.2%
40	Idaho	22	0.1%
NA	Illinois**	NA	NA
17	Indiana	297	2.0%
35	Iowa	44	0.3%
30	Kansas	108	0.7%
28	Kentucky	129	0.9%
8	Louisiana	544	3.6%
45	Maine	14	0.1%
9	Maryland	515	3.4%
23	Massachusetts	169	1.1%
6	Michigan	618	4.1%
31	Minnesota	105	0.7%
24	Mississippi	166	1.1%
15	Missouri	316	2.1%
42	Montana	19	0.1%
37	Nebraska	37	0.2%
22	Nevada	170	1.1%
43	New Hampshire	18	0.1%
13	New Jersey	392	2.6%
29	New Mexico	120	0.8%
4	New York	875	5.8%
11	North Carolina	428	2.8%
49	North Dakota	4	0.0%
10	Ohio	496	3.3%
25	Oklahoma	157	1.0%
33	Oregon	75	0.5%
5	Pennsylvania	619	4.1%
38	Rhode Island	26	0.2%
19	South Carolina	224	1.5%
48	South Dakota	7	0.0%
16	Tennessee	303	2.0%
2	Texas	1,308	8.7%
36	Utah	42	0.3%
46	Vermont	12	0.1%
14	Virginia	348	2.3%
21	Washington	181	1.2%
34	West Virginia	49	0.3%
27	Wisconsin	131	0.9%
47	Wyoming	9	0.1%

RANK ORDER

RANK	STATE	MURDERS	% of USA
1	California	2,368	15.7%
2	Texas	1,308	8.7%
3	Florida	918	6.1%
4	New York	875	5.8%
5	Pennsylvania	619	4.1%
6	Michigan	618	4.1%
7	Georgia	565	3.8%
8	Louisiana	544	3.6%
9	Maryland	515	3.4%
10	Ohio	496	3.3%
11	North Carolina	428	2.8%
12	Arizona	399	2.7%
13	New Jersey	392	2.6%
14	Virginia	348	2.3%
15	Missouri	316	2.1%
16	Tennessee	303	2.0%
17	Indiana	297	2.0%
18	Alabama	238	1.6%
19	South Carolina	224	1.5%
20	Colorado	197	1.3%
21	Washington	181	1.2%
22	Nevada	170	1.1%
23	Massachusetts	169	1.1%
24	Mississippi	166	1.1%
25	Oklahoma	157	1.0%
26	Arkansas	149	1.0%
27	Wisconsin	131	0.9%
28	Kentucky	129	0.9%
29	New Mexico	120	0.8%
30	Kansas	108	0.7%
31	Minnesota	105	0.7%
32	Connecticut	79	0.5%
33	Oregon	75	0.5%
34	West Virginia	49	0.3%
35	Iowa	44	0.3%
36	Utah	42	0.3%
37	Nebraska	37	0.2%
38	Hawaii	26	0.2%
38	Rhode Island	26	0.2%
40	Alaska	22	0.1%
40	Idaho	22	0.1%
42	Montana	19	0.1%
43	New Hampshire	18	0.1%
44	Delaware	17	0.1%
45	Maine	14	0.1%
46	Vermont	12	0.1%
47	Wyoming	9	0.1%
48	South Dakota	7	0.0%
49	North Dakota	4	0.0%
NA	Illinois**	NA	NA
	District of Columbia	198	1.3%

Source: Morgan Quitno Press using data from Federal Bureau of Investigation
"Crime in the United States 2004" (Uniform Crime Reports, October 17, 2005)
*Estimated totals for urban areas, defined by the F.B.I. as Metropolitan Statistical Areas and other cities outside such areas. National total includes those states listed as not available. Includes nonnegligent manslaughter.
**Not available.

Urban Murder Rate in 2004

National Urban Rate = 5.7 Murders per 100,000 Population*

ALPHA ORDER

RANK	STATE	RATE
14	Alabama	6.3
22	Alaska	5.0
5	Arizona	7.4
8	Arkansas	7.2
10	California	6.7
26	Colorado	4.6
36	Connecticut	2.6
40	Delaware	2.4
17	Florida	5.6
7	Georgia	7.3
33	Hawaii	2.9
43	Idaho	2.0
NA	Illinois**	NA
17	Indiana	5.6
43	Iowa	2.0
25	Kansas	4.7
27	Kentucky	4.5
1	Louisiana	14.3
47	Maine	1.3
2	Maryland	9.6
36	Massachusetts	2.6
9	Michigan	7.0
38	Minnesota	2.5
3	Mississippi	9.0
11	Missouri	6.5
30	Montana	3.7
35	Nebraska	2.7
4	Nevada	8.0
46	New Hampshire	1.4
27	New Jersey	4.5
5	New Mexico	7.4
24	New York	4.8
13	North Carolina	6.4
49	North Dakota	0.9
23	Ohio	4.9
20	Oklahoma	5.4
40	Oregon	2.4
19	Pennsylvania	5.5
40	Rhode Island	2.4
11	South Carolina	6.5
47	South Dakota	1.3
16	Tennessee	6.2
14	Texas	6.3
45	Utah	1.9
32	Vermont	3.0
21	Virginia	5.2
31	Washington	3.1
29	West Virginia	4.0
33	Wisconsin	2.9
38	Wyoming	2.5

RANK ORDER

RANK	STATE	RATE
1	Louisiana	14.3
2	Maryland	9.6
3	Mississippi	9.0
4	Nevada	8.0
5	Arizona	7.4
5	New Mexico	7.4
7	Georgia	7.3
8	Arkansas	7.2
9	Michigan	7.0
10	California	6.7
11	Missouri	6.5
11	South Carolina	6.5
13	North Carolina	6.4
14	Alabama	6.3
14	Texas	6.3
16	Tennessee	6.2
17	Florida	5.6
17	Indiana	5.6
19	Pennsylvania	5.5
20	Oklahoma	5.4
21	Virginia	5.2
22	Alaska	5.0
23	Ohio	4.9
24	New York	4.8
25	Kansas	4.7
26	Colorado	4.6
27	Kentucky	4.5
27	New Jersey	4.5
29	West Virginia	4.0
30	Montana	3.7
31	Washington	3.1
32	Vermont	3.0
33	Hawaii	2.9
33	Wisconsin	2.9
35	Nebraska	2.7
36	Connecticut	2.6
36	Massachusetts	2.6
38	Minnesota	2.5
38	Wyoming	2.5
40	Delaware	2.4
40	Oregon	2.4
40	Rhode Island	2.4
43	Idaho	2.0
43	Iowa	2.0
45	Utah	1.9
46	New Hampshire	1.4
47	Maine	1.3
47	South Dakota	1.3
49	North Dakota	0.9
NA	Illinois**	NA

District of Columbia	35.8

Source: Morgan Quitno Press using data from Federal Bureau of Investigation
    "Crime in the United States 2004" (Uniform Crime Reports, October 17, 2005)
Estimated rates for urban areas, defined by the F.B.I. as Metropolitan Statistical Areas and other cities outside such areas. National rate includes those states listed as not available. Includes nonnegligent manslaughter.
***Not available.*

Percent of Murders Occurring in Urban Areas in 2004

National Percent = 93.2% of Murders*

ALPHA ORDER				RANK ORDER		
RANK	STATE	PERCENT		RANK	STATE	PERCENT
21	Alabama	93.7		1	Delaware	100.0
46	Alaska	59.5		1	Massachusetts	100.0
12	Arizona	96.4		1	New Hampshire	100.0
32	Arkansas	84.7		1	New Jersey	100.0
6	California	99.0		1	Rhode Island	100.0
10	Colorado	97.0		6	California	99.0
29	Connecticut	86.8		7	Maryland	98.8
1	Delaware	100.0		7	Nevada	98.8
10	Florida	97.0		9	New York	98.4
24	Georgia	92.2		10	Colorado	97.0
37	Hawaii	78.8		10	Florida	97.0
41	Idaho	73.3		12	Arizona	96.4
NA	Illinois**	NA		13	Michigan	96.1
20	Indiana	94.0		14	Ohio	95.9
16	Iowa	95.7		14	Texas	95.9
28	Kansas	87.8		16	Iowa	95.7
47	Kentucky	54.7		17	Washington	95.3
19	Louisiana	94.8		18	Pennsylvania	95.2
38	Maine	77.8		19	Louisiana	94.8
7	Maryland	98.8		20	Indiana	94.0
1	Massachusetts	100.0		21	Alabama	93.7
13	Michigan	96.1		22	Minnesota	92.9
22	Minnesota	92.9		23	Nebraska	92.5
42	Mississippi	73.1		24	Georgia	92.2
26	Missouri	89.3		25	Utah	91.3
45	Montana	63.3		26	Missouri	89.3
23	Nebraska	92.5		27	Virginia	89.0
7	Nevada	98.8		28	Kansas	87.8
1	New Hampshire	100.0		29	Connecticut	86.8
1	New Jersey	100.0		30	Tennessee	86.3
44	New Mexico	71.0		31	Wisconsin	85.1
9	New York	98.4		32	Arkansas	84.7
36	North Carolina	80.5		33	Oklahoma	84.4
48	North Dakota	44.4		34	Oregon	83.3
14	Ohio	95.9		35	Wyoming	81.8
33	Oklahoma	84.4		36	North Carolina	80.5
34	Oregon	83.3		37	Hawaii	78.8
18	Pennsylvania	95.2		38	Maine	77.8
1	Rhode Island	100.0		38	South Carolina	77.8
38	South Carolina	77.8		40	Vermont	75.0
49	South Dakota	38.9		41	Idaho	73.3
30	Tennessee	86.3		42	Mississippi	73.1
14	Texas	95.9		43	West Virginia	72.1
25	Utah	91.3		44	New Mexico	71.0
40	Vermont	75.0		45	Montana	63.3
27	Virginia	89.0		46	Alaska	59.5
17	Washington	95.3		47	Kentucky	54.7
43	West Virginia	72.1		48	North Dakota	44.4
31	Wisconsin	85.1		49	South Dakota	38.9
35	Wyoming	81.8		NA	Illinois**	NA
					District of Columbia	100.0

*Source: Morgan Quitno Press using data from Federal Bureau of Investigation
"Crime in the United States 2004" (Uniform Crime Reports, October 17, 2005)*
*Estimated percentages for urban areas, defined by the F.B.I. as Metropolitan Statistical Areas and other cities outside such areas. National percent includes those states listed as not available. Includes nonnegligent manslaughter.
**Not available.

Murders in Rural Areas in 2004

National Rural Total = 1,099 Murders*

ALPHA ORDER					RANK ORDER			
RANK	STATE		MURDERS	% of USA	RANK	STATE	MURDERS	% of USA
22	Alabama		16	1.5%	1	Kentucky	107	9.7%
23	Alaska		15	1.4%	2	North Carolina	104	9.5%
23	Arizona		15	1.4%	3	South Carolina	64	5.8%
15	Arkansas		27	2.5%	4	Mississippi	61	5.6%
17	California		24	2.2%	5	Texas	56	5.1%
35	Colorado		6	0.5%	6	New Mexico	49	4.5%
28	Connecticut		12	1.1%	7	Georgia	48	4.4%
45	Delaware		0	0.0%	7	Tennessee	48	4.4%
14	Florida		28	2.5%	9	Virginia	43	3.9%
7	Georgia		48	4.4%	10	Missouri	38	3.5%
34	Hawaii		7	0.6%	11	Pennsylvania	31	2.8%
32	Idaho		8	0.7%	12	Louisiana	30	2.7%
NA	Illinois**		NA	NA	13	Oklahoma	29	2.6%
20	Indiana		19	1.7%	14	Florida	28	2.5%
42	Iowa		2	0.2%	15	Arkansas	27	2.5%
23	Kansas		15	1.4%	16	Michigan	25	2.3%
1	Kentucky		107	9.7%	17	California	24	2.2%
12	Louisiana		30	2.7%	18	Wisconsin	23	2.1%
38	Maine		4	0.4%	19	Ohio	21	1.9%
35	Maryland		6	0.5%	20	Indiana	19	1.7%
45	Massachusetts		0	0.0%	20	West Virginia	19	1.7%
16	Michigan		25	2.3%	22	Alabama	16	1.5%
32	Minnesota		8	0.7%	23	Alaska	15	1.4%
4	Mississippi		61	5.6%	23	Arizona	15	1.4%
10	Missouri		38	3.5%	23	Kansas	15	1.4%
29	Montana		11	1.0%	23	Oregon	15	1.4%
41	Nebraska		3	0.3%	27	New York	14	1.3%
42	Nevada		2	0.2%	28	Connecticut	12	1.1%
45	New Hampshire		0	0.0%	29	Montana	11	1.0%
45	New Jersey		0	0.0%	29	South Dakota	11	1.0%
6	New Mexico		49	4.5%	31	Washington	9	0.8%
27	New York		14	1.3%	32	Idaho	8	0.7%
2	North Carolina		104	9.5%	32	Minnesota	8	0.7%
37	North Dakota		5	0.5%	34	Hawaii	7	0.6%
19	Ohio		21	1.9%	35	Colorado	6	0.5%
13	Oklahoma		29	2.6%	35	Maryland	6	0.5%
23	Oregon		15	1.4%	37	North Dakota	5	0.5%
11	Pennsylvania		31	2.8%	38	Maine	4	0.4%
45	Rhode Island		0	0.0%	38	Utah	4	0.4%
3	South Carolina		64	5.8%	38	Vermont	4	0.4%
29	South Dakota		11	1.0%	41	Nebraska	3	0.3%
7	Tennessee		48	4.4%	42	Iowa	2	0.2%
5	Texas		56	5.1%	42	Nevada	2	0.2%
38	Utah		4	0.4%	42	Wyoming	2	0.2%
38	Vermont		4	0.4%	45	Delaware	0	0.0%
9	Virginia		43	3.9%	45	Massachusetts	0	0.0%
31	Washington		9	0.8%	45	New Hampshire	0	0.0%
20	West Virginia		19	1.7%	45	New Jersey	0	0.0%
18	Wisconsin		23	2.1%	45	Rhode Island	0	0.0%
42	Wyoming		2	0.2%	NA	Illinois**	NA	NA
						District of Columbia	0	0.0%

Source: Federal Bureau of Investigation
    "Crime in the United States 2004" (Uniform Crime Reports, October 17, 2005)
*Estimated totals for nonmetropolitan areas, defined by the F.B.I. as other than Metropolitan Statistical Areas and other cities outside such areas. National total includes those states listed as not available. Includes nonnegligent manslaughter.
**Not available.

410

Rural Murder Rate in 2004

National Rural Rate = 3.6 Murders per 100,000 Population*

ALPHA ORDER

RANK	STATE	RATE
30	Alabama	2.1
4	Alaska	7.1
10	Arizona	4.6
16	Arkansas	4.0
14	California	4.2
36	Colorado	1.7
29	Connecticut	2.3
45	Delaware	0.0
21	Florida	3.1
12	Georgia	4.4
32	Hawaii	2.0
22	Idaho	2.8
NA	Illinois**	NA
30	Indiana	2.1
44	Iowa	0.3
17	Kansas	3.6
2	Kentucky	8.3
14	Louisiana	4.2
37	Maine	1.5
22	Maryland	2.8
45	Massachusetts	0.0
32	Michigan	2.0
42	Minnesota	0.9
5	Mississippi	5.8
13	Missouri	4.3
26	Montana	2.6
43	Nebraska	0.8
41	Nevada	1.0
45	New Hampshire	0.0
45	New Jersey	0.0
1	New Mexico	17.6
39	New York	1.4
6	North Carolina	5.6
28	North Dakota	2.4
37	Ohio	1.5
8	Oklahoma	4.8
19	Oregon	3.3
22	Pennsylvania	2.8
45	Rhode Island	0.0
3	South Carolina	8.2
8	South Dakota	4.8
10	Tennessee	4.6
18	Texas	3.5
25	Utah	2.7
35	Vermont	1.8
7	Virginia	5.2
32	Washington	2.0
20	West Virginia	3.2
27	Wisconsin	2.5
39	Wyoming	1.4

RANK ORDER

RANK	STATE	RATE
1	New Mexico	17.6
2	Kentucky	8.3
3	South Carolina	8.2
4	Alaska	7.1
5	Mississippi	5.8
6	North Carolina	5.6
7	Virginia	5.2
8	Oklahoma	4.8
8	South Dakota	4.8
10	Arizona	4.6
10	Tennessee	4.6
12	Georgia	4.4
13	Missouri	4.3
14	California	4.2
14	Louisiana	4.2
16	Arkansas	4.0
17	Kansas	3.6
18	Texas	3.5
19	Oregon	3.3
20	West Virginia	3.2
21	Florida	3.1
22	Idaho	2.8
22	Maryland	2.8
22	Pennsylvania	2.8
25	Utah	2.7
26	Montana	2.6
27	Wisconsin	2.5
28	North Dakota	2.4
29	Connecticut	2.3
30	Alabama	2.1
30	Indiana	2.1
32	Hawaii	2.0
32	Michigan	2.0
32	Washington	2.0
35	Vermont	1.8
36	Colorado	1.7
37	Maine	1.5
37	Ohio	1.5
39	New York	1.4
39	Wyoming	1.4
41	Nevada	1.0
42	Minnesota	0.9
43	Nebraska	0.8
44	Iowa	0.3
45	Delaware	0.0
45	Massachusetts	0.0
45	New Hampshire	0.0
45	New Jersey	0.0
45	Rhode Island	0.0
NA	Illinois**	NA

District of Columbia   0.0

Source: Morgan Quitno Press using data from Federal Bureau of Investigation
  "Crime in the United States 2004" (Uniform Crime Reports, October 17, 2005)
*Estimated rates for nonmetropolitan areas, defined by the F.B.I. as other than Metropolitan Statistical Areas and
other cities outside such areas. National rate includes those states listed as not available. Includes nonnegligent
manslaughter.
**Not available.

Percent of Murders Occurring in Rural Areas in 2004

National Percent = 6.8% of Murders*

ALPHA ORDER			RANK ORDER		
RANK	STATE	PERCENT	RANK	STATE	PERCENT
29	Alabama	6.3	1	South Dakota	61.1
4	Alaska	40.5	2	North Dakota	55.6
38	Arizona	3.6	3	Kentucky	45.3
18	Arkansas	15.3	4	Alaska	40.5
44	California	1.0	5	Montana	36.7
39	Colorado	3.0	6	New Mexico	29.0
21	Connecticut	13.2	7	West Virginia	27.9
45	Delaware	0.0	8	Mississippi	26.9
39	Florida	3.0	9	Idaho	26.7
26	Georgia	7.8	10	Vermont	25.0
13	Hawaii	21.2	11	Maine	22.2
9	Idaho	26.7	11	South Carolina	22.2
NA	Illinois**	NA	13	Hawaii	21.2
30	Indiana	6.0	14	North Carolina	19.5
34	Iowa	4.3	15	Wyoming	18.2
22	Kansas	12.2	16	Oregon	16.7
3	Kentucky	45.3	17	Oklahoma	15.6
31	Louisiana	5.2	18	Arkansas	15.3
11	Maine	22.2	19	Wisconsin	14.9
42	Maryland	1.2	20	Tennessee	13.7
45	Massachusetts	0.0	21	Connecticut	13.2
37	Michigan	3.9	22	Kansas	12.2
28	Minnesota	7.1	23	Virginia	11.0
8	Mississippi	26.9	24	Missouri	10.7
24	Missouri	10.7	25	Utah	8.7
5	Montana	36.7	26	Georgia	7.8
27	Nebraska	7.5	27	Nebraska	7.5
42	Nevada	1.2	28	Minnesota	7.1
45	New Hampshire	0.0	29	Alabama	6.3
45	New Jersey	0.0	30	Indiana	6.0
6	New Mexico	29.0	31	Louisiana	5.2
41	New York	1.6	32	Pennsylvania	4.8
14	North Carolina	19.5	33	Washington	4.7
2	North Dakota	55.6	34	Iowa	4.3
35	Ohio	4.1	35	Ohio	4.1
17	Oklahoma	15.6	35	Texas	4.1
16	Oregon	16.7	37	Michigan	3.9
32	Pennsylvania	4.8	38	Arizona	3.6
45	Rhode Island	0.0	39	Colorado	3.0
11	South Carolina	22.2	39	Florida	3.0
1	South Dakota	61.1	41	New York	1.6
20	Tennessee	13.7	42	Maryland	1.2
35	Texas	4.1	42	Nevada	1.2
25	Utah	8.7	44	California	1.0
10	Vermont	25.0	45	Delaware	0.0
23	Virginia	11.0	45	Massachusetts	0.0
33	Washington	4.7	45	New Hampshire	0.0
7	West Virginia	27.9	45	New Jersey	0.0
19	Wisconsin	14.9	45	Rhode Island	0.0
15	Wyoming	18.2	NA	Illinois**	NA
				District of Columbia	0.0

Source: Morgan Quitno Press using data from Federal Bureau of Investigation
     "Crime in the United States 2004" (Uniform Crime Reports, October 17, 2005)
*Estimated percentages for nonmetropolitan areas, defined by the F.B.I. as other than Metropolitan Statistical Areas and other cities outside such areas. National percent includes those states listed as not available. Includes nonnegligent manslaughter.
**Not available.

Rapes in Urban Areas in 2004

National Urban Total = 87,263 Rapes*

ALPHA ORDER

RANK	STATE	RAPES	% of USA
17	Alabama	1,595	1.8%
39	Alaska	417	0.5%
13	Arizona	1,854	2.1%
26	Arkansas	1,034	1.2%
1	California	9,475	10.9%
12	Colorado	1,918	2.2%
35	Connecticut	640	0.7%
42	Delaware	289	0.3%
3	Florida	6,282	7.2%
9	Georgia	2,261	2.6%
45	Hawaii	222	0.3%
37	Idaho	506	0.6%
NA	Illinois**	NA	NA
16	Indiana	1,678	1.9%
34	Iowa	736	0.8%
28	Kansas	1,002	1.1%
33	Kentucky	796	0.9%
19	Louisiana	1,463	1.7%
43	Maine	286	0.3%
24	Maryland	1,281	1.5%
15	Massachusetts	1,799	2.1%
4	Michigan	4,614	5.3%
14	Minnesota	1,830	2.1%
32	Mississippi	890	1.0%
22	Missouri	1,356	1.6%
46	Montana	171	0.2%
36	Nebraska	558	0.6%
30	Nevada	913	1.0%
38	New Hampshire	441	0.5%
23	New Jersey	1,331	1.5%
29	New Mexico	921	1.1%
6	New York	3,361	3.9%
11	North Carolina	2,024	2.3%
47	North Dakota	140	0.2%
5	Ohio	4,430	5.1%
21	Oklahoma	1,406	1.6%
25	Oregon	1,189	1.4%
7	Pennsylvania	3,207	3.7%
40	Rhode Island	317	0.4%
20	South Carolina	1,427	1.6%
41	South Dakota	309	0.4%
10	Tennessee	2,054	2.4%
2	Texas	8,102	9.3%
31	Utah	892	1.0%
48	Vermont	115	0.1%
18	Virginia	1,592	1.8%
8	Washington	2,674	3.1%
44	West Virginia	254	0.3%
27	Wisconsin	1,024	1.2%
49	Wyoming	86	0.1%

RANK ORDER

RANK	STATE	RAPES	% of USA
1	California	9,475	10.9%
2	Texas	8,102	9.3%
3	Florida	6,282	7.2%
4	Michigan	4,614	5.3%
5	Ohio	4,430	5.1%
6	New York	3,361	3.9%
7	Pennsylvania	3,207	3.7%
8	Washington	2,674	3.1%
9	Georgia	2,261	2.6%
10	Tennessee	2,054	2.4%
11	North Carolina	2,024	2.3%
12	Colorado	1,918	2.2%
13	Arizona	1,854	2.1%
14	Minnesota	1,830	2.1%
15	Massachusetts	1,799	2.1%
16	Indiana	1,678	1.9%
17	Alabama	1,595	1.8%
18	Virginia	1,592	1.8%
19	Louisiana	1,463	1.7%
20	South Carolina	1,427	1.6%
21	Oklahoma	1,406	1.6%
22	Missouri	1,356	1.6%
23	New Jersey	1,331	1.5%
24	Maryland	1,281	1.5%
25	Oregon	1,189	1.4%
26	Arkansas	1,034	1.2%
27	Wisconsin	1,024	1.2%
28	Kansas	1,002	1.1%
29	New Mexico	921	1.1%
30	Nevada	913	1.0%
31	Utah	892	1.0%
32	Mississippi	890	1.0%
33	Kentucky	796	0.9%
34	Iowa	736	0.8%
35	Connecticut	640	0.7%
36	Nebraska	558	0.6%
37	Idaho	506	0.6%
38	New Hampshire	441	0.5%
39	Alaska	417	0.5%
40	Rhode Island	317	0.4%
41	South Dakota	309	0.4%
42	Delaware	289	0.3%
43	Maine	286	0.3%
44	West Virginia	254	0.3%
45	Hawaii	222	0.3%
46	Montana	171	0.2%
47	North Dakota	140	0.2%
48	Vermont	115	0.1%
49	Wyoming	86	0.1%
NA	Illinois**	NA	NA
	District of Columbia	222	0.3%

Source: Morgan Quitno Press using data from Federal Bureau of Investigation
    "Crime in the United States 2004" (Uniform Crime Reports, October 17, 2005)
*Estimated totals for urban areas, defined by the F.B.I. as Metropolitan Statistical Areas and other cities outside such areas. National total includes those states listed as not available. Forcible rape is the carnal knowledge of a female forcibly and against her will. Attempts are included. However, statutory rape without force and other sex offenses are excluded. **Not available.*

Urban Rape Rate in 2004

National Urban Rate = 33.2 Rapes per 100,000 Population*

ALPHA ORDER

RANK	STATE	RATE
15	Alabama	42.2
1	Alaska	94.2
26	Arizona	34.2
5	Arkansas	49.7
40	California	26.8
10	Colorado	45.2
46	Connecticut	21.5
18	Delaware	41.3
23	Florida	38.1
33	Georgia	29.2
41	Hawaii	24.5
9	Idaho	45.9
NA	Illinois**	NA
30	Indiana	31.4
28	Iowa	33.4
12	Kansas	43.3
37	Kentucky	27.9
22	Louisiana	38.4
39	Maine	27.4
42	Maryland	24.0
36	Massachusetts	28.0
4	Michigan	51.9
13	Minnesota	43.1
7	Mississippi	48.1
38	Missouri	27.8
27	Montana	33.5
19	Nebraska	40.4
14	Nevada	42.8
25	New Hampshire	35.5
49	New Jersey	15.3
3	New Mexico	56.7
48	New York	18.4
31	North Carolina	30.2
29	North Dakota	32.6
11	Ohio	44.0
6	Oklahoma	48.2
24	Oregon	37.8
35	Pennsylvania	28.4
32	Rhode Island	29.3
17	South Carolina	41.7
2	South Dakota	57.2
15	Tennessee	42.2
21	Texas	38.8
20	Utah	39.8
34	Vermont	28.6
42	Virginia	24.0
8	Washington	46.5
47	West Virginia	20.8
45	Wisconsin	22.3
44	Wyoming	23.6

RANK ORDER

RANK	STATE	RATE
1	Alaska	94.2
2	South Dakota	57.2
3	New Mexico	56.7
4	Michigan	51.9
5	Arkansas	49.7
6	Oklahoma	48.2
7	Mississippi	48.1
8	Washington	46.5
9	Idaho	45.9
10	Colorado	45.2
11	Ohio	44.0
12	Kansas	43.3
13	Minnesota	43.1
14	Nevada	42.8
15	Alabama	42.2
15	Tennessee	42.2
17	South Carolina	41.7
18	Delaware	41.3
19	Nebraska	40.4
20	Utah	39.8
21	Texas	38.8
22	Louisiana	38.4
23	Florida	38.1
24	Oregon	37.8
25	New Hampshire	35.5
26	Arizona	34.2
27	Montana	33.5
28	Iowa	33.4
29	North Dakota	32.6
30	Indiana	31.4
31	North Carolina	30.2
32	Rhode Island	29.3
33	Georgia	29.2
34	Vermont	28.6
35	Pennsylvania	28.4
36	Massachusetts	28.0
37	Kentucky	27.9
38	Missouri	27.8
39	Maine	27.4
40	California	26.8
41	Hawaii	24.5
42	Maryland	24.0
42	Virginia	24.0
44	Wyoming	23.6
45	Wisconsin	22.3
46	Connecticut	21.5
47	West Virginia	20.8
48	New York	18.4
49	New Jersey	15.3
NA	Illinois**	NA
	District of Columbia	40.1

Source: Morgan Quitno Press using data from Federal Bureau of Investigation
"Crime in the United States 2004" (Uniform Crime Reports, October 17, 2005)
*Estimated rates for urban areas, defined by the F.B.I. as Metropolitan Statistical Areas and other cities outside such areas. National rate includes those states listed as not available. Forcible rape is the carnal knowledge of a female forcibly and against her will. Attempts are included. However, statutory rape without force and other sex offenses are excluded. **Not available.

Percent of Rapes Occurring in Urban Areas in 2004

National Percent = 92.2% of Rapes*

RANK	STATE	PERCENT		RANK	STATE	PERCENT
22	Alabama	91.6		1	Massachusetts	100.0
46	Alaska	74.7		1	New Jersey	100.0
6	Arizona	97.8		3	Rhode Island	99.1
33	Arkansas	88.7		4	California	98.5
4	California	98.5		5	Colorado	98.1
5	Colorado	98.1		6	Arizona	97.8
35	Connecticut	88.4		7	Maryland	97.3
40	Delaware	83.8		8	Texas	96.6
13	Florida	95.0		9	New Hampshire	96.1
14	Georgia	94.7		10	Nevada	95.7
47	Hawaii	66.7		11	Utah	95.6
32	Idaho	88.8		12	Ohio	95.4
NA	Illinois**	NA		13	Florida	95.0
18	Indiana	93.1		14	Georgia	94.7
16	Iowa	93.2		15	Washington	93.6
24	Kansas	90.8		16	Iowa	93.2
48	Kentucky	64.3		16	New York	93.2
27	Louisiana	90.5		18	Indiana	93.1
24	Maine	90.8		19	Oregon	92.7
7	Maryland	97.3		20	Tennessee	92.5
1	Massachusetts	100.0		21	Missouri	91.7
39	Michigan	84.1		22	Alabama	91.6
38	Minnesota	86.2		23	South Dakota	91.4
44	Mississippi	76.7		24	Kansas	90.8
21	Missouri	91.7		24	Maine	90.8
49	Montana	62.6		26	Pennsylvania	90.7
31	Nebraska	90.0		27	Louisiana	90.5
10	Nevada	95.7		28	Oklahoma	90.3
9	New Hampshire	96.1		29	Virginia	90.1
1	New Jersey	100.0		29	Wisconsin	90.1
34	New Mexico	88.6		31	Nebraska	90.0
16	New York	93.2		32	Idaho	88.8
37	North Carolina	86.5		33	Arkansas	88.7
36	North Dakota	88.1		34	New Mexico	88.6
12	Ohio	95.4		35	Connecticut	88.4
28	Oklahoma	90.3		36	North Dakota	88.1
19	Oregon	92.7		37	North Carolina	86.5
26	Pennsylvania	90.7		38	Minnesota	86.2
3	Rhode Island	99.1		39	Michigan	84.1
41	South Carolina	83.1		40	Delaware	83.8
23	South Dakota	91.4		41	South Carolina	83.1
20	Tennessee	92.5		42	West Virginia	79.4
8	Texas	96.6		43	Wyoming	76.8
11	Utah	95.6		44	Mississippi	76.7
45	Vermont	75.7		45	Vermont	75.7
29	Virginia	90.1		46	Alaska	74.7
15	Washington	93.6		47	Hawaii	66.7
42	West Virginia	79.4		48	Kentucky	64.3
29	Wisconsin	90.1		49	Montana	62.6
43	Wyoming	76.8		NA	Illinois**	NA

District of Columbia   100.0

Source: Morgan Quitno Press using data from Federal Bureau of Investigation
    "Crime in the United States 2004" (Uniform Crime Reports, October 17, 2005)
*Estimated percentages for urban areas, defined by the F.B.I. as Metropolitan Statistical Areas and other cities
outside such areas. National percent includes those states listed as not available. Forcible rape is the carnal
knowledge of a female forcibly and against her will. Attempts are included. However, statutory rape without force
and other sex offenses are excluded. **Not available.

Rapes in Rural Areas in 2004

National Rural Total = 7,372 Rapes*

ALPHA ORDER

RANK	STATE	RAPES	% of USA
17	Alabama	147	2.0%
18	Alaska	141	1.9%
36	Arizona	42	0.6%
20	Arkansas	132	1.8%
19	California	140	1.9%
39	Colorado	38	0.5%
30	Connecticut	84	1.1%
34	Delaware	56	0.8%
3	Florida	330	4.5%
21	Georgia	126	1.7%
26	Hawaii	111	1.5%
32	Idaho	64	0.9%
NA	Illinois**	NA	NA
22	Indiana	125	1.7%
35	Iowa	54	0.7%
27	Kansas	102	1.4%
2	Kentucky	442	6.0%
15	Louisiana	153	2.1%
42	Maine	29	0.4%
41	Maryland	35	0.5%
48	Massachusetts	0	0.0%
1	Michigan	872	11.8%
6	Minnesota	293	4.0%
9	Mississippi	271	3.7%
23	Missouri	123	1.7%
27	Montana	102	1.4%
33	Nebraska	62	0.8%
37	Nevada	41	0.6%
46	New Hampshire	18	0.2%
48	New Jersey	0	0.0%
24	New Mexico	118	1.6%
10	New York	247	3.4%
5	North Carolina	315	4.3%
45	North Dakota	19	0.3%
11	Ohio	216	2.9%
16	Oklahoma	151	2.0%
29	Oregon	94	1.3%
4	Pennsylvania	328	4.4%
47	Rhode Island	3	0.0%
7	South Carolina	291	3.9%
42	South Dakota	29	0.4%
14	Tennessee	166	2.3%
8	Texas	286	3.9%
37	Utah	41	0.6%
40	Vermont	37	0.5%
13	Virginia	174	2.4%
12	Washington	183	2.5%
31	West Virginia	66	0.9%
25	Wisconsin	112	1.5%
44	Wyoming	26	0.4%

RANK ORDER

RANK	STATE	RAPES	% of USA
1	Michigan	872	11.8%
2	Kentucky	442	6.0%
3	Florida	330	4.5%
4	Pennsylvania	328	4.4%
5	North Carolina	315	4.3%
6	Minnesota	293	4.0%
7	South Carolina	291	3.9%
8	Texas	286	3.9%
9	Mississippi	271	3.7%
10	New York	247	3.4%
11	Ohio	216	2.9%
12	Washington	183	2.5%
13	Virginia	174	2.4%
14	Tennessee	166	2.3%
15	Louisiana	153	2.1%
16	Oklahoma	151	2.0%
17	Alabama	147	2.0%
18	Alaska	141	1.9%
19	California	140	1.9%
20	Arkansas	132	1.8%
21	Georgia	126	1.7%
22	Indiana	125	1.7%
23	Missouri	123	1.7%
24	New Mexico	118	1.6%
25	Wisconsin	112	1.5%
26	Hawaii	111	1.5%
27	Kansas	102	1.4%
27	Montana	102	1.4%
29	Oregon	94	1.3%
30	Connecticut	84	1.1%
31	West Virginia	66	0.9%
32	Idaho	64	0.9%
33	Nebraska	62	0.8%
34	Delaware	56	0.8%
35	Iowa	54	0.7%
36	Arizona	42	0.6%
37	Nevada	41	0.6%
37	Utah	41	0.6%
39	Colorado	38	0.5%
40	Vermont	37	0.5%
41	Maryland	35	0.5%
42	Maine	29	0.4%
42	South Dakota	29	0.4%
44	Wyoming	26	0.4%
45	North Dakota	19	0.3%
46	New Hampshire	18	0.2%
47	Rhode Island	3	0.0%
48	Massachusetts	0	0.0%
48	New Jersey	0	0.0%
NA	Illinois**	NA	NA
	District of Columbia	0	0.0%

Source: Federal Bureau of Investigation
    "Crime in the United States 2004" (Uniform Crime Reports, October 17, 2005)
*Estimated totals for nonmetropolitan areas, defined by the F.B.I. as other than Metropolitan Statistical Areas and other cities outside such areas. National total includes those states listed as not available. Forcible rape is the carnal knowledge of a female forcibly and against her will. Attempts are included. However, statutory rape without force and other sex offenses are excluded. **Not available.

Rural Rape Rate in 2004

National Rural Rate = 24.2 Rapes per 100,000 Population*

ALPHA ORDER				RANK ORDER		
RANK	STATE	RATE		RANK	STATE	RATE
26	Alabama	19.5		1	Michigan	71.0
2	Alaska	66.3		2	Alaska	66.3
38	Arizona	12.9		3	Delaware	42.6
25	Arkansas	19.6		4	New Mexico	42.3
17	California	24.7		5	Washington	40.7
43	Colorado	10.6		6	South Carolina	37.5
33	Connecticut	16.1		7	Florida	36.8
3	Delaware	42.6		8	Kentucky	34.3
7	Florida	36.8		9	Minnesota	34.2
41	Georgia	11.6		10	New Hampshire	31.9
11	Hawaii	31.2		11	Hawaii	31.2
20	Idaho	22.0		12	Pennsylvania	29.3
NA	Illinois**	NA		13	Utah	28.1
36	Indiana	13.9		14	Mississippi	25.7
46	Iowa	7.2		15	New York	25.1
19	Kansas	24.3		16	Oklahoma	25.0
8	Kentucky	34.3		17	California	24.7
21	Louisiana	21.6		18	Montana	24.5
43	Maine	10.6		19	Kansas	24.3
32	Maryland	16.2		20	Idaho	22.0
47	Massachusetts	0.0		21	Louisiana	21.6
1	Michigan	71.0		22	Virginia	21.0
9	Minnesota	34.2		23	Oregon	20.9
14	Mississippi	25.7		24	Nevada	20.4
36	Missouri	13.9		25	Arkansas	19.6
18	Montana	24.5		26	Alabama	19.5
30	Nebraska	16.9		27	Wyoming	18.2
24	Nevada	20.4		28	Texas	17.8
10	New Hampshire	31.9		29	North Carolina	17.1
47	New Jersey	0.0		30	Nebraska	16.9
4	New Mexico	42.3		31	Vermont	16.8
15	New York	25.1		32	Maryland	16.2
29	North Carolina	17.1		33	Connecticut	16.1
45	North Dakota	9.3		33	Tennessee	16.1
35	Ohio	15.6		35	Ohio	15.6
16	Oklahoma	25.0		36	Indiana	13.9
23	Oregon	20.9		36	Missouri	13.9
12	Pennsylvania	29.3		38	Arizona	12.9
47	Rhode Island	0.0		39	South Dakota	12.6
6	South Carolina	37.5		40	Wisconsin	12.3
39	South Dakota	12.6		41	Georgia	11.6
33	Tennessee	16.1		42	West Virginia	11.1
28	Texas	17.8		43	Colorado	10.6
13	Utah	28.1		43	Maine	10.6
31	Vermont	16.8		45	North Dakota	9.3
22	Virginia	21.0		46	Iowa	7.2
5	Washington	40.7		47	Massachusetts	0.0
42	West Virginia	11.1		47	New Jersey	0.0
40	Wisconsin	12.3		47	Rhode Island	0.0
27	Wyoming	18.2		NA	Illinois**	NA
					District of Columbia	0.0

Source: Morgan Quitno Press using data from Federal Bureau of Investigation
   "Crime in the United States 2004" (Uniform Crime Reports, October 17, 2005)
*Estimated rates for nonmetropolitan areas, defined by the F.B.I. as other than Metropolitan Statistical Areas and other cities outside such areas. National rate includes those states listed as not available.   Forcible rape is the carnal knowledge of a female forcibly and against her will. Attempts are included. However, statutory rape without force and other sex offenses are excluded. **Not available.

Percent of Rapes Occurring in Rural Areas in 2004

National Percent = 7.8% of Rapes*

ALPHA ORDER

RANK	STATE	PERCENT
28	Alabama	8.4
4	Alaska	25.3
44	Arizona	2.2
17	Arkansas	11.3
46	California	1.5
45	Colorado	1.9
15	Connecticut	11.6
10	Delaware	16.2
37	Florida	5.0
36	Georgia	5.3
3	Hawaii	33.3
18	Idaho	11.2
NA	Illinois**	NA
32	Indiana	6.9
33	Iowa	6.8
25	Kansas	9.2
2	Kentucky	35.7
23	Louisiana	9.5
25	Maine	9.2
43	Maryland	2.7
48	Massachusetts	0.0
11	Michigan	15.9
12	Minnesota	13.8
6	Mississippi	23.3
29	Missouri	8.3
1	Montana	37.4
19	Nebraska	10.0
40	Nevada	4.3
41	New Hampshire	3.9
48	New Jersey	0.0
16	New Mexico	11.4
33	New York	6.8
13	North Carolina	13.5
14	North Dakota	11.9
38	Ohio	4.6
22	Oklahoma	9.7
31	Oregon	7.3
24	Pennsylvania	9.3
47	Rhode Island	0.9
9	South Carolina	16.9
27	South Dakota	8.6
30	Tennessee	7.5
42	Texas	3.4
39	Utah	4.4
5	Vermont	24.3
20	Virginia	9.9
35	Washington	6.4
8	West Virginia	20.6
20	Wisconsin	9.9
7	Wyoming	23.2

RANK ORDER

RANK	STATE	PERCENT
1	Montana	37.4
2	Kentucky	35.7
3	Hawaii	33.3
4	Alaska	25.3
5	Vermont	24.3
6	Mississippi	23.3
7	Wyoming	23.2
8	West Virginia	20.6
9	South Carolina	16.9
10	Delaware	16.2
11	Michigan	15.9
12	Minnesota	13.8
13	North Carolina	13.5
14	North Dakota	11.9
15	Connecticut	11.6
16	New Mexico	11.4
17	Arkansas	11.3
18	Idaho	11.2
19	Nebraska	10.0
20	Virginia	9.9
20	Wisconsin	9.9
22	Oklahoma	9.7
23	Louisiana	9.5
24	Pennsylvania	9.3
25	Kansas	9.2
25	Maine	9.2
27	South Dakota	8.6
28	Alabama	8.4
29	Missouri	8.3
30	Tennessee	7.5
31	Oregon	7.3
32	Indiana	6.9
33	Iowa	6.8
33	New York	6.8
35	Washington	6.4
36	Georgia	5.3
37	Florida	5.0
38	Ohio	4.6
39	Utah	4.4
40	Nevada	4.3
41	New Hampshire	3.9
42	Texas	3.4
43	Maryland	2.7
44	Arizona	2.2
45	Colorado	1.9
46	California	1.5
47	Rhode Island	0.9
48	Massachusetts	0.0
48	New Jersey	0.0
NA	Illinois**	NA
	District of Columbia	0.0

Source: Morgan Quitno Press using data from Federal Bureau of Investigation
   "Crime in the United States 2004" (Uniform Crime Reports, October 17, 2005)
*Estimated percentages for nonmetropolitan areas, defined by the F.B.I. as other than Metropolitan Statistical Areas
and other cities outside such areas. National percent includes those states listed as not available. Forcible rape
is the carnal knowledge of a female forcibly and against her will. Attempts are included. However, statutory rape
without force and other sex offenses are excluded. **Not available.

Robberies in Urban Areas in 2004

National Urban Total = 396,599 Robberies*

ALPHA ORDER

RANK	STATE	ROBBERIES	% of USA
19	Alabama	5,959	1.5%
42	Alaska	420	0.1%
13	Arizona	7,677	1.9%
30	Arkansas	2,314	0.6%
1	California	61,664	15.5%
26	Colorado	3,735	0.9%
23	Connecticut	4,145	1.0%
35	Delaware	1,160	0.3%
4	Florida	29,723	7.5%
7	Georgia	13,440	3.4%
38	Hawaii	818	0.2%
44	Idaho	226	0.1%
NA	Illinois**	NA	NA
18	Indiana	6,173	1.6%
37	Iowa	1,121	0.3%
33	Kansas	1,774	0.4%
28	Kentucky	3,007	0.8%
17	Louisiana	6,390	1.6%
43	Maine	274	0.1%
9	Maryland	12,708	3.2%
14	Massachusetts	7,467	1.9%
10	Michigan	11,234	2.8%
24	Minnesota	4,033	1.0%
31	Mississippi	2,277	0.6%
16	Missouri	6,563	1.7%
45	Montana	207	0.1%
36	Nebraska	1,128	0.3%
22	Nevada	4,875	1.2%
41	New Hampshire	499	0.1%
8	New Jersey	13,076	3.3%
32	New Mexico	1,991	0.5%
3	New York	33,431	8.4%
11	North Carolina	11,124	2.8%
49	North Dakota	38	0.0%
6	Ohio	17,357	4.4%
27	Oklahoma	3,058	0.8%
29	Oregon	2,685	0.7%
5	Pennsylvania	18,316	4.6%
39	Rhode Island	731	0.2%
21	South Carolina	4,950	1.2%
46	South Dakota	108	0.0%
12	Tennessee	8,736	2.2%
2	Texas	35,630	9.0%
34	Utah	1,230	0.3%
47	Vermont	66	0.0%
15	Virginia	6,749	1.7%
20	Washington	5,810	1.5%
40	West Virginia	705	0.2%
25	Wisconsin	4,027	1.0%
47	Wyoming	66	0.0%

RANK ORDER

RANK	STATE	ROBBERIES	% of USA
1	California	61,664	15.5%
2	Texas	35,630	9.0%
3	New York	33,431	8.4%
4	Florida	29,723	7.5%
5	Pennsylvania	18,316	4.6%
6	Ohio	17,357	4.4%
7	Georgia	13,440	3.4%
8	New Jersey	13,076	3.3%
9	Maryland	12,708	3.2%
10	Michigan	11,234	2.8%
11	North Carolina	11,124	2.8%
12	Tennessee	8,736	2.2%
13	Arizona	7,677	1.9%
14	Massachusetts	7,467	1.9%
15	Virginia	6,749	1.7%
16	Missouri	6,563	1.7%
17	Louisiana	6,390	1.6%
18	Indiana	6,173	1.6%
19	Alabama	5,959	1.5%
20	Washington	5,810	1.5%
21	South Carolina	4,950	1.2%
22	Nevada	4,875	1.2%
23	Connecticut	4,145	1.0%
24	Minnesota	4,033	1.0%
25	Wisconsin	4,027	1.0%
26	Colorado	3,735	0.9%
27	Oklahoma	3,058	0.8%
28	Kentucky	3,007	0.8%
29	Oregon	2,685	0.7%
30	Arkansas	2,314	0.6%
31	Mississippi	2,277	0.6%
32	New Mexico	1,991	0.5%
33	Kansas	1,774	0.4%
34	Utah	1,230	0.3%
35	Delaware	1,160	0.3%
36	Nebraska	1,128	0.3%
37	Iowa	1,121	0.3%
38	Hawaii	818	0.2%
39	Rhode Island	731	0.2%
40	West Virginia	705	0.2%
41	New Hampshire	499	0.1%
42	Alaska	420	0.1%
43	Maine	274	0.1%
44	Idaho	226	0.1%
45	Montana	207	0.1%
46	South Dakota	108	0.0%
47	Vermont	66	0.0%
47	Wyoming	66	0.0%
49	North Dakota	38	0.0%
NA	Illinois**	NA	NA
	District of Columbia	3,202	0.8%

Source: Morgan Quitno Press using data from Federal Bureau of Investigation
   "Crime in the United States 2004" (Uniform Crime Reports, October 17, 2005)
*Estimated totals for urban areas, defined by the F.B.I. as Metropolitan Statistical Areas and other cities outside such areas. National total includes those states listed as not available. Robbery is the taking or attempting to take anything of value by force or threat of force.
**Not available.

Urban Robbery Rate in 2004

National Urban Rate = 150.7 Robberies per 100,000 Population*

ALPHA ORDER

RANK	STATE	RATE
14	Alabama	157.8
31	Alaska	94.9
17	Arizona	141.7
25	Arkansas	111.3
6	California	174.6
33	Colorado	88.0
18	Connecticut	138.9
12	Delaware	166.0
4	Florida	180.1
7	Georgia	173.7
32	Hawaii	90.2
45	Idaho	20.5
NA	Illinois**	NA
24	Indiana	115.6
41	Iowa	50.9
37	Kansas	76.6
26	Kentucky	105.3
10	Louisiana	167.9
44	Maine	26.3
1	Maryland	237.9
23	Massachusetts	116.4
20	Michigan	126.4
30	Minnesota	95.0
21	Mississippi	123.1
19	Missouri	134.7
42	Montana	40.5
36	Nebraska	81.7
2	Nevada	228.4
43	New Hampshire	40.1
15	New Jersey	150.3
22	New Mexico	122.6
3	New York	183.3
11	North Carolina	166.1
49	North Dakota	8.8
8	Ohio	172.4
27	Oklahoma	104.8
35	Oregon	85.4
13	Pennsylvania	162.3
38	Rhode Island	67.6
16	South Carolina	144.7
46	South Dakota	20.0
5	Tennessee	179.5
9	Texas	170.7
40	Utah	54.8
48	Vermont	16.4
28	Virginia	101.8
29	Washington	101.0
39	West Virginia	57.8
34	Wisconsin	87.6
47	Wyoming	18.1

RANK ORDER

RANK	STATE	RATE
1	Maryland	237.9
2	Nevada	228.4
3	New York	183.3
4	Florida	180.1
5	Tennessee	179.5
6	California	174.6
7	Georgia	173.7
8	Ohio	172.4
9	Texas	170.7
10	Louisiana	167.9
11	North Carolina	166.1
12	Delaware	166.0
13	Pennsylvania	162.3
14	Alabama	157.8
15	New Jersey	150.3
16	South Carolina	144.7
17	Arizona	141.7
18	Connecticut	138.9
19	Missouri	134.7
20	Michigan	126.4
21	Mississippi	123.1
22	New Mexico	122.6
23	Massachusetts	116.4
24	Indiana	115.6
25	Arkansas	111.3
26	Kentucky	105.3
27	Oklahoma	104.8
28	Virginia	101.8
29	Washington	101.0
30	Minnesota	95.0
31	Alaska	94.9
32	Hawaii	90.2
33	Colorado	88.0
34	Wisconsin	87.6
35	Oregon	85.4
36	Nebraska	81.7
37	Kansas	76.6
38	Rhode Island	67.6
39	West Virginia	57.8
40	Utah	54.8
41	Iowa	50.9
42	Montana	40.5
43	New Hampshire	40.1
44	Maine	26.3
45	Idaho	20.5
46	South Dakota	20.0
47	Wyoming	18.1
48	Vermont	16.4
49	North Dakota	8.8
NA	Illinois**	NA
	District of Columbia	578.5

Source: Morgan Quitno Press using data from Federal Bureau of Investigation
   "Crime in the United States 2004" (Uniform Crime Reports, October 17, 2005)
*Estimated rates for urban areas, defined by the F.B.I. as Metropolitan Statistical Areas and other cities outside such areas. National rate includes those states listed as not available. Robbery is the taking or attempting to take anything of value by force or threat of force.
**Not available.

Percent of Robberies Occurring in Urban Areas in 2004

National Percent = 98.8% of Robberies*

ALPHA ORDER

RANK	STATE	PERCENT
25	Alabama	98.6
42	Alaska	94.0
12	Arizona	99.4
31	Arkansas	97.6
4	California	99.8
8	Colorado	99.6
28	Connecticut	98.2
37	Delaware	95.2
15	Florida	99.1
27	Georgia	98.4
49	Hawaii	86.7
41	Idaho	94.2
NA	Illinois**	NA
35	Indiana	96.9
7	Iowa	99.7
29	Kansas	97.8
43	Kentucky	92.0
34	Louisiana	97.3
38	Maine	94.8
8	Maryland	99.6
1	Massachusetts	100.0
14	Michigan	99.2
15	Minnesota	99.1
45	Mississippi	91.0
19	Missouri	99.0
47	Montana	88.8
15	Nebraska	99.1
12	Nevada	99.4
4	New Hampshire	99.8
1	New Jersey	100.0
36	New Mexico	96.6
4	New York	99.8
40	North Carolina	94.4
33	North Dakota	97.4
23	Ohio	98.9
19	Oklahoma	99.0
31	Oregon	97.6
15	Pennsylvania	99.1
1	Rhode Island	100.0
46	South Carolina	90.9
39	South Dakota	94.7
24	Tennessee	98.8
10	Texas	99.5
10	Utah	99.5
48	Vermont	86.8
30	Virginia	97.7
19	Washington	99.0
44	West Virginia	91.8
19	Wisconsin	99.0
26	Wyoming	98.5

RANK ORDER

RANK	STATE	PERCENT
1	Massachusetts	100.0
1	New Jersey	100.0
1	Rhode Island	100.0
4	California	99.8
4	New Hampshire	99.8
4	New York	99.8
7	Iowa	99.7
8	Colorado	99.6
8	Maryland	99.6
10	Texas	99.5
10	Utah	99.5
12	Arizona	99.4
12	Nevada	99.4
14	Michigan	99.2
15	Florida	99.1
15	Minnesota	99.1
15	Nebraska	99.1
15	Pennsylvania	99.1
19	Missouri	99.0
19	Oklahoma	99.0
19	Washington	99.0
19	Wisconsin	99.0
23	Ohio	98.9
24	Tennessee	98.8
25	Alabama	98.6
26	Wyoming	98.5
27	Georgia	98.4
28	Connecticut	98.2
29	Kansas	97.8
30	Virginia	97.7
31	Arkansas	97.6
31	Oregon	97.6
33	North Dakota	97.4
34	Louisiana	97.3
35	Indiana	96.9
36	New Mexico	96.6
37	Delaware	95.2
38	Maine	94.8
39	South Dakota	94.7
40	North Carolina	94.4
41	Idaho	94.2
42	Alaska	94.0
43	Kentucky	92.0
44	West Virginia	91.8
45	Mississippi	91.0
46	South Carolina	90.9
47	Montana	88.8
48	Vermont	86.8
49	Hawaii	86.7
NA	Illinois**	NA

District of Columbia 100.0

Source: Morgan Quitno Press using data from Federal Bureau of Investigation
   "Crime in the United States 2004" (Uniform Crime Reports, October 17, 2005)
*Estimated percentages for urban areas, defined by the F.B.I. as Metropolitan Statistical Areas and other cities outside such areas. National percent includes those states listed as not available. Robbery is the taking or attempting to take anything of value by force or threat of force.
**Not available.

Robberies in Rural Areas in 2004

National Rural Total = 4,727 Robberies*

ALPHA ORDER

RANK	STATE	ROBBERIES	% of USA
17	Alabama	83	1.8%
34	Alaska	27	0.6%
28	Arizona	44	0.9%
24	Arkansas	58	1.2%
14	California	104	2.2%
36	Colorado	15	0.3%
18	Connecticut	77	1.6%
24	Delaware	58	1.2%
3	Florida	274	5.8%
6	Georgia	216	4.6%
13	Hawaii	126	2.7%
38	Idaho	14	0.3%
NA	Illinois**	NA	NA
7	Indiana	200	4.2%
43	Iowa	3	0.1%
30	Kansas	39	0.8%
4	Kentucky	261	5.5%
10	Louisiana	174	3.7%
36	Maine	15	0.3%
27	Maryland	53	1.1%
47	Massachusetts	0	0.0%
16	Michigan	86	1.8%
31	Minnesota	37	0.8%
5	Mississippi	226	4.8%
21	Missouri	67	1.4%
35	Montana	26	0.6%
39	Nebraska	10	0.2%
33	Nevada	30	0.6%
44	New Hampshire	1	0.0%
47	New Jersey	0	0.0%
20	New Mexico	71	1.5%
19	New York	75	1.6%
1	North Carolina	658	13.9%
44	North Dakota	1	0.0%
9	Ohio	186	3.9%
32	Oklahoma	32	0.7%
22	Oregon	66	1.4%
11	Pennsylvania	158	3.3%
47	Rhode Island	0	0.0%
2	South Carolina	496	10.5%
41	South Dakota	6	0.1%
14	Tennessee	104	2.2%
8	Texas	187	4.0%
41	Utah	6	0.1%
39	Vermont	10	0.2%
12	Virginia	157	3.3%
26	Washington	56	1.2%
23	West Virginia	63	1.3%
29	Wisconsin	40	0.8%
44	Wyoming	1	0.0%

RANK ORDER

RANK	STATE	ROBBERIES	% of USA
1	North Carolina	658	13.9%
2	South Carolina	496	10.5%
3	Florida	274	5.8%
4	Kentucky	261	5.5%
5	Mississippi	226	4.8%
6	Georgia	216	4.6%
7	Indiana	200	4.2%
8	Texas	187	4.0%
9	Ohio	186	3.9%
10	Louisiana	174	3.7%
11	Pennsylvania	158	3.3%
12	Virginia	157	3.3%
13	Hawaii	126	2.7%
14	California	104	2.2%
14	Tennessee	104	2.2%
16	Michigan	86	1.8%
17	Alabama	83	1.8%
18	Connecticut	77	1.6%
19	New York	75	1.6%
20	New Mexico	71	1.5%
21	Missouri	67	1.4%
22	Oregon	66	1.4%
23	West Virginia	63	1.3%
24	Arkansas	58	1.2%
24	Delaware	58	1.2%
26	Washington	56	1.2%
27	Maryland	53	1.1%
28	Arizona	44	0.9%
29	Wisconsin	40	0.8%
30	Kansas	39	0.8%
31	Minnesota	37	0.8%
32	Oklahoma	32	0.7%
33	Nevada	30	0.6%
34	Alaska	27	0.6%
35	Montana	26	0.6%
36	Colorado	15	0.3%
36	Maine	15	0.3%
38	Idaho	14	0.3%
39	Nebraska	10	0.2%
39	Vermont	10	0.2%
41	South Dakota	6	0.1%
41	Utah	6	0.1%
43	Iowa	3	0.1%
44	New Hampshire	1	0.0%
44	North Dakota	1	0.0%
44	Wyoming	1	0.0%
47	Massachusetts	0	0.0%
47	New Jersey	0	0.0%
47	Rhode Island	0	0.0%
NA	Illinois**	NA	NA
	District of Columbia	0	0.0%

Source: Federal Bureau of Investigation
"Crime in the United States 2004" (Uniform Crime Reports, October 17, 2005)
*Estimated totals for nonmetropolitan areas, defined by the F.B.I. as other than Metropolitan Statistical Areas and other cities outside such areas. National total includes those states listed as not available. Robbery is the taking or attempting to take anything of value by force or threat of force.
**Not available.

Rural Robbery Rate in 2004

National Rural Rate = 15.5 Robberies per 100,000 Population*

ALPHA ORDER

RANK	STATE	RATE
24	Alabama	11.0
21	Alaska	12.7
19	Arizona	13.5
28	Arkansas	8.6
14	California	18.3
39	Colorado	4.2
16	Connecticut	14.8
2	Delaware	44.1
5	Florida	30.6
12	Georgia	19.8
4	Hawaii	35.4
35	Idaho	4.8
NA	Illinois**	NA
9	Indiana	22.2
46	Iowa	0.4
27	Kansas	9.3
11	Kentucky	20.2
7	Louisiana	24.5
33	Maine	5.5
7	Maryland	24.5
47	Massachusetts	0.0
31	Michigan	7.0
38	Minnesota	4.3
10	Mississippi	21.5
29	Missouri	7.6
32	Montana	6.2
41	Nebraska	2.7
15	Nevada	15.0
43	New Hampshire	1.8
47	New Jersey	0.0
6	New Mexico	25.5
29	New York	7.6
3	North Carolina	35.7
45	North Dakota	0.5
20	Ohio	13.4
34	Oklahoma	5.3
17	Oregon	14.7
18	Pennsylvania	14.1
47	Rhode Island	0.0
1	South Carolina	63.9
42	South Dakota	2.6
26	Tennessee	10.1
23	Texas	11.6
40	Utah	4.1
36	Vermont	4.6
13	Virginia	19.0
22	Washington	12.5
25	West Virginia	10.6
37	Wisconsin	4.4
44	Wyoming	0.7

RANK ORDER

RANK	STATE	RATE
1	South Carolina	63.9
2	Delaware	44.1
3	North Carolina	35.7
4	Hawaii	35.4
5	Florida	30.6
6	New Mexico	25.5
7	Louisiana	24.5
7	Maryland	24.5
9	Indiana	22.2
10	Mississippi	21.5
11	Kentucky	20.2
12	Georgia	19.8
13	Virginia	19.0
14	California	18.3
15	Nevada	15.0
16	Connecticut	14.8
17	Oregon	14.7
18	Pennsylvania	14.1
19	Arizona	13.5
20	Ohio	13.4
21	Alaska	12.7
22	Washington	12.5
23	Texas	11.6
24	Alabama	11.0
25	West Virginia	10.6
26	Tennessee	10.1
27	Kansas	9.3
28	Arkansas	8.6
29	Missouri	7.6
29	New York	7.6
31	Michigan	7.0
32	Montana	6.2
33	Maine	5.5
34	Oklahoma	5.3
35	Idaho	4.8
36	Vermont	4.6
37	Wisconsin	4.4
38	Minnesota	4.3
39	Colorado	4.2
40	Utah	4.1
41	Nebraska	2.7
42	South Dakota	2.6
43	New Hampshire	1.8
44	Wyoming	0.7
45	North Dakota	0.5
46	Iowa	0.4
47	Massachusetts	0.0
47	New Jersey	0.0
47	Rhode Island	0.0
NA	Illinois**	NA

District of Columbia — 0.0

Source: Morgan Quitno Press using data from Federal Bureau of Investigation
    "Crime in the United States 2004" (Uniform Crime Reports, October 17, 2005)
*Estimated rates for nonmetropolitan areas, defined by the F.B.I. as other than Metropolitan Statistical Areas and
other cities outside such areas. National rate includes those states listed as not available. Robbery is the taking
or attempting to take anything of value by force or threat of force.
**Not available.

Percent of Robberies Occurring in Rural Areas in 2004

National Percent = 1.2% of Robberies*

ALPHA ORDER

RANK	STATE	PERCENT
25	Alabama	1.4
8	Alaska	6.0
37	Arizona	0.6
18	Arkansas	2.4
44	California	0.2
41	Colorado	0.4
22	Connecticut	1.8
13	Delaware	4.8
32	Florida	0.9
23	Georgia	1.6
1	Hawaii	13.3
9	Idaho	5.8
NA	Illinois**	NA
15	Indiana	3.1
43	Iowa	0.3
21	Kansas	2.2
7	Kentucky	8.0
16	Louisiana	2.7
12	Maine	5.2
41	Maryland	0.4
47	Massachusetts	0.0
36	Michigan	0.8
32	Minnesota	0.9
5	Mississippi	9.0
28	Missouri	1.0
3	Montana	11.2
32	Nebraska	0.9
37	Nevada	0.6
44	New Hampshire	0.2
47	New Jersey	0.0
14	New Mexico	3.4
44	New York	0.2
10	North Carolina	5.6
17	North Dakota	2.6
27	Ohio	1.1
28	Oklahoma	1.0
18	Oregon	2.4
32	Pennsylvania	0.9
47	Rhode Island	0.0
4	South Carolina	9.1
11	South Dakota	5.3
26	Tennessee	1.2
39	Texas	0.5
39	Utah	0.5
2	Vermont	13.2
20	Virginia	2.3
28	Washington	1.0
6	West Virginia	8.2
28	Wisconsin	1.0
24	Wyoming	1.5

RANK ORDER

RANK	STATE	PERCENT
1	Hawaii	13.3
2	Vermont	13.2
3	Montana	11.2
4	South Carolina	9.1
5	Mississippi	9.0
6	West Virginia	8.2
7	Kentucky	8.0
8	Alaska	6.0
9	Idaho	5.8
10	North Carolina	5.6
11	South Dakota	5.3
12	Maine	5.2
13	Delaware	4.8
14	New Mexico	3.4
15	Indiana	3.1
16	Louisiana	2.7
17	North Dakota	2.6
18	Arkansas	2.4
18	Oregon	2.4
20	Virginia	2.3
21	Kansas	2.2
22	Connecticut	1.8
23	Georgia	1.6
24	Wyoming	1.5
25	Alabama	1.4
26	Tennessee	1.2
27	Ohio	1.1
28	Missouri	1.0
28	Oklahoma	1.0
28	Washington	1.0
28	Wisconsin	1.0
32	Florida	0.9
32	Minnesota	0.9
32	Nebraska	0.9
32	Pennsylvania	0.9
36	Michigan	0.8
37	Arizona	0.6
37	Nevada	0.6
39	Texas	0.5
39	Utah	0.5
41	Colorado	0.4
41	Maryland	0.4
43	Iowa	0.3
44	California	0.2
44	New Hampshire	0.2
44	New York	0.2
47	Massachusetts	0.0
47	New Jersey	0.0
47	Rhode Island	0.0
NA	Illinois**	NA

District of Columbia 0.0

Source: Morgan Quitno Press using data from Federal Bureau of Investigation
    "Crime in the United States 2004" (Uniform Crime Reports, October 17, 2005)
*Estimated percentages for nonmetropolitan areas, defined by the F.B.I. as other than Metropolitan Statistical Areas and other cities outside such areas. National percent includes those states listed as not available. Robbery is the taking or attempting to take anything of value by force or threat of force.
**Not available.

424

Aggravated Assaults in Urban Areas in 2004

National Urban Total = 806,800 Aggravated Assaults*

ALPHA ORDER

RANK	STATE	ASSAULTS	% of USA
23	Alabama	10,417	1.3%
39	Alaska	2,343	0.3%
13	Arizona	17,878	2.2%
25	Arkansas	9,073	1.1%
1	California	122,735	15.2%
21	Colorado	10,825	1.3%
32	Connecticut	4,775	0.6%
38	Delaware	2,677	0.3%
2	Florida	82,864	10.3%
9	Georgia	21,771	2.7%
42	Hawaii	1,441	0.2%
40	Idaho	2,160	0.3%
NA	Illinois**	NA	NA
20	Indiana	11,035	1.4%
31	Iowa	5,596	0.7%
28	Kansas	6,516	0.8%
33	Kentucky	4,427	0.5%
15	Louisiana	17,697	2.2%
47	Maine	636	0.1%
8	Maryland	23,771	2.9%
12	Massachusetts	20,002	2.5%
5	Michigan	30,511	3.8%
27	Minnesota	6,874	0.9%
35	Mississippi	3,302	0.4%
14	Missouri	17,760	2.2%
43	Montana	1,282	0.2%
34	Nebraska	3,350	0.4%
26	Nevada	7,899	1.0%
44	New Hampshire	1,161	0.1%
16	New Jersey	16,144	2.0%
24	New Mexico	9,185	1.1%
4	New York	45,485	5.6%
11	North Carolina	20,144	2.5%
49	North Dakota	262	0.0%
17	Ohio	15,786	2.0%
19	Oklahoma	11,566	1.4%
29	Oregon	6,064	0.8%
6	Pennsylvania	27,417	3.4%
41	Rhode Island	1,586	0.2%
10	South Carolina	21,452	2.7%
45	South Dakota	742	0.1%
7	Tennessee	26,751	3.3%
3	Texas	72,818	9.0%
36	Utah	3,288	0.4%
48	Vermont	359	0.0%
22	Virginia	10,665	1.3%
18	Washington	11,893	1.5%
37	West Virginia	2,888	0.4%
30	Wisconsin	5,643	0.7%
45	Wyoming	742	0.1%

RANK ORDER

RANK	STATE	ASSAULTS	% of USA
1	California	122,735	15.2%
2	Florida	82,864	10.3%
3	Texas	72,818	9.0%
4	New York	45,485	5.6%
5	Michigan	30,511	3.8%
6	Pennsylvania	27,417	3.4%
7	Tennessee	26,751	3.3%
8	Maryland	23,771	2.9%
9	Georgia	21,771	2.7%
10	South Carolina	21,452	2.7%
11	North Carolina	20,144	2.5%
12	Massachusetts	20,002	2.5%
13	Arizona	17,878	2.2%
14	Missouri	17,760	2.2%
15	Louisiana	17,697	2.2%
16	New Jersey	16,144	2.0%
17	Ohio	15,786	2.0%
18	Washington	11,893	1.5%
19	Oklahoma	11,566	1.4%
20	Indiana	11,035	1.4%
21	Colorado	10,825	1.3%
22	Virginia	10,665	1.3%
23	Alabama	10,417	1.3%
24	New Mexico	9,185	1.1%
25	Arkansas	9,073	1.1%
26	Nevada	7,899	1.0%
27	Minnesota	6,874	0.9%
28	Kansas	6,516	0.8%
29	Oregon	6,064	0.8%
30	Wisconsin	5,643	0.7%
31	Iowa	5,596	0.7%
32	Connecticut	4,775	0.6%
33	Kentucky	4,427	0.5%
34	Nebraska	3,350	0.4%
35	Mississippi	3,302	0.4%
36	Utah	3,288	0.4%
37	West Virginia	2,888	0.4%
38	Delaware	2,677	0.3%
39	Alaska	2,343	0.3%
40	Idaho	2,160	0.3%
41	Rhode Island	1,586	0.2%
42	Hawaii	1,441	0.2%
43	Montana	1,282	0.2%
44	New Hampshire	1,161	0.1%
45	South Dakota	742	0.1%
45	Wyoming	742	0.1%
47	Maine	636	0.1%
48	Vermont	359	0.0%
49	North Dakota	262	0.0%
NA	Illinois**	NA	NA

District of Columbia 3,968 0.5%

Source: Morgan Quitno Press using data from Federal Bureau of Investigation
    "Crime in the United States 2004" (Uniform Crime Reports, October 17, 2005)
*Estimated totals for urban areas, defined by the F.B.I. as Metropolitan Statistical Areas and other cities outside such areas. National total includes those states listed as not available. Aggravated assault is an attack for the purpose of inflicting severe bodily injury.
**Not available.

Urban Aggravated Assault Rate in 2004

National Urban Rate = 306.5 Aggravated Assaults per 100,000 Population*

ALPHA ORDER

RANK	STATE	RATE
21	Alabama	275.9
4	Alaska	529.2
16	Arizona	329.9
8	Arkansas	436.3
14	California	347.4
22	Colorado	255.2
38	Connecticut	160.1
10	Delaware	383.0
5	Florida	502.2
20	Georgia	281.3
39	Hawaii	158.9
32	Idaho	195.8
NA	Illinois**	NA
29	Indiana	206.7
23	Iowa	254.2
19	Kansas	281.4
41	Kentucky	155.0
6	Louisiana	464.9
48	Maine	61.0
7	Maryland	445.0
17	Massachusetts	311.8
15	Michigan	343.4
36	Minnesota	162.0
35	Mississippi	178.5
12	Missouri	364.5
24	Montana	251.1
27	Nebraska	242.6
11	Nevada	370.1
46	New Hampshire	93.4
34	New Jersey	185.6
2	New Mexico	565.4
25	New York	249.4
18	North Carolina	300.7
48	North Dakota	61.0
40	Ohio	156.8
9	Oklahoma	396.2
33	Oregon	192.9
26	Pennsylvania	242.9
42	Rhode Island	146.8
1	South Carolina	627.0
44	South Dakota	137.4
3	Tennessee	549.5
13	Texas	348.8
43	Utah	146.6
47	Vermont	89.4
37	Virginia	160.8
29	Washington	206.7
28	West Virginia	236.6
45	Wisconsin	122.8
31	Wyoming	203.8

RANK ORDER

RANK	STATE	RATE
1	South Carolina	627.0
2	New Mexico	565.4
3	Tennessee	549.5
4	Alaska	529.2
5	Florida	502.2
6	Louisiana	464.9
7	Maryland	445.0
8	Arkansas	436.3
9	Oklahoma	396.2
10	Delaware	383.0
11	Nevada	370.1
12	Missouri	364.5
13	Texas	348.8
14	California	347.4
15	Michigan	343.4
16	Arizona	329.9
17	Massachusetts	311.8
18	North Carolina	300.7
19	Kansas	281.4
20	Georgia	281.3
21	Alabama	275.9
22	Colorado	255.2
23	Iowa	254.2
24	Montana	251.1
25	New York	249.4
26	Pennsylvania	242.9
27	Nebraska	242.6
28	West Virginia	236.6
29	Indiana	206.7
29	Washington	206.7
31	Wyoming	203.8
32	Idaho	195.8
33	Oregon	192.9
34	New Jersey	185.6
35	Mississippi	178.5
36	Minnesota	162.0
37	Virginia	160.8
38	Connecticut	160.1
39	Hawaii	158.9
40	Ohio	156.8
41	Kentucky	155.0
42	Rhode Island	146.8
43	Utah	146.6
44	South Dakota	137.4
45	Wisconsin	122.8
46	New Hampshire	93.4
47	Vermont	89.4
48	Maine	61.0
48	North Dakota	61.0
NA	Illinois**	NA

District of Columbia   716.9

Source: Morgan Quitno Press using data from Federal Bureau of Investigation
    "Crime in the United States 2004" (Uniform Crime Reports, October 17, 2005)
*Estimated rates for urban areas, defined by the F.B.I. as Metropolitan Statistical Areas and other cities outside such areas. National rate includes those states listed as not available. Aggravated assault is an attack for the purpose of inflicting severe bodily injury.
**Not available.

Percent of Aggravated Assaults Occurring Urban Areas in 2004

National Percent = 94.4% of Aggravated Assaults*

ALPHA ORDER				RANK ORDER		
RANK	STATE	PERCENT		RANK	STATE	PERCENT
25	Alabama	92.3		1	Massachusetts	100.0
47	Alaska	75.2		1	New Jersey	100.0
18	Arizona	94.5		3	Rhode Island	99.4
29	Arkansas	90.5		4	California	98.7
4	California	98.7		5	Maryland	97.7
10	Colorado	96.0		6	New Hampshire	97.3
15	Connecticut	95.6		7	New York	97.0
39	Delaware	85.3		8	Pennsylvania	96.7
9	Florida	96.1		9	Florida	96.1
24	Georgia	92.4		10	Colorado	96.0
46	Hawaii	75.7		10	Utah	96.0
41	Idaho	84.0		12	Ohio	95.9
NA	Illinois**	NA		13	Texas	95.8
20	Indiana	93.5		13	Washington	95.8
23	Iowa	92.6		15	Connecticut	95.6
30	Kansas	90.4		16	Michigan	95.0
42	Kentucky	81.8		17	Nevada	94.6
35	Louisiana	88.1		18	Arizona	94.5
37	Maine	85.7		19	New Mexico	93.6
5	Maryland	97.7		20	Indiana	93.5
1	Massachusetts	100.0		21	Nebraska	93.2
16	Michigan	95.0		22	Virginia	92.8
25	Minnesota	92.3		23	Iowa	92.6
48	Mississippi	70.6		24	Georgia	92.4
33	Missouri	89.9		25	Alabama	92.3
49	Montana	58.6		25	Minnesota	92.3
21	Nebraska	93.2		27	Oregon	91.9
17	Nevada	94.6		28	Wisconsin	91.1
6	New Hampshire	97.3		29	Arkansas	90.5
1	New Jersey	100.0		30	Kansas	90.4
19	New Mexico	93.6		31	Oklahoma	90.3
7	New York	97.0		31	Tennessee	90.3
38	North Carolina	85.4		33	Missouri	89.9
34	North Dakota	88.2		34	North Dakota	88.2
12	Ohio	95.9		35	Louisiana	88.1
31	Oklahoma	90.3		36	South Dakota	87.1
27	Oregon	91.9		37	Maine	85.7
8	Pennsylvania	96.7		38	North Carolina	85.4
3	Rhode Island	99.4		39	Delaware	85.3
40	South Carolina	84.2		40	South Carolina	84.2
36	South Dakota	87.1		41	Idaho	84.0
31	Tennessee	90.3		42	Kentucky	81.8
13	Texas	95.8		43	Vermont	79.4
10	Utah	96.0		44	West Virginia	76.6
43	Vermont	79.4		45	Wyoming	76.3
22	Virginia	92.8		46	Hawaii	75.7
13	Washington	95.8		47	Alaska	75.2
44	West Virginia	76.6		48	Mississippi	70.6
28	Wisconsin	91.1		49	Montana	58.6
45	Wyoming	76.3		NA	Illinois**	NA
					District of Columbia	100.0

Source: Morgan Quitno Press using data from Federal Bureau of Investigation
    "Crime in the United States 2004" (Uniform Crime Reports, October 17, 2005)
*Estimated percentages for urban areas, defined by the F.B.I. as Metropolitan Statistical Areas and other cities outside such areas. National percent includes those states listed as not available. Aggravated assault is an attack for the purpose of inflicting severe bodily injury.
**Not available.

Aggravated Assaults in Rural Areas in 2004

National Rural Total = 48,111 Aggravated Assaults*

ALPHA ORDER

RANK	STATE	ASSAULTS	% of USA
20	Alabama	869	1.8%
22	Alaska	774	1.6%
14	Arizona	1,043	2.2%
16	Arkansas	950	2.0%
10	California	1,560	3.2%
34	Colorado	451	0.9%
40	Connecticut	220	0.5%
32	Delaware	463	1.0%
3	Florida	3,335	6.9%
8	Georgia	1,790	3.7%
33	Hawaii	462	1.0%
37	Idaho	412	0.9%
NA	Illinois**	NA	NA
23	Indiana	767	1.6%
36	Iowa	447	0.9%
24	Kansas	689	1.4%
15	Kentucky	983	2.0%
6	Louisiana	2,393	5.0%
43	Maine	106	0.2%
28	Maryland	563	1.2%
48	Massachusetts	0	0.0%
9	Michigan	1,617	3.4%
27	Minnesota	571	1.2%
12	Mississippi	1,375	2.9%
7	Missouri	2,003	4.2%
18	Montana	905	1.9%
38	Nebraska	245	0.5%
35	Nevada	449	0.9%
46	New Hampshire	32	0.1%
48	New Jersey	0	0.0%
26	New Mexico	626	1.3%
11	New York	1,426	3.0%
2	North Carolina	3,447	7.2%
45	North Dakota	35	0.1%
25	Ohio	671	1.4%
13	Oklahoma	1,236	2.6%
30	Oregon	536	1.1%
17	Pennsylvania	922	1.9%
47	Rhode Island	10	0.0%
1	South Carolina	4,018	8.4%
42	South Dakota	110	0.2%
5	Tennessee	2,862	5.9%
4	Texas	3,167	6.6%
41	Utah	136	0.3%
44	Vermont	93	0.2%
21	Virginia	831	1.7%
31	Washington	524	1.1%
19	West Virginia	880	1.8%
29	Wisconsin	548	1.1%
39	Wyoming	231	0.5%

RANK ORDER

RANK	STATE	ASSAULTS	% of USA
1	South Carolina	4,018	8.4%
2	North Carolina	3,447	7.2%
3	Florida	3,335	6.9%
4	Texas	3,167	6.6%
5	Tennessee	2,862	5.9%
6	Louisiana	2,393	5.0%
7	Missouri	2,003	4.2%
8	Georgia	1,790	3.7%
9	Michigan	1,617	3.4%
10	California	1,560	3.2%
11	New York	1,426	3.0%
12	Mississippi	1,375	2.9%
13	Oklahoma	1,236	2.6%
14	Arizona	1,043	2.2%
15	Kentucky	983	2.0%
16	Arkansas	950	2.0%
17	Pennsylvania	922	1.9%
18	Montana	905	1.9%
19	West Virginia	880	1.8%
20	Alabama	869	1.8%
21	Virginia	831	1.7%
22	Alaska	774	1.6%
23	Indiana	767	1.6%
24	Kansas	689	1.4%
25	Ohio	671	1.4%
26	New Mexico	626	1.3%
27	Minnesota	571	1.2%
28	Maryland	563	1.2%
29	Wisconsin	548	1.1%
30	Oregon	536	1.1%
31	Washington	524	1.1%
32	Delaware	463	1.0%
33	Hawaii	462	1.0%
34	Colorado	451	0.9%
35	Nevada	449	0.9%
36	Iowa	447	0.9%
37	Idaho	412	0.9%
38	Nebraska	245	0.5%
39	Wyoming	231	0.5%
40	Connecticut	220	0.5%
41	Utah	136	0.3%
42	South Dakota	110	0.2%
43	Maine	106	0.2%
44	Vermont	93	0.2%
45	North Dakota	35	0.1%
46	New Hampshire	32	0.1%
47	Rhode Island	10	0.0%
48	Massachusetts	0	0.0%
48	New Jersey	0	0.0%
NA	Illinois**	NA	NA
	District of Columbia	0	0.0%

Source: Federal Bureau of Investigation
   "Crime in the United States 2004" (Uniform Crime Reports, October 17, 2005)
*Estimated totals for nonmetropolitan areas, defined by the F.B.I. as other than Metropolitan Statistical Areas and other cities outside such areas. National total includes those states listed as not available. Aggravated assault is an attack for the purpose of inflicting severe bodily injury.
**Not available.

Rural Aggravated Assault Rate in 2004

National Rural Rate = 158.1 Aggravated Assaults per 100,000 Population*

ALPHA ORDER

RANK	STATE	RATE
30	Alabama	115.1
3	Alaska	364.0
6	Arizona	321.1
23	Arkansas	141.1
8	California	274.8
27	Colorado	125.6
43	Connecticut	42.3
4	Delaware	352.4
2	Florida	371.9
17	Georgia	164.1
26	Hawaii	129.7
22	Idaho	141.9
NA	Illinois**	NA
33	Indiana	85.3
39	Iowa	59.4
17	Kansas	164.1
35	Kentucky	76.2
5	Louisiana	337.4
45	Maine	38.7
9	Maryland	259.9
47	Massachusetts	0.0
24	Michigan	131.7
37	Minnesota	66.6
25	Mississippi	130.6
10	Missouri	227.0
13	Montana	217.4
36	Nebraska	66.9
12	Nevada	223.8
40	New Hampshire	56.7
47	New Jersey	0.0
11	New Mexico	224.5
21	New York	144.7
16	North Carolina	187.1
46	North Dakota	17.1
41	Ohio	48.3
14	Oklahoma	204.4
28	Oregon	119.0
34	Pennsylvania	82.4
47	Rhode Island	0.0
1	South Carolina	517.3
42	South Dakota	47.7
7	Tennessee	277.1
15	Texas	196.6
32	Utah	93.2
43	Vermont	42.3
31	Virginia	100.4
29	Washington	116.6
20	West Virginia	147.9
38	Wisconsin	60.0
19	Wyoming	162.1

RANK ORDER

RANK	STATE	RATE
1	South Carolina	517.3
2	Florida	371.9
3	Alaska	364.0
4	Delaware	352.4
5	Louisiana	337.4
6	Arizona	321.1
7	Tennessee	277.1
8	California	274.8
9	Maryland	259.9
10	Missouri	227.0
11	New Mexico	224.5
12	Nevada	223.8
13	Montana	217.4
14	Oklahoma	204.4
15	Texas	196.6
16	North Carolina	187.1
17	Georgia	164.1
17	Kansas	164.1
19	Wyoming	162.1
20	West Virginia	147.9
21	New York	144.7
22	Idaho	141.9
23	Arkansas	141.1
24	Michigan	131.7
25	Mississippi	130.6
26	Hawaii	129.7
27	Colorado	125.6
28	Oregon	119.0
29	Washington	116.6
30	Alabama	115.1
31	Virginia	100.4
32	Utah	93.2
33	Indiana	85.3
34	Pennsylvania	82.4
35	Kentucky	76.2
36	Nebraska	66.9
37	Minnesota	66.6
38	Wisconsin	60.0
39	Iowa	59.4
40	New Hampshire	56.7
41	Ohio	48.3
42	South Dakota	47.7
43	Connecticut	42.3
43	Vermont	42.3
45	Maine	38.7
46	North Dakota	17.1
47	Massachusetts	0.0
47	New Jersey	0.0
47	Rhode Island	0.0
NA	Illinois**	NA

District of Columbia 0.0

Source: Morgan Quitno Press using data from Federal Bureau of Investigation
    "Crime in the United States 2004" (Uniform Crime Reports, October 17, 2005)
*Estimated rates for nonmetropolitan areas, defined by the F.B.I. as other than Metropolitan Statistical Areas and
other cities outside such areas. National rate includes those states listed as not available. Aggravated assault is
an attack for the purpose of inflicting severe bodily injury.
**Not available.

Percent of Aggravated Assaults Occurring in Rural Areas in 2004

National Percent = 5.6% of Aggravated Assaults*

ALPHA ORDER

RANK	STATE	PERCENT
24	Alabama	7.7
3	Alaska	24.8
32	Arizona	5.5
21	Arkansas	9.5
46	California	1.3
39	Colorado	4.0
35	Connecticut	4.4
11	Delaware	14.7
41	Florida	3.9
26	Georgia	7.6
4	Hawaii	24.3
9	Idaho	16.0
NA	Illinois**	NA
30	Indiana	6.5
27	Iowa	7.4
20	Kansas	9.6
8	Kentucky	18.2
15	Louisiana	11.9
13	Maine	14.3
45	Maryland	2.3
48	Massachusetts	0.0
34	Michigan	5.0
24	Minnesota	7.7
2	Mississippi	29.4
17	Missouri	10.1
1	Montana	41.4
29	Nebraska	6.8
33	Nevada	5.4
44	New Hampshire	2.7
48	New Jersey	0.0
31	New Mexico	6.4
43	New York	3.0
12	North Carolina	14.6
16	North Dakota	11.8
38	Ohio	4.1
18	Oklahoma	9.7
23	Oregon	8.1
42	Pennsylvania	3.3
47	Rhode Island	0.6
10	South Carolina	15.8
14	South Dakota	12.9
18	Tennessee	9.7
36	Texas	4.2
39	Utah	4.0
7	Vermont	20.6
28	Virginia	7.2
36	Washington	4.2
6	West Virginia	23.4
22	Wisconsin	8.9
5	Wyoming	23.7

RANK ORDER

RANK	STATE	PERCENT
1	Montana	41.4
2	Mississippi	29.4
3	Alaska	24.8
4	Hawaii	24.3
5	Wyoming	23.7
6	West Virginia	23.4
7	Vermont	20.6
8	Kentucky	18.2
9	Idaho	16.0
10	South Carolina	15.8
11	Delaware	14.7
12	North Carolina	14.6
13	Maine	14.3
14	South Dakota	12.9
15	Louisiana	11.9
16	North Dakota	11.8
17	Missouri	10.1
18	Oklahoma	9.7
18	Tennessee	9.7
20	Kansas	9.6
21	Arkansas	9.5
22	Wisconsin	8.9
23	Oregon	8.1
24	Alabama	7.7
24	Minnesota	7.7
26	Georgia	7.6
27	Iowa	7.4
28	Virginia	7.2
29	Nebraska	6.8
30	Indiana	6.5
31	New Mexico	6.4
32	Arizona	5.5
33	Nevada	5.4
34	Michigan	5.0
35	Connecticut	4.4
36	Texas	4.2
36	Washington	4.2
38	Ohio	4.1
39	Colorado	4.0
39	Utah	4.0
41	Florida	3.9
42	Pennsylvania	3.3
43	New York	3.0
44	New Hampshire	2.7
45	Maryland	2.3
46	California	1.3
47	Rhode Island	0.6
48	Massachusetts	0.0
48	New Jersey	0.0
NA	Illinois**	NA
	District of Columbia	0.0

Source: Morgan Quitno Press using data from Federal Bureau of Investigation
   "Crime in the United States 2004" (Uniform Crime Reports, October 17, 2005)
*Estimated percentages for nonmetropolitan areas, defined by the F.B.I. as other than Metropolitan Statistical Areas
and other cities outside such areas. National percent includes those states listed as not available. Aggravated
assault is an attack for the purpose of inflicting severe bodily injury.
**Not available.

Property Crimes in Urban Areas in 2004

National Urban Total = 9,813,811 Property Crimes*

ALPHA ORDER

RANK ORDER

RANK	STATE	CRIMES	% of USA		RANK	STATE	CRIMES	% of USA
20	Alabama	172,873	1.8%		1	California	1,216,231	12.4%
45	Alaska	17,815	0.2%		2	Texas	984,619	10.0%
8	Arizona	299,907	3.1%		3	Florida	707,275	7.2%
28	Arkansas	101,173	1.0%		4	New York	407,834	4.2%
1	California	1,216,231	12.4%		5	Ohio	399,055	4.1%
19	Colorado	175,819	1.8%		6	Georgia	352,147	3.6%
32	Connecticut	87,260	0.9%		7	North Carolina	311,566	3.2%
43	Delaware	23,391	0.2%		8	Arizona	299,907	3.1%
3	Florida	707,275	7.2%		9	Michigan	288,736	2.9%
6	Georgia	352,147	3.6%		10	Washington	288,706	2.9%
37	Hawaii	44,121	0.4%		11	Pennsylvania	284,465	2.9%
39	Idaho	34,752	0.4%		12	Tennessee	233,551	2.4%
NA	Illinois**	NA	NA		13	Missouri	211,505	2.2%
15	Indiana	200,173	2.0%		14	New Jersey	211,313	2.2%
34	Iowa	80,347	0.8%		15	Indiana	200,173	2.0%
27	Kansas	101,343	1.0%		16	Maryland	198,655	2.0%
31	Kentucky	87,562	0.9%		17	Virginia	187,855	1.9%
18	Louisiana	185,271	1.9%		18	Louisiana	185,271	1.9%
41	Maine	27,817	0.3%		19	Colorado	175,819	1.8%
16	Maryland	198,655	2.0%		20	Alabama	172,873	1.8%
22	Massachusetts	157,825	1.6%		21	South Carolina	163,521	1.7%
9	Michigan	288,736	2.9%		22	Massachusetts	157,825	1.6%
24	Minnesota	141,447	1.4%		23	Oregon	156,767	1.6%
33	Mississippi	85,107	0.9%		24	Minnesota	141,447	1.4%
13	Missouri	211,505	2.2%		25	Oklahoma	141,168	1.4%
44	Montana	20,727	0.2%		26	Wisconsin	135,715	1.4%
36	Nebraska	57,403	0.6%		27	Kansas	101,343	1.0%
30	Nevada	93,842	1.0%		28	Arkansas	101,173	1.0%
42	New Hampshire	26,254	0.3%		29	Utah	95,183	1.0%
14	New Jersey	211,313	2.2%		30	Nevada	93,842	1.0%
35	New Mexico	73,839	0.8%		31	Kentucky	87,562	0.9%
4	New York	407,834	4.2%		32	Connecticut	87,260	0.9%
7	North Carolina	311,566	3.2%		33	Mississippi	85,107	0.9%
49	North Dakota	10,707	0.1%		34	Iowa	80,347	0.8%
5	Ohio	399,055	4.1%		35	New Mexico	73,839	0.8%
25	Oklahoma	141,168	1.4%		36	Nebraska	57,403	0.6%
23	Orogon	156,767	1.6%		37	Hawaii	44,121	0.4%
11	Pennsylvania	284,465	2.9%		38	West Virginia	36,698	0.4%
40	Rhode Island	31,132	0.3%		39	Idaho	34,752	0.4%
21	South Carolina	163,521	1.7%		40	Rhode Island	31,132	0.3%
47	South Dakota	13,795	0.1%		41	Maine	27,817	0.3%
12	Tennessee	233,551	2.4%		42	New Hampshire	26,254	0.3%
2	Texas	984,619	10.0%		43	Delaware	23,391	0.2%
29	Utah	95,183	1.0%		44	Montana	20,727	0.2%
48	Vermont	11,281	0.1%		45	Alaska	17,815	0.2%
17	Virginia	187,855	1.9%		46	Wyoming	14,567	0.1%
10	Washington	288,706	2.9%		47	South Dakota	13,795	0.1%
38	West Virginia	36,698	0.4%		48	Vermont	11,281	0.1%
26	Wisconsin	135,715	1.4%		49	North Dakota	10,707	0.1%
46	Wyoming	14,567	0.1%		NA	Illinois**	NA	NA
						District of Columbia	26,896	0.3%

Source: Morgan Quitno Press using data from Federal Bureau of Investigation
   "Crime in the United States 2004" (Uniform Crime Reports, October 17, 2005)
*Estimated totals for urban areas, defined by the F.B.I. as Metropolitan Statistical Areas and other cities outside
such areas. National total includes those states listed as not available. Property crimes are offenses of burglary,
larceny-theft and motor vehicle theft.
**Not available.

Urban Property Crime Rate in 2004

National Urban Rate = 3,728.3 Property Crimes per 100,000 Population*

ALPHA ORDER

RANK	STATE	RATE
13	Alabama	4,579.2
24	Alaska	4,023.4
1	Arizona	5,534.4
6	Arkansas	4,865.1
30	California	3,442.9
22	Colorado	4,144.5
38	Connecticut	2,925.0
31	Delaware	3,346.4
19	Florida	4,286.4
14	Georgia	4,550.4
5	Hawaii	4,866.7
34	Idaho	3,150.7
NA	Illinois**	NA
27	Indiana	3,750.0
29	Iowa	3,649.4
17	Kansas	4,376.5
35	Kentucky	3,065.9
4	Louisiana	4,867.2
42	Maine	2,666.9
28	Maryland	3,719.1
46	Massachusetts	2,460.1
33	Michigan	3,249.8
32	Minnesota	3,332.7
12	Mississippi	4,600.9
18	Missouri	4,341.1
23	Montana	4,059.5
21	Nebraska	4,157.1
16	Nevada	4,397.2
49	New Hampshire	2,112.0
47	New Jersey	2,429.2
15	New Mexico	4,545.6
48	New York	2,235.8
11	North Carolina	4,651.0
45	North Dakota	2,493.1
26	Ohio	3,962.6
7	Oklahoma	4,836.2
3	Oregon	4,986.1
44	Pennsylvania	2,520.4
39	Rhode Island	2,880.9
9	South Carolina	4,779.5
43	South Dakota	2,554.3
8	Tennessee	4,797.7
10	Texas	4,715.9
20	Utah	4,243.2
41	Vermont	2,807.7
40	Virginia	2,832.4
2	Washington	5,017.3
36	West Virginia	3,007.0
37	Wisconsin	2,952.8
25	Wyoming	4,001.7

RANK ORDER

RANK	STATE	RATE
1	Arizona	5,534.4
2	Washington	5,017.3
3	Oregon	4,986.1
4	Louisiana	4,867.2
5	Hawaii	4,866.7
6	Arkansas	4,865.1
7	Oklahoma	4,836.2
8	Tennessee	4,797.7
9	South Carolina	4,779.5
10	Texas	4,715.9
11	North Carolina	4,651.0
12	Mississippi	4,600.9
13	Alabama	4,579.2
14	Georgia	4,550.4
15	New Mexico	4,545.6
16	Nevada	4,397.2
17	Kansas	4,376.5
18	Missouri	4,341.1
19	Florida	4,286.4
20	Utah	4,243.2
21	Nebraska	4,157.1
22	Colorado	4,144.5
23	Montana	4,059.5
24	Alaska	4,023.4
25	Wyoming	4,001.7
26	Ohio	3,962.6
27	Indiana	3,750.0
28	Maryland	3,719.1
29	Iowa	3,649.4
30	California	3,442.9
31	Delaware	3,346.4
32	Minnesota	3,332.7
33	Michigan	3,249.8
34	Idaho	3,150.7
35	Kentucky	3,065.9
36	West Virginia	3,007.0
37	Wisconsin	2,952.8
38	Connecticut	2,925.0
39	Rhode Island	2,880.9
40	Virginia	2,832.4
41	Vermont	2,807.7
42	Maine	2,666.9
43	South Dakota	2,554.3
44	Pennsylvania	2,520.4
45	North Dakota	2,493.1
46	Massachusetts	2,460.1
47	New Jersey	2,429.2
48	New York	2,235.8
49	New Hampshire	2,112.0
NA	Illinois**	NA
	District of Columbia	4,859.1

*Source: Morgan Quitno Press using data from Federal Bureau of Investigation
    "Crime in the United States 2004" (Uniform Crime Reports, October 17, 2005)*
Estimated rates for urban areas, defined by the F.B.I. as Metropolitan Statistical Areas and other cities outside such areas. National rate includes those states listed as not available. Property crimes are offenses of burglary, larceny-theft and motor vehicle theft.
***Not available.*

Percent of Property Crimes Occurring in Urban Areas in 2004

National Percent = 95.0% of Property Crimes*

<table>
<tr><td colspan="3">ALPHA ORDER</td><td colspan="3">RANK ORDER</td></tr>
<tr><td>RANK</td><td>STATE</td><td>PERCENT</td><td>RANK</td><td>STATE</td><td>PERCENT</td></tr>
<tr><td>16</td><td>Alabama</td><td>94.8</td><td>1</td><td>Massachusetts</td><td>100.0</td></tr>
<tr><td>46</td><td>Alaska</td><td>80.3</td><td>1</td><td>New Jersey</td><td>100.0</td></tr>
<tr><td>7</td><td>Arizona</td><td>97.8</td><td>3</td><td>Rhode Island</td><td>99.9</td></tr>
<tr><td>34</td><td>Arkansas</td><td>91.6</td><td>4</td><td>California</td><td>99.1</td></tr>
<tr><td>4</td><td>California</td><td>99.1</td><td>5</td><td>New Hampshire</td><td>99.0</td></tr>
<tr><td>8</td><td>Colorado</td><td>97.5</td><td>6</td><td>Maryland</td><td>98.2</td></tr>
<tr><td>16</td><td>Connecticut</td><td>94.8</td><td>7</td><td>Arizona</td><td>97.8</td></tr>
<tr><td>37</td><td>Delaware</td><td>89.0</td><td>8</td><td>Colorado</td><td>97.5</td></tr>
<tr><td>11</td><td>Florida</td><td>97.3</td><td>8</td><td>Utah</td><td>97.5</td></tr>
<tr><td>25</td><td>Georgia</td><td>93.5</td><td>10</td><td>Texas</td><td>97.4</td></tr>
<tr><td>49</td><td>Hawaii</td><td>72.9</td><td>11</td><td>Florida</td><td>97.3</td></tr>
<tr><td>36</td><td>Idaho</td><td>89.3</td><td>12</td><td>New York</td><td>96.5</td></tr>
<tr><td>NA</td><td>Illinois**</td><td>NA</td><td>13</td><td>Washington</td><td>96.0</td></tr>
<tr><td>19</td><td>Indiana</td><td>94.5</td><td>14</td><td>Nevada</td><td>95.5</td></tr>
<tr><td>24</td><td>Iowa</td><td>93.6</td><td>15</td><td>Pennsylvania</td><td>94.9</td></tr>
<tr><td>28</td><td>Kansas</td><td>93.2</td><td>16</td><td>Alabama</td><td>94.8</td></tr>
<tr><td>44</td><td>Kentucky</td><td>83.2</td><td>16</td><td>Connecticut</td><td>94.8</td></tr>
<tr><td>29</td><td>Louisiana</td><td>93.0</td><td>16</td><td>Ohio</td><td>94.8</td></tr>
<tr><td>40</td><td>Maine</td><td>87.6</td><td>19</td><td>Indiana</td><td>94.5</td></tr>
<tr><td>6</td><td>Maryland</td><td>98.2</td><td>20</td><td>Oklahoma</td><td>94.4</td></tr>
<tr><td>1</td><td>Massachusetts</td><td>100.0</td><td>21</td><td>Missouri</td><td>94.2</td></tr>
<tr><td>26</td><td>Michigan</td><td>93.4</td><td>21</td><td>Oregon</td><td>94.2</td></tr>
<tr><td>35</td><td>Minnesota</td><td>91.2</td><td>23</td><td>Virginia</td><td>94.1</td></tr>
<tr><td>43</td><td>Mississippi</td><td>84.3</td><td>24</td><td>Iowa</td><td>93.6</td></tr>
<tr><td>21</td><td>Missouri</td><td>94.2</td><td>25</td><td>Georgia</td><td>93.5</td></tr>
<tr><td>48</td><td>Montana</td><td>76.2</td><td>26</td><td>Michigan</td><td>93.4</td></tr>
<tr><td>27</td><td>Nebraska</td><td>93.3</td><td>27</td><td>Nebraska</td><td>93.3</td></tr>
<tr><td>14</td><td>Nevada</td><td>95.5</td><td>28</td><td>Kansas</td><td>93.2</td></tr>
<tr><td>5</td><td>New Hampshire</td><td>99.0</td><td>29</td><td>Louisiana</td><td>93.0</td></tr>
<tr><td>1</td><td>New Jersey</td><td>100.0</td><td>30</td><td>South Dakota</td><td>92.6</td></tr>
<tr><td>32</td><td>New Mexico</td><td>92.4</td><td>31</td><td>Wisconsin</td><td>92.5</td></tr>
<tr><td>12</td><td>New York</td><td>96.5</td><td>32</td><td>New Mexico</td><td>92.4</td></tr>
<tr><td>39</td><td>North Carolina</td><td>87.7</td><td>33</td><td>Tennessee</td><td>91.9</td></tr>
<tr><td>38</td><td>North Dakota</td><td>88.1</td><td>34</td><td>Arkansas</td><td>91.6</td></tr>
<tr><td>16</td><td>Ohio</td><td>94.8</td><td>35</td><td>Minnesota</td><td>91.2</td></tr>
<tr><td>20</td><td>Oklahoma</td><td>94.4</td><td>36</td><td>Idaho</td><td>89.3</td></tr>
<tr><td>21</td><td>Oregon</td><td>94.2</td><td>37</td><td>Delaware</td><td>89.0</td></tr>
<tr><td>15</td><td>Pennsylvania</td><td>94.9</td><td>38</td><td>North Dakota</td><td>88.1</td></tr>
<tr><td>3</td><td>Rhode Island</td><td>99.9</td><td>39</td><td>North Carolina</td><td>87.7</td></tr>
<tr><td>41</td><td>South Carolina</td><td>86.5</td><td>40</td><td>Maine</td><td>87.6</td></tr>
<tr><td>30</td><td>South Dakota</td><td>92.6</td><td>41</td><td>South Carolina</td><td>86.5</td></tr>
<tr><td>33</td><td>Tennessee</td><td>91.9</td><td>42</td><td>Wyoming</td><td>86.3</td></tr>
<tr><td>10</td><td>Texas</td><td>97.4</td><td>43</td><td>Mississippi</td><td>84.3</td></tr>
<tr><td>8</td><td>Utah</td><td>97.5</td><td>44</td><td>Kentucky</td><td>83.2</td></tr>
<tr><td>47</td><td>Vermont</td><td>78.7</td><td>45</td><td>West Virginia</td><td>80.7</td></tr>
<tr><td>23</td><td>Virginia</td><td>94.1</td><td>46</td><td>Alaska</td><td>80.3</td></tr>
<tr><td>13</td><td>Washington</td><td>96.0</td><td>47</td><td>Vermont</td><td>78.7</td></tr>
<tr><td>45</td><td>West Virginia</td><td>80.7</td><td>48</td><td>Montana</td><td>76.2</td></tr>
<tr><td>31</td><td>Wisconsin</td><td>92.5</td><td>49</td><td>Hawaii</td><td>72.9</td></tr>
<tr><td>42</td><td>Wyoming</td><td>86.3</td><td>NA</td><td>Illinois**</td><td>NA</td></tr>
<tr><td></td><td></td><td></td><td></td><td>District of Columbia</td><td>100.0</td></tr>
</table>

Source: Morgan Quitno Press using data from Federal Bureau of Investigation
    "Crime in the United States 2004" (Uniform Crime Reports, October 17, 2005)
*Estimated percentages for urban areas, defined by the F.B.I. as Metropolitan Statistical Areas and other cities outside such areas. National percent includes those states listed as not available. Property crimes are offenses of burglary, larceny-theft and motor vehicle theft.
**Not available.

Property Crimes Occurring in Rural Areas in 2004

National Rural Total = 514,444 Property Crimes*

ALPHA ORDER

RANK	STATE	CRIMES	% of USA
23	Alabama	9,467	1.8%
35	Alaska	4,357	0.8%
28	Arizona	6,840	1.3%
24	Arkansas	9,291	1.8%
21	California	10,963	2.1%
33	Colorado	4,523	0.9%
32	Connecticut	4,786	0.9%
41	Delaware	2,881	0.6%
8	Florida	19,866	3.9%
4	Georgia	24,509	4.8%
10	Hawaii	16,404	3.2%
36	Idaho	4,181	0.8%
NA	Illinois**	NA	NA
19	Indiana	11,756	2.3%
31	Iowa	5,489	1.1%
27	Kansas	7,351	1.4%
9	Kentucky	17,647	3.4%
14	Louisiana	13,882	2.7%
38	Maine	3,923	0.8%
39	Maryland	3,671	0.7%
48	Massachusetts	0	0.0%
7	Michigan	20,472	4.0%
15	Minnesota	13,572	2.6%
11	Mississippi	15,873	3.1%
16	Missouri	13,124	2.6%
29	Montana	6,488	1.3%
37	Nebraska	4,109	0.8%
34	Nevada	4,373	0.9%
46	New Hampshire	257	0.0%
48	New Jersey	0	0.0%
30	New Mexico	6,056	1.2%
13	New York	14,900	2.9%
1	North Carolina	43,762	8.5%
44	North Dakota	1,451	0.3%
5	Ohio	21,855	4.2%
26	Oklahoma	8,304	1.6%
22	Oregon	9,708	1.9%
12	Pennsylvania	15,146	2.9%
47	Rhode Island	34	0.0%
3	South Carolina	25,592	5.0%
45	South Dakota	1,110	0.2%
6	Tennessee	20,572	4.0%
2	Texas	26,083	5.1%
42	Utah	2,424	0.5%
40	Vermont	3,062	0.6%
18	Virginia	11,813	2.3%
17	Washington	12,131	2.4%
25	West Virginia	8,799	1.7%
20	Wisconsin	10,995	2.1%
43	Wyoming	2,322	0.5%

RANK ORDER

RANK	STATE	CRIMES	% of USA
1	North Carolina	43,762	8.5%
2	Texas	26,083	5.1%
3	South Carolina	25,592	5.0%
4	Georgia	24,509	4.8%
5	Ohio	21,855	4.2%
6	Tennessee	20,572	4.0%
7	Michigan	20,472	4.0%
8	Florida	19,866	3.9%
9	Kentucky	17,647	3.4%
10	Hawaii	16,404	3.2%
11	Mississippi	15,873	3.1%
12	Pennsylvania	15,146	2.9%
13	New York	14,900	2.9%
14	Louisiana	13,882	2.7%
15	Minnesota	13,572	2.6%
16	Missouri	13,124	2.6%
17	Washington	12,131	2.4%
18	Virginia	11,813	2.3%
19	Indiana	11,756	2.3%
20	Wisconsin	10,995	2.1%
21	California	10,963	2.1%
22	Oregon	9,708	1.9%
23	Alabama	9,467	1.8%
24	Arkansas	9,291	1.8%
25	West Virginia	8,799	1.7%
26	Oklahoma	8,304	1.6%
27	Kansas	7,351	1.4%
28	Arizona	6,840	1.3%
29	Montana	6,488	1.3%
30	New Mexico	6,056	1.2%
31	Iowa	5,489	1.1%
32	Connecticut	4,786	0.9%
33	Colorado	4,523	0.9%
34	Nevada	4,373	0.9%
35	Alaska	4,357	0.8%
36	Idaho	4,181	0.8%
37	Nebraska	4,109	0.8%
38	Maine	3,923	0.8%
39	Maryland	3,671	0.7%
40	Vermont	3,062	0.6%
41	Delaware	2,881	0.6%
42	Utah	2,424	0.5%
43	Wyoming	2,322	0.5%
44	North Dakota	1,451	0.3%
45	South Dakota	1,110	0.2%
46	New Hampshire	257	0.0%
47	Rhode Island	34	0.0%
48	Massachusetts	0	0.0%
48	New Jersey	0	0.0%
NA	Illinois**	NA	NA
	District of Columbia	0	0.0%

Source: Federal Bureau of Investigation
    "Crime in the United States 2004" (Uniform Crime Reports, October 17, 2005)
Estimated totals for nonmetropolitan areas, defined by the F.B.I. as other than Metropolitan Statistical Areas and other cities outside such areas. National total includes those states listed as not available. Property crimes are offenses of burglary, larceny-theft and motor vehicle theft.
**Not available.*

434

Rural Property Crime Rate in 2004

National Rural Rate = 1,690.5 Property Crimes per 100,000 Population*

ALPHA ORDER

RANK	STATE	RATE
39	Alabama	1,253.9
12	Alaska	2,048.9
11	Arizona	2,105.5
33	Arkansas	1,380.4
15	California	1,930.9
38	Colorado	1,259.2
42	Connecticut	919.8
7	Delaware	2,192.8
6	Florida	2,215.1
5	Georgia	2,247.2
1	Hawaii	4,604.6
29	Idaho	1,440.3
NA	Illinois**	NA
37	Indiana	1,306.7
43	Iowa	729.1
16	Kansas	1,750.7
35	Kentucky	1,368.1
14	Louisiana	1,957.3
30	Maine	1,430.6
17	Maryland	1,694.6
47	Massachusetts	0.0
18	Michigan	1,667.3
22	Minnesota	1,584.1
26	Mississippi	1,507.1
27	Missouri	1,487.2
24	Montana	1,558.6
41	Nebraska	1,121.5
8	Nevada	2,179.4
46	New Hampshire	455.7
47	New Jersey	0.0
9	New Mexico	2,171.5
25	New York	1,511.5
4	North Carolina	2,375.4
44	North Dakota	708.1
23	Ohio	1,573.9
34	Oklahoma	1,373.5
10	Oregon	2,155.0
36	Pennsylvania	1,352.8
47	Rhode Island	0.0
2	South Carolina	3,294.6
45	South Dakota	480.9
13	Tennessee	1,991.6
21	Texas	1,618.9
19	Utah	1,661.7
32	Vermont	1,394.3
31	Virginia	1,427.5
3	Washington	2,698.6
28	West Virginia	1,479.0
40	Wisconsin	1,204.4
20	Wyoming	1,629.4

RANK ORDER

RANK	STATE	RATE
1	Hawaii	4,604.6
2	South Carolina	3,294.6
3	Washington	2,698.6
4	North Carolina	2,375.4
5	Georgia	2,247.2
6	Florida	2,215.1
7	Delaware	2,192.8
8	Nevada	2,179.4
9	New Mexico	2,171.5
10	Oregon	2,155.0
11	Arizona	2,105.5
12	Alaska	2,048.9
13	Tennessee	1,991.6
14	Louisiana	1,957.3
15	California	1,930.9
16	Kansas	1,750.7
17	Maryland	1,694.6
18	Michigan	1,667.3
19	Utah	1,661.7
20	Wyoming	1,629.4
21	Texas	1,618.9
22	Minnesota	1,584.1
23	Ohio	1,573.9
24	Montana	1,558.6
25	New York	1,511.5
26	Mississippi	1,507.1
27	Missouri	1,487.2
28	West Virginia	1,479.0
29	Idaho	1,440.3
30	Maine	1,430.6
31	Virginia	1,427.5
32	Vermont	1,394.3
33	Arkansas	1,380.4
34	Oklahoma	1,373.5
35	Kentucky	1,368.1
36	Pennsylvania	1,352.8
37	Indiana	1,306.7
38	Colorado	1,259.2
39	Alabama	1,253.9
40	Wisconsin	1,204.4
41	Nebraska	1,121.5
42	Connecticut	919.8
43	Iowa	729.1
44	North Dakota	708.1
45	South Dakota	480.9
46	New Hampshire	455.7
47	Massachusetts	0.0
47	New Jersey	0.0
47	Rhode Island	0.0
NA	Illinois**	NA

District of Columbia   0.0

Source: Morgan Quitno Press using data from Federal Bureau of Investigation
    "Crime in the United States 2004" (Uniform Crime Reports, October 17, 2005)
*Estimated rates for nonmetropolitan areas, defined by the F.B.I. as other than Metropolitan Statistical Areas and other cities outside such areas. National rate includes those states listed as not available. Property crimes are offenses of burglary, larceny-theft and motor vehicle theft.
**Not available.

Percent of Property Crimes Occurring in Rural Areas in 2004

National Percent = 5.0% of Property Crimes*

ALPHA ORDER

RANK	STATE	PERCENT
32	Alabama	5.2
4	Alaska	19.7
43	Arizona	2.2
16	Arkansas	8.4
46	California	0.9
41	Colorado	2.5
32	Connecticut	5.2
13	Delaware	11.0
39	Florida	2.7
25	Georgia	6.5
1	Hawaii	27.1
14	Idaho	10.7
NA	Illinois**	NA
31	Indiana	5.5
26	Iowa	6.4
22	Kansas	6.8
6	Kentucky	16.8
21	Louisiana	7.0
10	Maine	12.4
44	Maryland	1.8
48	Massachusetts	0.0
24	Michigan	6.6
15	Minnesota	8.8
7	Mississippi	15.7
28	Missouri	5.8
2	Montana	23.8
23	Nebraska	6.7
36	Nevada	4.5
45	New Hampshire	1.0
48	New Jersey	0.0
18	New Mexico	7.6
38	New York	3.5
11	North Carolina	12.3
12	North Dakota	11.9
32	Ohio	5.2
30	Oklahoma	5.6
28	Oregon	5.8
35	Pennsylvania	5.1
47	Rhode Island	0.1
9	South Carolina	13.5
20	South Dakota	7.4
17	Tennessee	8.1
40	Texas	2.6
41	Utah	2.5
3	Vermont	21.3
27	Virginia	5.9
37	Washington	4.0
5	West Virginia	19.3
19	Wisconsin	7.5
8	Wyoming	13.7

RANK ORDER

RANK	STATE	PERCENT
1	Hawaii	27.1
2	Montana	23.8
3	Vermont	21.3
4	Alaska	19.7
5	West Virginia	19.3
6	Kentucky	16.8
7	Mississippi	15.7
8	Wyoming	13.7
9	South Carolina	13.5
10	Maine	12.4
11	North Carolina	12.3
12	North Dakota	11.9
13	Delaware	11.0
14	Idaho	10.7
15	Minnesota	8.8
16	Arkansas	8.4
17	Tennessee	8.1
18	New Mexico	7.6
19	Wisconsin	7.5
20	South Dakota	7.4
21	Louisiana	7.0
22	Kansas	6.8
23	Nebraska	6.7
24	Michigan	6.6
25	Georgia	6.5
26	Iowa	6.4
27	Virginia	5.9
28	Missouri	5.8
28	Oregon	5.8
30	Oklahoma	5.6
31	Indiana	5.5
32	Alabama	5.2
32	Connecticut	5.2
32	Ohio	5.2
35	Pennsylvania	5.1
36	Nevada	4.5
37	Washington	4.0
38	New York	3.5
39	Florida	2.7
40	Texas	2.6
41	Colorado	2.5
41	Utah	2.5
43	Arizona	2.2
44	Maryland	1.8
45	New Hampshire	1.0
46	California	0.9
47	Rhode Island	0.1
48	Massachusetts	0.0
48	New Jersey	0.0
NA	Illinois**	NA
	District of Columbia	0.0

Source: Morgan Quitno Press using data from Federal Bureau of Investigation
    "Crime in the United States 2004" (Uniform Crime Reports, October 17, 2005)
*Estimated percentages for nonmetropolitan areas, defined by the F.B.I. as other than Metropolitan Statistical Areas
and other cities outside such areas. National percent includes those states listed as not available. Property crimes
are offenses of burglary, larceny-theft and motor vehicle theft.
**Not available.

Burglaries in Urban Areas in 2004

National Urban Total = 1,976,080 Burglaries*

<table>
<tr><td colspan="4">ALPHA ORDER</td><td colspan="4">RANK ORDER</td></tr>
<tr><td>RANK</td><td>STATE</td><td>BURGLARIES</td><td>% of USA</td><td>RANK</td><td>STATE</td><td>BURGLARIES</td><td>% of USA</td></tr>
<tr><td>13</td><td>Alabama</td><td>41,286</td><td>2.1%</td><td>1</td><td>California</td><td>241,908</td><td>12.2%</td></tr>
<tr><td>45</td><td>Alaska</td><td>2,505</td><td>0.1%</td><td>2</td><td>Texas</td><td>209,698</td><td>10.6%</td></tr>
<tr><td>10</td><td>Arizona</td><td>54,683</td><td>2.8%</td><td>3</td><td>Florida</td><td>160,055</td><td>8.1%</td></tr>
<tr><td>24</td><td>Arkansas</td><td>26,871</td><td>1.4%</td><td>4</td><td>Ohio</td><td>90,120</td><td>4.6%</td></tr>
<tr><td>1</td><td>California</td><td>241,908</td><td>12.2%</td><td>5</td><td>North Carolina</td><td>83,140</td><td>4.2%</td></tr>
<tr><td>21</td><td>Colorado</td><td>32,112</td><td>1.6%</td><td>6</td><td>Georgia</td><td>76,094</td><td>3.9%</td></tr>
<tr><td>35</td><td>Connecticut</td><td>14,433</td><td>0.7%</td><td>7</td><td>New York</td><td>66,634</td><td>3.4%</td></tr>
<tr><td>43</td><td>Delaware</td><td>4,423</td><td>0.2%</td><td>8</td><td>Michigan</td><td>57,551</td><td>2.9%</td></tr>
<tr><td>3</td><td>Florida</td><td>160,055</td><td>8.1%</td><td>9</td><td>Washington</td><td>56,323</td><td>2.9%</td></tr>
<tr><td>6</td><td>Georgia</td><td>76,094</td><td>3.9%</td><td>10</td><td>Arizona</td><td>54,683</td><td>2.8%</td></tr>
<tr><td>38</td><td>Hawaii</td><td>7,240</td><td>0.4%</td><td>11</td><td>Tennessee</td><td>52,924</td><td>2.7%</td></tr>
<tr><td>39</td><td>Idaho</td><td>6,367</td><td>0.3%</td><td>12</td><td>Pennsylvania</td><td>49,521</td><td>2.5%</td></tr>
<tr><td>NA</td><td>Illinois**</td><td>NA</td><td>NA</td><td>13</td><td>Alabama</td><td>41,286</td><td>2.1%</td></tr>
<tr><td>16</td><td>Indiana</td><td>39,040</td><td>2.0%</td><td>14</td><td>Louisiana</td><td>41,191</td><td>2.1%</td></tr>
<tr><td>33</td><td>Iowa</td><td>16,264</td><td>0.8%</td><td>15</td><td>New Jersey</td><td>41,030</td><td>2.1%</td></tr>
<tr><td>31</td><td>Kansas</td><td>17,788</td><td>0.9%</td><td>16</td><td>Indiana</td><td>39,040</td><td>2.0%</td></tr>
<tr><td>30</td><td>Kentucky</td><td>19,173</td><td>1.0%</td><td>17</td><td>Missouri</td><td>35,896</td><td>1.8%</td></tr>
<tr><td>14</td><td>Louisiana</td><td>41,191</td><td>2.1%</td><td>18</td><td>South Carolina</td><td>35,725</td><td>1.8%</td></tr>
<tr><td>41</td><td>Maine</td><td>5,053</td><td>0.3%</td><td>19</td><td>Maryland</td><td>35,665</td><td>1.8%</td></tr>
<tr><td>19</td><td>Maryland</td><td>35,665</td><td>1.8%</td><td>20</td><td>Massachusetts</td><td>34,469</td><td>1.7%</td></tr>
<tr><td>20</td><td>Massachusetts</td><td>34,469</td><td>1.7%</td><td>21</td><td>Colorado</td><td>32,112</td><td>1.6%</td></tr>
<tr><td>8</td><td>Michigan</td><td>57,551</td><td>2.9%</td><td>22</td><td>Oklahoma</td><td>32,058</td><td>1.6%</td></tr>
<tr><td>26</td><td>Minnesota</td><td>23,937</td><td>1.2%</td><td>23</td><td>Oregon</td><td>27,307</td><td>1.4%</td></tr>
<tr><td>28</td><td>Mississippi</td><td>21,412</td><td>1.1%</td><td>24</td><td>Arkansas</td><td>26,871</td><td>1.4%</td></tr>
<tr><td>17</td><td>Missouri</td><td>35,896</td><td>1.8%</td><td>25</td><td>Virginia</td><td>26,078</td><td>1.3%</td></tr>
<tr><td>46</td><td>Montana</td><td>2,441</td><td>0.1%</td><td>26</td><td>Minnesota</td><td>23,937</td><td>1.2%</td></tr>
<tr><td>36</td><td>Nebraska</td><td>8,829</td><td>0.4%</td><td>27</td><td>Nevada</td><td>21,748</td><td>1.1%</td></tr>
<tr><td>27</td><td>Nevada</td><td>21,748</td><td>1.1%</td><td>28</td><td>Mississippi</td><td>21,412</td><td>1.1%</td></tr>
<tr><td>42</td><td>New Hampshire</td><td>4,828</td><td>0.2%</td><td>29</td><td>Wisconsin</td><td>20,410</td><td>1.0%</td></tr>
<tr><td>15</td><td>New Jersey</td><td>41,030</td><td>2.1%</td><td>30</td><td>Kentucky</td><td>19,173</td><td>1.0%</td></tr>
<tr><td>32</td><td>New Mexico</td><td>17,252</td><td>0.9%</td><td>31</td><td>Kansas</td><td>17,788</td><td>0.9%</td></tr>
<tr><td>7</td><td>New York</td><td>66,634</td><td>3.4%</td><td>32</td><td>New Mexico</td><td>17,252</td><td>0.9%</td></tr>
<tr><td>5</td><td>North Carolina</td><td>83,140</td><td>4.2%</td><td>33</td><td>Iowa</td><td>16,264</td><td>0.8%</td></tr>
<tr><td>49</td><td>North Dakota</td><td>1,560</td><td>0.1%</td><td>34</td><td>Utah</td><td>14,571</td><td>0.7%</td></tr>
<tr><td>4</td><td>Ohio</td><td>90,120</td><td>4.6%</td><td>35</td><td>Connecticut</td><td>14,433</td><td>0.7%</td></tr>
<tr><td>22</td><td>Oklahoma</td><td>32,058</td><td>1.6%</td><td>36</td><td>Nebraska</td><td>8,829</td><td>0.4%</td></tr>
<tr><td>23</td><td>Oregon</td><td>27,307</td><td>1.4%</td><td>37</td><td>West Virginia</td><td>8,307</td><td>0.4%</td></tr>
<tr><td>12</td><td>Pennsylvania</td><td>49,521</td><td>2.5%</td><td>38</td><td>Hawaii</td><td>7,240</td><td>0.4%</td></tr>
<tr><td>40</td><td>Rhode Island</td><td>5,464</td><td>0.3%</td><td>39</td><td>Idaho</td><td>6,367</td><td>0.3%</td></tr>
<tr><td>18</td><td>South Carolina</td><td>35,725</td><td>1.8%</td><td>40</td><td>Rhode Island</td><td>5,464</td><td>0.3%</td></tr>
<tr><td>44</td><td>South Dakota</td><td>2,839</td><td>0.1%</td><td>41</td><td>Maine</td><td>5,053</td><td>0.3%</td></tr>
<tr><td>11</td><td>Tennessee</td><td>52,924</td><td>2.7%</td><td>42</td><td>New Hampshire</td><td>4,828</td><td>0.2%</td></tr>
<tr><td>2</td><td>Texas</td><td>209,698</td><td>10.6%</td><td>43</td><td>Delaware</td><td>4,423</td><td>0.2%</td></tr>
<tr><td>34</td><td>Utah</td><td>14,571</td><td>0.7%</td><td>44</td><td>South Dakota</td><td>2,839</td><td>0.1%</td></tr>
<tr><td>48</td><td>Vermont</td><td>2,246</td><td>0.1%</td><td>45</td><td>Alaska</td><td>2,505</td><td>0.1%</td></tr>
<tr><td>25</td><td>Virginia</td><td>26,078</td><td>1.3%</td><td>46</td><td>Montana</td><td>2,441</td><td>0.1%</td></tr>
<tr><td>9</td><td>Washington</td><td>56,323</td><td>2.9%</td><td>47</td><td>Wyoming</td><td>2,316</td><td>0.1%</td></tr>
<tr><td>37</td><td>West Virginia</td><td>8,307</td><td>0.4%</td><td>48</td><td>Vermont</td><td>2,246</td><td>0.1%</td></tr>
<tr><td>29</td><td>Wisconsin</td><td>20,410</td><td>1.0%</td><td>49</td><td>North Dakota</td><td>1,560</td><td>0.1%</td></tr>
<tr><td>47</td><td>Wyoming</td><td>2,316</td><td>0.1%</td><td>NA</td><td>Illinois**</td><td>NA</td><td>NA</td></tr>
<tr><td></td><td></td><td></td><td></td><td></td><td>District of Columbia</td><td>3,946</td><td>0.2%</td></tr>
</table>

Source: Morgan Quitno Press using data from Federal Bureau of Investigation
   "Crime in the United States 2004" (Uniform Crime Reports, October 17, 2005)
*Estimated totals for urban areas, defined by the F.B.I. as Metropolitan Statistical Areas and other cities outside such areas. National total includes those states listed as not available. Burglary is the unlawful entry of a structure to commit a felony or theft. Attempts are included.
**Not available.

Urban Burglary Rate in 2004

National Urban Rate = 750.7 Burglaries per 100,000 Population*

ALPHA ORDER

RANK	STATE	RATE
5	Alabama	1,093.6
34	Alaska	565.7
11	Arizona	1,009.1
1	Arkansas	1,292.1
24	California	684.8
20	Colorado	757.0
41	Connecticut	483.8
32	Delaware	632.8
15	Florida	970.0
13	Georgia	983.3
18	Hawaii	798.6
33	Idaho	577.3
NA	Illinois**	NA
23	Indiana	731.4
21	Iowa	738.7
19	Kansas	768.2
26	Kentucky	671.3
7	Louisiana	1,082.1
40	Maine	484.5
27	Maryland	667.7
37	Massachusetts	537.3
29	Michigan	647.7
35	Minnesota	564.0
3	Mississippi	1,157.5
22	Missouri	736.8
42	Montana	478.1
30	Nebraska	639.4
10	Nevada	1,019.1
47	New Hampshire	388.4
43	New Jersey	471.7
8	New Mexico	1,062.1
48	New York	365.3
2	North Carolina	1,241.1
49	North Dakota	363.2
16	Ohio	894.9
4	Oklahoma	1,098.3
17	Oregon	868.5
45	Pennsylvania	438.8
39	Rhode Island	505.6
9	South Carolina	1,044.2
38	South Dakota	525.7
6	Tennessee	1,087.2
12	Texas	1,004.4
28	Utah	649.6
36	Vermont	559.0
46	Virginia	393.2
14	Washington	978.8
25	West Virginia	680.7
44	Wisconsin	444.1
31	Wyoming	636.2

RANK ORDER

RANK	STATE	RATE
1	Arkansas	1,292.1
2	North Carolina	1,241.1
3	Mississippi	1,157.5
4	Oklahoma	1,098.3
5	Alabama	1,093.6
6	Tennessee	1,087.2
7	Louisiana	1,082.1
8	New Mexico	1,062.1
9	South Carolina	1,044.2
10	Nevada	1,019.1
11	Arizona	1,009.1
12	Texas	1,004.4
13	Georgia	983.3
14	Washington	978.8
15	Florida	970.0
16	Ohio	894.9
17	Oregon	868.5
18	Hawaii	798.6
19	Kansas	768.2
20	Colorado	757.0
21	Iowa	738.7
22	Missouri	736.8
23	Indiana	731.4
24	California	684.8
25	West Virginia	680.7
26	Kentucky	671.3
27	Maryland	667.7
28	Utah	649.6
29	Michigan	647.7
30	Nebraska	639.4
31	Wyoming	636.2
32	Delaware	632.8
33	Idaho	577.3
34	Alaska	565.7
35	Minnesota	564.0
36	Vermont	559.0
37	Massachusetts	537.3
38	South Dakota	525.7
39	Rhode Island	505.6
40	Maine	484.5
41	Connecticut	483.8
42	Montana	478.1
43	New Jersey	471.7
44	Wisconsin	444.1
45	Pennsylvania	438.8
46	Virginia	393.2
47	New Hampshire	388.4
48	New York	365.3
49	North Dakota	363.2
NA	Illinois**	NA

District of Columbia	712.9

Source: Morgan Quitno Press using data from Federal Bureau of Investigation
    "Crime in the United States 2004" (Uniform Crime Reports, October 17, 2005)
*Estimated rates for urban areas, defined by the F.B.I. as Metropolitan Statistical Areas and other cities outside such areas. National rate includes those states listed as not available. Burglary is the unlawful entry of a structure to commit a felony or theft. Attempts are included.
**Not available.

Percent of Burglaries Occurring in Urban Areas in 2004

National Percent = 92.2% of Burglaries*

ALPHA ORDER				RANK ORDER		
RANK	STATE	PERCENT		RANK	STATE	PERCENT
18	Alabama	92.4		1	Massachusetts	100.0
48	Alaska	66.4		1	New Jersey	100.0
9	Arizona	96.1		1	Rhode Island	100.0
29	Arkansas	89.3		4	California	98.4
4	California	98.4		5	Colorado	97.3
5	Colorado	97.3		6	Maryland	97.2
16	Connecticut	92.7		6	New Hampshire	97.2
39	Delaware	82.2		8	Florida	96.2
8	Florida	96.2		9	Arizona	96.1
19	Georgia	91.7		10	Utah	95.7
47	Hawaii	66.9		11	Texas	95.3
37	Idaho	83.5		12	New York	94.3
NA	Illinois**	NA		13	Nevada	94.0
17	Indiana	92.6		14	Ohio	93.0
27	Iowa	89.5		15	Washington	92.9
30	Kansas	88.9		16	Connecticut	92.7
45	Kentucky	74.0		17	Indiana	92.6
22	Louisiana	90.8		18	Alabama	92.4
42	Maine	79.7		19	Georgia	91.7
6	Maryland	97.2		20	Oklahoma	91.0
1	Massachusetts	100.0		20	Pennsylvania	91.0
28	Michigan	89.4		22	Louisiana	90.8
35	Minnesota	85.3		22	Oregon	90.8
43	Mississippi	77.4		24	Virginia	90.6
31	Missouri	88.7		25	South Dakota	90.2
46	Montana	69.4		26	Nebraska	89.9
26	Nebraska	89.9		27	Iowa	89.5
13	Nevada	94.0		28	Michigan	89.4
6	New Hampshire	97.2		29	Arkansas	89.3
1	New Jersey	100.0		30	Kansas	88.9
33	New Mexico	86.6		31	Missouri	88.7
12	New York	94.3		32	Tennessee	87.9
39	North Carolina	82.2		33	New Mexico	86.6
41	North Dakota	81.7		34	Wisconsin	85.6
14	Ohio	93.0		35	Minnesota	85.3
20	Oklahoma	91.0		36	Wyoming	84.6
22	Oregon	90.8		37	Idaho	83.5
20	Pennsylvania	91.0		38	South Carolina	82.3
1	Rhode Island	100.0		39	Delaware	82.2
38	South Carolina	82.3		39	North Carolina	82.2
25	South Dakota	90.2		41	North Dakota	81.7
32	Tennessee	87.9		42	Maine	79.7
11	Texas	95.3		43	Mississippi	77.4
10	Utah	95.7		44	West Virginia	76.0
49	Vermont	66.3		45	Kentucky	74.0
24	Virginia	90.6		46	Montana	69.4
15	Washington	92.9		47	Hawaii	66.9
44	West Virginia	76.0		48	Alaska	66.4
34	Wisconsin	85.6		49	Vermont	66.3
36	Wyoming	84.6		NA	Illinois**	NA
					District of Columbia	100.0

Source: Morgan Quitno Press using data from Federal Bureau of Investigation
    "Crime in the United States 2004" (Uniform Crime Reports, October 17, 2005)
*Estimated percentages for urban areas, defined by the F.B.I. as Metropolitan Statistical Areas and other cities
outside such areas. National percent includes those states listed as not available. Burglary is the unlawful entry
of a structure to commit a felony or theft. Attempts are included.
**Not available.

Burglaries in Rural Areas in 2004

National Rural Total = 167,376 Burglaries*

RANK	STATE	BURGLARIES	% of USA
20	Alabama	3,380	2.0%
33	Alaska	1,268	0.8%
29	Arizona	2,202	1.3%
21	Arkansas	3,228	1.9%
17	California	3,995	2.4%
41	Colorado	896	0.5%
36	Connecticut	1,137	0.7%
40	Delaware	960	0.6%
9	Florida	6,277	3.8%
5	Georgia	6,898	4.1%
18	Hawaii	3,587	2.1%
34	Idaho	1,259	0.8%
NA	Illinois**	NA	NA
23	Indiana	3,128	1.9%
30	Iowa	1,910	1.1%
28	Kansas	2,211	1.3%
8	Kentucky	6,729	4.0%
14	Louisiana	4,168	2.5%
32	Maine	1,288	0.8%
38	Maryland	1,017	0.6%
48	Massachusetts	0	0.0%
6	Michigan	6,843	4.1%
15	Minnesota	4,111	2.5%
10	Mississippi	6,249	3.7%
12	Missouri	4,576	2.7%
37	Montana	1,074	0.6%
39	Nebraska	997	0.6%
31	Nevada	1,394	0.8%
46	New Hampshire	138	0.1%
48	New Jersey	0	0.0%
26	New Mexico	2,672	1.6%
16	New York	4,062	2.4%
1	North Carolina	18,053	10.8%
44	North Dakota	350	0.2%
7	Ohio	6,834	4.1%
22	Oklahoma	3,186	1.9%
24	Oregon	2,765	1.7%
11	Pennsylvania	4,922	2.9%
47	Rhode Island	1	0.0%
3	South Carolina	7,700	4.6%
45	South Dakota	310	0.2%
4	Tennessee	7,281	4.4%
2	Texas	10,420	6.2%
42	Utah	650	0.4%
35	Vermont	1,140	0.7%
25	Virginia	2,715	1.6%
13	Washington	4,309	2.6%
27	West Virginia	2,625	1.6%
19	Wisconsin	3,444	2.1%
43	Wyoming	422	0.3%

RANK	STATE	BURGLARIES	% of USA
1	North Carolina	18,053	10.8%
2	Texas	10,420	6.2%
3	South Carolina	7,700	4.6%
4	Tennessee	7,281	4.4%
5	Georgia	6,898	4.1%
6	Michigan	6,843	4.1%
7	Ohio	6,834	4.1%
8	Kentucky	6,729	4.0%
9	Florida	6,277	3.8%
10	Mississippi	6,249	3.7%
11	Pennsylvania	4,922	2.9%
12	Missouri	4,576	2.7%
13	Washington	4,309	2.6%
14	Louisiana	4,168	2.5%
15	Minnesota	4,111	2.5%
16	New York	4,062	2.4%
17	California	3,995	2.4%
18	Hawaii	3,587	2.1%
19	Wisconsin	3,444	2.1%
20	Alabama	3,380	2.0%
21	Arkansas	3,228	1.9%
22	Oklahoma	3,186	1.9%
23	Indiana	3,128	1.9%
24	Oregon	2,765	1.7%
25	Virginia	2,715	1.6%
26	New Mexico	2,672	1.6%
27	West Virginia	2,625	1.6%
28	Kansas	2,211	1.3%
29	Arizona	2,202	1.3%
30	Iowa	1,910	1.1%
31	Nevada	1,394	0.8%
32	Maine	1,288	0.8%
33	Alaska	1,268	0.8%
34	Idaho	1,259	0.8%
35	Vermont	1,140	0.7%
36	Connecticut	1,137	0.7%
37	Montana	1,074	0.6%
38	Maryland	1,017	0.6%
39	Nebraska	997	0.6%
40	Delaware	960	0.6%
41	Colorado	896	0.5%
42	Utah	650	0.4%
43	Wyoming	422	0.3%
44	North Dakota	350	0.2%
45	South Dakota	310	0.2%
46	New Hampshire	138	0.1%
47	Rhode Island	1	0.0%
48	Massachusetts	0	0.0%
48	New Jersey	0	0.0%
NA	Illinois**	NA	NA
	District of Columbia	0	0.0%

Source: Federal Bureau of Investigation
  "Crime in the United States 2004" (Uniform Crime Reports, October 17, 2005)
*Estimated totals for nonmetropolitan areas, defined by the F.B.I. as other than Metropolitan Statistical Areas and other cities outside such areas. National total includes those states listed as not available. Burglary is the unlawful entry of a structure to commit a felony or theft. Attempts are included.
**Not available.

Rural Burglary Rate in 2004

National Rural Rate = 550.0 Burglaries per 100,000 Population*

ALPHA ORDER				RANK ORDER		
RANK	STATE	RATE		RANK	STATE	RATE
29	Alabama	447.7		1	Hawaii	1,006.9
15	Alaska	596.3		2	South Carolina	991.3
11	Arizona	677.8		3	North Carolina	979.9
26	Arkansas	479.6		4	Washington	958.5
8	California	703.7		5	New Mexico	958.1
42	Colorado	249.5		6	Delaware	730.7
44	Connecticut	218.5		7	Tennessee	704.9
6	Delaware	730.7		8	California	703.7
9	Florida	699.9		9	Florida	699.9
13	Georgia	632.5		10	Nevada	694.7
1	Hawaii	1,006.9		11	Arizona	677.8
33	Idaho	433.7		12	Texas	646.7
NA	Illinois**	NA		13	Georgia	632.5
36	Indiana	347.7		14	Oregon	613.8
41	Iowa	253.7		15	Alaska	596.3
20	Kansas	526.6		16	Mississippi	593.3
21	Kentucky	521.7		17	Louisiana	587.7
17	Louisiana	587.7		18	Michigan	557.3
27	Maine	469.7		19	Oklahoma	527.0
28	Maryland	469.5		20	Kansas	526.6
47	Massachusetts	0.0		21	Kentucky	521.7
18	Michigan	557.3		22	Vermont	519.1
25	Minnesota	479.8		23	Missouri	518.5
16	Mississippi	593.3		24	Ohio	492.2
23	Missouri	518.5		25	Minnesota	479.8
40	Montana	258.0		26	Arkansas	479.6
39	Nebraska	272.1		27	Maine	469.7
10	Nevada	694.7		28	Maryland	469.5
43	New Hampshire	244.7		29	Alabama	447.7
47	New Jersey	0.0		30	Utah	445.6
5	New Mexico	958.1		31	West Virginia	441.2
34	New York	412.1		32	Pennsylvania	439.6
3	North Carolina	979.9		33	Idaho	433.7
45	North Dakota	170.8		34	New York	412.1
24	Ohio	492.2		35	Wisconsin	377.3
19	Oklahoma	527.0		36	Indiana	347.7
14	Oregon	613.8		37	Virginia	328.1
32	Pennsylvania	439.6		38	Wyoming	296.1
47	Rhode Island	0.0		39	Nebraska	272.1
2	South Carolina	991.3		40	Montana	258.0
46	South Dakota	134.3		41	Iowa	253.7
7	Tennessee	704.9		42	Colorado	249.5
12	Texas	646.7		43	New Hampshire	244.7
30	Utah	445.6		44	Connecticut	218.5
22	Vermont	519.1		45	North Dakota	170.8
37	Virginia	328.1		46	South Dakota	134.3
4	Washington	958.5		47	Massachusetts	0.0
31	West Virginia	441.2		47	New Jersey	0.0
35	Wisconsin	377.3		47	Rhode Island	0.0
38	Wyoming	296.1		NA	Illinois**	NA
					District of Columbia	0.0

Source: Morgan Quitno Press using data from Federal Bureau of Investigation
"Crime in the United States 2004" (Uniform Crime Reports, October 17, 2005)
*Estimated rates for nonmetropolitan areas, defined by the F.B.I. as other than Metropolitan Statistical Areas and other cities outside such areas. National rate includes those states listed as not available. Burglary is the unlawful entry of a structure to commit a felony or theft. Attempts are included.
**Not available.

Percent of Burglaries Occurring in Rural Areas in 2004

National Percent = 7.8% of Burglaries*

ALPHA ORDER

RANK	STATE	PERCENT
32	Alabama	7.6
2	Alaska	33.6
41	Arizona	3.9
21	Arkansas	10.7
46	California	1.6
45	Colorado	2.7
34	Connecticut	7.3
10	Delaware	17.8
42	Florida	3.8
31	Georgia	8.3
3	Hawaii	33.1
13	Idaho	16.5
NA	Illinois**	NA
33	Indiana	7.4
23	Iowa	10.5
20	Kansas	11.1
5	Kentucky	26.0
27	Louisiana	9.2
8	Maine	20.3
43	Maryland	2.8
47	Massachusetts	0.0
22	Michigan	10.6
15	Minnesota	14.7
7	Mississippi	22.6
19	Missouri	11.3
4	Montana	30.6
24	Nebraska	10.1
37	Nevada	6.0
43	New Hampshire	2.8
47	New Jersey	0.0
17	New Mexico	13.4
38	New York	5.7
10	North Carolina	17.8
9	North Dakota	18.3
36	Ohio	7.0
29	Oklahoma	9.0
27	Oregon	9.2
29	Pennsylvania	9.0
47	Rhode Island	0.0
12	South Carolina	17.7
25	South Dakota	9.8
18	Tennessee	12.1
39	Texas	4.7
40	Utah	4.3
1	Vermont	33.7
26	Virginia	9.4
35	Washington	7.1
6	West Virginia	24.0
16	Wisconsin	14.4
14	Wyoming	15.4

RANK ORDER

RANK	STATE	PERCENT
1	Vermont	33.7
2	Alaska	33.6
3	Hawaii	33.1
4	Montana	30.6
5	Kentucky	26.0
6	West Virginia	24.0
7	Mississippi	22.6
8	Maine	20.3
9	North Dakota	18.3
10	Delaware	17.8
10	North Carolina	17.8
12	South Carolina	17.7
13	Idaho	16.5
14	Wyoming	15.4
15	Minnesota	14.7
16	Wisconsin	14.4
17	New Mexico	13.4
18	Tennessee	12.1
19	Missouri	11.3
20	Kansas	11.1
21	Arkansas	10.7
22	Michigan	10.6
23	Iowa	10.5
24	Nebraska	10.1
25	South Dakota	9.8
26	Virginia	9.4
27	Louisiana	9.2
27	Oregon	9.2
29	Oklahoma	9.0
29	Pennsylvania	9.0
31	Georgia	8.3
32	Alabama	7.6
33	Indiana	7.4
34	Connecticut	7.3
35	Washington	7.1
36	Ohio	7.0
37	Nevada	6.0
38	New York	5.7
39	Texas	4.7
40	Utah	4.3
41	Arizona	3.9
42	Florida	3.8
43	Maryland	2.8
43	New Hampshire	2.8
45	Colorado	2.7
46	California	1.6
47	Massachusetts	0.0
47	New Jersey	0.0
47	Rhode Island	0.0
NA	Illinois**	NA
	District of Columbia	0.0

Source: Morgan Quitno Press using data from Federal Bureau of Investigation
"Crime in the United States 2004" (Uniform Crime Reports, October 17, 2005)
*Estimated percentages for nonmetropolitan areas, defined by the F.B.I. as other than Metropolitan Statistical Areas
and other cities outside such areas. National percent includes those states listed as not available. Burglary is the
unlawful entry of a structure to commit a felony or theft. Attempts are included.
**Not available.

442

Larcenies and Thefts in Urban Areas in 2004

National Urban Total = 6,640,998 Larcenies and Thefts*

ALPHA ORDER

RANK	STATE	THEFTS	% of USA
20	Alabama	118,417	1.8%
45	Alaska	13,648	0.2%
9	Arizona	190,703	2.9%
29	Arkansas	68,552	1.0%
1	California	723,021	10.9%
19	Colorado	119,952	1.8%
30	Connecticut	62,294	0.9%
44	Delaware	16,962	0.3%
3	Florida	470,349	7.1%
6	Georgia	233,836	3.5%
37	Hawaii	29,512	0.4%
38	Idaho	25,983	0.4%
NA	Illinois**	NA	NA
15	Indiana	140,893	2.1%
32	Iowa	59,136	0.9%
27	Kansas	75,568	1.1%
31	Kentucky	61,303	0.9%
18	Louisiana	125,159	1.9%
40	Maine	21,666	0.3%
17	Maryland	127,406	1.9%
25	Massachusetts	101,303	1.5%
11	Michigan	181,846	2.7%
23	Minnesota	105,108	1.6%
33	Mississippi	56,952	0.9%
13	Missouri	150,692	2.3%
43	Montana	17,138	0.3%
36	Nebraska	43,580	0.7%
34	Nevada	49,847	0.8%
42	New Hampshire	19,496	0.3%
16	New Jersey	139,977	2.1%
35	New Mexico	49,299	0.7%
4	New York	300,694	4.5%
8	North Carolina	204,832	3.1%
49	North Dakota	8,384	0.1%
5	Ohio	269,656	4.1%
26	Oklahoma	97,018	1.5%
22	Orogon	111,901	1.7%
7	Pennsylvania	205,089	3.1%
41	Rhode Island	21,592	0.3%
21	South Carolina	114,274	1.7%
47	South Dakota	10,187	0.2%
12	Tennessee	157,992	2.4%
2	Texas	682,836	10.3%
28	Utah	73,105	1.1%
48	Vermont	8,649	0.1%
14	Virginia	145,273	2.2%
10	Washington	190,154	2.9%
39	West Virginia	25,525	0.4%
24	Wisconsin	104,722	1.6%
46	Wyoming	11,597	0.2%

RANK ORDER

RANK	STATE	THEFTS	% of USA
1	California	723,021	10.9%
2	Texas	682,836	10.3%
3	Florida	470,349	7.1%
4	New York	300,694	4.5%
5	Ohio	269,656	4.1%
6	Georgia	233,836	3.5%
7	Pennsylvania	205,089	3.1%
8	North Carolina	204,832	3.1%
9	Arizona	190,703	2.9%
10	Washington	190,154	2.9%
11	Michigan	181,846	2.7%
12	Tennessee	157,992	2.4%
13	Missouri	150,692	2.3%
14	Virginia	145,273	2.2%
15	Indiana	140,893	2.1%
16	New Jersey	139,977	2.1%
17	Maryland	127,406	1.9%
18	Louisiana	125,159	1.9%
19	Colorado	119,952	1.8%
20	Alabama	118,417	1.8%
21	South Carolina	114,274	1.7%
22	Oregon	111,901	1.7%
23	Minnesota	105,108	1.6%
24	Wisconsin	104,722	1.6%
25	Massachusetts	101,303	1.5%
26	Oklahoma	97,018	1.5%
27	Kansas	75,568	1.1%
28	Utah	73,105	1.1%
29	Arkansas	68,552	1.0%
30	Connecticut	62,294	0.9%
31	Kentucky	61,303	0.9%
32	Iowa	59,136	0.9%
33	Mississippi	56,952	0.9%
34	Nevada	49,847	0.8%
35	New Mexico	49,299	0.7%
36	Nebraska	43,580	0.7%
37	Hawaii	29,512	0.4%
38	Idaho	25,983	0.4%
39	West Virginia	25,525	0.4%
40	Maine	21,666	0.3%
41	Rhode Island	21,592	0.3%
42	New Hampshire	19,496	0.3%
43	Montana	17,138	0.3%
44	Delaware	16,962	0.3%
45	Alaska	13,648	0.2%
46	Wyoming	11,597	0.2%
47	South Dakota	10,187	0.2%
48	Vermont	8,649	0.1%
49	North Dakota	8,384	0.1%
NA	Illinois**	NA	NA
	District of Columbia	14,542	0.2%

Source: Morgan Quitno Press using data from Federal Bureau of Investigation
    "Crime in the United States 2004" (Uniform Crime Reports, October 17, 2005)
*Estimated totals for urban areas, defined by the F.B.I. as Metropolitan Statistical Areas and other cities outside
such areas. National total includes those states listed as not available. Larceny and theft is the unlawful taking of
property without use of force, violence or fraud. Attempts are included. Motor vehicle thefts are excluded.
**Not available.

Urban Larceny and Theft Rate in 2004

National Urban Rate = 2,523.0 Larcenies and Thefts per 100,000 Population*

ALPHA ORDER

RANK	STATE	RATE
16	Alabama	3,136.7
18	Alaska	3,082.3
2	Arizona	3,519.2
7	Arkansas	3,296.5
40	California	2,046.7
24	Colorado	2,827.6
38	Connecticut	2,088.1
29	Delaware	2,426.7
23	Florida	2,850.5
22	Georgia	3,021.6
12	Hawaii	3,255.3
31	Idaho	2,355.7
NA	Illinois**	NA
27	Indiana	2,639.5
25	Iowa	2,686.0
10	Kansas	3,263.4
36	Kentucky	2,146.4
8	Louisiana	3,288.0
39	Maine	2,077.2
30	Maryland	2,385.2
48	Massachusetts	1,579.0
40	Michigan	2,046.7
28	Minnesota	2,476.5
19	Mississippi	3,078.9
17	Missouri	3,092.9
3	Montana	3,356.5
15	Nebraska	3,156.0
32	Nevada	2,335.7
49	New Hampshire	1,568.3
47	New Jersey	1,609.1
21	New Mexico	3,034.9
46	New York	1,648.4
20	North Carolina	3,057.7
43	North Dakota	1,952.2
26	Ohio	2,677.7
5	Oklahoma	3,323.7
1	Oregon	3,559.1
45	Pennsylvania	1,817.1
42	Rhode Island	1,998.1
4	South Carolina	3,340.1
44	South Dakota	1,886.3
13	Tennessee	3,245.5
9	Texas	3,270.5
11	Utah	3,259.0
35	Vermont	2,152.7
34	Virginia	2,190.4
6	Washington	3,304.6
37	West Virginia	2,091.5
33	Wisconsin	2,278.5
14	Wyoming	3,185.8

RANK ORDER

RANK	STATE	RATE
1	Oregon	3,559.1
2	Arizona	3,519.2
3	Montana	3,356.5
4	South Carolina	3,340.1
5	Oklahoma	3,323.7
6	Washington	3,304.6
7	Arkansas	3,296.5
8	Louisiana	3,288.0
9	Texas	3,270.5
10	Kansas	3,263.4
11	Utah	3,259.0
12	Hawaii	3,255.3
13	Tennessee	3,245.5
14	Wyoming	3,185.8
15	Nebraska	3,156.0
16	Alabama	3,136.7
17	Missouri	3,092.9
18	Alaska	3,082.3
19	Mississippi	3,078.9
20	North Carolina	3,057.7
21	New Mexico	3,034.9
22	Georgia	3,021.6
23	Florida	2,850.5
24	Colorado	2,827.6
25	Iowa	2,686.0
26	Ohio	2,677.7
27	Indiana	2,639.5
28	Minnesota	2,476.5
29	Delaware	2,426.7
30	Maryland	2,385.2
31	Idaho	2,355.7
32	Nevada	2,335.7
33	Wisconsin	2,278.5
34	Virginia	2,190.4
35	Vermont	2,152.7
36	Kentucky	2,146.4
37	West Virginia	2,091.5
38	Connecticut	2,088.1
39	Maine	2,077.2
40	California	2,046.7
40	Michigan	2,046.7
42	Rhode Island	1,998.1
43	North Dakota	1,952.2
44	South Dakota	1,886.3
45	Pennsylvania	1,817.1
46	New York	1,648.4
47	New Jersey	1,609.1
48	Massachusetts	1,579.0
49	New Hampshire	1,568.3
NA	Illinois**	NA

District of Columbia 2,627.2

Source: Morgan Quitno Press using data from Federal Bureau of Investigation
"Crime in the United States 2004" (Uniform Crime Reports, October 17, 2005)
*Estimated rates for urban areas, defined by the F.B.I. as Metropolitan Statistical Areas and other cities outside such areas. National rate includes those states listed as not available. Larceny and theft is the unlawful taking of property without use of force, violence or fraud. Attempts are included. Motor vehicle thefts are excluded.
**Not available.

Percent of Larcenies and Thefts Occurring in Urban Areas in 2004

National Percent = 95.6% of Larcenies and Thefts*

ALPHA ORDER

RANK	STATE	PERCENT
14	Alabama	95.8
45	Alaska	84.5
7	Arizona	98.0
34	Arkansas	92.8
5	California	99.2
11	Colorado	97.3
18	Connecticut	95.2
37	Delaware	90.5
10	Florida	97.5
29	Georgia	93.7
49	Hawaii	71.8
36	Idaho	90.9
NA	Illinois**	NA
23	Indiana	94.8
21	Iowa	95.0
26	Kansas	94.2
43	Kentucky	86.9
33	Louisiana	93.3
39	Maine	89.9
6	Maryland	98.2
1	Massachusetts	100.0
30	Michigan	93.6
35	Minnesota	92.6
42	Mississippi	87.0
18	Missouri	95.2
48	Montana	77.6
27	Nebraska	93.9
20	Nevada	95.1
4	New Hampshire	99.5
1	New Jersey	100.0
24	New Mexico	94.7
12	New York	96.7
38	North Carolina	90.2
40	North Dakota	89.7
17	Ohio	95.3
14	Oklahoma	95.8
22	Oregon	94.9
16	Pennsylvania	95.7
3	Rhode Island	99.9
41	South Carolina	87.9
31	South Dakota	93.4
31	Tennessee	93.4
7	Texas	98.0
9	Utah	97.8
46	Vermont	83.3
24	Virginia	94.7
13	Washington	96.5
47	West Virginia	82.8
27	Wisconsin	93.9
43	Wyoming	86.9

RANK ORDER

RANK	STATE	PERCENT
1	Massachusetts	100.0
1	New Jersey	100.0
3	Rhode Island	99.9
4	New Hampshire	99.5
5	California	99.2
6	Maryland	98.2
7	Arizona	98.0
7	Texas	98.0
9	Utah	97.8
10	Florida	97.5
11	Colorado	97.3
12	New York	96.7
13	Washington	96.5
14	Alabama	95.8
14	Oklahoma	95.8
16	Pennsylvania	95.7
17	Ohio	95.3
18	Connecticut	95.2
18	Missouri	95.2
20	Nevada	95.1
21	Iowa	95.0
22	Oregon	94.9
23	Indiana	94.8
24	New Mexico	94.7
24	Virginia	94.7
26	Kansas	94.2
27	Nebraska	93.9
27	Wisconsin	93.9
29	Georgia	93.7
30	Michigan	93.6
31	South Dakota	93.4
31	Tennessee	93.4
33	Louisiana	93.3
34	Arkansas	92.8
35	Minnesota	92.6
36	Idaho	90.9
37	Delaware	90.5
38	North Carolina	90.2
39	Maine	89.9
40	North Dakota	89.7
41	South Carolina	87.9
42	Mississippi	87.0
43	Kentucky	86.9
43	Wyoming	86.9
45	Alaska	84.5
46	Vermont	83.3
47	West Virginia	82.8
48	Montana	77.6
49	Hawaii	71.8
NA	Illinois**	NA

District of Columbia   100.0

Source: Morgan Quitno Press using data from Federal Bureau of Investigation
    "Crime in the United States 2004" (Uniform Crime Reports, October 17, 2005)
*Estimated percentages for urban areas, defined by the F.B.I. as Metropolitan Statistical Areas and other cities outside such areas. National percent includes those states listed as not available. Larceny and theft is the unlawful taking of property without use of force, violence or fraud. Attempts are included. Motor vehicle thefts are excluded.
**Not available.

Larcenies and Thefts in Rural Areas in 2004

National Rural Total = 306,687 Larcenies and Thefts*

ALPHA ORDER

RANK	STATE	THEFTS	% of USA
25	Alabama	5,233	1.7%
37	Alaska	2,511	0.8%
29	Arizona	3,853	1.3%
23	Arkansas	5,322	1.7%
22	California	5,666	1.8%
30	Colorado	3,319	1.1%
31	Connecticut	3,157	1.0%
40	Delaware	1,780	0.6%
7	Florida	12,135	4.0%
3	Georgia	15,590	5.1%
8	Hawaii	11,566	3.8%
35	Idaho	2,600	0.8%
NA	Illinois**	NA	NA
17	Indiana	7,777	2.5%
32	Iowa	3,122	1.0%
27	Kansas	4,692	1.5%
11	Kentucky	9,232	3.0%
13	Louisiana	8,921	2.9%
38	Maine	2,430	0.8%
39	Maryland	2,380	0.8%
48	Massachusetts	0	0.0%
6	Michigan	12,413	4.0%
15	Minnesota	8,345	2.7%
14	Mississippi	8,488	2.8%
18	Missouri	7,572	2.5%
26	Montana	4,944	1.6%
33	Nebraska	2,819	0.9%
36	Nevada	2,591	0.8%
46	New Hampshire	107	0.0%
48	New Jersey	0	0.0%
34	New Mexico	2,770	0.9%
10	New York	10,342	3.4%
1	North Carolina	22,315	7.3%
44	North Dakota	958	0.3%
5	Ohio	13,447	4.4%
28	Oklahoma	4,253	1.4%
21	Oregon	5,967	1.9%
12	Pennsylvania	9,110	3.0%
47	Rhode Island	31	0.0%
2	South Carolina	15,777	5.1%
45	South Dakota	723	0.2%
9	Tennessee	11,177	3.6%
4	Texas	13,671	4.5%
43	Utah	1,630	0.5%
42	Vermont	1,733	0.6%
16	Virginia	8,191	2.7%
19	Washington	6,818	2.2%
24	West Virginia	5,301	1.7%
20	Wisconsin	6,760	2.2%
41	Wyoming	1,755	0.6%

RANK ORDER

RANK	STATE	THEFTS	% of USA
1	North Carolina	22,315	7.3%
2	South Carolina	15,777	5.1%
3	Georgia	15,590	5.1%
4	Texas	13,671	4.5%
5	Ohio	13,447	4.4%
6	Michigan	12,413	4.0%
7	Florida	12,135	4.0%
8	Hawaii	11,566	3.8%
9	Tennessee	11,177	3.6%
10	New York	10,342	3.4%
11	Kentucky	9,232	3.0%
12	Pennsylvania	9,110	3.0%
13	Louisiana	8,921	2.9%
14	Mississippi	8,488	2.8%
15	Minnesota	8,345	2.7%
16	Virginia	8,191	2.7%
17	Indiana	7,777	2.5%
18	Missouri	7,572	2.5%
19	Washington	6,818	2.2%
20	Wisconsin	6,760	2.2%
21	Oregon	5,967	1.9%
22	California	5,666	1.8%
23	Arkansas	5,322	1.7%
24	West Virginia	5,301	1.7%
25	Alabama	5,233	1.7%
26	Montana	4,944	1.6%
27	Kansas	4,692	1.5%
28	Oklahoma	4,253	1.4%
29	Arizona	3,853	1.3%
30	Colorado	3,319	1.1%
31	Connecticut	3,157	1.0%
32	Iowa	3,122	1.0%
33	Nebraska	2,819	0.9%
34	New Mexico	2,770	0.9%
35	Idaho	2,600	0.8%
36	Nevada	2,591	0.8%
37	Alaska	2,511	0.8%
38	Maine	2,430	0.8%
39	Maryland	2,380	0.8%
40	Delaware	1,780	0.6%
41	Wyoming	1,755	0.6%
42	Vermont	1,733	0.6%
43	Utah	1,630	0.5%
44	North Dakota	958	0.3%
45	South Dakota	723	0.2%
46	New Hampshire	107	0.0%
47	Rhode Island	31	0.0%
48	Massachusetts	0	0.0%
48	New Jersey	0	0.0%
NA	Illinois**	NA	NA
	District of Columbia	0	0.0%

Source: Federal Bureau of Investigation
   "Crime in the United States 2004" (Uniform Crime Reports, October 17, 2005)
*Estimated totals for nonmetropolitan areas, defined by the F.B.I. as other than Metropolitan Statistical Areas and other cities outside such areas. National total includes those states listed as not available. Larceny and theft is the unlawful taking of property without use of force, violence or fraud. Attempts are included. Motor vehicle thefts are excluded. **Not available.

446

Rural Larceny and Theft Rate in 2004

National Rural Rate = 1,007.8 Larcenies and Thefts per 100,000 Population*

ALPHA ORDER

RANK ORDER

RANK	STATE	RATE		RANK	STATE	RATE
41	Alabama	693.1		1	Hawaii	3,246.6
14	Alaska	1,180.8		2	South Carolina	2,031.0
13	Arizona	1,186.0		3	Washington	1,516.7
35	Arkansas	790.7		4	Georgia	1,429.5
21	California	998.0		5	Delaware	1,354.8
26	Colorado	924.0		6	Florida	1,353.1
42	Connecticut	606.7		7	Oregon	1,324.6
5	Delaware	1,354.8		8	Nevada	1,291.3
6	Florida	1,353.1		9	Louisiana	1,257.8
4	Georgia	1,429.5		10	Wyoming	1,231.5
1	Hawaii	3,246.6		11	North Carolina	1,211.3
27	Idaho	895.7		12	Montana	1,187.7
NA	Illinois**	NA		13	Arizona	1,186.0
30	Indiana	864.5		14	Alaska	1,180.8
44	Iowa	414.7		15	Kansas	1,117.4
15	Kansas	1,117.4		15	Utah	1,117.4
39	Kentucky	715.7		17	Maryland	1,098.7
9	Louisiana	1,257.8		18	Tennessee	1,082.0
29	Maine	886.1		19	New York	1,049.1
17	Maryland	1,098.7		20	Michigan	1,010.9
47	Massachusetts	0.0		21	California	998.0
20	Michigan	1,010.9		22	New Mexico	993.2
24	Minnesota	974.0		23	Virginia	989.8
34	Mississippi	805.9		24	Minnesota	974.0
31	Missouri	858.1		25	Ohio	968.4
12	Montana	1,187.7		26	Colorado	924.0
37	Nebraska	769.4		27	Idaho	895.7
8	Nevada	1,291.3		28	West Virginia	891.0
46	New Hampshire	189.7		29	Maine	886.1
47	New Jersey	0.0		30	Indiana	864.5
22	New Mexico	993.2		31	Missouri	858.1
19	New York	1,049.1		32	Texas	848.5
11	North Carolina	1,211.3		33	Pennsylvania	813.7
43	North Dakota	467.5		34	Mississippi	805.9
25	Ohio	968.4		35	Arkansas	790.7
40	Oklahoma	703.5		36	Vermont	789.1
7	Oregon	1,324.6		37	Nebraska	769.4
33	Pennsylvania	813.7		38	Wisconsin	740.5
47	Rhode Island	0.0		39	Kentucky	715.7
2	South Carolina	2,031.0		40	Oklahoma	703.5
45	South Dakota	313.2		41	Alabama	693.1
18	Tennessee	1,082.0		42	Connecticut	606.7
32	Texas	848.5		43	North Dakota	467.5
15	Utah	1,117.4		44	Iowa	414.7
36	Vermont	789.1		45	South Dakota	313.2
23	Virginia	989.8		46	New Hampshire	189.7
3	Washington	1,516.7		47	Massachusetts	0.0
28	West Virginia	891.0		47	New Jersey	0.0
38	Wisconsin	740.5		47	Rhode Island	0.0
10	Wyoming	1,231.5		NA	Illinois**	NA
					District of Columbia	0.0

Source: Morgan Quitno Press using data from Federal Bureau of Investigation
   "Crime in the United States 2004" (Uniform Crime Reports, October 17, 2005)
*Estimated rates for nonmetropolitan areas, defined by the F.B.I. as other than Metropolitan Statistical Areas and
other cities outside such areas. National rate includes those states listed as not available. Larceny and theft is
the unlawful taking of property without use of force, violence or fraud. Attempts are included. Motor vehicle thefts
are excluded. **Not available.

Percent of Larcenies and Thefts Occurring in Rural Areas in 2004

National Percent = 4.4% of Larcenies and Thefts*

RANK	STATE	PERCENT
35	Alabama	4.2
5	Alaska	15.5
42	Arizona	2.0
16	Arkansas	7.2
45	California	0.8
39	Colorado	2.7
31	Connecticut	4.8
13	Delaware	9.5
40	Florida	2.5
21	Georgia	6.3
1	Hawaii	28.2
14	Idaho	9.1
NA	Illinois**	NA
27	Indiana	5.2
29	Iowa	5.0
24	Kansas	5.8
6	Kentucky	13.1
17	Louisiana	6.7
11	Maine	10.1
44	Maryland	1.8
48	Massachusetts	0.0
20	Michigan	6.4
15	Minnesota	7.4
8	Mississippi	13.0
31	Missouri	4.8
2	Montana	22.4
22	Nebraska	6.1
30	Nevada	4.9
46	New Hampshire	0.5
48	New Jersey	0.0
25	New Mexico	5.3
38	New York	3.3
12	North Carolina	9.8
10	North Dakota	10.3
33	Ohio	4.7
35	Oklahoma	4.2
28	Oregon	5.1
34	Pennsylvania	4.3
47	Rhode Island	0.1
9	South Carolina	12.1
18	South Dakota	6.6
18	Tennessee	6.6
42	Texas	2.0
41	Utah	2.2
4	Vermont	16.7
25	Virginia	5.3
37	Washington	3.5
3	West Virginia	17.2
22	Wisconsin	6.1
6	Wyoming	13.1

RANK	STATE	PERCENT
1	Hawaii	28.2
2	Montana	22.4
3	West Virginia	17.2
4	Vermont	16.7
5	Alaska	15.5
6	Kentucky	13.1
6	Wyoming	13.1
8	Mississippi	13.0
9	South Carolina	12.1
10	North Dakota	10.3
11	Maine	10.1
12	North Carolina	9.8
13	Delaware	9.5
14	Idaho	9.1
15	Minnesota	7.4
16	Arkansas	7.2
17	Louisiana	6.7
18	South Dakota	6.6
18	Tennessee	6.6
20	Michigan	6.4
21	Georgia	6.3
22	Nebraska	6.1
22	Wisconsin	6.1
24	Kansas	5.8
25	New Mexico	5.3
25	Virginia	5.3
27	Indiana	5.2
28	Oregon	5.1
29	Iowa	5.0
30	Nevada	4.9
31	Connecticut	4.8
31	Missouri	4.8
33	Ohio	4.7
34	Pennsylvania	4.3
35	Alabama	4.2
35	Oklahoma	4.2
37	Washington	3.5
38	New York	3.3
39	Colorado	2.7
40	Florida	2.5
41	Utah	2.2
42	Arizona	2.0
42	Texas	2.0
44	Maryland	1.8
45	California	0.8
46	New Hampshire	0.5
47	Rhode Island	0.1
48	Massachusetts	0.0
48	New Jersey	0.0
NA	Illinois**	NA
	District of Columbia	0.0

Source: Morgan Quitno Press using data from Federal Bureau of Investigation
   "Crime in the United States 2004" (Uniform Crime Reports, October 17, 2005)
*Estimated percentages for nonmetropolitan areas, defined by the F.B.I. as other than Metropolitan Statistical Areas and other cities outside such areas. National percent includes those states listed as not available. Larceny and theft is the unlawful taking of property without use of force, violence or fraud. Attempts are included. Motor vehicle thefts are excluded. **Not available.

Motor Vehicle Thefts in Urban Areas in 2004

National Urban Total = 1,196,733 Motor Vehicle Thefts*

ALPHA ORDER

RANK	STATE	THEFTS	% of USA
24	Alabama	13,170	1.1%
43	Alaska	1,662	0.1%
4	Arizona	54,521	4.6%
35	Arkansas	5,750	0.5%
1	California	251,302	21.0%
14	Colorado	23,755	2.0%
28	Connecticut	10,533	0.9%
41	Delaware	2,006	0.2%
3	Florida	76,871	6.4%
7	Georgia	42,217	3.5%
31	Hawaii	7,369	0.6%
40	Idaho	2,402	0.2%
NA	Illinois**	NA	NA
19	Indiana	20,240	1.7%
37	Iowa	4,947	0.4%
29	Kansas	7,987	0.7%
33	Kentucky	7,086	0.6%
20	Louisiana	18,921	1.6%
45	Maine	1,098	0.1%
10	Maryland	35,584	3.0%
18	Massachusetts	22,053	1.8%
5	Michigan	49,339	4.1%
25	Minnesota	12,402	1.0%
34	Mississippi	6,743	0.6%
13	Missouri	24,917	2.1%
44	Montana	1,148	0.1%
36	Nebraska	4,994	0.4%
17	Nevada	22,247	1.9%
42	New Hampshire	1,930	0.2%
11	New Jersey	30,306	2.5%
32	New Mexico	7,288	0.6%
8	New York	40,506	3.4%
15	North Carolina	23,594	2.0%
47	North Dakota	763	0.1%
9	Ohio	39,279	3.3%
26	Oklahoma	12,092	1.0%
21	Oregon	17,559	1.5%
12	Pennsylvania	29,855	2.5%
38	Rhode Island	4,076	0.3%
23	South Carolina	13,522	1.1%
46	South Dakota	769	0.1%
16	Tennessee	22,635	1.9%
2	Texas	92,085	7.7%
30	Utah	7,507	0.6%
49	Vermont	386	0.0%
22	Virginia	16,504	1.4%
6	Washington	42,229	3.5%
39	West Virginia	2,866	0.2%
27	Wisconsin	10,583	0.9%
48	Wyoming	654	0.1%

RANK ORDER

RANK	STATE	THEFTS	% of USA
1	California	251,302	21.0%
2	Texas	92,085	7.7%
3	Florida	76,871	6.4%
4	Arizona	54,521	4.6%
5	Michigan	49,339	4.1%
6	Washington	42,229	3.5%
7	Georgia	42,217	3.5%
8	New York	40,506	3.4%
9	Ohio	39,279	3.3%
10	Maryland	35,584	3.0%
11	New Jersey	30,306	2.5%
12	Pennsylvania	29,855	2.5%
13	Missouri	24,917	2.1%
14	Colorado	23,755	2.0%
15	North Carolina	23,594	2.0%
16	Tennessee	22,635	1.9%
17	Nevada	22,247	1.9%
18	Massachusetts	22,053	1.8%
19	Indiana	20,240	1.7%
20	Louisiana	18,921	1.6%
21	Oregon	17,559	1.5%
22	Virginia	16,504	1.4%
23	South Carolina	13,522	1.1%
24	Alabama	13,170	1.1%
25	Minnesota	12,402	1.0%
26	Oklahoma	12,092	1.0%
27	Wisconsin	10,583	0.9%
28	Connecticut	10,533	0.9%
29	Kansas	7,987	0.7%
30	Utah	7,507	0.6%
31	Hawaii	7,369	0.6%
32	New Mexico	7,288	0.6%
33	Kentucky	7,086	0.6%
34	Mississippi	6,743	0.6%
35	Arkansas	5,750	0.5%
36	Nebraska	4,994	0.4%
37	Iowa	4,947	0.4%
38	Rhode Island	4,076	0.3%
39	West Virginia	2,866	0.2%
40	Idaho	2,402	0.2%
41	Delaware	2,006	0.2%
42	New Hampshire	1,930	0.2%
43	Alaska	1,662	0.1%
44	Montana	1,148	0.1%
45	Maine	1,098	0.1%
46	South Dakota	769	0.1%
47	North Dakota	763	0.1%
48	Wyoming	654	0.1%
49	Vermont	386	0.0%
NA	Illinois**	NA	NA
	District of Columbia	8,408	0.7%

Source: Morgan Quitno Press using data from Federal Bureau of Investigation
    "Crime in the United States 2004" (Uniform Crime Reports, October 17, 2005)
*Estimated totals for urban areas, defined by the F.B.I. as Metropolitan Statistical Areas and other cities outside such areas. National total includes those states listed as not available. Motor vehicle theft includes the theft or attempted theft of a self-propelled vehicle. Excludes motorboats, construction equipment, airplanes and farming equipment. **Not available.

Urban Motor Vehicle Theft Rate in 2004

National Urban Rate = 454.6 Motor Vehicle Thefts per 100,000 Population*

ALPHA ORDER

RANK	STATE	RATE
27	Alabama	348.9
22	Alaska	375.4
2	Arizona	1,006.1
34	Arkansas	276.5
5	California	711.4
7	Colorado	560.0
25	Connecticut	353.1
33	Delaware	287.0
13	Florida	465.9
10	Georgia	545.5
3	Hawaii	812.8
43	Idaho	217.8
NA	Illinois**	NA
20	Indiana	379.2
41	Iowa	224.7
29	Kansas	344.9
37	Kentucky	248.1
12	Louisiana	497.1
48	Maine	105.3
6	Maryland	666.2
30	Massachusetts	343.7
9	Michigan	555.3
32	Minnesota	292.2
23	Mississippi	364.5
11	Missouri	511.4
40	Montana	224.8
24	Nebraska	361.7
1	Nevada	1,042.4
46	New Hampshire	155.3
28	New Jersey	348.4
15	New Mexico	448.7
42	New York	222.1
26	North Carolina	352.2
45	North Dakota	177.7
19	Ohio	390.0
17	Oklahoma	414.3
8	Oregon	558.5
35	Pennsylvania	264.5
21	Rhode Island	377.2
18	South Carolina	395.2
47	South Dakota	142.4
14	Tennessee	465.0
16	Texas	441.0
31	Utah	334.7
49	Vermont	96.1
36	Virginia	248.8
4	Washington	733.9
38	West Virginia	234.8
39	Wisconsin	230.3
44	Wyoming	179.7

RANK ORDER

RANK	STATE	RATE
1	Nevada	1,042.4
2	Arizona	1,006.1
3	Hawaii	812.8
4	Washington	733.9
5	California	711.4
6	Maryland	666.2
7	Colorado	560.0
8	Oregon	558.5
9	Michigan	555.3
10	Georgia	545.5
11	Missouri	511.4
12	Louisiana	497.1
13	Florida	465.9
14	Tennessee	465.0
15	New Mexico	448.7
16	Texas	441.0
17	Oklahoma	414.3
18	South Carolina	395.2
19	Ohio	390.0
20	Indiana	379.2
21	Rhode Island	377.2
22	Alaska	375.4
23	Mississippi	364.5
24	Nebraska	361.7
25	Connecticut	353.1
26	North Carolina	352.2
27	Alabama	348.9
28	New Jersey	348.4
29	Kansas	344.9
30	Massachusetts	343.7
31	Utah	334.7
32	Minnesota	292.2
33	Delaware	287.0
34	Arkansas	276.5
35	Pennsylvania	264.5
36	Virginia	248.8
37	Kentucky	248.1
38	West Virginia	234.8
39	Wisconsin	230.3
40	Montana	224.8
41	Iowa	224.7
42	New York	222.1
43	Idaho	217.8
44	Wyoming	179.7
45	North Dakota	177.7
46	New Hampshire	155.3
47	South Dakota	142.4
48	Maine	105.3
49	Vermont	96.1
NA	Illinois**	NA

District of Columbia   1,519.0

Source: Morgan Quitno Press using data from Federal Bureau of Investigation
   "Crime in the United States 2004" (Uniform Crime Reports, October 17, 2005)
*Estimated rates for urban areas, defined by the F.B.I. as Metropolitan Statistical Areas and other cities outside such areas. National rate includes those states listed as not available. Motor vehicle theft includes the theft or attempted theft of a self-propelled vehicle. Excludes motorboats, construction equipment, airplanes and farming equipment. **Not available.

Percent of Motor Vehicle Thefts Occurring in Urban Areas in 2004

National Percent = 96.7% of Motor Vehicle Thefts*

ALPHA ORDER

RANK	STATE	PERCENT
27	Alabama	93.9
47	Alaska	74.2
9	Arizona	98.6
36	Arkansas	88.6
4	California	99.5
8	Colorado	98.7
21	Connecticut	95.5
28	Delaware	93.4
11	Florida	98.1
22	Georgia	95.4
41	Hawaii	85.5
37	Idaho	88.2
NA	Illinois**	NA
19	Indiana	96.0
33	Iowa	91.5
24	Kansas	94.7
45	Kentucky	80.8
19	Louisiana	96.0
42	Maine	84.3
6	Maryland	99.2
1	Massachusetts	100.0
15	Michigan	97.6
32	Minnesota	91.7
40	Mississippi	85.6
17	Missouri	96.2
48	Montana	71.0
26	Nebraska	94.5
10	Nevada	98.3
5	New Hampshire	99.4
1	New Jersey	100.0
31	New Mexico	92.2
7	New York	98.8
38	North Carolina	87.4
43	North Dakota	84.2
18	Ohio	96.1
29	Oklahoma	93.3
24	Oregon	94.7
16	Pennsylvania	96.4
1	Rhode Island	100.0
39	South Carolina	86.5
35	South Dakota	90.9
33	Tennessee	91.5
13	Texas	97.9
11	Utah	98.1
49	Vermont	67.1
23	Virginia	94.8
14	Washington	97.7
46	West Virginia	76.7
30	Wisconsin	93.0
44	Wyoming	81.9

RANK ORDER

RANK	STATE	PERCENT
1	Massachusetts	100.0
1	New Jersey	100.0
1	Rhode Island	100.0
4	California	99.5
5	New Hampshire	99.4
6	Maryland	99.2
7	New York	98.8
8	Colorado	98.7
9	Arizona	98.6
10	Nevada	98.3
11	Florida	98.1
11	Utah	98.1
13	Texas	97.9
14	Washington	97.7
15	Michigan	97.6
16	Pennsylvania	96.4
17	Missouri	96.2
18	Ohio	96.1
19	Indiana	96.0
19	Louisiana	96.0
21	Connecticut	95.5
22	Georgia	95.4
23	Virginia	94.8
24	Kansas	94.7
24	Oregon	94.7
26	Nebraska	94.5
27	Alabama	93.9
28	Delaware	93.4
29	Oklahoma	93.3
30	Wisconsin	93.0
31	New Mexico	92.2
32	Minnesota	91.7
33	Iowa	91.5
33	Tennessee	91.5
35	South Dakota	90.9
36	Arkansas	88.6
37	Idaho	88.2
38	North Carolina	87.4
39	South Carolina	86.5
40	Mississippi	85.6
41	Hawaii	85.5
42	Maine	84.3
43	North Dakota	84.2
44	Wyoming	81.9
45	Kentucky	80.8
46	West Virginia	76.7
47	Alaska	74.2
48	Montana	71.0
49	Vermont	67.1
NA	Illinois**	NA

	District of Columbia	100.0

Source: Morgan Quitno Press using data from Federal Bureau of Investigation
   "Crime in the United States 2004" (Uniform Crime Reports, October 17, 2005)
*Estimated percentages for urban areas, defined by the F.B.I. as Metropolitan Statistical Areas and other cities
outside such areas. National percent includes those states listed as not available. Motor vehicle theft includes
the theft or attempted theft of a self-propelled vehicle. Excludes motorboats, construction equipment, airplanes and
farming equipment. **Not available.

Motor Vehicle Thefts in Rural Areas in 2004

National Rural Total = 40,381 Motor Vehicle Thefts*

ALPHA ORDER					RANK ORDER			
RANK	STATE	THEFTS	% of USA		RANK	STATE	THEFTS	% of USA
21	Alabama	854	2.1%		1	North Carolina	3,394	8.4%
28	Alaska	578	1.4%		2	South Carolina	2,115	5.2%
25	Arizona	785	1.9%		3	Tennessee	2,114	5.2%
26	Arkansas	741	1.8%		4	Georgia	2,021	5.0%
9	California	1,302	3.2%		5	Texas	1,992	4.9%
36	Colorado	308	0.8%		6	Kentucky	1,686	4.2%
30	Connecticut	492	1.2%		7	Ohio	1,574	3.9%
44	Delaware	141	0.3%		8	Florida	1,454	3.6%
8	Florida	1,454	3.6%		9	California	1,302	3.2%
4	Georgia	2,021	5.0%		10	Hawaii	1,251	3.1%
10	Hawaii	1,251	3.1%		11	Michigan	1,216	3.0%
35	Idaho	322	0.8%		12	Mississippi	1,136	2.8%
NA	Illinois**	NA	NA		13	Minnesota	1,116	2.8%
22	Indiana	851	2.1%		14	Pennsylvania	1,114	2.8%
32	Iowa	457	1.1%		15	Washington	1,004	2.5%
33	Kansas	448	1.1%		16	Missouri	976	2.4%
6	Kentucky	1,686	4.2%		16	Oregon	976	2.4%
23	Louisiana	793	2.0%		18	Virginia	907	2.2%
39	Maine	205	0.5%		19	West Virginia	873	2.2%
38	Maryland	274	0.7%		20	Oklahoma	865	2.1%
48	Massachusetts	0	0.0%		21	Alabama	854	2.1%
11	Michigan	1,216	3.0%		22	Indiana	851	2.1%
13	Minnesota	1,116	2.8%		23	Louisiana	793	2.0%
12	Mississippi	1,136	2.8%		24	Wisconsin	791	2.0%
16	Missouri	976	2.4%		25	Arizona	785	1.9%
31	Montana	470	1.2%		26	Arkansas	741	1.8%
37	Nebraska	293	0.7%		27	New Mexico	614	1.5%
34	Nevada	388	1.0%		28	Alaska	578	1.4%
46	New Hampshire	12	0.0%		29	New York	496	1.2%
48	New Jersey	0	0.0%		30	Connecticut	492	1.2%
27	New Mexico	614	1.5%		31	Montana	470	1.2%
29	New York	496	1.2%		32	Iowa	457	1.1%
1	North Carolina	3,394	8.4%		33	Kansas	448	1.1%
43	North Dakota	143	0.4%		34	Nevada	388	1.0%
7	Ohio	1,574	3.9%		35	Idaho	322	0.8%
20	Oklahoma	865	2.1%		36	Colorado	308	0.8%
16	Oregon	976	2.4%		37	Nebraska	293	0.7%
14	Pennsylvania	1,114	2.8%		38	Maryland	274	0.7%
47	Rhode Island	2	0.0%		39	Maine	205	0.5%
2	South Carolina	2,115	5.2%		40	Vermont	189	0.5%
45	South Dakota	77	0.2%		41	Wyoming	145	0.4%
3	Tennessee	2,114	5.2%		42	Utah	144	0.4%
5	Texas	1,992	4.9%		43	North Dakota	143	0.4%
42	Utah	144	0.4%		44	Delaware	141	0.3%
40	Vermont	189	0.5%		45	South Dakota	77	0.2%
18	Virginia	907	2.2%		46	New Hampshire	12	0.0%
15	Washington	1,004	2.5%		47	Rhode Island	2	0.0%
19	West Virginia	873	2.2%		48	Massachusetts	0	0.0%
24	Wisconsin	791	2.0%		48	New Jersey	0	0.0%
41	Wyoming	145	0.4%		NA	Illinois**	NA	NA
						District of Columbia	0	0.0%

Source: Federal Bureau of Investigation
    "Crime in the United States 2004" (Uniform Crime Reports, October 17, 2005)
*Estimated totals for nonmetropolitan areas, defined by the F.B.I. as other than Metropolitan Statistical Areas and other cities outside such areas. National total includes those states listed as not available. Motor vehicle theft includes the theft or attempted theft of a self-propelled vehicle. Excludes motorboats, construction equipment, airplanes and farming equipment. **Not available.

Rural Motor Vehicle Theft Rate in 2004

National Rural Rate = 132.7 Motor Vehicle Thefts per 100,000 Population*

ALPHA ORDER

RANK	STATE	RATE
21	Alabama	113.1
3	Alaska	271.8
4	Arizona	241.6
26	Arkansas	110.1
5	California	229.3
39	Colorado	85.7
35	Connecticut	94.6
29	Delaware	107.3
13	Florida	162.1
11	Georgia	185.3
1	Hawaii	351.2
24	Idaho	110.9
NA	Illinois**	NA
35	Indiana	94.6
43	Iowa	60.7
30	Kansas	106.7
16	Kentucky	130.7
23	Louisiana	111.8
41	Maine	74.8
18	Maryland	126.5
47	Massachusetts	0.0
33	Michigan	99.0
17	Minnesota	130.3
28	Mississippi	107.9
25	Missouri	110.6
22	Montana	112.9
40	Nebraska	80.0
10	Nevada	193.4
46	New Hampshire	21.3
47	New Jersey	0.0
7	New Mexico	220.2
44	New York	50.3
12	North Carolina	184.2
42	North Dakota	69.8
20	Ohio	113.4
15	Oklahoma	143.1
8	Oregon	216.7
32	Pennsylvania	99.5
47	Rhode Island	0.0
2	South Carolina	272.3
45	South Dakota	33.4
9	Tennessee	204.7
19	Texas	123.6
34	Utah	98.7
38	Vermont	86.1
27	Virginia	109.6
6	Washington	223.3
14	West Virginia	146.7
37	Wisconsin	86.6
31	Wyoming	101.8

RANK ORDER

RANK	STATE	RATE
1	Hawaii	351.2
2	South Carolina	272.3
3	Alaska	271.8
4	Arizona	241.6
5	California	229.3
6	Washington	223.3
7	New Mexico	220.2
8	Oregon	216.7
9	Tennessee	204.7
10	Nevada	193.4
11	Georgia	185.3
12	North Carolina	184.2
13	Florida	162.1
14	West Virginia	146.7
15	Oklahoma	143.1
16	Kentucky	130.7
17	Minnesota	130.3
18	Maryland	126.5
19	Texas	123.6
20	Ohio	113.4
21	Alabama	113.1
22	Montana	112.9
23	Louisiana	111.8
24	Idaho	110.9
25	Missouri	110.6
26	Arkansas	110.1
27	Virginia	109.6
28	Mississippi	107.9
29	Delaware	107.3
30	Kansas	106.7
31	Wyoming	101.8
32	Pennsylvania	99.5
33	Michigan	99.0
34	Utah	98.7
35	Connecticut	94.6
35	Indiana	94.6
37	Wisconsin	86.6
38	Vermont	86.1
39	Colorado	85.7
40	Nebraska	80.0
41	Maine	74.8
42	North Dakota	69.8
43	Iowa	60.7
44	New York	50.3
45	South Dakota	33.4
46	New Hampshire	21.3
47	Massachusetts	0.0
47	New Jersey	0.0
47	Rhode Island	0.0
NA	Illinois**	NA
	District of Columbia	0.0

Source: Morgan Quitno Press using data from Federal Bureau of Investigation
   "Crime in the United States 2004" (Uniform Crime Reports, October 17, 2005)
*Estimated rates for nonmetropolitan areas, defined by the F.B.I. as other than Metropolitan Statistical Areas and other cities outside such areas. National rate includes those states listed as not available. Motor vehicle theft includes the theft or attempted theft of a self-propelled vehicle. Excludes motorboats, construction equipment, airplanes and farming equipment. **Not available.

Percent of Motor Vehicle Thefts Occurring in Rural Areas in 2004

National Percent = 3.3% of Motor Vehicle Thefts*

ALPHA ORDER

RANK	STATE	PERCENT
23	Alabama	6.1
3	Alaska	25.8
41	Arizona	1.4
14	Arkansas	11.4
46	California	0.5
42	Colorado	1.3
29	Connecticut	4.5
22	Delaware	6.6
38	Florida	1.9
28	Georgia	4.6
9	Hawaii	14.5
13	Idaho	11.8
NA	Illinois**	NA
30	Indiana	4.0
16	Iowa	8.5
25	Kansas	5.3
5	Kentucky	19.2
30	Louisiana	4.0
8	Maine	15.7
44	Maryland	0.8
47	Massachusetts	0.0
35	Michigan	2.4
18	Minnesota	8.3
10	Mississippi	14.4
33	Missouri	3.8
2	Montana	29.0
24	Nebraska	5.5
40	Nevada	1.7
45	New Hampshire	0.6
47	New Jersey	0.0
19	New Mexico	7.8
43	New York	1.2
12	North Carolina	12.6
7	North Dakota	15.8
32	Ohio	3.9
21	Oklahoma	6.7
25	Oregon	5.3
34	Pennsylvania	3.6
47	Rhode Island	0.0
11	South Carolina	13.5
15	South Dakota	9.1
16	Tennessee	8.5
37	Texas	2.1
38	Utah	1.9
1	Vermont	32.9
27	Virginia	5.2
36	Washington	2.3
4	West Virginia	23.3
20	Wisconsin	7.0
6	Wyoming	18.1

RANK ORDER

RANK	STATE	PERCENT
1	Vermont	32.9
2	Montana	29.0
3	Alaska	25.8
4	West Virginia	23.3
5	Kentucky	19.2
6	Wyoming	18.1
7	North Dakota	15.8
8	Maine	15.7
9	Hawaii	14.5
10	Mississippi	14.4
11	South Carolina	13.5
12	North Carolina	12.6
13	Idaho	11.8
14	Arkansas	11.4
15	South Dakota	9.1
16	Iowa	8.5
16	Tennessee	8.5
18	Minnesota	8.3
19	New Mexico	7.8
20	Wisconsin	7.0
21	Oklahoma	6.7
22	Delaware	6.6
23	Alabama	6.1
24	Nebraska	5.5
25	Kansas	5.3
25	Oregon	5.3
27	Virginia	5.2
28	Georgia	4.6
29	Connecticut	4.5
30	Indiana	4.0
30	Louisiana	4.0
32	Ohio	3.9
33	Missouri	3.8
34	Pennsylvania	3.6
35	Michigan	2.4
36	Washington	2.3
37	Texas	2.1
38	Florida	1.9
38	Utah	1.9
40	Nevada	1.7
41	Arizona	1.4
42	Colorado	1.3
43	New York	1.2
44	Maryland	0.8
45	New Hampshire	0.6
46	California	0.5
47	Massachusetts	0.0
47	New Jersey	0.0
47	Rhode Island	0.0
NA	Illinois**	NA
	District of Columbia	0.0

Source: Morgan Quitno Press using data from Federal Bureau of Investigation
"Crime in the United States 2004" (Uniform Crime Reports, October 17, 2005)
*Estimated percentages for nonmetropolitan areas, defined by the F.B.I. as other than Metropolitan Statistical Areas and other cities outside such areas. National percent includes those states listed as not available. Motor vehicle theft includes the theft or attempted theft of a self-propelled vehicle. Excludes motorboats, construction equipment, airplanes and farming equipment. **Not available.

Crimes Reported at Universities and Colleges in 2004

National Total = 92,455 Reported Crimes*

RANK	STATE	CRIMES	% of USA
26	Alabama	1,240	1.3%
41	Alaska	240	0.3%
6	Arizona	3,548	3.8%
30	Arkansas	871	0.9%
1	California	13,548	14.7%
18	Colorado	2,150	2.3%
27	Connecticut	1,100	1.2%
38	Delaware	389	0.4%
5	Florida	3,942	4.3%
14	Georgia	2,583	2.8%
NA	Hawaii**	NA	NA
NA	Idaho**	NA	NA
NA	Illinois**	NA	NA
15	Indiana	2,484	2.7%
34	Iowa	703	0.8%
28	Kansas	1,028	1.1%
21	Kentucky	1,421	1.5%
13	Louisiana	2,629	2.8%
39	Maine	388	0.4%
17	Maryland	2,183	2.4%
8	Massachusetts	3,077	3.3%
3	Michigan	4,237	4.6%
29	Minnesota	1,026	1.1%
32	Mississippi	832	0.9%
19	Missouri	1,550	1.7%
NA	Montana**	NA	NA
36	Nebraska	491	0.5%
33	Nevada	720	0.8%
NA	New Hampshire**	NA	NA
11	New Jersey	2,876	3.1%
25	New Mexico	1,311	1.4%
9	New York	3,053	3.3%
10	North Carolina	3,023	3.3%
40	North Dakota	342	0.4%
4	Ohio	3,964	4.3%
24	Oklahoma	1,329	1.4%
NA	Oregon**	NA	NA
31	Pennsylvania	846	0.9%
37	Rhode Island	465	0.5%
16	South Carolina	2,310	2.5%
NA	South Dakota**	NA	NA
12	Tennessee	2,869	3.1%
2	Texas	9,683	10.5%
22	Utah	1,374	1.5%
NA	Vermont**	NA	NA
7	Virginia	3,081	3.3%
23	Washington	1,342	1.5%
35	West Virginia	522	0.6%
20	Wisconsin	1,536	1.7%
42	Wyoming	149	0.2%

RANK	STATE	CRIMES	% of USA
1	California	13,548	14.7%
2	Texas	9,683	10.5%
3	Michigan	4,237	4.6%
4	Ohio	3,964	4.3%
5	Florida	3,942	4.3%
6	Arizona	3,548	3.8%
7	Virginia	3,081	3.3%
8	Massachusetts	3,077	3.3%
9	New York	3,053	3.3%
10	North Carolina	3,023	3.3%
11	New Jersey	2,876	3.1%
12	Tennessee	2,869	3.1%
13	Louisiana	2,629	2.8%
14	Georgia	2,583	2.8%
15	Indiana	2,484	2.7%
16	South Carolina	2,310	2.5%
17	Maryland	2,183	2.4%
18	Colorado	2,150	2.3%
19	Missouri	1,550	1.7%
20	Wisconsin	1,536	1.7%
21	Kentucky	1,421	1.5%
22	Utah	1,374	1.5%
23	Washington	1,342	1.5%
24	Oklahoma	1,329	1.4%
25	New Mexico	1,311	1.4%
26	Alabama	1,240	1.3%
27	Connecticut	1,100	1.2%
28	Kansas	1,028	1.1%
29	Minnesota	1,026	1.1%
30	Arkansas	871	0.9%
31	Pennsylvania	846	0.9%
32	Mississippi	832	0.9%
33	Nevada	720	0.8%
34	Iowa	703	0.8%
35	West Virginia	522	0.6%
36	Nebraska	491	0.5%
37	Rhode Island	465	0.5%
38	Delaware	389	0.4%
39	Maine	388	0.4%
40	North Dakota	342	0.4%
41	Alaska	240	0.3%
42	Wyoming	149	0.2%
NA	Hawaii**	NA	NA
NA	Idaho**	NA	NA
NA	Illinois**	NA	NA
NA	Montana**	NA	NA
NA	New Hampshire**	NA	NA
NA	Oregon**	NA	NA
NA	South Dakota**	NA	NA
NA	Vermont**	NA	NA
	District of Columbia**	NA	NA

Source: Morgan Quitno Press using data from Federal Bureau of Investigation
   "Crime in the United States 2004" (Uniform Crime Reports, October 17, 2005)
*Includes murder, rape, robbery, aggravated assault, burglary, larceny-theft and motor vehicle theft. Total is only for states shown separately. Many states had incomplete reports.
**Not available.

Crime Rate Reported at Universities and Colleges in 2004

National Rate = 1,580.0 Reported Crimes per 100,000 Enrollment*

ALPHA ORDER

RANK	STATE	RATE
28	Alabama	1,380.8
39	Alaska	1,021.1
3	Arizona	2,383.0
11	Arkansas	1,884.1
23	California	1,526.4
15	Colorado	1,784.8
4	Connecticut	2,315.6
13	Delaware	1,827.2
31	Florida	1,336.8
14	Georgia	1,808.1
NA	Hawaii**	NA
NA	Idaho**	NA
NA	Illinois**	NA
7	Indiana	2,016.5
40	Iowa	979.6
34	Kansas	1,201.7
24	Kentucky	1,443.0
8	Louisiana	1,969.4
21	Maine	1,557.2
6	Maryland	2,024.5
9	Massachusetts	1,952.7
33	Michigan	1,241.1
16	Minnesota	1,754.1
26	Mississippi	1,426.6
29	Missouri	1,355.7
NA	Montana**	NA
19	Nebraska	1,671.0
25	Nevada	1,438.4
NA	New Hampshire**	NA
18	New Jersey	1,694.1
1	New Mexico	3,017.7
2	New York	2,879.4
17	North Carolina	1,694.2
32	North Dakota	1,315.0
20	Ohio	1,578.7
36	Oklahoma	1,065.6
NA	Oregon**	NA
38	Pennsylvania	1,023.4
5	Rhode Island	2,106.7
10	South Carolina	1,933.8
NA	South Dakota**	NA
12	Tennessee	1,857.8
22	Texas	1,541.7
37	Utah	1,026.8
NA	Vermont**	NA
27	Virginia	1,394.1
30	Washington	1,353.9
42	West Virginia	826.5
35	Wisconsin	1,135.8
41	Wyoming	977.9

RANK ORDER

RANK	STATE	RATE
1	New Mexico	3,017.7
2	New York	2,879.4
3	Arizona	2,383.0
4	Connecticut	2,315.6
5	Rhode Island	2,106.7
6	Maryland	2,024.5
7	Indiana	2,016.5
8	Louisiana	1,969.4
9	Massachusetts	1,952.7
10	South Carolina	1,933.8
11	Arkansas	1,884.1
12	Tennessee	1,857.8
13	Delaware	1,827.2
14	Georgia	1,808.1
15	Colorado	1,784.8
16	Minnesota	1,754.1
17	North Carolina	1,694.2
18	New Jersey	1,694.1
19	Nebraska	1,671.0
20	Ohio	1,578.7
21	Maine	1,557.2
22	Texas	1,541.7
23	California	1,526.4
24	Kentucky	1,443.0
25	Nevada	1,438.4
26	Mississippi	1,426.6
27	Virginia	1,394.1
28	Alabama	1,380.8
29	Missouri	1,355.7
30	Washington	1,353.9
31	Florida	1,336.8
32	North Dakota	1,315.0
33	Michigan	1,241.1
34	Kansas	1,201.7
35	Wisconsin	1,135.8
36	Oklahoma	1,065.6
37	Utah	1,026.8
38	Pennsylvania	1,023.4
39	Alaska	1,021.1
40	Iowa	979.6
41	Wyoming	977.9
42	West Virginia	826.5
NA	Hawaii**	NA
NA	Idaho**	NA
NA	Illinois**	NA
NA	Montana**	NA
NA	New Hampshire**	NA
NA	Oregon**	NA
NA	South Dakota**	NA
NA	Vermont**	NA
	District of Columbia**	NA

Source: Morgan Quitno Press using data from Federal Bureau of Investigation
    "Crime in the United States 2004" (Uniform Crime Reports, October 17, 2005)
*Includes murder, rape, robbery, aggravated assault, burglary, larceny-theft and motor vehicle theft. National rate is only for states shown separately. Many states had incomplete reports.
**Not available.

Crimes Reported at Universities and Colleges as a Percent of All Crimes in 2004

National Percent = 0.85% of Crimes*

ALPHA ORDER				RANK ORDER		
RANK	STATE	PERCENT		RANK	STATE	PERCENT
36	Alabama	0.61		1	North Dakota	2.70
22	Alaska	0.91		2	Massachusetts	1.64
16	Arizona	1.06		3	New Mexico	1.41
33	Arkansas	0.70		4	Virginia	1.40
21	California	0.95		5	Rhode Island	1.37
13	Colorado	1.09		6	Utah	1.33
14	Connecticut	1.08		7	Delaware	1.26
7	Delaware	1.26		8	Kentucky	1.23
40	Florida	0.46		9	New Jersey	1.19
35	Georgia	0.62		10	Michigan	1.18
NA	Hawaii**	NA		11	Maine	1.17
NA	Idaho**	NA		12	Louisiana	1.15
NA	Illinois**	NA		13	Colorado	1.09
15	Indiana	1.07		14	Connecticut	1.08
31	Iowa	0.75		15	Indiana	1.07
24	Kansas	0.86		16	Arizona	1.06
8	Kentucky	1.23		17	South Carolina	1.04
12	Louisiana	1.15		17	West Virginia	1.04
11	Maine	1.17		19	Tennessee	0.97
23	Maryland	0.90		19	Wisconsin	0.97
2	Massachusetts	1.64		21	California	0.95
10	Michigan	1.18		22	Alaska	0.91
36	Minnesota	0.61		23	Maryland	0.90
30	Mississippi	0.76		24	Kansas	0.86
36	Missouri	0.61		24	Ohio	0.86
NA	Montana**	NA		24	Texas	0.86
32	Nebraska	0.73		27	Wyoming	0.83
34	Nevada	0.64		28	Oklahoma	0.80
NA	New Hampshire**	NA		29	North Carolina	0.77
9	New Jersey	1.19		30	Mississippi	0.76
3	New Mexico	1.41		31	Iowa	0.75
39	New York	0.60		32	Nebraska	0.73
29	North Carolina	0.77		33	Arkansas	0.70
1	North Dakota	2.70		34	Nevada	0.64
24	Ohio	0.86		35	Georgia	0.62
28	Oklahoma	0.80		36	Alabama	0.61
NA	Oregon**	NA		36	Minnesota	0.61
42	Pennsylvania	0.24		36	Missouri	0.61
5	Rhode Island	1.37		39	New York	0.60
17	South Carolina	1.04		40	Florida	0.46
NA	South Dakota**	NA		41	Washington	0.42
19	Tennessee	0.97		42	Pennsylvania	0.24
24	Texas	0.86		NA	Hawaii**	NA
6	Utah	1.33		NA	Idaho**	NA
NA	Vermont**	NA		NA	Illinois**	NA
4	Virginia	1.40		NA	Montana**	NA
41	Washington	0.42		NA	New Hampshire**	NA
17	West Virginia	1.04		NA	Oregon**	NA
19	Wisconsin	0.97		NA	South Dakota**	NA
27	Wyoming	0.83		NA	Vermont**	NA
					District of Columbia**	NA

Source: Morgan Quitno Press using data from Federal Bureau of Investigation
   "Crime in the United States 2004" (Uniform Crime Reports, October 17, 2005)
*Includes murder, rape, robbery, aggravated assault, burglary, larceny-theft and motor vehicle theft. National
percent is only for states shown separately. Many states had incomplete reports.
**Not available.

Violent Crimes Reported at Universities and Colleges in 2004

National Total = 2,534 Reported Violent Crimes*

ALPHA ORDER

RANK	STATE	CRIMES	% of USA
22	Alabama	37	1.5%
35	Alaska	18	0.7%
11	Arizona	96	3.8%
27	Arkansas	25	1.0%
1	California	328	12.9%
18	Colorado	46	1.8%
30	Connecticut	24	0.9%
34	Delaware	20	0.8%
3	Florida	138	5.4%
16	Georgia	51	2.0%
NA	Hawaii**	NA	NA
NA	Idaho**	NA	NA
NA	Illinois**	NA	NA
15	Indiana	67	2.6%
26	Iowa	28	1.1%
21	Kansas	39	1.5%
27	Kentucky	25	1.0%
10	Louisiana	99	3.9%
37	Maine	11	0.4%
6	Maryland	112	4.4%
5	Massachusetts	124	4.9%
8	Michigan	103	4.1%
38	Minnesota	9	0.4%
39	Mississippi	5	0.2%
17	Missouri	47	1.9%
NA	Montana**	NA	NA
40	Nebraska	4	0.2%
22	Nevada	37	1.5%
NA	New Hampshire**	NA	NA
4	New Jersey	135	5.3%
25	New Mexico	32	1.3%
18	New York	46	1.8%
12	North Carolina	83	3.3%
41	North Dakota	2	0.1%
13	Ohio	73	2.9%
24	Oklahoma	33	1.3%
NA	Oregon**	NA	NA
20	Pennsylvania	45	1.8%
36	Rhode Island	14	0.6%
14	South Carolina	71	2.8%
NA	South Dakota**	NA	NA
9	Tennessee	101	4.0%
2	Texas	208	8.2%
33	Utah	21	0.8%
NA	Vermont**	NA	NA
7	Virginia	106	4.2%
27	Washington	25	1.0%
32	West Virginia	22	0.9%
30	Wisconsin	24	0.9%
42	Wyoming	0	0.0%

RANK ORDER

RANK	STATE	CRIMES	% of USA
1	California	328	12.9%
2	Texas	208	8.2%
3	Florida	138	5.4%
4	New Jersey	135	5.3%
5	Massachusetts	124	4.9%
6	Maryland	112	4.4%
7	Virginia	106	4.2%
8	Michigan	103	4.1%
9	Tennessee	101	4.0%
10	Louisiana	99	3.9%
11	Arizona	96	3.8%
12	North Carolina	83	3.3%
13	Ohio	73	2.9%
14	South Carolina	71	2.8%
15	Indiana	67	2.6%
16	Georgia	51	2.0%
17	Missouri	47	1.9%
18	Colorado	46	1.8%
18	New York	46	1.8%
20	Pennsylvania	45	1.8%
21	Kansas	39	1.5%
22	Alabama	37	1.5%
22	Nevada	37	1.5%
24	Oklahoma	33	1.3%
25	New Mexico	32	1.3%
26	Iowa	28	1.1%
27	Arkansas	25	1.0%
27	Kentucky	25	1.0%
27	Washington	25	1.0%
30	Connecticut	24	0.9%
30	Wisconsin	24	0.9%
32	West Virginia	22	0.9%
33	Utah	21	0.8%
34	Delaware	20	0.8%
35	Alaska	18	0.7%
36	Rhode Island	14	0.6%
37	Maine	11	0.4%
38	Minnesota	9	0.4%
39	Mississippi	5	0.2%
40	Nebraska	4	0.2%
41	North Dakota	2	0.1%
42	Wyoming	0	0.0%
NA	Hawaii**	NA	NA
NA	Idaho**	NA	NA
NA	Illinois**	NA	NA
NA	Montana**	NA	NA
NA	New Hampshire**	NA	NA
NA	Oregon**	NA	NA
NA	South Dakota**	NA	NA
NA	Vermont**	NA	NA
	District of Columbia**	NA	NA

Source: Morgan Quitno Press using data from Federal Bureau of Investigation
   "Crime in the United States 2004" (Uniform Crime Reports, October 17, 2005)
*Includes murder, rape, robbery and aggravated assault. Total is only for states shown separately. Many states had incomplete reports.
**Not available.

Violent Crime Rate Reported at Universities and Colleges in 2004

National Rate = 43.3 Reported Violent Crimes per 100,000 Enrollment*

ALPHA ORDER

RANK	STATE	RATE
23	Alabama	41.2
5	Alaska	76.6
10	Arizona	64.5
15	Arkansas	54.1
27	California	37.0
26	Colorado	38.2
16	Connecticut	50.5
2	Delaware	93.9
18	Florida	46.8
28	Georgia	35.7
NA	Hawaii**	NA
NA	Idaho**	NA
NA	Illinois**	NA
13	Indiana	54.4
25	Iowa	39.0
20	Kansas	45.6
34	Kentucky	25.4
6	Louisiana	74.2
21	Maine	44.1
1	Maryland	103.9
4	Massachusetts	78.7
31	Michigan	30.2
38	Minnesota	15.4
40	Mississippi	8.6
24	Missouri	41.1
NA	Montana**	NA
39	Nebraska	13.6
7	Nevada	73.9
NA	New Hampshire**	NA
3	New Jersey	79.5
8	New Mexico	73.7
22	New York	43.4
19	North Carolina	46.5
41	North Dakota	7.7
32	Ohio	29.1
33	Oklahoma	26.5
NA	Oregon**	NA
13	Pennsylvania	54.4
11	Rhode Island	63.4
12	South Carolina	59.4
NA	South Dakota**	NA
9	Tennessee	65.4
30	Texas	33.1
37	Utah	15.7
NA	Vermont**	NA
17	Virginia	48.0
35	Washington	25.2
29	West Virginia	34.8
36	Wisconsin	17.7
42	Wyoming	0.0

RANK ORDER

RANK	STATE	RATE
1	Maryland	103.9
2	Delaware	93.9
3	New Jersey	79.5
4	Massachusetts	78.7
5	Alaska	76.6
6	Louisiana	74.2
7	Nevada	73.9
8	New Mexico	73.7
9	Tennessee	65.4
10	Arizona	64.5
11	Rhode Island	63.4
12	South Carolina	59.4
13	Indiana	54.4
13	Pennsylvania	54.4
15	Arkansas	54.1
16	Connecticut	50.5
17	Virginia	48.0
18	Florida	46.8
19	North Carolina	46.5
20	Kansas	45.6
21	Maine	44.1
22	New York	43.4
23	Alabama	41.2
24	Missouri	41.1
25	Iowa	39.0
26	Colorado	38.2
27	California	37.0
28	Georgia	35.7
29	West Virginia	34.8
30	Texas	33.1
31	Michigan	30.2
32	Ohio	29.1
33	Oklahoma	26.5
34	Kentucky	25.4
35	Washington	25.2
36	Wisconsin	17.7
37	Utah	15.7
38	Minnesota	15.4
39	Nebraska	13.6
40	Mississippi	8.6
41	North Dakota	7.7
42	Wyoming	0.0
NA	Hawaii**	NA
NA	Idaho**	NA
NA	Illinois**	NA
NA	Montana**	NA
NA	New Hampshire**	NA
NA	Oregon**	NA
NA	South Dakota**	NA
NA	Vermont**	NA
	District of Columbia**	NA

Source: Morgan Quitno Press using data from Federal Bureau of Investigation
    "Crime in the United States 2004" (Uniform Crime Reports, October 17, 2005)
*Includes murder, rape, robbery and aggravated assault. National rate is only for states shown separately. Many states had incomplete reports.
**Not available.

Violent Crimes Reported at Universities and Colleges
As a Percent of All Violent Crimes in 2004
National Percent = 0.20% of Violent Crimes*

ALPHA ORDER

RANK	STATE	PERCENT
27	Alabama	0.19
6	Alaska	0.43
14	Arizona	0.33
30	Arkansas	0.18
31	California	0.17
17	Colorado	0.27
21	Connecticut	0.24
7	Delaware	0.42
36	Florida	0.11
34	Georgia	0.13
NA	Hawaii**	NA
NA	Idaho**	NA
NA	Illinois**	NA
14	Indiana	0.33
12	Iowa	0.35
10	Kansas	0.38
19	Kentucky	0.25
13	Louisiana	0.34
1	Maine	0.81
16	Maryland	0.29
7	Massachusetts	0.42
25	Michigan	0.21
38	Minnesota	0.07
40	Mississippi	0.06
31	Missouri	0.17
NA	Montana**	NA
38	Nebraska	0.07
18	Nevada	0.26
NA	New Hampshire**	NA
5	New Jersey	0.44
21	New Mexico	0.24
41	New York	0.05
23	North Carolina	0.22
9	North Dakota	0.40
27	Ohio	0.19
27	Oklahoma	0.19
NA	Oregon**	NA
37	Pennsylvania	0.09
2	Rhode Island	0.52
23	South Carolina	0.22
NA	South Dakota**	NA
19	Tennessee	0.25
31	Texas	0.17
11	Utah	0.37
NA	Vermont**	NA
2	Virginia	0.52
35	Washington	0.12
4	West Virginia	0.45
25	Wisconsin	0.21
42	Wyoming	0.00

RANK ORDER

RANK	STATE	PERCENT
1	Maine	0.81
2	Rhode Island	0.52
2	Virginia	0.52
4	West Virginia	0.45
5	New Jersey	0.44
6	Alaska	0.43
7	Delaware	0.42
7	Massachusetts	0.42
9	North Dakota	0.40
10	Kansas	0.38
11	Utah	0.37
12	Iowa	0.35
13	Louisiana	0.34
14	Arizona	0.33
14	Indiana	0.33
16	Maryland	0.29
17	Colorado	0.27
18	Nevada	0.26
19	Kentucky	0.25
19	Tennessee	0.25
21	Connecticut	0.24
21	New Mexico	0.24
23	North Carolina	0.22
23	South Carolina	0.22
25	Michigan	0.21
25	Wisconsin	0.21
27	Alabama	0.19
27	Ohio	0.19
27	Oklahoma	0.19
30	Arkansas	0.18
31	California	0.17
31	Missouri	0.17
31	Texas	0.17
34	Georgia	0.13
35	Washington	0.12
36	Florida	0.11
37	Pennsylvania	0.09
38	Minnesota	0.07
38	Nebraska	0.07
40	Mississippi	0.06
41	New York	0.05
42	Wyoming	0.00
NA	Hawaii**	NA
NA	Idaho**	NA
NA	Illinois**	NA
NA	Montana**	NA
NA	New Hampshire**	NA
NA	Oregon**	NA
NA	South Dakota**	NA
NA	Vermont**	NA
	District of Columbia**	NA

Source: Morgan Quitno Press using data from Federal Bureau of Investigation
     "Crime in the United States 2004" (Uniform Crime Reports, October 17, 2005)
*Includes murder, rape, robbery and aggravated assault. National percent is only for states shown separately.
Many states had incomplete reports.
**Not available.

Property Crimes Reported at Universities and Colleges in 2004

National Total = 89,921 Reported Property Crimes*

ALPHA ORDER

RANK	STATE	CRIMES	% of USA
26	Alabama	1,203	1.3%
41	Alaska	222	0.2%
6	Arizona	3,452	3.8%
30	Arkansas	846	0.9%
1	California	13,220	14.7%
17	Colorado	2,104	2.3%
27	Connecticut	1,076	1.2%
39	Delaware	369	0.4%
5	Florida	3,804	4.2%
13	Georgia	2,532	2.8%
NA	Hawaii**	NA	NA
NA	Idaho**	NA	NA
NA	Illinois**	NA	NA
15	Indiana	2,417	2.7%
34	Iowa	675	0.8%
29	Kansas	989	1.1%
21	Kentucky	1,396	1.6%
14	Louisiana	2,530	2.8%
38	Maine	377	0.4%
18	Maryland	2,071	2.3%
9	Massachusetts	2,953	3.3%
3	Michigan	4,134	4.6%
28	Minnesota	1,017	1.1%
31	Mississippi	827	0.9%
20	Missouri	1,503	1.7%
NA	Montana**	NA	NA
36	Nebraska	487	0.5%
33	Nevada	683	0.8%
NA	New Hampshire**	NA	NA
12	New Jersey	2,741	3.0%
25	New Mexico	1,279	1.4%
7	New York	3,007	3.3%
10	North Carolina	2,940	3.3%
40	North Dakota	340	0.4%
4	Ohio	3,891	4.3%
24	Oklahoma	1,296	1.4%
NA	Oregon**	NA	NA
32	Pennsylvania	801	0.9%
37	Rhode Island	451	0.5%
16	South Carolina	2,239	2.5%
NA	South Dakota**	NA	NA
11	Tennessee	2,768	3.1%
2	Texas	9,475	10.5%
22	Utah	1,353	1.5%
NA	Vermont**	NA	NA
8	Virginia	2,975	3.3%
23	Washington	1,317	1.5%
35	West Virginia	500	0.6%
19	Wisconsin	1,512	1.7%
42	Wyoming	149	0.2%

RANK ORDER

RANK	STATE	CRIMES	% of USA
1	California	13,220	14.7%
2	Texas	9,475	10.5%
3	Michigan	4,134	4.6%
4	Ohio	3,891	4.3%
5	Florida	3,804	4.2%
6	Arizona	3,452	3.8%
7	New York	3,007	3.3%
8	Virginia	2,975	3.3%
9	Massachusetts	2,953	3.3%
10	North Carolina	2,940	3.3%
11	Tennessee	2,768	3.1%
12	New Jersey	2,741	3.0%
13	Georgia	2,532	2.8%
14	Louisiana	2,530	2.8%
15	Indiana	2,417	2.7%
16	South Carolina	2,239	2.5%
17	Colorado	2,104	2.3%
18	Maryland	2,071	2.3%
19	Wisconsin	1,512	1.7%
20	Missouri	1,503	1.7%
21	Kentucky	1,396	1.6%
22	Utah	1,353	1.5%
23	Washington	1,317	1.5%
24	Oklahoma	1,296	1.4%
25	New Mexico	1,279	1.4%
26	Alabama	1,203	1.3%
27	Connecticut	1,076	1.2%
28	Minnesota	1,017	1.1%
29	Kansas	989	1.1%
30	Arkansas	846	0.9%
31	Mississippi	827	0.9%
32	Pennsylvania	801	0.9%
33	Nevada	683	0.8%
34	Iowa	675	0.8%
35	West Virginia	500	0.6%
36	Nebraska	487	0.5%
37	Rhode Island	451	0.5%
38	Maine	377	0.4%
39	Delaware	369	0.4%
40	North Dakota	340	0.4%
41	Alaska	222	0.2%
42	Wyoming	149	0.2%
NA	Hawaii**	NA	NA
NA	Idaho**	NA	NA
NA	Illinois**	NA	NA
NA	Montana**	NA	NA
NA	New Hampshire**	NA	NA
NA	Oregon**	NA	NA
NA	South Dakota**	NA	NA
NA	Vermont**	NA	NA
	District of Columbia**	NA	NA

Source: Morgan Quitno Press using data from Federal Bureau of Investigation
    "Crime in the United States 2004" (Uniform Crime Reports, October 17, 2005)
Includes burglary, larceny-theft and motor vehicle theft. Total is only for states shown separately. Many states had incomplete reports.
**Not available.*

Property Crime Rate Reported at Universities and Colleges in 2004

National Rate = 1,536.7 Reported Property Crimes per 100,000 Enrollment*

ALPHA ORDER

RANK	STATE	RATE
28	Alabama	1,339.6
40	Alaska	944.5
3	Arizona	2,318.5
11	Arkansas	1,830.0
23	California	1,489.4
14	Colorado	1,746.6
4	Connecticut	2,265.1
16	Delaware	1,733.3
32	Florida	1,290.0
13	Georgia	1,772.4
NA	Hawaii**	NA
NA	Idaho**	NA
NA	Illinois**	NA
6	Indiana	1,962.2
41	Iowa	940.6
34	Kansas	1,156.1
25	Kentucky	1,417.6
8	Louisiana	1,895.2
21	Maine	1,513.1
7	Maryland	1,920.6
10	Massachusetts	1,874.0
33	Michigan	1,210.9
15	Minnesota	1,738.7
24	Mississippi	1,418.0
30	Missouri	1,314.6
NA	Montana**	NA
17	Nebraska	1,657.4
26	Nevada	1,364.5
NA	New Hampshire**	NA
19	New Jersey	1,614.6
1	New Mexico	2,944.1
2	New York	2,836.0
18	North Carolina	1,647.6
31	North Dakota	1,307.3
20	Ohio	1,549.6
36	Oklahoma	1,039.1
NA	Oregon**	NA
39	Pennsylvania	969.0
5	Rhode Island	2,043.3
9	South Carolina	1,874.4
NA	South Dakota**	NA
12	Tennessee	1,792.4
22	Texas	1,508.6
37	Utah	1,011.1
NA	Vermont**	NA
27	Virginia	1,346.1
29	Washington	1,328.7
42	West Virginia	791.7
35	Wisconsin	1,118.0
38	Wyoming	977.9

RANK ORDER

RANK	STATE	RATE
1	New Mexico	2,944.1
2	New York	2,836.0
3	Arizona	2,318.5
4	Connecticut	2,265.1
5	Rhode Island	2,043.3
6	Indiana	1,962.2
7	Maryland	1,920.6
8	Louisiana	1,895.2
9	South Carolina	1,874.4
10	Massachusetts	1,874.0
11	Arkansas	1,830.0
12	Tennessee	1,792.4
13	Georgia	1,772.4
14	Colorado	1,746.6
15	Minnesota	1,738.7
16	Delaware	1,733.3
17	Nebraska	1,657.4
18	North Carolina	1,647.6
19	New Jersey	1,614.6
20	Ohio	1,549.6
21	Maine	1,513.1
22	Texas	1,508.6
23	California	1,489.4
24	Mississippi	1,418.0
25	Kentucky	1,417.6
26	Nevada	1,364.5
27	Virginia	1,346.1
28	Alabama	1,339.6
29	Washington	1,328.7
30	Missouri	1,314.6
31	North Dakota	1,307.3
32	Florida	1,290.0
33	Michigan	1,210.9
34	Kansas	1,156.1
35	Wisconsin	1,118.0
36	Oklahoma	1,039.1
37	Utah	1,011.1
38	Wyoming	977.9
39	Pennsylvania	969.0
40	Alaska	944.5
41	Iowa	940.6
42	West Virginia	791.7
NA	Hawaii**	NA
NA	Idaho**	NA
NA	Illinois**	NA
NA	Montana**	NA
NA	New Hampshire**	NA
NA	Oregon**	NA
NA	South Dakota**	NA
NA	Vermont**	NA
	District of Columbia**	NA

Source: Morgan Quitno Press using data from Federal Bureau of Investigation
    "Crime in the United States 2004" (Uniform Crime Reports, October 17, 2005)
*Includes burglary, larceny-theft and motor vehicle theft. National rate is only for states shown separately. Many states had incomplete reports.
**Not available.

Property Crimes Reported at Universities and Colleges
As a Percent of All Property Crimes in 2004
National Percent = 0.94% of Property Crimes*

ALPHA ORDER				RANK ORDER		
RANK	STATE	PERCENT		RANK	STATE	PERCENT
38	Alabama	0.66		1	North Dakota	2.80
23	Alaska	1.00		2	Massachusetts	1.87
17	Arizona	1.13		3	New Mexico	1.60
33	Arkansas	0.77		4	Virginia	1.49
20	California	1.08		5	Rhode Island	1.45
14	Colorado	1.17		6	Delaware	1.40
14	Connecticut	1.17		7	Utah	1.39
6	Delaware	1.40		8	Michigan	1.34
40	Florida	0.52		9	Kentucky	1.33
36	Georgia	0.67		10	New Jersey	1.30
NA	Hawaii**	NA		11	Louisiana	1.27
NA	Idaho**	NA		12	Maine	1.19
NA	Illinois**	NA		13	South Carolina	1.18
16	Indiana	1.14		14	Colorado	1.17
31	Iowa	0.79		14	Connecticut	1.17
26	Kansas	0.91		16	Indiana	1.14
9	Kentucky	1.33		17	Arizona	1.13
11	Louisiana	1.27		18	West Virginia	1.10
12	Maine	1.19		19	Tennessee	1.09
22	Maryland	1.02		20	California	1.08
2	Massachusetts	1.87		21	Wisconsin	1.03
8	Michigan	1.34		22	Maryland	1.02
38	Minnesota	0.66		23	Alaska	1.00
30	Mississippi	0.82		24	Texas	0.94
36	Missouri	0.67		25	Ohio	0.92
NA	Montana**	NA		26	Kansas	0.91
31	Nebraska	0.79		27	Wyoming	0.88
35	Nevada	0.70		28	Oklahoma	0.87
NA	New Hampshire**	NA		29	North Carolina	0.83
10	New Jersey	1.30		30	Mississippi	0.82
3	New Mexico	1.60		31	Iowa	0.79
34	New York	0.71		31	Nebraska	0.79
29	North Carolina	0.83		33	Arkansas	0.77
1	North Dakota	2.80		34	New York	0.71
25	Ohio	0.92		35	Nevada	0.70
28	Oklahoma	0.87		36	Georgia	0.67
NA	Oregon**	NA		36	Missouri	0.67
42	Pennsylvania	0.27		38	Alabama	0.66
5	Rhode Island	1.45		38	Minnesota	0.66
13	South Carolina	1.18		40	Florida	0.52
NA	South Dakota**	NA		41	Washington	0.44
19	Tennessee	1.09		42	Pennsylvania	0.27
24	Texas	0.94		NA	Hawaii**	NA
7	Utah	1.39		NA	Idaho**	NA
NA	Vermont**	NA		NA	Illinois**	NA
4	Virginia	1.49		NA	Montana**	NA
41	Washington	0.44		NA	New Hampshire**	NA
18	West Virginia	1.10		NA	Oregon**	NA
21	Wisconsin	1.03		NA	South Dakota**	NA
27	Wyoming	0.88		NA	Vermont**	NA
					District of Columbia**	NA

Source: Morgan Quitno Press using data from Federal Bureau of Investigation
    "Crime in the United States 2003" (Uniform Crime Reports, October 25, 2004)
*Includes burglary, larceny-theft and motor vehicle theft. National percent is only for states shown separately.
Many states had incomplete reports.
**Not available.

Crimes in 2000

National Total = 11,608,070 Crimes*

ALPHA ORDER

RANK	STATE	CRIMES	% of USA
21	Alabama	202,159	1.7%
46	Alaska	26,641	0.2%
12	Arizona	299,092	2.6%
32	Arkansas	110,019	0.9%
1	California	1,266,714	10.9%
25	Colorado	171,304	1.5%
31	Connecticut	110,091	0.9%
42	Delaware	35,090	0.3%
3	Florida	910,154	7.8%
9	Georgia	388,949	3.4%
38	Hawaii	62,987	0.5%
40	Idaho	41,228	0.4%
5	Illinois	526,474	4.5%
18	Indiana	228,135	2.0%
35	Iowa	94,630	0.8%
29	Kansas	118,527	1.0%
28	Kentucky	119,626	1.0%
17	Louisiana	242,344	2.1%
44	Maine	33,400	0.3%
15	Maryland	255,085	2.2%
22	Massachusetts	192,131	1.7%
7	Michigan	408,456	3.5%
24	Minnesota	171,611	1.5%
30	Mississippi	113,911	1.0%
16	Missouri	253,338	2.2%
43	Montana	35,005	0.3%
37	Nebraska	70,085	0.6%
36	Nevada	85,297	0.7%
45	New Hampshire	30,068	0.3%
14	New Jersey	265,935	2.3%
33	New Mexico	100,391	0.9%
4	New York	588,189	5.1%
8	North Carolina	395,972	3.4%
50	North Dakota	14,694	0.1%
6	Ohio	458,874	4.0%
27	Oklahoma	157,302	1.4%
26	Oregon	165,780	1.4%
10	Pennsylvania	367,858	3.2%
41	Rhode Island	36,444	0.3%
19	South Carolina	214,515	1.8%
48	South Dakota	17,511	0.2%
13	Tennessee	278,218	2.4%
2	Texas	1,033,311	8.9%
34	Utah	99,958	0.9%
47	Vermont	18,185	0.2%
20	Virginia	214,348	1.8%
11	Washington	300,932	2.6%
39	West Virginia	47,067	0.4%
23	Wisconsin	172,124	1.5%
49	Wyoming	16,285	0.1%

RANK ORDER

RANK	STATE	CRIMES	% of USA
1	California	1,266,714	10.9%
2	Texas	1,033,311	8.9%
3	Florida	910,154	7.8%
4	New York	588,189	5.1%
5	Illinois	526,474	4.5%
6	Ohio	458,874	4.0%
7	Michigan	408,456	3.5%
8	North Carolina	395,972	3.4%
9	Georgia	388,949	3.4%
10	Pennsylvania	367,858	3.2%
11	Washington	300,932	2.6%
12	Arizona	299,092	2.6%
13	Tennessee	278,218	2.4%
14	New Jersey	265,935	2.3%
15	Maryland	255,085	2.2%
16	Missouri	253,338	2.2%
17	Louisiana	242,344	2.1%
18	Indiana	228,135	2.0%
19	South Carolina	214,515	1.8%
20	Virginia	214,348	1.8%
21	Alabama	202,159	1.7%
22	Massachusetts	192,131	1.7%
23	Wisconsin	172,124	1.5%
24	Minnesota	171,611	1.5%
25	Colorado	171,304	1.5%
26	Oregon	165,780	1.4%
27	Oklahoma	157,302	1.4%
28	Kentucky	119,626	1.0%
29	Kansas	118,527	1.0%
30	Mississippi	113,911	1.0%
31	Connecticut	110,091	0.9%
32	Arkansas	110,019	0.9%
33	New Mexico	100,391	0.9%
34	Utah	99,958	0.9%
35	Iowa	94,630	0.8%
36	Nevada	85,297	0.7%
37	Nebraska	70,085	0.6%
38	Hawaii	62,987	0.5%
39	West Virginia	47,067	0.4%
40	Idaho	41,228	0.4%
41	Rhode Island	36,444	0.3%
42	Delaware	35,090	0.3%
43	Montana	35,005	0.3%
44	Maine	33,400	0.3%
45	New Hampshire	30,068	0.3%
46	Alaska	26,641	0.2%
47	Vermont	18,185	0.2%
48	South Dakota	17,511	0.2%
49	Wyoming	16,285	0.1%
50	North Dakota	14,694	0.1%
	District of Columbia	41,626	0.4%

Source: Federal Bureau of Investigation
"Crime in the United States 2001" (Uniform Crime Reports, October 28, 2002)
Revised figures. Includes murder, rape, robbery, aggravated assault, burglary, larceny-theft and motor vehicle theft.

Percent Change in Number of Crimes: 2000 to 2004

National Percent Change = 0.8% Increase*

ALPHA ORDER				RANK ORDER		
RANK	**STATE**	**PERCENT CHANGE**		**RANK**	**STATE**	**PERCENT CHANGE**
22	Alabama	(0.2)		1	Nevada	32.0
27	Alaska	(1.2)		2	Colorado	15.3
5	Arizona	12.2		3	Arkansas	12.9
3	Arkansas	12.9		4	California	12.5
4	California	12.5		5	Arizona	12.2
2	Colorado	15.3		6	Wyoming	10.9
39	Connecticut	(7.3)		7	Texas	9.6
45	Delaware	(11.7)		8	Georgia	7.2
37	Florida	(6.5)		9	Washington	7.1
8	Georgia	7.2		9	West Virginia	7.1
19	Hawaii	1.2		11	Oregon	6.9
16	Idaho	2.7		12	Oklahoma	6.2
44	Illinois	(9.9)		13	Tennessee	6.1
18	Indiana	1.8		14	South Carolina	3.5
25	Iowa	(0.8)		15	Utah	3.3
20	Kansas	0.3		16	Idaho	2.7
30	Kentucky	(3.6)		16	Virginia	2.7
36	Louisiana	(5.9)		18	Indiana	1.8
26	Maine	(0.9)		19	Hawaii	1.2
35	Maryland	(5.4)		20	Kansas	0.3
29	Massachusetts	(2.5)		20	Ohio	0.3
46	Michigan	(12.2)		22	Alabama	(0.2)
28	Minnesota	(1.7)		22	Missouri	(0.2)
31	Mississippi	(3.8)		24	North Carolina	(0.6)
22	Missouri	(0.2)		25	Iowa	(0.8)
49	Montana	(14.5)		26	Maine	(0.9)
32	Nebraska	(4.5)		27	Alaska	(1.2)
1	Nevada	32.0		28	Minnesota	(1.7)
33	New Hampshire	(4.6)		29	Massachusetts	(2.5)
43	New Jersey	(8.9)		30	Kentucky	(3.6)
41	New Mexico	(7.4)		31	Mississippi	(3.8)
47	New York	(13.7)		32	Nebraska	(4.5)
24	North Carolina	(0.6)		33	New Hampshire	(4.6)
48	North Dakota	(13.8)		34	Pennsylvania	(4.7)
20	Ohio	0.3		35	Maryland	(5.4)
12	Oklahoma	6.2		36	Louisiana	(5.9)
11	Oregon	6.9		37	Florida	(6.5)
34	Pennsylvania	(4.7)		38	Rhode Island	(7.1)
38	Rhode Island	(7.1)		39	Connecticut	(7.3)
14	South Carolina	3.5		39	South Dakota	(7.3)
39	South Dakota	(7.3)		41	New Mexico	(7.4)
13	Tennessee	6.1		42	Wisconsin	(8.1)
7	Texas	9.6		43	New Jersey	(8.9)
15	Utah	3.3		44	Illinois	(9.9)
50	Vermont	(17.3)		45	Delaware	(11.7)
16	Virginia	2.7		46	Michigan	(12.2)
9	Washington	7.1		47	New York	(13.7)
9	West Virginia	7.1		48	North Dakota	(13.8)
42	Wisconsin	(8.1)		49	Montana	(14.5)
6	Wyoming	10.9		50	Vermont	(17.3)
					District of Columbia	(17.2)

Source: Morgan Quitno Press using data from Federal Bureau of Investigation
   "Crime in the United States" (Uniform Crime Reports, 2001 and 2004 editions)
*Revised figures. Includes murder, rape, robbery, aggravated assault, burglary, larceny-theft and motor vehicle theft.

Crime Rate in 2000

National Rate = 4,124.0 Crimes per 100,000 Population*

ALPHA ORDER

RANK	STATE	RATE
15	Alabama	4,545.9
21	Alaska	4,249.4
1	Arizona	5,829.5
23	Arkansas	4,115.3
31	California	3,739.7
28	Colorado	3,982.6
36	Connecticut	3,232.7
17	Delaware	4,478.1
2	Florida	5,694.7
13	Georgia	4,751.1
6	Hawaii	5,198.9
38	Idaho	3,186.2
22	Illinois	4,239.2
30	Indiana	3,751.9
35	Iowa	3,233.7
19	Kansas	4,408.8
45	Kentucky	2,959.7
4	Louisiana	5,422.8
46	Maine	2,619.8
12	Maryland	4,816.1
42	Massachusetts	3,026.1
24	Michigan	4,109.9
32	Minnesota	3,488.4
27	Mississippi	4,004.4
16	Missouri	4,527.8
29	Montana	3,880.0
25	Nebraska	4,095.5
20	Nevada	4,268.6
48	New Hampshire	2,433.1
39	New Jersey	3,160.5
3	New Mexico	5,518.9
40	New York	3,099.6
9	North Carolina	4,919.3
50	North Dakota	2,288.1
26	Ohio	4,041.8
14	Oklahoma	4,558.6
11	Oregon	4,845.4
43	Pennsylvania	2,995.3
33	Rhode Island	3,476.4
5	South Carolina	5,346.8
49	South Dakota	2,319.8
10	Tennessee	4,890.2
8	Texas	4,955.5
18	Utah	4,476.1
44	Vermont	2,986.9
41	Virginia	3,028.1
7	Washington	5,105.6
47	West Virginia	2,602.8
37	Wisconsin	3,209.1
34	Wyoming	3,298.0

RANK ORDER

RANK	STATE	RATE
1	Arizona	5,829.5
2	Florida	5,694.7
3	New Mexico	5,518.9
4	Louisiana	5,422.8
5	South Carolina	5,346.8
6	Hawaii	5,198.9
7	Washington	5,105.6
8	Texas	4,955.5
9	North Carolina	4,919.3
10	Tennessee	4,890.2
11	Oregon	4,845.4
12	Maryland	4,816.1
13	Georgia	4,751.1
14	Oklahoma	4,558.6
15	Alabama	4,545.9
16	Missouri	4,527.8
17	Delaware	4,478.1
18	Utah	4,476.1
19	Kansas	4,408.8
20	Nevada	4,268.6
21	Alaska	4,249.4
22	Illinois	4,239.2
23	Arkansas	4,115.3
24	Michigan	4,109.9
25	Nebraska	4,095.5
26	Ohio	4,041.8
27	Mississippi	4,004.4
28	Colorado	3,982.6
29	Montana	3,880.0
30	Indiana	3,751.9
31	California	3,739.7
32	Minnesota	3,488.4
33	Rhode Island	3,476.4
34	Wyoming	3,298.0
35	Iowa	3,233.7
36	Connecticut	3,232.7
37	Wisconsin	3,209.1
38	Idaho	3,186.2
39	New Jersey	3,160.5
40	New York	3,099.6
41	Virginia	3,028.1
42	Massachusetts	3,026.1
43	Pennsylvania	2,995.3
44	Vermont	2,986.9
45	Kentucky	2,959.7
46	Maine	2,619.8
47	West Virginia	2,602.8
48	New Hampshire	2,433.1
49	South Dakota	2,319.8
50	North Dakota	2,288.1
	District of Columbia	7,276.5

Source: Federal Bureau of Investigation
"Crime in the United States 2001" (Uniform Crime Reports, October 28, 2002)
*Revised figures. Includes murder, rape, robbery, aggravated assault, burglary, larceny-theft and motor vehicle theft.

Percent Change in Crime Rate: 2000 to 2004

National Percent Change = 3.4% Decrease*

ALPHA ORDER				RANK ORDER		
RANK	STATE	PERCENT CHANGE		RANK	STATE	PERCENT CHANGE
19	Alabama	(2.1)		1	Nevada	13.0
28	Alaska	(5.5)		2	Arkansas	9.6
12	Arizona	0.3		3	Wyoming	8.1
2	Arkansas	9.6		4	Colorado	7.8
6	California	6.2		5	West Virginia	6.7
4	Colorado	7.8		6	California	6.2
37	Connecticut	(9.9)		7	Oklahoma	4.0
48	Delaware	(16.7)		8	Tennessee	2.3
46	Florida	(14.1)		9	Oregon	1.7
13	Georgia	(0.6)		9	Washington	1.7
21	Hawaii	(2.9)		11	Texas	1.6
26	Idaho	(4.6)		12	Arizona	0.3
43	Illinois	(12.0)		13	Georgia	(0.6)
15	Indiana	(0.8)		14	Ohio	(0.7)
18	Iowa	(1.8)		15	Indiana	(0.8)
17	Kansas	(1.4)		16	South Carolina	(1.1)
31	Kentucky	(6.0)		17	Kansas	(1.4)
34	Louisiana	(6.9)		18	Iowa	(1.8)
25	Maine	(4.1)		19	Alabama	(2.1)
37	Maryland	(9.9)		20	Virginia	(2.5)
24	Massachusetts	(3.6)		21	Hawaii	(2.9)
45	Michigan	(13.7)		22	Missouri	(3.0)
27	Minnesota	(5.2)		23	Utah	(3.5)
30	Mississippi	(5.8)		24	Massachusetts	(3.6)
22	Missouri	(3.0)		25	Maine	(4.1)
49	Montana	(16.8)		26	Idaho	(4.6)
33	Nebraska	(6.5)		27	Minnesota	(5.2)
1	Nevada	13.0		28	Alaska	(5.5)
35	New Hampshire	(9.3)		29	Pennsylvania	(5.6)
42	New Jersey	(11.9)		30	Mississippi	(5.8)
41	New Mexico	(11.5)		31	Kentucky	(6.0)
47	New York	(14.8)		32	North Carolina	(6.3)
32	North Carolina	(6.3)		33	Nebraska	(6.5)
44	North Dakota	(12.8)		34	Louisiana	(6.9)
14	Ohio	(0.7)		35	New Hampshire	(9.3)
7	Oklahoma	4.0		35	South Dakota	(9.3)
9	Oregon	1.7		37	Connecticut	(9.9)
29	Pennsylvania	(5.6)		37	Maryland	(9.9)
37	Rhode Island	(9.9)		37	Rhode Island	(9.9)
16	South Carolina	(1.1)		40	Wisconsin	(10.5)
35	South Dakota	(9.3)		41	New Mexico	(11.5)
8	Tennessee	2.3		42	New Jersey	(11.9)
11	Texas	1.6		43	Illinois	(12.0)
23	Utah	(3.5)		44	North Dakota	(12.8)
50	Vermont	(19.0)		45	Michigan	(13.7)
20	Virginia	(2.5)		46	Florida	(14.1)
9	Washington	1.7		47	New York	(14.8)
5	West Virginia	6.7		48	Delaware	(16.7)
40	Wisconsin	(10.5)		49	Montana	(16.8)
3	Wyoming	8.1		50	Vermont	(19.0)

District of Columbia (14.4)

Source: Morgan Quitno Press using data from Federal Bureau of Investigation
"Crime in the United States" (Uniform Crime Reports, 2001 and 2004 editions)
Revised figures. Includes murder, rape, robbery, aggravated assault, burglary, larceny-theft and motor vehicle theft.

Violent Crimes in 2000

National Total = 1,425,486 Violent Crimes*

ALPHA ORDER

RANK	STATE	CRIMES	% of USA
20	Alabama	21,620	1.5%
40	Alaska	3,554	0.2%
18	Arizona	27,281	1.9%
29	Arkansas	11,904	0.8%
1	California	210,531	14.8%
24	Colorado	14,367	1.0%
31	Connecticut	11,058	0.8%
39	Delaware	5,363	0.4%
2	Florida	129,777	9.1%
9	Georgia	41,319	2.9%
43	Hawaii	2,954	0.2%
41	Idaho	3,267	0.2%
5	Illinois	81,196	5.7%
21	Indiana	21,230	1.5%
35	Iowa	7,796	0.5%
33	Kansas	10,470	0.7%
30	Kentucky	11,903	0.8%
15	Louisiana	30,440	2.1%
46	Maine	1,397	0.1%
8	Maryland	41,663	2.9%
16	Massachusetts	30,230	2.1%
6	Michigan	55,159	3.9%
25	Minnesota	13,813	1.0%
34	Mississippi	10,267	0.7%
17	Missouri	27,419	1.9%
44	Montana	2,807	0.2%
38	Nebraska	5,606	0.4%
32	Nevada	10,474	0.7%
45	New Hampshire	2,167	0.2%
14	New Jersey	32,298	2.3%
26	New Mexico	13,786	1.0%
4	New York	105,111	7.4%
11	North Carolina	40,051	2.8%
50	North Dakota	523	0.0%
12	Ohio	37,935	2.7%
23	Oklahoma	17,177	1.2%
28	Oregon	12,000	0.8%
7	Pennsylvania	51,584	3.6%
42	Rhode Island	3,121	0.2%
13	South Carolina	33,225	2.3%
48	South Dakota	1,259	0.1%
10	Tennessee	40,233	2.8%
3	Texas	113,653	8.0%
37	Utah	5,711	0.4%
49	Vermont	691	0.0%
22	Virginia	19,943	1.4%
19	Washington	21,788	1.5%
36	West Virginia	5,723	0.4%
27	Wisconsin	12,700	0.9%
47	Wyoming	1,316	0.1%

RANK ORDER

RANK	STATE	CRIMES	% of USA
1	California	210,531	14.8%
2	Florida	129,777	9.1%
3	Texas	113,653	8.0%
4	New York	105,111	7.4%
5	Illinois	81,196	5.7%
6	Michigan	55,159	3.9%
7	Pennsylvania	51,584	3.6%
8	Maryland	41,663	2.9%
9	Georgia	41,319	2.9%
10	Tennessee	40,233	2.8%
11	North Carolina	40,051	2.8%
12	Ohio	37,935	2.7%
13	South Carolina	33,225	2.3%
14	New Jersey	32,298	2.3%
15	Louisiana	30,440	2.1%
16	Massachusetts	30,230	2.1%
17	Missouri	27,419	1.9%
18	Arizona	27,281	1.9%
19	Washington	21,788	1.5%
20	Alabama	21,620	1.5%
21	Indiana	21,230	1.5%
22	Virginia	19,943	1.4%
23	Oklahoma	17,177	1.2%
24	Colorado	14,367	1.0%
25	Minnesota	13,813	1.0%
26	New Mexico	13,786	1.0%
27	Wisconsin	12,700	0.9%
28	Oregon	12,000	0.8%
29	Arkansas	11,904	0.8%
30	Kentucky	11,903	0.8%
31	Connecticut	11,058	0.8%
32	Nevada	10,474	0.7%
33	Kansas	10,470	0.7%
34	Mississippi	10,267	0.7%
35	Iowa	7,796	0.5%
36	West Virginia	5,723	0.4%
37	Utah	5,711	0.4%
38	Nebraska	5,606	0.4%
39	Delaware	5,363	0.4%
40	Alaska	3,554	0.2%
41	Idaho	3,267	0.2%
42	Rhode Island	3,121	0.2%
43	Hawaii	2,954	0.2%
44	Montana	2,807	0.2%
45	New Hampshire	2,167	0.2%
46	Maine	1,397	0.1%
47	Wyoming	1,316	0.1%
48	South Dakota	1,259	0.1%
49	Vermont	691	0.0%
50	North Dakota	523	0.0%
	District of Columbia	8,626	0.6%

Source: Federal Bureau of Investigation
"Crime in the United States 2001" (Uniform Crime Reports, October 28, 2002)
*Revised figures. Violent crimes are offenses of murder, forcible rape, robbery and aggravated assault.

Percent Change in Number of Violent Crimes: 2000 to 2004

National Percent Change = 4.1% Decrease*

ALPHA ORDER				RANK ORDER		
RANK	STATE	PERCENT CHANGE		RANK	STATE	PERCENT CHANGE
41	Alabama	(10.6)		1	Nevada	37.3
3	Alaska	17.0		2	Colorado	19.6
7	Arizona	6.1		3	Alaska	17.0
4	Arkansas	15.4		4	Arkansas	15.4
36	California	(5.9)		5	Hawaii	8.8
2	Colorado	19.6		6	Texas	7.0
39	Connecticut	(9.3)		7	Arizona	6.1
44	Delaware	(12.0)		8	South Dakota	5.0
33	Florida	(4.6)		9	Idaho	4.4
26	Georgia	(2.7)		10	Ohio	3.2
5	Hawaii	8.8		11	Virginia	3.1
9	Idaho	4.4		12	Missouri	2.9
48	Illinois	(15.0)		13	Iowa	2.7
31	Indiana	(4.4)		13	Oklahoma	2.7
13	Iowa	2.7		15	Tennessee	2.0
22	Kansas	(2.1)		16	Vermont	0.7
47	Kentucky	(14.7)		17	New Hampshire	0.1
35	Louisiana	(5.2)		18	Minnesota	(0.4)
24	Maine	(2.4)		19	South Carolina	(0.9)
37	Maryland	(6.6)		20	Pennsylvania	(1.1)
25	Massachusetts	(2.6)		21	Utah	(1.3)
40	Michigan	(10.1)		22	Kansas	(2.1)
18	Minnesota	(0.4)		22	Washington	(2.1)
49	Mississippi	(16.5)		24	Maine	(2.4)
12	Missouri	2.9		25	Massachusetts	(2.6)
27	Montana	(3.0)		26	Georgia	(2.7)
29	Nebraska	(3.8)		27	Montana	(3.0)
1	Nevada	37.3		28	North Dakota	(3.6)
17	New Hampshire	0.1		29	Nebraska	(3.8)
30	New Jersey	(4.2)		30	New Jersey	(4.2)
34	New Mexico	(5.1)		31	Indiana	(4.4)
50	New York	(19.2)		32	North Carolina	(4.5)
32	North Carolina	(4.5)		33	Florida	(4.6)
28	North Dakota	(3.6)		34	New Mexico	(5.1)
10	Ohio	3.2		35	Louisiana	(5.2)
13	Oklahoma	2.7		36	California	(5.9)
41	Oregon	(10.6)		37	Maryland	(6.6)
20	Pennsylvania	(1.1)		38	Wisconsin	(9.1)
46	Rhode Island	(14.4)		39	Connecticut	(9.3)
19	South Carolina	(0.9)		40	Michigan	(10.1)
8	South Dakota	5.0		41	Alabama	(10.6)
15	Tennessee	2.0		41	Oregon	(10.6)
6	Texas	7.0		43	Wyoming	(11.6)
21	Utah	(1.3)		44	Delaware	(12.0)
16	Vermont	0.7		45	West Virginia	(14.0)
11	Virginia	3.1		46	Rhode Island	(14.4)
22	Washington	(2.1)		47	Kentucky	(14.7)
45	West Virginia	(14.0)		48	Illinois	(15.0)
38	Wisconsin	(9.1)		49	Mississippi	(16.5)
43	Wyoming	(11.6)		50	New York	(19.2)
					District of Columbia	(12.0)

Source: Morgan Quitno Press using data from Federal Bureau of Investigation
      "Crime in the United States" (Uniform Crime Reports, 2001 and 2004 editions)
*Revised figures. Violent crimes are offenses of murder, forcible rape, robbery and aggravated assault.

Violent Crime Rate in 2000

National Rate = 506.5 Violent Crimes per 100,000 Population*

ALPHA ORDER

RANK	STATE	RATE
20	Alabama	486.2
10	Alaska	566.9
14	Arizona	531.7
22	Arkansas	445.3
9	California	621.6
31	Colorado	334.0
33	Connecticut	324.7
6	Delaware	684.4
2	Florida	812.0
16	Georgia	504.7
44	Hawaii	243.8
43	Idaho	252.5
8	Illinois	653.8
29	Indiana	349.1
41	Iowa	266.4
24	Kansas	389.4
37	Kentucky	294.5
7	Louisiana	681.1
49	Maine	109.6
3	Maryland	786.6
21	Massachusetts	476.1
11	Michigan	555.0
39	Minnesota	280.8
27	Mississippi	360.9
19	Missouri	490.0
35	Montana	311.1
32	Nebraska	327.6
15	Nevada	524.2
46	New Hampshire	175.4
25	New Jersey	383.8
4	New Mexico	757.9
12	New York	553.9
18	North Carolina	497.6
50	North Dakota	81.4
30	Ohio	334.1
17	Oklahoma	497.8
28	Oregon	350.7
23	Pennsylvania	420.0
36	Rhode Island	297.7
1	South Carolina	828.1
47	South Dakota	166.8
5	Tennessee	707.2
13	Texas	545.1
42	Utah	255.7
48	Vermont	113.5
38	Virginia	281.7
26	Washington	369.7
34	West Virginia	316.5
45	Wisconsin	236.8
40	Wyoming	266.5

RANK ORDER

RANK	STATE	RATE
1	South Carolina	828.1
2	Florida	812.0
3	Maryland	786.6
4	New Mexico	757.9
5	Tennessee	707.2
6	Delaware	684.4
7	Louisiana	681.1
8	Illinois	653.8
9	California	621.6
10	Alaska	566.9
11	Michigan	555.0
12	New York	553.9
13	Texas	545.1
14	Arizona	531.7
15	Nevada	524.2
16	Georgia	504.7
17	Oklahoma	497.8
18	North Carolina	497.6
19	Missouri	490.0
20	Alabama	486.2
21	Massachusetts	476.1
22	Arkansas	445.3
23	Pennsylvania	420.0
24	Kansas	389.4
25	New Jersey	383.8
26	Washington	369.7
27	Mississippi	360.9
28	Oregon	350.7
29	Indiana	349.1
30	Ohio	334.1
31	Colorado	334.0
32	Nebraska	327.6
33	Connecticut	324.7
34	West Virginia	316.5
35	Montana	311.1
36	Rhode Island	297.7
37	Kentucky	294.5
38	Virginia	281.7
39	Minnesota	280.8
40	Wyoming	266.5
41	Iowa	266.4
42	Utah	255.7
43	Idaho	252.5
44	Hawaii	243.8
45	Wisconsin	236.8
46	New Hampshire	175.4
47	South Dakota	166.8
48	Vermont	113.5
49	Maine	109.6
50	North Dakota	81.4

District of Columbia	1,507.9

Source: Federal Bureau of Investigation
    "Crime in the United States 2001" (Uniform Crime Reports, October 28, 2002)
*Revised figures. Violent crimes are offenses of murder, forcible rape, robbery and aggravated assault.

Percent Change in Violent Crime Rate: 2000 to 2004

National Percent Change = 8.0% Decrease*

ALPHA ORDER

RANK	STATE	PERCENT CHANGE
40	Alabama	(12.3)
3	Alaska	11.9
22	Arizona	(5.2)
2	Arkansas	12.1
36	California	(11.2)
4	Colorado	11.8
39	Connecticut	(11.8)
46	Delaware	(16.9)
41	Florida	(12.4)
33	Georgia	(9.7)
5	Hawaii	4.3
17	Idaho	(3.0)
48	Illinois	(17.0)
28	Indiana	(6.8)
8	Iowa	1.7
19	Kansas	(3.8)
45	Kentucky	(16.8)
27	Louisiana	(6.2)
24	Maine	(5.6)
35	Maryland	(10.9)
18	Massachusetts	(3.6)
38	Michigan	(11.7)
20	Minnesota	(4.0)
49	Mississippi	(18.2)
10	Missouri	0.1
24	Montana	(5.6)
26	Nebraska	(5.8)
1	Nevada	17.5
21	New Hampshire	(4.8)
30	New Jersey	(7.3)
32	New Mexico	(9.3)
50	New York	(20.3)
34	North Carolina	(10.0)
16	North Dakota	(2.5)
7	Ohio	2.3
9	Oklahoma	0.5
44	Oregon	(14.9)
14	Pennsylvania	(2.1)
46	Rhode Island	(16.9)
23	South Carolina	(5.3)
6	South Dakota	2.8
13	Tennessee	(1.7)
11	Texas	(0.8)
31	Utah	(7.7)
12	Vermont	(1.3)
15	Virginia	(2.2)
29	Washington	(7.0)
43	West Virginia	(14.3)
37	Wisconsin	(11.5)
42	Wyoming	(13.8)

RANK ORDER

RANK	STATE	PERCENT CHANGE
1	Nevada	17.5
2	Arkansas	12.1
3	Alaska	11.9
4	Colorado	11.8
5	Hawaii	4.3
6	South Dakota	2.8
7	Ohio	2.3
8	Iowa	1.7
9	Oklahoma	0.5
10	Missouri	0.1
11	Texas	(0.8)
12	Vermont	(1.3)
13	Tennessee	(1.7)
14	Pennsylvania	(2.1)
15	Virginia	(2.2)
16	North Dakota	(2.5)
17	Idaho	(3.0)
18	Massachusetts	(3.6)
19	Kansas	(3.8)
20	Minnesota	(4.0)
21	New Hampshire	(4.8)
22	Arizona	(5.2)
23	South Carolina	(5.3)
24	Maine	(5.6)
24	Montana	(5.6)
26	Nebraska	(5.8)
27	Louisiana	(6.2)
28	Indiana	(6.8)
29	Washington	(7.0)
30	New Jersey	(7.3)
31	Utah	(7.7)
32	New Mexico	(9.3)
33	Georgia	(9.7)
34	North Carolina	(10.0)
35	Maryland	(10.9)
36	California	(11.2)
37	Wisconsin	(11.5)
38	Michigan	(11.7)
39	Connecticut	(11.8)
40	Alabama	(12.3)
41	Florida	(12.4)
42	Wyoming	(13.8)
43	West Virginia	(14.3)
44	Oregon	(14.9)
45	Kentucky	(16.8)
46	Delaware	(16.9)
46	Rhode Island	(16.9)
48	Illinois	(17.0)
49	Mississippi	(18.2)
50	New York	(20.3)

District of Columbia (9.1)

Source: Morgan Quitno Press using data from Federal Bureau of Investigation
    "Crime in the United States" (Uniform Crime Reports, 2001 and 2004 editions)
*Revised figures. Violent crimes are offenses of murder, forcible rape, robbery and aggravated assault.

Murders in 2000

National Total = 15,586 Murders*

ALPHA ORDER

RANK	STATE	MURDERS	% of USA
18	Alabama	329	2.1%
41	Alaska	27	0.2%
15	Arizona	359	2.3%
27	Arkansas	168	1.1%
1	California	2,079	13.3%
30	Colorado	134	0.9%
33	Connecticut	98	0.6%
42	Delaware	25	0.2%
4	Florida	903	5.8%
7	Georgia	651	4.2%
40	Hawaii	35	0.2%
45	Idaho	16	0.1%
5	Illinois	898	5.8%
16	Indiana	352	2.3%
36	Iowa	46	0.3%
25	Kansas	169	1.1%
23	Kentucky	193	1.2%
9	Louisiana	560	3.6%
46	Maine	15	0.1%
11	Maryland	430	2.8%
32	Massachusetts	125	0.8%
6	Michigan	669	4.3%
28	Minnesota	151	1.0%
21	Mississippi	255	1.6%
17	Missouri	347	2.2%
44	Montana	20	0.1%
35	Nebraska	63	0.4%
31	Nevada	129	0.8%
43	New Hampshire	22	0.1%
20	New Jersey	289	1.9%
29	New Mexico	135	0.9%
3	New York	952	6.1%
9	North Carolina	560	3.6%
50	North Dakota	4	0.0%
12	Ohio	418	2.7%
24	Oklahoma	182	1.2%
34	Oregon	70	0.4%
8	Pennsylvania	602	3.9%
38	Rhode Island	45	0.3%
19	South Carolina	291	1.9%
49	South Dakota	7	0.0%
13	Tennessee	410	2.6%
2	Texas	1,238	7.9%
39	Utah	43	0.3%
48	Vermont	9	0.1%
14	Virginia	401	2.6%
22	Washington	196	1.3%
36	West Virginia	46	0.3%
25	Wisconsin	169	1.1%
47	Wyoming	12	0.1%

RANK ORDER

RANK	STATE	MURDERS	% of USA
1	California	2,079	13.3%
2	Texas	1,238	7.9%
3	New York	952	6.1%
4	Florida	903	5.8%
5	Illinois	898	5.8%
6	Michigan	669	4.3%
7	Georgia	651	4.2%
8	Pennsylvania	602	3.9%
9	Louisiana	560	3.6%
9	North Carolina	560	3.6%
11	Maryland	430	2.8%
12	Ohio	418	2.7%
13	Tennessee	410	2.6%
14	Virginia	401	2.6%
15	Arizona	359	2.3%
16	Indiana	352	2.3%
17	Missouri	347	2.2%
18	Alabama	329	2.1%
19	South Carolina	291	1.9%
20	New Jersey	289	1.9%
21	Mississippi	255	1.6%
22	Washington	196	1.3%
23	Kentucky	193	1.2%
24	Oklahoma	182	1.2%
25	Kansas	169	1.1%
25	Wisconsin	169	1.1%
27	Arkansas	168	1.1%
28	Minnesota	151	1.0%
29	New Mexico	135	0.9%
30	Colorado	134	0.9%
31	Nevada	129	0.8%
32	Massachusetts	125	0.8%
33	Connecticut	98	0.6%
34	Oregon	70	0.4%
35	Nebraska	63	0.4%
36	Iowa	46	0.3%
36	West Virginia	46	0.3%
38	Rhode Island	45	0.3%
39	Utah	43	0.3%
40	Hawaii	35	0.2%
41	Alaska	27	0.2%
42	Delaware	25	0.2%
43	New Hampshire	22	0.1%
44	Montana	20	0.1%
45	Idaho	16	0.1%
46	Maine	15	0.1%
47	Wyoming	12	0.1%
48	Vermont	9	0.1%
49	South Dakota	7	0.0%
50	North Dakota	4	0.0%
	District of Columbia	239	1.5%

Source: Federal Bureau of Investigation
   "Crime in the United States 2001" (Uniform Crime Reports, October 28, 2002)
*Revised figures. Includes nonnegligent manslaughter.

Percent Change in Number of Murders: 2000 to 2004

National Percent Change = 3.5% Increase*

ALPHA ORDER

RANK	STATE	PERCENT CHANGE
45	Alabama	(22.8)
8	Alaska	37.0
18	Arizona	15.3
23	Arkansas	4.8
19	California	15.1
5	Colorado	51.5
37	Connecticut	(7.1)
48	Delaware	(32.0)
23	Florida	4.8
35	Georgia	(5.8)
34	Hawaii	(5.7)
3	Idaho	87.5
42	Illinois	(13.6)
40	Indiana	(10.2)
28	Iowa	0.0
47	Kansas	(27.2)
15	Kentucky	22.3
25	Louisiana	2.5
17	Maine	20.0
16	Maryland	21.2
10	Massachusetts	35.2
32	Michigan	(3.9)
46	Minnesota	(25.2)
41	Mississippi	(11.0)
27	Missouri	2.0
6	Montana	50.0
49	Nebraska	(36.5)
11	Nevada	33.3
44	New Hampshire	(18.2)
9	New Jersey	35.6
13	New Mexico	25.2
36	New York	(6.6)
33	North Carolina	(5.0)
2	North Dakota	125.0
14	Ohio	23.7
26	Oklahoma	2.2
12	Oregon	28.6
21	Pennsylvania	8.0
50	Rhode Island	(42.2)
29	South Carolina	(1.0)
1	South Dakota	157.1
43	Tennessee	(14.4)
20	Texas	10.2
22	Utah	7.0
4	Vermont	77.8
30	Virginia	(2.5)
31	Washington	(3.1)
7	West Virginia	47.8
39	Wisconsin	(8.9)
38	Wyoming	(8.3)

RANK ORDER

RANK	STATE	PERCENT CHANGE
1	South Dakota	157.1
2	North Dakota	125.0
3	Idaho	87.5
4	Vermont	77.8
5	Colorado	51.5
6	Montana	50.0
7	West Virginia	47.8
8	Alaska	37.0
9	New Jersey	35.6
10	Massachusetts	35.2
11	Nevada	33.3
12	Oregon	28.6
13	New Mexico	25.2
14	Ohio	23.7
15	Kentucky	22.3
16	Maryland	21.2
17	Maine	20.0
18	Arizona	15.3
19	California	15.1
20	Texas	10.2
21	Pennsylvania	8.0
22	Utah	7.0
23	Arkansas	4.8
23	Florida	4.8
25	Louisiana	2.5
26	Oklahoma	2.2
27	Missouri	2.0
28	Iowa	0.0
29	South Carolina	(1.0)
30	Virginia	(2.5)
31	Washington	(3.1)
32	Michigan	(3.9)
33	North Carolina	(5.0)
34	Hawaii	(5.7)
35	Georgia	(5.8)
36	New York	(6.6)
37	Connecticut	(7.1)
38	Wyoming	(8.3)
39	Wisconsin	(8.9)
40	Indiana	(10.2)
41	Mississippi	(11.0)
42	Illinois	(13.6)
43	Tennessee	(14.4)
44	New Hampshire	(18.2)
45	Alabama	(22.8)
46	Minnesota	(25.2)
47	Kansas	(27.2)
48	Delaware	(32.0)
49	Nebraska	(36.5)
50	Rhode Island	(42.2)

District of Columbia   (17.2)

Source: Morgan Quitno Press using data from Federal Bureau of Investigation
    "Crime in the United States" (Uniform Crime Reports, 2001 and 2004 editions)
*Revised figures. Includes nonnegligent manslaughter.

Murder Rate in 2000

National Rate = 5.5 Murders per 100,000 Population*

ALPHA ORDER

RANK	STATE	RATE
5	Alabama	7.4
26	Alaska	4.3
10	Arizona	7.0
14	Arkansas	6.3
17	California	6.1
34	Colorado	3.1
36	Connecticut	2.9
32	Delaware	3.2
21	Florida	5.6
4	Georgia	8.0
36	Hawaii	2.9
47	Idaho	1.2
8	Illinois	7.2
19	Indiana	5.8
45	Iowa	1.6
14	Kansas	6.3
25	Kentucky	4.8
1	Louisiana	12.5
47	Maine	1.2
3	Maryland	8.1
41	Massachusetts	2.0
12	Michigan	6.7
34	Minnesota	3.1
2	Mississippi	9.0
16	Missouri	6.2
40	Montana	2.2
28	Nebraska	3.7
13	Nevada	6.5
44	New Hampshire	1.8
30	New Jersey	3.4
5	New Mexico	7.4
23	New York	5.0
10	North Carolina	7.0
50	North Dakota	0.6
28	Ohio	3.7
22	Oklahoma	5.3
41	Oregon	2.0
24	Pennsylvania	4.9
26	Rhode Island	4.3
7	South Carolina	7.3
49	South Dakota	0.9
8	Tennessee	7.2
18	Texas	5.9
43	Utah	1.9
46	Vermont	1.5
20	Virginia	5.7
31	Washington	3.3
38	West Virginia	2.5
32	Wisconsin	3.2
39	Wyoming	2.4

RANK ORDER

RANK	STATE	RATE
1	Louisiana	12.5
2	Mississippi	9.0
3	Maryland	8.1
4	Georgia	8.0
5	Alabama	7.4
5	New Mexico	7.4
7	South Carolina	7.3
8	Illinois	7.2
8	Tennessee	7.2
10	Arizona	7.0
10	North Carolina	7.0
12	Michigan	6.7
13	Nevada	6.5
14	Arkansas	6.3
14	Kansas	6.3
16	Missouri	6.2
17	California	6.1
18	Texas	5.9
19	Indiana	5.8
20	Virginia	5.7
21	Florida	5.6
22	Oklahoma	5.3
23	New York	5.0
24	Pennsylvania	4.9
25	Kentucky	4.8
26	Alaska	4.3
26	Rhode Island	4.3
28	Nebraska	3.7
28	Ohio	3.7
30	New Jersey	3.4
31	Washington	3.3
32	Delaware	3.2
32	Wisconsin	3.2
34	Colorado	3.1
34	Minnesota	3.1
36	Connecticut	2.9
36	Hawaii	2.9
38	West Virginia	2.5
39	Wyoming	2.4
40	Montana	2.2
41	Massachusetts	2.0
41	Oregon	2.0
43	Utah	1.9
44	New Hampshire	1.8
45	Iowa	1.6
46	Vermont	1.5
47	Idaho	1.2
47	Maine	1.2
49	South Dakota	0.9
50	North Dakota	0.6

| | District of Columbia | 41.8 |

Source: Federal Bureau of Investigation
    "Crime in the United States 2001" (Uniform Crime Reports, October 28, 2002)
*Revised figures. Includes nonnegligent manslaughter.

Percent Change in Murder Rate: 2000 to 2004

National Percent Change = 0.0% Change*

ALPHA ORDER				RANK ORDER		
RANK	STATE	PERCENT CHANGE		RANK	STATE	PERCENT CHANGE
45	Alabama	(24.3)		1	South Dakota	155.6
9	Alaska	30.2		2	North Dakota	133.3
21	Arizona	2.9		3	Idaho	83.3
22	Arkansas	1.6		4	Vermont	73.3
18	California	9.8		5	West Virginia	48.0
7	Colorado	41.9		6	Montana	45.5
35	Connecticut	(10.3)		7	Colorado	41.9
48	Delaware	(37.5)		8	New Jersey	32.4
28	Florida	(3.6)		9	Alaska	30.2
41	Georgia	(13.8)		10	Massachusetts	30.0
35	Hawaii	(10.3)		11	Oregon	25.0
3	Idaho	83.3		12	Ohio	21.6
42	Illinois	(15.3)		13	New Mexico	20.3
38	Indiana	(12.1)		14	Kentucky	18.7
24	Iowa	0.0		15	Maine	16.7
46	Kansas	(28.6)		16	Maryland	16.0
14	Kentucky	18.7		17	Nevada	13.8
22	Louisiana	1.6		18	California	9.8
15	Maine	16.7		19	Pennsylvania	6.1
16	Maryland	16.0		20	Texas	3.4
10	Massachusetts	30.0		21	Arizona	2.9
29	Michigan	(4.5)		22	Arkansas	1.6
47	Minnesota	(29.0)		22	Louisiana	1.6
40	Mississippi	(13.3)		24	Iowa	0.0
24	Missouri	0.0		24	Missouri	0.0
6	Montana	45.5		24	Oklahoma	0.0
49	Nebraska	(37.8)		24	Utah	0.0
17	Nevada	13.8		28	Florida	(3.6)
44	New Hampshire	(22.2)		29	Michigan	(4.5)
8	New Jersey	32.4		30	South Carolina	(5.5)
13	New Mexico	20.3		31	Washington	(6.1)
32	New York	(8.0)		32	New York	(8.0)
37	North Carolina	(11.4)		33	Wyoming	(8.3)
2	North Dakota	133.3		34	Virginia	(8.8)
12	Ohio	21.6		35	Connecticut	(10.3)
24	Oklahoma	0.0		35	Hawaii	(10.3)
11	Oregon	25.0		37	North Carolina	(11.4)
19	Pennsylvania	6.1		38	Indiana	(12.1)
50	Rhode Island	(44.2)		39	Wisconsin	(12.5)
30	South Carolina	(5.5)		40	Mississippi	(13.3)
1	South Dakota	155.6		41	Georgia	(13.8)
43	Tennessee	(18.1)		42	Illinois	(15.3)
20	Texas	3.4		43	Tennessee	(18.1)
24	Utah	0.0		44	New Hampshire	(22.2)
4	Vermont	73.3		45	Alabama	(24.3)
34	Virginia	(8.8)		46	Kansas	(28.6)
31	Washington	(6.1)		47	Minnesota	(29.0)
5	West Virginia	48.0		48	Delaware	(37.5)
39	Wisconsin	(12.5)		49	Nebraska	(37.8)
33	Wyoming	(8.3)		50	Rhode Island	(44.2)
					District of Columbia	(14.4)

Source: Morgan Quitno Press using data from Federal Bureau of Investigation
    "Crime in the United States" (Uniform Crime Reports, 2001 and 2004 editions)
*Revised figures. Includes nonnegligent manslaughter.

Rapes in 2000

National Total = 90,178 Rapes*

ALPHA ORDER

RANK	STATE	RAPES	% of USA
22	Alabama	1,482	1.6%
38	Alaska	497	0.6%
19	Arizona	1,577	1.7%
34	Arkansas	848	0.9%
1	California	9,785	10.9%
14	Colorado	1,774	2.0%
35	Connecticut	678	0.8%
40	Delaware	424	0.5%
3	Florida	7,057	7.8%
13	Georgia	1,968	2.2%
43	Hawaii	346	0.4%
42	Idaho	384	0.4%
6	Illinois	3,926	4.4%
15	Indiana	1,759	2.0%
36	Iowa	676	0.7%
29	Kansas	1,022	1.1%
28	Kentucky	1,091	1.2%
21	Louisiana	1,497	1.7%
45	Maine	320	0.4%
20	Maryland	1,543	1.7%
16	Massachusetts	1,696	1.9%
4	Michigan	5,025	5.6%
10	Minnesota	2,240	2.5%
30	Mississippi	1,019	1.1%
25	Missouri	1,351	1.5%
46	Montana	308	0.3%
39	Nebraska	436	0.5%
33	Nevada	860	1.0%
37	New Hampshire	522	0.6%
24	New Jersey	1,357	1.5%
31	New Mexico	922	1.0%
7	New York	3,530	3.9%
12	North Carolina	2,181	2.4%
48	North Dakota	169	0.2%
5	Ohio	4,271	4.7%
23	Oklahoma	1,422	1.6%
26	Oregon	1,286	1.4%
8	Pennsylvania	3,247	3.6%
41	Rhode Island	412	0.5%
17	South Carolina	1,660	1.8%
47	South Dakota	305	0.3%
11	Tennessee	2,186	2.4%
2	Texas	7,856	8.7%
32	Utah	863	1.0%
50	Vermont	140	0.2%
18	Virginia	1,616	1.8%
9	Washington	2,737	3.0%
44	West Virginia	331	0.4%
27	Wisconsin	1,165	1.3%
49	Wyoming	160	0.2%

RANK ORDER

RANK	STATE	RAPES	% of USA
1	California	9,785	10.9%
2	Texas	7,856	8.7%
3	Florida	7,057	7.8%
4	Michigan	5,025	5.6%
5	Ohio	4,271	4.7%
6	Illinois	3,926	4.4%
7	New York	3,530	3.9%
8	Pennsylvania	3,247	3.6%
9	Washington	2,737	3.0%
10	Minnesota	2,240	2.5%
11	Tennessee	2,186	2.4%
12	North Carolina	2,181	2.4%
13	Georgia	1,968	2.2%
14	Colorado	1,774	2.0%
15	Indiana	1,759	2.0%
16	Massachusetts	1,696	1.9%
17	South Carolina	1,660	1.8%
18	Virginia	1,616	1.8%
19	Arizona	1,577	1.7%
20	Maryland	1,543	1.7%
21	Louisiana	1,497	1.7%
22	Alabama	1,482	1.6%
23	Oklahoma	1,422	1.6%
24	New Jersey	1,357	1.5%
25	Missouri	1,351	1.5%
26	Oregon	1,286	1.4%
27	Wisconsin	1,165	1.3%
28	Kentucky	1,091	1.2%
29	Kansas	1,022	1.1%
30	Mississippi	1,019	1.1%
31	New Mexico	922	1.0%
32	Utah	863	1.0%
33	Nevada	860	1.0%
34	Arkansas	848	0.9%
35	Connecticut	678	0.8%
36	Iowa	676	0.7%
37	New Hampshire	522	0.6%
38	Alaska	497	0.6%
39	Nebraska	436	0.5%
40	Delaware	424	0.5%
41	Rhode Island	412	0.5%
42	Idaho	384	0.4%
43	Hawaii	346	0.4%
44	West Virginia	331	0.4%
45	Maine	320	0.4%
46	Montana	308	0.3%
47	South Dakota	305	0.3%
48	North Dakota	169	0.2%
49	Wyoming	160	0.2%
50	Vermont	140	0.2%
	District of Columbia	251	0.3%

Source: Federal Bureau of Investigation
"Crime in the United States 2001" (Uniform Crime Reports, October 28, 2002)
*Revised figures. Forcible rape is the carnal knowledge of a female forcibly and against her will. Assaults or attempts to commit rape by force or threat of force are included. However, statutory rape without force and other sex offenses are excluded.

Percent Change in Number of Rapes: 2000 to 2004

National Percent Change = 4.9% Increase*

ALPHA ORDER			RANK ORDER		
RANK	STATE	RATE	RANK	STATE	RATE
6	Alabama	17.5	1	Idaho	48.4
11	Alaska	12.3	2	Nebraska	42.2
5	Arizona	20.2	3	Arkansas	37.5
3	Arkansas	37.5	4	Georgia	21.3
37	California	(1.7)	5	Arizona	20.2
14	Colorado	10.3	6	Alabama	17.5
27	Connecticut	6.8	7	Iowa	16.9
48	Delaware	(18.6)	8	Mississippi	13.9
44	Florida	(6.3)	9	Kentucky	13.5
4	Georgia	21.3	10	New Mexico	12.7
41	Hawaii	(3.8)	11	Alaska	12.3
1	Idaho	48.4	12	Nevada	10.9
25	Illinois	7.4	13	South Dakota	10.8
32	Indiana	2.5	14	Colorado	10.3
7	Iowa	16.9	15	Missouri	9.5
23	Kansas	8.0	15	Oklahoma	9.5
9	Kentucky	13.5	17	Virginia	9.3
24	Louisiana	7.9	18	Michigan	9.2
36	Maine	(1.6)	19	Pennsylvania	8.9
47	Maryland	(14.7)	20	Ohio	8.8
29	Massachusetts	6.1	21	Vermont	8.6
18	Michigan	9.2	22	Utah	8.1
42	Minnesota	(5.2)	23	Kansas	8.0
8	Mississippi	13.9	24	Louisiana	7.9
15	Missouri	9.5	25	Illinois	7.4
45	Montana	(11.4)	26	North Carolina	7.2
2	Nebraska	42.2	27	Connecticut	6.8
12	Nevada	10.9	27	Texas	6.8
46	New Hampshire	(12.1)	29	Massachusetts	6.1
38	New Jersey	(1.9)	30	Washington	4.4
10	New Mexico	12.7	31	South Carolina	3.5
33	New York	2.2	32	Indiana	2.5
26	North Carolina	7.2	33	New York	2.2
43	North Dakota	(5.9)	34	Tennessee	1.6
20	Ohio	8.8	35	Oregon	(0.2)
15	Oklahoma	9.5	36	Maine	(1.6)
35	Oregon	(0.2)	37	California	(1.7)
19	Pennsylvania	8.9	38	New Jersey	(1.9)
49	Rhode Island	(22.3)	39	Wisconsin	(2.5)
31	South Carolina	3.5	40	West Virginia	(3.3)
13	South Dakota	10.8	41	Hawaii	(3.8)
34	Tennessee	1.6	42	Minnesota	(5.2)
27	Texas	6.8	43	North Dakota	(5.9)
22	Utah	8.1	44	Florida	(6.3)
21	Vermont	8.6	45	Montana	(11.4)
17	Virginia	9.3	46	New Hampshire	(12.1)
30	Washington	4.4	47	Maryland	(14.7)
40	West Virginia	(3.3)	48	Delaware	(18.6)
39	Wisconsin	(2.5)	49	Rhode Island	(22.3)
50	Wyoming	(30.0)	50	Wyoming	(30.0)

District of Columbia   (11.6)

Source: Morgan Quitno Press using data from Federal Bureau of Investigation
"Crime in the United States" (Uniform Crime Reports, 2001 and 2004 editions)
*Revised figures. Forcible rape is the carnal knowledge of a female forcibly and against her will. Assaults or attempts to commit rape by force or threat of force are included. However, statutory rape without force and other sex offenses are excluded.

Rape Rate in 2000

National Rate = 32.0 Rapes per 100,000 Population*

ALPHA ORDER

RANK	STATE	RATE
24	Alabama	33.3
1	Alaska	79.3
28	Arizona	30.7
26	Arkansas	31.7
31	California	28.9
11	Colorado	41.2
47	Connecticut	19.9
2	Delaware	54.1
7	Florida	44.2
42	Georgia	24.0
33	Hawaii	28.6
29	Idaho	29.7
27	Illinois	31.6
31	Indiana	28.9
43	Iowa	23.1
17	Kansas	38.0
35	Kentucky	27.0
23	Louisiana	33.5
40	Maine	25.1
30	Maryland	29.1
36	Massachusetts	26.7
4	Michigan	50.6
6	Minnesota	45.5
21	Mississippi	35.8
41	Missouri	24.1
22	Montana	34.1
39	Nebraska	25.5
8	Nevada	43.0
9	New Hampshire	42.2
50	New Jersey	16.1
3	New Mexico	50.7
48	New York	18.6
34	North Carolina	27.1
38	North Dakota	26.3
19	Ohio	37.6
11	Oklahoma	41.2
19	Oregon	37.6
37	Pennsylvania	26.4
14	Rhode Island	39.3
10	South Carolina	41.4
13	South Dakota	40.4
16	Tennessee	38.4
18	Texas	37.7
15	Utah	38.6
44	Vermont	23.0
45	Virginia	22.8
5	Washington	46.4
49	West Virginia	18.3
46	Wisconsin	21.7
25	Wyoming	32.4

RANK ORDER

RANK	STATE	RATE
1	Alaska	79.3
2	Delaware	54.1
3	New Mexico	50.7
4	Michigan	50.6
5	Washington	46.4
6	Minnesota	45.5
7	Florida	44.2
8	Nevada	43.0
9	New Hampshire	42.2
10	South Carolina	41.4
11	Colorado	41.2
11	Oklahoma	41.2
13	South Dakota	40.4
14	Rhode Island	39.3
15	Utah	38.6
16	Tennessee	38.4
17	Kansas	38.0
18	Texas	37.7
19	Ohio	37.6
19	Oregon	37.6
21	Mississippi	35.8
22	Montana	34.1
23	Louisiana	33.5
24	Alabama	33.3
25	Wyoming	32.4
26	Arkansas	31.7
27	Illinois	31.6
28	Arizona	30.7
29	Idaho	29.7
30	Maryland	29.1
31	California	28.9
31	Indiana	28.9
33	Hawaii	28.6
34	North Carolina	27.1
35	Kentucky	27.0
36	Massachusetts	26.7
37	Pennsylvania	26.4
38	North Dakota	26.3
39	Nebraska	25.5
40	Maine	25.1
41	Missouri	24.1
42	Georgia	24.0
43	Iowa	23.1
44	Vermont	23.0
45	Virginia	22.8
46	Wisconsin	21.7
47	Connecticut	19.9
48	New York	18.6
49	West Virginia	18.3
50	New Jersey	16.1
	District of Columbia	43.9

Source: Federal Bureau of Investigation
    "Crime in the United States 2001" (Uniform Crime Reports, October 28, 2002)
*Revised figures. Forcible rape is the carnal knowledge of a female forcibly and against her will. Assaults or attempts to commit rape by force or threat of force are included. However, statutory rape without force and other sex offenses are excluded.

Percent Change in Rape Rate: 2000 to 2004

National Percent Change = 0.6% Increase*

ALPHA ORDER				RANK ORDER		
RANK	STATE	PERCENT CHANGE		RANK	STATE	PERCENT CHANGE
4	Alabama	15.6		1	Nebraska	39.2
14	Alaska	7.3		2	Idaho	37.7
13	Arizona	7.5		3	Arkansas	33.8
3	Arkansas	33.8		4	Alabama	15.6
41	California	(7.3)		4	Iowa	15.6
25	Colorado	3.2		6	Georgia	12.5
23	Connecticut	4.0		7	Mississippi	11.7
48	Delaware	(23.3)		8	Kentucky	10.7
45	Florida	(14.0)		9	South Dakota	8.4
6	Georgia	12.5		10	Pennsylvania	8.0
42	Hawaii	(7.7)		11	New Mexico	7.7
2	Idaho	37.7		11	Ohio	7.7
21	Illinois	5.1		13	Arizona	7.5
29	Indiana	0.0		14	Alaska	7.3
4	Iowa	15.6		14	Oklahoma	7.3
20	Kansas	6.3		16	Michigan	7.1
8	Kentucky	10.7		17	Louisiana	6.9
17	Louisiana	6.9		18	Missouri	6.6
36	Maine	(4.8)		19	Vermont	6.5
47	Maryland	(18.6)		20	Kansas	6.3
22	Massachusetts	4.9		21	Illinois	5.1
16	Michigan	7.1		22	Massachusetts	4.9
43	Minnesota	(8.6)		23	Connecticut	4.0
7	Mississippi	11.7		24	Virginia	3.9
18	Missouri	6.6		25	Colorado	3.2
44	Montana	(13.5)		26	Utah	1.3
1	Nebraska	39.2		27	New York	1.1
37	Nevada	(4.9)		27	North Carolina	1.1
46	New Hampshire	(16.4)		29	Indiana	0.0
38	New Jersey	(5.0)		30	Washington	(0.6)
11	New Mexico	7.7		31	Texas	(1.1)
27	New York	1.1		32	South Carolina	(1.2)
27	North Carolina	1.1		33	Tennessee	(2.1)
35	North Dakota	(4.6)		34	West Virginia	(3.8)
11	Ohio	7.7		35	North Dakota	(4.6)
14	Oklahoma	7.3		36	Maine	(4.8)
39	Oregon	(5.1)		37	Nevada	(4.9)
10	Pennsylvania	8.0		38	New Jersey	(5.0)
49	Rhode Island	(24.7)		39	Oregon	(5.1)
32	South Carolina	(1.2)		39	Wisconsin	(5.1)
9	South Dakota	8.4		41	California	(7.3)
33	Tennessee	(2.1)		42	Hawaii	(7.7)
31	Texas	(1.1)		43	Minnesota	(8.6)
26	Utah	1.3		44	Montana	(13.5)
19	Vermont	6.5		45	Florida	(14.0)
24	Virginia	3.9		46	New Hampshire	(16.4)
30	Washington	(0.6)		47	Maryland	(18.6)
34	West Virginia	(3.8)		48	Delaware	(23.3)
39	Wisconsin	(5.1)		49	Rhode Island	(24.7)
50	Wyoming	(31.8)		50	Wyoming	(31.8)
				District of Columbia		(8.7)

Source: Morgan Quitno Press using data from Federal Bureau of Investigation
  "Crime in the United States" (Uniform Crime Reports, 2001 and 2004 editions)
Revised figures. Forcible rape is the carnal knowledge of a female forcibly and against her will. Assaults or attempts to commit rape by force or threat of force are included. However, statutory rape without force and other sex offenses are excluded.

Robberies in 2000

National Total = 408,016 Robberies*

RANK	STATE	ROBBERIES	% of USA
22	Alabama	5,702	1.4%
42	Alaska	490	0.1%
16	Arizona	7,504	1.8%
34	Arkansas	2,001	0.5%
1	California	60,249	14.8%
28	Colorado	3,034	0.7%
25	Connecticut	3,832	0.9%
35	Delaware	1,394	0.3%
3	Florida	31,809	7.8%
11	Georgia	13,250	3.2%
38	Hawaii	1,123	0.3%
45	Idaho	223	0.1%
5	Illinois	25,641	6.3%
18	Indiana	6,282	1.5%
39	Iowa	1,071	0.3%
33	Kansas	2,048	0.5%
27	Kentucky	3,256	0.8%
15	Louisiana	7,532	1.8%
44	Maine	247	0.1%
9	Maryland	13,560	3.3%
20	Massachusetts	5,815	1.4%
8	Michigan	13,712	3.4%
26	Minnesota	3,713	0.9%
30	Mississippi	2,703	0.7%
14	Missouri	7,598	1.9%
46	Montana	203	0.0%
37	Nebraska	1,147	0.3%
23	Nevada	4,543	1.1%
43	New Hampshire	453	0.1%
10	New Jersey	13,553	3.3%
32	New Mexico	2,499	0.6%
2	New York	40,539	9.9%
12	North Carolina	12,595	3.1%
50	North Dakota	56	0.0%
7	Ohio	15,610	3.8%
31	Oklahoma	2,615	0.6%
29	Oregon	2,888	0.7%
6	Pennsylvania	18,155	4.4%
40	Rhode Island	922	0.2%
19	South Carolina	6,220	1.5%
47	South Dakota	131	0.0%
13	Tennessee	9,465	2.3%
4	Texas	30,257	7.4%
36	Utah	1,242	0.3%
48	Vermont	117	0.0%
17	Virginia	6,295	1.5%
21	Washington	5,812	1.4%
41	West Virginia	749	0.2%
24	Wisconsin	4,537	1.1%
49	Wyoming	70	0.0%

RANK	STATE	ROBBERIES	% of USA
1	California	60,249	14.8%
2	New York	40,539	9.9%
3	Florida	31,809	7.8%
4	Texas	30,257	7.4%
5	Illinois	25,641	6.3%
6	Pennsylvania	18,155	4.4%
7	Ohio	15,610	3.8%
8	Michigan	13,712	3.4%
9	Maryland	13,560	3.3%
10	New Jersey	13,553	3.3%
11	Georgia	13,250	3.2%
12	North Carolina	12,595	3.1%
13	Tennessee	9,465	2.3%
14	Missouri	7,598	1.9%
15	Louisiana	7,532	1.8%
16	Arizona	7,504	1.8%
17	Virginia	6,295	1.5%
18	Indiana	6,282	1.5%
19	South Carolina	6,220	1.5%
20	Massachusetts	5,815	1.4%
21	Washington	5,812	1.4%
22	Alabama	5,702	1.4%
23	Nevada	4,543	1.1%
24	Wisconsin	4,537	1.1%
25	Connecticut	3,832	0.9%
26	Minnesota	3,713	0.9%
27	Kentucky	3,256	0.8%
28	Colorado	3,034	0.7%
29	Oregon	2,888	0.7%
30	Mississippi	2,703	0.7%
31	Oklahoma	2,615	0.6%
32	New Mexico	2,499	0.6%
33	Kansas	2,048	0.5%
34	Arkansas	2,001	0.5%
35	Delaware	1,394	0.3%
36	Utah	1,242	0.3%
37	Nebraska	1,147	0.3%
38	Hawaii	1,123	0.3%
39	Iowa	1,071	0.3%
40	Rhode Island	922	0.2%
41	West Virginia	749	0.2%
42	Alaska	490	0.1%
43	New Hampshire	453	0.1%
44	Maine	247	0.1%
45	Idaho	223	0.1%
46	Montana	203	0.0%
47	South Dakota	131	0.0%
48	Vermont	117	0.0%
49	Wyoming	70	0.0%
50	North Dakota	56	0.0%
	District of Columbia	3,554	0.9%

Source: Federal Bureau of Investigation
"Crime in the United States 2001" (Uniform Crime Reports, October 28, 2002)
Revised figures. Robbery is the taking or attempting to take anything of value by force or threat of force.

Percent Change in Number of Robberies: 2000 to 2004

National Percent Change = 1.6% Decrease*

ALPHA ORDER				RANK ORDER		
RANK	STATE	PERCENT CHANGE		RANK	STATE	PERCENT CHANGE
15	Alabama	6.0		1	Massachusetts	28.4
35	Alaska	(8.8)		2	Colorado	23.6
18	Arizona	2.9		3	Arkansas	18.5
3	Arkansas	18.5		4	Texas	18.4
19	California	2.5		5	Oklahoma	18.2
2	Colorado	23.6		6	Maine	17.0
10	Connecticut	10.2		7	Montana	14.8
40	Delaware	(12.6)		8	Ohio	12.4
30	Florida	(5.7)		9	New Hampshire	10.4
17	Georgia	3.1		10	Connecticut	10.2
44	Hawaii	(15.9)		11	Virginia	9.7
14	Idaho	7.6		12	Minnesota	9.6
38	Illinois	(12.1)		13	Nevada	8.0
22	Indiana	1.4		14	Idaho	7.6
16	Iowa	4.9		15	Alabama	6.0
37	Kansas	(11.5)		16	Iowa	4.9
24	Kentucky	0.4		17	Georgia	3.1
42	Louisiana	(12.9)		18	Arizona	2.9
6	Maine	17.0		19	California	2.5
31	Maryland	(5.9)		19	West Virginia	2.5
1	Massachusetts	28.4		21	Pennsylvania	1.8
46	Michigan	(17.4)		22	Indiana	1.4
12	Minnesota	9.6		23	Washington	0.9
34	Mississippi	(7.4)		24	Kentucky	0.4
41	Missouri	(12.7)		25	Utah	(0.5)
7	Montana	14.8		26	Nebraska	(0.8)
26	Nebraska	(0.8)		27	New Jersey	(3.5)
13	Nevada	8.0		28	Wyoming	(4.3)
9	New Hampshire	10.4		29	Oregon	(4.7)
27	New Jersey	(3.5)		30	Florida	(5.7)
47	New Mexico	(17.5)		31	Maryland	(5.9)
45	New York	(17.3)		32	North Carolina	(6.5)
32	North Carolina	(6.5)		33	Tennessee	(6.6)
49	North Dakota	(30.4)		34	Mississippi	(7.4)
8	Ohio	12.4		35	Alaska	(8.8)
5	Oklahoma	18.2		36	Wisconsin	(10.4)
29	Oregon	(4.7)		37	Kansas	(11.5)
21	Pennsylvania	1.8		38	Illinois	(12.1)
48	Rhode Island	(20.7)		39	South Carolina	(12.4)
39	South Carolina	(12.4)		40	Delaware	(12.6)
43	South Dakota	(13.0)		41	Missouri	(12.7)
33	Tennessee	(6.6)		42	Louisiana	(12.9)
4	Texas	18.4		43	South Dakota	(13.0)
25	Utah	(0.5)		44	Hawaii	(15.9)
50	Vermont	(35.0)		45	New York	(17.3)
11	Virginia	9.7		46	Michigan	(17.4)
23	Washington	0.9		47	New Mexico	(17.5)
19	West Virginia	2.5		48	Rhode Island	(20.7)
36	Wisconsin	(10.4)		49	North Dakota	(30.4)
28	Wyoming	(4.3)		50	Vermont	(35.0)
					District of Columbia	(9.9)

Source: Morgan Quitno Press using data from Federal Bureau of Investigation
   "Crime in the United States" (Uniform Crime Reports, 2001 and 2004 editions)
*Revised figures. Robbery is the taking or attempting to take anything of value by force or threat of force.

Robbery Rate in 2000

National Rate = 144.9 Robberies per 100,000 Population*

ALPHA ORDER

RANK	STATE	RATE
21	Alabama	128.2
33	Alaska	78.2
15	Arizona	146.3
37	Arkansas	74.8
6	California	177.9
38	Colorado	70.5
22	Connecticut	112.5
6	Delaware	177.9
5	Florida	199.0
10	Georgia	161.9
26	Hawaii	92.7
48	Idaho	17.2
4	Illinois	206.5
23	Indiana	103.3
43	Iowa	36.6
34	Kansas	76.2
32	Kentucky	80.6
8	Louisiana	168.5
45	Maine	19.4
1	Maryland	256.0
27	Massachusetts	91.6
17	Michigan	138.0
36	Minnesota	75.5
25	Mississippi	95.0
20	Missouri	135.8
44	Montana	22.5
39	Nebraska	67.0
2	Nevada	227.3
42	New Hampshire	36.7
11	New Jersey	161.1
19	New Mexico	137.4
3	New York	213.6
12	North Carolina	156.5
50	North Dakota	8.7
18	Ohio	137.5
35	Oklahoma	75.8
31	Oregon	84.4
14	Pennsylvania	147.8
29	Rhode Island	88.0
13	South Carolina	155.0
47	South Dakota	17.4
9	Tennessee	166.4
16	Texas	145.1
40	Utah	55.6
46	Vermont	19.2
28	Virginia	88.9
24	Washington	98.6
41	West Virginia	41.4
30	Wisconsin	84.6
49	Wyoming	14.2

RANK ORDER

RANK	STATE	RATE
1	Maryland	256.0
2	Nevada	227.3
3	New York	213.6
4	Illinois	206.5
5	Florida	199.0
6	California	177.9
6	Delaware	177.9
8	Louisiana	168.5
9	Tennessee	166.4
10	Georgia	161.9
11	New Jersey	161.1
12	North Carolina	156.5
13	South Carolina	155.0
14	Pennsylvania	147.8
15	Arizona	146.3
16	Texas	145.1
17	Michigan	138.0
18	Ohio	137.5
19	New Mexico	137.4
20	Missouri	135.8
21	Alabama	128.2
22	Connecticut	112.5
23	Indiana	103.3
24	Washington	98.6
25	Mississippi	95.0
26	Hawaii	92.7
27	Massachusetts	91.6
28	Virginia	88.9
29	Rhode Island	88.0
30	Wisconsin	84.6
31	Oregon	84.4
32	Kentucky	80.6
33	Alaska	78.2
34	Kansas	76.2
35	Oklahoma	75.8
36	Minnesota	75.5
37	Arkansas	74.8
38	Colorado	70.5
39	Nebraska	67.0
40	Utah	55.6
41	West Virginia	41.4
42	New Hampshire	36.7
43	Iowa	36.6
44	Montana	22.5
45	Maine	19.4
46	Vermont	19.2
47	South Dakota	17.4
48	Idaho	17.2
49	Wyoming	14.2
50	North Dakota	8.7
	District of Columbia	621.3

Source: Federal Bureau of Investigation
   "Crime in the United States 2001" (Uniform Crime Reports, October 28, 2002)
*Revised figures. Robbery is the taking or attempting to take anything of value by force or threat of force.

Percent Change in Robbery Rate: 2000 to 2004

National Percent Change = 5.7% Decrease*

ALPHA ORDER

RANK	STATE	PERCENT CHANGE
13	Alabama	4.1
34	Alaska	(12.8)
28	Arizona	(8.1)
4	Arkansas	15.2
21	California	(3.3)
3	Colorado	15.6
9	Connecticut	7.1
43	Delaware	(17.5)
37	Florida	(13.4)
23	Georgia	(4.4)
46	Hawaii	(19.3)
17	Idaho	0.0
39	Illinois	(14.2)
18	Indiana	(1.1)
14	Iowa	3.8
36	Kansas	(13.0)
19	Kentucky	(2.2)
38	Louisiana	(13.7)
5	Maine	12.9
32	Maryland	(10.3)
1	Massachusetts	27.1
45	Michigan	(18.9)
10	Minnesota	5.7
29	Mississippi	(9.3)
41	Missouri	(15.2)
6	Montana	11.6
20	Nebraska	(2.8)
27	Nevada	(7.6)
11	New Hampshire	4.9
24	New Jersey	(6.7)
47	New Mexico	(21.2)
44	New York	(18.4)
33	North Carolina	(11.9)
49	North Dakota	(29.9)
7	Ohio	11.3
2	Oklahoma	15.7
30	Oregon	(9.4)
16	Pennsylvania	0.7
48	Rhode Island	(23.2)
42	South Carolina	(16.3)
40	South Dakota	(14.9)
31	Tennessee	(10.0)
8	Texas	9.8
25	Utah	(7.0)
50	Vermont	(36.5)
12	Virginia	4.2
22	Washington	(4.1)
15	West Virginia	2.2
34	Wisconsin	(12.8)
25	Wyoming	(7.0)

RANK ORDER

RANK	STATE	PERCENT CHANGE
1	Massachusetts	27.1
2	Oklahoma	15.7
3	Colorado	15.6
4	Arkansas	15.2
5	Maine	12.9
6	Montana	11.6
7	Ohio	11.3
8	Texas	9.8
9	Connecticut	7.1
10	Minnesota	5.7
11	New Hampshire	4.9
12	Virginia	4.2
13	Alabama	4.1
14	Iowa	3.8
15	West Virginia	2.2
16	Pennsylvania	0.7
17	Idaho	0.0
18	Indiana	(1.1)
19	Kentucky	(2.2)
20	Nebraska	(2.8)
21	California	(3.3)
22	Washington	(4.1)
23	Georgia	(4.4)
24	New Jersey	(6.7)
25	Utah	(7.0)
25	Wyoming	(7.0)
27	Nevada	(7.6)
28	Arizona	(8.1)
29	Mississippi	(9.3)
30	Oregon	(9.4)
31	Tennessee	(10.0)
32	Maryland	(10.3)
33	North Carolina	(11.9)
34	Alaska	(12.8)
34	Wisconsin	(12.8)
36	Kansas	(13.0)
37	Florida	(13.4)
38	Louisiana	(13.7)
39	Illinois	(14.2)
40	South Dakota	(14.9)
41	Missouri	(15.2)
42	South Carolina	(16.3)
43	Delaware	(17.5)
44	New York	(18.4)
45	Michigan	(18.9)
46	Hawaii	(19.3)
47	New Mexico	(21.2)
48	Rhode Island	(23.2)
49	North Dakota	(29.9)
50	Vermont	(36.5)

District of Columbia (6.9)

Source: Morgan Quitno Press using data from Federal Bureau of Investigation
   "Crime in the United States" (Uniform Crime Reports, 2001 and 2004 editions)
*Revised figures. Robbery is the taking or attempting to take anything of value by force or threat of force.

Aggravated Assaults in 2000

National Total = 911,706 Aggravated Assaults*

<table>
<tr><td colspan="4">ALPHA ORDER</td><td colspan="4">RANK ORDER</td></tr>
<tr><th>RANK</th><th>STATE</th><th>ASSAULTS</th><th>% of USA</th><th>RANK</th><th>STATE</th><th>ASSAULTS</th><th>% of USA</th></tr>
<tr><td>19</td><td>Alabama</td><td>14,107</td><td>1.5%</td><td>1</td><td>California</td><td>138,418</td><td>15.2%</td></tr>
<tr><td>41</td><td>Alaska</td><td>2,540</td><td>0.3%</td><td>2</td><td>Florida</td><td>90,008</td><td>9.9%</td></tr>
<tr><td>16</td><td>Arizona</td><td>17,841</td><td>2.0%</td><td>3</td><td>Texas</td><td>74,302</td><td>8.1%</td></tr>
<tr><td>26</td><td>Arkansas</td><td>8,887</td><td>1.0%</td><td>4</td><td>New York</td><td>60,090</td><td>6.6%</td></tr>
<tr><td>1</td><td>California</td><td>138,418</td><td>15.2%</td><td>5</td><td>Illinois</td><td>50,731</td><td>5.6%</td></tr>
<tr><td>25</td><td>Colorado</td><td>9,425</td><td>1.0%</td><td>6</td><td>Michigan</td><td>35,753</td><td>3.9%</td></tr>
<tr><td>32</td><td>Connecticut</td><td>6,450</td><td>0.7%</td><td>7</td><td>Pennsylvania</td><td>29,580</td><td>3.2%</td></tr>
<tr><td>39</td><td>Delaware</td><td>3,520</td><td>0.4%</td><td>8</td><td>Tennessee</td><td>28,172</td><td>3.1%</td></tr>
<tr><td>2</td><td>Florida</td><td>90,008</td><td>9.9%</td><td>9</td><td>Maryland</td><td>26,130</td><td>2.9%</td></tr>
<tr><td>10</td><td>Georgia</td><td>25,450</td><td>2.8%</td><td>10</td><td>Georgia</td><td>25,450</td><td>2.8%</td></tr>
<tr><td>44</td><td>Hawaii</td><td>1,450</td><td>0.2%</td><td>11</td><td>South Carolina</td><td>25,054</td><td>2.7%</td></tr>
<tr><td>40</td><td>Idaho</td><td>2,644</td><td>0.3%</td><td>12</td><td>North Carolina</td><td>24,715</td><td>2.7%</td></tr>
<tr><td>5</td><td>Illinois</td><td>50,731</td><td>5.6%</td><td>13</td><td>Massachusetts</td><td>22,594</td><td>2.5%</td></tr>
<tr><td>22</td><td>Indiana</td><td>12,837</td><td>1.4%</td><td>14</td><td>Louisiana</td><td>20,851</td><td>2.3%</td></tr>
<tr><td>34</td><td>Iowa</td><td>6,003</td><td>0.7%</td><td>15</td><td>Missouri</td><td>18,123</td><td>2.0%</td></tr>
<tr><td>30</td><td>Kansas</td><td>7,231</td><td>0.8%</td><td>16</td><td>Arizona</td><td>17,841</td><td>2.0%</td></tr>
<tr><td>29</td><td>Kentucky</td><td>7,363</td><td>0.8%</td><td>17</td><td>Ohio</td><td>17,636</td><td>1.9%</td></tr>
<tr><td>14</td><td>Louisiana</td><td>20,851</td><td>2.3%</td><td>18</td><td>New Jersey</td><td>17,099</td><td>1.9%</td></tr>
<tr><td>48</td><td>Maine</td><td>815</td><td>0.1%</td><td>19</td><td>Alabama</td><td>14,107</td><td>1.5%</td></tr>
<tr><td>9</td><td>Maryland</td><td>26,130</td><td>2.9%</td><td>20</td><td>Washington</td><td>13,043</td><td>1.4%</td></tr>
<tr><td>13</td><td>Massachusetts</td><td>22,594</td><td>2.5%</td><td>21</td><td>Oklahoma</td><td>12,958</td><td>1.4%</td></tr>
<tr><td>6</td><td>Michigan</td><td>35,753</td><td>3.9%</td><td>22</td><td>Indiana</td><td>12,837</td><td>1.4%</td></tr>
<tr><td>28</td><td>Minnesota</td><td>7,709</td><td>0.8%</td><td>23</td><td>Virginia</td><td>11,631</td><td>1.3%</td></tr>
<tr><td>33</td><td>Mississippi</td><td>6,290</td><td>0.7%</td><td>24</td><td>New Mexico</td><td>10,230</td><td>1.1%</td></tr>
<tr><td>15</td><td>Missouri</td><td>18,123</td><td>2.0%</td><td>25</td><td>Colorado</td><td>9,425</td><td>1.0%</td></tr>
<tr><td>42</td><td>Montana</td><td>2,276</td><td>0.2%</td><td>26</td><td>Arkansas</td><td>8,887</td><td>1.0%</td></tr>
<tr><td>37</td><td>Nebraska</td><td>3,960</td><td>0.4%</td><td>27</td><td>Oregon</td><td>7,756</td><td>0.9%</td></tr>
<tr><td>35</td><td>Nevada</td><td>4,942</td><td>0.5%</td><td>28</td><td>Minnesota</td><td>7,709</td><td>0.8%</td></tr>
<tr><td>45</td><td>New Hampshire</td><td>1,170</td><td>0.1%</td><td>29</td><td>Kentucky</td><td>7,363</td><td>0.8%</td></tr>
<tr><td>18</td><td>New Jersey</td><td>17,099</td><td>1.9%</td><td>30</td><td>Kansas</td><td>7,231</td><td>0.8%</td></tr>
<tr><td>24</td><td>New Mexico</td><td>10,230</td><td>1.1%</td><td>31</td><td>Wisconsin</td><td>6,829</td><td>0.7%</td></tr>
<tr><td>4</td><td>New York</td><td>60,090</td><td>6.6%</td><td>32</td><td>Connecticut</td><td>6,450</td><td>0.7%</td></tr>
<tr><td>12</td><td>North Carolina</td><td>24,715</td><td>2.7%</td><td>33</td><td>Mississippi</td><td>6,290</td><td>0.7%</td></tr>
<tr><td>50</td><td>North Dakota</td><td>294</td><td>0.0%</td><td>34</td><td>Iowa</td><td>6,003</td><td>0.7%</td></tr>
<tr><td>17</td><td>Ohio</td><td>17,636</td><td>1.9%</td><td>35</td><td>Nevada</td><td>4,942</td><td>0.5%</td></tr>
<tr><td>21</td><td>Oklahoma</td><td>12,958</td><td>1.4%</td><td>36</td><td>West Virginia</td><td>4,597</td><td>0.5%</td></tr>
<tr><td>27</td><td>Oregon</td><td>7,756</td><td>0.9%</td><td>37</td><td>Nebraska</td><td>3,960</td><td>0.4%</td></tr>
<tr><td>7</td><td>Pennsylvania</td><td>29,580</td><td>3.2%</td><td>38</td><td>Utah</td><td>3,563</td><td>0.4%</td></tr>
<tr><td>43</td><td>Rhode Island</td><td>1,742</td><td>0.2%</td><td>39</td><td>Delaware</td><td>3,520</td><td>0.4%</td></tr>
<tr><td>11</td><td>South Carolina</td><td>25,054</td><td>2.7%</td><td>40</td><td>Idaho</td><td>2,644</td><td>0.3%</td></tr>
<tr><td>47</td><td>South Dakota</td><td>816</td><td>0.1%</td><td>41</td><td>Alaska</td><td>2,540</td><td>0.3%</td></tr>
<tr><td>8</td><td>Tennessee</td><td>28,172</td><td>3.1%</td><td>42</td><td>Montana</td><td>2,276</td><td>0.2%</td></tr>
<tr><td>3</td><td>Texas</td><td>74,302</td><td>8.1%</td><td>43</td><td>Rhode Island</td><td>1,742</td><td>0.2%</td></tr>
<tr><td>38</td><td>Utah</td><td>3,563</td><td>0.4%</td><td>44</td><td>Hawaii</td><td>1,450</td><td>0.2%</td></tr>
<tr><td>49</td><td>Vermont</td><td>425</td><td>0.0%</td><td>45</td><td>New Hampshire</td><td>1,170</td><td>0.1%</td></tr>
<tr><td>23</td><td>Virginia</td><td>11,631</td><td>1.3%</td><td>46</td><td>Wyoming</td><td>1,074</td><td>0.1%</td></tr>
<tr><td>20</td><td>Washington</td><td>13,043</td><td>1.4%</td><td>47</td><td>South Dakota</td><td>816</td><td>0.1%</td></tr>
<tr><td>36</td><td>West Virginia</td><td>4,597</td><td>0.5%</td><td>48</td><td>Maine</td><td>815</td><td>0.1%</td></tr>
<tr><td>31</td><td>Wisconsin</td><td>6,829</td><td>0.7%</td><td>49</td><td>Vermont</td><td>425</td><td>0.0%</td></tr>
<tr><td>46</td><td>Wyoming</td><td>1,074</td><td>0.1%</td><td>50</td><td>North Dakota</td><td>294</td><td>0.0%</td></tr>
<tr><td></td><td></td><td></td><td></td><td></td><td>District of Columbia</td><td>4,582</td><td>0.5%</td></tr>
</table>

Source: Federal Bureau of Investigation
"Crime in the United States 2001" (Uniform Crime Reports, October 28, 2002)
*Revised figures. Aggravated assault is an attack for the purpose of inflicting severe bodily injury.

Percent Change in Number of Aggravated Assaults: 2000 to 2004

National Percent Change = 6.2% Decrease*

ALPHA ORDER			RANK ORDER		
RANK	STATE	PERCENT CHANGE	RANK	STATE	PERCENT CHANGE
46	Alabama	(20.0)	1	Nevada	68.9
3	Alaska	22.7	2	Hawaii	31.2
8	Arizona	6.1	3	Alaska	22.7
5	Arkansas	12.8	4	Colorado	19.6
40	California	(10.2)	5	Arkansas	12.8
4	Colorado	19.6	6	Missouri	9.0
48	Connecticut	(22.6)	7	Vermont	6.4
41	Delaware	(10.8)	8	Arizona	6.1
25	Florida	(4.2)	9	Tennessee	5.1
32	Georgia	(7.4)	10	South Dakota	4.4
2	Hawaii	31.2	11	Texas	2.3
19	Idaho	(2.7)	12	New Hampshire	2.0
45	Illinois	(18.2)	13	South Carolina	1.7
33	Indiana	(8.1)	14	North Dakota	1.0
15	Iowa	0.7	15	Iowa	0.7
16	Kansas	(0.4)	16	Kansas	(0.4)
50	Kentucky	(26.5)	17	Oklahoma	(1.2)
21	Louisiana	(3.6)	17	Virginia	(1.2)
35	Maine	(9.0)	19	Idaho	(2.7)
31	Maryland	(6.9)	20	Minnesota	(3.4)
42	Massachusetts	(11.5)	21	Louisiana	(3.6)
39	Michigan	(10.1)	22	Montana	(3.9)
20	Minnesota	(3.4)	22	Utah	(3.9)
49	Mississippi	(25.6)	24	New Mexico	(4.1)
6	Missouri	9.0	25	Florida	(4.2)
22	Montana	(3.9)	25	Pennsylvania	(4.2)
36	Nebraska	(9.2)	27	North Carolina	(4.5)
1	Nevada	68.9	28	Washington	(4.8)
12	New Hampshire	2.0	29	New Jersey	(5.6)
29	New Jersey	(5.6)	30	Ohio	(6.7)
24	New Mexico	(4.1)	31	Maryland	(6.9)
47	New York	(21.9)	32	Georgia	(7.4)
27	North Carolina	(4.5)	33	Indiana	(8.1)
14	North Dakota	1.0	34	Rhode Island	(8.4)
30	Ohio	(6.7)	35	Maine	(9.0)
17	Oklahoma	(1.2)	36	Nebraska	(9.2)
43	Oregon	(14.9)	37	Wisconsin	(9.3)
25	Pennsylvania	(4.2)	38	Wyoming	(9.4)
34	Rhode Island	(8.4)	39	Michigan	(10.1)
13	South Carolina	1.7	40	California	(10.2)
10	South Dakota	4.4	41	Delaware	(10.8)
9	Tennessee	5.1	42	Massachusetts	(11.5)
11	Texas	2.3	43	Oregon	(14.9)
22	Utah	(3.9)	44	West Virginia	(18.0)
7	Vermont	6.4	45	Illinois	(18.2)
17	Virginia	(1.2)	46	Alabama	(20.0)
28	Washington	(4.8)	47	New York	(21.9)
44	West Virginia	(18.0)	48	Connecticut	(22.6)
37	Wisconsin	(9.3)	49	Mississippi	(25.6)
38	Wyoming	(9.4)	50	Kentucky	(26.5)
				District of Columbia	(13.4)

Source: Morgan Quitno Press using data from Federal Bureau of Investigation
    "Crime in the United States" (Uniform Crime Reports, 2001 and 2004 editions)
*Revised figures. Aggravated assault is an attack for the purpose of inflicting severe bodily injury.

Aggravated Assault Rate in 2000

National Rate = 324.0 Aggravated Assaults per 100,000 Population*

ALPHA ORDER

RANK	STATE	RATE
18	Alabama	317.2
10	Alaska	405.1
15	Arizona	347.7
16	Arkansas	332.4
8	California	408.7
31	Colorado	219.1
37	Connecticut	189.4
7	Delaware	449.2
2	Florida	563.2
20	Georgia	310.9
45	Hawaii	119.7
35	Idaho	204.3
9	Illinois	408.5
33	Indiana	211.1
34	Iowa	205.1
22	Kansas	269.0
38	Kentucky	182.2
6	Louisiana	466.6
49	Maine	63.9
5	Maryland	493.3
14	Massachusetts	355.9
12	Michigan	359.7
42	Minnesota	156.7
30	Mississippi	221.1
17	Missouri	323.9
24	Montana	252.3
27	Nebraska	231.4
25	Nevada	247.3
47	New Hampshire	94.7
36	New Jersey	203.2
3	New Mexico	562.4
19	New York	316.7
21	North Carolina	307.0
50	North Dakota	45.8
43	Ohio	155.3
11	Oklahoma	375.5
28	Oregon	226.7
26	Pennsylvania	240.9
39	Rhode Island	166.2
1	South Carolina	624.5
46	South Dakota	108.1
4	Tennessee	495.2
13	Texas	356.3
41	Utah	159.5
48	Vermont	69.8
40	Virginia	164.3
29	Washington	221.3
23	West Virginia	254.2
44	Wisconsin	127.3
32	Wyoming	217.5

RANK ORDER

RANK	STATE	RATE
1	South Carolina	624.5
2	Florida	563.2
3	New Mexico	562.4
4	Tennessee	495.2
5	Maryland	493.3
6	Louisiana	466.6
7	Delaware	449.2
8	California	408.7
9	Illinois	408.5
10	Alaska	405.1
11	Oklahoma	375.5
12	Michigan	359.7
13	Texas	356.3
14	Massachusetts	355.9
15	Arizona	347.7
16	Arkansas	332.4
17	Missouri	323.9
18	Alabama	317.2
19	New York	316.7
20	Georgia	310.9
21	North Carolina	307.0
22	Kansas	269.0
23	West Virginia	254.2
24	Montana	252.3
25	Nevada	247.3
26	Pennsylvania	240.9
27	Nebraska	231.4
28	Oregon	226.7
29	Washington	221.3
30	Mississippi	221.1
31	Colorado	219.1
32	Wyoming	217.5
33	Indiana	211.1
34	Iowa	205.1
35	Idaho	204.3
36	New Jersey	203.2
37	Connecticut	189.4
38	Kentucky	182.2
39	Rhode Island	166.2
40	Virginia	164.3
41	Utah	159.5
42	Minnesota	156.7
43	Ohio	155.3
44	Wisconsin	127.3
45	Hawaii	119.7
46	South Dakota	108.1
47	New Hampshire	94.7
48	Vermont	69.8
49	Maine	63.9
50	North Dakota	45.8

	District of Columbia	801.0

Source: Federal Bureau of Investigation
"Crime in the United States 2001" (Uniform Crime Reports, October 28, 2002)
*Revised figures. Aggravated assault is an attack for the purpose of inflicting severe bodily injury.

Percent Change in Aggravated Assault Rate: 2000 to 2004

National Percent Change = 10.2% Decrease*

ALPHA ORDER

RANK	STATE	PERCENT CHANGE
46	Alabama	(21.5)
3	Alaska	17.4
19	Arizona	(5.3)
5	Arkansas	9.5
41	California	(15.3)
4	Colorado	11.9
48	Connecticut	(24.7)
42	Delaware	(15.8)
38	Florida	(12.0)
40	Georgia	(14.2)
2	Hawaii	25.9
27	Idaho	(9.6)
45	Illinois	(20.1)
30	Indiana	(10.4)
11	Iowa	(0.3)
12	Kansas	(2.1)
50	Kentucky	(28.4)
16	Louisiana	(4.7)
37	Maine	(11.9)
33	Maryland	(11.3)
39	Massachusetts	(12.4)
34	Michigan	(11.7)
22	Minnesota	(6.8)
49	Mississippi	(27.1)
6	Missouri	6.0
21	Montana	(6.5)
31	Nebraska	(11.1)
1	Nevada	44.6
14	New Hampshire	(3.1)
25	New Jersey	(8.7)
24	New Mexico	(8.3)
47	New York	(23.0)
28	North Carolina	(10.0)
8	North Dakota	2.2
23	Ohio	(7.5)
15	Oklahoma	(3.2)
44	Oregon	(19.0)
17	Pennsylvania	(5.2)
31	Rhode Island	(11.1)
13	South Carolina	(2.9)
8	South Dakota	2.2
10	Tennessee	1.3
17	Texas	(5.2)
29	Utah	(10.2)
7	Vermont	4.2
20	Virginia	(6.2)
26	Washington	(9.5)
43	West Virginia	(18.3)
34	Wisconsin	(11.7)
34	Wyoming	(11.7)

RANK ORDER

RANK	STATE	PERCENT CHANGE
1	Nevada	44.6
2	Hawaii	25.9
3	Alaska	17.4
4	Colorado	11.9
5	Arkansas	9.5
6	Missouri	6.0
7	Vermont	4.2
8	North Dakota	2.2
8	South Dakota	2.2
10	Tennessee	1.3
11	Iowa	(0.3)
12	Kansas	(2.1)
13	South Carolina	(2.9)
14	New Hampshire	(3.1)
15	Oklahoma	(3.2)
16	Louisiana	(4.7)
17	Pennsylvania	(5.2)
17	Texas	(5.2)
19	Arizona	(5.3)
20	Virginia	(6.2)
21	Montana	(6.5)
22	Minnesota	(6.8)
23	Ohio	(7.5)
24	New Mexico	(8.3)
25	New Jersey	(8.7)
26	Washington	(9.5)
27	Idaho	(9.6)
28	North Carolina	(10.0)
29	Utah	(10.2)
30	Indiana	(10.4)
31	Nebraska	(11.1)
31	Rhode Island	(11.1)
33	Maryland	(11.3)
34	Michigan	(11.7)
34	Wisconsin	(11.7)
34	Wyoming	(11.7)
37	Maine	(11.9)
38	Florida	(12.0)
39	Massachusetts	(12.4)
40	Georgia	(14.2)
41	California	(15.3)
42	Delaware	(15.8)
43	West Virginia	(18.3)
44	Oregon	(19.0)
45	Illinois	(20.1)
46	Alabama	(21.5)
47	New York	(23.0)
48	Connecticut	(24.7)
49	Mississippi	(27.1)
50	Kentucky	(28.4)

District of Columbia   (10.5)

Source: Morgan Quitno Press using data from Federal Bureau of Investigation
   "Crime in the United States" (Uniform Crime Reports, 2001 and 2004 editions)
*Revised figures. Aggravated assault is an attack for the purpose of inflicting severe bodily injury.

Property Crimes in 2000

National Total = 10,182,584 Property Crimes*

ALPHA ORDER

RANK	STATE	CRIMES	% of USA
21	Alabama	180,539	1.8%
46	Alaska	23,087	0.2%
12	Arizona	271,811	2.7%
32	Arkansas	98,115	1.0%
1	California	1,056,183	10.4%
25	Colorado	156,937	1.5%
31	Connecticut	99,033	1.0%
44	Delaware	29,727	0.3%
3	Florida	780,377	7.7%
9	Georgia	347,630	3.4%
38	Hawaii	60,033	0.6%
40	Idaho	37,961	0.4%
5	Illinois	445,278	4.4%
18	Indiana	206,905	2.0%
34	Iowa	86,834	0.9%
28	Kansas	108,057	1.1%
29	Kentucky	107,723	1.1%
17	Louisiana	211,904	2.1%
43	Maine	32,003	0.3%
16	Maryland	213,422	2.1%
22	Massachusetts	161,901	1.6%
8	Michigan	353,297	3.5%
24	Minnesota	157,798	1.5%
30	Mississippi	103,644	1.0%
15	Missouri	225,919	2.2%
42	Montana	32,198	0.3%
37	Nebraska	64,479	0.6%
36	Nevada	74,823	0.7%
45	New Hampshire	27,901	0.3%
14	New Jersey	233,637	2.3%
35	New Mexico	86,605	0.9%
4	New York	483,078	4.7%
7	North Carolina	355,921	3.5%
50	North Dakota	14,171	0.1%
6	Ohio	420,939	4.1%
27	Oklahoma	140,125	1.4%
26	Oregon	153,780	1.5%
10	Pennsylvania	316,274	3.1%
41	Rhode Island	33,323	0.3%
20	South Carolina	181,290	1.8%
48	South Dakota	16,252	0.2%
13	Tennessee	237,985	2.3%
2	Texas	919,658	9.0%
33	Utah	94,247	0.9%
47	Vermont	17,494	0.2%
19	Virginia	194,405	1.9%
11	Washington	279,144	2.7%
39	West Virginia	41,344	0.4%
23	Wisconsin	159,424	1.6%
49	Wyoming	14,969	0.1%

RANK ORDER

RANK	STATE	CRIMES	% of USA
1	California	1,056,183	10.4%
2	Texas	919,658	9.0%
3	Florida	780,377	7.7%
4	New York	483,078	4.7%
5	Illinois	445,278	4.4%
6	Ohio	420,939	4.1%
7	North Carolina	355,921	3.5%
8	Michigan	353,297	3.5%
9	Georgia	347,630	3.4%
10	Pennsylvania	316,274	3.1%
11	Washington	279,144	2.7%
12	Arizona	271,811	2.7%
13	Tennessee	237,985	2.3%
14	New Jersey	233,637	2.3%
15	Missouri	225,919	2.2%
16	Maryland	213,422	2.1%
17	Louisiana	211,904	2.1%
18	Indiana	206,905	2.0%
19	Virginia	194,405	1.9%
20	South Carolina	181,290	1.8%
21	Alabama	180,539	1.8%
22	Massachusetts	161,901	1.6%
23	Wisconsin	159,424	1.6%
24	Minnesota	157,798	1.5%
25	Colorado	156,937	1.5%
26	Oregon	153,780	1.5%
27	Oklahoma	140,125	1.4%
28	Kansas	108,057	1.1%
29	Kentucky	107,723	1.1%
30	Mississippi	103,644	1.0%
31	Connecticut	99,033	1.0%
32	Arkansas	98,115	1.0%
33	Utah	94,247	0.9%
34	Iowa	86,834	0.9%
35	New Mexico	86,605	0.9%
36	Nevada	74,823	0.7%
37	Nebraska	64,479	0.6%
38	Hawaii	60,033	0.6%
39	West Virginia	41,344	0.4%
40	Idaho	37,961	0.4%
41	Rhode Island	33,323	0.3%
42	Montana	32,198	0.3%
43	Maine	32,003	0.3%
44	Delaware	29,727	0.3%
45	New Hampshire	27,901	0.3%
46	Alaska	23,087	0.2%
47	Vermont	17,494	0.2%
48	South Dakota	16,252	0.2%
49	Wyoming	14,969	0.1%
50	North Dakota	14,171	0.1%
	District of Columbia	33,000	0.3%

Source: Federal Bureau of Investigation
"Crime in the United States 2001" (Uniform Crime Reports, October 28, 2002)
*Revised figures. Property crimes are offenses of burglary, larceny-theft and motor vehicle theft.

Percent Change in Number of Property Crimes: 2000 to 2004

National Percent Change = 1.4% Increase*

ALPHA ORDER

RANK	STATE	PERCENT CHANGE
19	Alabama	1.0
31	Alaska	(4.0)
4	Arizona	12.9
6	Arkansas	12.6
2	California	16.2
3	Colorado	14.9
39	Connecticut	(7.1)
45	Delaware	(11.6)
38	Florida	(6.8)
9	Georgia	8.3
20	Hawaii	0.8
17	Idaho	2.6
43	Illinois	(9.0)
18	Indiana	2.4
26	Iowa	(1.1)
21	Kansas	0.6
28	Kentucky	(2.3)
36	Louisiana	(6.0)
25	Maine	(0.8)
34	Maryland	(5.2)
29	Massachusetts	(2.5)
46	Michigan	(12.5)
27	Minnesota	(1.8)
30	Mississippi	(2.6)
24	Missouri	(0.6)
49	Montana	(15.5)
32	Nebraska	(4.6)
1	Nevada	31.3
33	New Hampshire	(5.0)
44	New Jersey	(9.6)
40	New Mexico	(7.7)
46	New York	(12.5)
23	North Carolina	(0.2)
48	North Dakota	(14.2)
22	Ohio	0.0
13	Oklahoma	6.7
9	Oregon	8.3
35	Pennsylvania	(5.3)
37	Rhode Island	(6.5)
14	South Carolina	4.3
42	South Dakota	(8.3)
12	Tennessee	6.8
8	Texas	9.9
15	Utah	3.6
50	Vermont	(18.0)
16	Virginia	2.7
11	Washington	7.8
7	West Virginia	10.0
41	Wisconsin	(8.0)
5	Wyoming	12.8

RANK ORDER

RANK	STATE	PERCENT CHANGE
1	Nevada	31.3
2	California	16.2
3	Colorado	14.9
4	Arizona	12.9
5	Wyoming	12.8
6	Arkansas	12.6
7	West Virginia	10.0
8	Texas	9.9
9	Georgia	8.3
9	Oregon	8.3
11	Washington	7.8
12	Tennessee	6.8
13	Oklahoma	6.7
14	South Carolina	4.3
15	Utah	3.6
16	Virginia	2.7
17	Idaho	2.6
18	Indiana	2.4
19	Alabama	1.0
20	Hawaii	0.8
21	Kansas	0.6
22	Ohio	0.0
23	North Carolina	(0.2)
24	Missouri	(0.6)
25	Maine	(0.8)
26	Iowa	(1.1)
27	Minnesota	(1.8)
28	Kentucky	(2.3)
29	Massachusetts	(2.5)
30	Mississippi	(2.6)
31	Alaska	(4.0)
32	Nebraska	(4.6)
33	New Hampshire	(5.0)
34	Maryland	(5.2)
35	Pennsylvania	(5.3)
36	Louisiana	(6.0)
37	Rhode Island	(6.5)
38	Florida	(6.8)
39	Connecticut	(7.1)
40	New Mexico	(7.7)
41	Wisconsin	(8.0)
42	South Dakota	(8.3)
43	Illinois	(9.0)
44	New Jersey	(9.6)
45	Delaware	(11.6)
46	Michigan	(12.5)
46	New York	(12.5)
48	North Dakota	(14.2)
49	Montana	(15.5)
50	Vermont	(18.0)

District of Columbia (18.5)

Source: Morgan Quitno Press using data from Federal Bureau of Investigation
"Crime in the United States" (Uniform Crime Reports, 2001 and 2004 editions)
*Revised figures. Property crimes are offenses of burglary, larceny-theft and motor vehicle theft.

Property Crime Rate in 2000

National Rate = 3,618.3 Property Crimes per 100,000 Population*

ALPHA ORDER

RANK	STATE	RATE
15	Alabama	4,059.7
23	Alaska	3,682.5
1	Arizona	5,297.8
24	Arkansas	3,670.0
33	California	3,118.2
25	Colorado	3,648.6
38	Connecticut	2,908.0
19	Delaware	3,793.6
3	Florida	4,882.7
11	Georgia	4,246.4
2	Hawaii	4,955.1
37	Idaho	2,933.7
27	Illinois	3,585.4
30	Indiana	3,402.8
36	Iowa	2,967.3
18	Kansas	4,019.4
42	Kentucky	2,665.2
5	Louisiana	4,741.7
46	Maine	2,510.2
17	Maryland	4,029.5
44	Massachusetts	2,550.0
29	Michigan	3,554.9
31	Minnesota	3,207.6
26	Mississippi	3,643.5
16	Missouri	4,037.7
28	Montana	3,568.9
20	Nebraska	3,767.9
21	Nevada	3,744.4
48	New Hampshire	2,257.8
40	New Jersey	2,776.6
4	New Mexico	4,761.0
45	New York	2,545.7
9	North Carolina	4,421.8
49	North Dakota	2,206.6
22	Ohio	3,707.7
14	Oklahoma	4,060.8
8	Oregon	4,494.7
43	Pennsylvania	2,575.3
32	Rhode Island	3,178.7
7	South Carolina	4,518.7
50	South Dakota	2,153.0
13	Tennessee	4,183.0
10	Texas	4,410.4
12	Utah	4,220.3
39	Vermont	2,873.4
41	Virginia	2,746.4
6	Washington	4,736.0
47	West Virginia	2,286.3
35	Wisconsin	2,972.3
34	Wyoming	3,031.5

RANK ORDER

RANK	STATE	RATE
1	Arizona	5,297.8
2	Hawaii	4,955.1
3	Florida	4,882.7
4	New Mexico	4,761.0
5	Louisiana	4,741.7
6	Washington	4,736.0
7	South Carolina	4,518.7
8	Oregon	4,494.7
9	North Carolina	4,421.8
10	Texas	4,410.4
11	Georgia	4,246.4
12	Utah	4,220.3
13	Tennessee	4,183.0
14	Oklahoma	4,060.8
15	Alabama	4,059.7
16	Missouri	4,037.7
17	Maryland	4,029.5
18	Kansas	4,019.4
19	Delaware	3,793.6
20	Nebraska	3,767.9
21	Nevada	3,744.4
22	Ohio	3,707.7
23	Alaska	3,682.5
24	Arkansas	3,670.0
25	Colorado	3,648.6
26	Mississippi	3,643.5
27	Illinois	3,585.4
28	Montana	3,568.9
29	Michigan	3,554.9
30	Indiana	3,402.8
31	Minnesota	3,207.6
32	Rhode Island	3,178.7
33	California	3,118.2
34	Wyoming	3,031.5
35	Wisconsin	2,972.3
36	Iowa	2,967.3
37	Idaho	2,933.7
38	Connecticut	2,908.0
39	Vermont	2,873.4
40	New Jersey	2,776.6
41	Virginia	2,746.4
42	Kentucky	2,665.2
43	Pennsylvania	2,575.3
44	Massachusetts	2,550.0
45	New York	2,545.7
46	Maine	2,510.2
47	West Virginia	2,286.3
48	New Hampshire	2,257.8
49	North Dakota	2,206.6
50	South Dakota	2,153.0
	District of Columbia	5,768.6

Source: Federal Bureau of Investigation
   "Crime in the United States 2001" (Uniform Crime Reports, October 28, 2002)
   *Revised figures. Property crimes are offenses of burglary, larceny-theft and motor vehicle theft.

Percent Change in Property Crime Rate: 2000 to 2004

National Percent Change = 2.8% Decrease*

ALPHA ORDER				RANK ORDER		
RANK	STATE	PERCENT CHANGE		RANK	STATE	PERCENT CHANGE
16	Alabama	(0.9)		1	Nevada	12.3
34	Alaska	(8.1)		2	Wyoming	10.0
12	Arizona	0.8		3	California	9.6
5	Arkansas	9.3		3	West Virginia	9.6
3	California	9.6		5	Arkansas	9.3
6	Colorado	7.4		6	Colorado	7.4
37	Connecticut	(9.7)		7	Oklahoma	4.5
48	Delaware	(16.6)		8	Oregon	3.0
47	Florida	(14.4)		8	Tennessee	3.0
13	Georgia	0.5		10	Washington	2.4
22	Hawaii	(3.3)		11	Texas	1.9
27	Idaho	(4.7)		12	Arizona	0.8
41	Illinois	(11.1)		13	Georgia	0.5
14	Indiana	(0.2)		14	Indiana	(0.2)
19	Iowa	(2.1)		15	South Carolina	(0.3)
18	Kansas	(1.1)		16	Alabama	(0.9)
28	Kentucky	(4.8)		16	Ohio	(0.9)
33	Louisiana	(7.0)		18	Kansas	(1.1)
25	Maine	(4.0)		19	Iowa	(2.1)
37	Maryland	(9.7)		20	Virginia	(2.5)
24	Massachusetts	(3.5)		21	Utah	(3.2)
46	Michigan	(14.0)		22	Hawaii	(3.3)
29	Minnesota	(5.3)		22	Missouri	(3.3)
26	Mississippi	(4.5)		24	Massachusetts	(3.5)
22	Missouri	(3.3)		25	Maine	(4.0)
49	Montana	(17.7)		26	Mississippi	(4.5)
32	Nebraska	(6.6)		27	Idaho	(4.7)
1	Nevada	12.3		28	Kentucky	(4.8)
36	New Hampshire	(9.6)		29	Minnesota	(5.3)
43	New Jersey	(12.5)		30	North Carolina	(5.9)
42	New Mexico	(11.8)		31	Pennsylvania	(6.2)
45	New York	(13.6)		32	Nebraska	(6.6)
30	North Carolina	(5.9)		33	Louisiana	(7.0)
44	North Dakota	(13.1)		34	Alaska	(8.1)
16	Ohio	(0.9)		35	Rhode Island	(9.3)
7	Oklahoma	4.5		36	New Hampshire	(9.6)
8	Oregon	3.0		37	Connecticut	(9.7)
31	Pennsylvania	(6.2)		37	Maryland	(9.7)
35	Rhode Island	(9.3)		39	South Dakota	(10.2)
15	South Carolina	(0.3)		40	Wisconsin	(10.4)
39	South Dakota	(10.2)		41	Illinois	(11.1)
8	Tennessee	3.0		42	New Mexico	(11.8)
11	Texas	1.9		43	New Jersey	(12.5)
21	Utah	(3.2)		44	North Dakota	(13.1)
50	Vermont	(19.7)		45	New York	(13.6)
20	Virginia	(2.5)		46	Michigan	(14.0)
10	Washington	2.4		47	Florida	(14.4)
3	West Virginia	9.6		48	Delaware	(16.6)
40	Wisconsin	(10.4)		49	Montana	(17.7)
2	Wyoming	10.0		50	Vermont	(19.7)
					District of Columbia	(15.8)

Source: Morgan Quitno Press using data from Federal Bureau of Investigation
    "Crime in the United States" (Uniform Crime Reports, 2001 and 2004 editions)
*Revised figures. Property crimes are offenses of burglary, larceny-theft and motor vehicle theft.

Burglaries in 2000

National Total = 2,050,992 Burglaries*

ALPHA ORDER

RANK	STATE	BURGLARIES	% of USA
18	Alabama	40,331	2.0%
45	Alaska	3,899	0.2%
13	Arizona	51,902	2.5%
31	Arkansas	21,443	1.0%
1	California	222,293	10.8%
24	Colorado	27,133	1.3%
34	Connecticut	17,436	0.9%
43	Delaware	5,216	0.3%
3	Florida	172,898	8.4%
9	Georgia	68,488	3.3%
37	Hawaii	10,665	0.5%
40	Idaho	7,330	0.4%
7	Illinois	81,850	4.0%
17	Indiana	41,108	2.0%
35	Iowa	16,342	0.8%
30	Kansas	21,484	1.0%
28	Kentucky	25,308	1.2%
14	Louisiana	46,289	2.3%
41	Maine	6,775	0.3%
20	Maryland	39,426	1.9%
22	Massachusetts	30,600	1.5%
8	Michigan	69,790	3.4%
26	Minnesota	26,116	1.3%
25	Mississippi	26,918	1.3%
16	Missouri	41,685	2.0%
46	Montana	3,624	0.2%
38	Nebraska	10,131	0.5%
33	Nevada	17,526	0.9%
44	New Hampshire	4,992	0.2%
15	New Jersey	43,924	2.1%
32	New Mexico	21,339	1.0%
6	New York	87,946	4.3%
4	North Carolina	97,888	4.8%
49	North Dakota	2,093	0.1%
5	Ohio	88,636	4.3%
21	Oklahoma	31,661	1.5%
27	Oregon	25,618	1.2%
11	Pennsylvania	54,080	2.6%
42	Rhode Island	6,620	0.3%
19	South Carolina	40,319	2.0%
48	South Dakota	2,896	0.1%
10	Tennessee	56,344	2.7%
2	Texas	188,975	9.2%
36	Utah	14,348	0.7%
47	Vermont	3,501	0.2%
23	Virginia	30,434	1.5%
12	Washington	53,476	2.6%
39	West Virginia	9,890	0.5%
29	Wisconsin	25,183	1.2%
50	Wyoming	2,078	0.1%

RANK ORDER

RANK	STATE	BURGLARIES	% of USA
1	California	222,293	10.8%
2	Texas	188,975	9.2%
3	Florida	172,898	8.4%
4	North Carolina	97,888	4.8%
5	Ohio	88,636	4.3%
6	New York	87,946	4.3%
7	Illinois	81,850	4.0%
8	Michigan	69,790	3.4%
9	Georgia	68,488	3.3%
10	Tennessee	56,344	2.7%
11	Pennsylvania	54,080	2.6%
12	Washington	53,476	2.6%
13	Arizona	51,902	2.5%
14	Louisiana	46,289	2.3%
15	New Jersey	43,924	2.1%
16	Missouri	41,685	2.0%
17	Indiana	41,108	2.0%
18	Alabama	40,331	2.0%
19	South Carolina	40,319	2.0%
20	Maryland	39,426	1.9%
21	Oklahoma	31,661	1.5%
22	Massachusetts	30,600	1.5%
23	Virginia	30,434	1.5%
24	Colorado	27,133	1.3%
25	Mississippi	26,918	1.3%
26	Minnesota	26,116	1.3%
27	Oregon	25,618	1.2%
28	Kentucky	25,308	1.2%
29	Wisconsin	25,183	1.2%
30	Kansas	21,484	1.0%
31	Arkansas	21,443	1.0%
32	New Mexico	21,339	1.0%
33	Nevada	17,526	0.9%
34	Connecticut	17,436	0.9%
35	Iowa	16,342	0.8%
36	Utah	14,348	0.7%
37	Hawaii	10,665	0.5%
38	Nebraska	10,131	0.5%
39	West Virginia	9,890	0.5%
40	Idaho	7,330	0.4%
41	Maine	6,775	0.3%
42	Rhode Island	6,620	0.3%
43	Delaware	5,216	0.3%
44	New Hampshire	4,992	0.2%
45	Alaska	3,899	0.2%
46	Montana	3,624	0.2%
47	Vermont	3,501	0.2%
48	South Dakota	2,896	0.1%
49	North Dakota	2,093	0.1%
50	Wyoming	2,078	0.1%
	District of Columbia	4,745	0.2%

Source: Federal Bureau of Investigation
    "Crime in the United States 2001" (Uniform Crime Reports, October 28, 2002)
*Revised figures. Burglary is the unlawful entry of a structure to commit a felony or theft. Attempts are included.

Percent Change in Number of Burglaries: 2000 to 2004

National Percent Change = 4.5% Increase*

ALPHA ORDER

RANK	STATE	PERCENT CHANGE
12	Alabama	10.7
35	Alaska	(3.2)
15	Arizona	9.6
1	Arkansas	40.4
13	California	10.6
4	Colorado	21.7
48	Connecticut	(10.7)
24	Delaware	3.2
37	Florida	(3.8)
5	Georgia	21.2
28	Hawaii	1.5
22	Idaho	4.0
45	Illinois	(7.2)
26	Indiana	2.6
11	Iowa	11.2
43	Kansas	(6.9)
27	Kentucky	2.3
31	Louisiana	(2.0)
40	Maine	(6.4)
44	Maryland	(7.0)
9	Massachusetts	12.6
46	Michigan	(7.7)
19	Minnesota	7.4
25	Mississippi	2.8
32	Missouri	(2.9)
33	Montana	(3.0)
33	Nebraska	(3.0)
2	Nevada	32.0
30	New Hampshire	(0.5)
41	New Jersey	(6.6)
41	New Mexico	(6.6)
50	New York	(19.6)
23	North Carolina	3.4
47	North Dakota	(8.7)
16	Ohio	9.4
10	Oklahoma	11.3
6	Oregon	17.4
29	Pennsylvania	0.7
49	Rhode Island	(17.4)
18	South Carolina	7.7
17	South Dakota	8.7
20	Tennessee	6.9
7	Texas	16.5
21	Utah	6.1
36	Vermont	(3.3)
39	Virginia	(5.4)
8	Washington	13.4
14	West Virginia	10.5
38	Wisconsin	(5.3)
3	Wyoming	31.8

RANK ORDER

RANK	STATE	PERCENT CHANGE
1	Arkansas	40.4
2	Nevada	32.0
3	Wyoming	31.8
4	Colorado	21.7
5	Georgia	21.2
6	Oregon	17.4
7	Texas	16.5
8	Washington	13.4
9	Massachusetts	12.6
10	Oklahoma	11.3
11	Iowa	11.2
12	Alabama	10.7
13	California	10.6
14	West Virginia	10.5
15	Arizona	9.6
16	Ohio	9.4
17	South Dakota	8.7
18	South Carolina	7.7
19	Minnesota	7.4
20	Tennessee	6.9
21	Utah	6.1
22	Idaho	4.0
23	North Carolina	3.4
24	Delaware	3.2
25	Mississippi	2.8
26	Indiana	2.6
27	Kentucky	2.3
28	Hawaii	1.5
29	Pennsylvania	0.7
30	New Hampshire	(0.5)
31	Louisiana	(2.0)
32	Missouri	(2.9)
33	Montana	(3.0)
33	Nebraska	(3.0)
35	Alaska	(3.2)
36	Vermont	(3.3)
37	Florida	(3.8)
38	Wisconsin	(5.3)
39	Virginia	(5.4)
40	Maine	(6.4)
41	New Jersey	(6.6)
41	New Mexico	(6.6)
43	Kansas	(6.9)
44	Maryland	(7.0)
45	Illinois	(7.2)
46	Michigan	(7.7)
47	North Dakota	(8.7)
48	Connecticut	(10.7)
49	Rhode Island	(17.4)
50	New York	(19.6)

District of Columbia (16.8)

Source: Morgan Quitno Press using data from Federal Bureau of Investigation
   "Crime in the United States" (Uniform Crime Reports, 2001 and 2004 editions)
*Revised figures. Burglary is the unlawful entry of a structure to commit a felony or theft. Attempts are included.

Burglary Rate in 2000

National Rate = 728.8 Burglaries per 100,000 Population*

ALPHA ORDER

RANK	STATE	RATE
11	Alabama	906.9
31	Alaska	621.9
5	Arizona	1,011.6
16	Arkansas	802.1
26	California	656.3
29	Colorado	630.8
40	Connecticut	512.0
24	Delaware	665.6
3	Florida	1,081.8
15	Georgia	836.6
13	Hawaii	880.3
34	Idaho	566.5
25	Illinois	659.1
23	Indiana	676.1
35	Iowa	558.4
17	Kansas	799.1
30	Kentucky	626.2
4	Louisiana	1,035.8
37	Maine	531.4
21	Maryland	744.4
41	Massachusetts	482.0
22	Michigan	702.2
38	Minnesota	530.9
8	Mississippi	946.3
20	Missouri	745.0
48	Montana	401.7
32	Nebraska	592.0
14	Nevada	877.1
47	New Hampshire	404.0
39	New Jersey	522.0
2	New Mexico	1,173.1
43	New York	463.4
1	North Carolina	1,216.1
50	North Dakota	325.9
18	Ohio	780.7
9	Oklahoma	917.5
19	Oregon	748.8
44	Pennsylvania	440.4
28	Rhode Island	631.5
6	South Carolina	1,005.0
49	South Dakota	383.7
7	Tennessee	990.4
12	Texas	906.3
27	Utah	642.5
33	Vermont	575.0
45	Virginia	429.9
10	Washington	907.3
36	West Virginia	546.9
42	Wisconsin	469.5
46	Wyoming	420.8

RANK ORDER

RANK	STATE	RATE
1	North Carolina	1,216.1
2	New Mexico	1,173.1
3	Florida	1,081.8
4	Louisiana	1,035.8
5	Arizona	1,011.6
6	South Carolina	1,005.0
7	Tennessee	990.4
8	Mississippi	946.3
9	Oklahoma	917.5
10	Washington	907.3
11	Alabama	906.9
12	Texas	906.3
13	Hawaii	880.3
14	Nevada	877.1
15	Georgia	836.6
16	Arkansas	802.1
17	Kansas	799.1
18	Ohio	780.7
19	Oregon	748.8
20	Missouri	745.0
21	Maryland	744.4
22	Michigan	702.2
23	Indiana	676.1
24	Delaware	665.6
25	Illinois	659.1
26	California	656.3
27	Utah	642.5
28	Rhode Island	631.5
29	Colorado	630.8
30	Kentucky	626.2
31	Alaska	621.9
32	Nebraska	592.0
33	Vermont	575.0
34	Idaho	566.5
35	Iowa	558.4
36	West Virginia	546.9
37	Maine	531.4
38	Minnesota	530.9
39	New Jersey	522.0
40	Connecticut	512.0
41	Massachusetts	482.0
42	Wisconsin	469.5
43	New York	463.4
44	Pennsylvania	440.4
45	Virginia	429.9
46	Wyoming	420.8
47	New Hampshire	404.0
48	Montana	401.7
49	South Dakota	383.7
50	North Dakota	325.9
	District of Columbia	829.5

Source: Federal Bureau of Investigation
"Crime in the United States 2001" (Uniform Crime Reports, October 28, 2002)
*Revised figures. Burglary is the unlawful entry of a structure to commit a felony or theft. Attempts are included.

Percent Change in Burglary Rate: 2000 to 2004

National Percent Change = 0.2% Increase*

ALPHA ORDER				RANK ORDER		
RANK	**STATE**	**PERCENT CHANGE**		**RANK**	**STATE**	**PERCENT CHANGE**
11	Alabama	8.7		1	Arkansas	36.3
36	Alaska	(7.4)		2	Wyoming	28.4
25	Arizona	(2.1)		3	Colorado	13.7
1	Arkansas	36.3		4	Nevada	13.0
16	California	4.4		5	Georgia	12.4
3	Colorado	13.7		6	Oregon	11.7
48	Connecticut	(13.2)		7	Massachusetts	11.5
26	Delaware	(2.6)		8	Iowa	10.2
47	Florida	(11.6)		9	West Virginia	10.1
5	Georgia	12.4		10	Oklahoma	9.0
26	Hawaii	(2.6)		11	Alabama	8.7
30	Idaho	(3.4)		12	Ohio	8.4
41	Illinois	(9.4)		13	Texas	8.0
21	Indiana	0.0		14	Washington	7.7
8	Iowa	10.2		15	South Dakota	6.5
39	Kansas	(8.5)		16	California	4.4
22	Kentucky	(0.2)		17	Minnesota	3.6
29	Louisiana	(3.0)		18	Tennessee	3.0
41	Maine	(9.4)		19	South Carolina	2.9
46	Maryland	(11.3)		20	Mississippi	0.7
7	Massachusetts	11.5		21	Indiana	0.0
40	Michigan	(9.3)		22	Kentucky	(0.2)
17	Minnesota	3.6		23	Pennsylvania	(0.4)
20	Mississippi	0.7		24	Utah	(0.8)
34	Missouri	(5.6)		25	Arizona	(2.1)
34	Montana	(5.6)		26	Delaware	(2.6)
31	Nebraska	(5.0)		26	Hawaii	(2.6)
4	Nevada	13.0		26	North Carolina	(2.6)
33	New Hampshire	(5.4)		29	Louisiana	(3.0)
43	New Jersey	(9.6)		30	Idaho	(3.4)
45	New Mexico	(10.8)		31	Nebraska	(5.0)
50	New York	(20.7)		32	Vermont	(5.2)
26	North Carolina	(2.6)		33	New Hampshire	(5.4)
37	North Dakota	(7.6)		34	Missouri	(5.6)
12	Ohio	8.4		34	Montana	(5.6)
10	Oklahoma	9.0		36	Alaska	(7.4)
6	Oregon	11.7		37	North Dakota	(7.6)
23	Pennsylvania	(0.4)		38	Wisconsin	(7.8)
49	Rhode Island	(19.9)		39	Kansas	(8.5)
19	South Carolina	2.9		40	Michigan	(9.3)
15	South Dakota	6.5		41	Illinois	(9.4)
18	Tennessee	3.0		41	Maine	(9.4)
13	Texas	8.0		43	New Jersey	(9.6)
24	Utah	(0.8)		44	Virginia	(10.2)
32	Vermont	(5.2)		45	New Mexico	(10.8)
44	Virginia	(10.2)		46	Maryland	(11.3)
14	Washington	7.7		47	Florida	(11.6)
9	West Virginia	10.1		48	Connecticut	(13.2)
38	Wisconsin	(7.8)		49	Rhode Island	(19.9)
2	Wyoming	28.4		50	New York	(20.7)
					District of Columbia	(14.1)

Source: Morgan Quitno Press using data from Federal Bureau of Investigation
   "Crime in the United States" (Uniform Crime Reports, 2001 and 2004 editions)
*Revised figures. Burglary is the unlawful entry of a structure to commit a felony or theft. Attempts are included.

Larcenies and Thefts in 2000

National Total = 6,971,590 Larcenies and Thefts*

ALPHA ORDER

RANK	STATE	THEFTS	% of USA
20	Alabama	127,399	1.8%
46	Alaska	16,838	0.2%
12	Arizona	176,705	2.5%
32	Arkansas	69,740	1.0%
1	California	651,855	9.4%
25	Colorado	112,843	1.6%
33	Connecticut	68,498	1.0%
44	Delaware	21,360	0.3%
3	Florida	518,298	7.4%
7	Georgia	240,440	3.4%
38	Hawaii	43,254	0.6%
39	Idaho	28,545	0.4%
5	Illinois	313,161	4.5%
18	Indiana	144,707	2.1%
34	Iowa	65,118	0.9%
28	Kansas	80,077	1.1%
30	Kentucky	73,141	1.0%
19	Louisiana	144,345	2.1%
42	Maine	23,906	0.3%
17	Maryland	145,423	2.1%
26	Massachusetts	105,425	1.5%
9	Michigan	227,783	3.3%
23	Minnesota	118,250	1.7%
31	Mississippi	69,758	1.0%
13	Missouri	159,539	2.3%
41	Montana	26,678	0.4%
36	Nebraska	49,118	0.7%
37	Nevada	44,125	0.6%
45	New Hampshire	20,761	0.3%
14	New Jersey	155,562	2.2%
35	New Mexico	57,925	0.8%
4	New York	340,901	4.9%
8	North Carolina	232,767	3.3%
50	North Dakota	11,092	0.2%
6	Ohio	293,277	4.2%
27	Oklahoma	96,116	1.4%
24	Oregon	114,230	1.6%
10	Pennsylvania	225,869	3.2%
43	Rhode Island	22,038	0.3%
21	South Carolina	125,385	1.8%
48	South Dakota	12,558	0.2%
15	Tennessee	154,111	2.2%
2	Texas	637,522	9.1%
29	Utah	73,438	1.1%
47	Vermont	13,184	0.2%
16	Virginia	146,158	2.1%
11	Washington	190,650	2.7%
40	West Virginia	28,139	0.4%
22	Wisconsin	119,605	1.7%
49	Wyoming	12,318	0.2%

RANK ORDER

RANK	STATE	THEFTS	% of USA
1	California	651,855	9.4%
2	Texas	637,522	9.1%
3	Florida	518,298	7.4%
4	New York	340,901	4.9%
5	Illinois	313,161	4.5%
6	Ohio	293,277	4.2%
7	Georgia	240,440	3.4%
8	North Carolina	232,767	3.3%
9	Michigan	227,783	3.3%
10	Pennsylvania	225,869	3.2%
11	Washington	190,650	2.7%
12	Arizona	176,705	2.5%
13	Missouri	159,539	2.3%
14	New Jersey	155,562	2.2%
15	Tennessee	154,111	2.2%
16	Virginia	146,158	2.1%
17	Maryland	145,423	2.1%
18	Indiana	144,707	2.1%
19	Louisiana	144,345	2.1%
20	Alabama	127,399	1.8%
21	South Carolina	125,385	1.8%
22	Wisconsin	119,605	1.7%
23	Minnesota	118,250	1.7%
24	Oregon	114,230	1.6%
25	Colorado	112,843	1.6%
26	Massachusetts	105,425	1.5%
27	Oklahoma	96,116	1.4%
28	Kansas	80,077	1.1%
29	Utah	73,438	1.1%
30	Kentucky	73,141	1.0%
31	Mississippi	69,758	1.0%
32	Arkansas	69,740	1.0%
33	Connecticut	68,498	1.0%
34	Iowa	65,118	0.9%
35	New Mexico	57,925	0.8%
36	Nebraska	49,118	0.7%
37	Nevada	44,125	0.6%
38	Hawaii	43,254	0.6%
39	Idaho	28,545	0.4%
40	West Virginia	28,139	0.4%
41	Montana	26,678	0.4%
42	Maine	23,906	0.3%
43	Rhode Island	22,038	0.3%
44	Delaware	21,360	0.3%
45	New Hampshire	20,761	0.3%
46	Alaska	16,838	0.2%
47	Vermont	13,184	0.2%
48	South Dakota	12,558	0.2%
49	Wyoming	12,318	0.2%
50	North Dakota	11,092	0.2%
	District of Columbia	21,655	0.3%

Source: Federal Bureau of Investigation
"Crime in the United States 2001" (Uniform Crime Reports, October 28, 2002)
*Revised figures. Larceny and theft is the unlawful taking of property without use of force, violence or fraud. Attempts are included. Motor vehicle thefts are excluded.

Percent Change in Larcenies and Thefts: 2000 to 2004

National Percent Change = 0.3% Decrease*

ALPHA ORDER				RANK ORDER		
RANK	STATE	PERCENT CHANGE		RANK	STATE	PERCENT CHANGE
24	Alabama	(2.9)		1	Nevada	18.8
28	Alaska	(4.0)		2	California	11.8
3	Arizona	10.1		3	Arizona	10.1
9	Arkansas	5.9		4	Tennessee	9.8
2	California	11.8		5	West Virginia	9.5
7	Colorado	9.2		6	Texas	9.3
30	Connecticut	(4.4)		7	Colorado	9.2
45	Delaware	(12.3)		8	Wyoming	8.4
38	Florida	(6.9)		9	Arkansas	5.9
12	Georgia	3.7		10	Oklahoma	5.4
32	Hawaii	(5.0)		11	Virginia	5.0
20	Idaho	0.1		12	Georgia	3.7
40	Illinois	(7.8)		12	South Carolina	3.7
16	Indiana	2.7		14	Washington	3.3
30	Iowa	(4.4)		15	Oregon	3.2
19	Kansas	0.2		16	Indiana	2.7
26	Kentucky	(3.6)		17	Utah	1.8
39	Louisiana	(7.1)		18	Maine	0.8
18	Maine	0.8		19	Kansas	0.2
44	Maryland	(10.8)		20	Idaho	0.1
27	Massachusetts	(3.9)		21	Missouri	(0.8)
47	Michigan	(14.7)		22	Rhode Island	(1.9)
29	Minnesota	(4.1)		23	North Carolina	(2.4)
36	Mississippi	(6.2)		24	Alabama	(2.9)
21	Missouri	(0.8)		25	Ohio	(3.5)
49	Montana	(17.2)		26	Kentucky	(3.6)
34	Nebraska	(5.5)		27	Massachusetts	(3.9)
1	Nevada	18.8		28	Alaska	(4.0)
35	New Hampshire	(5.6)		29	Minnesota	(4.1)
42	New Jersey	(10.0)		30	Connecticut	(4.4)
43	New Mexico	(10.1)		30	Iowa	(4.4)
41	New York	(8.8)		32	Hawaii	(5.0)
23	North Carolina	(2.4)		33	Pennsylvania	(5.2)
48	North Dakota	(15.8)		34	Nebraska	(5.5)
25	Ohio	(3.5)		35	New Hampshire	(5.6)
10	Oklahoma	5.4		36	Mississippi	(6.2)
15	Oregon	3.2		37	Wisconsin	(6.8)
33	Pennsylvania	(5.2)		38	Florida	(6.9)
22	Rhode Island	(1.9)		39	Louisiana	(7.1)
12	South Carolina	3.7		40	Illinois	(7.8)
46	South Dakota	(13.1)		41	New York	(8.8)
4	Tennessee	9.8		42	New Jersey	(10.0)
6	Texas	9.3		43	New Mexico	(10.1)
17	Utah	1.8		44	Maryland	(10.8)
50	Vermont	(21.3)		45	Delaware	(12.3)
11	Virginia	5.0		46	South Dakota	(13.1)
14	Washington	3.3		47	Michigan	(14.7)
5	West Virginia	9.5		48	North Dakota	(15.8)
37	Wisconsin	(6.8)		49	Montana	(17.2)
8	Wyoming	8.4		50	Vermont	(21.3)
					District of Columbia	(32.8)

Source: Morgan Quitno Press using data from Federal Bureau of Investigation
"Crime in the United States" (Uniform Crime Reports, 2001 and 2004 editions)
*Revised figures. Larceny and theft is the unlawful taking of property without use of force, violence or fraud.
Attempts are included. Motor vehicle thefts are excluded.

Larceny and Theft Rate in 2000

National Rate = 2,477.3 Larcenies and Thefts per 100,000 Population*

ALPHA ORDER

RANK	STATE	RATE
16	Alabama	2,864.8
22	Alaska	2,685.8
2	Arizona	3,444.1
24	Arkansas	2,608.7
40	California	1,924.5
23	Colorado	2,623.5
39	Connecticut	2,011.4
20	Delaware	2,725.9
5	Florida	3,242.9
13	Georgia	2,937.0
1	Hawaii	3,570.2
35	Idaho	2,206.0
26	Illinois	2,521.6
30	Indiana	2,379.9
33	Iowa	2,225.2
11	Kansas	2,978.6
44	Kentucky	1,809.6
7	Louisiana	3,229.9
41	Maine	1,875.1
19	Maryland	2,745.7
49	Massachusetts	1,660.5
31	Michigan	2,291.9
29	Minnesota	2,403.7
28	Mississippi	2,452.2
17	Missouri	2,851.3
12	Montana	2,957.0
15	Nebraska	2,870.3
34	Nevada	2,208.2
47	New Hampshire	1,680.0
42	New Jersey	1,848.8
8	New Mexico	3,184.4
45	New York	1,796.4
14	North Carolina	2,891.8
46	North Dakota	1,727.2
25	Ohio	2,583.2
18	Oklahoma	2,785.4
3	Oregon	3,338.7
43	Pennsylvania	1,839.2
37	Rhode Island	2,102.2
9	South Carolina	3,125.2
48	South Dakota	1,663.7
21	Tennessee	2,708.8
10	Texas	3,057.4
4	Utah	3,288.5
36	Vermont	2,165.5
38	Virginia	2,064.8
6	Washington	3,234.6
50	West Virginia	1,556.1
32	Wisconsin	2,229.9
27	Wyoming	2,494.6

RANK ORDER

RANK	STATE	RATE
1	Hawaii	3,570.2
2	Arizona	3,444.1
3	Oregon	3,338.7
4	Utah	3,288.5
5	Florida	3,242.9
6	Washington	3,234.6
7	Louisiana	3,229.9
8	New Mexico	3,184.4
9	South Carolina	3,125.2
10	Texas	3,057.4
11	Kansas	2,978.6
12	Montana	2,957.0
13	Georgia	2,937.0
14	North Carolina	2,891.8
15	Nebraska	2,870.3
16	Alabama	2,864.8
17	Missouri	2,851.3
18	Oklahoma	2,785.4
19	Maryland	2,745.7
20	Delaware	2,725.9
21	Tennessee	2,708.8
22	Alaska	2,685.8
23	Colorado	2,623.5
24	Arkansas	2,608.7
25	Ohio	2,583.2
26	Illinois	2,521.6
27	Wyoming	2,494.6
28	Mississippi	2,452.2
29	Minnesota	2,403.7
30	Indiana	2,379.9
31	Michigan	2,291.9
32	Wisconsin	2,229.9
33	Iowa	2,225.2
34	Nevada	2,208.2
35	Idaho	2,206.0
36	Vermont	2,165.5
37	Rhode Island	2,102.2
38	Virginia	2,064.8
39	Connecticut	2,011.4
40	California	1,924.5
41	Maine	1,875.1
42	New Jersey	1,848.8
43	Pennsylvania	1,839.2
44	Kentucky	1,809.6
45	New York	1,796.4
46	North Dakota	1,727.2
47	New Hampshire	1,680.0
48	South Dakota	1,663.7
49	Massachusetts	1,660.5
50	West Virginia	1,556.1
	District of Columbia	3,785.4

Source: Federal Bureau of Investigation
   "Crime in the United States 2001" (Uniform Crime Reports, October 28, 2002)
*Revised figures. Larceny and theft is the unlawful taking of property without use of force, violence or fraud.
Attempts are included. Motor vehicle thefts are excluded.

Percent Change in Larceny and Theft Rate: 2000 to 2004

National Percent Change = 4.4% Decrease*

ALPHA ORDER				RANK ORDER		
RANK	STATE	PERCENT CHANGE		RANK	STATE	PERCENT CHANGE
21	Alabama	(4.7)		1	West Virginia	9.1
35	Alaska	(8.2)		2	Tennessee	5.8
14	Arizona	(1.7)		3	Wyoming	5.7
6	Arkansas	2.9		4	California	5.5
4	California	5.5		5	Oklahoma	3.2
7	Colorado	2.1		6	Arkansas	2.9
29	Connecticut	(7.1)		7	Colorado	2.1
48	Delaware	(17.2)		8	Nevada	1.7
43	Florida	(14.5)		9	Texas	1.3
19	Georgia	(3.8)		10	Indiana	0.2
36	Hawaii	(8.9)		11	Virginia	(0.4)
28	Idaho	(7.0)		12	South Carolina	(0.9)
38	Illinois	(9.9)		13	Kansas	(1.5)
10	Indiana	0.2		14	Arizona	(1.7)
25	Iowa	(5.3)		15	Oregon	(1.8)
13	Kansas	(1.5)		15	Washington	(1.8)
26	Kentucky	(6.0)		17	Maine	(2.4)
33	Louisiana	(8.1)		18	Missouri	(3.5)
17	Maine	(2.4)		19	Georgia	(3.8)
46	Maryland	(15.0)		20	Ohio	(4.4)
23	Massachusetts	(4.9)		21	Alabama	(4.7)
47	Michigan	(16.2)		22	Rhode Island	(4.8)
30	Minnesota	(7.5)		23	Massachusetts	(4.9)
33	Mississippi	(8.1)		23	Utah	(4.9)
18	Missouri	(3.5)		25	Iowa	(5.3)
49	Montana	(19.4)		26	Kentucky	(6.0)
30	Nebraska	(7.5)		27	Pennsylvania	(6.1)
8	Nevada	1.7		28	Idaho	(7.0)
40	New Hampshire	(10.2)		29	Connecticut	(7.1)
41	New Jersey	(13.0)		30	Minnesota	(7.5)
42	New Mexico	(14.1)		30	Nebraska	(7.5)
38	New York	(9.9)		32	North Carolina	(8.0)
32	North Carolina	(8.0)		33	Louisiana	(8.1)
44	North Dakota	(14.7)		33	Mississippi	(8.1)
20	Ohio	(4.4)		35	Alaska	(8.2)
5	Oklahoma	3.2		36	Hawaii	(8.9)
15	Oregon	(1.8)		37	Wisconsin	(9.3)
27	Pennsylvania	(6.1)		38	Illinois	(9.9)
22	Rhode Island	(4.8)		38	New York	(9.9)
12	South Carolina	(0.9)		40	New Hampshire	(10.2)
45	South Dakota	(14.9)		41	New Jersey	(13.0)
2	Tennessee	5.8		42	New Mexico	(14.1)
9	Texas	1.3		43	Florida	(14.5)
23	Utah	(4.9)		44	North Dakota	(14.7)
50	Vermont	(22.8)		45	South Dakota	(14.9)
11	Virginia	(0.4)		46	Maryland	(15.0)
15	Washington	(1.8)		47	Michigan	(16.2)
1	West Virginia	9.1		48	Delaware	(17.2)
37	Wisconsin	(9.3)		49	Montana	(19.4)
3	Wyoming	5.7		50	Vermont	(22.8)
					District of Columbia	(30.6)

Source: Morgan Quitno Press using data from Federal Bureau of Investigation
   "Crime in the United States" (Uniform Crime Reports, 2001 and 2004 editions)
*Revised figures. Larceny and theft is the unlawful taking of property without use of force, violence or fraud.
Attempts are included. Motor vehicle thefts are excluded.

Motor Vehicle Thefts in 2000

National Total = 1,160,002 Motor Vehicle Thefts*

ALPHA ORDER | | | | RANK ORDER

RANK	STATE	THEFTS	% of USA		RANK	STATE	THEFTS	% of USA
28	Alabama	12,809	1.1%		1	California	182,035	15.7%
42	Alaska	2,350	0.2%		2	Texas	93,161	8.0%
7	Arizona	43,204	3.7%		3	Florida	89,181	7.7%
33	Arkansas	6,932	0.6%		4	Michigan	55,724	4.8%
1	California	182,035	15.7%		5	New York	54,231	4.7%
21	Colorado	16,961	1.5%		6	Illinois	50,267	4.3%
27	Connecticut	13,099	1.1%		7	Arizona	43,204	3.7%
41	Delaware	3,151	0.3%		8	Ohio	39,026	3.4%
3	Florida	89,181	7.7%		9	Georgia	38,702	3.3%
9	Georgia	38,702	3.3%		10	Pennsylvania	36,325	3.1%
36	Hawaii	6,114	0.5%		11	Washington	35,018	3.0%
44	Idaho	2,086	0.2%		12	New Jersey	34,151	2.9%
6	Illinois	50,267	4.3%		13	Maryland	28,573	2.5%
19	Indiana	21,090	1.8%		14	Tennessee	27,530	2.4%
37	Iowa	5,374	0.5%		15	Massachusetts	25,876	2.2%
34	Kansas	6,496	0.6%		16	North Carolina	25,266	2.2%
30	Kentucky	9,274	0.8%		17	Missouri	24,695	2.1%
18	Louisiana	21,270	1.8%		18	Louisiana	21,270	1.8%
46	Maine	1,322	0.1%		19	Indiana	21,090	1.8%
13	Maryland	28,573	2.5%		20	Virginia	17,813	1.5%
15	Massachusetts	25,876	2.2%		21	Colorado	16,961	1.5%
4	Michigan	55,724	4.8%		22	South Carolina	15,586	1.3%
25	Minnesota	13,432	1.2%		23	Wisconsin	14,636	1.3%
32	Mississippi	6,968	0.6%		24	Oregon	13,932	1.2%
17	Missouri	24,695	2.1%		25	Minnesota	13,432	1.2%
45	Montana	1,896	0.2%		26	Nevada	13,172	1.1%
38	Nebraska	5,230	0.5%		27	Connecticut	13,099	1.1%
26	Nevada	13,172	1.1%		28	Alabama	12,809	1.1%
43	New Hampshire	2,148	0.2%		29	Oklahoma	12,348	1.1%
12	New Jersey	34,151	2.9%		30	Kentucky	9,274	0.8%
31	New Mexico	7,341	0.6%		31	New Mexico	7,341	0.6%
5	New York	54,231	4.7%		32	Mississippi	6,968	0.6%
16	North Carolina	25,266	2.2%		33	Arkansas	6,932	0.6%
47	North Dakota	986	0.1%		34	Kansas	6,496	0.6%
8	Ohio	39,026	3.4%		35	Utah	6,461	0.6%
29	Oklahoma	12,348	1.1%		36	Hawaii	6,114	0.5%
24	Oregon	13,932	1.2%		37	Iowa	5,374	0.5%
10	Pennsylvania	36,325	3.1%		38	Nebraska	5,230	0.5%
39	Rhode Island	4,665	0.4%		39	Rhode Island	4,665	0.4%
22	South Carolina	15,586	1.3%		40	West Virginia	3,315	0.3%
49	South Dakota	798	0.1%		41	Delaware	3,151	0.3%
14	Tennessee	27,530	2.4%		42	Alaska	2,350	0.2%
2	Texas	93,161	8.0%		43	New Hampshire	2,148	0.2%
35	Utah	6,461	0.6%		44	Idaho	2,086	0.2%
48	Vermont	809	0.1%		45	Montana	1,896	0.2%
20	Virginia	17,813	1.5%		46	Maine	1,322	0.1%
11	Washington	35,018	3.0%		47	North Dakota	986	0.1%
40	West Virginia	3,315	0.3%		48	Vermont	809	0.1%
23	Wisconsin	14,636	1.3%		49	South Dakota	798	0.1%
50	Wyoming	573	0.0%		50	Wyoming	573	0.0%
						District of Columbia	6,600	0.6%

Source: Federal Bureau of Investigation
"Crime in the United States 2001" (Uniform Crime Reports, October 28, 2002)
*Revised figures. Includes the theft or attempted theft of a self-propelled vehicle. Excludes motorboats, construction equipment, airplanes and farming equipment.

Percent Change in Number of Motor Vehicle Thefts: 2000 to 2004

National Percent Change = 6.6% Increase*

ALPHA ORDER				RANK ORDER		
RANK	STATE	PERCENT CHANGE		RANK	STATE	PERCENT CHANGE
16	Alabama	9.5		1	Nevada	71.8
31	Alaska	(4.7)		2	Colorado	41.9
9	Arizona	28.0		3	Hawaii	41.0
33	Arkansas	(6.4)		4	Wyoming	39.4
5	California	38.8		5	California	38.8
2	Colorado	41.9		6	Oregon	33.0
45	Connecticut	(15.8)		7	Idaho	30.6
50	Delaware	(31.9)		8	Kansas	29.8
40	Florida	(12.2)		9	Arizona	28.0
13	Georgia	14.3		10	Maryland	25.5
3	Hawaii	41.0		11	Washington	23.5
7	Idaho	30.6		12	Utah	18.4
46	Illinois	(19.7)		13	Georgia	14.3
28	Indiana	0.0		14	Mississippi	13.1
25	Iowa	0.6		15	West Virginia	12.8
8	Kansas	29.8		16	Alabama	9.5
32	Kentucky	(5.4)		17	New Mexico	7.6
34	Louisiana	(7.3)		18	North Carolina	6.8
29	Maine	(1.4)		19	South Dakota	6.0
10	Maryland	25.5		20	Missouri	4.9
44	Massachusetts	(14.8)		20	Oklahoma	4.9
36	Michigan	(9.3)		22	Ohio	4.7
25	Minnesota	0.6		23	Nebraska	1.1
14	Mississippi	13.1		24	Texas	1.0
20	Missouri	4.9		25	Iowa	0.6
42	Montana	(14.7)		25	Minnesota	0.6
23	Nebraska	1.1		27	South Carolina	0.3
1	Nevada	71.8		28	Indiana	0.0
37	New Hampshire	(9.6)		29	Maine	(1.4)
39	New Jersey	(11.3)		30	Virginia	(2.3)
17	New Mexico	7.6		31	Alaska	(4.7)
48	New York	(24.4)		32	Kentucky	(5.4)
18	North Carolina	6.8		33	Arkansas	(6.4)
35	North Dakota	(8.1)		34	Louisiana	(7.3)
22	Ohio	4.7		35	North Dakota	(8.1)
20	Oklahoma	4.9		36	Michigan	(9.3)
6	Oregon	33.0		37	New Hampshire	(9.6)
42	Pennsylvania	(14.7)		38	Tennessee	(10.1)
41	Rhode Island	(12.6)		39	New Jersey	(11.3)
27	South Carolina	0.3		40	Florida	(12.2)
19	South Dakota	6.0		41	Rhode Island	(12.6)
38	Tennessee	(10.1)		42	Montana	(14.7)
24	Texas	1.0		42	Pennsylvania	(14.7)
12	Utah	18.4		44	Massachusetts	(14.8)
49	Vermont	(28.9)		45	Connecticut	(15.8)
30	Virginia	(2.3)		46	Illinois	(19.7)
11	Washington	23.5		47	Wisconsin	(22.3)
15	West Virginia	12.8		48	New York	(24.4)
47	Wisconsin	(22.3)		49	Vermont	(28.9)
4	Wyoming	39.4		50	Delaware	(31.9)
					District of Columbia	27.4

Source: Morgan Quitno Press using data from Federal Bureau of Investigation
  "Crime in the United States" (Uniform Crime Reports, 2001 and 2004 editions)
*Revised figures. Includes the theft or attempted theft of a self-propelled vehicle. Excludes motorboats,
construction equipment, airplanes and farming equipment.

Motor Vehicle Theft Rate in 2000

National Rate = 414.2 Motor Vehicle Thefts per 100,000 Population*

ALPHA ORDER

RANK	STATE	RATE
32	Alabama	288.0
24	Alaska	374.8
1	Arizona	842.1
36	Arkansas	259.3
7	California	537.4
21	Colorado	394.3
23	Connecticut	384.6
20	Delaware	402.1
5	Florida	558.0
11	Georgia	472.8
8	Hawaii	504.6
45	Idaho	161.2
18	Illinois	404.7
26	Indiana	346.8
42	Iowa	183.6
39	Kansas	241.6
40	Kentucky	229.5
10	Louisiana	475.9
50	Maine	103.7
6	Maryland	539.5
15	Massachusetts	407.6
4	Michigan	560.7
34	Minnesota	273.0
38	Mississippi	245.0
14	Missouri	441.4
41	Montana	210.2
29	Nebraska	305.6
2	Nevada	659.2
44	New Hampshire	173.8
17	New Jersey	405.9
19	New Mexico	403.6
33	New York	285.8
28	North Carolina	313.9
46	North Dakota	153.5
27	Ohio	343.7
25	Oklahoma	357.8
16	Oregon	407.2
30	Pennsylvania	295.8
13	Rhode Island	445.0
22	South Carolina	388.5
49	South Dakota	105.7
9	Tennessee	483.9
12	Texas	446.8
31	Utah	289.3
47	Vermont	132.9
37	Virginia	251.6
3	Washington	594.1
43	West Virginia	183.3
35	Wisconsin	272.9
48	Wyoming	116.0

RANK ORDER

RANK	STATE	RATE
1	Arizona	842.1
2	Nevada	659.2
3	Washington	594.1
4	Michigan	560.7
5	Florida	558.0
6	Maryland	539.5
7	California	537.4
8	Hawaii	504.6
9	Tennessee	483.9
10	Louisiana	475.9
11	Georgia	472.8
12	Texas	446.8
13	Rhode Island	445.0
14	Missouri	441.4
15	Massachusetts	407.6
16	Oregon	407.2
17	New Jersey	405.9
18	Illinois	404.7
19	New Mexico	403.6
20	Delaware	402.1
21	Colorado	394.3
22	South Carolina	388.5
23	Connecticut	384.6
24	Alaska	374.8
25	Oklahoma	357.8
26	Indiana	346.8
27	Ohio	343.7
28	North Carolina	313.9
29	Nebraska	305.6
30	Pennsylvania	295.8
31	Utah	289.3
32	Alabama	288.0
33	New York	285.8
34	Minnesota	273.0
35	Wisconsin	272.9
36	Arkansas	259.3
37	Virginia	251.6
38	Mississippi	245.0
39	Kansas	241.6
40	Kentucky	229.5
41	Montana	210.2
42	Iowa	183.6
43	West Virginia	183.3
44	New Hampshire	173.8
45	Idaho	161.2
46	North Dakota	153.5
47	Vermont	132.9
48	Wyoming	116.0
49	South Dakota	105.7
50	Maine	103.7
	District of Columbia	1,153.7

Source: Federal Bureau of Investigation
   "Crime in the United States 2001" (Uniform Crime Reports, October 28, 2002)
*Revised figures. Includes the theft or attempted theft of a self-propelled vehicle. Excludes motorboats,
construction equipment, airplanes and farming equipment.*

Percent Change in Motor Vehicle Theft Rate: 2000 to 2004

National Percent Change = 1.7% Increase*

ALPHA ORDER				RANK ORDER		
RANK	STATE	PERCENT CHANGE		RANK	STATE	PERCENT CHANGE
15	Alabama	7.5		1	Nevada	47.1
34	Alaska	(8.8)		2	Wyoming	35.9
11	Arizona	14.3		3	Hawaii	35.3
35	Arkansas	(9.1)		4	Colorado	32.6
5	California	31.0		5	California	31.0
4	Colorado	32.6		6	Kansas	27.6
44	Connecticut	(18.2)		7	Oregon	26.6
50	Delaware	(35.7)		8	Idaho	21.3
45	Florida	(19.3)		9	Maryland	19.6
16	Georgia	6.0		10	Washington	17.3
3	Hawaii	35.3		11	Arizona	14.3
8	Idaho	21.3		12	West Virginia	12.4
46	Illinois	(21.6)		13	Mississippi	10.8
25	Indiana	(2.5)		14	Utah	10.7
23	Iowa	(0.4)		15	Alabama	7.5
6	Kansas	27.6		16	Georgia	6.0
32	Kentucky	(7.8)		17	South Dakota	3.8
33	Louisiana	(8.3)		18	Ohio	3.7
28	Maine	(4.6)		19	New Mexico	2.9
9	Maryland	19.6		20	Oklahoma	2.8
42	Massachusetts	(15.7)		21	Missouri	1.9
36	Michigan	(10.8)		22	North Carolina	0.7
26	Minnesota	(2.9)		23	Iowa	(0.4)
13	Mississippi	10.8		24	Nebraska	(1.0)
21	Missouri	1.9		25	Indiana	(2.5)
43	Montana	(16.9)		26	Minnesota	(2.9)
24	Nebraska	(1.0)		27	South Carolina	(4.1)
1	Nevada	47.1		28	Maine	(4.6)
38	New Hampshire	(14.0)		29	Texas	(6.4)
39	New Jersey	(14.2)		30	North Dakota	(7.0)
19	New Mexico	2.9		31	Virginia	(7.2)
48	New York	(25.4)		32	Kentucky	(7.8)
22	North Carolina	0.7		33	Louisiana	(8.3)
30	North Dakota	(7.0)		34	Alaska	(8.8)
18	Ohio	3.7		35	Arkansas	(9.1)
20	Oklahoma	2.8		36	Michigan	(10.8)
7	Oregon	26.6		37	Tennessee	(13.3)
41	Pennsylvania	(15.6)		38	New Hampshire	(14.0)
40	Rhode Island	(15.2)		39	New Jersey	(14.2)
27	South Carolina	(4.1)		40	Rhode Island	(15.2)
17	South Dakota	3.8		41	Pennsylvania	(15.6)
37	Tennessee	(13.3)		42	Massachusetts	(15.7)
29	Texas	(6.4)		43	Montana	(16.9)
14	Utah	10.7		44	Connecticut	(18.2)
49	Vermont	(30.4)		45	Florida	(19.3)
31	Virginia	(7.2)		46	Illinois	(21.6)
10	Washington	17.3		47	Wisconsin	(24.3)
12	West Virginia	12.4		48	New York	(25.4)
47	Wisconsin	(24.3)		49	Vermont	(30.4)
2	Wyoming	35.9		50	Delaware	(35.7)
					District of Columbia	31.7

Source: Morgan Quitno Press using data from Federal Bureau of Investigation
   "Crime in the United States" (Uniform Crime Reports, 2001 and 2004 editions)
*Revised figures. Includes the theft or attempted theft of a self-propelled vehicle. Excludes motorboats,
construction equipment, airplanes and farming equipment.

Hate Crimes in 2004

National Total = 7,649 Reported Hate Crimes*

ALPHA ORDER

RANK	STATE	CRIMES	% of USA
48	Alabama	3	0.0%
44	Alaska	9	0.1%
12	Arizona	224	2.9%
20	Arkansas	93	1.2%
1	California	1,393	18.2%
28	Colorado	59	0.8%
17	Connecticut	116	1.5%
36	Delaware	33	0.4%
9	Florida	274	3.6%
38	Georgia	29	0.4%
NA	Hawaii**	NA	NA
34	Idaho	37	0.5%
13	Illinois	187	2.4%
26	Indiana	63	0.8%
41	Iowa	23	0.3%
32	Kansas	49	0.6%
22	Kentucky	71	0.9%
42	Louisiana	22	0.3%
24	Maine	68	0.9%
10	Maryland	245	3.2%
6	Massachusetts	346	4.5%
3	Michigan	556	7.3%
11	Minnesota	239	3.1%
49	Mississippi	2	0.0%
22	Missouri	71	0.9%
30	Montana	56	0.7%
27	Nebraska	62	0.8%
21	Nevada	81	1.1%
33	New Hampshire	48	0.6%
2	New Jersey	769	10.1%
43	New Mexico	21	0.3%
4	New York	386	5.0%
25	North Carolina	66	0.9%
45	North Dakota	8	0.1%
5	Ohio	353	4.6%
31	Oklahoma	51	0.7%
15	Oregon	155	2.0%
18	Pennsylvania	105	1.4%
38	Rhode Island	29	0.4%
18	South Carolina	105	1.4%
46	South Dakota	7	0.1%
16	Tennessee	136	1.8%
7	Texas	309	4.0%
28	Utah	59	0.8%
40	Vermont	28	0.4%
8	Virginia	307	4.0%
14	Washington	175	2.3%
37	West Virginia	31	0.4%
34	Wisconsin	37	0.5%
47	Wyoming	4	0.1%

RANK ORDER

RANK	STATE	CRIMES	% of USA
1	California	1,393	18.2%
2	New Jersey	769	10.1%
3	Michigan	556	7.3%
4	New York	386	5.0%
5	Ohio	353	4.6%
6	Massachusetts	346	4.5%
7	Texas	309	4.0%
8	Virginia	307	4.0%
9	Florida	274	3.6%
10	Maryland	245	3.2%
11	Minnesota	239	3.1%
12	Arizona	224	2.9%
13	Illinois	187	2.4%
14	Washington	175	2.3%
15	Oregon	155	2.0%
16	Tennessee	136	1.8%
17	Connecticut	116	1.5%
18	Pennsylvania	105	1.4%
18	South Carolina	105	1.4%
20	Arkansas	93	1.2%
21	Nevada	81	1.1%
22	Kentucky	71	0.9%
22	Missouri	71	0.9%
24	Maine	68	0.9%
25	North Carolina	66	0.9%
26	Indiana	63	0.8%
27	Nebraska	62	0.8%
28	Colorado	59	0.8%
28	Utah	59	0.8%
30	Montana	56	0.7%
31	Oklahoma	51	0.7%
32	Kansas	49	0.6%
33	New Hampshire	48	0.6%
34	Idaho	37	0.5%
34	Wisconsin	37	0.5%
36	Delaware	33	0.4%
37	West Virginia	31	0.4%
38	Georgia	29	0.4%
38	Rhode Island	29	0.4%
40	Vermont	28	0.4%
41	Iowa	23	0.3%
42	Louisiana	22	0.3%
43	New Mexico	21	0.3%
44	Alaska	9	0.1%
45	North Dakota	8	0.1%
46	South Dakota	7	0.1%
47	Wyoming	4	0.1%
48	Alabama	3	0.0%
49	Mississippi	2	0.0%
NA	Hawaii**	NA	NA
	District of Columbia	49	0.6%

Source: Federal Bureau of Investigation
"Crime in the United States 2004" (Uniform Crime Reports, October 17, 2005)
Figures are for reporting law enforcement agencies. Participating agencies covered 87 percent of the U.S. population. Fifty-four percent of the incidents were motivated by racial bias; 16.7 percent by religious bias; 15.6 percent by sexual-orientation bias; and 13.2 percent by ethnicity/national origin bias.
***Not available.*

Rate of Hate Crimes in 2004

National Rate = 3.0 Hate Crimes Reported per 100,000 Population*

ALPHA ORDER				RANK ORDER		
RANK	STATE	RATE		RANK	STATE	RATE
47	Alabama	0.6		1	New Jersey	8.8
20	Alaska	3.3		2	Michigan	6.2
14	Arizona	4.0		3	Montana	6.0
5	Arkansas	5.7		4	Massachusetts	5.9
16	California	3.9		5	Arkansas	5.7
40	Colorado	1.3		6	Maine	5.2
20	Connecticut	3.3		7	New Hampshire	5.1
14	Delaware	4.0		8	Minnesota	4.7
36	Florida	1.6		9	Vermont	4.6
33	Georgia	1.8		10	Maryland	4.4
NA	Hawaii**	NA		11	Oregon	4.3
24	Idaho	2.7		12	Nebraska	4.2
18	Illinois	3.7		13	Virginia	4.1
29	Indiana	2.1		14	Arizona	4.0
44	Iowa	0.8		14	Delaware	4.0
27	Kansas	2.3		16	California	3.9
32	Kentucky	1.9		16	Ohio	3.9
47	Louisiana	0.6		18	Illinois	3.7
6	Maine	5.2		19	Nevada	3.5
10	Maryland	4.4		20	Alaska	3.3
4	Massachusetts	5.9		20	Connecticut	3.3
2	Michigan	6.2		22	Utah	3.2
8	Minnesota	4.7		23	Washington	2.8
49	Mississippi	0.2		24	Idaho	2.7
30	Missouri	2.0		24	Rhode Island	2.7
3	Montana	6.0		26	South Carolina	2.5
12	Nebraska	4.2		27	Kansas	2.3
19	Nevada	3.5		27	Tennessee	2.3
7	New Hampshire	5.1		29	Indiana	2.1
1	New Jersey	8.8		30	Missouri	2.0
33	New Mexico	1.8		30	New York	2.0
30	New York	2.0		32	Kentucky	1.9
44	North Carolina	0.8		33	Georgia	1.8
37	North Dakota	1.4		33	New Mexico	1.8
16	Ohio	3.9		35	West Virginia	1.7
37	Oklahoma	1.4		36	Florida	1.6
11	Oregon	4.3		37	North Dakota	1.4
42	Pennsylvania	0.9		37	Oklahoma	1.4
24	Rhode Island	2.7		37	Texas	1.4
26	South Carolina	2.5		40	Colorado	1.3
42	South Dakota	0.9		41	Wyoming	1.1
27	Tennessee	2.3		42	Pennsylvania	0.9
37	Texas	1.4		42	South Dakota	0.9
22	Utah	3.2		44	Iowa	0.8
9	Vermont	4.6		44	North Carolina	0.8
13	Virginia	4.1		46	Wisconsin	0.7
23	Washington	2.8		47	Alabama	0.6
35	West Virginia	1.7		47	Louisiana	0.6
46	Wisconsin	0.7		49	Mississippi	0.2
41	Wyoming	1.1		NA	Hawaii**	NA
					District of Columbia	8.9

Source: Morgan Quitno Press using data from Federal Bureau of Investigation
   "Crime in the United States 2004" (Uniform Crime Reports, October 17, 2005)
*Figures are for reporting law enforcement agencies. Participating agencies covered 87 percent of the U.S.
population. Fifty-four percent of the incidents were motivated by racial bias; 16.7 percent by religious bias; 15.6
percent by sexual-orientation bias; and 13.2 percent by ethnicity/national origin bias.
**Not available.

Consumer Fraud Complaints in 2005

National Total = 371,448 Complaints*

ALPHA ORDER

ALPHA ORDER

RANK	STATE	COMPLAINTS	% of USA
25	Alabama	4,840	1.3%
43	Alaska	1,654	0.4%
13	Arizona	9,789	2.6%
36	Arkansas	2,155	0.6%
1	California	48,707	13.1%
18	Colorado	7,551	2.0%
26	Connecticut	4,688	1.3%
46	Delaware	1,091	0.3%
2	Florida	24,796	6.7%
11	Georgia	10,285	2.8%
40	Hawaii	1,852	0.5%
39	Idaho	1,899	0.5%
6	Illinois	14,885	4.0%
15	Indiana	9,572	2.6%
33	Iowa	2,981	0.8%
32	Kansas	3,323	0.9%
27	Kentucky	4,149	1.1%
31	Louisiana	3,724	1.0%
42	Maine	1,714	0.5%
16	Maryland	8,413	2.3%
19	Massachusetts	7,363	2.0%
8	Michigan	11,618	3.1%
23	Minnesota	6,224	1.7%
37	Mississippi	2,114	0.6%
17	Missouri	7,912	2.1%
44	Montana	1,253	0.3%
34	Nebraska	2,278	0.6%
30	Nevada	3,770	1.0%
38	New Hampshire	2,008	0.5%
12	New Jersey	10,180	2.7%
35	New Mexico	2,168	0.6%
4	New York	20,868	5.6%
14	North Carolina	9,765	2.6%
50	North Dakota	632	0.2%
7	Ohio	14,075	3.8%
28	Oklahoma	3,917	1.1%
24	Oregon	5,938	1.6%
5	Pennsylvania	15,996	4.3%
45	Rhode Island	1,127	0.3%
21	South Carolina	6,312	1.7%
47	South Dakota	709	0.2%
22	Tennessee	6,261	1.7%
3	Texas	23,184	6.2%
29	Utah	3,829	1.0%
49	Vermont	651	0.2%
9	Virginia	11,234	3.0%
10	Washington	11,008	3.0%
41	West Virginia	1,849	0.5%
20	Wisconsin	7,215	1.9%
48	Wyoming	679	0.2%

RANK ORDER

RANK	STATE	COMPLAINTS	% of USA
1	California	48,707	13.1%
2	Florida	24,796	6.7%
3	Texas	23,184	6.2%
4	New York	20,868	5.6%
5	Pennsylvania	15,996	4.3%
6	Illinois	14,885	4.0%
7	Ohio	14,075	3.8%
8	Michigan	11,618	3.1%
9	Virginia	11,234	3.0%
10	Washington	11,008	3.0%
11	Georgia	10,285	2.8%
12	New Jersey	10,180	2.7%
13	Arizona	9,789	2.6%
14	North Carolina	9,765	2.6%
15	Indiana	9,572	2.6%
16	Maryland	8,413	2.3%
17	Missouri	7,912	2.1%
18	Colorado	7,551	2.0%
19	Massachusetts	7,363	2.0%
20	Wisconsin	7,215	1.9%
21	South Carolina	6,312	1.7%
22	Tennessee	6,261	1.7%
23	Minnesota	6,224	1.7%
24	Oregon	5,938	1.6%
25	Alabama	4,840	1.3%
26	Connecticut	4,688	1.3%
27	Kentucky	4,149	1.1%
28	Oklahoma	3,917	1.1%
29	Utah	3,829	1.0%
30	Nevada	3,770	1.0%
31	Louisiana	3,724	1.0%
32	Kansas	3,323	0.9%
33	Iowa	2,981	0.8%
34	Nebraska	2,278	0.6%
35	New Mexico	2,168	0.6%
36	Arkansas	2,155	0.6%
37	Mississippi	2,114	0.6%
38	New Hampshire	2,008	0.5%
39	Idaho	1,899	0.5%
40	Hawaii	1,852	0.5%
41	West Virginia	1,849	0.5%
42	Maine	1,714	0.5%
43	Alaska	1,654	0.4%
44	Montana	1,253	0.3%
45	Rhode Island	1,127	0.3%
46	Delaware	1,091	0.3%
47	South Dakota	709	0.2%
48	Wyoming	679	0.2%
49	Vermont	651	0.2%
50	North Dakota	632	0.2%
	District of Columbia	1,243	0.3%

Source: Federal Trade Commission, Consumer Sentinel
"Consumer Fraud and Identify Theft Complaint Data (January 2006)
*Figures are for individuals filing complaints. Some complaints result in multiple infractions. The total number of complaints is 431,118. Total does not include identity theft or "Do Not Call" registry complaints.

Rate of Consumer Fraud Complaints in 2005

National Rate = 125.3 Complaints per 100,000 Population*

ALPHA ORDER

RANK ORDER

RANK	STATE	RATE		RANK	STATE	RATE
38	Alabama	106.2		1	Alaska	249.2
1	Alaska	249.2		2	Washington	175.1
3	Arizona	164.8		3	Arizona	164.8
49	Arkansas	77.5		4	Oregon	163.1
16	California	134.8		5	Colorado	161.9
5	Colorado	161.9		6	Nevada	156.1
18	Connecticut	133.5		7	Utah	155.0
24	Delaware	129.3		8	New Hampshire	153.3
14	Florida	139.4		9	Indiana	152.6
33	Georgia	113.4		10	Maryland	150.2
13	Hawaii	145.2		11	Virginia	148.5
20	Idaho	132.9		12	South Carolina	148.3
30	Illinois	116.6		13	Hawaii	145.2
9	Indiana	152.6		14	Florida	139.4
44	Iowa	100.5		15	Missouri	136.4
28	Kansas	121.1		16	California	134.8
45	Kentucky	99.4		17	Montana	133.9
48	Louisiana	82.3		18	Connecticut	133.5
22	Maine	129.7		19	Wyoming	133.3
10	Maryland	150.2		20	Idaho	132.9
31	Massachusetts	115.1		21	Wisconsin	130.3
32	Michigan	114.8		22	Maine	129.7
27	Minnesota	121.3		23	Nebraska	129.5
50	Mississippi	72.4		24	Delaware	129.3
15	Missouri	136.4		25	Pennsylvania	128.7
17	Montana	133.9		26	Ohio	122.8
23	Nebraska	129.5		27	Minnesota	121.3
6	Nevada	156.1		28	Kansas	121.1
8	New Hampshire	153.3		29	New Jersey	116.8
29	New Jersey	116.8		30	Illinois	116.6
35	New Mexico	112.4		31	Massachusetts	115.1
37	New York	108.4		32	Michigan	114.8
34	North Carolina	112.5		33	Georgia	113.4
46	North Dakota	99.3		34	North Carolina	112.5
26	Ohio	122.8		35	New Mexico	112.4
36	Oklahoma	110.4		36	Oklahoma	110.4
4	Oregon	163.1		37	New York	108.4
25	Pennsylvania	128.7		38	Alabama	106.2
40	Rhode Island	104.7		39	Tennessee	105.0
12	South Carolina	148.3		40	Rhode Island	104.7
47	South Dakota	91.4		41	Vermont	104.5
39	Tennessee	105.0		42	West Virginia	101.8
43	Texas	101.4		43	Texas	101.4
7	Utah	155.0		44	Iowa	100.5
41	Vermont	104.5		45	Kentucky	99.4
11	Virginia	148.5		46	North Dakota	99.3
2	Washington	175.1		47	South Dakota	91.4
42	West Virginia	101.8		48	Louisiana	82.3
21	Wisconsin	130.3		49	Arkansas	77.5
19	Wyoming	133.3		50	Mississippi	72.4
					District of Columbia	225.8

Source: Federal Trade Commission, Consumer Sentinel
    "Consumer Fraud and Identify Theft Complaint Data (January 2006)
Figures are for individuals filing complaints. Some complaints result in multiple infractions. Does not include identity theft or "Do Not Call" registry complaints.

Average Amount Paid by Consumers to Fraudulent Organizations in 2005

National Average = $2,412*

ALPHA ORDER

RANK	STATE	AVERAGE
43	Alabama	$1,356
49	Alaska	1,062
12	Arizona	2,359
20	Arkansas	2,000
10	California	2,460
29	Colorado	1,736
36	Connecticut	1,600
9	Delaware	2,670
18	Florida	2,042
16	Georgia	2,112
41	Hawaii	1,409
19	Idaho	2,041
26	Illinois	1,784
42	Indiana	1,374
47	Iowa	1,185
44	Kansas	1,354
6	Kentucky	3,336
15	Louisiana	2,208
38	Maine	1,466
25	Maryland	1,815
39	Massachusetts	1,463
32	Michigan	1,638
23	Minnesota	1,913
30	Mississippi	1,679
2	Missouri	6,412
5	Montana	3,378
40	Nebraska	1,434
14	Nevada	2,209
4	New Hampshire	3,439
17	New Jersey	2,073
7	New Mexico	3,210
11	New York	2,379
28	North Carolina	1,754
50	North Dakota	1,004
35	Ohio	1,607
21	Oklahoma	1,982
3	Oregon	5,439
33	Pennsylvania	1,630
45	Rhode Island	1,340
34	South Carolina	1,618
48	South Dakota	1,176
24	Tennessee	1,876
8	Texas	2,908
31	Utah	1,673
27	Vermont	1,768
22	Virginia	1,926
36	Washington	1,600
13	West Virginia	2,333
46	Wisconsin	1,310
1	Wyoming	12,504

RANK ORDER

RANK	STATE	AVERAGE
1	Wyoming	$12,504
2	Missouri	6,412
3	Oregon	5,439
4	New Hampshire	3,439
5	Montana	3,378
6	Kentucky	3,336
7	New Mexico	3,210
8	Texas	2,908
9	Delaware	2,670
10	California	2,460
11	New York	2,379
12	Arizona	2,359
13	West Virginia	2,333
14	Nevada	2,209
15	Louisiana	2,208
16	Georgia	2,112
17	New Jersey	2,073
18	Florida	2,042
19	Idaho	2,041
20	Arkansas	2,000
21	Oklahoma	1,982
22	Virginia	1,926
23	Minnesota	1,913
24	Tennessee	1,876
25	Maryland	1,815
26	Illinois	1,784
27	Vermont	1,768
28	North Carolina	1,754
29	Colorado	1,736
30	Mississippi	1,679
31	Utah	1,673
32	Michigan	1,638
33	Pennsylvania	1,630
34	South Carolina	1,618
35	Ohio	1,607
36	Connecticut	1,600
36	Washington	1,600
38	Maine	1,466
39	Massachusetts	1,463
40	Nebraska	1,434
41	Hawaii	1,409
42	Indiana	1,374
43	Alabama	1,356
44	Kansas	1,354
45	Rhode Island	1,340
46	Wisconsin	1,310
47	Iowa	1,185
48	South Dakota	1,176
49	Alaska	1,062
50	North Dakota	1,004

District of Columbia — 1,633

Source: Federal Trade Commission, Consumer Sentinel
  "Consumer Fraud and Identify Theft Complaint Data (January 2006)
Average amount is based on the total number of fraud complaints where amount paid was reported by consumers.
Organizations include internet auctions, foreign money offers, catalog sales, prizes, lotteries and other internet
services. In 2005, 49 consumers each reported an amount paid of $1 million or more.

Identity Theft Complaints in 2005

National Total = 248,524 Complaints*

ALPHA ORDER

RANK	STATE	COMPLAINTS	% of USA
26	Alabama	2,675	1.1%
45	Alaska	421	0.2%
6	Arizona	9,320	3.8%
33	Arkansas	1,617	0.7%
1	California	45,175	18.2%
16	Colorado	4,535	1.8%
29	Connecticut	2,313	0.9%
43	Delaware	583	0.2%
4	Florida	17,048	6.9%
7	Georgia	7,918	3.2%
38	Hawaii	810	0.3%
39	Idaho	745	0.3%
5	Illinois	11,137	4.5%
17	Indiana	4,201	1.7%
36	Iowa	1,090	0.4%
34	Kansas	1,606	0.6%
30	Kentucky	1,815	0.7%
24	Louisiana	2,831	1.1%
44	Maine	491	0.2%
15	Maryland	4,848	2.0%
18	Massachusetts	3,999	1.6%
10	Michigan	7,139	2.9%
22	Minnesota	3,015	1.2%
35	Mississippi	1,458	0.6%
19	Missouri	3,920	1.6%
46	Montana	398	0.2%
37	Nebraska	919	0.4%
21	Nevada	3,144	1.3%
41	New Hampshire	645	0.3%
11	New Jersey	6,582	2.6%
32	New Mexico	1,634	0.7%
3	New York	17,387	7.0%
12	North Carolina	5,830	2.3%
50	North Dakota	158	0.1%
9	Ohio	7,155	2.9%
28	Oklahoma	2,403	1.0%
23	Oregon	2,973	1.2%
8	Pennsylvania	7,908	3.2%
42	Rhode Island	626	0.3%
27	South Carolina	2,416	1.0%
47	South Dakota	233	0.1%
20	Tennessee	3,412	1.4%
2	Texas	26,624	10.7%
31	Utah	1,668	0.7%
49	Vermont	201	0.1%
14	Virginia	5,163	2.1%
13	Washington	5,810	2.3%
40	West Virginia	677	0.3%
25	Wisconsin	2,782	1.1%
48	Wyoming	224	0.1%

RANK ORDER

RANK	STATE	COMPLAINTS	% of USA
1	California	45,175	18.2%
2	Texas	26,624	10.7%
3	New York	17,387	7.0%
4	Florida	17,048	6.9%
5	Illinois	11,137	4.5%
6	Arizona	9,320	3.8%
7	Georgia	7,918	3.2%
8	Pennsylvania	7,908	3.2%
9	Ohio	7,155	2.9%
10	Michigan	7,139	2.9%
11	New Jersey	6,582	2.6%
12	North Carolina	5,830	2.3%
13	Washington	5,810	2.3%
14	Virginia	5,163	2.1%
15	Maryland	4,848	2.0%
16	Colorado	4,535	1.8%
17	Indiana	4,201	1.7%
18	Massachusetts	3,999	1.6%
19	Missouri	3,920	1.6%
20	Tennessee	3,412	1.4%
21	Nevada	3,144	1.3%
22	Minnesota	3,015	1.2%
23	Oregon	2,973	1.2%
24	Louisiana	2,831	1.1%
25	Wisconsin	2,782	1.1%
26	Alabama	2,675	1.1%
27	South Carolina	2,416	1.0%
28	Oklahoma	2,403	1.0%
29	Connecticut	2,313	0.9%
30	Kentucky	1,815	0.7%
31	Utah	1,668	0.7%
32	New Mexico	1,634	0.7%
33	Arkansas	1,617	0.7%
34	Kansas	1,606	0.6%
35	Mississippi	1,458	0.6%
36	Iowa	1,090	0.4%
37	Nebraska	919	0.4%
38	Hawaii	810	0.3%
39	Idaho	745	0.3%
40	West Virginia	677	0.3%
41	New Hampshire	645	0.3%
42	Rhode Island	626	0.3%
43	Delaware	583	0.2%
44	Maine	491	0.2%
45	Alaska	421	0.2%
46	Montana	398	0.2%
47	South Dakota	233	0.1%
48	Wyoming	224	0.1%
49	Vermont	201	0.1%
50	North Dakota	158	0.1%
	District of Columbia	842	0.3%

Source: Federal Trade Commission, Consumer Sentinel
   "Consumer Fraud and Identify Theft Complaint Data (January 2006)
*Figures are for individuals filing complaints. Some complaints result in multiple infractions. The total number of complaints is 255,565. Total does not include consumer fraud or "Do Not Call" registry complaints.

Rate of Identity Theft Complaints in 2005

National Rate = 83.8 Complaints per 100,000 Population*

ALPHA ORDER				RANK ORDER		
RANK	STATE	RATE		RANK	STATE	RATE
30	Alabama	58.7		1	Arizona	156.9
26	Alaska	63.4		2	Nevada	130.2
1	Arizona	156.9		3	California	125.0
33	Arkansas	58.2		4	Texas	116.5
3	California	125.0		5	Colorado	97.2
5	Colorado	97.2		6	Florida	95.8
23	Connecticut	65.9		7	Washington	92.4
16	Delaware	69.1		8	New York	90.3
6	Florida	95.8		9	Georgia	87.3
9	Georgia	87.3		9	Illinois	87.3
25	Hawaii	63.5		11	Maryland	86.6
38	Idaho	52.1		12	New Mexico	84.7
9	Illinois	87.3		13	Oregon	81.7
22	Indiana	67.0		14	New Jersey	75.5
47	Iowa	36.7		15	Michigan	70.5
32	Kansas	58.5		16	Delaware	69.1
43	Kentucky	43.5		17	Virginia	68.2
27	Louisiana	62.6		18	Oklahoma	67.7
46	Maine	37.2		19	Missouri	67.6
11	Maryland	86.6		20	Utah	67.5
28	Massachusetts	62.5		21	North Carolina	67.1
15	Michigan	70.5		22	Indiana	67.0
30	Minnesota	58.7		23	Connecticut	65.9
40	Mississippi	49.9		24	Pennsylvania	63.6
19	Missouri	67.6		25	Hawaii	63.5
44	Montana	42.5		26	Alaska	63.4
37	Nebraska	52.3		27	Louisiana	62.6
2	Nevada	130.2		28	Massachusetts	62.5
41	New Hampshire	49.2		29	Ohio	62.4
14	New Jersey	75.5		30	Alabama	58.7
12	New Mexico	84.7		30	Minnesota	58.7
8	New York	90.3		32	Kansas	58.5
21	North Carolina	67.1		33	Arkansas	58.2
50	North Dakota	24.8		33	Rhode Island	58.2
29	Ohio	62.4		35	Tennessee	57.2
18	Oklahoma	67.7		36	South Carolina	56.8
13	Oregon	81.7		37	Nebraska	52.3
24	Pennsylvania	63.6		38	Idaho	52.1
33	Rhode Island	58.2		39	Wisconsin	50.3
36	South Carolina	56.8		40	Mississippi	49.9
49	South Dakota	30.0		41	New Hampshire	49.2
35	Tennessee	57.2		42	Wyoming	44.0
4	Texas	116.5		43	Kentucky	43.5
20	Utah	67.5		44	Montana	42.5
48	Vermont	32.3		45	West Virginia	37.3
17	Virginia	68.2		46	Maine	37.2
7	Washington	92.4		47	Iowa	36.7
45	West Virginia	37.3		48	Vermont	32.3
39	Wisconsin	50.3		49	South Dakota	30.0
42	Wyoming	44.0		50	North Dakota	24.8

District of Columbia   152.9

Source: Federal Trade Commission, Consumer Sentinel
   "Consumer Fraud and Identify Theft Complaint Data (January 2006)
Figures are for individuals filing complaints. Some complaints result in multiple infractions. Does not include consumer fraud or "Do Not Call" registry complaints.

Criminal Victimization in 2003-2004

Each year the Bureau of Justice Statistics conducts the National Criminal Victimization Survey (NCVS). Unlike the FBI's Uniform Crime Reports, which collects crime data from law enforcement agencies, the NCVS information is obtained through interviews with victims of crime. The numbers and rates below are two-year annual averages for 2003-2004.

Type of Crime	Number of Victimizations	Victimization Rates*
All crimes	24,136,970	NA
Personal crimes	5,496,580	22.9
Crimes of violence	5,292,195	22.0
Completed violence**	1,695,995	7.1
Attempted/threatened violence	3,596,200	15.0
Rape/Sexual Assault	204,365	0.9
Rape/attempted rape	108,945	0.5
Rape	65,510	0.3
Attempted rape	43,435	0.2
Sexual assault	95,415	0.4
Robbery	548,975	2.3
Completed/property taken	338,555	1.4
With injury	135,200	0.6
Without injury	203,355	0.9
Attempted to take property	210,425	0.9
With injury	62,180	0.3
Without injury	148,250	0.6
Assault	4,538,850	18.9
Aggravated	1,065,595	4.4
With injury	369,720	1.5
Threatened with weapon	695,875	2.9
Simple	3,473,255	14.4
With minor injury	833,540	3.5
Without injury	2,639,715	11.0
Personal theft**	204,385	0.9
Property crimes	18,640,390	162.2
Household burglary	3,411,655	29.7
Completed	2,859,830	24.9
Forcible entry	1,055,940	9.2
Unlawful entry without force	1,803,890	15.7
Attempted forcible entry	551,825	4.8
Motor vehicle theft	1,023,620	8.9
Completed	771,360	6.7
Attempted	252,270	2.2
Theft	14,205,115	123.6
Completed**	13,651,390	118.8
Less than $50	4,152,170	36.1
$50-$249	4,799,355	41.8
$250 or more	3,318,020	28.9
Attempted	553,725	4.8

Source: U.S. Department of Justice, Bureau of Justice Statistics
  "Criminal Victimization 2004" (Bulletin, September 2005, NCJ-210674)
*Rates are per 1,000 persons age 12 or older or per 1,000 households and reflect two-year annual averages. **Completed violent crimes include rape, sexual assault, robbery with or without injury, aggravated assault with injury, and simple assault with minor injury. The NCVS is based on interviews with victims and thus cannot measure murder. Personal theft includes pick pocketing, purse snatching and attempted purse snatching not shown separately. Completed theft includes thefts with unknown losses.

VIII. APPENDIX

Population in 2005

National Total = 296,410,404*

ALPHA ORDER

RANK	STATE	POPULATION	% of USA
23	Alabama	4,557,808	1.5%
47	Alaska	663,661	0.2%
17	Arizona	5,939,292	2.0%
32	Arkansas	2,779,154	0.9%
1	California	36,132,147	12.2%
22	Colorado	4,665,177	1.6%
29	Connecticut	3,510,297	1.2%
45	Delaware	843,524	0.3%
4	Florida	17,789,864	6.0%
9	Georgia	9,072,576	3.1%
42	Hawaii	1,275,194	0.4%
39	Idaho	1,429,096	0.5%
5	Illinois	12,763,371	4.3%
15	Indiana	6,271,973	2.1%
30	Iowa	2,966,334	1.0%
33	Kansas	2,744,687	0.9%
26	Kentucky	4,173,405	1.4%
24	Louisiana	4,523,628	1.5%
40	Maine	1,321,505	0.4%
19	Maryland	5,600,388	1.9%
13	Massachusetts	6,398,743	2.2%
8	Michigan	10,120,860	3.4%
21	Minnesota	5,132,799	1.7%
31	Mississippi	2,921,088	1.0%
18	Missouri	5,800,310	2.0%
44	Montana	935,670	0.3%
38	Nebraska	1,758,787	0.6%
35	Nevada	2,414,807	0.8%
41	New Hampshire	1,309,940	0.4%
10	New Jersey	8,717,925	2.9%
36	New Mexico	1,928,384	0.7%
3	New York	19,254,630	6.5%
11	North Carolina	8,683,242	2.9%
48	North Dakota	636,677	0.2%
7	Ohio	11,464,042	3.9%
28	Oklahoma	3,547,884	1.2%
27	Oregon	3,641,056	1.2%
6	Pennsylvania	12,429,616	4.2%
43	Rhode Island	1,076,189	0.4%
25	South Carolina	4,255,083	1.4%
46	South Dakota	775,933	0.3%
16	Tennessee	5,962,959	2.0%
2	Texas	22,859,968	7.7%
34	Utah	2,469,585	0.8%
49	Vermont	623,050	0.2%
12	Virginia	7,567,465	2.6%
14	Washington	6,287,759	2.1%
37	West Virginia	1,816,856	0.6%
20	Wisconsin	5,536,201	1.9%
50	Wyoming	509,294	0.2%

RANK ORDER

RANK	STATE	POPULATION	% of USA
1	California	36,132,147	12.2%
2	Texas	22,859,968	7.7%
3	New York	19,254,630	6.5%
4	Florida	17,789,864	6.0%
5	Illinois	12,763,371	4.3%
6	Pennsylvania	12,429,616	4.2%
7	Ohio	11,464,042	3.9%
8	Michigan	10,120,860	3.4%
9	Georgia	9,072,576	3.1%
10	New Jersey	8,717,925	2.9%
11	North Carolina	8,683,242	2.9%
12	Virginia	7,567,465	2.6%
13	Massachusetts	6,398,743	2.2%
14	Washington	6,287,759	2.1%
15	Indiana	6,271,973	2.1%
16	Tennessee	5,962,959	2.0%
17	Arizona	5,939,292	2.0%
18	Missouri	5,800,310	2.0%
19	Maryland	5,600,388	1.9%
20	Wisconsin	5,536,201	1.9%
21	Minnesota	5,132,799	1.7%
22	Colorado	4,665,177	1.6%
23	Alabama	4,557,808	1.5%
24	Louisiana	4,523,628	1.5%
25	South Carolina	4,255,083	1.4%
26	Kentucky	4,173,405	1.4%
27	Oregon	3,641,056	1.2%
28	Oklahoma	3,547,884	1.2%
29	Connecticut	3,510,297	1.2%
30	Iowa	2,966,334	1.0%
31	Mississippi	2,921,088	1.0%
32	Arkansas	2,779,154	0.9%
33	Kansas	2,744,687	0.9%
34	Utah	2,469,585	0.8%
35	Nevada	2,414,807	0.8%
36	New Mexico	1,928,384	0.7%
37	West Virginia	1,816,856	0.6%
38	Nebraska	1,758,787	0.6%
39	Idaho	1,429,096	0.5%
40	Maine	1,321,505	0.4%
41	New Hampshire	1,309,940	0.4%
42	Hawaii	1,275,194	0.4%
43	Rhode Island	1,076,189	0.4%
44	Montana	935,670	0.3%
45	Delaware	843,524	0.3%
46	South Dakota	775,933	0.3%
47	Alaska	663,661	0.2%
48	North Dakota	636,677	0.2%
49	Vermont	623,050	0.2%
50	Wyoming	509,294	0.2%
	District of Columbia	550,521	0.2%

Source: U.S. Bureau of the Census
"Population Estimates" (December 22, 2005, http://www.census.gov/popest/estimates.php)
*Resident population.

Population in 2004

National Total = 293,656,842*

ALPHA ORDER

RANK	STATE	POPULATION	% of USA
23	Alabama	4,525,375	1.5%
47	Alaska	657,755	0.2%
18	Arizona	5,739,879	2.0%
32	Arkansas	2,750,000	0.9%
1	California	35,842,038	12.2%
22	Colorado	4,601,821	1.6%
29	Connecticut	3,498,966	1.2%
45	Delaware	830,069	0.3%
4	Florida	17,385,430	5.9%
9	Georgia	8,918,129	3.0%
42	Hawaii	1,262,124	0.4%
39	Idaho	1,395,140	0.5%
5	Illinois	12,712,016	4.3%
14	Indiana	6,226,537	2.1%
30	Iowa	2,952,904	1.0%
33	Kansas	2,733,697	0.9%
26	Kentucky	4,141,835	1.4%
24	Louisiana	4,506,685	1.5%
40	Maine	1,314,985	0.4%
19	Maryland	5,561,332	1.9%
13	Massachusetts	6,407,382	2.2%
8	Michigan	10,104,206	3.4%
21	Minnesota	5,096,546	1.7%
31	Mississippi	2,900,768	1.0%
17	Missouri	5,759,532	2.0%
44	Montana	926,920	0.3%
38	Nebraska	1,747,704	0.6%
35	Nevada	2,332,898	0.8%
41	New Hampshire	1,299,169	0.4%
10	New Jersey	8,685,166	3.0%
36	New Mexico	1,903,006	0.6%
3	New York	19,280,727	6.6%
11	North Carolina	8,540,468	2.9%
48	North Dakota	636,308	0.2%
7	Ohio	11,450,143	3.9%
28	Oklahoma	3,523,546	1.2%
27	Oregon	3,591,363	1.2%
6	Pennsylvania	12,394,471	4.2%
43	Rhode Island	1,079,916	0.4%
25	South Carolina	4,197,892	1.4%
46	South Dakota	770,621	0.3%
16	Tennessee	5,893,298	2.0%
2	Texas	22,471,549	7.7%
34	Utah	2,420,708	0.8%
49	Vermont	621,233	0.2%
12	Virginia	7,481,332	2.5%
15	Washington	6,207,046	2.1%
37	West Virginia	1,812,548	0.6%
20	Wisconsin	5,503,533	1.9%
50	Wyoming	505,887	0.2%

RANK ORDER

RANK	STATE	POPULATION	% of USA
1	California	35,842,038	12.2%
2	Texas	22,471,549	7.7%
3	New York	19,280,727	6.6%
4	Florida	17,385,430	5.9%
5	Illinois	12,712,016	4.3%
6	Pennsylvania	12,394,471	4.2%
7	Ohio	11,450,143	3.9%
8	Michigan	10,104,206	3.4%
9	Georgia	8,918,129	3.0%
10	New Jersey	8,685,166	3.0%
11	North Carolina	8,540,468	2.9%
12	Virginia	7,481,332	2.5%
13	Massachusetts	6,407,382	2.2%
14	Indiana	6,226,537	2.1%
15	Washington	6,207,046	2.1%
16	Tennessee	5,893,298	2.0%
17	Missouri	5,759,532	2.0%
18	Arizona	5,739,879	2.0%
19	Maryland	5,561,332	1.9%
20	Wisconsin	5,503,533	1.9%
21	Minnesota	5,096,546	1.7%
22	Colorado	4,601,821	1.6%
23	Alabama	4,525,375	1.5%
24	Louisiana	4,506,685	1.5%
25	South Carolina	4,197,892	1.4%
26	Kentucky	4,141,835	1.4%
27	Oregon	3,591,363	1.2%
28	Oklahoma	3,523,546	1.2%
29	Connecticut	3,498,966	1.2%
30	Iowa	2,952,904	1.0%
31	Mississippi	2,900,768	1.0%
32	Arkansas	2,750,000	0.9%
33	Kansas	2,733,697	0.9%
34	Utah	2,420,708	0.8%
35	Nevada	2,332,898	0.8%
36	New Mexico	1,903,006	0.6%
37	West Virginia	1,812,548	0.6%
38	Nebraska	1,747,704	0.6%
39	Idaho	1,395,140	0.5%
40	Maine	1,314,985	0.4%
41	New Hampshire	1,299,169	0.4%
42	Hawaii	1,262,124	0.4%
43	Rhode Island	1,079,916	0.4%
44	Montana	926,920	0.3%
45	Delaware	830,069	0.3%
46	South Dakota	770,621	0.3%
47	Alaska	657,755	0.2%
48	North Dakota	636,308	0.2%
49	Vermont	621,233	0.2%
50	Wyoming	505,887	0.2%
	District of Columbia	554,239	0.2%

Source: U.S. Bureau of the Census
   "Population Estimates" (December 22, 2005, http://www.census.gov/popest/estimates.php)
*Resident population. Revised estimates.

Population in 2000 Census

National Total = 281,421,906*

ALPHA ORDER

RANK	STATE	POPULATION	% of USA
23	Alabama	4,447,100	1.6%
48	Alaska	626,932	0.2%
20	Arizona	5,130,632	1.8%
33	Arkansas	2,673,400	0.9%
1	California	33,871,648	12.0%
24	Colorado	4,301,261	1.5%
29	Connecticut	3,405,565	1.2%
45	Delaware	783,600	0.3%
4	Florida	15,982,378	5.7%
10	Georgia	8,186,453	2.9%
42	Hawaii	1,211,537	0.4%
39	Idaho	1,293,953	0.5%
5	Illinois	12,419,293	4.4%
14	Indiana	6,080,485	2.2%
30	Iowa	2,926,324	1.0%
32	Kansas	2,688,418	1.0%
25	Kentucky	4,041,769	1.4%
22	Louisiana	4,468,976	1.6%
40	Maine	1,274,923	0.5%
19	Maryland	5,296,486	1.9%
13	Massachusetts	6,349,097	2.3%
8	Michigan	9,938,444	3.5%
21	Minnesota	4,919,479	1.7%
31	Mississippi	2,844,658	1.0%
17	Missouri	5,595,211	2.0%
44	Montana	902,195	0.3%
38	Nebraska	1,711,263	0.6%
35	Nevada	1,998,257	0.7%
41	New Hampshire	1,235,786	0.4%
9	New Jersey	8,414,350	3.0%
36	New Mexico	1,819,046	0.6%
3	New York	18,976,457	6.7%
11	North Carolina	8,049,313	2.9%
47	North Dakota	642,200	0.2%
7	Ohio	11,353,140	4.0%
27	Oklahoma	3,450,654	1.2%
28	Oregon	3,421,399	1.2%
6	Pennsylvania	12,281,054	4.4%
43	Rhode Island	1,048,319	0.4%
26	South Carolina	4,012,012	1.4%
46	South Dakota	754,844	0.3%
16	Tennessee	5,689,283	2.0%
2	Texas	20,851,820	7.4%
34	Utah	2,233,169	0.8%
49	Vermont	608,827	0.2%
12	Virginia	7,078,515	2.5%
15	Washington	5,894,121	2.1%
37	West Virginia	1,808,344	0.6%
18	Wisconsin	5,363,675	1.9%
50	Wyoming	493,782	0.2%

RANK ORDER

RANK	STATE	POPULATION	% of USA
1	California	33,871,648	12.0%
2	Texas	20,851,820	7.4%
3	New York	18,976,457	6.7%
4	Florida	15,982,378	5.7%
5	Illinois	12,419,293	4.4%
6	Pennsylvania	12,281,054	4.4%
7	Ohio	11,353,140	4.0%
8	Michigan	9,938,444	3.5%
9	New Jersey	8,414,350	3.0%
10	Georgia	8,186,453	2.9%
11	North Carolina	8,049,313	2.9%
12	Virginia	7,078,515	2.5%
13	Massachusetts	6,349,097	2.3%
14	Indiana	6,080,485	2.2%
15	Washington	5,894,121	2.1%
16	Tennessee	5,689,283	2.0%
17	Missouri	5,595,211	2.0%
18	Wisconsin	5,363,675	1.9%
19	Maryland	5,296,486	1.9%
20	Arizona	5,130,632	1.8%
21	Minnesota	4,919,479	1.7%
22	Louisiana	4,468,976	1.6%
23	Alabama	4,447,100	1.6%
24	Colorado	4,301,261	1.5%
25	Kentucky	4,041,769	1.4%
26	South Carolina	4,012,012	1.4%
27	Oklahoma	3,450,654	1.2%
28	Oregon	3,421,399	1.2%
29	Connecticut	3,405,565	1.2%
30	Iowa	2,926,324	1.0%
31	Mississippi	2,844,658	1.0%
32	Kansas	2,688,418	1.0%
33	Arkansas	2,673,400	0.9%
34	Utah	2,233,169	0.8%
35	Nevada	1,998,257	0.7%
36	New Mexico	1,819,046	0.6%
37	West Virginia	1,808,344	0.6%
38	Nebraska	1,711,263	0.6%
39	Idaho	1,293,953	0.5%
40	Maine	1,274,923	0.5%
41	New Hampshire	1,235,786	0.4%
42	Hawaii	1,211,537	0.4%
43	Rhode Island	1,048,319	0.4%
44	Montana	902,195	0.3%
45	Delaware	783,600	0.3%
46	South Dakota	754,844	0.3%
47	North Dakota	642,200	0.2%
48	Alaska	626,932	0.2%
49	Vermont	608,827	0.2%
50	Wyoming	493,782	0.2%
	District of Columbia	572,059	0.2%

Source: U.S. Bureau of the Census
"First Census 2000 Results" (December 28, 2000, http://www.census.gov/main/www/cen2000.html)
*Resident population as of April 2000 Census.

Population 10 to 17 Years Old in 2004

National Total = 33,601,158

ALPHA ORDER

RANK	STATE	POPULATION	% of USA
24	Alabama	505,632	1.5%
45	Alaska	89,738	0.3%
16	Arizona	676,806	2.0%
33	Arkansas	308,118	0.9%
1	California	4,378,361	13.0%
23	Colorado	524,398	1.6%
27	Connecticut	397,143	1.2%
47	Delaware	88,831	0.3%
4	Florida	1,850,424	5.5%
9	Georgia	1,031,374	3.1%
42	Hawaii	133,168	0.4%
39	Idaho	169,081	0.5%
5	Illinois	1,469,360	4.4%
13	Indiana	732,334	2.2%
31	Iowa	319,344	1.0%
32	Kansas	311,739	0.9%
26	Kentucky	447,945	1.3%
22	Louisiana	533,465	1.6%
41	Maine	142,078	0.4%
17	Maryland	651,618	1.9%
15	Massachusetts	679,166	2.0%
8	Michigan	1,203,349	3.6%
21	Minnesota	581,039	1.7%
30	Mississippi	342,193	1.0%
18	Missouri	646,169	1.9%
44	Montana	102,231	0.3%
37	Nebraska	197,997	0.6%
35	Nevada	266,410	0.8%
40	New Hampshire	151,472	0.5%
10	New Jersey	989,643	2.9%
36	New Mexico	229,711	0.7%
3	New York	2,112,746	6.3%
11	North Carolina	948,626	2.8%
49	North Dakota	66,963	0.2%
7	Ohio	1,302,745	3.9%
29	Oklahoma	388,806	1.2%
28	Oregon	394,734	1.2%
6	Pennsylvania	1,373,028	4.1%
43	Rhode Island	116,899	0.3%
25	South Carolina	474,156	1.4%
46	South Dakota	89,353	0.3%
19	Tennessee	634,070	1.9%
2	Texas	2,740,726	8.2%
34	Utah	304,498	0.9%
48	Vermont	69,200	0.2%
12	Virginia	825,465	2.5%
14	Washington	698,675	2.1%
38	West Virginia	181,588	0.5%
20	Wisconsin	625,891	1.9%
50	Wyoming	56,233	0.2%

RANK ORDER

RANK	STATE	POPULATION	% of USA
1	California	4,378,361	13.0%
2	Texas	2,740,726	8.2%
3	New York	2,112,746	6.3%
4	Florida	1,850,424	5.5%
5	Illinois	1,469,360	4.4%
6	Pennsylvania	1,373,028	4.1%
7	Ohio	1,302,745	3.9%
8	Michigan	1,203,349	3.6%
9	Georgia	1,031,374	3.1%
10	New Jersey	989,643	2.9%
11	North Carolina	948,626	2.8%
12	Virginia	825,465	2.5%
13	Indiana	732,334	2.2%
14	Washington	698,675	2.1%
15	Massachusetts	679,166	2.0%
16	Arizona	676,806	2.0%
17	Maryland	651,618	1.9%
18	Missouri	646,169	1.9%
19	Tennessee	634,070	1.9%
20	Wisconsin	625,891	1.9%
21	Minnesota	581,039	1.7%
22	Louisiana	533,465	1.6%
23	Colorado	524,398	1.6%
24	Alabama	505,632	1.5%
25	South Carolina	474,156	1.4%
26	Kentucky	447,945	1.3%
27	Connecticut	397,143	1.2%
28	Oregon	394,734	1.2%
29	Oklahoma	388,806	1.2%
30	Mississippi	342,193	1.0%
31	Iowa	319,344	1.0%
32	Kansas	311,739	0.9%
33	Arkansas	308,118	0.9%
34	Utah	304,498	0.9%
35	Nevada	266,410	0.8%
36	New Mexico	229,711	0.7%
37	Nebraska	197,997	0.6%
38	West Virginia	181,588	0.5%
39	Idaho	169,081	0.5%
40	New Hampshire	151,472	0.5%
41	Maine	142,078	0.4%
42	Hawaii	133,168	0.4%
43	Rhode Island	116,899	0.3%
44	Montana	102,231	0.3%
45	Alaska	89,738	0.3%
46	South Dakota	89,353	0.3%
47	Delaware	88,831	0.3%
48	Vermont	69,200	0.2%
49	North Dakota	66,963	0.2%
50	Wyoming	56,233	0.2%
	District of Columbia	46,419	0.1%

Source: Morgan Quitno Press using data from U.S. Bureau of the Census
"Population Estimates Data Sets" (http://www.census.gov/popest/datasets.html)

IX. SOURCES

Administrative Office of the U.S. Courts
Office of Public Affairs
Washington, DC 20544
202-502-2600
www.uscourts.gov

Bureau of the Census
4700 Silver Hill Road
Washington, DC 20233-0001
301-457-2800
www.census.gov

Bureau of Justice Assistance
810 Seventh Street, NW
4th Floor
Washington DC 20531
202-616-6500
www.ojp.usdoj.gov/BJA/

Bureau of Justice Statistics
810 Seventh Street, NW
Washington, DC 20531
202-307-0765
www.ojp.usdoj.gov/bjs/

Children's Bureau
Administration for Children & Families; HHS
370 L'Enfant Promenade, SW
Washington, DC 20201
202-401-9215
www.acf.dhhs.gov

Death Penalty Information Center
1101 Vermont Ave, NW
Suite 701
Washington DC 20005
202-289-7336
www.deathpenaltyinfo.org/

Drugs and Crime Clearinghouse of the Office of National Drug Control Policy
PO Box 6000
Rockville, MD 20849-6000
800-666-3332
www.whitehousedrugpolicy.gov

Federal Bureau of Investigation
J. Edgar Hoover Building
935 Pennsylvania Avenue, NW
Washington, DC 20535
202-324-3000
www.fbi.gov

Juvenile Justice Clearinghouse
PO Box 6000
Rockville, MD 20849-6000
800-851-3420
www.ojjdp.ncjrs.org

National Archive of Criminal Justice Data
ICPSR
University of Michigan
P.O. Box 1248
Ann Arbor, MI 48106
734-647-5000
www.icpsr.umich.edu/NACJD/

National Association of State Alcohol and Drug Abuse Directors, Inc.
808 17th Street, NW
Suite 410
Washington, DC 20006
202-293-0090
www.nasadad.org

National Center for State Courts
300 Newport Avenue
Williamsburg, VA 23185-4147
800-616-6164
www.ncsconline.org/

National Institute of Justice
810 Seventh Street, NW.
Washington, DC 20531
202-307-2942
www.ojp.usdoj.gov/nij

National Clearinghouse on Child Abuse and Neglect
330 C Street, SW
Washington, DC 20447
800-394-3366
http://nccanch.acf.hhs.gov/index.cfm

National Criminal Justice Reference Service (NCJRS)
Box 6000
Rockville, MD 20849-6000
800-851-3420
www.ncjrs.org

Office for Victims of Crime Resource Center
PO Box 6000
Rockville, MD 20849-6000
800-851-3420
www.ojp.usdoj.gov/ovc/

Substance Abuse and Mental Health Services Administration
U.S. Department of Health and Human Services
1 Choke Cherry Road
Room 8-1036
Rockville, MD 20857
240-276-2000
www.samhsa.gov

X. INDEX

X. INDEX (continued)

X. INDEX (continued)

X. INDEX (continued)

CHAPTER INDEX

Arrests

Corrections

Drugs and Alcohol

Finance

Juveniles

Law Enforcement

Offenses

HOW TO USE THIS INDEX

Place left thumb on the outer edge of this page. To locate the desired entry, fold back the remaining page edges and align the index edge mark with the appropriate page edge mark.